Infantry. UNIFORMS OF REGULAR CONFEDERATE TROOPS. Cavalry. Artillery. Louisiana Zouave

Volunteer Infantry of Virginia. 1st Regiment Maryland Line. South Carolina Light Infantry. Hampton Legion. Rockingham Rangers Artillery. Gentlemen of the Road Independent Cavalry. Black Horse Cavalry.

UNIFORMS OF THE CONFEDERATE A

Louisiana Zouaves. Washington Artillery of New Orleans. Mississippi Rifles. Heavy Infantry of Georgia. Alabama Light Infantry. Marine Battery, Manassas Junction.

Black Horse Cavalry. Dragoon Guards, 14th Regt., Va. Cavalry. Mounted Rifles, North Carolina. Virginia Cadets. Grayson Dare-devils. Kentucky Rifle Brigade. Tennessee Sharp-shooters.

IFORMS OF THE CONFEDERATE ARMY.

The Confederate Soldiers and Sailors of Moore County, NC

Volume II

Civil War Letters, Confederate Pensions, Conscription Papers, Petitions for Amnesty, Deserters and Outliers, Civil War Reunions and Cemetery Census

Researched and
Compiled by

Morgan Jackson
www.MooreCountyWallaces.com

Inside Front & Back Covers: Confederate Uniforms as depicted in Harper's Weekly, August 17, 1861
Courtesy of www.CivilWar.com
https://www.civilwar.com/media/Confederate_Uniforms.jpg

Back Cover: 1855-1861 Map of NC and VA showing roads, plank roads and *railroad (edited to focus on Moore County)*
Courtesy of the State Archives of North Carolina
https://dc.lib.unc.edu/cdm/singleitem/collection/ncmaps/id/5207/rec/152

ISBN 979-8-9932029-2-1

Published by Morgan Jackson
Raleigh, North Carolina
www.MooreCountyWallaces.com
morganjackson_1997@yahoo.com
919-624-7281

Printed by IngramSpark
www.IngramSpark.com

Table of Contents

To Thurman D. Maness [1909-2010], my great-uncle, who spent much of his life researching the Moore County companies in the Civil War and the soldiers who served. He worked diligently to assemble the histories of soldiers and units in a time when records were much less accessible than now. This volume is dedicated to your many years of work and your memory.

To Lacy A. Garner, Jr., who not only continued Thurman's work but has had a life-long desire to document Moore County's contributions to the Civil War and the sacrifices of the men who served and the families they left behind. Lacy's detailed research on the 26th Regiment, Company H of the "Moore Independents" was a direct inspiration.

And to my family...Shawn, Emsley, Colt and my mother, Pat. Thank you for the love and support that you have tirelessly given as I have pursued my life-long devotion to history and genealogy.

Introduction

The Civil War was one of the most tragic events in our nation's history and discussing the great war brings with it many difficult and complicated feelings. These volumes are not meant to glorify the Civil War, to spark debates, open old wounds or create new ones. It is merely an attempt to document the soldiers and sailors from old Moore County that served and to create a resource for current and future generations. I think there is room in our heads and our hearts to commemorate those that served and at the same time regret and condemn the unjustness of the war and the stain that slavery left on our country.

The goal of these volumes is to provide as comprehensive of a listing as possible of all Confederate soldiers and sailors that were born, enlisted or received a pension in Moore County and Lee County.

This work would have been possible without the incredible resources of *The Civil War Roster Project* and its volumes, *North Carolina Troops 1861-1865: A Roster, Vols. I-XXII.* The enormous undertaking began when the North Carolina Centennial Commission began to compile the rosters of Confederate soldiers in 1961 on the 100th anniversary of the Civil War and this work has continued over the years through the Office of Archives and History, the State Archives, the Historical Publications Office and now the Historical Research and Publications Section. The rosters published in this volume are curated directly from those volumes courtesy of *The Civil War Roster Project.* As they begin the second part of the series, they will shift their focus to documenting the Union soldiers and sailors from North Carolina, both White and African American, who served. [1]

Utilizing personal research and a multitude of information from numerous sources, the following two volumes are a collection of abstracts of service records, company and unit rosters, bounty payrolls, pension records, newspapers accounts, letters from soldiers and their families, accounts of reunions of soldiers in Moore and genealogical data detailing the Confederate soldiers and sailors of Moore County and Lee County. These abstracts were collected over many years from courthouses, libraries, the North Carolina Office and Archives and History, the National Archives, the Moore County Historical Association and other researchers as well as from *Fold3.com, Newspapers.com, Ancestry.com, Familysearch.org* and other amazing web-based repositories. I have strived to be as accurate as possible but readily admit that there are likely errors and omissions. Please contact me at ***morganjackson_1997@yahoo.com*** and I will gladly make any corrections to future editions, paper and online.

This collection was inspired by, and I hope continues to add to the volumes of genealogical research that came before. No discussion of Moore County, NC history and

[1] Beehler, Carly and Chris Meekins, Editors. *The Civil War Roster Project.* (Raleigh, NC: Historical Research and Publications Section, Department of Natural and Cultural Resources).

genealogy can be complete without paying tribute to *Miscellaneous Ancient Records of Moore County, NC* by Rassie E. Wicker; *A Guide to Moore County Cemeteries* by Anthony E. "Tony" Parker; *Moore County 1747-1847* by Blackwell Robinson and *Moore County 1847-1947* by Manly Wade Wellman. As always, a special praise and word of thanks to my longtime friend, mentor, and master genealogist James Vann Comer, whose volumes of work have documented too many families, communities and institutions across Central North Carolina to list them all here.

Morgan Jackson – November 1, 2025
www.MooreCountyWallaces.com

Civil War Letters from Soldiers, Family and Friends

The following letters provide first-hand accounts from soldiers on their experiences, successes and hardships faced during the War. These letters are an invaluable resource and provide a bird's eye view of life on the battlefront, in prisoner of war camps and the home front and have been curated from historical archives, libraries, family histories, websites and private collections across the state and country. A tremendous thanks to the generations who have preserved these incredible historical accounts. Small edits were required on some letters to create an easier experience for readers.

1861, February 6
Mastin C. Phillips (*Trinity College*) to sister **Emeline Phillips**. General wartime correspondence with brief mentions of the beginnings of war, father Rev. **Lewis Phillips Jr**., uncle Rev. **Charles H. Phillips** and wife **Lizzie Skeen Phillips**, cousin **Louis C. Phillips,** cousin **Malphus S. Phillips, Dr. Dunlap** and mother **Nancy Edwards Phillips**. [1]

Dear Sister, I take the present opportunity to drop you a few lines[.] your letter which came to hand in due time after it was mailed[.] truly glad to hear from you and that all were well. I was not well for some time after I arrived here. I thought that I was going to have fever. I feel very thankful that I did not have fever. I do not want to be sick while I am here. I hope God will giv me health while I am from home. About the time I recovered from the illness above mentioned, I was vacinated. I soon found that the matter was taking effect and at the end of a week I was nearly helpless and remained quite sick for several days. If the small pox is not really a fatal disease and nothing more than ordinary disease, the remedy is worse than the disease. I don't reckon it makes all as sick as I was. My arm is not quite well yet, though it has not pained me in several days. We have 165 boys in school now. There are more than we expected at the opening of the term. I guess that we will have two hundred by the commencement. We have very little excitement about here with regard to political affairs. We have several South Carolinians, some of whom volunteered to defend South Carolina this winter when they were at home. They are allowed to come back to school on condition that they would go back to S.C., if needed, at one minute warning. I wish they were in S.C. now and would stay there. I do not like to look upon a traitor and hear them boast, what he will do if the Federal officers don't give up the ports on her coasts. I wish they were hanged, the last one, both North and South Carolina and I would like to do it, at least I want to be there to see it done. I don't think there will be much fighting for a month or two. I am studying very hard now, but I am afraid that I am doing no good, or at most, not much. I am making 5 recitations a day. These are too many to recite with, but I believe I will hang on to them all as long as I can, if I do not recite very well. I guess that Pa has had a letter from Uncle Charles before this time as I mailed one here last Friday for him. Uncle Charles was quite well when it was mailed and said that Aunt Lizzie and Lewis were improving fast. I hope they will have good health from this time. But I must close. You must excuse this letter. I am something over half asleep and have written in haste. Give the enclosed scab to Malphus and tell him if he wants to use it to ask Dr. Dunlap and he will tell him how. Write soon, give me all the news. My love to all. Tell Ma to keep well and think that I am well also. Goodnight. This leaves me well.
Your brother, Mastin

1861, May 4
Donald Street (*Kienzi, Tishomingo County, MS*) to brother **Richard Street**. General wartime correspondence between brothers with brief mentions of the beginnings of war, companies forming in Mississippi, **Hugh McQueen Street** and wife **Charlotte Prindle**, **Archibald McBride Street**, **Mary Street**, Mr. **Drake** and **Jim Rees**. [2]

My Dear Brother. Your very welcome letter was recd a few days ago from the United States. When is tethered a Foreign Country by the State of Tish. I see you are [illegible] as of old on the political question of the day tho you are more unanimous for union, than suits my views at present, I done my best to preserve it, but we are now out, in spite of all conservative men. tho Tish sent 4 of the 15 that voted against secession, I would like to see all the slave states in our Confederacy. I think the North would back from their coercion policy[.] It perhaps save us from a civil war. If we should get into one, I would advise a Northern man not to place his foot on Southern soil with the expectations of going back alive, public sentiment is such there that it would be a war of extermination so far as lay in the power of the South. I believe no quarter would be asked & none granted, it would be more like a war among savages than a civilized nation. Hugh, Archy & Mary are out & out Secessionists. I have been all the time for union but now it is broken to pieces, I see no chance of its preservation & the North or black Republicans of Congress seem determined to make no concession, Reading the Washington union papers has almost made me an open secessionist. the Remarks of the black rascals in Congress makes me feel desperate, it would not do for one to pop in, at such times. He would bite the dust quick, for the olive branch the offer looms, the breach seems to be widening every day, old Abe seems determined not to back down from the Chicago platform & I would not be surprised if he was not allowed to see Washington City or be inaugurated if he does, We have had a great deal of rain one of the highest drenches ever known in the creeks up here, but no snow to lie on the ground & not enough to cover it if it had[.] The Iron horse has been hauling Rienzi to Corinth since the 13 Jany/1st passenger, tho it passes at one & 2 o'clock at night there been two break, near twenty mile creek 15 or 20 miles South. Caused by heavy rains the last on Friday 1st inst[.] Archy went to Corinth on last night on a freight for Hugh & wife they were with us as usual & will spend the summer with us[.] finished sowing oats on 31st Jany, the second sowing come up better than the 1st days[.] the ground seemed to be green together very Close in low places[.] Mr Drake has recd his so Jim Rees said last week, twice all cause to hand[.] Glad to hear from Paddy[.] When you come out again bring him along[.] my Respects to him[.] I saw his bro a few days ago all well[.] I have been looking for a letter from the Dr for some time he is due me one[.] Matters & things in genl are going just the same as if we were in the United States except cotton is up & down & we are making great preparations for war. 2 Companies in Corinth, 1 in Jacinto & Rienzi 65 men[.] Some of the men can hit the bottom of a pint tin at 400 yards, guns made at Harpers ferry, we have all sorts of rumors of Battles every day or two[.] you did not say how many bales of cotton made[.] I have packed 26 & have two to gin[.] All well join in much love to you & all relatives. Respects to all enquiring friends your affect, Brother D. Street

1861, May 6-7

Donald Street (*Kienzi, MS*) to brother **Richard Street**. General wartime correspondence between brothers with brief mentions of North Carolina joining the war, companies forming in Mississippi, **Hugh McQueen Street**, **Archibald McBride Street**, the **Buchanans**, Dr. **Shields**, and **Lydia McBryde Street**. [3]

My Dear Brother. I have not had a letter from you lately, but events transpired so fast I have concluded to write you a line or two[.] I am glad to see the old North State dissociated & at last took on the abolition, black, lincoln vandals[.] I told our folks Mr Hale would come out on the picket side after a while[.] did you ever see such a greater contrast in the same paper than in the observer 15 & 22 Apl[.] The Military Spirit is at the highest notch[.] here there has been no more companies formed & offered[.] These has been accepted by the by the government of this county[.] Several with over the number allowed[.] 100 is the no. by law but they make up 104 & 6 & 8 & have to refuse many[.] those are companies already called out[.] I was in Corinth a few days ago went down to see the soldiers there were then I think 2700 or 3000 & arriving everyday[.] they concentrate there to drill & be ready to go to any point, Many companies are the best drilled I ever saw[.] all were anxious to get a hop at old Abe, I heard many say they did not intend to return without a bag full of Black Republicans scalps in a fair fight. I think every man can whip three[.] They will fight with a brave determination to conquer or die, We formed two more companies in Rienzi the other day[.] one has gone from there & Jacinto 108 men & many joined one of the Corinth Companies & have been at Pensacola sometime. Hugh is 1st Lieutenant and Archy 2nd & the other Company is comprised entirely of married men[.] Some over 70 years old to which I belong, home guards. The troops at Corinth suppose they are going to Washington City but it is all companies[.] it is said there will be troops there during the war as a place of general rendezvous[.] Old Abe will find us all union men now all united against him & his black villains, three fourths of the volunteers are slave holders, & many very wealthy[.] I heard of one young man said to be worth $300,000, one company at Corinth have $7000 in their private treasury, many of this large sums, I saw many darkies with their uniform & side arms on, they were prouder than their masters & walk about large with their belts & pistols on, I never saw the negroes more quiet and obedient & attention to their work than they are now. They seem as much enraged at old abe as the whites, & I do not think their in as much danger of an insurrection now as at a more quiet time[.] though I cannot tell how it is in other Sections all is reported light every whear I can hear from[.] One of four Buchanans sons was Lieutenant of the Chickasaw guards, a fine company. Tom was there himself but I did not see him. only learned he was there a few minutes before I left[.] I came from Corinth to Rienzi in 23 minutes & C is a warlike city at present. Dr. Shields & family were well[.] He is surprised that Pa or some of his family does not answer his letters. I sent you a few papers lately tho I do not know whether you will get them as your mails only come by a slauret, (what sort of weather have you had for the last month or two, I do not think I ever knew as much rain in the same lenght of time[.]

finished planting cotton last Friday[.] it has been raining ever since. would have finished 29 Apl if it had not rained 26th and 27th[.] I have not touched my bottom land plowed over some corn, not much grass, weeds plenty, it has been so wet the weeds have nearly taken our garden[.] Provisions of all kinds advanced rapid in the last 10 days. The bacon corn & flour are dull & prices in favor of buyers in Memphis a day or two ago, large arrivals from St. Louis caused the decline[.] it is said the wheat crop in Texas is ruined with rust. & the rust reported south of this[.] it is very early for it I see some fields in full bloom mine is just leading, Mary was very ill two days last week I thot she had or was threalused with a congestive chill[.] the Dr said not[.] She is up and about tho not very well. Several have colds tho not severe, Lydia is very busy over her Poultry, 400 young chickens & 40 goslings 30 turkeys & 3 or 4 hens to hatch & tend. Such a gitten up & pruning when a cloud is coming up you never didnt see[.] an Irishman was taken up at Baldwin in this County M&O.R.R. thrashed and ordered to leave, at Corinth he was telling they whipped him for falling in love with a negro woman, They shaved over his head put a coat of Tar & Cotton & sent him on rejoicing[.] I have just heard 2000 troops left Corinth for Lynchburg, VA preparatory to a visit to old abe the he will run, May 7th, it is fair this morning the ground very wet. Cool this morning. All join in love to you and all relatives & enquiring friends. Write soon & often[.] lines getting tight[.] Your Attached B. Donald Street [P.S.] Mary says She will write you soon.

1861, May 17
Mary J. Ray to cousin **Hugh M. Ray** (*Wadesboro, NC*). General wartime correspondence between cousins with brief mentions of brother **Joseph Ray**, Capt. **Hall**, cousin **Christian Lewis** and father **Archibald Ray.** [4]

Dear Cousin, It was with much pleasure that I received you most welcome letter of the 8th which came to hand this eavning. it found us all quite well[.] I was very much gratified to hear that you wer well. Cousin I wish have to begin to make excuses for this letter for I do not feel like I can write any at all this eavning but I thought I would make a try if I failed in writing it. I am so very sleepy this eavning[.] Cousin we have heard from Brother Joseph several times since he left home[.] say that he has bin very sick but Sis received a letter from him this week and he sayed that he had not bin sick but he had a cold he spoke of coming home next week[.] Capt Hall & seven (7) of the company arrived hear last Sunday & they will return nigt Monday & then some of the rest will come home if they do not start to begin[.] I so hope they will not have to fight for some time yet or not at all. Cousin there was two (2) letters came to you since you left[.] one of them was from Cousin Christian Lewis[.] I will send it in this letter to you if I dont forget it. We have so much trouble with the P.O. that sometimes I dont know what I am doing[.] Papa has quite the U.S. postage stamps & he has ten (10) for every letter sent & received[.] he will not make any thing at all keeping the office now. Cousin I havent got any thing more to tell you at this time. you cant imagin how lonesome I get sometimes up hear. I want you to write to me often where ever you go to write to[.] if it is the end of the wourld for I do love to get a letter from you or anybody else[.] the family all join me in much love to you[.] I will come to a close by begging you to please write to me very often & I will answer every letter I get from you. So please excuse my bad writing and spelling write soon soon soon soon. Your cousin Mary J.

1861, May 18
Artemus S. Caddell to Miss **Martha M. Sullivan**. General personal correspondence. [5]

The greate love I have hitherto expressed for you increases daily[.] the more I see you the more I feel myself every way disposed and determined to Love [.] our last conversation has given me the most exalted idea of your character and if we are reunited I shall experience nothing but pleasure in living with you[.] I have indeed a heart of service[.] I could not give it to one more worthy or capable to do "honor to" myself and friends[.] I speak sincerely and sentimently as you will do me a favor to answer this[.] Adieu Adieu believe me to be your most affectionate friend til Death. I hope you will excuse me for writing to you as our intevues[?] are but few and fare apart[.] I hope you will answer this soon. Yours Resp. Artemas S. Caddell

1861, June 6
Mastin C. Phillips (*Trinity College*) to father Rev. **Lewis Phillips Jr.** General wartime correspondence with brief mentions of the beginnings of war, sister **Emeline Phillips**, brother **Malphus S. Phillips,** uncle **Rev. Charles H. Phillips** and Uncle **Jabaz ?**. [6]

Dear Pa, I have seated myself to drop you a few lines, I have written to Emeline and Malphus recently and I hope that the letters have been received before this time. I am inclined to believe that the most of the letters, which I have written for the last two months, have never reached you. I know that I have written several for which I have had no answers. I guess they have been delayed on the way. Our Commencement is close at hand. I think that we will have a nice time in spite of the war. We were making preparation for the occasion as fast as we can. I do not think that we will have as many spectators as have been here formerly at Commencement, but enough for hot weather and hard times. Malphus wrote me that he was coming, but did not say whether you were or not. I have expected you to come all the time, and I expect it yet. So, I hope you will not disappoint me. You can come with Malphus and then we can all go back together. I intend to go home if "Old Abe" does not invade the State before Commencement. Bring something along for me to carry a change of clothes home. I shall let my books and the most of my clothes remain here as I intend to return at the opening of the next session if all things are favorable. I came here to get an education and I will not give it up yet. I am studying closely now, and learning some I think. I heard from Uncle Charles last Tuesday. He and all were well then. I expect to see him tomorrow as I understand that he is going to pass here. We are having fine seasons now and the crops look well, especially wheat and oats. I want you to have your hooks in time for I intend that we shall fish some when I get home. But, I must stop now. You must come to the Commencement. Get here the 19th inst. I borrowed five dollars from Uncle Jabaz it has satisfied my wants for the present. Eleven hundred troops passed on the road today for the seat of war. I guess blood will be shed soon, but I think that we can whip the rascals (we must do it). This leaves me well. I could write more but haven't time. My love to all. Your unworthy son, Mastin

1861, June 9
W.B. Clegg (*Garysburg, NC*) to **Richard Street**. General wartime correspondence discussing buildup of troops, training in Garysburg and the anticipation of war, **John M. Edwards** and **Nick P. Smith**. [7]

Dear friend, I have been thinking for some days that I would write to you but my opportunities have been very short[.] So I hope you will forgive me for writing on Sunday[.] We have few duties to perform today than on other days though we are not entirely free. We have to appear on dress parade morning & evening. I had rather drill an hour than to be on parade thirty minutes. Pardon me for so long a preamble. We left Raleigh on friday morning & arrived at his place on the same day time enough to get our tents up[.] But unfortunately we had nothing to eat[.] there was some mistake made in regard to our bagage & our provisions were left behind. They mess luckily had some loaf bread ham & coffee along & that all saved us from sharing the fate of the company[.] There has been considerable compliant in our company since we left home though we have had no severe case of sicking mostly diarrhea. we left one at Raleigh he said to have bilous fever[.] we have not heard from him since we left. Our friend J.M. Edwards was sick a few days at Raleigh. He has recovered & sends you his respects. There are between three and thousand troops here. One regiment is to leave here Tomorrow. they are preparing here by the thousands daily from the South. Some of them desperate looking fellows especially the Zouaves from New Orleans. One regiment passed through here yesterday who have taken an oath to ask no quarter nor give any. It is reported here that there has been a fight at Phillipi VA. but the accounts are so contradictory that I hardly know what to believe, all the accounts nearly agree as to the number killed[.] We lost six & old Abe Lincoln sixty to seventy. They out numbered us by about four to one. A fight is expected at Manassas shortly[.] Such news as this I suppose you will get by the papers sooner than by letter. Our company belong to the fifth regiment[.] I understand that we will have to elect our Colonel this week[.] we have not received our arms yet. I reckon they will give us some before they sends us to the battlefield if they don't I shall run and I may run anyhow. The prospects are that we will be put to the test in a few weeks. There is something out I can't what it is[.] So many men preparing going to Virginia[.] shows conclusively that the war is to be commenced in ernest & that shortly[.] A regiment has first pass from South Carolina & I understand there is another at Weldon – which will pass in a few minutes. Loud & prolonged cheers sound the air as they pass from camp & cars – The other regiment has pass which makes two in about twenty minutes. You will please excuse this poor apologe for a letter as it has been written amidst the greatest confusion. My best respects to Nick & my acquaintances of your company & write soon to your friend. W.B. Clegg, Address Care of Capt Ihrie, Chatham Rifles, Garysburg, NC

1861, July 23
Noah Deaton (*Garysburg, NC*) to father **William Deaton**. General wartime correspondence with brief mentions of travel from home and the battle of Manasses Gap. [8]

Dear father[,] I take the opportunity of droping you a few lines to let you know that I am well and hope these few lines will find you all well[.] We were received with respect by the sitizens all the way from home to [illegible] place[.] we met with a fine dinner at Jonesborough and supper and breakfast in Fayetteville[.] we went on the cars from Jonesborough to Fayetteville and then went on the steamboat to Wilmington and then we got on the rail road and went to Weldon about 164 miles[.] the rout we traveled is about 310 mils from Carthage[.] all the way cittizens thronged the road with cheers and shouts and waveing ther hats and handkerchiefs in the air as the cars went by flying as fast as a bird, the ladies would come running out and throw flowers and cedar boughs to us to show their respect for the company[.] Companys are pass this place ever day[.] there was five or six companies passed us yesterday while we were at Weldon waiting for the car[.] trains are passing dily crowded with volunteers to Virginia[.] the greatest battle that has accurd since the battle of watterloo was last Sunday at Manasses gap in which their was about one hundred and twenty thousand engaged[.] the fight continued 10 hours[.] the confederates killed about 10,000 of the yankes with a loss of 1,300 and capturing some 30 pieces of artillery and about 1,200 prisoners of the enemy[.] great victory on our side[.] the yankes were totaly whiped and routed and were persued by our cavalry for several miles when stoped at last and returned to camp[.] I have not time write much at this time[.] I cannot tell how long we will stay here so answer this as soon as you can[.] direct your letter to Garysburg N.C. Northhampton County, yours truly, Noah Deaton

1861, July 28
Noah Deaton (*Garysburg, NC*) to sister **Sarah Bethune Deaton**. General wartime correspondence with brief mentions of travel from home, the battle of Manasses Gap and **John P. Leach** and **Emsley H. Owen**. [9]

I again take the pleasure of droping you a few lines to let you know that I am well and have been well ever since I left home and I hope this may find you all well. the company is well with exception of two or three[.] I was deceived in the fare for it is good enough we have corn meal and flour & rice & bacon & fish & sugar coffee & molasses and other things plenty[.] we pitched our tents in a nice grove wher we can make ourselves comfertable and the boys all seem in fine spirit[.] about five hundred troops left here today[.] it is thought that about 30,000 troops will pass here this week[.] about 1000 passed yesterday but we are likely to remain here for some time yet[.] the Montgomery company is here[.] I saw J. P. Leach & E. Owens today[.] there was preaching at our camp to day and apointed agan next Sunday and one good thing I can say the company has all been sober ever since we come here because they cant get liquor here and in fact the camp seems as much like a camp meeting and more than like a camp of warriors[.] the great victory at menases has revived the people all about here[.] It cannot be ascertained how many of the enemy was engaged but they confess their loss to be 20,000 of which over 10,000 wer killed and the rest missing and our loss is not moore than five or six hundred[.] our armies are surely protected by a devine providence so far and I hope the north will soon see their folly and let us a lone[.] I am about 360 miles from here home[.] If providence will permit hope the war will soon be over and we will all be sent home[.] If I no more see you here I hope we will meet in heaven where parting is no more[.] No more at present[.] only I remain true to you all[.] please answer this as soon as you can, Noah Deaton

1861, July 30
Christian Ray (*Moore County, NC*) to brother **Hugh M. Ray**. General wartime correspondence between siblings with brief mentions of cousin **Neill Ray**, **Malcolm Ray**, cousin **William M. Black**, cousin **William B. Monroe**, **Archibald Blue, Daniel Blue, Burrell Bailey**, **William Whitlock**, **John McLean**, Mr. **Tyson**, **Nancy Ray** and **Kenneth Black**. [10]

Dear Brother I seat myself this morning to drop a few lines to let you know that we are all well and hope this will find you cousin Neill and all the company in perfect health[.] you requested me to wright soon that you would hear from us[.] I would hav written last week if I had known where to direct my letter[.] you can not imagine how much satisfaction it was to us to hear from you and that you were well and that you wer well satis fied and had comfortable tents to sleep in not exposed to the damp ground[.] I hardly know what to wright that would be of satisfaction to you at your distant stations[.] you must wright son and tell me how times pass with you all[.] Malcom says to tell you he would wright but if he had time he has volunteered[.] cousin William Black is making up company and I hav not heard how many he has on his list[.] cousin William B. Monroe, Archibald Blue, Daniel B and the two Balys is all that has their names on yet except Malcom in this neighborhood[.] tell Mr Whit too that his mother is well and I hav not heard of any of the companys frend being sick since you left here][.] Mr John McLean has the misfortune of geting his arm broke and put out of Joint thursday eaving on his way home from court[.] his horse sprang and when he found that he could not recover he bent ove and lit on his lef hand[.] his arm broke just above the joint put the rist out of joint[.] he is geting allong as well as he could expect with a broken bone[.] Hugh you must wright soon and I can giv more satisfaction[.] I am anxious to hear[.] Mr Tyson sayd that Cousin Neill had a chill and that he was up and about the next day[.] tell Cousin Neill that I saw his gall last Sunday[.] she was up at church and she ll looks as well as ever[.] I was not thier but though she was her and I am in hopse that it will not be long till you well all be at home again[.] I must close[.] you must wright as often as you can[.] your letters will be welcom at any time or any place[.] sarah says must giv that apple to the one sh told you to[.] giv my love to all and receive a portion yourself[.] aunt Nancy and all the family sends their love to you all[.]

I remain your affectionate sister. Christian Ray [P.S.] I have said nothing about Uncle Kenneth. His family is well.

1861, July 31

John Parsons (*Weldon, NC*) to Rev. **Lewis Phillips Jr.** General wartime correspondence with brief mentions of the beginnings of war. [11]

Dear Friend, I take the pleasure of writing you a few lines to inform you that I am well and hope these lines find you and the family well. We reached this part of the country on last Monday as a week ago in the hardest rain I thought I ever saw[.] though we put up our tents at Louisburg and on last evening we left that place and came over to this place where we are now. After leaving Fayetteville on Saturday morning, we reached Wilmington on that night at 11:00 o'clock. We then left that place at 2:00 o'clock on Sunday and reached this place that night, a distance of 165 miles by railroad conveyance. There is about six or seven thousand soldiers in this region around here. I will state to you that there has been a great deal of confusion in our company about the way we have been treated and by the Coln. of the 14th regiment. After coming to this place, our company was a large company and a strong, robust set of men, and he took the advantage of our officers and Coln. Clark, after seeing this, he went to Raleigh and took one of his companies out of his regiment and put our company in without the consulting of either officers or privates, ready to start with the regiment[.] we with no guns nor nothing to defend ourselves better than knives. It has been [illegible] by the officers and Coln. to leave to a vote whether we shall go to Norfolk or Raleigh to join the 15th regiment. The vote was taken in favor of going to Raleigh and get our arms and take an even start. There has been no fighting since the fighting at Mannasses and Bull Run, though there will be plenty of it to do if we succeed in our undertaking. I will write to you in a few days concerning our transfer. I hope it will all be right without dishonor, coming home with nothing. I'm through if our officers leave. We will be compelled to leave and reorganize and start again, but I think it will all be solved without more difficulty. I will state that I have plenty to eat and I have the stomach to eat it. I shall state that I bought feathers over at Louisburg in the [illegible]. When I left that place I had to leave them and now I have to lie on the ground. I should like for Mastin and Baxter to come and help relieve the country of its distress. Tell the old general and the boys that I am well and I will write to them soon. I have nothing more to write at present, though I never saw as many people going on to Richmond [illegible] drove from all parts of the Confederate States. Remember my love to all the family and those who shall inquire for me. John Parsons

1861, July 31

Richard Street (*Weldon, NC*) to **Candace Phillips**. General wartime correspondence with brief mentions of the beginnings of war and **William W. "Buck" Edwards** and **Callie**, **Mastin C. Phillips** and **Malphus S. Phillips**. [12]

My dear Candace, I have intended writing for several days but having a good deal of news have postponed until this time hoping that I would have something interesting to tell you. We have been in a constant state of bustle and excitement ever since we left home. We arrived in Fayetteville in about three hours after we left Jonesboro. Were hospitably entertained by the citizens of that ancient town that night, and next morning when we left for Wilmington on the steamboat North Carolina, where arrived Sunday morning at two o'clock. Some of our Company were very lively and had slept none up to that time. When we landed at the wharf some stretched out on piles of lumber where they slept until day light. Some, among whom was myself, had secured berths in the cabin of the steamboat from which they were driven out as they said by fleas. I had no fleas but was saturated with water in the shape of a leak overhead. I awoke during a hard rain and found myself almost floating in water. I jumped out, dressed myself, I was sleeping with half my clothes on, and dried myself as well as I could by the boiler. Fell in a dry place and slept very comfortably till morning. Part of us attends church in Wilmington that morning in our red jackets. Some spent the morning not so profitably. We were on the same train with us. We were to have left at three o'clock that evening for Weldon, but did not get off until five o'clock. A Company from Georgia was on the same train with us. A noble set of fellows. We traveled with them to Weldon and we arrived Monday morning at three o'clock. Having slept but little for two nights and some of the Company having eaten nothing since breakfast the morning before. You may be sure we were pretty well worn out with hunger and fatigue. We could not find the Company who had to provide breakfast for me until nine o'clock. However he was found at last and a bountiful breakfast was soon gotten ready and quickly dispatched. We left Weldon for Garysburg where we stayed a week and a day and returned to Weldon to encamp with the 14th Regiment which received orders to be in readiness to march to Virginia today. It will however remain several days longer at this post. It is very uncertain whether we will go with the Regiment on account of the manner in which we were put in. I think of you very often. Write soon. Tell me all the news. How are the new married folks getting on, Buck and Callie. I will direct this letter to Mastin and put a private mark on the corner. When you see that mark on a letter break it. Write soon. Get Mastin or Malphus to direct your letter to the care of Captain Martin. I could not say all that I would say in this letter as I was surrounded by a crowd while writing. Yours truly, Richard Street

1861, August

C.D. Caddell to brother **A.S. Caddell**. General local correspondence between brothers with brief mentions of **Rip Moore**, **Mary E. Moore**, **Absalom Fry**, **Jerry Davis**, **Martha McIntosh, Barrett** and **Sowell's** company with Capt. **S.W Sowell**, 1st Lt. **Wm. Ashley Barrett**, 2nd Lt. **Alexander Barrett**, 1st Sgt. **Charles Sowell**, 1st Corp. **A.B. Dowdy**, church at Bethlehem and Pleasant Hill and teaching school at Pleasant Hill. [13]

Dear Brother. I take the opportunity of writing you a few lines[.] we are all well at present hoping these few lines may find you well[.] I have rec several letters from you which gave me much pleasure to hear from you[.] I have roe to you 4 times since you left[.] I am going to commence teaching school at Pleasant Hill the 18 day of Aug[.] I have a verry good school all in the district will send but old Rip Moore[.] Miss M.E. Moore tried to get a school and did not get the first scholar and it mad old Rip made and she [torn...]. She was pleased I know is when she got to them[.] She said she did not know you was a going to give her your likeness[.] She said she loved it better than anything walking about in these digins[.] She has got to be the pretiest gal in our settlement except mine[.] Miss A. and I fly around all of the McIntoshes and Miss Martha in particular[.] We had a very good meeting at Bethlehem, we had a verry good sing and meeting once evry 2 weeks on Sunday night at Pleasant Hill. Mr. Barrett and Mr. Sowell's Company is in a verry flourishing condition[.] Sowell is Co-Captain and Ash 1st lieutenant[.] they have got about 50 on their list Linctum may watch out[.] Mr. Sandy Barrett is 2 lieut Mr. Charles Sowell is first seg Mr. A.B. Dowdy is first coperal[.] I wish you could see them a drilling[.] I would be drafted Jerry Davis before I would go with them[.] David is coming out some[.] I want you to write to mee where I shall have his tripes taken off or not[.] Absalom Fry wants to sell mee his colt and tell mm where you would buy or not [torn....] of wheat I think I can spare ½ of the corn[.] I want you to kill a Lincolnite and sen me his repiter[.] write as soon as this gets to hand[.] I remain your affectionate brother until death[.] C.D. Caddell [P.S.] I want you to quit writing to Miss M.E. Moore if you please for sha has told hit to evry body in moore.

1861, August 7

Noah Deaton (*Weldon, Halifax County, NC*) to **Sarah Jane McDonald** (*Reedybranch PO, Moore County, NC*). General wartime correspondence with brief mentions of travel from home, the battle of Manasses Gap and Col. **W. J. Clark**. [14]

Madam, We the Moore County Indipendents arrived at Garysburg on Monday[.] after we lef Carthage we pitched our tents in a pleasent grove on the west side of the rail road and we remained their untill Tuesday the 30th ult., when we by order of Col W. J. Clark and adjutant of that post we moved our tents to Weldon and were placed in an open field where we are exposed openly to the sun shine and I am sorry to say that it's verry sickly place[.] the companys here has sufferd a great deal with the fever and measels[.] ours is the healthiest company in camp about here[.] we are in camp wit the 14th Regiment but we do not belong to any regiment yet[.] we will stay here a while but I cannot tell how long[.] we have got to guard the rail road bridge across the Ronoke River[.] We hear from the seat of war every day[.] there is no important movement since the great Battle at Mannassas[.] the nuse came here today tha lincon wants for him and his cabinet to study about the war question the term of 60 days but Jeff Davis we learn has granted him only 20 days[.] it is rumord that Lincon begins to want to make peace[.] Whether it be so or not we fear it is only to reorgamze his armies[.] The Lincolnites met with such a perfect defeat at Mannassas that we allow they would need some time to think before they undertake to give us another trial[.] I have seen some of the men that was in the battle[.] they state that it is the terrblest scene of horror that can be immagined[.] may God grant that I may never behold such a scene of slaughter[.] the camp seems to almost demoralized[.] it is a place that tries morality in almost every form[.] it almost a continual hum of profane language. O may we be remembered by all the praying christians[.] please remember me and all rest of our company at your prayer meetings[.] nothing more at present[.] please answer this that I may hear from you all Yours respectfuly Noah Deaton

1861, August 9
C.D. Caddell to brother **A.S. Caddell**. General local correspondence between brothers with brief mentions of **Zacheus Hogan**, **Martha M. Sullivan** and beginning to teach school at Pleasant Hill. [15]

Dear Brother. I seat myself this morning to let you know that we are all well at present. I have nothing strange to write to you[.] [T]ell Hogans that I give the letter to his gal. [T]ell him she loves him the best [illegible] and said she would write to him[.] I have done as you directed me to do[.] if I was you I would write to M.M.S. tolerable often[.] I shall commence a school Monday week at pleasant hill[.] write as soon as this gets to hand. I remain your affectionate Brother until Death. C. D. Caddell

1861, August 9
A.S. Caddell (*Weldon, NC*) to brother **C.D. Caddell**. General wartime correspondence between brothers listing duty of company to guard the town and the bridge across the Roanoke River with brief mentions of **Jane McIntosh**, Capt. **William P. Martin**, cousin **Lydia F. Seawell**, **Mary E. Moore**, **Malcolm P. Davis**, **Stephen Davis**, **Noah F. Muse**, **Silas D. Crook** and church at Bethlehem. [16]

Dear Brother[,] I take my seat again to write you a few lines to inform you that I am well at this time[,] hoping this will find you all well. Our company is generally well except a few cases of measles and mumps[.] we are all in good spirits[.] I Recd one letter from you which gave me much pleasure to hear that you was all well[.] I think you ought to write oftener[.] I have wrote 10 or 12 letters to you and I think you might answer them[.] I wrote to several of the girls and enclosed their letters in yours[.] I want to know if you Recd them[.] I wrote to Jane and want to know if she recd her letter[.] I was call out and guard yesterday at 8 and served till 8 to day[.] I have done nothing but shot a dog and put one drunkard in in the guard house[.] we have to guard the town and Bridge across Rowanok which is 2/3 of a mile long[.] I want you to tell me how my gal is geting along[.] tell her to write to me[.] they may think that Capt Martin has to see them but it is not so[.] they are only directed in his care in order that they will not be lost[.] I wrote to Cousin L. F. Seawell & Miss M.E. Moore[.] tell them to answer my letters[.] I shal enclose in this a letter give to the owner[.] tell M P Davis to write to me[,] also Stephen[.] tell N. F Muse to write[.] I want you to tell me all the news and who is a flying around[.] I do not expect to write any more until you write to me[.] give my best Resp to all enquiring friends if any[.] I would be glad to be at Bethlehem tomorrow but while I am far distant in Body I am present in mind[.] I hope I will not be forgotten in that congregation. I wrote to S D Crook tell to write to me soon as he can. Resp. yours. A.S. Caddell

1861, August 10
W.L. Sullivan (*Moore County, NC*) to **A.S. Caddell**, **Zacheus Hogan**, **William Whitlock**, **W.H.H. Davis**, **James N. Caddell**, **Neill McIntosh** and **Samuel Jackson McIntosh**. General local correspondence with brief mentions of **John A. Jackson**, **Devotion Davis**, **Alexander M. Dunlap**, **D. Shaw** and their location at Garysburg, NC, Weldon, NC and muster from Jonesboro, NC and church at Bethlehem. [17]

Dear Friends[,] It is for the first time that I have seated my Self since you left Moore Cty For The purpose of droping you a few lines to inform you that I and the Family is enjoying very good health[.] and I hear that you are all well at garysburg and I am glad to hear Such good news from you all[.] Tho I have not Received a line from Any of you since I parted with you at Jonesborough and I never Experienced Such a day in my Life[.] I have no nuse to write to you since more than Cadell is elected[,] But this will Be no nuse to you[.] I have Bin Looking for Letters from you all But have not Recd[.] I Send my love and Respects to you all Z. Hogan, A.S. Caddell, J.A. Jackson, J.N. Caddel, Jackson McIntosh, Neil McIntosh, W.H.H. Davis, Wm. Whitlock, A.M. Dunlap, J.L. Caddell & all of the company[.] I want to see you all if things continue as they are you may look out Shortly For the Rest of we Moore Cty Boys[.] our company organizes Saturday next if we are provided that time[.] we hear that there has Bin some hard Battles fought Lately and Glorious victory won[.] if we obey the god of Battle we need not Fear tho our Enemy Be strong[,] we go on[.] My prayer is that god will preserve you from all danger that you all may Be so fortunate as to prove victorious in Battle and all Returned home without the Loss of one[.] But if any of you should Fall and never return I trust god will Receive you where troubles never come[.] Be Sure and write Soon[.] tell all the rest of them to write to me[.] give my Love to all Inquiring Friends. Yours truly. Remember me tho many miles apart we Be no more[,] write soon. W.L. Sullivan

Dear friends[,] I have Just Received a letter since I Began to write that was dated July 31st on August 10th which gave me great satisfaction to hear from you that you was all well[.] I would answered you then but I thought from what you said you would Be gone from Weldon Before it could get there[.] But I saw a letter [by Mr. D. Shaw] from you yesterday stating that you was yet at Weldon so I am going to send these Lines on In hast[.] I was in hope that you was Coming to Raleigh But your Letter to S.D.C. says you are going Norfolk[.] I want to see you all very Bad[.] if you had come on to Raleigh I intended to go there and see you all[.] I have Know [no news] nuse of much importance to write to you[.] we are neading Rain and our corn is fading fast and Every other growin vegetable[.] Zacheus[,] you told me to get your fine shirt too warred homespun shirts and your Black pants[.] But I Can't hear no tell of your Blk pants nor your two shirts[.] I want you to tell me where they are[.] I must get this together[.] I want you to write to me wherever you may Be on land or on see[,] and let W.L.S. know how you are Enjoying yourselves if you are in a battle[.] Send me the Result[.] I trust god will be with you all in Every Battle and will guide and direct so that all will be Rite so that you may Be able to put the Enemy to flight[.] I must Close By saying I Remain your friend until death[.] Yours Respectfully yours. W. L. Sullivan

Zacheus Hogan[:] I have Know [no news] nuse to write to you of much importance[.] Zacheus[,] your little girl is well and as prety as Ever[.] I wish you & A.S. Cadell and all the Rest could be here next Sabath[.] There is a protracted meeting at Bethlehem and were it feasible for you to Be here I should rejoice to see you[.] the little girls hearts would Rejoice to see you here[.] There is not Any thing could give me such pleasure as to see you all there[.] But I hope you have a meeting where Ever you ma[y] Be with god who is able Bless[.] and Every man shall sit under his vine and under his fig tree and none shall make them afraid; all tho we are parted and seated a Broad we will pray for each other and trust in the Lord[.] I want you to write to me one and all of you[.] know we would Be more thankfull to receive a letter from Any of you[;] than I would to shure and write and tell me how you are getting along how you are Enjoying yourself when this you see[.]Remember me tho many miles apart we Be[.] ok let not this our friendship Chill tho mountains Rise Between us[.] Lett trooth and Justice gide our will and god from Evil serean us your company sweet your union as your words delighful to my Ear[.] But when I saw we had to part you draw like cord around my heart if we on Earth do meet no more[,] I hope we meet on Canaans Shore[.] So no more[.] I must close By Saying I Remain your friend until death. W.L. Sullivan to Zacheus Hogan & A.S. Caddell Wm. Whitlock, W.H.H. Davis, J.N. Caddell, N. McIntosh Jackson McIntosh, as your friend this I write. W. L. Sullivan

1861, August 11
C.D. Caddell (*Carthage, NC*) to brother **A.S. Caddell**. General local correspondence between brothers with brief mentions of **Zacheus Hogan**, school at Pleasant Hill and the death of **John R. Ritter**. [18]

Dear Brother[,] I seat my Self this morning to drop you a few lines & that you have not Recd no letters[.] I have written twice to Garysburg[.] wee are all well at present hoping these few lines may find you well[.] I done as you directed me with the Ring letter & likeness[.] She was glad to get them I know[.] She said what you sent She wanted me to give her my Self[.] I am going to Start to meeting in a few minutes[.] John R. Ritter is dead[.] I am going to Commence a School a Monday at pleasant hill[.] we are suffering for Rain very bad at this time[.] tell Hogans that I wrote to him tell him that his gal Said She would be true for ever and was glad to hear from him[.] She told me she loved him[.] tell all to Rite to me[.] I have Rote several letters since you bin gone[.] write soon[.] I Remain your affectionate[,] Brother CD Caddell

1861, August 14
A.S. Caddell (*Weldon, NC*) to Miss **Martha M. Sullivan**. General wartime correspondence with brief mentions of some of the Company in Carthage next week and the Company being sent back to Raleigh to form a regiment and brief mentions of Capt. **Clement Dowd** and **Robert W. Goldston** and church at Bethlehem. [19]

Fair Miss. I devote these few linnes to the when this you read[.] Oh, think of me[.] I am well at this time hoping that this will find you enjoying good health[.] I have nothing of interest to write to you[.] this makes the 3 or fourth time that I have wrote to you and I have received no answer[.] I want you to answer this and tell me how you are getting along if you pleas[.] their will be several of our company at Carthag next week[.] I want you to write and you can make it convenient to send your letter by Mr Dowd or Mr. Goldston[.] let me know if you received any word from me[.] I will not write nomore at present as I have not heard from you[.] when I hear from you[,] I will explain my self more fully[.] so I will close by saying I Remain your friend. our company is going to return back to Raleigh in order to form a regiment[.] It may be probable that we may stay their for some time[.] if we do I may go home for a while[.] if I do so I will try to make it convenient to see you[.] I shall not write nomore until I hear from you[.] Remember our bet and don't spoil my hankerchief[.] tell me about the meeting at Bethlehem[.]

1861, August 14
Unknown soldier (*Weldon, NC*) to **Baxter Clegg Phillips**. General wartime correspondence with brief mentions of the beginnings of war and **William Henry Harrison Davis** and **William B. Clegg**. [20]

Dear Sir, We are still at this place, but expect to leave tomorrow. Not for the seat of war, but to take the back track and go a little nearer home. In other words, we have been ordered to Raleigh where we should have gone first. It was a great blunder in to have sent us to Garysburg as all the troops stationed there[.] we organized into Regiments and a great number of them were sick with measles and mumps. We were put into camp with the companies which had those diseases[.] and as a natural consequence, our men who have not had them will have them. So you may have heard we were put in the 14th Regiment by the chicanery of Col. Clark[.] but by showing a determined front we were transferred and I suppose will go in the 15th. It was a very happy riddance for from what I have seen of the field officers regiment[,] I know that their knowledge of military tactics is very limited. A great many of the privates have the greatest contempt for the Col.[,] and I understood[,][,] sneered at him a few days ago while he was addressing them. The regiment is on the point of open rebellion. I had my information from a commissioned officer of the regiment who stated seven of the regiments were in for disbanding and holding a new election, so you see we got clear of it in good time. It will not do to go into battle with officers in whom the men have not full confidence, both as to courage and ability. A man can't fight if he thinks he is being led by a coward or a fool. I see a good many sick and wounded soldiers returning home every day. One man passed through yesterday who been shot through the face and the ball came out of the back of his neck. His face was very much disfigured, but he was nearly well. What is more melancholy a number of the dead are daily carried home by their friends, both those who have died of their wounds and those who have died of disease. I saw a young man from Yorktown yesterday who was in the same regiment with Harrison and Billy Clegg. He did not show them and could give no information concerning them, but sad there was a great deal of sickness in that regiment. All the movements of the army are keep very secret. We hear a great many rumors and officers passing through make many surmises as to what will be done next, but at the same time confess that they do not know anything of the plans of our leaders. It is stated that an officer asked Beauregard if he did not intend to take Washington. He answered, taking hold of his coat at the same time. If my coat knew what my intentions are, I would pull it off and throw it in the fire. So[,] you can see that all that is in the papers, as to what will be done, is mere guess work. An officer told me yesterday that he thought some stirring news would be heard in a few days and perhaps a battle would be fought today, that his regiment was ordered to Acquia Creek and that wages are being collected. It is thought that our troops will be sent into Maryland in large numbers this week. It is reported that thirty thousand men will join us in Maryland as soon as we cross the river. The government at Washington is said to be very much alarmed and have been busily preparing for defense. Over two thousand trees have been cut down around Arlington Heights and trimmed so as to leave all the limbs pointed and placed with the laps out to form a (battis?) so as to impede the progress of our troops if they make an attack on that point. I send you a diagram of the camp of the 14th regiment while we were in it. The captains' tents were placed in a line. The tents of the privates were pitched in two lines in front of each captain's tent with a pass of about thirty feet wide between each line of tents where the company was formed each morning for drill on parade[.] and at the tap of a drum all marched out to a forty acre field to drill. The col's tent was pitched about the center, the lieut, col. On one side, the major on the other side. Cook's tent at the lower end of the line and all the fires were made in line. Guards were placed all round and were selected in the following manner. There were ten posts around the camp and ten posts at the bridge and in town to guard. It required sixty men, two corporals and a sergeant. The companies sent out men in proportion to their numerical strength, commencing in alphabetical order. Thus[,] the company having the most men fit for duty sends out the most for guard. Our company being the largest is enjoying the best health furnished most generally ten while some furnished only five, and one which had a good many sick only three. The sixty men were divided into two squads, one for town the other for camp duty. Each squad of thirty were divided into three reliefs of ten each. The guards are detailed for twenty-four hours. The first relief is put on at 8 o'clock in the morning and stands till 10 o'clock when the second relief comes on and stands till 12 o'clock. At 12 o'clock the third relief is put on and stands till 2 o'clock when the rest relief comes in again, so that each relief stands two hours and is off four, serving in all eight hours out of twenty-four....(The last page of this letter is missing. Do not know who the writer was).

1861, August 19
Jane McIntosh (*Carthage, NC*) to uncle **A.S. Caddell**. General local correspondence between niece and uncle with brief mentions of church at Bethlehem, **Isom Wallace's** wife being sick with fits and "people are saying it was because he bit her", **Samuel W. Sowell** and **William A. Barrett** are organizing a company with **S.W. Sowell** as captain, her brother **William McIntosh**, **C.D. Caddell**, **William Caddell**, **Raney Caddell**, **Sam Wallace** and **Sarah F. McIntosh**. [21]

Dear uncle[,] it is with pleasure that [I] take present opportunity writing you a few lines to let you know that we are all in very good health and I hope when this comes to hand that it may find you well and hearty[.] we had a very good meeting at Bethlehem[.] I received your letter which gave me great satisfaction to hear from you and that you was well[.] I gave that whitch was in my letter to the one that it was directed to the same day I got it[.] it seemed to pleas her very well[.] I have nothing strang to write[,] the people is comonly well[.] Isom Walices wife is sick[.] she has somthing like fits but people says that he bit her what is the matter[.] Your old julalky is swell[.] I went home with her from M Meeting last Sunday night and we seen the most fun ever you went any where[.] you may not know who I am speaking of[.] she lives near Bethlehem church[.] I tell you Tim that the gals is very sorow about your leaving[.] they go by companies to see your likeness and I am afraid that they will ruin it a looking at it before you come home[.] SW Sowel and W.A. Barret has got enough volunteers to be organized. S W Sowel is thier captain[.] I tell you that we don't have sutch singing as we had before you left hear[.] We had a sing yesterday[.] I will tell you a Joke ther was a young man to see a girl a few day ago and when the old folks went to bed[,] he seated himself by her and said how would you like to live with me[.] she said not atal[.] then he said may I come to see you[.] she said that would never do[.] he said if that was the way she talked that she would never see him and old doc ther any more[.] William told me to tell you that he had went home with one girl for you[.] he is gone to school now to CDC[.] I had better come to a close for I recon you dont want no more of sutch[.] you must write to as often as you can[.] grandmother and papy is well[.] you must excus me for writing you this bad letter and bad writing and spelling and I will try to do better next time so write me soon[.] so nothing more at present[,] only I remain you afectionate niece until Death[.] Jane McIntosh [P.S.] *I will tell you who old doc is[.] he is Sam Walices horse and the lady was Sarah F Mc[Intosh][.]*

1861, August 20
Lydia [Seawell] (*Carthage, NC*) to cousin **Artemus S. Caddell**. General local correspondence between cousins with brief mentions of church at Bethlehem and his father **William Caddell**. [22]

Dear Cousin[,] with pleasure I seat my self to drop you a few lines in return to your double welcome letter which I read after along time[.] I was glad to hear from you and know that you was well and in good spirit[.] I recon you would like to know how all of your friends is coming on[.] they are all doing as well as well as thay can I believe[.] we have bin going to meeting and sings[.] I went to the sing last Sunday and thare I saw your little girl[.] she was the pretiest one that was there and we both sung your favorit song in remembrance of you[.] sunday week is the last day of the sing[.] I was at your fathers last Sunday bout a dousin other girls[.] you ought to abeen there[.]

thay went down there to see your likeness[.] oh how thay did prase it. I want you to write to me and write every thing you can think of[,] and if you do not come home while you are so close at home[,] we shal think that you do not want to see us[.] pleas excuse this and write as soon as you can fore I cannot write any more. your Cousin Lyd

1861, August 24
Mary E. Moore (*Broadway, NC*) to **Artemus S. Caddell**. General local correspondence between cousins with brief mentions of Capt. **Samuel W. Seawell**, **Bethuel Coffin**, **Harrison Davis**, **Alexander M. Dunlap**, **Ann M. Dowd** and church at Bethlehem. [23]

I received your letter a few days since[.] I was very much pleased to hear you all were in fine spirit. I am from home at this time and have been for the last week, therefore you must not expect me to say much. I suppose you are all at Raleigh and expect to remain there some time. I think you might come home before you leave there, or do you think it would be worse leaving home the second time than the first. Our fishings has gone down since you all left[.] I have not fished the first bit since that evening[.] There is a death at home today. Captain Seawell's company[.] I dont know how many he has but I dont think he is making it up very fast[.] There was a diner given them at Cofins last Saturday. I would like very much like for these companies to join your regiment. Our meeting did not continue. broke up Sunday night. Our sing still continues just about the same it was when you left. There was a protracted meeting commenced on Serat yesterday. Mr. Dean and several other ministers are expected. You wished to know who was married and who was trying to marry[.] well it is just about the same as it was when you left[,] all flying around as thick as ever but dont seem to marry, but I think there will be a few marriages before the company starts. I believe all of you volunteers have written to me that promised except Harrison Davis[.] I think very hard of him for not writing. I suppose you all have a very nice time cooking washing fetching etc[.] I hope you will have a nice time killing the Yankees, that is of nothing else will satisfy them. I would much rather you would make peace without any more fighting if you could. Tell Mr. A.M. Dunlap Miss Ann M. Dowd says to remind what he promised. I must close as I have nothing else to say. Excuse this short letter and I will try to do better next time. my very best respects to all. write soon to your friend and cousin. M. E. Moore

1861, August 25
C.D. Caddell to brother **A.S. Caddell**. General local correspondence between brothers with brief mentions of teaching school, **James Horner** and **Jane Wallace's** marriage, church at Bethlehem, **Jane McIntosh**, **Zacheus Hogan**, **Benjamin Gilliam Hollingsworth**, **Samuel Jackson McIntosh** and **W.H.H. Davis**. [24]

I seat my self again to write you a few lines[.] I am a teaching Scholl and has a bout from 25 to 30 schollars[.] My school is worth a bout $1.35 per day[.] Since I am in need I think it is tolerable good business[.] James Horner and Jane Wallis is married[.] I have nothing to write to you of much in fact[.] I wrote to you the other day[.] Since you wrote to me I have Recd all the letters that you Sent since[.] and Jane recd one from you to Kitty[.] they have had a meeting at Bethlehem for 5 days and Knights they had supper. tell Hogans to write to me and to his gall for she is all write[.] tell Gilem to write. and Jack and W.H.H[.] write to me as Soon as this Comes to hand and let me know when you Recd my letter or not[.] I am a coming next week if I Can get the chance[.] write soon I remain your affectionate Brother untill Death. I would write more only I don't like the male boys. C.D. Caddell.

1861, August 26
Noah Deaton (*Raleigh, NC*) to father **William Deaton**. General wartime correspondence with brief mentions of uncle **Hiram Deaton**. [25]

Dear father[,] I take my pen in hand to drop you a few words[.] I am not well[.] I have the measles[.] I think I feel some better today than I have felt in three or four days[.] I am broke out all over with the measles[.] I hope this may find you all in good health and I think I'll be up in a few days[.] there is several of our company down with the measles[.] I have written four or five letters home and have not received any answer yet[.] I heard that uncle Hiram Deaton was dead and I was sorry to hear it[.] we are in camp at Raleigh in a very pleasent place[.] please answer this soon[.] Yours truely Noah Deaton

1861, August 26
Noah F. Muse (*Moore County, NC*) to **A.S. Caddell**. General local correspondence with mentions of Capt.

Bryant trying to form a Company, **Ashley Barrett** and **S.W. Sowell** trying the same with officers **S.W. Sowell** (Capt.), **A. Barrett** (1st Lt.), **Z.B. Moore** (2nd Lt.) and **Charles Seawell** (1st Sgt.) and brief local mentions of church at Bethlehem including upcoming wedding of **James Horner** and **Jane Wallace** by **Jesse Muse** on Sunday the 27th, trip to Guilford County, death of **John R. Ritter**, and requests for letters from **Zacheus Hogan**, **Kelly Williamson**, **John J. McIntosh**, **Neill McIntosh**, **John A. Medlin**, and **Benjamin Gilliam Hollingsworth**. [26]

Well friend A.S.Caddell[,] I write you a few lines[.] I am well this morning & all the neighbors is well so far as I know[.] I've nothing of interest to write[.] Times is about as they was when you was here[.] they are trying to make up a company on two of volunteers[.] Capt. Bryant has got his Company made up[.] Ashley Barrett and SW Sowell is trying to make up a Company[.] how much they lack I dont know[.] they have Elected Their officers S.W.Sowell, Capt. A. Barrett, 1 Lieut Z.B. Moore 2 Lieut and well you know Mr Charles Sowell is first Sergeant and so on down. Well Boys I will tell you more when I see you on matters of importance. Well Tim if I could see you I would tell you something about the Girls[.] I saw your Pullit Last Sunday[.] She is as pretty as ever[.] I was talking with her and her again[.] Tim[,] I think of you Oh often & to go to church and see your seat vacant[.] it almost makes me shed tears of grief and joy too[.] I think of the fun we have seen together[.] I was at old Bethlehem[.] I call it old for I do love old Bethlehem where we have spent so many hours of pleasure[.] well I was there when you write or was writing your Letter to me among the Girls[.] But not without thinking of you[.] well there hasnt been any weddings since you left but there is to be one on the 27 Sunday[.] James Horner to Miss Jane Wallace to be joined by Mr Jesse Muse[,] and others flying around strong[.] watch for Squlls before Long[.] Tim[,] I did want to see you start but I was gone up into Guilford after a thrasher[.] I didnt expect you to start before I come back though[.] I recon you didnt much care for it for I realy think hard of you for not writing to me[.] I know Tim you must have a bad chance so to write. But I think you if you was disposed to write to me[,] you could find as much time to write me as to others as I thought I was as good a friend to you as others you wrote to in all I want[.] I would have wrote but didnt know where to direct my Letters to. Tim[,] I want you tell Z. Hogans to write & kiss him for me[.] tell K. Williamson to write, also J.J. McIntosh & Neil McIntosh, J.A. Medlin, B.G. Hollingsworth[.] I want to hear from all[.] one thing I Reckon you have not heard[,] By J.R. Ritter died[.] N.F. Muse

1861, September 2
Richard Street (*Camp Carolina near Raleigh, NC*) to Rev. **Lewis Phillips Jr.** General wartime correspondence with brief mentions of **John Parsons**. [27]

Dear Sir, We were ordered to leave this place for New Bern yesterday evening. We have now struck our tents and have everything packed up and are now putting them on the cars. We go to meet the enemy who has landed on our coasts to prevent them from coming into the country. With a firm reliance on God, I believe we can drive them back[.] Pray for us. We leave John Parsons and twenty-three others here. John has been very sick since I wrote and his life has been despaired of[,] but is now thought to be in a fair way to recover. All that are left have the measles and are now going about[,] but it is not thought prudent to take them out as we may have much exposure to undergo. Remember me to all inquiring friends. Yours truly, Richard Street P.S. I have no idea of going home and raising another Company. Can I do so? Is their Spirit enough in the people to raise another? Yours, R. Street

1861, September 3
A.S. Caddell (*Bogue Island, NC*) to father **Wm. Caddell**. General wartime correspondence from son to his father with details of a dreadful storm and enemy vessel blown ashore that led to the capture of 80 prisoners and brief mention Mr. **Lawhon**. [28]

Dear father, I drop you a few lines to let you know that I am well and in high spirits[.] I hope this will find you well and doing well I write this in order to let you know that we had some good fun here to day[.] we had a dreadful storm the night before last which raged until to day[,] and the fun of it was that there was a report of the enemy blown on shore this morning and we got 80 prisoners[.] you ought to a seen us marched in to camp with them[.] we had some good fun[.] one of them told me that there was 75000 of them by old point—for this place and he thought that they was nearly all lost—they men we taken was good looking men well dressed and looked they could do good fighting though we taken them without any trouble[.] they did not seem to mind it[.]

they said if they could get something to eat and that they would not ask for any thing els[.] we got five really good horses and I suppose we will get something worth talking about when we examine the rest[.] I will tell you all in the next[.] Mr. Lawhon left here this morning[.] I sent you a letter by him[.] I got $31 of my wages[.] I wish you had $20 dollars of it[,] but I dont know where to send it or not[.] so no more at this time[.] write soon to your affectionate son. AS Caddell

1861, September 3
John A. Jackson (*Morehead City, NC -- reply to Capt. **W. Martin***) to **Richard A. Cole**. General wartime correspondence between brothers-in-law regarding military life around Fort Macon and brief mentions of **Martin McKinnon** and Lt. **Clement Dowd.** [29]

Dear Brother. I take the presant opertunity of riting you a few lines to let you now where I am. I am at moorehead sity on the sound inside the Fort. The sand nearly nee deep. I can see the ships sailing on the ocean and there is an English ship landed at this place now loaded with salt. There is another ship here. I dont now what it is tho. I was at it Yesterday and saw them loading Rosin[,] and I asked one of the sailors where it was bound[,] and they said only the captain new that so I said no more. There is a large ship lying off the coast in sight. I saw it yesterday. Some say it is a yankey and others say an English man of war and for my part I dont now which but one thing. Some seamed very uneasy and some did not pay much attention to it. Some of our boys was over at the Fort yesterday and they said the men over at the Fort told them it was a Lincolnite so they are expecting an attack[,] or that they will try to land at some other point if they can take advantage[.] they are certain to so so. I do not now how long we will stay at this place. There is some talk of moving to an island neare Fort Macon but it is uncertain. We can get as many fish heare as we want fresh or pickeld. I can go round the edge of the sound and see the fish sport[,] and our boys go and fish and some times they have right good luck. They can go in the sound and get clams and oyesters as many as they want and take morning and evening baths. It wont do to go in any time in the heat of the day[,] and morning is the hot part of the day. The most of our company in tolerable good health at present. One or two sick heare. We left our sick at camp carolina something about 20 or 25 but none considerd it dangersous. I heard from them this morning. Martin McKinon he staid with them the night before last and said they were doing very well. I understand from Lieutenant Dowd since I commenced riting that it is certain that we will be stationed on an island some 3 to 4 times away from Fort Macon. I do not now what direction. They say it will be a pleasant place. So I must come to a close by saying I am well at presant[,] hoping these few lines may come to hand and find you all the same and mother and her family. So no more. J. A. Jackson [P.S.] Direct your letter to moorehead sity in care of Capt W. Martin.

1861, September 3
C.D. Caddell [*Carthage, NC*] to brother **A.S. Caddell**. General local correspondence between brothers with brief mentions of **Catherine "Kitty" McIntosh, Sarah C. McIntosh, Zacheus Hogan, Silas D. Crook**, the birth of **Archibald Buckley Muse's** son **James C.B. Muse, Samuel Jackson McIntosh** and **W.H.H. Davis.** [30]

Dear brother, I take my pen in hand to write you a few lines to let you now I am well at present[,] hoping these few lines may find you well[.] I have nothing of interest to write to you[.] I have read all the letters you spoke of in your letter and done as you directed[.] let me know who all you get letters from and where you have got any one from Sary or not and where you have got any one from Kitty or not[.] tell me if Hogans got the letter from his gal that I sent him[.] ask Hogans how many days he sung that counted before he left[.] Crook Said he counted 4 days that Hogans Sung and if Hogans did not count & what time he sung[,] I wont pay them a cent[.] they have sung 3 Sundays and Says that the Sing is out[,] and if Hogans dont count I want to know it[.] I want you to Rite Soon[.] I was a going to Raleigh but I heard you was gone from there[.] I Should a went if I could a got a cariage before you left[.] Mr A. B. Muse had got a him a big boy[.] it came in to this world last Knight[.] my School is very good[.] I have taught 12 days and it has bin worth $14.30[.] I think it will pay[.] I have whiped a few of them for pugalism if you know what it is[.] as old dow says life is short there is hardly a nought pleasure in it to pay[.] I should like to see you a while and talk a while with you[.] tell Jack and Hogan the same[.] I want you to keep out of all mill[?] company and do what it rite[.] I will write no more at present [...] let me know where you are[.] I hope God shall see you again on their earth but if not[,] I trust you wee will meet in heaven[.] I remain your most affectionate brother until Death. C.D. Caddell. [P.S.] tell W.H.H. Davis that I have nothing of interest to write to him[.] I have not seen his guardian angel since I Recd his letter[.] tell him to write and I will rite to him as soon as I see his gal.

1861, September 4
Mary A. McIntosh (*Moore County, NC*) to **A.S. Caddell**. General local correspondence between niece and uncle with brief mentions of **Jim Horner** and **Jane Wallace's** wedding, **Benjamin Gilliam Hollingsworth**, **Martha McIntosh, Catherine "Kitty" McIntosh, Samuel Jackson McIntosh** and **Neill McIntosh**. [31]

Dear Sir. I take my pen in hand to drop you a few lines in answer to those from which I received from you last week[.] This leaves us all well at present[.] hopin that these few lines may reach you and family the same[.] I have a little news to write you but it is such a little[,] I almost shamed to put it in as I am very bashful[.] anyhow best I can shut my eyes and put it in[.] well here it goes[.] Mr Jim horner has got married to somebody up at Mr. Wallaces[.] I recon it is to Jane[.] the sing down at the road and was out last Sunday[,] but there is sing there next sunday to finish off[.] return my love and best respects to Mr B G Hollingsworth and Martha McIntosh says to return her love and best respects to him and Kitty never said nothing[.] you may tell Jack McIntosh I am much obliged to him for his letter that he promised to write to me[.] I have not got the first letter from none of them but that one you and Neill wrote to me and it was so long that it like to a took me all day to read[.] I would like to see you all getting dinner some time[.] I must hush my foolishness[.] So[,] nothing more at present[,] but you must excuse bad writing and spelling and all mistakes for I have had to write in a hurry for it is getting late[.] please write soon[.] you shall not lack for an answer[.] Mary A McIntosh

1861, September 8
A.S. Caddell (*Bogue Island, NC*) to brother **C.D. Caddell**. General wartime correspondence between brothers with anticipation of attack by northern armies and building breastworks in defense, mention of **Raleigh P. Allen**, Capt. **W.P. Martin** and **Martha Sullivan**. [32]

Dear Brother, I seat myself to drop you a few lines to let you know that there is considerable excitement in camp and has been ever since 12 yesterday[.] there is four Northern vessels lying in five miles of us[.] we are ingaged in throwing up breastworks[.] we expect an atact every hour from their vessels[.] we have our arms all in order[.] we have about thirty cannons on our shores[.] we lay an our arms last night[.] some of our company is panic struck[.] they are like RP Allen was before he professed religion[.] they think they are going rite strate to eternity[.] as for myself[,] I am ready for a fight[.] two poor fellows run away from the Regiment[.] I expect they have gawn to Moore Cty to join the Home gard[,] but there is no danger of any more of them leaving[.] we have every landing garded and special orders for no one to pass under pain of death[.] we are all in the hot sun[.] we had to take down our tents to keep the enemy from seeing our position[.] thou we ar not in any danger of any thing unless they throw their shells on us[.] we are in a position that we can whip three to one if they undertake to land[.] Fort Macon is in about 4 miles of us and they say that 2000 Yankees cannot whip them[.] we expect to be joined by another Regiment today from new bern[.] I wrote you a letter and I did not have the opportunity of poastin it[.] I will put it in this[.] answer this as soon as it comes to hand[.] give my best Resps to all my friends[.] it may be the last you will Recd from me though I hope not for I shal trust in God and keep my my powder dry[.] I would be glad to hear from Miss M.M.S[.] I have not heard from her since the 16th of Aug[.] I would be glad to Receive a few lines from her[.] direct your letters to Moorhead Citty care of Cap W.P. Martin[.] I will close by saying I will be happy to hear from you all[.] give my special respects to the home gards of Moore. Your affectionate Brother til Death. A.S. Caddell

1861, September 14
Noah Deaton (*Carolina City, NC*) to sister **Sarah Bethune Deaton**. General wartime correspondence with brief mentions of travels. [33]

I set my self down to drop you a few lines in answer to you very kind letter that came to hand since I came to this place[,] and I was much pleased to hear from you all and to hear that you were all well[.] my health is tolerable good at present and the company is in tolerable good health at this time[.] and I hope this may find you enjoying the same state of health[.] I have seen many strange things since I left home and may see many more before I return[,] but I hope the time till my return will be short[.] I have seen several towns and thing[.] I'll give the names of some of the towns Fayetteville, Elizabeth City & Wilmington on Cape fare River, Wilson, Goldsboro and on the Rhonoke River, Weldon & Garysburg, Raleigh & Kinston & Newbern on the Nuse River, Moorehed City &

Carolina City on Bogue sound[.] the state house in Raleigh is the finest house that I have seen[.] I went all through it and saw the musium and book library and went up at the top of it and took a look at the town[.] We are now on Bogue Island[.] the Island is about 45 miles long and about 50 yards from Atlantic Ocean[.] we are faned here continually by the sea breeze and we get very good water here to drink[.] we can see the ships every day sailing about on the ocean[.] there was three ships in sight to day and two of them got fireing cannons at each other but we could not find out what they meant[.] we have been alarmed twice since we came here by the near aproach of a war vessel[.] we were called to our arms the other night at 11 oclock and after we found there was but little danger[,] we all retired to our tents and lay the remainder of the night with our muskets in our arms[.] there is about 17000 men in camp here with us[.] We have an advantageous position and I hope the lord will protect and preserve us and deliver our enemies into our hands if they attact us[,] but I have hopes that we will not get into a fight soon if ever[.] if the yankees attempt to land [,] they will meet with a warm reseption[.] I must come to a close by saying may god save us in heaven for crist sake[,] Amen[.] Give my respects to all the neigbors, accept the best wishes of a friend. Write soon[.] Yours truly[,] Noah Deaton

1861, September 16
Wm. A. McIntosh (*Moore County, NC*) to uncle **Artemas S. Caddell**. General local correspondence between nephew and uncle with brief mentions of **Riley Muse**, **Martha McIntosh**, the birth of **Archibald Buckley Muse's** son **James C.B. Muse**, **Commodore G. Muse**, **Mark Cockman**, **Alexander Wallace**, **Sampson Delaney Wallace**, **Samuel Jackson McIntosh** and **Zacheus Hogan**. [34]

Dear uncle[,] it is with pleasure that I take the present opertunity of dropping you a few lines to let you no that I am well at present[,] hoping that when thease lines ma reach you that tha ma find you enjoying the same like blessing[.] I havent any thing to write only the gals is as pretty as they was before you left[.] you just ought to be her to see[.] Mr Riley muse is flying around with Martha McIntosh[.] he does gather ever Sunday night and I expect to be invited to the weding before long if nothing dont haphen me[.] and the gals is giting a long very well but I asked one the other day if She doesnt ***out*** *me to tote her umberelar[,] and she said that she could tote it her self and I guess I got away from there[.] I saw your gal the other day and I will tell you that She looked powerful pretty[.] I hadnt guessed none of them till they holerd calf rope yet but will be fore long if they dont mind[.] Archy B Muse has got a larg son...ther is a good many left hear since you did[.] CG Muse and Archy and Mark Cockman and Alexander and Lany Wallice and several moore[.] it isent worth while to name them[.] you must excuse me for mistake and bad writing if you please for it is the first letter that I ever undertuck to writ you[.] tell S.J.McIntosh to writ to me if you please[,] and also Hogans[.] So[,] I will close by saying write to me soon and give me all the nuse. Resp yours, Wm. A. McIntosh*

1861, September 19
Louis H. McLeod to wife **Eliza Jane Walker McLeod**. General wartime correspondence with brief mentions of **David P. Morris, Capt. William Swann** and **Francis Moore**. [35]

I have got safe home to our camp at Crabtree and have just got our tents put up and all hands [are] writing [letters] this evening. We havent drilled any yet. We had a jolly time coming here. we got to Fayetteville that eavening and went right on down the River. traveled all knight and got down to Willmington at one oclock the next day. we stayed there too ours and started for golesborough [Goldsboro]and got ther at ten oclock and was all marched up in a too story brick house and stade ther till four when we started for Raleigh and got there at nine the next mourning. we were marched to the Rock church and stade there one knight and started next mourning and marched three miles to our camp. ther came three companyes here to day we dont lack but too companys having enough to fill out the Rejiment. we wont stay here but about too weeks and then we will go to Fort Caswell. Eliza I havent nothing moore to write only my feet is so sore that I cant hardly walk. our company is all well but David P. he got a little foxy last knight and is sick to day. I stade at Pullin' last night and three or four others and they were all well but the youngest one was sick. I had to leave befour breakfast this mourning. Elize I had mighty bad luck in Willmington. I lost every sent of money I had but three Dollars and twenty five cents. I was with the Captain and Moore wher thay was getting there uniforms. I bought a little purs and put all the paper money I had in it and we started up to the cars to get on when I missed it not twenty five minutes [after I bought it. I went back but in vane. I could not her any thing of it. I have got too Dollars and eighty five cents is all the money I have in the world. some of my friends has promised to lend me as long as they have any. Eliza I am truly sorry to write you any such thing but it is so. Nothing moore at present. write to me as soon as you can and direct your letter to L. H. MacLeod, Cpt Swanns Company Raleigh

1861, September 22
Evander Caddell and **Barbara A. Caddell** (*Moore County, NC*) to cousin **A.S. Caddell**. General local correspondence between cousins with brief mentions of **Jenny Caddell, Nancy Caddell, Zacheus Hogan, William Caddell** and **William Whitlock**. [36]

Dear cosan[,] I seat myself down this mrning for the purpose of answering your letter Which I rec last sunday and to let you no how I am getting a long Dear cosan[.] We are well at this time hoping that When these few lines reaches you tha Will find you and your company being all Well. Dear cosan I have no more to rite to you mor these people are generally Well through this part of the country[.] Well Tim I would be glad to see you to talk with you about old times[.] I saw one of the prettyest girls riting one of the prettyest letters to you that I nearly ever saw but Whether you got the letter or not I can not tel...you red something about the prayer meetings[.] We have bin surrounded With prayer meetings and some five or six profest and When I go to meeting as I go up to the schoolhouse it seems like I ought to hear your voice[.] Well Tim if We are not permitted to se each other any more in this World[,] I hope We Will meat in a better World Where hurting Will be no more[.] tel Mr. hogans I Would love to se him and drink cider With him one nite more in our lives[.] tel him to rite to me and let me no how he likes to se the northern vessels standing round the sea[.] no more at present[.] Jinny and nancy misses you[.] must rite to them soon as you can[.] no more at present[.] rite soon. Evander Caddell

Dear cousin[,] I was glad to hear from you and to hear that you was well[.] it gav me great pleasure to read a letter from you but it would be more to see you than to hear from you Tim[.] I have no nuse to rite to you more than I ingoying very good health at the present time[,] hoping you are too[.] Mr Caddell family are all well Tim[.] we all heard that you was All taken prisoners which troubled me very mutch but then I heard it was not so and I am glad[.] give my best love and respects to Mr Hogans W. Whitlock[.] tell them both to rite us[.] Tim I tell you all had better make hast and make peace an come back if you dont the girls will all mary[.] tell Z. Hogans that his little girl is just as pretty as she was when She received his hart[.] So[,] no more at this time but write soon. B.A.C.

1861, September 22
Noah Deaton (*Carolina City, Bogue Island, NC*) to father **William Deaton**. General wartime correspondence between father and son. [37]

Dear Father[,] I take my seat this time to answer your kind and welcom letter that came to hand to day[.] it finds me in good health and the company are all in tolerable good[.] only one of our company is in the hospital and that with measels[.] there are a few that there health is not fully restord from the measels for them to drill but I think that if no other gets sick that it will not be long before they will all be able to do service[.] I trust that this may find you and all the rest of the family enjoying a reasonable portion of health. I have writen two letters before this home since I came to this place. I have recived three letters from home[,] two since I came here one last week the other today[.] I am glad to hear that you had a tolerable good crop this season. the commissary gives us a plenty of flour and some corn meal plenty of bacon & coffee & sugar[.] we can get a plenty of fish when we want them just as they are caught out of sea[.] As I have before wrote[,] we are stationed on Bogue Island between Bogue sound and the Atlantic Ocean[.] this Island is about 500 yds wide here[.] our camp is about 200 yds from the ocean where we can see the ships every day[.] this part of the island is without a single tree upon it nothing but grass is growing on it[.] the island is composed of shells and sand[.] we have our wood to toat about ¼ of a mile from the thickest place of bushes I ever saw[.] it is impossible to go through but few places without cutting your way out[.] there are several kinds of growth[.] there but only very little of it any but cedar that is large nough for fire wood and a small dwarfish kind of oak to look at the woods[.] it looks like a mat of cedar boughs and apears to be a little higher than ones head[,] and nothing only cedar can be seen at a distance only the surrounding rushes in the marshes[.] there are two ships in view this evening[.] we have been expecting a battle ever since we came here and it may be that we will have a fight before we leave here[.] there is between 1700 & 2000 men here and I think if we will trust in God and keep our powder dry that we nead not fear the yankees[.] there is some of us meets together almost every day to ask the favours and mercies of our maker wile others will not show respect enough towards God to go ten steps hear preaching[.] I just took up pen to finish my letter after hearing good sermon which was from the words because God does not execute judement spedily for sin[.] the heart of man is prone to do evil[.] May God hear our petitions and grant us such thing as he seeith[.] we need pardn our many sins and give praying hearts that we may die dily unto sin and live unto righteousness and when he has finished his portion the he hath aloted to us here[,] may he save us in Heaven where we will praise him more perfect in a world without end Amen[.] I must come to a close, Yours truely Noah Deaton

1861, September 23
Mastin C. Phillips (*Trinity College*) to sister **Emeline Phillips.** General wartime correspondence with brief mentions of father **Rev. Lewis Phillips Jr., Malphus S. Phillips, Celia Gilbert Phillips, Nancy Edwards Phillips** and **Mary "Polly" Phillips.** [38]

Dear Emeline, Your kind letter came to hand a few days ago. I was truly glad to hear from you. I had begun to think that I was forgotten by you all when your letter came informing me that one at least still remembered me. I cannot understand why it is that the boys will not write to me. It is no trouble to get a letter to me now and I will not receive the excuse that they do not have time to write. You tell them I will not send them another line until I hear from them and tell Pa I would like to hear from him also. Tell him to send me some money if he can do so as I am writing some just now a little of the worst. Tell him (ie. Pa) to send me, (well, I do not know how much it will take). I want enough to get my wedding suit, license and some other little fixings that I shall need, if the old lady concludes to come home this winter. And I shall need, if the old lady concludes to come home this winter. And I rather think she will, for I think she is about to conclude that a piece of a man is better than no man at all these hard times. This is not all foolishness. I was glad to learn that your health was improving. I hope all are well at Pa's. I was glad to hear that they are going ahead with their work. What is the reason that Malphus is not building? Tell him for me to go to building and keep at it until he gets a wall covered[,] and them take Celia and go into it and work like the notion. These are extraordinary times and it is essential that extraordinary work shall be done. Tell him if he wants any more of my advice to write and let me know it[,] and I will give him a full supply. I am studying about all that I can these times. Think I am learning some. We have about 55 boys now. Will not have many more I reckon. The drilling goes on with a vim. We will all be soldiers if we stay here long enough. There are about fifteen hundred soldiers at High Point at this time. I guess a regiment will leave there soon for the war. I don't believe that I have any news go give you tonight. I will close for the present. Write soon. Give me all the news. Tell Ma that I am not going to the war until after Christmas and that I expect to see her before I go. Tell Pa that I have been with the lady three times since I left home and expect to go again soon. Give my love to Aunt Polly and tell her that I expect to want her house after Christmas[,] and that she had better to be ready to move. I can't come to the meeting the second Sunday in October, though I would like to do so. Give my love to all my friends and tell them to write to me. Good night. Write soon. My love to all. Your brother, (In haste) M.C. Phillips

1861, September 25
Julia A. Caddell to cousin **A.S. Caddell**. General local correspondence between cousins with brief mentions of the marriage of **Thomas P. Maness** and **Eliza Stuart**, church at Bethlehem and Flint Hill, **Barrett**, **Noah Muse**, **Riley Muse** and **Martha McIntosh.** [39]

Dear cousin, I tak my pen this evening to let you know that I had not forgotten you yet[,] but I suspect you think I have by my not writing to you but I never received your letter till last Sunday[.] I was glad to here from you for I would give any thing in the world to see you and spend a day or too with you for I have not seen a bit of fun since you all lef here[.] their isent any Boys here that is worth a notice but since you all left[.] they think that they is all hifluten stock[.] there has Been too or three married since you left[.] Tom maner to Miss Eliza Stuard was married las thursday night[.] if you could see him[,] you would think that she had a pill. Cousin Tim[,] he is not a comparison to the Clarks offis and you may know that he is hansom[.] Tim, R Muse is pitching around Miss Martha Mcintosh & expect the will get married[.] I do wish that you was here to see the Catham puks a flying around the girls[.] But if they was all of my nocion they would not succeed[.] Tim[,] I saw your julark last Sunday[.] she was well but Mary sends her best respects to you and ses for you to not get up a conspute with nun of your friends[.] you will know what that means[.] it is some thing that you and her was talking a bout the nigh you sat at our house[.] Tim[,] he preach at flint hill last sunday night and all of murdering grammar that you ever herd in you life[.] he beat all Tim[.] we are goin to have a protracted meeting at friendship and I expect he and Brother Barrett will be ther[.] I do wish that you and some more of my friends was her to go[.] if you was we would see fun[.] Tim[,] if you was here we would fly around like five hundred[.] Tim[,] their is another thing I must tell you[.] Noh Muse run for Captain at ritters and got beat[.] he only got six votes and I was glad of it for they wont volunteer and go to the war[.] I heard today that he sed he had too much invested to go to the war[.] Tim[,] you know that he's like we ar, he is a big bug but I think if he dont mind he will get his wings cropt[.] Tim[,] I expect you will think that I composed my letter about Muses[,] but[,] Tim[,] if you could see them since you all left you would not blame me to write about them[.] I must Bring my letter to a Close for I know when you read it you will think of the fun that we have seen together[.] give my best respects to all of my friends and relatives and tell them that I have not forgotten them[.] cousin Tim[,] Please dont show this letter to any person for it is badly written[.] write to me as soon as you get this and give me all the nuse[.] I remain your true Cousin un till death[.] write soon and fail not[.] good Bye Tim. Julia A Caddell

1861, September 27
Jesse Muse (*Moore County, NC*) to **A.S. Caddell**. General local correspondence with brief mentions of son **Commodore Muse**, Capt. **J.L. Bryant**, Capt. **W.P. Martin**, school at Pleasant Hill, death of **Leonard Lawhorn's** son **Lemuel Lawhorn** and burial at Bethlehem, **Harrison Davis**, **Zacheus Hogan**, **Neill McIntosh**, **Jack McIntosh**, **William L. Wallace**, **Daniel McIntosh**, **William Caddell**, **Raney Caddell**, **John Jackson** and the marriages of **James W. Horner** and **Lovedy J. Wallace**, **Thomas P. Maness** to **Eliza Stewart**. [40]

Dear Brother[,] I take the opportunity of writing you a few lines to in form you that I am well at present and my family for which blessings I thank God[.] hoping when these few lines reaches you that they will find you all well[.] I received a letter from you a few days ago which gave me great satisfaction to hear that you was well[.] I was in hope that you would come home when you was at Raleigh so I cood see you and hear you tell your travels[.] I have nothing strange to write at this present time[.] I can inform you that my son Commodore has joined Captains Bryants company and is now at the kitrel springs in granville county[.] you dont know how heart rending it is to me[.] he left the 10 Day september 1861[.] it was a serious time you may depend it seems like to me that cant git over it quick but we was born to see trouble[.] we get the news that captain martin and his company was taken prisoners & when that news reached the fathers and mothers such a time you hardly seen[.] thougth we soon heard it was not so and you may depend there was Joy a most unspeclbe[.] as for my part[,] my feelings I could not express[.] I want you write as often as you can if you please for if I know my own heart[.] I wish you well and I wish you may have the pleasure of treading your own native soil and that we may meet at pleasant hill school house where we have spent many happy hours[,] but if we never meet in this world lets try to meet where parting is no more[.] I can inform you that Leonard Lawhons son Lemuel was brought home from kitrell springs a corpse on the 24th day of this instant[,] and was buried at Bethlehem church[.] he died with the typhoid fever[.] that was a solem thing you may depend but that the way we all have to go for death is a break in the land[.] tell H Davis that I shant forget him and Hogans to remember his promis[.] Neil McIntosh and Jack McIntosh, William L Wallace and all inquiring friends the neighberhood is all well as fare as I know at this time[.] A. S. Caddell[,] your old father and mother is well and all the rest of the family[.] A big day at Daniel Mcintoshs when your father heard that you were all taken prisoners[,] he told me he did not know how he felt at a fathers love to his child[.] you must excuse me for I cant write half as much as I want to so farewell my brother in the love till we meet again. Jesse Muse [P.S.] I can inform you that people is still in the notion of marring James W Horner to Miss Lovedy J Wallice, Thomas Manas to a Miss Stewart and some of them wating for you no doubt[.] I want you to write me a full letter of all your travels[.] you dont know half how much I want to see you and all of my frends and acquaintances[.] tell cousin John Jackson to write to me[.] I am glad when I hear that you all are getting along well[.] So[,] nothing more at present[,] But remaining your frend untill death. Jesse Muse

1861, September 27
Ashley.F. Muse (*Moore County, NC*) to **A.S. Caddell**. General local correspondence with brief mentions of **Commodore G. Muse**, Capt. **J.L. Bryant** and school in Chatham County. [41]

dear sir[,] I take the pleasure of writing you a few lines to let you no that I am well at present[.] hoping when these few lines comes to hand that this will find you in good health and in fine spirit and all my fellow asociates all in good hart. I have nothing of mutch importance to relate to you – people up this way is in as good helth as could be expected[.] there has bin a few wedings up here since you left but I gess you have herd of them[.] I would like to see you and spend awhile in talking about our scrimages and tiet places which with difficulty we have come threw[.] but as we are destitute of this privilege of talking face to face and perhaps may ever be on earth. Should it be so that we should never meet on earth[,] I hope that we will meet where parting is no moore, and where there is no war nor rhumors of war, where we will be saved from all fears and doubts in that eternal City, where it need no light of the sun nor of the moon nor stars, but where Christ is the light thereof. I have quit going to school in Chatham and are at home now working about the farm with the old man Pete[.] they keep volunteering[.] some has gone[.] C. G. Muse is gone with Capt J.L. Briant but I hope you will all come out victorious. It bin many a pleasure hour we have spent together but I fear that we will never spend many moore together here in this earthly tabernacle[.] if not[,] be a good boy A.S.C.[.] for those hours we have spent together I will never forget[.] in the remembrance of our past Joys and the doubtfulness of meeting again[,] I will utter prayer in yore behalf to our protecting god. may god be with you in all time of trouble and bless you in all time of need and give you Strength that you may walk and not get wary run and not faint. and that he may be with you in time of danger & in the time of battle and protect you with his protecting power and shield you from the hurt of your enemy[,] and stand by you in the hour of death that he may save your soul from the power of the wrath to come with an everlasting salvation threw Christ our redeemer[,] amen[.] A.F. Muse

1861, September 28

Noah F. Muse (*Moore County, NC*) to **A.S. Caddell**. General local correspondence with brief mentions of **Kelly Williamson, S.W. Seawell, S. Barrett, Bethuel Coffin** and **William Caddell**. [42]

Old friend[,] I once more take the time to write you a few lines to let you know matters & things is in your old neighberhood[.] people is all well, they are all well at your fathers[.] I said at your father Last Sunday night you ought to see me & Dr Aaron fly around among the girls[.] we make them stand about they want us to marry[.] Oh! the worst[.] Tim I heard that you & all was taken prisoners[.] that was one of the times I asked around some to find out[.] you cant tell how I felt for I cant myself. Well Tim people dont get any better here yet[.] we had a muster Wednesday[.] Oh! such fighting. Just ask K. Williamson[.] Something about it he will tell you some[.] Tim I saw your gall not long since[.] well she looked charming there[.] people is making up volunteers companies well rite smart S.W. Sowell is S--- & dabled in it[.] he cant make up a Company no more than dry rain in my way of thinking[.] S Barrett & B Coffin is making up a Company[.] it is likely Coffin will do to make up a Company. Tim[,] you cant tell half how bad I want to see you[.] there is something singlar Tim that you never write to me[.] I hear from you very often through somebody else[.] I wrote a short letter when you was at Raleigh but never got one in return[.] Ill try you again if you feel disposed to write, write[.] if not just let it alone is my remarks[.] N.F. Muse

1861, September 28

Louis H. McLeod to wife **Eliza Jane Walker McLeod**. General wartime correspondence with brief mentions of **John** ?, **Catherine** ?, **Elizabeth Hinton Brewer McLeod, Anne Elizabeth McLeod, Nancy Ann McLeod, Thomas Bragg McLeod**, and **Emily Franklin.** [43]

My Dear Wife I receaved your letter this mourning and was moor than glad to hear from you and all the children. Eliza I never was so glad to here from you in my life. John, Cat, and Mother came to our camp this mourning and I was you know moore than glad to see them. Eliza I was glad to here from you. But above all things I drouther see you and the children. Eliza I send some little books to the children, and some candy. Eliza take the candy and gave some to Liss and divide the balance. Eliza I havent much time to write to you. We have orders to leave by times in the mourning and I have the worst chance you ever saw to write and you must excuse me. Eliza remember me. Eliza we are agoing to leave this place soon in the mourning and agoing down the same way we came to Willmington and down the River to the coast. where I am in hopes I can here from you every week. Eliza write to me and I will bee glader than you ever saw mee. Just if you could see this boy. you never saw such a feller in your life. I have got on a knew soot of close and feel big. A new cap too. My feet is got well, I have been to town to day and eat diner with Nancy and Mother. the best diner you ever saw. Eliza I havent nothing worth writing. If I could see you I could tell you a grate many things. Some, Eliza you never heard tele of before. Eliza I want to see you varry bad and kiss perticuley.Tell Bragg to bee a good boy I will send you and him some nice shills when I get down in the sea coast. If the yankees dont kill me. God bee with you all and Remember me. Eliza, we are all packing up and getting ready to leave. The Captain ses we cant stop in Raleigh at all. We are gone. Elize good bie.

A few lines to Emely. I was glad to here from you but Emely I am sorry to let you know how unwell I am at this time. Emely I have too of the worst biles you ever saw. One of them is right on one side of my ass and the other is just between my cod and ass hole in the worst place in the world. I hardly can sit on the stool to write you a few lines. Emely bee a good girl and write to me as soon as you and Eliza gets another from me and kno where I will bee. Eliza I never will forget you. and I want you to remember you have a husband in the War. Eliza I dont expect to see you any moore for twelve month. Eliza do every thing you think best and remember me. Elize I have the worst chance you ever saw to write. you must excuse me for bad writing and spelling. Eliza a fare well. our time is out the drum has roald and we have to put oud the light. Louis H. McLeod

1861, October 2
C.D. Caddell (*Pleasant Hill School, Moore County, NC)* to brother **A.S. Caddell**. General local correspondence with brief mentions of **Kelly Williamson**, **Martha McIntosh**, **William R. Muse**, **Mary Ann McIntosh**, **Malcom Morrison**, **S. McIntosh**, **Sarah Frances McIntosh**, **Sarah McIntosh**, **Liz McIntosh**, **Julia A. Caddell**, **Martha M. Sullivan**, **Neill Caddell**, **Zacheus Hogan**, **Ed Love**, **Presley Caddell**, **John Sowell**, **Daniel Caddell**, **John Caddell**, **W.H.H. Davis** and **Caroline Dowdy**. [44]

Dear Brother[,] I again seat myself to inform you that I am well at present[,] hoping these pen lines may find you well[.] Recd your letter this day which gave me mutch satisfaction to hear you was well. I have sent you a blanket and a pair of socks by Cel Williamson and I will send you a pair of Shoes as soon as I can also your fiddle shep skins[.] you said something about the[.] you wanted to know something about the Miss McIntoshes[.] Well Martha has got a beau W.R. Muse but I dont think She likes him any at all[.] Miss Mary Ann is a going to get married to Mr. Macom Morrison[.] I squired Miss S.F. once and awhile[.] Miss S and Liz is the same and has got no beaus[.] If you rite to Julia A. Caddell[,] [s]end them to me and don't put anything in it but what she can show[,] for She wants to show them to the old...She said for you to answer it when you rite to me[.] tell me if you have quit riting to Miss M.M.S.[.] I tell you that you can not rite to one who loves you better[.] I can hear tell of her saing She loves you and dont cear who knows it[.] I would rite to her evry week or break a trace[.] She is the smartest gal I ever saw[.] I don't care whos gal she might bee[.] tell Hogans to write to me[.] I have got Ed love hired to plow[.] I give him 25 cts per day[.] I have got 8 bushels of oats sowed[.] I have teached School 20 days and it has bin worth $21.50[.] They are all good that I counted[.] if there comes a draft[,] I shal come to that company but I will rite to you again first[.] I shal stay at home as long as I can but I should like to be there with you all. Uncle Neill Said to tell you to write to him and that you must excuse him for not riting to you[.] he said he could not rite any[,] he was so nervous[.] I see a right smart of fun & fly around all particular of A.J.B. but dont you tell anybody[.] I can shine among the best of them[.] write to me and tell me if you want Davids [David was a horse] tripes taken or not[.] I went a coon hunting with Presley and caught one of the largest coons you ever saw[.] I went a possum hunting last night and me and John Sowell, Daniel Caddell and John Caddell. We caught a possum[.] Scot has caught two coons this fall[.] I will come down some night and bring my dog for I expect there is possums in them woods[.] Give W.H.H. Davis his letter that is in yours[.] I have got two letter from Caroline Dowdy since commencing school[.] I will send one of them to you next time I write[.] Write soon as this gets to home[.] I remain your most affectionate brother until death. C.D. Caddell.

1861, October 2
Louis H. McLeod to wife **Eliza Jane Walker McLeod**. General wartime correspondence. [45]

Dear wife. I take this opertunity this day to informe you that I am at this time well and heartyexcept thim biles that I wrote to you [about] when I was at Raleigh. I sufered very much with them. I could not sit down nor stand up nor lie down for too or three days, but they have broke and has got better. I can sit down with a little uneasiness. Eliza. We left Raleigh on saturday eavening and traveled all knight. We got to Willmington on sunday mourning one hour [err ? son] . We rode in a boxe car wher ther had been horse [hauled?] hall and smelt verry bad and every place was seraushed to the hanur (Hames?). We was put through as quik as possible. We never stopt to get any thing to eat at all untill we got to Willmington. and when we got there it was on sunday and there was so many that there wont enough of vituals in Willmington for us. We all was discharged to get our breakfast and pay our own bill. Then we went back into camps. all went in the depot and put out gards to ceep our men in and stade there until eavening and all went then in the warehouse and stade there until mourning.

and then we all marched one mile from and stuck up our tents. and last knight there came another rejiment eleven hundren and fifty men and pitched there tents joinings ours. and I wish you could see the tents and men. there is some twenty five hundred on one field, and there is soldiers trane long every trane one way or other. No moore about the war only we dont no when we will leave here. the Conel was elected would not except and they have to elect another. When we leave here we will go down some eighteen miles from here right on the sound where we can gett aplenty of fish and oysters. Our rejiment is all willing to go and agetting ancious to meet the yankees. If we can get our guns. we have no guns nor the rejiment that came last knight. and since we cant get guns soon. we dont no when we can leave her. some says we will stay here some three or four weeks but no boddy knows. We may have to go in a weeke and we may not have to go at all. Some says the fighting is all done. We have plenty to eat. plenty of baken and flowir and corn bread and shughar and coffee and beef. There is measles and hooping cough. the cough is the worst I ever saw. I was on gard last knight. and I never herd as much coughing in my life I never slep any at all and you must excuse me for bad writing and I have a mighty bad chance. the tent is full and I have to write on my napsack. Eliza remember me and tell the children howdy for me. I would bee glad to see you and them. Louis H. MacLeod. Eliza. write as soon as you get this and let me no how you are a getting along. I am ancious to here from you and the children. Direct your letters to Wilmington in care of Captain Swann. Your affectionate husband until kill by the yankees. Louis H. McLeod

1861, October 5

Louis H. McLeod to wife **Eliza Jane Walker McLeod**. General wartime correspondence with brief mentions of **Francis Moore**, **Captain Moore, Archibald McIntosh, Thomas Bragg McLeod, Anjalett McLeod, Emily Franklin** and **Abner Flynn Harrington**. [46]

Dear Wife, I take another opertunity of droping you a few lines to let you know that I am gone again. We are going to leave here to morrough sunday as it will be for Smithville. both Regiments is going down the river to gether. we are washing up and fixing to start in the mourning There is no Sunday with us nor has been since I left home Sunday is just like any other day with us. We are agoing to get our guns this eavening we have got all the rest of our things. Some of our Captains is grumbling like any thing. [They] Says they dont get enough to eat. but we cant. so we have plenty to eat so far of every thing but molasses. and we havent had any since we have been here. only what I eat with Lieutenant Moore to day at dinner. Eliza I am well and hearty as ever I was in my life. them biles has got in about well. I have suffered very much with thim. but I am up in the land of the living again thank god. Eliza we are agoing right amongst the yankees. and all of our men is ancius for that time to come when we can have the chance of handling them as we think best. and I think that we have enough of men on this field to whip all the yankees that can come to our land if they will weight untill we can get down there and get our fixing put in order. I expect we will have lots of heard wirk to do when we get down on the sound. we will be stationed right down on the sound where we can get plenty of fish and oysters and sea brease. we will get there time enough to go in the sirf bathing. I have been in bathing to day in the tide water. the nicest place I ever saw Captain Moore with his artillery. came over last eavening to our camp and shot a few rounds of canons which farely shuck the ground. I never saw any thing like it. [they] went through all ther maneuvirs with six pieces of canon with some eighty horses to carry all the wagons that was requird. They would go just as hard as they could run. I thought they would tear every thing to pieces. I saw such a tangted up mess in my life [but] every thing was done to the hammer. [they] never run over no one nor tuched one or others wagons. It was done splended. Eliza. I receaved your letter yesterday mourning by Archibald McIntosh. and I was very glad to hear from you and the children and moore so to here that you was all well and the children was glad to receave there boks and that Bragg had locked up his knife to save it untill I came home. tell him to take it out and whittle with it but not loose it untill I come home and I will bring him a new one. Tell Siss I was glad to here that she was glad to get the candy and called it war candy. Tell her that I will come back about Christmass. if the yankees dont kill me. and I will bring her some moore candy. and I will bring her some pretty nice little shells from the Sea. I will send some home before I go if i can get the opertunity. Eliza. this is one of the hotest days that I have felt in a long time It is so hot here to day and yesterday that we cant drill any at all only in the eavening. We have not drilled any at all to day yet nor wont, only we will bee mustered into the Confederet serviss this eavening and get our guns. and then we will be ready to leave in the mourning. no moore about the war only about the sick. there is none of our company sick yet except bad colds. some of them is very bad off with colds. There is some forty or fifty in the horsspittle at this time. Eliza. I dont know where to tell you to send your letters. send me one or too when Flin comes back and tell him that we will be gone down to Smithville. I will write to you as soon as I get down ther and let you now whire to send your letters. I was glad to here that you was going to the camp meeting and stay untill Monday. Eliza. I will be glad to hear from you everry week. I would like to bee with you awhile but my chance is mighty bad to ever come to see you I dont expect the Captain will let me off untill the years is out. he wont let me go to Willmington now only when I can slip off the [illegible] (there) make a long mark you will understand it. Tell Emely that them biles broke them selves. and I didnt have to pick them at all. We have lots of ladies to see us every eavening. we are at the Place called Hardscrabble [one] mile from town right [Wilmington] on the rail road. no moore at this time. only your loving husband untill dath. may god bless and bee with you at the camp meeting and at last save you in heaven is the praris [prayers] of your beloved husband until dath. whether I ever see you or not. Louis H. McLeod

1861, October 6

Jane McIntosh (*Carthage, NC*) to uncle **A.S. Caddell.** General local correspondence between niece and uncle with brief mentions of church at Bethlehem, wedding of **Mary Ann McIntosh** and **Malcom Morrison**, **Martha McIntosh**, **Wm. R. Muse**, **Wm. A. Barrett**, Miss **Sarah Frances McIntosh**, **Artimus McIntosh**, **Neill McIntosh**, and **Betty McIntosh**. [47]

Dear uncle[,] it is with pleasure that I take my pen in hand to write you a few lines to inform you that I am well at this time[,] and hope when this may come to hand that they may find you well and hearty[.] the people is comonly well hear[.] I received your letter day before yesterday whitch gave me mutch pleasure to hear from you and that you was well and doing well[.] I have not got nothng new to write, only Miss Mary Ann McIntosh is married to Mr. Malcom Morrison[.] they was married last thursday night the 3 instant[.] I do not know of any other wedding to be shortly[.] you told me to tell Miss Martha not to get married to Mr. Wm. R. Muse untill Christmas and you would attend[,] but I dont think that there is mutch danger[.] I do not know whether she has turned him off or not[,] but I think he has near quit goin[.] whatever is the matter I dont know[.] without Mr Wm. A. Barrett has cut him out[.] Miss S. F McIntosh is not married yet[.] she was hear this morning and she is as bad as ever[.] I dont expect you have forgot the sugar shilling yet[.] well Tim I was just thinking about taking my knitting and staying with you a week[,] but there is sutch big spiders there that I am afraid that they would kill me before I could get to see you and sutch long snakes that they would swallow me[.] I would like to see you[.] you dont know half how glad I would be to see you and talk with you awhile[.] I could tell you a heap more than I can write[.] you said that you wanted me to tell you how Tim and Neil and Betty was coming on[.] they are all well and has been well ever since you left[,] only Betty was sick last week[.] I tell you that Tim is uneasy about you[.] he wants me to no nearly every day when you are a coming home[.] you wanted to know how I liked your ugliness[.] I tell you Tim I think you are getting fat and I liked it very well[.] you wanted me to tell you who I seen kiss it and you would claim one from them but I dont think you would[.] she lives on the way to Bethlehem church[.] you know that there is but one house this side of ritchland creek where there is two gals and it was one of them I wrote to you the 22nd of September[.] I want you to write soon and let me know if you got it and you must forgive me for writing you sutch a letter[.] so[,] I must close my few remarks by saying write to me soon and give me the news and I will do the same[.] excuse all mistakes and bad writing[.] yours truly from Jane McIntosh

1861, October 6

Noah F. Muse to **A.S. Caddell.** General correspondence between friends with brief mentions of **William Caddell, A.W. Maness, Commodore Muse, Riley Muse, Ashley F. Muse, Jesse Muse, C.D. Caddell, T.W. Ritter, W.H.H. Davis, Mary Ann McIntosh's** marriage to **Malcolm Morrison, Jesse Bean** Esq. and the **Muse** girls. [48]

Old Friend. I take my pen in hand to drop you a few lines I am well and all is well and all the neighbors is well[.] Tim[,] I have nothing to write that will amuse you[.] times is hard up here in Moore County[.] such times I never experienced in my born days[.] people is hardly like they use they was[.] Tim[,] I have wished 100 times I had a went with you[.] I know if you enjoy yourself any[,] you see as much or more pleasure than people does up her[.] people is stirred up so bomable and they are just a getting mixed well, Tim[.] J.S – R[,] well there is no use swearing now but I don't know what to do. I don't know whether to volunteer or to try to make a farm the ensuing year[.] I think I know which would do the best for our future welfare would be to go and fight the Yankees[.] I have rented out my Stutts place to A.W. Maness again[.] I've only got the high place to work an Jane thought I would tend a part of that and put me up a still[,] but times is so troublesome[.] I am a feard to go into anything that takes money[.] Tim[,] I would be more than glad to see you[.] I could tell you some monstrous ups & downs certain[.] I staid at your fathers house last night[.] me and Dr Aaron talked over old times[.] they are well. Cptn. Scott[,] he be bad off to go a opossom hunting[.] well AS I got a letter on she from you[.] I was so glad to here from you[.] I get to standing on the past until sometimes I am a good notion to start for you[.] I would like to be with you ASC very well if I could fix my arrangements to my notion[.] Tim[,] I cant fix my mules of anywhere as I would like without giving them away[.] Rileys got more than he wants to help so has Pa[.] Commodore is gone[.] Ashley is going to school though I think we will have to go to fighting somewhere from what I can here of the war news[.] Tim[,] if is true I dont much want to leave Rite off now but I expect I will have to go soon somewhere[.] me and C.D. Caddell was talkin that if we had to go and wanted to go in your company[,] if there was any chance to get in[.] AS I want you to write me about the chance if we do have to go[.] Tim, I want you to write them if the malitia is called out[.] Mr. T.W. Ritter is Captain in Dist. No. 9 now[.] I had just as leave go with somebody – AS[,] dont neglect writing all about what the chance will be for if time gets much worse[.] I tell you we will be off shure[.] well Tim[,] now for the galls they all want to marry in the worst[.] they will take any body in the shape of a man[.] they are marrying rite peart now[.] Miss Mary Ann McIntosh took a man Thursday night[,] one Malcom Morrison[.] Muses girls is all new & looks as pretty as ever[.] I charge among them a few shure. AS[,] I want to know whats become of WHH[.] Ive wrote 3 or 4 times & don't heare nothing of him[.] if he is there[,] ask him if he remembers that big suck in Esq Bean's lane[.] Id bet if he ant too sick[,] he Laughs[.] tell him I saw his bird & talked with her some[.] well[,]JSR[,] I cant go about that old meating house without I feel like I am lost and a heap other ways & feel all damp about the eyes. write soon[.] be shure to write as soon as this gets to hand[.] write a long letter[.] I will write you a letter so long as you can remember[.] Your most truly[.] Noah F. Muse

1861, October 7

Noah Deaton (*Carolina City, NC*) to Miss **Christian Ray**. General wartime correspondence with brief mentions of local surroundings, warships, **Neill Ray** and Gen. **Hill**. [49]

Dear friend. I resume my seat this morning to answer your very kind and most welcome letter that came to hand last Friday[,] and was much pleased to hear from you and all the rest. Neill is well and I think well satisfied. My health is very good at present and the company in tolerable good health[.] there only two in the hospital now. We are surrounded by water on all sides two miles to the nearest point of main land. But from what I can learn we will not be apt to stay here long[.] where we may go I have no idea. We are under the command of Gen. Hill and he don't let it be known weeks early what he intends to do. We are hemed up here in this place so that if the enemy comes we will have to fight[.] be taken on take water the general has ordered as I hear for lumber to make a gang way across the sound[.] and I guess that we will be moved across the sound shortly if not sent to some other place. I hear some of the private saying this morning that will get orders today to cook three days rations[.] and[,] if so[,] we will be sent to some other point[,] but I doubt the truth as it very much for the hundred tongued deceivers is a doing such an active business now a days[,] that truth so rarely tells her tale that we cannot believe it when we hear it with out proof that it is so. I hear various reports about the war movements[,] but nothing late that is reliable or interesting. There was three war ships in sight of us yesterday and one of them was near enough for us to see them drilling on their deck but they are gone today[.] and if they know what is the best for themselves[,] they will stay away from here or at least keep out of reach of us. You cannot think how much pleasure it would give me could I get back to Moore County again there to remain in peace where I could enjoy the company of friends as before I left there[.] and see the ladies smile and hear their voices which seem so charming. There are is a great many young fellows that have no cares to keep them from going out in defense of their country[,] but are such cowards that they would suffer subjugation rather than fight[,] and I trust the ladies will not countenance such fellows. I hope therefore remark will be no offense but if it does? any one let them take best remedy to get rid of it. That's to take up arms to defend their homes and not wait for others to do what they should do. I must close. Please write to me soon as you can. I remain your affectionate friend. Noah Deaton

1861, October 8

Louis H. McLeod to wife **Eliza Jane Walker McLeod**. General wartime correspondence with brief mentions of **Tandy Walker, Emily Franklin, Catty ?, Archibald McIntosh, Francis Moore** and **Abner Flynn Harrington**. [50]

Dear Wife, I sat down last Saturday and wrote you to you [sic] dated October 5 and I could not put it in the office untill I found out that I would not leave on Sunday so I stopt the letter untill know, and I thought I would write a few lines to let you no that I am yet at Wilmington and to be surtain whin we would leave[.] It is said that we will leave here to morrough. There is four of our companys agoing to day down the River thirty five miles to a place called Smithville we have got to be Sworne into the Confedret Service to day and to morrough we will leave here, Tan is setting here smoking the long stem pipe and told me to say to you that he is most dead[.] he went to town last knight and ses to Emely and Catty to come over some eavening and stay untill after supper and if they chuse stay all knight[.] Tell all the galls that is enquiring about me that I am as well and harty as ever and that I would be verry glad to see them all. Eliza I receaved your letter by Mr McIntosh and was moore than glad to here from you[.] I was glad to here that you and all the rest of the family was going to the campmeeting[.] I hope you had a good time. I want to here from there verry bad. I want you to write to me all about the campmeeting. Eliza I though[t] of you moore last Saturday Knight and Sunday than I have since I left home. I knew you was at the meeting and I knew you would think of me. Eliza I thought of the prayers you was rendering for me. Eliza I never will forget the prayers you have put up for me and I no [know] you divent forg[it] me alltho I was so far from you. I hope the Lord will spare both of us and all the children to live untill we can meet again. You needent [needn't] look for me untill you see me and I wont no Eliza when that time will evar come not untill the twelve months is out. Eliza dont think long of the time. I will come some time if the Lord is willing. Eliza I went over home with Frances Moore on sunday mourning and we stade untill Monday eavening and then returned to the camp. I enjoyed myself firstrate Frances is one of the best fellers in the world he is the best officer we have got. Eliza I am afraid I will worry your patience reeding. I was sorry to here of your headake. write by Flin and tell him to come on to Smithville. my paper is scarse and money is all most gone so write as every chance you can good bie Eliza and children. L. H. McLeod

1861, October 12
C.D. Caddell to brother **A.S. Caddell** (*Bogue Island, NC – in care of Mr. **Davis***). General local correspondence with brief mentions of **Julia A. Caddell**, horses David and Lucy and the meeting at Dover Church. [51]

Mr. AS Caddell[,] I seat myself to write you a few lines to let you know I am well[.] hoping these few lines may find you well[.] I have not got the first letter from you in two weeks[.] I want you to write to me if you hant forgotten me[.] tell me about the war and ever thing els[.] you had art to write to your gal[.] I will give her as many letters as you will send or anything els you want to[.] I will send you anything I can[.] I will send you a pare of Shoes as soon as I can[.] I hant got no letter[.] Rite to me and let me know have got what I Sent you[.] tell me about J.A. Caddells letter and what she Rote to you[.] I have got 11 bush of oats sowd if any thing should happen[.] I ride David or Lucy[.] I wount be surprised to see the gals[.] David aces rite a long. I am a going to the Sociation at Dover[.] My Schollars all sends you the best Respects[.] rite soon, your most affectionate Brother till Death[,] C.D. Caddell. Remember creator in the days of thy youth, While the will day come not[.]

1861, October 13
Neill A. Ray (*Carolina City, NC*) to cousin **Christian Ray**. General wartime correspondence between cousins with brief mentions of Fort Macon, Shackelford Banks and **Hugh Ray**. [52]

Cousin Christian, I take this operrtunity to drop you few lines to inform you that I am well and hope this will find you and all the rist likewise[.] the company is in very good health[.] there is only two cases in the Hospital from our company[.] We are going to move tomorrow about two miles nearer to Ft. Macon where we will be in 1½ mile of the Ft. and it will be in beautiful cedar grove – where if we stay[.] it will be a good place for winter quarters[.] One of our company will go to Shackleford which is about two miles north of fort macon[.] there was forty traitors taken the other day at Shackleford who were passing as fishermen and are secured in the fort to await their destiny[,] which I think will be death for they have in their posession weapons and hand cuffs that was given them by the yankees[.] they hav also been selling fish to the enemy[.] the enemy is lurking about here every day[.] there was four vessels in some four or five miles of us on friday and fired about a dosen cannon[.] it is thought they were only shooting of their guns to relode them – there is only one in view of us today[.] there has been a fight expected here and it is probable that there will be[,] but I dont think it will be apt to come on soon[.] tell cousin Hugh to come as soon as he can[.] please write soon[.] direct your letter to carolina city N.C. 26th regit, nc. and in car of Capt W.P. Martin[.] accept the best wishes of a friend[.] give my respect to all[.] I remain yours most affectionately, N.A. Ray

1861, October 14

Jane McIntosh to uncle **Artemus S. Caddell**. General wartime correspondence from niece to uncle with brief mention of rumor of confederates capturing Washington and local news from Bethlehem church including funeral of cousin **Mary J. Hunsucker** on 3rd Sunday in November. [53]

Dear uncle[,] it is with pleasure that I take my pen in hand to write you a few lines to inform you that I am well at this time[.] hoping when these few lines may come to hand that they may find you well and hearty[.] the people is comonly well at this time[.] I recived your letter that you wrote the 3rd of Oct the 12th whitch gave me mutch pleasure to hear that was well[.] I have nothing new to write it seems the news is stoped[.] I herd that the Southern men had taken the city of Washington but I dont know how true it is[.] We have a sing next sunday though I think they had about as well quit having them appointed for the people has nearly all quit goin[,] and them that does go[,] just go for to laugh and you know that will not do[.] cousin Mary G. Hunsuckers funeral is to be preached at Bethlehem the third Sunday in November[.] I must come to a close for I can write no longer now[.] I want you to write soon and give me the news and I will write more next time[.] you must look over mistakes and bad writing[.] so[,] I close by saying I hope if we meet no more on earth[,] we will meet in a better world where parting is no more[.] Yours with respects[,] Jane McIntosh

1861, October 14

Wm. A. McIntosh to uncle **A.S. Caddell**. General wartime correspondence from nephew to uncle with brief mentions of rumor of confederates capturing Washington, skirmishes near Ft. Hatteras, a new company forming in Moore, local news from Bethlehem church with brief mentions of **James H. Muse** and **Rill Lacys** wife and upcoming association meeting at Dover. [54]

Dear uncle[,] I tak the present opportunity riting to you to let you no that I am well at present[.] hoping that when this comes to hand that tha will find you in good helth[.] I have not much to write[.] I was at Bethlehem yesterday and ther was five baptisms, ther was three sermons and James H. Muse and Pill/Rill Lacy's wife[.] we dont very good meetings now[,] it seems that everbody has got tired goin[.] ther is going to be a sociation next Sunday at dover[.] I herd that tha had struck the city of Washington but I am doubtful that it is not so for I have herd it so often[.] we hav got a new hors[.] pap got him from [illegible][.] he is a racer[.] he can rack faster than yourn can trot[.] ther is another company a going to start from Carthag next Thursday[.] I would like to see you but I cant[.] The gals all sa that tha are not goin to get married without that company comes back[,] but I dont bliev them for one has got married already[.] I recon you no who it is[.] I herd that J.L. Briants company had to be garded when tha had to leav Raleigh[.] I want you to write to me and tell me all the nuse[.] I herd that ther was a battle close to wher you are[,] and that the Sothern men took the canons that the yanks got at fort hatteras and a bout few hundred dolars worth[.] besides[.] so I must come to a close[.] Wm. A. McIntosh

1861, October 15

Jane Caddell, **Nancy A. Caddell** and **Mary Caddell** to cousin **A.S. Caddell**. General wartime correspondence between cousins with brief mentions of church at Bethlehem, **Zacheus Hogan** and **Martha Sullivan**. [55]

Dear cousin[,] I for the first time seat myself down for the purpos of writing you a few lines to let you no that I am Well at this time[.] hoping that When these few lines reaches you there Will find you and your company well[.] Well Tim you must not think hard of me for not riting to you no sooner for my chance was bad to rite[.] Well Tim I have no new nuse to rite to you more than people are generly Well in this part of the country[.] We have had a very good meeting at Bethlehem[.] there was five baptised last Sunday[.] Well Tim I have not forgeten the happy hours that We has spent together and I hope it Will not belong before We can spend a few more[.] Well Tim When I heard that you Were all took prisoners[,] I Was troubled but then I heard better and I hope there is no danger[.] I hope that you Will serv out your time and come back home safe and sound Without the loss of one[.] giv my best respects to all my friends well[.] Tim[,] I see your sweet oh gal at last sunday and she Was just as pretty as ever[.] and I Want you to come back and I think I will get to go to another wedin pretty soon and I could say more about the girls but I Will stop[.] and I Want you to tel me something about the boys down there for these all gone from a bout hear[.] tel Mr Hogans that I hav not forgeton him yet[.] Well Tim I Want you to come up next thursday and help us shuck corn and my soles[.] Tim What a time We Will hav[.] We Will hav the most good things to eat my soles[.] Well I recon that I had better come to a close[.] you must excuse bad riting and spelling[.] if We are never more permitted to see each other in this World[,] I hope We Will meet in a better place[.] rite as soon as you can[.] Jane Caddell

Dear cosen[,] I must rite to you for if I was to liv and dye hear with old age I dont beleave that you Would ever rite to me[,] but for dear cosen sake[,] I Will rite to you[.] Well Tim I am afrade that you Will go Wild away down there[.] you had better come back home and leav that bugory place Where the spiders groes as big as the old pepper box[.] Well Tim you must come up to our corn scheckin and tel Mr Hogans too come too[.] Dear cosen[,] I Will not say very much more this time[,] but you must rite to me and let me know how you like to stay in them buggory places[.] Well[,] I must come to a close[.] giv my love to all my friends[.] rite soon[.] Nancy A. Caddell

A. S. Caddell Dear sir[,] I seat myself down for the purpos of riting you a few lines to let you no that I am well[.] hoping these few lines may find you enjoying the same blessing[.] I hav no nuse to rite to you more than people are generally Well through this section of the country[.] Dear cosen[,] I must tell you some funny little storys[.] old folly love is not ded yet[,] but just so yet[.] Well there is one thing I Want to no[.] I Want to no if you love possum as good as ever for I love coon mighty good[.] Well[,] I Will quit my foolishness and talk about something good[.] Well[,] I Want to no if there is any pretty boys down there tha hav all left hear[.] Dear cosen[,] if I could see you I could tel you a heap of funny things[.] Dear cosen[,] I would love to hear your voice once more at our little meetings for your voice sounded sweet to my ears[.] Well[,] I must come to a close[.] you must rite to me[.] Without fail[,] give my love to one and all[.] tel them they must all rite to us[.] Mary Caddell

1861, October 21
Malcom P. Davis to **A.S. Caddell**. General wartime correspondence with brief mentions of **Caroline Dowdy**, **Neill Caddell**, **Sarah McIntosh**, **Harrison Davis**, **John Dunlap** volunteering with Captain **James O.A. Kelly's** company. [56]

I drop a few lines to let you know that I am well[,] hoping these few lines may find you enjoying good health[.] Tim you must excuse me for not writing to you before now nor I have nothing to write now[.] Your folks are well as common[.] King David will be ready for you to ride a Christmas to see the dals but I believe the gals are about to dry up[.] you ought to see the letters that Caroline Dowdy sent to Neil. She sent thre the loveinest letters you ever saw[.] She has poped the question to him certain. She told him if he was ready just to print the time[.] She would be ready any time. Sarah Mc has got that letter you wrote for another fellow but didnt get the chance to see how[.] it took nothing more[.] write to me soon[.] Your Friend, M.P. Davis

I have no envelopes and will put this in Harrisons[.] John Dunlap has Volunteered in Kellys Company & I heard that his father was gone off tradeing and if that is so I expect he done without his fathers consent[.] they have orders to leave soon[.] Malcom

1861, October 23
Noah Deaton (*Carolina City, NC*) to sister. General wartime correspondence with brief mention of **William McKinnon**, **John McKinnon** and **Hugh M. Ray**. [57]

Dear sister, I am well at present and hope this will find you and all the rest enjoying the same blessing[.] the company is in very good health at present[.] the yankees are still lurking about here and from what I can learn we will be apt to have a fight before long[.] there came orders last night for us to cook three days rashions and it is thought that we will have a plenty to do in a few days[.] there was some of the yankees landed yesterday not far from this place[,] but I dont think they remained on shore long. Our fare is as good as could be expected[.] we have plenty of bacon & flour some com meal & sugar & coffee twice every day and fish as often as we want them[.] we can get beef and potatoes[.] somtimes there is no spring on this Island but we can get very good water by diging three or four feet deep which is not very cold[,] but I think as healthy as the water in moore county. we have had very cold rainy wether for a few days[,] but we have not had any frost yet for the weather is not cold enough[.] W. & J. McKinnon & H. M. Ray all landed here safely saturday the 19 and were gladly received by the company[.] they brought me 1 pair pants and one pair sock which I was glad to get for such things ar dificult to be had here and if atall not at any reasonable price[.] for which I send my thanks to you and Mother[.] I must come to a close though there is a plenty of rumors here but they are with little foundation therefore I will close[.] plese write soon as you have the opertunity[.] yours truly, Noah Deaton

1861, October 24
Mary A. Caddell to cousin **A.S. Caddell**. General wartime correspondence between cousins with brief mentions of church at Bethlehem, **Martha Sullivan, William Caddell** and **Raney Caddell**. [58]

Dear Cousin[,] I write you a few lines to let you know that we are all well or as much so as common[,] and hope this may reach and find you all in the best of health[.] I havent anything new to write[.] times are hard and dull here and not much prospects of their getting much better at present though[.] I hope it will not be long till things will be strait again and we can all see each other once more[.]—I saw your gal at Bethlehem the other week[.] she looks as pretty as ever and I know she want to see you very bad if all things are true[.] for I suppose you and her were getting along very well[.]—I shall prepare myself for going to a heap of weddings when you all get home if providence permits[.] if you all wont think I am too old for such as that but I Can see as good now as ever I could[.] and I believe better for you know there is none so blind as Them[.] Thats got good eyes and cant see[.]—I saw your father and Mother yesterday[.] they are all well and says they want to see you very bad[.]—I must bring this short letter to a close[.] write soon and I will write you a great long letter next time and give you all the news[.] nothing more from Your Affectionate Cousin. M. A. Caddell

1861, October 28
Hugh M. Ray (*Camp Burgwyn, Bogue Island, NC*) to sister. General wartime correspondence between siblings with brief mentions of guarding the coast and **Neil Thompson, Nathan L. Fry, John L. Caddell, Andrew J. Kimbrel**, Lt. **Robert W. Goldston's** death, Capt. **Pender**, Capt. **Martin**, Capt. **Carraway** and **William Whitlock**. [59]

Dear Sister, I now take my pen in hand to drop you a few lines to let you know that I am well at this time and have been ever since I left home[.] I reached carolina city on Friday night after I left home and met with John R. Keith who was waiting[.] Neil Thompson and N.L. Fry at the hospital[.] On Saturday morning I came over to the camp where I found the company all in very good health except John L Caddell and D. Kimbrel[.] Lieutenant R.W. Goldston was also sick and on thursday night he died at carolina city[.] Two of Lincoln's vessels have been in sight ever since I came here untill last Friday[.] we have not seen them since then[.] we heard on wednesday night that a large fleet was on the way to make an attack on Fort macon[,] but we have not seen it yet nor I dont think we will son[.] if they will attempt to land here they will find that there is trouble before them[.] Capt Penders artillery is about a mile up from our camp and this morning we moved two cannons from Penders camp down about a mile below here[.] there is but two companies in this encampment[,] Captain Martins and Captain Caraways company from Anson County[.] the balance of the Regiment is two miles nearer the fort and the seventh Regiment is at carolina city[.] we expect to move the other encampment tomorrow[.] as I have no news to write I must come to a close[.] please write soon[.] Mr. Whitlock sends his best respects to you all[.] give my respects to all my friend and accept a portion to yourself[.] No more at present[.] only remaining your affectionate brother until death[.] Hugh M. Ray

1861, October 30
C.D. Caddell to brother **A.S. Caddell**. General wartime correspondence between brothers with brief mentions of economic hardships, farming, church meetings are Dover and Pleasant Hill, **Dowd, Davis** girls, **Devotion Davis, W.L. Sullivan, Zacheus Hogan, Jack McIntosh,** uncle **Joe Caddell, Capt. James O.A. Kelly's** company and **Martha M. Sullivan.** [60]

Dear Brother[,] I seat myself to drop you a few lines to let you know I am well at present[,] hoping that these few lines will find you well[.] I Recd your letter today that Mr. Dowd brought which gave me much pleasure to hear from you[.] you say you dont get any letters from me[.] I have rote every week but last and I dont get your letters if you rite more than I do[.] I went to the sociation last week at Dover[.] I saw the most pretty gals I ever saw &

flew around so[.] me and WL Sullivan went home with two of Miss Davises saw fun enough[.] I have finished gathering corn today but I and done halling[.] I will make 50lbs of corn[.] I have got the 11 ½ bush of oats sowed[.] I shal comence sowing wheat on Monday[.] I shal sow a bit wheat[.] I can take myself leave if with me yet[,] but I shant keep him[,] only till I get done sowing wheat[.] I had to pay $4.50 tax[.] I had to pay your poll tax and I cant get no money at all[.] Salt is 10.00 a sack in Fayetteville[.] it is the hardest times her I ever saw[.] I was a going to get your a pair of shoos but I had to pay four ten and I cant get a bit of money[.] I cant get a pair for less than $2.50 and the cash has to be me or no shoes[.] leather is 50cts a pound[,] but if you are ablige to have a pair I will sell something and get them[.] let me know if you got your things from D. Davis that I sent you[.] when the things comes that that the women is a makin up you will get a heap of things[.] you must watch and see what your name is on[.] I your gal at last Sunday at pleasant hill and heard her saying she could not enjoy herself there as well as she last spring[.] tell me if you rite to her in your next letter[.] if you don't[,] you had ort to for she is the smartest gal in Moore or any where els[.] I have caught 20 possums this fall[.] I wish you was here to night to go with me a huntin for some times I catch a pos and some times a gal[,] but [illegible] is the bes on the gals this fall[.] do what I told you in that letter you get from D. Davis[.] I will close by saying I want you to help me shuck corn a Friday[.] rite soon as this gets to hand[.] your most affectionate Brother till Death[.] C.D. Caddell [P.S] tell me what going on with Hogans if you can[.] tell him his gal is well[.] tell him to rite to me[.] tell Jack McIntosh to write to me[.] us and uncle Jo has got friendly[.] I had been there one[.] Papy and mother sends their best respects and says for you to rite to them[.] Come home if you get the chance at Christmas and we will see some fun[.] mother says she will have you a pair of pants made if you need them[.] Kelleys company is a going to leave today[.] if you get sick come home if you can[.] let me know if you get any letters from your gal[.] no more at present[.] CDC

1861, October 30

Louis H. McLeod (*Smithville, NC*) to wife **Eliza Jane Walker McLeod**. General wartime correspondence with brief mentions of **Francis Moore, Tandy Walker, Emily Franklin, John Lewis Cox, Green Berry Cole, Benjamin Knight, Dr. Campbell, Catty ?** and **Mary** ?. [61]

My Dear and Beloving Wife. I receaved your welcomb letter last knight the 29 that was dated the 24 I was moore than glad to hear from you all and moore than glad to get them five Dollars you sent me. Eliza I had to barrough money from my friends to get along with I have some of the best friends here in the wirld when I lost my money they told me I needent lack for any thing they would divide the last sent they had with me. and I beleave they would. Thank God for that much[.] Eliza my friend Frances Moore has give me room in his tent for this Winter[.] he bought him a little stove the other day and we put it up in his tent and has cooking utincils so we can do our one cooking. He sayed it was no use of talking I had to stay in the tent with him and lie by the stove where we could keep warm[.] I havent movd yet I have to send to Wilmington to get me a cot and matress that will cost me seven or eight dollars but that is not much money to spend for the comfurt during the winter. I want you to make me a new sack or cumfort or what ever you call it and put aplenty of cotton in it and tack it well and send it by the first oportunity and if you think you can send me some provisions I would like to have ham meete and eggs and butter. I tell you every thing we get from Moore to eat does go mighty well We have eaten nearly out here. Yesterday and last knight we had nothing. But I was along with my friend Frances. We cooked oysters and faired first rate. I never will perish as long as I am with him. I will stick to him as long as I can stick to my self. We are together all the time. I want you to send us anything you can get and think would do us good. If you ever can send us any thing I want you to send some whisky. We cant bye a quart of any thing here for less than seventy five cents. When we come here they sold it at fifty cents [per quart] . now sell it at seventy five. Eliza We cant live here without a little whisky to mix with our watter I think a little will help us but our men cant bye whisky and the prices here. Eliza I am well at this time as ever I was. I have just got over the cold only my neck is alittle sore yet but it will be well in a few days. Eliza Tan is in the tent with me again reading the thirty first chapter of Jobe. He is not verry well but he goes about where he is not verry well but he goes about where he wants to go. He went up to Wilmington the other day with the Captain and the wind was so strong it throwd him back alittle. John Louis is got nearly over the measles. I wish you could have seen him he was the uglest men I ever saw in my life. I had to laff at him. John sayed it was not fun to him to laff at. All John wanted was brandy. All of our men has gotten over the measles only some eight or ten. there is some with the feavr. Green Cole and Benjamin Knight is the worst off. the Captain is going to send thim home as soon as they get so they can go and the Doctor Campbell is going with thim. If they go in a week or to I will rite to you when they start so you can send any thing you want to send back by the doctor. Eliza I want you to write to me oftener. I thought it along time since I herd from you

Eliza it a great satisfaction to here from you. May the God of (sic) spar us to meete again in this wirld if the prairs of your unworthy frien. Tan sends his love and respects to Emely and wants her to write to him and let him know all the nuse about the times and hoo is about to get married and ho is not and tell Catty that he would like to see her verry much Tell her and Mary to come down some knight and bring there knitting and stay a week and eat fish and oysters and get fat No more for Tan. Eliza I was glad to here that you was getting fat and hearty. I would like to see you fat again in my life I recon you would look so funny I would have to laff at you right out.|Eliza I think of you everyknight when I lie down to sleep.to think where I use to lie on a good bead and you by my side and now think where I have to lie now on a small bed tick with a small partion of pine straw in it and my over coat for a heading. hoo [who] would have thought it Eliza I have got use to itbut I am afraid our men will suffer from cold this winter if they dont get moore bed close. Eliza I am well satisfied. I feel that my country calls me and I must be satisfied. Eliza I dont want to alarm you there is a great excitement about Wilmington and this time all the militia is ordered out down here and will all bee ordered or drafted up there in a short time if things goes on like they are now Your loving Husband until death L.H. McLeod. Eliza write as soon as you get this.

1861, November [undated estimate]
Unknown to **A.S. Caddell**. General wartime correspondence betweens friends with brief mentions of **Harrison Davis**, the Captain's race for 51st Regiment NC Militia, **Noah F. Muse**, **Thomas W. Ritter**, **William McSwain Cockman**, **Zacheus B. Moore**, **William Wesley Wallis**, **Emsley Wallis**, **Nicholas A. Shields**, **Ike Wallis**, and the **Moore** family. [62]

A.S. Caddell. tell Harrison to rite to me. we had a race in district No 8 for a captain. N.F. Muse, T.W. Ritter, Swain Copmon, Z.B. Moore. Ritter was elected. He got 82, N.F 45, Swain 7, Z.B. Moore 1. they fought some. the Moores and Wes Wallis, Ems Wallis, Nick Shields, Ike Wallis. you never saw such a time.

1861, November
Hugh M. Ray *(Bogue Island, NC)* to father **Nevin Ray**. General wartime correspondence between father/son with brief mentions of **Major Hugh C. McLean**, **Dr. Hector Turner**, **Duncan Keith**, **Isaac Seawell**, **Neal Ray**, **William Whitlock**, **Noah Deaton**, **John McKinnon**, **Martin A. McKinnon**, **William McKinnon**, **Dr. Daniel W. Shaw**, **Neill Thompson**, **Capt. William P. Martin**, **Lewis Lawhon** and included a brief note from **William Whitlock** to **Nevin Ray** with mentions of **Alexander H. McNeill** and **Whitlock**'s mother. [63]

Dear Father, I now embrace the opportunity of writing you a few lines which will inform you that I received your kind letter of 10th inst by the hand of Major H.C. McLean on yesterday[,] which gave me much satisfaction to hear that you were all well. I also received at the same time a blanket and a pair of shoes from you[.] Mr. McLean, Dr. Turner, Duncan Keith and Isaac Sewell is all down here at this time. I have been here about one month now and have well ever since I left home. Neal, Whitlock, Deaton, and the McKinnons are all well. The company is in very good health this time except Dr. Shaw, Neal Thompson. Thompson has been in the hospital ever since I came here. Dr. Shaw has been in the hospital about two weeks very sick but he is getting some better. We have moved up nearer the fort. We are in about a mile and a half of the fort now. The Yankees have paid us a visit down here two weeks since we went about fifteen miles down the beach where the steamer Union was wrecked[.] and there a week moving the machinery from the wreck. Lincoln's vessels passing us everyday. Some of the men came out one day with a flag of truce[,] and talked with the Major and Captain Martin. Then left us. On the next week, they fired about twenty times at the men at work there one day[,] but hurt no one. I think we will save about sixty thousand dollars worth of machinery and other property. When Mr. Lewis Lawhorn left here two weeks ago, I sent twenty dollars by him for you[.] and at the same time I also sent a barrel of fish which he was to haul from Jonesboro to Carthage. Please write and let me know if they came to you yet. As I have nothing new to write, I must come to a close. No more at present. Only remaining your affectionate son. Hugh M. Ray

Mr. Neven Ray, Dear Sir, I now embrace the opportunity of writing you a few lines to let you know that I am well at this time[,] hoping that these few lines may find you and family enjoying the same blessing. Mr. Ray, I want you if you please, to do a little favor for me. Please call on A.H. McNeill at Carthage and get thirty-five dollars in money that was to be lodged in his hands by Mr. L. Lawhorn[,] three ten dollar bills on the Bank of Charlotte, one five dollar on the State Bank of N.C. and hand it over to my mother and tell her to take care of it for me. And in so doing, you will oblige your friend William Whitlock. So no more at present[,] but remain yours most respectively. William Whitlock

1861, November 1
Noah Deaton (*Carolina City, NC*) to father **William Deaton**. General wartime correspondence with brief mentions of **Daniel McKinnon, William McKinnon, John McKinnon** and **Lewis Lawhon.** [64]

Dear Father, I seat myself to drop you a few lines to let you know that I am well at present and hope this may find you and all the rest well[.] I have no news to write to you at present[.] we received part of our wages today up to the 31st of august[.] I received $31.00 and think it best to send a part home to you to keep for me until I return if I be so lucky as to be spared or to use it for yourself if you need it[.] I would send more but I think it best to keep some on hand in case I may need it for it takes a goodeal to do one here[.] I send it to the care of Mr Daniel McKinnon[.] William and John McKinnon send some home and I thought best to send it all together[.] Mr Louis Lawhon[,] is here and he will leave in the morning and will carry our money and letters to Carthage[.] I would send it in a letter to you but Mr Lawhon will not take any money sealed up in letters[.] the amount that I send you is $20.00 Dollars[.] as it is late I must close[.] write to me soon and let me know whether you get the $20.00 that I send you[.] Yours truely Noah Deaton

1861, November 3
Louis H. McLeod (*Smithville, NC*) to wife **Eliza Jane Walker McLeod**. General wartime correspondence with brief mentions of **Francis Moore, Dr. Campbell, Alexander Hamilton McLeod. F.J. Swann, Miss Hill, Emily Franklin, William ?, Fanny ?, Henry ?, Peg ?, Nelson ?, Cate?, Jack ? and Dup?** [65]

My Dear Wife, I seat my self down this Sunday knight to drop you a fiw lines to let you know that I am well at this time hoping when those lines reaches you [they] will find you and family all enjoying the same blessings. Eliza my self and friend Lieutenant Moore is just as well fixed in our tent as we can bee. We sent up to Wilmington and got me one of the nicest Buregard camp cots you ever saw and then I moved in his tent where we have a nice little stove where he lies on one side of the stove and me onthe other. he is just 1a down on his bead and left me writing. he sends his verry best love and respects to you. Eliza I send you those few lines by Dr.Campbell to let you know that I want you to send me something to eat. I want you to call on Mother and Sand to box up one or too ham and eggs and butter if they will and if not I want you to be sure [to do so] and send them by Moore and we want every thing that I mentioned. We have got tired eating old tuff beef. We have plenty of potatoes. We have one barrel of potatoes in our tent at this time. Moore can bet plenty of them from home. They sell here at seventy [cents] per bushel. Pork twelve and half cents per pound. dear eating. We have plenty of coffee and sugar and molasses. Eliza you must send me some moore money I have had to borroug money to get along with up to this time Eliza I dont know what you will do for salt I dont here any thing sayed about salt. If you can't get it you better get F. J. Swann to get it for you. Eliza I wrote to you to send me a new tack. I want you to see Miss Hill and tell her to send me a good blanket to keep me from freasing this winter When you box up the things get old Swann to mark it for you so they will cone strate. Eliza there is verry much excitement down in this country at this time. ther is all of the old malitie ordered out. there is for or hundred [hundred or so] of them here now and they looks like they are scerid half to death. but here is what ant scerd we are all anxious to fight. we want to do it at once and go home. I was out last Friday knight on picket gard and I thought the fight had commenced.The canons begant to rore some seven or eight [of them] and the small arms begane to tell the nuse. I could see them firing on the water as plane as day, But it was fals alarm. It was too miles off over at Fourt Caswell. there is [union?] vessels in sight every day.We expect an attact soon but I dont beleave we will ever have to fight here. Eliza I never have enough paper when I begin to wright you must excuse me for not writing moore. give my best love and respect to Emely and the children and William and Fanny, Henry and Peg (?) and Netson (?) and Cate and Jack and Dup (?) Good bye Eliza Tak good of your self you must quit eating so mich I am afraid you will get too fat. I would like to sea you verry much Your affectionate Husband untill Death, Louis H. McLeod

1861, November 6
Mastin C. Phillips (*Trinity College*) to brother **Malphus S. Phillips.** General wartime correspondence with brief mentions of **Rev. Lewis Phillips Jr., Bowman, Skeen** and **Nancy Edwards Phillips.** [66]

Dear Brother, I have just time to write you a few lines. Your letter came to hand in due time. I was happy to hear from home and that all were well. Tell Pa that the two dollars he sent me kept me from doing a desperate crime. I do not believe that I I love money, but a little is indispensable[,] and I had reached the point when I had to have some[.] and the day before it came to hand I was thinking about whetting up my old knife and trying my luck on the highways and hedges. But now I have given up that idea for the present, hoping that I will not be reduced to such a strait again. There is some sickness in the country at this time. One of our students died a few days ago. Bowman was his name, a very fine young man, a member of my class and the best in the freshman class. He lived only three miles from college. His family is a very interesting one. They mourn their loss very much. I have heard from Mr. Skeen since I wrote before. I hope he is well by now. We have some measles among the boys at this time but no bad cases. I have been quite well most of the time. I feel very thankful that I am blessed with health while others are afflicted. I hope my health will remain good while I am from home as it is hard work[.] hope my health will remain good while I am from home as it is hard work to get along smoothly at best in this stingy hardhearted community. I was glad to hear that your corn turned out so well. I guess you have plenty to do. Have you many hogs to fatten? I guess you will do well to make all the bacon you can, for I am of the opinion that it will bring the money next year. It is worth 25 cents per pound at High Point at this time. I hope it will not be that high long, for if it does many will have to do without it. I am getting along with my studies now just about as fast as a cat can gnaw a rock. I get discouraged sometimes and have been on the eve of quitting a time or two lately[,] but I reckon I shall stay a while longer as I have stayed until now. But I think that I shall quit at Christmas. Times are so hard that I cannot get money to pay my way. I do not know yet what I shall do. I intend to marry soon as I can if I don't get kicked which by the way is not improbable at this time. I came very near getting blown up the other night and matters are not quiet yet. I shall not be surprised if I get my papers in a few days. I would have been hurled overboard the other night but just at the critical moment when all seemed lost, I succeeded in drawing the young lady into a [illegible][.] and before she was aware of my intentions, I attacked her in the rear, and carried the fort by storm. But she is prolific in resources and is drumming up recruits for another combat. The end is yet to come. I cannot guess at this issue, though I am determined to make her pay dearly for the victory if she gains it. This is not foolishness but the truth. I have found the road to the [illegible] altar a confounded crooked concern. Thus far I have come very near quitting the field more than one time and may have it to do yet. If I do not love the little witch I would quit and if you ever caught me in another such scrape- (well, no difference what). She does not object to me in any respect. But her objections (well, I can't tell you now)[.] I have refused to acknowledge them as objections and shall continue to do so until I find that she will not give then I will have to quit. If I have to give up this business, I shall not come home this winter and it is a little doubtful whether I'm ever seen in Moore again. I shall leave here but where I shall go is uncertain. And if I shall marry I expect to do so before I come home again. Tell Pa that I will write him definitely about the matter in a week or ten days as I am going to see the lady in a short time to settle the matter one way or another. I can't tell to save my life how it will go now, but whether I marry or not[,] I want some money to get my license and such other little fixings as will be indispensable. And if not, I must have some to run away on as I am determined to leave here soon as I can after I get kicked. I am in earnest about this business. If you hear any grumbling about me not writing[,] tell them that I would write but have no money to pay for the postage. I hope you will all be prosperous and happy. Give my love to Ma and all. Write soon. I am quite well. Yours, Mastin C. Phillips

1861, November 6
William Worth "Buck" Edwards (*Camp Wilkes*) to cousin **Emeline Phillips.** General wartime correspondence with brief mentions of **John M. Edwards, Frank ?, Powell Edwards** and **Candace Phillips.** [67]

I now take my pen in hand to write you a few lines to let you know how I am getting along. I am well and enjoying tolerable good health and I hope these few lines will find you well and enjoying the same good blessings. Miss, I have but little news to communicate. We are all as well as could be expected. I heard from Brother John the other day. He is well as for common. You must excuse me for not writing sooner, for I am a very sorry scribe and don't have much to write. But I have a little good news to tell you at this time. We took 80 Yankee prisoner last Sunday evening. But I will tell you no more as Frank is writing and will tell you all about it. I must tell you something about a soldier's life. It is hard one, and I berit easy and say nothing about it, for I think I am in a good cause, and I feel like it is every mans duty to be here, and when I look back behind me and see how many big, hardy strong men are at home lying on the cold earth and make a pillow of their knap-sacks and are exposed to all the work and fatigue of camp life. I cannot look upon them as patriotic men. Many a dark and lonesome night when you are all asleep and hardly know that war is in our land, we are rambling from post to post in our country and casting fond remembrance back home to our dear fathers and mothers who are sending their prayers to heaven on the behalf of their dear sons who are surrounded by so many dangers. You may look upon it as nothing, but I never experienced such a life before. The time has been therefore that when we lay our weary limbs down to rest, we did not expect to be around till day, but here we do not know what minute we will be called to face the wide mouthed cannon. But I never have regretted the day when I volunteered for I am in a good cause and I believe that God is on our side. And if He is, I fear no enemy that can approach us, and here I shall stay until death before I will see my country imposed on. So I will close as you will be tired of reading my bad written letter. John is at Culpepper Town. They are all getting along as well as could be expected. You must write soon. Please give my love to Cousin Powell Edwards and tell him to write. Give my love to Candace and your mother and father and all the rest. Tell them all to write to me as I will be very glad to hear from them. So this leaves me in good spirit hoping I shall receive an answer soon. Excuse all mistakes, bad writing and spelling as I am in a hurry. Yours truly until death. W. W. Edwards

1861, November 14
Eliza Jane Walker McLeod (and **Emily Franklin**) to husband **Louis H. McLeod**. General wartime correspondence with brief mentions of **Abe Douglas, Emily Franklin, Tandy Walker, William Underwood, Sandy Kelly, Sandy Brown, John A. Walker, Elizabeth Hinton Brewer McLeod, Sam ?, Fanny ?, William ?, Henry ?, Amy ?, Nellie ?, Kate ?, Puk ?, Jack ?, Anjalette McLeod, John Lewis Cox, James Deaton** and **David P. Morris.** [68]

*Dear Louis mc. i sete my self to drop you a few lines to let you no that we ar all wel at this time hoping thes few lines may find you in the same blessing. I rcevd your leter last friday and was mor then glad to her from you and to her you were well. I hope you may remain so[,] go grat [great.] i hird [heard] your leter red to day you sent to Abe and you had moved and i want to see you mity bad. it dos seme so long since I sine [seen] you. my lord have mercy on you and kee[p] you from danger. may the god of battle be with you all. Louis we have got in our corn and have made the crib fool [full] and hav dug our patatos and have made about seventy five bushels. we are now soing whete as hard as we can. we hav som seven or eight bushels sode. we hav up our hogs and getting along the bes we can but not like if you wer her. My dear I want to no wher [whether] you got the last leter I sent you or not. Emley sent you an tan one dolar a pese [piece] and I want to no where you got it or no. Louis I sent you a baxe [box] of something to eat and a half galen of whisky by underwood and ccavat and I wil send the compfert by the doctor if I can no when he starts and I want to no where San has sent you enny mony or*1861, *Not and if he has not i will send you five mor dolars. that is all I hav got to spar until i can go to town [and] sell somthin and then i will send you more. tel tan i wan to her from him and I want you to rite how Sandy Kelley is geting along and i want to hoo [who] nate is staing with[,] if he is staing with Sandy brown or not. we herd he had the mesels. I want you to rite. ifele sorey for him. i herd from John laste Sunday and he wanted to no wher you all wer. he hadent herd nothing from you all sence you lefte Raley [Raleigh] he is in edton chowan. he sais it is no whar. tha hav not to ther horses yet nor has not got enny thing to fight with but their fist he sais that luck of [r]esineing. no more about John. your mother is rite smart. I sent her and San the work you sent. fanny sais for you to com home crismas. she has two chicken up and has won [one] dozen of eges [eggs] an she will save them for you. wiliam sends his lov to you and all of the children. Sis tel pap howdy for them and tel him tha want to see you very bad. tha are all the time talking about you. Louis I wish you would come home and see uss all won time more. if you think you can com crismis rite to me. Henry and Ary and Nelee all like for you to. Kate and Puk (?) and Jack is wel. Jack is won of the smar dogs you ever saw. hehe will set the birds. I wold [would] do you good to see him. nothing more. giv my lov to Francis and tel him i wish him all the good luck in the worle for being so good to you. I never will get him. devide [the food I sent] with him I hope his cole will so get wel. my dear Louis I long to see the time when you will cum home and say her. San(?) syd tha think I had beter keep Wiliam. i want to no what you think a bout it. and giv him part of the crap [crop.] rite what you think. I most clos. rite as soon as you get this. may god bless you and save you is my pras. your der loving wife Eliza McLeod Anjalett sends her lov to Tan an John Cox.*

Mr McLeod I heard your letter read this morning an was glad to hear you was well. I hope you will remain so untill you come home. i send my love to you an to Tan an San Kelly an James Deaton an Davy P an tell him i am not married yet nor want be untill he cones back to be at the weding),tell him the cherry is red the stem gren the time is past that we have seen. Emily Franklin

November 17

Louis H. McLeod (*Camp Wyatt*) to wife **Eliza Jane Walker McLeod.** General wartime correspondence with brief mentions of **Francis Moore, Alexander Waddell, William Underwood** and **William M. Swann.** [69]

Dear and loving Wife I am sorry to say to you that I feel so bad.| I have got the Big measles at this time once more in life. Eliza on last Wednesday my eyes aked like they vould burst open for one or too days. Thurisday knight the measles broke out on ne in the big order. I got up the next mourning and went out to the roal [role] call and all the boys was laughfing at me because I had the measles when I did not no I had them. I went back to my tent and tuck [took to] my bed where I have been ever since. I hasrnt been sick a bit only my head and eyes aked verry bad. To day is Sunday at Dinner and I feel first rate Thank god. The Captain want [won't] let me go out of the tentat all for fear of cetching cold. the Doctor came round this mourning and he said I would not bee fit for duty for three weeks but it is not so. I am going out from here in a few days. There is a talk now in the Rejiment of going out to sea to take a yankee vessel by the name of Sante park that used to run from Wilmington to N. York that has been botheren us ever since we have been down here. We are determined not to take it no longer. I am one of the men that is a going on the old Uncle Ben a war stamer that happened [to be] at Wilmington about the time the war commenced. Eliza I am not surtain it will be so. but if it dois and I am well I will be one amongst them. No moore about the yankees. Eliza I am sorry to tell you that my friend Lieutenant Moore was taken down sick abead [a bed] last sunday and remained sick here untill Friday when he lift here to go up to Alexander Waddells at or near Wilmington. he was attactedd with the Belious Feaver. I never was so sorry to see a man leave me in my life. Ah my wife he is moore than a brother ever was to me. He told me when he left me lying on the bead that If I did get bad off he would send for me as soon as his farther came down and take me over to his place where the greatest attention would bee givin me. My paper is small I cant write as much as I would if it was larger. Eliza Mr. Underwood arrived here on Saturday mourning and he was welcomed of course in the company. Every baddy was glad to see him. But the opossoms and chickens was all spoiled. We had them all to threw away. The whisky you sent me came to hand in a good time to keep the measles out. the day before billy came I never wanted a dram worse in my life and the next day billy came and I had no tast for whisky at all. I was right mad with my self becuase I could not drink any. No moore at present. The Captain sends his best love and respects to you and for you to tell his folks that he is well and you may tell them it is a fine thing he is well. He can eat moore than any man I ever saw. only when I was well I could stand him on everything only patatoes and there he would get. He could eat too to my one. No moore Good by Eliza. I will send you a few lines by Billy. You ar [not?] verry punctual in writing to me. I haven't receavd a letter from you since the third of this month. If you dont write to me oftener I will quit a corespondence with you.

1861, November 19

Mary E. Moore (*Plank Road*) to cousin **A.S. Caddell.** General wartime correspondence between cousins with brief mentions of church at Bethlehem, **Sarah Moore, Mary Caddell, W.R. Muse, Martha McIntosh, Sarah Frances McIntosh, Noah Muse, Alice Fry, Neill Caddell, William Caddell, Raney Caddell, H.B. Muse** and Rev. **Noah Richardson's** sermon for Mrs. **Hunsucker** at Bethlehem Church. [70]

Dear Cousin, I will now try to give you the most interesting newse and that will not be mutch for newse is not something that falls threw this section of the country. It seemed to be newse to you about your having a sweetheart[.] I am very mutch surprised to think you didnt know her name[.] you said for me to tell you her name and you would write to her[.] if you was to write to her it would not be the first time. I believe I will tell you her name now for if you dont know her name I know she is no sweetheart of yours. Well there is not any prospects of a wedding in this settlement at present but if some of them dont marry before long[,] I dont know what will be the reason for if some of the boys dont want to marry there is no truth in them[.] I know Sarah sends her very best respects to you, and wishes you to write to her. Mary Caddell says for you to answer her letter she wrote to you. You say you will not come home until your time is up unless you get a ticket to some of our weddings[.] I tell you now if anybody marries about here[,] I will try to get them to send you a ticket. Do you expect to remain there on the Island this winter[.] you told me what you had for breakfast now I would like to know who cooked it. Christmas will soon be here but when it comes how can we enjoy it. I know it will be the dulest Christmas we ever remember of[.] I believe I have told you about all. You must excuse this badly written and spelt letter[.] for my sake never show to any person. If you ever was tired of stuff in your life I know you want to know who the boys are flying around here[.] I will try to tell you as near as I can. W.R. Muse is flying around Martha McIntosh, Noah [-] Alice Fry, Neil [-] Sarah Frances McIntosh. They fly around many more but they pay their respects mostly to these girls[.] Well enough of my foolishness[.] I was at Bethlehem Saturday and Sunday[.] Mrs. Hunsuckers funeral was preached on sunday by Mr Richardson[.] he preached an splendid sermon & his tixt was For the great day of wrath is come and who will be able to stand. We have prair meeting at our School house Saturday night & sing sunday. Oh! if you could be there you would enjoy it so much. I have been making you some pants tonight. It is getting late but I will write some before I retire. Your Mother is with us to night, but she is gone to bed. Your father is up here at H.B. Muses. Noah is over with Neil. We hear there is fighting there where you are but I hope it is not true[.] Oh! it is trouble trouble and nothing but trouble in this wourld at the best: but as it is so it must be, we must pass it off the best we can. We have ejoyed ourselfs better in this wourld than we ever will again I fear for it is more pleasure to me to think upon the past than the future. How can we look forward for happiness in this distracted country. The chickens is now crowing & I must close for tonight[.] in truth of this for it is nothing but stuff[.] for my mind is not composed enough to write a letter fit for any person to read. but bad as it is I will keep trying to write as long as I can get a letter. Do not fail to write as soon as you get this, write a long letter. Nothing more at present. Write soon very soon to your friend & cousin. Mary E. Moore [P.S.] My very best respects to all enquiring friends if there be any & tell them to write to me.

1861, November 20
Sarah McIntosh to **A.S. Caddell.** General local correspondence. [71]

Mr. A. S. Caddell, I take my pen in hand to rite you a few line to let you no that I am well[,] hoping this will find you well[.] i was glad to here that you was well[.] you musn let the yankeys run[.] you save all them that come to you like you did them others[.] i would like to see you all once more[.] i want to see the spring come[.] i hope you all will live so we can have another fishing party[.] we has not had nary one since you left here[.] you said that you herd that i was a going to get married[.] i never herd it before i want to no who told you[.] but if i do i will send you a ticket[.] dont you get married to that old man gal that live down there[.] if you do you must send me a ticket[.] the home stayers is herer[,] yet they are worst than here they have disbanded[.] shed not a teare or your friend erly beare[.] When I am gone & so no more at present[.] rite when you get this[.] Sarah McIntosh

1861, November 20
Louis H. McLeod (*Camp Wyatt*) to wife **Eliza Jane Walker McLeod**. General wartime correspondence with brief mentions of **John Lewis Cox, W.W. Cox, Emily Franklin, Tandy Walker, Sandy Kelly, James Deaton, Jarret Graham** and **Elizabeth Hinton Brewer McLeod.** [72]

[First page missing] If this comes to hand before John L. Cox starts back I want you to send me leather enough to half sole my shoes Eliza since I commenced writing this I examined the box good, the pone of bread was spoilt mildued all through. I was moore than glad to get those hickry nuts and walnuts I expect that was the childrens vorks. Eliza tell them I never will forget them there is never a day passe but what I think of them May God bless and save them if I never see them any moore. I would bee moore than glad to see them and bee with you and then about one week. Since I have bee riting this letter there was one of our men died by the name of W. W. Cox he was off in a house about one quarter of a mile from camp you must excuse me for not riting no moore and also for bad spelling Tell Emely I never will forget her for her kind favor she bestoed on me and Tan Tan is on the hatchets [?]running about with his belly in his hand and cant get over the line and the sentinal make him double quick out of the gap to the sink before he can ease himself Sandy Kelley is well and a getting as fat and harty as ever. Sand is grumbling about bead cloas he says he has not but one blanket I think his folks ought to send him some bad close Jim Deaton is well and the worst off man ever saw to go home he wanted to go home ever since he left never Saw such a fool He went on and made such a fuss at Smithville because he did not get a letter some of the boys rote him one and give it [to] Graham and he handed it to Jim and that cooled him Jim never says letter since I am agoing to walk about the camp this eavening for the first time in three days Give Mother my best love and respects and tell her that I am getting along verry well. Eliza you wanted to no whether Sandy sent me anymoney or not I have not receaved one sent from him yet I looked for some when billy come but non The balance of our company what is here is tolerable well at this time one or too down and some of the rest moping about thought I would close in severel places but I helt on untill I rote up allthe paper I had and now I am oblige to stop Your loving husband untill the last hour of my life. Louis H. McLeod

1861, November 21
W.L. Sullivan to cousin **A.S. Caddell** (*Bogue Island*). General wartime correspondence between cousins with brief mention of **Lawhon**. [73]

Mr A.S.Caddell. Dear sir[,] I seat myself to drop you a few lines which will inform you that I am well and the rest of the family people I generaly well[,] and I hope when these few lines comes to your hands they will find you enjoying the same blessing[.] I can inform you that I received your welcome letter by Mr Lawhon which I was glad to receive[.] I was glad to hear that you was well and had the pleasure of taking some of the yankees prisoners without any trouble or danger[.] I hope that will be the hardest task you will have to contend with on the Island[.] I have know nuse to write to you of much importance[.] it is hard to think of our condition in this world[.] But we dont have to live always in this world[.] So let us prepare to die as well as to live[.] I hope we will meet and talk with each other and spend many peacefull hours together as well as we once could do[.] But while we are parted and hatred abroad we will pray for each other and trust in the lord[.] I think I will come and see you all this winter[.] I should like the best sort to see my old associats my old friends again[.] God bless you all[.] take care of you all till you come home hapy[.] home is sure I love the[.] A.S. the girls is prety as ever[.] I wish you was here to fly around them[.] I pitch round little some times[.] Mr A.S.C[,] you said i did not know how bad you wanted to se the little girls[.] you dont want to see them more than they want to see you[.] Mr A.S. I wish I could be with you all awhile at Bogue Island and se the Yankees sailing on the Big Branch[.] I would help bust their heads if it was needed if they did not get mine[.] But I hope peace will be in our land soon[.] But the prospect is gloomy at this time[.] we all want to see you all my old Friend[.] I dont want you to forget WL tho far from you[.] I'll remember you till the sun shall godown behind the western hills to rise no moore[.] give my love and Respects to all my old friends and keep a portion yourself[.] tell the rest of the boys to write to me[.] I must come to a close for this time hoping to hear from you shortly again[.] I hope you will excuse bad writin on my knee by fire lite[.] give my respects to all enquiring friend if there be any[.] Yours respectfully your friend till death[.] W.L. Sullivan [P.S.] When this you see[,] remember me tho many miles apart we be[.] look at this and think of me. Write soon.

1861, November 23
Noah Deaton (*Carolina City, NC*) to sister **Sarah B. Deaton**. General wartime correspondence with brief mentions of **Daniel McKinnon** and **Lewis Lawhon**. [74]

Well Sarah[,] I seat myself to answer your letter that came to hand yesterday[.] It gives me satisfaction to hear from you and all the rest. I am well and hope this may reach and find you and all enjoying the same blessing[.] I received the bundle of clothes you sent to me and the letter that com with it and wrote to you in a day or two afterwards[.] I was glad to get them though I was not in need of them at the time[.] you need not send any more to me this winter unless I send for something for I think I have near about enough of clothing to do me this winter[.] I am glad to hear that you have all gatherd a fine crop this fall and that Father was geting along tolerable well a sowing small grain (sow all you can)[.] you said you wished me to come home and help you eat some of your rice[,] but I tell you that we have rice here almost every day until I am tired eating it. I woud be glad to get the chance to go home but I don't much expect to get an opportunity this winter. our fare is tolerable good for the last two or three weeks we have had take rye coffee but we have sugar to sweeten it and the most of us likes it tolerable well[.] we can git thousands of sweet potatoes at from .40 to .50 cents per bu. &c[.] I shall not say much about the wreck this time as I have writen to you about it before. We served their one week and then relieved by other 2 companys. two days after we left a larg ship came near and fired many bomb shells at our men their[.] our boys took shelter behind the sand banks and let the vandals shoot til they got tired of the fun[.] some shells fell near our men but done no harm only one fell about the cookery and broke one plate and scaterd sand among the dishes[.] we had no larg guns at the wreck or we could have sunk their ship. we will move in a day or so across the sound out on the main land where I expect we will take up our winter quarters. The blocking vessels are about here as usual[.] on the night of the 22 inst[.] 6 negros runaway from Beaufort[.] the got on a small boat and it is thought they went out and got a board of a yankee vessel that was anchord out some 4 miles from shore. nothing more at present only I send my best wishes to every one of you, Noah Deaton [P.S] Father[,] I sent $20.00 to you to Carthage by Mr L Lawhon in care Mr Daniel McKinnon[.] I have wrote to you twice to let me know whether you receivd it or not and have not heard from it yet[.] their was two ten dollar bills[.] I want you to let me know about it as soon as you can[.]

1861, November 24

Eliza Jane Walker McLeod to husband **Louis H. McLeod**. General wartime correspondence with brief mentions of **Angelet McLeod, Elizabeth Hinton Brewer McLeod, John Lewis Cox, Wiley ?, ? Jordan, Francis Moore, Tandy Walker, Swann, Sandy Kelly, Miss Hill, Tempy Thomas, Abe Douglas, Thomas Bragg McLeod, Alexander McNeill and Nelly ?.** [75]

I sete my self this evning to drop you a few lines to let you no that we are all wel at this tine but Angelet [who is] rite sick this evning with the cole[. i rcevd your letter last Friday and was sorey to her you was sick . i hop you wil soon get wel. Louis if you ant no beter i want you to com home and stay until you get well. my dear you rote about going on the water to fite. Louis i never can give up for that.now for your sake never go. for if you go thar i never shal expect to see you again. Louis i beg you not to go. the children all say tha hope pap will be too sick to go. when i red that we all cold [could]not help crien to think you wold go Louis i pry [pray] that you may not goo. fite them on land but for my sake and the childrin sake and your mother sake dont go in the see. your mother was her to day an told me to beg you not goo. she sade she had rather her [hear] you wer ded then her you wer takin prisner and i had too. Louis if you goo i never expect to see you again. my lord hav mercy on you. i had a live [I had lived] in hope that i wold see you again in this life but if you go on the osian [ocean] i never shal see you again. i hope you will not goo. Louis i have not pot [put] it out of my mind sinc i herd [since i heard] it i cant thing of nothing else. my dear dont goo for i want to se you won time more in my life. Louis i want you to com home as soon as you can, you rote to me you hadent got nary leter from me sine the therd[.] i hav rote evry weke only this weke and i thot [thought] i wold send [the letter]by John LouisSwan back them and he sais he dont no how it is that my leters dont go[.] Louis dont blame me for not riting for i hav rote evry weke and Swan pack them and if you dont get them i dont no how it is[.] he sase he pack them like he did wiley [?] Louis i am glad to get a leter from you and i recken you are so too if i cold rite like you i wold rite evry ofner but it take me so long to rite and i cant think of nothing to rite and the i spel so bad i dont no how you can rede it[.] Louis times is mity hard up her[.] i hav livd harder sence you went of the [then] i ever did in my life[.] we hav to liv on white cofey and dos goo mity hard with me[.] i havt had a drop of whisky in my house since you left[.] i am going to town if my helth wil admit weke after this and i am going to get a few pound of cofee if it is fifty cents, and som whisky[.] i am sorey that i hav nothing to send you by John[.] i hav ten dolars and i send you five of that and the other five i hav to giv for won bushel of sault and dont no wher i can get it for that or not[.] i hav nothing to sel but a few bushel of otes and little flower, the coten i wil keep tel you com home[.] if you can com crismas and if you want the money you can sel the coten and hav the money[.] it is no use to take to San[.] i never shal ask him eny more[.] wil a sell a horse before i wil[.] i can liv withthout him and i now, you can[.] you shal hav as long as ther is eny thing her whe you wantet eny thing rite to me[.] i went to Jordens yestirday to giv in war taxies[.] i told som of them i didnen think it was rite for me to pay such taxas as the for the [them] for that Louis was worth as much as eny other man to me an he was fiting for his contry and tha dident feed me. so that is to pay in may. it wil bee but ten dolars. Louis i was mity sorey to her of Francis being sick. i was so wel plesd about you and him living to gether. i hope he may son get wel. i never shal for ge[t] him for being so good to you. may the god of heven bless him and save him is my [prayer. Give my] lov to him when you rite to him. giv him my best lov and til [tell] him i never wil forget him. Louis i her yesterday the Captan was sick is it so or no. Swan red my leter and sade he cold not beleiv it. we ar all mity sorey if it is so. it seenes you all have a hep of sikeness. i was in hopse when the wether got cold the sickess wold be over. sorry to her Tan wont wel. tel Tan i remember him an Sandy too. Louis i her Swan is going to send you some whisky by John. giv Tan San and Sam [same] pore felow i hope his mother wil send him bedclose. if she wont rite to me and i will send him a quilt. i send you the comfert by John the blanket is the won miss Hil sent to you. she sade she had but won more but she most send that to you so i quilted them to gether and think it will keep you warm and i send your pilow too. giv my lov to Swan and tel him i wil tri to make another lofe and if i can i wil send it by John. i never cold make good lofe bred [loaf bread] in the winter. is you staing with the Captin now or hoo[?] rite to me. timpy Thomas stade with me last nite and sends all of her lov to you. i red the leter to her and she had to cri alitle and say pore felow. you sem like won of her one children. Abe comover and most [must] ride [read] all of your leter and ole Swan too and miss Hil too. tha say you rite so much stisfaction in your leter. miss hil most rede the leters you sen to Abe too evry body wants to her from you. your long leders dont werey [worry] me tha are the sort tha i like to get. Louis i am glad to get a leter from you and i recken you are so too. if i cold rite like you i wold rite ofner but it take me so long to rite and i cant think of nothing to rite and the i spel so [pleased] it plising them so much to her you praise Francis. tha like you so much. the leter you herd old Swan baby was ded i was mity sorey for them. tha seme to hete it so bad. my dear Louis i am geting veri fat. tha hav coments bringin me litle thing over aredy [already] and tha tel me to take good cer of my self. tha say i ot [ought] to take beter car of my self then i ever did. it had bin so long since i had any won. if you rite eney thing about it rite it on a litle slip for tha most rede all of your leters. i hope i may doo well. may god spar you to liv to com home and see us all won time mor in this world. Louis i most close it is very cole and the childrin all a slep. no bod[y] up but myself. the childrin all sends howdy to pap and say tha hope you wil come home crismas tha all thaut tha saw you coming yeterday threw the file [field,] all run in and sade yander comes pap up and look out. i told it want you but Brag thow [thought] it was you and run away down to mete you but it ander McNeil. i recken tha wold hav a fit if tha could see you com all the time talking about you. it make me sorey for them. Nelee said i most rite to you that he could plow and he was worken mity hard to make you biskit to eat when you com home. no more onley take good cer of yourself dont go out and take cole. Louis bee cerful. may god bless you and sav you is my prar. so good bey your loving wife until deth rite as soon as you get this. Eliza McLeod

1861, December [undated estimate]
Malcom Ray to brother. General wartime correspondence between brothers with brief mentions of **James W. McDonald, Aaron Davidson, Ruffin Wallace, James Dowdy, Daniel L. McDonald** and **William B. Monroe**. [76]

Dear brother[,] I receaved your letter and was very much pleasd to here from you[.] I have nothing new to write to you[.] we are geting a long here the best we can and that is not very well[.] I hope when thes few lines will reach you it will find you all well and doing well[.] I have nothing new to write to you[.] there is 4 of our men in the hospital in Raleigh[—]James McDonald, Daveson, R. Wales, J. Dowdy is very sick, D.L.McDonald has been very sick[.] I thot he would die the night he was take but he is nearly well now[.] he was out of his senses about two our that nite[.] he would get up and say he would die, he said he woudent mend dein[,] only his people wod hait it so bad[.] cousen W.B. Monroe is geting some better[.] he cant speak out of a whisper yet but he keaps up and about all the time[.] I must close by sending my best respects to you all[.] I still remain your afectionate brother, Malcom Ray [P.S.] excuse bad writing and mistakes[.] write soon and tell me the nuse[.]

1861, December 1
Mary Caddell to cousins **A.S. Caddell** and **James N. Caddell**. General wartime correspondence between cousins with brief mentions of **Will Barrett, Absalom Fry**, old aunt **Polly, Ashley F. Muse** and **Mary Caddell's** father **Joseph Caddell**. [77]

Dear cosen[,] I again seat myself down for the purposes of answering your very kind letter which I rec last Sunday[.] affectionate cosen[,] I red your letter with pleasure[.] I was glad to hear that you was well and I am well myself and fathers family is Well and the people are generally Well through this section of country[.] Dear cousen[,] I have no nuse to rite to you moore than I was at a quilting the other day at cousin Will Barett and was ask to another at Absalom Fry but I did not go[.] Tim you ought to be at home just about now for thare is frolicks almost every night of some sort[,] but Tim old aunt Poly has not had turn yet[.] you said you loved possum[.] come over and we will go a hunting well[.] I must quit my badness for I am a going to hear A.F. Muse preach today[.] Tim father sends his best love to you and wants you to rite to him[.] well I must stop my few lines by saing rite soon to your cousin[.] Mary Caddell

A few lines to cousin J.N.C. dear cousin[,] I received your few lines which found me well[,] hoping these few lines may reach you and find you well an engoying yourself[.] Well I hav no nuse to rite to you for you no times hard in deed about here[.] when the boys are all gon for the company of the boys are all the engoyment the girls ingoy[.] you must excuse bad riting and spelling[.] I must bring my letter to a close by saing rite soon[.] Mary Caddell

1861, December 1
John A. Walker to brother **Tandy Walker** and nephew **Louis H. McLeod**. General wartime correspondence with brief mentions of **James A. Cole, Archibald Black, Richard M. Jackson, Isaiah Matthews, Sandy Kelly, Jarret Graham, W.W. Cox, John Arnold** and **Thomas Durham**. [78]

My Dear Brother & Nephu, I recvd yours of the 24th and was glad to here from you and to here that you was well But was sorry to learn that so many of your men was sick. Louis I have nothing of any importance to rigt to you at presant only those lines leaves me well at presant. I have not bin down sick nary day since I left home and hope that I will remain well untill I go home to stay if the damn each [itch] dont kill me and Jim. Sandy Cole big as a dam dog give me and Cole the dam each [itch] but that wont kill me. we have bin mooving a good many times and I dont no how long before we will have [our]orders to leave here as soon as practible and go to little Washington we have only five comp (companies) here and none of them equipt yet. we have nothing more to fight with than when we left home. we have not lost but three of our men R. Jackson, A. Black and I. Mathes but a great many sick and goan [gone] home there has three men dyed in camp this weak. we are in camp on a ridge between two big swamps and you cannot get out without crossing over the water about one mile wide the sound is twelve miles wide against Edenton. we are one mile from Edenton and wood is devilish scan[re] and the wind comes keen and the hardest winds you ever herd blau. But for eating we cannot grumble we have good beef bacon corn & flour bread peas rice sugar molases vinegar but no coffe. we have not had none since we left Camp Clark I have got so I can quit drinking whisky for we cant get it without paying from 50 [cents] to 1 dollar per qt and you no we dont drink much for we have not got one cent of money yet not eaven our bounty money. Louis I want to no what has become of Sandy Kelley & if he is wel and how many times he has bin in the gard house. If I could see you I could tell you a dam sight about own travles. Louis John Arnold says if you let such a man as Jaret Grimes keep you in side of the line you are no man. John Arnold says he feels right wooly today for he was over town yesterday steaming most to much. Louis who is W. W. Cox that you sai dyed. I dont no him. Since I commenced this letter I have taken the netter rash what we call at home the mad each and it like to of killed me. I had four men detailed for to scratch and curry me and of all sights it was [on] me in great whaels as big as your finger. But I am up again and about. we expect to go to Newbern in ten days so sayes presant orders. you need not right to me until I right to you for we may be goan from this place on the 9th [inst] we have got a man to try for his life for striking one of his officers some say they will shoot him his name is Durham, — Thomas Durham [you no him] I will bring my letter to a close by saying I remain your loving brother until death. J. A. Walker

1861, December 1

Eliza Jane Walker McLeod (and daughter **Anjalett McLeod**) to husband **Louis H. McLeod**. General wartime correspondence with brief mentions of **William ?, Fanny ?, Frances ?, Tandy Walker, David P. Morris, Elizabeth Hinton Brewer McLeod, William Underwood, Alex ?, Henry ?, Mary ? , Nelly?, Emily Franklin, David Kelly** and **Delilah McLeod.** [79]

My der Louis it is with pleser i sete my self this morning to drop you a few lines to let you no that we ar all well at this time hoping these few lines may find you in the same blesing. i hope you hav got wel. i was afraid you wold venter [venture] too fer and take the backswet and wold be wors then at first. my der doo take good cer of your self someney (?)of your men is dide i am unesy all of the time about you. i hope you wil take good cer of your self and tri to cum home crismas. want to see you very bad. i hav nothing moch to rite only we hav got doon soing whete and ots at last. tha had along time of it we sod fiften bushel of whet and twenty bushel of otes and we hav got the coten out. we hav getherd all in at last. i am going to start to Fayetteville if nothing hapens wensday with what otse we had lefte and too barles of flower to tri to get somthing to eat. i dred the trip but it seemes like i cant doo without going. I hop it wont hurt me for i most hav somthing. if you wer her i wont hav to goo. Louis it is mity bad chances to hav to depend on other folks for foo enything. if i cant doo my self it gose [goes] andoon [undone.] i think i wil discharg Wiliam when we com back from town i think we can tend what lan we hav ourself unles we cler a new ground and i dont no wher to cler if you want us to cler enny perticker place rite wher as soon as you get this. it wll be mity bad doing without enny man on the plantation but if you com home when your time is out it will bee time enof to soo whet. Louis i dont no what William is going to doo big fed(?) wants him to liv with him but Fanny dont want to goo. She wants him to bild on the land wher you tole him to bil and i think he had beter. i herd from Frances last friday and he was beter and the Captin was able to rite his self. i hope he wil soon get wel Louis tel Tan i want to her from him an i want to no wher he is coming home with you or not. tel him tocom [to come] if he can. David P. is very low tha dont think he wil ever be able to goo back. your mother is rite smart at this time. i hope these few lines will find you in good health. i hope your finger is beter. i hope you hav got out of the notion of going on the see to fite. i sent six dolars by John and too chickins. i recken you hav got them. rite to me. Billy and Ileck got home last thirsday and tha had a hepe to tel. i dont recken Biley wil ever get doon teling. you no it take him so long to tel enny thing. the childrin all sends ther best lov to you and Henry and Ary and Nelee and Fanny and William all want you to com home crismas. i wil send the six when i send the boots. i wil send them as soon as i can. we hav no cash and i dont see no cansh [chance] of geting non soon. the childrin ot [ought] to be going every day. Louis i hav nthng more to rite only your loving wife until deth may the god of heven bless you and save you is my prar until we shal meet again in this life. i hop for that time. i long to see that time and god grant that we may both liv to see that time. good by my loving husban until deth. Eliza McLeod

Dear Pap I take pen in hand to let you know how Emely and Dave is com on. he com down every uther sunday night and Delely say the set up in corner till the chickens crows. be shore and com home crismas and we will hav a big wedding with Emely and Dave. Mother says the shant married here. they will hafter go to the school house nothing more at presand. Anjalett McLeod

Mr McLeod I am very sorry you have to lye by youre self but if you come home Eliza is so fat there will be no room for you to lye with her without we put down the matress. Mr McLeod tell Tan i am very much oblige to him for writing to me to let me know what he said about the money i sent him. Emily Franklin.

1861, December 2
Louis H. McLeod (*Camp Wyatt*) to wife **Eliza Jane Walker McLeod**. General wartime correspondence with brief mentions of **Thomas Buchanan, Abner Flynn Harrington, Tandy Walker, Sandy Kelly, John Lewis Cox, Dr. Campbell, Francis Moore, Miss Hill, Archibald Kelly, Dick Wicker, F.M. Blalock, Eli Brafford.** [80]

Dear Wife, I receaved your welcomb letter on Saturday knight that was dated the 24. I was verry glad to hear from you and that you and all the children was well. Eliza I am as well and hearty at this time as ever I was in my life. But there is a good manny of our company that cant say that. There is about twenty of our company sikk or not able to drill at this time. There is none of them seriously sick. Thomas Buchanan and A. F. Harrington is the worst off. Harrington has been verry sick but is a good deal better. He thought a while of going to the Harspital at Wilmington but he got better. He is now so he can go about a little. There is a good many cases of mumps. Tandy has had them but he has got over them. he is a going out to drill to day for the first time since he had the mumps. Sandy Kelley is well and fat and can eat moore patatoes than any man you ever saw. Eliza there was twelve of our men came down when John L. Cox came and we was verry glad to see them. We looked for them on friday knight but they dident come. The boat was so late a going up that mourning that it could not get back so our men had to lay over one day and knight in Wilmington so they came down on saturday eavening. It was dark befour they got off the boat. When the tide is down the boat cant get nearer than one mile and a half of the shore on our side of the river. So it takes a long time when the tide is up the steam boad can cum up to the warf and is no trouble. There is twenty of our men at home now. we expect some of them the last of this week. The Doctor Campbell is here now. I think our men will all soon get well. After they get over this spell I think they will stay well. The Regimant that left here was as well and hearty as ever I saw men. They dident have a sick man in it. I like to stay here first rate. We have verry good water and mighty handy and a plenty of it. You sayed in your letter you wanted to no for surtain whether the Captian was sick or not. He was sick and the sickest sort. He was staying in the tent with me at the time he was taken sick. He was taken Monday knight the 18th of November with a hard aguer. I never saw a man have a harder aguer than he did. he woke me up about four oclock to make a fire in the stove to ceep him from freasing. he stade here untill Thursday. I rote a note for him up to his Brother to come to see him the Doctor came down on Thursday or Friday and taken him up home with him. The Captain has got in about well. He is coming home to day. He would have come home Saturday but Doctor Campbell stade with him on Friday knight so the Doctor and his Brother cep him from coming. I want to see him verry bad, but I am a fraid he will turn out too soon. The last I herd from my friend Lieutenant Moore he was verry sick. He was a going up to Chatxham. I hope he will soon get well and return. I miss him so much. I had rather any body else was sick than him. We were together all of the time when he was here. And if we ever got into a fight we will be to gether. we had don made up our minds to fight side by side. if one got shot down the other was to shoot down the man that don it or die in the attempt. I wish he was well and back here now. You wanted to no where I was staying. I am staying in the same tent lying on the same cot and has now a plenty of bead close to ceep me warm. Tell Mrs Hill I am a thousand times oblige to her for being so good as to give me a blanket, and then to you for quilting them together. It is a splendid thing. I am not afraid of freasing now. Tandy is staying in the tent with me now. We have the stove to set by when the wither is cold enough. I live first rate a good little tent and every thing fixed off nicely one riting table and one table to eat often. You wanted to no wher Sandy Kelley stayed. He stayed in the tent with Arch Kelley and Dick Wicker, Blalock and Brafford. Our rules is mighty tite on us now but it is just there is so manny men here if the cornmal want tight on them he could not do any thing with them. our men has don pretty well. there hasent been but four in the gard house. Our Regiment is about to bee pade off now. just as soon as the Captian gets so he can ten to it. we will get our money. some of the company has heer don and got thern. I think we will get ours this week up to the thireth of October. It will come in a mighty good time. I never herd men grumble so much about tabacco. None of them had any money to buy tabacco with. When they get their money they will all buy tabacco. There is some left here in the camp to sell that is all they can buy. there ant nothing else here to buy unless oysters. As to something to eat we have a plenty of good baken and some good beef but some of the beef is verry bad. it looke like it was some old steers that was halling up corn or something else on Saturday and on Monday comes to our camp for us to eat. We have plenty of flower and corn bread but no coffe only meal coffe and that is first rate. We havent had any coffe in some time we have quit thinking about it. We have no molasses at all. We have plenty of sugar. We dont get any candles now only as we can buy them. there is one company that makes some tallow candles and sells them at five cents a piece. We git some potatoes. We draw 2 quarters of beef each day six days out of ten. We would like mightyly to get holt of some poark. We have no reasen in the wirld to complain of eating. I must close the paper has give out. It is verry doubtfull about my coming home. I cant give you any idez about coming. I will come as soon as I can get off. give my respects to all enquiring friends your husband, Louis H. McLeod

1861, December 5
Harrison Davis (*Devils Den, Fort Macon*) to **A.S. Caddell**. General wartime correspondence with brief mentions of **Zack Hogan**, **Neill Caddell, Samuel Jackson McIntosh, Raleigh P. Allen, Alexander M. Dunlap** and others **Jim** and **Laky**. [81]

Dear Friend Tim, as Sandy come over I will drop you a few lines[,] but you may be assured that this is no place together news[.] Tim I would like to pay you all a visit but I don't expect that I could get off handy and I don't like to be bothersome no how[.] The fort is not the thing it is cracked up to though not as bad as I expected[.] we get plenty of rye tea to drink and it sweetened at that bread meat & c[.] Tim if I get back to the camp I think it will take a coon dog to ketch one next time[.] Sandy told me that you Jim & Laky had a contract for ten days[.] if so get through it as easy as possible[.] the less you say the better it will be[.] Tim if there comes any letters for me be certain and send them over[.] if there comes anything from my gal don't send it unless you think it will be in good hands and be sure to get to me. Tim you fellows must keep dark or we all might get more lies told and make the matter worse than it really is[.] it is bad enough at best, but it is our first offence and I don't think they ought to be rough with us[.] Tell Zack and Jack to watch or they might break over into the guard house[.] Tell Neill that if our cigars comes to sell them at 1.50 per box & no less. Tim the next passing send me a clean shirt, some envelopes & paper[.] drop me a few lines any chance[.] I got a letter from RPA but no news no more[.] from your friend Harrison

1861, December 6
C.D. Caddell to brother **A.S. Caddell**. General wartime correspondence between brothers regarding Christmas and brief mention of **J.A.B. Blue**, **Martha Sullivan**, **Harrison Davis** and **Devotion Davis**. [82]

Dear Brother, I seat myself again to write you a few lines to let you know that I am well at present[.] hoping these few lines will find you well[.] I wrote to you the 2d of this inst[.] though I recd a letter today that J.A.B. Blue brought and I was glad to hear from you[.] you talk like you write everyday but I dont get the letters if you do[.] I am a coming to see you about Christmas if nothing happens[.] write as soon as you get this and I will come and bring my next letter[.] get what things you can for nothing and I will go prepared to bring them home[.] I will start the 26 of December if nothing breaks so you can look for me about that time[.] I will rite no more at present you must write two letter before I go[.] rite one as quick as you can and the other to get here about the 22 of Dec before I start[.] if there is nothing the matter I shall go certain[.] I want you to fix a plan to make some money[.] I got the things D. Davis brought[.] I expect all your likeness looks verry well and I will give your gal, the big likeness if you say so[.] tell Harrison I wrote to him[.] I will close by saying I am your Loving Brother till Death, C.D.C

1861, December 8
Eliza Jane Walker McLeod (and **Emily Franklin**) to husband **Louis H. McLeod**. General wartime correspondence with brief mentions of **Tandy Walker, Abe Douglas, John A. Walker, David Kelly, Fanny Morris, Fanny ?, Delilah McLeod, Elizabeth Hinton Brewer McLeod, Anjalett McLeod** and **Rory ?.** [83]

Der and loving Louis i set down this evening to drap my you a few lines to let you no that we ar all wel at this time hoping thes few lines may find you in the same blesing. i recved your leter dated the third and was more the glad to her you was wel and harty agan and to her the captin had got wel enof to go back to his company agin. i recken you was mity glad, and to her the rest of your men was on the mend. i hope you all will get well and harty again. i was very sorey to her that Tan was sick again. i hop he wont hav the fever if he dos i want you to tend to him. i fele very sorey for tan. Louis i hav bin to town and hav got home safe. i got fifty cents [per bushel]for otes six dolars and a haf for flower and i paid eighteen cents[per pound] for shuger and i bot four[bought four] pound of cofee and paid too dolars for it. Abe said he was coming over to drink cofee and i told him he wol [would] not yeit [yet]. when you com home he mout [might] cam over and he wold get a drink of cofee. i am going to keep it until you com home. i wil hav a drink of it every sunday morning. my hogs is getting very fat but i don expet to kill them til crismas. i want to hav the sparribs to ete when you com home. Louis i hav got your bots [boots] fixt and i wil send them the first chanc i get and your sox too. if you think you can doo without them until you com rite to me. i red your leter you sent to Abe to day and i was more then glad to her from you and to her the capten had got home and Tandy was beter. Louis i herd you wer all expected to bee orderd to Kantucky and i was mity unesy until i red Abe leter and then i felt beter satisfid. i hop you wil never hav to goo that far from home. now i can her from you every weke and that is grate satisfaction to me and if you wer way thar i cold not her. i shold be all of the time unesy. i herd from John today and he is not very wel. he has the yeler jaudies [yellow jaundice.] he said tha are going to mov to newberge, about one hundre an twenty mile ner, tha hav got the horses and are going to start to marow and tha hav got ther gun es. tel Tan dave was her last Saterday nite but dave Kelly was her and he had a bad chance. Louis i hav kep the fouder [fodder] yet but it is the hardest thing i ever don tha com and shake the money at me most everyday but i tel them it is no use tha cant get it. the lither [leather] is the same way. you never said nothing about the money i sent you nor the chickengs did you get them or not. Louis you said you new me and fany moris wold doo something soon as you left. i think we both don it before you left. i recken you k her it in all most every leter you get. it tickes ther fun her but it is no fun to me i dreed to have to go enny wher and i dont go onley whar i hav bisness. Louis you most com home crismas and if i cant doo enny thing for you i hope the gales will take pity on you and let you hav alitle. your mother is creping boudy to pap and sais you most com home crismas. fanny sase so too. i want you to rite in the niret(?) where you wil com or not. i hope the god of heven will bless yo with helth and life to met again in this life. I trust in god for all things. i hope god wil bee with you in all of your trobles and keep you from all harm. i hope god wil bee with me in my troble. i most close by saing good by your der and loving wife until deth & my god bless you and love you. Eliza McLeod

Mr McLeod while Mr Douglas an the rest of them is writing so mutch about me an Dave i will tell you something about Anjalett and roery(?) they are riding about to meeting together very often. it will be them that will marry chrismas i expect if you dont come home an stic it. McLeod we want you to come home verry bad. Emily

1861, December 10
Louis H. McLeod (*Camp Wyatt*) to wife **Eliza Jane Walker McLeod.** General wartime correspondence with brief mentions of **John Lewis Cox, Elizabeth Hinton Brewer McLeod, William M. Swann, William Underwood, Dr. Campbell, Buie, Henry ?, Anjalett McLeod and Emily Franklin.** [84]

Dear Wife I seat my self down this mourning to drop you a few lines to let you know that I am well at this time hoping those few lines will find you and family all well particular after your trip to Fayetteville. Eliza I havnt nothing of importance to write to you. I receavd every thing that you sent by John Cox and was verry glad to get them Sandy Brown got back last Saturday and mother sent me some beef and butter and bisquet and corn bread and I was verry glad to get it I have been eating butter eversince Billy Underwood was down here all the time the Captin was sick there was no boddy to eat on that you sent me but me and Tan until the Doctor came back and then he brought some and we all eat togea ther myself and Tan and Doctor Campbèll and the Captian when he is hear. I think he will bee with us all the time now. he came from Wilmington last knight and brought our money. he never stopt untill he pade off every one except them that was on gard and the cooks which he will pay to day. We drawed too months and a half up to the thirty first of October. I receaved twenty eight dollars after paying my part for the cook and paying Doctor Campbell his part. I think I can do with what money I have got now. I ow some in the company which I must pay but I think I will have money enough to do me untill the next pay day and that is not far off if they pay up every too months. I tell you the company is well pleased plenty money in there pockets and plenty to eat and that is what a good manny up in your country cant say. Our men is all well satisfied. The pay day will come off the last day of this month as they say but I think it is too soon if we can draw every three months it will be often enough. We have got lots and cards of money on this poore sand hill now if the yankees does come and kill us or take us they will get the money. It taken twenty eight hundred dollars to pay off our company. some of the rest got a good deal moore than we did because they were in the sirvis longer. some of them has been in the sirvis nearly seven months. Nothing moore about the war only the blockade hasent been seen for sevirel days and every boddy thinks that they are fixing to attack us and will do it in a few days. Well we are anxious to see them that is just what we are here far and if they ever do land here they will have something to do if they whip us. Eliza you wanted to know where to clear a new ground. I think that you cant do without wood to burn and that you had better have them to cut wood over the branch towards Bowies(?) to get wood to burn whether you can take it in or not. I want you to hav Henry to cut them ditches one in that little swamp below Angays(?) patch and one other one down in that branch where the new ground was last year begining down at the Barrowes at the low grounds and run it up to where the branch goes though the fence. I am afraid you havnt sowed enough of wheet and oats. I thought it would have taken moore to have sowed the ground. Eliza the chance is very bad about coming home Christmas. I dont think there is any chance for me to come home untill six months is out. the Counral has got orders to let no men go home on a furlough not even the sick. so my chance is bad about going home. if I go at all it will bee after christmas. I am in hopes them orders will be countermanded by that time so I can go home to see you all Christmas and get something good to eat. Eliza I havent got time to write Mr Cole is just about to start, you must excuse me for bad writing and spelling for I am in a hurry. look over all mistakes and dont grumbel. give my love and respects to the children and tell them howdy and tell Anjalett I was glad to see that she had improved so much in writing Tell Emely that I was much oblige to her for the few lines that she send to me. Louis H. McLeod

1861, December 11

William P. Martin (*Camp Vance*) to **Hugh Leach**. General wartime correspondence with brief mentions of **H.L. Muse, Maj. Carmichael, Col. White, Lawhon, Dr. John Shaw, Oren Smith, Will Thompson, John L. Caddell, Kelly Williamson, Nathan Fry, John D. Tyson, Robert Willcox, John W. Corrum** and **Eliza Leach.**

85

My Dear Friend, I feel under many obligations to you for your kindness and attention to me, In writing whether I answer your letter or not. I feel under more obligation to you and H. L. Muse than any other person in the county. Neither of you dont stand on etiquett like a great many do. I have written some, and requested them to write as often as they could, and I would answer their letters as soon as I could convenienlly, but I have received no letters from any person except yourself and Muse, only where I have written them first. A great many I suppose think I have nothing to do but write, but they are very mistaken. I was down at the wreck of the steamer "Union" when I received your letter, or I would have answered it immediately. I got so far behind in answering letters that I received while at the wreck that I have never caught up yet. And since we got back from there we have had to move twice, and there is generally two or three days at everytime we move that I cant write any. We had a hard time while at the wreck. We staid there a weak, and had no tents or blankets, and but very little to eat and had to work in the water all the time. I thought while there that I would have the honor of being commander in one battle, but I was disappointed. I had about 80 men, 50 of my company and thirty of the Pee Dee Wild Cats under my command until the third night. I was reinforced with another company and one small field piece. On tuesday evening after we got there a steamer came right up to us, with her guns run out, and came within about four hundred yards of us and cast anchor. I had ordered the men over the bank before they got within a mile of us. We had first rate plan for protection. The bank is about fifteen feet high, and from forty to fifty feet thick, with depressions in it that could [?] up [?] under and we felt perfectly safe from shell as long as we could stay there. I had to remain on the bank and watch the movements of the yankees. I had a spy glass and could see every thing done. The deck was covered with men, and I could see their arms glisting in the sun, and their gunners on the upper deck standing ready to match them off at a moments notice. They had not cast anchor more than a minute or two before they began to lower a boat and soon began to fill with men. I then thought we were in for a fight then, as I expected they intended to try and effect a landing under the protection of their guns. I went under the hill to give some more orders, and went back on the bank, and saw the boat was nearly half way to the beach, but as soon as they discovered me, they hoisted a flag of truce, but could not effect a landing on account of the breakers being two high. They returned to the vessel and steamed off, but next morning renewed their visit, and the same maneuvers were gone through on both sides. I had received my reinforcements that night, and felt a little better prepared if they made an attempt to land, as I had my field piece planted upon the bank so we could rake them if they did land, and had it masked so it could not be seen, but they again hoisted their white flag and succeeded in getting to shore. Major Carmachael came up that morning, him and myself went down to know what they wanted, the officer came forward, but was scared so bad he could hardly tell. He was the most excited man I have seen in a long time, he shook like he had an asue(?). He wanted to know the name of the vessle, and what had become of the men. He returned in a few minutes to his vessle and steamed off. I sent a messenger to the Fort that evening, with a note to Col. White requesting him to send me up a rifled cannon, as I knew they had been rifling out some, and not mounted them all. But he didnt send me one, for the reason he had no cartridges to fit. If I would have got one that night, and got it up I would have had another prize, as they came along next day in about three hundred yards of us. On tuesday after I left their two different vessles came along, one in the morning and the other in the evening and gave the companys that went up to releive me ten rounds each, but without any damage, although the shell bursted right over where the men were. They came very near hitting the cannon we had planted on the bank. The wreck didn't turn out to be as valuable as was reported in the papers. We got twenty four horses, two small engines, and a great many other valuable things off of it, and could have saved a great many more if it had not been that there was a heavy wind on the third day which caused the vessle to settle at one end, and the water got in so deep that we were obliged to leave a great many articles of value that we could have gotten out of it had not been for her settling down. We never got the cannon that Lawhon reported we got. How it is a man can manufacture such a tale as Lawhon did I cant see. He stated that he had been to the wreck when the was not in fifteen miles of it. The fact is he didn't know the vessle was wreck until after he left for home- -[.] Weare hard at work fixing up our winter quarters, and hope we will be comfortably situated in a week or two, we ten frames up one hundred feet each, by 18 ft, they are to be divided into four rooms each, with two chimneys each. We will have a butiful encampment when we get it finished. The encampment is square, the officers quarters will be at one end and the encamp will nearly be enclosed. It will only require three senteniles to guard the camp, one at the end next to the rail road and two on each side, in the space between the officers and the soldiers quarters. I am in hopes the health of the regiment will improve since we have got off this beach out of the bleak winds that we were exposed to from the ocean. It was enough to have killed the men standing picket on the beach, it was so cold, and the atmosphere so damp. Their clothes would be almost wet through in the morning after standing three hours. The health of my company has been better than any other company in the Regiment recently. I think the reason is they took the meassles sooner, and got through earlier than any other company in the Regiment recently, and were better able to stand the chilling winds, than those who were having theirs late in the fall. The Drs. said if we had remained there was no doubt we would have lost half the regiment with typhoid pneumonia & fever together. Every case of typhoid fever from that side has proven fatal, while other cases in the 7th Regiment, stationed at Carolina have got well. Death has again visited our ranks and taken from our midts one of our best companions. I mean Dr. Shaw. He is a great loss to the regiment, as well as to his friends and relatives. Since his death I have lost another member of my company. Orron Smith of Chatham, he has been in Webster's company (since) the last of August, with his father and brother but had not been regularly transfered. I I have made application to have Will Thompson, John L. Caddell, Kelly Williamson and Nathan Fry discharged. John D. Tyson got a discharge about two weeks ago. The other four have not been able to perform any service for two months, and don't seem to improve any, and thought it best for them to go home. With the exception of those named Robert Willcox the health of my company is pretty good. Some few are complaining of cold. I am very uneasy about Robt. He is very sick with fever, I fear he will have a hard time of it if he gets over it. I was truly sorry to hear of the death of John W. Corrum(?). It must have given his relatives a great shock when they heard it. Mr. Ruple spent four days with us, and preached for us four times while hear. I wish we had him with us, if you had somebody else in his place. I think he would do a great deal of good if he was here, as he had twice the number out to hear him that I have ever seen out at one time. I wish you to remember me to all my friends in your neighborhood. Give my respects to your wife. I hope when I hear from you again you, you may be enjoying your usual good health. Let me hear from you as often as you conviently can. I remain your sincere friend, W. P. Martin

1861, December 11

Alexander McDonald (*Camp Mangrum, near Raleigh, NC*) to unidentified brother. General wartime correspondence between brothers with brief mentions of **McBlue**, Capt. **John M. Kelly**, **Neill McDonald** and the death of cousin **James W. McDonald**. [86]

Dear Brother and friend, I take this opportunity of informing you all that I am well at this present time[,] hoping these lines to find you all enjoying the same comfort. I would write home oftener than I do only there are so many passing between here and home. McBlue and some others reached our camp last night. They brought a large amount of bed clothing and provisions. They brought potatoes that was damaged by being out so long. I got my bed tick. I would you and all that anything to camp to send it in the care of the captain and the regiment. The turnips you sent me reached camp next Wednesday after they left home. All of Capt. Kelly's company was in Raleigh that day getting arms[,] and the men could not find any owner and he carried the turnips back to Raleigh and I have not got my turnips yet. Anything that is to be carried by a stranger must be well marked or it may get lost. A good many of the company is complaining but none bad off—only cousin James W. McDonald. He has got the typhoid fever. It is expected that the regiment will leave here before Christmas. As to where we will go is not known. I received a letter from brother Neill some 12 days ago[,] of which he stated that he was well. We have the promise of overcoat and if I don't get a coat before we leave here, I will send home for one. There are nearly three regiments in camp here. I have some letter wafer in my trunk. I want you to send some of them to me by some person that will pass by here. Elias Harrington was in camp here the 3rd night of this month on his way to Norfolk, Virginia, to get salt and I sent 5 dollars to get some salt. I heard since he left that a man from Raleigh came from that place and he said that 800 hundred wagons was waiting at the place so I think it is a doubtful case that I will get any at all. If he does get any, you can find out very soon. I heard that none in this regiment will not get to go home after the 20th of this month. I thought I would go home but I see a bad chance for it now. Some think that peace will be made before two weeks and some say we will never have peace till the South go over to the North and fight there. Nothing more at present. I must close. - Alex McDonald

1861, December 14
Neill A. Ray *(Carolina City, NC)* to cousin **Mary A. Ray**. General wartime correspondence with brief mentions of **Hugh Ray, Robert P. Wilcox, John L. Caddell, Neill Thompson, Peter M. Campbell, Nancy Ray, Nevin Ray, Jane Ray, John McKinnon, Martin A. McKinnon, William McKinnon, Noah Deaton** and **William Whitlock.** [87]

Miss Mary A Ray, Dear cousin, I take my pen in hand this evening to communicate to you a few lines to inform you that I and Hugh is well at present[,] and hope this will find you and all the family enjoying good health. When it comes to hand, this company is all in tolerable good health with the exception of two or three[,] viz R.P. Willcox has got the fever, J.L. Caddell and N. Thompson is both rather feeble but not serious. I have nothing of much importance to write to you at this time, only we have got out of Bogue Island. We are in camp now between Morehead and Carolina cities ¾ of a mile from the latter place. This is a very nice and pleasant situation. We are busy building our winter houses. I think we will have them completed in a short time if nothing happens to hinder our work. Mr. P.M. Campbell arrive here last night from Moore County with a number of barrels and boxes that our Moore County friends sent to this company consisting of provisions and clothing. I believe I have nothing more that would interest you at this time and therefore I will conclude by saying another word. I have wrote to Cousin Jane to know whether the shells that I sent to Aunt Nancy got home or not, but I have not received as answer as yet. Tell Uncle Niven that I would like to hear from him and all the rest of you as often as I can. I suppose that times is very dull up there at present[,] that salt is very scarce and dear it is dear down here it is $4.00 per bu. (or box). There are many of the citizens about here a making salt but they are not in for making much yet but I respect that often a while that some of them will get to making a good sale. The water here is only part salt in Bogue Sound. The McKinnon boys, Deaton and Whitlock are all well. I send my best wishes and respects to you all. Give my respects to all the neighbors. Please write soon as you can for I would like to hear from you anytime. I am your affectionate cousin. N.A. Ray

1861, December 15
Malcom Ray *(Wake County, NC)* to sister **Christian Ray**. General wartime correspondence between siblings with brief mentions of **William B. Monroe**, Mr. **Blue, John W. McCaskill, James W. McDonald** and **Nancy Ray.** [88]

Dear sister, I tak the privleg of writing you a few lines to let you no that I am in tolerable health at this time and hope these few lines will find you all engoying the same blessing[.] I have not been well for the last weak but have no reason to complain[.] I have the measles but I dont mind them much[.] I am not sick[.] I can eat anything[.] I heard from home the 10 when Mr Blue got back he had a letter from home and a box for Cousen W.B. Monroe and I found two shuck of butter in his box and a letter[.] both lettors came to hand at the same time[.] I was very glad to get boath the lettor and the butter[.] It came to hand in very good time[.] Just when the Measles was about comencing[,] me cousen W.B. Monroe has not got over the measles yet he had tolerable bad spell of them but think he is geting better now[.] he cannot speak out of a whisper yet but he is up and about all the time[.] J. McCaskill is got the measles two[.] he is up and about[.] he dont seam to mind them[.] he got a box of provision from home but it was all eat up[.] it seams lik anything from home is better than anything we have here all tho we get a planty we get tolerable good beaf now[.] we have mooved into our house yesterday we will fare some beter now we can keap dry of wet days and have a fire to sit bay[.] if we will stay here all winter I think I will goe home about Christmas but I dont no how lone we will stay here[.] the colonel was here yesterday and said he had the chance of going to three places[,] Manases Willmington or South Carolina[.] it is thot we will be sent to Willmington[.] if we will go there I expect we will go in a weak or two at the farthest[.] James W. McDonald is in the hospital in Raleigh[.] he has the feavor[.] I saw him yesterday[.] he is geting better[.] he has fell a way till there is nothing but skin and bone[.] I have nothing new to write so I must close bye sending my best respects to you and all the rest[.] I remain your affectionate brother till death, Malcom Ray [P.S.] write soon as you can when you get this and tell me all the news[.] give my love to Aunt Nancy[.] tell her I have not forgoten her[.] give my respects to all enquiring friends[.] So I must close for the time[.]

1861, December 19
Noah Deaton (*Camp Vance, Carolina City, NC*) to sister **Sarah B. Deaton** and father **William Deaton**. General wartime correspondence with brief mentions of **Tyson** and **Robert P. Willcox.** [89]

Dear sister[,] I take my pen in hand to pen you a few words[.] I am on guard to day and have not time write much but I have not much important news to write this time[.] only I am well at present and hope this may reach and find you and all the rest enjoying the same blessing[.] Mr Tyson from Carthage is down here and will leave in the morning for home and I thought it proper to write a few lines home[.] Our co. are in tolerable good health at present[.] We have only one case that is serious[.] Mr R. P. Willcox has the Typhoid Fever but I think he is mending[.] Well I have not much news to write this time[.] one day this week the blockade seized a schooner that attempted to come into this harbour and we supose robed it of its load and then let it go. the next night heavey firing was heard by us in the vicinity of Macon which is 8 miles from this place[.] it was between a Lincoln blockade and a British man of war[,] but we have not heard anything of the result as yet. we heard heavy firing in the direction of Newbern this morning continueing about 3 hours and then seased[.] we have not heard of the meaning of the shooting[.] it is reported in todays news that Lord Lyons of England has demanded of Lincoln a surrender of our ministers to Eng. Messrs Mason and Slidell and also ample apologies for the insult offerd to the British Flag by the Federal navy I hope there will soon be a change for the better. Well Sarah[,] I must soon close this hastly letter[.] I have wrote home once since I received any answer from them. I take pleasure in the chance to send you a stran of shells by Mr Tyson[.] such shels as are in great plenty on the coast here[,] but they sell from fifty to sixty cents per strann[.] if I had a small box I would send home a variety of shells but as I have no box I must be excused[.] I am your affectionate Brother[,] Noah Deaton

Dear father, I have not time to write to you now but I will write before long[.] I supose salt is from $20 to $30 per sack up there[.] it is four Dollars per bushel down here[.] there is many of the sitizens at work at salt and I think the price will soon come down. if I could see any safe chance I would buy some and send it home[.] I must close[.] please write soon. May the God of heaven bless you all is my prayer[.] I remain affectionate to you all, Noah Deaton

1861, December 20
Duncan C. Blue *(Camp Vance, Carolina City, NC)* to **Frances Anna V. Patterson** General wartime correspondence with brief mentions of **Robert P. Willcox**, **James A.N. McLeod** and **William H. Patterson.** [90]
Miss F. A. V. Patterson, It is with pleasure I take my pen in hand this morning to communicate a few lines to you in the form of a letter[.] your letter came to hand in due time and you cannot imagine the pleasure it affords me in [?]. I am at the present time inthe enjoyment of very good health, and my sincere wish is that these lines may reach in good health and the enjoyment of all other desirable blessings. The general health of our Co. is very good with the aception of Robert P. Willcox and James A. N. McLeod. Willcox has the fever very bad but I think he is on the mend. McLeod has something like pneumonia but he is not very bad off. We have good(news) here[,] if it be true[,] that England has or will at an early day acknowledge the independence of our Southern Republick and is making preparation to blow out Lincoln's blockade. I hope it is a fact. Well Miss F. A. V.[,] christmas is coming

near and I dont expect that I can have any fun in camp[.] and I want you to write to me by the next mail and let me have a christmas letter to read for the last letter I got from you gave me more pleasure thatn any thing I have seen since I left home. I thought that I could go home at that time and see you all in that section but it is impossible for me to go that soon[.] but I think I will get off about the middle of January and then I am going home in double quick time[,] but you must write me that christmas letter and tell me some thing that will make me a christmas gift. Tell your brother that I rec'd his letter in dur time but had not time to answer it. I will answer by next mail. Dear Miss[,] I must stop writing for this time. Please excuse all mistakes etc. I remain your most affectionately[,] Duncan C. Blue

1861, December 22
Noah Deaton (*Camp Vance, Carolina City, NC*) to father **William Deaton** and mother **Flora Deaton**. General wartime correspondence with brief mentions of **John McKinnon, William McKinnon, Robert P. Willcox, Jonathan A. Britt, N. McDuffie, John L. Martin, M.J. McLeod, Allen E. McDonald** and Capt. **John M. Kelly**. [91]

Dear Father and Mother[,] I take my pen in hand to answer your most welcom letter that came to hand today[.] it afforded me much satisfaction to hear that you were all in good health. I am in tolerable good health at present[.] the McKinnon boys are also well[.] the health of our Company is remarkably good at present[.] there is only one in this company sick[.] Mr R. P. Willcox is down with the Typhoid Fever he has been sick near about a month[.] we cannot tell whether he is mending or not yet. I have no news to write at present[.] nothing of intrest has occurd of late about here and therefore you must be content with such news as I have[.] I regret to learn that cousin J.A. Britt is no better yet and also I regret to hear of Mr N. McDuffie Mr J.L. Martin and Mr M.J. McLeod being sick and hope they will soon recover there health[.] I heard from Mr Kellys Company yesterday[.] they are in camp near Raleigh[.] there is about one half of them sick[.] I heard from cousin A.E. McDonald and have wrote to him[.] he was well at that time and I hope he will keep his health while he stays in camp[.] (I learn from your letter that the money that I sent to you got home safe[.] as times is hard and salt is so dear[,] one cannot get along with some money so use it as you see fit if you need it.)[.] We are at work now building our winter houses[.] they are framed and weatherboarded with brick chimneys[.] I think we will have our house done in three or four days[.] the blockade is still kept up at Bogue Inlet but if news that we hear is true I expect the blockade will see some trouble before long[.] We hear that the Queen of England has proclaimed war against Lincoln but the report is not fully confirmed here yet. You requested me to let you know if we had any Religious Society in the Regiment. We have a Society known as the Christian Association but the members are few for out of the whole Regt there is I think not 100 church members[.] and very seldom that out of about 1000 men that as many as 75 will go ten steps to hear preaching[.] many of them spend the Sabath playing cards and in like manner. Some of them got so bold as to play cards one Sunday in five steps of the preacher when he preachin[.]g the chaplain give them such a talking they have been a little shy ever since. Our Society is composed of Baptists, Presbyterians Methodists these denominations principally make out our small number of professors[.] there is no reference to sect and any member acting improperly to common church rules will be excluded from this Society[,] it being the only way to enjoy religious privileges here[.] I have become a member of the Society[.] I hope the Lord will bless us and revive the work of Grace in this Regt, though the prospect gloomy at this time[.] Rev. G.A. Russel was down here about a week ago[.] he preached five sermons for us which I think had great influence on the Regiment. our present Chaplain is not as influential as our first Chaplain was[,] but he is a very intelligent (he is a Methodist)[.] in conclusion[,] I will say my prayer is that may the God of heaven bless you all and give us all hearts to feel our need of him and forgive our many short comeings towards him[,] and fit and prepare us for the many shifting scenes of this life[.] may he stand by us in the hour of danger and shield us from all harm and at last save us in heaven for Christ sake. I must close by saying that I trust this may reach and find you and Mother and all the family and neighbors enjoying common good health. Pleas write as soon as you can make it convenient. I am your affectionate son until Death[,] Noah Deaton

1861, December 24
Noah Deaton (*Camp Vance, Carolina City, NC*) to **Sarah Jane McDonald**. General wartime correspondence with brief mentions of **Kelly Williamson** and **Robert P. Willcox**. [92]

Dear Miss, with pleasure I resume my seat to day to drop you a few lines in answer to your very kind and most welcom letter that came to hand the 20th inst. I was much pleased with its contents, yes[,] better pleased with it than with any letter that I have seen yet because it revealed a more feeling sympathy for me than any other and I return my thanks most cordialy to you for your kindness in making such a liberal offer but I believe that I have clothing aplenty to do me this winter[.] I recd the towel that you sent me most thankfully. (I received a box of clothing from home about 1 month ago). you said boys was scarse about Reedy Branch but I expect they are as plenty as the girls is about here[.] I have not spoke to a girl since I left More county. I would like to spend christmas about Reedy Branch if I could but I see that we will have no holidays this Christmas[.] I sent my likeness to you by Mr Kelly Williamson to Carthage, but it is not very pretty[.] if you will put it on a stump about the house it will keep hawks off for I dont think they can stand the looks of it[.] if you don't like the loocks of it please do not make fun of it for the artist done the best he could and it is rough enough after all[.] this leaves me and all the company in tolerable good health except three or four[.] Mr R. P. Willcox has Typhoid Fever but he is mending[.] one or two others has the Dyspepsa[.] it is likely they will be discharged from the Co. I have no news of importance to write this time[.] nothing of intrest has occurd in this vicinity[.] We have got out of Bogue Island[.] we are in camp between Morehead and Carolina Cities near the latter place[.] we are busily at work building our winter houses which we will finish in a day or two. I reckon I'd better close this badly writen letter as I have nothing more to write and will soon have to go to drill[.] please excuse bad writing and all mistakes[.] write soon as you can for I will be pleased to hear from you often[.] Your affectionate friend[,] Noah Deaton [P.S.] my faithful heart shal still renew that faithful look of thine, though many miles apart we be[,] when this you see remember me[.]

1861, December 28
Neill A. Ray *(Camp Vance near Carolina City, NC)* to **Christian Ray**. General wartime correspondence with brief mention of **Robert P. Wilcox**, **Samuel P. Short**, Christmas in camp, the blockade around Bogue Island, cousin **John B. Ray** and the marriage of **Cornelius Dowd Hudson** and **Edith Bradley.** [93]

Miss Christian Ray, Dear Cousin[,] With pleasure I take my pen in hand to drop you a few words to let you know that I and Hugh are both in tolerbable good health[.] and I hope this will reach and find you all enjoying the same blessing[.] Our co. are all in tolerable good health except two or three[.] Mr. R.P. Willcox has the Typhoid Fever but he is mending since a few days[.] Mr S.P. Short was taken sick yesterday[.] the Dr said he had the fever[.] there is a few slight cases of the Mumps in our co. We have not got our houses finished yet by there not being enough of sent at first[.] we can finish in two or three days if the lumber will come[.] There was a rowdy tim here at christmas[.] there is 5 days allowed that we are exempt from all duty except guard munting and Roll call[.] but some of our men must spend there christmas in the guard house for there misbehavior[,] but I can boast so fare that none of my tent mates or mess mates has got in the guard house yet[.] The Blockade is still lying about Bogue inlet but they take care to keep out of range of guns at the Ft.[.] there is nothing of importance around about here of late and therefore you must be content with such news as I have at present[.]— There was a weding in this Regt. last Thursday (day after christmas) in the company caled the Chatham guards. Mr D. Hutson to a lady from Wake county[.] she had come down to wait on her brother in the hospital and concluded to marry before she would go back[.] Please write soon and give all the news[.] tell cousin John that I will write to him before long. I send my best respects to you all. Your affectionate cousin, N.A. Ray

1861, December 28
Malcom Ray *(Wake County, NC)* to sister **Flora Jane Ray**. General wartime correspondence between siblings with brief mentions of the death of **James Dowdy, Archibald Ray, Capt. John M. Kelly, Capt. Haliburton, William Ray, John B. Ray, Celia McCaskill Ray, Hugh Ray** and the death of cousin **Mar Ray.** [94]

Dear sister[,] I take my pen in hand this morning to inform you that I am in tolerable good health at this time and I hope when thes few lines will reach you[,] it will find you all engoying the same blessing of health[.] I have nothing of importance to write to you at this[.] there has bin a gret deal of sickness in this regement[.] there has bin severl death here sens we came in to camp[.] Mr James Doudy died last thursday knight about two oclock[.] there is five or six of the company very sick yet as long as you will sea cousin Archibald[.] I shal say no more about them[.] he can tell moore than I can write at this time[.] you sent me a par of pantaloons by him and I all most had a notion to send them back with him for I had two good pare but I believe I will keap them[.] I can not write such a letter to you as I would like to[,] but for ther would not be space to doe so[.] we hve a troublesom time here[.] there was an old man and his wife beat nearly to death last wednesday knight by a part of our regiment[.]

it took place a bout one oclock[.] the alarm came in to the camp an the role was called to se hoe was missing[.] [Capt J.M. Kelly went reached every man in his company[.] there was not one of them a msing[.] about four oclock the Magor calld for three men from every company in the regement to go in search of the men[.] the magor and part of the men went to the house and found three of them hve a quarrel[.] they had broak all the dishes and one glass window[.] they took them up and guarded them back to the camp[.] the men all be long to Capt Haliburtons company[.] they have bin under guard ever senc[.] there trial has not come off yet[.] the punishment will be bad I think [.]the balanc they wer acused of doing is not fiten for me to write to you[.] you may no it was tolerable bad if so[.] but there is so many things said here that is not so[.] we doe not no when we hear the truth but there is some truth in this for they broak all the dishes and one glass window and throad a galon of whiskey in the fier and it smoakt the right black[.] I must not tell you any more about our men now[.] I saw 175 yankees christmas day in raleigh that had ben taken prisoners they war[.] all good looking large men and well drest[.] they all had good cloath and shoes and very good over coats[.] they wer going to take them to Salisbury[.] I heard them talking and saw bulet holes in some of ther coats larg a nuf to put a hen egg through[.] I believe if they war bac that they would come wrigh back to fight us agane[.] they said that we out numberd them in every battle that had ben fought yet about thre to one[.] they maid out like they had only about 40 killed at manases and one of them said the sothern papers published nothing but lies an they dare not publish the truth for if they did[,] there men would all leave them[.] they got to such a peach the guard ordered them to quit talking to them and we left[.] that is all I can tell you about the yankees now[.] I think that is all the news I have to write to you now[,] only all the neighbors in the the camp is well[.] there is none in our house sick[,] only cousin William and I think he is some better than he was[.] I am in hope he will go home and you all sea him[.] our cook has left us and gon home[.] some of ourselvs have to do the cooking now and I believe we can doe beter without him than with him[.] it counts up money prety fast at fifty cents a mouth[.] now I have told you everything I can think of at present[.] I want you to write to me as son as you can and let me no how you are geting along[.] you may tell Cela that John is well and geting very well[.] I got the cakes you sent to me[.] I havenot heard from Hugh this weak yet[.] I heard from him las wek and he was well[.] I heard that cousen Mar Ray was dead and I was sory to hear there was so muc sickness in the neighborhood[.] I must come to a close by sending my best respects to you and all the rest of the family so I close[.] I still remain your most affectionate brother till death. Malcom Ray [P.S] excus bad writing and mistakes[.] give my respects to all enquiring friends[.] I want you to write soon all of you[.] I can not write all of you at once[.] all of you write to me as son as you can.

1861, December 31
John A. Walker (*New Bern*) to brother **Tandy Walker** and nephew **Louis H. McLeod**. General wartime correspondence. [95]

Dear Brother & Nepheu I take my seat to let you no where and how I am geting along. I have nothing that will interest you only we have bin mooving all the time and will moove this week again about 2 miles from town. our Company is in the fare ground the damndes coldest place you ever saw. we have bin here about ten dayes and got two cords of wood in the time. you no fences and houses fared bad.But I tell you the wind blow moore and harder down here than any place I ever saw. We have got our horses and sadles but no sabers. you had aught to see us riding and runing races and jumping fences on our horses. we look 1ike we would run over creation if it war in the shape of a yankee but ther is no danger of them I dont think. There came nuse here on christmas day that they war down the river and that ten men had to be sent out of evry company to see as scouts. You had aught to of seen our men. they was all most fit to fight one & a other because all could not go. some offering ten dollars to go and some five but whin I come to find out how the garden (?) hoped it was done to see how our men should stand. all stood but two or three got sick on the occasion. that was a christmus tk trick played on us but before I wory you I will tell you about the helth of our company. there is 35 hone sick and on ferlow but I am here yet and well only & last week I took on too much steam and was devlish sick for one or two days but am over that now. we got our bounty and pay last wik up to the 31 th of Octbr and dt come in good time for there was not ten dollars in the company so you may no we waas dam poor. Louis I would like to see you and Tan but I dont no vhen that will bi for I cant get to go home let alon coming to see you. if you can come to see me I would be glad and if I can ever get of. will come to see you all. Right to me soon boath of you and give me the nuse. give my respects to all the comp[any] and receve a portion your selves. Nothing more only [I] remain your friend until Death. John A Walker. Direct your to Newbern N. C, and it will come to hand.

1862, January 5
A.S. Caddell (*Camp Vance, NC*) to Miss **Martha M. Sullivan**. General personal correspondence with brief mention of **C.D. Caddell.** [96]

Miss Martha, I take the pleasure of dropping you a few lines to let you know that I landed safe to my quarters in good health but my spirits are somewhat lingering[.] though you could not expect much els after parting with the one I prefer to all others in this world[,] besides many affectionate rellatives and warm friends[.] though Miss Martha when I think of you[,] my hope brightens and if you would just a went by the Esqs. I would a ben better satisfied thang[.] you must not think hard of my jokes. I must bring my short letter to a close for I have not been here long enoug to gotten any news[,] though there is one thing I will say to you and that is I had a likeness that I intended to give you though[.] I never thought of it when I was with you though[.] I will send it with this letter and if you want it you can get it from C.D. and if you dont want it[,] you can let him keep it[.] so I will close as I am about to freese[.] I want you to write to me as soon as you get this without fail[.] I shal await your answer with impatience. Yours truly[,] AS Caddell [P.S.] I thought I would stop but I could not close without asking you if you had seen any more pretty folks since the quiltin[.] I will close if you will forgive my bad spelling and writing[.] pleas write as soon as you get this.

1862, January 9
Louis H. McLeod (*Camp Wyatt*) to wife **Eliza Jane Walker McLeod**. General wartime correspondence with brief mentions of **Daniel ?, David H. Sloan, John A. Sloan, William M. Swann, Archibald Kelly, Andrew Brown, James Kelly, Hardy Matthews, Tandy Walker, Sandy Kelly, James Mashburn and John A. Walker.** [97]

Dear Wife, I seate my self down to let you know that I reached home safe. We stade all knight in Fayettevill on monday knight and the next mourning we left at nine oclock on the Cate McLaren and that knight between twelve and one oclock we arived at Wilmington. We stade all knight on the boat and next mourning we went to Bishops Hotell. While we was eating breakfast the Captain came in to his breakfast when we was verry glad to see each other. We had to stay there all that day and the next knight and the next mourning at nine oclock we started to our camp and the Captin came with us so we all got home safe. Daniel and the Sloan Boys liked there trip first rate. Daniel was verry scerd when we first got on the steam boat at Fayetteville. It made his head swim so bad but he soon got over that. that knight he could not sleep on the boat. We reached here yesterday eavning about too oclock. Daniel and the boys looked about and the Captian gave them close and fixed them off in tents. Daniel went in the tent with Arch Kelly. Arch was on gard and came in late in the knight to take a nap and ast Daniel if he had sleep any. Daniel sayed no damned if he ever expected to sleep any. more for the sea cep such a roaring that he never could sleap. he sayed every time he got in a dose it seamed as if the water was a going to run over him. Daniel is very much fraid he wil do something rong. Eliza it cost me nearly all the money that I had to get home, there was six of us and I had all the expences to pay it cost me fifty cents apiece on the cars and then in town it cost me four dollars and fifty cents for our board and what things I had cost me sixty cents to get thim halled to the river and then our pashage on the river to Wilmington cost me eaven ten dollars and then breakfast the next mourning cost me one dollar and fifty cents and then fifty cents for halling my things again from one boat to the other. the captin then pade the balance of our board at Wilmington. To take it all round it cost me eighteen dallars and sixty cents and we had to take a little whisky which made it about eaven twenty dollars which was all I had and dont no whether I ever will get any of it back only Daniels will bee good so I did not get you the salt at Wilmington. I thought I would get here before Cozen Andrew left and if he was agoing to get any salt in Wilmington I would get the money from the Captain and send it to you by him. But he was gone before we got here. I will send you the salt by James Kelley next monday or tuesday. he says he will start home. I think that will bee soon enough for you. I can get it for four dolars per bushel. Eliza there is not nothing new in the camp. the men is all nearly well some few cases of yellow Janders and Hardy Matthis has got the mumps The Captin has got nearly over his Janders and is as peart as ever. The wirkmen has got our houses nearly ready for our men to move in and take possession. Tandy is well and hearty at this time and is wirking on the houses. he says he had a lively time christmas and was well & sattisfied he was on gard chrismas day and the captian was officer of the day. Sandy Kelley is well and fat as you please. he was very glad to get them sauchage that Fanny sent him he eat them for breakfast this mourning. The Captin got some coffee & brought with him and we will live well aslong as our goodies lasts. Eliza there is too and three vessels in sightevery day but no prospect of a fight. There isent but one of our men inthe gard house at this time and that is James Mashburn. he got drunk on his post and had his canteen full of whisky and then left his post and came up in our street and fired off his gun twice he was then put in the gard house amediately and since was courtmashald and sentanced imprisonment for fifteen days and to waer ball and chain for ten day and hard labor the ball not weighing less than six pounds. Eliza I have nothing worth writing to you at present I hope those lines will find you and your family all well. Eliza I want you to write to me Every weeke any how and let me no how you are a getting a long with your troubles. Eliza I have thought moore a bout you since I left than I have since I have been in the serves. I want to here from you ofteen for I shall bee uneasy about you untill your troubles will be over. I want you to take the verry best care of your self that you posibly can and never go lifting to heavy things. I wish you all the good luck in the world. you loving husband untill death. Eliza when I got here there was a letter here for me from John Walker. he sayed he was well and hearty and that he was in a mighty cold place and had not had but too cords of wood since they have been at newburn and he sayed they were a going to move in a few days some too miles from where they are now. Eliza I must tell you something about Cozen Andrew and the speculation chickens. as soon as I got to Wilmington and the people saw my coop of chickens they began to talk about the man that had such a big coop of chickens carrying down to the soldiers and that he had don so much for them. they thought it was all right but they soon found out that he was carrying them down for a speculation he sold too of his chickens for four dollars so they told him he should not seil no moore there and they would make him pay for carrying them down to the camp and the Captin made him pay five dollars for carrying them. the Captains mate told me that it taken fifteen negroes to lift the coop. but the funnyest part was when he wint to start he went round and made the through in fifteen cents apiece enough to make up him five dolars for fetching down the chickens to Sandy. And now none of them cant buy one of them for not less than thirty five or fourty cents apiece. That shows what he done for the soldiers. No moore about him. I will close by saying rite to me as soon as you get this. Tell sis and all the children howdy and that I never will forget them as long as life lasts your loving husband Louis H. McLeod

1862, January 11
William Wade Fry to brother **Daniel Fry** and sister **Lydia Shields Fry.** General wartime correspondence with brief mentions of **James McDonald**. [98]

Dear Brother and Sister: I take my seat to write you again to let you know that I am well, and I hope that when these few lines reach you[,] they may find you well. I received your letter yesterday which afforded me much pleasure to hear that you are well. I have no news of interest to write to you. Well, I heard since I left Raleigh that James McDonald died in the hospital at Raleigh. We came to this place last Saturday. We are at the fair grounds near Newbern. We get fish and oysters here. We can't get whiskey under four dollars per gallon, they say. I have not tried to get any yet, nor I don't intend to buy at that price unless I get sick and need it. So I will come to a close by saying excuse my short letter, for I have not time to write at present. I am going to get some whiskey and some store coffee before long.

1862, January 14
Eliza Jane Walker McLeod to husband **Louis H. McLeod**. General wartime correspondence with brief mentions of **Jim Brown, William Buchanan, Fanny ?, William ?, Alexander Hamilton McLeod, Tandy Walker, Sandy Kelly, Andrew Brown, John Lewis Cox, Isaac Buchanan, John A. Walker, Daniel ?** and **Elizabeth Hinton Brewer McLeod.** [99]

My dear husband, I sete my self this morning to drop you a few lines to let you no tha I recved your welcom leter last nite and was morr then glad to her from you and to her that you got home safe I was mity unesy you wold hav to stay in town too or three dayes Louis me and famley is all wel at this time hoping thes few lines will find you in the same blesing may god grant it so to be this is a very cole day it is haling and sleeting i am afraid we wil hav a bad winter the balence of the time Louis i was so glade whei i got you leter and redit tho i cold not help crien and then i felt beter i saw Jim brown an willam buchanan thaa cam by our house last sater day an tole me you had got home that was the first neuse i had herd from you tha got to fayett Saterday morning and tha hird the car to bring them to Swan Station but cosin ander wold not pay his bil an so he stade tel monday tha giv five dolars for the car to bring them Louis tha told me such tailles i was unesy all of the time untill i got your leter tha said ther was eight vesels in site evry day and tha dident no but what you wer fiting them and if tha ever had to fite you wold all bee takin prisners for thar was no other chanc and tha said tha herd in wilmington that the yankes had taken the salt works and broke the kitles and taken the men i was so unesy i never felt so bad in my life i pray god to be with you and protect in all of your trobles and spar you from the boolet and from sord Louis i was in hops you wold git won of them boyes you card down withyou to take your plase and you wold com home my dear Louis i hav thaut more about you since you left then i ever did befor you hav not bin out of my mind twenty five minetes sence you lef only when i was a slepe my lord hav mercy on you and me and spar us to liv until the time is out so wa may liv to gether in this life a gain and injoy this lif to gether and if it is not gods wil so to be god grant it so to be that we may liv to gether in heven wher parting is none no more the prare of your loving wife ever remains with you for you wel far capten trust in him and you wil com out near the conker my der i wil trito take the best cer of my self i can for i fele so clomsey i cant get about much and i dont inten to tri to doo much al onley lite worke such ans i no wont hert me for i cant stand up to doo much fanny and willam moved last thirsday and we has bin very lonsom since tha went of we ar douing the best we can glad to her tan was wel and Sandy an the captin giv my lov to the capten and tan and Sandy cosen ander and the chickens was enof for me to no we herd he cared down sparibs and backbone to sel to the solders i wonder how he got aloin with them i expect your brther San wil bee down with a lode of chickes an sparibs an backbone to keepe up with cose ander how did John Louis get a long with his spectilon an the chicken line i hope the solders want by won from him the yankes ot to got cosin ander and his chicken. Louis i hav nothing much to rite to you i want you to say something about issack buchanan in you next leter i hav not herd much nuse since you left i was glad to her from John Walker your nuse was the latis dilen rote to his wife last friday and said tha wer all orderd to newbern the nite before tha expeecd to hav a fite thar but tha had not gon when he rote he was sick his self and we hav not herd from thar since i am ancis to her Abe came over and took the pipe the other is on the firebord. yet and the childrin say it most stay thar tel you com home i hav not herd from you mother since you left to no what she had to say about the salt i hope you can send it by kelly it is eleven dolars in fayettville per bushel i dont want you to send it without you can send it by som body I am a fraid it wold get lost the hogs ot to be kild this weke but i most wait tel kelly com and if he dont hav the salt i most giv the price for it was won thing i cant doo without tel danil i want to her from him to rite to me how he likes and evry thing he can think of i want you to rite all about the times down thar and if you think you wilk hav to fite soon and if ther takin of the salt works was so or not rite evry thing you can think of it is grate satisfaction to me for i dont no when to belive any thing i her onley when you rite i believ you wil rite the truth when i rede a leter from you I belev what you rite my der living Louis i hav nothing more to rite this is won of them cold dayes i hope your houses is don by now if you hav to stay in tents now you wil sufer now i hope you ar in them. Louis i cant think of nothing more to rite onley the childrin sends ther lov to pap and sayes tha hope he will liv to com home and stay so good by my dear loving husban until deth your loving wife until deth. Eliza McLeod. rite as soon as you get this.

1862, January 14, 18

C.D. Caddell to brother **A.S. Caddell**. General wartime correspondence with brief mentions of Miss **A.J.**, **Haywood Caddell** and **Mary Ann Caddell's** son [**Charles Caddell**], the **Moore** girls, **Zacheus Hogan**, **Benjamin Gilliam Hollingsworth, Samuel Jackson McIntosh, William Henry Harrison Davis, Nathaniel Fry, William L. Sullivan, Tom Jackson, Morrison, William Caddell** and **Raney Caddell**. [100]

January 14 - Dear Brother[,] it is with pleasure I seat my self to drop you a few lines[.] we are all well at present and hoping these few lines will find you well[.] I have not recd no letter from you since you went back nor heard from you[.] I want you write as soon as this gets to hand[.] I have nothing strange to write[.] I am a getting a long about write with the feminines in this vicinity[.] I went to meeting last Sunday and staid all night at your old daddy inlaws[.] your gal has been sick but is on the mend[.] I saw my gal[.] Miss A.J. I went to the old Esqs. and got a long verry well[.] Mary Ann, Haywood has got a boy[.] the Miss Moores is mad because you did not go to the quiltin[.] tell Hogans, Harrison, Gilam & Jack to write to me[.] if they don't[,] I shal get mad[.] Nathaniel Fry has told that W.H.H. Davis shot a man[.] Tell me what W.H.H. Davis says about his gal[.] dont show this letter to nobody but burn it[.] write to your gal in my letter and I will give her your likeness as you Said[.] pappy and Mother sends you their love and best Resp and says for you to write to them[.] let me know if you got your money or not[.] Take good care of it or Send it to me and I will pay your dets with it[.] write soon[.] your affectionate Brother till death, CD. Caddell [P.S.] we have bad weather here since you started[.] we have one big sleet[.] There is sleet on the trees now and it is a snowing besides[.] tell me what you think of the war[.]

January 18 - Dear Brother[,] I seat my self again to drop you a few lines to let you know that we are all well at present[,] hoping these lines will find you well[.] I have not recd the first letter from you since you left home and I would be glad to hear where you have writen or not[.] if you have written and sent your gal one in it, it is lost, and I shal give her the Likeness[.] you must write to her and tell her you sent it to her, and told me to give it to her[.] I want you to write to pap and mother for I am going off a trading with W.L. Sulivan[.] we are a going to start the 20 of this month which is a Monday[.] I want you to be certain and write to them[.] Send all your letters in paps name till I tell you to stop for I shant be at home before the 15 of Feb[.] write one to me to get to carthage by that time the 15 of Feb[.] Tell Mr W.H.H. Davis to write to me so it will come by the 15 of Feb[.] tell him I recd his letter the 17 inst[.] and was glad to hear from him[.] tell him I have not seen his gal since you was at home and if there is anything wrong I dont know it[.] I will write to you and him Both in 7 or 8 days and let you know how I am a getting a long selling ardent spirits and beer for me[.] and Linsey is in with Tom Jackson & Morrison in thir still and has got license to sell any where in N.C. Tell Jack and Zach & Gilam not to write me before the 15 of Feb[.] dont tell them what I am a doing nor nobody els[.] I shall give your gal the likeness if you must write a letter to suit the case[.] write soon to pap and Mother[.] no more at present[,] only I remain your lovin Brother till Death. CD Caddell

1862, January 15

Louis H. McLeod (*Camp Wyatt*) to wife **Eliza Jane Walker McLeod**. General wartime correspondence with brief mentions of **William M. Swann, Daniel ?, John A. Sloan, David H. Sloan, Tandy Walker, Francis Moore, D. Wicker, F.J. Swann, Louis M. Wicker, Jesse Wicker, Dr. Campbell, Ben Gunter, Mary McNeill, Jim Hight, Nancy Ann McLeod** and **Jackson Taylor.** [101]

Mrs. McLeod, Dear Madam I seat my self down this knight to drop you a few lines to let you know that I am well at this time hoping those few lines will find you and all the rest of the family well and hearty Eliza I havent nothing much to rite to you. Our company is tolerable well at this time the mumps hangs on to some of thim yet Our Captain is well and Hearty as ever but looks a little yellow from the Janders We have had some severe weather down here last Monday it turned cloudy and verry cold and the wind did blow the hardest sort all the eavening and all knight it looked like it would blow our tents sway in spite of us. It did blow down one or to of our tents and the wind split the cloth all about. I was corprel of the gard that knight. But the Counral had pitty on us and taken the gard all off about eight oclock and divent put thim on no moore untill day brake the next mourning. I got up befour day to put on my relief and you better believe the wind blew and the sand flew thex the parade ground looked just like snow and itcep our eyes so full of sand that we could hardly see but last knight the wind camed off and is as still now as it can bee and looks like settled wether. On Monday our company drew their over coats and you better believe they came in a good time and yesterday we drew shoes also some of the men got splendid coats and some wasent so good Little Daniel and the Sloan Boys got over coats and was verry glad to get thim. They seeme to bee verry well satisfied. Our company moved into there winter quarters yesterday and is verry well fixed too men lies in one bunk and the bunks is fixed one abov another but I am yet in the same tent and Tan is with me yet the officers quarters is not finished yet as soon as they get them don we all will move in and I will take the room that will bee lade off for Lieutent Moore Tan is at wirk on the houses and Sandy Brown and they both is gone up to Wilmington to knight to get lumber they will retur to morrough Eliza I told you in the last letter that I would send you the salt by James Kelley but he sliped of yesterday mourning befour I got off of the gard and I dident no when he started he told me that he wasent a going untill to day I had spoke to him about it he sayed he was a going to get salt and would carry the salt for me with the greatest pleasure I cant sent it by its self you had better get it up there if you can, and if not send me a letter as quick as you can Mr, Dy Wicker will bee here this week and will return next and if you cant get it I can send it by him If you have not got money enough tell F. J. Swann to get the salt for you he can send down on the rail road and get it any time for you. Eliza vhen I cone to look into ny truck of eggs I found then nearly every one broke with then sauchage on the top The Captain liked thim cakes you put in splended he said he rather eat them than any sort of poun cake he ever sav. He said he wouldent care if you would send down a box full of thim. When I told him about the butter he said good thing good thing He said the saucidge was the best he ever eat there is so manny of us eats together now we have something good to eat all the time Louis and Jess Wicker and Doctor Caupbell and they all got something from home We have no reason in the wirld to grunble We have been looking ever since I cone back for a battle but the yankees havnt Landed yet It is thought they vill & land sone where on this cost befour long. the captian and nyself was over at the beach last Sunday eavening and sav three large vessles about two miles off and one of thin cane to the other too while we vas there. We thought she cane to bring the mall to the rest she went off while we was over there when she started she histed a white flag and went clear out of sight but the wind blew them off and they havent returned yet there is not been a flag up on our pole to day. I receaved a letter from Ben Gunter dabefour [day before] yesterday and he is well at this time and from the letter he rote he must fell verry joly he filled a sheet plum full as he coudd stick it he said he would send me a bag of coffe they get a plenty. Well I have nothing moore that will enterest you I want you to rite to me as soon as you get this and let me now how you and all the rest of the children is coming on particular yourself I feel verry uneasy about you I want to hear from you as oftin as you can rite when you cant rite get Abe to rite for you I want a letter any how every week. Your loving husband untill death. Louis H. McLeod. Tell Mary McNeill that I want to bee at her and Jim Hights weading and not get married untill we all cone back home and we will have a big time give all my respects to all enquiring friends Tell Sis I want to see her verry bad tell her tom come down to sleep with me I have to sleep by my self and to knight I am right by my self Tan is gone and I am verry lonsum Tell Abe I would like to hear from him once in a while Rite to me how Jackson Tailor is coming on whether he is a coming back or not No moore at present only you will here from me again soon. I remain yours verry truly. L. H. McLeod

1862, January 17
W.M. Black *(Raleigh, NC)* to cousin **Christian Ray**. General wartime correspondence between cousins with brief mentions of **Malcom Ray** and **Archibald Ray.** [102]

Dear Cousin, at the request of Cousin Archibald I drop you a few lines in regard to the health of Cousin Malcom[.] I think he is improving slowly[.] I can not say that he is any stronger but think he is getting clear of the Disease[.] he rested better last night than usual and should he take no back set[,] he will be up as soon as could be expected[.] The Dr says he is on the mend. Cousin Archibald is well and is staying at the same house I am staying at. I can not tell when I shall leave here but shall do so as soon as I can git the business transacted for which I stayed. I Shall then go to Newbern. We have very little news about hear[.] the Malitia is ordered out in thirty counties. I can not tell whether this will include Moore or not but I hardly think it will. There is some prospect of getting in to a fight about Newbern as Yankee fleet has sailed in that direction. I should like to see some short in that way. I think it will all turn out stiff. Such things genrl do so. Cousin Christian[,] I believe I have nothing more to write that would interest you. I think I shall be at home in two or three weeks if should I shall give all my adventures since I left home. Nothing more. Yours truly[,] W.M. Black

1862, January 17
John E. Phillips to **Mary E. Shields; Gerry G. Brewer** to **Robert Shields;** General wartime correspondence with brief mentions of **Alpha Phillips.** [103]

Miss Mary Shields: I received your kind letter of the 12th of January and was glad to hear you were tolerably well. As for myself, I am well and well satisfied. The rest of the company is well, except for a few cases of the mumps, and some colds. They seem to be in very good heart. I will also state that we have not had any fight yet, and I don't know if we will have hard fighting to do next spring. If we have them to fight[,] we will try to give them the best we have got in our shop. You stated in your letter that you wanted me to get back against harvest, but if I do I am too big and fat to our wheat, for I weigh two hundred and five pounds. I do not reckon you would know me if you were to see me for I have not shaved since the first of July. I should be glad to come home, and if I were there I should be certain to go see Miss Alpha before long. You may, if you please, tell Miss Alpha I should be glad to see her and all the rest of the girls in that part of the country. As I have nothing to write, I remain your affectionate friend til death. From John E. Phillips to Miss Mary E. Shields.

Gerry G. Brewer to Robert Shields: Our fare is tolerably good but was very scarce a few days ago, but we have plenty now. You stated you were going to have an exhibition: I should be very glad to be at it though I can't be there. I may be fighting Yankees that day as far as I know. But if nothing happens to me[,] I shall be home the 28th of May. If I could see you I could tell you a great deal. I have seen several curious things since I left home. We have got our houses done and moved in them. They are a great deal better than tents. I reckon if you were to see me you would hardly know me. I am tolerably fleshy and I haven't shaved since I volunteered.

1862, January 21
Noah Deaton (*Camp Vance, Carolina City, NC*) to sister **Sarah B. Deaton**. General wartime correspondence with brief mentions of **John McKinnon, William McKinnon, Allen E. McDonald, Catharine Deaton, Margaret Deaton** and **John Deaton.** [104]

Dear sister[,] with pleasure I take my pen in hand to answer your kind letter that came to hand last night which give me pleasure to hear that you were all in tolerable good health. this leaves me in tolerable good health though I was a little sick two or three days ago[.] I am hearty as ever now. The McKinnons are well[.] well Sarah I have not much news to write at present only there is a little excitement down here at present[.] there came news here last night that there was 53 yankee ships in side of the shoals at Hatteras and it is thought they intend sailing up the Nuse River to attact Newbern[,] and we are holding ourselves in readiness to march at a moments warning to assist at Newbern if there is an attempt made[.] there can be 12,000 of our boys there in a short time which is sufficient to keep a good many of the Abes at bay on the river[.] I would not be surprised to hear orders at any moment for it is likely that there will be a brush at Newbern soon[,] though I hope not. we are living in our houses at present and are doing very well if it was not for guard duty[,] a duty that cannot be dispensed with[.] the 35 Regt is at Newbern[,] the Regt that cousin A. E. McDonald is in[.] I recd a letter from him not long since he was well then[.] we drill 4 hours a day 2 hours Battallion and 2 hours Company drill. you said there was a sleet up there but it was only a cold rain here at that time we have not had much ice down here[.] there came 2 very light sprinkles of snow here in the night but melted fast as it fell we have had no sleet at all some frosty nights[.] I have three or four strans of shells and also a bunch of nice shells which I will send home if I can get the chance[.] I believe I will send two strans in this letter one to Catharine, one to Margaret that costs .60 cents per stran. I will send John some shells the first chance I get[.] tell them to attend to their books at school and at home and learn all they can[.] you said for me to write you some of the fun but I say fun is scarse down here[.] only our boys enjoys themselves very well at playin cat and bullpen &c[.] well I will come to a close as I have no more news at present[.] may the god of heaven bless you all is my prayer[.] write soon[.] give all the news[.] I send my best wishes to you all[.] your affectionate brother, Noah Deaton

1862, January 21

Eliza Jane Walker McLeod to husband **Louis H. McLeod**. General wartime correspondence with brief mentions of **Tandy Walker, John A. Walker, Sandy Kelly, Absalom Kelly, Henry ?, Polly Yarborough, Isaiah Buchanan, Andrew Brown, Annie Elizabeth McLeod, Thomas Bragg McLeod, William ?, Jack ?, John A. Sloan, David H. Sloan, Emily Franklin, William M. Swann** and **Daniel ?.** [105]

Der Louis I ste my self down this evning to drop you a few lines to let you now that me and famley is wel at this time hoping thes few lines will find you in the same blesing i hav injad very good helth since you left her and i hop my helth wil bee good untill my troble will bee over god grant it i recvd your leter yesterday and was more then glad to her from you and to her you wer well and the capten was wel and Taney you sade nothing about my leter i sent you i started won last wensday i recken you had not gotit you rote to me to rite evry weeke and i am going to doo it as long as i stand up i hav nothing much to rite but it wil bee nuse to you i hav not herd a word from John Walker since you rote to me i want to her mity bad i hope tha hav got wod befor now if tha hant tha most sufer you said you got a leter from ben gunter i was very glad to her from him and to her he had plenty of coffee. when he sends you the bag of cofee i wold like to hav a drink of it that is what we dont hav her you most save som tel i come down thar Louis i was very much disapinted whe Kelley came up and did not bring me the salt i did not no what to do i cold not borrey won single bit and so i hav not kild the hogs yet So i sent to Ab Kelley to day and got a haf bustel and i shall kill them to marow that wil save them tel i can get more Abe isin going to fayettville this weke or next and i wel send and get a bushel and that will doo me the wether is very unsette her we ar not doing much henry has coverd the shop and the rest is haling [hauling] pine straw we hav had a hepe of ran Louis i hav nothing new to rite to you onley poley yarber is ded and Isaih buchanan tels evry thing cosand ander don he said he will tel it he wants evry body to no how he don he said cosen and cared down whisky and sold it out by the dram at fifty cents a dram i her cosn ander wont say nothing about the chicken speckulation he wont say chicen atall Louis i was glad to her you all got over cots and shuse I hope you wont sufer for close i was also glad to her the yankey has not troble you i hope tha will never attact you thar this is my pras all of the time I hope god is on our side and if he is we can stand them i was glad to her your houses was so ni don in you can doo so much beter my der Louis you ar all of the time a on my mine the weter is so bad when i ly down and think wher you hav to ly it make me fele so sorey to think you hav a good bed her and cant bee her to li on it may the god of heven bless you and keep you in this life until your time is out so you can com home and liv with me and the children again Sis ses she cant com down thar she dont no the way you most com home and she wil sleep with you then Sis talks a gardle about you when she herse the car blow She sais pap is coming now brag did like william taken his gun he sad when pap cam home the gun wold hav to com home then william has took Jack to keep until you com hom and i was very glad Louis i was in hops you wold put won of them Slones boyes in your place and com home it is so long it semes like you hav bin gone too monts since you went of the last time the time seme so long to me becaise i hav to stay her all of the tim i hav not bin of sinc you left Saterday nits and Sonday ware me clene out Emley gon somtimes and the childrin som tims and me by my self to deth my work keeps my mind to gether Louis tel tan i want to her from him i was glad to her he had gais [?] to wer i hope he is satisfide the time will run out sometime til Sandy Kelley i hav not for got him i want to her from him tel danil he is not riting fast to his swethart very fast i want to her from him giv my best lov to the capten and tel him i wold be very glad to see him somor sasges if i cold so nothing mor at present onley rite to me good by my der loving husband until deth your der wife Eliza McLeod

1862, January 24
John A. Jackson (*Carolina City – Camp Vance*) to his brother-in-law **Richard A. Cole** and sister **Mary Ann Margaret Cole**. General wartime correspondence between brother/brother-in-law regarding military life and the anticipation of an attack at New Bern with brief mentions of Capt. **Pender**, **James Martin**, **Edward Graham** and **Tom Jackson**. [106]

Mr. R. A. Cole and M. A M. Cole, Dear brother and sister and family[,] I received your letter this morning and you may be shure that it done me a greateal of good to hear from you and family[,] and that you was well and the neighbors also. I am well at presant and the rest of the company is in very good health. A few are just geting over the mumps[.] they are what I call in good health. I hope these few lines will come safe to hand and find you and family all the same. I have no newse of intrest to rite you only we have been expecting to be caried to Newbern. It was reported that there was thirty or forty vesels in side the bar at Hateras and bound for newbern[,] and the people down hear are very uneasy and it is reported that a great many have left newbern and gone west. Everytime they expect this place or newbern attacted[,] they leave and when the excitement is over they come back and wait for the next time. It is reported that there was a man taken up at morehead that was tring to make his way to the lincoln fleet[.] and that capt Pender who was a capt of an artillery company and resigned sometime since was also tring to do the same. They stoped the vesel and would not let her leave the port. Her Capt is suspected of something not right[.] I do not know what they will do with him and if he is guilty it dont make much difference. They dont let him go without he gives some good evidence of his loyalty to the confederacy or wont try to convey off traitors and rascals. I must come to a close as I have nothing to rite that is worth while. I was very glad to hear from James Martin and that he was well again, I was very uneasy a while about him. I should like to have been there to a went around with him. I think we could have had some fun but I dont expect to come home til my time is out[,] but I am lucky then we will see about whether we go home or not. They wont grant furlows to any person now and still they want us to Volunteer for 2 years more[,] but I dont think they will get many out of this regiment until the second relief comes on. Especialy as long as they are so clever to grant furlows. There is several of us that has never been home yet and some that has went two or three times and when we ask anything about going hom we can get no satifaction or some short answer so I don't expect to come home til I get free. I should like to know Edward Grahams post office so I could rite to him and hear the VA newse. So[,] no more at present. You must excuse bad riting and mistakes. I remain you brother. John A. Jackson [P.S]. Richard do you thinnk that Tom is going to make any money at his still or not. I fear it is a bad operation.

1862, January 26
Louis H. McLeod (*Camp Wyatt*) to wife **Eliza Jane Walker McLeod**. General wartime correspondence with brief mentions of **Tandy Walker, William M. Swann, Francis Moore, Price, Sion Campbell, Dr. Campbell, John Lewis Cox, Sandy Brown, John A. Walker, Alfred Kelly, Emily Franklin** and **Annie Elizabeth McLeod.** [107]

Dear Wife, I seat myself this Sunday knight to answer your kind and wilcomb letter that came to hand last Friday knight which I was moore than proud to get. You said that you had started one on the Wednesday befour I have received too letters from you since I left Home. Your letter was dated the twenty first and I received it the twinty fourth. Eliza I was glad to here that you and all the rest was well. This leaves me well and tolerable hearty but not so hearty as I have been I have no room to complain. Tandy has been verry bad off with the bowel complaint but he has got nearly over it. He is a getting strong again He is setting on the other side of the table riting a letter to Jo and has too ritten to send to the girls. Our company is in tolerable good health but not so good as it has been. The Regiment is in verry good health considering the weather has been verry baddown hear and the wind did blow so hard we could hardly stay in our tents. All the men has moved in their houses except the officers houses is not don yet. As soon as they are finished they will move in them and myself and Tan will have to go in the quarters with all the rest and that is one thing I dont want to do I had rather stay in the tents all the winter than to go in the houses where is such a fuss and so nasty. I think it will make us all sick. I am afraid so any how. Eliza I havent nothing new to right to you about the yankees only we are cep here Every boddy is thinking that the Burnside Fleete will land here or some where near here No boddy can get a furlough to go home nor any where else. There was some of the Captains started home on Friday to recruit and I got to Wilmington and was ordred back. There is one vessel in sight I was over at the beach this evening and saw one off about twelve or fifteen miles and it was a shooting canons. We can here them rouring here most every day some while another I cant see that there is any nearer a fight here than when we first came here. The people in Wilmington is verry bad scared They are a drafting there and in Sampson Duplin and all the other counties on the cost and I expect there will soon bee a draft up there. You better tell every one you see they had better come down and join our company the Captian ses he will take a few moore enough to make out his company to one hundred and ten men. If they want to get in the sooner they come the better. No moore about the war Eliza the Captain liked that wheete coffee so much he wanted me to righte to you to send us some moore if you can see any boddy that will bee coming down here you may parch us about a peck and grind it and send it down. If Frances Moore is up there you can send it by him and if he is up you can send me any thing else you wish and have to spair and if Francis is up there I want you to tell him I want him to come home verry bad I dont know what to do about moving untill he comes back I am afraid I will bee cut out of a room with him Eliza I want you to send me my likness that Price taken for me down here there is a man here that is the best I ever saw to take likeness of such looking men as I am. I want to have him to take that over, and if you will send your picture down I will have them both taken in that fraim of mine together Send them as quick as you can then I will send them back again. If you cant send them by any boddy send them by the mail it will will cost fifteen or twenty cents and send them as soon as you get this. Which I expect you will get on Wednesday and if you will right and send it on the Friday Train I will get it Saturday knight Sion Campbell is a coming down here soon so the Doctor says John Louis and Sandy Brown has got through with their chickens and I think that coop of chickens will last them for they will never hear the last of them. There was too other lots of chickens sent down at the same time that has never been Heard of since There has letters been sent here to that effect Eliza I received a letter from John Walker last Wednesday and he said he was well and hearty and as fit as he could bee he said he had the finest Christmas he ever did in his life he said he had only three fights a chistmas and the worst hurt he got was when he fell down over the rail rode iron a running after Chisam he said he had a hel of a time and had the steam pretty high but he said he had cooled off. He said he had to dig dirt about one our for thumping Chisam but that dident hurt him much. Alfred kelley was here and he had just came from there he saw John and he said he was fatter than he ever saw him in his life and that he dident think he would come home untill his time was out that they were a looking for a fight every day No moore about John it is a gettäng late and Tan has finished his letter so I must come to a close Right as soon as you get this give my best love and respects to Emely and all the children tell Siss I want to see her verry bad but she here the cars blow a heepe of times befour she will see pap come again. God bless and save you and the children in all your tryals and troubles is the prayers of your unworthy husband. Louis H. McLeod. P.S. Eliza Inclosed you will find five letter stammps that will last you a while and when you get most out I will send you some moore if I can get them.

1862, January 27
A.S. McIntosh (*Moore County, NC*) to **A.S. Caddell**. General local correspondence. [108]

Middle old friend, I take my pen in hand to inform you that I am well at this time hoping when this come to hand it may find you well[.] i was glad to here that you was well and got home safe[.] i started to town last Tuesday and I received your letter[.] when i got to the court house i had not time to rite then and you must excuse me[.] i have not to much to rite[.] time is hard[.] i not seane much fun since you were here[.] i had a little fun but the way i dont kiss them is a little and do it & it is so sweet I can not tell[.] Tim wornt it sweet to give me a chaw tobacco[.] i wish i had a bole of mam honey and [illegible] and my Charley horse and the way we would go but he didden go did he[.] i hope you wont have to go from there but if you do i hope you will not get in no worst plase than that you have been in[,] but if you have to fight i hope the lord will be with you[.] in the morning i left your place you was asleep[.] i would like to aseene you but i no that you would loos sleep and would nead to sleep then[.] so[,] i must close my remarks[.] excuse my short letter and i will give you a full history in my next rite[.] when you get this give me the news. Your friend. A.S. McIntosh

1862, January 29

William P. Martin (*Camp near Fort Thompson, New Bern, NC*) to **George W. Foushee**. General wartime correspondence with brief mentions of **Susan Foushee, Giles Foushee, Robert Willcox, Richard Street, Murchison, William C. Campbell, Paisely, J.T. Clegg** and **Tyson**. [109]

Dear Sir, I received Mrs. Fooshee's very welcome letter yesterday morning, and feel under many obligations to her for writing me. I was truly glad to hear that you were neither lost or mislaid, that you are still enjoying the comforts of home, but fear if this unrighteous war continues, you may be called out in defence of these rights that we all left our homes to fight for. On last Sunday about one o'clock the train came down to Carolina a snorting, after us, and we had to pack up in a hurry, and get off about four o'clock, and arrived at this place, or at least opposite this place, about ten o'clock[.] and I can assure some of our men were very cold, as they had to ride in open flats all the way. We built fires and cooked supper and then slept the best we could in the open air, expecting probably before we could get our breakfast the yankees would be upon us, from the various reports we had heard, and didn't know whether we would make a breakfast for them, as we had heard their were one hundred and fifty vessels on their way to Newbern, but they havent made their appearance yet. I expect they have heard that the 26th had got up here and that they they were a dangerous sett to encounter, and have turned back. It is reported that twenty of their gun boats a about one thousand of their men were lost in the late storm. The race is not always to the swift nor the battle to the strong. If it be true that they have lost that number of boats and men, who can doubt but it was the Lords doing, and if he be for us we need not care who is against us. I felt more strongly convienced that he was on our side, than I did before, when they started out their other great fleet, when it was scattered to the four winds and several of their vessels were wrecked. Some of the prisoners we captured said if they could get back home they would never fight against us any more, for they believed the Lord was on our side and there was no use in fighting against us. One of them said that they devil had been before them, and hell behind them ever since started, that the boat they came down the Potomac on came very near sinking before they reached Fortress Monroe and immediately after leaving, the storm came up and continued until they were wrecked – I dont think there is much prospect of a fight here at this time, I am afraid so at least. I think we could give them a decent thrashing if they would only land, even if their numbers were ten to one, I would be willing to risk it with the entrenchments we have thrown up. I have never been anxious to get into a fight like some make our they are, but would be willing now to try them a few rounds, for putting us to the trouble of coming up here, and having to leave our comfortable quarters. I feel more independent at present than I have here to fore, from the fact that I have something to fight with. I bought a handy little Maynard rifle yesterday that I can swing over my shoulder and not be in my way, and can take a yankee from two to three hundred every fire. I could do some executions with it if I had the chance, as I could load and shoot as often as I pleased almost, as it is a break loading piece. I don't know whether we will go back to Carolina or not, even if the excitement dies out, without a fight at this place. I am afraid they entend to try and get possession of our Rail Road about Weldon, and if they should suceed in taking it will be a sad blow to the Southern Confederacy, as all communication from the south would be cut off from Richmond except by the Tennessee and Virginia Road. I fear we are going to have a hot time of it, for some time, if they can only raise the means to carry on the war. If this last fleet they have sent out should prove a failure[,] I wouldn't be surprised if it didn't cause a crack in their finances as they have their all as it were, staked on the sweep of this expedition. Friday Evening 31st. I haven't learnt anything definite in regard to the movements of the enemy since writing the above. It is reported at Newbern yesterday by a man who had gone down for the purpose of reconnoitering, that they are still at [?] as getting their vessels over the bar, that they had suceeded in getting about fifty in the sound. They find it a troublesome business, as they have to unload all there vessels over the bar. There is some heavy firing toward Fort Macon now, and it may be that they have attached that place, if so I expect we will have to go back. I wouldn't care if the yankees would get some of the people that live near our camp, they have no conscience at all when it comes to pricing anything they have for sale. I sent out yesterday to get a chicken for a sick negro, and couldn't get one for less than a dollar. If I could prevent the yankees from capturing him I wouldn't do it. Yesterday they were asking sixty cents for potatoes, and today some of my company went to get some and they asked them a dollar a bushel. Such prices ought not to be tolerated, and wont be by me. We came up here defending their property and themselves, and because they think we will have such things, they ask any sort of price they please. I sent back again after potatoes and told the men to tell them that we were willing to pay a fair price for any thing they had to sell, and if they are not willing to take a fair price I would march my company down and take every potatoe they had. They came back with plenty at sixty cents per bushel. Mrs. Fooshee said you were wishing the other morning that you could hand me over a place of sausages and chittilings. I wish it was so you could do so, nothing would please me better. She said she reckoned we were fareing better than you were, eating oysters and fish. I got tired of both, but could eat some fresh fish now if I could get them as we havent had any for more than two months, as the fishing season is over for a while. You can tell her that we have been feasting on bacon since we came up here that weighs from 75 to 80 pounds to the piece. I hope we will get some shad soon if we remain here. Mrs. Fooshee wanted to know how Robert Willcox has got. He is nearly well enough to go to duty again. He came up with us but I sent him back on tuesday night as it looked like we were going to have bad weather. I fear we are going to have a bad night as it has commenced raining. My tents are too sorry for wet weather, and I fear some of us will fair bad. I had all my tents condemed today and will make a requesition for new ones which I hope I will get right a way. I would like very much to see you down here, if you think you could stand our fare. I would like very much to go up to see you all, but dont suppose I can do so soon, if at all before my time is out, if I should be spared that long. My company is in very good health. Last week every man was on foot for the first time since we were at Gettysburg. There is one case of pneumonia, and two cases of mumps in the company now. Mr. Davis has the pneumonia. He was taken last week, and I left him at a private house near Carolina, and left Dr. Street with him. I heard this morning that he was some better, but is quite sick yet. I will bring this uninteresting scroll to a close, but not without reminding you to write me immediately when you receive this, and direct your letter to Carolina, as we get our mail from there yet. We can get it sooner than we could from Newbern although we are in four miles of the latter place[.] you may think that strange, but the mail dont get to Newbern at night until between six and seven o'clock and it would be impossible to get it at night, and we get it here next morning from Carolina by nine O clock[,] which is sooner than we could go to Newbern after it. Give my best respects to Mrs. Fooshee, and tell little Giles I would like very much to see him. Give my respects to Mr. Murchinson, W. C. Campbell & Lady, Mr. Paisely, T.J. Clegg and Lady, and Mr. Tyson and any other person you may see fit. I remain as ever[,] your friend W. P. Martin

1862, January 30
Eliza Jane Walker McLeod (and **Emily Franklin**) to husband **Louis H. McLeod**. General wartime correspondence with brief mentions of **Francis Moore, Tandy Walker, Joseph Walker, John A. Walker, Emily Franklin, Thomas Bragg McLeod, Swann, Miss Hill, Alexander Waddle, Annie Elizabeth McLeod, John Cox, Andrew Brown** and **Mary McNeill.** [110]

Der husban I ste my self this evning to drop you a few lines to let you now that me and famley is all wel at this time hop those few lines may find you in the same like blessin Louis I recvd your welcom leter last nite and was mor then glad to her from you and to her you wer wel and tolerble harty I hope your helth wil contin good i recken Louis you dont hav nothing you can eat i wt wish you had som of my saribs and sausage i hav I now you cold eat them but i see no chanch to send you enny you said if francis more was up her I cold send enny thing by him but he is not up her nor hant bin if he coms up i wil send somthing by him for you to eat and wil send som wheat coffy to you that is what i drink i was sorey to her tan was not very wel tel tan to take good cer of his self for if he can liv the time wil bee out soon time and then he can com to see all of us and get somthing he can eat tel tan Jo (?) that ((thought???)) very hard of him for not riting to him wher he got the ham and Sausay and whisky he sent him or no he ot to rite to Jo ofner Louis you said you diden like to go in with Somey [somebody] i dont think i wold if i cold stay in the cloth tent i wold i no i had rather bee by my self then in with Sommy (?) Louis John sent me a few lines in Jo (?) leter last weke and i was very glad to her from him me and Emley sent him won wensday and he said he wanted to her from you and tan and solded me for not riting to him he said he dident hav the chance to rite my der i am unesy all of the time now we her somthing bad evry day about the yankes i am a fraid a evry time i her from down lounther (?) i wil her tha hav kild all of you or taken you all prisners or herd you ar all ordred off somwher else it is bad enoff now but it mout bee hepe wors i can her from you evry weke and that is grate satisfaction if you wher i cold not her it goo hepe harder with me it giv me grat satis faction to rede a leter and no you rote it your self i thank my god that you can rite and i can so you can redit my der Louis i hav nothing much to rite to you you rote to me to send down yor picter and mine and you wold hav thim taken together i wil send them but when you hav them takin i want you to take good cer of my little won and if you want to keep it you may and send me the other and if you dont wat to keep it may send it back when you send the other Louis I hav no bady to send them by i wil send them with the leter and i am afraid tha wel get lost if you get them you had beter keep them until you can send them by sombody brag is gon down to spend this weke with faney he went with mister Swan and he told me to rite to you miss hill is gon down to spend the winter and i dont recken francis will com now Alaxander wadle is up now bying meules to send to the armey he cut big shines he stade from saterday until tuesday evning at tirkles and bot John too mules and wagan Sis sase you must bring her som candy and little plate and friping pay when you com hom the childrin sends ther lov to you Louis if you think the yankes will take you jump in the river and swim out. Louis i was mity glad you sent me them stamps i had abut won cixpene in the world and did not no how i wold get eny mor my der i hav nothing more to rite onley it is raning to day we hav mity rany wether not so cole as it has bin we had won for day sunday and I went up to John carses (?) and spent the day i had not ben of since you left before John sase he wold com down to see you all but he is afraid he wold doo somthing for somebody. to talk a bout like cosen ander i most close i cant think of nothing more to rite onley my time is drawin ni and i dred that time i long to se the time over i trust in god i hope he will deliver me out of my troblos and spar me to liv to see you a gain in this life my god hav mercy and save us both in heven if we never mete again in this life to mete me in heven wher parting is no [known] no nor So good by my der loving husban until deth your der wife. Eliza McLeod

Dear sir i seat my self to drop you a few lins to let you know that Mary says she cant wait untill you come back she is a fraid he will have to go to war an then what will she do Mr McLeod we all want to see you very bad that i am a fraid the yankeys wil get you an all of the pretty boys if they do what wil we girls do we will have to come down an take your places an if they do get you all i will be so mad i wont no what to do so ferwell Mr McLeod. Emily Franklin

1862, January 31
Noah Deaton (*Ft. Thompson*) to **Sarah Jane McDonald**. General wartime correspondence with brief mentions of **William Henry Harrison Davis,** Capt. **John M. Kelly, Daniel L. McDonald, Daniel Currie, Martin Currie** and **Daniel Arnett**. [111]

Dear Miss, after a long delay I take my pen in hand to answer your very welcom letter which came to hand in due time[,] which gave me much satisfaction to bear from you and I here beg pardon for not writing sooner[.] I am in tolerably good health at present and all of our company is tolerable well[,] only W.H.H. Davis he is very sick. I hope this will reach and find you and all enjoying good health[.] Well Sarah I have not much news to write at present. we have moved and from our winter quarters and are in camp now 5 miles below Newbern between the raill road and the Nuse River ½ mile from Ft. Thompson[.] there is a breast work from the rail road to the river about 1 mile long. I have seen some of Capt Kelly's Co since we came here day before yesterday[.] I saw your brother and you cousin Daniel Currie and Martin Currie and Arnitt and they all looked better I ever saw them look[.] I saw Mc Blue on yesterday he is well and hearty. we were orderd here last Sunday with the expectation of meeting the enemy here but we have not seen anything of them yet and we are very much unsettled[.] we don't know whether we will stay here or not[.] some think we will stay here and some think we will be sent to Weldon or Roanoke Island but I hope and expect that we will go back to our winter quarters in a short time[.] our boys are all fat as pigs[.] I have gained 15 lbs since I came in to camp. I recd the pair of gloves you sent to me with my thanks to you for them[.] you said you would send me your likeness if there was any artist about there to draw it[.] I would like to see it very much but I have your likeness in my memory so that I can carry it with me where ever I go[.] as I have nothing of intrest to write I will come to a close[.] please excuse my badly writen letter[.] I will try to do better next time[.] please write soon and give all the news. Address Carolina City N.C. 26 Reg N.C. Vol. Co. H. When this you see remember me[,] Though many miles apart we be, I love thee, your affectionate friend, N. Deaton

1862, February 1
Jane McIntosh, **Wm. A. McIntosh** and **Danl. McIntosh** to their uncle **A.S. Caddell**. General wartime correspondence between uncle and niece/nephew/brother-in-law with brief mentions of the Burnside Expedition, **C.D. Caddell**, **W.H.H. Davis**, **Devotion Davis**, **William Caddell** and **Raney Caddell**. [112]

Dear uncle[,][.] it is with pleasure that I take my pen in hand to drop you a few lines to let you know that I am well hoping this may find you in good health[.] I have nothing of importance to write this time only I have hear that part of the Burnside expedition has been lost[.] the people is generaly well[.] granpapy and grand mother is complaining but is so as to be about well[.] Tim there is now a powerful pretty gal hear today[.] I wish you had just a been here and we would have had a heap of fun[,] but I dont see verry mutch and what I do is not worth sending so far as it would not be worth any thing after its geting there[.] I wrote to you the 20th of last month but I have not got no answer yet[.] I heard that the stage driver had broke the letters and if you wrote I expect he broke it well[.] Tim I do want to see you the worst in the world but I cannot[.] I would like to talk with you awhile so I will come to a close by saying write soon and give me the if any[.] so[,] nothing more only I remain your affectionate niece until Death[.] yours[,] Jane McIntosh

Mr A.S. Caddell[,] after my respects not having anything new to write nor room to rite[.] I shall just say that if you can send that shirk skin by D. Davis[,] I will satisfy you for it[.] so[,] nothing more[.] yours Respectfully[,] Danl. McIntosh

Dear uncle[,] it is with that I take my pen in hand to let you know that we are all well hoping that these few lines ma find you in good health[.] I have nothing to write and say that times is hard yet[.] C. D. C has not come back yet and I dont no when he will[.] I hav not seen no fun since you left[.] I hant got nery kiss yet[.] I am a giving a most sick for one I must git a little smarter or I will forgit how and I dont want to fogit[.] Finely[,] the galls dont seme so liveley as they did when you was amung them[.] I hav not seen none of them tell I have a most forgot how they looked[.] I herd that you had moved and all the galls was mighty bad of about it[.] they was skerd that you as in a battle[.] we have not got letter from since 17th of last month[.] granmother and granpap is gitting mighty skerd about you[.] we herd that all the news was soped and that they would not let no one go in[,] or if they went in the camp that they would not let them out in three year[,] but D. Davis said that he would risk his life in going in[.] he said that if he went that he would see W.H.H. So[,] I will come to a close saing wright soon[.] yours truly[,] Wm. A. McIntosh

1862, February 1
Neill R. Kelly *(New Bern, NC)* to sister **Mrs. H. (Rachel) Gilchrist** General wartime correspondence with brief mentions of **John G. Ferguson, Margaret Robertson** and **Kate Robertson**. [113]

Dear Sister, According to promise I take pen in hand to drop you a few lines to let you know that I and John are still in the land of the living, and doing about as usual. We both have had very bad colds, but are nearly well of them now. We have enjoyed ourselves much better than I anticipated at first[.] We have got use to our plank beds now, and they fell nearly as pleasant now as fathers bed used to feel. I have no news of importance to write this time. We have been looking for a fight every day for the last week but we have now concluded that we will not have one soon. It was thought by most every body that the Burnside expedition was to attempt to take Newbern, but it delayed coming so long that they have concluded that it is for Wilmington or some other Seaport town further south. You must not think because we were looking for the Yankees that we were almost scared to death for we were not, but were anxious to see them; for we have concluded that Newbern is not a very easy place taken and I fear the Yankees have too much sense to undertake it. Our company is in only tolerably health. We have 6 in the hospital at Newbern and 18 in quarters besides 9 sick at home. Making in all 33 out of 85 sick. John G. Ferguson is complaining a little, he has the headache and a bad cold. Neill is as fat and saucey as ever. I received a letter from Cousin Margaret and Kate Robertson this week. They gave me all the general news in your neighborhood. They said that you were complaining of a bad cold, but never said how your cough was getting. I hope to hear that it is at least getting no worse. You must be sure and answer this and return good for evil for I am kept so busy these times that had I the news[,] I have scarcely no time to write long letters. If they would let us set up as long as we please at night we might write then[,] but we have to put out our lights at nine o'clock just about the time I get through my other business, consequently[,] I have no time for writing only what few moments I get between drills. I expect I will have to begin to write on Sundays like the other boys, then I will write you a long letter. So[,] you may conclude the first long letter you get from me that it was written on Sunday if not otherwise dated. There is a preacher here today. I suppose he is our chaplain but am not certain. I must close. You must be sure and write soon. I remain your bro, Neill R. Kelly

1862, February 9
Eliza Jane Walker McLeod to husband **Louis H. McLeod**. General wartime correspondence with brief mentions of **Tandy Walker, John Lewis Cox, Elizabeth Hinton Brewer McLeod, Sloan, Kelly, Sandy Kelly, Swann, John McNeill, Dave Kelly, Henry Sivy, Pane, William M. Swann, Louis Wicker, Andrew Watson, Douglas** and **Annie Elizabeth McLeod.** [114]

Dere husban i sete my self this morning to anser your kind litter that cam to han friday and i was more than glad to her from you and to her you were wel Louis thes lines leve me and the rest of the famley wel at this time hoping this may find you in the same blessing i am troubled a little with my hed but no rom to grumble i cant expect to be well all of the time Louis i dident rite last weke for i dident gete your leter until friday and did not no what to rite we have had the worst whether i ever saw this weke it rand all of the weke i dont no how you standet it down thar i am clene out of hart we cant doo nothing only make fires and cook and eat i am afraid we wil care everything we have if the whether holds on much longer my dere loving husban you rote to me to no wher i would bee wiling for you to join during the war or no Louis i am not wiling for you to jine it is the hardest thing i ever did in my life to give up for you to stay the twelve months and how could i bar to think of you having to stay eny longer god grant that we may both liv to see the twelve monts out and you can come home and live to gether in this life in pese Louis i cant bare it it is all i can doo to keep my mind now and if you go in during the war you may expect to have a loving wife in the Silom i hav more to stan than eny other body enny how and i now [know] i never can stand that while i am riting the ters moves down my cheak i cant help it i am her by my self and see soo meny lonsom Sunday if you were her it would bee so much sistfaction to me the children awl [all] say to write to pap not join tha want you to com home for tha dont think tha ever wil get to go to scool until you come home tha wil have to work for something to eat until you com home Louis I think twelv monts wil bee dooing your duty and then come home and let alters [others] take your place We want to live and hav something as wel as every body else and we cant doo it and you gone all or the time twelve monts is long enough for eny man let those that is staying at home enjoying ther sef take some of the hardship of the war as wel as you and ther wifes see troble as wel as me tel tan i am not wiling for him to goo and the childrin sad for tan not to goo never mind what the girls say remember he has a mother living and she want him to com home you no tan you are not helthy and if you can liv the twelve monts out we all want you to com home and tel us all about the time you have had tan you fel like a brother to me and for my sake dont goo i want you and Louis to come home to gether tel the balence of my frends down thar not to join for if tha can liv the twelve monts that is long enof Louis you rote me to no something about your mother i hav not herd a word about what she said only John Cox was up thar and he said she wasent very wel plesed with me you no if ennything happens the blame must bee laid on me i exspect she blames me for all ov it and if she dos i cant help it it wil be som time before she will see me unles she come to see me i hav not done nothing nor sad a word about San only John sade San shode [showed] him the leter he had rote to send to you if he hadent sen you at Slones he said it was wel don he said his feeling never was hurt so bad in his life as tha wer at Keleys that evening he said he com by on perps [purpose] to invite you home with him and you com out and talk so to him he never was soo put out in his life he went home and told his mother he said he had allways treeted you like a gentleman and he wold doo so yet if you wold come to see him. Louis i rote to you i sent the picters with the leter i did but mister Swan thout tha wold be safer to send them by John McNeil I did [didn't] no John was going until he was gon i diden no but what he sent the picters with the leter until i got your leter and i told him you did not get the picter and then he told me he sent them by John and i was mity glad so i am in hopse you hav got them i never no when enny body is going until tha as gon i never nod dave kelly was going until last Sunday nite i think he did bad thing to go way down thar and not take San nothing i never wold went if i cold not don better then that tel tan henry Sivy [?] and Pane [?] stade with me last Sunday night and tha were wel and mother was wel and tha left Monday morning soon as tha cold get tha brecfast and went to Jose and it rand all day and tha stade tel nex morning Louis i saw the likeness of the company the captain sent to his brother and it was the worst I ver saw if kelly cant doo beter he had beter say [stay] at home and go to work i cold not no but the capten and Louis Wicker and Ander Watson the childrin all said the outside man was you the face look like you but it did not stan like you rite if that was you so i may no tel the capten i wil send the white coffey with the grtes [greatest] pleasuer as soon as i can get the chances i never no when enny lad is going until tha ar gon Mister Swan said he was going to send somthing to him and when he sent he wold let me no and i cold send some thin Louis i wil tri to send you something to eat tha wold like to no what you hav to eat wher [whether] you hav got enny pork or not rite and let me know how you liv and if you have enny whisky or no timeis souer [sour] up here corn is seling won dolar and twenty five cents per bushel i sent fitten bushels of otes by Mister Dougles last weke and got sixey too and a haf cents per bushel and got me won bushel of sault and giv three dolars and a haf for it der sault i most close for i hav nothing mor to rite onley nelce sade to tel you he was wel and harty and Sis sade i most put her name down as Elizabeth McLeod. this is Sisis work Bragg was wel plesed at his trip down at Williams nothing more at present so good by my der loving husban until death you der wife, Eliza McLeod. rite as soon as you get this for i was unesy when i did not get a leter wensday you will her something from me befor long

My time is most out and i shal be mity goad if i can liv i dont sleep good thes nites for i am thinken of you all of the time.

1862, February 10
Daniel L. McDonald (*New Bern, NC*) to sister **Sarah Jane McDonald**. General wartime correspondence with brief mentions of **Capt. William P. Martin** and **Hugh McDonald**. [115]

Dear Sister, I embrace the present opportunity of droping you a few lines to inform you that I am well at this time and hope these few lines to reach you in good health[.] I have nothing of importance to write to you at this time[.] We have some verry cold rough weather here for some time past and not much likelyhood of getting much better[.] Capt Martins Co. has moved up within four miles of here[.] Some of them comes up to see us every day[.] you wanted to know if I received my drawers I forgot to mention it in my letters, I recd 2 prs flannel drawers[.] I should like to hear from you all verry much[.] Hugh is mending verry fast but has not got out of the hospital yet[.] [torn] good many of our company [torn] this time there is a heap [torn] got the mumps [torn] the tyfoid feaver[.] I want you to write to me as soon as you get this for I would be particular glad to hear from you any time[.] give my best respects to the rest of the family & tell them I want to see them very much[.] Nothing more for this time[,] only I remain your most affectionate brother untill death, D.L. McDonald

1862, February 13
D. Frank Wilkie (*Camp Branch near New Bern, NC*) to **Emeline Phillips.** General wartime correspondence with brief mentions of fighting at Vicksburg, Elizabeth City and Roanoke. [116]

Dear Miss E., It is with pleasure that I again seat myself to write you a few lines. I am well at present, hoping these few lines may reach you all well. The health of our company is very good and has been for some time. We have noone in the hospital nor has been for three months and the health of the regiment is much better. We have left our winter quarters and are in camp near New Bern. We have been looking for a fight now for some time but have not had any luck, though I have some bad news to write. They have had a fight at Vicksburg and the yankees have possession of it and they have taken 3,000 men though they did not kill but 300 of them[,] and have burned Elizabeth City and our men killed two to one of the yankees. And I wish that they had killed the last one of them. This is enough to make the young men that have not volunteered to flee to this army. Their help is needed for we have but few troops and have so many places to guard and the yankees can overpower us. We are very well prepared to guard and the yankees can overpower us. We are very well prepared for them here, We have three new forts here in two miles and have blockaded the river with old vessels. There was fifty of our men got away from Ronoak and they say that our men ran the yankees back three times. Our men got out of ammunition. There was six yankees to one of our men. We heard one of the best speeches delivered on yesterday I ever heard by our colonel. There is a great deal of talk of reenlisting for the war. I cannot tell how many will reenlist though I reckon that the young men wish we all would. Miss E., your kind letter came to hand in due time and I was proud to hear from you all. I would have written sooner but I did not have anything worth writing and have not at this time. We were on a agreeable view on last Saturday at New Bern. All the troops that were near were there. It was a beautiful sight. Write soon. Direct your letters as you have here to fore. Give my love to all. I shall remain yours, D. Frank Wilkie.

1862, February 15
A.S. Caddell (*Camp Branch, NC*) to **Martha Sullivan**. General wartime correspondence with brief mentions of coming draft in Moore County. [117]

Miss Martha, I drop you a few lines to let you know I am well hoaping these may find you in good health[.] I have been unwell for a while though I believe my health has returned again[.] I recd a few lines from you a few days since[.] I was glad to hear from you and to hear that you was well[.] I shall not be able to interest you for I have no news[.] times are somewhat dull in camp[.] we have no fighting to do here though we may not be idle long but I cannot tell[.] I would like to see you and engoy your company a while though as I have not the opportunity of seeing you[.] I have one consolation[.] my time is short that I shal have to stay here and then I think I will have the pleasure of enjoying the presence of my friends and relatives for a while at least[.] I want you to write to me[.] give me all the news[.] I suppose there will be a draft in Moore Cty next Wednesday[.] I expect you will loose some of your particulars[.] I think you slited me or you would of asked me to your quiltin yesterday[.] I will close[.] write as soon as you get this[.] Yours affectionately, A.S. Caddell

1862, February 19

W.L. Sullivan (*Moore County, NC*) to **A.S. Caddell**. General wartime correspondence with brief mentions of **Neill A. Fry, Zacheus Hogan, William Whitlock, Samuel Jackson McIntosh, Neill McIntosh, John A. Jackson, William J. Dowd, Nicholas P. Smith, Noah Deaton, William McKinnon, John McKinnon,** and the burial of **Thomas Cox** at Bethlehem. [118]

I seat myself to drop you a few lines which will inform you that I am well and the rest of the family[.] Mr A.S.[,] I have know news to write to you moore than we expect to be drafted next Tuesday[.] times is hard enough but not like they will be when we all have to leave home tho we are no better to leave home than you who have gone before[.] I received your welcome letter by N.A. Fry which I was glad to receive to hear that you was getting along very well[.] I wat to see you all the worst sort[.] give my love to Z.H. and tell him to write to me soon for haint herd anything from him lately[.] C.D. is well, me and him is together frequently[.] Me and C.D. Caddell ma be drafted[.] if we are together we will go together[.] we will fight if nesesary[.] I hope we all meet with you all in good health[.] A.S. remember me to Z. Hogans, Wm. Whitlock, S.J. McIntosh, N. McIntosh, J.A. Jackson, W.J. Dowd, N. Smithe, N. Deaton, Wm. Mcinen & brother and all your company[.] I saw Thomas Cox yesterday at Bethlehem[.] it was the best looking corpse I ever saw[.] AS, I have quit flying around the girls since the draft came[.] I have a good reason for saying so they wont let me fite clost by and I thought it time to quit[.] the girls as pretty as ever[.] I must come to a close by saying I remain your cincere friend until death. Yours respectfully. A.S. Caddell write soon as you can, give my love to all enquiring friends if eny[.] when this you see[,] remember me[.] WL Sullivan

1862, February 23

Louis H. McLeod (*Camp Wyatt*) to wife **Eliza Jane Walker McLeod**. General wartime correspondence with brief mentions of **Sandy Brown, Tandy Walker, Sandy Kelly, William M. Swann, Hardy Harris, Bass, Abe Douglas, John McNeill, John A. Walker, Benjamin Gunter, Alvin Buchanan** and **Elbert Patridge.** [119]

Dear Wife I seat my self this Sunday eavening to answer your kind letter that came to hand on Friday knight which I was moore than glad to hear from you and the rest of the Family but I was sorry to hear that you I was troubled so with your head. Eliza I was sorry that you think hard of me for not riting to you every weeke I have rote every weeke since I came back I started one last saturday mourning which I thought you would bee surtain to get on Monday but from your letter you did not get it our male gets rong here sometimes that our letters wont get off in a day or too. Eliza this leaves me well and hearty only I havent got over the bad cold that has been anoying me ever since I came back home. The rest of our company is in verry good health considering the bad rainy wether there is nothing much the matter now but colds and cough Sandy Brown has got the mumps. Tandy has got over his boils and is well and hearty and so is Sandy Kelley The Captain is well and has gond to Wilmington on horseback to over take Hardy Harris and Bass that ran a way last knight. Eliza the news that you heard about the fight at Ronake wasent as bad as you heard it was it was to the contrary our men killed and wounded six thousand of the yankees and our side lost twenty seven hundred killed and wounded This was at Fourt Donilson if they dont look sharp we will give them seet (?) yet When all them drafted men comes down on the cost we will have a pretty strong fource and that is just what we ought to have. I am glad the draft is coming on in Moore [county] If I just had the calling out of the men I would pick them about right. Tell Abe to not bee like John McNeill take the woods and crack ticks all the summer Tell him to stick to it like a man. Eliza you wanted to know if I ever hear from John I havent heard from him in a good while I rote to him since he did to me and he never answered my letter. Tandy sent him a letter last weeke but has not got an answer. I havent got but one letter frøjm Benjamin Gunter since I came home. Eliza you said you had nine lambs and expected the old bell weather would have too. Hura for the Southan Confedracy I think your flock will increase verry much this year if you will have luck and take care of them Eliza we have no room to grumble about our eating we have a plenty pickle pork and beef and flower and corn bread and sometimes molasse but it is badly cooked but we can make out with it first rate. We fair a good deal better here than a heap of the soldiers in other places Eliza you said you would send me any thing I wanted. you nedent trouble your self about sending me any thing I can stand what the rest can. Dont send any thing without you have a good chance. Alvin Buchanan is down here now he is a going to start home to morough We heard Elbert Patridge was a coming down to see us befour long Eliza I hopet those lines will find you well and remain well as could bee expected through all your troubles. My wife dont get out of heart dont greave for me if the God of heaven will spar me to live untill my time is out I will come home where we canjoin hand and heart once moore in this life your husband. L. H. McLeod

1862, February 25

Eliza Jane Walker McLeod to husband **Louis H. McLeod**. General wartime correspondence with brief mentions of **Sandy Kelly, Tandy Walker, Alexander Hamilton McLeod, Elizabeth Hinton Brewer McLeod, Abe Douglas, Henry ?, Ary ?, Thomas Bragg McLeod** and **Nelly ?.** [120]

Der and lovin husband, i recvd your welcom leter last wensday and was more then glad to her from you and to her you wer well onley to the cole. i hope you will soon get over the cole and the sty you had on your eye. my der these lines leve me and the rest of the famley wel hoping tha may find you in the same blesing. i was glad to her Sandy was so fat but was sorey to her tandy was troble so meuch with biles. i hope he will soon get over them. Louis i was more then glad to her the favor Sandy did. i hope you and him will bee frenley enny more it is no time for such as that i want you to rite to him. i herd he did not like your riting to them felows up thar and not riting to him. i hope you will rite to him and your mother too, forgiv all that was past when you wer up her. Louis ther is grate excitment up her now the draft is in more (Moore) to day and evry body ganl tha hav the chanch to volentur and if tha dont tha will bee drafted. tha hav got a larg company of volenturs in harnet Abe sais he is on the top ov the fence and he dont no which way to fall to morow. tha hav to doo won way or tother. he talks of volentur. Louis Abe said you ought to bin down at illington. he said tha dinent mind poling(?) down and sauing(?) it did tickle him and he said them that wont busen(?) tha wold take too focks and beet it til it was sweld up as big as a mans hed. he said befor he wold doo that he wold goo and fite tel tha kild him. no more abott them. my der i am unesy all of the time now. i want to her from down thar and am fraid to her. i never was sow out ov hart in my life. i don't think of eny thing els hardley. i fer tha will kill you all or take you all prisners. Louis if tha ever dos attack you doo the best you can to tri to save your self, if times gets too hot tri to make your ascape in somway or other. may the god of heven bee with you is all my pras all of the time. my lord hav mercy on you and save you from the bulet or sord. trust in god if he dont help we ar a conkerd people. i hope our pepel will giv up and make pese if tha dont evry body will bee kild. thar never was such times in our world befor. evry body think if englantt and franse dont join us and doo it quick we will hav to giv up. rite to me what you all think about it down thar and if you hav got eny more men. tha ar mity scerd in fayettvill tha ar hunting them homes to goo too. tha hav tride me for houses room but i hav denied them. Louis we hav had too pirty dase and i hope the wether will bee setle a little while now. we comens plowing to day and i hope we can kepon a little while. tha givs me som satisfaction when we can all werk. i want to tri to make bed [bread] for you to eat if you ar so fornate as to get hom. our whete look very wel at this time. i dont no how you liv dow thar. the wether has bin so bad. Louis i was glad to her you did not sufer for somthing to eat. i was afraid you did. get eny thing you cod [could] eat. Louis if you hav eny mony i want you to by eny thing you can eat for it is such a bad chanch for me to send you eny thing but if you cant get it rite to me. i want you to hav somthing you can eat as long as i hav eny. nothing more the childrin sends howdy to pap. henry and ary an nelee. helee was mity wel plesed at what you rote. brag sade nelee wondent bee over ser over him. my der loving husban i wel say a few words about my self. i dont expect to bee able to rite to you eny more. my time is out now and i dont no what minit i shal bee down. i hope i will hav a goo tim. if you wer her i won think so much abot it. if anny thing dos hapen and i dont liv i want you to com home and take cer ov the childrem. my der i never wanted to see you so bad in my life. i dreme of you evry nite. i dont sleep good. I hope when you her from me it will be over. may the god ov heven bee with me and spar me until you com home. no more onley your loving wife until deth. goob by rite as son as you gethis. my der loving husband, Eliza McLeod

1862, February/March

Lizzie Skeen Phillips (*Randolph, NC*) to **Emeline Phillips.** General wartime correspondence with brief mentions of **R. Harris Skeen, Nancy Harris Skeen, Martha "Mat" Skeen** and **Louis C. Phillips.** [121]

My Emeline, I now have an opportunity of dropping you a line though I have nothing of a cheering nature to write you at this time. Oh, our troubles in this country are great. Brother Harris is going to war. We all are in trouble about it for it is something so hard to give up. But my daily prayer and trust in God is that He will provide and take special care of him and all other innocent persons and that we may soon have peace given us again. My path has been one on continual trouble since I saw you. God has given grace to bear up under it so far. I will trust Him for time to come. We are tolerably well except Ma. She has been complaining for some time. I fear she will get down sick, she is in so much trouble about Harris. I shall not go to Guilford until he leaves home. Louis grows and talks most plain anything. I would like so much to see you all again, but don't know when I shall have an opportunity of so doing but hope to see you again. Have any of your brothers gone to war yet? Oh, how I wish for peace. I hope and pray we may soon have it, but I fear not soon. I must close with a short note this time. Excuse me for so doing. Sister Mat has come down since I commenced writing. She is very well. You must write me soon. I love to hear from you. Remember me kindly to all my friends. Write soon and let no one see this for I am writing on my lap and Louis is around me so I can't write with correct. Yours truly, Lizzie

1862, March 2

Louis H. McLeod (*Camp Wyatt*) to wife **Eliza Jane Walker McLeod**. General wartime correspondence with brief mentions of **John W. Ellis, Kelly, Grissom, William McAulay, Thomas Harrington, Francis Moore** and **Jesse Wicker.** [122]

Dear and Loving Wife I once moore seat myself to drop you a few lines to let you know that I am well and hearty. Eliza I have looked and looked for a letter from you but alass every male no letter. Every boddy getting letters and I could get nerer one from you. You know that I am verry anxious to hear from you. There is too letters that you have never answered at all. I hope you will not qiet writing to me for maby you wont have me to write to you before my time is out. there is no telling where I will bee in that time. There is great indusements here at this time for men to go in during the War. There was able speaches here in camp yesterday by our brave Colonel and John W. Ellis and Major Kelly and Cpt. Grissom able speaches Incouraging their men to go in far the war. I dont think there will bee any one of our company that will go in untill our time is out. If we would go in betweext this and fifteenth of this month we can get a furlough of thirty days and one Hundred Dollars Bounty to take home in our pockets so they say but we have been folled about furloughs to go home and all the men is afraid they mout bee fooled again. There will bee a meeting on to morrough to see what we will do I dont think there will bee any of our men that will go in untill their time is out and then they will all go in again if times dont get any better. Eliza I watied all day thinking I would get a letter to hear something about the men that was drafted. William McAuley got a letter and stated some that was drafted and there was one that I was sorry that He was drafted and that was Thomas Harrington. I am anxious to here all the names that was drafted. I recen there was a scared set of men up there. Eliza I commenced this letter yesterday but there was an election came off to day and I was nominated to fill Lieutenant Moores place and I was beaten by nine votes by J. Wicker and there was an election held to see how many would go in during the war and there wasent the first man that would go in. Eliza I will stay my time out here if I dont get killed and then I am a going to see you and my loving children and all my aquaintance if the God of Heaven will spaire me to live untill the tenth of September next. No moore at present only your loving Husband untill Death. Louis H. McLeod. Rite soon as you get this.

1862, March 3

Eliza J. Berryman (*Lick Creek*) to **Louis H. McLeod**. General wartime correspondence with brief mentions of **James O.A. Kelly, Nathan Douglas, Alex Bolin, Malcolm Watson, Robert Thomas, Terry Bud, Billy Buchanan, Joseph Buchanan, David Thomas, Buck Brooks, Clark Oliver, John Walden, Benjamin Hunter, John G. Hunter, Malcolm Dalrymple, Thomas Harrington, Sandy Cox, John Campbell, John Thomas, Elias Cox, Benjamin Muckle, John Buchanan, Henry Godfrey, John Godfrey, Andrew Wicker, James L. Sheppard, Fred Swann, James Scarborough, Joseph Avent, Ben Avent, Jonas Parham, Ambrose Gunter, Absalom Kelly, E. Wicker** and **Ann E. Berryman.** [123]

Dear Sir, I received your kind favors per Mr Buchanan and was turely glad to here from you and here that you were all enjoying good health. This leaves myself and family in tolerbly good health but their is great confusion up here since the draft come off. I fell realy sorry for some of them but there is some I dont care for. they might have volunteered and not had any draft at all. If they had been patriotic but their was too much cowardice amongst thim or els they were scared so bad they hardly knew what they were doing. The day the draft come off the big men in this district [they] dont think best to get them to volunteer. Their was large money offered to them if they would make up the number without a draft but they didnt suceede and finaly had to stand the draft but their was not very many drafted for the largest portion of the men in this district had volunteered before the draft came off. James Kelly had made up a company. He has about 75 men and expect to get them that was drafted. they had a meeting yesterday and elected their officers James Kelly was elected Capt. Nathan Douglass 1st Lieutenant Alex Bolen 2nd Malcom Watson 3rd Lieutenant Kelly is going to Raleigh this week. They expect to commence drilling next Friday. Mr. McLeod I will give you a list of the volunteers that I am acquainted with Robert Thomas, Terry Bud, Billy Buchhanan and both of the Jo Buchhanans, David Thomas, Buck Brooks, Clark Oliver, John Waldon, Ben Hounten & John Henton, Malcom Dalrimple. I will now give you a list of the men that were drafted Thomas Harrington, Sandy Cox, John Campbell, John Thomas, Elias Cox, Ben Michie, John Buchhanan, Henry Godfrey, John Godfrey, Andrew Wicker, Dr Sheppard and Mecan, Fred Swann. Mr Swann has hired a man to go in his place and so has Thomas Harrington. I am not acquainted with the man that Thomas Harrington hired, he has one of the railroad hands. Mr Swann hired Scarborough he gave him seventy five dollars. I heard yesterday that Mr Joseph Avent was offering 3 hundred & fifty dollars to any one that would go in his son Bens place. Ben was drafted & so was Jonas Parham & Ambros Gunter. Mr McLeod it is not worth while to speak about the times up here for you of course must know its distressing. I heard yesterday that Elias Cox said he would not care if his horses would runaway & kill him on his way from Carthage. He is goine to Raleigh now to see if he can get off. Mr Absalom Kelly went with him. I would hate to be such a coward. I wish he had my spunk; if I am a woman I would fight as long as I had life for my country. Mr. McLeod there was one of the prisoners that was taken on Ronoke Island passed Aunt E. Wickers last Wednesday and said he was in the fight, his account was quit different from the account in the papers; he stated only ten of our men killed & thirty three hundred of the yankees. he said their wasnt but three hundred of our men in the fight and their was about 2000 held in reserve. he said that it took a thousand men three days to bury their dead. he staid with them two weeks and his fair was but poor, he was glad to get away. he said he talked to some of the privates & they told him that they would take volenteres for thirty days for they were going to do what they had to do right away, their is several of the prisoners about Haywood that was in fight. I have told you all the news I can think of at present, you must give my best respects to all of my friends & relatives in the company & reserve a portion for yourself please excuse this badly written letter and write when you think proper. I will be glad to her from you at any time. A. E. B. send her respects to you & Tandy. Yours respectfully, E. J. Berryman

1862, March 5

Louis H. McLeod (*Camp Wyatt*) to wife **Eliza Jane Walker McLeod**. General wartime correspondence with brief mentions of **William M. Swann, John Lewis Cox, Sandy Kelly, James P. Deaton, John W. Ellis** and **Tandy Walker.** [124]

I seat my self once moore to drop you a few lines to let you know how I stand in this troubleson wirld. Eliza This will inform you that I am yet spaired with good health. The rest of our company is tolerable well. There is only three that is sick withe the feavar, Sandy Brown is a good deal better he will soon bee up. there was one man died in camp day befour yesterday that belonged to the Duplin Turpentine Boys. verry little sickness in the Regiment at this time. Eliza I just send you those few lines to let you know the facts I never was put out so much in my life as I was yesterday and the day befour. Our company has split up the worst sort. There has fourty of them gone in for the War and because they couldent but twenty go home at a time some of them got mad and taken their names of. I dident now what in the wirld to do. I thought all the company at once was a going in and what would I do. I studed and studed till I thought I would have to go in any how. I consulted my best friends and finally we all concluded to all stay out and serve out our time for the twelve months and bee free once moore and if the times did not get any better we would all stick to gether after going home and stay a while and them we would all volenteer again and recrut up a full company again for the war. There was no man in the Company that knew what to do for the best. Probably it might have been the best for all of us to have went in and thin it might have not. There was some of the men swore they never will go in again under Captain Swann there never was a Captain that could please everry boddy. It is a great Inticement for some of them to go in. they get thirty days furlough and one hundred dollars but ten dollars taken out of the hundred which leaves them ninety which is moore than a heap of them could make in one or too years. I thought John Louis would run crasy because he could go home and so was Sand Kelley and Deaton. They are all the joylest in the wirld. I never saw such fools n my life. I will bee glad when they are gone. I am afraid they wont bee so when they came back. As John W. Ellis said the other day in his speach go home and stay them thirty days and arrange your matters and then shake hands with your wives and children and sweethearts for the last time and come back to the battle field to fight for their protection keep off the Envaders from their homes and fire sides. And if they never see them again they will no they died in a just cause. David Peg [?] is in for the War and is a going home again. Tandy and my self Bool Rocks will hold on untill our time is out and then We all will go home together. The Captain is a going home with them. All the best of the Company is here yet to stay their time out. I expect we will have to go to aitchen (ditching) to day but a trench to fight in from the ocean to the river. I went in bathing in the sea the last day of February and it cured my cold. Your Husband untill death, L. H. McLeod

1862, March 12
Jane McIntosh, **Wm. A. McIntosh** (*Carthage, NC*) to their uncle **A.S. Caddell**, and Danl McIntosh (*Carthage, NC*) to his brother A.S. Cadell. General wartime correspondence between uncle and niece/nephew/brother-in-law with brief mentions of uncle **Joseph Caddell's** marriage to **Margaret McMillan, A.B. Muse's** wife's aunt in Bladen County on March 6, **C.D. Caddell**, **Ashley F. Muse**, **Wm. A. Barrett**, Widow **Moore**, **William Caddell**, **Raney Caddell**, the birth of **John A. Barrett's** son [**Jesse Samuel Barrett**], Mr. **Hogan**, **Sarah Frances McIntosh**, **Cornelius Alexander Stutts**, **Duncan Black**, **Susan Muse Wallace**, **Lock Wallace**, **Hiram Wallace** and church at Bethlehem and Pleasant Hill. [125]

Dear uncle[,] it is with pleasure that I take the present opportunity of writing you a few lines to let you know that I am still in the land of the living well and hearty and hope that these few lines may find you enjoying the same[.] I have nothing strang to write more than you know[.] only uncle Joseph Caddell is married to A. B. Muses wifes aunt[.] I do not know how she writes her name[.] C. D. C. went with him down in Bladen City after her they were married the 6th inst[.] well Tim very near all the men is drafted in the settlement[.] we had meeting last sunday and A. F. Muse and Wm. A. Barret preached for the last time for awhile and perhaps forever[.] ther was a quilting party held at the Widow Moores last night[.] I was not there and I do not know whether they had mutch big times or not but I expect that it is doutfull[.] the people is comonly well[.] hear grandmother about as comon but I think grand papy is geting worse if any difference[.] Mr John A. Barret has a fine son[.] your gal is very well though she seemes not to be so funny since the draft as her brother has go[.] I should like to see you[.] I think that if you was to come home that we could have some more fun[.] I supose they were a goin to raise the union flag at Carthage but they did not do it[.] Mr Hogans sings at pleasant hill the 5th sunday in this month[.] Miss S.F. McIntosh has give Mr C.A. Stutts walking papers. So[,] I will come to a close for the present[.] pleas excuse all mistakes and bad writing and write soon and give me the news if any[.] Yours affectionly, Jane McIntosh

Dear uncle[,] it is with plesure that I take my pen in hand to drop you a few lines to let you know that we are all well at present hoping that these will find you well[.] I have nothing to and [?] that Duncan Black is a goine to go to the war in paps place[.] he is to give him a 100 Dolar and Duncan has volunterd in Black's company[.] the drafted men has to start tomorrow[.] I dont know whether the volunteers will start then or not[.] I hav not got a letter from you since you was at home[.] you said in paps letter that you wrote to me but I have not got it[.] I wrote to you I have got a few kisses since I wrote and I hope me powerful[.] I am a fatning[.] I weigh a hundred fifty[.] A.F. Muse preached his farewell sermon last sunday at pleasant hill[.] I want you to write to me as soon as you get this and tell me all the fun[.] I havnt had no fun since the draft[.] they say that Susan Wallace has rubed all the skin of her face and crying and wiping the tears of since Lock was drafted[.] Hiram Wallace started to war last Tuesday[,] was a week and he has got back[.] So[,] I will come to a close by saing write sone and give me the nuse[.] yours truly, Wm. A. McIntosh

Dear Brother I onst mor seat myself for the purpose of writing you a few lines to let you no that we are in whel health and hope when it comes to hand that it will find you well[.] I receive youre very kind letter of the 3rd and was glad to here from you[,] and to here that you had got in whel helth again[.] I havnt anything to write of interest[.] I was drafted and thought a while I should be to go tho I shall send a man in my place[.] I divent think I could stand there fare[.] you said that you was thinking of joining an Artillary company[.] I dont think I should[.] it as well as the other tho I suppose that you will come home before you join other[.] So[,] I will close[.] yours truly untill Death. Danl. McIntosh

1862, March 13
Martha M. Sullivan to **A.S. Caddell**. General wartime correspondence with brief mention of **Zach Hogan** and the marriage of uncle **Joseph Caddell** to Miss **McMillan** of Bladen County and **W.L. Sullivan**. [126]

I am blest with the opportunity of writing you a few lines which will inform you that I am well hoping these lines will find you well and injoying yourself[.] I hav no nuse to you moore than times is sum what dull and trouble[.] Tim people is stiring about hear at this time[.] you must excuse me for not writing to you no sooner for I hav bin sum what in a dull state, jus no I am[.] I cant contented long enough to write to you[.] my will is good to rite to you if could you must rite to me and tell me what to rite[.] Mr Z. Hogans is staying us a night[.] I was glad to see him in old Moore once more[.] I would bee glad to see you[.] that is something I never expect to see in sum time if you volunteer again[,] but you must not do that[.] if you do times will change[.] your uncle Joseph Caddell is married to a Miss McMillan from Bladen city[.] that is bad for the girls about hear to think off[.] I want you to use your pleasure about volunteering[.] I dont want you to do so but use your pleasure[.] dont mind what I say[.] I heard that sum person said if any of you com home without volunteering that you would be drafted rite off[,] but that is hard to heare[.] you write to me what you aim at doing[.] tell me the truth[.] I must close for this time[.] excuse bad writing and spelling for it is giting late[.] I will send this in WL letter for the last one I ever expect to send with him to you if he leaves hear[.] if I dont rite often[,] you must not think hard of me[.] write soon[.] yours truly, M.M. Sullivan

1862, March 13
W.L. Sullivan to **A.S. Caddell**. General wartime correspondence with mention of **C.D. Caddell**. [127]

Dear friend I am trying to write you a few lines which will inform you that we are all well as comon only colds[.] I received your welcome letter which gave me great pleasure to know that you was well[.] I have know newse to write to you of much interest[.] I am fixin to start for Raleigh the morning[.] I hate to start but we must start[.] I have know newse to write to you moore than the Confed gun killed a heap of us[.] But I hope we leave and do well yet[.] we will get on the wagon at twelve o'clock and I recken we will all take a ride[.] I havnt time to write much since I ought to be fixing to start[.] But I wont to write you a few lines which I now must come to a close by saying I remain your friend untill death[.] Neill is well, he staid here last night[.] I Remain your friend untill death, your friend W.L. Sullivan

1862, March 13
Mary E. Moore (*Carthage, NC*) to cousin **A.S. Caddell**. General wartime correspondence between cousins with brief mention of **Noah Muse**, the marriage of **Joseph Caddell** and **Peggy A. McMillan**, **Kate McMillan**, **Archy Muse**, **Exer Moore**, **Sarah Moore** and **Ashley Muse**. [128]

Dear Cousin: I received you very welcome letter yesterday, I had nearly come to the conclusion that you was not going to write to me anymore. I wrote a few lines to you the other day giving you a scolding for not writing. I ought not to have done it but I will now take it back. I have just bid some of my best friends farewell[.] I feel very sad on this occasion[.] This is the day they all must start[.] Three people are all now going by[.] I have never seen Noah Muse look so sad in my life. He come in here crying & went off the same way. I dont mind seeing the boys go when they go cheerful; but when they go weeping[,] it makes me feel awful. I tell you it will be lonesome times about here, for a while; but the time is not far when some of you return home, to stay. I hope. I suppose some of you has volunteered[.] have you or are you going too[.] I think you all ought to come home & let some go that has never been. but I know they had mutch rather have you all that is prepared for fighting. though the rest can prepare as well as you all did. I am about to forget Mr Joseph Caddell[.] he returned home sunday knight with his wife Miss Pegy A McMillan[.] her sister Kate is now at Archys[.] Miss Kate, Exer, Sarah & I all went to Mr Muses yesterday[.] I tell you Ashley was pitching around Miss Kate about rite[.] We give the boys a quilting Tuesday eavening[.] we had a very nice time about 15 of each[.] Oh I do wish you could have been here. If you had I dont suppose you would have enjoyed it, as your intended was not here[.] That is if I am not mistaken in the one. If I am please tell me she is. I suppose you know who I am looking to. It is Miss M. S.[.] Exer sends her respects to you[.] I believe I have told you about all the newse & I don't expect anything I have told you is newse to you for you have so many correspondens that can give you the newse mutch better than I can. I hope you dont think that I would be any way but sincere in my wishes in regard to your personal welfare[.] I would be very sorry if I thought you formed such an opinion of that of me, I cannot think you do. Nothing more. I hope to hear from you soon. Write soon. your friend & Cousin M.E.M. [P.S] Sarah is covered up in the bed[.] she has not spoken a word since They all comenced going on.

1862, March 13
Richard Street (*Camp Branch, near New Bern, NC*) to **Candace Phillips.** General wartime correspondence with brief mentions of **Mastin C. Phillips** and **Baxter C. Phillips.** [129]

My dear Candace, I have intended writing to you ever since I came down, have been waiting to hear from home and the effects of the draft before writing. Tell Mastin and Baxter that I am sorry to hear that they have not a man in Moore smart enough for Captain but have to send to Fayetteville for one. But I need not send such a message as they may be gone long before this reaches you. I know that you and that you parents are deeply distressed at the idea of parting with them, and I truly sympathize with you in your distress. However, you have the satisfaction of knowing that their characters are formed and that they will not be led astray by the enticement and frivolties of which young men are exposed to in the life of a solider. We are expecting a great battle tomorrow. I do not know that I shall get to fight any but I will be in as much or more danger than those who are engaged, as I shall have to take care of the wounded and have them carried off from the field. From what I can learn, the enemy have about six men to our one. But then we are looking for about as many more tomorrow and that will make out three to one against us. I think we can whip that number easily, but we may be whipped and taken prisoner, or killed by the Yankees. Or how would you like to see me come home with one arm or leg? You will certainly hear of the battle before this reaches you. Before you receive this, all will be over. Victory or death will be ours. Should we fall, shed a tear over our grave. An should we never meet again, may you be happy. I hope your correspondence with me may never cause you the least unhappiness . It has been my desire to elevate and enlarge your mind to adorn and enable your character. I must now bid your goodbye as it is getting late and I have the prospect of a hard days work tomorrow. It has been pouring down rain with slight intermission since dark and nearly all day. The soldiers are out in it all waiting for the foe. I hear the axes still going. Many a man will be wrapped in his winding sheet before another setting sun. Good night. Yours truly, R. Street

1862, March 20
Noah Deaton (*Fairgrounds Hospital, Goldsboro, NC - reply to 26th Reg. N.C.V., Kinston, NC*) to father **William Deaton**. General wartime correspondence from son to father detailing skirmishes and battles on Neuse River, New Bern and Kinston. Mentions of General **Burnside**, Capt. **Kelly**, the death of Major **Abner Carmichael**, the 7th, 26th, 33rd and 35th Regiments and wounds to Capt. **William P. Martin**, **Lewis Brock Tysor**, **Charles Jones**. [130]

Dear Father, I seat myself to pencil you a few lines. I am in the hospital yet but as I have gained my health, I expect to start to the regiment tomorrow or next day. I am in the Fairground at Goldsboro, North Carolina. I hope this may reach and find you all well. I wrote you a few imperfect lines the other day — and as yet I am unable to give any correct account about the battle. On the 13th of March, Burnside with his fleet of about 120 vessels sailed up the Neuse river throwing large quantities of shot and shell to both sides of the river[,] and routed the 35th Regiment North Carolina volunteers, wounded 2 of Capt. Kelly's men from Moore County. They retreated just before the 26th Regiment reached the place. It was five miles below our camp which was 5 miles below Newbern. The enemy landed large forces that day[,] and our forces all gathered to the entrenchments and — notwithstanding the wet and disagreeable night — our men remained in the trenches until overpowered and driven back by the invading host next day. The fight lasted about 3½ hours but with what loss on either side I am unable to say. The enemy's loss is very heavy and our loss is said to not be very great in killed[,] but we lost most of our clothing and baggage and a great many arms. I believe if all of our men had displayed the same valor that was done by the 26th, 33rd, and 7th Regiments, that the enemy would have been defeated. The 26th Regiment held their position about 1 hour after all the rest of our men had retreated and come within an inch of being taken prisoners. When they reached Newbern, the bridges was burnt down and they were forced to swim a creek or be taken. They tried swimming and lost nearly all their guns and everything else. After a long and tiresome travel, they reached Kinston and joined our army. Our company was most wonderfully lucky to come out from such showers of balls. Capt. Martin was shot through the head and Brock Tysor was shot in the thigh. And while Dr. was dressing his wound, he was shot in the head. There was only 1 wound. Mr. Charles Jones was hit on the side of the head, glancing the bone but the would is not dangerous. Our Major was killed. He was shot through the head. There was one of Capt. Kelly's men killed and 4 or 5 wounded. The Yankees are living in Newbern now.

There has been reinforcements coming in to Kinston ever since the fight and I think if the invaders come up there, they will get into a hornet's nest. Our men was truly shielded by Providence or our loss would certainly have been great. I must close by saying God help us all and shield our heads in the hour of danger and at last save us in Heaven for the Redeemer's sake. I remain your affectionate son till death, — Noah Deaton

1862, March 25
C.D. Caddell to brother **A.S Caddell**. General wartime correspondence between brothers with brief mentions of Capt. **William P. Martin**'s death and local news of the death of **Evander Caddell's** wife **[Barbara Sullivan]** on March 19, uncle **Joseph Caddell** marriage to **Margaret McMillian** in Bladen County, news of the local militia and talk of a new draft. [131]

It is with much pleasure I take the present opportunity of writing you a few lines to let you know I am well hoping these few lines will find you well[.] Recd your letter which gave me much satisfaction to hear from you and that you was not killed nor taken prisoner. I hated to hear of your defeat and the death of Capt Martin though I am glad it is no worse than what it is[.] Evander Caldwell's wife is dead[.] She died the 19 of this inst[,] She was not sick but 3 days[.] Uncle Jo is married to a Miss McMillian in Bladen County[.] I was at his wedin and saw a heap of fun[.] I wrote to you and Harrison the day you was a filing and I dont expect you got the letters[.] tell Jack to write to me[.] I saw your gal last night[.] She said to write to her for she was afraid you was killed[.] you had better come home if you can try to get off and I will meet you any where you want mee too. the Malitia is a going to start from here tomorrow[.] there is 8 companies of them[.] there is a talk of another draft but I dont belive it[.] write soon and send one to your girl[.] I have a heap of fun some times[.] certain I saw fun for certain at old Jo wedding[.] I will close write soon[.] your affectionate Brother till Death. CDC

1862, March 26
Noah Deaton to father **William Deaton**. General wartime correspondence with brief mentions of **Alexander Kelly, John McKinnon, William McKinnon, Daniel McKinnon,** Capt. **William P. Martin, Brock Tysor, William Whitlock, Hugh M. Ray, Charles E. Jones, Col. Avery** and Capt. **Rand.** [132]

Dear Father, I take this opportunity to drop you a few words to inform you that I sent $40.00 to you by Mr Alex Kelley for you to save for me. the McKinnon boys sent some also and I expect if Kelly sees Mr D. McKinnon he will send the money by him to you[.] if not you had better go down and get it as I have given Sarah a small skech about the fight[.] I will close my remarks with saying a few words. loss in our company Capt W. P. Martin killed by a minie ball passing through his head[.] Brock Tysor was wounded in the thigh and left on the field with two of my tent mates with him trying to take care of him viz. W. Whitlock and H. M. Ray we have not heard from any of them as yet[,] and also Mr C.E. Jones was slightly wounded in the head. Our Maj. was severly wounded by a ball passing throug both his legs and Col Avery was take prisoner while trying to resue Capt Rand from the enemy. our loss is about 350 and the enemys loss is about 2,000[.] our force was from 4,000 to 5,000 and the enemys 27,000[.] if I could see you I could tell you lots[.] I must close[.] please write soon[.] your affectionate son, N. Deaton [P.S.] our Regt will be disbanded the 17th of May next.

1862, March 30
Noah Deaton to father **William Deaton**. General wartime correspondence with brief mentions of **Alexander Kelly, Lewis Lawhon, Daniel McKinnon,** Gen. **Branch,** and Gen. **Ransom.** [133]

Dear Father, I was very much gratified this morning when I received the little note from Sarah and the bundle of clothing that came to me by the hand of Mr L. Lawhon[.] it is true that we lost all of our clothing but the Ladies of Raleigh on hearing of our destitute condition[,] they bought clothing and sent them to us which did not come before we kneeded them[.] we will be ever thankful to them for their kindness to us and we are equally thankful to our old Moore county friends for sending us so much clothing[.] there came several boxes of clothing yesterday evening which we are oblige to send the most of it back. we are travling almost every day and cannot carry any thing[,] only what we can on our backs in our knapsacks and as I have as much as I care about carrying, I will send back the bundle you sent to me[.] I will send it back to Mr Lawhons where you can get it, so that you can send it to me if I want it at any other time. if I want it I will let you know. I have ben very much surprised that I got no letters from home and also that you dont get letters from me[.] this make the 4th letter since I received *any letter from you. we camped in Kinston night before last, and last night at this place[.] we are 5 miles below Kinston[.] our regt is out on picket now and we are traveling under sealed orders and we will not know when we will leave untill we get orders to strike our tents[.] our pickets and the enemies pickets are frequently running in contact with each other. I am in hopes our Gen. is better than the other we had, Branch is not much better than an old woman. I think that Ransom will do to depend on. he dont tell every body what he intends to do. there over thousand troops about here and more coming in every day. our time will be out the 17 of May but I expect we will be in another fight before then, and probably before 3 weeks. I supose Old Burnside has a printing office in Newbern and our General (Ransom) got a paper by some means in which it was stated that Burnside said the Rebels fought like devils and that nothing but an overwhelming number could have done any thing with us. I think he guessed very well that time for they had about 27,000 while our force did not number 5,000 and at that we repulsed them three difrent times at point of the bayonet[.] you cannot imagine how much our boys are cheerd up by receiving such liberal suplies from our friends and surely it is gratifying for us to know that we have friends behind us that will stand to us in time of kneed. it inspires us with new courage. As the mails are out of order[,] I dont know where to tell you to write to[.] if you see no chance to send a letter by hand that you may direct to Kinston N.C. 26. Regy N.C. Vol Co H[.] I sent $40.00 to you to keep for me by the hand Mr Alex. Kelly you had better go down and get it as soon as you can if Mr Kelley dont send it to you by Mr D. McKinnon[.] I wrote to before now about it and not knowing that you got the letter is why I mention it again[.] I must close by saying may god be merciful to us all and suport us by his mighty arm and shield and protect us in the hour of danger[.] O may the hand of divine Providence guide and direct us through every shifting scene in life and merciful God help us to live as we should and at last save us in heaven for christ sake[,] Amen. I am your affectionate Son untill death[,] N. Deaton. P. S. Give my respects to all. I am in good health at present.*

1862, March 30

Louis H. McLeod (*Camp French*) to wife **Eliza Jane Walker McLeod**. General wartime correspondence with brief mentions of **Campbell, Tandy Walker, David P. Morris, Joseph Walker, Thomas Bragg McLeod, Henry?** and **John McFarlane.** [134]

Dear Wife, I send you the balence of the things that I have to send by Mr. Campbell. Myself and Tandy and David P. Morris sends our close in one box together. you can tell all them by the labil that is on them. All that has Tandys and David Ps on you can send them up to Joseph Walker and all mine you can keep untill I come home. I sent the cap for Bragg. Tell sis I havent nothing to send her but I will fetch her something whin I come home. The shoes that I wore of hurt my feet so bad I could not stand them. you can give them to Henry or Ary if they need them and if not save them untill next fall. We have drawed our uniform dress got them yesterday and they are splendid. our coats are just like the others we had only they are lined through and through. our pants is all brown and they are lined with the thickest sort of homspun or Arsenburgs [?]. The verry best of cloth I send you my shirt and drawers you can see a sample of all the rest. All the company got caps but me and Tandy. Eliza you will find my bovie knife in the box. I want you to make Henry rub it up so it will look bright and send it to John B. MacFarlane and he will pay you one dollar and thirty five cents for the case that I had put on it if John is gone you can keep it to kill yankees with if they ever get up their. I have no use for it for I cant toat it no how. Eliza I havent found my bead close yet nor I dont think I ever will. I will get one blanket and that is as much as I am alowed to have after we leave this place and that will bee in a few days I expect. it is thought we will bee ordred to Swanns Borough Sixty Miles from this place which we will have to walk. That will try our faith. There is canons herd that way to day if they are a fighting there we will bee ordred there before mourning. The yankees has landed there. If they will stay untill we get there we will soon make hash meete of them. We are all anxious for a fight. If we have it to do we want to do it at once and go home. The Cournal is verry tight on us he wont let us go out of Camp hardly at. We cant go in Wilmington and if we could get in the town we could not get out without a pass. We have pickets out all round the camp out side the gard that wont let no man come in without a permit from the Promost Marshal nothing moore only we are all well and enjoying our selves first rate. Something to eat is a getting scarse we havent only half rashions this week. Write as soon as you get this and let me no whether you get the close or not. L. H. McLeod. Direct your letters to Wilmington in care of Cpt. Swann 30 Regiment and they will come safe. Louis H. McLeod

1862, April 4

Louis H. McLeod (*Camp Holmes*) to wife **Eliza Jane Walker McLeod**. General wartime correspondence with brief mentions of **Thomas Bragg McLeod**, **Anne Elizabeth McLeod**, **Francis Moore Parker McLeod**, **General French**, **Duncan Moore**, **Henry J. McNeill**, **Horace Morrison**, **Tandy Walker**, **Dave ?**, **John D. Sinclair**, **J.M. Campbell**, **Emily Franklin** and **William M. Swann**. [135]

Dear Wife, I receeved your kind and welcomb letter this evening that was dated the first. Eliza I was moore than glad to hear from you and to hear that you were all well but poor Bragg I was truly sorry to here that he was no better and that he had not set up since I left and his apetite was not good. Eliza if the Doctor can do him any good send and get him at once. I am verry uneasy about him. I was moore than glad to hear Parker was a getting along first rate but his eyes had not get well. I am in hopes when I hear from him and Bragg again they will both bee well and doing well. Tell Sis I am glad to hear that she was well and trotting about with them too cats after her where ever she goes. Eliza I havent nothing worth your attention at this time only this (time) leaves me well only a bad cold. I have that bad enough and there is a good many of our company that has bad colds and cough. Eliza we are down here in the piny woods yet and we dont know how long we will stay here we heard to day that old General Frinch sayed he would keep us here sometime This is a nice place we all like to stay here first rate Plenty of wood and litewood But we have to get our water out of the creeke We havent dug any wells yet for we dont know how long we will stay here. Duncan Moores Artillery has mooved to ajoining our line We are verry glad to have his company attached to our regiment but it is thought we wont be moved away from about Wilmington unless the Yankees comes on to Goldsborough and then we will bee moved on to meet them. We expect to move round about Wilmington If we move at all or maby we will have to go back towards Camp Wyatt If the Yankees will attempt to come up the river. I dont think the yankees ever can take Wilmington without they can come up the River. There is batries throne up all around the town about too miles off and canons mounted all round in sight of each other and them the bigest sort and the men is a cutting down all the trees that is in shooting distance of the batries. Eliza I havent heard nothing of my bead close yet nor never will. you needent mind sending me any H. J. McNeill gave me one and I got another so I have got too now and that is just as many as I want to tote. The General wont let us have no moore than we can toat on our backs. I have been doing first rate since I came back. I ly with Harris Morrison and we sleep first rate. We ly close together when the knights is cold Tan and Dave lies together. I have my cot with me but it has been too cold to ly on that without cover I thought I would bring it along it would bee first rate to ly on in the sumer when the weather gets hot. But I expect to loose it the next time we move I wish I had sent it home when I sent that last bax for Bragg to ly on I will send it by the first opertunity and some moore of my close for I have got moore than I want Tell Bragg that I will be surtain to bring him a fife the next time I come home I will come home in a month or too The good man Colonel ses all the reinlisted men shal have the balance of thim thirty days when times get a little better. Eliza I have gone in three years or during the war and yesterday my self and Sinclar and J. Campbell went with the Captain to Wilmington and got our bounty. I have the money and I want to send it to you as soon as I can get a chance. The Colonel says he dont think the War will last moore than too months if it does it will bee ever lasting. As to France I never heard of its coming over to join us I take the Journal every day and I never saw any thing of it in the papers nor heard any tell of it. Tell Emely I would like verry well to see her down here in this deep sand and wire grass Lolling along with her gun on her sholder. Eliza you wanted to know how many men we had here we havent but our one regiment and moores company which makes eleven companys that is about twelve or fourteen hundred men We had a long string when we marched to this place our company was befour and a heap of the time we couldent see the other end and we in four rank Eliza wanted to know about our fair it is not verry good We dont get nothing but the fastest sort of this pickle pork and a plenty of corn and flower bread. I eat yet with the Captian and the balence of the officers We live tolerable well we by fish aplenty right out of the water. No moore at this time only I remain your loving husband untill death Tan and Dave sends their respects to you and says they will put in something in the next one I rite Write to me soon and let me no how you are getting along. Louis H. McLeod

1862, April 4
Sallie A. Moore and **Mary E. Moore** (*Plank Road*) to their cousin **A.S. Caddell**. General wartime correspondence between cousins with brief mention of **Noah F. Muse**, **Eli P. Seawell** and **Ashley F. Muse**. [136]

Dear cousin, I answered your letter but I dont recon you ever got it and I will write you a few lines to let you know I am yet living and flying around[.] you had better believe I fel in love with one of your company at the quilting the other nite and you out to have bin there to see me flying around hin and all the other boys. I no you are getting home sick. Oh Tim do come home when your time is out[.] I would be glad to see you and I no your sweetheart would be so glad[.] I think all the boys will soon leave these digins and then what wil we all do. I have already nearly cryed my eyes out and I soon expect to finish then. Tell S. W. B. that I ans his letter and have not herde from him since[.] So[,] write to me soon if you please. Sallie A. Moore [P.S.] Tell all the boys to write me soon.

Cousin Tim, I must say a few more words. The boys did not get off today. Noah was here a few minutes ago[.] he is to be back here to knight until midnight[,] then he is going back to Carthage. He is not certain yet whether or not he will go[.] he is an officer perhaps he will get off[.] I spent the eavening over at your house this eavening[.] your Father is not getting any better. They are both very mutch opposed to you volunteering again & I do not think you ought to do it. Stay until your time is out & got a final discharge to come home to stay. The boys come & I did not finish this last knight. I will write a few more lines before I send this off. I suppose the most of the men volunteered yesterday & it is supposed the rest will today[.] the volunteers are going to start in about 3 weeks[.] all that does not volunteer started to day. Eli Sowell, Ash Muse & several more of our neighbors volunteered. I know if you ever tired of a letter in your life you are tired of this, for when I get to writing to a particular friend I never know which to stop[.] I always write a long muse & it all amounts to nothing. I hope you will excuse me for this. I will close by saying I hope I shall see you in June at home to stay for[.] Write soon very soon. M.E.M.

1862, April 4
C.D. Caddell to brother **A.S Caddell**. General wartime correspondence between brothers with brief mentions of **Joseph Caddell, J.J. McIntosh, T.W. Ritter** and **Zacheus Hogans.** [137]

it is with pleasure I seat myself to drop you a few lines to let you know we are all well at present hoping these few lines will find you well[.] I recd the $20 you sent home and tell me what you want done with it for you did not say[.] I have ben at 3 frolicks in a week one at uncle Joes and one at J.J. McIntoshes and one at T.W. Ritters[.] I had fine times at them me and Zack has had a heap of fun[.] since he came he will tell you all about it[.] dont you volunteer but come home for I should like to see you[.] write soon [.] I would write more only I havnt got no paper[.] C.D Caddell

1862, April 6
W.L. Sullivan (*Moore County, NC*) to **A.S. Caddell**. General wartime correspondence with brief mention of sister's **Barbara Sullivan Caddell** death, her son **Willy Caddell**, battle at Carolina City, trip to Raleigh, **Zacheus Hogan**, **Silas D. Crook**, **W.A. Barrett**, **Dave Barrett**, **William Lawhon**, **Ashley F. Muse** and **Eli P. Seawell**. [138]

I seat myself to drop you a few lines to let you know how we are geting a long[.] Mr A. S. Caddell[,] we are all about but not well[.] I have to say to you that sister Ann is gon from this world[.] she has paid the det we all have to pay[.] She was taken on monday night and died thursday morning[.] She did not Know anything from monday morning till she died[.] I never saw anybody in any such a fix before. She could not speak a word[.] Little Willy[,] her baby is at our house, mother took the baby[.] A.S. I wrote you a letter in the time of your fight at New Bern to Carolina City but I recin you did not get it[.] I herd from you since then[.] I was glad to hear from you[.] A. S. I started to Raleigh with the Company and they all volunteered and I Came back home[.] Mr A.S. I wont two see you the worst sort[.] I have bin with Z. hogans for some time and he has seen a heap of good fun[.] I think I wish you could bin with us A.S.[.] Zachus would give you his file if he could stay here[.] I wont you to come home and stay when your time is out for the buoys is but few here now[.] But girls is plenty[.] I herd you was not well But you was getting better[.] I am glad to heare that was getting better[.] A.S. the girls is prety as ever[.] I am sorry for the girls the buoys is so scarce[.] Zacheus is going to leave us tomorrow and I am sorry for that I was glad to see him come home and sorry to see him leave[.] I long to see[.] S.D. Crook is gone withe the rest of the volunteers[.] I am sorry to think we are in such a condition as we are and yet I glad we are alive[.] W.A. Barett, Dave Barett is gone, Wm. Lawhon is gone, A.F. Muse, E.P. Sowell is gone[.] I hate to see them have to leave for they are like myself[,] they dont wont the fun with the the yankees. I am in hopes that you wont have no more fun with them[.] they tell me it is not mutch fun fighting the Yankees[.] I was glad to hear that you fared as well as you did[.] I was uneasy about you all[.] I was affraid you was all kild and woundid and taken prisoners[.] I have know news to write to you of much interest[.] I am affraid we will come to starvation soon if this wore does not stop[.] the men is so few I am affraid there wont be support mad for the army and those at home[.] AS I wont you to come home and if we live[,] we ma see some pleasure withe the girls[.] I dont want you to forget to write to me give me the newse in your Camp[.] give my love and respects to all of your boys and you have my love and respects[.] sure I would be glad to seeing of you[.] I hope we will meet each other soon and spend our time together in peace as we have in time past[.] I must come to a close by saying I remain your friend till death[.] I want you to write soon[.] tell the other boys to write to me for I have not forgoten you tho we are parted and seated abroad[.] we will pray for each other and trust in the Lord[.] give my love to all engagin friends if there be eny[.] excuse Bad writin then this you see[.] Write to me[.] W.L. Sullivan

1862, April 13

Abel Douglas (*Harnett County, NC*) to **Louis H. McLeod.** General wartime correspondence with brief mentions of **Dillon J. Gaster, Hinton Franklin, Crockett Sloan, James O.A. Kelly, Jordan, Thomas Bragg McLeod, Francis Moore Parker McLeod** and **Henry ?.** [139]

Mr. McLeod, Dear Sir it is with a trimbling hand I sit dom to write you a few lines to let you no how I ema geting a long I have got a very bad cold and nearly all the rest of my famley has got them Mr. McLeod I did not answer your very welcom letter as soon as I should to of done on the account of my geting of on a little spree I thought a little drop would be good for my cold but it has left me a little nervus I hope when these fev lines reaches you they may find you injoying good health Louis I started to Kinston the wednesday after you left up here Mondy with Rosey to see Dillon J. Caster we got to Hinton Franklins a wedensday knight and the next morning we went to Raleigh and we had to stay at Raleigh untill nearly Sunset be fore train came to go to golds Borro [Goldsboro] and got there a bout 8 oclock in the knight and I went in the Hotel end T could not get any place to sleep only on the floor the next morning I went to both of the hospittes to see if I could find Dillon there he was not in either of them but he had bin there and they had sent him up to Raleigh the day before wee got to goldsboro and then wee got on the train at 2 oclock in evening end sent up to Releigh and found him in the Hospitle in the Fare ground reading of a newspaper and there was nothing the matter with him only a bowell complaint Louis I never expect to see as many sick people in the seme length of time again as I saw in goldsborro and in Raleigh I think I must to of seen a thousand in the three Hospittles it has nearly put me out of the notion of volenteering I saw a most any number of soldiers a bout goldstorro and Raleigh No more a bout goldsborro Louis the weather keeps very cold and vet up here yet. There has not bin mutch corn planted in this settlement yet I have planted my Hill field but it keeps so wet and cold I mxmex exspect I shall have to plant it over a gain. Crockett Sloan ran away with James Kellys companey last Thursday and Jordan is a bout to run mad a bout it. Louis I was over at your house to day Sunday your folks are a geting a long pritty well now Brag is mending very fast he can go all over the house in a chair I think he will be a walking a bout in three or four days. Parker is a groing finely he is as fat as he art to be and his eyes is a geting a great deal better. the rest of your famley are well Henry has planted some corn I must close I remain your friend Abel Douglass

1862, April 13

Louis H. McLeod (*Camp Holmes*) to wife **Eliza Jane Walker McLeod.** General wartime correspondence with brief mentions of **Lauchlin McNeill, Dr. Campbell, David H. Sloan, John A. Sloan, Thomas Bragg McLeod, Francis Moore Parker McLeod, Andrew Brown, Tandy Walker, David P. Morris, Pasly Campbell, Henry ?, William M. Swann, John A. Walker, Bryant, Louis Wicker, Emily Franklin, Anjalette McLeod, Delilah McLeod** and **Anne Elizabeth McLeod.** [140]

Dear and Loving wife, I receaved your kind letter last eavening thet you dated the eighth and you said you receaved mine on Friday and you dident wirte untill Tuesday It is no wonder I dident get a letter no sooner than I did When you never wrote from Frydey untill Tuesdey I dont serv you so as soon as I get a letter from you I ansver it by the next mail I think verry hard of it I looked and looked for a letter untill I gave it out and thought your letters had been misplaced and when this came to hand it vas bact to Lauchlin McNeill after he broke it open he found it was to me so he brought it in tome. Write as soon as you get a letter from me. Eliza this leaves me tolerable well at this time but I have been verry sick the day after the Cpt left here I was taken down and has not drilled any since. The Doctor said I had a slite [slight] tuch [touch] of the billious feavar But Tan all right now will go to drilling in the mourning if nothing happens. Our company is tolerable well at present only bad colds and cough The Sloan boys has the measles I am sorry to hear Bragg has been bad off so long but I was glad to hear his leg had broke I am in hopes when I hear from him again he will bee well. I was sorry to hear Parkers eyes had not got well I am in hopes they will soon get well and bee one of the finest sons in the County of Moore you never said whether he had grone any or not I hope he is. Eliza you said you receaved all the things that I sent. You never said any thing about the box that me and Tan sent our close in I sent the tin box and my truck by cozen Andrew Brown and thin myself and Tandy and David P. sent one box by Pasly Campbell. The Captain told me I could take my cot along with us before Camel left but soon €fter I found out that it would bee a bad chance but I managed to get to the place where we now is. I found out it would bee too troublesom to carry about so I congluded to send it up by the captien so I sent it 1 thought it would be verry good for Bragg to ly on this summer espeshely if he Was confined to his bead It will be first rate if you can put it up there is holes in the ends of the side peaces that fits on them pegs in the sides of the stools. I dident have no matres to the cot Tell Bragg that I sent that to him to ly on m untill I came home and tell Siss I sent her that new tin bucket to pick black berris in this summer As to sleeping I have faired first rate only I have no heading only pine straw that answers first rate. When the Captain went off he got me to stay in his tent and sleepe in his bead untill he returnxs so I fair first rate any how I stay in there by myself. I was sorry to here it rained and stoped you from planing corn I was in hopes you was most don. Eliza tell Henry to ster everry thing that he can and get the corn in the ground and then to wirk hard and make a heap of corn If he dont make it he will perrish next summer Eliza We havent heard from John since we have been back Tan sent him a letter but havent receaved an answer. Bryants company is at Kinston Archa Jackson got a letter from one of Bryants men to day but dident say any thing about John Eliza our eating is verry inferaeour at this time nothing but picle pork and that the fatest sort once in a while one quarter of old tuff poor beef flower bread scarse plenty corn bread. Tan came in just now and said tell you he was nearly perished but it is not supper time yet I fair in the eating line tolerable well yet. I eat with the officers and shall continve to do so if I do have a little moore to pay for the cooks Louis Wicker quit on that account the pay for the cook was too high for him But I want back [torn] for I get better eating than I would if I eat with the rest of the men. Eliza you said you was out of heart Dont giv up too soon I am hear yet I am in good heart yet Cheer up and dont bee so chicken hearted as long as we have so manny of our bravest men on the field I think we can whip the yankees and we can do it quick if they ever will leave the water There is a large vissel in sight of the beach everry day. Eliza I was so confused whin I sent my truck I sent severel things that I had aughter cep [kept]. I want you to send them back by the Captian you will find too little vices in the truck I had one of them wih me when I was up there send them both back by the Captian and that round file that has got a handel on it and my pins and neadles and thread send thin back too. And you can rop up my book and send it back I thought me and Tan could do with one but we cant by any paper at all in the town of Wilmington at any price our men will has to by books and them any sort they can get nothing moore Tell Emely and Anja and Delilah I would like to here from them once in a while I saw the Captain had severel letters going to my house when he went home. Tell Abe I will give him ten dollars if he will tell me hoo put that spirits turpentine in my horses wope wope you ser Give my best respects to all the family particular to my loving wife a full portion and Bragg and Sis and Parker. L. H. McLeod

1862, April 15

Eliza Jane Walker McLeod to husband **Louis H. McLeod**. General wartime correspondence with brief mentions of **Thomas Bragg McLeod, Anne Elizabeth McLeod, Francis Moore Parker McLeod, Dr. McIver, William Hughes, John A. Walker, Tandy Walker, David P. Morris, Sandy Kelly, Joseph Walker** and **James Monroe.** [141]

Der and loving husband, I recvd your kind and welcom leter and was more then glad to her from you and to her you wer well onely the colde I hope you will son get over that Louis thes lines leve me and famley all wel onley brag he is getting beter he can set up alitle and has got to eating a plenty I hope he wil soon get wel his lage is runing a little yet he is liing on your cot he was the prodest thing you ever saw when he cold set up and now he can drag over the house in the little cher and to day he sat to the table to diner i hope he will soon walk you beter belev I was more than glad to see him up i thank god for it brag said for you to rite if he mout hav the cot tha all want it sis is troting a bout and geting egges and her too cats after her frances parker is geting a long very wel his eyes is beter and he is groing very fast i hav never bin of ar the place yet I think I shal get awef som of these dayes i hav got to go to given in taxes this weke or nexe again i think tha will hav a nof ov it Louis I receved all the thing you sent and the sixety dolares you sent by the capten and the twenty fore for tan but i was more then sorey to her you had gon in durin the war but if the war dont last more then too monts i dont cer but no such good luck as that i hope it will not god grant it to end in won month my der it semes like you dont want to com home ore you wont went in during the war we ar geting along very slow plan[t]ing the ground is bin so wet i hope it will stay dri a little so we can plant our corn the wheat look very wel i hope we will make a good wheat crop if you can com home i want you to com at harvest i hav got up the hog for harvest and if the old cowes will keep out ov the mire i shal hav buter for you to eat I hav fore cowes and i hope i will get milk an buter after a little i cant get no shoger [suger] without giving twenty five cents and i intend to hav som if it dont get enny hire [higher] i cant doo without som Louis I think I had beter pay docter McIver [MacIver] and Wiliam Huse with som of the money you sent and if you think so rite in your nex leter so if the war ends the money will bee no count and the det wold bee paid i think we can get along with out the forty dolares i hav twenty dolars my self Louis i am glad to her you can get fish to eat times is mity hard up her we cant get eny thing onley what we hav i hope times will get beter after a little my der I wish you all the good luck in the world and I hope the lord will spar you to liv to com home and liv at home with me and your der little children. Louis I hav herd from John since i rote to you and he was wel and he said he had not bin in many fite yet but it was a hel ov a wonder tel tan and dave and San to rite to me in your next tel tan i giv the money to Joseph and all the rest ov the thing he sent Louis rite in your nex somthing about James Monrow his mother is all ways inquerin in your leters the childrin all sends howdy to pap and say for you to com home as soon as you can I most com to a close by giving you my best lov your der loving wife until deth com at harvest if you cant com before take good cer ov your self i hop we may both liv to met again in this life So fare you well my der So fare you well my lov my der loving husban until deth Eliza McLeod

1862, April 15
Rev. **W.S. Chaffin** (*Oxford, Granville County, NC*) to Rev. **Lewis Phillips, Jr.** General wartime correspondence with brief mentions of **Jimmie Chaffin, Emory Capers Phillips, Nancy Edwards Phillips, Sarah Abbie Chaffin, Martha Chaffin, Robert Chaffin, Mastin C. Phillips, Malphus S. Phillips, Baxter C. Phillips, William P. Martin, William Cole, Lewis Brock Tysor, Harris Tysor, Robert Phillips** and **Harris Williamson**. [142]

Dear Brother Phillips, it has been almost a year since I wrote to or heard directly from you. In that time multitude of changes have taken place in our land. Some, who then were in the enjoyment of life and health are now returning to the dust as they were. It has fallen to my lot to lose a loving and lovely child. Our little Jimmie after suffering six months died in November last. I know not how I could have given him up but for the troubles of the country. Abbie nursed him with unwearried diligence and when he died[,] she reminded me most forcibly of my much esteemed Sister Phillips when death forced Capers from her. But we try to bow in humble submission to the will of God. But ruin is in our land. I see no remedy, no ceasing of hostility between North and South. Things are pretty much as I supposed they would be, but I hoped against them. No land ever suffered more for the same period of time. Husbands and sons have been torn away from the bosoms of their families and homes. But the contemplation of the scene sickens my heart and I turn from it in horror. May God interpose. We are in Granville Circuit. There are twelve appointments, abundance of wealth, a beautiful country and productive. The farmers were making money almost as fast as they wanted before the war. The roads have been very muddy through the winter, but Kate keeps fat. We are boarding at a most excellent house, no child but Mattie. She is enjoying life finely. She has begun to learn her books, is spelling pretty well in three letters, is sewing-has commenced her a bedquilt-has sewed some ten or more pieces together. She is very happy, is forming quite regular habits. Never sleeps in the day, but as soon as supper is over she goes to sleep and sleeps all night. Abbie's health is not good, but better than it was last year. Hope she will soon have good health. Bobbie is at Trinity. I was up to see him a week or so ago. I was up to see him a week or so ago. There were some thirty students there. The war has ruined our schools. Bobbie was very well and spoke a good deal of you and your family. I suppose Mastin has volunteered and gone to war. I guess you have not let Baxter go, nor do I suppose that Malphus has gone. The death of Brother W. P. Martin was sad news to me. He was my friend. Please give me a list of those who fell in his company at New Berne. Has any of Brother William Cole's sons gone to war? Has Brock Tysor been recovered? I found the churches in my charge in a torn to piece condition. The preacher who was here volunteered and left the circuit and went to the war. Many members from this circuit are in the camp, some very prominent members, good and true. The whole church is in ruins, schools, commerce and everything. If God fails to help us[,] we are in a most pitiable condition. My trust is in Him and to Him is my daily prayer for peace. Let us pray for it. I was in possession of no news that would be so to you, I presume, by the time my letter reaches you. Your family is not infrequently the subject of conversation between Mrs. Chaffin and myself, and I can assure you it would be a source of pleasure to spend a few hours with you and interchange view upon the various topics connected with our present troubles. But of this we must be denied at present. Spring seems to be opening upon us, but how different two years ago. One year ago the country was I a bliss of political excitement., now overwhelmed by war, the end of which is unseen by man. Poor Brother Tysor, I heard he was at Kingston looking after his son who was *wounded at New Berne. I have seen a good many refugees from New Berne since the battle there. I do wish I could write without writing about the war. Well, this is a tobacco and wheat country, especially tobacco. They make the finest article of tobacco here and sell it at tremendous prices. The people are generally attentive to the preaching of the word, and almost every house is a home for our preachers and the people are very kind indeed. I think if there was no war Abbie would be well pleased in this circuit. All our church houses are new, save two, and last year they had $1,800.00 subscribed to build in one of these places and by some slip failed to build. At the other they had some $1,500.00 a few years ago, but some bad management lost that, so at these places they use their old houses. They have the finest country church that I know of in the state on this circuit. Bobbie is lazy and tired of going to school, and I have some idea of stopping him for a season after the present session. If I do, I want to have his work somewhere. I have tried to buy me a little farm but have failed to do so, so far. I do not wish to put him to work with negroes. He is 14 years old last December. I do not wish to hire him out, but if he goes to your house[,] I wish him to be treated as your child in food, clothes, and work, etc. And if he falls to earn what he could consume in food and clothes, I would pay you. I want him to have good clothes, you understand me. Now if you would like to have him upon these terms and would send to Trinity at or after commencement for him[,] you will please write me immediately and let me know as I must make some arrangements concerning him. Abbie joins me in kindest regards to yourself, Sister Phillips and all your children, to Uncle Robert Phillips and his family. We wonder what he does for coffee now a days. Remember us in your prayers. Our address is Oxford, Granville County, N.C. May God bless you all abundantly is the prayer of your sincere friend. W. S. Chaffin P.S. Brother Willamson Harris lives in my circuit and is making bowie knives.*

1862, April 17

Eliza Moore (*Plank Road*) to cousin **A.S. Caddell**. General wartime correspondence between cousins with brief mention of parents **William Caddell** and **Raney Caddell**, **Neill Caddell**, and her sister **Sarah Moore**. [143]

Dear Cousin: It is with pleasure I take the opportunity of writing to you. I received your kind & interesting letter some time ago, I would have written before now but I had first written you a long letter & I thought I would wait until I could get some newse to tell you but I fear if I wait forever I shall wait a while for that is a thing that does not pass by here[.] it may pass but that is all I dont get any. I was over at your house this evening[.] your Mother was gone down to Mrs Sowell, Neill was a plowing, your Father was alone he is very well, halped up with the idea of seeing you in about a month[.] I am going fishing Monday that you know is easter Monday[.] I do wish you was here to go with us. I would have a fishing party if all you boys was at home but as you are [,]I will part from it until you return. I know you remember the fishing you all had before you left home[.] I hope we will see them some more this summer, but I fear there is some of the boys with us that that we will never have with us again. We can never enjoy ourselfs a fishing or anything else as we have. I have began to think that there is no enjoyment for any of us in this wourld but I hope all persons does not think as I do. Sarah says to tell you she is yet living & doing well. You may know why it is she is doing so well, her sweethearts is left at home[.] Several of them is here but I think she has some in your company. you would think so too if you could see a letter she received this morning. Do you know who of your company is writing her love letters. Tell A.F. Muse I have just written to him that I think he ought to write to me[.] We had prair meeting at our school house last Sunday[.] We are going to have it there again next Sunday[.] Oh I do wish you would be there for I tell you it is lonesome times up there since the boys all left. but I hope it will not be so long. As it is getting late I must close[.] They are all a sleep except me & I a nearly[.] Neill was to have come here toknight but he didnot come[.] I know you will never read this letter, if you come to any part[,] you cant read pass it unnoticed & think it of no importance. Please excuse this badly written enclosed letter & write soon[.] I will apologize when I see your good friend. Eliza

1862, April 18

Mastin C. Phillips (*Camp Mangum, near Raleigh, NC*) to sister **Emeline Phillps.** General wartime correspondence with brief mentions of Lt. **James C. Dowd,** Dr. **B. Craven, Anderson Willard Smith, Baxter C. Phillips, Nathan Paschal, Malphus S. Phillips,** Rev. **Lewis Phillips Jr., Nancy Edwards Phillips** and **Celia Gilbert Phillips.** [144]

Dear Sister, Yours by Lt. Dowd was received a few days since. I was glad to hear from home and that all were well. I was not surprised at any of the news contained in your letter. I am quite well, have been improving all the time since I left home. I sprained or hurt my left foot. Came down and for several days it pained me very much, but I believe it is about well now. I like camp life so far well enough. I think I can endure it. The monotony of the thing is the worst, but I think our Coln. has an eye on that thing for on yesterday we moved our tents for the third time. This you know gives us variety. I think our Coln. is an excellent officer thus far. All are pleased with him but those who think that they know more about the business than the Coln. does himself. I am glad that he is stern and prompt. I would not willingly serve under any other sort of a man. I am becoming quite unpopular in our Company for promptly and energetically performing my duty. This is probably attributable to the drilling I received from Dr. B. Craven while at Trinity College. This is no idea sport, but a real reality. I feel it so, our men must understand it. This and to that end the reigns must be held with a firm grasp. When the men shall have learned their duty and that I am doing mine. I shall regain all that I have lost. Human nature is a curious thing, but few boys know anything about it. Perhaps I don't but I am trying to learn. This is three o'clock P.M. I was up all night last night attending to the guard. Went on yesterday at eight A.M., was not dismissed until 10:00 A.M. today. Did not sleep one moment. The guard was quite unprepared for their business and of course needed much instruction. I walked and talked all day and all night, but I do not feel worsted. I reckon you think instructors are scarce in these parts or I would not be used this early on such business. Well, they better prepared for my duty than any of our officers except Lt. Anderson Willard Smith, but I don't care one straw for it. I can make my way independent of them all. I may do that which no one expects if this war should last long, but do not anticipate. For the present I shall remain quiet. Baxter's thumb is well, cured immediately after it was lanced. He is one of the boys and is at the heart of everything. The boy has more [illegible]about him than any of the officers in the regiment, but can't get an office, yet he does his duty. Such boys are kept out if possible by the masses. He will get a place after a while. A few of our Company are on the sick list, but none very sick. I don't think Nathan Paschal will stand it very well, but he is better now than he was a few days ago. I guess you have the war news. It is very interesting at present. Some indication now that it will soon end. God grant that it may be so. I have had interesting news from a young lady recently. More of this anon. I must stop now. I want some of you to write every week. Tell Malphus I will write to him in a day or so. When is Pa coming? We have received our uniform suit, the roughest, ugliest you ever saw. I don't know when we will get our bounty money and dress suit, soon I should hope. I want Pa to come for them when we get them. I will try to let him know. Tell Ma to keep cheerful, I think all will end well. Remember us in your prayers. Our love to all, to Malphus and Celia and to all our friends. Good day. We are both quite well. Your brother, Mastin

1862, April 20
Matthew C. Yow (*Camp Mangrum, NC*) to his in-laws **Joseph** and **Nancy Albright** and family. General wartime correspondence with brief mentions of his wife **Nancy Catherine Albright Yow,** brothers-in-law **Henry A. Albright** and **John E. Albright**. [145]

Deer Father Mother and Family I now sit down to rite you a few lines to let you no ware I am at this time. I am at Camp Mangum. I am well at this time hoping when this comes to hand may find you enjoying the same blesing. I could get any man in my plase so I had to go. I cannot when I can come home. Our colonel is vary tight on us. I am in the 48 regiment NC state troops under Colonel Hill. I hav not hear from home since I left. I hav rote 3 letters and no answer yet. I want to here vary bad from you all. There are a great deal of sicknes in this camp and the worst caugh I ever herd. We have moved out about a mile from our old camp. I do not no how long we will stay here. We hav not got our money yet. We think we will get it soon. I want you to go and see my wife and little children when you can. Catharine is troubeld bad when I left. When I think of her the children it fils my hart with greaf for I love them. Well I wrote a few lines to Henry and John but hav got no answer yet. Our regiment is rite on the railrode now. I hav bin to Raleigh once since I come to Camp Mangum. We here that the men from 18 to 35 had to inlist. If this be so it will be a bad chanc at home. We hav plenty to eat. We hav bacon beef sugar rice flour no corn. I want corn bread. We get soap and candles but I am not satisfied at all. Camp life is a hard and troublesome life to me. We are learning to drill vary fast. I want to come home at harvest if I can but donot no how it will be. If I donot come I hope my friends will save my wheat and oats. I hav drawn one suit clothes one blanket two caps one canteen one haversack and one pare of shoes. I want you to soon direct your letters to Camp Mangum in care of Capt Clegg. You must look my bad hand. If I never see you no more on earth I hav a good hope that I may meet you all in heven. When this you see remember me tho fare apart we be so fairwill. Matthew C. Yow

1862, April 20

Lydia Brown (*Moore County, NC*) to husband **William A. Brown**. General wartime correspondence with brief mentions of **Lucy Brown** and **Franklin Burns**. [146]

Dear husband[,] I can inform you that I recd your letter the 15th of this month and when I recd it and seed that you were sick[.] it maid me Sory but I cant be there to help you in your Sickness and I hant sean no satisfaction sence and I want you to write to me as soon as you can and let me no how you are[,] but I can inform you that we are all at present and I havent herd from your mother sence you left[.] but as soon as I hear from them[,] I will write to you and let you no how tha are and I want you to write to me as soon as you can and write all your letters to me and let no how you are[.] I shall be glad to see you my deer[.] I want you to remember me and your dear little children and I want you to be shore to take good care of yourself I am trying to do the best I can[.] I have planted a little corn but god knows how we are to get a long in this world so wen we are parted and scattered abroad[,] let us pray for each other and be with god[.] I can in form you that I have not got that note from Franklin Burns yet and as soon as you can[,] send me your money for the times will be hard about getting corn hear[.] So[,] nothing more but I still remaing your loving wife until death[,] Lydia Brown

1862, April 20
Louis H. McLeod (*Camp Holmes*) to wife **Eliza Jane Walker McLeod**. General wartime correspondence with brief mentions of **William M. Swann, Colonel Parker, Thomas Bragg McLeod, Anne Elizabeth McLeod, Emily Franklin, Anjalette McLeod** and **Delilah McLeod.** [147]

Dear Wife, I received your welcomb letter last knight and you better believe I was glad to get it for I hadent receaved one from you since the eight of this month Eliza I did not think you would bee so long righting to me as soon as I get a letter from you I set down and answer it by the next mail and you ought to do that too. Eliza I have been sick ever since the Captain left here with the Billous Feavar When I wrote to you last I thought I was in about well I went out on Monday to drill and it throwed me up again and I havent don any thing since but I am as well at this time as I ever was Aperently our men has been ordred off and too other companys to Jqckson ville in Anslow County some sixty miles from this place Our men left here last Friday evening at too oclock. With the Lieutenant Colonel with them. The good Colonel Parker is here with us. Eliza I never hated any thing so bad as I did to see our men start off and I could not go with them They went off lively all hands holering and rejoicing but the poor fellers I reckon is not so jaly to knight to get to their journys end and after they get there no dout will have to go right into a fight The yankees is all about Jacksonville doing all kind of meenxess and every thing that is meen and taking every thing befour them The balance of the regiment will leave her on Wednesday or Thursday next to go on there to join the rest of our fellow soldiers I want the time to com when we can all get together and face the enemy at one time. There is thirteen of us here some of them has got the measles and will have to go in the Horspital when we leave this place. It is a long ways to march but as colonel Parker told our men when they started they would have to endure hardships and we have just entered into that point now We are not lowed to carry any thing but what we could toat. There was four wagons went with them to take cooking impliments and provisions for twelve days. Eliza We are agoing where we will bee bound to fight or bee taken prisoners and I dont think we willever bee taken. Our men has all become blood thirsty and the yankees had better keepe out of the way no moore about the war your letter was so long a coming I thought if I dident get one befour I left here I mounht not never get one from you. Tell Bragg he can ly on the cot untill I come home and tell Siss to get a heepe of eggs and set the hens and rais me I [a] heepe of chickens. Tell Emely and Anjaan and Delilah to think where I am and for them to wirk hard to make something to eat Write as soon as you get this and direct your letter to Wilmington untill further orders. No moore only your loving Husband, L. H. McLeod

1862, April 21
H.B. Bryan (*Tarboro, Edgecombe County, NC*) to **Neill R. McDonald**. General wartime correspondence regarding **Daniel L. McDonald**'s hospitalization. [148]

Mr. N.R. McDonald, Mr. D. L. McDonald is now in the Hospital in this place & wishes me to say to you that he is wounded in the left leg, the calf of the leg being taken out by the explosion of a bomb shell at the battle at Newbern. He is now safe from the Yankees & in the hands of friends & I know he is well attended for my wife has taken him charge & does everything to render him comfortable. He is doing well & hopes soon to be well. Respectfully yours, H.B. Bryan

1862, April 23
H.B. Bryan (*Tarboro, Edgecombe County, NC*) to **Ann McDonald**. General wartime correspondence regarding her son's **Daniel L. McDonald**'s hospitalization. [149]

Your letter dated the 18th has been received by your son today. I have seen him today. He is improving & will be able to go home in two or three weeks, so the Dr says who is attending him[.] I will write to you when he will be able to go & what time for you to come for him. I think your son is a very good young man. He reads his bible constantly. My wife has taken charge of him & sends him his meals from our table three times ago & also attends to his washing & his bed. Do not be uneasy about him as he says he is perfectly satisfied. Respectfully Yours, H. B. Bryan

1862, April 25
Catharine Sloan (Moore County, NC) to sons **David H. Sloan** and **John A. Sloan**. General wartime correspondence with brief mentions of **Dalrymple's** slave **Dread, Kearney Buchanan, A.T. Campbell** and **Mary Campbell**. [150]

Dear Sons, I with pleasure embrace this present time to write you a few lines to let you know myself and family are in moderate health, hoping when this comes to hand it may find you both well and doing well. I have nothing interesting to write you alone than the measles and mumps are raging in this neighborhood. There are some very bad off with them. I am getting very uneasy about you as I have got no letter since the 11th of April. I will say that I want you to write as soon as this comes to hand. They caught Dalrymple's Dread last week. He has already taken three severe whippings and if he runs away again[,] they intend to shoot him if they can get in sight of him. He broke open Kearney Buchanan's smoke house a few days before he was caught and stole a good chance of bacon, but they took it from him and carried it back to Kearney's wife. He is gone in Kelley's company. I heard you was gone to Jacksonville in Onslow County, but I have heard since you was ordered back so I do not know where you are at this time. Your relations are generally well except the measles. The most of them is getting better. The neighbors sends their love to you. The children all wish to be remembered to you. My dear sons, let me admonish you to put your trust in God and pray to him to guide and protect you through the dangers and tribulations you have to encounter through this troublesome world[.] if you will but give yourself to him he will shield you from all harm and fight the battles for you and gain the great victories for which so many is struggling and falling victims to the ground. I beseech to remember your God in the days of thy youth while the evil days come not[,] nor the years draw nigh when thou shalt say I have no pleasure in them. Thy name Almighty God shall sound through distant lands. Great is thy grace and sure thy word. Thy throne forever stands. Far be thine honour spread and long thy praise endure till morning light and evening shade shall be exchanged no more. My dear sons, read this and think of your dear mother. I will say to you I want you to come to see me as soon as you can as I want to see you very bad. Dear sons, try and take the best care of yourselves as you can. I am anxious for your good welfare in this world and the world to come. I close by asking you to write often. I remain your most affectionate mother till death. Catharine Sloan. To D and J Sloan. Tell A.T. Campbell, Mary and family is well. She sends her love and respect to both of you[.]

1862, April 26
Matthew C. Yow (*Camp Mangrum, NC*) to his wife **Nancy Catherine Albright Yow** and children. General wartime correspondence with brief mentions of his brothers **Issac Yow** and **Simeon Jones Yow,** father-in-law **Joseph Albright,** father **Henry C. Yow** and brother-in-law **William N. Brower**. [151]

Deer Wife and Little Children[,] I now take my pen in hand to inform you that I am well with the exception of cold and caugh hoping when this comes to hand my find you all injoying the same blesing. There are a great deal of sicknes here. Several hav died and I am vary about you at home. I hav riten five letters and no answer yet. There must be something rong. I want to here so bad I cant rest. We got fifty dollars appease and I want to send it to you if I can. I donot want to keep it here. Tel the boys if they hav to come I want them to come to me but stay if you can. If Jones does hav to come[,] you must try to get some body to stay with you and the children. I rote one letter to your father one to my father and one to W.N. Brower and two to you and no answer yet. I can tel you I am not satisfied when I think of you and my children. My hart is ful for a soldires life is a hard one. It is raining to day[,] vary cold from the north east. I must tel you that I work as hard evry day as I would at home. Drilling is hard work you may be sure. We hav to run the double quick. That is vary hard. We hav bacon beef flour sugar but we want something elce but we cant get anything with out paying double the worth. Eggs are 20 to 25 cents. Chickens 50 cents each. I cant eate them. Pies 20 to 25 cents. I hav bin to Raleigh one time. I want to go again and get my likenes taken and send it to you if I can. I cannot tel you when I can come home. I want to come about the tenth of June if I can. If I dont come you must do the best you can. I want you to tel me how you are geting along with your crop. When you rite direct your letter to Camp Mangum near Raleigh in cear of Capt Clegg[,] the 48 regiment[,] NC troops. Give my best respect to all inquiring friends. I want to here from you all. If you need any moore corn you buy it. So I must close. When this you see[,] remember me tho many miles apart we be[.] so fairwell to you all. M.C. Yow

1862, April 26
Martha M. Sullivan (*Moore County, NC*) to **A.S. Caddell.** General wartime correspondence. [152]

your very welcom letter is safe at hand[.] I was happy to hear from you[.] your letter found mee enjoying myself very well[.] I hope these lines may find you well[.] I hav nothing to write to you moor than there is a heap of sickness about[.] hear you did Something about geting sum April fools. I would like to no where they cam from[.] I hav not seen merry this Spring[.] ther has bin a heap of starnns about hear[.] I hav not bin to any of them[.] you said you would like to of bin at some of them[.] they hav fine times at them[.] you said you was coming home in may[.] perhaps you get to go to some of them and starrn[.] all of them[.] I no you will hav a big starrn when you can[.] I would like very much to see you up this way very well[.] you said you had not reinlisted for the war[.] I do not want you to volunteer untill you com hom and then not go[,] for it seems that it has bin 25 months since I saw you tho it has not bin very long since[.] you must look over bad writing and spelling[.] write soon[.] I must cum to a close[.] yours affectionat and missus[.] Martha M. Sullivan

1862, April 26
Wm. L. Sullivan (*Moore County, NC*) to **A.S. Caddell.** General wartime correspondence with brief mention of **Willy Caddell, Zaccheus Hogan, Peter M. Campbell, John A. Jackson, John Hale McGilvary, Neill McIntosh, Samuel Jackson McIntosh, John H. Warner, Ashley F. Muse** and **Eli P. Seawell.** [153]

I am permited again to drop you a few lines in answer to your welcome letter which I received last week[.] your letter found me in modrat health and the rest of the family[.] we have very bad colds, little Willy[,] the baby is very sick[.] I am affraid will never get any Better[.] Mr A.S. I am sorry that I have nothing that will intrest you[.] I am glad to hear you have got able to get about again and I hope these few lines will find you well and doing well[.] I was happy to hear from you[.] nothing gives me more satisfaction than to hear from you[.] you said that you had the pleasure of engagin the Company of some of the fare sects[.] I was glad to hear of you enjoying yourself for I know if I had bin there[,] I would ben glad to had the opertunity of being withe the fare sects[.] I know there is a heap of people there[.] I hope you will never get in to a battle[.] I hear that they have past an act that you all have to stay 3 years[,] and all is under 35 and over 18 years[.] it is a nough to make you twelve months volunteers rebellif they dont let you come home[.] you have served your times which if you wer two[.] if men clothed in a little authority will do so[,] they have shone there tyrany milatary despotism very soon to there friends[.] we thought very hard of the Yankees for there despotism[.] But o when we think of our sothern people acting so ungeneros to want there citizens, people will have to depend on themselves some[.] A.S. it is a disheartning time have withe the people; if god dont save us[,] we are lost but it is worse than a monarch goverment[.] the lord knows what will become of us for I don't[.] A.S we have a good deal of sickness heare and now the baby is sick[.] may be there is no hopes of any pleasure in this world and I fear our hopes in the will be blasted god forbid that it should[.] I recon Zacchus could tell you of his fun with the little girls in old moore[.] the girls is glad to see any of the soldiers come home[.] tell Campbell I herd the pretyest little girls talking about him[.] Remember me to Camel, J.A. Jackson John Hale Magilbery, N. McIntosh, S.J. McIntosh, J.H. Warner, Eli P. Sowell, A.F. Muse all of your buoys[.] give my love and Respects to all enquiring friends if any[,] if none[,] excuse me[.] I must come to a close for this time[.] hoping to hear from you soon[.] excuse my neglect of writing[.] I remain your friend untill death[.] Your friend, Wm. L. Sullivan

1862, April 27

Noah Deaton (*Camp near Kinston, NC*) to **Sarah Jane McDonald**. General wartime correspondence with brief mentions of **Hugh McDonald, Malcom Ray, Zebulon B. Vance, Henry K. Burgwynn, Clement Dowd, James D. McIver, Murdo McLeod** and **George Willcox**. [154]

Dear friend, I received your very welcom letter of the 17th which give me much pleasure to hear from you once more and to hear that you were in good health. my health is very good at present. the health of our Company is only tolerable at present but is improveing some. I hope this will find you in good health. I have nothing of intrest to communicate to you as we hear nothing but war news and that is so common and I suppose you get ever thing of intrest as soon as we do here[.] Our pickets and the Yankees are frequently having little skirmishes down between here and Newbern[.] our men have brought in several prisoners[.] the enemies lines are about 15 miles from here. Our Regiment has reorganised[,] unanimously re-elected Z. B. Vance for Col., H.K. Burgwynn Lieut. Col, our company officers are C.C. Dowd capt, Lieut's J. D. Mclever 1st, M. McLeod 2nd, G. Willcox 3rd[.] our Col. will soon have a legion made up[.] he wants 2 Regts of infantry 2 companies of cavilry and one of artillery[.] he only wants one more company of infantry to make out the 2 Regts. I cannot see far into the future but the present state of things looks very gloomy and seems to tell that we have not had the worst yet[.] and seems like there must be much bloodshed yet before peace though the present gloom will may soon be followed by peace[.] I fear it will not. your cousin Hugh McDonald and Mallcom Ray was here today[.] they are well and as lively as crickets[.] you said you didnt think our retreat was funny and certainly it was not[.] but the boys can laugh at each other about how they come off and did not think to bring their clothes[.] well there was no time for swaping horses at that time[.] ever one thought it prudent to take care of number one[.] I wish I could be back at Little River and go down to Prare meeting where I could enjoy myself in your presence as I once did and hear all you girls sing them old songs[,] but I dont have much hopes of seeing Moore County untill times change[.] if I live and keep strong for the enemy is now upon our soil and must be driven back[.] I must close my badly writin letter[.] please write the first opportunity and give me the news[.] from your affectionate friend, N. Deaton. Yours with much respect[.]

1862, April 28

Eliza Jane Walker McLeod to husband **Louis H. McLeod**. General wartime correspondence with brief mentions of **William M. Swann, Thomas Bragg McLeod, Francis Moore Parker McLeod, Anne Elizabeth McLeod, Anjalette McLeod, Delilah McLeod, Tandy Walker, Sandy Kelly, David P. Morris, Elizabeth Hinton Brewer McLeod, McNeill, Joseph Walker, John A. Walker** and **John Gaster.** [155]

Der and loving husban once more I sete my self to anser your kind and welcom leter that came to han to day and was more then glad to her g from you and to her you had got wel i was mity unesy about you fore i was afraid you wold not rite how bad of you wer I hope you may remain well enny more but you hav a bad chance no bed close and then no tens [tents] how are you to stan such fare as that I think mity hard ov your cernel I think he ot to doo beter then that for how can you stand that Louis the capten left this leter to me this morning and he red it he said he hadnot herd from down thar and he wanted to her I recvd your leter wensday and I started won to you and I am afraid you hav not got it as you hav moved you said in your wensday leter direct my leters to wilmington I sent too last week and I dont recken you hav got any won so i shal send this by the capten Louis i am sory to say to you the capetn disapinted me very much he told me he was going last friday and he wold take eny thing i wanted to send to you so i fixet a boxe and put all your thing in and i thot i wold send you somthing to eat fore maby you wold never eat eny more ov my cooking and so i sent it to the station and now he cant going until next wensday and I had to send and bring it back he said he dident no how he wold get from wilmington and he said I had beter not send it i was very sorey fore i no you liv hard but since you hav got well I hope you can stand it as well as the reste Louis I think very hard on the capten fore staing up her so long at such a time fore i think he ot to bee with his men i think he is staing fore the worst ov the time to get over i dont think it is rite Louis I am more then sory to her you hav moved rite in amonse the yankes wher you will hav to fite or bee taken prisner may the god ov batles bee with you is my prar and I hope he may spar your life and all the reste ov your company I still liv in hops that you wont hav to fit but if you doo pray god to bee with you Louis this is the trings (tryingest) time in this world to think how we have bin to gether and now we are parted maby never to see eachother again in this life it nerley takes my very harts blod o god hav mercy on us and save us as a nation hasten the time when this trublesom war may bee to a end Louis if i never see you again tri to meet me in heven whar we may never part again may the god ov heven bee with you is my prar der and loving husban all now these lines leve me and famley all well brag is getting about his leg is not quite well yet it is not strate yet but i think it wil get strait he can go now without a stick frances parker is groing very fast his eyes is wel now if you cold see him now you wold nurs him I recken Sis is geting eggs yet and is as pert as ever anjalett an lila is in the feld tring to make bred for you if ever you com home and if you don't we wil hav to eat our selves I was sorey to her tan giv out, pore tan giv her lov to tan and San and dave tel them i never for get them may the god ov heven be with them rede this to them for it rele for all ov my blood that is in servest may tha think on ther later dend [?] Louis your mother stade down last weke and i sent her home an she said for me to say somthing for her in this she is as wel as you cold expect and is niting sox for you i had won pare [pair] in the box so i will keep them until you need them i hope you will com home before you need them Louis if you had not gon in during the war you cold com home now in ninty dase for you are thirty six the law now is from nineteen to thirty five and you wold bee cler i tel you that giv them bringer [?] up [?] her this gets the mack neils [MacNeills] i am sory for Jo Walker he dont no what to doo unles John wold get of and com home i hope he wil i recken you herd John Gasterd [Gaster] getin wonded and his fauther went after him but he was so badley wounded tha cold not bring him he brot the bolet to show and he saw John Walker and he said he was well he was staning by John when he was shot John said it was the mercy ov god that he was not kild he said when tha tird to run the yankes said run you dam rebels John was shot thou the sholder an the bolet lodg in the brest ov his cote tha are at kinston Louis i am doing the best i can we are don planting corn onley the swamp and we wil plant our little coten i wil tri mity hard to make somthing to eat this yar and if we fail i canthelpit Louis the whete looks promising now and i hope we wil hav plenty ov bisquit for you to eat when you com home Louis i am going up on the ceak to morow if nothing hanes [?] for the first time nothing more i was oferd eighty dolars fore the mule if you think i had beter sel him rite to me i most close by saing rite soon fare well my der loving husban if i never see you again god bee with you i send the little things to you by the capten your loving wife until deth. Eliza McLeod

1862, April 28

Louis H. McLeod (*Onslow County, NC*) to wife **Eliza Jane Walker McLeod**. General wartime correspondence with brief mentions of **Sanders, John A. Walker, John Gaster, Hiram Barber** and **Daniel ?.** [156]

Dear Wife, I seat my self to knight to drop you a few lines to let you know that I am well at this time. I dident write to you how bad off I was I fell off so much I have lost ten potunds but I feel as well now as I ever did. I have got with our company again We left Camp Holmes on last Thursday mourning and got to the company on Sunday evening and joined in with our other men about the next morning we started and went ten miles farther in the and a half miles or White bak River We are in camp to knight at Mrs Sanders where the yankes has been you red of it in the papers where they taken her mules and carrige horses and six negroes and seven head of horses and three hundred dollars worth of juelry. Eliza we are agoing to Swanns Borough to mourrow twelve miles from this place right in amongst the yankees We are bound to fight now or bee taken prisesers Eliza we had a lively time coming here We had to walk all the way and the distant is seventy five miles from Wilmington and now have twelve miles to go to morrow Eliza you wanted to know if I ever had heard from John Walker I got a letter from him last weeke he said he was well as to health but he was troubled with hisfoot He said he had been in a deavel of a fight but he did not get hurt but John Gaster was shot through the sholder I expect he was in a nother fight yesterday there was a fighting some eight or ten mils from here with Spruels Regiment and that is the Regiment that John and his company was in. We havent heard the particulars of it yet. Hiram Barber was taken prisener in the fight they had his hors was killed under him and fell on his leg and he could not get it out. No moore about the War. We had to leave five of our men at the camp at Wilmington. There is several of our men got the meesles at this time Little Daniel has got them now and is verry bad off. Tan continues to have boils yet but he has got nearly over them one gets well another one comes Eliza I will try to write to you every weeke if I can and I want you to do the same and I will bee verry much oblige to you Send your letters to Wilmington Just as you have been sending them Eliza My verry best respects to you and all the family L. H. McLeod Good by Eliza and children and Emely

1862, May

Baxter C. Phillips (*Goldsboro, NC*) to sister **Emeline Phillps.** General wartime correspondence with brief mentions of Rev. **Lewis Phillips, Jr.** [157]

Dear Sister Emeline, This morning I will answer yours which I received a few days since. When I got it, I was so sick that I could hardly read it, but did and it gave me some comfort in my sickness to know that you were all well at home. This morning I feel well as common although I am weak yet. I hope son to be able to go out in camp again. Pa got here the day I went in the hospital. I have been improving ever since then. I tried to get furlough but could not, it not being necessary for my health. I was most pleased with Pa's coming when he did. He has done me more good, his presence, than almost anything else that has been done. But he must start home in the morning. I can't ask him to stay any longer. His affairs at home need him there. I think I can get along here now very well. I wish I could see you all but I can't tell when I will. I hope soon the war will be over and we all return home and enjoy each other once more in this life. If not, let us meet in Heaven where there is no such thing as war. It does me much good to learn that you all seem so cheerful at home[.] I enjoy myself very well here. I often think of you all and I think you do the same by me. I am glad that you have a fine crop of fruit at home. I hope it will do well and you save a great deal of it. I want you to keep cheerful as you can. You don't know how much good it does me to know it is so. I have heard Duty is dead. Poor fellow, I did not expect to see him anymore when I left home. Was he ready to die or not? If he was, happy is he. All the regiments have left here but ours and one more, and I don't know whether it will go or not. It will go to Virginia, if it does. There is some talk of it staying here now. We don't know one hour what we will do the next. I am willing to stay here a while anyhow till I get well, which God grant may soon be for I desire health very much if it is consistent with God's will that I should. My sickness has done me much good. I want to see old Fair Promise once mor and hear the gospel preached in its walls. God grant that we may do so once more. Oh, it would be such pleasure to me. I think the health of our company is improving. I want you all to meet in prayer for us in all our conditions. Pray that we may yet meet again and that we may be better Christians than we have been. Take care of your health. I close. I remain. Your brother, Baxter

1862, May 2
A.S. Caddell (*Kinston, NC*) to **Martha Sullivan**. General wartime correspondence. [158]

Miss M.M. Sullivan, I receive yours kind letter a few days since which gave me pleasure to hear that you was well[.] my health is good at this time[.] I hope this will reach you in possesion of the same blessing[.] times appears to be lively in camp and our term of service will soon expire that we set in to serve[.] it was to that time I looked forward with sweet anticipations of meeting with you (but alas) I regret verry much to say to you that I am not only deprived of returning at that time but I fear forever[.] any person would be fortunate to survive this war as we are exposed to so many dangers[.] I will say to you that I can not return when I promised you to although I much regret it[.] you know what your promises was[.] you said if I did not return when my time was out that things would change[.] so probably you want to be released from your former promises[.] I can only say that I hold you bound no longer if it is your wish though it is with much regret that I say so[.] if I never see you again[,] I will say that my affections is as they ever were towards you[.] pleas drop me a few lines as soon as you get this and let me know if your mind has really changed[.] I shall await your answer in suspence[.] Yours until Death, A.S. Caddell

1862, May 5
Raney G. Caddell to son **A.S. Caddell**. General wartime correspondence between mother and son with brief mentions of his father's **William Caddell** poor health, the likelihood of his brother **C.D. Caddell** going to war and **W.H.H. Davis**, **Eli P. Seawell**, **Zacheus Hogan** and **Samuel Jackson McIntosh**. [159]

Dear son[,] I once more take my pen in hand to write you a few lins to let you know that we are yet alive but I cannot say that we are well[.] your papa is very poorly with his head and ses he gets wors[.] we received your very kind letter and was glad to hear from you once more and glad to hear your health was good[.] I hope it will remain so[.] I have nothing strange to write[.] the people is in greate trouble about the war[.] it look like disalation on every han[.] we was very sorry that you could not come home when your time is out[,] and it had got so near that it look like I could almost see you and hear you walk in the yard but we are disapoind[.] I fear it will be a long time before you can come home[.] we all want to see so bad and if Neil has to leave[,] I do not know what what we should do for I cant work mutch[.] I am now in my 60th year[.] you want to know if we knead any thing[.] we dont knead any thing that you can do for us[.] we knead your presents[.] I was glad you thought enough of us to want to know what we nead[.] we have a plenty to live on as yet[.] but if we should live till another year rools around[,] I do not know what we shall do but we must do the best we can[.] I want you to take care of yourself the very best you can and dont forget pray and keep in that Strait and narrow path[.] give my respects to Harrison Davis and Eli and Hogans and Jack[.] be shore to get in to drive a wagon if you can[.] I think it will be best for you[.] be shore to come home as soon as you can[.] if you could see your pritty horse and sheep and hogs[.] I must close[.] I remain your loving mother until death. Rany G. Caddell

1862, May 6
Daniel McIntosh to brother-in-law **A.S. Caddell**. General wartime correspondence between brothers-in-law with brief mentions of **C.D. Caddell**. [160]

Dear Brother, I take the presant opportunity of answering your very kind letter of the 26 which I received last nite which gave us satisfaction to hear that you was well[.] tho sorry if you cant get a furlow to come and see us all before you have to commence serving the other two years tho I think that you certainly will get a furlow shortly[.] we are all very anxious to se you come home again and was in hope that you could come to stay tho I suppose sircumstances has ordered it otherwise and it must be submited to[.] there is some few that express some disaffection concerning the conscription bill tho to no grate extent[.] I think that they are becoming more reconciled to it[.] some of them are volunteering[.] you said that you dident no what they would do at home when Neil left[.] the chance is bad tho I am willing to do what I can for them as either of you[.] and if he dose have to go and expect that he will[,] we must all work together so as to help them all that we can[.] you also said that if he left[,] you wanted me to take your horse untill you come home[.] I will do so and attend to anything in my power for you and you also wanted me to tell you how would be the best to manage youre business at home[.] as to that I dont no what to tell you tho I think that the chance of hiring one that would do to depend on is bad[.] tho if you and Neill cant find no better chance[,] I will do all I can in attending to it for you[.] we are all well and hope this will find you enjoying the same like blessing[.] I remain youse respt. Until deth. Danl McIntosh

1862, May 7
C.D. Caddell (*Moore County, NC*) to brother **A.S. Caddell**. General wartime correspondence between brothers with brief mentions of **Neill Stuts'** marriage to **Jane Yow** and **Harrison Davis**, **Devotion Davis** and Capt. **Clement Dowd**. [161]

It is with pleasure I seat myself to drop you a few lines[.] wee are all well at present hoping thes few lines will find you well[.] I recd your letter and money which D. Davis brought for you[.] I mailed a letter to you the 2nd of May and I want you to do as I said[.] I will pay your debts with your money as far as it will go[.] I expect to have to go to the war and I want to go to that company[,] and I want you to tell Capt Dowd to let me in if I am bound to go[.] but I am not a going unless I am bound to go and I want you to tell him my condition[,] and see if he wont preserve a place for mee without my volunteering till I no I have to go[.] he could send meea passport and if I ant bound to go it will be nothing against him[.] it will be a bad chance for mee to go or I would go now[.] tell Harrison I would a thought he would a wrote to me by Devotion[.] Neill Stuts is maried to Jane Yow[.] I am a geting along with the one I spoke of in my last letter all rite[.] write as soon as this comes to hand and let me no what Dowd says[.] no more at present[.] Your Loving Brother till Death., CDC

1862, May 7
Lydia Sowell (*Moore County, NC*) to cousin **A.S. Caddell**. General wartime correspondence between cousins. [162]

Dear Cousin[,] with pleasure I seat myself to drop you a few lines and in the first place I will ask you why you have forgotten to write to me[.] I received a letter from you but it has been so long ago[.] I don't know when it was and I wrote you one in return to it and that is the last[.] I have been looking for you to write me this long time[,] but it seems you wont write so I thought I would make you think of your duty. Weel Tim everything is going rong up here[.] if evry I seed people tring to be old it is now. Thay all about to be 35 but some of them cant mak it out[.] and if thay don't drane their purse to the bottom that will have think now what camp life is yet though I think it will go very hard with them[.] Tim I wish I could see you & tell you things you never thought of in your life[.] I saw your little girl the other day[.] she is as prety as ever and I want you to take care of yourself on the account but time you was only here[,] you could see one of the prettiest girls you ever put your peepers on in all your life[.] she is on her way to Fayettville[.] she is a native of Philadelphia[.] he is pretty indeed and when she went to bed[,] I told her I was going to write to you and so she sends her love to you for being a soldier[.] you must excus this fore it is now late in the knight. I want you to write to me before long so good knight my dear Cousin[,] Lyd Sowell

1862, May 11
Jane McIntosh (*Moore County, NC*) to uncle **A.S. Caddell**. General wartime correspondence between niece/uncle with mention of death of **Evander Caddell's** son **William M. Caddell** and **Mary Caddell McIntosh**. [163]

Dear uncle[,] it with pleasure that I seat myself to drop you a few lines to let you know that I am still in the land of the living[,] well and hearty and hopes that these few lines may find you enjoying the same like blessing[.] I have no news to write that would interest you oh only Evander Caddell has lost his child now so he is left alone[.] ther was a sunday school organized today[.] I was appointed a teacher over the Bible class[.] you must come over and hear me question my scholars[.] I will make them mind right as I know off[.] well Tim I was in hopes that you would git to come home and stay but I suppose that you bound for two more years[,] but I think they will surly give you furlough[.] well Tim I heard a gal say that she would give a sugar shiling to see brother moderater[.] she said it would not do for her to see you coming[.] the people is comonly well hear[,] only a few cases of the measels[.] mother has got the measels but is some better[.] so I will close by saying write soon and give me all the news if any[.] yours affectionately, Jane McIntosh

1862, May 11
Sarah McIntosh to **A.S. Caddell**. General wartime correspondence with brief mention of her brother **Neill McIntosh, C.D. Caddell, T.B. Tyson, William Caddell** and **Neill Caddell**. [164]

Most Esteemed and affectionate friend and neighbour, I this evening imbrace this opportunity of returning you my thanks for receiving your kind letter[,] which gave me great satisfaction of hearing from you that you was well[.] and was glad to hear that you were attending to my poor sick brother and I want you to continue your kindness to him as much as you can spare from your duty[,] and I want you to right how he is, if he is a getting better or worse[.] I can hear that he is getting better some times and that he is not dangerous[,] but I cannot tell how he is by what I can hear[.] I would be glad for you or some of you to right every mail or twice a weeke while he is sick or till he gets better[,] and I will be under lasting obligations to you or any of you for your kind favours to my sick brother[.] I am yours respectfully, Sarah McIntosh

Sir[,] I was at your father today[.] I got CD Caddells tutor from Mr TB Tyson yesterday eveng[.] your father was not home[,] he went to your Uncle Neills yesterday[.] your Mother and CD was at home and was well and in good part as common[.] as for news we have none of importance ondly the war[.] some is a making ready to go before the conscription takes them and some is bound to stay as long as posible and then beg to be excused by some craft or other[.] some is a making up schools and began to teach and has no scholling but how they will git alon[?] it is yet to found out for they are old unionist and not for the war[.] But I expect that if the call comes before harvest that wheat and oats will no be saved if it should not be blacked[.] there is a report that has the rust in many places[.] I am well at this times and hoping that this may find also well.

1862, May 11
Mary E. Moore (*Plank Road*) to cousin **A.S. Caddell**. General wartime correspondence between cousins. [165]

Dear Cousin, I am very sorry you have so many corresponders[.] you cannot answer all their letters yourself, as you employ some person to write to me for yours[.] I dont think it is necessary for me to write to you anymore. All I ask of you is to tell me why you do not write to me yourself. I hope you will excuse me for writing these few lines to you & yet believe me as ever your friend & cousin. M.E.M.

1862, May 11
Eliza Jane Walker McLeod to husband **Louis H. McLeod**. General wartime correspondence with brief mentions of **Francis Moore Parker McLeod, William M. Swann, John Cox, Abel Douglass, John Kelly, Sandy McLeod, Joseph Kelly, Tandy Walker, Sandy Kelly, David P. Morris, Thomas Bragg McLeod, Douglas, Emily Franklin** and **Francis Moore** [166]

Der and loving husban Louis McLeod once more i sete my self to anser your leter that was dated the first and i was more then glad to her from you and to her you wer wel and on the land amonest the living these lines leve me and all ov the reste of the famley well at this [time] hoping tha may find you in the same blesing to day is sunday and nobody her but me and frances M parker and he is a slepe Louis i was more then sorey to her the capten Swan was ternd out ov ofice fore i am a fraid your dos not no a nof [know enough] but I did not like the way he was dooing up her for i thot he ot to bin with his men at such a time as this i recken the men node him best or tha wold not ternd him out dident he hate it mity bad rite to me how he looked when he got thar Louis i am glad to her you got your old ofice agin now try to doo the best you can and be smarte but dont bee too smart bee good to your men and take good cer ov your self i am afraid you ar all kild or taken prisner before now this is a pirty day and i expect when i her from you you hav bin fiting i wish you wer somwher wharels for i think you are in a danges [dangerous] place i rather you wer in a batle then in those services i think the are more danger thar thin in a batle field Louis i never saw such times in my life up her i cant see no men but John Cox and Abeeke(?) douglass all gon and how we are to get our whete cut i dont no Sam (some) few hird [heard] John Keley and San McLeod giv five hundred dolars to ole harpe Louis corn is mity little we never got a stan yet and wormes eates it down as fast as it comes up im afrait it will not bee a good crop yer but we wil doo the best we can and if we fail we cant help it Louis i hav sold the mule and got one hundred dolars in cash for him i thot we wold not make on of to winter them all and i cold not sel nary won ov the others and i thot i had beter let him go for we cant run the thraser no how for if Jo Walker has to go i am going to put big to la [?] Jack and tri to raise another mule and if you think i beter pay your dets i wil doo so for if you never com back i will hav them to pay and if god spars you to liv to com back you can start ov a new may the god ov heven spar me and you to liv to meete in this life and liv in pese if you wer her to day and pese was made it wold bee a hapy time but no hapinss to bee serve in this life and I fer a no more in my life may god hasten the time to com when man and wife can mete and liv together again in pese that time will never com until sin and pride is put down it is sin and pride has brot this war on i think and in stidyovgeting [instead of getting] beter tha get wors Louis dont forget your god pray god to bee wit you in all ov your trobles for witout help from him we are a lost peple he most fite the gratle batle or we ar a whip nation ov peple if we ar in the rite god will be with us and if we ant he will forsake us i hope the war wil soon bee over an you all com home Louis i sent them things you wanted by the capten and a pece ov dride beefe rite if you got them tel tan i stil reman his loving ant and I want to her from him bee good to your self tandy tel San an dave I never for get them in my leter i want to her from them evry time i get a leter the childrin wishs to bee remember to you in this leter and wants you to say somthing to them in your next brag is gon to mister douglas to day fore the first time Louis Abe rote to you som time a goy an he has not got ary anser and told me to say somthing about it in mine Louis i red the leter you sent Emeley and i never saw such a won in my life. i dont no how you ever thot ov such things it was so good i had to sho it to Abe and you ought to herd him laff he said that was good advice to Emley Louis i want you to rite how meny men you hav thar and if duncin more is thar and evry thing you can think ov Louis i am geting beter now and i wish you cold hav som to eat too when you com home I will hav a big plate fool frances more is up her now and his father too tha brot thirty or forty negos up her i think the negeres wil take this setlement i don't like no such a way Louis i hav nothin mor to rite to you onley i expect thar is som town bernning up to day for it is mity smokey today i her tha ar fiting at yorktown i moste close by saing if i never see you agen tri to mete me in heven whar parting is none no more good by my der loving husban Eliza McLeod my hart is with you until the end ov my life. Com home harvest if you can excuse bad ritin don in a hery

1862, May 13

John Francis Williamson (*46 Reg Company F, Goldsboro, NC*) to father **Wyatt Williamson**. General wartime correspondence from son to his father with brief mentions of relatives/friends **Isaac**, **Mary** and **Mary E.** [167]

Dear Father, I seat myself this beautiful morning to try to anser yore very kind letter which I recevied not long since[.] I was more than glad to hear from you all[.] We are ar Goldsboro doing finely[.] we have no news to write that will interest you in the least[.] you say that I must come home if I can the chance[.] there is no chance to get a furlow hear[.] It is most impossible for the suck to get one[.] I would be more than glad to come home if I cood[.] I would be glad to see you out hear[.] I hant got much time to write[.] I think it will be [illegible] for me to stop[.] I am very well sufice and injoy camp life as well as cood be expected[.] I getting very fat[.] I think I will stand it very well[.] I want you to have my wheat sowed and my hogs[.] you must do th ebest you can with them and feed him more then[.] glad to receive them socks but I did not get them[.] Tell Isaac and Mary to write to me and tell me how they are getting along[.] Tell Mary E. that I woodbe glad to see her[.] tell her howdy for me[.]

write very soon and long[.] I hope you all joy and peas of mind[.] I hope I will meat you all again[.] give my love to all the friends[.] Your son[,] J.F. Williamson. [P.S.] Pleas addres me at Goldsboro NC 46 Reg Company F in care of Captin McAlester.

1862, May 14
John A. Sloan (*Wilmington, NC*) to mother **Catharine Sloan**. General wartime correspondence with brief mention of **David H. Sloan, John Wesley Love, William Andrew Love, Mary Campbell, Thomas Campbell** and uncle **J.M.** [168]

Dear Mother, I seat myself to inform you that I hav bin sick and I hav bin in the hospital a week[,] but I am able to go to the camp. David is well[.] he company left us at Wilmington and went to Jacksonville and as soon as we got able to go[,] we went and they had left and we mist them and so we are back to Wilmington ad found them there and we had a bad travil at it. I expect we will moov in a day or too and I don't know where we will go to[,] but we will not leave Wilmington tho aim all spirit to deth her and a movin out everyday[.] you wanted us to come hom[.] we can not get a furlo[.] we will com as soon as we can. I want you to tell Wes Lov and Andrew to com to this company. Tell Mis Mary Campbell that Thomas is well and harty. Tell uncle J.M. to right to us for I have not herd from him in a long time. Right soon and direct your letter to Wilmington in car of Capt. Wicker. J.A. Sloan[.]

1862, May 16
J.L. Stuart (*Goldsboro, NC*) to mother **Mary A. Harper** and cousin **Emily C. Nall**. General wartime correspondence with brief mentions of **John Harper**. [169]

Miss Mary A. Harper, Dear mother[,] I received a letter from you to day[.] when it come I was afraid to open it for fear that it would tell me that you was dead but I was glad to hear that you was a live[.] but I was very sorry to hear that John Harper was sick[.] I hope that I will hear that he is better[.] I hope that he will get well. I was to hear that many of you was dead and I should greave to death about it[.] I do believe that I shall see old Moore again[.] yesterday the 16th we went to church[.] it was fast day[.] the preacher said it would not be long before it would be decided[.] He talked very pretty about the ones we had left. there is prair meeting ever night.

Miss E.C. Nall, Dear cousin[,] for the first time I am in the hospital[.] now I come here a Sunday morning[.] this is the 21 so some of them told me they give medicine & then I do the best I can for I cannot eat[.] they have boild meet rice coffee baked bread & corn. Do you stay at our house[?] if you do[,] I need you to John Harper cure him as quickly as you can so he can come after me.

Dear mother[,] I send you a few lines to in form you that I am well as common[.] I have been sick but I can drill now[.] we are goin throe the manuel of armes[.] I am about as good as any[.] I hope these line will find you all well[.] I have sent you two letters an I have not receive no answer from you yet[.] if you have not got them[,] write to me any how for I want to kno if you are all alive or not[.] direct your letters to Goldsboro NC 49 regt Co D and troops in care of Capt Black[.] our capt has not got home yet. when I get a letter from you[,] I will send you a good Big letter and tell you how I am getting along Drilling[.] this paper is so sorry I cant write[.] I want to see you all mightily[.] I think I can come after awhile. J.L. Stuart

1862, May 17
Matthew C. Yow (*Goldsboro, NC*) to his brother **Simeon Jones Yow**. General wartime correspondence with brief mentions of his brother **Isaac Yow, William Pool, Andrew John Stutts** and **David D. Yow**. [170]

Deer Brother[,] I take my pen in hand to inform you that I am well with the exception a risen in my yer which makes my head ach hoping when this comes to hand it may find you injoying the same great blesing. I receivd your kind letter to day. It giv me great satisfaction to here from you that you was getting along with your work so well. Jones when you rite to me rite with ink. I could hardly reed your letter it had rubd out so bad. Deer brother you said you had not drank any spirits sinc I left. I was glad to here that for I hav seen trouble about you. I hope the good Lord will bles and save you forever. I am looking for a letter from father. I hav rote to him and no answer yet. I want you all to rite. I want you to rite me when you get this. I hav bin vary uneasy about you. I was afraid you would hav to come to the war. I want you to stay if you can. Dont come as long as you can stay. I want you to rite to me about what the people say about coming. Several hav come to our company now and if you hav to come I want you to come to me. Jones take good of my little children. Poor little children[,] I want to see them so bad. I rote a letter to Isaac. I suppose he has got it. William Poole is well and as wicked as ever. He says he wants to see you all. A.J. Stuts is well also. David D. Yow is sick. I must close my letter by saying May the good Lord bles and save us all forever. Your affectionate brother[,] M.C. Yow so fairwell[.] Simeon J. Yow

1862, May 19
A.S. Caddell (*Camp Magruder, NC*) to Miss **Martha M. Sullivan**. General personal correspondence. [171]

Miss Martha, it again I have recorse to my pen to answer your kind response[.] It came to hand a few days since[.] I was highly interested with its contents[.] It found me in possesion of good health as I hope this will find you enjoying the same blessing[.] I was well pleased with your sentiments[.] they was jus as I wished them to be[.] you spoke of my givings you a final discharge[.] that was a sentence which I dont think was contained in my last letter (it is a misunderstanding on your part)[.] I only said as I say now that if it is life[.] I want you to write as soon as you get this[.] give me a relation of all that is passing in that part of the country (and if you hear anybody say anything about me[,] tell them my motto is Right, Face File Right March. Your affectionate lover, A.S. Caddell

1862, May 21
Asa S. McIntosh (*Goldsboro, NC*) to **A.S. Caddell.** General wartime correspondence with brief mentions of **Neill Caddell**, **Zacheus Hogans** and of **Neill Branson Caddell** and **John Stewart** being sick. [172]

Dear friend[,] I seat myself to inform you that I am well at this time[,] hoping these few lines may find you all of your mess mates well. I have no news to write at this time only we have grait times here a puting men in the guard house[.] I believe I had rather be at home at some of our old fishing partyes or at home any how[,] but my buisness is so I cant leave as I no off[.] I want you to write to me[.] It seames that I cant get any more letters from you & all the rest[.] I want you to write and let me no how Neill is a getting along[.] I would like for you to write if he should get worst to let me no[,] if you please[.] I shall look for and answer in a few days[.] tell Jackson to write to me & Hogans[.] give my best respect to all of my friends if any[.] so write soon and give me the news and I will do the same or try in my next[.] I will give you a list of the sick N.B. Caddell & J. Stewart[.] I dont think they will get over it[.] so no more[.] rite soon[.] tell Neill to rite if he is able[.] write soon. A.S. McIntosh

1862, May 23
Matthew C. Yow (*Goldsboro, NC*) to his wife **Nancy Catherine Albright Yow** and children. General wartime correspondence with brief mentions of his brother **Simeon Jones Yow,** father **Henry C. Yow,** brothers-in-law **Henry A. Albright**, **John E. Albright, David D. Yow, Peter Moody** and children **William Henry Yow**, **Nancy E. Yow, Mary Jane Yow** and **Joseph Gibbs Yow**. [173]

Deer Wife and Little Children[,] I now take my pen in hand to let you no that I am well at this time hoping when this comes to hand it may find you all injoying the same great blesing. I must tel you that we hav to leav here tomarrow to go to Weldon[,] stil futher from home but I hope the good Lord will be with me there. I want you to pray for me. I expect we shal hav to fight before long. Catharine do the best you can. I hope and pray we will meet again but if we dont I hope we will in haven whare we will part no more. Catharine try to rais the little children to love the Lord who can save them forever. Lord bless my little children. Catharine when I think about the day we parted it fils my hart with sorrow. I do want to see you the worst I ever did. I cant rite like I could talk if I could see you. I rote to you and Jones. I hope you will get them. I rote father a letter yesterday. Catharine I saw your brothers. They ware both well. I was vary glad to see them. I must tel you that there is a greateal of sicknes here. Some die every day. David D Yow is sick and I think he will get off. I expect to send this letter by him if he comes. Catharine I will rite as soon as I get to Weldon if I can and tel you no wher to rite. I will come home as soon as I can if I live but I cant tel you when that will be. Catharine and little children fairwell if I never see you any more. Catharine if get in a battle and get kild[,] I dont want you to greev about me. I hope I shal be prepard. I will rite as soon as I can when I get to Weldon. I have bin looking for letters from some of you. I rite vary often. I am glad to here that you are geting along so well with your work. William Henry my deer little son you said you wanted to rite me a letter. I wish you could. Henry you must be a good boy and help your mother and dont fight your little sisters. I want to see you all so bad but I cant see you soon. Catharine take good cear of what you hav got. I cant tel when I can help you any more. I want you to get what you need Catharine. I am riting and in trouble you may be sure. Catharine I thought I would get my likenes taken but I hav not yet. I will as soon as I can. You said you went with Jones to your fathers. I am glad you went. Go when you can leav. Jones deer brother do the best you can for my wife and children and you shant loose nothing if I live. Jones I hope you will not hav leav home. If you do rite to me and I want you to come to me but stay if you can. Jones we parted in tears but I hope we will meet again. So fairwell brother. Catharine another word to you and the children if nevere see you no more I hope you will all remember me. Nancy C. Yow William Henry Yow Nancy E. Yow Mary J. Yow Joseph G. Yow Fairwell to you all. Catharine I will send this letter David D Yow. I hav too shilling of silver I will send by him. I receivd a few lines from Peter Moody. He said you was all well. Tel him I will rite as soon as I can. I said we was going to Weldon but I dont no where we shal go. We shal leav in the morning the 24 of May. I must close. I hav not forgoten you yet. So fairwell. Matthew C. Yow

1862, May 23
Louis H. McLeod (*Camp McRae*) to wife **Eliza Jane Walker McLeod**. General wartime correspondence with brief mentions of **Emily Franklin, John A. Walker, Henry J. McNeill, Archibald A. Jackson, B.C. Jackson** and **Abe Douglass.** [174]

Mrs L. H. McLeod, I seat myself to drop you a few lines to let you know that I am yet spaired with good health Eliza I receaved a letter last knight from your and Emely that was written to John Walker you must have made a bad mistake and have sent the letter you entended for me to John. Eliza there is nothing enteresting down here at this time we have moved again since I wrote to you last we moved wright on the sound we get splendid water right out of the edge of the sound when the tide is up the salt water is all round the spring We can get a plenty of fish at this place and the nicest place we have ever been at yet a good shady place and a plenty of pine straw Myself and H. J. McNeill and A. A. Jackson and Bird Jackson just moved in a tent to our selves we put up forks in the ground and then put little pine poles a cross to ly on we rested first rate last knight. Our company is all well except bowel complaint but they are a getting a great deal better now no moore at this time for I am in a hurry it is now drill hour is at hand now you must excuse me for this time my verry best respects to the children and Emely you ought to have not shode Abe that letter that I sent to Emely, L. H. McLeod

1862, May 24
Mary Ann Harper to son **John L. Stuart**. General wartime correspondence with brief mentions of **E. Davis, Spivey** and **J. Sheffield.** [175]

Mr John L Stuart Dear son[,] I now rite my letter to you since I left you[.] we hav recevd from you your last was on the 20 by Davis letter us[.] we are anxious to here from you again[.] I hope these few lines will find you well[.] We understand the yankeys has raised an white flag at new bern[,] and do not want to fite with Carolina[.] how true this is[,] we can not[.] tell your mother she is complaining and is bad and her eyes sighte is mighty Well[.] she complains hard on your account[.] we are in formed by a letter from E. Davis that you all that you all was a going to start from goldsborough to Virginia to hunt the yankeys[.] rite if it so[.] tell Capt Black he promised his men a furlo at home and I want him to be as good as his word[.] I am shor you ask but I am doing moor then I ought to do[.] I am getting in [illegible] of that new ground to make a little corn and peas[.] I hope you will rite how you like and some cheering words to your mother[.] We keep the horses as strong as possible[.] her hole complaint is if I has done as she wanted me to[,] you would not have been where you are[.] this is her greatest grief[.] I tell her I may a hav don rong but I do not now[.] it then I thought I could get off by inspection[,] but I found I could not[.] and now the thing is as it is and we muste get thru with it the beste we can[.] and to grief will do no good it is in the nuse before that all the sick soldiers is to be sent home to get well[.] So if you get sick or am not able to[.] I will remember your captn. of that and tell him you claim your rites. When Spivey is at home and plowing and J. Sheffield[,] They say if their captain will send some of his men after them[,] they will go to him but they will not be taken by anybody here. our wheat looks well if the rain does not hurt it[.] the oats is coming out and heading somewhere good seasons yet. We all wish you well and hope good luck will attend you and a hearte cheering feeling in you to lift your mind a bov trouble or fear you[.] now your mother grievs hard on your account and thinks she will never see you again[,] but She is still praying for you and wants you to to prepare to meete her in heaven when parting is no more[.] She wants you to not state your condition in sooth to her how you satisfied for the days if she was able she would go and see you[.] I would like to now if all the men over there by furlows to be sent home in 90 days or not[.] of if it is the first volunteers. yours with greate affections[,] Mary A. Harper

1862, May 26
Louis H. McLeod (*Camp McRae*) to wife **Eliza Jane Walker McLeod**. General wartime correspondence with brief mentions of **Henry ?, Ary ?, Nelse ?, Emily Franklin** and **Nancy Ann McLeod.** [176]

Mrs L. H. McLeod, I drop you once moore a few lines to let you know that I am in the land of the living and spaired with tolerable good health Eliza we have moved a great deal since we have been in the servis. But we have the worst move to maken now I have been to Wilmington today and it rained on me half the day and has got everry thing wet and it is still pooring down rain and just dark and we have just got orders from the colonel to cook three days rashions and leave here to knight to go to South Carolina We are to get to Wilmington by mourning so we can take the train to Fair Bluff on the River that runs by George Town We will bee stationed at Fair Bluff. The Yankees is going up the river and the people are burning up the rice mills all on the river what the yankees havent burnt. our men all raired and hollerd when they got the news that we had to leave altho it was raining. I would not mind the trip if it was good weather The road is full of water from hear to Wilmington we will have to wade the swamps as we come to them you must excuse this blotted specte there was so many in the tent scrounging I couldent help it Eliza we have got those orders to go to South Caroline and about the time we get there we will bee ordred back if not when we get to Wilmington I think the order will bee countermanded. We heard all the soldiers from Raleigh and Goldsborough was ordred to Richmond and away goes the Moore Countyans I want them to see some of the hardship in this war for I think our Regiment has seen a good portion Eliza I want you to keepe in good heart and never give up to any thing as long as you can have your health. May the god of Heaven help us to drive back the invaders from off our land so we may all go home to stay with our wives and children Eliza direct your letters to Wilmington and they will bee sent on to the regiment if we have to stay out there this summer I want you to write to me as soon as you get this and tell me all about how you are coming on farming and how the wheet looks. Tell Henry and Ary and Nelse I think of them verry oftin and I want them to think where I am and I want them to try and make a plenty to eat My verry best respects to Emely and the children Tell Sis I will come home to see her some time before long your husband L. H. McLeod

1862, May 27
Louis H. McLeod (*Camp Lamb*) to wife **Eliza Jane Walker McLeod**. General wartime correspondence with brief mentions of **Dave Kelly, Tandy Walker, Sandy Kelly, Anjalette McLeod, Delilah McLeod** and **Thomas Bragg McLeod.** [177]

Dear and Loving Wife just as I expected I wrote the last letter to you that we was ordard to South Carolina and so we was We got as far as Wilmington and the order was countermanded and we wint in the quarters at Camp Lamb where we will stay untill further orders. We dont know where we will go next. I wouldent bee at all surprised if we will have to go to Richmand next. There is a Regiment here now that came from South Carolina that is agoing on to Richman this evening. I cant see into such business want to send us to South Carolina and sending South Carolinians on to Richman. I had rather they would send us to Richman at once. Where I expect we will have to go at last. It will bee moore healthy for us than at home. I havent nothing to wright to you at this time only I am well and hearty at present and I hope those few lines will find you and family all well and hearty and enjoying yourselves as well as sircumstances will admit. I dont want you and family to get out of heart ceep in good spirit and bee lively like we soldiers is in camp dont mind the wether so the wind dont blow. Our company is all in tolerable good health none verry sick Dave Kelley is a little puny Tan is well and so is Sand Kelley Sand is driving the wagon now and has been at it some time It takes betwixt thirty and thirty five wagons to move us when we move from one place to another when we are so far that the wagons cant go backwards and forwards in one day Eliza We have plenty to [eat] such as meete and bread I eat dinner at the hotel the other day and it was as good as I ever eat in my life. It was at Bishops Hotell They had fresh pork and chicken meete and greens and twenips and peas and beats squashed irish potatoes new and sweete potatoes and everry thing that was good and you better belief I set to it like a bline kitten to a pan of milk I eat there every time I go to Wilmington but I have to pay seventy five cents for it. It seams very high but the dinner is verry good and money plenty as the old saying. We havent been pad our monthly wages yet which we ought to have drawn too or three weeks ago all the men that dinent reinlist when we did under the ages of thirty five have drawn fifty dollars of their bounty.

But we dont know when we ever will get the balance. I think we will get our wages in a few days. No moore at this time only I must draw your attention to write as soon as you get this I sent you some stamps in the letter before this. Eliza tell Anja and Delilah to studdy their books and practice writing and keep at it every time they have nothing else to do and learn Bragg all they can make him try to learn and I will bring him a top whin I come home. Eliza I want to see you and all the family and bee with you a while I remain your loving husband until death, Louis H. McLeod.

1862, May 27
C.D. Caddell to brother **A.S. Caddell**. General wartime correspondence between brothers. [178]

I seat myself to drop you a few lines to let you know I am well at present[.] this makes 3 letters I have wrote since I have got any one from you[.] write soon and post one in for your gal[.] I expect to have to go to the war before long[.] If I go[,] I expect to join the Rangers and I want to no what you think of it[.] I have no news[,] only what you saw in my last letter[.] I am in a hurry[.] Write soon to your loving Brother, C.D. Caddell

1862, May 28
Raney G. Caddell (*Moore County, NC*) to son **A.S. Caddell**. General wartime correspondence between mother/son with brief mention of **Joseph Fry**. [179]

Dear son[,] I take the pleasure this evning of writing you a few lins to let you know how we are a coming on[.] we are as well as common[.] I am a going to send you a dozen eggs and a little butter. I want you to write soon[.] I have not time to write as wait is going to start[.] So I will conclude your eggs is in with Joseph Frys[.] Hope you can get them from him[.] So no more at present[.] wee would send you more if wee had a chance[.] I will say no more[.] R.G. Caddell

1862, June 2
Baxter C. Phillips (*Goldsboro, NC*) to sister **Candace Phillps.** General wartime correspondence. [180]

Dear Candace, I often think of you and the many happy hours we have enjoyed all together. Their recollection still lingers like a pleasant dream in my memory and I delight to retrospect those days. Happiness could [illegible] me sometimes. You would know I had the blues, but [illegible]. I have but often when people think I am in the blues. It is then that I enjoy some of the most pleasant hours of my life. I am so disposed naturally and few persons know it. There are many things that transpire in camp that make me melancholy as appear [illegible]. I am not always when people think I am. Dear Sister, these days of pleasure_with us seem to cast off for the present anyway. Is it so that we will never meet again in life? I can't think it is. Somehow[,] I am persuaded that we shall meet again. I trust in God for it. We may not if we are unfaithful. I have as you have heard been sick[,] but feel as well as ever I did in my whole life now. I am weak yet. Am gaining my strength as fast as I can. I have improved very fast since Pa left me. I am not able for duty yet, nor in several days. I will stay here until I feel able. I will close as I have written a good deal. Pray for us. Baxter Clegg Phillips

1862, June 2
James Kelly *(Kinston, NC)* to sister **Mrs. Rachel Gilchrist** General wartime correspondence with brief mentions of **John M. Kelly, Neill R. Kelly, Green Cox, Hugh Moore, Robert Smith, John Smith, Neill McInnis, Duncan Thompson, Alex McDonald, John McDonald, William Fry** and **Andrew Medlin**. [181]

Dear Sister: I take my pen in hand to drop you a few lines in order to let you know how I am coming along. John has been very puny for the last week or two. I am also not very well, John was tolerably sick last week with diareah but it now near about over it, I was taken with it the day after I reached camp but it does not make me sick much. I was pretty sick a while yesterday evening but feel very well today[,] only I am weak. Neil is well. A great many in camp have the diareah and some the flux, a great (many) died with the latter, some also have the typhoid fever. There are fewer sick now than were last week and the week before. Green Cox died last Friday night, he died of typhoid fever. Our company has four men who are pretty sick. Hugh Moore (flux) Robert & John Smith, (flux), Neill McInnis, Duncan Thompson (consumption he has a final discharge). Alex McDonald is John McDonald, William Fry are also sick and in the hospital[,] but not very sick. I have not commenced drilling yet so

I cannot give you any idea of the hard ship of a soldiers life. But can guess it is pretty hard to drill in an open field in the hot sunshine these hot days, when they come in they look wetter than if they came out of the harvest field. This morning Johns company was detailed as provost guard[.] the other companies were sent on picket. But few of us are in camp, Gen. Ransom left here Saturday for the big fight in Richmond which commenced Saturday and is in progress yet, according to last dispatches received here. Gen. Martin who has charge of this brigade since Gen. Ramsom left-received a telegraphic despatch yesterday morning stating that we fought them Saturday[,] drove them from their brest works, slept in their camps Saturday night. Commenced the fight again Saturday morning. This morning he received another despatch stating we routed the yankees[,] taking fifteen thousand prisoners. I do hope it will turn out to be the truth but fear this report is premature. It caused great rejoicing in camp, which was as a refreshing shower after a long dry spell. For there was so much sickness in camp for the last few weeks[,] the soldiers were somewhat gloomy. They have been trying the deserters here lately, old Andy Medlin came clear. The soldiers who took him up had gone to Richmond before his trial came off and there was no witness to appear against him, so he came off unhurt, he is doing pretty well now[,] can hear as well as any one, is cheerfull and is cooking for his mess. But some of the other men did not come of as well. Two were condemmed to be shot, but the sentence was remitted by Gen. Holmes[.] two others were drummed out of service. You have no idea how bad it looked to see men with half their head shaved, their hats in their hands, a large piece of past board tacked to their backs with deserter written on it in large letters, marching round every regiment, followed by a plattoon of soldiers with drawn bayonetts and the ugliest and most confused noise, for it was not music, which could be made with drums, horns, and fifes, I tell you when old Andy saw them[,] he rejoiced at his happy escape, and well he might. I do not think he will try it ever again. Well[,] I know you wish to know how I am pleased with camp life. I cannot tell yet how I shall like it, but I fear it will not suit me well for I shall have to eat meat or perish and I never eat but very little meat in the summer, perhaps when I commence hard work I can eat it. We get a plenty good meat, flour, corn meal, and a little rice, a little sugar and rye [?]. We have received no beef since I came[,] bacon all the time, But it is very fine. Also[,] the planks feel very hard before day in the morning but I am getting used to that and do not mind it. And hope I shall get used to it all soon so I shall not mind it. Give my love to all and write soon, As ever your affectionate brother[,] James Kelly. John and Neill send their love to you and the rest-

1862, June 8

Matthew C. Yow (*Petersburg, VA*) to his wife **Nancy Catherine Albright Yow** and children. General wartime correspondence with brief mentions of his brother **Simeon Jones Yow,** father **Henry C. Yow** and children **William Henry Yow, Nancy E. Yow, Mary Jane Yow** and **Joseph Gibbs Yow**. [182]

Deer Wife and Little Children[,] I one more time take my pen to rite to you. I am well this blesed Sabbath morning. I hope when this comes to hand it will you injoying the same great blesing. We hav just got back from our jurney. We left our camp Friday morning to meet the Yankies. We went about 40 miles towards Norfolk but we did not see them. Then we commenct tearing up the rail rode. We turnd it over about 15 miles. It was the best railrode I ever saw. It is the Norfolk and Petersburg rode. It belongs to the Yankies. It rained all day Friday and rained Saturday evning again. There is the most rain I ever saw. It dont look like there will be anything made here. All the wheet I see is red with rust and thers not much wheet here. Catharine if it rains as much up there as it does here it will be a bad chanc about your work but you must do the best you can and be saving for there will be hard times I am afraid. Take good cear of your salt and do the best you can for I cant tel you when I can come home. I am afraid not soon if ever. Catharine I do want to see you and the children so bad. I do hope and pray that we will meet again before long. I dont no what hour we shal be called to the battle field. The cannons was herd here yesterday[,] supposed to be at Richmond. If hav to go I hope the good Lord will be with me there. Catharine I dont want you to greav so much about me. I no you are in trouble but bare it the best you can and pray to the Lord for my protection. Catharine there will be no chanc for me to come home at harvest. You must get your wheet savd if you can. It seems like there is no chanc of peace til we shal all perish. I think thats what will end the war for there is not much a making. There is hundreds of acres here lying idol and what is planted is always coverd in water. Catharine I rote you a letter since I came here the 3 and one to father the 4. I hope you hav got them. I am looking for letters from you but we mov so much I am afraid I shal not get them all. I want you to rite when you get this. It may be that I will get your letters. Direct to M.C. Yow[,] Co D[,] 48 regiment[,] NC Troops[,] General Ransoms Brigade[,] Petersburg VA. Simeon J Yow deer brother[,] I hav bin looking for a letter from you. How are you geting along with your crop. Jones you must do the best you can. I cant come to help you any. I do want to come to come home and help you cut wheet so bad. Jones try to save all the wheet you can. Dear brother fairwell. M.C. Yow. Catharine deer wife I must close my letter and I dont no what to say to you. My hart is ful. This may be my fairwell letter. If I never see you on earth I hope we will meet in haven where we shal part no more. Catharine try to rais my poor little children the best you can. Henry you must be a good boy. Nancy E. Yow Mary J. Yow Joseph G. Yow fairwell to you all. Nancy C. Yow deer wife fairwell. Matthew C. Yow your affectionate husband. Rite soon.

1862, June 10
Louis H. McLeod (*Camp Lamb*) to wife **Eliza Jane Walker McLeod**. General wartime correspondence with brief mentions of **Lawrence, Cox, Sandy Kelly, Dave Kelly, James Monroe, John Johnson, Emily Franklin, Anne Elizabeth McLeod, Thomas Bragg McLeod, Francis Moore Parker McLeod** and **William M. Swann.** [183]

Dear and Loving Wife I seat myself to inform you that I am not verry well at this time I have had the bowel complaint for about three days so bad that I was not able to drill at all But I feel a little better to day. Eliza I send some of my close by Mr. Lawrence and Cox. I have had to by new close alltogether and had to pay verry high for them. You can do as you please with the things that I have sent. You can send to Swanns Station for them as soon as you get this I expect to get a letter from you tomorrow mourning I want you to answer this as soon as it comes to hand. I havent nothing of enterest to write to you at this time only I want to hear form you often and know how you are a getting on farming and all about the wheete and oats and the peaches and apples and everry thing you have about the plantation. Eliza I would like to come up home first rate our bead and planks is a getting mighty hard the bones has gone nearly through the skin. We have had cold weather ever since knight befour last we had a fire in the house all day yesterday and last knight and to day I never saw as cold a time for the time of year in my life and it continues cool yet and clowdy and a little rain. Tan has been bad off a good while with the bowel complaint but he is a getting better know Sand and Dave Kelley is a grunting about there is not moore than half of our regiment that is able for duty owing to the bowel disease there is not many that is verry sick We havent but too in the horspitile James Monroe and John Johnson James Monroe is nearly well our colonel has not come back yet. If he had been here we would have been in Virginia befour now. There is regiments a going on there every day almost There was one regiment went on this mourning befour day with twelve hundred men and Sunday there was another went on to Virginia and they are a going every day from Georgia and South Carolina. I am afraid they will send all there troops from South Carolina and then the yankees will brake out here and then we will bee the first that will bee sent there and that is a place that non of us wants to go We are all willing to go to Virginia at any time if our Colonel was with us. We dont know when he will come back Eliza nothing moore only give my best respects to Emely and the children and tell Bragg and Sis and Parker howdy and tell them I will come to see them some of this long times. Eliza I am in hopes those lines will find you well and hearty and as fas and as like as you as you was when Cpt Swann came down here he said you was as fat and looked better than he ever saw you in his life and I am in hopes you will remain so untill I come home I want to see you moore Look like you use to when I first begin to fly round you My loving wife and children from Louis H. McLeod

1862, June 11
Robert B. Stewart (*Petersburg, VA*) to father **William Stewart**. General wartime correspondence between father/son with brief mentions of brothers **Enoch Stewart** and **George Stewart**. [184]

Dear father, I take my pen in hand to inform yu that I am wel at presant hoping these lines ma find yu wel. I have nothing of importance to rite more than yo have herd[.] I have not recieved a liter since I left Golsburoug[.] I have not herd whether Eanoch got home or not[,] and I want to here from yo all very bad and lern how evry thing is going on in that part of the world[.] I wan sum of yo to rite evry weak and not neglect it for it dos a great eal of good to here from home[.] as to the war[,] I dont no when it wil end[.] we cant lern as mucha bout it here as you can at home tho are fighting evry day[.] and it looks like it cant last long tho one stil fighting yet at Richmon and we are looking out evry moment for a call to go thare[.] evry thing is very [illegible] here and looks like times is going to be very hard[.] it rains here evry day and corn loks sorry[.] wheat is ruind with the rust[.] it is cold today[.] a cow and calf sels here for eighty dolars[.] I want yo to take good cear of mi things till I come home if I ever doo[.] Tel Gorge never to come to the war[.] I wod li out first[.] I wont to se yo all very bad[.] Eanoch can tel yo how bad it is to be here and no yo cont go home[.] I want yo to go on and make all yo can[.] want to se all the children very bad[.] thare is never a day nor a night be what I am studing about yo all[.] I want yo a to pray for mi safe return home[.] I tel the boys to be smart as tha can for tha dont no anything about hard times with tha war here[.] so I must bring leter to a close by saing rite soon, I remain your un son til deth. R.B. Stewart [P.S.] direct your letter to Petersburg Virginia[,] Forty Eight Regiment[,] company D in cear of Captin Clage[,] Generals Ronsoms brigade[,] North Carolina volunteers[.]

1862, June 11

Matthew C. Yow (*Petersburg, VA*) to his brother **Simeon Jones Yow**. General wartime correspondence with brief mentions of his father **Henry C. Yow**, brother **Isaac Yow, William Pool** and **Andrew John Stutts**. [185]

Deer Brother[,] I one time more sit down to drop you a few lines to let you no that I am well at present hoping when this comes to hand it may find you injoying the same great blesing. I receivd your kind letter the 10 which giv me great satisfaction to here that you was all well and geting along so well with your work. I am so glad to here that you are trying so hard to make somthing to liv on. It will be needed. Jones father says you work hard. I no I want to be with you. I red your letter and cride all the time. I am riting with tears in my eys. Work on brother and do the best you can. I am praying that we may meet again. I hope and trust that my prayers will be answerd. I believ you are all praying for me and I hop your prares will be answerd. I am afraid I cant come home soon. I am trying to get to come. It seems like there is no chanc to get a furlow but I hop that times will alter soon. I could the cannons roaring yesterday evning. I cant tel how long we shal stay here. We all want to come back to NC again for we dont get as much to eat here as we did there. We have drawn some now. William Pool says he will rite you a letter today. He is as wicked as ever. A.J. Stutts is well. Jones dear brother I hav prayd for you and I hop you will quit all of your wicked ways and try to serv the Lord for the time to come. Tel Isaac to rite to me. I rote to him and I got no answer. I must close by saying may the Lord bles and sav us all forever. Fairwell. Matthew C. Yow

1862, June 15

Louis H. McLeod (*Camp Lamb*) to wife **Eliza Jane Walker McLeod**. General wartime correspondence with brief mentions of **Stonewall Jackson, Henry ?, Ary ?, Nelse ?, Anjalette McLeod, Delilah McLeod, Thomas Bragg McLeod** and **Emily Franklin.** [186]

Mrs. L. H. McLeod, Dear Madam I seat myself to drop you a few lines to let you know that I am yet spaired breath amongst the brave ones of good old North Carolina sons are [torn] but it has been all I could do the last week but I am up and first rate to day. I have had the bowel complaine until I have worne it out or verry near it. On last Friday about [torn] oclock we got orders to move to Virginia [torn] at nine that knight the train blew a long whistle and [torn] went with the train and the fools all hollering you ever heard they done it. but that is the case with every regiment that goes by hear. Myself and twenty one of the company was left besides what was in the horspittal [there] is some of our men mending verry [torn] I think we will leave here sometime[next] week to follow the regiment. Eliza dont let this alarm you at all it is just the place we have been wanting [torn] to for sometime I understood we would [torn] Stonewall Jackson Peace will bee made in a week or too England and France has declared the Southern Independence and will bee over on the Southern shours [torn] a few days so the Richman Dispatch says [torn] the fourteenth. I red that much to day Eliza I am in hopes you have got all of your wheet saved and you corn [is] in good fix Tell Henry and Ary and Nelse I am coming home about the [torn] of August and I want to see some [of] the best corn in that plantation & that I will see while I will bee up there [torn] everry thing in good fix and the hogs fat and a plenty to eat on the table [when] I set down. For there will bee no telling [how] much I can eat when it is put on a [table] and I have a chair to set on Eliza you ought to see our table we have had [to eat] offten since we have been hear it is [torn] such a one as your old meete bench [in the] smokehouse only a little wider and [torn] bit as greasy and dirty and moore [torn] than seemed ever to bee in the wirld [torn] saw the life in my life. No moore to [torn] only tell Sis she ought to come down and keep the flies of the table while Im eating my bite. Tell the children all [howdy] Tell Anja and Lila and Bragg to learn [torn] books and to learn to write and when [torn] home I will send them all to school but they must keepe trying at home [torn] they can learn some and & everry bit is a help as the old woman said she pissed in the sea give my respects to Emely and all enquiring girls and [tell] them I will come home as soon as I can— I ever remain your sincear and loving husband untill the last breath [of] my one life good by Eliza Your husband. My hand for ever

1862, June 15
Martha Sullivan to **A.S. Caddell**. General wartime correspondence. [187]

Dear absent Friend[,] I hav taken my seat once to answer your letter which came safe as Sam time since it found me enjoying myself very well and I truly hope when these lines comes to hand[,] they may find you enjoying good health[.] I nothing worth responding to you[.] times are very troublesome heare tho I am getting so that I can bear with troubles right & well[.] I am geting along first rate[.] I would bee glad to see you if it so that I could[.] I will liv in hopes if I die in despaire I no I will as no of[.] well I would like to no what yours are doing at your home these days[.] if you see eney fun ar not[.] I quit this subject and begin on something worse[.] I want to no where you are at for dont no where to rite to[.] you must excuse me for not writing to beefore now for I did no where to write to[.] I heard that you was gon from Kinston...but I hear that I am not going[,] but I think that you will heare from mee as soon as you want to[.] I wont you to write to me since I must come to a close[.] excuse bad writing for I am in a [.] there is no person nose when I am riting this. Marth Sullivan

1862, June 16-17
J.L. Stuart (*Petersburg, VA*) to mother **Mary A. Harper** and brother **Charles Harper**. General wartime correspondence with brief mentions of **David S. Barrett, Joseph Fry, Neill Fry** and **Fox**. [188]

Dear mother[,] I once more take to my seat to writ to you to inform you that I am in the land of the living yet I am not very strong yet[.] But I have got to the regt[.] we are stationd about ½ a mile from the edge of the city of Petersburge[.] this is the Best town I ever saw[.] I left the hospital Saturday evening at 8 oclock and landed at the camp about 12[.] They was very glad to see me[.] D.S. Barett was as glad as any of them[.] I thought if I staid at thesick hole I was in[,] I should take some kind of a disease so I thought I would leave there[.] 3 & 4 died a day. I truly hope these lines will reach yourself alive and better than you was than the last account I had[.] the regt got orders to be ready to march in 2 hours or 9 oclock[.] I recon I shall stay if they leave their tents[.] I do not know where they will go[.] some says to NC[,] some says to city point[.] I have seen a great Deal since I left home. June 17 I have just taken a fine batc of catfish & corn bread. I stand sentinel today[.] our regiment march for city point or some whare else yesterday with two days rations[.] about 11 oclock yesterday I heard heavy firing of canon[.] I went to the Dr yesterday morning and told him I was just from the hospital & he said go stay in your quarters to day[.] in about 1 hour orders came for us to cook two days rations[.] I made myself contented[.] 12 of us staid in camp[,] 9 sick. 3 on guard[.] we are told that our Boys camped in 1 1/2 miles of the enemy[.] the 48th went also[.] I understand that we must go to Stonewall[.] 49th 48th & 24th NC[,] we will do them some for Jackson taken 3500 prisoners at one point and 1000 at another not long since[.] it would do me a great deal of good to receive a letter from you[.] I told David Barett that mother wrote to me that she was almost dead[,] that that she was going blind and that she wanted to see me one time more. well sayes he John[,] you could a got off better at the hospital than you can here[.] it is a hard thing to get away from here[.] I think it made him sorry but never mind mother[.] I think I will get to come after awhile and then I will tell you more than you have any idea off[.] I have wrote several letter to you[.] I hope that you will receive them[.] I think we will have peace Before long[.] I want to hear from you all and I want to see you all the rest worst in this world and everbody else that I am acquainted with[.] Joseph Fry and Neill and two more are in the hospital at Petersburg & Neill has got the fever[,] and they was very bad off[.] I recon I shall get to shoot at the yankees before long if I do I want to bring one ever[.] When I came in camp I thought they would run me mad[,] they made so much fuss to night[.] we shall have meeting in our street by one of the Co men[.] his name is Fox. I will close[.] I remain your loving son until Death and will remember you also.

Charles Dear Brother[,] I have not forgot you yet & I will say all of you I must send you Howdy and I am four hundred miles from you[.] I wish we all was only four feet apart we would talk and laugh a week without stoping[.] what a time we would have[.] we would Kill old speck and have a pie[.] I will tell you a joke that heard yesterday evening[.] five of us was in a tent and a little boy came in and got to talking[,] and one of us asked him how many single men they was in the tent[,] he pointed his finger at one and said you are married & done the same at two more[,] and turned to me and said you are not married[,] and we wanted to know which was the best looking man and he looked at me and said this is the best looking man[.] I had the joke then[.] When this you see[,] remember me and tell all my friends Howdy[.] tell them to write to me. J.L. Stuart

1862, June 19
Matthew C. Yow (*Petersburg, VA*) to his wife **Nancy Catherine Albright Yow** and children. General wartime correspondence with brief mentions of his brother-in-law **John E. Albright** and father-in-law **Joseph Albright.** [189]

Deer Wife and Little Children[,] By the kind hand of Providence I sit down to rite you a few lines to let you no that I am well at present hoping when this comes to hand it may find you injoying the same great blesing. On Monday the 16 we got orders to march. We marht about 12 miles to City Point and took up camp at dark. Company D with 3 other companys was orderd down to the river on picket which we did and stayd nearly all night. We could here the Yankie pickets hollow all night. We went back to our camp and eat our crackers and broild beef for our brakefast then we was orderd to march down to the river to attack the Yankies which we did. We had 2 peaces of artlery. Tha fired on the gun boats and fired about 2 hours and tha commenct sheling of us so hard that our major orderd us to retreat which we did in double quick time. The shels was bursting all around us but nobody was hurt vary bad. I was sorter scard when tha fel so fast. We got back to our camp the 18 all tired and hungry. I expect we shal hav to go back before long and try them again. Catharine I cant tel you all this time your brother John come to see me last Sunday. He was well. I want to go to see them if I can. Catharine I hav bin looking for a letter from you. I want to be at home so bad now to see you all and help you save the wheet and eat peas and onions but I cant come yet. I hav to stay here in trouble. But I do hope and pray that I will get home to see you and the deer little children again. I believ you are praying for me and I hope your prares will be herd. Catharine dont greav so much about me for I do hope and pray that I will come to you again. I want you to rite soon and let me no how you are geting along with the wheet and the oats. I will rite evry chanc I get. I want to here from you every day if I could. I rote your father a letter the 15. I must close for this time. When this you see[,] remembr me tho often times I think of you. M.C. Yow

1862, June 22
Leonard W. Lawhon (*Postmaster, Lawhons Hill, Moore County, NC*) to **Governor Henry Toole Clark**. Correspondence notifying the Governor of **Alexander Wallace** and **Isham Wallace** desertion from their companies. [190]

Governor Clark[.] sir, this is to inform you that there is two men that has left the camps on furlows[.] the time is out and they will not return (viz Alexander Walis & Isom Walis)[.] they are in this neighborhood[.] Alexander belongs to Col. Vance's ridgement Capt. Martins company[.] I think had left before the battle of newbern[.] We the citizens of the neighborhood simply wish to be instructed what to do with them[.] your most obedient, L.W. Lawhon, Postmaster at Lawhons Hill

1862, June 22
Louis H. McLeod (*near Richmond, VA*) to wife **Eliza Jane Walker McLeod.** General wartime correspondence with brief mentions of **John W. Thomas, Captain Grissom, Captain Holmes, Dennis Carr, Benjamin Gunter, Dillon Morris, David H. Sloan** and **Anjalette McLeod.** [191]

Dear and Loving Wife, Once moore I seat myself to answer you Verry kind and welcom letter that come to hand yesterday eavening which I read with the greatest anxiety. I have been looking for a letter from you for sometime. Eliza oftimes do I think of thee tho manny miles apart we bee. I left Wilmington on the too oclock train last Wednesday and on thirsday at ten oclock I was in Richman distance too hundred and fifty miles. I was not able at the time to come on with the regiment so I was left with the sick at Wilmington. I got furlough for all that was sick much and sent them home and myself and six others came on to our company. We are stationed about too miles east from Richman on a rocky hill side it is so steep when we ly down to sleep the next mourning we have sliped out of the tent. We are all over in amongst the yankees here and any quantity I expect. But of all the men I ever saw we have got them here, the hole face of the land is covered with men and tents horses and wagons. The land is in a perfect wirk with them. We are stationed within too miles of the yankee picket line where they are shooting at each other everry day and some killing on each side but we get the best of them everry time. I havent done any duty since I came here. Our men and the rest of the division had to go on picket last Saturday mourning and wont get off untill twelve to day Monday. The yankees commenced bombarding them in the four part of the day and late in ther eavening they poored shell grape and canister on them like all rain for about one hour. The balls sung all round them in all direction They were fighting across a swamp our men could not see the yankees so they did not shoot and god would have it non of our little company was just one ball struck John W. Thomas on his blanket that was roaled up and was hung on his back but did not hurt him. The shell burst all over and around them. There was three of our regiment wounded. Cpt Grissom was shot through the right shoulder one Lieutent Pitt was struck in the back with part of a shell the round part struck next to him so it cripper him but verry little. There was one of Cpt. Holmes men shot through the right arm that was all the damage that was don on our side There was several of the yankees that we know was killed. One of our men Dennis Car killed as dead as hector it is the thickest swamp I ever saw where our picket line is there came orders down the line to put out twenty of our men as scurmishers advance fifty yards in the swamp and Car was one of thes men he sliped in to his post as easy as he could and the reckly he saw a yankee climming a tree about fifty yards of him with his gun in his hand so Car lade his gun up against a saplis and droped him off like a squirrel. That was all the fire that was made by our men up to twelve oclock yesterday. I went down there to see them and to take some provisions for the Captian and Lieutenants but I did not feel able to stay out in the hot sun and the knight air untill I get stronger. I havent herd from thim since I left them at twelve yesterday I am looking for them everry minnet. Our men came in so I had to stop writing to hear the nuse. They had it hot and heavy Sunday eavening but as God would have it none of them got hurt. They think they killed some twelve or fifteen of the enemy. I thought I would close my letter in the eavening but the firing commenced of a new in the eavening. The long rool was beat all hans that was well enough to fight was in ranks and off we went to a battry some mile from the camp. The firing ceaced so we came back to our tents and it rain verry hard through the knight and just about day this mourning the firing commenced again. Just like burning a read pack we havent heard any thing from them since our boys left. We have too hundred and thirty thousand men round about Richman no moore about the war. Ben Gunter came over to see us last Friday and stade all day he is stationed too miles from us Ben is well and as fat as he can bee he looks better than I ever saw him only he is verry badly sun burnt for they are exposed to all the son and rain their regiment havent had a tent since March Ben has seen hard times in the servis and has been in too battles. There is a good manny men here that we know Dillarn Morris and D. Sloan is close to us but we havent see them yet No moore about the times here only we get a plenty of meat and bread to eat meat is worth sixty cents per pound coffee too dollars and a half sugar eighty cents per pound every thing is very high Eliza direct your letters to Richman Virginia I ever remain your loving husband Louis H. McLeod

Analett I receave your letter which I was mooore than glad to hear and see a letter form you to see how you had improved in writing I want you to continue to write and what ever you do learn to spell That is the main thing in writing Anja I was glad to hear you was getting along with the crop so well and the oats was so good I want you to ceep everry thing moving I will right a gain soon L.H. McLeod

1862, June 22
Jane McIntosh (*Moore County, NC*) to uncle **A.S. Caddell**. General wartime correspondence between niece/uncle with brief mentions of church at Bethlehem, Mrs. **Person**, **Charles Sowell, Devotion Davis** and **Samuel J. McIntosh**. [192]

Dear uncle[,] it is with pleasure that I seat myself to drop you a few lines to inform you that I am in the land of the living yet[,] and in first rate health[.] and I hope that these few lines may reach you will and find you enjoying the same like blessing[.] I have no news to write that would interest you any[.] I received your very kind letter and was glad to hear from you that you was well[.] I have nothing funy to write[.] I see some fun but it is sutch that it would not be funny to go so far[.] well Tim you said that there was one of your Regs. married the other day[.] well I think his bride must have been a rite sort of principaled lady but every to there own notion as the old woman said[.] and you said you wanted me to tell you about our Sunday School[.] we have a very nice school especialy the female class[.] me and Mrs Persons take the Bible class[.] the males has not got up to it yet but I think they will all work together for good[,] that we will have a good school but it will not do if do not Charles Sowell is superentender[.] Well Tim you just ought to be hear[.] there is the most pretty girls comes[.] you ever went anywhere to stay all night[,] they come far and near[.] I wrote to you and sent by D. Davis and I put one in it for S.J.Mc. and I have not got no answer yet[.] what is the mater[?] I do not know[.] I want you to write and let me know whether he is a writing or not[,] if you can find out[.] I take you as a sincere friend and please find out if you can[,] and let me know just how he seemes or if you have heard him say anything about me[.] pleas let me know every thing[.] you can find out for if it does no good[.] it will do no harm as the old women said when she greesed the the old man for the fish bone[.] if he has quit writing[,] he may think I can get no one else[,] but as the proverb says the love of one is the gain of two and choice out of twenty more[.] you must not let him nor no one else know that I wrote this to you[.] if you do[,] it will caus me to be thought hard of[.] I would like to see you the best in the world[.] I could tell you a heap of funy things[.] your jularkys is well so far as I know[.] at least they look like they was there one in particular[.] she lookes the best I ever saw her look and I expect that is the one you would like to hear from[.] so as I have nothing of importance to write[,] I will close by saying please excuse all mistakes and bad writing and spelling[.] write soon and give me all the news if any[.] so nothing more. I remain your affectionate niece. Jane McIntosh

1862, June 22
A.S. Caddell (*Petersburg, VA*) to Miss **Martha M. Sullivan**. General personal correspondence with brief mentions of battles and **S.D. Crook** and **W.L. Sullivan**. [193]

Miss Martha, I recd your kind letter this morning & now have the pleasure of answering your responce[.] I am in possesion of good health hoping this will find you well[.] I have no interesting news more than we have left Old N.C.[.] I was truly sorry to leave my native state though we had a pleasant ride[.] we landed safe at this place last night[.] we expect to leave here in the morning bound for Richmond[.] there is no doubt but what we will have fighting to do in a few days[.] I met with several of my old friends today[.] I saw SD Crook and others that I was happy to meet with[.] I wish I could see you and spend a few hours with you[.] Oh, it would be pleasant but I fear the time of our meeting is far distant if even the happyness I once enjoyed[.] how sweet there memory still but this season of joy is past[.] I fear to return now or when you hear from me again[,] I have no doubt you will hear of my being in a battle[.] I hope you will remember me in your petitions at the throne of grace[.] I will close[.] write soon[.] please dont be so long next time[.] tell WL I wrote to him sometime ago and recd no answer[.] I also sent one to you in it[.] I recon it long lost[.] Yours, A.S. Caddell

1862, June 19
Matthew C. Yow (*Petersburg, VA*) to his wife **Nancy Catherine Albright Yow** and children. General wartime correspondence with brief mentions of his brother-in-law **John E. Albright** and father-in-law **Joseph Albright**. [194]

Deer Wife and Little Children[,] By the kind hand of Providence I sit down to rite you a few lines to let you no that I am well at present hoping when this comes to hand it may find you injoying the same great blesing. On Monday the 16 we got orders to march. We marht about 12 miles to City Point and took up camp at dark. Company D with 3 other companys was orderd down to the river on picket which we did and stayd nearly all night. We could here the Yankie pickets hollow all night. We went back to our camp and eat our crackers and broild beef for our brakefast then we was orderd to march down to the river to attack the Yankies which we did. We had 2 peaces of artlery. Tha fired on the gun boats and fired about 2 hours and tha commenct sheling of us so hard that our major orderd us to retreat which we did in double quick time. The shels was bursting all around us but nobody was hurt vary bad. I was sorter scard when tha fel so fast. We got back to our camp the 18 all tired and hungry. I expect we shal hav to go back before long and try them again. Catharine I cant tel you all this time your brother John come to see me last Sunday. He was well. I want to go to see them if I can. Catharine I hav bin looking for a letter from you. I want to be at home so bad now to see you all and help you save the wheet and eat peas and onions but I cant come yet. I hav to stay here in trouble. But I do hope and pray that I will get home to see you and the deer little children again. I believ you are praying for me and I hope your prares will be herd. Catharine dont greav so much about me for I do hope and pray that I will come to you again. I want you to rite soon and let me no how you are geting along with the wheet and the oats. I will rite evry chanc I get. I want to here from you every day if I could. I rote your father a letter the 15. I must close for this time. When this you see[,] remembr me tho often times I think of you. M.C. Yow

1862, June 22
William Wadsworth Shields (*Confederate Hospital, Petersburg, VA*) to brother **Duncan P. Shields**. General wartime correspondence with brief mention of being in the hospital at Petersburg and **Hagins**, **Stewart**, **Richard Goins**, and their parents **Benjamin J. Shields** and **Mariah Shields**. [195]

Dear Brother, it is the greatest of pleasure that I do drop you theas few lines[,] but not so good a nuse to rite you but I cant help it[.] I am sick and in the hospital at Petersburg[.] Dunk[,] I would a rote you before now[.] I got sick 4 or 5 days a go and then we moved[.] old Hagins hauled me to sity pint an rack[.] an our brigade was ordred to Richmond[.] I ant in no pane a tall[.] I am just weeke, our doctor told me he though it was the dirair I had[.] he though mi hed is dub wase & swimming[.] I like the place where I am very well and the rest of it shot is with me[.] an Stuard out of our Co is with me to and Rich Goins[.] So I must close[.] I will rite oftan an let you here[.] don't be oneasy for God is just as ni me here as there[.] any take it and rite[.] give me love to Pap an Mard an to Sim an to any of me friends. Bill Shields

1862, June 22
Matthew C. Yow (*Petersburg, VA*) to his wife **Nancy Catherine Albright Yow** and children. General wartime correspondence with brief mentions of **Christopher Columbus Harrison**, grandfather **Andrew Yow**, **Nancy Harrison**, brothers-in-law **Henry A. Albright**, **John E. Albright,** his brother **Simeon Jones Yow** and son **William Henry Yow.** [196]

Deer Wife and Little Children[,] By the kind hand of Providence I one more time take my pen in hand to inform you that I am well at present hoping when this comes to hand it may find you all injoying the same great blesing. I receivd your kind letter the 21 which giv me great satisfaction to here from you all again and to here that you was all well but I was sorrow to hear that the wheet was so sorry. I am afraid you will not hav enough for bread but you must take good cear of it and do the best you can for I hope and pray to the Lord that I will get home again to see you and my poor little children. I want to see you all so bad it seems like I cant bare it. I red your letter and tears dropt from my eyes all the time. Catharine I expect we shal hav another battle before long[;] for the last week there has come 6 or 7 regiments here from NC and tha keep coming. The 26 has just come this morning. That is the one Columbus Harrison is in but I hav not bin to them. Catharine I expect we shal hav to leav here before long. We are orderd to cook three days rations and I no we will hav to leav. I expect there will be a big battle before long and I hope that will end the war. If it dont stop before long we shal all suffer at home and in the army. Catharine I told you not to greav but you say you cant help it. I no you cant for I am in as much trouble as anybody ever was but I put my trust in the good Lord. Catharine I hav prayd all the time that I might be savd and get home to my wife and poor little children. For I do want to see them so bad I dont no what to do. Catharine I believ you are praying for me. Dear wife pray on and if I never see you on earth any more I hope we will meet in haven where we will part no more. Catharine I shed tears of greaf evry day. Catharine I dont no what to rite for I am in a great deal of trouble about you and the poor little children for I am afraid I never shal see you all again. I am riting today. It is the Sabbath. I got fathers letter when I got yours. I want to rite to you both today if I can. I must stop and go to preaching. We hav preaching evry Sunday. I hav bin to preaching and I will try to rite some more. Catharine tel old granfather that I want to see him mity bad. I am glad to here that he is well and that he is praying for me. I hope and pray to the Lord that his prares will be answerd and tell Nancy that Columbus is here now and is well. I expect we will all hav to fight together. It is hard to think of but I will put my trust in the good Lord. Catharine I rote you a letter about our battle on James River but let that not scear you. But we was all in a close place. The shels was bursting all over us like thunder but we all escapt unhurt but I cant tel how it will be next time. I thought I would go and see Henry and John today but I cant go today. I must rite to you and the children for it may be the last time but I hope not. I want you to rite to me as often as you can and I will do the same. Jones I want you to stay at home if there is any chanc for I dont want you to come to this bad place. Do the best you can. I hope I shal come to see you all again. Jones I am in trouble but I put my trust in the Lord. I read your letters and cry all the time. Rite soon and fail not. I was glad to here that you was geting along so well with your crop. I remain your brother until death[,] so fairwell. Catharine I must say a word to you and my deer little children. Dear wife continue your prares for me. You may be sure I hav not forgotten you. William Henry[,] be a good boy. May the Lord bles the children. I must close. My hart is ful so fairwell deer wife and children. Matthew C. Yow

1862, June 22
Joel J. Lawhon (*Confederate Hospital, Petersburg, VA*) to cousin **Duncan P. Shields**. General wartime correspondence with brief mention of being in the hospital at Petersburg and **William Wadsworth Shields, Ann McLauchlin Shields** and **Lewis Lawhon**. [197]

Dear Cousin, I will drop you a few lines in your bro. Bill's letter[.] we are in the Confederate Hospital in Petersburg[.] We both got here yesterday. Bill came from his Regt. And I came from Blacks & Whites Hospital. The Dr. sent me here to try and get a furlough but I can as yet tell nothing about it. It maybe a week or two before I find out whether I get one or not. I am improving but I am very feeble yet. Bill is very sick but I hope it is nothing more than a bowel complaint. Dunk[,] I will stop writing as I want this to start in the morning mail. Give my love to Ann and father and family, also to all my relations. Please write soon. I remain your affectionate cousin. J.J. Lawhon [Confederate Hospital, Petersburg, VA, in care of Dr. Claiborne]

1862, June 23

Daniel McIntosh and **William A. McIntosh** (*Moore County, NC*) to uncle **A.S. Caddell**. General wartime correspondence with brief mention of **C.D. Caddell** and of his father **William Caddell** being ill. [198]

I seat myself to answer your very kind letter of the 10th which you gave us satisfaction to hear that you was well and hope that this will find you well and doing well[.] we are all in tollerable helth at present[.] tho a good smart chance of grass to contend with the wet wether help us out of our crops untill the grass got the start of us[;] since we havnt got it in rite order since our corn looks the sorrowest you ever saw and our wheat was spoiled with the rust[.] and crops is ginerly so with very few exceptions and oats is also injured with rust [.]C.D. got rite smart of corn washed up with the fresh and the land injured[.] a good deal people is of the opinion now that they wont make enough to do them in this settlement tho I hope that crops will come out yet[.] peoples wheat was about half filled and had fell so that they ondly could gather about half of it[.] they have made about one fourth of a crop of wheat tho there is some few crops that is no good as common where the rust did not hurt it[.] youre Papy has bin very porly all this Spring[.] he has not been able to do anything and sometimes hardly able to come up to see us tho he is as pirt as could be expected now[.] the sore has got rite smart larger since you was here[.] he may out live many of us tho at the same time I shouldnt be supprised to here of his deth at any time[.] the rest of them is in good helth and doing very well[.] So not having anything new to wright I shall close by telling you to wright soon and give us all the news[.] So I remain yourse respectfully, Danl McIntosh

Dear uncle[,] it is with pleasure that I take the present opportunity of dropping you a few lines to let you know that I am well at present hoping that these may find you well[.] I have nothing mutch to write ondley I was with some rite purty galls yesterday[.] you just ought to have bin with me[.] I saw a right smart of fun[.] I received your letter the other day for the first one since I saw you and I hav wrote three or four to you[.] you said something about the baked turkey[.] I hav got in to another one of them and of them purty little gals since I saw you but wee did not see as mutch fun as we did when you was ther[,] but wee saw a right smart of fun[.] wee had the same crowd of gals[.] you said something about your horse[.] he works splendid[;] he is more of a horse than he was when you wase at home[.] I think that if you would listen right good some day when I go to mill that you could hear him squeal a way down to your house[.] you must wright soon and giv me all the nuse[.] our paper said that it was reported that the frintch had declared the south independent and I hope that it is so[,] for I will come to a close by saing wright soon as you get this[.] yourse affectionately, Wm. A. McIntosh

1862, July 4

Matthew C. Yow (*Petersburg, VA*) to his wife **Nancy Catherine Albright Yow** and children. General wartime correspondence with brief mentions of the Seven Days Battle, the death of **Isaac Brady** and wounds received by **Andrew John Stutts**, Lt. **John H. Anderson**, Maj. **Benjamin R. Huske** and brief mentions father **Henry C. Yow**, brothers-in-law **Henry A. Albright, John E. Albright,** his brothers **Simeon Jones Yow, Isaac Yow and John Francis Williamson.** [199]

Dear Wife and Little Children[,] By the kind hand of Providence I take my pen in hand to rite you a few lines to let you no that I am well and unhurt yet and I do hope these lines may find you injoying the same great blesing. I receivd your kind letter today. It giv me great plesure to here from you all one time more. I must tel you about my travels for the last ten days. We left Petersburg the 24 and went to Richmond and Wensday the 25 we went into the battle field and about one hour by sun in the evning we had a hard battle. We had five hundred men and we fought five thousand 25 minuts when we was orderd to retreat and then the Georgians come in and helped us and we drove them back. We lost one hundred and four of our regiment kild and wonded 20 kild and 84 wonded. A.J. Stuts got his leg broke by a ball and it had to be cut off. Isaac Brady was kild dead on the field. Our captain was badly wonded in the thigh and Lieutenant Anderson was wonded in leg. Major Husk wonded in the foot. I can tel you it was an awful sight. We kild a heep of the Yankies. I some of them lying on the field on Friday after the battle. I shot 6 times at them with good aim. I expect I kild some body and I dont want to fight anymore. That was enough for me. I suppose we hav taken a hundred pecies of artilary in the 8 days fiting and we hav whipt them all out from there and I dont no were tha will try next. We hav evry place ful of prisnors. We 25 or 30 thousand. Some of them come and giv them selvs up. Some thinks tha wont fight much more. I hope tha will not. Catharine I no you think I am ded for I haint had no chanc to rite tel now. I got fathers letter to day and all them you sent. Your brothers is both alive and well. John was here when I was reding your letter. He said he rote you a letter. He said he was noch dow by a bom shel. Catharine you said tha had savd all the wheet and you must pay the hands for there work. I was glad to here that the grain was all cut and in the barn. I red all of the letters and shed many tears. I was seting studing about you and the pore little children when the letters come and I was so glad that sat rite and red them and cried all the time. I no you are in trouble about me for I hav not in many days but dont be troubled for I alive and I thank the Lord for it. For I hav bin praying all the time for the Lord to sav me that I might get home to my wife and blesed little children again and I hope our prares hav herd and answerd. Tel my poor old granfather that I hav not forgoten him yet. I want to see him mity bad. Tel him to pray for me. I do hope and pray to the Lord that I shal see you all again in this world. I hope we will get back to NC again before long I hope. I hope that times will get better and I can get to come home to see you all again. Catharine tel father that I will rite to him before long. We are not at Petersburg now. We are about 11 miles from there on the rode a resting. I think we will go back to our camp before long. Send your letters to Petersburg VA General Walkers Brigade[,] Co D[,] 48 regiment[,] NC Troops. We joined another brigade. Colonel Hill and General Ransom fel out and he left him. Jones I will rite to you before long when I get back to the camp and if you hav to come I want you to come to me. Tel Isaac the same but stay if you can. So deer brother Fairwell. M.C. Yow. John Williamson says he wants his people to rite to him. Catharine my deer wife I must a word to you. Continue your prars for me. I am praying all the time. Lord, save us all I pray. We hav to march now. So fairwell deer wife and little children. Matthew C. Yow

1862, July 8
Noah Deaton (*Richmond, VA*) to father **William Deaton**. General wartime correspondence with mentions of travels from Kinston, Petersburg and Richmond, skirmishes and injuries to Captain Thomas Clegg and Raleigh Allen. [200]

Dear father[,] this morning affords me an opportunity of drop in you a few line which I hope will find you all well[.] my health is tolerable good except that I feel very much jaded and worn out from much loss of sleep and fatigue[.] we are about 6 miles east of Richmond fronting the enemy[.] we left Kinston, NC and came to Petersburg, VA and left all our tents there and all of our surpus baggage[.] there is heavy skirmishing here everyday and night[.] we have been in several skirmishes since we came here but luckily none of our compnay has been killed yet[,] though teo are wounded slightly[.] we were about 2 days and nights without daring to close our eyes for sleep for us and the enemy were firing on each other at every corner and form behind trees[.] we have driven the enemy into to their trenches but it take much force to keep them back[.] there are 4 moore county compnays here and all have had fighting[.] Capt Clage got his thigh broke and Raleigh Allen was hit a glancing shot on the neck but only inflicted a slight wound[.] it is impossible for me to give you a satisfactory account of the state of thing here[.] our men has gined a great victory on the line north of us[,] capturing about 100 cannon and several thousand prisioners[,] sweeping everythign before them[.] there is a general engagement expected every hour[.] here may god help us and save from the hand of the enemy and protect us from all the dangers that surround us and save us in heaven for christ sake[.] I wish I could write more but the mail is going to start and I must stop short off[.] I cannot tell you whether it is worth will to write or not for it is doubtful whether it would come or not[.] your affectionate son[.] Noah Deaton [P.S.] if you write address Co H[,] 26 Regt[,] NCT, 1st NC Brigade, Richmond, VA

1862, July 10
J.L. Stuart (*near Richmond, VA*) to mother **Mary A. Harper**. General wartime correspondence. [201]

My Dear Mother[,] thanks Be to God I am a live yet and with my co. I think that I am taking the mumps[.] I hope that this will reach you all doing well[.] I received a letter about 4 Days ago which gave me great satisfaction to hear that you all was yet a live[.] But very sorry to hear your condition[.] I cannot write half what I want to and if I was at home I could not tell with my tongue[.] I have been in a battle or so we left Petersburg less than two week ago on Wednesday about nine o'clock attention to forwards march[.] you never heard such a volley after volley about a mile[.] I recon I expected to be marched right to firing[.] we went by the breast work a double quick[.] no one could tell my feelings the distant roar of canon[.] we went about ½ mile and we was ordered to be down[.] we did it the quickest you ever saw[.] the gen came and ordered us double quick to about 3 or 4 hundred yards to our right[.] the enemy was trying to flank us so we got in an old road and lay flat down and staid tell about sundown[.] the balls would whistle by us[.] the bombs would fall about 3 & 4 hundred yard off[.] some burst over us[.] it was terrible to new hands[.] the wounded was Brought by us but not very many[.] there was skirmishes until Sunday[.] the 26th NC. passed the enemy Breast works[.] no enemy there[,] But lots of plunder commissary & we followed on after the enemy[.] Sunday and Tuesday night come on them

1862, July 10

Matthew C. Yow (*Petersburg, VA*) to his wife **Nancy Catherine Albright Yow** and children. General wartime correspondence with brief mentions of the Seven Days Battle, the death of **Capt. Thomas J. Clegg** and wounds received by **Andrew John Stutts** and brief mentions of Capt. **James C. Dowd**, father **Henry C. Yow**, grandfather **Andrew Yow** and brother **Simeon Jones Yow.** [202]

Dear Wife and Dear Little Children[,] I one time more take my pen in hand to rite you a few lines to let you no that I am well at present and unhurt and I do hope when this comes to hand it may find you all in good helth. I receivd your letters of the 28 the 4 of July and I no that you hav sent me a letter but I hav not got it yet. I expect tha hav gon to Ransoms brigade and I am afraid that I will not get them. We belong to Walkers brigade now. We are at our camp at Petersburg. I want to here from you all vary bad. We hav to pay 10 cents on a letter now but I rite as long as I can get any money. I am scears of money now. I think we shal get some money before long. I want you to rite as often as you can. I will send you some stamps if I can to mail letters. Catharine I no you was uneasy about me but I went through safe thank the lord. I praid for the Lord to save me and I hope my prares was herd. The balls came as thick as hail around me but none of them hit me. I no you hav red about the battle. The line of battle is said to be 15 miles long. I wish you could see what I hav seen. It is awful to think of to see dead men lying all over the ground not buried and a great many of them was never buried at all. I saw some that had bin dead 2 days the same ones we kild. I must you that Captain Clegg is dead. James Dowd will be our capt now. I do hop and pray that the war will soon close so I can come home to see you all again. I do want to see you all so bad. It fils my hart when I try to rite to rite to you but I hop the good Lord will be with me to the end. Catharine your brothers come out safe. John said he rote you a letter before the battle. A.J. Stuts was wonded and he is at Richmond in the hospital. His leg was cut off. I am mity sorrow for him. Catharine I am afraid that Jones will hav to leav you. I hav herd that the conscript will hav to come the 15 of this month. I do hope he will not. I dont think tha can mak them come. If I was there I wold try them awhile. Any how Jones stay if you can for I want you to stay with my wife and little children til I come back. Jones I believ you are good to them and will tak cear of them. I do want to come home so bad to get somthing to eat. I want beans and potatoes and milk and butter. We cant get these things here. Butter is one dollar a pound. Tobacco 5 cents a plug. Milk 10 cents a quart. Catharine I want you to rite to me all about your things how tha are geting along. You dont no how bad I want to see you. I do hope and pray that I can com home again to see you and the blesed little children. It seems like I could take them all in my arms at one time. Lord bles and save my dear wife and little children. May the good Lord bles and sav us all forever is my prare. Direct your letters to Petersburg VA[,] General Walkers brigade[,] 48 regiment[,] NC Troops[,] Co D in cear of Capt Dowd. Catharine do the best you can and be saving with what you hav got. Take good of your wheet. Dont sell none of the wheet if you can help it. Keep it for bread. I do hope I can come home before long. Some says the last battle is fought and I think tha will giv furlows after a while. Tha wont give none now. Catharine giv my best respect to all of my friends and relations. Tel father to rite when he can for it revivs me when I get your letters. Tell old granfather that I hav not forgoten him yet. Tel him to pray for me. Catharine I must close for this time. Pray for me and I hope and believ your prares will be answerd. May the Lord bles and save us all. So fairwell for this time[.] Nancy C. Yow M.C. Yow

1862, July 10

A.S. Caddell (*Petersburg, VA*) to Miss **Martha M. Sullivan**. General personal correspondence with brief mention of **S.D. Crook** and **C.D. Caddell**. [203]

Miss Martha, I devote theses few lines to this to let you know that I am in possesion of usul health[,] truly hoaping this will find you enjoying good health[.] this is the second letter that I have written sine I have heard from you[.] I would like to hear much oftiner from you than I do though you may not have a good chance to write[.] If I knew this was the case I would be satisfied. Miss M[,] we have had a great battle and have been fortunate in whipping the great army of McLeland[.] I was not in the battle[.] I was attending to a team at Petersburg[.] I am still remaining at this place[.] I cannot tell when I will have the pleasure of joining my company again though I hope it will not be long[.] none of our co was killed[,] four or five of them was likely wounded[.] the general impression of the people about here is that this war will soon close[.] I hope their conjectures are true[.] These is six co. here from Moore County[.] I saw S.D. Crook & many others of my acquaintance which I was glad to meet with[.] I am getting impatient to Return back to NCarolina[.] This part of the woods I dont like[.] I hope we will be ordered back there soon[.] I suppose the conscripts has to leave there the 15th of this month[.] I know they dread to see that day arrive and I can not blame them for a soldiers life is dreadful[.] you must write to me as soon as they all leave and let me know if they left in good spirits[.] you must let me know how I must arrange my letters to get them to you for if C.D. has to leave I will be without a confidant[.] let me know if their is any person that you would be wiling for me to make my confidential friend[.] if not I shal be at a loss what to do and I fear you will be in the same condition[.] I cannot tell you how glad I would be to see you and spend a few hours in your presence though the prospects of our meeting soon is gloomy yet[.] as you said in your last letter I will live in hopes if I die in despir[.] I have bloched my papper so bad that I must stop for this time[.] write as soon as you get this[.] give me all the news in general[.] Your affectionate friend, A.S. Caddell

1862, July 13
J.L. Stuart (*near Richmond, VA*) to mother **Mary A. Harper** and stepfather **John Harper**. General wartime correspondence with brief mentions of **William Teague, Devotion Davis, Isaac Dunn** and **Silas D. Crook**. [204]

Mr J. Harper & Wife & Family Dear Father & Mother & C: Once moore I take my seat to drop you a few lines to inform you by gods good mercy I am still alive[,] but I have got the mumps[.] I truly hope these few lines will reach you all alive and doing well[.] mother I am very sorry to hear your condition[.] But I hope you will get better[.] I received a letter yesterday Dated June 15th[,] one last Sunday I think dated June 27 & one Friday dated 20 June & one from Wm Teague the same day I have wrote one to you[,] I stated about our fight. I gave it to Devotion Davis last Friday[.] I told him to put it in the office at Carthage as soon as he got there[.] you said that you wanted a pare of spects[.] I wish I could get them But I am 8 miles from Richmond and 12 from Petersburg and it is a bad chance unless I am sent there for some thing for me to get them[,] but may be it will be so I can shortly[.] if I hav them[,] I could send them by Isaac Dunn[.] I saw this by him[.] there is lots of soldiers here or about there. Mr Harper[,] Silas D. Crook sends his Best respects to you. This is Drewys Bluff[.] it is Pretty well fortified with canon[.] I am told it is a mile or so from here[.] the yanks cant do much with their boats[.] the banks is so high they will have to come with in two or 3 hundred yards before they will discover us[.] I think peace is not far off[.] the enemy got such a good whiping at Richmond[.] we folow them twenty miles below Richmond until they got in reach of ther gunboats[.] it was sight ful to look at to see the dead men[.] when I get home I will tell you all about it[.] I want you all to com fort yourselves as well as you can[.] I think and hope peace will come off before long[.] if it does[,] what a happy time there will be over the country. husband will go to their wives, fathers to their children and sons to their parents & Lovers to their sweethearts[.] what an embracing ther will Be & how I wish to see the time[.] I want you to write as often as you can[.] it Does me good to hear from you[.] Direct your letters to Petersburg VA[.] I remain your true son untell Death[,] J.L. Stuart

1862, July 13
J.L. Stuart (*near Richmond, VA*) to cousin **Emily C. Nall**. General wartime correspondence with brief mentions of **John Nall, William Nall, Nicholas Nall, Lydia Williamson Nall, Polly Nall** and **Nancy Nall**. [205]

Miss E. C. Wall and all of you[,] I will say a few words to you[.] I have the mumps at present[.] I hope these few lines will reach you all all well[.] you must excuse me for not writing sooner and a better letter for my chance is bad[.] I want you to write[.] I want to know if John is gone back[,] if Wm is gone into the service[.] I want to see uncle Nick and Aunt Lydia and all the ret[.] I want to know how your crops is & I recon you Dont like to give up your jularks[,] but you and Polly can keep yours[.] But Nancy will have to give up hers[.] I mean the ones you was with that night at our house the night I sliped off out of the shed[.] ha ha ha, We have seen a heap of pleasure together[.] I wish it would be so again[.] I wish I was in moore county to eat apples and c. we have hard times here[.] You have heard me say it was hard times[,] but it was not hard times then[,] but it is now[.] but I hope hard times will be over now[.] write me about the girls and all about ever thing[.] I will write when I have time and paper[.] Direct your letters to Mr J. L. Stuart[,] Petersburg VA[.] 49 regt[,] N.C. Troops in care of Capt W.M. Black[,] Co D[.] tell all my Friends to write to me if they please[.] tell the girls to all to write[.] I must Bring my letter to a close[.] I remain Yours Truly[,] John L. Stuart

1862, July 13
J.L. Stuart (*near Richmond, VA*) to cousins **William Teague** and **Nancy Teague**. General wartime correspondence. [206]

Cousins[,] I will say a word to you[.] I have fought a [.] I am about But I have the mumps[.] I hope these few lines will reach you well and doing well[.] I want you to write to me if you will[.] I am very sorry to here that all the young men has to leave[.] But you must Bare it like I did[.] I hope peace will Be made and that we all can get to go home[.] When this you see[,] remember me though many miles apart we Be[.] I am yours truly[,] J.L. Stuart

1862, July 13
J.L. Stuart (*near Richmond, VA*) to brother **Charles Harper**. General wartime correspondence. [207]

Dear Brother[,] I hope you are Doing well[.] now is the time to fly round go to see the Prettyest girls you Know off[.] it makes one shed tears to read your letter[.] But Do the Best you can and I will[.] tell sis and Granny Howdy[,] tell them to Do the Best they can[.] I want to see you all the worst in this world[,] J L Stuart

1862, July 13
J.L. Stuart (*near Richmond, VA*) to **Cynthia Teague** and **Lydia Comer**. General wartime correspondence with brief mentions of **Henry [?]** and **Archy [?]**. [208]

I have been in the fights[.] we made the yanks go it double quick[.] my jaws look fat with the mumps[.] if I could see you[,] I could tell a big tale[.] now if you know anything about men being shot through the head[,] ther heads shot off[,] some all to pieces and something about bumps a bursting over our heads & ball flying all around and go buzlike bees[.] I hope you are both well[.] I should like to see you all[.] Cyntha[,] I want to know how you and Henry gets along and[,] Lydia[,] I want to Know how you and Archy gets along[.] you all must writeif you will[.] Direct to me Petersburg Va[,] 49 regt[,] N.C.T. in care of cap Wm Black[,] Co D [.]I wish I could write moore But the paper is scarce[.] I must close[.] save me some Apples and Peaches[.] I am yours. J. L. Stuart

1862, July 14
Wm. L. Sullivan and **C.D. Caddell** (*Moore County, NC*) to C.D. Caddell's brother, **A.S. Caddell**. General wartime correspondence with brief mentions of trips to Raleigh and Jonesborough, teaching school, battle at Richmond, **Eli P. Sowell** and **Zacheus Hogans**. [209]

Dear Sir, I seat myself to drop you a few lines in answer to your kind letter which I received sometime ago which I was glad to receive[.] I am sorry to think that I not answered before now[.] I can inform you the conscrips is cald out[.] C.D. Caddell starts tomorrow to Raleigh and I expect to take him to Jonesborough[,] I am sorry to sa so far Neill is my best friend[.] Mr. A.S. Caddell[,] I am teachin School which they say it clares me from the conscription[.] and Mr A.S. you have had big fighting and gaind a larg amount of goods of one sort or other withe your victory[.] I am glad to hear of such a victorious Battle in Richmond VA[.] I have know more to coment to you[.] Mr AS Caddell[,] I would be glad to see you and E.P. Sowell, Z Hogans[.] Mr A.S. I sent you a few lines in Mr Z. Hogans today[.] the conscrips had to leave old Moore and am sorry to see them leave there farms to go to fight insted of farming to make Bred[.] A.S. Caddell[,] I can inform you that I hate for C.D.Caddell to leave his pap and mother but I think he will be sent back to stay with his father[.] he could got of by the school law and other ways besides that of school[.] I wish you and all the rest of the boys could come home and see your friends once moore[.] I must come to a close by saying write soon to your friend, Wm.L. Sullivan. I remain your friend till death[.]

Dear Brother[,] it is with pleasure I seat myself to drop you a few lines[.] I am on my way to Camp Carolina and if you should write[,] I will be at Raleigh[.] I have to leave everything in a bad condition at home[,] but I hope they may get a long[.] Mother and papy said for you to write to them as soon as you get this letter[.] I will write to you as soon as I get to Raleigh[.] I will conclude by saying I hope the time may not be long before I shal see you. I remain your lovin brother[,] CDC

1862, July 19
Rany G. Caddell (*Moore County, NC*) to **A.S. Caddell**. General wartime correspondence between mother/son brief mentions of brother **Neill Caddell,** father **William Caddell, Eli P. Sowell** and **W.H.H. Davis.** [210]

Dear son[,] I take my pen to drop you a few lins to let you know that we are yet a live tho very infirm[.] and I hope when this reaches you this finds you in good health[.] I have no news to write that is good[.] it is all bad with me for Neil is gone and we are in great trouble[.] to think that this cruel war has bereaved us of both our sons and and we are left here alone and o the hard ship and trouble I see[.] I cannot express tho we have good friends and that itself is some consolation[.] I have worked in the field all the spring and summer and am now in my 60th year[.] we are now laying by corn[.] it will be a few weeks before we are done[,] our crop is good tho we had a bad beginning[.] I don't feel afraid but what we shore make a plenty to do us if nothing happens from now. I want you to write to inform me and papa for we have not had a line from you since you left NC[.] your papa can not do annything at all and some knights he dont sleep any at all[.] Tim we would give any thing to see you but as I can not see you[.] I can pray for you and I want you to try to live up to your duty for when you in the path of duty[,] you are in the path of safety[.] be brave and faithfully discharge your duty in all things[.] give my love and and respct to Eli P. Sowell and Harison[.] write soon to your affectionate parent[,] Rany G Caddelll

1862, July 19
Mastin C. Phillips (*Second NC Hospital*) to parents Rev. **Lewis Phillips Jr.** and **Nancy Edwards Phillips.** General wartime correspondence with brief mentions of **Baxter C. Phillips.** [211]

My Dear Parents, I again write a few lines to let you know how I am. I am still in the hospital, but I am improving and I think in a week more I will be able to go to the Regiment, though I am very weak yet. I have not been out of the hospital but once since I cam here, and then I did not get ten steps from the house before I found it necessary to return quick as I could. For the last three days it has been cool and raining and I have kept close. I think when the weather gets fin I will try to stir out. I think it will help me in gaining strength. I received Baxter's letter day before yesterday. I was proud to hear from home, and especially was I rejoiced to hear that Malphus did not have to go with the conscripts. Tell him for me to drive ahead with all the work, for I fear it will be a long, long time before Baxter and I are with you again[,] and it may be that we may never see home again. But I humbly pray that God will see proper to preserve our lives and permit us to return to you all again. There are three of our Co. in this and two in the First Hospital, but all are doing well at this time. The Yankees were terrible beaten in the fight below Richmond. We took nine thousand prisoners, and killed and wounded about twice that number. They acknowledge a loss of 30 thousand. Our loss was very heavy as we had to storm scores of the most destructive [illegible] that ever was erected for man's obstruction. I have had many serious thoughts since I have been sick. I have read my testament and tried to pray a great deal since I have been sick. I think my afflications will be a benefit to me, but I am not satisfied yet. I have not received what I have been praying for. I am afraid I shall become discouraged. I have not been able to exercise living further in God's promises. I beg you all to intercede for me that I may have faith to receive all his precious promises. But goodbye. Mastin [P.S.] I would write more but it tires me so bad that I must stop. I beg you all to pray for me in that I must have religion and shall never stop praying until I get right and my request is answered.

1862, July 20
C.D. Caddell (*Camp Carolina*) to brother **A.S. Caddell**. General wartime correspondence between brothers with brief mentions of **C.D. Caddell's** discharge by **Maj. Mallett** because of their father's **William Caddell** illness and Col. **William B. Richardson.** [212]

Dear and most affectionate Brother[,] I seat myself to drop you a few lines[.] I am well at present hoping these few lines will find you well[.] I have some news to write to you[.] I have got a discharge from the Conscription act[.] I sent in a pertition to Maj. Mallett & he discharged mee on the acct of the condition of papy[.] I shall ever feel under obligations to Col. Richardson for he done all he could to get mee cleard[.] I am a going to start home this morning[.] give my best respects to all the boys in your company and tell them to write to mee[.] Tim this trip has hurt mee $0.50 at least[,] but I am glad to get off at that[.] wee went down an N.C. steamboat and then to Goldsboro and then to Raleigh[.] I saw Sion Ellen and got accuainted with him[.] he is the funies fellow I ever saw & mee and my gal is all rite[.] your gal cried when I saw her last[.] she said she thought I was her best friend in some respects[.] I want you to write as soon as you get this so I will close by saying I am your loving Brother forever. CD Caddell

1862, July 24
H.F. Craven (*Camp Holmes, Raleigh, NC*) to **Emeline Phillips.** General wartime correspondence with brief mentions of Col. **Thompson** and Col. **William B. Richardson**. [213]

Miss E.P., The object of these lines is to bear you in mind that we and all [illegible] of life called the camp of instruction. It should have been destruction. One week tomorrow in a heavy rain we came in camp. Col. Thompson and Col. Richardson of the Moore County boys followed us in. We lived from Friday noon til Tuesday eve in the open air without any shelter but the blue canopy of Heaven to shelter us from beating rains and hot sunshine. We are now in our tents. Yesterday we passed our examination. Four out of one hundred and eight men were exempted. The Moore County regiment was also examined. Four of their men were exempted. I knew none of them. The news in camp this morning is that fifty men from Pitt County deserted[,] and about one hundred more from the whole camp. I cannot [illegible]. I have been appointed Seargent of the 50th Regiment and I am sick of my appointment. Sure we draw rations for two days at a time. Some of the men say they do not get half enough even of sour flour and pertrified bacon. I get enough of that kind of diet and some to spare for the next meal. Your Moore County boys are deeply agitated and some time talk of marching out the whole regiment and going home. On a certain evening three or four sergeants sent runners to me to know if I would march my regiment out. If so, four of five others would follow me. But I told them to hold on a while longer and see how we should get along. But I believe they will march out yet. As for my own part I do not know when I shall run away but I hope never. We are in for the war, long or short, exposed to all the [illegible] of camp life, cook our own eatings, draw wood on our waggons, sleep upon the ground and get a pass from the seargeants of the regiments to go after a bucket of water. This is confinement in deed. You who are at home with one meal per day, couch to sleep on and roof under and privileges to go outside of the house are a happy people. Think of us who are tied down by the strong fetters of tyrannism, despotism and cruelty. The ladies sometime come into our camp to see us but they bring us no snaps, cucumbers, apples, pies or cider, consequently, I can not [illegible] be released from prison walls of this gloomy cell and hear audibly the sound what the heroes of Seventy-six did and which filled a nation's heart with rejoicing. Please look over all simplicity, pardon errors and for the sake of a prisoner write me soon. Direct to Camp Holms near Raleigh 50th Regiment in care of Lieut. Hill. Your ever well wishing friend. H. F. Craven

1862, July 26
Lydia Fry (*Moore County, NC*) to cousin **A.S. Caddell**. General wartime correspondence between cousins with brief mention of uncle **Simon Phillips** who is in hospital at Petersburg and very sick, **Nan Hill**, **Neil Caddell**, **Neil McIntosh** and **Alice Fry**. [214]

Cousin Tim, As much as I dislike to write[,] I believe I had better answer your letter which I received last May than to do anything that is in my power to do this morning[.] if I had anything worth writing, but I tell you everybody is so dull about here it is a hard matter to live. The ladies south of here are looking like they had run away from the grave yard the cause of this I cannot tell without it is grieving so much about their beaus who are in the war[.] I am truly sorry for them but know how to sympathise with them aright for I am in love with every brave and patriotic Southern boy that have gone to drive the Yankees from our coast[,] and secure for us peace and freedom which will make glad every heart on our rainy soil. Who could love one only when there are so many noble hearts equely engaged in securing this great independence. May every Southern soldier live long to enjoy the many comforts and pleasure which only this soon anticipated independence can give. What a flattering future! you all will forget the many risks and fatigues which you have endured when wellcomed home by many kind friends and relations who will ever be proud of you, whom the world will praise and the nation bless. All this may never be, yet I cannot help painting bright pictures and framing them with the golden light of the future. Well Tim I am not gone south yet, and it is very doubtful whether I go at all or not, once I recon after all it would be the best for me that I go. I do not care as much about going as I did[.] my attention has been drawn in another direction altogether. I received a letter from uncle Sim the other day. He was in the hospital at Petersburg, but not very sick, he is carried away with the ladies there I am afraid he is just pretending to get the ladies to wait on him[.] I have such a funy joke to tell you on uncle Sim and Nan Hill but it is too long to pen down and I would hardly do to trust on paper[.] Your duck is a funny as ever or was the other day[.] I recon you would be glad to see her[.] Niel Caddell has got home safe again, I was very glad that they let him off, for I tell you the conscript has taken all the boys except a few who are afraid that they will die before then their time comes that they have hid in the school houses[.] dont you think it would be funny if some of the old houses were to fall on them and almost if not quite kill them[.] if it was leap year I would know right where to go to find them boys[,] but as usual my dish is always bottom upwards when it rains pudding[.] I think it is a great pity that postage is so high and paper so scarce, for there is so many postmasters that they all cannot get employ, and you know this is not time for people to be idle[.] I supose some of the conscripts are determined not to go, I heard of one man the other day eating dinner with his sword lying on the table by him. dont you think if a company of cavalry were to see him they would be frighten about to death[.] I will hush about what is left behind for they want a place to hide when peace is made worse than they do now. I want you all to make hast and give the yankees one more good whipping, and I think that will do for them. I tell you I am tired of this war, and dont think I am alone. Niel McIntosh is going back to camp in a few days[.] when you see him ask him and he hot, but for my sake do not tell him who wrote it, for I do not know the meaning of the word, if it has any. Well Tim my thinking faculties is are absent t day, as I will be oblige to stop writing for the want of something to write. I hope that I may have something interesting to write next time[.] My respects to all that I am acquainted with[.] Please write soon and all the news, and I will not be so lazy next time. Allice says to tell you to take good care of all her sweet hearts, for the conscrip has taken her every day sweet heart off[.] since then she complains of feeling better, but I dont think she need too, for Sarah Moore had taken him before. Many good wishes for you all[.] Write soon. I remain your affectionate cousin, Lyd Fry

1862, July 26
Jane McIntosh (*Moore County, NC*) to uncle **A.S. Caddell**. General wartime correspondence between niece/uncle with brief mentions of **C.D. Caddell, Artemus McIntosh** and conscripts hiding in the woods. [215]

Dear uncle[,] it is with pleasure that I take my pen in hand to drop you a few lines to let you know that I am well[,] hoping that these few lines may find you enjoying the same like blessing[.] I have nothing strange to write that would interest you any[.] times is hard and is likely to get harder[.] there is some of the conscripts taken the woods and some has hid behind the school houses and some has went[.] C.D.C. went but has come back[.] you dont know how glad we was to see him come home[.] I should like to see you two and I hope that it will not be long before you will have the pleasure of coming home and staying with us awhile[,] if not all the time[.] well Tim I see a heap of fun[.] I tell you we do have some powerful times[.] we have Sunday School and meeting every Sunday and you just ought to be here to see the little boys a flying around the gals is all as bad as ever and as prety your gall is[.] I seen her last Sunday and she looked as prety as ever you saw[.] well Tim you wanted to know how the children was a coming on[.] they are all well[.] Tim is as fat as ever[.] we are done hilling corn we finished the 23rd of July[.] some of our corn looks very well but some of it is very sorry[.] so as I have nothing of importance to write[,] I will close by saying write soon without fail and give me all the news if any. yours affectionately, Jane McIntosh

1862, July 26
William Caddell and **Raney Caddell** (*Moore County, NC*) to their son **A.S. Caddell**. General wartime correspondence between parents/son with brief mention of **Eli P. Sowell**. [216]

Dear Son, I take my pen this beautiful Sunday morning to drop you a few lins to let you know that we are as well as what tho your papa sas he gets worse every day[.] we received your very kind letter last evning and was truly glad to hear from you and hear you was well and I hope when these lines reached you[,] they would find you in good health[.] I have nothing strange to write to you[.] the prospect of our crop[,] I think[,] is very good at this time[.] everything looks promising at this time[.] we have moor potatos planted than we ever had and they a vary likely[.] I hope we shall make a plenty[.] we all will be done laying the corn in about two days[.] I have wish you could see it[.] CD has got off and come home and we was very glad[.] I want you to write to let us know how you fare about something to eat[.] we cannot send you anything now[.] the wether is so warm but your papa ses he will send you some fresh meat as soon as the wether turns cooler[.] we want to see you vary bad[,] but we would rather not see you in five years than for you to be a skulking about here and lying in the bushes as some is without a furlow[.] we want to see our son as bad as anyboddy ever did[,] but when we see you we want to see you come in honor and not in shame[.] we want you to be there to true to your truist[.] take care of yourself and do the thing that is write then[.] we hope to see you one day a orniment to your country[.] we are pleased that you got to drive the wagon[.] write if you will have that chance. I shall have your clothes maid by the coming of fall and could wether so when perhaps you will have the to come home on furlow[.] so no more at preset[.] we remain your loving parents until death[.] give my respects to Eli P. Sowell. William Caddell and Rany G. Caddell

1862, July 26

Lizzie Skeen Phillips (*Guilford, NC*) to **Emeline Phillips.** General wartime correspondence with brief mentions of **Delinda Skeen Kearns, Julius Kearns, Harris Skeen** and **Baxter C. Philips.** [217]

My Dearest Em, No doubt you are ere this becoming anxious to receive some intelligence from me. I hope not many days will pass away until shall have the pleasure of so doing. This morning finds us well as usual. I received a letter from home not long since and in its contents I found sad news, the death of Sister Kurnes little Julius. He is no longer an inhabitant of earth but is now numbered with million of happy spirits that compose the family of God. Poor Sister, I do sympathize with her, for she is in such feeble health. Trouble seems to hurt her very much, but still she has more fortitude than any weakly person I ever saw. The doctor went down to see Harris last week, found him in Petersburg. He was well and said he looked better than he had seen him for some time. But he has seen hard times of late. He wrote me he had to march nearly all night one night through mud and water[,] half leg deep and lay on the bare ground and a fence rail for his pillow. That was when they were marching. Poor fellow, I can't see how he can stand such as that, but he is cheerful under it all and perfectly resigned to the will of God. He says if its His will to lay him on the bleaching field all will be right and if he is brought safely through, it will all be for his good. But, oh, I do pray that he may returned home again with all of our friends. But when, Oh when will peace be unfurled on our banners to wave over our southern homes? God speed the day when every invader may be driven from our soil and leave to civilized people. You ought to see me with my Homespun on. I feel quite grand with it. I have made me one dress since I left home. I send you a specimen of it though it is not pretty but suits me at this time. Everyone is in the spirit of making cloth. I believe we have it to do for callico is 15 cents per yard up here. I can't afford much at that price[.] Lewis is very interesting now. Talks plain. I would like to see you all, think I will soon. Sorry to hear Baxter was wounded. Write me soon. I love to get letters from you often. I have no more now. Love to all, Lizzie Phillips

1862, July 27

C.D. Caddell to brother **A.S. Caddell.** General wartime correspondence between brothers with brief mention of **W.H.H. Davis.** [218]

Mr A. S. Caddell, It is with pleasure I seat myself to drop you a few lines[.] wee are all well at present[,] hoping these few lines will find you well[.] I have got back from the war & I hope I never will have to start any more[.] if it had not have been for my friends[,] I might have staid[.] shal ever feel under obligations to them[.] it cost mee right smart but I am glad it is no worse[.] evry boddy wanted mee to stay[.] I think that is anybody[.] I have got a right pretty crop if the seasons dont fail[,] I will make anough to do us[.] I have paid Josiah that mate and it was a most $15 that and your take is all your money I have spent yet[.] mee and my gal is all right[.] every time I see your gal she is a talking about you[.] she loves you as good as she can[.] she has wrote to you several letters lately for I mailed some of them[.] Send her one in mine when you write & I will take it too her[.] W.H.H. has not writen to mee since he left Kinston[.] tell mee if you and him hasnt fell out[.] I never expect to do any more for some people[.] I told her so and she said she was out of it[.] I think a heap of her but she wont pay[.] I wish I could see you and tell you some things & wee have got 2 of the smartest gals in N.C. write soon to your loving brother. CD Caddell

1862, July 27
Mastin C. Phillips (*Second NC Hospital*) to father Rev. **Lewis Phillips Jr.** General wartime correspondence with brief mentions of **J. Tillman** and **Nancy Edwards Phillips.** [219]

Dear Father, I have just put a letter on the office asking you to come to see me. But as Mr. J. Tillman is here and going to start for home in the morning, he says he will carry this note to you. I want you to come to see me. I am worse than when I wrote you last, but I don't think I am dangerous. Still[,] I want you to come to see me. You will find me in the second N.C. Hospital on the second story and 5th ward. Come if you please. Tell Mother and all not to be uneasy about me. Pray for me. Your son, Mastin C. Phillips

1862, August 4
Matthew C. Yow (*Petersburg, VA*) to his wife **Nancy Catherine Albright Yow** and children. General wartime correspondence with brief mentions of **Lewis Grant Maness** and brother-in-law **John E. Albright.** [220]

Dear Wife and Little Children[,] I one more time take my pen in hand to rite you a few lines to let you no that I am well at this time hoping when this comes to hand it may find you all in good helth. Catharine I will tel you what I am going to do. I am going to send my likenes to you by Lewis Maness and I will send you some money. I will send you 60 dollars now and you can keep it tel you need it and I will send you some more invelops. He said he wold take all to you and I know he will do what he says. I haint got time to rite much this tim. I will rite before long again. Catharine you sent me some butter and I was glad to get it. I cold sold it for one dollar a pound if I wold. Butter sels here for one dollar a pound and unions ten cents a peac. I cold hav sold them that John sent me at 20 cents a peac. Apples sel for 15 and 25 cents a dosen but I dont buy them. I hire my washing don and I hav to pay 10 to 15 cents for a shirt and not half washt at that. I got them washt at Goldsboro for 5 cents. Catharine my loving wife I must close for this time. May the good Lord bles and sav you is my prare. Catharine I want you to rite as often as you can. Catharine my dear wife do the best you can. May the Lord bles and sav you and my blesed little children forever is my prare. Matthew C. Yow to his dear wife Nancy C. Yow So fairwell for this time.

1862, August 6
Matthew C. Yow (*Petersburg, VA*) to his wife **Nancy Catherine Albright Yow** and children. General wartime correspondence with brief mentions of **Lewis Grant Maness** and brothers-in-law **Henry A. Albright** and **John E. Albright, Isaac Williams,** father **Henry C. Yow, Samuel D. Stewart,** brothers **Simeon Jones Yow** and **Isaac Yow**, Miss **Cox** and children **William Henry Yow, Nancy Elizabeth Yow, Mary Jane Yow** and **Joseph Gibbs Yow** [221]

Deare Wife and Little Children[,] I now tak my pen in hand to rite you a few lines to let you no that I am well at this time and I do hop when this comes to hand it find you all well. Catharine I got a letter from your father tha was rote the 4 July and I got it the 5 of August. It was a long time a coming. I had bin to Richmond. Henry and John is well as far as I no. I herd from them yesterday. Catharine I hav sent my liknes by Lewis G Maness and my money also. I put in the letter that I sent by Lewis 60 dollars but I sent 67 dollars to you and if you are afraid to keep it at home you can get some body to keep it for you. Catharine I think you had beter pay Isaac Williams for your cow. You can get father to do that for you. Catharine I am afraid that we shal hav another battle before long. Tha are fixing for it now and we shal fight if the Yankees comes out to us. I do hope tha will let us alone. I can here some cannon down the river every day. Tha had a little skirmish last Sonday. There was some two or three kild. Catharine the boys has not come yet and I dont no what to think. Samuel Stewart went after them and he has never come back yet. The boys said in there letter of the 28 that he come and took there names and went to Raleigh and tha had not seen him sinc. I hav herd that there has went a great many through Petersburg going to Richmond and I am afraid tha will go there. I do wish tha cold come here for I do want to see them so bad. Catharine when Lewis Maness shook hands with me I shed tears. I hated to see him leav. He eat dinner with me and I told to tel you that was some of my cooking. I can make up wheet dough and bake rite good bread. Catharine I hav one hundred and forty five dollars of money sinc I come in camp and I hav sent you one hundred and seven dollars and I hav 18 dollars now. It taks so much money to by paper and stamps and invelops and washing my cloths. Catharine there is no chanc for me to come home now but I hope there will be after a while if I am spard to liv. I do hop and pray that I shal get home to see my loving and blesed little children again. May the good Lord help me I pray. Catharine I am so uneasy about you now. You hav so much to do. I am afraid you will hurt your self. Catharine do the best you can. I do hope you will hav friends when you need them. I do hop that Miss Cox will come and stay with you when you need her. I do wish I cold come home then but I am afraid I cant. I do hop you can get some body to stay with you and help you when you cant help your self. May the good Lord help you I pray. Rite soon and fail not. Catharine the Negros comes in the camp with baskets with pies and apples and any thing that you want but tha ask more for them than I will giv. Tha want all of our money and all of our help. I dont like these Viginians much. I think tha are cowards. Catharine I shal need some cloths after a while if I dont get to come home. It seems like I shant get any more here. William Henry my dear little son you must be a good and help your mother and feed your little horse tel I come home. My dear little son I want to see you so bad. Nancy Elizabeth my dear little daughter be a good girl. Mary Jane my dear little daughter be a good girl. Joseph Gibs my blesed little bab[.] Lord bles the children I pray. My dear loving wife and little fairwell for this time. Pray for me. Matthew C. Yow to Nancy C. Yow

1862, August 7
W.L. Sullivan (*Moore County, NC*) to **A.S. Caddell**. General wartime correspondence with brief mentions of **Zachus Hogan**, **Z.B. Vance**, **K.H. Worthy**, **C.D. Caddell**, **Asa S. McIntosh**, the death of **W.H.H. Davis** and teaching school at Bethlehem. [222]

Mr. A.S. Caddell[,] I seat myself this morning to drop you a few lines in answer to your kind letter which I received a few days since which I was glad to receive from your hands and know that you are well[.] I understand that Mr Zachus H went to the hospitle last week[.] I should be glad to hear from him but he has quit writing to me[.] I don't know what is the reason unless it is case I have knot sent him anything[.] I am sorry that I haint don so, I have tried to send him something but when I woud I get something for him then they would not take it and when they would take anything[,] I would knot know till it would be too late for me to get it for him[.] But tell him that I shal try to send him something soon[.] Mr A.S. Caddell[,] I have know nuse to write to you of much importance moore than we are today making Mr Z.B. Vance the govener of N.C.[.] we think K.H. Worthy will be the sherif[.] we are well as common[.] C.D. Caddell says tell you he is not well[.] you wanted to know what for school I have got[.] my school is small[.] I have twenty 23 or 24 subscribers[.] I am teachin at Bethlehem Acadamy[.] I wish I could see you and Z. hogans[.] I was sorry to hear of W.H.H.D death[.] I thought a heap of him. But he thought a heap of a prety girl that lives in moore and so do I[.] She is prety as a pink[.] If you was here[,] we would fly around some[.] I hope you will not think hard of me for keeping out of the war as long as possible[.] Mr A.S. Caddell[,] I thought I had rather teach school than to go to the war tho I would like to be with you all[.] But I hope you will not think hard of me for not being withe you[.] A.S.[,] I recin you think I am not going to pay you that 2 Dollars but I intend to pay it before I die if I live long[.] I must close by saying write soon to your friend W.L. Sullivan [P.S] tell A.S. McIntosh I was glad to receive his letter and I will answer it soon[.] tell him I received his letter[.] no moor[.] hoping to hear from you soon[.]

1862, August 12
Jesse Brown *(Camp near Richmond, VA)* to wife **Mary E. Brown** and father **Isaiah Brown.** General wartime correspondence with brief mentions of **Jones**. [223]

Dear Wife, and little child, I take the pleasure of writting you a few lines to inform you that I am in good health. I have not been able to do nothing today, but I feel a little better this evening. I hope when these lines come to hand will find you and my little child well at this time. Dear wife[,] I got a letter from you yesterday which made me proud to hear from you, but I was sorry to hear that you were in so much trouble about me, and I got one from Jones the same time, and they was both in the same envelope and I got that to, and I want to know when you got mine or not. I wouldn't take five dollars for it and[,] dear wife[,] I got something to tell you now. I have seen great sight today[.] O Lord God[,] forbid that I ever shall witness it again. Dear wife[,] I saw a man shot for running away. They shot five holes through him, they tied his hands and blindfolded him. He was a Irishman, and he was on gard and tried to get to the Yankees and was caught. I can't tell in two days what I could tell you. Dear wife, I want you to pray for me and perhaps the Lord will bless my poor soul. Lord God of Heaven and Earth have pity on my soul and save me. Dear wife[,] we have orders to march now and it is raining now and we don't know when we will have to go. Write to me soon and tell me about the baby. Good, good by for this time and kiss the baby for me.

Dear Father[,] I am in ten thousand troubles about my wife and child, I never shall forget you. Tell all to write to me. I shall have to stop our time is short. Send your mail in the way of Richmond, Va. Reg.[,] Co. H.[,] C/o Lieutenant Mr. C. Nair Trumps[.]

1862, August 12, 14

J.L. Stuart (*Petersburg, VA*) to mother **Mary A. Harper,** brother **Charles Harper,** sister **Mary Ann Harper,** grandmother **Nancy Glass Nall** and stepfather **John Harper**. General wartime correspondence with brief mentions of **John Nall, Martin L. Nall, Allen Shields, Joseph P. Thomas, David S. Barrett, Elijah B. Burroughs, Jesse Thomas, Duncan Black, A.R. McDonald,** and **Matthew Williamson**. [224]

Mrs Harper Dear mother[,] I again seat myself to drop a few lines to you to inform you I am well[,] hoping these few lines will reach you enjoying the pleasures of this present life or as well as your pains will admit of[.] I received a letter last night the dated the 9th. It was dark but I read enough by fire light to find out you was alive[.] you cannot tell the pleasure it gave me[,] but it makes me so sorry to read how you suffer & when I get a letter it is so much like mother a talking[,] it does me good to the bottom of my heart[.] I wrote a letter to you yesterday[.] the letter I got was the 18 letter the 49D[.] 26th is gone to day to city point after corn[.] But they left John[.] he is on Brigade guard[.] yes[,] I am under an apple tree guarding fruit[.] uncle John Nall was at the 26 to see Martin & Martin is at Richmond sick[.] Allen Shields has got to his Com. we understand Jackson is running Pope and taking his men. August 14th 1862 - I am well today[.] I am improving very fast since I came to this camp[.] I hope you all are getting along well[.] our regt came back the same night[.] they did not fight But got 16 loads of corn. J.P. Thomas is Dead[.] David Barett is trying to get a furlow[.] if he does[,] I want you to send me a jug of honey. Honey is good. We are slinging up breastworks all about here. E.B. Buroughs & Jesse Thomas & Duncan Black has deserted but I shall stick to them as long as I can[.] I give McDonald fifty Dollars for to take to you & I started a letter to you the other day so if you do not get that this[,] will tell you he lives at Carthage[.] I shall get about $40 more[.] I want to see you all the worst in this world[.] I have got paper plenty in and good tho don't pester about envelopes[.] I can get plenty. Va is the greatest grain country I have ever seen[.] I want you all to write and give me all the nuse[.] tell all my friends to write[.] I do write about every week when I have a chance[.] how glad I would be to be at home see you all one more time and I want to see Ginny too[.] if I just was at home I would ride about pretty large[.] tell all the girls god bless them[.] I want to kiss them[.] if you want my likeness I will have it taken[.] write if you want it[.] do not greave about me[.] I think I will get a furlow before long[.] I shall try after a while[.] it is hard to get a furlough now we understand three of the northern states refuses to send their quota of men[.] Lincoln wants 300,000 more men[.] I hope he will draft them and send them on[.] they wont hurt us bad for they wont make soldiers until they are drilled[.] the ones that are out now is their best soldiers Lincoln can send and[.] the best fit of you could jest a saw what they flung away beyond Richmond[,] it would astonish[.] my paper is so bad I cant write good. Charles & sis and Granny & J. Harper[,] howdy to you all[.] I want to see you all you cant tell how Bad[.] you all must write to me[.] I will send a lock of my hare to you[.] ever time I get a letter[.] I am afraid to open it for fear of some of you being dead[.] do the best you can and I will[.] cider is from one to 1½ dollars per gallon[.] tell everybody howdy for me. M Williamson is well. We do not drill any but work some[.] I work half an hour today[.] your affectionate son until death. J.L. Stuart

1862, August 13

Daniel McIntosh (*Moore County, NC*) to **A.S. Caddell**. General personal correspondence with brief mentions of his parents **William** and **Raney Caddell**, **Neill Caddell**, the Lawhon Spring Branch, **J.J. McIntosh**, **S. McIntosh**, **William McIntosh** and **Alexr. Kelly**. [225]

I seat myself for the purpos of writing you a few lines to let you no that we are all well and hope this will find you enjoying the same like blessing[.] I received youre kind letter and was glad to here that you was well[.] I have no nuse to write that would intrest you[.] youre papy and mother is as well as usual[.] you said you wanted to no what was the prospect for a crop down there[.] they have got the ground that you and Neill clard on the branch in corn[,] and that pece between the house and the Lawhorn Sprang Branch and it is all tollerable good corn there[.] wheat was hurt with the rust[.] Some tho there oats was tollerable good there[.] corn is tollerable late and they was not done working it when Neill went off with the conscrips[,] and I went and worked it over with the help of J.J. & S. McIntoshs,[.]Williams one day since they let him off and he got back the nite after we finished plowing over his corn[.] he has bin trading horses some since he sold his mare for $150 Dollars and bought a *horse 2 years old for 85 Dollars[.] he said that his colt was so young that if I had no particular use for youre horse that he would take him and I let him take him the day before yesterday[.] you dident say that you wanted me to keep him unless he went to the war tho if you want me to keep him at any time[,] I will do so by youre letting me no about it[.] we have had our election over and went strong for Vance for Governor, Worthy was elected for Sheriff and Alexr. Kelly in the commons[.] So not having anything of intrest to write I shall close[.] you must write soon, yourse respectfully, Danl. McIntosh*

1862, August 13
Raney G. Caddell to son **A.S. Caddell**. General wartime correspondence between mother and son with brief mentions of **William Caddell** and **Neill Caddell**. [226]

Dear son[,] I have the pleasure of writing you a few lines to let you know that we are as ushal half a live and I do sincerely trust that thes few lins will find you well[.] I have nothing of intrest to write to you[.] we all want to see you very mutch[.] we are vary uneasy for fear you will get sick[.] I want you to take as good care of yourself as you can and if you get sick[,] we want you to let us know it so some boddy can come and take care of you[.] if Niell ant well enough to come[,] we will get some boddy to come and wait on you[.] I want you live as easy as you can to perform your duty[,] all the leisure time you have from service[,] rest all you can[.] I hope the almighty will be with you and guide you through and to the end of this cruell war[.] pray without seasing[.] clave to that good and shun evil[.] I shall send you some little thing by Mr Muse[.] I am sorry I cant send a horse but they wont take it[.] I will try to send something[.] any chance your papa ses you have got some good mutons and it is a good price[.] he ses to write whether you want any of them sold or not[.] I must come to a close and if we meet no more on earth[,] I hope we will meet in heaven where wars will be no more. Rany G. Caddell

1862, August 13
C.D. Caddell to brother **A.S. Caddell**. General wartime correspondence between brothers with brief mentions of **Eli P. Seawell** and **Martha Caddell Seawell**. [227]

It is with pleasure I seat myself to day to drop you a few lines[.] I am not well[.] I have got a bad cough and a pain in my breast & has had evry since I went to Raleigh[.] Mother and papy is well as common[.] I hope these few lines will find you well[.] I have not got but one letter from you in about 3 weeks and hit was the one you sent by Black[.] I got it & your money at the election[.] it had bin rite about 2 weeks[.] you said something in it about my taking your place for a while and I dont know what to say for I am not well a enough now or I should a come to see you before now[,] only I hant binable to do anything hardly at home. I hate that you cant come home for I know you want to[,] but if I was to take your place they would not let me off any[.] if I knowed they would[,] I would tryit a while when the weather gets cool but I expect there will be a draft before long[,] but if I can[,] I will stay out of it[.] your gal said she had not heard from you in a long time[.] she said she would love to hear from you[.] mee and my gal is all rite[.] I should have written before now[,] only I dont know where to male my letters[.] this makes 3 I have sent by hand since I have got but one so I will conclude by sayin write soon to your loving brother, C.D. Caddell [P.S.] Give E.P. Sowell my best resp and tell him Martha is well[,] and the rest of his people.

1862, August 15
A.S. Caddell (*Petersburg, VA*) to Miss **Martha M. Sullivan**. General personal correspondence. [228]

Miss Martha, with pleasure I drop you a few lines to let you know that I am in moderate health (only)[.] I recd your welcome letter this morning[.] I was truly glad to hear that you was well and enjoying yourself[.] I have nothing of interest to communicate[.] our Co. is generaly in good health and getting along fine though I have been in places that I would perfer to this. Miss M.[,] I would like to pay you Moore Cty. girls a visit[.] I think I could enjoy myself first rate though I have no idea that it would add anything to the happings of any other person except myself[.] Miss M.[,] I heard that their was a going to be two or three wedings in your settlement which are to be solomised in a few days[.] well[,] if I don't received a ticket from some of them[,] I sure would think I ought to[.] their was one of the marrying party which I have just spoken of that paid us a visit sometime not long since[.] he told me that he was only waiting for cool weather to come on[.] he says the weather is to (hot) to emerge into lifetime business[.] I will stop my foolishness[.] I can only say that I would like to a few days in your company[.] nothing would give me more pleasure[.] I can only exclaim with this Poet. Yours affectionately[,] A.S. Caddell. I love thee gentle and; With a lovers holy love; Symbolic of affections; Which angels feel above; And though I seldom see thee; Yet in my inmost heart; The waters of affections; Will ever ever start[.]

1862, August 19
Sarah McIntosh (*Moore County, NC*) to **A.S. Caddell**. General wartime correspondence with brief mention of marriage of Mr. **Crook.** [229]

Mr Caddell[,] sir[,] I take my pen in hand to let you know that I am well at this time[,] hoping when this come to hand may find you enjoying the same blessing[.] I was glad to here from you that you was well[.] you wanted to us girls come on we are all well now[.] I want to know how you gentlemen come on tell me in the next letter[.] you wanted to know if any of the girls had got maried no they have not[.] the last was Mr Cruck[.] I would be glad to see you all[.] I hope that the war will stop and you all get home[.] so nothing moore at present[.] rite soon[.] excuse bad spelling[,] riting[.] I will you in the next. Sarah McIntosh

1862, August 20
Archibald McNeill (*2nd NC Hospital, Petersburg, VA -- reply to Capt.* ***McInnis****, Co. H. 26th Reg.*) to wife Mrs. **Jane Brewer McNeill**, daughter **Mary McNeill** and cousin **Murdock McKenzie**. General wartime correspondence with brief mentions of children **Daniel McNeill**, **Martha McNeill**, **Elizabeth McNeill**, **John Robert McNeill**, **Alexander McNeill** and **Nancy Jane McNeill;** and **Hardy Sanders.** [230]

Mrs. Jane McNeill, Dear wife[,] you no doubt have heart that I have been in the hospital for the last two or three weeks. I have geen quite sick, suffered a great deal but am improving now, and hope to be well soon, though I am quite weak yet. I am passing some of my time walking about in the house and yard, but I am very slow and sore, yet tired. I have suffered a great deal with risings under my right arm. I have had a half a dozen lanced, but I am not clear of them yet. You wish me at home to eat white cabbage. I assure you that nothing would afford me more pleasure, for I have been craving them for some time, but in my fares it would not do for me to eat them, in my condition, and I fear it will be sometime before I can come home, but I hope to return to you safe and sound sometime.

To Mary, I saw my Daniel a few days ago and was happy to see him, and would be equally happy to see you. He was well when I saw him, and little Martha, if I could just have hold of her and give her one good kiss, I think it would almost cure me. Give my love and best respects to Elizabeth McNeill, tell her I often think of what she said to me before I left home[,] and feel very thankful to her. John Robert, I love you as well as I ever did. I want you to obey the instructions I have given you, be kind to your sisters and brothers[,] and obey your mother. You did not state in your letter any thing about little Alexander, whether he could talk or not. It would afford me untold pleasure to see him. Nancy Jane, do not think that I have forgotten you, no, I love you as well as I can. My best love to the other three little ones, be good children.

To Cousin Murdic McKinsey, You will learn from this letter where I am and how I am. I hope when you get these lines that you may be enjoying good health. I want to know if you are still at my house, and if so, I want you to attend to my business until my oats are all sowed, and more ground broke up. I also want you to have all the hay, and feed you can cut of all descriptions. I want them to get somebody to do that piece of ditching just as soon as possible. I want it well done, the ground properly drained.

Dear wife, I have understood that you have bought my brother's mare. I am well pleased, take all that you will let me have at that price. I wish that times were as they used to be so that I could be with you and drink some of your good cider[,] and I would like to have a meal out of a good fat turkey. I want my friend Hardy Sanders to see to getting me a one horse wagon, one that will be suitable, if I should conclude not to keep in when I come home. My love to my dear wife and children and all my friends. Arche McNeill [P.S.] Send your letters to Petersburg, Virginia, care of Capt. McInes, Company H[,] 26th N.C. Infantry[.]

1862, August 25

J.L. Stuart (*Camp Pontoon Bridge near Richmond, VA*) to mother **Mary A. Harper,** stepfather **John Harper,** brother **Charles Harper,** sister **Mary A. Harper** and grandmother **Nancy Glass Nall**. General wartime correspondence with brief mentions of **Isaac Teague, A.R. McDonald** and **William Barrett**. [231]

Dear mother[,] I again take my seat to drop you a few more lines to inform I am well truly[,] hoping these lines will reach you all alive and doing well[.] I have nothing of importance[,] only we have not go clear gone yet[.] I thought last week that we would be carried to Jackson[.] But we were stopped at Richmond and lay by two days and marched back five or six miles to a bridge on the James[,] and picked our camp and we are put to drilling[.] this is the fourth letter I have wrote since I have recd one[.] I now there is some on the way but I do get them[.] you said the last account you had of me was a letter I sent to Isaac Teague[.] I gave A.R. Mc Donald one Fifty Dollar bill and I wrote for you to go and get it[.] and I gave Wm. Barret one twenty Dollar Bill for you[.] I also gave him a letter for him to put in the office in Carthage[,] and I stated for you to go and get the money[.] day before yesterday[,] I wrote a letter to you[.] I think you will be certain to get of them[.] I recd Eighty nine dollars and Twenty three cents and sent seventy dollars to you by the two above named men[,] and I gave John Harper seventeen Dollars when he started home and he had fifty Dollars[,] making one hundred and thirty seven Dollar and I have got fifteen Dollars and some stamps and paper & I owe over one dollar[.] I have been saving you known it I heard to keep money several of the comp. has not got ten cents[,] but Stewart does better than that[.] Mother[,] try and console yourself and do the best you can[.] I want to see you very much so let us hope for the Better[.] I hope we will meet again[.] your affectionate son[,] J.L. Stuart

Mr J. Harper step father[,] dear sir[,] I will say a few words to you[.] I hope you are doing well[.] I would be very glad to see you[.] we are at a good camp[.] I think we have some very good spouts to get water like them at Mangrum[.] last week we got order to cook three days ration and be ready at ten o'clock[.] we started and marched through Petersburg at 12 and camped at the Bluff next day[.] we got in sight of Richmond at 12[.] staid there two days and turn back six miles on the James at the Pontoon Brig[.] the General say we may stay here some time[.] we hear troops have been passing through Richmond for three weeks Brigade after Brigade[.] Jackson has more men than he can use[.] I hope me dear Pope advancing on Washington and Jackson is falling Back after him[.] last Saturday[,] Jackson captured four hundred Prisoners[.] write soon[.] your truly[,] J.L. Stuart Direct to Richmond Va[,] 49th regt[,] N.C. Troops[,] Co D in Ransoms Brigade[.]

Brother Charles and sister M.A.[,] I hardly know what to write[.] I want to see you so bad[.] it would please me more if I could see you than all the money I ever saved[.] I cannot write enough to you all so I will write but little[.] I hope I will get thru before long but I am doing very well[,] better than you think for[.] tell all the girls I want to see them[.] I am going to send you both a present as soon as I get the chance[.] I want you to write soon[.] I am your true Brother[,] JL. Stuart

Dear grandmother[,] I hope you are doing well[.] I want to see you mightily and I want to see all the family and everybody else[.] give my best respects to ever Body[.] the 46th & 48th is 8 or ten miles from here[.] the 44th is two miles[.] all of you write soon[.] your J.L. Stuart is in old VA[.]

1862, August 26
Neill A. Ray (*Petersburg, VA*) to cousin. General wartime correspondence with brief mention of cousin **William Ray.** [232]

Dear Cousen, I take the present opportunity of writing you a letter as it has bin sometime cence I have riten to you or heard from you. I have no news to write of any enportince. I am at work at my traid. I think that I will git cousen William to strike for me as soon as I can[.] he is very ansus to git out of the regiment. I am very well contented now if I can remain so. The bregaid has lef to hear[.] thay are at James river a bout too miles above Drewry Bluff. I dont think thay will stay ther long. I do hope that this reched war will soon cloas for I think very body tired of it. I must cloas my letter by asken you to writ soon. Remember me ever as yours truly, N. A. Ray [P.S.] Derect your letters to Petersburg va in the care of Majer Simmons[,] quarter master of ginerl brigaid[.]

1862, August 27

J.L. Stuart (*Petersburg, VA*) to mother **Mary A. Harper**. General wartime correspondence with brief mentions of **Dugald McFarland, William A. Brown, S.D. Crook, Eli C. Bean, A.R. McDonald, John Harper, D.S. Barrett, E.A. Davis, Martin L. Nall, Eli Teague** and **Allen Shields**. [233]

Dear mother[,] I take my seat this morning to Drop you a few lines to inform you that I am well at this time[.] I am not to strong as I was[.] I was very poorly for a week or so but now I am hearty[.] I hope these lines will reach you all a live[,] and that your health is improving and that all of the family is well[.] I[,] for over a week[,] was sick and a severe head ache and I suffered four days[.] and then I went to the Doctor and he gave me a Dose of calonce and dovers powders in the evening[,] and it lay until next morning[,] and he gave me a large dose of rhubarb and something else and I rested over a week[.] the regt left and I come to the new camp last Thursday[,] and I am a great deal now at Drury's Bluff[.] was the sicklys place we have been at. We now are about two miles from Petersburg. McFarling is dead[.] Wm A Brown is dead[.] S.D. Crook is dead[,] and we hear E.C. Bean is dead but I do not know whether it is so or not[.] about half of our Co. was sick[.] We have drawn our money or part of it[.] I got one fifty dollar bill and I have sent it to you by A.R. McDonald[.] he lives at Carthage[.] he put John Harpers name on the bill[.] I want him to go and get it as soon as you get this[.] I would have sent more but it the bill was fifty dollar bill and the Lieut could not make the change[.] But I shall get a bout thirty nine Dollars as soon as D.S. Barett get able to go to town to get it changed[.] he is sick and so is the capt. Buy land or any thing you please[.] I want you to get shet of it while it is good. I received a letter from you about two weeks ago[,] number sixteenth letter[.] the other day I received a letter from E.A. Davis[.] you can tell her it came safe it does me a great deal of good to get a letter from anybody[.] I have received fifteen letters since the fight from Moore County[.] I want to see you all very bad and I hope I shall before long[.] I saw Eli Teague yesterday evening[.] he looks dried up he is about[.] it is supposed Martin L. Nall is Dead & Allen Shields is in the hospital at Richmond[.] yours truly[,] J. L. Stuart

1862, August 28

John Lane Stuart (*Rapidan Station, VA*) to mother **Mary Harper**. General wartime correspondence with brief mentions of General **Stonewall Jackson**, General **Ransom**, **William Brewer, Henry Brewer, Wesley Brewer, George Davis, Matthew Williamson, Sandy Johnson, John Nall, Isaac Teague** and others. [234]

Dear mother, I take my seat to drop you a line to inform you that I am well as this time[,] hoping these few lines will find you all alive and doing well. We are at Rhapodan Station, VA[.] it is a splendid place here. We have a splendid view of the Blue Ridge[.] it is the prettiest you ever saw[.] it reminds me of thunder head close[.] last Saturday and Sunday[,] Stonewall had an engagement with the enemy[.] he made them get further we are told[.] he[,] Jackson[,] is eighty miles from here[.] he is after the yankees hard up. I do not doubt but that he will try Washington. The yankees burnt the bridge here on the Rhapodan[.] the cars have to stop here. I think it ninety miles to Richmond rail track from High Point here. The 46th and 48th is here. I saw Wm. & Henry & Wesley Brewer yesterday. Wm. is about but he looks very poorly. George Davis stopped at Richmond[.] they told me he was very danger. I tell you I felt like I had got home[.] hurrah for plenty & sundry[,] Moore cty here[.] in one mile around is four companies. The 26th has left our brigade[,] but it does not differ[.] they played at cards night & day[.] before yesterday General Ransome send orders around and to the four regt[,] his order was to be ready to march to Richmond[,] and to the 26th[,] his order was to go to hell[.] hahaha[.] that is what I heard. I am in the heart[.] I have been since I left home. We are at a mountainous country but water is good. I cannot express myself with a pen. I received a letter the other day the 21 letter by [illegible]. I was very sorry to part from the 26th[,] I cannot tell my doom[.] I may return safe and may not[,] but I am in pretty fare heart now[.] if it be the orders for us to go to New York[,] I will follow my regt. If I live & keep my strength, I will not desert. I am better satisfied than you would suppose[,] but the further I go[,] the moore I think if home & it would be a great pleasure to be at home [,] but we must defend our country. I do hope I shall return home again and see you all. I think when we put up Winter quarters[,] we will get furloughs, Write often and I will do the same. I started a letter to you as we came through Richmond but I did not have the chance to get my likeness taken. We staid half a day but we did not know what minute we would have to start. We made watermelons get [illegible]. It is as familiar for me to here the cars as it is for you to here the cowbell as any other thing. Excuse me [illegible]. M. Williamson is a hearty chap at present, Sandy Johnson is along[.] he has been on duty the hole time[,] but two days as we came through the city[,] one of the artillery wagon run over his foot and hurt his toes[,] but he keeps along. it is getting dark[.] I will have to stop. Tell Emmy I will try to be at her wedding. The Moore cty conscripts was in a mile of here when we got here. John Nall came with the 46th to this place[,] he went to the 3rd to see Martin's boys and the rest the day before we got here. Wm. Brewer was looking for him yesterday the 10th. Alex is before somewhere with Stonewall. I recon I was sorry to hear old Fly was dead. Please give these lines to from Mack to Isaac Teague. You may direct to Richmond, VA[,] 49th Regt[,] NC Troops in care of Black Co. D. in Ransoms Brigade, I want to see all the girls and everybody else. I will send money as I get it. You must have two good horses. It is so dark I cannot see to write. J.L. Stuart

1862, September 4
Jane McIntosh (*Moore County, NC*) to uncle **A.S. Caddell**. General wartime correspondence between uncle/niece with brief mentions **Neill McIntosh** and the marriage of **Martha McIntosh** and **Wm. R. Muse.** [235]

Dear uncle[,] it is with pleasure that I take my pen in hand to drop you a few lines to inform that I am in the land of living but I have a very bad cough and I am afraid it is the whooping cough that is in the settlement[.] [A]nd I hope these few lines may reach you and find you well[.] well Tim I have nothing of importance to write[,] only was at a wedding last night[.] cousin Martha McIntosh and Mr. Wm. R. Muse was married you just ought to a been there to a seen them. They looked mighty well and of all the fun that you ever seen[.] I reckon you never seen as mutch as small a crowd of all the flying around of little boys[.] I never seen the like since the conscrpts was called for[.] Tim I heard you was sick I am sorry to hear of it but I hope you will soon you well and have the opportunity of coming to see us all[.] I would like to spend awhile with you[.] I could tell you a heap that I can not write[.] I wrote to you and sent by Neill McIntosh but I never got any answer[,] but it seemes that I can not get any letters that comes to me[.] well Tim and I did not sleep mutch last night and cough so bad[.] I must come to a close by saying write soon and give me all the news if any[.] tell me how all of my friends and relaions is coming on[.] so nothing more at present[,] only I remain your affectionate niece until death, Jane McIntosh

1862, September 5
Daniel. McIntosh (*Moore County, NC*) to **A.S. Caddell**. General wartime correspondence with brief mentions of deserters **Ira Lane Maness, Cornelius A. Stutts** and **George Dumas Stutts**, his father **William Caddell, Neill Caddell, Blackstreet** and **Barrett.** [236]

I onst more seat myself to drop you a few lines to let you know that we are all well with the exceptions of the cough and hope this will find you well[.] I have nothing that is new to write to you[,] only youre deserters have come home[.] I have herd some say they have seen Irey Maner and Neill Stutts and Doom Stutts and several others that has left the army[.] there is some conscripts that is talking of fiting at home[.] what fiting they do and they are claming the deserters as recruts in there number[.] there is some talk of the Colonel and Shirreff having orders to take the conscrips tho they havnt commenced it yet as I know of [.] they are all about at youre Papys tho I thin youre papy has bin some worse for some days[.] Neill has sold his horse or swap him for a buggy[.] he got a buggy and sixty dollars for him[.] you said that you wanted me to tell you what I thought that youre horse would pitch here if he was sold[.] I dont no tho I think that he would bring $150 or $175 if he was put in market tho the price of horses is so unsettled I cant tell what he would bring[.] we have had very good season latly and corn and potatoes is a going to be so good[.] I havnt heard from Blackstreet but write to me and let me no what they have done with him[.] they went back of there own acord and Barrett being in company with give them up and clamed the reward I suppose[.] write soon and give me the nuse[.] So I will close[.] yourse truly, Danl. McIntosh

1862, September 5
William A. McIntosh (*Moore County, NC*) to uncle **A.S. Caddell**. General wartime correspondence between nephew/uncle with brief mentions conscripts hiding, **Robert W. Barrett** and **Jinney Muse.** [237]

Dear uncle[,] it is with pleasure that I seat myself to drop you a few lines to let you know that I am well and hoping that these may find you well[.] I have nothing mutch to wright ondley I was at a weding last night and they had a mighty fine supper[;] they had baked turkeys[.] porsels of them one enny how and I recon that ther was more and all that was needed was you and two or three more gals[.] I got my supper and breakfast and dinner and have just got home[.] I trotted some of them throo the doble quick[.] Neill was not asked so he was out that scrape[.] well Tim the conscripts has not all gone yet they is are a taken the bushes[.] ther was about a half a dozen lay out up abut one night and they got a shamede of themselvs and went back home next morning[.] they say that the school teachers has to go[.] Bob Burrett is clear of the ware all his life time[.] Jinney Muse has a pointed him debuty[.] So I will come to a close by saing wright soon[.] you must look over mistakes for it is a giting so dark that I cant see[.] yours truly, Wm. McIntosh

1862, September 16
Martha M. Sullivan (*Moore County, NC*) to **A.S. Caddell**. General wartime correspondence. [238]

its again that I have taken my pen in hand to inform you that I am well at present truly hoping these lines may reach you enjoying your health tho I heard that you was sick but I hope not dangerous[.] I nothing to rite to you of much importance[.] I received your letter som time ago[.] it found me well[.] you must excuse me for not answering it before now for I could not it was conveniently for me to do so[.] I would like to hear from you very well at present[;] if I could tho you seemed to think in your last letter that you would like to pay the moor cty girls a visit as to the benefit of your own happiness but no other persons except yourself well[.] I am willing for you to enjoy all the happyness that you can no this wourld[.] So I must com to a clos[.] wright to me if it goes well with you and tell if are getting tired of reading my letters[.] if you are tell me and I will trouble you no moor[.] So no news[.] I offer this heart of mine; If I could love thee less; hearts as warm and pure as thine; should never no distress[.] yours truly, M.M. Sullivan

1862, September 21
J.L. Stuart (*Martinsburg, VA*) to mother **Mary A. Harper**. General wartime correspondence with brief mentions of **Hiram Wallace, Randolph McDonald, Kenneth McDonald, William Brewer, Henry Brewer** and **Wesley Brewer**. [239]

Mrs M.A. Harper[.] thank god I am yet a live and well and I do hope that this will reach my Dear mother and the rest all alive and well. I have waded the Potomac 6 times and been in a severe fight last week Sunday and by with the good mercy of god I came throe safe[.] I think I have marched 300 miles since I wrote last[.] we are on the river about 80 miles above Washington[.] the large battle was fought at Sharpsburg Maryland[.] 8 of our regt got Killed and the field about that many more died. Hiram Walis died, R. McDonald his leg broke, K. McDonald hit bad. Our brigade held there position and drove the enemy back three times. We made tremendous charges[.] the 49th run a 5 regt and our brigade run a diversion. We lay in a line of battle the next day and that night one fell back across the river[.] the enemy loss was heavy and our right smart the soldiers told me it was the greatest battle that had been fought and he had been in seven[.] if I ever get home I can tell ten thousand times moore than I can write[.] I have been hearty the whole time but one day I was [.] Wm & Henry & Wesley Brewer is safe[.] I saw Wm and Wesley yesterday[.] I wish I had time and paper[;] I would write more[.] we get flour and beef cook and travel day and night[.] I have kept up all the time[.] write to me[.] I can get letter when you can not[.] there is passing here and but little back was[,] we to the Meridan post office Va[.] J.L. Stuart

1862, September 23
J.L. Stuart and **John Nall** (*Martinsburg, VA*) to mothers **Mary A. Harper and Emily C. Nall**; she is also cousin to J.L. Stuart. General wartime correspondence with brief mentions of **Hiram Wallace, Randolph J. McDonald, Kenneth M. McDonald, William Brewer, Henry Brewer, Wesley Brewer, Stephen Davis, Isaac Sheffield** and **Sandy Johnson**. [240]

Mrs M.A. Harper[.] Dear mother[,] I was over joyd yesterday by receiving two letters from you but very sorry to here you suffering so much[.] my health is good at present and it has been good for some time[.] I hope these lines will reach you all alive and well[.] I started a letter to you the other day that will inform you that I have been in the largest battle that been fought[.] it was long at Sharpsburg Maryland[.] I did not get hurt[.] we went in under a heavy fire of grape and canister and we made three heavy charges and made the enemy fall back ever time[.] Hiram Walis was short through the side and died that night[;] R.J. McDonalds leg was Broke and cut off above his knee[;] K.M. McDonald was wounded in the breast and several of the rest was slightly wounded[.] I came out with not a brake in me[.] we lay a line of battle that night and next day and the next night[.] we fell back across the Potomac[.] I have waded the Potomac four times[.] our forces taken taken Harper Fery and about 1200 prisoners and seventy pieces of canon[.] the Battle in Maryland was fought the 17th[,] about 15 of our regt was Killed. Wm & Henry & Wesley Brewer came out safe they are well. John Nall is with me now[,] he is well[.] he was not in the fight. Isaac Sheffield and Stephen Davis and some of the rest of the conscripts were taken prisoners in the fight[.] we suppose By what we saw the Yankees lost ten to our one[.] I do not Know the enemies movement now. We marched twenty days in succession day and night[.] we did not get six night sleep in the twenty for when we stoped we had to cook our bread and beef ever night[;] some nights traveled all night[.] I lost my knapsack blanket and one shirt and my paper[.] some person stole my blanket or I should a know it now. Our officers are making out the recisition for shoes and a suit out and out and blankets knapsacks[,] etc. We have Been at this place two dayes[.] I think we will get good rested Before we have to march. I will tell you the rout we marched[.] we left Richmond and thence to Rapidan thence to Culpepper CH, Amosville, Warenton, Gainsville thence across the Potomac to Fredrickstown & then back across the river at Point Rocks[,] and then we went to the Louden Heights in Va and then we left there and then we crossed the Potomac at Shephardstown and then to Sharpsburg[;] where there fought and then we fell back and now we are near Martinsburg Va[.] try and get a map and you can see the rout we went[.] it was not my foot the wagon run over[;] it was Sandy Johsons foot[.] he got drum or he would not got hurt[,] but his foot is swell[.] Sandy Did not go in the fight[.] we pleg him some.

Miss E. C. Nall[.] Dear Cousin[,] I am hearty truly hoping these lines reach you well[.] I received a few lines from you yesterday[.] I would be very glad to see you[.] do give my love to all inquiring friends[.] Mother[,] do not greave about me[.] I will take care of myself[.] I should have wrote sooner But I had no chance to send the letters[.] Direct your letters to Richmond as usual untell further orders[.] Farewell to you all[.] I am your loving son J.L. Stuart

A few lines from John Nall to you all[.] I am well as usual hoping these lines may find you all well and doing well[.] tell father & family that where I am tell them[.] I wrote a few lines yesterday which I will start todays[.] J.L. is as best as ever & got. no moore at present[.] J. Nall

1862, October 5

Matthew C. Yow to his wife **Nancy Catherine Albright Yow** and children. General wartime correspondence with brief mentions of Capt. **James C. Dowd**, his father **Henry C. Yow,** brothers **Simeon Jones Yow** and **Isaac Yow.** [241]

Dear Wife and Little Children[,] I one more time take my pin in hand to rite you a few lines to let you no that I am alive yet but not vary well. I hav had a bad spel of the yellow jangers. We left the Rappadan River the first day of September for Manasses and when we got there the battle was over. We then started for Maryland and I got in four miles of the Potomac River and I giv out and tha sent me back to the hospital and it has bin 4 weeks to day sinc I left them and I am on my way to them now. I am in the vally over Blue Ridge. I hav had chanc to rite to you so long[.] I no you think I am dead but thank the Lord I am alive yet and I do hop and pray when this comes to hand it may find you all well. Catharine I receivd your letter of the 23: the 7 of September and fatheres the same time. When I turnd back I met Capt Dowd and he giv them to me and I want to here from you so bad I dont no what to do. I think when I get to the regiment tha will be a letter there for me. I hop tha will. My regiment is at Winchester now and I am on my way there and I sat down to rest and I thought I wold rite for I am in so much trouble. It seems lik I cant stand it much longer. I dream so much about you and the dear little children. It seems lik it will brak my hart. It seems lik I never shal get home any more. Catharine my loving wife I do want to see you and my dear little so bad. I dont no what I shal do if I cant get to see you all one time more. I am praying day and night for you. Catharine I will rite again as soon as I can and I want you and father to rite to me as often as you can. Direct your letter to Winchester VA. But I cant tel how long tha will stay there. Tha may be gon when I get there. I am in so much trouble that I dont no what to rite to you now. I can tel you that I am brok down and I dont think I can do much more. The men is nearly all brok down and I am afraid the Yankees will whip us yet. I expect there will be a battle at Winchester before long. Catharine I do want to here from you so bad I cant rest day nor night. Catharine I hav not seen your brothers in a long time and I haint herd from my brothers sinc I got fathers letter. I want to here from them. Catharine My dear wife I am praying that we may meet again in this world and I hop you are praying for me that I may liv to get home to see you all one time more in this world. May the Lord bles and sav us all forever. So fairwell my dear wife and little children. Matthew C. Yow to Nancy C. Yow

1862, October 6

John Lane Stuart (*Rapidan Station, VA*) to mother **Mary Harper,** stepfather **John Harper,** siblings **Charles Harper** and **Mary Harper** and grandmother **Nancy Nall**. General wartime correspondence with brief mentions of church at Dover, **William Brewer** and **Matthew Williamson**. [242]

Dear mother, I once more seat myself to inform you that I am still in the land of the living & I am hearty[.] a day or so back I was unwell in my bowels but all is rite now. I do hope these lines will reach you all alive and doing well. I received a letter the 3rd[,] dated September 21st which gave me great satisfaction to hear from you but paper is so scarce[.] dear mother do excuse me for not writing much. I write enough to let you now how I get along & c. I have started 3 letters to you since the fight at Sharpsburg. I do consider myself a very lucky boy and if I only could see my dear mother and the rest of you how would I feel[,] and if I live until Christmas[,] I think I will get to come home. It has been more than five long months since I saw you. I want you to write often[.] every time I get a letter[,] I am scared to read it for fear some of you are dead. I would like to go your Dover meetings but my seat there must be vacant[.] and I others Wm. Brewer & bros. are well[.] I was with them awhile last night. M. Williamson is well. I think we will be sent back to Richmond in a short time. We are over two hundred miles from there. I want to see you all so bad. I will not try to explain it to you. When this you see[,] remember me for you can look at this when you cannot see. J.L. Stuart

Dear stepfather, I was very glad to recd[] Those lines from you. I hope you will have your health better than you do[.] try and do the best you can. I cannot help you work now[.] you had better not buy a horse if you do not need one for if I get to come home if peace if made[,] I will buy one to suit me. Horses may get cheaper a mare & a mule colt sold here the other day for fifteen dollars. It was confederate property. Wait until spring anyhow. Feed Jim good. It would please me to come home but we munst live take all things in patience & live in hope[.] if we die in despair[,] I hope you and your family will live and enjoy all the pleasure of this present life and that we all may meet on earth once more and spend our days in peace. J.L. Stuart

Dear brother, sister & granny, I must send you my best respects. I am highly pleased to think I have a little brother at home that thinks enough of me to alwaise write something home. I want to see that little brother & sis and talk and tell them how the canons roar and what a lucky being I am that I have escaped so far and that I enjoy my health so good heare of late. We must give all the praise to him who danels above. I am glad to here of your meetings at Dover where I have spent so many pleasant hours. I want to know the names of the girls that inquires so about me and I want to know your war nuse. I would write more but paper is so scarce[,] you must excuse me at this. Your loving brother until death.

1862, October 9
Bryant Green Dunlap (*Goldsboro, NC*) to Sheriff **Richard Bray Paschal**. General wartime correspondence with mention of death of **John A. Phillips**. [243]

Sheriff R. B. Paschal, Dear friend, I have the pleasure of acknowledging the reception of your kind letter which came duly to hand. It found me with no particular news, having passed through no thrilling scenes[,] not made no hair breadth escapes. I am not prepared as the most of the soldiers and in these times to interest my friends in a correspondence. But as I wrote to a young lady once,"will presume that it is me you want to hear from instead of news that you want" and proceed to tell you something of my own life and how I enjoy it. I am in tolerable good health. The most of my time I have spent since I left home has been attending to the sick and I am now in Goldsboro on my way to Garysburg with ten sick men in [my] charge. I am stopping with them at the hospital until the Battalion can get to Garysburg and be prepared to do something with them. I have been acting Steward of the Hospital ever since I came to Goldsboro, but I do not know whether I will hold my office any longer or not as we are going into a regiment and I do not know who will be our surgeon. There is no responsibility in the office and take it every way. I think if I can get the permanent appointment, I shall be satisfied to hold it. One of our company died the other night. His name was John A. Phillips of Moore county - a son of Martin Phillips. He was a good soldier and clever man. He leaves a wife and six children to mourn the loss. He died with Typhoid Fever. We have some other sickness in camp and some hard cases of Typhoid Fever. Well, you spoke of the association. I should have been highly ratified to have been there - especially with so many inducements to enjoyment as you promised me, all of which I am very fond of. And[,] as you know[,] a soldier's life is by no means a life of luxury and ease, it makes the enjoyment greater when they have an occasional chance of refreshments and fair Ladies. But I must beg to differ with you in one case and that is Miss Mag Fox thinking anything of your humble servant. I imagined on one occasion that, notwithstanding, "I was a youth unknown to fame and fortune," that I would be bold enough to write to her. I did so and silent contempt was my only response. That is, she never answered my letter. I did not blame her for there is such a mania for letter writing with young men in the army that I was ashamed of myself after I did the act, and could not keep from feeling like a poor man at a frolic. But enough of this. I hope I have convinced you that I am neither insensible to the fair ladies charms or to your good opinion of my living in her affections, but that my only response to the case is what the man said about the Bull - Can't quite come it. As I shall be in Garysburg after this, I shall be pleased to get a letter from you at any time. Direct to Garysburg, Col. Evans' Regt., Partizan Rangers. Care of Capt. Harris, and remember me as ever your friend, - B. G. Dunlap

1862, October 14
David H. Sloan (*Northern VA*) to mother **Catharine Sloan**. General wartime correspondence with brief mention of **John A. Sloan.** [244]

Dear Mother, I take my pen in hand to inform you John has got back and we are both well. I have been well ever since I came back[,] and have been in two battles since I came back but I come out alive. A bomb shell struck me on the shoulder but did not hurt me very bad. When this comes to hand I hope it may find you all well[.] as you wrote about that razor[,}It is mine and I don't know how to get it home and my pistol too[;} and you wanted to know about something to eat. We get enough to make out on and that is all that I can say. We don't get anything but beef and flour bread. I have not ate any corn bread since I left home. I will say to you that you may look for John in about three or four weeks for I think he will get a discharge by then[,] but I can't say when I can come home. You need not to look for me until you see me. I will come as soon as I can.

1862, October 28
Matthew C. Yow to his wife **Nancy Catherine Albright Yow** and children. General wartime correspondence with brief mentions of Capt. **James C. Dowd**, his father **Henry C. Yow,** sons **John Matthew Yow** and **William Henry Yow.** [245]

Dear Wife and Little Children, I one time more take my pen in hand to rite you a few lines to let you no that I am well at this time and I do hop and pray that this may find you all well. I receivd your kind letter yasterday the 27. I was so glad to here from you again for I was so uneasy I cold not rest night nor day. I am going to send this letter by Capt Dowd. He is coming to see you and get some cloths for me. I want you to send me one good suit of cloths and my overcoat. I want 2 pare of galloos for I am almost naked and nearly perrish. I dont get half enogt to eat and it goes hard with me for I always had plenty at home. You may no it is a bad chanc here. Catharine I want you rite a letter and send back by Dowd and tel me all about the cloths. Catharine my dear wife I cant rite much this time. You said you wanted to name the baby Matthew. I am willing. I hav rote to you what to name him. If it wold suit you John Matthew. I do want to see him so bad and all the rest of the dear little children but seems lik I never shal get there any more. I pray to the Lord night and day that I may get home to see you all again and I hop you will pray for me. I am in a heep of trouble about you and the children. I am here in the mountians and the wether vary cold. Catharine tel my dear old father to rite me a ful letter and send by Dowd. I want to here all about the times there. Catharine I want you to get lether and hav shoes made for you and the children. I want them to hav shoes. Henry must hav shoes. I want you to rite to me all about your things your hogs and cattle and how much corn you made. I want to no if you are out of bacon yet and how much meet you can mak this fall. You must do the best you can and be saving for the hard times has not come yet. I dont no what you will do for salt. You and father must try to get some if you can. Catharine I will rite again as soon as I can and tel you more than I can now. William Henry my dear little son you must be a good boy and help your mother and reed your book. Lord bles the dear children. Catharine I must close for this time by saying I stil remain your husband tel death. pray for me my dear wife. So fairwell for this time. Nancy C. Yow rite as often as you can.

1862, November 14
Neill R. Kelly *(Camp near Madison Court House, VA)* to sister **Rachel Gilchrist.** General wartime correspondence with brief mentions of **John M. Kelly, Andrew Medlin, Martin Currie, John C. Ferguson** and **James Gilchrist.** [246]

My Dear Sister, I have at last concluded to drop you a few lines to let you know that I am yet in the land of the living and doing tolerable well. I have been in very good health ever since I saw you- Johns health is also as usual very good. I have no news of importance. We have never been able to learn anything of [?] fate – I fear he has gone the way of all the earth – he is either dead or very badly wounded I think, or we would have heard something from him before now. I can not but hope though that he is yet spared and will be permitted to return to his family where he is so much needed. I can't imagine how his family will get along without him. I have no war news. You can learn more from the papers than from any other source, for I assure you we know now nothing at all except what we do ourselves[.] we hardly ever get a paper and when we do get one it is generally so old that we will hardly read them. We march & countermarch so much that it is almost impossible to get anything. We were in hopes that we would get to spend the winter in North Carolina[,] but we have given up the idea now. I was very much in hopes that we would get to go somewhere we could get to buy some sweet potatoes. There is none of them made in this part of the world[.] sometimes we find a few for sale at 4 dollars per bushel but I cant eat potatoes at that price. We can get apples up here cheaper than anything else[.] we get them for 1.25 per bushel. There are two men or rather one man and one boy in our company who have gotten their discharges or we have time for them[,] old Andrew Medlin and Martin Currie. Medlin too old and Currie too young, John C. Ferguson can not get one[;] he is not forty yet. I was afraid a while that the 40 set would make a widow of you but when I thought a little I concluded that Jas. was over 40. I know that he rejoices in his sleve that he is too old. Tell him not to make too much to do over it he may have to come yet. Rachel[,] we don't get one thing to eat here but wheat bread and beef. I tell you I am getting particular tired of it[,] so tired that it makes me mad to see it. You no doubt heard of my loosing my pocket book and my money[.] if I had had any chance in Richmond[,] I would have sent you the money you wanted but I could see no chance. I drew all the money that was due me in Richmond but as good luck would have it when I got to the company the boys all out of money and I suceeded in lending all out but 65 40/100 dollars[.] if I had not[,] I would have lost it all. Some grand rascal stole it from me but I can't find out exactly who done it. I have nothing else of importance to write. You need not write until you hear from us again. I have no idea that we will stay here long neither have I any idea where we will go. I hope we will go to Weldon but have no reason to hope so. I have nothing else to write. Write as soon as you can. Give my love to Jas. and all the children. I remain your affectionate Brother. N. R. Kelly

1862, November 16
Noah Deaton (*Camp near Petersburg, VA CO H 26 Regiment, NC*) to **Sarah Jane McDonald**.
General wartime correspondence with brief mentions of **Neill** [no last name], Gen. **Hill**. [247]

Dear friend. I resume my seat this morning to answer your very kind and most welcome letter that came to hand last Friday and was much pleased to hear from you and all the rest. Neill is well and I think well satisfied. My health is very good at present and the company in tolerable good health[.] there only two in the hospital now. We are surrounded by water on all sides[;] two miles to the nearest point of main land. But from what I can learn we will not be apt to stay here long[.] where we may go I have no idea. We are under the command of Gen. Hill and he don't let it be known weeks early what he intends to do. We are hemed up here in this place so that if the enemy comes[,] we will have to fight[,] be taken on take water[.] the general has ordered as I hear for lumber to make a gang way across the sound and I guess that we will be moved across the sound shortly if not sent to some other place. I hear some of the private saying this morning that will get orders today to cook three days rations and[,] if so[,] we will be sent to some other point[.] but I doubt the truth as it very much for the hundred tongued deceivers is a doing such an active business now a days that truth so rarely tells her tale that we cannot believe it when we hear it with out proof that it is so. I hear various reports about the war movements but nothing late that is reliable or interesting. There was three war ships in sight of us yesterday and one of them was near enough for us to see them drilling on their deck[,] but they are gone today and if they know what is the best for themselves they will stay away from here or at least keep out of reach of us. You cannot think how much pleasure it would give me could I get back to Moore County again[.] there to remain in peace where I could enjoy the company of friends as before I left there and see the ladies smile and hear their voices which seem so charming. There are is a great many young fellows that have no cares to keep them from going out in defense of their country but are such cowards that they would suffer subjugation rather than fight[.] and I trust the ladies will not countenance such fellows. I hope therefore remark will be no offense but if it does? any one let them take best remedy to get rid of it. That's to take up arms to defend their homes and not wait for others to do what they should do. I must close. Please write to me soon as you can. I remain your affectionate friend. Noah Deaton

1862, November 16
Noah Deaton *(26th Infantry, Company H, near Petersburg, VA)* to friend. General wartime correspondence detailing travels from Petersburg, VA to Beaufort County, NC, Washington, NC, Tarboro, NC, Rawls Mills, Martin County, NC and Williamston, NC and battles and skirmishes in eastern NC and Governor **Z.B. Vance**. [248]

Dear Friend, I take the present opportunity to drop you a few lines[.] it has been some months since I received a letter from you and not knowing that you recd my last[,] I proceed to write a second time. I have seen much hard service since I wrote to you last. We left this place about 4 weeks ago for N.C. and after about 20 days of marching and exposure to all the weather without shelter even in time of the snow[,] we reached our old camp here last Friday for the purpose of resting a short time but I expect we will soon be out on another expediton to hunt yankees[.] 5 companies of our regt were stationed at old Ford Mills Beaufort county N.C.[,] 6 miles from Washington, N.C. Our Co. was there and was on picket at the time the yankees advanced on us but no loss on our sid at that place only 1 man of Co. E was wounded[.] the enemy had a larg force and we had to fall back to Rawls Mills[,] Martyn county[,] where we joined the rest of our regt.[.] we got thair ½ hour before the enemy and as we got a very good position[,] our regiment without any artillery held in check and drove back 3 Regiments of infantry and two Batteries of Artillery[.] the fight lasted 1½ or 2 hours[.] the enemy loss was about 100 killed while ours was 4 killed and some 10 or 12 wounded[.] our men had a position in the swamp at a ford and the enemies shot and shell passed over without much effect[.] we would wait till they got in 20 steps[,] then rise and fire on them and cut them down so fast that that but few of them evn reached this side the swamp[.] after the fight ceased[,] we were informed by the 17th Regt and a batterie of Artillery and 2 peices wer brought in position and give the enemy several rounds of shot and shell[,] but they seemed satisfied for the night and would not return a a single shot. we learned that they were sending a large force to Williamston to cut us of and so we had to resume our march so as to pass Williamston that night[,] which we did abut the time there boats arrived. next day we marched about 20 miles towards Tarboro where we met reinforcements to cope with the enemy[.] we turned upon him and aftere a little skirmish in which the yankees lost five and not a man of ours hurt[,] we pursued them to thir gunboats[.] Govener Z. B. Vance was with us in this winding up[.] I must close this badly writin letter[.] please write soon for it gives me much pleasure to hear from you at any time[.] your friend truly, Noah Deaton

1862, November 21
Charles A. Gilchrist *(Point of Rocks, VA)* to aunt **Catherine Gilchrist** and uncle **Randall Gilchrist.** General wartime correspondence with brief mentions of **Goodman, Charles Gilchrist, Cattie Gilchrist,** uncle **James** and aunt **Jennett**. [249]

Dear ant[,] I this morning seat myself to drop you a few lines to let you no that I am well at this time hoping when these few lines come to hand they will find you and all the rest of the family well and harty. I have no newse to rite at this time only we are a working very hard now on our winter quaters[.] we will soon have them done now and they say that they will give us furlow then[.] I hope it so but I dont know wether it is true or not[.] we dont hear no talk of any more fighting this winter about hear. You said something about the Goodman girls and you must not let mary tell I get back and tell them not to be uneasy for we all will soon be back.again and then we will leg them a bout rite[.] and you need not be uneasy about geting you one now for you can wait tell we all get back and then you can get a good one for yourself[.] and you be shore to get a volenteer for the concriots will run when they think they will have to fight. Shore I have sen the Goodman boys one time since I have been here in Va. it was just after the 7 days fight befor Richmond[.] they was at Mechanics factory[.] I have not heard from them since. Tell grandfather and mother houdy and Uncle James family too and ant Jinnetts family houdy too – no more at present so I must close by saying rite soon. I remain as ever, C. A. Gilchrist

Uncle Rondol Gilchrist, I seat myself to let you no that I am well and harty hoping these few lines will find you well and harty[.] I have no newse to rite at this time only we have to work very hard upon our houses but we will soon be done with them. We have bull beef and cake bread to eat and I am afraid to meet a cow or bull in the road for fear they will claim cin with me[.] so I close for this time, C. A. Gilchrist

1862, November 26

Mother **Mary A. Harper**, stepfather **John Harper** and brother **Charles Harper** to **J.L. Stuart**. General wartime correspondence with brief mentions of **Granny Shields, Levi Davis, Marshal Williams, Stephen Davis, Dempsy Sheffield, Peter Shamburger, Isaac Cagle, Hamon Miller, Bill Owens, James W. Stephens, Cynthia Teague, Lydia Comer, S.L. Davis, Lutitia Davis, Mathany Teague, L.F. Teague, M.S. Teague, Sinthia Davis, M.P. Nall, Emily C. Nall, N.N.P.N., Aletha Owen, D. Spivy, P. Spivy, S. Spivy, Anlisa Davis** and **Susan Teague**. [250]

Mr. J.L. Stuart[.] Dear Sone[,] I again rite in an Swore to your letter dated 17th[.] I was glad to see you was well and I truly hope these few lines will reach you in good health[.] we are all about like common in common health[,] but granny Shields took her bed with bowel complainte and dos like she used to[.] I was truly glad to here yesterday that you remembered your mother advice not to curse and not to play cards[.] it filled my heart with such joy that the tears fell from my eyes as by as big as bullets. I truly hope you will not let your morals splayed with wicked associates as a great many men will not keeping in vice that they hav to dec and giv an accounte for he deeds done in the boddy[.] I now you are wore out with the fatigue of work and being away from your home. I wish you could come home but you do not want to do it if you cant get to come other ways. Levi Davis & Marshall Williams has deserted[;] one has got home and are lying out Stephen Davis & [?] Allen has deserted and come home[.] they was paroled. Dempes Shuffel is trying to get clear of going by his house[.] the men here keeps on hunting conscripts. Peter Shamburger has had about 35 men garding him & Isaac Cagle and Hamon miller & Bill Owens[,] it is said threatened to kill them and burn there property for hunting him and his crowd and abusing his wife[.] we are looking for the cavalry to make a hunt. Peter Shamburger sent to the court house for the cavalry to help hunte[.] they has not come yet we think these will be some were in our land before long[.] James W. Stephens sent me a letter this morning[.] he wishes to now when you are here are Petersburg. He want you to rite to him[,] 26 Reg[.] I never wanted to see anybody so bad as I want to see you[.] it looks like I cante stand it mutch longer[.] I am wore out with the horribles of this war. I never was so sorry for anybody in my life as I am for you and I pity you with all my heart and I can not find in the nuse any hopes of peace[.] and god only knows when it will be and if all the soldiers would lay down their arms and come home[,] there might be peace but if the Yankey holds on they will perish us all out after a while[.] the people in our State will not sell corn at any price now and the governor & legislature is laying the embargo on a great many [?] in our state[.] and he says in his message that the state must raise 10 regiments to defend the state[.] they are to leave 4 months and to go home and make there corps[.] this is part of his message[.] I must conclude my letter to a close[,] to remain your loving mother on till death. Mary A. Harper. If you got back to Petersburg or Richmon[,] I will go and see you or send you any things that you want if I have it. John Harper.
Dear brother[,] it is with much pleasure for me to seat[.] I am as well as common[.] you wanted to now if we thought Jin was with food or no. I dont think she is. You wanted to no what girls talked about you. I will tell you of a few but I cant name half a quarter of them[,] forget all of them[:] C. Teague, L. Comer, S.L. Davis, Lut. Davis, Thany Teague, L.F. Teague, M.S. Teague, Sinthia Davis, M.P. Nall, E.C. Nall, N.N.P.N., Aletha Owen, D. Spivy, P. Spivy, S. Spivy, Anlisa Davis, Susan Teague[.] that about half[.] no more at present[.] rite to me as soon as you can[.] Charley E. Harper to J.L. Stuart

1862, November 30
Matthew C. Yow (*Fredericksburg, VA*) to his wife **Nancy Catherine Albright Yow** and children. General wartime correspondence with brief mentions of Capt. **James C. Dowd**, his father **Henry C. Yow,** grandfather **Andrew Yow** and children **William Henry Yow, Nancy Elizabeth Yow, Mary Jane Yow, Joseph Gibbs Yow** and **John Matthew Yow**. [251]

Dear Wife and Little Children[,] I this blesed Sabbath day tak my pen to rite you a few lines to let you no that I am well at this time and I do hop when this comes to hand it may find you all in good helth. Catharine Capt Dowd has come back and brought me a letter from you and father. I was so glad to here from you all one time more. He did not bring our cloths to us. He left them in Richmond and I dont no when we shal get them. We hav bin here 9 days expecting a battle and it has not come on yet and I hop it wont. Catharine am in a heep of trouble sinc fathers barn was burnd. I am afraid tha will do somthing to your things. I do hop tha will not pester you but I no they are not two good to burn your barn and wheet. I hav rot 2 or 3 letters to you and father sinc Dowd went home. I hop you hav got them. We hav hard times here and I think you hav bad times there. We are all in trouble. Some times I get so bad out of hart that I dont no what to do when I think of you and the pore little children. It seems like it will brak my hart for it seems like there is no chanc for me to come home soon. Tha wont giv no furlows to well men and if tha dont tha will all runaway. The men sa tha will go home to see there people and I can tel you the men will not fight as tha hav fought the way tha treted. We dont enough to eat and the flour we get is sour and it is not fit to eat but we hav to eat it or none. Catharine I hate to tel you as bad as it is. I no it hurts your feelings. Catharine do the best you can and put your trust in the good Lord for all our help must come from him. Pray for me which I beleiv you do and I hop your prares will be herd and answerd. Catharine my dear wife I do hop and pray that we may meet again in this world. If we never see each other on earth I do hop we will meet in haven. Catharine I shed tears and pray for you all. I never close my eys at night without asking the good Lord to bles and tak cear of me and I do thank the Lord that my helth has bin as good as what it has. Catharine I am in trouble but I trust in the Lord for my help. Catharine I do want to get the things that you sent to me and the potatoes and unions that the dear little children sent to me. Bles there dear soles. I do want to see them so bad. I do hop that we will get back to NC but I am afraid we shal hav to out here all winter without any tents and it will kil us all. there is lots of men here barefoot and the wether is vary cold. I can tel you a soldiers life is a hard one you may be sure. Catharine I was sorrow when you said you had no wheet sowd yet. I am a fraid you wont get none sowd. I dont no what you will if you dont. Father said in his letter that you did not hav half corn enough to do you. He said he wold hav to go to Stanly to buy corn for you or let the children sufer. Catharine you hav got money and you must giv it to him to buy corn. I no he will do the best he can for you. Catharine tel my old granfather that I hav not forgoten him yet. I do want to see him. Tel him to pray for me. May the lord bles and sav you all is my prare so no more. Catharine giv my best respect to all my friends. Tel them I want to see them all. Tel all of my brothers and sisters that I hav not forgoten them. I want to see them. If I cold I wold rite them all a letter. O that I cold see you all and talk with you one more time in this world. I shal never die satisfied without I do see you all again. I cant rite as I cold talk to you. Catharine when this you see[,] remember me though many miles apart we be. Catharine tel your father I dont get any letters from him. I hav rote several and got no answer from them. Catharine I must bring my letter to a close for this time by saying I stil remain your affectionate husband until death shal part us. Matthew C. Yow To Nancy C. Yow William H Yow Nancy E. Yow Mary J. Yow Joseph G. Yow John M. Yow My dear wife and dear little children fairwell for this time.

1862, December 19
William A. Ray to sister **Mary A. Ray**. General wartime correspondence between siblings with brief mentions of **Anderson Smith** and **John A. Cox** being wounded, **Sandy Johnson** and brother **John B. Ray**. [252]

Deare Sister, I now seat myself to write you and at the rest at home that I am well at this time and came out of the fight on hurt[.] we may be thankful we cam out as well as we did[.] there was too of the copany wounded[.] Anderson Smith, Mr Jac. A. Cox was wounded by shell[.] we are marching in line of battle when Smith was wounded[.] there was three or four work down[.] cox was wounded on the head[.] the shell busted about fifty yards from us[,] then fell another shell in about fifteen steps of our copany and thowed the dirt over us[.] it did not hurt anybody[.] I not time to write much[.] I comenced writeing yesterday and had to fall in for marching[.] it turnt out to be a fals alarm[.] we are still at the old camp and have to carry wood a long wais[.] it is rite cold today[.] I was tired and sleaping after the fight[.] some of the boxes came and I got a mess of potatoes which hop us very much[.] they have got Sandy Johnson under gard about leaving the copany in time of the fight[.] my time is geting out and I must close by asking you to write as soon as you can[.] I have writin a letter or too[.] I got no answer for yet[.] I received a letter from Brother J.B. Ray and have not answered it yet[.] I will write as soon as I can[.] I cannot tell whether or not they a pear to carry the war on thou the winter as well summer[.] I still remain your affectionate brother till death, W.A. Ray [P.S.] the co is general well except cold[.]

1862, December 19-20
Noah Deaton (*Co H 26th Regt, Goldsboro, NC*) to father **William Deaton**. General wartime correspondence with mentions battles of Goldsboro and Kinston, the burning of Neuse River bridges, the destruction of the Wilmington Railroad, **Sam Morrison**, **Neill Leach**, **James Leach**, **John C. Morrison** and Governor **Zebulon B. Vance**. [253]

Dear Father[.] I have the pleasure this morning of penciling you a few lines which will inform you that I am in good health at present time and hope these few lines may find you all in good health[.] Stop for drill and review[.] Saturday morning the 20th[.] we left Petersburg last Monday for Kinston NC[,] but the enemy had taken it before we got there and we were stopped at Mosley Hall[.] and after we burned about 150 bales of cotton[,] we turned back to Goldsboro[.] the yankees came up in the west side of the nuse river in heavy force and succeeded in reaching the Bridge at Goldsboro and burned it, cut the telegraph wire and tore up about 5 miles of the railroad (Wilmington Railroad)[.] our forces met them here and after a sharp fight[,] our forces drove them back with heavy loss on both sides[.] our pickets report that the enemy is throwing up breastworks about 10 miles from here but I doubt whether it is so or not[.] they destroyed all the bridges on the river as the came up to prevent our men from crossing from the north side and getting in their rear[.] we had no forces in this vicinity at the time the yankess made their dash but the troops got here in time to save Goldsboro and stop the yankees advance[.] troops have been pouring into this place till now[.] there are several thousand here and around here[.] the Raleigh guard got into the fight at Kinston and was completely scattered[.] there was 150 of them taken prisioner[.] Sam Morrison was among the number[.] Neill Leach, James Leach and John C. Morrison came out safe[;] I saw them[.] Gov. Z.B. Vance was here amongst us[.] we are ready for movement at any moment but I have no idea were or which way we may go[.] it depends upon which direction the yankees go[.] I muse close[.] may God assist us and shield our defenceless forms from every danger and bless us for the redeemers sake[.] your obedient son, Noah Deaton.

1862, December 25
Henry W. Stutts *(Soldier's Hospital, Richmond)* to **Kenneth B. Kelly**. General wartime correspondence with brief mention of **Sandy**. [254]

Dear Friend, I take this opportunity of writing to you to let you know that I am well at present and hope these few lines may find you all well and enjoying a happy Christmas. I have no news of importance to communicate to you. I am getting well of the small pox and have hardly anything else to do at the hospital but to sit down and smoke the pipe, chew tobacco or else lounger about the house. I have sent twenty dollars to my wife in a letter I wrote to her yesterday Christman Eve and[,] if she get it[,] I want you to take the money and lay it out for the benefit of the family for such things as they need. If you get this money[,] I want you to write directly back to me and let me know so that I can send you more and if you do not get it[,] I would very much like for you to come to Richmond after some money as I have about ninety dollars. I would like for my wife to have but I am afraid to send by letter. Write me what kind of [?] you and my wife have made. I would not have begrudged twenty dollars if I could have been at home with you all this Christmas[,] but I suppose it is no use to grumble about because it is too late now. I have had my eggnog though for all that. Write me word whether Sandy has ever come home or not or whether he has sent his wife any money or not. Regard my word how trim comes on. I will close this letter wishing you all a happy Christmas. I still remain your devoted friend. Henry W. Stutts

1863, January 11
J.L. Stuart (*Camp near Petersburg, VA*) to mother **Mary A. Harper,** stepfather **John Harper,** brother **Charles Harper,** sister **Mary A. Harper** and grandmother **Nancy Glass Nall**. General wartime correspondence with brief mentions of **Matthew Williamson, John Harper, Isaac Teague** and **Peter Comer**. [255]

Dear Mother[,] I seat myself to inform you that I am still alive and well and hearty and I truly hope these few lines may come to hand in due time and reach you all alive and getting along as well as this life will afford[.] this is the third letter I have wrote to you this year[.] this morning Mathew Williamson received a letter from John Harper and he stated that he had not heard from me in five weeks[,] and that you very uneasy about me[.] I am very sorry that my letters does not come safe to you[.] I never fail in writing once a week if no more[.] But I think our letters will come safe now we have got back to Petersburg[.] You stated in your letter to M. that Isaac Teague and Peter Comer was dead which I was very sorry to hear[.] the letter stated that they died at Petersburg[.] I want you to write to me as soon as this letter comes to hand for I want to hear from you all[.] we left Fredericksburg last Saturday week and now we are eighty five miles from there[.] we are waiting for orders to come and I expect we will be ordered to North Carolina if there is much fighting to do there[.] if we get back to Goldsboro[,] I would like for John Harper to pay us a visit[.] But if we put up winter quarters[,] I think that we will get furloughs[.] But I hope that this bad war will soon com to a close[.] our soldiers are in very high spirit here[.] we laugh and talk and hale[.] if you was here to see us[,] you would think that we do like we did when we was at home I mean any of ourselves as well[.] but I want to come home the worst in this world[,] but it is not my fault that I do not come[.] all the soldiers are very tiard of the war[.] I sometimes think that peace will be made by spring[.] But it may not be made in ten year[.] I can inform you that I have been vaccinated in my arm for the Small Pox[.] it taken very well[.] all of our Regiment have been vaccinated[.] the Small Pox is in all the larg town but I hope that I will not have it[.] I want you to write what illment Isaac & Peter died with[.] I hope this letter will come safe to you this time and I want you to write soon[.] Direct your letters to Petersburg Va[,] 49th regt[.] N.C. troops in care of Capt Black[,] Co. D[.] I must bring my letter to a close[.] I remain your affectionate son[,] Jno. L. Stuart

Mr Jno. Harper[.] Dear stepfather[,] I recd a letter from you this mornin[.] I was very glad to hear that you was yet alive[.] I want you to write to soon and let me know how you are getting along[.] I was very sorry to hear that Isaac & Peter Comer was dead[.] write-when they died. Jno. L Stuart

Dear Brother Charles[,] I am well and hearty and I hope that you are well[.] I want to see you very Bad[.] I want you to write me a big letter this morning[.] we drawd a drink of whiskey apiece[.] I sold mine for one Dollar. Sis[,] I want to see you mity bad[.] I want you to write to me[.] I am your Brother[,] J.L.S

Grandmother[,] I want to see you very Bad[.] I hope that you are well. When this you see[,] remember me[,] John L. Stuart

1863, January 12

Mary A. Harper mother and stepfather **John Harper** to **J.L. Stuart**. General wartime correspondence with brief mentions of **William Dunn, Isaac Teague, Peter Comer, Banister Hogans, William Nall** and **Nicholas Nall**. [256]

Mr J.L. Stuart[.] Dear Son[,] I now write you answer your last letter received by us[.] we received 3 letters January and none sense. I was glad to find that you was well and in good heart after fiting that the great battle at Fredericksburg and with the good luck to come of on hurt. Thank you for that with all and with all other blessings[.] I have answered your letters before this but I do not no that you had received it. I want you to be mity careful about the Small Pox and not get init the papers[.] state there is near a thousand cases of Small Pox at Petersburg and at Richmond and I want you to be careful and keepe out of it or get noculated and it mite go easy with you if you get it[.] and if you should get nearer home and was to get sick let me now[,] and I would send you something good to eat[.] I wish you could get a furlow and come home a while. We understand the 26 Regiment is guarding the Weldon and it is expected the yankees is trying to get in possession of the railroad. We look for troublesome times in our state[.] rite off there is a large army of yankees at New Bern and the papers state they are on an onward march for the railroad and Wilmington. Our men was called to meet at the court house at Carthage yesterday and none went from our end of the county[,] and they swear they wont go[.] the woods is full of conscripts and deserters and they are doing mischief and threatening to kill or destroy the property of any of their neighbors that speaks against them. We are afraid to say anything against them[.] they are inquiring who does speak against them. There was 400 armed men last week in Chatham hunting for deserters and conscripts and were looking for a company from Raleigh to hunt these reaches up[.] but there is not enough of men now at Raleigh to guard the city and our state lacks men to defend her soil[,] and it is to be feared the State will suffer by the enemy. William Dun deserted and is at home[.] he deserted at Petersburg by changing cars. Isaac Teague is dead & Peter Comer dead & Banister Hogins is dead at Petersburg[.] William Nall had his leg shot in the knee joint and it was cut off. Nick went to Goldsborough and saw him and he is mending and will soon be at home. I rote these things in your other letters but I do not now whether you got it. I keep about the rumatism hurts me some. The health of the family is as good as common[.] I want to see you the worst in the world[.] I can not tell yo how anxious my mind is to see you. You are ever present in my mind[.] many times I go to the door and look a way towards the north[,] thinking mabe my son is that way and my eager mind casts a sigh that you are in the care of god. His mercies is ever shure to those that fear him. My son[,] look to god and he will save you out of all harm. I tryed to get you som stamps but there was none at the office. No more[.] only your dear mother and her husband[.] love[,] Mary A. Harper John Harper

1863, January 18

Matthew C. Yow (*Goldsboro, NC*) to his wife **Nancy Catherine Albright Yow** and children. General wartime correspondence with brief mentions of Capt. **James C. Dowd**, his father **Henry C. Yow** and father-in-law **Joseph Albright**. [257]

Dear Wife and Little Children[,] I tak my pen in hand to let you no where I am. I am at Goldsboro NC one time more and I am well and I do hop when this comes to hand it may find you well. We landed here yesterday but cant tel how long we shal stay. I think we shal go to Wilmington. Tha say the Yankees is going to try that place and if tha do[,] there will be some hard fiting done for we hav a great many men here now. Catharine I got a letter from you the 2 of January --- that I hav had sinc Dowd come back and --- letters and I am afraid you never get them. The chanc has bin bad to get letters from you for we hav bin marching so much. I do hop you will get this and I think we will get letters now. I got a letter from your father the same day that I got yours. I hav not got no letter from my father sinc Dowd come back. I want him to rite and let me no how he is geting along these hard times. Catharine I herd this morning that there was 5 regiments of Yankees at New Burn laid down there arms and said tha wold not fight no more against us. I cant tel how true it is. Catharine I cant tel you when I can come home. It seems like I never shal get to see you and my dear little children any more. I want you to do the best you can and pray for pore me that I may get home to see you all one more time in this world. I have praid for the good Lord to protect and save me and I do hop he will hear and answer my prares. May the good Lord bles and save us all forever. Catharine rite when you get this[.] so fairwell my dear wife Nancy C. Yow.

1863, January 31
Mastin C. Phillips (*Winder Hospital*) to sister **Emeline Phillips**. General wartime correspondence with brief mentions of **Malphus Phillips, Baxter Phillips** and parents **Lewis Phillips** and **Nancy Phillips**. [258]

Dear Sister, Your very lengthy letter was received today. I was truly happy to hear from home and that all were well. I was not surprised to hear of the sickness in N. C. I do hope that you all will be spared. I was uneasy about the small pox for a while, but I am not much now although I may have it yet, as it is still raging in this city and many are dying. When you write again[,] I want you to use ink. I can not decipher a part of this letter. I guess I have made out the most important. have written to Malphus and Baxter. I was glad to hear where they were, but was sorry to hear that Malphus was so unwell. I hope ere this he is quite well again. I suppose my regiment is in N. C. I expect to go there soon, perhaps I may see him. I know not what to say about my clothes. I reckon though you had better have them ready and send them to me soon as I get to the Regiment. I will let you know when I get there. Make them the best you can. I guess you will have to make my uniform coat for I shall need it, and you can make the overcoat quite easy. Make it a close bodied coat and then put the cape on it. Make it a loose fit for Pa and it will do for me. I guess I shall need the flannell clothes too. The letter you spoke about from Mrs. Johnson, where is it? Did you mail it or did you forget it, or do you intend to keep it until I get home? I wish to know more about it. I have written to her since I came here, but did not give her my address. If I get the letter you spoke of[,] I will write again. I will devote the rest of this sheet to Ma. I hope you will continue to pray for me. I think I will see you again. Mastin

1863, February
Neill A. Baker (*Camp near Goldsboro, NC*) to wife **Sarah Jane Baker**. General wartime correspondence between husband/wife with brief mentions of **Neill T. Watson, Jack Thomas, John Godfrey, William J. Kelly, John B. McFarland, Robert B. Thomas, David Thomas, Absalom Kelly, Getty Cox, John Buchanan, Jasper Thomas** and the blockade at Charleston. [259]

Dear Jane, Having a good opportunity of sending you a few lines by N.T. Watson, I embrace it. This leaves me in my usual health. Hope that this will reach you & the babies enjoying the same blessing. Mr. Watson goes home on furlough for 14 days—also Jack Thomas & Sergeant John Godfrey. Again[,] I am acting quartermaster[.] sergeant "vice" William J. Kelly gone home upon furlough for 14 days. John B. McFarland got an indefinite detail to work in Goldsboro upon guns for government and I am pretty certain that he will get a furlough too to go after his tools. One man for every twenty-five gets furloughs[,] but you see Sergt. W. J. Kelly or J. B. McF's furloughs has nothing to do with the furloughs of those of the company. We have a good many visitors. Rob & David Thomas' wives & mother, Absalom Kelly & Petty Cox came today, John Buchanan & daughter & Jasper Thomas' wife came last evening and some others that came before. We have good news in today's papers, some of which I will mention.

Our little navy pitched into the blockading vessels at Charleston, SC and cleared the ranch—raised or opened the blockade without any loss on our side. I still have very flattering hopes that we will soon have peace again in our land. I have a very strong opinion that in a few days the number of furloughs will be increased for because if they are not[,] you see one for every twenty-five men—it would take nearly or quite all the year for all to get home at that rate. If there is no threatening movement of the enemy soon[,] I am confident that the number will be increased. I want to go in this or the first of next month[,] if possible. Nothing more worth your attention. Yours truly – Neill A. Baker

1863, February 1
Matthew C. Yow (*New Hanover County, NC*) to his wife **Nancy Catherine Albright Yow** and children. General wartime correspondence with brief mentions of Capt. **James C. Dowd**, his father **Henry C. Yow,** uncle **John Henry Stutts, John Lewis Maness, William Nicholas Brower, Col. Robert C. Hill** and **James Goodwin Morgan**. [260]

My Dear Wife and Little Children[,] I one more time take my pen to rite you a few lines to let you no that I am well at this time and I do hop when this comes to hand it may find you all well. Catharine I rote you a letter the 18 of January when I was at Goldsboro and I hav bin looking for a letter from you for some time and I hav not got no answer yet. I hav not had no letter from you sinc the 2 of January and I do want to here from you so bad I dont no what to do. Catharine I cant tel what is the matter. We left Goldsboro the 17: and marcht to a place called South Washington ---- miles from Willmington and this morning we marcht 6 or 7 miles nearer to Willmington on the railrode and I cant tel how long we shal stay here but not long I no. I expect we shal get into a fight before long but I cant tel what we are going to do. We are always marching through rain and mud and water. We see hard times you may be sure but sinc we come to NC we hav enough to eat such as bread and meat and we hav some potatoes. We hav bin drawing fresh pork and it eats mity good to me. Catharine I am fat. Uncle John Stuts says I am fatter than he ever seed me. I am as harty as I ever was in my life and I am so thankful that I am for it is so bad to be sick in camp. Catharine I cant tel you where you had beter direct your letters but I think you had beter send them to Goldsboro and tha will come to me. Direct to Goldsboro NC[,] General Cooks Brigade[,] Co D[,] the 48 regiment[,] NC Troops in cear of Capt Dowd. Catharine if you get this letter I want you to rite to me and I want father to rite to me and John Manes and W.N. Brower. I want to here from them all. Catharine I think there be some chanc to get to come home this spring. Colonel Hill says if them that has runaway will come back by the 10 of this month tha will not be punisht and if tha dont tha will be shot without any trial. And tha had beter come. If tha will come back we will get furlows. James Morgan is at home now. Colonel Hill has come back again and he says we all shal go home to see our families. I do hop and pray that I can come to see you and the children one more time in this world. May the good Lord bles and sav us all for ever. Catharine dont forget to pray and pray for me that I may be spard to get back again. Catharine I want rite to me whether brother Jones is gon back or not. I want to rite to them and I dont no where to rite. But I suppose tha hav gon bak to Raleigh. I do want to see them so bad. Your brothers has come to NC but I dont no where tha are. We dont stay in one plac long enough to here from any of you. Catharine I want you to right as often as you can. I want to here from you. If I cold get to any place that I cold stay any time I cold rite to you where to send your letters. I must close for this time. Catharine My dear wife do the best you can. I am praying for you and my dear little children that you may not suffer. May the good Lord bles and sav us all for ever is my prare. Matthew C. Yow to Nancy C. Yow fairwell.

1863, February 6
Willis A. Nall (*camp near Fredericksburg, VA*) to uncle **John Harper,** aunt **Mary A. Harper,** and cousins **Charles Harper** and **Mary Ann Harper**. General wartime correspondence with brief mentions of **Nancy Glass Nall, John Lane Stuart, Isaac Teague** and **Peter Comer.** [261]

Dear uncle[,] it is with great pleasure that I seat my self to answer your letter dated January the27th which give me great pleasure to hear from you all[.] and hear that you was all well[,] truly hoping may all remain in good health[.] I am well at this time. (illegible) I have been in the best health since I left home[.] the last time that I have been since I had the fever[.] there is no talk of a fight hear now[.] the yankees still remain on the other of the river and we on this side in sight of each other[.] they lack a strong force on the other side of the river and we have a strong force on this side[.] We are reddy to meet them any time when they feal like crossing[.] and if they dont mind[,] they will lose more men than they did when they crossed before[.] We fought below[.] We can whip them and forth if a keep up of help[.] we have whipt them so much when we are drawn up in line of battle[,] we can hear all the boys crying out[.] We will whip them[.] Just let them come but I will tell you[,] uncle John[,] they shoot well but we look a little to much of spunk for them[.] We have colde weather here[.] it is almost always snowing or raining We have[.] tell grand mother I send her my best respects and love and I would be glad to see her one more time in this world which I hope I will[.] tell her that I am well tell the girls not to git out of heart for me[.] and[,] John[,] I hope will get to come home before long[.] plenty to eat and not much to do at the present time[.] you said ther was several of my friends and relations dead which I was sorry to here[.] I had heard of Isaac Teague and Peter Comer being dead but I had not heard of the rest of the deaths. the health of the comp is very good now[.] ther is some small pox hear but I dont think it is as bad as if it was a month or so back[.] So I will close for this time[.] Write soon and give me all the news you can[.] So no more[.] I remain yours truly[,] W. A. Nall to John Harper

A few lines to aunt Mary[.] I am well hoping these lines may find you well[.] Dear aunt[,] I would be glad to see you and talk with you but I dont know when I shall[.] but I hope the time will not be long before we all can come home and stay[.] I dont think this war can last much longer[.] you must not grieve yourself to much about John[.] I hope he will return home safe and unhurt[.] when you write to him you must tell him I have not forgotten him yet and I would be glad see him and talk with him[.]

A few lines to Charles and Mary an Harper[.] you must be smart and work hard to try to make something for the soldiers to eat for I think that provision will be spent by another year[.] and when your papy and mother tell you to do any thing[,] you might think of your cousin Arin and your brother John who is fighting for you[,] and think they have to have something to eat[.] if you cant do no fighting[,] you can do your part in this war by work and it will be of much honor to you if you had a fought[.] So I will close[.] so no more from[,] W. A. Nall to his aunt Mary Harper and Charles and Mary an Harper) be good children[.]

1863, February 8
J.L. Stuart (*camp near Kenansville, NC*) to mother **Mary A. Harper** and stepfather **John Harper**. General wartime correspondence with brief mentions of **Charles Harper, Martha Nall** and **John Teague.** [262]

Dear mother[,] I seat myself to answer your letter of 3 inst[.] I was pleased to hear from you all one more time for I was getting very uneasy about you all for it is the 2nd letter I have received from you since we came to NC[.] Mother[,] you had something to say about me taking the Snows & bad weather but I fare a great deal better than you might suppose[.] I beg of you not to greave so much about me[.] my health has been very good ever since the first of August[.] I was sorter poorly a few dayes back with cold but I Kept on foot].] I am very hearty and well at present[.] I am able to eat my allowance[.] I hope this letter will come to hand and find you all getting along well[.] you stated that you was very poorly[.] I hope that you will get better and get so that you can go about your business[.] we have had one little snow here about a week ago[.] it was three or four inches deep[,] not so cold here as it is with you[.] you stated that you had only received one letter from me since we came back to NC[.] I have wrote you three or four letters and I wrote one to Charles[.] I started a letter to Martha Nall this morning and I wrote one to John Teague yesterday to know what was the mater with you as I did not get no letter from you. I have no stamps and I have to frank my letters but I did not send it for I could not get no stamp[,] but I received your letter yesterday evening[.] I have Just came from church it was the first sermon I have heard since last July[.] it was a Baptist church[.] to day was their seacrament day[.] there was some as pretty gals as common[.] there it appears like a have bad luck writing to the girls when it comes to the old folks at home finding it out[.] I want to see you very bad but I do not know when I can get to come home[.] I hope this war will close this spring so we all can get to go home[.] some of us could get furloughs if it was that all our company was present[,] but we have some absent with out leave and that keeps us from getting furloughs[.] it is heard that men that have their duty cannot get to go home because some is absent without leave[.] I hope I will get to see you soon[.] I think I will get to come after a while[.] Do the best you can[.] I think I will be along after a while but I should stick to my post[.] let the regt go where it will I will go if I am able[,] but I want a furlough mity bad.

Mr John Harper[,] I was glad to hear from you[.] you stated that was going to start to see me but heard that we had moved from Warsaw[.] we are at Kenansville[,] the county seat at Duplin[,] about twelve miles from

Warsaw[.] I should be very glad to see you[.] if you aim to come[,] you had better come soon[.] We may move from hear[.] write soon as this comes to hand[.] J.L. Stuart[,] Co D[,] 49[.]

1863, February 9
William Henry Patterson (*Warsaw, NC*) to sister **Frances Anna V. Patterson**. General wartime correspondence between siblings with brief mentions of **Sam McLeod, Jones, Rufus Gloven, Calvin Blue** and **William Blue**. [263]

Dear Sister, I have concluded to drop you a line to let you know of my safe arrival here(Warsaw). I left Fayetteville yesterday at 2 o'clock[.] after a very tiresome ride[,] we arrived at this place at 4 o'clock this morning. The stage was very much crowded and we had 11 passenger and you will know that we were very much crowded. Though I enjoyed the trip as well as I expected. Sam McLeod came with to Clinton, Mrs. Jones from Carthage came with us to this place. Rufus Gloven came on the stage to this place. He is the young man that went off in the Partisan Rangers but he has been transfered to Capt. Starr's Artillery Company now at Goldsboro. My Regt. is still at Magnolia. I expect I will have to wait here till evening before the train will come down from Goldsboro. It should have been here at 6 o'clock this morning but it is now between 7 and 8 and it has not arrived yet and it is said that the train will not come along till evening. Magnolia is 9 miles below here on the R. road. Mrs. Jones told me that she understood that our company is to be sent back to Moore County to catch conscripts and deserters and Calvin Blue said that his brother William said some thing about that in his letter. If our Co. is sent back to Moore[,] it will be likely that it will be sent pretty soon. The train is now running by this place from Wilmington to Goldsboro. I did not sleep any last night and consequently I feel rather green. I write these few to you to let you know where our regt. is as I believe this will reach you by this weeks mail, as the stage will leave here this evening for Fayetteville and if I would not write until I get to the Regt. I think it very doubtful whether it will reach you this week or not. I told Pa that I would probably write to him this week and direct Fayetteville as he said he intended to go there this week. I may write after I get to Regt. and direct to Fayetteville if I think that it will get to Fayetteville soon enough for him to get it[.] I had to pay $6.50 on the stage. My hand is so cold and there is so much confusion here that I cannot write. So I will close for the present. Your Afft. Brother W. H. Patterson

1863, February 15
Baxter C. Phillips (*Hospital, Danville, VA*) to sister **Emeline Phillips**. General wartime correspondence with brief mentions of parents **Lewis Phillips** and **Nancy Phillips**. [264]

Dear Sister, Yours came to hand last night, money and all safe. It is sufficient for my personal need. I was truly thankful to hear you were all well. It does me good to hear such news from dear old home. I pray God to continue to you these blessings. He has seen fit to afflict me, I trust. I try to improve under his counseling hand. It is all for my good and I feel it so. I feel better today than I have since I came here, but I am not well yet. It is dyspepsia that ails me, I suppose, and you know how curious it works. I have no idea of ever standing camp life any more, still I reckon I must try it soon if I get no worse. I don't know yet when I will go to the Regiment. The Dr. may not let me leave this winter, or I may go this week. I will just as soon as I get able and if I get worse I intend to report at hospital in Raleigh where I will be closer home, and in my own state. I am getting tired of Danville, that is sure. I have heard my Regiment has gone to South Carolina. I don't know whether it is true or not. It was in North Carolina the last time I heard from it. We have had some bad weather here, though it is nice now and I hope will stay so. I wish your country was clear of conscripts and run-aways. It is a shame to the state that such is the case. The path of duty is the only path of safety and honor. One thing I want to know, has all forgotten me but you? I don't hear a word from anyone else. I have asked them to write me but they don't seem to do it. (I don't mean Ma and Pa)[;] They won't forget me. I shall not ask anyone to write any more. It is for them to write fist, and then I will answer them. I think you will write, but please get some better paper. It is more than I can do to make out part of it. Tell Pa not to come until he hears from me again. The war will soon be over and I pray God to let me live and see you all again. There is no chance of getting up here, that is a settled fact. I have got used to disappointment, and am satisfied with my situation. Give my love to Pa and Mother. Tell them I am trying to do as they advised me, and I find great comfort in it. I can almost adopt the language of Christ and say, "Thy Will Be Done." This is what I want to feel in my heart and speak in my conduct in life. Tell them to continue to pray for me. I will send you a ring. You will keep it in remembrance of me, though it is a trifling thing, yet keep it. Address:

B. C. Phillips[,] Co. D.[,] 48th Regt. NC, Div. Cen.[,] Hospital No. 2, Danville, VA, I may be gone, and it will follow me. B. C. Phillips

1863, February 15
J.L. Stuart to mother **Mary A. Harper,** stepfather **John Harper,** brother **Charles Harper,** sister **Mary Ann Harper** and grandmother **Nancy Glass Nall**. General wartime correspondence. [265]

Mrs Mary A. Harper[.] Dear Mother[,] I seat myself tonight to inform you that I am well at present & I truly hope these lines may come to hand in due time and find you all getting along as well as this present life will afford[.] I have nothing of interest to write to you only we are getting along very well but we have to stand guard once a week if not oftener[.] I have Just come off guard[.] I hardly know whether to write to you or not for I can not get no letters nor answers from any of you[.] I write one and two letters to you ever week[.] I want to hear from you very bad[.] the latest account I had was the 3 of inst[.] Dear mother[,] I want to see you all the worst in the world and it will be some time before I get to come there from our co on a fourteen dayes furlough[.] we get one furlough to every twentyfive[.] we have only thirty three men present but my time will be along after a while[.] Dear mother[,] I think I shall see you after awhile if we live[.] I think perhaps peac will be made By the last of may[.] I hope so at any rate[.] the 49th is comeing out[.] she wrastler and jump and has all kind of sport. I hope to see you all soon and I want you to write[.] any how I the world if I do not get a letter by Sunday[,] I shall have to quit writing to you[.] be certain to write for I want to hear from you[.] Yours aft[,] J.L. Stuart

Mr John Harper, I am looking for you ever day but I may not see you quick[.] it appears like I can not no letters from you indeed of seeing you[.] the last letter I received from you was dated the 3rd inst[.] write how you are getting along and how things are in gener all[.] I would be Pleased to see you if you come down but if you are too long[,] I will not insist[.] I have heard it often said a body could go home when they could not go nowhere yet but that is a mistake for I have been both in Va & MD[,] but they have never let me go home[.] your obedient[,] J.L. Stuart

A few lines to Charles[.] Dear Brother[,] I want to see you very bad and I hope I will go to see you soon[.] my health is pretty good I hope this letter will find you well[.] I want to know all your times and sprees and how your julark is[.] write me all your nuse and tell the girls I shall be along after awhile[,] to have their shoes well tallowed[.] Charles give me all your nuse and times and try to write it and so I can read it[.] your Dear Brother[,] J.L. Stuart

Dear sister and grandmother[,] I want to see you very bad but I can say is I send you my best respects and wants to see you very bad[.] Direct your letters to Kenansville NC[,] 49 regt[,] and at troops co D in care of Capt Black[.] J.L. Stuart

1863, February 15
David H. Sloan to mother **Catharine Sloan**. General wartime correspondence with brief mention of **John A. Sloan**. [266]

Dear Mother, I seat myself to drop you a few lines to inform you that I am well at present and heavier than I ever was in my life. Hoping when this comes to hand it may find you and all well. I drop you those few lines to inform you that I heard from John the other day. He is at Richmond in the hospital. I would write to him if I knew what hospital to write to. I am going to try to find out what hospital he is in[.] and[,] if I do, I will write to him and I will write to you also and let you know about him. So nothing more. D.H. Sloan

1863, February 15
Matthew C. Yow (*New Hanover County, NC*) to his wife **Nancy Catherine Albright Yow** and children. General wartime correspondence with brief mentions of **James G. Morgan, George B. Campbell, Col. Robert C. Hill** and son **John Matthew Yow**. [267]

Dear Wife and Little Children[,] I one more time tak my pen in hand to drop you a few lines to let you no that I am well at this time and I do hop when this comes to hand it may find you all in good helth. Catharine I receivd your vary kind letter last night wich was great satisfaction to me to here from you one time more. I was so uneasy that I cold not rest at all. I hav not had no letter from you sinc the 2 day of January and you may no that I was uneasy. I rote you a letter the 1 of this month and on the 8 and I hop you will get them all. Catharine you said that you wanted me to come home. I think I will get a furlo to come before long. I do not want to runaway if tha will giv me half a chanc. James Morgan and Georg Camel is at home on furlo and some is going every day. Colonel Hill says we shal all go to see our families but I am a fraid we shant all get to go. Catharine I will tel you where we are now. We are in camp on the railrode at a place cald Burgaw 22 miles from Wilmington and I herd that we was under marching orders but I cant tel how true it is. Catharine you said that you was in so much trouble. I no you are. I want you to do the best you can and put your trust in the good Lord and he will help you in time of trouble. Catharine I am praying for you and the dear little children and I hop and believ that he will here and answer my prare. I can tel you I am in trouble but I trust in the good Lord for help and all that trust in Him[,] He will bless. I am amongst all sorts of people and I hav hard trials but let others do as tha may I will serv my God. I hav one Testament and two him books and I read them every chanc I get. You said you wisht I cold see little John. I do wish I cold see him and all the rest. M.C. Yow

1863, February 17
Mastin Phillips (*Winder Hospital, Richmond, VA*) to sister **Emeline Phillips**. General wartime correspondence between siblings with brief mentions **Baxter C. Phillips**, father **Lewis Phillips**, **Candace Phillips** and husband **Richard Street**, and **Billy**[?]. [268]

Dear Sister[.] Yours of the 11 inst came to hand to day. I was truly glad to hear from home. You will have learned ever this reaches you that I have been confined to my bed again[.] I am still suffering, but happy to inform you that I am improving though it will be several days & perhaps weeks before I shall be able to take the field again. I wrote to Baxter the same day I did to you but have received no answer yet. I guess I did not get the address right. That letter was so badly marked out that it was very unsatisfactory to me. You ask again about what I need[.] Well I have written that I would try to make out with what I have while I am here. I drew a pr pants, drawers & shirt some time ago, but I have no shoes or hat yet. I wrote to Pa the other day[.] I thought then that I would get a pair of shoes, but I have not got them yet & the prospect is very good that I shall not, but as I am confined to the house all the time[,] it has not made so much diference[.] I cant get away from here untill I get well and when I get able to leave if they do not give me shoes[,] they will find some difficulty in getting that of me, the fact is I'll fight no more untill I am shod. Make my clothes & keep them untill I call for them. I may call for them in a few weeks or I may never call at all. Mrs Johnson's letter came to hand the day after I wrote to you, I was very glad to hear from her[.] She always sends me words of cheer[.] Have you ever thought that this (to some a strange proceeding) may lead to some thing real one of these days? Dont try to imagine what I mean for you cant guess in a month but perhaps you will understand some day. Where is Candace and what shall I call him? I have not heard one word from them since I heard they were married – in fact I do not know that they are married. Please let me know something definitely about them. I was glad to learn that Billy had reached home, I was afraid he was dead. If you see him tell where I am and tell him to take care of himself. Tell Pa that I will go to the regiment when I am all right. I will let him know. You all want me to come home & I want to come but I tell you again not to look for me for I never expect to try again untill the war is over. I expect to come there if living. But do not be uneasy about me, I hope the good Lord will carry me safely through[.] Do the best you can all of you, I think we will meet again, My love to you all & to my friends. Pray for me. Your affectionate brother, Mastin [P.S.] Write as soon as you get this.

1863, February 20
Mary A. Harper and **John Harper** to son (and step-son) **J.L. Stuart**. General wartime correspondence with mentions of deserters, conscripts, **Elijah Spivey, Temple Spivey, Murphy Owens, William Deaton, Willis Aaron Nall, Levi Deaton, John Brewer, Polly Brewer, John Teague, Permelia Teague** and the death of a deserter **Morgan.** [269]

Dear son[,] I again rite in answer to your letter 15th this instant[.] I was glad to find that you was well but I sorry to here that you can not get letter from me for I make one to you every week but some times two[,] and I fear they keepe the money and letter[.] I took it the poste office[.] if they was sent rite[,] you wonte get them[.] my health is bad and it fore days but I keep trying So all I can[.] it is gitting to be hard times here[.] the people has got very little corn to sell in the contry and at the price 2 to 3 dollars a bushel and there is about one horse in cavalry[.] men in our neighborhood hunting conscripts and Deserters and they are to feed and they are taking all the horses from the deserters and the men that Joins them deserters[.] they took two from Lige Spivey[,] 3 from Temple Spivey[,] from Murphy Owens and 3 from Wm Deaton[.] and they say they will take all the horses from the Deserters if they dont come in and giv themselves up[.] they say they will hunt for year or get them[.] The deserters is close[.] they hav not got none in our neighborhood yet. I saw 42 of the cavalry yesterday morning a paste our house[.] they look poorly. you State that you thought you would be a long after a while to see us[.] I want to see that time come mity bad So that I can get to see you for I cante got to a letter to you[,] and that upsets me because a letter from Oren [Aaron] Nall yesterday an[.] he say he is well and hearty and sends his best respects to you and tells you not to griev for too hard bout you[.] he thinks we will see him and you at home before long and he thinks he will be man soon. He is at Fredericksburg yet and says if the yankeys will come over they will get them a worser whipping than they got before. the rest of our family is all well as common. I stated in a letter to you 2 weeks ago that about 3 weeks past there come a deserter from Raleigh home with Levi Deaton[,] both deserters. Deaton left the man names Morgan at John Brewers in the nite. Seek and gave out and he went home. Morgan stayed all nite at John Brewers[.] he complained of the matris and say nothing else about him. Brewer had him near my house next day and he beg to Stay all nite and I can not get shot of him[.] he begs me to let him lye in the home and I don ot but he could not walk and in the nite I brought him in and let him ly on a bed in the shed that nite[.] about 2 oclock I heard him praying and calling me[.] I wente to him and saw a braking out in his fase[.] I gav him some tea and Started him with mair and got him to Bill Deatons and Deaton let him stay all nite and next morning[.] Deaton took him to (illegible) on his way home and that nite he died and they said they did not now what else from[,] but the truth is he had the small pox for one of Deatons children has dyed with pox and Polly Brewer has got the pox now. We have escaped the pox yet and 20 days has passed and I hope we may not take it but if we escape it will be good luck. Morgin told us nothing but lyes. He said he had not been in the army and he was run away from the (illegible) in Raleigh, I must tell you my dreem. I dreamed last Wednesday nite that I saw my poor son come home from the army and you comin and sat down by the fire and I was lying on the bed and John Teagues wife was setting by the fire and you and her was talking and I did not now who you was and you talked awhile[,] and I said Meary ant that John my son and she said yess. I sprang from the bed and came to you and you looked at me and I fell on my nees at your chare and threw my arm around your neck[.] and I thot you dropped your head on your nees and your color changed and the dollars stove in your eyes like sparkles but you never spoke to me and I waked crying and I happen asked you what was the matter. I saw you as plain as I ever did. I was in hopes you had (illegible)...a dream but if we don't meet again no more on this earth but hav to meet in heaven and there we will part no more. I must close by hoping you may get this letter. Your absent mother. M.A. Harper. [followed by short and illegible note from John Harper]

1863, February 27
Matthew C. Yow (*Pocotaligo, SC*) to his wife **Nancy Catherine Albright Yow** and children. General wartime correspondence with brief mentions of **James Monroe Garner,** his brothers **Simeon Jones Yow, Isaac Yow,** uncle **John Henry Stutts** and son **Henry W. Stutts,** father **Henry C. Yow,** stepmother **Elizabeth Randall Maness Yow** and children **William Henry Yow, Nancy Elizabeth Yow, Mary Jane Yow, Joseph Gibbs Yow** and **John Matthew Yow.** [270]

Dear Wife and Little Children[,] I one more time tak my pen in hand to drop you a few lines to let you no that I am well at this time and I do hop when this comes to hand it may find you and the dear little children well. Catharine I receivd your vary kind letter yesterday the 26 that you rote the 15. Catharine I was so glad to here that you was all well. I shal look for more letters soon. I hav Rote 4 or 5 in this month and I hop tha all will get to you. I Rote one sinc I come to this place the 24. I hop you will get it. Catharine you said in your letter that Monrow Garner wanted to By Henrys colt Colonel Walker. I dont want you to sel him yet. I do hop and pray that I will get home again. Henry wants to keep him and I want him to keep his colt. Catharine you said that you wanted me to come home and help you plant your Irish potatoes. I am a fraid I cant get home that soon. We hav got so far off down here in the swamps. Our regiment is vary helthy at this time but I am a fraid it wont be so long in these moosy swamps. Catharine you said that you made a good crop of Irish potatoes last year. You said that you thought you had 11 bushels now. Take cear of them. Tha will bring you 4 or 5 dollars per bushel this spring. Catharine we dont fare as well in South Carolina as we did in NC. We get beef here and not much of that. We hav got some pork. I think if we hav to stay here long we shal see hard times. But that is what we are use to is hard times. I cant tel whether we shal hav any fight here or not. Some thinks we will and if we do it will be in a few days. I do hop the fiting is nearly over. I dont think it can last much longer. Catharine, Jones said in his letter that he was going back to his company and I was glad to here that for I want him to go to his company. He said that Isaac was not going back if he cold help it. I think he had beter go. If he dont tha will tak him up and punish him and tha may kill him. I want them both to go back and do there duty as soldiers. I started home one time but I was perswaded to do that and if I had got home I did not aim to try to stay there. I was sick and I wanted to see you and the dear little children and try to get some body to sow some wheet for you. But I did not get to see you at that time. But I do hop that the good Lord will spare my life that I may get home to see you all one time more. That has bin my prare all the time and I do hop that the Lord has herd my prares. Catharine I belev you are praying for me. Catharine I will say to you that my Uncle John H. Stuts and his son Henry W. Stuts is here with me and tha are both well at this time. Henry W. Stuts has had the smallpox vary bad. Catharine said in your letter that you was so lonsom. I no you are. I am so sorrow for you that I cant hardly stand it. Catharine my dear and loving wife put your trust in the Lord who can sav you. Tel father to rite to me as soon as he can. Tel Elisabeth R. Yow that I hav not forgoten her yet. It has bin 11 months sinc I saw her. So I must close for this time. Dear father and Mother[,] fairwell for this time. Catharine my dear wife and dear little[,] fairwell for this time. Matthew C. Yow William Henry[,] Be a good and obey your Mother. Catharine, Cousin Henry W. Stuts is here with me and he has had the smallpox and if you get I will tel you what he said tha don for him. He said that you must not eat no greas from the time it begins to brak out tel the scabs get dry. Eat wheet bread and coffee and be sure to keep warm. Dont let the are get to you at all. Uncle John H. Stuts is here and him and Henry is both well at this time. Give my love to all my friends. Tel father to rite. Catharine My dear wife I do want to see you and the dear little so bad but it seems like I never shal get home any more. But I shal hop and pray to the good Lord that I may come to you again in this world. William Henry my dear little son obey your mother and be a good boy. Read your book. Nancy E. Yow Mary J. Yow Joseph G. Yow John M. Yow so my dear little children fairwell. Matthew C. Yow

1863, February 28
Mastin C. Phillips (*Winder Hospital, Richmond, VA*) to father Rev. **Lewis Phillips Jr**. General wartime correspondence with brief mentions of **Baxter Phillips**, **Malphus Phillips** and uncle **Charles Phillips**. [271]

Dear Pa, Yours of the 23rd inst. came to hand this morning and I hasten to reply[.] I am happy to learn that you all are well at home. Hope it will always be so when I hear from you. I have improved in some respects since the date of my last, though I am still suffering. I am being treated at this time for dropsey and chronic diarrhea. I also take fever mixture. I have strong symptoms of fever part of the time, but hope I shall keep it off. I don't think the dropsey is doing me much harm, but the diarrhea gives me fits and so far has resisted all attempts to stop it. My side and breast are about as they have been ***[sore?]*** *for some time. I have no hope that they will be cured soon. We have rough weather, though not very cold. We had a fall of snow a few days ago near a foot deep, but it was followed by heavy rains and abatement in the weather which soon carried it all off. Today it is quite cold and raining, but I think it will turn to snow by night. I was glad to learn that you are making preparations for a crop. Don't care anything about the work, but would like to be there to have it carried out for you. I believe this war will end in time for me to help gather your next crop. But whether I shall be living at that time, the events of the future will disclose. There will be much hard fighting before the close, but I think the most of it will be done early in the Spring, though if King Abraham gets his three millions of conscripts upon us, the struggle will be prolonged. But our ultimate success will be none the less severe on that account. The end of all our trouble is determined by the continued assistance of Almighty God. We shall subdue all our enemies and establish our independence. I am sorry that the deserters and conscripts are causing so much trouble in the country. Fools! They will repent of this when they are led out to be shot. This fate awaits many of them, judging from the way they are shooting them in these parts. It was mistaken leniency on the part of the Government to allow them so much liberty in the outset, but it is beginning to lessen. For the future I guess the reins will be held suficiently tight. Now if it would release it's grip upon the sick and disabled confined in the hospitals, it would be acting from the dictates of common sense. I believe they are furloughing from every other place except this. I had thought that I would try no more, but since you wish it, if I see any chance, I will try again. I am not able for duty and will not report until I am. I am still without shoes and no prospect of getting any, but I can make out while I am in doors. Baxter has not answered my letter yet. I was glad to hear that he is improving, also that Malphus was well. I wrote to Uncle Charles a few days ago, but did not give him my address. But I must stop, though I could say much. I may write more before I send this. I will try to follow your advice. I desire to place entire* *confidence in God that He may carry me safe through all and permit me to return home. My love to all. Pray for me. Your son, Mastin*

1863, February 28

J.L. Stuart (*Wilmington, NC*) to mother **Mary A. Harper**. General wartime correspondence with brief mentions of **Alexander H. Barrett, William Barrett, George Moore, John Moore, Bartes Maness, Neill Warner, Swain Warner, Sandy Johnson, Elkin Jones, Elijah Boroughs, Thomas Fry, Rachel Barber Warner, John Thrower, Elizabeth Warner Thrower, John Harper, Cynthia Teague, Lydia Comer, Martha Nall** and **Emily Nall.** [272]

Mrs Mary A. Harper[.] Dear Mother[,] I seat myself today to inform you that I am well truly hoping these lines may reach you and family well[.] I know that you are not well but I hope your are so that you can attend to your business. I Do not know anything of interest[.] all things are quite here as far as I know[.] we got with the regiment yesterday eveng[.] tha was three companies that could not get on the cars[.] When the regiment got on I wrote a letter to Wm Teague while we was at Magnolia and I post a few lines in it to you[.] if Wm & John Teague does not get a letter from me tell the I wrote to them[.] any how I have a new pare of shoes and a pare of pants and one pare of Drawers[.] I have never wore any. there was ten men came to our company yesterday[:] Sandy & Wm Barett[,] George Moore's son John[,] & Bartes Manes, Neill & Swain Warner that have never Been in service & Sandy Johnson & Elkin Jones & Burroughs come also[.] our co numbers 44 men[.] John Patterson in from furlough[.] Burroughs Deserted from the co in August 62[.] the rest was sick furlough[.] We are in camp in about two miles before Wilmington[.] I do not think we will not stay here long[.] I think we will go about 18 miles below here or else to Charleston S.C. if they dont send us to Charleston[,] I do not think they will fight for they send us ever where there is fig thing to be Done[.] Pettigroes Brigade is about Goldsboro the 26th is in it[.] I rather think we will stay about here[.] I hear that there is only our Brigd and Evans Brigd here. Thomas Fry has come back to our Co[.] he was Discharged at Camp Mangrum[.] he told me he passed by your house the other day but he said he did not know how you all was getting along[.] I understand there is Cavelry in Moore County[.] write how they come on catching Deserters & conscripts. Edward Warner & John Throers[Thower] Wifes came to see them[.] they got to them Monday at Magnolia[.] I have been looking for John Harper for some time but I recon he is too busy[.] if he dont come I shall not think hard of him for I know he has got a great deal to do[,] but I should be very glad to see him come[.] I think I shall get to come now after awhile[.] you must do the best you can[.] I know you see a great deal of trouble[.] I wish I could be with you but cannot[,] you know[,] and I had a great deal rather be here than to be in the woods hiding about. I may die or be killed and never see you but if I Do[.] you can say your son Died in defence of his country and if I live to see our independence won I can say that I was one the did not flinch from helping to do my part[.] I do hope that peace will be made soon[.] It greaves my heart to hear the pitiful condition of my own county settlement & people but do the best you can is all I can say[.] and I will I expect to get a letter from you soon as the mail can come from Kenansville[.] I wrote a letter to Ema last week & I some time ago wrote a letter to Cynthia and Lydia and Martha Nall that they do not answer[.] I am going to commence and write to all the girls in Moore County and see how many will answer me[.] Dyrect to Wilmington NC[.] J.L. Stuart[,] Co D[.]

1863, March

Baxter C. Phillips to sister **Elmira Phillips**. General wartime correspondence with brief mentions of **Candace Phillips**. [273]

Dear Elmira, Your letter was not very hard to read nor understand (and pardon me)[.] it was very well spelled and composed. I was glad you did write to me and I wish you all would write every week. I will read all yours and answer it all to boot. Reading letters is the only conversation I can have with you now and you know I love to talk. Then you can't wonder if I do want you to write to me. All you wrote is of interest to me and especially what you tell with regard to your having a better Lord. There is a consolation in this. It is what I have long prayed for and can I forget you now? No, Never. Elmira[,] live faithful and show forth the virtues of a Christian. There is nothing so lovely on earth as a Christian. Be faithful to the grace given and you will yet overcome all and be saved. I would like it very much if Candace would write me. I want to know why she don't. She is too busy I reckon, but I think she ought to spare time enough to convince me that she cares for me. I have not heard one word from her since she was married. I don't like it much and I reckon she will think I am quite impatient about writing. This is a low swampy country full of alligators, frogs and almost all kinds of ugly things, mosquitoes, gnats and flies. There is not many people living where we are. It is too low down, nothing but negroes. Don't forget to write to me as soon as this reaches you. Give my love to Candace. Be a good girl. Goodbye. Your brother, B. C. Phillips

1863, March 1
J.L. Stuart (*camp near Wilmington, NC*) to mother **Mary A. Harper,** stepfather **John Harper,** brother **Charles Harper,** sister **Mary A. Harper** and grandmother **Nancy Glass Nall**. General wartime correspondence with brief mentions of the death of **William A. Ray, David Samuel Barrett, Rev. Mark Russell, Capt. William M. Black** and **Emily Nall.** [274]

Mrs Mary A Harper[.] Dear Mother[,] I seat myself to inform you that I am well and hearty truly hoping these few lines may reach you and family well[.] I have nothing of interest to write to you at this time[.] all things are quite here as far as I know[.] I have received one letter from you since we came here Dyrected to Kenansville dated about the 25 Feb[.] I started an answer to you about the 26th[.] we are in camp about about four miles below Wilmington[.] I do not know how long we will stay here[.] it is thought we will go to Charleston S.C. but I cannot tell[.] I believe I had rather stay here[.] I am hoping for a letter from you ever day now I am very uneasy for fear you will all take the Small Pox[,] but I hope that none of you will take it[.] but it seems to strike me that some of you will take the pox and Die before I shall get to see you[.] if any of you does[,] take it try and get over it[.] if you all have not been vaxcinated[,] you had better be[.] one of our men has got a very bad case of pox now at Danville Va. and another one is there Just getting over the pox and another one of our Co Died a few dayes ago at Goldsboro with Pneumonia[.] his name is Wm. A. Ray. Dear mother[,] I hope I shall live to see you all again on earth[.] I would give anything I ever am if I in fact(?) could go home and see you but Dear mother we must take all things patiently[.] I was in good heart until I got that letter that stated the pox was in the settlement and ever since I have been very uneasy for fear you all will take but I hope you will not[.] if one is vaccinated there is not so much danger taking it[.] J.L. Stuart. D.S. Barett has not got in yet[.] we look for him now[.] I want you to write to me often[.] I love to hear from you[.] there came in three or four English vessel here a few dayes ago loaded with salt & shoes & leather & c. we had preaching today by Russell of Carthage[.] I want to see the time come when I can go to the meeting as I use to[.] I hope peace will be made soon so I can come home[.] if any of you get very sick write to me and I will show the letter to the Captain and he may try to get me a furlough[.] I hope I shall get to come before long[.] I shall look for a letter from you soon[.] Farewell Mother[.] you old son[,] J.L. Stuart

Mr John Harper[.] Dear stepfather[.] after my best respects to you I want to see you very bad and see how you are getting along[.] write and let me know how you are getting along with your work and if you make much money[.] I am nearly out of money[.] twenty Dollars is my crop[.] if any of you get sick the best way for you to do is to write a letter to Capt Black that some of you is very bad off and if he can get me a furlough to do so and not let him know that I had any to do with it[,] but if you all keep about[.] I will try and wate tell my time comes if any of you get Real bad off anyhow[,] write it to the Captain[,] I I think he will try and me off[.] J.L. Stuart

Dear Charles & Sis & granny[,] I want to see you very bad[.] I hope you are getting along pretty well[.] Charles[,] I wrote a letter to you about three weeks ago that you never answer[.] tell Emmy I wrote her a letter about a week ago[.] Direct your letters to Wilmington NC[,] J.L. Stuart[,] Co D[.]

1863, March 7
William Henry Patterson (*Camp near Goldsboro, NC*) to sister **Frances Anna V. Patterson**. General wartime correspondence between siblings with brief mentions of **Kelly Williamson**, Lt. **Geo. Wilcox, Shields, William M. Person, Harmon H. Wilcox, Issac Maness,** Capt. **James D. McIver, John R. Keith, Neill C. Graham, Daniel McCaskill, Daniel McDonald, N.D.J. Black, W.D. Patterson, Iver D. Patterson** and **William P. Blue**. [275]

Miss F. A. V. Patterson, Dear Sister[,] I received your letter included in one I received from Pa on the 5th Inst. I was truly glad to receive the letter as I had not received a letter from (with the exception of the one I recd. from Pa that he wrote in Fayettiville) since I left. I am in the enjoyment of health and I hope these few lines will find you and all the rest of the family similarly blessed. I have stood camp life a great deal better than I expected. So far I have been in camp very near a month and strange to say I have enjoyed better health than I have for the same length of time since I got sick at Kinston[.] I have a pretty bad cold at this time but with that exception my health is good. When I came to camp I was fearful that that pain in my side would be aggravated by exposure and get a great deal worse but it has troubled me but little since I came to camp and I am in hopes that it will wear off altogether after a while. Tis true that it has troubled me some since I came to camp[,] but it has not troubled me near so much (as) when when I was at home. I am thankful to have it to say that I have at all times been able to discharge the duties required at my hands. I have not missed an hours duty since I returned to camp[.] the general health of the company is good. Kelly Williamson is sick in a private home[.] Leut. Geo. Wilcox has come back to camp[.] he did not bring back any of the deserters but one[,] a fellow by the name of Shields. W, M. Person (Billy Button) and Wilcox brother[,] H. H. Wilcox[,] came with him and I learn they intend joining the company. I understand that some of the deserters from the 47th Regt. have received firty lashes each the other day and I have seen 2 or 3 carring blocks of wood which I learn they have to carry fourteen days; this looks like rather rough punishment to inflict on men but deserting is a great and growing evil and should be stopped if possible. But notwithstanding all this Isaac Maness deserted this company on the 5th Inst. he has got himself into business[.] certain for if he is caught he will be shot. The other day while we were out on drill he would not go through the manuel of arms right & Capt. McIver put him on two hours extra duty and I guess that offended the gentleman. John R. Keith, Neill C. Graham, Daniel McCaskill & Daniel McDonald have drawn to go home[.] they will start the 13 or 14th Inst.[,] provided that those that are at home on furlough will return at the proper time. Pa stated in his letter that he would try and come down to see me about the 20th of this month. I wrote to Pa last Sunday[.] there are several things that I told him I wanted him to bring to me and there are some that I omitted[.] I should like to have my hair brush & tooth brush and that little red cravat that bought from N. D. J. Black. I would like also to have that black coat that Jenny made, the one I had at Kinston. I want a colored cotton shirt and when it is made[,] I want you to put a breast pocket on the outside. Pa said that he was in hopes that he would kill some turkies and that he would bring me some. I am in hopes that he will kill some[.] I tell you it would be a treat for me. to get something good to eat from home & when he comes[,] I am in hopes he will bring me something good. Well, Anna, we have just received orders to be ready to march at any time but I do not know where we are going. We may not go far and we may not leave here in some days but I cannot tell if we leave here[.] I will write to Pa the very first opportunity & let him know I am. W. D. Patterson I understand has gone home on furlough. I saw William last Sunday but he did not tell me he was going home[,] but I understand he has gone. Some of the boys in the camp think that we will probably go to Tarboro or Washington but as for my part I do not know where we will go. I could write you a good deal but I must close as my space is nearly exhausted. Write to me soon Anna and I want you or Pa to write to me every week, So I will close. Your Afft. Brother[,] Wm. H. Patterson. [P.S] Wm. P. Blue is well.

1863, March 8
Matthew C. Yow (*Pocotaligo, SC*) to in-laws **Joseph Albright** and **Nancy Albright**. General wartime correspondence with brief mentions of wife **Nancy Catherine Albright Yow**, and brothers-in-law **John E. Albright** and **Henry A. Albright**. [276]

Matthew C. Yow to Joseph Albright[.] Dear Father and Mother[,] It is with plesure that I seat myself to drop you a few lines to inform you that I am well at present truly hoping when this comes to hand it may find you all in good helth. I receivd your vary kind letter the 6 inst which giv me great satisfaction to here from you all one time more. I hav receivd several letters from Catharine sinc I hav bin here. She rits to me that she sees hard times and I am so sorrow for her. I no that she is in much trouble for she never was use to having every to see two and I am afraid that she will try to do more than she is able to do. I study a greateal about them. I do not no what tha will do if I cant soon get home before long. You said in your letter that the conscripts and deserters is stil doing mischief yet[.] I wish tha wold all come to the army and not hav so much fus in the contry. It seems lik the people is trying to see what tha can do. I am looking for a letter from Catharine to day. We herd here yesterday that the Yankees was firing on Fort Sumter all day and I hav herd some heavy cannoning to day but I hav not herd what was don. I hop that if tha come out here we will whip them and I hop that will end the war. The war commenct at Charlston and I hop it will end ther. I hav no news of any importanc to rite to you at this time. I am afraid that this to swampy contry will not agree with me if we stay here much longer. The wether is vary changeable for some times it is vary and in a short time it will be cold enough to freeze. But the woods here is green now. Last Sunday morning there was a big frost here and it is vary cool to day. I want to rite to Henry and John but I dont no wher to rite. We hav hard time here. We hav to drill twise every day one company drill and one battalion drill and parade in the evening and not much to eat here. The men greiv vary bad at the fare. So I must close for this time by saying pray for me when it goes well with you. Yours truly[,] so fairwell for this time[.] M.C. Yow to Mr Joseph Albright

1863, March 18
J.L. Stuart (*camp near Topsail Sound, NC*) to mother **Mary A. Harper** and brother **Charles Harper**. General wartime correspondence with brief mentions of **Capt. William M. Black.** [277]

Mrs M. A. Harper[.] Dear Mother[,] by the good mercies of god I avail of the opportunity of writing you a few lines to inform you that I am well truly hoping this line may find you in Better health than you was when you last wrote[.] I received a letter from you the 13th March at Carthage the 10th stating that you was very bad off which I was very sorry to hear[.] I should be very glad to get to come to see you but I cannot tell when I shall get to come[.] two of the co is gone home[.] there time will be out the 19th but I do not know who will get to go next[.] ever body wants to go next but I do not know who will go[.] we have not draw no money yet[.] when I am I want to buy the balance of that land[,] I shall be 21 years old now the 5 of April[.] so if you think it will be best I will buy the balance of the tract[.] I shall try to come and see you soon[.] you must write often[.] if you want to[,] you can write Capt Black a letter that you are very bad off and wants to see me[.] We are throwing up breast works here but I do not think we will stay here long[.] I am out of paper so I cannot write much more[.] J.L. Stuart[,] Co D[.]

Dear Brother and all of you[,] I want to see you very bad[.] we are int two miles of the sound[.] I have eat about 7 oyters[.] some of our boys eats them mitty[.] you must also write and I will do the same[.] give my respects to all inquiring friends[.] Direct to Wilmington NC[.] yours truly[,] J.L. Stuart to M A Harper

1863, March 19
Matthew C. Yow (*Pocotaligo, SC*) to his wife **Nancy Catherine Albright Yow** and children. General wartime correspondence with brief mentions of **Mary Myrick Williamson**, **John Francis Williamson**, his brothers **Simeon Jones Yow** and **Isaac Yow**. [278]

Mrs Nancy C. Yow[.] My Dear Wife and Little Children[,] It is with plesure I seat myself to try to rite you a few lines to let you no that I am well at this time truly hoping when this comes to hand it may find you all well. Catharine I receivd your vary kind letter the 17 that you the 9 and 22 Febu. I was so glad to here from you again. Catharine I rote you a letter the 17 and sent it off and got yours the same day. You said that I did not tel you where to direct your letters. Direct to Pocotaligo SC. I cant tel how long we shal stay here. We are throwing up breastworks here every day and tha say it will take us 10 days. Yet I do not think that we shal hav a fight here tho we may. Catharine you said that Mrs. Williamson wanted to no if I knew any thing of her son John. he was taken sick and sent to the hospital at Petersburg and I haint herd sinc. My dear wife I cant tel you when I can come home. Tha wil not giv furloes now. It seems like tha dont intend to let us go home any more. I dont think tha use us right. We hav bin out here almost 12 months and cant get to go to see our wives and dear little children. I think that's rong. I now tha cold let us come if tha wold but the big men dont cear for us. Tha go home when tha pleas. Catharine you said that the boys was gon back. I am glad tha went. I now tha cold not stay there in peac. I do hop that peac will be made before long so we pore suffering soldiers can return to there homes and lovd ones. Catharine you said that you seed so much trouble. I no you do. I want you to try to bear it as well as you can. I see trouble two but I trust in the good Lord for help. I do thank my god for giving me good helth. It seems like I hav bin blest. I do hop by the aid of your prares I shal return to you again my dear wife[.] Nancy C. Yow.

1863, March 21
J.L. Stuart to mother **Mary A. Harper** and brother **Charles Harper**. General wartime correspondence with brief mentions of **William W. Hunsucker, Asa S. McIntosh, Nancy Glass Nall, Alexander Fry** and **Archibald Currie.** [279]

March 21st[.] I wrote a this letter the other night and next morning we had to march 12 miles[.] we was orderd before day to go to a station 9 miles from Wilmington to take the brain to Goldsboro[,] but the order was countermanded so we came back to the old camp yesterday[.] I do not know when I can come home but as soon as I can[.] it may be better for me after a while to come than to come now[.] Hunsucker & McIntosh got back yesterday[.] they Brought one recruit with them[.] this leaves me well and I hope I will find you all well[.] I hope granny will get well[.] I received a letter yesterday dated 14th[.] I am very uneasy about you and granny[.] I hope you both will get better[.] I can not come yet but I hope I will get to see you all yet[.] I guess at A. Fry and A. Currie will go home next[.] write to me soon[.] your truly[,] J.L. Stuart

Charles[,] you said you would tell me why your julark is when I come home[.] my best love to you and is all I can say[.] give my respects to all my friends[.] J.L. Stuart to M. A. Harper

1863, March 22
Mary A. Harper to son **J.L. Stuart**. General wartime correspondence with brief mentions of clashes between deserters and of **Haywood Nall, Elijah Spivey, Murphy Owens, James Phillips, Bill Owens, Mark Spivey** and **John Brewer.** [280]

Mr J.L. Stuart[.] Dear son[,] I now rite and answer to your letter dated 12[.] I was glad to find that you was well[.] I am on foot but along with all my complaints[,] my eyes is getting so that I cant see but little and I fear they will loose site in time. the rest of the family is as well as common and I truly hope these few lines may find you well and doing well. Haywood Nall is at the salt works at Wilmington[.] the cavalry and foot troops is still in our neighborhood hunting deserters. Elige Spivey has 2 sons & Murphy Owens and his two sons, James Phillips and Bil Owen is the crowd that is hunted & Bill Owens with a company of about 12 men is all that the men is hunting for & they say they will halt them if they see them[,] and if they do not halt[,] they will shoot them down[.] if they fetch them[,] they mean to appoint a day for their execution and for all to come in out of the neighborhood that has had anything stole from them and see them whip these deserters to death and make them tell all they has stole from. they shot at Lige Spivey & Mark. Constable went and did not hit them. I hear they take them in after awhile but I fear not soon enough. We hav had a cold streak for the last 4 days heavy enough to brake the limbs of our [illegible] trees and dead trees. John[,] my Son[,] I do want to see you come home mity bad[.] I often fear I never shall but hold up your leave. There is a better day a coming when the soldiers will get to return home. The small pox has not spred none from John Brewers. His family is all so that they can do about home but they are not allowed to visit ther neighbors yet. No neighbors has went to Brewers house yet but they do his milling and take it to his house and he gets[,] but we have kept clear of the pox and I hope we wont yet by taking care of ourself. We are trying to farm a little[.] we hav planted a big batch of [illegible] potatoes and hav planted our garden with onions and [illegible] beans and hav commenced taking up corn ground and hav cabbag plants growing and if the war would stop and you could get to come home[,] I think we could be yet. you stated you thought you could get a furlow and come home soon[.] I wish you could for I want to see you as bad as ever said and if I can not get to see you[,] I muste keepe riting to you and you must do as you hav done for it is some satisfaction to here from you[,] but I am mity bad you will be in a fite at new bern soon[.] I donte want you to be in no moor fites if it can be helped[.] I am out of paper now and must conclude and Stop my letter by saying I am your affectionate Mother on till death. M.A. Harper

1863, March 22
J.L. Stuart (*camp near Topsail Sound, NC*) to mother **Mary A. Harper,** stepfather **John Harper,** sister **Mary A. Harper** and brother **Charles Harper**. General wartime correspondence with brief mentions of **Nancy Glass Nall** and **McLeod.** [281]

Dear Mother[,] I seat myself to drop you a few lines to inform you that I am hearty truly hoping your health is better than when I heard last[.] I was very sorry to hear granny was sick[.] I hope she will get well[.] I have nothing of interest to write at present[.] I started a letter to you this morning[;] I hope none of you will take the Pox[.] I shall get a furlough after a while but they come very slow[,] only two get to go over 14 dayes[.] when I come[,] I shall want to Bring back a bag of dried fruit[.] when I come[,] it will be unexpected to you[.] it may be at the hour of midnight but I shall stay untell I get a furlough.

Mr. Harper[.] Dear Stepfather[,] after my best respects to you[.] I can inform you I am well truly hoping this letter may find you well[.] I hope you are getting along pretty well with your work & I want to see you very bad[.] I hope you will have a nice start on the far when I come home[.] I must close by giving you my best respects.

Dear Sis[,] I want to see you very bad[.] you must be smart[.] I shall come to see you after a while[.] give my respects to all my friends[.] your affectionate Brother[,] John L. Stuart

Dear Brother[,] I seat myself this pleasant Sabbath evening to inform you that I am in the land of the living and well truly hoping these lines may reach you well[.] the last letter I received stated Grandmother was very poorly[.] I fear I never shall see her any more and Mother stated she was very bad off which I am very sorry to hear[.] I hope she will get better[.] I shall be home after a while[.] when I come I shall be twentyone and I shall buy one hundred acres of land from McLeod[.] when I come[,] I shall have a great deal to tell you. You stated you would tell me who your julark now[,] said she was pretty[.] I cannot imagine who she is but I will say this[,] you may tell the girls they may look out when I come for I guess I shall Break some of there bones but none of them will write to me[.] give my respects to all the girls & friends & I started a letter to Mother this morning[.] I hope none of you will not take take the Pox[.] I hope I shall see you all again yet[.] you must write to me often[.] Dyrect your letters to Wilmington N.C[.] start your on Monday and I will get them right off[.] I have nothing of interest to write so I will close[.] give me all your nuse[.] it may be my time to come home[,] will come in a better time than the present. Yours affectionate Brother[,] J.L. Stuart

1863, March 22
David H. Sloan (*Camp near Fredericksburg, VA*) to mother **Catharine Sloan**. General wartime correspondence regarding the death of his brother, **John A. Sloan**, with brief mention of Lt. **John McNeill.** [282]

Dear Mother, I seat myself this morning to inform you that I am well at this time and I hope when this comes to hand it may find you and all the rest of the family enjoying good health. I will say to you that I got Lieutenant McNeill to write to the army intelligence office at Richmond concerning John, and he got an answer on yesterday, and it stated that he died in Stanton, Virginia, on the 4th day of November [1862]. This is the first time I have heard anything concerning him since he left camp. Lieutenant McNeill will write you a letter and tell you all about it and give you instructions how to collect the money that was due him. Give my love to all the children and accept a good portion yourself. Don't know no more at present. Write soon, Yours Truly, D.H. Sloan

1863, March 24
J.L. Stuart (*Goldsboro, NC*) to mother **Mary A. Harper**. General wartime correspondence with brief mentions of the death of **Noah Brown** and **Nancy Glass Nall.** [283]

Mrs Mary A. Harper[.] I seat myself to drop you a few lines to inform you that I am well truly hoping these few lines may come to hand in due time and find you and the rest as well as usual[.] I have nothing of interest to write to you at the present[.] the last letter I received from you was dated 15[.] I have wrote two to you since[.] I want to hear from all of you very bad[.] you must write ever chance for I want to hear from you often[.] we are at Goldsboro N.C[.] we left Wilmington last night and landed here this morning[.] we will not stay here long I do not think but I should like to stay here At this place very well[.] the 26th regt is at Greenville[.] they had a fight some time ago[.] Noah Brown was killed[.] I cannot get to come see you yet a while but I hope I shall get to come before long[.] I cannot write much at this time[.] paper is scarce and I nothing much to write this time[.] you must write and let me know how you are and how Granny is and how you all are getting along[.] our Co numbers about 44 men[.] give my best respects to all my friends[.] send your letters By high point[.] I truly hope you are getting along well I hope I shall get to come and see you before long[.] tell all my friends to write[.] Dyrect to Goldsboro N.C[,] 49th NCT[.] your affectionate son[,] J. L Stuart

1863, April 1
J.L. Stuart (*Goldsboro, NC*) to mother **Mary A. Harper,** stepfather **John Harper** and brother **Charles Harper**. General wartime correspondence with brief mentions of **Emily C. Nall, John Teague, Mary A. Harper** and **Nancy Glass Nall.** [284]

Mrs Mary A. Harper[.] Dear Mother[,] I seat myself to drop you a line to inform you that I am well truly hoping this line may come to hand in due time and find you all a live and doing well[.] I received a letter from you yesterday Dated 22nd which gav me pleasure to hear from you. you stated that you was in pretty good heart[.] I am in pretty good heart too[.] I fear in too good heart[.] I expect we will have a fight soon[.] we are all so lively and our three months time is for we have had a fight ever three months[.] and our time is out for another one but I hope we will not have any more to do[.] I have nothing of interest to write to you[.] I cannot tell how long we will stay here[.] we may leave here in a day or so and we may stay here some time[.] I had rather stay here than any other place[.] Goldsboro is a very public place to be a small place[.] we get plenty to eat here but while we was at Wilmington we did not get half enough[.] I want to see you all very bad[.] I shall come and see you as soon as I can[.] I shall try to be at the exhibition[.] if I cannot come before[,] you must all do the best you can and I will do the same[.] we have we have drawd a supply of clothes[.] I chose a hat & shirt & Drawers canteen and haver sack[.] I have got plenty to carry on a march[.] I also received a letter from Emmy[.] I hope peace will be made so we all can come home to stay[.] you all must do the best you can[.] I was glad to hear you was getting a long pretty well[.] I hope I shall live to see you all yet[.] I have a great deal to talk about if I ever get to see you[.] give my respects to all my friends[.] tell J. Teague I am well and hearty[.] he wrote me a letter but I could not read it with any satisfaction[.] you stated the cavalry was in the neighborhood yet[.] I wish that I belong to a cavalry for they see better times than we do[.] I must close my letter[.] I want to see you very bad[.] I shall come home as soon as they will let me[.] I wish I was at home to day[.] I would write some of the girls some April fool[.] Farewell yours affct son[,] J.L. Stuart

Mr John Harper[.] Dear step father[,] I seat myself to drop you aline to inform you that I am well truly hoping you are doing well[.] you stated you was going to go off with a load of wheels to buy corn[.] do the best and try to make enough to do you another year[.] if the war does not stop[,] it will be hard time another year[.]

Charles Dear Brother[,] I want to see you very bad[.] I hope I shall get to see you before long[.] four dayes from to day I shall be twenty one[.] if the war would Just stop[,] I should be free[.] tell sis and granny I want to see them very bad[.] I must close my letter[.] you must write soon[.] Dyrect your letter to Goldsboro NC[,] 49 regt[,] NCT Co D[,] in care of Capt Black[.]

1863, April 4
J.L. Stuart (*Camp at Kinston, NC*) to mother **Mary A. Harper**, stepfather **John Harper**, brother **Charles Harper**, sister **Mary A. Harper** and grandmother **Nancy Glass Nall**. General wartime correspondence with brief mentions of desertions by **Alexander Johnson Sr., Elijah Boroughs, Bartis Maness, Eli Bean, Wyatt Williamson, Patrick Williamson** and **William S. Moore.** [285]

Mrs M A Harper[.] Dear mother[,] I seat myself to drop you a few lines to inform you that I am in very good health at this time truly hoping these lines may find you all alive and well[.] we left Goldsboro the 1st[.] we came in on the train[.] Kinston is twenty six miles below Goldsboro[.] I do not know what hour we will get orders to leave here[.] we have heard cannonading ever since we have been here[.] I suppose it is at Washinton but we have not heard from there[.] I hope thy will flog the yankees without our help[.] I guess the 26th is there but I do not know[.] J.L. Stuart. I have to tell you some bad nuse about Co. D[.] seven men run away last night[.] there names is as follows Sandy Johnson Sr., Buroughs, Bartis Manes, Eli Bean, Wiatt & Tad Williamson and S Moore all went from our CO last night[.] I call that bad nuse from Co. D[.] I guess they got scared for they hear canons at a Distance. I have heard cannons several times but now I am on Brigade guard leaning against the fence but I will not run away[.] I don't think but I Dread them canons but we must put our trust in god and if it is his will for us to be killed we must not murmer[.] I do not get but few letters from you[.] I wrote two letters to you while we was at Goldsboro[.] I want to see you very bad but I cannot tell when I shall get to come[.] for the last two or three days we have had some right Cold wether. tomorrow is Easter & how I wish I was at home but I hope the time will come when I shall get back home to my Dear mother and Brother and little sister and all of my friends[.] my health is very good and they call me very fat[.] if you see any of them fellows they can tell you about John Stuart[.] I must close[.] Dear mother do the best you can[.] Farewell[,] J.L. Stuart[,] Co D[.]

Mr Harper[.] Dear stepfather[,] after my respects to you I will inform you that I am hearty[.] I have nothing much to write[.] you must try and get along the best you can[.] I wish I was at home to help you work but I have to stay here yet a while[.] try & plant your corn and make all the corn you can for it will be needed[.] write ever chance you get[.] Dyrect your letters to Kinston NC[,] 49th regt[,] NC Troops[,] Co. D[.]

Dear Brother & sister and grandmother[,] I hope you are well[.] I want to see you all very bad[.] you must write often and I will do the same[.] give my best respects to all my friends[.] your affectionate Brother[,] J.L. Stuart

1863, April 5
Mary A. Harper (*Good Spring Post Office*) to **Capt. William M. Black**. General wartime correspondence with brief mentions of **John L. Stuart** and his ailing grandmother **Nancy Glass Nall.** [286]

Mr Wm B Black Capt. Dear Sir[,] offer my beste compliments to you hoping you well and wishing you good success[.] my greatest request for you is that you try and get a fur low for my sone John L. Stuarte and send him home[.] his grand mother is living with me and she is 88 years old and is helpless and suffering greatly [illegible][,] but short time and her greatest request is to see her grand son J.L. Stuart before she dies[.] and I pray you send him and see is for the desire of the suffering grandmother, I am bad off with my lingering corn planted which which I had lose for many years[.] scarcely able to get a bout and I am moore than anxious to see my son J.L. Stuart come home and see us all once more in the land of the living[.] no more[,] only I remain your friend[,] M.A. Harper

1863, April 5
Mary A. Harper to son **J.L. Stuart**. General wartime correspondence with brief mentions **Capt. William M. Black, McLeod, Nancy Glass Nall** and **Charles Harper.** [287]

Mr J.L. Stuarte[.] Dear Son[,] I now write a few lines in answor to your letter Dated about 27th which I was glad to receive[.] I rote to you at Willmington last week and you stated you hav not received it[.] I find you are at Goldsboro and well which I was glad to here[.] I rote a letter in your to Capt Black stating your grandmothers helth and her presente condition and in case you doe not get it[,] I will write a nother to him and send it in your letter and if you get it and the other giv one[.] and let him try to get you a fur low and let you come home and see us all[.] I all so rote in to your requeste about the s and your money[.] I am willing for you to to hav the same and I think it is better than confederate money[.] and it is well nown by us all that the confederate money will not liv at [illegible] any longer than the wore lasts. I stated that I had a deed for the other hundred acres and McLeod has my note for one hundred and forty dollars[,] but I think I can get it for a hundred dollars and if you get a fur low and can come home we will fix it all rite[.] I have nothing too good for you[.] my greateste desire is for your well fare and I want to see you in the worst in the world and so does all the family[.] and I hope and trust you may liv to returne home and for the wore to stop and this a new stash to bye to live. I am glad to here that you are well and I hope you may stay well[,] but I am not well[.] my head is mity bad at present and I see a great [illegible] of trouble. your old granny looks bad and I donte think she will liv long[.] she is nearly helpless. Charles had to go by by laste weeke with his baler. he had only 20 bels on him at on but I hope he will plow some week. the rest of the family is a bout in common fix[.] no more[,] only rite soon and I will rite moore next time. M.A. Harper

1863, April 5
Matthew C. Yow (*Pocotaligo, SC*) to his wife **Nancy Catherine Albright Yow** and children. General wartime correspondence with brief mentions of his father **Henry C. Yow**, brother-in-law **William Stockard Albright**, **John Lewis Maness**, children **Nancy Elizabeth Yow** and **Mary Jane Yow**. [288]

My Dear Wife and Little Children[,] Through the mercies of our hevenly father I this blesed Sabbath evning I seat myself to drop you a few lines to inform you that I am well at present truly hoping when this comes to hand it may find you all in good helth. Catharine I receivd your vary kind letter under date of the 24 March. I was truly glad to here from you and the dear little children. You said in that letter that you didnot get a letter that week but father got one and sent it to you to read and then you rote that letter. I receivd your letter when I was riting to father and I made mension of it in his letter of the 1 April. Catharine I expect we shal leav here in a short time. We hav marching orders now to be ready at any time to go to Charlston. It is thought that the Yankees is going to make an atact on Charlston but I cant tel how it will be yet. Catharine you said in your letter that you see hard times. I no you do. I am sorrow for you and I want to be there to do my things again but it seems like I never shal get home any more but I stil hav a hop that I may get bak to you and the dear little children again. That is my prare and has bin all the time and I believ that you are praying for me all the time. Catharine today is Easter I suppose. O that I cold be with you and my dear little children. Pore little children[,] I expect tha hav forgotten me almost. I hav bin gone so long. Catharine father says the children looks so well. Lord bles them I pray. I cant rite much this time. I will rite as often as I can. I rote your father a letter sinc I come here and I rote one to your brother William and one to John Maness. I rote you a letter the 24 and I put a ring in it and 50 cents in money. I want to no if you get them. If you get them I will send Nancy and Jane one. So I must close by saying to you to remember me in your prares. I stil remain your affectionate husband until death parts us. So Fairwell[.] Nancy C. Yow.

1863, April 5
David H. Sloan to mother **Catharine Sloan**. General wartime correspondence with brief mention of **John A. Sloan**. [289]

Dear Mother, I take my pen in hand to inform you that I received your kind letter about a hour ago and was glad to hear from you all. I am well at this time. Hoping when this comes to hand, it may find you all well. Mother, you wanted to know how far I was from John. It is about one 100 and 45 miles Northern. There is no chance to get him home and he has been dead five months now, and you know it would do no good to get him home now. So don't study no more about him than you can help for there is no good in it. So nothing more about John. We have bad weather here now. It snowed all night here last night[.]

1863, April 9
J.L. Stuart (*Kinston, NC*) to mother **Mary A. Harper,** stepfather **John Harper,** brother **Charles Harper,** sister **Mary A. Harper** and grandmother **Nancy Glass Nall**. General wartime correspondence. [290]

Mrs Mary Harper[.] Dear Mother[,] I seat my self to day to drop you a few lines to inform you that I amwell truly hoping these lines may find you all alive & well as usual[.] we have Just returned from a march the 6th[.] we went 12 miles below here and came back yesterday evening[.] we started back about one oclock and got here about five[.] we understood that 12,000 yankees were comeing up toward Kinston[,] but when the found out Ransoms got cavalry was comeing to meet them they took another notion[.] I rather think we will stay about here this spring[.] I want to come and see you very bad but I do not know when I can get off[.] furloughs is stopped for awhile[.] I will tell you our quantity of rations per day[.] we get 1 pound and am eight of meal or flour and quarter of a lb of Bacon[.] we grumble mitly sometimes[.] I want to see you very bad but if I cannot see you I will write often[.] I wrote a letter to you the 6th and as I was able[,] I thought I would write to you today[.] I don't get letter from you as often as I would like[.] it has been nine dayes since I have heard rom you or the last letter was dated March 30[.] I shall have to close my few remarks to you[.] I hope I shall live to see your yet[.] you must write[.] Your affectionate son[,] J.L. Stuart[,] Co D[,] 49th regt[.]

Dear stepfather[,] after my best respects to you I will inform you I am hearty. I should be very glad to see you and hope I shall soon[.] you stated you was doing pretty well in many maters which I am pleased to know[.] I have to spend right smart of money here[.] we have not drawn no money in five month[.] the most of the boys are out[.] I have got 18.00 and some owing to me when I draw[.] I will send some home[.] I ought to send more than I do but you must not think hard of me[.] I have to pay high for ever thing I buy[.] you said you had a deed for that land and if could come home we would fix it if you can[.] hold it all right[.] if this war wont stop[,] I could call my self a free man[.] try and make out the best you can[.] J. L Stuart

Dear Brother sister & granny[,] I want to see you very bad[.] I am very sorry to hear poor old granny is so bad off[.] if shedding tears would cause me to see you[,] I would not stay away long but it will do no good[.] so Dear Granny[,] try and spend your dayes in peace and prepare your self for a better world. Charles[,] I was sorry to hear you was so crippled up with boils[.] try and cure them and work heard (hard?) to make corn[.] sis[,] I am pleased to her you are so smart[.] I would give you any sum if I could see you[.] when I see little girls and boys[,] it makes me mity sorry that I cannot see my little Brother and sis but we must hope for the day to come when we shall see each other again[.] Dyrect your letter to Kinston NC[,] 49th regt[,] NCT[,] Co D in care of Capt Black. write to me soon and tell all the girls and boys to write to me[.] tell the girls if they dont write[,] I will not speak to them when I come home[.] J. L Stuart

1863, April 12

Neill A. Ray *(Goldsboro, NC)* to cousin **Sarah Ray**. General wartime correspondence between cousins with brief mentions of rumors of General **Hill** capturing Washington, DC and fighting at Charleston, SC. [291]

Dear Cousin, I take the present opertunity to writing to you once more to let you no that I am well and hope that when this will come to hand it will find you all well[.] I hav no nuse to write at this time[.] therr is varius reports in town today[.] I dont no whether it tis correct or not[.] they say Gineral Hill has taken Washington[.] I dont no whether it is so ornot but I hope it will soon be so[.] they hav bin fighting at Charleston[.] I dont no what the result[.] I hope we will hear tomor and if we whip them at Charleston and at Vixburg[,] I think the war will son close[.] I think their will be a hard fight down on black water before many days[.] Nothing more at present[,] only remaines your cousin til death. N.A. Ray [P.S] Write soo as you get this fo I want to hear from home very much.

1863, April 15

Mary A. Harper, John Harper and **Charles Harper** to son and brother **J.L. Stuart**. General wartime correspondence with brief mentions **Dempsey Sheffield, Will Teague, James Stephens, Capt. William M. Black, John Teague, Eli Teague, James** and **Mart.** [292]

Mr J L. Stuart[.] Dear Son[,] I rite in answer to your letter Dated 9th this inst[,] which came to hand to day stating that you was well which I was glad to here[.] you stated your allowance in rations which is not enough to keepe you a liv and strong which I am sorry to here[.] for I now you muste suffer with hunger and it is grievous and bad yes disheartening to you and me to think our soldiers has to starve or nearly starv[.] and so long befor there will be a full supply of provsions for them[,] but god nowes what is beste suited for his glory and this wore will end to the glory of god[.] if man is tis appointed[,] I wish you was nearer home . I about to start John Harper with some thing to eate to you for it seems like I cante stand it[.] I am not well yet but I am a little about[] my leggs and sinus pain me so bad and weekeness over my system[.] the reste of the family is a bout in common health. granny is better a little[.] the people in the neighborhood is well[.] Dempsey Shuffel is getting better, Will Teage was in the horse battle on 4th March. James Stephens stated in his letter and he has not rote home and many thinks Will is dead[.] So they hav not herd from him since march. the Deserters has come back which left with the cavalry and they Say they had to run a way to keepe from perishing[.] that is bad news to here from our head men that ther men has to run a way to keepe from perishing[.] tell Captain black to furlow you home to get something to eate[.] I wante to see you there worst of all things in the worste[,] but I am out of hearte[.] for it appears that the time goes no nearer for you to return home to me for I donte be leav the war will end and as long as they can get men to fight[.] our wheate looks promising and our oates is turning green now[.] our garden is in goodfix with a heape of onions planted and our Fresh potatoes is coming up and we hav planted Some corn and will plante moore soon. John Harper and the children is working hard to trye to liv. I saw that you Started to meete the yankeys but did not meete them which I was glad to here . I wish you could Stay oute of the the battlefield and hav your helth and hav patience to bare what is your lot[.] and may god bless you and his presence be with you throo all the troubles of this on [illegible] wore fore if life[.] and bring you up in spirit with greater faith to be leav that he is a god that is able to Save your Lot from Destruction and your contry from yankee slavery[.] your neighbors are all anxious to here from you[.] John Teage and family Says they had rather here from you than any man in the army but Ely[.] So I must close my letter by Saying rite oftene and I will rite the same way. your obed iente mother untill Death[,] M.A. Harper

Dear stepsone[,] I will rite moore in the next letter[.] I am harty and very busy and doing all I can and I hope we will liv if we keep our helth[,] I could make lots of money. if I cante work in shops the but I shall get aples this week and goe to the farm[.] J Harper. do the best you can[.]

Mr J.L. Stuart[.] Dear Brother[,] it is with pleasure that I have the present opertunity of riting you a few lines to let you no that I am well & want to see you the wirst I ever did in my life[.] I was sorry to hear that you got so little to eat[.] I wish you was at home So that you could get Something to eat[.] I went a fishing last Saturday night[.] I killed 24 pretty good ones & me & James & Mart went in again a monday night[.] I killed 23 some of them was large & good[,] not toat them more than one hundred yards with out resting[.] no more at this time[.] rite soon[.] Yours truly[,] C. E. Harper to J.L.S.

1863, April 17
J.L. Stuart (*camp on the Trent River*) to mother **Mary A. Harper**. General wartime correspondence. [293]

Dear mother[,] I seat myself this evening to inform you that I am well and hearty but hoping these lines may find you all well as usual[.] I am very anxies to hear from you all and hear how you are getting along[.] we are about eighteen miles below Kinston on the trent Riveradvance Pickets[.] we have good fortifications here this morning[.] a little after eight o clock this morning our pickets fired at[.] was answered by the yankees with a small piece of Artillery they fired twice[.] I think our men fired on the yankees and fell back and the yankees fell back also[.] a Major Chambers our Maj the company sent Co H out skirmishing[.] they advanced about a mile and found the yankees were gone[.] they learnt that two Co. of cavalry came up with one piece of canon but our Pickets wounded[.] two of there men[,] one Artillery man & one cavalry man[,] but the yankees got them and we learnt at a house where our skirmishes went[,] the yankees Brought there two wounded men in the house and Dressed there wounds and said that one of the men were mortally wounded[.] they said they would try another rout and go and they would burn Kinston and go on to Raleigh[,] but they will get mistaken[.] Gen Ransom sent down a squad of cavalry Down here this evening and they caught one horse and one mule that came this side[.] our Scripts[,] they had the US brand on them[.] the house was worth about $200.00 and the mule $500.00 the way horses sells[.] I shall have to stop writing[.] it is getting Dark[.] if I do not have to go on Picket tomorrow[,] I will write more[.] as I said Co H was sent out skirmishing[.] Co. H was sent out also[.] Dyrect your letters to Kinston as usual[.] I shall have to close[.] one of our men were hurt in the skirmish[.] write soon[.] Give my best respects to all and my best wishes for your own wel fare[.] I am yours obed son[,] J.L. Stuart

1863, April 19
J.L. Stuart to mother **Mary A. Harper** and stepfather **John Harper**. General wartime correspondence. [294]

April 19th 1863 Mrs Harper[,] I am well to day and have Just come off Picket[.] no yankee came in sight yesterday[.] I understand the yankees have fallen back but I do not know whether it is so or not[.] I received a letter from you yesterday evening Dated the 12th which I was very glad to received but it made me very sorry to get word of grannies farewell[.] it made my heart ache yesterday[.] I stood from 8 oclock untell 12 and went on at eight last night and came off at 12 in the night[.] I want to see you all the worst in the world but furloughs are stoped for a while[.] the weather is very warm[.] it made me sweat[.] it is so hot[.] I wish I could be at home to be ploughing[.] I am glad to hear you have planted some corn[.] try and make all you can and Do the best you can and I will do the same[.] I shall write ever week[.] give my respects to all[.] When this you see[,] remember me. J.L. Stuart

Mr Harper[,] I was glad to hear from you[.] Do the best you can[.] you said you could buy a horse if I thought it would be best[.] all that I shall say is you know your own business better than I do so do what you think will be the most benefit to the family[.] what money I have sent home I sent it for the benefit of the family so spend it as you please[.] and when we draw again[,] I will give you some moore if they pay us all that is Due and I will send you enought to make out the five hundred[.] I spend right smart of money for some thing to eat & other things[.] tell all my friends I want to see them and I hope I shall see you all again but I may not[.] that is unknown[.] spend the money I sent for what you think best[,] mother[.] try & keep in[.] maybe I will get furlough sometime[.] farewell[,] J.L. Stuart to J Harper

1863, April 19
J.L. Stuart to brother **Charles Harper** and mother **Mary A. Harper**. General wartime correspondence with brief mention of **William Spinks Moore.** [295]

April 19th 1863 to Charles[,] I am well and hope these few lines may find you all well[.] you said you caught a good many fish[.] I should like to be at home to help you eat them[.] I am sitting in five foot of the water in Trent River[.] the water is nearly fifteen foot deep and about thirty or forty foot wide[.] you must attend to the girls about Right for I now they love to be hugged[.] I would hug them if was at home[.] none of the girls will not write to me but they can let it alone[.] you must write to me all about your sprees[.] write if Spinks Moore has got back[.] seven run away from our co one night[.] write if they have got back[.] you must make all the corn you can and hug the gals of a Sunday[.] you must be smart and mind your pa and mother and Poor old granny[.] Poore mother and granny[,] I wish I could see them them[.] When this you see[,] think of me for often times I think of the[.] write to me[.] Your affectionate Brother[,] J.L. Stuart

To sis[,] I want to see you very bad[.] I wish I was at home to eat them Potatoes but eat them your self and think of me and that will do[.] Oh my dear little sister[,] I want to see the time come when I can come home[.] I shall have to close to send my letter[.] tell granny I want to see her very bad and hope I shall live to see her yet[.] you must all write to me[.] Dyrect your letters to Kinston NC. give my respects to all inquiring friends[.] When this you see[,] remember me[.]

I just received a letter from you dated the 15[,] stating John Harper was coming. I am making out pretty well Do not be uneasy about me.

1863, April 19
Capt. James O.A. Kelly (*near Greenville, NC*) to wife **Nannie Sloan Kelly**. General wartime correspondence with mentions of General **Ransom**, **John B. Kelly**, uncle **William J. Kelly,** aunt **Betty Kelly** and his children **Oscar, Edith** and **Mattie Kelly**. [296]

Dear wife, we have got back from Washington and I don't think we accomplished much. I am mending slowly. I hope this may find you and the children well. I have nothing of interest to write to you[.] if I could see you[,] I would and could tell you somethings that would interest you about our marches, shellings, & c. but suffice it to say[,] that there was nobody hurt in our company. We are now in camp at this place. I suppose we will stay here a few days. I don't know how long perhaps sometime. I learn that the yankees are advancing on Kinston. There was a battle fought at Core Creek. We hear that Gen. Ransom fought with small armies for 4 hours and run them back, I also learn the yankees are advancing from Washington on this place[,] but our pickets maid a stand about 14 miles below here and whipped them back. I don not know what they are doing now. We have a pretty strong force in Eastern NC now and if we have a few days notice[,] we can meet them with a strong force anytime. We have several VA Brigades here together with 5 NC Brigades that I know of. Nannie[,] I would like very well to see you now. I want to see you about as bad as I ever did and I hope and trust I will be favored with the blessed privates[?] soon. I dropped a sleep today and dreamed of you and you may be sure it was a pleasant dream. I have lost oo much sleep[.] I can sleep in the daytime now. We marched nearly all night before last over the worst land I ever saw almost. John B. Kelly is some better, he is in a private house in Greenville. I have not had a letter from you now in a few days. I would be glad to hear from you. You will continue to address me at Kinston as I can get them from there or I do not know what the better place would be to direct them as the envelopes are closed. Nannie, write to me[,] tell me all the news and everything you think would interest me. The most of the company is well. Nannie[,] it is bedtime and the light is bad consequently I must close. My love to Edith, Oscar and Mattie, Uncle Bill & Betty and retain a large portion for yourself. If any of the neighbors come here to see their family and you feel like coming with them to see me[,] come ahead anytime. Be sure to let me know you will start for the soon – believe me yours always. Jim

1863, April 20
Noah F. Muse to **A.S. Caddell** and **W.H.H. "Harrison" Davis**. General personal correspondence. [297]

Well Tim it is almost with tears I seat myself this eaving to write you a few short lines[.] Tim I am well as far as health is conserned but my feelings is mortally wounded just to think I and you have spent so many pleasureful hours together and to think you have go off & has deserted me[.] Tim little did I think by being absent a few months you would forget me[.] Tim Ive wrote you one or two letters and no answer yet[.] Ive not forgotten you neither will if you prove the friend to me as you have[.] if I fall a victim to the bloody rebels of the North[,] I will always esteem yo was one of my best friends Tim[.] what to write I dont know[.] I could tell you of several little antics that would amuse you if I only knowed that you would like to read something of the kind[.] But Tim if you will be so kind to wright to me[,] I will give you a full letter[.] so farewell[,] old friend[.] if I never more see you on earth[,] I hope we will meet in a better wourld where parting is no more[.] N F Muse

Tim I send a few lines to my play mate W.H.H. Davis if he is not dead[.] I want you to give this to him[.] Harrison 25th wrote to you and has got no answer[.] I will write a few lines to let you know that I am in the land of the living yet anocking along very well[.] Harrison I started to the war once with the Malitia but they all volunteered and I turned back[.] I need not tell you anything about such as that for you have seen our boys & as I suppose you would like to know something about the fair sex[.] I wish you could only be here some sunday just to fly around[.] I see your girls sometimes[,] they are all right[.] I saw so many pretty girls yesterday I don't know which to love though if you were here I recon you would[.] Harrison I only write this to see if you will write to me[.] write soon and I will write you a full letter giving all the particulars[.] so farewell[,] old schoolmate, Noah F. Muse

1863, April 21
Matthew C. Yow (*Pocotaligo, SC*) to his wife **Nancy Catherine Albright Yow** and children. General wartime correspondence with brief mentions of **David D. Yow**, his brothers **Simeon Jones Yow, Isaac Yow,** father **Henry C. Yow,** and children **William Henry Yow**, **Nancy Elizabeth Yow, Mary Jane Yow** and **Joseph Gibbs Yow**. [298]

My Dear Wife and Little Children[,] It is with much plesure that I tak my pen to drop you a few lines to inform you that I am well at present truly hoping when this comes to hand it may find you all well. Catharine I receivd a letter from you last week the one you rote the 6 of April and I did not rite bak to you tel now. I sent a letter by David D. Yow and he did not get off as soon as I expected and I thought I wold rite this morning and see which wold get home first[,] David or the letter. He is going to leav this morning. Catharine I hav sent my overcoat by him and 50 cents worth of pins and one dollars worth of needles and one dollars worth of stamps and one camp him book and a cap for little Joseph Gibbs. And I sent father and William Henry 20 buttons to put on there coats and David Yow did not hav money to tak him back and I let him 3 dollars and if he dont spend it[,] he will giv it to you. I told him to pay himself for his troubles with my things. I hav nothing to send to Nancy and Jane but some pins and needles. Catharine I will say to you that my brother Isaac come to see me last Sunday the 19. I was so glad to see him. Jones did not get to come. He was detaild to go to Charlston on some bisnis. I want to go to see him before long. The boys seems to be vary well satisfied now more so than tha was at Camp Homes. Catharine I must tell you what I way 155 pounds yesterday. that is 20 pounds more than when I left home. I am in good helth at this time and I am so thankful for it. All is quiet here now and I do hop that peac will be made soon so we pore soldiers can come home to those that is near and dear to us. O that I cold come to see you all again. I do want to come to see you and help you plant corn. I do hop tha will giv furlows again before long. I no tha cold if tha wold. I want you to rite me all the news and rite as often as you can. I am looking for a letter from you now. Catharine sinc I commenct this letter I hav herd that there going 4 men out of every company home on furlows. If that be so I think I will get to come before long. So I must close for this time by saying I stil remain your affectionate until death. So fairwell dear wife[.] Nancy C. Yow.

1863, April 26
John Harper to stepson **J.L. Stuart**. General wartime correspondence with brief mention of deserters stealing from **John Comer, Adam Comer** and **Aaron Davis.** [299]

I now rite in answor to our letter Dated 12[.] We are all on foot and able to ete our allowance[.] I hope you are well and may stay well and I hope you may still has good luck[.] and I hope you may still hav good luck[,] the good mercy of god to return home[.] I am now starting off after corn and will be gone this week[,] and I will rite you more when I return. the Deserters is very troublesome in our neighbourhood[.] they come about 30 of them on friday night to John Comers house and asked to now where Adam Comers bacon was and it was in John Comers house[.] left and they went up and took a bout 500 lbs of all of it and Say they in tend to kill him yet they stole Aron Davis corn last week[.] and they are getting bold enough to goe and take what they want before peoples faces[.] I donte think the people can shame them and I hope they will be taken up and punished no more[.] only I am trying to doe the best I can[.] trust in god[,] John Harper

1863, April 26
Charles Harper (*Good Spring Post Office*) to brother **J.L. Stuart**. General wartime correspondence with brief mention of **William Spinks Moore, Wyatt Williamson, Mary A. Harper** and **Nancy Glass Nall.** [300]

Mr J.L. Stuart[.] dear brother[,] it is with pleasure that I have the present opertunity of riting you a few lines to inform you I am[.] you said you wanted to now the S More & Wiatt Williamson & the rest of them fellows got home. We ar told that tha got back last monday as 2 weekes a go at breakfast time[.] a day or will be 2 weaks in the morning. today I found the morning & it is a beautiful morning[.] sis sends her love to you & sayes she wants to see you mity bad[.] granny sends her best respects to you[.] you must excuse my bad hand rite[.] no more at present[.] rite soon[.] I want to hear from you if I cant see you[.] C. E. Harper

1863, May 1
J.L. Stuart (*camp near Kinston, NC*) to mother **Mary A. Harper**. General wartime correspondence. [301]

Dear mother[,] I seat myself to drop you a line to inform you that I am well. Truly hoping these lines may find you all doing well. I received a letter from you yesterday which I was very glad to hear from you. We are in camp about two or three miles below Kinston. We have been looking for the yankees to come. We are told that they got in five miles of us. I heard the guns. We have throwed u a pretty good string of breastworks and if that had a came up here[,] we would a give them some of our shills. I hear that the 25th regt made the yankees get yesterday down below here[.] the 25th regt is some of Ransoms boys[.] they are a severe set they do not flinch. Our regt had a skirmish with the yankees[,] but only three co was at the place[.] if all of the old 49th had a been together[,] they would a been glad if they stayed away. I was very glad to har from you. You said you thought it was a bad idea to buy that blind horse[.] if you think so[,] do not buy him. You may trade to the best for your welfare. If I was at home[,] I would know what would be best but as it is I cannot tell but I want the land paid for. I want to see you the worst in the world. we have throwed up over one mile of Breastworks[.] if the yankees do come[,] they will get hurt[,] but I understand that the Petigrews Brigade left to day for Va[.] this paper cost one ten cents a sheet[.] it is rules too wide[.] Mother[.] I hope I shall get to see you yet[.] be in good heart[.] I hardly know what to write[.] it makes my heart ache to think of your condition and how Moore County is doing. my writing is bad on account of my ink. we are getting half a lb meat a day while we are at work and we get Molasses[.] I shall come home assoon as I can[.] I have a heavy knapsack[.] I wish I could send some of my things home[.] I have got about a heap of letter[.] I shall have to burn them[.] we will draw money soon $44[.] I will send you some[.] I have got fifteen soldiers[.] I must close[.] write soon[.] my best respects to all the family. Kinston NC[,] Co D[,] J.L. Stuart

1863, May 4
Capt. James O.A. Kelly (*Kinston, NC*) to wife **Nannie Sloan Kelly**. General wartime correspondence with mentions of General **Ransom**, **Alexander Bolin**, **Mrs. Tull** and his children **Oscar, Edith** and **Mattie Kelly**. [302]

Dear Nannie, I again seat myself to inform you that I am reasonably well hoping that these few line may find you and the children enjoying good health. I have nothing of interest to write to you at this time. We are now resting preporiatory to going somewhere else[.] it is likely we will go back to VA. I am almost certain that our Brigade or Ransom[;] one will be sent back to the VA and somehow I am afraid it is to be ours though I hope not. I would not have minding going back so bad if they had let me go home and stay awhile[.] but as it is[,] I don't like it much[.] I can assure you Liet. Bolin is going to Wilson tomorrow after our trunks. I never wanted some clean clothes so bad in my life. Nannie[,] the first time you can[,] I wish you to send me some cotton socks and I have not seen in my trunk in some time but I know I lost a pr drawers on our last march. I have forgot how many I had[.] I recon you know whether I send need any or not better than I[.] as unless I had my trunk here so I could see[.] I would give almost anything to see you now before I go to VA[,] that if we do go. I wish you were here or could meet us at Goldsboro if I knew we would go and when I would write to you to meet me there. The company is enjoying good health at present. The boys are grumbling a little about their rations being short[,] but I hope they will get longer soon. I have not been to see Mrs. Tull since I come back as our camp is over the river and I have not felt like walking about only when I am obliged to go. I learn from your letter that you have bought a puppy and want me to send you a name for it. I propose to call him Battle as that winds up the dog business. I will proceed to another subject. I have wrote to you so often lately that I have not got much to write[,] but if I could only see you I could tell you lots in a short time though I have got to be very sleepy headed for the last few days since I have got better. I get sleepy as soon as the dark comes. Two weeks ago[,] I could not sleep at all. The woods have put out down here more and will soon by very thick. It is quite warm down here. Is the fruit all killed or not did my peach trees boom this year? I see any number of men off with their shirts off catching fish. I guess I could get a few if I was to take the trouble to look. I want to get my clothes and feel like I am clear of the Confederate dress. Now don't let this scare you nor don't let anybody know though I expect everybody knows it already for I don't believe that there is a man in the Regt.[,] but what has some on him. Tell Edith she has not sent me that plot of hair yet. I would be very glad to get it now. Also tell Oscar that he may grow and fatten as much as he pleases but I will know him when I see him if he don't mind. Just give Mattie Lee a few sweet kisses for me. I think that will suit her best. Write soon, come if you can and believe me as even your own. Jim

1863, May 5
J.L. Stuart (*Kinston, NC*) to mother **Mary A. Harper,** stepfather **John Harper,** brother **Charles Harper,** sister **Mary A. Harper** and grandmother **Nancy Glass Nall**. General wartime correspondence with brief mentions of **Generals Stonewall Jackson, Hooker, A.P. Hill, Paxton, D.H. Hill, Emily Nall** and **Mathany Teague.** [303]

Mrs M. A. Harper[.] Dear Mother[,] I seat myself this morning to write you a line to inform you that I am well[.] I received a letter from you night before last stating that you was very bad off[.] I had to work yesterday or I should have wrote then[.] it made me mity sorry to hear that you are so bad off[.] I would give any thing in this world if I could only see you but we must suffer Gods will to be done[.] I do not know whether I shall get to come home soon or not[.] I shall try and if it is gods will for us to see each other again[,] I can tell you a great deal[.] Dear mother[,] it hurts me to think you are so bad off and I am so far away from you and may be at this time you are of being cold[.] I can hardly keep from starting home but that is something I never wanted to disgrace my self and county by running away[.] I truly hope these lines may find you better[.] I shall expect a letter to night and I am very anxious to hear[.] you must write often you must try and get better and if you ever get better you must take care of your self[.] Dear mother[,] if I was to hear that you was Dead[,] I do not know what I should do for you are the best friend that I have in the world[.] and if it had not been that I am helping to defend our country and could not get to see you[.] I never should have stayed away from you this long but we must suffer gods will to be done and not ours[.] we had been a fight at Fredericksburg and Gen. Jackson got in the rear of Hookers army and killed and taken agood many prisoners[.] Gen Paxton was killed[.] Gen Jackson was badly wounded and A.P. Hill and another gen was slightly wounded[.] we will hear the particulars soon the fight come off[.] I think it was last Sunday[.] it had been rumord that we had to start to VA to day but there is nothing of it[.] Pettigrews Brigade is gone to VA[.] times are quite here at this time[,] but we do not know when the enemy may come[,] but if they do come[,] there will be some very hard(?) fighting for our men say they will fight to the last and there are a good many Troops about here and there is a great general here. D.H. Hill[,] he is a very plain looking man[.] I hope that the yankees will find out that we will not be subjugated by them and go home[.] so we all that is living can return to our once peaceful homes and friends to live in peace for the remainder of our dayes[.] I received a letter from Emmy but I have forgotten whether I answerd it or not[.] tell her I am well and to write to me[.] I hope I shall get to see you soon[.] we must suffer gods will to be done and not ours[.] Fare well[,] J.L. Stuart

Mr Harper[.] Dear stepfather[,] after my best respects to you[,] I hope you are well & I want to hear how you succeeded in your trip[.] you must do the best you can[.] you must take care of mother and try to get her better for I am very uneasy about her[.] you must write often and let me know how she is getting[.] I do not know what I should do if I was to hear that she was dead[.] we shall draw money soon[.] they say we will draw this week[.] they have made out the flag rolls for 4 months[.] you must all do the best you can[.] Farewell[.]

Dear Brother and sister and granny[,] I hope you are well[.] I want to see you very bad and hope I shall get to see you after awhile[.] you must all do the best you all can[.] take care of yourselves and try and take care of mother and try and cure her and try and make all the corn you can for it will be needed[.] Charles[,] I bought my half quire papers at one Dollar[.] this morning it is noble. I wish you had some[.] I want to be at home ploughing[.] it is such nice weather[.] I must close my letter[.] you must write soon[.] Dyrect your letter to Kinston as usual[.] give my respects to all my friends[.] tell Mathany Teague I got a letter from here the other day[.] John Stuart

1863, May 9
John A. Jackson (*Hanover Court House, VA*) to sister **Martha R. Jackson**. General wartime correspondence between brother/sister regarding military life and discussion of the battle of Fredericksburg with brief mentions of **Richard A. Cole**, **Catherine Ritter Jackson**, **Tom Jackson** and **Benjamin W. Stutts.** [304]

Miss Martha R. Jackson, Dear sister[,] I rec'd your kind letter yesterday morning and it was a welcome visitor. You may depend I was more than glad to hear from you and all the rest of the family and Cole and family and the Neighbors generaly[,] and that you were all well. I am well at presant and hope these few lines will soon come to hand and find you all the same. The company is in very good health at presant[,] but very few sick in it. We have very near 100 men for duty[.] at any rate we draw rations for 99 and they are all able for duty. I havnt much news to write you at this time[,] only they say that General Lee has whipt the yankeys again at Fredricksberg and taken about then thousand prisoners and several peaces of artillery and drove them back across the rapahaoc with heavy loss. There is suposed to be some where about 40 thousand kild[,] wounded and mising[,] and our loss 10 thousand. 17 I saw yesterday 2000 prisoners pass the bridge that we are garding[,] and some 1200 more this morning passed down the Railroad in about the ½ of mile of where we are standing. Some of our boys saw them this morning. I did not see them[.] I was off fishing when they passed this morning. I hear there is a great many behind yet. They say it was one of the hardest fought battles that has been fought since the war commenced. So I shal say no more about the battle for some body else can give a better description than I can and that will be put in the papers for every body to read. I have no newse of importance more than what I have wrote that is worth spoiling paper with. You said Mother wanted to know how I was geting along in the army. Well just as I always have only I dont get but a ? pound bacon per day but I got shugar now in the place of meat ? of a pound per day. Times is hard here[,] but if they dont get any worse I think I can stand it[.] at least I intend to try it a while longer before I do like B. Stutts. So I must close by saying write soon and airect your letters to Richmond Va.[,] 26 Regt[,] NC Co H[,] in care of Capt J. D. McIver Pettigrews Brigade. Give my love to Mother and Brother and my respects to the rest of the family & all enquiring friends. Your ever loving Brother[,] J. A. Jackson

1863, May 11

John A. Jackson (*Hanover Court House, VA*) to brother **Samuel Thomas "Tom" Jackson**. General wartime correspondence between brothers regarding military life and discussion of the battle of Fredericksburg, the death of General **Stonewall Jackson** with brief mentions of **Richard A. Cole**, **Catherine Ritter Jackson** and **Martha Jackson**. [305]

Dear Brother, I take the presant opertunity of droping you a few lines to let you know that I have not fogotten you. If you have me it seames that you dont intend to write to me any more or if you do I dont get you letters. I want to know what is the matter that you dont write or have I done any thing to keep you from writing. If so[,] let me know what it is so no more on that subject at presant. I am well at presant and hope these few lines will come safe to hand and find you and all the family well and Cole & family. I have no newse of much importance to write you[,] only General Jackson departed this life yesterday. He rec'd a wound in the last battle at Fredrickberg in his left arm. Our own men done it[,] but I heard today that is was a bumshell that struck him and that he never recovered from the shock. It is a great loss to us and I fear that it will bother us to find a man to fill his place thought I hope we will and soon (god can give us a man to stand in his place)[.] I hope it is for the better if it is gods will for us to gain our independence[,] it is all right. I saw about 2000 yankey prisoners yesterday going to Richmond. There has went some 5000 by us to Richmond and a good many others so no more on that subject. You need not send them shoes that I wrote to you for I have bought a pair since and dont need them at presant. So I must close for the presant by saying write soon and direct your letters to Richmond Va[,] 26 Regt[,] N.C. Troops Co H[,] General Pettigrews Brigade. Give my love to mother and Martha and all the family and Cole and family. No more at present[,] only I remain your loving brother. J.A. Jackson

1863, May 14

Noah Deaton (*Hanover Junction on the North Anna River, VA*) to **Sarah Jane McDonald**. General wartime correspondence with brief mentions of the company movements from Kinston to Richmond, battles and skirmishes at Hanover Courthouse, positions at Fredericksburg, Richmond, West Point on the York River, Generals **Robert E. Lee**, **Stonewall Jackson**, **Stephen W. Brewer** and others being detailed to engage deserters in Moore and Capt. **Evander Blue's** Company C 35th Regiment. [306]

Dear friend, I had the pleasure of receiving a letter from you today which came in hand in due time and it afforded me much pleasure to hear from a dear friend once more[.] it was the first intelligence that I have heard from old Moore since we left NC. We came by railroad from Kinston to this place[.] we are encamped near the Railroad Bridge across the North Anna guarding the Bridge[.] 5 companies from the Regt. Reached here about 1 o'clock one night[.] our company was one of them[.] the remaining companies discharged until the next day evening[.] they passed at Ashland but a short time before the yankee cavilry made a dash on that part of the road[.] our general was at Hanover C.H. and came within 15 minutes of being captured[.] the enemy in their Cavilry raid[,] I supose have made their way back to their own lines[.] they have been successful in far as escapring our clutches[,] but they done very little damage[.] all in which was repaired in a few days[.] as for the great battle on the Rappahannock[,] I only know what appears in the papers that God has again been pleased to crown our army with another great victory[,] perhaps the greatest of the war[.] while every hart gladened with the victory[,] every heart mourns the loss of the hero of the days[.] Genl. Jackson's corps passed here day before yesterday[.] it is rumored here today that [illegible] is evacuating his old position at Fredericksburg[.] it is also rumored that the navy is landing at or about West point on the York River[.] it is the general opinion that they will advance on Richmond by the same rout they did last year[,] that is last spring[.] Gen. R.E. Lee considered the greatest military mind of the age by the yankees and I guess he will meet them at any point they make their appearance. I learn from a letter to this company today[,] the the men detailed from the Brigade are in Moore playing havock with the deserters[.] it was stated that S.W. Brewer from our company has shot two of them[.] Mr. Brewer is a good and expert soldier and willing for his duty underall cirumstances[.] The fields and forest are putting forth their verdue and are clothed in green[.] Spring is in two weeks later before than at Kinston, NC. I had the pleasure of seeing Mr. Blue's company as we were about leaving Kinston and and was glad to see many of my old friends in good health[,] but alas there were some missing that we will see no more in this life[.] Of that this cruel war would soon end for I am tired! tired! tired! of it[.] I saw about 4000 yankees pass this Bridge on their way to Richmond. The truth is they are as tired of the war as any of us (prisioners)[.] I am in excelent health at present and also the health of the company is very good[.] please write soon and give all the news[.] address to Richmond VA, Co. H.[,] 26 NCT[,] Pettigrews Brigade[.] Excuse my haste and badly manufactured letter[.] your affectionate friend[.] N. Deaton

1863, May 18

Baxter C. Phillips *(Kinston, NC)* to sister **Elmira Phillips**. General wartime correspondence with brief mentions of **Emeline Phillips**. [307]

Dear Sister, I received yours with Emeline's. I was pleased with it as much so as any I have ever got. I wish I was with you to go to Sunday School and intend to, but this can't be so now. But I hope the time is not far distant when we shall dwell in peace plenty. They have kept us moving up and down 'til they have got us to Kinston. There is not much in the town nor in the vicinity to make it pleasant, but in time of peace it may be and is quite a pleasant place. Yet the hand of the invader has polluted it. Now it looks desolate compared with its former appearance. We are in camp about one mile from the town. I don't much like this country. The water is not so good as I would like and there is not enough shade, too many swamps and gnats. Our Regiment is the largest in the Brigade and we have the best Colonel I ever saw, but his health is not good and he can't stay with us all the time. We may stay in the country some time. I hope we ill not have to leave North Carolina any more, but just where the enemy is, there we will go no matter where that is. There is some of the nicest corn crops growing here I have seen. It makes me think of what I have seen at home and which I hope I will see again. Elmira, I have no news to write you this time so you must excuse me and I will do better next time. But because I don't write[,] that's no reason why you should not. At least I don't want you to think so. Do the best you can and I will do the same. Continue to pray for us. B. C. Phillips

1863, May 21

J.L. Stuart (*Kinston, NC*) to mother **Mary A. Harper**. General wartime correspondence with brief mentions of **James Dunn, Martha Nall** and **Emily Nall**. [308]

Mrs Mary A. Harper[.] Dear mother[,] I seat myself to day to drop you a few lines to inform you that I am well and hoping these few lines may reach you as well as usual and all the family well[.] I have nothing to write of Interest at this time[.] I received a letter from you the other day dated the 14 and I also received one from James Dunn[.] you may tell him I received his letter[,] but I cannot write to him now[.] I also received a letter from Martha Nall the other day and one from Emily Nall yesterday[.] Mother[,] it appears like some of our Moore County friends will not read my letters after I sent letter to them but they can do as they like[.] I am going to write to all my acquaintances and see who will write back to me[.] the can use there pleasure about writing I shall come home after a while and then I will Settle with them[.] is the talk that we will go back to Virginia but I do not know[.] tell ever body you see I am going to write them[.] we are about twelve miles below Kinston on picket now on the Neuse river where Moses Creek enters into the river[.] we came here last Sunday and will leave about next Sunday[.] my knapsack is back at the Camp and paper and all my clothes[.] I left ever thing but my Blanket[.] I though if the Yankees did come[,] I would not have any thing for them to get[.] I hope that your health is improving and I hope I shall get to come home before long[.] I expect to get a letter from you this evening and my chances is bad to write to this evening for my paper & c. are at camp[.] I want to see you all very bad but I will say but little this time[.] give my best respects to all that inquires about me[,] and them that do not want to read my Letters[,] let them stay along with the buffaloes[.] Dyrect your letters to Kinston[.] fare well[,] John L Stuart to MA Harper

1863, May 21
J.L. Stuart (*Kinston, NC*) to stepfather **John Harper**. General wartime correspondence with brief mentions of **Mary A. Harper** [309]

Mr John Harper[.] Dear step father[,] I seat myself to drop you a line to inform you that I am well truly hoping these lines may find you well[.] I am very sorry to hear of Mothers bad health[.] I wish I was at home but I cannot tell when I can come[.] I received a letter this evening dated the 3rd[.] I should have got it last night but wee about 16 miles below here[.] we advanced that far below here about twenty miles below Kinston towards Newbern[.] felt we did not see the Yankees[.] our regt went one road and our Brigade and General Daniels Brigade went down another road[,] but I have not heard what they done[.] we marched about sixteen miles to day[.] I am sorter tierd[.] it is dark[.] I will stop for the night[.] you said you could get a track of land worth $1000 if you would go in a mans place[.] do you remember that text what profit is it to a man to Join the whole world and loose his own soul[.] you know nothing about being in the army while you staid at Raleigh[,] you had fine time[.] we do not have such times now[.] I will just say stay at home if I was at home and did not have to come[.] I could not be fraid to come[.] I want you to stay at home and take care of Mother as long as she lives and if anybody says tha want you go for them[,] tell them you had the chance to stay in the army[,] but you can stay and your stay at home stay at home[.] I ask of you do not leave mother[.] I hope I may get to come home soon[.] write soon[.] take good care of yourself and family[,] J.L. Stuart

1863, May 25
William Henry Patterson (*Camp near Hanover Junction, VA*) to sister **Frances Anna V. Patterson**. General wartime correspondence between siblings with brief mentions of **Iver D. Patterson, William P. Blue, W.S. McDonald, C.B. McKinnon, Daniel R. McKinnon, Archibald B. McDonald**, **John D. McDonald, Lauchlin C. McKinnon, Gen. Robert E. Lee, Gen. Pettigrew** and **Eliza J. McDonald.** [310]

Miss F. A. V. Patterson, Dear Sister, I seat myself for the purpose of writing you a few lines to let you know that I am in possession of usual health and I sincerely hope these few lines will find you similarly blessed. Pa arrived here yesterday and you may depend I was glad to see him and besides I was very glad to receive the clothing and provisions he brought me for I was nearly destitute for pants and the 2 pairs he brought to me suit me very well. I was also pleased to get the box of provisions. Pa says he will start back home tomorrow evening I would be glad if he could remain with me longer but I know his presence is very much needed at home particularly at this season of the year. The health of the company and in fact the entire Regiment is very good. We have most excellent water here. It is very cool and good water. The weather is very cool to day. Yesterday was a very warm day but the weather has taken a considerable change since yesterday evening The night have been very cool here ever since we came to Virginia. William P. Blue is well and so are all our friends in camp. W. S. McDonald is in this Regt. though he does not belong to our company he is in good health. C. B. McKinnon is in good health and is as lively as ever, his brother Daniel R. was badly wounded in his right hand at Fredericksburg. He is in one of the hospitals in Richmond and Pa says that if he will have time when he goes through Richmond on his way home that he will try and call at the Hospital and see poor Daniel. I suppose from what Pa tells me that A. B. McDonald will keep of the service of his country by being Shepard. I am sorry that Archibald has acted in this way. I expect the name of Shepard will cling to him as long as he lives and John D. too has acted very cowardly in my openion it is true that the army is a bad place but I believe that it is every man's duty who has no more to confine him at home than he has to come and join in the conflict to assist in driving the miserable vandals from our soil and when this war is over and the South has gained her Independence those that have managed to evade the law and keep out of the service of their bleeding country will hardly be respected as friends to their country. I am in hopes that some of our boys will get furloughs to go home Genl. Pettigrew approved furloughs for 4 of our company but the Prevost board would not let them get on the train because their furloughs were not approved by Genl. Lee so their furloughs have been sent to Genl. Lee for approval which I am in hopes will be granted and if their furloughs should get back in time (and if approved by Genl. Lee) Pa will have company part of the way home. I have not received that shirt that was sent by Lauchlin C. McKinnon yet as his Regiment the 52nd is encamped 3 or 4 miles from here and I have not had an opportunity of going after it. Will Anna I like to stay in Virginia very well so far. If they will let us stay here I can get along very well. But I think it very uncertain wheather we will remain here much longer or not – It is rumored here that we will be sent to Gordonsville and if we should leave here I would not be surprised that we will be sent to Gordonsville or Fredericksburg and I do not wish to go to either place. I suppose that Miss Eliza J. McDonald is staying with you while Pa is gone for which I am much obliged to her. Well Anna I have no news of importance to write to you so I will come to a close as Pa can tell you all the news. Write to me on the recipt of these? Few lines and give me all the news you have. Give my kindest regards to all enquiring friends and accept the warmest Brother's love for yourself. Your affectionate Bro. W. H. Patterson. address me at Richmond, VACo H 26th Regt. Pettigrew's Brigade

1863, May 26
Mastin C. Phillips *(Kinston, NC)* to father Rev. **Lewis Phillips Jr.** General wartime correspondence with brief mentions of **Cornelius Lawhon, General J.H. McNeill** and **Baxter C. Phillips.** [311]

My Dear Father, I will send this by Cornelius Lawhon to Carthage. Perhaps you will get it as soon as if I were to send it by mail. I received yours yesterday. Was happy to hear from you and that all were well. We have had a rough time of it for the past few days. I guess there is more in store for us soon. Last Thursday night the Yanks captured about one hundred and fifty of our piquetts. We heard of it soon the next morning. We cooked rations for one day and set out after them. We cam in sight of them the same evening, but they would not stop to fight. We kept after them all night and until noon the next day, by which time we had driven them to their fortifications in eight miles of New Bern. General J. H. McNeill then made an attempt to find where they were, but did not get a fight that evening. They would not come where we could reach them. We opened upon the fort with our artillery, with what effect I do not know[,] except that we killed the Coln. Cmdr. of the Post. We then threw out skirmishes. These soon became engaged with the Yankee advance, but the Yanks retreated and the prospects for a fight that night disappeared. We then fell back five miles in haste to a position, but they would not follow us. Sunday and yesterday we came back to this place which is about five miles below Kinston. We had men enough to make a strong fight, but I am afraid we did not get engaged. Troops are arriving here from Virginia. I do not know the object, but I guess to march on New Bern or to relieve us so that we can go to Virginia. You do not want us to leave the State, but I am ready to go anywhere to get out of these swamps. I can not live long here. The water, diet and hot sun make it the most disagreeable place I ever saw. I hope we will go to Virginia. I know we will have to fight there, but we can get the best water in the world and the sun is not so hot. I still hope to live through all this and get home when the war is over. I have but little hope of coming before. Baxter stood the march very well, but I gave out Sunday morning and went to the front. I am no better today, but hope to be soon. I suffer with my breast and hear nearly all the time, but I don't think I am worse than I have been for some time, except for the effects of this march. Please send me a suit of clothes ready. I may have a chance to get them sometime. I send my type to Carthage by Lawhon so you can get it. Mastin

1863, May 26
J.L. Stuart (*Kinston, NC*) to mother **Mary A. Harper**. General wartime correspondence with brief mentions of **William Brewer, Henry Brewer, Emory Davis** and **John Teague**. [312]

Mrs MA Harper[.] Dear Mother[,] I seat myself to drop you a few lines to inform you that I am well truly hoping these lines may reach you all a live and as well as usual[.] I must write a short letter this time[.] the yankees came up last Friday and got around the 56th regt and taken several of them[.] we runn them back nearly to Newbern[.] Ransoms Brigade and Cooks and our Co and two more did not go as far as the rest of the troops[.] we were on picket and did not overtake our regt untell the turned back[.] we march about 20 or 25 miles saturday trying to get to the regt[,] but they turned back and we got orders to turn back before we got up with them[.] there was little fighting done[.] I saw Wm Brewer and his Brother and Emra Davis and several that I knew in the 48th regt[.] I cannot tell when I shall get to come home but I think if we can get furloughs[,] I will get home before long[.] I think I shall get to come in a good time[.] I received your letters posted on the two but since I cannot write much this time[,] I will write when Mack gets back[.] It is thought we will be sent to virginia but I do not know nor care much[.] I hope I shall get to see you all some of these time but I do not now[.] I think but say nothing about it now. give my respects to all my friends[.] tell John Teague I sent a letter to him by M.C[.] I received a few lines from him yesterday[.] tell all inquirers that I am well[.] I must close by saying my best respects to you all[.] write soon[.] your afec son[,] John Stuart[.] all of you write[.]

1863, May 27

J.L. Stuart (*Kinston, NC*) to mother **Mary A. Harper,** stepfather **John Harper** and brother **Charles Harper**. General wartime correspondence with brief mentions of **Generals Ransom** and **Hill,** the death of Union **Col. Jones,** and **James Dunn, Martin Comer, John Teague, Nancy Teague, Cynthia Teague** and **Nancy Glass Nall**. [313]

Mrs Mary A Harper[.] Dear Mother[,] I seat my self to day to drop you a line to inform you that Im well at this time truly hoping these lines may find you so you can get about and the rest all well[.] I received a letter from you yesterday by the hands of Mr Williamson[,] stating that you was about as usual[.] I also received the butter and fruit and socks and tobacco and forth[.] I was highly pleased me and my mess had a fine Breakfast this morning[.] when one of us gets any thing from home[,] we all eat untell it is gone[.] some of my mess gets a right smart of things[.] we are like a family[.] one of my mess has sent up a furlough[.] if he goes home[,] he will bring back a good deal of provision[.] my time to get off will come after a while[.] I hope in a better time than the present[,] if furloughs are not stoped the. for I saw the glimse of the back of it[,] but about the man that will go next had the furlough promised to him some time[.] Dear Mother[,] I want to see you the worst in the world[.] it made me so sorry when I saw what you had sent to me[.] I even thought poore mother fingers tied them strings but[,] alas[,] I am here and I do not know how long I am to stay in this war but to Desert will not do after I have been in what the 49th has for twelve long months[.] I wrote a short letter to you yesterday[.] say major want to see my letters[,] if you secrets to write them on a strip of paper[,] so it selfres and then I can show the letter[,] if any person wants to see it[.] I hope I shall get to see you all again but we must do the Lords will[.] I write very often to you and get letter pretty often[.] I have got sixty Dollars Cash[.] I will send some of it home the first chance if I do not get to come[.] I must close my letter[.] I remain your affectionate son untell Death[,] John L. Stuart[.] I have got a great deal to tell you if I ever see you[.] Your aft son[,] John L. Stuart. we had 20 pieces artillery and shell at the enemy a right smart Saturday evening[.] our co was in the rear[.] I cannot tell all of it[.] John L Stuart

Mr John Harper[.] after my best wishes for your welfare &c I will tell you about our last few dayes work[.] last sunday as aweek ago our Company Co C &. H. was sent about eight miles below Comp on the Neuse river road on picket Duty and we was getting along finely fishing &c untell Friday about 10 oclock[.] orders came to us to get back to comp the best way we could[.] that we was about to be cut off by Yankees some started and went up the river about one mile and crossed the river in canoes and came up on the other side untell we got even with our camps[,] and then we crossed again in the same Kind of Boats and reached the comp about Dark[.] and our rest was gone next morning[.] order came to march on after the regt in the direction of Newbern so we march a bout twenty miles to with out overtaking our rest[.] and by this time it was dark and we got orders to march back about four miles and wait untell our Brigade came back[.] they came next morning and we staide all day at Core Creek and left at 5 oclock that evening and next morning and came about ten miles[.] and next morning we came back camp... well[,] last Friday[,] the yankees came up to gum swamp on the Dover road and Gen Ransom had sent the 25th to support the 56th that was on picket[.] and gen Ransom himself rode down that morning and passed where the 25th was halted and went pretty close to the 56th and saw yankees in the wood[.] and he turned back and passed the 25th and found the yanks had got in there rare and they fired at him[,] about two Co of them and he went throe the swamp and got away[,] and the 25th all got out without loss[,] but the 56th lost over 100 men[,] prisioner and Gen Hill taken gen Ransoms and Cooks Brigades and run them in four or five miles of Newbern and we was told that the yankees lost[.] Col Jones a great yankee officer[.] I must close[.] you can see that there was not much done[.] we do not know how many we killed Saturday.

May 27th 1863[.] Mr Charles E Harper[.] Dear Brother[,] I seat my self to write a line to you[.] I have received two or three letter from you lately[.] I want to see you very bad[.] you said that you did not get mad at me for writing what I did[.] Charles[,] I get letters occaisonly from the girls[.] Wm Brewer told me you had grown a good deal but did not say whether you were pretty boy or not[.] I have not had time to talk CNC(?) yet for I am on guard at a house a bout a mile from Camp Charles[.] we gave the yankees scare enough to run them to there breastworks last week[.] tell sis and granny I want to see them very bad[.] I hope I shall get to come home soon[.] tell James Dunn I received his letter and will write to him as soon as I get the chance[.] tell Martin Comer I received a letter from him[,] but I have not time to write to him now[.] tell John Teague I received his letter also[.] tell all my friends to write to me[.][.] John L Stuart

tell Nancy Teague I will write to her as soon as I get the chance I recon you and Mart and Jim do have some mitty times but if I ever get back[,] I will cut your leather for you all if you dont mind[.] but you or mart or James Dunn can have Cynthia Teague for she said that she did not want to see my letters and she does not want to see me[.] tell Poore old granny I have not forgot her and none of you[.] I would give anything if I Could see you all[.] I hope I shall see you all yet[.] tell mother and granny not to get out of heart[.] I hope the war will soon stop[.] I must stop writing[.] I have so many to write too to day[.] tell little sis I think of her as often as any and I do want to see her very bad[.] I must close[.] Charles[,] you must tell me what girls you think wants to see me the worst and I will write to her[.] Kinston NC[,] Care Capt Black[,] Co D[,] 48 regt[,] NCT

1863, June 2

William Henry Patterson (*Camp near Hanover Junction, VA*) to sister **Frances Anna V. Patterson**. General wartime correspondence between siblings with brief mentions of **J.T. Warwick, Nathan L. Fry, Noah Deaton, W.H. McDonald, Neill McDonald, B. Gilliam Hollingsworth, Capt. James D. McIver, Iver D. Patterson, Murdoch McLeod, Daniel R. McKinnon, Colin McKinnon, William P. Blue, Lauchlin C. McKinnon, W.D. Patterson, James A.J. Buchan, Denson, A.B. Fry** and **John M. Graham.** [314]

Dear Sister, with the greatest pleasure I seat myself to write you a few lines to inform you that I am in enjoyment of usual health and I sincerly hope these few lines will find you and the rest of the family enjoying the same. The health of the company is pretty good, J. T. Warwick and Nathan L. Fry are sick but neither of them are in a dangerous condition. I am enjoying very good health myself at this time. I have no news to write you[.] we are still at the same place though I have no idea how long we will remain here. Noah Deaton, W. H. McDonald , Neill McDonald and B. G. Hollingsworth are gone home on furlough. Capt. McIver has gone home also. I wrote a letter to Pa and gave it to Gilliam Hollingsworth and him to mail it in Fayetteville. Our company is comanded by our 1st Leuit. Murdoc McLeod[.] he is a very fine man and I wish he was Captain. I dont care if I never see Jim McIver again but- I guess he will be back at the expiration of his furlough[,] which is only about 20 days. Daniel R. McKinnon is still in the hospital at Richmond Va. Colin had a letter from him a few days ago, he said his hand was improving pretty fast- but he said that it will be a good while before he will be fit for duty[.] he also said that there is no chance for him to get a furlough to go home[.] he did not think that his hand would be amputated. Colin is enjoying excelent health and is as lively as ever. William P. Blue is in very good health. I went to the 52nd Regiment last Sunday and got that shirt that L. C. McKinnon had of mine. I saw W. D. Patterson last Sunday when I was at the 52nd Regt. William is enjoying good health. I was very glad to get the box of provisions that Pa brought me from home. I have some the dried turkey yet. I dont know what I would give to be at home now to get milk and butter. I begin to want to go home to see you all very bad but I do not suppose that there is any chance for me to go home soon. If furloughs continue[,] James A. J. Buchan will get to go home the next time and I hope that Jimmy will get off for he out when the company first came out[,] and he has not been at home since. I beleive that all of the boys have been at home since the company came out[,] but Jas. Buchan and a fellow by the name of Denson and he has sold the chance of his furlough to A. B. Fry. I have no news of interest to comunicate so I will come to a close but before I close I will request you to write to me on the receipt of these few lines. I have not had a letter from hoe since I got that one the L. C. McKinnon brought me from Pa[.] when you write[,] let me know how John M. Graham is getting along wheather his leg has got well or not. I forgot to ask Pa about him when he was here. Your Afft. Bro.[,] Wm. H. Patterson

1863, June 3
Baxter C. Phillips to sister **Elmira Phillips.** General wartime correspondence with brief mentions of **Mastin C. Phillips** and **David Paschal.** [315]

Dear Elmira, You must excuse me for not writing sooner. I could not write until things got better as now you have heard that the enemy was coming close to Richmond and at first was expected here. It has come off but not as bad as we were looking for. On yesterday our forces moved closer and attacked them, but they made no effort to generate anything. We chose not to pursue them. I don't think that there will be much fighting here at this time although there may be. We have now returned to camp and it will be our business to watch the enemy. If he moves, we will move to him. We have men enough here to take care of Richmond unless they move more men against us than at this time. My health is as good as it has been since I was at home. I think I possibly will recover. Mastin is better off now. He has been some sick several days, but I think he will get well now. I have no news to write this time. Tell mother I will write to her soon. All of you keep in good heart at home. We are doing well here. David Paschal is well. All the regiment are in good health now. Do the best you can and always remember us. All will be well with us yet. Write soon. Address me at Richmond, Virginia[.] May God be with you all. Baxter

1863, June 6
Lizzie Skeen Phillips *(Randolph County, NC)* to **Emeline Phillips.** General wartime correspondence with brief mentions of **Milton Skeen, Louis C. Phillips** and **Louisa Skeen.** [316]

My dear Em, No doubt you have long been looking for some intelligence from me. I now attempt to drop you a line though nothing of great importance to communicate. Times are somewhat dull about here. Nothing but deserters can be heard of scarcely. Brother Milton just returned from Raleigh last evening. They carried several dozen to camp. Oh, it is so unpleasant to have to force men into duty. Wounded soldiers are passing here daily from the Fredericksburg fight. Some ruined for lifetime. When, oh when will this cruel war stop? I fear it will yet be a long time. I hope your brothers have been home ere this time. I don't see why they can't get a furlough. I hope they may some time. I know it is hard to be separated from them so long. I am anxious to visit you all but can't tell when the time may come. Louis is well and lively and talks of you all often. I will close for the present. Write soon and give me all the news. My love to all. Sis Louiser sends you much love. Lizzie Phillips

1863, June 9
David H. Sloan (*Lynchburg, VA*) to mother **Catharine Sloan**. General wartime correspondence with brief mention of **John B. Cole.** [317]

Dear Mother, I take my pen in hand to inform you that I am well except my hand that is no better than it was when I wrote last. I hope when this comes to hand it may find you and all of the children well. I have been looking for a letter from you for the last three weeks, but I have not got it yet. J.B Cole is with me yet we fare splendid here. I want you to write how you are getting along, and I want to know if the fruit was killed or not, and I want to know if you have got a horse to work or not. I would be glad to be at home to help cut the rye, but if I was there[,] I would do no good for I can't use my hand. I believe that I will make Lynchburg my home till the war is ended for they won't let me come home[,] and I intend to stay here as long as I can. So I must close. Write soon, fail not. Direct your letter to Lynchburg, VA, General Hospital, No.2.[,] 2 Division, 2 Ward. D.H. Sloan

1863, June 14
Exer L. Ritter and **Mary M. Ritter** (*Oak Dale, NC*) to **A.S. Caddell**. General wartime correspondence with brief mentions of **Brewer**, **Gunter**, **Eliza Moore**, **Mollie Elliott**, **H.C. Tyson**, **Ashley F. Muse**, **C.D. Caddell**, **William Caddell** and **Raney Caddell.** [318]

Last evening my heart was made glad by the reception of your welcome letter and I hasten to reply to it --- home is full of excitement as you know it is almost crowded with men from the army after these cowardly conscripts and deserters[.] The Cavalry though are ordered back to this regiment and leave today[.] We girls have great times with some of those boys from the army[.] There is some nice looking along as I ever saw[.] Mr. Brewer[,] a member of your company[,] called on us not long since[.] he had a very nice looking young man along with him who he introduced to me as a Mr Gunter[.] I think he is right nice. he is very interesting in conversation[.] You say you are on the rule of the unfortunate and to think your case a hopeless one as the boys says[.] now what that little darling of yours been doing to cause this sorrow[.] I deeply sympathise with you in your deep distress[.] This miserable war cannot last always[.] the darkest night will have an end and these dark clouds will all soner or latter reveal this silver lining[.] then let no bode and trust and pray waiting for the brighter day[.] I wish you had been with us last week we had the greatest time[.] Eliza Moore (your old sweetheart) and Miss Mollie Elliott from Franklinvile spent the week with us - we had a grand picnic at Goldstons Mills while they come down and such a splendid time we did have[.] Mollie is a great little pie[.] She is all life[.] they left Friday and how I do miss the little piece of mischief[.] I hope you will excuse my short letter by replying to it with a long one soon[.] Give my respects to Mr. H.C. Tyson, cousin Ash and all my friends[.] Your devoted friend, Exer.

Mr Caddle, As sister is riting[,] I will write you a few lines to let you now I am well and hope these few lines will reach you safe and find you well[.] Tim I havent seen any fun since we stade at Mr Caddles[.] I stade there last monday night and oh how I wish you was there for we dint so have such a Tim as we hade when you was there[.] I went to see your Mother a tusdy she was with Neal[.] [illegible] to come up this week and I hop he will come b fore he starts to the war[.] rite to me soon and write a long letter and tell me all the nuse[.] your friend[,] Mary M. Ritter

1863, June 17-18
Matthew C. Yow to his wife **Nancy Catherine Albright Yow** and children. General wartime correspondence with brief mentions of **Andrew John Stutts**, cousin **Henry W. Stutts**, father **Henry C. Yow,** and children **William Henry Yow, Nancy Elizabeth Yow, Mary Jane Yow, Joseph Gibbs Yow** and **John Matthew Yow**. [319]

My Dear Wife and Little Children[,] Through the kind hand of Providenc I hav bin spard to seat myself to drop you a few lines to let you no that I am well at present truly hoping when this comes to hand it may find you and the dear little children well and harty. Catharine I hav not herd from you sinc I left you at High Point and I want to here vary bad. I am looking for a letter from you now. I hop I will get one soon. I wrote to you the day I got to the company and I wrote to father sinc and I thought I wold write to you again to day and let you no where I am now. We are in camp about 4 miles east of Richmond near the 7 pines where we fought the Yankees last June. But I dont here any tel of a fight here now. I dont no what we come here for but I suppose to wach for them. Catharine I here some nuse in camp to day that we shal hav to go to Vicksburg in Missisippi and I can tel you that I dont want to go there you may be sure. We hav bin sent here to gard this point. It was thought that the Yankees wold mak another rade run here. Tha come out down here and stold some horces and cattle and sheep and burnt some houses and then tha went back and tha may come out again. I cant tel. Our boys has bin down on the old battlefield and brought some old Yankee bones to camp. Tha say that the Yankees is lying down there any where dryd. I no that looks bad. I hav not bin to the battlefield yet. I am going down if we stay here. I think I will tomorrow and see the place where pore Andrew Stuts got his leg shot off. Catharine I study so much about you and the dear little. It seems like I cant stand it now.
June 18. Catharine I will say to you that I hav bin on the battle field today and I saw 7 skul bones in one pile besids may others ling about. Any wheres it is an awful looking sight you may be sure. Catharine, Henry W. Stuts is going to start home to day and he may go to see you. I cant tel. He talks like going by High Point and if he does he will go by fathers I expect. Catharine I will say to you that my 2 brothers will be in our company before tomorrow night. There is 2 men in our company that is going to the 15. I think it will be a swap this time if nothing happens more than I no. Catharine I hav sent for a pocket Bible. I hav red my testament all the time and I thought I wold get a Bible and read that. It is some satisfaction to read the blesed promises in this Bible. My book and hart shal never part. Catharine I suppose there has bin a big in western Va over in the vally at Winchester. I no the place vary well. We whipt them bad. We taken 8 thousand prisnors and 70 pecies of artillery and every thing that tha had. We hav a heep of camp nuse here. Some think we will go to Vicksburg and some say we will go to South Carolina again but I dont no where we will go. Catharine I hav nothing more to rite at this time. I stil remain your true and loving husband untel death. Matthew C. Yow to Mrs Nancy C. Yow. I hav nothing at this time. I am looking for a letter from you. I want to here so bad. So fairwell my dear wife[.] Nancy C. Yow. M.C. Yow William H Yow Nancy E. Yow Mary J. Yow Joseph G. Yow John M Yow My dear little children so fairwell. Lord bles the children.

1863, June 18
Jane McIntosh (*Moore County, NC*) to uncle **A.S. Caddell**. General wartime correspondence between uncle/niece with brief mentions of deserters at Meadow Branch including **Jefferson Williams**, the birth of uncle **Joseph Caddell's** son **William Neill Caddell**, **Archibald B. Muse's** son **William Ashley Muse**, **Neill Caddell,** grandmother **Raney Caddell** and the death of grandfather **William Caddell**. [320]

Dear uncle[,] it is with pleasur that I take my pen in hand to write a few lines to you to inform you that I am well and that this may reach you and find you in good health[.] I have nothing of interest to write to you[.] times is hard and not likely to get any better[.] the cavalry and infantry is a takin in some of the conscripts and deserters[.] they have not caught any of the meadow branch company but Jeff Williams[.] I hope that they will get them all before long[.] uncle Jo Caddell has another son and as A.B. Muse[.] well Tim I wish I could see you now and talk over old times[.] I hope it will not be long before you are permited to come home and stay[.] I tell you it will be a lonesom looking place when Neill leaves as he will start this evening or in the morning[.] if nothing happens it has looked lonesom ever since you left and then more so when Grandpapa died and now Neill[.] though I suppose we will meet again on earth[,] if not I hop we will in that uper and better world wher parting will be known no more[.] Grandmother is about as well as comon and that people gneraly is in comon good health[.] As I have nothing of importance to write I will close by saying write soon[.] I have not wrote to you since I received any from you[.] It seems like my letters will not go to you[.] When this you see[,] remember me though many miles apart we be[.] so nothing more at present only I remain your affectionate neice until Death. Jane McIntosh

1863, June 18
Mastin C. Phillips *(Richmond, VA)* to sister **Emeline Phillips.** General wartime correspondence with brief mentions of Generals **Lee** and **Early, Rev. Lewis Phillips Jr., Baxter C. Phillips, Malphus Phillips** and **Catherine Livingston Johnson**. [321]

My Dear Sister, We are in camp several miles below the city on the Williamsburg road. We have been to several places since we came to Virginia, but have not met the enemy yet and I hope we will not while the war lasts. General Lee had a fight in Winchester two days ago. It was a grand affair. I do not know the extent of our loss, heavy though I expect as the works were very formidable. The victory was complete. Troops that can storm such works as those will do to depend on any where. It was General Early's division that stormed the works. I think the Yanks had better quit fighting if they can't hold such places. The Yanks can't take it from us. Vicksburg is still standing. I hope it will not fail, but I have my doubts. How would you like for me to go home? You need not be surprised if my next is dated somewhere in that country. We are going to leave this State and I would not be surprised if we go to Vicksburg. I had rather stay here, but I will go anywhere. I read your last a few days ago. Was happy to hear from you and that all were doing well. I hope you have had rain before now and that the growing crops are doing well. I hope Pa will save all his wheat. Wish I could be with him. I could not do much work, but I should like to be there, but this is out of the question just now. I don't expect to come home while the fighting is going on. I still hope to live through all and get home. If so and you are all living, I shall not regret that I was absent from you so long. The weather is quite warm and dry now, but our troops are quite healthy and I hope will remain so. I think the war will end next fall if we shall be able to hold the enemy in check through the summer. I think we shall be able to do so and perhaps more. There is a movement in the North not developed yet, which hope will result in good. I am so nervous this morning I can hardly write. My health is not good, but I have to keep at my post. Baxter is well and will write you soon. He had a letter from Malphus a few days ago. He was well and said he was trying to get a furlough. I hope he will get home. I will write to Mrs. Johnson soon. I wrote to her just before we left South Carolina, and I have not heard from her since. You will not make my coat until you hear from me again. I drew one the other day that will do me until winter. We all have clothes enough and good enough. We also get enough to eat. With regard to these matters, you need not be uneasy. I will come home if I get an opportunity. But if I do not, all of you do the best you can. Pray for me. I am trying to live a better boy than when you knew me. My love to all. Mastin

1863, June 20
Isaac Thompson to **N.G. Cameron.** General wartime correspondence with brief mentions of **George McDavis, Angus Smith** and **Daniel Smith**. [322]

Dear Sir: When you left me at Burgaw Station, I promised to write to you some time, but owing to our continued moving from one place to another I have neglected to until now, for I have scarcely had time to write my wife, but hope you will excuse me for not fulfilling that promise sooner. We remained at Burgaw after you left us until that night. We then started for Charleston after waiting at the warf in Wilmington until midnight for transportation[.] we set out for Charleston, after two days and a half travel[.] we reached the place expecting to fight immediately, but found no indications of a fight there after stacking arms and resting for two hours[.] we took the train for Pocodaligo Station near Savannah, this being about the 20th of February, we found peach trees in full bloom, and gardens of the finest kind, and everything showed that summer was high, there were cabbage leaves as large as a palm leaf and Irish potatoes knee high. We took up camp at this station in an old field surrounded by rice fields, every side entirely covered by water, this of course was called a sickly place, yet we enjoyed good health. The sickly season had not come on here. We stayed for 8 weeks throwing up breastworks all the time and was expecting an attack by the Yankees all the time, yet it was never made. After finishing the work necessary to defend the place which was breastwork of dirt three miles long, we were ordered back to Charleston, where we got on the train and started. You ought to have heard the boys hollering. Such a fuss you never heard in your life, they thought we were coming back to North Carolina, but when we reached Charleston we marched 4 miles to this side and took up camp in a beautiful grove between the Cooper and Ashely rivers where we remained two weeks resting, we then came back to Wilmington which place all was glad to see[.] we remained there but a short time before we were ordered to Topsail Sound, when we reached that place we were all delighted with it and were in hopes that we would stay there this summer. There we could get fish a plenty and had boats to go across the sound to the beach and look at the ocean and nearly everything beautiful was there to behold. But scarsely two weeks had elapsed when we had to leave that beautiful place and go. Knew was making a start back to Va. and therefore little hollering was done. After staying there two days we left for Goldsboro which was inching on to Va. Two weeks passed by and we were at Kinston. Here I saw the first man killed that I ever saw in my life, he had made the attempt to go to the Yankees for which crime he was shot. A few days after this the Yankees came up near Kinston and surprised General Ransoms brigade earring off a good many prisoners[.] conseguently[,] we were ordered to persue them. Opening upon them with our cannons whenever we would get in sight of them. We followed them within 7 miles of Newbern,but could not get them to show fight at all. We then returned back near Kinston and repaired our breastworks which the Yankees had torn down. After finishing this we came on here to Richmond. After marching 75 or 80 miles we came back to the seven pines where the fight took place last June, and is now in camp here. We can see plenty of dead men laying here on the ground now and there bones are scattered in every direction. Mr. Cameron, since I saw you I have been through enough to kill a man. I have worked hard all day with but one meal of victuals. I have had to eat beef so poor it would stick to my fingers and I could scarecly get clear of it. I have marched through dust that would rise up in my face till I could write my name on my face. I have marched 30 miles a day in this kind of dust yet you can not conceive the hardships I've been through. Mr. Cameron, I've given you a very brief history of my travels and hardships since I saw you last, but time will not permit me to go into greater detail at present. I will just say that not with standing all my hardships, I injoyed as good health as I ever did in my life. The regiment generally has been in good health. George McDavis of our company died a few weeks ago. I had forgotten to tell you that. One of our men was shot near Petersburg as we came in here. The cort marshall having sentenced him to be shot on that day for running away five times. He was shot in less than a hundred yards of me. When they fired upon him he fell instantly, crying out "Lord have mercy" and died without a struggle or groan. We had a fine rain here nigh before last. I hope you had it also for it was needed. Though there is nothing making here. It does look like starvation is at the door and prices indicate the same. You can buy two eggs here for one dollar and everything high in proportion. I would like to say something about the length of this war if I knew what to say. When I came back I thought starvation would have ended it before now yet it is not so, the end looks farther off than it did there. Yet I hope the Lord will look upon us in mercy will take us out of the hands of those wicked rulers who is now trying to get the last poor man killed to get him out of the way. Oh that the hand of the destroyers would ever take them and remove them from our midst that peace and prosperity might again pervail ever our once happy country but now miserable country. Our leaders are getting so bold in wickedness that I can but think that God will crush them for their deeds. I beleive that all the soldiers nearly in the Confederacy is for peace. Let it come as it will. I believe myself it would be better to be subjugated and quit now than to fight on two years longer and gain our independence. For before that time starvation will visit our land with great destruction and if my family has to suffer and die for want of something to eat what good would it do me to gain independence? For if I fight at all let me fight for my family's rights. I am a southern man with southern principals yet I'm not in favor of fighting until we are worse off than we would be to be subjugated. I leave this subject now knowing that man's rath has got to such a pitch unless Divine Providence interfers neither party will give it up until compelled to do so for the want of means to carry it on. I saw Angus Smith a few days since and was glad to see him yet was sorry to hear of the death of Daniel though he had not quite recovered from his wound. I will close my letter hoping this will find you and family well and the neighbors generally. The men in our Co. is generally well. We are getting some better than we have done. Please write soon and tell me all the news and everything else for anything does me good that I have from that part of the country. Excuse bad writing and spelling and all other mistakes for I am in such a hurry. I cannot write scarcely at all. Your very truly and sincerely, Isaac Thompson.

1863, June 23 and June 30
Noah Deaton *(Wilmington, NC and Winchester, VA) to* **Sarah Jane McDonald***. General wartime correspondence with details of travel from Little River to Jonesboro to Fayetteville to Wilmington to Richmond, VA and Staunton, VA and brief mentions of church in Fayetteville, raids in Virginia and the Blue Ridge Mountains.* [323]

My Dear friend, While I am idle here waiting for the train which will leave at 7pm I have concluded to commence this letter but will not finish it now[.] The day I left Little River I arrived to Jonesboro in good time 2 hours before the train left[.] Mr. Whitlock carried me within a few miles of the place[.] I remained in Fayetteville until Monday morning and was at church twice and also Sunday school[.] on Saturday night I went to the Presbyterian church to hear the choir which was performed by ladies[.] it was the best musick I ever heard except some I heard in the Presbyterian church in this place[.] I went to sleep last night in the early part of the night some 35 miles from here[.] when I awoke this morning the boat was lying at the wharf[.] I suppose we reached here at one o'clock last night[.] I hear no news of importance today[.] June 30th, Winchester, VA...We have left Wilmington went to Richmond them to Staunton west of the Blue Ridge[.] we came through 4 tunels through the mountains the one through the Blue Ridge is 7/8 of a mile and it is the darkest place I ever saw[.] we set out from Staunton on last Friday for this place distance 92 miles and have a hard march making 20 miles a date[.] the road runs on the west side of the Blue Ridge[.] this is the richest portion of country that I have seen[. The yankees has been all through this section and have laid waist to many fine farms and burned much fence but there is a good deal of fence[.] they can do nothing but through down gaps where they want to pass[.] many farms are enclosed in stone walls which the yankees cannot burn[.] we will set off from here in the morning to hunt our regiment[.] it is either in Maryland or Pennsylvania[.] it will take us three of four days of march to Pennsylvania[.] it will probably be difficult to get to our Regt. as the enemy are constantly making raid between here and our troops and have captured some that were making their way to their command[.] these is stirring times over in here now[.] our forces are invading the enemy country now as well as them invade us[.] I am in a hotel here tonight and it is getting late and my candle is dim so you must excuse my hasty and badly written letter[.] think of me when I am far away and write soon for I wish to hear from you as often as I can. Truly yours. N. Deaton [P.S.] address as follows Co H[,] 26th[,] NCT, Pettegrews Brig. Heth's Division, A.P. Hills corps, Richmond, VA

Soldiers Farewell, June 23, 1863
The time is now fast coming on; When we poor soldiers must be gone; And leave our homes and native land; Now give to me your lilly hand; Farewell, farewell my dear sweet heart; The time has come we now must part; Perhaps we'll never meet again; While on this earth we do remain; My dearest dear lovely dove; You are the only one I love; It is for you I risk my life; You are my own intended wife; When I am on the Battle field; And I think of you how shall I feel; And you so many miles from me; What would I give could you I see; Though I am on the Battle field; Your love to me I yet believe; By the help of almighty hand; I will return to you again[.]

1863, June 30
J.L. Stuart (*Seven Pines near Richmond, VA*) to mother **Mary A. Harper,** stepfather **John Harper,** brother **Charles Harper,** sister **Mary A. Harper** and grandmother **Nancy Glass Nall**. General wartime correspondence with brief mentions of **W.W. Wood, John W. Maness, William Monroe, Murdock Fry, Jacob Fry, Levi Davis** and **John Teague.** [324]

Mrs Mary A Harper[.] Dear Mother[,] I seat myself to drop you a few lines to day to inform you that I have landed back safe to the company. W.W. Wood, John W. Maness, Wm. Munroe and Murdock Fry and Jacob Fry have been sent to the hospital since I left[.] I am well and hope these lines may find you all as well as when I left you[.] I got *to Petersburg at 3 oclock[.] we started march and heard my regt was at Below Richmond and night before last a Brige broke down between Petersburg and Richmond so I walked to the regt[.] I got with several more men and Boxes[.] I got my Box along[.] It cost $50 and I maid my way to Weldon 500 so I paid $50 to get to my regt[.] the boys were all very glad to See me[.] all of them had to shake hands with me[.] I do not know whether we will have a fight or not[.] we have a right smart force here[.] I am very well satisfied but I had a rather a bee at home but I will make out pretty well. It hurt my feelings to here you a crying so when I left[.] I hope shall live to see you again[.] we are where the fight was at the Seven Pines before Richmond[.] I have not been out to day[;] it has been raining so today but when it dries off I want to go and see the battle field[.] Dyrect your letters to Richmond Va[.] tell all that inquires about me where I am and where to Dyrect the letters to Richmond[.] tell all my friends to write to me for I want to hear from them and write to me soon[.] give me all the nuse[.] your affectionate son untell Death[,] J L. Stuart*

Mr John Harper[.] sir[,] I have landed back safe yesterday evening the 29th[.] there have been six of our company to the Hospital since I left[.] do the best you can all of you and do not think too much about me for I will do noble[,] but I want to be at home and be with the girls very bad but tell the girls the next time I come home[,] I shall go to see them all[.] I must close[.] do the best you can[.] we are going to get mony shortly[.] give me all the nuse[.] yours[,] John L Stuart

Charles sis and granny[,] I hated to leave you very bad but do not care too much about me[.] I got back yesterday evening[.] all was glad to see me[,] nearly as glad as any of the girls was at home to see me and all of them was shaking hands with me like they had not seen me in a month or so. The pies were spilt when I opened the box[.] Charles tell all the girls to write to me[.] tell them I wish I could have staid with them[.] Charles there was four letters for me when I got back[.] one was from Levi Davis[,] one from M.A. Nalll[,] one from you and one[.] I hardly know what to write this time[.] I have no news only you must all write to me and tell me all the friends to write to me[.] Dyrect to Richmond Va 48th regt[,] care Capt Black[,] Co.D. Charles you must tell me if you have and fly around[.] tell John Teague I havent heard from Eli since I got back. J.L. Stuart

1863, July 3
Matthew C. Yow to his wife **Nancy Catherine Albright Yow** and children, and stepmother **Elizabeth Randall Maness Yow**. General wartime correspondence with brief mentions of his grandfather **Andrew Yow** and **Henry Maness.** [325]

My Dear Wife and Little Children[,] I one time more seat my self to drop you a few lines to let you no that I am well at present truly hoping when comes to hand it may find you all well and harty. Catharine I receivd your vary welcom letter yesterday the 2 inst under date of June the 23 and you said in your letter that that you had riten 3 letters to me sinc I left you and I hav not got but 2 of them. Your 2 letter has not come to me yet and I was geting so uneasy I cold not rest. Wensday the 1 our company was sent off on picket down on Chickahomine River and I was there when I got the letter which give me great releif. But I was vary sorrow to here that your wheet was ripe and you cold not get it cut. If you cant get it saved I dont no what you will do. I am afraid you and the dear little children will suffer and I cant stand that you no. Catharine the same day that we went off on picket[,] the regiment was orderd off two. And we expect to hav a big battle here again but the Yankees wold not fight much. General Cooks brigade did not get in the skirmish. Tha had some vary heavy cannonding but not much harm don. Tha Yankees ran and we hav just got bak to camp. But tha may try us again. I cant tel. I hav not seen my 2 brothers in 3 days. I saw the regiment to day but there company was on picket. I dont no whether tha hav come yet or not. I am going to see if tha have come this eavning. I hav bin looking for a letter from father but he has had so much to do that he cold not write. I want to here how tha are geting on taking the out liers. Tel my old granfather that I hav not forgoten him yet. I want him to pray for me when it goes well with him. Our company is in vary good helth at this time. I do hop it will remain so while we are here in old Va. Catharine I am so glad that you hav got some beter. You said that had a bad risen under your arm. I no how bad that is but it will get well I hop soon. Catharine you are vary week and I dont want you to try to do so much and lay your self up. You say that you are in so much trouble and I bliev you are. I no I am my self. But I dont want you to greav so much about me. I am afraid you will injure your self. I no it is hard enough to brak our harts to be seperated like we are now. But I do hop and pray that the good Lord will spare my life and yours two[,] that we may meet again in this world. Catharine you and the children is on my mind so much that I dream of seeing you every night. I saw you all last night as plain as I ever did. when I dream so much it makes me uneasy about you and my dear little children.

Catharine I want to no if you hav had much rain. It has bin raining here for the last 2 weeks and crops looks well here. Catharine I hav nothing more to rite at present. I will close my letter by saying to you rite soon. Also dont forget to pray. I stil remain your affectionate husband until death parts us. So fairwell for this time[.] Nancy C. Yow.

A few lines to Elisabeth R. Yow[.] Dear Mother[,] I seat my self to drop you a few lines to let you no that I am well at present truly hoping when this comes to hand it may find you and family well. Betsy I will say to you that I saw your brother Henry Maness the 1 day of July. I staid with him nearly all day. He told me to rite to you and say to you that he was well now but he had bin sick. He said his family was well the last he herd from them. He said that he wold rite to you before long. He belongs to the cavalry from SC[,] 50 Halcamess legion[,] Co A. So I must close for this time. Rite soon[,] so fairwell for this time. Elisabeth R. Yow M. C. Yow

1863, July 4
J.L. Stuart (*4 miles below Richmond, VA*) to mother **Mary A. Harper**. General wartime correspondence. [326]

Mrs Mary A. Harper[.] Dear mother[,] I seat myself to write you a few lines to inform you that I am alive and well truly hoping these few lines may come safe to hand and find you all alive and well as you were when I left home. Mother I know you are worse off about seeing me than ever for it seemed like I did not talk any to you[,] but mother I hope I shall live to come home and see you all before we die I cannot express my self by writing so I will say no more on this subject the fight. Well mother I got back in time for the little fight the second of July[.] Gen Hill advanced on the enemy about twenty miles from Richmond and put out skirmishers[,] a sharp picket fight[.] General Jenkins Brigade went in and we went in on the left of his Brigade as we were going to form in line of battle[.] our Batterys opened on the yankees and they fired three times with grape shot and killed one man in the 24th and wounded one man and wound one man in the 49[,] Co C[,] but little damage done in Jenkins Brigade one man or so wounded[.] the yankees loss ten killed and eleven prisoners[.] the yankees would not stand to fight[.] they got away as soon as possible and we run them under cover of their gun boats[.] I do not know how strong the yankee force was but I know one thing[,] they could not not run over us they have not got Richmond yet[.] I expect the next fight will be at hanover Junction but it may be on the Chickahomeny where we were[.] the 2nd we have very warm weather and rain[.] plenty news is good from Vicksburg and good from Gen Lees army in Maryland and PA[.] our men are all right but the yankee people are very uneasy[.] I wish you could see some of the Richmond papers and had me to read them for you Mother[.] I think we are all right but July is the fighting season it seems but Mother you must look to God for our protection[.] some body mayst die and we do not know no who it will be[,] but mother I hope shall come through it safe[.] I hope the months of July and August will Deside[.] I want to hear from you very bad[.] I have wrote one letter to you since I came back[.] I hope will get it[.] Dyrect your letters to Richmond Va[,] 49th regt[,] NC[,] Co D[,] Ransoms Brigade[.] give me all the news and give my to all inquiring friends this morning as aweek ago I left you cry ing but do not greave about me Dear mother[.] we get plenty to eat more meat and Bread than we can eat and some sugar peas and rice[.] I wish you all well and comfort of mind and hope I will see you all again[.] fare well[,] John L. Stewart

1863, July 8
Noah Deaton (*Near Orange Court House, VA*) to **Sarah Jane McDonald**. General wartime correspondence with mentions of Battle at Gettysburg and the heavy losses sustained, company movements and skirmishes on the way back to Virginia, concerns about morale and support among the troops fading (especially in the 11th Regiment), injuries to **Daniel C. Ferguson**, **Lauchlin W. Currie**, **William J. McNeill** and deaths of **James A.N. McLeod**, **Colin B. McKinnon**, **Archibald A. Clark** and General **J.J. Pettigrew.** [327]

Miss Sarah Jane, My Dear friend, Nothing give me more pleasure out here in the army than to get a letter from a dear friend or relative[.] your kind favor of the 27th has been received and was highly cherished by me and gratifying to learn that you are were still enjoying the blessings of good health[.] my health is excelent and also the rest of the company is well with the exceptionof D.C. Ferguson has been at his sickest for a few days[.] he is able to go about sime yet and hope he will soon recover[.] my mind is so confused with the hundreds of flying rumors contradicting each other that I realy know not what to say[,] but from what I can learn I fear there is a disatisfaction brewing among the soldiers from some cause[.] there has been a meeting held in some of the regiments here and to my regrett[,] it is found that there is some who advocate the doctrine of the Raleigh

Standard[.] if it does nothing more[,] it will encourage the enemy and weaken us[.] there is 1 company in the 11th NCT who are nearly all in favour of going back in the Union[.] lest I worry you[,] I will say no more about this cowardly and submissive spirit that has found place to send of our people! What to think of submitting to Old Abe after sacrificing so many valuable lived, property and money. I say never never! better to join France or any other foreign power if it be necessary than to submit to old Abe, you cannot tell my feelings as I was on my way back to the army[.] the first I heard of the company was when I met some of the wounded who told the sad story of the Battle of Gettysburg PA[.] there has went sad news to many a person from that memorable field[.] we must all soon die and let us striuve to meet our God in peace[.] Mr. W.J. McNeill has returned to the company and several others but our company is very small yet[.] the last I heard of L.W. Currie he was at Richmond[.] he is probably at home by this time[.] J.A.N. McLeod, Wm. & John & C.B. McKinnon and A.A. Clark were killed (they were mess mates)[.] I reached my command near Hagertown, MD when Lee fell back to the south bank of the Potomac[.] our brigade was left as rear guard to cover the retreat and as we waited to give the army time to cross[.] we were overtaken and chargered on by a party of yankee cavilry which nut very few made their escape from us[.] it was in this fight that Genl. J.J. Pettigrew feel mortally wounded[.] otherwise our loss was slight in killed but the enemy reinforced heavily and attempted to surround us and did succeed in capturing 63 of our Regt.[.] The Regt had only 80 men for duty when it reached virginia's shore out of 800 that went into PA. We had been traveling all night[.] it was very rainy and dark and the worst road I ever saw[.] as we crossed the mountain we were harrassed and bushwhacked by a party of yankess[.] I must close my uninteresting and badly written letter[.] please excuse my scribling and write soon[.] address as before[.] from your admirer[.] N. Deaton

1863, July 10

Mary Patterson (*Carthage, Moore County, NC*) to stepson **Duncan A.W. Patterson**. Correspondence between stepson and stepmother with mentions of death of soldier **Samuel D. Patterson** in Staunton, VA, family members **Daniel Patterson**, **Mary Patterson**, **Barbara Patterson**, **Christian Patterson**, **Daniel Black**, **John**, **Peggy** and **Betsy**. [328]

Dear Son, I take the present opportunity to write you a few lines from which you will learn that I am in totally good health – The neighbors are well. I am sorry to have to announce to you the death of my son – Sam. D. Patterson – who was taken sick between Culpepper court house and Winchester. Va, and continued sick till the 22d of last Decr. when he died at Staunton, VA, he was taken ill on the march into Maryland – Samuel sent me a copy of a letter written by you to him while he was sick at Mount Jackson hospital VA...Your uncle Danl. Patterson died some three or four years previous to your father's death[.] your uncle Danl's family are all married except Mary, two of them are dead (viz) Barbara and Christian...Dan'l Black is dead, John is living, has a large family of daughters[.] his two sons are dead. Peggy and Betsy are living, and single yet....My house was burned this winter two years ago. I lost all that was in the house. I am not able to make my living by labor, being too feeble, there is not enough cleared land to enable me to rent the land, and live on the rest. I shall therefore be driven to the necessity of quiting housekeeping, and I wish to give permission to sell the land, I would rather if it is so that you can that you would come and see to it yourself. I wish you to write to me as soon as this comes to hand and let me know what I had better do[.] affectionately[,] Mary Patterson P.S. Your stepmother earnestly wishes you to come and see her. write to me at Carthage, NC[.]

1863, July 11

Joseph C. Fry (*Winchester, VA*) to parents **Absalom** and **Chery Fry** (*Caledonia, NC*). Wartime correspondence between son and parents with mentions of marches through MD and PA, Hanover Junction, PA and the battle of Gettysburg, PA and soldiers **Auley McAuley**, **Samuel Jackson McIntosh**, **Thomas Johnson**, **Samuel Short**, **Ashley Muse**, **Dumas Brewer**, **Daniel Malone**, **James McLeod**, **Colin McKinnon**, **John McKinnon**, **Neill A. Currie**, **Archibald Clark**, **Harmon Wilcox**, Lieut. **Murdoch McLeod**, Lieut. **George Wilcox**, Lieut. **John McGilvary**, **Absalom Fry**, **Thomas Fry**, **Nelson Hunsucker**, **Neill Caddell** and death of **Marshall Brown**. [329]

Dear Parents: Impressed with a great sense of the deep gratitude I owe you, for the unspeakable favors I have received, I cannot express it in a more suitable way than in writing you a few lines. We are such a great distance from each other that it is the only way we can communicate our thoughts and be informed of each others welfare, which cannot fail to give us great satisfaction since we are in a world abounding with disappointments, troubles and afflictions, which it becomes us to bear and submit unto with a humble resignation, as we know not but they be for our own good and will finally tend to our high advantage; both in this life and that which is to come. Numberless temptations, also, are presenting themselves to our minds, and renders it necessary for us to seriously reflect in order to determine what is to us of the most importance, and after this is attained[,] it requires our greatest exertions to resist those things that are most pleasing but which leads to destruction. Our short and uncertain stay in this life ought to fill every mind with the most serious considerations, who we are, whence we came, and whither we are going. But in a state of health and happiness, how little do these important thoughts dwell in our minds. And how many do we see pursuing pleasure and seem to think they have found it to perfection. I believe that all my past troubles have been for my good, though, leaving home at so early an age may have caused you some uneasiness, fearing that I should fall into some evil or meet with misfortunes in a strange land; yet I believe that it was ordered for the best. I am persuaded that if I had continued to live in the land of my nativity I should never have been as I am now. I am thankful for all that has passed. Dear Parents, you may think the time long since I wrote you before, but do not conclude from my delay in writing that I have forgotten you or that my affection is less for you. The delay was occasioned by a long march over Maryland and Pennsylvania. We left Hanover Junction on the 7th of June and marched to Gettysburg, Pa. There we were met by the enemy in full force. We suffered greatly; I have not time to write all. I will only say what I can to make known to you the situation in our own company. We went into the charge with about ninety men and came out with only eight on the first day. The second day two or three more of the company were killed and wounded. I will tell you as near as I can who were killed and wounded. Sergt. A. McAuley, Jack McIntosh, Thomas Johnson, Samuel Short, Ashley Muse, Dumas Brewer, Daniel Malone, James McLeod, Colin McInen were killed on the first day. On the second day John McInen, Neill A. Currie, Arch Clark, Harmon Wilcox were killed and some others either killed or taken prisoners. Lieut. McLeod was shot in the side, Lieut. Wilcox in the foot, Lieut. McGilvary in both legs. Ab Fry was shot through the left breast, he is yet alive I believe. Thomas Fry was shot in the belly, he is yet alive. Several were shot through the thighs and legs, some in the head. N. Hunsucker was shot through the seat. I was wounded by a gun bursting in my hand. I gave them forty rounds and shot the stock off my gun so that I had to throw it down and I took up a rifle lying by a dead Yankee and when it fired[,] the barrel flew upwards and the stock struck me on the arm, tore my fingers some and dislocated my shoulder. I am thankful that it is no worse. We are now back in Winchester, Va., that is, all who could get here. I have not seen half of them since we left Pennsylvania. I met Neill Caddell at the Potomac River and he gave me a letter from you which I was glad to get. You sent your respects to Marshall Brown but he could not hear it for he was killed and left far from this place. I must close, may this soon find you all well. I remain as ever Yours. J. C. Fry

1863, July 11
Mastin C. Phillips *(Winder Hospital, Richmond, VA)* to sister **Emeline Phillips.** General wartime correspondence with brief mentions of **Baxter C. Phillips** and **Malphus Phillips.** [330]

My Dear Sister, I write to let you know that yours of the 28th of June has reached me. It went to the Regiment and then Baxter sent it to me. I was glad to hear from home once more. I do not want any of you to give yourselves any uneasiness about me. It is true that I am unfit for active duty in the field, but I am not confined to my bed and hope I shall not be. I think now that the danger of fevor has passed for the present and I am gaining in flesh and strength slowly. I am diseased, perhaps incurable, but if I take good care of myself, I think I would be some account yet. But what my condition will be when I am liberated from this war, the future alone can determine. The disease in my breast is pronounced by the surgeons here to be Bronchitis. They may be correct. I only know that they are able to do very little to relieve me. If I get no worse I shall leave for the Regiment in a few days. I don't think I shall hold out long at a time when the weather is so warm but all are needed in the field at this time, and I am not satisfied to be here when our all is at stake. The fighting in Pennsylvania and Maryland has been most obstinate and [?]; the truth is we have not had our usual success. We have not been whipped, but our proceedings have been checked for the present. Our loss is very great in killed and wounded, but as yet no lists of casualties have come to hand. Vicksburg has certainly fallen, but we have been expecting this for a long time. Consequently it's fall has affected matters but little. But these things have encouraged the enemy and he is putting forth every means in his power to crush us. But he will fail. We have only to stand firm, meet and repel his last and most desperate effort and the end will follow. Think not that this is an idle whim of a diseased mind. I have watched the progress of events with intense interest and I have good reason for this conclusion. I know that to secure this and that it may be decisive, satisfactory and glorious, all praying people, yes the whole nation, must humble itself before God, which it never yet has done. This I am persuaded must be done. The fathers, mothers, sisters and wives who have sons, husbands and brothers in the army can't help it. They have nothing else left them and I think the soldiers in the field will see the necessity of this and act accordingly. I believe God intends to make an independent nation of us, but we must first repent of our national sins, and the sooner this is done, the sooner will the end come. Believe me, the continuation of this war is caused by our own sins. When God sees that the great heart of the nation is right before him, He will stay the hand of the destroyer and give us peace. I could write a week about this matter, but I will stop for the present. You speak in such terms with regard to the conduct of Baxter and myself. Would that I was a worthy recipient of such expression. You need not be uneasy that I will desert. I may be stricken down by disease. I may be taken and executed by the enemy, or I may fall on the field of carnage and war, but Desert, never, never. I still hope to see you all again. True the future looks dark and ominous, the shock of battle is again heard in the distance, thousands are wending their way to the scene of the conflict. I shall soon be among them. I may be swept away. I beg you all (if this shall be so) to pray that I may find rest and happiness on the peaceful shore of the Heavenly Command where war will be no more. I was happy to learn that Malphus had reached home. I wish he could stay all the time. You need not to look for Baxter and myself without we outlive the war, and this I hope we will do. Baxter was well day before yesterday. I will write again soon. I will try to be a good boy. I know that none but God can bring me safely out of these troubles. I will try to trust Him. Pray for me. My love to you all. Mastin

1863, July 18
Matthew C. Yow to his wife **Nancy Catherine Albright Yow** and children. General wartime correspondence with brief mentions of **Hiram Williamson**, **David Williamson** and **Lewis Grant Maness.** [331]

My Dear Wife and Little Children[,] Through the kind merces of our heavenly Father[,] I hav bin one time more permited to drop you a few lines to inform you that I am well at present and I do hop and pray when this comes to hand it may find you and the dear little children all well and harty. Catharine I receivd your vary welcom letter the 16 that you wrote the 7. I was so glad to here that you was well and harty one more time. I am some beter satisfied now than I hav bin. When I can here that you are all well it chers me up. I do hop you will be well now and can attend to your things. Catharine I was writing to my dear old father when I got your letter and I did not write to you that day. I am looking for a letter from father now. I hav not had but one from him sinc I left. He said in that letter that he had rote one to me before that and I never got it. I hav got all of your letters I think. Catharine you said that you expected that old Hy had kild my boar. I do hate to here that but I no he is mean enough to do any thing. I do hop and pray to the good Lord that I may be spard to get home again. Any man that will do that may will do any thing. I think tha will steal as tha hav done. And there is big Dav. That great lawyer is going to law me as long as I liv. If he had wanted to law me so bad he ought come to see me when I was at home and I wold giv him something to law for. But I will stop this for such a tory as Dav Williamson is not worth talking about. Catharine I am vary glad that you hav got some corn plowd at last. I am afraid it was hurt but it has raind so much that you cold not work. You say you hav got your potatos all planted. I was glad to here that. Catharine do the best you can and dont work two hard for I no you are not able to work much. You said that you had drawd 24 dollars sinc I left. I no Lewis Maness will attend to you right. I believ he is a friend to me and he is to you. I will say to you that I hav drawd 25 dollars sinc I came back. Catharine I want you to rite to me how all your things is geting on. I hav vary uneasy about your wheet. It raind so much and I was afraid it was not hauld in when the weet got in. M.C. Yow

1863, July 22
J.L. Stuart (*Petersburg, VA*) to mother **Mary A. Harper,** stepfather **John Harper,** brother **Charles Harper** and sister **Mary A. Harper**. General wartime correspondence. [332]

Mrs Mary A. Harper[.] Dear mother[,] I seat myself to drop you a line this evening to inform you that I am well and very hearty truly hoping these lines may come to hand in due time and find you all doing well[.] I received your letter of the 17th yesterday 21st[.] I was very glad to hear from you all am hope your health will get better soon[.] I was sorry to hear granny was unwell[.] I have nothing of much importance to write at this time[.] we are in camp 2 miles from Petersburg Va[.] our co came in Monday night from Piquet[.] the negro Woman Keeps bringing in this greens and all sorts of stuff but I do not buy very much[.] I started a letter yesterday morning to Charles[.] I was sick four or five dayes and takend some medicine but I have got well and very hearty yours[.] Jno L Stuart

Mr John Harper[.] Dear stepfather[,] I hope these lines will find you well and getting a long well at present and we get plenty to eat &c we have got to drilling again[.] I do not know how long we will stay here[.] it may be that we will go to North Carolina soon[.] two regt of our Brigade are gone to NC[,] the 24 & 25 regiments[.] I have no war news to write for I hardly know what to think of the war at this time will soon end for I think from what I learn the North had got the head fever on them about now[.] I must close[.] write to me and let me know how you get along & Dyrect your letters to Petersburg Va[,] 49th regt[,] Co D[,] Ransoms Brig[,] NCT[.] yours Truly[,] J.L. Stuart

Dear Brother Charles[,] I hope you are well and getting along well[.] I have no news of Interest to write this time[.] Charles yesterday some Negros Broughtin some fresh meat stew[.] Pig meat they calld it and it was condemned to be Day so two of them Woman was taken up and flogged with a leather strap about 39 lashes each[.] I don't think they will bring any more Dog stew to the 49th soon again[.] Charles I started a small song book to you yesterday in a letter Dixie land songster a sorry book but I give 50 cents for it[.] give my respects to all my friends and to all the girls[,] but I will not say anything about the girls for I have not heard from any of them since I was at home[.] write to me and let me know how you are getting along[.] your[,] John

Dear sister[,] I will write a few lines to you[.] I want to see you all very bad[.] it seemes like along time since I was at home but I hope I will live to see you all again[.] sis you must be smart you and Charles and mind what Mother tell you[.] sis I will send you a fifty cent shinplaster for a little present[.] I started Charles a little book and you the money[.] it is a little present but you can keep it ti remember me[.] tell all the girls howdy for me[.] sis you must write soon[.] tell granny I want to see her very bad[.] I hope she will get better and get well & we have got a preacher in our regiment[.] he preaches ever night[.] I must close[.] I received all three letters from home[.] fare well to you all[,] J.L. Stuart

1863, July 25
William Henry Patterson (*Hospital, Lynchburg, VA*) to sister **Frances Anna V. Patterson**. General wartime correspondence between siblings with brief mentions of **Iver D. Patterson, William P. Blue** and **Daniel McCaskill.** [333]

Dear Sister[,] I seat myself to inform you that Pa has arrived at this place[.] he got here this morning . I was very glad to see him for I have had a very lonesome time here in the Hospital. Pa intends to go to Richmond and try to get me discharged. A good many men are getting furloughs to go home. The board met yesterday. I did not go before it – The Dr. that attendes to this ward did not recomend me. I am in great hopes that I will get a discharge and be permitted to go home a while to recover my health. William P. Blue was slightly wounded in the great battle in Pensylvania. He was left at Winchester, Va. all of those that were wounded very slightly were stopped at Winchester. Ann I cannot tell you when Pa will get home[.] he may possibly reach home by the last of the week but – if he does not you need not be uneasy; when he gets home I am in hopes that I will be with him. Daniel McCaskill has died of his wound. I have no more news to write you so I will close. Your Affectionate Bro. William H. Patterson, 6# Ward[,] 2nd Division[,] Genl. Hospital No 2, Lynchburg, Va.

1863, July 30
Matthew C. Yow to wife **Nancy Catherine Albright Yow** and children. General wartime correspondence. [334]

Mrs Nancy C. Yow[.] My Dear Wife[,] I am one more time permited to drop you a few lines informing you that I am not well but I feel some better than I did when I wrote last. I hav not bin well for several days and I hav fel at away tel I am as pore as you was when I was at home. I do hop when this comes to hand it may find you and the dear children well and harty. I was so glad to here that you had got wel and harty again. I do hop you will be well now. Catharine I wil say to you that I did not get no letter to day. I got one last Sunday but I answerd it and I thought I wold write to day. I am afraid I dont get all your letters. Catharine I haint much to write to you now. we are stil at the same camp yet and all is quiet now but I cant tel what a day may bring forth. I hav herd that tha are fiting in NC about Weldon. We may hav to go their yet. Catharine I am here not wel and you may no that I am not satisfied here in this troublesom place. when I study so much about you and our dear little children it seems like I cant sta here much longer. You may be sure that I dont see any satisfaction here. The men is all out of hart and tha are runing away in a huree now and I dont care if tha all go and that wold brak this unholy war.

Catharine I am afraid that it is going to be sickly here. It rains so much. It rains here every day. I cant rite much at this time. I am looking for a letter now. I think I will get one soon. Catharine my dear wife do the best you can for your self and our dear little ones. Catharine dont forget to pray. May the good Lord bles and save us all forever. I stil remain your affectionate husband untel death. Mrs Nancy C. Yow fairwell. Rite soon and fail not.

1863, July 30
Jacob Gaster (*Rollins Store, NC*) to Surgeon in Charge, Chimborazo Hospital. General wartime correspondence requesting information on his son **John C. Gaster**. [335]

Dear Sir, I want some information about my son John C. Gastor of Company H[,] 30th Regt.[,] NCT who left his company about the last of March 1863 and I understood he went to some hospital in Richmond. His Captain says he is in the Chimborazo Hospital. I wish to know whether he is in that hospital or not. Pleas right to me whether he is or not and how to direct letters to him. Address me at Rollins Store, Moore Co. NC. Yours very respectfully, Jacob Gastor. Note on the back states that he was admitted April 1, 1863 and died May 9, 1863 of Typhoid fever and left no effects.

1863, August
Matthew C. Yow to his wife **Nancy Catherine Albright Yow** and children. General wartime correspondence with brief mentions of brothers-in-law **John E. Albright** and **Henry A. Albright,** his brothers **Simeon Jones Yow, Isaac Yow, Cornelius Alexander Stutts** and children **William Henry Yow, Nancy Elizabeth Yow, Mary Jane Yow, Joseph Gibbs Yow** and **John Matthew Yow**. [336]

Catharine, I cant here nothing from your brothers sinc that great battle in Penn. I am afraid tha are kild or wounded. My 2 brothers is both well but tha are not satisfied. Tha are so tiard of the war. The soldiers is all tiard of it. Tha are running away from here. Like any thing the pore soldiers is out of hart the worst now that I hav out of hart now that I ever saw them. Yet tha all think we will have to giv it up and I think so myself. It looks so at any rate. I am out of hart myself at this time. Catharine I had 2 little rings made and I put them in a letter to Nancy Elisabeth and Mary Jane. I do hop tha will get them. C. A. Stutts made them. Tha will pleas the dear little children. I also sent you 2 sheets of good paper in an envelop this week. I hop you will get it. It is good paper. I sent William Henry a peac of poetary in a letter this week. I want him to read that and be a good boy. I wish I cold send little Joseph Gibs and little John Matthew some thing but I haint nothing to send to them now. Lord sav my dear little children I pray. M. C. Yow

William Henry Yow[.] My Dear Little Son[,] I drop you a few lines in answer to your letter. Henry you said that you eat a heep of peaches. I expect you do and I do want to be their to eat peaches with you. You said that Bet and Walker had mended sinc you got them in the pasture. I am glad to here that tha hav mended. Do the best you can with your colt and you will hav to sel him this fall and I want you to get all you can for him. You must get your granpapy to help you sel him. He will do all he can for you. Henry you must be a good boy and be good to your mother and little brothers and sisters. May the good Lord bles and save you forever William Henry Yow. Matthew C. Yow Catharine, Isaac and Jones is both well. Tha are on picket now. Tha will stay tel Saturday morning. I hop tha will hav good luck.

Nancy Elisabeth Yow and Mary Jane Yow My Dear Little Daughters[,] I must drop you a few words in answer to your kind little letter. Nancy you said you was sick with the tooth ach. Pore little girl I am so sorrow for you. I hop you wil soon get wel and be harty. Nancy you must be a good girl and mind your mother. Mary Jane you said that you was rocking little Johny. That is rite Jane you must be a smart girl and mind your mother and be good to your little brothers. May the good Lord bles and sav my dear little children forever I pray. Matthew C. Yow to Nancy E. Yow and Mary J. Yow and Joseph G. Yow and John M. Yow my dear little sons and daughters. So fair well for this time[.] M.C. Yow to Nancy E. Yow.

1863, August 3
Baxter C. Phillips to sister **Emeline Phillips.** General wartime correspondence with brief mentions of General **Lee** and **Malphus Phillips**. [337]

Dear Sister, Yours has just been received and I will answer it immediately. It found me close to the old battlefield at this place. We came her on Friday night and we are here for the purpose of guarding this point for the present. I think though, in a short time, that we will go back to Richmond as we are the nearest troop to that point at this time. I can see no signs of fighting here for there is no enemy in thirty miles, that we know of, yet they can soon come. I don't think that we will join General Lee's Army soon, if ever, as we are designed for defense of Richmond. There is no news stirring here. I spent the day yesterday in Fredericksburg. It is the worst torn up place that I ever saw. Nearly every house in it has from one to twenty bombs shot into it. Things look badly. The weather is very warm. We are in camp near our old camp. If we move soon to Lee's Army I will write you. I want you to be of good cheer and always pray for me. I think all will be well. I can't write you much this time. Mastin is improving. He will join us soon, I trust, as there is no chance for him to get home. Tell Malphus I congratulate him on his success. I am in his stead. I do not repent it. Tell him to do all he can at home. My love to all. I ask the special prayer of all, and give you mine. May God bless you. Direct as before. This leaves me well. Baxter Clegg Phillips

1863, August 9
J.L. Stuart (*Garysburg, NC*) to mother **Mary A. Harper**. General wartime correspondence. [338]

Mrs Mary A.Harper[.] Dear mother[,] I seat myself to day to write you a few lines to inform you that I am well truly hoping these lines may find you all well as usual[.] I have now news of importance to write to you at this time[.] we are at Garys burg NC[.] I do not think that we will [be] here long[.] I think we will either go to Charleston NC or to Gen Lees army in Virginia[.] I received a letter from you the 7th dated the 3[.] you said that you has some very nice Cabbage & Potatoes[.] I wish I was at home to eat some of them but I cannot be there[.] you must all get along the best you can for it is hard case these times[.] make the best of it[.] I have no idea when this war will stop but the darkest time is Just before day[.] the people are getting very tired of the war but that does not stop[.] it you said that you was very poorly[.] I hope that you will mend this fall so that you can get about[.] we have some very warm weather[.] we drill 3 hours aday and then play the remainder of the day[.] I do not suppose we will stay there long[.] I heard the yankees were coming in about Tarboro[,] the 35th regt ment to Rocky mount yesterday morning[.] that is between Weldon and Goldsboro[.] write ever chance[.] Dyrect your letters to Weldon NC[,] Co D[,] 49th regt[,] NCT[,] Ransoms Brigade[.] give my respects to all inquiring friends and relations[.] tell them to write to me[.] I wish I was at home with you all but I cannot be there[.] you need not be uneasy about me[.] if any thing gets the mater I will let you know it[.] tell sis I want to see her mity bad[.] tell her to be as smart girl and maybe if I will live to see her again[.] excuse bad writing[.] I must close[.] farewell. J.L. Stuart

1863, August 11
Baxter C. Phillips *(Hamilton Crossing, Fredericksburg, VA)* to parents Rev. **Lewis Phillips Jr.** and **Nancy Phillips.** General wartime correspondence with brief mentions of **Mastin Phillips, Malphus Phillips, Emeline Phillips, Elmira Phillips** and **Reuben Maness.** [339]

My Dear Parents, I feel a disposition this morning to converse with you. The Regiment is out and I am somewhat lonely. I will attempt to interest you for a while. It has been near twelve months since I parted with you at home. In this time I have gone through many dangers. My sufferings never came to you, for I knew it would make you too anxious for me. Consequently, I kept it secret. But now I am happy to tell you my health is good as in former days, for which I feel very thankful. Since I left you, I have been nearly to the extremes of the Confederacy. I have seen the mountains high and the valley low with their variety of productions. I have traveled the rough pikes of the Blue Ridge barefoot (as good as so) and I have lain the swamps of South Carolina sick. Sometimes I would nearly despair, but then I would remember your lessons to me and I would take courage and try it again. But I must tell you something about the country in which I have lived for the past year. Virginia has a name for high lands and good water, and the land though high is well adapted to meadows. It is superior to any that ever I saw for wheat, oats, clover and all such grains. It has naturally a beauty that I never saw in any section before. When I first crossed the ridge, I and Mastin were together and just took our own time for it. We had the chance of looking at it well. Yet, it don't possess half its former beauty for the demon of war has been there and when it visits, beauty must vanish. Everything delightful, everything lovely and prosperous leaves and desolation takes its place. Society is thrown into a state of anarchy and misery. Sin and trouble take the day. Yet notwithstanding all this, the country around the Blue Ridge has some chasm, in peace it must be delightful. We pass through Virginia and enter North Carolina. This bears no semblance to Virginia's high and fertile lands, but it more productive in regard to corn than any land I have ever seen. I mean the lower section of the state. Now the North Carolina bottoms, it will do for rice where it is not too wet, and cotton also, but North Carolina will heat it for corn. I have seen a good deal of this Confederacy and find that no place has more charm for me than old Moore County, though not so [?] as the Virginia and Southern farms. Yet there is something else [?] brings the balance even with them. And quietness, society I think is better at home than anywhere else that I have been because it is more on equality and the standard there is just as high as here. There is more wealth in Virginia and South Carolina and consequently more aristocracy which is a fatal thing to society because none are good enough for such themselves. They measure themselves by themselves showing that they are not wise. But I must make some exceptions to that for I have seen the young lady of eighteen give her Sunday meeting snack to battle worn soldiers. I have met with some who would give me the last morsel they had, but these are like angel's visits, they don't come often. So I conclude that home has more charm than any other place for me. I reckon you want to know my feeling in regard to the condition of affairs militarily. I feel just the same as I did before I left home. You know I told you I had well considered the thing and then I was prepared for anything that might come. I am so yet. I know that sometimes things change, but this is only for a season. I continuously believe that if our course is right, we will prevail though God may hid his face for a season. But when he sees that we trust him as we ought, then He comes when our enemies don't expect Him and crowns us with what we are striving for. This may be our condition at this time. But if we are in the wrong, God will not help us, for He cannot sin and that would be sin. Though He may intend bringing us to our senses by this now and make both sections render homage to him and give victory to neither. Man does not know God's purpose anytime. He may have made the North and South scourge for each other yet let us humble ourselves that He may be entreated for us and turn from the fierceness of His wrath. Let us remember that we must expect chastisements and not despond when we are undergoing them. God intends them all for our good. God has not given us up yet for there is now more religion shown in camp than I have ever seen before. I have seen soldiers get religion here, which is evidence taken that our God has not left for if He had He would not hear our prayers. And, I think there is more humility at present than heretofore among our rulers. Let us all humble ourselves and God will hear and deliver for He has promised it. We have meetings in our company twice a week held by Reuben Maness which are well attended by all or mostly so. I saw in the Raleigh Standard, the proceedings of Moore County meetings which I endorse some of and yet, at the same time, it is giving aid and comfort to the enemy and prolonging this war. I do wish men at home would take care how they act. All that has gone to the Yankees, and now they are looking for commissioners at Washington to see under what terms North Carolina can go back into the Union. Papa, please have nothing to do with such meetings. I don't think you will for every one of these meetings, there adds just that much more suffering to us. And, I know you don't delight in my suffering. And then, it will cause more desertions from the army and when they get home they tell their own tale of fire and plunder, and these men are the cause. We men are cursed more here by the soldiers than some of these men are, not all of course. I wish I could forget some of the names connected with it, but cannot. Some of the rest will inform the enemy just as soon as an opportunity affords them a chance. There is hatred gathering in the bosoms of the soldiers which will finally break on the heads of three classes. And that is the skulker, the deserter and the speculator. Whether victorious or vanquished, it will come. If victorious, they will be cursed for not going, and if vanquished, they will allege that they are the cause. I don't want men who have lain at home taking the very life of our country, by speculating to dictate the terms of peace for me. They are the worst curse in our country. They have done more harm to soldiers than any other set of men and will join the enemy the quickest. That is hard, but it is the truth and they can't deny it. But I exonorate my father from all these things. You have a common sense view of the subject and consequently you are on safe ground. Just stand where you are and you will be safe. Let victory or defeat come, they can't change you with anything but what is honorable. But my paper gives out and I must close. We are yet at Fredericksburg, but it is said that we will go back to Petersburg as we don't belong to Lee's army but to [?] army. I heard from Mastin two or three days since. He was improving. The weather is very warm here, as hot as ever I felt in my life. Give my respects to all who may inquire after me. It seems that nearly all the people have forgotten me since I left. None write to me save you and Mother, Malphus, Emeline and sometimes Elmira. Tell them I am well whether they inquire or not. They don't know what comfort a word from them would give me. Tell them I hope to arouse them from their slumber with a "How do you do" some day and find them, if lost. They seem lost to me. My love to all. Pray for me, dear parents, that all will be well with us. May God take care of you. Love, Baxter

1863, August 12
Noah Deaton (*CO. H. 26th N.C.T., near Orange Court House, VA*) to unidentified sister. General wartime

correspondence with brief mentions of cousin **Margaret McDonald** and her mother's [**Flora Deaton**] poor health and brief reports from the 26th Regiment of the battle of Gettysburg, PA and station at Orange Courthouse, VA with brief mentions of generals **George G. Meade** and **Robert E. Lee**. Includes a note to **Martha Moore** regarding **B.B. Moore**, **Anderson Moore** and **W.C. Moore** [340]

Dear Sister, I feel thankful that by the providence of our maker[.] I am blessed with another opportunity to drop you a few imperfect lines in answer to your kind favor of the 1st Inst[.] I was much gratified to hear that you were all well for had a day or two before Recd a letter from cousin Margarett McDonald stating that mothers health was not good that her back was hurting her very much and your letter afforded me much relief[.] this leaves me in excellent health and I trust it will find you and she enjoying your usual good health[.] I am sorry to hear that the sore throat still prevails in that section[.] I have nothing very important to write at present – as to all of our boys that unfortunately fell into the hands of the enemy during the magnificent campaign into PA[,] we have heard nothing from them yet and may not for some time yet[.] It is with sorrow that I meditate uppon this sad fortune of our brave boys on this field of Gettysburg PA[,] the 26 N.C.T. Regt both for its bravery and the losses has scarcely a parallel in history[.] the army appears to be quite at present[.] A.P. Hill Corps is bivovaced near Orange C.H. VA[.] there has just been clothing issued to the troops here and as far as I know every man has as much as he needs for the present[.] it has been the opinion heretofore that another great battle was iminent in this region but it seemes at present that Meade (the yankee commander) has ceased following Lee and it may be some time before anything important occurs[.] I have heard nothing from our wounded that has been scattered about in the difrent hospitals for some time[.] The weather has been very hot for some time but fortunately we have not had much marching to do in some 3 or 4 weeks[.] there has been a great deal of rain here but since I returned[,] not more than 2 or 3 fair days at a time since the first July and generally rain every evening. I will stop for the present[.] the mail will not go out untill morning and if anything new occurs I will write it[.] Your brother truly untill Death[.] N Deaton [P.S.] I enclose in this letter a piece from the Fayetteville Observer complimenting the 26 N.C.T. as you know I was not with the Regt at the time of the battle but from what I have seen and heard of the Regt since[,] I know it suffered the losses reported and therefore know that the highest compliments is due to it[.] I want you to take care of this piece and let all see it that wants to[.]

To Martha Moore: I have heard nothing more from B.B. Moore[.] I have seen Anderson Moore two or three weeks ago[.] W.C. Moore has returned to camp from the hospital[.] they are both well[.] truly yours, N Deaton

1863, August 15

Matthew C. Yow to his wife **Nancy Catherine Albright Yow** and children. General wartime correspondence with brief mentions of **Wyatt Williamson**, brothers-in-law **John E. Albright** and **Henry A. Albright,** his brothers **Simeon Jones Yow, Isaac Yow,** father **Henry C. Yow,** grandfather **Andrew Yow** and son **William Henry Yow**. [341]

Mrs Nancy C. Yow[.] my Dear Wife[,] It with plesure that I seat myself to drop you a few lines to let you no that I am wel at present truly hoping when this comes to hand it may find you and the dear children well and in beter hart than I am at this time. Catharine I receivd your welcom letter the 14 that you wrote the 8. I am glad to here that you are as wel as what you are. Pore little Nancy I am so sorrow for her. It seems like she has a hard time. I hop she wil soon get beter. Catharine you said that you was scard to liv by your self now. If you can get any body to liv with you that will do you any good I hav no objection. But I do hop that no one will pester you. You said that some one brok open Mr Wiat Williamson house. It seems like tha wont let him alone. He ought to kil some of them. I dont no what will become of our contry. The people has got to be so mean. It is the same way here. Some of them dont ceare what tha do. Their is two much meanness going on that we cant do any good. Thire is traitors every where and we shal be subjugated in spite of all we can do. I hav giv it up for lost. Sometimes I hav a great mind to come home for I no that it will be no credit to me to sta here and get kild and then be subgated by the Yankee rouges. I will say to you that I am out of hart. I wrote a letter to your father and I told him what I thought about this war and I dont think I am mistaken and I think that he will agree with me now. Our soldiers is all out of hart and there is a big battle depending some where about here. The Yankees is on one side of the river and we on the other. Tha come in sight some times and look over on our side. Tha kild one of our men the other day. Catharine I was glad to here that your brothers was aliv and well. I was afraid tha was kild in that dredful battle. My 2 brothers is both well. Tha got a letter from father yesterday. I cant tel what is the matter that I cant get no letter from father. I hav wrote several letters to him and no answer from him. I cant help but think that he has rote to me and I hav not got them. Catharine you said that Henry was at his granpapies a helping them thrash wheet. Pore little Henry I am glad that he can do something to help. I hop you can get your wheet cut now. I want to tel me in your next letter how much old wheet you hav got yet. I do hop you wil hav plenty yet a while. Catharine tel my old granfather that I hav not forgoten him yet and I want to see him vary bad now but I cant tel when I shal see him again. I do hop it wont be long. I do hop and pray that my life will be spard so that I can return home you that is so near and dear to me. O that I cold see you all again and stay with you. Catharine Read the 3 chapter of Isaiah and it will tel you about [illegible] Spirts. Also Read the 11 chapter of Daniel and see if it dont suit these times of trouble. Catharine I want you to do the best you can and you had beter sel your colt this fal if you can get the worth of him. He ought to bring you one hundred dollars. Father said that had bin offerd one hundred dollars for his colt and I no you ought to get that for your colt. Get all you can for him and I want to no what you are going to do with your cow if you hav turned her dry. Yet if tha dont be no acorns to make the hogs fat you had beter make beef of that cow for I no you will need her for you and the children for you cant fatten hogs with corn I no. Write soon and fail not and giv me the nuse. So I must close by saying I stil remain your affectionate husband tel death. So fairwell[.] Nancy C. Yow.

1863, August 16
J.L. Stuart (*Rocky Mount, NC*) to stepfather **John Harper,** sister **Mary A. Harper,** brother **Charles Harper, mother Mary A. Harper and** grandmother **Nancy Glass Nall**. General wartime correspondence with brief mention of **Nicholas Nall**. [342]

Dear step Father[,] I seat myself to write you a few lines to inform you that I am well truly hoping these lines may reach and find you all well as usual. I have no news of Interest to write[.] we left Tarboro yesterday about 12 oclock and we marched about 15 miles and this morning we came two miles to Rocky Mount[,] a station on the railroad Between Weldon and Goldsboro[.] I do not know how long we will stay here but not long[.] I do not suppose Tarboro is the greatest place we have been at yet I should like if we could go back there and stay if necessary[.] Tarboro is the county seat of Edgecombe County on the Tar River[.] it is one of the greatest corn country I have ever seen anywhere in NCarolina and people were all very liberal to the soldiers[.] the yankees done a great deal of damage through this part of the country[.] at Tarboro they burnt several shops and depot and a gun boat that was on hand there[,] but if we had a been here they would have found a warm time of it before they had went through with there Roberry[.] I want to see you all very bad and hope I shall live to get home and see you all again[.] I hope the war will soon come to a close so we all can go home in peace[.] write to me ever chance you get and let me know how you are all getting along[.] I received letter from you yesterday morning dated the 9th[.] I was very sorry to hear about your corn being eat by them cows[.] of some Deserter turned them in they had better be here helping to keep the yankees Back[.] fare well[,] J.L. Stuart

Dear Mother[,] I want to see you very bad[.] I am sorry that you keep so bad off[.] I hope you will get better before long[.] I have nothing of interest to write to you at this time[.] we are at Rocky mount[.] we left Tarboro yesterday[.] it was the greatest place we have been at yet[.] I received your letter yesterday dated the 9th[.] I was very glad to hear from you[.] write every chance[.] Dyrect your letters to Rocky Mount NC[.] give my respect to all inquiring friends and tell them to write to me[.] excuse my short letter this time[.] I started a letter to you a few days ago[.] I hope I shall live to see you all again but I cannot tell when it will be[.] I must close[.] farewell. J.L. Stuart

Dear Brother Charles[,] I was sorry to hear that you are so bad off with boils[.] I hope they will get better soon[.] I am well and hearty[.] I hope I shall see you before long[.] give my respect to all Inquiring friends[.] tell uncle Nicks folks to write to me[.] I must close[.] write to me soon[.] your Brother[,] John

Dear sis and granny[,] I want to see you very bad[.] do the best you can[.] I hope I shall live to get home and see you all again[.] you must all do the best you can. John L. Stuart. When this you see[,] remember me[.] tell all my friends to write[.] farewell[,] J.L. Stuart

1863, August 21
Matthew C. Yow to his wife **Nancy Catherine Albright Yow** and children. General wartime correspondence with brief mentions of **Reuben Maness**. [343]

Catharine[,] I will say to you that this day the 21 day of August was set apart for humiliation and prare. We did not hav any duty to do at all. We read our Bibles and praid to the good Lord to help us in our troubles and bring peac on our distracted contry. O that the good Lord wold bring peac on our land and contry that we may return home to those that we love so well. Mr Reubin Manes comes to our company and sings and prays with us. Reubin is just the same man yet our company thinks a heep of him. I do wish that he belong to our company for we hav no meeting at all[,] only when he comes. He comes twice a week and prays with us. O, that the good Lord will here and answer our prares. We believ that you are all praying for us pore soldiers here in the army. I think this is a time that all ought to pray. But I fear that it is not don. O lord bles and sav us all I Pray. M.C. Yow

1863, August 23
Matthew C. Yow to wife **Nancy Catherine Albright Yow** and children. General wartime correspondence. [344]
Catharine[,] I wil tel you how tha do here. Friday the 21 was set apart for fasting and prare by Jef Davis and we had no duty to do that day and this the Sabbath[,] the Lords day[.] we hav to be rubing our guns and go out on inspection. That shoes to whos day tha respect the Lords day or Jef Davises day. I am afraid that it will be a bad chanc with some of our head men in time to come. I do wish tha wold try to do beter and I think we wold hav beter times than we do. M. C. Yow to Nancy C. Yow

1863, August 24
Matthew C. Yow to his wife **Nancy Catherine Albright Yow** and children. General wartime correspondence with brief mention of his father **Henry C. Yow.** [345]

Catharine[,] I will to you again that I cant get no letters from my father. The last letter I got from him was dated July the 12 and non sinc. Your letters comes and I cant tel why his dont come. I do want to here from him and his family so bad. May the good bles and sav you all forever I pray. Nancy C. Yow

1863, August 29
J.L. Stuart to mother **Mary A. Harper**. General wartime correspondence. [346]

Mrs Mary A. Harper[.] I have Jest received a letter from you dated 26th which I was very glad to hear from you but sorry to hear that you are so poorly[.] I hope you will soon get better[.] I did not get that letter that had all the news in it[.] dont Think I have nothing more to write[.] I have got a new pare of shues[.] we have breaching in our Brigade and some pretty good meetings at Tarboro[.] one man was Babtised in Tar River[.] he belonged to Co F[,] 49th NCT[.] I must close[.] farewell[,] J.L. Stuart to MA Harper

1863, August 29
J.L. Stuart (*camp near Weldon, NC*) to mother **Mary A. Harper**. General wartime correspondence with brief mention of **Anderson H. Smith, Alexander McDonald Williamson** and **Nancy Glass Nall.** [347]

Mrs Mary A Harper[.] Dear Mother[,] I seat myself to write you a few lines to inform you that I am well truly hoping these lines may reach and find you all well[.] I want to hear from you all mity bad[.] it has been ten days to day since I heard from you[.] the last letter I received was dated the 19th[.] I have been looking for a letter from you for three or four days[.] I want to see you all very bad but I cannot see you yet a while[.] A.H. Smith came in last night from home on furlough[.] I do not know who will go next[.] we are under marching orders now to be ready at a minuets warning[.] I do not know where we will go[.] if we do go some thinks to Richmond or Suffolk and some thinks towards Goldsboro[.] I expect we will have a brush before long some where[.] Mc Williamson got out of the guard house at Weldon the other night and the four Deserters also go out that I hope caught last Sunday[.] I want you to write to me and let me know what the people are doing in the upper end and give me all the news[.] tell Granny I want to see her very bad[.] tell her to do the best she can[.] I hardly know what to write about the war[.] it looks like there is no prospects of peace. I get out of heart some times and then again I think we will come out right[.] I am very uneasy about you all[.] I want to hear from you[.] I think something is done to the letters for I should get more letters than I do[.] I do not know whether you get my letters or not but I write ever week to you and some times oftener[.] there are several letters due me but I do not get but few[.] write soon[.] Dyrect your letters to Weldon NC[,] Co. D.[,] 49th[,] NC Troops[,] Ransoms Brigade[.] give my respects to all inquiring friends[.] do the best you can all of you[.] I remain your affectionate son untell Death[,] J L. Stuart

1863, August 30
J.L. Stuart (*Garysburg, NC*) to mother **Mary A. Harper**. General wartime correspondence with brief mention of **W.W. Wood, John Tucker** and **Willis Smith**. [348]

Dear mother[,] I embrace the opportunity to write you a few lines to inform you that I am well truly hoping these lines may reach and find you all well as usual[.] I received a letter to day from you dated 23[.] I am very sorry to hear how bad the times are[.] the peoples going home does not help the war any but makes it worse[.] I want this war to stop as bad as any body but I hear it will last a long time[,] and I may die on the Battle field but I hope I shall live to see the war end so I can come home and live with you all as we once have lived[.] I am sorry to hear that your health is so bad[.] I wish that I could com home to see you but I cannot come now[.] W.W. Wood started home do day on furlough[.] John Tucker has sent up a furlough[.] if he gets it[,] you will see him[.] I reckon we have about 40 forty men in our Co[,] only one man gone home at the time. Today I was at a baptizing[.] fifteen men was put under the water and four was sprinkled[.] there has been some mity meetings in the 25th and a good many Drafted eighteen of the men to day belonged to the 25th and one to the 24th[.] I think it was when we was at Tarboro about he 15th one man in our regt was Baptized[.] he I will venture to say was the biggest lier in the 49th except Willis Smith in Co. D. I suppose part of the men that was emurced to day used to be the Wickedest men out[.] I hope that times will soon other and if the people alters there waise[,] I think that the times will alter also[.] Do the best you can[.] I will do the same[.] Dyrect your letters to Weldon NC as usual[.] You son[,] J.L. Stuart

1863, August 30
Matthew C. Yow (*Taylorsville, VA*) to wife **Nancy Catherine Albright Yow** and children. General wartime correspondence with brief mention of father **Henry C. Yow**, father-in-law **Joseph Albright** and **Lawhon**. [349]

Mrs Nancy C. Yow[.] My Dear Wife[,] I hav bin one more time permited to drop you a few lines to let you no that I am well at present truly hoping when this comes to hand it may find you and my dear little children well and harty. Catharine I hav not had no letter from you in 10 days. I am looking for a letter from you every mail. I receivd a letter from your father the 26 and I hav rote a letter to him to day. I cant get no letter from father yet. I cant tel what is the matter. I think he has rote to me but I cant get them. Catharine I will say to you that we hav left Fredricksburg and come to Taylorsville about 20 miles north of Richmond at the same plac wher we was when we went to Fredericksburg. Catharine I hav some hop that we are going to NC again soon and it may be that we shal go to Charlston. I dont much want to go their now but I want to go to NC. I am tired of Va but it seems like we cant get away from here. I haint got no news to rite to you of any importanc. From what I can here from NC tha will be bad times their. I herd that Lawhon's croud had kild one man and he kild one of them. I herd a letter red to day from moor and it said that tha had a white flag up in fayatville NC and tha say tha will fight at home. Catharine I will send you 2 stamps and 2 fifty cents bills of mony and see if you get it. I hop you will. I cant rite much this time. Rite soon and fail not. I Stil remain your affectionate husband tel death parts us. So fairwell my dear wife[.] Nancy C. Yow.

1863, September 3
J.L. Stuart (*camp near Weldon, NC*) to mother **Mary A. Harper** and stepfather **John Harper**. General wartime correspondence with brief mention of **John Tucker** and **Nancy Teague**. [350]

Mrs Mary A Harper[.] Dear Mother[,] I embrace the opportunity to write you a few lines to inform you that I am well truly hoping these few lines may reach and find you all well as usual[.] I have nothing of interest to write[.] I Started a letter to you last Monday[.] by the hands of John Tucker I also sent my Knife by him for J.H. to mend and Bend it back by him[.] he is on ten days furlough. Our Brass band Came in yesterday evening[.] they do pretty well for the time they have been practicing[.] I want to see you all mity bad but I cannot tell when I shall get to see you[.] I want this war to stop very bad for I want to come home to live mity bad[,] but I see no hopes of this war stopping soon but we do not know what will be our end[.] write to me and give me all the news[.] I hope we will live to see each other again[.] I must close my short letter[,] J.L. Stuart

Mr Harper[.] sir[,] after my best wishes for your welfare I want to see you all very bad but I cannot tell when I shall get to come home[.] we will draw two moths wages shortly[.] the pay rolls are already made out and assigned[.] write to me and give me the news[.] if you can race enough silver to make a finger ring[,] make me one and send it in a letter as by John Tucker[.] I will send the measure[.] I must close write soon[.] yours[,] J.L. Stuart. hand Nancy Teague a letter to her[.] you will find enclosed in yours[.]

1863, September 7
Daniel McIntosh (*Moore County, NC*) to **A.S. Caddell**. General wartime correspondence with brief mentions of the changing of the conscription laws and mother **Raney Caddell**. [351]

Mr AS Caddell[,] I take the present opportunity of writing you a few lines to inform you that we are all in as good health as common and hope that these few lines ma reach you and find you well and doing well[.] we havent heard from you sense you wrote when your unit got to Richmond after you was paroled by then yankees[.] I should have rote before this time tho you said that you was a going to try to get a furlow home and if you did not get one that you would let us know[,] and we have been looking for you evry day sense or expecting to hear from you[.] tho both expectations have faild as yet and I have concluded to write these few lines to see if I can hear what has hapend to you that you dont write[.] your Mother is well except sick spells that she has evry day or two[.] She is very ancious to hear from you[.] She is afraide that your leg has got so bad that you cant get along by yourself[.] Wm. is staying with her yet he has just comenced getting fodder[.] the corn is tollerable good considering the drout and they made rite good wheat[.] my corn crop was planted late and the dry wether kilt it[.] the most of corn is injured by the dry wether in this settlement[.] the people is mitty put out about the war in this section[.] they have conscripted all up to forty five and the govener has had all from forty five to fifty and all the exemps inrold for state defense[.] some of the conscripts between forty and forty one says that they are not a going tho I cant tell whether they will or not tho[.] next Wednesday is the time that they have to select and we will see then whether they will go or not[.] you must rite as soon as you receive this and let me now how you are and if you got a furlow to come home, whehter you can gite along by your selfe or not you can get a furlow and need help about coming home[.] I will go and bring you as I rote before. So I shall close my short letter and expect to hear from you soon[.] your sincere friend and well wisher untill Death, Danl McIntosh

1863, September 10
Matthew C. Yow to his wife **Nancy Catherine Albright Yow** and children. General wartime correspondence with brief mention of his uncle **John Henry Stutts**, father **Henry C. Yow**, father-in-law **Joseph Albright** and **Eli N. Moffitt**. [352]

Mrs Nancy C. Yow[.] My Dear Wife[,] I seat myself to drop you a few lines to inform you that I am well at present truly hoping when this comes to hand it may find you and my dear little children well and harty. Catharine I rote a letter to you yesterday and I am going to drop you a few lines to send by Uncle John Stutts. He is going home on a furlo. I am going to send you some money. I will send you 25 dollars by him. I want to no how you are off for money now. Father said that you only draw (illegible) dollars per month. I want to no what is the number that tha hav reducd your pay. It was little enoughf any how. Catharine I want you to send me one pair of socks by Uncle John. I haint got but one pair now and I dont no when we will draw any. Catharine, Uncle John says he will go to see you and I hop he will. Catharine the mail has come and no letter for me to day. The last letter I got from you was dated 21 of August and this is the 10 of September. That is a long time without hering from you and my dear little children. Catharine I am going to send you some money and I dont want you to tel any body that I sent it to you. For you no that their is some mean enoughf to take it from you and when you go to spend any[,] dont show no more than you are going to spend. But you no who to sho your money to. Catharine if your father wold buy the colt it wold be paying for the land. If you dont need the money your self and if you do need the money dont pay no dets. I want the dets paid but I dont want you to suffer for the money and I no your father dont want you to suffer by no means. But I hop you hav money enoughf to by any thing that you need. I think you ought to try to get you some salt before it gets so hi. I no it will get higher than it is now. I no it taks a heep of money to get nothing now. You said in your letter that you had to pay ten dollars for one bunch of thred. That does look hard and I dont think it is fair. Catharine I hop Mr Moffitt will be a good friend to you as he has bin. I no you will hav corn to by and I think you can get from him if you can get it from any body. I dont think your neighbors will let you suffer as long as you hav any money but when the money is gon it will be a bad chanc.

1863, September 17
Matthew C. Yow to his wife **Nancy Catherine Albright Yow** and children. General wartime correspondence with brief mention of his uncle **John Henry Stutts**. [353]

Matthew C. Yow to Nancy C. Yow[.] Dear Wife and Little Children[,] A few more lines to you. I will send you this letter as I hav got it rote and you can read it and see what I was going to send to you by Uncle John Stutts. Catharine you said in one of your letters that you wanted me to send you a chew of my tobaco and I cold not think of it tel now and I will send it in this letter. Catharine I do want to here that peac is made so bad so that I and all thes pore soldiers can come home and sta with those that we lov so well and you that is always on our minds. Catharine do the best you can for your self and the dear little children. Some times I study so much about them and what is to become of them. I cant hardly stand it to sta here. It is hard and I dont think it is fair. So I must close for this time. Rite as often as you can and maby I will get some of your letters. May god bles you is my prare. So fairwell[.] Mrs Nancy C. Yow

1863, September 17
Matthew C. Yow (*Taylorsville Station, VA*) to his wife **Nancy Catherine Albright Yow** and children. General wartime correspondence with brief mention of his brother **Simeon Jones Yow** and **Isaac Yow**, uncle **John Henry Stutts, David S. Fairley, Samuel W. Howerton, Charles Carroll Dodson** and **Calvin Plyler**. [354]

Mrs Nancy C. Yow[.] my Dear Wife[,] I one time more seat my self to drop you a few lines to inform you that I am well at present truly hoping when this comes to hand it may find you and my dear little children well and harty. Catharine I will tel you that I am out of hart. I cant get no letters from you. The last I had from you was rote the 21 of August. I cant tel what is the matter. There is something rong some way. I cant tel whither you got my letters or not but I hop you do. Catharine when I cant here from you and the children I am out of hart for that is all the satisfaction that I can see is when I can here from you and here that you are all well and I think it is the same with you. Isaac and Jones dont get no letters and tha are out of hart as well as my self. Tha are both well exept bad cold Jones has. He cant hardly talk he is so horse and Isaac has a bad risen on his hand. Catharine I can inform you that we hav a great meeting going on here now. It is a brigade meeting. Their is a great prospect of doing a heep of good if we can sta here. Their has several profest now and the morners just goes in rouds. I am so glad to see such good attention as is here now. Their is great revivals going on in the army at this time and their is a great need of it here. I hop you hav good meetings at home. This meeting is held by Mr Fairly chaplin of the 27[,] Mr Howerton of the 15 and Mr Dodson of the 46. The 48 has no chaplin at this time. Its said that the Rev Mr Pliler is coming to our regiment and I hop it is so. Catharine I rote a letter to send by Uncle John and he did not get off and I will send it in this as long as I hav got it rote. So no more for this time. I stil remain your true and affectionate husband tel death. So fairwell dear wife.

1863, September 18
William J. McNeill (*Orange Courthouse, VA)* to brother **Angus McNeill**. General wartime correspondence between brothers with brief mentions of fighting at Culpepper Courthouse, **Ewell**, General **Sheridan**, **Martha**, and **W.W. Kirkland**. [355]

Dear brother[,] having received your letter last night I will seat myself this morning to answer yours. I was truly glad to hear from you and my friends at home. I am well at this time and I hope this may reach you and all the rest enjoying the same blessing. Angus I thought before this time I would be in a fight. On last Sunday evening while I was at preaching I could hear cannonading towards Culpeper C. H. About eleven o'clock that night we were ordered up to cook one day's rashings and to be ready by daylight[.] at daylight we had orders to move[.] we started for Orange C. H. about two miles we then changed our course for Culpeper. We got in one mile and a half when we heard them fighting down about Cedar Run[.] we could see the smoke from the cannon[.] we went to within one mile of the river at the rail road bridge[.] we could see them fighting that is the skirmishers[.] our men planted their cannon and give them a few rounds but they made no reply with their artillery[the pickets is still fighting. Ewell's corps. whipped them out down below here on Monday. I hear cannonading going on above here this evening. General Sheridan is above. I think there will be a general engagement here some of these days. Its principle cavalry scouts that is coming on[.] we have a permanent camp in sight of the Yankee camp[.] we do not feel alarmed, though we can see them and hear them. Angus you said that I did not state about the dissatisfaction that was in our army. What they are dissatisfied about is that they did not have a sharing in their big meeting that you scene[,] that our men held at Orange Court House sometime a go about going back in the union. The most of them think that we will be bound to go back on any sort of terms but they seem very quiet at this time. There is one man to be shot in the Forty Fourth Regiment next Saturday[.] that is a scene that I will have to witness. He will be shot before the brigade[.] his crime is for advising men to runaway. I am opposed to shooting our own men. Angus you said that you did not get but one letter from me since I left home[.] I am sure that I sent several letters to you as I had promised[.] I was very anxious to hear how Martha was getting for I felt from what I heard that she would hardly get over it for if I live to get home again[.] I want to see all my kindest friends once more. Angus I am truly glad that you have excused from coming out in this miserable war though some of your friends is not so. Angus I must this to a close we have a new brigade general[.] his name is W. W. Kirkland. Yours till death, Wm. J. McNeill. Write soon.

1863, September 20
Baxter C. Phillips *(Camp South, Ann Bridge, Richmond, VA)* to sister **Elmira Phillips.** General wartime correspondence with brief mentions of **Charles H. Phillips, Mastin Phillips, Emeline Phillips** and **Robert H. Phillips.** [356]

Dear Sister, Yours came in time to give me some comfort for I was not very well, nor am I yet. But your letter did me much good because it was so cheerful and encouraging. Hope the next I get from you that I will be well.
I have nothing of interest to write this time more than there is quite an extensive revival going on in our brigade and I hope it will continue 'till all of us are converted. I got a letter from Uncle Charles the day that I got yours. He was in a revival as usual. Mastin is getting better. I look for him up tomorrow. Rather he would go home but I don't think there's much chance for that. I received Emeline's last today. Tell her I will write in detail to her in a few days. Do the best you all can at home. I don't think the deserters will interrupt you at all. Continue to live right and pray for us, and God will bless us. We have a nice camp now, nothing much to do and plenty to eat and good water to drink. You must excuse me this time for not writing. Give my love to all at home, to Uncle Bob and family. Goodbye. B. C. Phillips

1863, September 20
Matthew C. Yow (*Taylorsville Station, VA*) to his wife **Nancy Catherine Albright Yow** and children. General wartime correspondence with brief mention of his sons **Joseph Gibbs Yow** and **John Matthew Yow**, brother-in-law **Willian Nicholas Brower**, father **Henry C. Yow, Hiram Williamson** and **Wesley Brower.** [357]

Mrs Nancy C. Yow[.] my Dear Wife[,] I am permited to drop you a few lines to inform you that I am wel at present truly hoping when this comes to hand it may find you and my dear little children all wel and harty. Catharine I receivd 2 letters from you today one dated the 8 and the other 12 which made me so proud to here from you again. It has bin nearly three weeks sinc I had a letter from you and you no that I wanted to here from you and my dear little children. You said that Joseph had got well but John was sick now. I am so sorrow to here that he has the thrush so bad. Pore little children. I am so sorrow for them and I want to see them so bad. I am so uneasy about them. I am so afraid that tha wil tak that sore throat and if tha do I fear that it wil kil some of them. You may no that I am in trouble. I study so much about you and them some times. It seems like I cant stand it much longer and I no that you are nearly scared to death sinc tha rob Brower. I dont no what will become of you all. You said that my pore old father was sick and had sent after the doctor and I no that he is bad off if he sent for the docter. I shant rest tel I here from him again. I got a letter from W N Brower the 18 and he said that father was sick and had sent for the docter and you said that some one had kild your sow and that made me vary mad when I red that. I no that it was old Hy Williamson for their is no body do that wold do that mean a trick but him and if I was their I wold try to make his back strait. I do hop and pray that I will get home again and I will help him kill my hogs. Any man that will such a trick as that will steal and I no he will do that. Catharine you said in one of your letters some time back that old Hy had kild my boar and I want to no if he did. It makes me so mad to think that any man will tak that mean a turn on you. but he noes that you cant help your self and I am gon now and I cant help my self but I cant my self now but I do hop I will get home again. It made me mad but I cant help it now. Such men as him wants you and your little children to suffer but I hop you will not. I suppose that ___ is dead and their is no body dead[.] he was not fit to die nor fit to liv without he had ___. Catharine you said that Wesley Brower had offerd you 75 dollars for the colt. I think you can get one hundred dollars for him. Get all you can and then old Hy will come and steal the money from you. He is mean enough to do it I no. Do the best you can. Catharine all is quiet here now. I dont here much tel of fiting about here. I hop tha wont be much more don in Va. You said you thought that we ought to come home and defend our homes and I think so two. We want to come and kil them all when we here how tha are doing their. It is hard to bear. You said that you was sorrow that me and your father cold not agree. He is all rite. He dont make me mad. He thinks that he nows all about the war but he is mistaken. He can read the papers but tha dont tel the truth. Tha talk to incourage the soldiers. Holden talks to suit me and all the soldiers is for him and Govener Vanc and old Sam Christian. We say baby for Sam. Catharine my dear wife rite soon[.] so no more at this time. May God bles you all. So fairwell.

1863, September 28
Matthew C. Yow to his wife **Nancy Catherine Albright Yow** and children. General wartime correspondence with brief mention of his father-in-law **Joseph Albright, Levi Wright, James Madison Wright** and brother **Simeon Jones Yow.** [358]

Catharine[,] We hav good meeting here yet we had to move but we hav commenct here again. I herd 2 sermonds preacht yesterday and a great many morners. Tha will be some Baptists here to day and preaching again to nite. It seems like the good Lord is working a mong his people now. I am so glad to see and here of so much good being don[,] not only here but all through the Confederate Army. I believ that we cold do more good by praying for peac than we cold do by fiting for peac. If we hav to fight for peac we shant hav it soon. I do hop that something will soon be don. Catharine I rote to your father and he did not answer me. I dont no what is the matter. I hop I did not make him mad. When I rote to him last I rote plain and he does the same. It all goes rite with me. I am glad to here from him and here what he thinks about this cruel war. It is so bad. Catharine I rote a letter to you the 24 about selling the colt. You said in your letter that you did not think that you cold get more than 80 dollars for him and Mr wright said that he wold giv 90 dollars for him without seeing him. He said he newd his mother and I rot to you to let his son James hav him if you cant do any beter. He said tha wold pay you 60 dollars their and he wold pay me 30 dollars here and I hop you hav got the letter. We both rote a letter the same time and sent them. Catharine maby I can get to send the money to you before you need it. Do the best you can and get some wheet sowd if you can. Catharine my dear wife I do want to see you so bad and my dear little children. Catharine Jones says I look the best he ever saw me. I weigh one hundred and 50 pounds. So no more for this time. May God bles all. So fairwell my dear wife[.] Nancy C. Yow

1863, October 8
J.L. Stuart (*Weldon, NC*) to stepfather **John Harper** and brother **Charles Harper**. General wartime correspondence with brief mention of **Mary A. Harper** and **Nancy Glass Nall.** [359]

Mr John Harper[.] Dear step father[,] I write you a few lines to inform you that I am well truly hoping these lines will reach and find you well[.] I was very sorry to hear that mother is so bad off[.] try and get her better if you can[.] you must do that best[.] you can try and buy wheat corn and stuff you[.] the sooner you buy[,] the better it will be[.] from all accounts Bragg has whiped the yankees in the west[,] in fact that General Lee will have a fight before long[.] the last account I had from his army[,] they were in line of battle ready for the word forward[.] I hope the war will soon end but I fear it will last another year yet[.] write to me ever chance[.] Dyrect to Weldon[,] Co D[,] 49th regt[,] NC T[.] give my respects to all inquiring friends[.] I remain as ever[,] J.L. Stuart To John Harper

Mr Charles E Harper[.] Dear Brother[,] I write you a few lines to inform you that I am well truly hoping these lines will find you well[.] you said you had had the shingles but was about well[.] you must be a smart boy[.] I hope I shall live to get home and see you all again[.] write to me and let me know how you are getting along[.] tell sis and granny I want to see them all very bad[.] you must all do the best you can[.] Charles you ought to hear our band today[.] give my respects & tell inquiring friends write to me and let me know how you are getting along[.] I must close[.] sis you and Charles must be smart and mind mother[.] I must close so I remain your brother as ever[,] J.L. Stuart to Charles & sis

1863, October 11
Matthew C. Yow (*Gordonsville, VA*) to his wife **Nancy Catherine Albright Yow** and children. General wartime correspondence with brief mention of his father **Henry C. Yow**, brothers-in-law **John E. Albright, Henry A. Albright, John Rich, Thomas Craven, Coffin, Dorsett,** brothers **Isaac Yow** and **Simeon Jones Yow, Eli N. Moffit, Hiram Williamson, Levi Wright,** and grandfather **Andrew Yow.** [360]

Mrs Nancy C. Yow[.] my Dear Wife[,] I one time more seat myself to drop you a few lines to inform you that I am well at present and I do hop and trust when this comes to hand it may find you and my dear little children all well and harty. Catharine I receivd your welcome letter to day that you rote the 27. It come to hand in due time. I hav bin geting letters regular for the last 2 weeks. You say that you get my letters regular. I am glad to here that you get my letters. I write vary often to you. No body do not write to me but you. My father cant rite to me. Catharine I will say to you that your brother John come to see me yesterday and he staid with me half of the night. He come here to get one of there guns brusht and he left here this morning. Henry was well and also John Rich. John looks well but he is like myself. He is tiard of the war. He told me how Thomas Craven treated him when he went home. I allways thought that Tom was mean and now you can tel what he will do. He is one of the tories. I reckon Coffin and Dorset is the same way. For he will do as tha do you no. John come to see me and he wanted to see Isacc and Jones and we went to see them and staid a long time and talk with them. Jones had such a bad cold that he cold not talk only whisper but he is some beter today. Catharine you said that you went to Mr Moffitt to get corn and did not see him. I think he will let you hav corn. You tel him that I said he must let you hav corn if he let any body hav any and I no that he will hav corn to sell. You said that you hav 2 hogs in the pen and tha was fat. That is the way for you to do. Keep some always in the pen if old Hy dont kill them all. He is mean enough to kill you and tak your money. Catharine dont let any body no that you hav much money. I expect you hav a good eal of money now and when you sel the colt you will hav more. I reckon you hav got my letter that I rote to you about the colt. Mr rite wants him vary bad and I am afraid that you cant feed what you will hav left. I am vary uneasy about you. I am afraid that you will suffer yet it greavs my hart that I cant be their to make somthing for you and my dear little kids to live on. I do hop and pray that their will be ___. May god help you to rais my dear children. Catharine dont forget me in your prares. I believ you do pray for me. I am always praying for you and my dear little children and my dear sick father. I hop he will bear his sickness with patience. May God bles and rais him up. Catharine I expect that I will hav to go into another battle before long. I think tha will be sure to fight on the Rappadan River. We are in 15 miles of that place. Johns camp is on the bank of the river. The Yankees on one side and our men on the other. If I do hav to go into battle with them I pray to the good Lord to be with me there and save me from all danger. Catharine from what I can here their is bad chanc at home now. I suppose tha are kiling some and sending some to the army. Tha go along here every day. Catharine giv lov and best respects to all my friends. Tel my old granfather that I hav not forgot him yet. I do want to see him and all the rest of you so bad I cant hardly stand it. So I must close for this time. I remain your affectionate husband tel death. M.C. Yow Fair well to Nancy C. Yow[.]

1863, October 17
Noah Deaton (*Washington City*) to father **William Deaton**. Wartime correspondence between son and father regarding injuries sustained at Bristol Station, VA and imprisonment in Washington along with **Levi Wright**, **Isaac Freeman**, **Rials Key**, **Edmund Morgan** and **W.C. Moore**. [361]

Dear Father, I am very thankful that I have an opportunity this morning of writing a few lines which I trust will reach you[.] I was wounded at Bristol Station, VA and captured and am now in prison in Washington City[.] my wound is slight – a piece of my ear shot off and a bruise on my shoulder – not serious[.] My health is good. Several of our boys are here, all well, sone with slight wounds[.] Those not wounded are Levi Wright, Isaac Freeman, R. Key, Edmund Morgan, W.C. Moore[.] We have been treated very kindly better than I expected to be[.] not a man has said a harsh word to me[.] yet do not be uneasy about me for I trust that I will be treated with the hospitality and respect that I have been and as a prisoner of war should be[.] Your obedient son until death. Do not be uneasy about me for I trust that I will be treated with the[.] Noah Deaton

1863, October 17
William Henry Patterson (*Gordonsville, VA*) to sister **Frances Anna V. Patterson**. General wartime

correspondence between siblings with brief mentions of **Gen. Lee, John M. Graham, William D. Patterson, James A.J. Buchan** and **William Kennedy.** [362]

Dear Sister, I embrace the present opportunity of writing you a few lines to let you know that I am in the enjoyment of usual health and I sincerely hope these few lines will find you in similar blessings. I have no news to write you[.] We have any number of reports here to day[.] Genl. Lee's Army but beleive they all want confirmation. I heard a few minutes ago that there was a general engagement some where near Manassas yesterday[.] it is also reported that our fources were victorious but that we lost more men than in any engagement during the war. This is only mere rumor and is not thought to be reliable though I have but little doubt but there has been heavy fighting. I have been here ever since Thursday and I cannot tell when I will be allowed to make my way on to the Regiment. Some of the soldiers here seem to think we will be sent on soon probably tomorrow, but I think it extremely uncertain when we will leave, though we may leave tomorrow. I staid in Richmond one day and night[.] I went out to the Winder Hospital to see John M. Graham and William D. Patterson. Poor William seems to be nearly sawed(?) out, he looks very bad indeed though he seems to be cheerful and is very anxious to go home but I think he is entirely too weak[.] John M. Graham expected to start home yesterday and William [?] to go with him but I told him I thought [?]. There are over a thousand soldiers here[.] they are coming in every train that comes from Richmond. I have been looking for James A. J. Buchan and William Kennedy but I have not seen either of them yet. If they started from home in the early part of this week[,] they must have been detained in Richmond. I have no acquaintance here with me but I am getting along very well as there are some very clever boys here. I wrote Pa yesterday and I am in hopes the letter will reach him by next weeks mail. I also wrote to him from the Winder Hospital and gave the letter to John M. Graham to carry to him. We have had a few days of very disagreeable weather but it has faired off today and I am in hopes it will not rain any more soon. As I have nothing of interest to communicate[,] I will come to a close hoping to be able to write you a more interesting letter before long. Give my respects to all inquiring friends and accept the best wishes of your afft. Bro. William H. Patterson

1863, October 18
Matthew C. Yow (*Rappahannock River, VA*) to his wife **Nancy Catherine Albright Yow** and children. General wartime correspondence with brief mention of his brother **Simeon Jones Yow** being severely wounded and **Isaac Yow** being slightly wounded, father **Henry C. Yow, William Nicholas Brower** and **Levi Wright.** [363]

Mrs Nancy C. Yow[.] my Dear Wife[,] I do thank my God that I hav one more opportunity of riting you a few lines one time more. I will say to you that I am well as I cold expect at this time. We hav bin marching 10 days and fiting together. Wensday the 14 we had a fight at Bristo Station 4 miles this side of Manasses Gap. I did not get hurt much. A ball hit me on the thigh but did not go through my cloths but I hav bad news to tel you. My Brother Simeon J. Yow is I fear mortaly wonded. He was shot through the left brest and the ball went out under the left shoulder blade. I do hop it will not kil him. I went to see him next day and he lookt vary bad but he said that it did not hurt him vary bad. He dont think that it will kil him. He was shot through the left hand also pore fellow. I am so sorrow for him. He was a good soldier. He was pushing on the Yankees when tha shot him. His captain hast it vary bad for he was such a good soldier. Isaac was hurt some. He is with Jones or was at last account. Isaac was not hurt so bad but what he cold take care of Jones. The Yankees repulst us one time but we held the battle field and tha left that night and went to Manasses and we did not follow them. Some followed them and fought them next day and drove them on. Catharine I cant rite much this time. We shal hav to march vary soon now. We are at the Rappahanoc River a wating to cros. It has raind so much that the river is vary high. We hav bin tearing up the railrode for the last 2 days. We are coming back as fast as we can. We aim to get to Culpeper today if we can cros the River. Catharine I hav seen hard times for the last 10 days. Your brothers was in the fight but did not get hurt. I think I will get some letters from you now. We haint had no mail in 10 days. It cold not get to us. I got a letter from W.N. Brower the day I left Gordonsville but I cold not answer it then. We had one man kild in our company and several wonded and 10 taken prisnors. Levi Right was taken prisnor. Catharine I will rite as soon as I stop and tel you more about the times here. Tel my father that I will rite to him soon as I can. I dont want him to greav so much about my dear brother. I do hop that he will get well. Jones is sent to Culpeper now. I want to see him when I get their. Jones was rite pert yesterday. Tha said that he cold walk a little. I am nearly brok down. My feet is all over blisters but I keep going yet. So I must close for this time. I will rite again as soon as I can. May God bles you all I pray. Catharine do the best you can. Write as often as you can. Fairwell. Matthew C. Yow

1863, October 20
J.L. Stuart (*Weldon, NC*) to mother **Mary A. Harper** and brother **Charles Harper**. General wartime correspondence with brief mention of **Neill C. Blue, Duncan Cole, Mary A. Harper** and **Nancy Glass Nall**. [364]

Mrs Mary A Harper. Dear Mother[,] I seat myself to write you a few lines to inform you that I am well truly hoping these lines will reach and find you all well as usual[.] I received a letter to day dated 16tg which gave me great pleasure to hear from you. you said something our pickets seeing men with white uniform on[.] I read of it a month ago[.] the sight has been been twice in[.] it stated in the Daily Richmond papers that Cooks Brigade has had a fight in V.A. and lost five pieces of artillery and about five hundred men[.] it is stated also that some of Lees army have takend several prisoners in Northern V.A. you said you wanted me to come home but I do not know when I shall get to come home[.] only two men out of one hundred men to get furlough so that will be slow getting furlough[.] two men out of one hundred to have 15 dayes[.] Lt N.C. Blue starts home to Day on furlough but you will not see him[.] he will not go any nearer than Carthage[.] our regt have all Brand new uniform[.] our coats are Blue and pants are grey, a very nice uniform[.] Gen Picket has command of us Gen Ransoms Brigade and Maj Gen Picket Division[.] I Believe I have wrote all the news. we are in the same camp[.] I do not know how long we will stay here[.] I have got only 20 Dollars[.] I have nearly spent all my money[.] I want to see you all very Bad. I hope I shall get to see you all again Before long but I cannot tell when I shall get to come home[.] I wish I could be at your quilting[.] last night three men were Baptised at night meeting By sprinkling[.] I must begin to close my letter By asking you to write ever chance[.] I hope I shall get to come home and see you all again[.] it may be that Duncan Cole will go home before long[.] if he does I shall want you to send me a Jug of syrup[.] give my respects to all inquiring friends[.] Dyrect your letters to Weldon N.C[,] Co. "D"[,] 49th regt[,] NC Troops[.] I will close by asking you to write soon. I remain your son as ever. J.L. Stuart

Mr Charles E Harper[.] Dear Brother[,] I seat myself to write you a few lines to inform you that I am well truly hoping these few lines will reach and find you all well[.] I want to see you all mity bad and hope I will get to see you after a while[.] you said if I would come home you would have a quilting but I am afraid it will be a long time before I shall get to come home[.] you said you were going to build a chimney to the big house this winter[.] try and doit if you can[.] give my respects to all inquiring friends[.] tell sis and granny I want to see them very bad[.] I want to see you all[.] I must close my letter[.] write to me ever chance[.] I remain your Brother as Ever[,] John L Stuart to Charles & all at home

1863, October
Matthew C. Yow to his wife **Nancy Catherine Albright Yow** and children. General wartime correspondence with brief mention of his brother **William Yow, Horner, Shaw**, and **Levi Wright.** [365]

Catharine[,] I am glad that William met with Horner. He giv more than Shaw would giv and more than Write wold giv. Write was taken prisnor. He has gon to sta with the Yankees awhile now. Catharine do the best you can and get corn as cheap as you can. I am so uneasy about you now. I thought you had got well. If you get sick I donot no what will becom of our little children. Pore little children. It greavs hart to think that I cant come to them and tha are so near to my hart. May God help you to keep them along rite and giv you helth to work and provide for them. O that I cold see you and them one time more in this world. May the good Lord bles and giv you helth I pray. So fairwell my dear wife and little children. M. C. Yow to Nancy C. Yow

1863, October 23
Matthew C. Yow to his father-in-law **Joseph Albright**. General wartime correspondence with brief mention of the battle of Bristoe Station, VA and his brothers-in-law **John E. Albright, Henry A. Albright** and brother **Simeon Jones Yow, Isaac Yow** and wife **Nancy Catherine Albright Yow.** [366]

Mr Joseph Albright[.] Dear [,] Through the kind hand of Providenc I am permited one time more to drop you a few lines to inform you that I am well at present truly hoping when these lines reaches you tha may find you and family enjoying good helth. I receivd your letter the 6 which come to hand in due time and was truly glad to here that you was all well. I hav not had the chanc to answer your letter tel now. We got marching orders the 8 and the 9 we left Gordonsville and the 6 day we over took the enemy at Bristo Station near Manasses. At about 2 oclock we opend fire on them. Grahams Battry opend the fire and it was a close time for a while. The enemy was hid behind the railrod and we cold not see them and we had no protection at all and the Yankee batteries was playing on us all the time. It was said that tha had 40 peaces. You may be sure that tha opend our ranks. Tha repulst one time but we held the battle field and lay their that night and the cowardly Yankees left under cover of night. Next morning tha was all gon. Tha was followed by our cavalry. We lost one man kild and 10 wonded[,] one mortaly wonded and 10 taken prisners. We lost 700 and 75 men out of the brigade. That was a bad loss for the time that we was their. It is said that it was badly managed and I think so myself. I am afraid that General Heath is not a good commander. Them that has bin under him say that he is not successful. General Cook was badly wonded. I herd that he was ded but I think it is a mistake. His leg has bin taken off. I suppose Colonel Hall is in command now. Henry and John was not hurt. I saw John next day. My 2 brothers was both wonded. Jones was badly wonded[,] I am afraid mortaly but I hop not. He was shot through the left brest and the ball come out under the left shoulder blade and he was shot through the left hand. I am vary sorrow for him. He was a good soldier. His captain hats it vary bad. He thought a heep of Jones and Isaac. Isaac was slitly wonded by a shel. He will soon be able for duty I think. I was hit on the thigh but the ball did not go through my cloths. We are on the south side of the Rappahanoc River. I cant tel how long we shal sta here. I got a letter from Catharine the 20 and she said that she was not well. She said that she had bin to the doctor again. I fear that she will get down sick yet. So no more. Your friend tel death. M. C. Yow Joseph Albright

1863, October 24
Baxter C. Phillips *(Culpepper Courthouse, VA)* to sister **Elmira Phillips.** General wartime correspondence with brief mentions of **Mastin Phillips, Rev. Lewis Phillips Jr., Tyler, Jasper Bray, Frank Wilkie, Meredith Rowan** and **Nancy Phillips.** [367]

Dear Elmira, Yours did not reach me until after I had written to Pa after we crossed the river. We are in camp about six miles from Culpepper Court House. There is not much talk about the enemy. I hope that we will not be in another fight, but can't tell what will come. My last informed you that Mastin was taken prisoner. He was in good health for him and had all clothes with him and his blanket too. I don't want you to be too uneasy about him, but give him, yourselves and me all into the hands of God. I am better satisfied about him than if he had been killed. As it is, he is not hurt. I have got rested since the march, which was very fatiguing and the weather was bad a good deal of the time. Our company lost twenty men. Most of them were captured, only one was killed, a man from Davidson. I feel thankful that I am not hurt. Continue to pray for me. Brother Tyler got to us yesterday. He is our Chaplain. Jasper Bray and Frank Wilky are well. Meredith Rowan is a prisoner now. I have no news to give you. I commend you all to the care of Almighty God,who is able to keep you and us. Be cheerful and content. Be humble, and God, for Christ's sake will hear and answer all your prayers as is best for you. Write soon and give me all the news. Give my love to Mother. This leaves me well. Baxter

1863, October 24
J.L. Stuart (*camp near Weldon, NC*) to mother **Mary A. Harper**. General wartime correspondence with brief mention of **Levi Davis, Richmond Nall, Charles Harper** and **Mary A. Harper**. [368]

Mrs Mary A Harper[.] Dear Mother. I write you a few lines to day to inform you that I am well truly hoping these lines will come to hand in due time and find you all well as usual. I received a letter to day dated 21st which gave me great pleasure to hear that you was all a live[.] you said you wanted to see me very bad[.] I want to see you all as bad as you want to see you[.] I reck on you said Levi Davis had moved[.] I did not know what to think of his moveing[.] you also said Uncle Richmond was a going to move[.] you said you had a good may little pigs[.] tell Charles & sis to feed them and try to rase them and if I ever get to come home you will have some nice hogs for me to see[.] Mother I want to see you mity bad but I cannot tell you when I shall get to come home[.] we moved from our old camp the 22[.] we are in a camp about a quarter from the River[.] Wood is very plenty hear[.] we are seeing a very easy time but I fear we will see a hard time yet[.] we have got a fine regiment[.] there is about 700 men in it and we have all got new coats and pants[.] the coats are Blue and pants are grey[.] yesterday we had General Review[.] there was a good many Ladies out to look at us[.] I wish you could a been there to a seen us[.] there was four regiments and about 10 pieces of artillery[.] if you hear who was killed in the 26th & 46th and 48th regiments[,] let me know for I saw in the papers that Cookes Brigade and Kirklands Brigade was in a fight[.] so you will hear who was killed or wounded and let me know. Give my respects to all inquiring friends and tell them all to write to me[.] tell Charles I want to see him very bad and tell sis and granny the same[.] tell Charles to be smart and tell sis I send her fifty cents[.] tell her she must be smart[.] I hope I shall live to come home and live with you all so I will close my letter by saying to you do the best you all can[.] write ever chance[.] I remain your son as ever[,] J.L. Stuart to Mary A Harper

1863, October 25
Matthew C. Yow to his wife **Nancy Catherine Albright Yow** and children. General wartime correspondence with brief mention of his brother **Simeon Jones Yow** and son **William Henry Yow.** [369]

Mrs Nancy C. Yow[.] my Dear Wife[,] With pleasure I seat my self to drop you a few lines inform you that I am well at this present time and I do trust when this comes to hand it may find you and my dear little children all well and harty. Catharine I hav not had no letter from you in several days but I am looking for a letter now and I thought I wold to you to day. It seems like I cant be satisfied with I am riting to you. I think that you want to here from me and I no I want to here from you as often as I can. I dont see anything but trouble now. My brother is so badly wonded and I cant here from him and I am so uneasy about you and the children that I dont see any satisfaction at all. I can here how things is going on about home and it greavs me for I no if this war last much longer you will suffer. The wether is geting cold and I study so much about you and pore little Henry. I dont no what you will do this winter and I see no chanc for me to come home to help you. O that the good Lord wold giv us peac one time more in this distracted country. I hav prayd for peac all the time and there is thousands of prares going up every day for peac and it seems to do no good. But I do thank my God that I am aliv and doing as well as I am. I am well and harty if I cold get enough to eat but I dont get enough but I dont mind that. I will freely suffer my self but I cant bear to think of you and my dear little children suffering. But it seems like their is no other chanc for you. Every thing is so clear that your money will not hold out long I am afraid. Do the best you can. May God help you I pray. God bles my dear little children I pray.

1863, October 25
J.L. Stuart to stepfather **John Harper**. General wartime correspondence with brief mention of **Charles Harper**. [370]

Mr. John Harper[.] Dear stepfather[,] I write you a few lines in answer to yours of the 21st[.] I was very glad to hear from you[.] well I have no news to write you at this time[.] I am of the same opinions about the war that you are[.] I think it will last a good while yet but I cannot tell[.] I hope I shall live to get back and see you all again[.] you must all do the best you can[.] give my respects to all inquiring friends[.] tell them to write to me[.] my address is Co D[,] 49th[,] N.C. Troops, Weldon NC. tell Charles to write to me and all of you. J.L. Stuart

1863, October 26
Henry C. Brown (*Old Capitol Prison, Washington, DC*) to **Bryan Tyson**. General wartime correspondence with brief mentions of **Rev. William Lineberry, William A. Lineberry** and **Eli Branson**. [371]

Dear Sir, I drop you this note to let you know that I am here a prisoner and would be glad to see you[.] also the Rev. Wm. Lineberry son is here and having heard his father speak of you[,] he desires to see you on acco of that intimate friendship that exist between you and him and also E. Branson[.] so no more[,] but I remain as ever your most affectionate friend. Henry C. Brown

1863, October 29
J.L. Stuart (*Weldon, NC*) to **Mary A. Harper**. General wartime correspondence with brief mention of **John N. Copeland** and **Cornelius Matheson**. [372]

Miss Mary A Harper[.] Dear Mother[,] I seat myself to writ you a few lines to inform you that I am well truly hoping these lines will come to hand in Due time and find you all as well as usual. I received a letter from you to day dated 27th which gave me great pleasure to hear from you all[.] you said times were very bad[.] I hope the war will soon stop for times will get no better as long as the war last but I do not have any idea the war will stop in twelve months[.] if it stops in that time there will be a many a man killed before the war ends. There has been some big fighting going on in the Trent[.] our men out done the enemy and captured a good many of them[.]

there have been some four or five thousand Brought by here on the way to Richmond in the last few days[.] I am told they are mity bad sorry clothed and sickly men[.] I hope the war will not last much longer for I want to come home very bad but you nead not look for me for there are agood many that have not been at home and they want to go home as bad as I do. John Copeland came in yesterday[.] he Brought some very good valuable Boxes to some of the company & Matherson will go next. We have preaching here every day and night and there are a good many mourners[.] if there was women here[,] there would be the greatest meetings you ever heard of but there is no women here nothing but the soldiers[.] you have no idea what a change there are in some of the soldiers[.] men that use to be heard hearted enough to do anything are now professors of religion[.] I hope it will last. from ever part of the army I hear of religious revivals[.] it looks like the war will soon come to a close if they are in earnest as some thing is a going to happen[.] our company have some cases of sickness chills is the complaint generally. I must close my letter for this time[.] I started a letter to you the other day with one of them rings in it for it to be made smaller and Broader[.] give my respect to all inquiring friends[.] write as soon as this come to hand[.] give my respects to all the family[.] I have not forgotten none of you yet I hope I shall live to see you all again[.] excuse me all of you for not writeing more. this time I will close by saying my best wishes for the welfare of you all[,] John L Stuart. Address me at Weldon N.C[,] Co. "D.[,]49th regt[,] NCT. When this you see[,] remember me your friend & son. John L Stuart

1863, November 2
William Henry Patterson (*Camp near Brandy Station, VA*) to sister **Frances Anna V. Patterson**. General wartime correspondence between siblings with brief mentions of **James A.J. Buchan, L.A. Currie, Isham Sheffield, James Beck, William P. Blue, John R. Keith, G.W. Shaw, W.J. McNeill, Neill T. Smith, Neill McDonald, Anderson S. Warner** and **J.C. Fry.** [373]

Dear Sister, I am again in the Army having reached the regiment on the 23rd inst. after having been detained at Gordonsville some 8 days and a day and a night in Richmond. Had I known how things were I would certainly have remained at home some 8 or 10 days longer and then I would have reached the regiment as soon as I did. James A. J. Buchan reached Camp on the night of the 25th inst. he was detained in Richmond several days[.] he and L. A. Currie came together. Dear Sister[,] I am glad to inform you that I am in the possession of more than ordinary health, Such a blessing should be appreciated at a time like the present. Sorrounded as we are by civil war and all its devastation and horror. Such a war as has no paralel in the annals of history and we ought to feel grateful to a kind Providence for permitting us to live and enjoy health while hundreds and thousands equally as good[.] as we are under going and have under gone sickness, sorrow, pain and death. But we hope and trust that the time is not far distant when our nationality will be recognized and wholesale slaughter will cease. Dear sister on yesterday I witnessed a sight that was anything but pleasent. It was the execution of a man for desertion. He belonged to this (Kirkland's) Brigade, to the 47th Regt. he was tied to a stake and shot in the presents of the Brigade. He was shot by 10 men though 5 of them had their guns loaded with blank cartridges; the object of this was to keep the men from knowing who killed him. It was an awful sight. Genl. Heath was present[.] I would not be surprised if there will be a man shot in this company for desertion. I understand that old Isham Sheffield who deserted at Greenville last spring has been caught[.] he deserted once before that and he will be apt to be shot when he is brought to the Regiment. Jas. Beck who deserted on the march to Pennsylvania has been sentenced to hard labor for 12 months. William P. Blue is in very good health as so are all the boys from our section of county. Jon. R. Keith and G. W. Shaw were slightly hurt at Bristow Station but neither were hurt bad enough to uncapicitate them for duty. W. J. McNeill, Neill T. Smith, Neill McDonald, Anderson S. Warner and J. C. Fry were killed.

1863, November 3
William K. Nunnery & Thomas Needham (*Point Lookout, MD*) to **Bryan Tyson**. General wartime correspondence with brief mentions of **Christopher Columbus Harrison**. [374]

Dear frind, we received you kind letter to day and wer glad to hear from you[.] you stated in you letter that you wer goin to New Bern an if you do I want yo to call on se seea us if you can[.] we will bea more than glad to sea you one time moor[.] you stated in you kind letter that you wanted us to hav one of your bookes an we wood bea glad to hav on of them[.] an you stated in you letter if we wanted eny money rite to you[.] we wood bea moor than glad if you can let us hav som money for we havt got eny that will pass hear[.] and if you will let us hav som it will obleg us very much[.] it will bea a favor that will never bea forgotten[.] It will bea a favor that will never be forgotten. So nothen moor at present. W.K. Nunery & Thomas Needham [P.S] Columbes Harison is wounded an now is at home.

1863, November 4

J.L. Stuart (*Weldon, NC*) to mother **Mary A. Harper**, stepfather **John Harper,** brother **Charles Harper** and sister **Mary A. Harper**. General wartime correspondence with brief mention of **Martha Nall, Martin Nall, Martha Harper Hardin, Duncan Cole** and **Henry Brewer**. [375]

Dear Mother[,] I avail myself the pleasure of writing you a few lines to inform you that I am well truly hoping these few lines will come to hand in due time and reach you all as well as usual. I received a letter to day from you dated the 29th Oct which gave me great pleasure to hear from you but I was mity sorry to hear that you was so unwell and I was very sorry to hear sis was so bad off[.] I shall be mity uneasy untell I hear from you again[.] we have got us a good place to stay in[.] we have got a chimney to our tent but we now are under marching order[.] we are ordered to Kinston[.] this morning we had preaching[.] a blind man preached and now there is preaching[,] but I am writing to you[.] if we go to Kinston I will write as soon as we get there[.] I received a letter to day from Martha & Martin Nall[.] they are all well but Martins wound. I wrote two or three times to Aunt Patsey but she will not write to me[.] I will close my letter this time but I have not wrote half enough[.] I think you paid a big price to get your butter to Fayetteville[.] give my respects to all inquiring friends[.] I hope I shall get to come home again[.] I do want to come the worst in this world. write soon[.] I remain your son as ever[,] J.L. Stuart

Mr John Harper[.] sir[,] I received a few lines from you to day which gave me great pleasure to hear from you[.] I hope these lines will find you all well[.] I have no news of interest to write[.] Our regiment is ordered to Kinston[.] we may start to day[.] I do not know what is to do there[.] we only get one furlough to ever fifty men. Duncan Cole sendes his best respects to you and says when you write to me again to state how Henry Brewer family is[.] he sayes he cannot here from them[.] I must close[.] I remain your son as ever[,] J.L Stuart. give my respects to all inquiring friends[.] Do the best you can all of you[.] farewell. John L. Stuart

Bro Charles[,] I write you a few lines[.] I want to see you very bad[.] I wish I could a been at that big quilting[.] you must tell me who was your sweetheart at the quilting[.] I hope these lines will find you well[.] write to me ever chance[.] tell granny I want to see her very bad[.] tell her to do the best she can[.] I must close[.] J.L. Stuart Dear Sister[,] I write a few lines to you[.] I hope they will find you well[.] I was mity sorry to hear that you was so sick[.] I hope you will get better soon[.] I want to see you very bad but I cannot tell when I shall get to come home[.] When this you see[,] Remember me[.] your Brother as ever[,] J.L. Stuart

1863, November 7

Henry N. Tomlinson (*Point Lookout, MD*) to cousin **Bryan Tyson**. General wartime correspondence with brief mentions of **Henry C. Tyson** and **John M. Tomlinson.** [376]

Dear Cousin, It is with pleasure this eav that I hav the oppertunity of droping you a few lines to let you no where I am and my condition[.] I am a Prisoner of War at Point Lookout Md. desitute of money. If possible I should like to hav some assistance from you. having seen a pamphlet of which you were the another[,] I found out your address. When you write let me no if you hav hurd or sean anything of Brother John[.] I am informed that he taken the oath at Washington. H.N. Tomlinson, Co. H.[,] 5th Division. [P.S.] H.C. Tyson is at home wounded.

1863, November 10

Matthew Manis (*Point Lookout, MD*) to **Bryan Tyson**. General wartime correspondence with brief mentions of **Joseph Moore** and **William Brady**. [377]

Dear Friend, I am here a prisoner of war, and am nearly destitute of clothing. You will oblige me very much by sending me the following articles. viz 1 Coat. 1 Pr pants. 1 Pr. Drawers 1 overshirt. 1 Pr. socks. Also two or three dollars in U.S. Treasury notes. I will reciprocate in any monies at the earliest moment possible and thereby consider it a great favor. Please let me know what has become of Joseph Moore & Wm. Brady[.] Very Respectfully, Matthew Manis (care of Capt N. Patterson)

1863, November 14
Mastin C. Phillips (*Point Lookout, MD*) to **Bryan Tyson**. General wartime correspondence with brief mention of **Lewis Phillips**. [378]

Dear Sir, You will no doubt be surprised when you see & learn the object of this note. Necesity often compells us to do a many disagreiable things. I am under the necesity at this time of asking you or someone else for assistance. I have decided to ask you believing that you will assist me. I am suffering very much with Bronchitis & Rheumatism[.] I am without shoes socks and flannel underclothing and also without the means to procure them. no 8 Shoes will fit me. I am also need of a blanket as I have had but one light one. I mention the things I most need. I request that you or some of your friends will assist me in this my time of greatest need and the day is not far distant—I hope when I shall be able to repay you. I ask you Mr. Tyson besides what I have mentioned above send me some money and chewing tobaco. Remember me in these troubles and your name shall ever be held in greatful remembrance by your friend & humble Servant. Address Serg't M. C. Phillips prisoner of war[,] Company H[,] 7th Division[,] NC. Believing that you and your friends will assist me, I anxiously await your response. Your friend, M.C. Phillips [P.S.] Keep a bill of the things you send and I will pay all or my father Lewis Phillips will be disavowed here[.] have no fears on this point if you shall be paied.

1863, November 14
William Henry Patterson (*Camp near Brandy Station, VA*) to sister **Frances Anna V. Patterson**. General wartime correspondence between siblings with brief mentions of **Iver D. Patterson, C.O. Roberts** and **Daniel S. Blue.** [379]

Dear Sister Annie, Enclosed I send you to splendid pieces of music viz, Little Bessie and The Southern Girl's Song. The former is suited to the air of The Dying Carolinian which you have heard me sing frequently and the Ballard of which I left at home. The latter is suited to the air of the Bonnie Blue Flag and I consider it an excellent piece of composition. Dear Sister I am happy to inform you that I am in possession of uninterupted good health for which I fell thankful to our all wise Providen. I wrote to Pa last Wednesday and I hope he will receive it this week. We have fallen back from the Rappahannock and are now encamped on the Rapidan Near Orange C. H. We have a pretty place for camp. We have wood a plenty and an excellent spring of water. Dear Sister the Regt. is off on Picket duty but I did not go with them. I and C. O. Roberts of this company were left in camp to take care of the things that were left. Such as the cooking utensils, etc. Daniel S. Blue is in camp in about ¼ of a mile of our camp[.] he is dismounted and he and several others of the 63rd Regt. are on Prevost Guard at Orange Court House. It is thought that there will be a fight before long if the weather continues favorable. Wheather it will be on the Rapidan or on the Rappahannock near Fredericksburg depends entirely on the movements of the enemy. Our cavalry drove the yankee cavalry back yesterday in the direction of Culpeper. Annie I want you and Pa to write me regulary as I am always glad to get a letter from home. Your affectionate Bro. William Henry

1863, November 19
Matthew C. Yow to his wife **Nancy Catherine Albright Yow** and children. General wartime correspondence with brief mention of his daughter **Nancy Elizabeth Yow**, **Christopher Columbus Harrison**, brother **Simeon Jones Yow** and brothers-in-law **John E. Albright** and **Henry A. Albright.** [380]

Mrs Nancy C. Yow[.] Dear Wife[,] I am truly thankful that I am one time more permited to drop you a few lines to inform you that I am well at this present time and I do hop when this letter reaches you it may find you and my dear little children wel and harty. Catharine I receivd your letter of the 9 the 15. I did not rite when I got your letter. I had just rote one to you the same day before I got yours. I was so glad to here from you all. I was sorrow to here that little Nancy was so bad off with the toothache. I hav had a hard spel of the toothach my self. It is bad I no. Catharine you said that you was troubled so bad about me not geting enough to eat. I dont want you to think much about that. I can bear that. I dont mind it for myself as bad as I do for you and my little children. That is what greavs me so bad to think that you hav to giv so much for corn and I am here fiting for them that you get corn from as wel as for myself. It looks hard for them to charg you so much and if tha wold consider the case tha wold not do so. Our people has got two hard harted to do the thing that is rite. It looks hard and I dont think it is fair. You said that Columbus was plowing for you yet and he got along mity slow. I do hop you can get your wheat sowd. I am afraid that your ground is not in good fix to sow. Maby it will make some wheat. Catharine you said that you had 4 hogs up and I am afraid that you cant get corn to make them fat. It will be a pity to kil them half fat. I fear that you will hav to do it. May God help you to provide for our dear little children. O that I cold see them now. I do want to see you all so bad. May God bles you I pray. Catharine, Jones will be at home before this letter gets their if he has good luck. I hop he will get home safe. I cant tel you when I can come to see you again. I fear it will be a long time if ever. I hop that my life will be spard to get through this cruel war and get home again but it looks like a bad chanc now but I hop it will get beter soon. But the prospect looks vary gloomy at this time tho it may soon close. I hop it may. I fear we shal have a hard battle here yet and I fear it will be soon tho it may not be. I hop it may not. Catharine I dont no what to rite to you. I hav nothing good to rite. I want you to rite to me as often as you can and let me no how you are geting along. I rote to your father and I got no answer from him. I dont no why he dont rite to me. I hav not seen your brothers sinc the battle at Bristo. Tha are not far from here. We are on the Rappadan River yet and we shal sta here tel the Yankees makes some move. I am looking for a letter from you and father now. Tel Jones when he gets home to rite to me. So I will close for this time by saying I stil remain your affectionate husband tel death. So fairwell[,] my dear wife[.] Nancy C. Yow.

1863, November 20
Matthew C. Yow to his wife **Nancy Catherine Albright Yow** and children. General wartime correspondence with brief mention of his sister **Sarah Yow**, and father **Henry C. Yow.** [381]

Catharine[,] the mail come last night and no letter for me. I will send this off this morning. I hav no stamps to put on my letters but I hop you can pay the postag and if you want to here from me as bad as I want here from you you will pay it freely. Catharine I am wel this morning. I hop this may find you wel. Catharine I dream so much about being at home. I hop I will get home before long. I was with you all night last[.] I saw you and the children as plain as I ever did in my life but when I awakd I was not with you. I cant help but study about my dream. Matthew C. Yow to Nancy C. Yow May God bles you I pray. Catharine giv my lov to my brothers and sisters. You said that Sarah was vary bad off. I am sorrow to here that for I expect it is hard times with them now as wel as your self. Tel father that I will rite to him before long. I want him to rite to me as often as he can and giv me the news. From what I can here their is bad times in Moor County. Tha are hunting and eating up every thing. It is a bad chanc I think any how. So fairwell.

1863, November 20
Baxter C. Phillips *(Orange Courthouse, VA)* to sister **Emeline Phillips.** General wartime correspondence with brief mentions of **Mastin Phillips, Charles H. Phillips, Plyler** and **Richard Street**. [382]

Dear Sister, Yours came to hand two days since. I was glad to get it as it gave me information with regard to Mastin, as well as from home. The day after I received yours I got one from Mastin myself written October 24th. He was still in Washington City. He was well but knew nothing about when he could get back to us. He said he was kindly treated. This is better than I feared he would get. Try to be cheerful and pray to God for what ever, He will direct all things well and for our good. We are still here but I do not think we will stay here long. At least there is a chance for me to come South this winter. The enemy don't show much disposition to fight as yet. But then, I can't say how soon they may try us. If they do attack us here, I don't fear the result is we are led right. I wish I could be at home to See Uncle Charles and family. If they don't leave before this reaches you[,] remember me to them. My health is not very good but don't be uneasy about me. No news in camp now. Brother Plyler is going to conference. If you could see him, he could fetch me some things if you have anything ready for me, socks, shirts and drawers. Send me a jar of syrup if you can conveniently do so. My love to all at home. Tell Street to come and see me and fetch me just what you have ready for me. I am not [?] in as yet. Pray for me. Baxter Clegg Phillips

1863, November 20
J.L. Stuart (*Kinston, NC*) to sister **Mary A. Harper,** brother **Charles Harper,** stepfather **John Harper** and grandmother **Nancy Glass Nall**. General wartime correspondence. [383]

Miss Mary Ann Harper[.] Dear sister[,] I write you a few lines to inform you that I am well truly hoping these lines will reach and find you well[.] I want to see you very bad but I do not know when I shall get to see you[.] you must be a smart little girl and mind poore mother[.] and it may be your Brother will get to come home and see you again but it may that he never will but if I never do I will think I have a smart little sister at home[.] I would get my likeness takend for you but it cost fifteen Dollars and that is too much[.] I want to see you very bad and hope I will soon[.] you must give my best respects to all inquiring friend and relations and to all the pretty girls[.] I am in Kinston[.] me and some more men cutting and hauling wood for the government & I maid one Dollar and thirty cents extra to day[.] I will send you some more nice money as soon as I get some[.] tell mother not to think too much about me[.] I am fat and hearty and as well as I ever was[.] write to me ever chance[.] I must close my letter[.] When this you see[,] remember me Your Brother untell Death. J.L. Stuart to Mary Ann Harper

Dear Brother[,] I write you a few lines[.] I hope they will find you well[.] I want to see you very bad but I do not know when I shall get to see you. you must be a smart Boy and try to get a long the best you can[.] I hope I shall get to see you all again[.] you must tell me who your sweatheart is and write about your sprees[.] I am in Kinston but I do not have anything to say to any of the girls[.] give my respects to all the girls and to all my inquiring friends and write to me ever chance[.] When this you see[,] remember me[.] your Brother[,] J.L. Stuart

Mr John Harper[.] Dear stepfather[,] I seat myself to night to write you a few lines to inform you that I am well truly hoping these lines will find you well[.] you said you was mity busy but you are making money[.] I understand that all the bank notes are put down[.] if that is so some men are hurt[.] I want to see you very bad[.] you must do the best you can all of you[.] write to me ever chance[.] Dyrect your letters to Kinston N.C.[,] Co "D"[,] 49th regt[,] N.C.T.

A few lines to granny[,] I want to see you very bad you must do the best you can[.] I hope I shall get to see you again[.] I must bring my letter to a close[.] write to me ever change[.] yours[,] J.L. Stuart

1863, November 20
J.L. Stuart (*Kinston, NC*) to his mother **Mary A. Harper**. General wartime correspondence with brief mentions of **Kindred Muse, Eliza Jane Bethune Muse, Flora McLean Hunsucker** and **William W. Hunsucker**. [384]

Mrs. Mary A. Harper. Dear Mother[,] I write you a few lines this evening to inform you that I am well truly hoping these lines will reach you all as well as usua[.]l I received a letter from you last night dated the 16th[.] I was very glad to hear from you all[.] I am still in Kinston cutting wood[.] all is quite down here at this time[.] our regiment is still in camp in houses but I do not know how long we will stay here[.] I have no news to write at present more than K. Muse wife has been to see him and is gone back home and to day Wm Hunsuckers wife starts to see him[.] there are a good many women coming to the 49th[.] these times we get one pound and an eight of flour or corn meal a day and one lb of Beef and some potatoes. I want to see you all the worst in the world but I do not know when I shall get to see you but I sorter think I shall got to come home yet[.] give my best respects to all inquiring friends[.] do not trouble your self too much a bout me[.] I am making out very well[.] you need not send me no paper[.] I can get plenty there in Kinston[.] write to me ever chance[.] I will do the same[.] I have got thirty four Dollars[.] I can have my likeness taken for fifteen but that is too much. Dear Yours[,] J.L. Stuart

1863, November 24
William Henry Patterson (*Camp near Orange Courthouse, VA*) to sister **Frances Anna V. Patterson**. General wartime correspondence between siblings with brief mentions of **Iver D. Patterson, Isham Sheffield, Evander McLeod** and **McNeill.** [385]

Dear Sister, Your much esteemed favor of the 15th inst. was received last Saturday evening was a week ago enclosed in a letter from Pa. I was happy to learn that you were all in the enjoyment of good health and I sincerely hope when it reaches you that it will find you and all similarly blessed. Dear Sister, Before I proceed any further I will remark that I have nothing new of interest to write. We are still encamped near Orange Court House, the Regiment is off on Picket duty today[.] it left camp yesterday evening, though I did not go with it. I am on guard here in camp guarding a prisoner old Isham Sheffield of our company[.] he is kept under guard closely *until he is court martialed for desertion. The general opinion is that he will be shot he has deserted so often. We are faring pretty well at at this time. We have chimneys to our tents and bed clothing a plenty so we are living pretty comfortable. The winter has been very mild so far though I think it will certainly get colder in a few days. Everything sells very high about here. Writing paper sells at from 3 to 5 dollars per quire[,] apples from 2 to 4 dollars per dozen[,] Tobbacco $2 a plug etc. You seem to be some what surprised how Evander McLeod stays home so long. Evander told me when I was at home that he was off on furlough that he had the offer of a discharge but refused for fear that he would conscripted. As I was returning to my Regt. on the boat between Riverside and Wilmington[,] I fell in conversation with a Mr. McNeill a young man from Robeson County who belongs to the same company Evander did. He told me that Evander left on furlough when he came home first but when he returned last spring or summer that he had been away so long that his officers gave him a discharge. So he is now at home on a discharge passing off as a furloughed soldier to avoid conscription. All the boys from our section of country in this company are well. We are getting flour to eat all the time. I have not eaten any corn bread since I left home. We get beef nearly all the time. As I have nothing worth your attention I will close. Hoping to receive a letter from you or Pa this week[.] I wrote to Pa last week which I hope he will receive this. Your Afft. Bro. William H.*

1863, November 25

Henry C. Brown (*Point Lookout, MD*) to **Bryan Tyson**. General wartime correspondence with brief mention of **Lewis Phillips.** [386]

Dear friend[,] I take the pleasure of writing you this note to let you know that I am not well at present. as I have had the chills since I came here. Although I am getting some better: Mr Tyson as I am destitute of money[.] a dollar or two would be thankfully received of you. and it will be returned again if ever permitted to do so. please write as soon as this comes to hand address. So I remain your friend until death. Henry C. Brown.

1863, November 26

Alexander K. Pearce (*Old Capitol Prison*) to **Bryan Tyson**. General wartime correspondence with brief mention of growing support for the union, **Gov Holden, Spelman, Kelly Trogdon, Thomas Macon, John Maness, John Chriscoe, Reuben Pearce, Riley Needham, James Beck,** the death of **Alfred Pearce, James Tyson, Thomas Pearce** and **John Pearce.** [387]

I have written to you concerning affairs at hom but probly you hav not received it[.] I wil first commence on the union[.] Ther is more union in Randolph than ther was when the war commensed tho people cannot not have a fair hearing but I know the sentiments many[.] and probaly you have hearde of the Holden and Spelman affair which shows the union is not forgotten and all or nothing for the Yankees to come if they would go through N.C. I believe they would get more men than Davis has[.] ther ar many lying out to keep from fighting[.] Kelly Trogdlin is at hom in the woods, his father is a strong union man and every tim the union army whip[,] it make the union that much more increasing[.] about the tim of the Getysburg battle nearly all the people was union[.] if a man said he was union[,] his life was threated and nearly all the men was union[.] but ther was men sent from the army to quel this union sentiment[.] and then thes turn coats were cecesh but the good old union men stand firm[.] they believe the union wil reesstablese and they share a love for the stars and stripes[.] often hav I heard them say how butiful it would be to see the old flag once more floating in the air. I saw uncl Thos Macon the day I left. he is yet a union man a strong as ever lived[.] he and all his family has joined the friends on quakers and laid out of the service[.] he is union and wil die in this state so is John Maness, John Criscoe, uncle Reuben, Rily Needham, James Beck and many others I could tel[.] you need not be uneasy about the old man Macon for I know his opinion after did we meet and talks about the Times and I do love that old man[.] As for the publication of your book I never heard much[.] tell of them in the army as the authority would not let them pass through[.] therefor ther is not many that knows them but the people at hom was glad to get them[.] all the union people said that all was correct and every one would need them and try to convince others that you was right[,] but th strong cecesh would not believe them and would say you wer a traitor to your country[.] I left hom with the intention of joining the union for I did not believe that the rebellion was right nor I never did and my friends told me to leave the first chance I got[.] so the first chance I left[.] Alfred was killed at Sharpsburg sept 17th 1862[.] I was not ther and I never could see any one that saw him after his death[,] but the report was that he was killed and I [illegible] he was he had first been in the service two months[.] your brother James was wounded near

Manasses Junction[.] he was badly wounded[.] it was thought minor at first but he was fairly and geting well the last I heard from him[.] The prices of provision ar veary high corn is worth $8.00 per bus, flour $60.00 per bar, bacon $2.50 per pound, Whiskey & Brandy $50.00 per gallon an everything is veary high[.] if I could be with you som fun day[,] I could tel you many things and I have a bad chance to write up wher I am as ther are many in this room[.] but I expect to remain in th [illegible] until this war ends and I hope that can help us to get[.] John, father and family ar all well and doing as well[.]Times wil allow my father and family wer well when I left home. A.K. Pearce

1863, December
Matthew C. Yow (near Orange Courthouse, VA) to his wife **Nancy Catherine Albright Yow** and children. General wartime correspondence. [388]

Catharine[,] I hav no news of interest to rite to you only we hav got to our winter quarters at last. We hav built us huts to sta in and hav chimneys to them. We are about 3 miles east of Orang C H So I must close for this time. Write as often as you can. I stil remain your affectionate husband tel death. M. C. Yow to Nancy C. Yow

1863, December
Matthew C. Yow (*near Orange Courthouse, VA*) to his wife **Nancy Catherine Albright Yow** and children. General wartime correspondence with brief mentions of brother **Simeon Jones Yow** and **Isaac Yow**, **George Moore**, **John Williamson** and father **Henry C. Yow.** [389]

Tel Jones that I said not to come here[.] tel he ___ and well. I want to see him as bad as I can but I dont want him to come here tel he gets well. I praid to the good for him to recover and I do hop he will. Tel him for my sake not to forget to pray for himself. Catharine I am praing for you all and I hop that my prare will be herd. I do hop and pray that ___ soon be made but I ___ expect at this time for it ___ for it to come ___ Isaac I rote to ___ not answerd ___ hop that he has gone ___ Catharine I rote to you to ___ something when ___ me to eat if he can bring it. I want something from home. Wold eat so good to me. I do want to come to see you so bad but I cant tel when I can. Catharine giv my best respects to all my brothers and sisters and all my friends ___. If any tel them all that I hav not forgoten them yet. You said that the hunters had shot Georg Moore and John Williamson. I recon that some is glad that Georg is dead. I no their is bad times their now but I hop tha will not pester you non. Nothing that you hav got dont let no body cheat ___ of any thing that you ___. I hop that father will ___ and help you to ___. Catharine as soon as you can ___ me no how you are so I must close by saying I stil remain your husband tel death parts us. M. C. Yow Nancy C. Yow[.] Fairwell.

1863, December 18
J.L. Stuart (*Weldon, NC*) to his mother **Mary A. Harper** and stepfather **John Harper**. General wartime correspondence with brief mentions of **Calvin Reddin, Wyatt Williamson, William Riley Barrett, Capt. David S. Barrett, Capt. William M. Black**, brother **Charles Harper**, sister **Mary A. Harper** and grandmother **Nancy Nall**. [390]

Dear Mother, I embrace the oppertunity to write you a few lines to inform you that I am well truly hoping these few lines will come to hand and find you all as well as usual. I received your letter dated the 12th[.] I was mighty pleased to hear from you all[.] we are all in camp near Weldon[.] our Brigade is under marching orders[.] two hundred and fifty of our regiment is gone down about Franklin but I do not know what is up[.] I am at the Brige at Weldon guarding the Bridge[.] I do not know whether I shall go if the Brigade is going or not[.] if we are not relived we will not go if the Brigade does not go[.] I do not know whether our Brigade will go any where or not. I want to see you very bad but I cannot tell when I ever get to see you[.] Calvin Redding is gone home from our Co. he will go some where close to Shields' Mills[.] do the best you can all of you. you said you heard that Confederate navy was killed but I haven't heard anything about it. Wiatt Williamson was brought in this morning to Weldon and sent to the guard house and another one of our co with him. W.R. Barrett was Brought in also this week. Lt Barrett takend him out of the guard hour. Capt Black has a (illegible) and gone home. Lt Barrett will be captain[.] I have not more news to write[.] I should have written sooner but I was on guard and haven't had chance to write. write soon and I will write sooner next time. give my regards to all inquiring friends[.] tell

Charles, sis and granny I want to see them very bad[.] I wish I could be home at Christmas but I cannot[.] I must close this 18th December. your affectionate son as ever[,] J.L. Stuart

Mr. John Harper[,] offer my best respects and well wishes for you all. I can inform you that I am well truly hoping these lines will reach & find you all well. Congress has passed an act to Bring in all the men that have furnished substitutes. they will try to scare you but you must do the best you can[.] none is exempt from the war in the last act[.] Wiatt Williamsson was Brought to the guard house in Weldon today. write soon and let me know the times. I hope I shall live to come home again[.] Dyrect to Weldon as usual. J.L. Stuart

1863, December 21
J.L. Stuart (*Weldon, NC*) to his mother **Mary A. Harper**, stepfather **John Harper**, brother **Charles E. Harper,** sister **Mary A. Harper** and grandmother **Nancy Nall**. General wartime correspondence with brief mentions of **Levi Sheffield**. [391]

Dear mother[,] I write you a few lines by which you will learn that I am well truly hoping these few lines will reach and find you all well as usual. Our regt to come down below Frankling Va[.] they started yesterday morning[.] the 25th regt went also[.] the 35th regt is here with three dayes rations cooked but I heard that our regt is coming back this evening or tomorrow. there was two Negro regts and one white regt of yankees down there I heard[,] but I hear the yankees are falling back. I am at the Bridge yet I received a letter from you last week but answered. next Friday is Christmas. I wish I could be at home but I cannot. I saw Levi Sheffield today[.] he is well[.] I would give a good deal if I could be at home at Christmas but if you will only have to read the letter and not see me. give my respects to all inquiring friends and write to me ever chance. I am getting out of heart[.] mainly it looks like the war will not end soon. I hear no news from the west nor Lees army lately. give my love to all the family and write to me all of you[.] Dyrect your letters to Weldon and Co. "D[,] 49th regt[,] NCT[.] I have been at the Bridge eight days today[.] I missed going to Frankling Va[.] When this you receive[,] remember me. Your son as ever. John L. Stuart

Mr John Harper[.] Dear stepfather[,] I write you a few lines to inform you I am well truly hoping these lines will reach you & find you all well[.] we are in camp at Weldon[.] our regt and the 25th regt is gone down to Frankling Va[.] they went yesterday morning the 20. I understand will that Congress is trying to pass a law a bout bring all the able boddied men from 16 to 60 years of age and is being on all the men able that have furnished substitutes. if that is so[,] you may look out but do not get scard and volunteer. I hope you will not have to come. I suppose there has been about seventy thousand substitutes furnished in this war. write to me and give me the news and let me know the times & C write soon[.] yours as ever[,] J.L. Stuart

Dear Brother[,] I write you a few lines to inform you that I am well and hope these lines will reach & find you well[.] you must have a good time at Christmas[.] I wish I could be at home then[.] you must write to me and let me know what kind of time you have at Christmas. Dear sis & granny[,] my love and write to me all of you[.] I must close my letter by asking you to write soon[.] When this you get[,] remember me[.] your Brother as ever[,] J.L. Stuart To C E Harper

1863, December 21
William Henry Patterson (*Camp near Orange Courthouse, VA*) to sister **Frances Anna V. Patterson**. General wartime correspondence between siblings with brief mentions of **Iver D. Patterson** and **James N. Caddell.** [392]

Dear Sister – Your letter was received in due time enclosed in one I received from Pa[.] I was Much gratified to receive letters from home and to learn that you were all in the enjoyment of good health. These few lines leave me in possession of usual health; I was very unwell for 8 or 10 days sometime ago and I was fearful that I was about to have another hard spell of sickness but I guess it was nothing more than a bad cold[.] I have got all right again. We have very cold weather for a few days. I expect we will suffer with cold over here in Va. this winter. It is so far North that it is a great deal colder here than in N. C. We had a very disagreeable time last thursday night. We were off on picket on the Rapidan and I beleive it was about as disagreeable a night as I ever was out. The rain fell in torrents and we stood out and took it like good fellows without any shelter at all. We have pretty good tents and chimneys to them but we have not got enough of them. They are too much crowded to have a good chance at the fire in the cold weather. I would like very much to be at home so I could get some thing good to eat[.] I have eaten beef and flour bread till I dont beleive I could look a cow straight in the face though I would rather have beef than old fat bacon. I begin to want some butter milk and potatoes very much. Dear Sister I want you to make me a heavy pair of socks. Perhaps you may have a chance of sending them to me by the time I will need them[.] I do not need them now but I will before the winter is over. Perhaps Jas N. Caddell or some of those that are off will be returning to the company after a while and you may have a chance of sending them. Write to me on the receipt of these few lines & give me all the news you have. Your affectionate Bro. William Henry P. It is said that we will move to a new camp in a day or two.

1863, December 30
Baxter C. Phillips *(Orange Courthouse, VA)* to unidentified friend. General wartime letter. [393]

My dear friend, Yours reached me two days since. I would have written sooner but had to go on picket which worsted me considerably. But I feel better this morning but am not well nor don't expect to be any more while in the army. I am reduced in flesh and very weak, yet I keep up all the time or nearly so yet you need give no uneasiness about me yet. We have had some very cold weather but it is not so cold now. We are doing picket every two days but expect to be relieved soon and some others will take our place. I think active operations are over here for this winter. At least, they ought to be for this army is in bad fix now. We are in worse condition than ever I saw it in my life. We don't have meat more than half the time and that sometimes one fourth to one fifth rations. This looks very much like the thing is, but we can survive a defeat better than this. I don't think we are gaining much now. Should this not teach us humility, lead us to repentence and newness of life? Things, in my opinion, bear an alarming aspect. May God save us from what now threatens us. I hope you will not be interrupted again by your adversaries and that they may be unable to blind things by falsehood, but that they may be brought to justice and made to acknowledge their evil designs. For if I know the men, they are doing our country no good at all when it needs their aid. There is nothing here worth writing now. I would like very much to see you but there is no chance unless you can come to see me for which I wish you would do if you can for I don't expect to get a furlough in twelve months under the present mode of furloughing. I'm in low spirits now, not well, and by all the girls turned off, forlorn in this respect. I think I will brush all females from my mind and turn my attention to something else[.] Give my love to all the family and don't forget to answer this. I trust to see you all again. May God bless you all is the prayer of your friend. Baxter

1864, January 3
J.L. Stuart (*Weldon, NC*) to his brother **Charles E. Harper**. General wartime correspondence with brief mention **Martha Teague.** [394]

Mr C. E. Harper[.] Dear Brother[,] I write to you a few lines by which you may learn that I am well truly hoping they will reach you and find you well. I want to hear from you and your Christmas spree. You write to me and tell me what fun times you had at Christmas and tell me what your girls names is and tell me how all the girls are getting along and if they want to see the dirty soldiers coming home and if they have forgotten us. I hear that you are having what is called snow storms in Moore County, I wish I could be at some of them kind of parties. I hear the girls and boys all go at night to some mans house and frolic until that all got tired. You must write ma a good long letter and tell me about your times. Tell Martha Teague that she owes me a letter[,] that I wrote to her since I received any letter from her. I received one from her when we was a Kinston and answered it. Tell everybody you see that they all owe me a letter for I have wrote to them all last. I must close my letter[,] hoping to get a long one from you soon. When this you see[,] remember your Brother until Death[.] J.L. Stuart

1864, January 4
Doctor Franklin Wilkie *(Orange Courthouse, VA)* to Rev. **Lewis Phillips Jr.** General wartime correspondence with brief mentions of **Mastin Phillips, Baxter Phillips, Nancy Phillips, Candace Phillips Street** and **Richard Street**. [395]

Dear Friend, Sitting and thinking of the happy and pleasant moments that I have spent in your dwelling and think of times at present. But it is enough, may it all be for the best. I am well at the present time and enjoy myself as well as could be expected. I truly hope these few lines may find you al in perfect health. I have but little to communicate at the present. We have gone in our winter quarters. We are four miles south of Orange Courthouse. We have some snow at this time, but the weather is a good deal warmer than it has been. Times seem quiet out here. I have not seen Baxter in some time as our camps are some distance apart. His brigade is on pickett. We will take their place soon. I suppose that Mastin is still in the hands of the Yankees. I hear from our boys that some of them are treated very badly. I wish that they could all get back. We have lost a good many of our regiment since he has been taken. Our rashions are tolerable good except rations of meat. It is some smaller than it has been. The most of us are very well prepared for winter. There are giving a good many furloughs at this time. I will get one after a while if I live. The health of the Company is very good. We have forty men present for duty. Mr. Phillips, it is a shame to see what we have to pay for everything here, but we have to live. I can't tell what is to become of us all. We will have to do the best we can and I am afraid that will be bad. I reckon I had better close unless I had something new to write. Remember my love to Mrs. Phillips and family and also to Mr. Street and wife. Write to me for I like to hear from my old friends. This from your friend, D. F. Wilkie

1864, January 5
Matthew C. Yow to his wife **Nancy Catherine Albright Yow** and children. General wartime correspondence with brief mentions of **Mrs. Pool** and son **Willian Henry Yow.** [396]

Dear Wife and Little Children[,] I one time more seat my self to drop you a few lines which will inform you that I am as well as I cold expect for what I hav bin through with. I was on picket the first day of January and it was the coldest day that I ever saw. I thought I should freez but I did not quite. Catharine I do hop when this reaches you it may find you all well. I am going to send this by __ Pool. I will send Henry 14 buttons and you a half pound of soda. She said that she would go to see you and tel you that she seed me. Catharine I wanted to send you somthing but I did not no what elc to send to you. I paid two dollars and 50 cents for the soda and one dollar for the buttons. The wether is vary cold. It is snowing now and it looks like we shal all freez. Catharine tha hav a new post offic at Richmond and I will tel you how to direct your letters Matthew C. Yow[,] Co D[,] 48 Regiment[,] N C Troops[,] Cooks Brigade[,] A N VA. This means the Army of Northern Virginia. Tha say that the letters will come quicker and better to us. Catharine I am riting this to send by Mrs. Pool. I dont no when she will leav here. I thought I wold rite to day. I may be off on picket when she leaves. I am looking for a letter from you and father now. It has bin snowing all day. I fear tha will be a deep snow here and it will be a bad chanc here. Wood is so scearc here. Catharine I study a heep about you. This wether may God help to get along and hav good luck. I no you see hard times and I am so sorrow for you. May God bles you all is my prare. So fairwell[.] Nancy C. Yow

1864, January 10
William Henry Patterson (*Camp near Orange Courthouse, VA*) to father **Iver D. Patterson**. General wartime correspondence with brief mentions of **Capt. James D. McIver** and **Tyson.** [397]

*My Dear Father, I avail myself of the present opportunity of communicating a few lines to you to inform you that I am well and I sincerely hope that these few lines may find you enjoying good health. I wrote a letter to you on the 6th Inst. and one to Ann on the 8th. I wrote to you that Capt. McIver had sent up an application for a furlough[.] his furlough came back approved and he will start in the morning. I wrote you that I wanted you to try and fix me up some sort of a pair of shoes and convey them to Carthage and leave them with Mr. Tyson & McIver will bring them. I think that the shoes you brought me at Hanover Junction would probably last me until I get some[.] if you have good leather to half sole them. Dear Father I wrote you in my last that I would probably send you the necessary papers to procure my state bounty. I was under a mistake about the bounty due me[.] it is the Confederate instead of the state bounty that is due me, and I can get that here when the company is paid off which will be in a few days. So I'm in hopes I will get my bounty at last. It is getting late and I have a dim light so I will close for this time but will write again this week[.] all the boys are well. We are faring pretty well now.
In haste your aft. Son[,] W. H. Patterson*

1864, January 11
Thomas Needham (*Point Lookout, MD*) to **Bryan Tyson**. General wartime correspondence with brief mentions of **William K. Nunnery.** [398]

Dear friend[,] I take my pen in hand to let you know that I am well & I rot a few lines to you in W. Nunnery letter but I never heard from you but I received a book from you an all[.] so W.K. received a book an I heard that he received a letter but I not certain of it[.] Mr Tyson you know we hafe all was ben nabors an you know mee an I want you to rite to me as soon as this comes to hand an giv mee your advise[.] I want to git out of this ware an I sentenctoo for some turmes[.] I am hear an cant git chewinng tobacco[.] Mr Tyson I hav read your book well an I find it troo[.] I would rote to you But I could not git a stamp[.] W.K. Nunery has got the Small pox[.] he has ben gon to the hospittal some time[.] I haf not heard from them sens he lef hear[.] I woud bea glad of you cood help mee to a few dollars[.] it will bea a favear that will never bea forgoten an moor that I will make it all rite with you[.] Rite as soon as this comes to hand[.] Back you letters to the Division Co I.T Needham. Your respect frind, Thomas Needham

1864, January 11
Henry C. Brown (*Point Lookout, MD*) to **Bryan Tyson**. General wartime correspondence with brief mentions of **Wright** and **William K. Nunnery**. [399]

Dear Sir, I received yours of the 21st of Dec last evening wich contain one dollar enclosed in it an was more than oblige to you for the same but I did not received the books or pamphlet. but as soon as I received them I will send them on to the same persons. you also stated that you sent a letter to Wright & Nunnery. I never knew any of it until last evening[.] I enquired if they had received it and they said they had. the most of the boys are in tolerable good health except Nunnery[.] he has gone to the Hospital with the small pox. I am getting very tired of this unjust and cruel war. please send me a pocket bible as I have none. So no more[.] write soon so I remain your friend until Death[.] Your Truly[,] H.C. Brown

1864, January 16
Alexander K. Pearce (*Old Capitol Prison*) to **Bryan Tyson**. General wartime correspondence with brief mention of **John Pearce**. [400]

Dear sir[,] I am yet in prison but think we will leave before long[.] I am veary anxious to lave this place[.] I received the artickles you sent me[.] I hope I shall be with you before long[.] I have not received any letters from John yet – write soon and give me as much information as you can. Very Respectfully Yours, A.K. Pearce P.S. I want some cloths. I find some friend in this land of strangers[.]

1864, January 16
Horace A. Bridges (*Point Lookout, MD*) to **Bryan Tyson**. General wartime correspondence.[401]

Dear Friend, it is with pleasure that I embrace the presente opportunity of writing you a few lines to let you here from me[.] my health is very good at the time and truley hoping these few lines may reach you and find you well[.] I would like to bee with you very much[.] I saw you at Washington but did not have the chance to speak to you tho I hope I shall have the chance of seeing you again[.] you wanted to no the principals of som of men[.] I can tell you for myself their no Secinestenes about me[.] if I can get out as a citizen I will do it for I am tyard of the war[.] I would like to have som assisteance if you pleas and oblige your friend[.] I want you to write to me as soon as you get these few lines and let me here from you[.] no more at presente, youres truly, H.A. Bridges

1864, January 16
Matthew C. Yow to his wife **Nancy Catherine Albright Yow** and children. General wartime correspondence with brief mentions of sons **John Matthew Yow, Joseph Gibbs Yow** and **Willian Henry Yow, James Hunsucker, William Nicholas Brower, Dorcas Maness Yow, Stephen M. Carter, Reuben Maness, Christopher Columbus Harrison** and **Eli N. Moffitt.** [402]

Dear Wife and Little Children[,] I do thank the Lord that I am one time more permited to drop you a few lines which will inform you that I am well and I do hop and trust when this reaches you it may find you all well and harty. Catharine I receivd your vary welcom letter last night the 15 that you rote the 6. It has bin a long time on the way. I was so glad to here from you for it had bin a long time sinc I had a letter from you. I was vary sorrow to here that little John was sick. I do hop that he is not dangerous. Catharine you said that you see so much trouble. I no it is hard to bear but try to bear it the best you can. I hav rote several letters to you that I hav not herd from. I sent 50 cents in one to Henry and 50 cent bills and some stamps for another to you and I fear you did not get them as you do not mention them. Catharine, James Hunsucker came back last night and he told a big tail. He told me that W. N. Brower told him that Dorcas went to Carters and she was bearfooted and she told Carter that she did not hav any bred in the hous and he said Matthews family was in the same fix. I told him that was a lie or you did not write the truth to me and I did not think that you wold do that. But I did not thank him for his news for I did not believ that was so. Catharine I hav sent you some money this morning by Mr Reubin Maness. I expect you will get the money before this letter comes to hand. Catharine I sent you 10 dollars. I cold hav sent you some moore but I may need it here. I think I shal get to come to see you this spring. There is 4 men gon from our company now. You said that Joseph sais he wants papy to come home. Pore little children. When I red that the tears dropt from my eys. Catharine I am sorrow to here that you had such bad luck with your cows. I am afraid that you cant get feed for them this winter. Do the best you can. You said that Columbus was haling hay. Then I do hop you can get feed. You said that Moffit said he cold not let you hav corn much longer. I do hop you can get corn some where. I thought that W. N. Brower was going to let you hav corn. I hav rote to him and I recon he is ashamed to rite to me sinc he told you about the corn and bread. I hop the good Lord will help you so no more at present. M. C. Yow to Nancy C. Yow

1864, January 17
J.L. Stuart (Weldon, NC) to his mother **Mary A. Harper**. General wartime correspondence with brief mentions of the death of his grandmother **Nancy Nall, Barrett** and **Nicholas Nall.** [403]

Dear Mother[,] I write you a few line to inform you that I am well truly hoping these lines will come safe to hand and find you all well[.] I receive yours of the day of the 13th[,] you stating Grandmother was dead. I hardly know what to say[.] first I was very sorry indeed to hear of her death[.] if I could have come home[,] I would have done it[.] I went to the Col but he would not let me go. Lt. Barrett would a let me a went if the Col. Would. I let him read my letter and I think he was sorry for me. I looked for a letter all the well and when it came today I was afraid to open it and so the sad news was in it. I wanted to see poor old granny once more but she is gone I hope to heaven where there will be no war no hurting of friends[.] you said she was willing to die[.] I was glad to hear it. Oh mother I feel mity sad this evening no one to tell my troubles to and nowhere to go and away from home and friends[.] you said no news[.] say love from all to me very lonesome at home. I know you are. I wish I could be at home to night but we must hope for the better days to come[.] it may all be for the best not our will be done but Gods who rules the heaven and earth[.] you said no one of Nick's folks at the burying. I was surprised to hear it for they did not live only four miles and I am am over two hundred and I would have come if they would have given me leav. if I would have started back in two hours. It was last sunday that I received the letter stating she was so hard off and I went to the Col. and he said I could not go for nothing[,] only to see a sick wife[,] but a man has to take a good deal here for Grandmother when I heard that she was dead. Say must thou conscious of the tears I shed knowing thy spirits over thy grandson. I wretch even these lives of sorrows just being perhaps thou gavest me though unfelt a kiss. Perhaps a tear if I could can reach in bliss. Oh that maternal smile is answering yes. J.L. Stuart. Mother cheer up and do not greave yourself too much. Do not badger yourself more than you can help[.] perhaps I will get to come home some time and see you all write soon J.L. Stuart

1864, January 18
J.L. Stuart (*Weldon, NC*) to his mother **Mary A. Harper** and stepfather **John Harper**. General wartime correspondence with brief mentions of **David S. Barrett**, **Alexander M. Fry**, **Neill B. Caddell**, **Jordan,** his brother **Charles E. Harper** and sister **Mary Ann Harper.** [404]

Dear Mother[,] I am well truly hoping these lines will find you all as well as usual[.] I want to see you all very bad but there is no chance for me to come home. Lt D.S. Barrett and orderly sergeant A.M. Fry is gone home to get recruits[.] all them that have furnished substitutes from the age of 18 to 45 has to come out. N.B. Caddell is also gone home on furlough and Jordan the officers cook is gone also. there is no mess here[.] only one man gets to go ever hundred in Lees army[.] eight men out of ever hundred goes home on furlough[.] give my respects to all[.] write soon[,] J.L. Stuart

Mr Harper[,] after my best respects to you I can inform you that I am well and hope these lines will find you well[.] I have no news[.] I hear that they will get you into the war but you must stay at home as long as you can[.] write to me and let me Know how you are all getting along ever chance[.] I have got sixty Dollars[.] we was paid off the other day[.] I would send you some paper if I could[.] this paper cost two Dollars a quire[.] I have plenty of it[.] tell Charles to write to me[.] tell sis I sent her a ten cent shinplaster[.] write soon all of you[.] J.L. Stuart to J Harper and family 1864

1864, January 19
William Henry Patterson (*Camp near Orange Courthouse, VA*) to sister **Frances Anna V. Patterson**. General wartime correspondence between siblings with brief mentions of **Iver D. Patterson, A. McNair, Archibald Hayes, Malcolm McNeill, Rev. J.C. Sinclair, Nancy Johnson, Nancy McLeod, John W. Graham** and **Charles Washington Shaw.** [405]

Dear Sister Annie – Your letter of the 10th Inst. was received on the 17th[,] also one from Pa enclosed with yours. I seat myself to drop you a few lines in response to your kind letter. These few lines leave me in the enjoyment of toberably good health. I have diarrhea pretty badly today but that is a very common thing in camp. I have no news of interest to write. The health of the company is pretty good at this time. We have had very much duty to perform since we have been at this camp. It is said that our Brigade will have to go over the Rapidan on Picket this week. I do not like the idea of leaving our comfortable quaters to go over there where wood is so scarce. It is some 5 or 6 miles from here to where we will have to go. I received the socks you made for me by A. McNair. I am very much obliged to you for them they are very good socks though they are rather large. I got a sort of a pair of shoes the other day but they are very poor shoes[.] they are full small for me but they are better than no shoes[.] perhaps they will last till I get shoes. I have been nearly without shoes for a good while. I suppose there another party at Arch'd Hays also one at Malcom McNeills. I guess there were few boys at either of them for there are but very few in that section of the county. I do not know where they could start young men enough to have a party. I learn that Rev. J. C. Sinclair and Mrs. Nancy Johnson are married[.] I also understand that Mrs. Nancy McLeod is about to get married to a widower from Chatham County who has 8 children; Hurrah for the widow and widower I say. I hear that John W. Graham has an idea facing the hymenial alter. I am some what surprised at John if it be true. I recd. a letter from him some time before Christmas and I have been looking for another letter from him for a few days. Dear Sister, We are getting very slim rations at this time. We have had but very little meat in about 2 weeks. We are getting some lard and a little sugar and coffee and a little rice but we do not get much of either. I would like very much to get a box of provisions from home if it were possible but I know of no chance at the present. C. W. Shaw expects to get a furlough in 8 or 10 days and if he does[,] perhaps he will bring some things for me. I would like very much to be at home a short time but it is useless to talk of going home it is impossible so I will try and content myself as well as I can. I beleive I enjoy myself about as well as any of the boys in camp. We have had a very cold winter and several snows but no very deep ones, we had a good deal of rain yesterday and the roads are in very bad condition. It has quit raining and it is turning cold very fast. I am in hopes that it will not be as cold any more this winter as it has been. You said in your letter that you had made some flannel to make me a shirt and pair of drawers, I beleive I have clothes enough to do me this winter and it is bad policy to have more clothes in camp than I can carry. I will close as my sheet is exhausted. Your Afft. Bro. W. Henry Patterson

1864, January 21
J.L. Stuart (*Goldsboro, NC*) to his mother **Mary A. Harper**. General wartime correspondence with brief mentions of sister **Mary A. Harper, Duncan Cole** and **John Tucker**. [406]

Mrs Mary A Harper[.] Dear Mother[,] I write to you a few lines this morning to inform you that I am well truly hoping these few lines will come to hand and find you all well as usual. We landed here at Goldsboro last night at 8 oclock. at one oclock yesterday morning we got orders to be ready to march By five A.M. I do not know how long we will stay here or which way we will go[,] some say to Kenansville and some say to Kinston[.] it is thought we are going to get forge down below our lines[.] only time will show us. We have some as pleasant weather now as April & May[.] we left very good quarters at Weldon. The 25th regt is ready now to start to Kinston so I must stop writing[.] we will leave soon[.] I will write again as soon as we get settled down in camp. Direct your letters to Kinston NC[,] care Lt Barrett[,] Co. D[,] 49th NC[,] G Ransoms Brigade[.] put the Brigade on the letter. tell sis and all the family I want to see them all very bad[.] write all of you[.] I wish you could hear our Brass bands. J.L.

Stuart. Some say the yankees are going to try Kinston and some say Wilmington[.] it is thought we will have some fighting in E.N.C. this Spring[.] we do not know the meaning of any of the moves until after it is completed. I want to see you all very bad[.] the last letter I received from you was to day as a week ago[.] Duncan Cole has sent up a furlough but it has not come back yet[.] the co is generally well[.] I do not know where to tell you to Direct too but to Goldsboro I reckon[.] I must close my letter[.] write soon and excuse my short letter[.] give my respects to all. J.L. Stuart

I have heard since writing we will go to Kinston[.] at any rate the order has come around that we will go to Kinston between this and morning so Direct your letters to Kinston N.C. the 56th regt marched by us from hunting in your part of the county but I have not said anything to them[.] they came from Raleigh this morning. I saw John Tucker this morning[.] he is well and looks the best you ever saw him and has got a heavy set of whiskers. there is something to be done below[.] there was a VA Brigade went on to Kinston this morning and we will go tonight. Monday 1st February[.] left at two A.M. being in line of Battle the over night and we went in two miles of the city here[.] we found the yankee pickets and we sent out our skirmishers and Killed one and captured five and advanced our skirmishers within three hundred yards of the Yankee Block house which contains a few rifle cannons[.] and we sent 4 pieces of Artillery and tried the Yankees[.] as soon as our men opend on them[,] they replied to them and wounded two Artillerymen and one Lt in the 24th regt and two Private and I learn one Died[.] our Artillery was brought out that evening and we remained in line of Battle all night with out any fire scarcely[.] mid morning at four oclock A.M. our company was sent out in front to relieve them that staid out all night and we staid out until Dark Tuesday evening. the most of our fellows had eat all their rations and had nothing to eat. I eat about 2 ounces of cold corn Bread that day[.] the yankees threw several shells and sollid Balls at us when ever they could see a man[.] we would listen for the shell was shore to come but one lay pretty low[.] I tell you for we could not shoot at them for we was too far off and we had to remain there for fear they would come out at Dark[.] we was brought out and found that our troop was falling back[.] I tell you I was relieved the most you ever saw for we thought we would have to charge the city but our Generals found it was too strongly fortified[.] so we fell back about fifteen miles that night over the muddiest road you ever saw[.] the mud was Knee deep all the way and it was dark but I traveled it very well[.] our company and about nine others was rear guard but the yankees did not follow us[.] if the had I would have shot at them all I could[.] so we came in about fifteen miles of Kinston and the next Day came to Kinston and left there last night and landed here this morning[.] the men that went down the Neuse road captured four or five hundred Prisoners and all there comp Baggage commissary and sutlerstores and Killed several[.] we lost on our side about thirty five killed and wounded[.] our men had three companies of Mariners that went down the river in small boats and captured one gun boat and burnt the boat up[.] as we went out on picket Tuesday morning[,] we saw the light of boat and heard the noise of...[letter cut off after]

1864, January 27

Matthew C. Yow to his wife **Nancy Catherine Albright Yow** and children. General wartime correspondence with brief mentions of **Reuben Maness, Mrs. Pool, John Crisco,** sons **Joseph Gibbs Yow** and **John Matthew Yow,** brother **Simeon Jones Yow,** father **Henry C. Yow,** uncle **John Henry Stutts, Dr. John Shaw** and father-in-law **Joseph Albright.** [407]

Mrs Nancy C. Yow[.] Dear wife[,] Through the mercies of our heavenly father I am one time moore permited to drop you a few lines which will inform you that I am well at this present time truly hoping when this reaches you it may find you and the dear little children all well and harty. You said in your letter which I receivd the 25 that you rote the 20 that the children had vary bad colds. That is vary common here. I hop that the dear little children will get well before this comes to hand. Catharine I am glad to here that you got the money that I sent by Reubin Maness and the soda that I sent by Mrs Pool. She told that she wold go to see you and take the things to you and I suppose she did and she told you that I was so fat and pretty. I am vary fleshy now and I feel well and I am vary harty. But I cant get enough to eat here. But it may be the best for me not to hav enough to eat here. Catharine I never saw so many baskets as come here now. Tha come by the hundreds from home to the soldiers. But you liv so far from the railrode that you cant send me any thing to eat. Catharine, Big John Crisco came to see me yesterday. It supprised me to see him here. I thought I wold this letter by him but I was on gard and did not hav the chanc to rite. Catharine I come in time to see a bad site. Their was a man shot here yesterday. He belong to the 48 Regiment Co. K from Forsyth County and their will be 3 shot next Saturday. Tha belong to the 46 N C Regiment. If I liv tel then[,] I shal hav to see them shot and it is a bad looking sight to see. Men had beter not runaway than to hav to be shot to death. I dont want my brothers to sta at home after their furlows are out or tha cant get them extended any longer. If tha do tha will be taken up in Richmond. Every man that come through there and his furlow is out tha take him up. I am looking for 3 letters from Jones and I think that I will soon. We haint movd from this camp yet. I suppose we will next week if nothing happens. Catharine you said that little Joseph wants his pap to come home so he can sit in his lap. Bles his dear little soul. I do want to see you all so bad. Father said in his letter that little John M. has bin sick and he went to see Doctor Shaw and paid one dollar for medicine for him. Catharine you said that you were going to send me something good to eat by Jones when he comes. I wold be more than glad to get something to eat from him if you can spare it without taking somthing from the children that tha need and I dont want you to do that. I do want to get to come home and eat some good food with you and Betsy. I expect you both hav some that is good. Catharine we hav nice wether here now. For the last 4 days it looks like spring. I told Uncle John today that you was planting your onions and peas if the wether was as pretty there as it is here. I no it cant sta so here long in these mountains. You said that you wanted me to come home to see your new garden. I will if I can and I hop I will get to come in March or April if not before. Catharine I do want to see you. It has bin most 7 months sinc I saw you. Lord send that happy time when we shal meet again. Some times I cant think that this war can last much longer but if it does last tel next summer[,] their will be the hardest fiting don that ever has bin don yet. But I do hop and pray that it will be stopt by March. If it dont we will all perish here and at home two. Catharine you said that your father was mistaken when he rote to me that you was in good hart. I new that wold not do. He allways tries to incourage me. I rote him a plain letter. I dont no what he will think and I dont much care. I dont like to here men speak up for this cruel war when I no that it is not just or I dont think it is. Catharine you never told whither Columbus was going to make a crop for you or not. I rote to you to let him in at his offer. You said that he wold work for one third of the crop and I expect that is the best chanc you will get. Let me no in your next letter. In conclusion I will to you to pray for me. I stil remain your affectionate husband tel death. Matthew C. Yow to Nancy C. Yow

1864, February 2
William Henry Patterson (*Camp near Orange Courthouse, VA*) to sister **Frances Anna V. Patterson**. General wartime correspondence between siblings with brief mentions of **William Stutts, Capt. Kryle, Gen. Hoke, Rev. Lacy, Capt. James D. McIver, Roberts, Iver D. Patterson, William P. Blue, Gen. Lee** and **Stephen W. Brewer.** [408]

My Dear Sister, I seat myself this morning to write you a few lines to let you know that I am well and I sincerely hope there few lines will find you enjoying a similar blessing. Dear Sister, on yesterday I witnessed a sight that was anything but pleasant[.] it was the execution of 2 men for desertion they belong to Co B – 52nd Regt.(Capt. Kryle's Company)[.] One of them was Willie Stutts of Randolph County, N. C. he deserted his company while at Magnolia last winter. The other deserted at or near Hookerton last April[.] I do not know his name[.] they were apprehended by Genl. Hoke last fall. It was an awful sight[.] they were brought out tied, and marched behind their coffins infront of the whole Brigade & then they were marched up to the stakes & tied to them and after prayer by Rev. Mr. Lacy (Chaplain of the 47th Regt.) the men who were about to shoot them were formed in front of them & fired[.] Stutts was not killed the first volley & some of the men had to reload, and one of them stepped up near him and placed his gun within a few inches of his breast and fired which soon put an end to his suffering. I have seen 3 men shot for desertion since I left home & have no desire to see another. Three was shot near the place where these men were one day last week but I did not see it done. He belonged to Davis' Brigade[.] they were all buried near where they were shot. Capt. McIver has not got back & Roberts went off together[.] their time was out last friday night[.] I am looking for them every day[.] I hope Capt. McIver will bring the shoes that Pa made for me as the trifling shoes I know will not last much longer. William P. Blue's furlong has been sent up to Genl. Lee. Wm will get off by the last of the week if everything works well, he will start when Stephen W. Brewer gets back[.] his time will out in a day or two. I would be very glad to get some provisions when Wm. comes back if he will bring a box or boxes. I have not said anything to him about it yet but will before he leaves[.] he will reach home as soon as this letter I guess. Dear Sister[,] if they continue granting furloughs at the rate they are now I will get home in April if I live[.] there are some 8 or 10 to go before me. We will leave this camp tomorrow & go over the Rapidan on picket[.] we will on picket duty 40 days. Write soon. Your afft. Bro. W. Henry

1864, February 5
Mastin C. Phillips (*Point Lookout, MD*) to **Bryan Tyson**. General wartime correspondence with brief mention of **Lewis Phillips**.[409]

Dear Sir[,] The object of this note is to inform you that I am in need of some money and to ask you to furnish me with some. I am in actual need of twelve or fifteen Dollars, but the smallest sum will be most thankfully received. If you can let me have some[,] I will acquaint my father Lewis Phillips with the fact and if I do note live to pay you, all that you will have to do will be to present your account to him. I hope that you will respond soon as convenient to this, and send me some money. I am kindly treated here, I am also done fighting in this war. I pray only for the end to come. Address Sergt. M.C. Phillips Prisoner of war[,] Co. H[,] 7th Division[,] Point Lookout Maryland[,] Care of Capt. Patterson[.] Truly yours[,] M.C.Phillips

1864, February 5
J.L. Stuart (*Kinston, NC*) to his mother **Mary A. Harper**. General wartime correspondence with brief mention of **Duncan Cole.** [410]

Dear Mother[,] I write you a few lines by which you will learn that I am well and hearty except being weary of Campaign[,] hoping these few lines will find you all well[.] we landed back to this place yesterday from Newbern[.] we went down on the south side of the Trent River[.] the Distance from Kinston to Newbern is 47 miles[.] the way we went we went in one mile of the Town and captured five yankees and Killed one that was on picket and takend five negros[.] we was orderd by the commanding gen to charge the Town but our general that was with us said it could not be done for there was two Bridges to cross and three Batteries to take[.] I have no time to write the whole affair[.] this time we are cooking rations and waiting for the train to go to Weldon. on monday at four oclock A. M. co "D was sent out on picket and we staid untell 7 P.M. when we fell back to where we left our regiment and they had fell Back[.] so we marched about 10 or 15 miles that night through mud Knee deep all the way[.] I never have saw such muddy roads in all my life and some of our men had not eat any thing that day[.] I eat about two ounces of cold corn Bread so we was on picket and marching togeather 24 hours[.] I could not help but laugh monday night to see the men fall down in the mud[.] the yankees threw several shells at us while we was on picket but did not hurt any of our Brigade[.] on sunday two of the 24 regt was wounded while on picket[.] Duncan Cole is well and none of the company was hurt on the Neuse river[.] our forces captured about 500 yankees and two gun boats and all the yankee Baggage and stores and 20,000 lbs Bacon. I heard we had one Col. killed and one private belonging to the 8th N.C.T and thirty wounded five mortally[.] some of the men that was captured was some o of our men that Deserted and takend armes against us[.] two of them was hung here today[.] as I have no time I will close[.] I received a letter from you here last Friday here as we started down[.] we will go to Weldon as soon as the trains comes[.] mother I reckon I am not thankful enough that I a live[.] I Know you will be pleased to hear I did not get hurt[.] J.L. Stuart

1864, February 7
J.L. Stuart (*Weldon, NC*) to his mother **Mary A. Harper**. General wartime correspondence. [411]

Dear Mother[,] I write you a few lines by which you will learn that I am well truly hoping these few lines will reach and find you all well as usual[.] I received a letter to day Dated 20th Jan with seven stamps in it and I received one the 6th dated the 3rd[.] I was very glad to hear from you all[.] I wrote a letter to you the 5th but I did not have time to write as much about our campaign as I wanted to so I will try and give you a small sketch[.] we left here on Thursday the 28th Jan and went to Goldsborough and went from there to Kinston Saturday 30th and took up line of march in the Direction of Newbern with four days rations cooked[.] the distance was 47 miles[.] we went about 18 miles and staid all night[.] next morning we crossed the Trent River on Pontoon Bridges and went in thirteen miles of Newbern without any opposition ...[letter cut off after]

1864, February 14-15
Matthew C. Yow to his father-in-law **Joseph Albright**. General wartime correspondence. [412]

Father and Family[,] With plesure I seat my self to drop you a few lines which will ___ that I am well at this present time truly hoping when this reaches you it will find you all well and harty. I received your letter in due time. It suprised me vary much the way you rote to me you must think that I am a disloyal man __ to my country at all. You must think that I had some notion of going to the Yankees by sending me the Abalishion Oath. I care nothing about that oath. I expect that me and you will hav to take that oath yet without __ what tha are at. You said that I was like some of my disrespected neighbors __ like to hav the disrespect throwd up to me that I __ and I no that I hav __ as well as any __ feelings to think that you thought such a thing as that about me just because I rote to you that I was out of hart. I am out of hart and I dont see any thing to put me in hart for what little money we get is no __ it wont by any thing hardly at all. You said the army rations was small. Tha seem not to agree with me. I hav a good part of them to by or I should suffer. You say that provisions is plenty. I dont see why we dont get it. General Lee sais that tha hav __ every exertion that tha can __ cant get it and he don't __ on that account __ that we must trust in God. If you go to the Bible about this war[,] I can tel you that it sais their shal be no Confederacy. I want to no what you think of that. You said somthing about the Revolution. If I knowd that we had the __ that tha had I could be in beter hart. But I __ think so it looks two much like __ people but this __ as for my part I am tired of this war and I want it to stop and I dont much care how. I hop and believe that the good Lord will take care of you. So I will close my letter by saying I stil remain your affectionate son tel death. Matthew C. Yow to Joseph Albright

1864, February 19
J.L. Stuart (*camp near Weldon, NC*) to his brother **Charles E. Harper** and mother **Mary A. Harper**. General wartime correspondence with brief mentions of sister **Mary A. Harper, Duncan Cole** and stepfather **John Harper**. [413]

Mr C.E. Harper[.] Dear Brother[,] I am Blest with the privilege of writing you a few lines to inform you that I am well truly hoping these few lines will reach and find you all well as common[.] I want to hear from all very bad[.] the last letter I received from Home was Dated the 3rd[.] I have wrote[,] thisis the fourth time since I do not Know what to think unless you have all forsaken me and I do not think you have[.] I send a letter by D. Cole home the other day and one quire of paper and twenty Dollars in money. I have Just Drawd a new Hat one new pare pants and Drawers[.] our regiment is well supplied with shoes. Clothing & blankets[.] I have a splendid Blanket worth one Hundred Dollars in Confederate[.] we have the Best quarter Master in the Confederacy to pay us off and clothe us well[.] I want to see you all very bad and hope I shall live to see you all again[.] I do not want you to Delay writing so long as you have any more. Charles I want to know how you and the girls are getting along and if you have sent any of the girls any Valentines and if you got any letters from your Dark skin girl at Franklinville but I suppose she is right pretty[.] give my respects to all inquiring friends and relatives. it is talked here that Congress has passed and act to call our all from 16 to 45 but I do not Know whether it is so or not. tell sis I want to see her very bad[.] tell her to be smart[.] I must close my letter by asking you to write as soon as this comes to hand[.] Direct to Weldon N.C. Co. D[,] 49th regt[,] NCT[,] Ransoms Brigade[.] farewell your Brother[,] John. To Charles[,] try and improve your self in writing[.] I think you can.

Mrs Mary A Harper. Dear mother[,] I write you a few lines by which you will learn that I am well truly hoping they will reach and find you all as well as usual[.] it has been some time since I received a letter from you[.] I fear you all have seceded from us here in the Army or I should get more letters from the people at home[.] but excuse me[,] we are under marching orders to some point in the compass. I know you have written but I have not received the letters[.] the soldiers have enlisted a good many During the War but I have not yet[.] but if we will all re-enlist[,] we will get twelve furloughs to the Hundred men[.] but we are getting one furlough to every twenty[.] I send twenty Dollars by Cole one quire paper and a letter[.] I would have sent more money but it cost me five Dollars to pay for my letter ever month but that is one of the soldiers great satisfaction to get letters[.] I want you to send me some sewing thread by Cole. no more at present[.] write soon[.] give my respects to John Harper[.] tell him to write[.] your affectionate son[,] John

1864, February 22
J.L. Stuart (*Weldon, NC*) to his mother **Mary A. Harper,** stepfather **John Harper,** brother **Charles Harper** and sister **Mary A. Harper**. General wartime correspondence with brief mentions of **Duncan Cole, Lt. Barrett** and **John Teague**. [414]

Dear Mother[,] I write you a few lines to inform you that I am well truly hoping these few lines will come to hand in due time and find you all well[.] I received yours of the 14th today[.] It had been three weeks since I received a letter from you[.] I was getting very uneasy about you all[.] I have no news to write of much importance[.] the 18th I think it was our Brigade was all marched out in a field to see a man shot[.] there was twelve men shot at him[.] he was tied to a stake[.] I was told four Balls hit him[.] he Deserted and killed his Cousin[.] he belonged to the 25th regt. I give out the idea of getting any letters from any more[.] you need not send me nothing by Cole but a pare of scocks and some sewing thread[.] the time we went to Newbern our company got thirteen Boxes with all Kinds of Provision and it was all stollen for the left them at Kinston with[.] Lt Barrett said the Provision was gone when we got back to Kinston[.] we have been expecting to leave here but we may stay here some time[.] I have wrote four letters and received only one from you[.] I want to see you very bad and hope I shall get to see you all again[.] excuse my short letter and write[.] Direct to Weldon N.C. Co. D[,] 49th regt[,] NCT[,] Ransoms Brigade[.] Yours[,] J.L. Stuart

Mr John Harper[.] Dear stepfather[,] to inform you that I am well truly hoping these few lines will reach and find you well[.] Congress has passed an ack to call out all from seventeen to fifty them from 17th 18th stay in there own state and from 18th to 46d(?) to go in the Confederate service and then from 46 d(?) to fifty to guard Bridges and commissary and to be town guards[.] They will let you stay a while yet I reckon[.] this is the Military Bill that I saw[.] I must close my letter[.] give my respects to all inquiring friends and tell them to write to me[.] I remain your ever affectionate step son[,] J.L. Stuart. I wrote to John Teague the other day[.] tell him.

Charles and sis[,] I want to see you very bad but I do not know when I shall get to see you[.] Charles you said you had fine times at quilting[.] I wish I could be at some of them[.] well Charles you left your axe and feed tropht at Franklinville for an excuse to go back and see your girl[.] there was a Boy told me she was too Dark to be pretty[.] I want to know her name[.] I suppose you are in Love with her[.] a Boy told me this and you do not Know who it was[.] give my respects to all the girls[.] I thought I would get some letters from the girls this year as it is leap year but I am mistaken[.] they won't write to the soldiers. Your brother[,] John

1864, February 26
Mastin C. Phillips (*Point Lookout, MD*) to **Bryan Tyson**. General wartime correspondence. [415]

Dear Sir, Yours of the 19th ult. is to hand. I was truly glad to hear from you, though very sorry that you were unable to assist me for I am really needy. I hope you have put my case befor the committee of which you spoke before now, but if you have not[,] I beg you to do so the first opportunity- for if by so doing you will be enabled to render me some assistance[.] you will have brought me under oblications to you that I shall take great pleasure in repaying when I am permited to do so. Besides money[,] I am in need of a shirt, pr of slips 8 a pr. socks. Can you procure these. You will also confer a great favor by sending me a few sheets of pape, envelups & stamps. I am not in good health, but doing as well as I can under the circumstances. Hoping to hear from you soon. I remain yours, very respectfully, M. C. Phillips

1864, February 26
Henry C. Brown (*Point Lookout, MD*) to **Bryan Tyson**. General wartime correspondence. [416]

Dear Sir, I received yours today informing me to make application to Board Corps for books[.] I have been supliede with books since I wrote to you[.] you stated that some prisoners had been exchanged & all probability that we would all be. I truly hope so. but I fear it will not be the case[.] you said you regreted that you could not grant me my request and sir I regretted it myself, owing to the condition that I am placed in and I think if you were in my condition and I in yours[,] I would have granted the request. but you know best. but if you had granted it[,] you would be amplyed rewarded for the same. you said you wanted me to attend to the busines you intrusted in my care. I will attend to that. and when I leave hear. I will drop you a line. So no more but I remain your friend until Death, H.C. Brown

1864, February 29
Daniel J. Shields (*Camp near Williamston, NC*) to father **Benjamin J. Shields**. General wartime correspondence with brief mention **Duncan P. Shields, William Wadsworth Shields, Mariah McIver**

Shields, John Vick, Katherine Ann McLauchlin Shields, Benjamin D. Shields, John W. Shields, William Joseph Shields, Lewis Lawhon and **Sims.** [417]

Dear father, yesterday I received your most gratifying letter the contents of which afforded me great pleasure to have from you all but was pained to learn that Dunk was still in a state of bad health but I hope and pray to the God of mercy that before this time he is better if not well. Oh, it would do me so much good to here he was well, it would do me as much good as any nuse I ever herd. I am so uneasy about hum but we must consider that Lord's will must be done and be as well satisfied as we can although we are a long wais a part[.] the same merciful God deals with us all. Well Father I have know nuse of interest to relate to you at this time[.] we are yet in the same place and fair as well as we could expect for soldier and I am as well satisfied as any place I have bin to in some time[,] but as for me I can stay anywhere anybody else can as long as I stay well and thank the Lord. I and Bill is both well...and we drawed our money yesterday and the first chance I get, I will send some home but I do not want to send it in a letter. The next set of men that goes home[,] I will send by them and you can do what you think best with it all. Spend it or fund it over and take bonds for it or buy land with it or do what you think best. You folks at home can tell what would be best to do with it. John Vick went home some time ago he promised me he would go see you and Dunk if he could and I hope he will so he can tell me how you all are when he comes back. I must close, tell all Uncle Johns Joes and Uncle Lewis and Richard and the gals howdy for me. Give my love and best respects to Mud, Dunk, Ann, Beny and to all my friends and relations and write soon. Tell Dunk I will write to him next time. I was glad to get the peace you sent me and Bill and I take a grate delite in reading it. I would be more than glad to see you all but I don't know when it will be. Bill sends his love to you all. Write soon and fail not, your affectionate son will death. D.J. Shields. [P.S.] Tell Sims howdy for me.

1864, March 3
Duncan Cole (*camp near Weldon, NC*) to **John Harper**. General wartime correspondence with brief mentions of **John Lane Stuart**. [418]

Mr John Harper. Dear Sir, This evening Seat myself for the purpose of droping you a few lines which will inform you that I am well[.] At the present. I have nothing new to write to you more then I arrived at camp safe last Sunday morning[,] but on my arrival I found The Regt gon. They have gon down in the Eastern part of this state[,] I suppose on a foreign Expedition. They have bin gon some our a week[.] I dont know how long They will be gon but I think they will be back in a few days. The reason I write to you now was that I thought you woud be uneasy about John as he has had no oportinity since he left. he was well when he went off[.] I have not went on to the Company yet. I was ordert by the lieut. colonel to stay at camp till the regt comes back[.] I got along with the things very well but I fear that some of the things will spoil if the boys don't come back soon. The was very warm and a few days after I get back I laid out all of the things that I thought would be any danger of spoiling. the air has turned some cooler so I am in hopes the things will not spoil. So for news I have non that is worth your attention. It is reported here that the yankees maid a raid on Richmond[.] they say the yankees get in a mile and a half of the town but I don't put much confidence in the report. I must now close[.] it is getting dark[.] I hope you will receive my bad writing letter[.] write soon and give me all the news[.] So nothing more. Very affectionately yours. Duncan Cole

1864, March 7
Matthew C. Yow to his wife **Nancy Catherine Albright Yow** and children. General wartime correspondence with brief mentions of his father **Henry C. Yow** and brother **Simeon Jones Yow.** [419]

Mrs Nancy C. Yow[.] Dear Wife[,] I this beautiful morning seat my self to drop you a few lines which will inform you that I am blest with tolerable good helth and I do hop and trust when this reaches you it may find you and my dear little children all wel and doing wel. Catharine I receivd your welcom letter the 4 that you rote the 28. I also receivd one from father the same time. Catharine I was so glad to here that you was all wel. Catharine I rote a letter to you the 3 and one to father the 4 before I got your letters. Tel father that I will rite to him soon. Jones got here last Sunday the 3. I was so glad to see him and I was sorrow two. He looks mity wel. Catharine it hurt my feelings vary bad to here how he don while at home. Father told me all about him in his letter. I do hate it vary much. He cant get any thing to drink here. Catharine tomorrow the 8 is a day set apart for fasting and prare. I hop that day will be holy. All is quiet here now. The wether has bin so bad that the Yankees could not do any thing. I expect that we shal hav bad times here this spring. I do dredit. I do hop that the good Lord will spare my life And take me through safe. Catharine do the best you can and pray for me that I may be savd from the hands of my enemies. So I will close by saying I stil remain your affectionate husband tel death. M. C. Yow to Nancy C. Yow

1864, March 9-10
Capt. James O.A. Kelly (*near Wilmington, NC*) to wife **Nannie Sloan Kelly**. General wartime correspondence with mentions of General **Whiting**, Comodore **Lynch, Alexander Bolin**, **Harwood**, father **Abner Kelly**, brother **John Kelly** and their children **Oscar, Edith** and **Mattie Kelly**. [420]

Dear Nannie, your note came safe to hand and I was truly glad to hear from you. I have written you one note since I recd. that one yours, but here goes again. I am tolerably well at present and still up here as witness in court martial in two cases. I have not been down to see the company yet. You can't imagine how bad I want to see them. I hope this may come to hand in due time cand find you and the children well. I have no news to write to you at present[.] things are tolerable quiet with the exception of a misunderstanding between Gen. Whiting and Comodore Lynch. I hope though they may settle their difficulty soon[.] things look a little squirrely though at present. There are a considerable number of the 50th reenlisting at present. I think the greater part of old "F" will reenlist for the war. All of them that I have seen seem willing to reenlist. Did the children get the picture I sent them? The one with the ships belongs to Oscar. You can give to Edith and Mattie the one you think will suit them but don't let them abuse them[,] but keep them hanging up and tell them to take care of them until I come home. Lt. Bolin has made an application to go home so I learn we shall hear from it in a few days. I hope you have recd. my cloth before this. I did have some idea of having my pants maid soon but don't know what to do about it. When they are maid I want a blue cord up the legs[.] be sure to recollect that. I will write more about it in a few days. How are you getting along plowing? Have you sowed my clover yet? And how are you getting along generally? Write me a long letter and give my the points. You may say to Papa or John that the Mary Annie the steamer I sent by for them that [?] is expected in this week though I think it uncertain whether she comes or not this week. I want to see you about as bad as I did before you come down. I believe that more I stay with you[,] the more I want to. I hope the time is not distant when I can see you again. Somebody has tried to trouble Mr. Harwood by writing down to Gen. Whitling that he is this and that and anything but a clever fellow, but I think he will come out all right as I am confident in my mind he is innocent of the charge. You may say to his friends that they may suffer no uneasiness. I am not uneasy on his acct but fear should his wife hear about it in her present state that she might lose her mind again. That's all I fear. Write soon and believe me as ever your loving husband. James

1864, March 12
Matthew C. Yow (*camp near Orange Court House, VA*) to his wife **Nancy Catherine Albright Yow** and children. General wartime correspondence with brief mentions of **John Lewis Maness**, his brother **Simeon Jones Yow,** father-in-law **Joseph Albright,** sister-in-law **Youtha Ann Albright, Christopher Columbus Harrison**, uncle **John Henry Stutts** and son **William Henry Yow.** [421]

Mrs Nancy C. Yow[.] Dear Wife[,] I hav bin one time more Permited to drop you a few lines which will inform you that I am wel at present and I do hop when this reaches you it may find you and my dear little children all wel and doing wel. Catharine I receivd your kind and welcome letter the 9 that you rote the 3. I was so glad to here that you and the children was wel for that is all the pleasure that I can see is when I can here that you are all wel. Catharine I dont see much satisfaction here but I no that it wont do to giv up. I try to do the best I can. I read a great deal in the Bible. I read the good promises of them that is faithful. Catharine I will say to you that John Manes has got to the army at last. He was attacht to the 27 regiment Co A. We are close to gether now. Jones has come but you no that before now he is wel as common he has a caugh. He has rote to you Catharine. I want to no how him and Youtha was geting on when he was at home. I never said any thing to him about it. He told me that he staid their the night that he left home. Catharine you don rite when you would not let Columbus work for you when he began to tryout. I dont want any of the deserters to sta about you. Tha had as wel come here as me. Catharine it seems lik your father wants to incourage me so much to sta and do my duty he would do more for you than he does. I dont get mad with him for riting as he does for he has his opinion and I hav mine. He sais he has rote to incourage me but he should quit and just rite about the helth of the family. Catharine do the best you can for I see no chanc to get to come home this spring. I do hate it so bad. I expect we shal hav bad times here before long. Tha are fixing every thing for to be ready to march at any time. The wether has bin so bad that tha could not move any way. As soon as the wether brakes tha will be somthing don. Catharine you may no that I do dred what I think will come on this spring but I will do the best I can and trust in the good Lord that has brought me though many dangers. Catharine you said that you was glad that I could send you paper. I will send you all that I can. I will send you some in this letter. I sent you some coffee and sugar by Uncle John. I hop that you got it all. You said you wanted me to use it. I am using what I got now. Catharine rite as often as you can and let me no how you are geting along. Jones sais that Henry can plow. I hop that you can make somthing this year. May God help you I pray. Tel Isaac to rite to me and let me no how he is geting along. Catharine if I never should see you any more in this world I hop that we will meet in haven where we shal part no more. So I must close by saying I stil remain your affectionate husband tel death. M.C. Yow to Nancy C. Yow

1864, March 15

Neill A. Baker (*Topsail Inlet*) to wife **Sarah Jane Baker**. General wartime correspondence between husband/wife with brief mentions of daughter Emma Baker **Neill T. Watson, Jack Thomas, John Godfrey, William J. Kelly, John B. McFarland, Robert B. Thomas, David Thomas, Absalom Kelly, Getty Cox, John Buchanan, Jasper Thomas** and the blockade at Charleston. [422]

Dear Jane, Today I will embrace the only means I have to communicate with you. My situation here is [a] good deal like yours in regard to mail facilities—that is, I have to trust a good deal to chance and Providence. This leaves me in my usual health, [and] I hope that this may reach you and the babies in the best of health but I do not suppose that Emma will admit that she is a baby. I have bought a pair of Yankee boot legs and if no person has stolen the old shoe soles that [I] left in camp, I can have a tolerable good pair of shoes made for her when I get back to camp. I have been making some envelopes since I came to this place. I bought a quire of large unruled paper that was saved off of some of those wrecked vessels. It made me 4 packs. Then I made up a quire for the telegraph operator for half and I made up a quire yesterday and have got another to make up tomorrow or someday upon the same conditions. I will send this in one of Baker's best, warranted to stick, as a sample of Southern enterprise and Southern manufacture. For the last few days I have been doing my own cooking. I baked myself some flour bread this morning for breakfast. As long as I have been in the service[,] I have not made up any flour dough until lately but I can work it finely. I have been remarking that I thought peace was going to be made soon since I had been in the service so long and had never baked any flour bread. I have some noble oyster stews here. You ought to see me eat oysters. Well, oyster soup is just good enough. I hear that our Band is gone to Fayetteville to practice. We have beautiful weather these days. Today is a most beautiful Sabbath. If I could but just be with you and the children this morning. Happy thought! But the stern reality is for the worse. Well, we must conform to the realities of the case and endeavor to enjoy it the best we can. Perhaps there is a better time coming for the true Patriotic Southerner when the sweet influences of the Holy Spirit shall have so softened grim visaged war as to permit Peace, gentle Peace, sweet Peace to ascend her throne in majesty and power to rule indefinitely. Yours Truly, - N. A. Baker PS - I was beginning to entertain the idea of sending for you to come see me in the course of a month or so, but they are getting the fare up so high that it looks like taking a person's whole pile to make a visit to Wilmington and return to Jonesboro - $35.00 for the passage to and from is tall figures for a soldier. But it is all in a lifetime. It is surely shameful for such prices to be asked. You need not read this to the old man and if you conclude to come at any time[,] you can get Mae to stay with him until you get back. You can broach the subject to him occasionally and see how he takes it. I think that he will consent for he appeared so much altered for the better. It is said that we will (our company) go into town as guard to relieve Company C. We have just got orders to go to town to start in the morning. I wish to see you and the babies worse than before I went home. I have felt very lonesome, etc., since I got back. Yours truly, — Neill

1864, March 15

William Henry Patterson (*Camp near Orange Courthouse, VA*) to sister **Frances Anna V. Patterson**. General wartime correspondence between siblings with brief mentions of **John A. Johnson, William Graham, Gen. Lee, John R. Keith Neill C. Graham, Daniel McDonald, William C. McDonald, Daniel Ferguson, Murdoch McLeod, J.J. McGilvary** and **C.W. Shaw.** [423]

My dear Sister, With the greatest of pleasure I seat myself this morning to write you a few lines in response to your letter of the 6th Inst. which came to hand last Saturday evening and found me in good health. May these few lines find you and all the rest of the family enjoying the same blessing. Dear sister I have no news of importance to communicate. The health of the company is very good at this time. We have but one sick man viz. John A. Johnson[.] poor John is in a bad condition he has the serofula(?) very bad. He certainly ought to have a discharge but he cannot get one[.] he has not done duty in more than twelve months and he will never be fit for service again. His face is swollen very bad[.] I would not have known him a few days ago if I had seen him when I was not expecting to, his face was swollen so much that it nearly shut his eyes. We moved back to our camp that we left on the 3rd of Feburary yesterday. Davis' Brigade took our place on picket. Yesterday was 12 months ago that we were lying under the shells of the enemy near Newberne, North Carolina. William Graham is with the company now[.] he came back about 2 or 3 weeks ago. He is not able for duty and I do not believe he will ever be. The doctor speaks of giving him and John A. Johnson a furlough but I do not know whether Johnson is able to go home or not if he had a furlough. Dear Sister, I have been in hopes a long time that I would get a furlough to go home some time in the spring but I have almost despaired of getting to go home. Furloughs have been stopped altogether. There was an order rec'd on Dress Parade last Saturday Evening from Genl. Lee to stop furloughs in consequence of the Quartermaster Department having preferred the Rail Roads. I understand that the Yankee prisoners that we have at Richmond are being moved South[.] probably that is the reason furloughs have been suspended. I am hopes that they will soon begin to give furloughs again. I do not think that Genl. Lee will them altogether for a while yet, though it may be possible that no more furloughs will be granted in this army. I will hate it very much if I cant get to go home this spring for I was almost confident that I would get a furlough before the order came to suspend them[,] but if I do not get a furlough I will have to try and content myself though I begin to want to see you all very much but I ought not to complain[.] there are some men in the company that have not been at home in twelve months and it has been only 5 months since I left home – if furloughs are resumed[,] there are some 5 or 6 to go before me, viz. John R. Keith, Neill C. Graham, Daniel McDonald, Wm. C. McDonald and Daniel Ferguson. The later has been home since I have but his father is very sick and Lt. McLeod gave him a furlough to go see him[.] he intended starting home last Saturday evening if the order had not come from Genl. Lee suspending furloughs. It was an awful circumstance you spoke of in your letter – the murder of Simmons and Sanders by those wretched robbers. Our country is in awful condition[.] no one knows when he is safe[.] if this war last much longer I fear that it will be a worse time at home than it is in the Army. Lt. J. H. McGilvary started home on furlough one day last week. I saw C. W. Shaw yesterday evening for the first time since he returned from home. Wash said that he enjoyed his furlough very much-only it was too short. Dear Sister I was very glad to hear that you had some cotton yarn made to make me a suit of clothes[,] but I dont know when I will get to go home and get them – but hold on to the cloth a while yet and if I get a furlough I will get some one to make me a short coat and pants that understands how to cut well. I must close for the present as my space is exhausted. Your Afft. Bro. W. H. Patterson

1864, March 20

J.L. Stuart (*camp near Weldon, NC*) to his mother **Mary A. Harper**. General wartime correspondence with brief mentions of **Duncan Cole** and **Bannister W. Hogan**. [424]

Mrs Mary A Harper[.] Dear mother. I write you a few lines to inform you that I am well truly hoping these few lines will reach and find you all well as usual[.] the latest news I have had from you was the 16th in a letter to Mr. Cole[.] our co and co was sent to Weldon last Monday for the purpose of unloading cars & c. we are in camp about half a mile of Weldon but we have but little to do. I hope we will get to stay here a good while[.] I want to hear from you very bad[.] I have been looking for a letter from you for the last few days[.] I received the socks and every thing you sent me but the slice pies and they spoilt before we go to camp[.] I want to see you very bad but it will be some time before I shall git to come home as there are a good many men that is before me[.] I wrote a letter to you last Monday and give you a Detail of our life in the Eastern part of NC & Va[.] you must all do the best you can[.] I hope I shall live to see you all again[.] give my respects to all inquirers and write ever chance[.] Direct to Weldon N.C. Co. D[,] 49th[,] N.C.T[,] Ransoms Brigade. Bannister Hogans grave is in fifty guards of our camp. it makes me mity sorry to see it. I must close. write soon[.] give my respects[.] I remain your son[,] J.L. Stuart

1864, March 20

J.L. Stuart (*camp near Weldon, NC*) to his stepfather **John Harper**. General wartime correspondence with brief mentions of **Alexander Johnson Jr., Levi D. Monroe, Richard A. Love, William Wesley Hunsucker, Kenneth McLean, Benjamin J. Medlin,** his brother **Charles E. Harper** and sister **Mary A. Harper**. [425]

Mr J Harper[.] after my last respects I hope these lines will reach and find you well and doing well[.] I am in very good health and doing pretty well. We get one third point Bacon and one and an eighth of meal and some peas per day[.] you said in your last letter you could make out pretty well if you did not have to come to the war[.] I think you can stay at home if you will work right in[.] I am not reported as a substitute here I think you can stay at home[.] I want to see you all very bad and hope I shall live to see you all again[.] it will be some time next summer before I shall get a furlough[.] three of our co is gone on furlough young Sandy Johnson, L.D. Munroe and Dick Love. W.W. Hunsucker was sent to the Hospital the other day sick[.] K. McLean and B. Medling also sick in camp[.] we are staying near Weldon to do fatigue Duty[.] I like to stay here very well[.] tell Charles and sis I want to see them very bad[.] excuse my short letter and all imperfection[.] write soon[.] tell sis and Charles I will write to them shortly[.] Direct to Weldon N.C. Co. D[,] 49th regt[,] N.C.T. Ransoms Brigade[.] yours with respects[,] J.L. Stuart

1864, March 25
Moore County citizens to the Enrolling Officer of the Seventh Congressional District. Petition on behalf to **A.S. Caddell** to be assigned light duty and returned to home. [426]

To the Enrolling Officer of the Seventh Congressional District, NC. We the undersigned being well acquainted with A.S. Caddell and believing him to be unable to do any active or heavy duty respectfully recommend that you assign him to some light duty, such as clerk or assistant in some of the departments in this District. Mr. Caddell is a respectable citizen of Moore County and have a widowed mother who would be blesses at his recurring appointment in this County or as near home as you, in the exercise of your power and discretion will be kind enough to place him. Devotion Davis, L.P. Tyson, A.M. Branson, W. Barrett, M.D. McNeill, G.S. Cole and A.H. McNeill.

1864, April 3
J.L. Stuart (*camp near Harrellsville, NC*) to his mother **Mary A. Harper**, stepfather **John Harper** and brother **Charles E. Harper**. General wartime correspondence with brief mentions of **Mary Diffie Spivey, Thomas Comer** and **Isaac Cagle**. [427]

Mrs Mary Ann Harper[.] Dear mother. excuse me for not writing sooner as we have moved from Weldon[.] we left there the 29th March and went by railroad twenty five miles and then marched the remainder of the way[.] we are a bout sixty miles below Weldon on the Charles River near a village called Harrellville[.] we came here for the purpose of guarding the fisheries in the River[.] I have been told they draw as many as twenty five hundred at one draw but worst is the yankees come up the River with there gun balls[.] I have seen some of their Cannon balls[.] they have threw out that weight one hundred pounds[.] we have some guns down here[.] I do not know what the yankees will do with us and what we will do with them but I had rather they would stay away[.] I received a letter at Weldon from you I did not answer dated the 20th March which is the last letter I have received from you[.] I was very glad to hear from you then but very sorry to hear you are so unwell[.] I want to hear from you very bad now as it has been two weeks since I have heard from you. you said that Mrs. Spiveys folks said they did not get no letters from me. I have wrote to them several times[.] if they do not get them they are mislaid. I saw Thomas Comer while on the Frankling march[.] he was unwell part of the time but kept a long. we were very glad to see each other[.] he belong to Co A[,] 56th N.C.T. Isaac Cagle also is in the 56th[.] I have not see him yet but her he is well so I am told the 30th[.] I want to see you very bad and hope I shall live to see you again but I cannot tell when I shall ever get to come and see you as there are several to go home before me but you must not get out of heart[.] I hope we will live to meet again[.] tell all the family I want to see them all very bad[.] tell sis she must be smart and learn to read and write[.] she said in your letter she was going to start to school[.] you must take care of yourself and not work too hard and over do yourself while sis is going to school[.] these lines leave me well truly hoping they will come to hand in due time and find you all well as usual and doing well[.] excuse me for not writing sooner[.] give my respects to all inquiring[.] J.L. Stuart

Mr J Harper[.] Dear stepfather[,] after my last respects to you I hope these lines will reach and find you usual & doing well[.] I hope you will be permitted to stay at home[.] write and let me know who has had to come to the war in your section and give me all the news. the mail leaves here twice a week and comes in twice[.] send your letters up the first of the week as the faster part. Direct to Weldon N.C. Co. D[,] 49th regt[,] N.C.T. Ransoms Brigade. John Stuart

Brother Charles, I hope you will excuse me for not writing to you but I will write in a few dayes to you if I am permitted to live[.] give my respects to all inquiring friends and to all the Ladies and write to me and give me all your news. Your brother[,] John

1864, April 4
Matthew C. Yow (*camp near Orange Court House, VA*) to his father-in-law **Joseph Albright**. General wartime correspondence with brief mentions of Lt. **Montraville D. Clegg**, brothers-in-law **Henry A. Albright** and **John E. Albright.** [428]

Mr Joseph Albright[.] Dear Father and Family[,] Through the mercies of our heavenly I hav bin one time more permited to drop you a few lines which will inform you that I am not in as good helth as I hav bin. I hav had a hard spel of thoothach and sore throat which hurt me vary bad. But I am now on the mend truly hoping when this reaches you it may find you all wel and doing wel. I receivd your letter some days back. I was truly to hear that you was all wel. The reason I didnot write no sooner I was not wel. Their is a good many sick here now and I dont no what is the caus. Some say that it is the water. I cant tel the caus of it. You rote me a long letter and it seems like from the way you write that you think that I hav no confidenc in you but you are mistaken. I ask your appinion and you giv it and I dont think hard of you for that. I will agree with you. I believ you are candid in what you say and I think you believ what you write and I do hop that it will come to pass that we may gain our independenc and be a free and happy people one time more. I believ that I am as true to my country as you or any other man but I am like a great many others. I hav becom tired of this war and some times I get out of hart and then I dont care how it goes so I can hav peac. Peac is what I want but I want it on fare terms and I dont want to fight any more. The more we fight the more we may fight. Govner Vanc come to see us and made a long speech. He sais that we must fight them tel hell freezes over. I call that a drab expression. I didnot like that at all. He is a great man if he was not so wicked. It seems that the most of our ruling men is wicked men and I believ that hurts our caus. All things will come rite some day and I hop it is not far distant. I didnot rite to you to insult you at all and if you rote to me to insult me you did not. You said you would not write any thing here after only about the health of your family. It all will be rite with me. My Lieutenant Cleg red the letter that you rote to me and he said that it was the best letter that he had seen sinc he had bin in the servis. He sais that it hurt. H. A. Albright come to see me the other day. He was wel and he said that John was wel. All is quiet here now but I cant tel what a day may bring forth. The wether has bin vary bad for some time. Pleas giv my lov and best respects to all my friends. So I must close. Rite soon and fail not. Your friend tel death. Matthew C. Yow Joseph Albright

1864, April 10
John Harper (*Good Spring Post Office*) to **Capt. David S. Barrett**. General wartime correspondence with brief mentions of wife **Mary A. Harper** and stepson **John Lane Stuart.** [429]

Lt. D.S. Barrett[.] Dear sir[,] after my best respects and compliments to you. I hope you are well and doing your Duty for your country in these troublesom times. I am Hearty and my family is well all[,] but my wife She is aleing and uneasy about J.L. Stuart. he has not rote to us Since 20 of march and we think something has happened to him and we are anxious to now what is the matter with him. we had Sent John L. Stuart 3 letters since 20 March and he has not answered these and we so all uneasy about him[.] please rite to me soon if any thing is the matter with John and if not tell him to write soon. Direct your letter to good Spring post office[,] Moor County[.] I have nothing of importance to ask[;] only winter is just passed and the whippoorwill come yesterday and laste nite herd them cry. We had afternoon of rain high waters today[.] giv all my friends in your company my best respects and tell them I would like to see them all but I am sorry they cannot be at hom[.] and peace be near on good terms but it seemes like peace is a great way off but we must still hope that it will come in its time. So be in courage is all I can say[.] no mor[,] only rite soon. your moste affect[,] John Harper

1864, April 12
J.L. Stuart (*Harrellsville, NC*) to his mother **Mary A. Harper**. General wartime correspondence with brief mentions of **Andrew J. Britt, John A. Cox, Levi D. Monroe** and **Matthew Teague**. [430]

Dear mother[,] I write you a line to inform you that I am well truly hoping these few lines will reach and find you all well[.] I received a letter from you yesterday dated the 3rd. I was very glad to hear from you[.] all you said you had not received no letter since the 20th March[.] I have wrote two or three letters to you since then[.] four of our co started home yesterday on furlough. A.J. Britt John Cox, M. McCaskill and Levi Munroe went also on a thirty dayes furlough[.] when he was at home he got a recruit and got a thirty dayes furlough[.] a man can get a thirty dayes furlough if he will get a recruit[.] I want to see you all very bad[.] I think I shall get to come home next fall if I live[.] you need not plague to send me any provision. While we are so far from the rail road we are getting a half pound of meat now[.] that is noble. excuse my short letter[.] I send it in a letter to Matthew Teague[.] I will write again in a few dayes[.] Direct your letters to Weldon NC[,] Co D[,] 49th regt[,] N.C.T. the mail only goes out her twice a week[.] give my compliments to all the family and to all my friends[.] J.L. Stuart

1864, April 14
J.L. Stuart (*camp near Harrellsville, NC*) to his mother **Mary A. Harper,** stepfather **John Harper** and brother **Charles E. Harper**. General wartime correspondence with brief mentions of **Matthew Teague, Martha Nall, Martin L. Nall, F.W. Tally, Leach, Foster** and **Ramsey**. [431]

Mrs Mary A Harper. Dear Mother[,] I write you a few lines to inform you that I am well truly hoping these few lines will reach and find you all well[.] I received a letter from you the first of the week dated 3rd[.] I was very glad to hear from you all[.] you said you had not heard from me since the 20th Mar[.] I wrote to you ever oppertunity but we left Weldon the last of the month which hinderd me from writing to you[.] we have been fortifying on the river for the cannons but about completed[.] to day we have been getting half a pound of meat part of the time while the work is been going on[.] but the work is done so we will come to the [illegible] again. I sent you a letter an one to Matthew Teague. I received a letter from Martha Nall today dated 4th[.] they were all well then but Martins wound was not well. William is gone to the war[.] he started the 26th march to the Co E 26th regt. She said times were very dull and sad at home. I want to see you all very bad and hope by the kind mercies of Providense I shall be spared to Come home and see you all again[.] There is fifteen of the county to go home before me yet that is present[.] we have four gone home on furlough now[.] I must close my letter[.] write ever opportunity[.] Direct to Weldon as usual[.] give my respects to all[.] I received a letter from F.W. Tally the other day[.] he was at home on furlough the first of the month. Your affectionate son[,] J.L. Stuart

Mr J Harper[.] Dear stepfather[,] I write you a line to inform you that I am well truly hoping these lines will find you in good health[.] our Election came off to day[.] Leach 44 Foster 4 Ramsey 0 nothing is the way the votes went. I want to see you all very bad but it will be some time before I shall get to go home. I hope you will succeed in all your business[.] do the best you can all of you[.] no more at present[.] write ever opportunity. yours aft. John L. Stuart

Dear Brother[,] I write you a line to inform you I received your letter of the 3rd[.] you said you heard we had had another fight but we have not[.] but I do not know how soon the yankees will pay us a visit with their gun boats but we are trying to get in fit for them. I want to see you very bad and hope I shall get to come home again[.] you must tell me how you are getting along with girls and tell me who your sweetheart is[.] give my compliments to all the girls and to my inquiring friends[.] tell sis I want to see her mity bad[.] tell her to learn all she can while going to school and try and spend your time well[.] I study at night and work in the day[.] I spent a good deal of my time in running about when I ought to been reading when I was of your age[.] study your Book when you are young and you will not repent it in your old age[.] J.L. Stuart

1864, April 17
J.L. Stuart (*camp near Harrellsville, NC*) to his mother **Mary A. Harper** and brother **Charles E. Harper**. General wartime correspondence with brief mentions of Aunt **Rebecca Perry** and **Eli Perry**. [432]

Mrs Mary A Harper. Dear mother[,] I write you a line this evening in response to yours of the 10th[.] I was very glad to hear from you all but mity sorry to hear you are so bad off[.] I fear your going to Carthage will lay your up and Probably cause your death[.] I had rather the Doctor would go to see you[.] I am willing to pay my hard earnd money willingly for your welfare for what pleasure would money be to me if my poore Mother was to die. for I never done half enough for your welfare but it is too late now[.] O Dear Mother you have no idea how bad I want to see you but I fear that happy day will never come if I was to be fortunate enough to survive this war and go home and you be not there[,] how unhappy would I be[.] I hope by Physical aid and Kind Providence you will live to see this war come to a close so if I am living I can return home to soothe you in your sorrows and rejoice when you laugh[.] I hope your trip will be a help to you[.] I shall be very uneasy until I hear from you again[.] write and let me know how you are getting along[.] I wish I could be with you this sabbath evening but our Country Calls me away[.] I can not be with you[.] we must trust to our Maker and hope for the better dayes to come when this cruel war will end[,] when all the soldiers can return to their homes and weeping friends they have left behind[.] excuse my short letter[.] your affectionate son[,] J.L. Stuart

Dear Brother Charles[,] I write you a line to inform you that that I am very well truly hoping these few lines will reach you in due time and find you well[.] I received your letter to day which caused me very unhappy to hear Mother was so bad off[.] I fear her going to Carthage will cause her death[.] I feel like somebody was dead at home but I hope we will all meet again[.] Charles you and sis must be good to Mother[.] do all you can to render her happy[.] do not spend your time in silliness[.] try to improve your time which I had done while I was rambling a bout[.] how much we benefit would it have renderd me[.] study of our Books at all your idle times and when you are grown up you will not regret it but will see your ignorant Brother[.] I wrote you the truth allwaise go to your Parents and aske their advice and alwaise do as your superiors tell you[.] I know how children are they think they know how to do but take good advice and try to improve your time[.] yesterday the yankees came up here with two gunbots and threw two shots at our Battery but our men replied to them with there Artillery with such vigor they did not want to get acquainted[.] and went back we know not at what hour they will come[.] you may listen out for active opperations in the army pretty soon[.] I received a letter to day from Aunt Rebecca she is well. Eli is dead and your girl is also dead[.] she died last Sunday. from J.L. Stuart to Charles and Mary Ann Harper

1864, April 18

J.L. Stuart (*Harrellsville, NC*) to his stepfather **John Harper**. General wartime correspondence with brief mentions of his mother **Mary A. Harper**. [433]

Mr John Harper[.] Dear stepfather, I write you a line to inform you that I am well truly hoping these lines will reach and find you well. I received your letter of the 16th yesterday[.] I was very sorry to hear Mother was so bad off[.] I fear her going to Carthage will cause her death[.] do not let her over do her self try and take care of her the best you can[.] I will try and send you money as I get it if you need it[.] you said was out of heart with your soul[.] I know times are very gloomy but Despair not as long as you can sit down to your own table[.] I hope to see you all again but the prospect looks gloomy[.] the 16th the yankees came up the River with two boats and fired twice at our Battery but done no damage[.] our men fired on them a few times and they went back[.]. they told some fishermen they would bring up a fleet in a few days and try us[.] we will not be surprised at their coming at any time[.] I expect to hear of some active operations in Lees army soon[.] I think this summer will decide and by next fall we can all go home but who we will be is the question for there are many men that will fall. I want you to write me as soon as possible for I want to hear from mother[.] give my love to all the family and all friends[.] Direct to Weldon N.C. Co D[,] 49th[,] N.C. Troops[.] give me all the news at home[.] your aft[,] J.L. Stuart

1864, May 14

Rebecca E. Perry (*Franklinville, NC*) to her nephew **Charles E. Harper**. General wartime correspondence with brief mentions of **Isham Thrift** and **York**. [434]

Dear nephew[,] I avail the present time to write to you to let you no how I am getting along[.] I am well and doing as well as I can but times is so hard that nobody can get along like they once could[.] I have no nuse to rite to you this time[.] there is a great deal of sickness in this place of measles but I think their they all are getting better now. theire has been three Died in this place[,] there was two of Mr. Thrift's children and one of Miss York's girls. I received a letter from you the other day and was more than glad to hear from you and to heare that you was well but sorrow to hear that you thought you would have to go to the army. If I could have my way ther would not another man go to the army. I have looked for you to come up and see me[.] I want you to come and see me if you have to go to the army and if you dont have to go I want you to come anyhow, So will close by saying I still remain your true friend unto Death[.] I want you to rite to me as son as you get this letter without faith[.] This from. R.E. Perry. Let Love abide till Death Divide.

1864, May 23
J.L. Stuart (*near Drewry's Bluff, VA*) to his mother **Mary A. Harper**. General wartime correspondence with brief mentions of battles at Drewry's' Bluff and the death of **John T. McDonald** and wounds received by **Duncan Cole, Neill B. Caddell, Neill Kennedy, Enoch Stuart** and **Alexander Johnson Jr.** [435]

Dear Mother[,] by the good mercies of God I am yet a live truly hoping these lines will find you all well[.] I received your letters three at one time & one yester day[.] we had a very heard fight at the Bluff and routed the enemy and now we are near the enemy fortifications and have put up entrenchments[.] the rebs worked in good earnest with there spades[.] our loss has been heavy. Gen Ransom wounded[,] Cols Clark and our Col is wounded[,] Lt Col. Johnson 35th wounded Lt. Col. of the 56th[,] our co lost Sergt. John T. McDonald killed & Cole wounded in thigh, N.B. Caddell in thigh, N. Kennedy in head, young Sandy Johnson in back very bad, E. Stuart in toe. the regt lost about 200 in all[.] our Brigade sustained a heavy loss in men and officers[.] Direct your letters to Petersburg Va[,] Ransoms Brigade. J.L. Stuart

1864, May 29
J.L. Stuart (*Battlefield near Bermuda Hundred, VA*) to his mother **Mary A. Harper**. General wartime correspondence with brief mentions of battles at Drewry's' Bluff and the deaths of **John T. McDonald** and **Thomas Comer** and wounds received by **Duncan Cole, Neill B. Caddell, Neill Kennedy, Enoch Stuart, Alexander Johnson Jr.** and **Isaac Cagle, Levi Sheffield** and **John Tucker**. [436]

Mrs Mary A Harper[.] Dear Mother[,] by the Blessing of our Heavenly Father I embrace the oppertunity of writing you a few lines to inform you that I am alive and unhurt so far truly hoping these lines will find you all well[.] I want to hear from you all very bad[.] the last letter from you was dated the 16th[.] I have wrote three letters to you since we came to Va but I cannot give you a full detail of the fight[.] but my chance is bad to write and paper scarce[.] we had some heard (hard?) fighting at Drewrys Bluff[.] the enemy takend our first five of Breast work and had our regiment and the 24th cut off and surrounded[.] but the Noble 35th and 56th let into the enemy and made them give away leaving their killed on the field which looked to be plenty[.] but we fell back to our inner line of fortifications leaving our dead in their hands[.] so we remain in the Breastworks 2 or 3 dayes and then we charged on the enemy and run them out of there fortifications and pursued them to their gun boats where they are now[.] our Breastworks and theirs are only three or four hundreds and from each other[.] we can see their Blue coats when we want to[.] all is quite[,] not a gun is fired on the picket line in the last day or so[,] but before I finish this letter the Din of Battle may be roaring at the highest pitch[.] we have very good Breast works here[.] last Friday week we had a severe fight here[.] we charged on the enemy[.] our Brigade last a good many men[.] I have been Ambulance Corps until after the fight to help carry off the wounded and Dead but I have got my gun again now[.] if I ever get to see you again[,] I can tell you all about these fights but I cannot for the want of paper. J.T. McDonald was killed, Duncan Cole wounded in thigh flesh wound, N. B. Caddell in thigh, Neill Kennedy in head, Enoch Stuart in foot, young Sandy Johnson in back very bad. this is the loss in our co. Isaac Cagle came thrue safe[.] he told me Thomas Comer was killed here in the fight on Friday. I have not had the time to se Thos Co. since Levi Sheffield and John Tucker came out safe. I do not know at what hour the fight will commence[.] I hope I will come out safe[.] write to me[.] be in good heart[.] give my love to ever Body[.] your affectionate son[,] John L. Stuart

1864, June 3
A.S. Caddell to **Martha Sullivan**. General wartime correspondence. [437]

Miss Martha, When I recd that last note from you I expected to have the pleasure of seeing you before this time but unfortunately havnt had the opportunity of doing so[.] Therefore I take the liberty of writing to you hoaping this may find you enjoying yourself[.] the letter recd from you seamed to signify that you wasn't sattisfied by some cause or other[.] you spoke of some persons telling you that I intended to fool you (but you seem strongly fortified as to that)[.] you say if I fool you it will be by fulfilling my former promises to you[.] I believe the one that told you this was the one that wrote me that fictitious letter so I care but little about it & it is lies to your own choice what you may believe about the affair[.] the letter I recd with the two first initials of your name assigned[.] I recd it at Carthage tho I didnt believe you wrote it[,] yet I wanted you to see it[.] I shall say no more about the matter being convinced that I have foes some where: you seamd to signify in your letter that you would be glad to be released from the promises that has been made between us[.] if you are dissatisfied do as I have always told you to do, as for my part I dont look on the matter quite so litely[.] the promises I made was done with the intention of fulfilling them & expect to do so yet if nothing prevented[.] as you now know my intentions please drop me a few lines and let me know yours[.] I expect to leave home the 5th of this Inst. not knowing when I will return but when I do[,] I hope to have the pleasure of seeing you[.] please answer and excuse this letter, Yours[,] AS Caddell

1864, June 6
William R. Jackson (*Clayton's Hospital, Lynchburg, VA*) to wife **Catherine Jackson**. General wartime correspondence detailing his wounds and hospitalization. [438]

Dear Catherine, I have just received yours of the 28th ult and was very glad to hear from you and the children and to hear that you all were well and doing well under the circumstances. I am doing very well now under the circumstances. I receive very good attention. The surgeon that attends to this house is a very nice young man and attends to his business very well and he is a good surgeon. You wish to know how I was wounded. The ball passed through the center of my rist breaking both bones and I suffered with a great deal for about 2 weeks and the Doctor done all he could to save it and for it to get well without amputation but could not so he had to amputate it above the elbow. I have not suffered half so much since with it as before. I have been rite sick but I am getting a great deal better now. I will get a furlough as soon as I am able to come home but don't look for me under 2 or 3 weeks as I will not be able to travel that far under 2 weeks but do not be uneasy. I hope I will be able to see you and the children before very long. I must bid you farewell until I see or hear from you again. Write as soon as you get this direct same as before. Your devoted husband. Wm. R. Jackson

1864, June 6
William R. Jackson (*Clayton's Hospital, Lynchburg, VA*) to **William McLeod**. General wartime correspondence from his hospital bed. [439]

Dear Sir, I have little space and will write a line to you. This leaves me improving and I hope I will soon be able to walk about some. It is useless for me to say anymore about my health as the above letter will answer for that. I am here without money and do not know when I can get away. You would do me a favor if you would let me have five dollars which you can send enclosed in a letter. I may get a chance to go to Rolley [Raleigh] and if I do I will write to you to come after me. Wm. R. Jackson

1864, June 7
Hugh M. McDonald (*Richmond, VA*) to cousin **Sarah Jane McDonald**. General wartime correspondence between cousins with brief mentions of the deaths of Lt. **Malcom Ray** and Lt. **John M. Kelly**. [440]

Dear cousin, I seat myself this morning to let you that I am still in the land of the living but not very well and am most broke down. I tell you we have been put through the last two months. We is at this time 12 miles below Richmond on the Chickahominy [River]. Our brigade came here last Sunday. Old Lee is still to our left fighting away. I think Lee will get Grant or I am in hopes of it. Grant is the Yankee general that is fighting Lee. There is some Negro soldiers against us on the opposite side of us but they had better lie low or we will put them in the same line we put them at Plymouth. We will kill every one we find under arms and dressed in soldier's clothes for we can't stand to look at them. I wrote a letter to you about the 6th of April but haven't received an answer as yet. I thought I would write you a few more lines to let you know that I am in the world. Our company have been cut up very bad since I wrote to you last, but I guess you have heard tell of it all. Lieut. M. Ray died last Saturday night nearly a week go from his wound & Lieut. Kelley died on the 2nd of this month from a wound he received in his leg. We is all very near worn down, I tell you. I am getting tired of this war and fighting. I think we will have hard times this summer and a great deal of fighting to do. I think the Yankees will try their best for Richmond this time but I hope the Lord will be with us and enable us to turn them back from our land. I would write more[,] only time is lacking. I want you to write as soon as you get this and tell me all the news that is passing. I remain your cousin till death - H. M. McDonald

1864, June 12
Stephen W. Brewer (*Johnsons Island, OH*) to Sheriff **Richard Bray Paschal**. General wartime correspondence with brief mentions of Lt. **Murdock McLeod**, **John J. Lambert**, **James O. Gilliand**, Col. **John T. Jones** and Capt. **N.G. Bradford**. [441]

Dear Sir, I have not heard from you in some time. I think it very strange that I did not receive a letter from you the last mail. Your last was the 19th March. I received a letter from Lieut. McLeod of our regiment. He was captured on the 6th of May and is now at Fort Delaware. Also seven of my company captured at the same time—John J. Lambert, James O. Gilliland and others. I have not been able to find out where they are. Lt.-Col. John Thomas Jones led the 26th North Carolina & was killed in the Battle of the Wilderness[.] Lieut. McLeod wrote that Col. Jones was wounded the 6th and died the 7th. We have not been able to learn anything from the regiment since. We are anxious to hear from our friends though it will be sad to some of us. I wrote you the same time ago that I had made arrangement with Capt. Bradford of our regiment to furnish me with anything that I might need[,] but I learn that he has not been sent through. I hope you have not neglected sending the tobacco that I wrote for. I am in better health now than I have been since I was captured. Give my best to all. Yours truly & fraternally, S. W. Brewer, 26 N. C. Regt.

1864, June 14
J.L. Stuart (*Battlefield near Bermuda Hundred, VA*) to his mother **Mary A. Harper**. General wartime correspondence. [442]

Mrs. M A Harper[.] Dear mother, I hope these lines will find you all alive and well as usual[.] the last letter I received from you was dated 4th,[.] I am very anxious to hear from you. I have been sick for four or five dayes but I am nearly well[.] I think I will be in a day or so[.] I am getting so I can eat cornbread. give my love to all the family and best respects to all friends[.] we are in very good houses and large Breastworks[.] there is over 100 guns in two miles of this place[,] what we call hundred pounders two hundred and so on[.] yester the enemy attacked our men below Malvern Hill and drew them back until our reinforcements came up. J.L. Stuart. I write you ever week[.] I want to you to write often[.] J.L. Stuart

1864, June 19
J.H. Siddons (*Clayton's Hospital, Lynchburg, VA*) to **Catherine Jackson**. General wartime correspondence reporting the death of her husband **William R. Jackson**. [443]

Mrs. Jackson, Madam, as I have been with Mr. Jackson ever since he came here I think it my duty to tell you the sad story of the death of Mr. Jackson. I am very sorry to have to do it but if I do not let you know it I don't know when you will hear of it. Mr. Jackson was doing very well until last Monday when he commenced getting weaker and has been growing worse ever since. Last night about 12 o'clock he expired. He had got so he could walk about the house and sit up rite smart but he was taking with a running off of the bowels and that weakened him very fast which was the cause of his death. He received all of the attention that we could give him but we could not raise him. I trust he is now in heaven as he appeared to be satisfied on that subject. Put your trust in the Lord and he will take care of you. He knows that is right. I send you the certificate that the Doctor gave him when he was received here. J.H. Siddons. P.S. He left one dollar and five cents. That was all the money he had which I will send in this letter.

1864, June 27
William Riley Barrett (*Point Lookout, MD*) to **Bryan Tyson**. General wartime correspondence with brief mention of **Short.** [444]

B. Tyson Esq[.] Dear sir[,] yours of the 22nd was received in due time and I should have answered it before[.] I have been quite unwell and am feeble yet[,] but able to sit up long enough to write a few lines. You wished me to say something concerning your publications if I had space. I am not able to do so at this time and do justice to your publications. I will say this much though at present. It was considered by all who read it as teaching sound doctrine and based upon the truest principles of American liberty. It was considered as being worthy the consideration of all who are for liberty and independence[.] I am only sorry that there are not enough such books in the South. I will give some names in my next in whom you may confide. Let me hear from you soon and what has been done concerning my case. I have not hesitancy in saying that Mr. Short is what he represents himself to be[.] Respectfully your friend, W.R. Barrett, Co "B"[,] 13th Division[,] Point Lookout Md[.]

1864, June 27
Daniel C. Wilson (*Point Lookout, MD*) to **Bryan Tyson**. General wartime correspondence with brief mentions of **Phillip Wilson, Enoch Stewart** and **Doctor C. Phillips** [445]

Sir[,] yours of the 24th Just come to hand and its contents was duly noticed. I was glad to hear from you[.] you spoke of wanting to know what Wilson I am[.] I'm the son Philip Wilson from More county[.] Enoch Stewart was wounded, Doctor Philips is hear sick & he wishes you to send him few postage stamps[.] The money that I wrote for[,] you need not be uneasy about it[.] I will pay it in gold or silver[.] I will write to you again soon and give you all the news in more county[.] write soon and direct as before, D. C. Wilson

1864, June 28
F.B. Fry to sister **Lydia Shields Fry**. General wartime correspondence with brief mentions of **Mrs. Muse, Ed Gardner, Daniel Fry, Ben Fry** and **Madison Fry.** [446]

F.B. Fry to Lydia Shields Fry: Dear Sister: I take my pen to answer yours of the 24th I received last Saturday. It found us well. I was at old Mrs. Muses's warping when Mr. Ed Gardiner came, and I tried that day to get some paper to answer you but they had none. I was glad to hear from you all, especially John. I have been so uneasy about him. I will save all the butter and eggs I can by the time he hears from his officer, and will send it to him and be glad to do so, and some honey too. I don't know who I can send it by; if you can find out[,] send me word. I cannot tell if Daniel will have to go or not. Today he has gone to Carthage and then he won't know until he hears from his (officer?)[.] I don't know how long that will be. I have got my dresses in the loom but I don't know when they will get out. Nothing strange down here. The Rogues are stealing all about constantly. They threshed several bushels of Ben Fry's wheat that was just cut at the (?). They bursted Madison Fry's mill but they did not get anything but his dinner that he had carried the day before and had not eaten. You must excuse this letter. The other side is an old letter from W.W. Fry. I will write again when I hear from Daniel's case. Your sister[,] F.B. Fry. Tell Kitty I will come as soon as I can; she must not think hard.

1864, July 6
Murdo McLeod (*Fort Delaware*) to **Bryan Tyson**. General wartime correspondence with brief mentions of **James Tyson, Henry C. Tyson** and **Thomas J. Hogan.** [447]

Dear Sir, Having been captured May 6th and now a prisoner of war at this place and being in straitening circumstances, destitute of money and all else that would add to my comfort, I have concluded to write you, hoping it may be in your power to do me a favor at this time by sending me some money[.] no difference how small the amount, If you can conveniently do this, I will replace the same, is tolerable while here, otherwise I will pay it to any of your friends in Moore whom you may designate, and be under many obligations to you. Your bro James Tyson of my Co. was wounded at Bristoe Station last Oct. –has not been able for duty since. H. C. Tyson was wounded at Gettysburg, and not fully able for duty at the time I left the co. Thos. J. Hogan was also wounded at Gettysburg – recovering from his wound, but was not with the co. where I was captured, he having been sent to the hospital a few days before the campaign opened. Hoping to hear from you soon. I remain Your Old Servant, Murdo McLeod, Lt. 26th N.C. Regt. Address me here, in care, Capt. G.W. Ahl.

1864, July 6
William Riley Barrett (*Prison Camp, Elmira, NY*) to **Bryan Tyson**. General wartime correspondence with brief mentions of Col. **Hoffman.** [448]

Dear sir[,] I intended writing some[?] after my arrival at this place but I have been quite unwell since I came here. I answered your letter before I left Point Lookout but I had not space to answer it satisfactorily. As for your pamphlets[,] I have not had the pleasure of seeing them. You wished to know if your book had been suppressed – it had not when I left home but was read with delight by all who love liberty and a free government and I can say that had enough such books been published at an earlier day[.] I think the Country would have been in a better condition Than it now is and I am satisfyed that if you could succeed in getting more of your publications through the lines[.] that they would do a great deal of good yet in restoring the union and in bringing back those who have been led astrays and prevailed an to rebel against their mother Country. I have never heard from my letter to Col Hoffman and I hope you will learn what disposition has been made of it as I am anxious to be relieved from Prison and become a citizen of the government to which I properly belong. – I am in the same condition that I was when I first wrote you concerning money matters[.] If you sent any to point Lookout let me know it and I can probably get it. if you have not and can accommodate me your favor will most assuredly be reciprocated[.] if you have not the means to spare[,] probably some of your acquaintances have who will be willing to relieve me who has been driven from his family and his home and compelled to take up arms against his now government contrary to practice and everything else that is right. Let me hear from you soon and oblige your friend, W. R. Barrett, Ward 20[,] Barracks No 3[,] Elmira New York[.]

1864, July 12
Baxter C. Phillips *(Greensboro, NC)* to mother **Nancy Phillips.** General wartime correspondence with brief mentions of **Henry Dorsett**, **Emily Dorsett, Thomas Dixon** and **Elmira Phillips**. [449]

Dear Mother, Before this reaches you I will be in Virginia. Our regiment is at Petersburg. We reached Henry Dorsett's Thursday night and stayed there until Saturday morning. Our kinfolks are all well in that region. We went fishing Friday with the girls, Caught a few. There is one thing that I wish to mention with regard to Cousin Em in respect to our conversation. Being with her, I have satisfied myself that she has been seriously wronged almost amounting to slander. So you may rest assured that you were right in disbelieving reports. She is much more steady than she used to be. I am sorry that I entertained such views of her as I did at the time of our conversation. I will try to be more careful in the future. In a word, Mother, I believe all that I heard about to be a lie, and that it was told maliciously too. Mother, just keep this to yourself. I hated to leave them. Had I been a brother parting, it would have hurt them but little worse. But being a soldier I had apparently to disregard their tears, yet it is a false exhibition, for it finds a reciprocal emotion in my breast. On Saturday night we stopped at Thomas Dixon's just above Snow Camp and yesterday we came to the Shops and this morning came to Greensboro. We will leave this evening for Raleigh as that road is the nearest open of any. I can't tell when we will reach the regiment. I want you to be cheerful and never despond. Continue in earnest suplication for us and, Mother, you will succeed. You need not write until you hear from me again. Tell Elmira I will write to her when I stop. I hope we will meet again. May God bless you. My love to all, Baxter

1864, July 12
Mastin C. Phillips *(Greensboro, NC)* to father Rev. **Lewis Phillips Jr.** General wartime correspondence with brief mentions of **Baxter Phillips**. [450]

Dear Father, I drop you a line as I promised to let you know that I have reached this place. We reached here a few minutes ago. I feel much worsted by the trip although we took our own time on the way. I don't know what to do for the best. I don't feel able for duty, but I can't see that I can do anything else but go to the Regiment. I have not seen nor do not see any prospect of getting employment on the way. If I can do better than go to the Regiment[,] I will let you know immediately, but you need not hope for anything of this sort. We will not leave here until morning[.] I reckon if I don't feel better by then I shall stay a day or two longer if I can get permission. There has been rain here recently and a fair prospect today for more. I hope you have had rain before now. Corn is good generally on the route. I hope there will be plenty made. I wish I could hear from you before I reach the army but this I cannot do. If we go straight tomorrow[,] I shall be in the fighting before you get this. I am not prepared for what awaits me in the future. I am not able for duty and I am unwilling to die. All I can promise is that I will do the best I can and if I die, I shall die praying. You can assist me by your prayers as you have heretofore. I hope we shall meet again. Baxter is waiting and I will stop. My love to you all. May God bless you all. Pray for me. Your son, Mastin

1864, July 27
Murdo McLeod (*Fort Delaware*) to **Bryan Tyson**. General wartime correspondence with brief mentions of **Lindsay Williams, Charles C. Roberts, Henry Harrington, William D. Harrington, John A.B. Blue, Neill Kelly, Malcom Ray, William T. Jones, Henderson Thomas, Roberts** and **Wesigier.** [451]

Dear Sir, Yours of the 21st inst. has been rec'd—I am pleased to hear from you and I thank you indeed, for your willingness to aid me when your precarious circumstances will admit--at any time, such a favor will be most acceptable. Lindsay Williams to whom you alluded, was not in my Co. but in a Mississippi reg't, if I have been correctly informed. Charles C. Roberts of my Co was killed May the 5th. Henry Harrington, son of Wm. D. Harrington was also killed, in a cavalry fight near Hanover CH. Lts. Jno. AB. Blue, Neill Kelly & Malcom Ray were killed in May. Our old county seems to have suffered several in the recent engagements. Capt. Blue and Lts. Thomas, Roberts & Jones of Moore were captured, and are here now,-- the latter (formerly of the farm of Tyson, Kelly &Co.) requests me to ask you if Weisiger, formerly of Fayetteville N.C. is in Washington City. I would be glad to receive copies of your recent publications. My health for sometime has been improving, but is yet bad, resulting as much from low spirits as anything else I imagine. I shall be pleased to hear from you at any time. Your Obd't Servant, Murdo McLeod.

1864, July 29
unknown soldier *(35th Infantry, Company C, Petersburg, VA)* to sibling **John B. Ray**. General wartime correspondence between siblings with brief mentions of constant engagements around Petersburg and **Daniel J. Shields**, **Thomas A. McDonald**, **D.C. Morris**, **Andrew Jackson Keith** and elections results for Sheriff and Governor. [452]

So I seat myself this morning to drop you a few lines to let you no that I am well at this time and hoping theas few lins may find you and your family in good health[.] the health of the company just tolerabel well at this time[.] D.J. Shields, Tomas McDonald, D Moris, A.J. Keath not well but they ar not not doing wors[.] their is about 20 men for duty in the company[.] we hav a very good officer in command of the company he is [illegible]. John thair has been a grate deal of work don hear sins lef old Boagard com[.] com as near going under as any jeneral[.] I think the yankees ar as near Petersburg as they will ever get I think and I think it imposibel for us to moov them from hear only they hav a mind to go[.] our men opend on them one evening to try thair strenth and they shot five tims to our once[.] thair is a continual sharpshootering at us from our brest works at each other[.] we hav to have trenches to cut to go after water & c. and they do too[.] thair is a continual shelling at us nearly all the time with mortrs but it is only once and a while[.] they can drop them our brest works and we drop ours in thair brest works thou[.] we are in just such a fix that neither sid has not much advantig! John I suppose you wold like to no how the election went in our company for Shireff, Worthy 16 McNeill 2, for governor Vans 12 Hoalden 8 Davis 8 Riter 1 Harington 2[.] thair was a good maney voted for Hoalden just to freact th oficers and aold sessionist[.] John we have a grate deal of work to do and gard[.] if I new as much as I no now when I was at hoam John I wold hav ben thair yet[.] if we wasnt so cloast to this enemy[,] thair wold be moar deserting than ever was but the man hate to run a way in the face of them[.] John honor is a grate thing but I am afraid we hav had vary dear for all we will get[.] John thair is not a man in the company but said if they was at hoam they wold stay[.] we hav to dig in our trenches day and knight rain os sine, hot or coald[.] thair is four killed or wounded moar or less evry day by morter shells or sharpshooters[.] the men hav becom so carless they don car much for anything[.] John I dont want to give any body bad advice but if I was at hoam[,] I wold stay thair till tims got beter[.] we get aplenty to eat of corn and bacon shugar and coffee and peas &c. the yankes shells the town sevear [rest of letter missing including the name of the sender]

1864, August 1
James R. Jones (*Prison Camp, Elmira, NY*) to cousin **Bryan Tyson**. General wartime correspondence with brief mentions of **Martha Jones.** [453]

Dear Cousin, I seat myself this morning to drop you a few lines from which you will learn that I am a prisoner of war, though I am enjoying my health tolerable well yet I do not like captivity[.] we fare tolerable well considering tho I am gitting very bear for clothes. I would like very well if you would be kind enough to send me some tobacco, clothing, a little money if you please. I remain, your true cousin. Jas. R. Jones, son of Martha Jones. Adress Jas. R. Jones[,] Prisoners Camp, Elmira N.York, Barracks no 3, Ward 24, Care of Maj Colt[.]

1864, August 2
Matthew Maness (*Point Lookout, MD*) to **Bryan Tyson**. General wartime correspondence with brief mentions of **Daniel Wilson** and **Phillip Wilson.** [454]

Dear Sir[,] I seat myself this morning to write you a few lines hoping it may reach you and find you well. My necessities are such that I am compelled to ask some friend to assist me and I thought I would ask you to send me a few dollars, as I am entirely out of both money and tobacco, which if you will comply with my request You will very much oblige me, indeed, besides I will be under many obligations to you, Daniel Wilson son of Phillip Wilson was here but has gone to another camp, as long as he was here I decided with him as long as I had[.] the people of our neighborhood was well generally when I heard from them. I will close. I remain Your Friend until death, Matthew Manes

1864, August 2
Noah Deaton (*Prisoners Camp Co. I 6th Division, Point Lookout, MD*) to father **Wm. Deaton** (*Caledonia, NC*). Wartime correspondence between son and father with brief mentions of fellow prisoners **Levi Britt**, **D. Martin**, **William Christopher Moore**, **Briton Saunders**, **A.M. Fields**, **John T. Warwick**, **Benjamin Gilliam Hollingsworth**, **Duncan Blue**, **Archibald Alexander Ray**, **John B. Clark**, **Neill Hannon**, Sergt. **Neill McIntosh** and **William Barrett**. [455]

Dear Father. After a long delay I again attempt to drop you a few lines in reply to your kind favor of June the 6th. It gave me great pleasure to hear that all was well at home. Although many are sickening and dyeing daily, by a kind providence I still enjoy good health and live in hope that I may return home some day to bask in the pleasant sunshine of peace. God speed the day. Levi Britt, D. Martin, W. C. Moore, Briton Saunders, A. M. Fields, Warwick & Hollingsworth are all with Duncan Blue, A. A. Ray, J. B. Clark, Mr. Hannon & Sergt. N McIntosh has gone from here to some other prison and also Wm Barrett. The old U.S. postage that is the stamp used before the war are dead and you may not trouble yourself about the US postage for I can pay that when the letter arrives here. I remain your affectionate son. N. Deaton

1864, August 2
C.D. Caddell to brother **A.S. Caddell**. General wartime correspondence between brothers with brief mentions of Col. **William B. Richardson, Vance, Holden, Lt. Little. A.M. Dunlap** and the marriage of **John B. Muse** and **Martha Cox.** [456]

I embrace the present opportunity of writing you a few lines in reply to yours which came to hand[.] I was glad to hear that you were well satisfied this leaves us all well[.] I have nothing strange to write[.] times is dull about here[.] There has nothing strange occured since you left of any interest[.] the deserters and conscrips is doing about the same[.] there is some of them at the Sunday School every Sunday[.] They will soon take the day unless something is done[.] I recd your things that you sent by Colonel Richardson[.] he told mee you had turned to be a strong Holden man[.] let mee know if it was so[.] let mee if that board is coming around soon or not tell me if you think there would be any chance of my being assigned to duty there with you by my going there to go before the board[.] do you think Pearson could have me assigned to the 7th district or not find out & let me know[.] I expect Vance will be elected if Holden is[.] I shant cry but I shant go to the election[.] your Horse is at Home[.] A.M. sent him home as soon as you left[.] I have not seen him since you left[.] I dont know why he did not keep him[.] Lt.

Little has left Carthage[.] I will close write soon as this comes to hand & give me all the news[.] I remain your Loving Brother untill Death, C.D. Caddell [P.S] J.B. Muse & Martha Cox is married[.]

1864, August 2
Alexander M. Dunlap (*Carthage, NC*) to **A.S. Caddell**. General wartime correspondence with brief mentions Lt. **Williamson**, Lt. **Little**, Capt. **Pearson**, **Pleasant Seawell**, **George Muse**, **Howard Muse**, **Harrington**, **Absalom B. Fry**, Capt. **Lilley**, Lt. **George Willcox**, **Bradley Brady** and the marriage of **Julia Caddell** and **Thomas W. Ritter**. [457]

Dear Sir, I have recd yours of a recent date[.] I see that you are safe at Lexington & seemes to be very well satisfied with your present situation. I am glad to hear that for it would be much worse if you were dissatisfied being away from home – I guess you have a very pleasant time of it carrying prisoners to Raleigh getting on big spreys but I expect money is wanting in this respect. We have a new enrolling officer in the place of Lt. Little – Lt. Williamson from Caswell Co. who has been acting as S.O. in the eastern part of the state is E.O. for this Council. he is a very nice fellow you would like him better than you did Little—I will endeavor in the mean time to have you sent back to this office[.] The S.O. says he will apply for you when Capt Pearson sends men here to hunt[.] Tim I would like to have you here very much, but my advice to you would be to stay where you are and as long as your are pleased with your situation because you will never be put any trouble to go before the Board but not withstanding this[.] if you still insist I will do my best but I think will succeed[.] I have just returned from our cousins wedding[.] we had quite a pleasant time of it. A "big ball crowd" at both places[.] Julia seemed to be satisfied with her husband & her husband I know was pleased with her[.] I have been calling on "our galls" as usual. I still have a hankering notion of feeling them in different spots[.] I saw Nancy last week, She seemed to be very much dejected at your absence. I often think of you when I am with them - I & Jack had a fin time yesterday eating water melons drinking cider[.] I eat two pieces for you & drank ½ gallon cider[.] Jack done likewise for Pleasant[.] Lt. Little did not seem to be very much displeased though he was a little angry. You has seen him yourself in this time of grief - I see that Vance is running clean ahead in the army & I pray that he may do the same in the state - Harrinton will give Ritter a race if he does not beate him[.] I have not seen Neill since you left but I suppose they are well at home— I sent your horse to Neill, Little did not want him – Give my respects to Pleasant & George Muse & tell Muse his family is well[.] I saw them Howard yesterday. I will be glad to hear from you at any time & will respond cheerfully, A.M. Dunlap [P.S] Little says he would get me a position as E.O. in the eastern part of the state[.] if he does this[,] I will take you along with me & try & work you into a position[.] A.B. Fry is home he is relieved for the war[.] I expect you could get relieved if you were back with the Brigad. If they bother me much I will go here & be relieved two. Brad Brady is at home[.] he deserted. who voted for Holden in Capt. Lilleys Co[.] I saw Lt. Wilcox last week[.] he is wounded badly in the shoulder but will get over it[.] he seems buoyant and hopeful

1864, August 8
Neil McIntosh (*Elmira, NY*) to **Bryan Tyson**. General wartime correspondence with brief mentions of **Sallie Moore**. [458]

Dear sir[,] I received your kind letter at the Point but faild to answer it on the account of being moved to this place[.] I am in tolerable health only at the present time but hopping that this may reach you and find you in good health[.] we get tolerable good fare here[.] we have good water as their is any need of drinking[.] all of your acquaintances here is in good health[.] Mr. Tyson if is is in your power to aid mee soon I will make it up to you or som of your relation that you say for mee to do[.] if Mr .Tyson is there a lady in your city by the name of Sallie Moore from Chatham[?] if you know her give me the number of her box[.] I remain yours, N McIntosh. Direct to Elmira N.Y[,] ward 33rd[,] in care of Magor Colt[,] Provost Marshal[.]

1864, August 9
James R. Jones (*Prison Camp, Elmira, NY*) to cousin **Bryan Tyson**. General wartime correspondence with brief mentions of **William Jones**. [459]

Dear Cousin, Your kind and most welcome letter of the 5th [illegible word] was duly received yesterday—I also received the money for which I am very much obliged to you[.] Brother William is dead[.] he was wounded and died in dec 1862[.] Father and Mother were well last May[,] also grandfathers folks— I have never seen any of your publications in N.C. but I have heard of them but I never heard them commented on. When I was at home last uncle James told me where you were[.] If you have any good literary works[,] I wish you would send me a copy. Hoping to hear from you soon[.] I will close. I remain your cousin, Jas. R. Jones, Ward 24[,] Barracks no 3[.]

1864, August 10
Baxter C. Phillips *(Division Hospital)* to sister **Elmira Phillips.** General wartime correspondence with brief mentions of **Mastin Phillips, Davis** and the death of **Reuben Maness.** [460]

Dear Elmira, Yours reached me and found me sick, but not dangerous, I trust. It is my old disease. I have been sick near two weeks. Came to hospital yesterday. Am much reduced in flesh and strength. Don't be uneasy, I will do the best I can. I trust in God and will be well. Mastin is doing well as could be expected for him. Nothing to write, Davis is with me but getting better. Reuben Maness died yesterday from a wound received the day before. I will let you know how I get along. Write soon. My love to all. Pray for me. Be cheerful. God will hear, for our good. Direct as before. Baxter

1864, August 10
J.L. Stuart (*Petersburg, VA*) to his mother **Mary A. Harper**. General wartime correspondence with brief mentions of the Battles of the Crater and the death of **William J. Monroe** and mentions of **William Brewer**, **Henry Brewer**, **William Dunn**, **Enoch Jordan**, **William Kennedy**, **Asa A. McIntosh, Mary Diffie Spivey**, **Anderson H. Smith** and **Eli Lambert.** [461]

Dear Mother[,] once more by the Blessing of God I am permitted to write you a few lines to inform you that I am well and unhurt truly hoping these lines may reach and find you all a live and well[.] we are in reserve now to rest a few dayes but we are at a very dangerous place for the yankees Mortar shells all about us[.] two men of our regiment was wounded to day[.] we have got us bunker proofd but I do not feel too safe in them[.] our company is getting to be very small[.] we have fourteen for duty the sixth of this month[.] Wm. J. Munroe of our co. was killed while going out on picket[.] he was hit in the hip and did not live but a short time[.] he has two Brothers in the company[.] one of them went out and saw him buried. he was put in a coffin[.] he never spoke a word I have seen[.] Wm. and Henry Brewer and Wm. Dunn and Enoch Jordan they was all well as usual[.] I also saw William Kennedy he was well ten dayes ago. It was a burying day from the great slaughter of the 30th July[.] according to the account in the papers our loss was about 1200 and the yankee loss about 2000[.] since then our men spring a mine under the yankee picket line but it did not amount to much[.] we do not know at what minuet the yankees will spring another mine on some part of our lines[.] the report is that Grant is a mining us again but he did not make any thing by the operation the other time[.] I received your letter dated the 31st July[.] I was very glad to hear from you all[.] I wish I could have been at home at your threshing to a eat potatoes and looked at the pretty girls[.] you had so many[.] Day before yesterday our co. went out to wash up[.] me and Sergt McIntosh had a fine Dinner[.] we bought us one qt of Irish potatoes at 2.00and we give two rations of meat for three pounds of flour we had Irish potatoes and Dumplings and we made us Apple pies and had sugar and coffee to go a long with the rest of our good things[.] give my respects to Mary Spivey. tell her we use to see funny times but all my fun is changed for I am far away from home and friends under the sound of the Booming cannons and rattle of muskets and do not know at what minuet I may receive the stroke that will take me to eternity. I must close write soon[.] I hope we will all meet again[.] give my love to all the family and respects to all inquiring friends. Direct to Petersburg as usual[.] A.H. Smith and Eli Lambert run away the other night. Yours, J.L. Stuart

1864, August 16
Wesley W. Gilliland to wife **Charity Brady Gilliland**. General wartime correspondence with brief mentions of **Barney Noodles** and **Owen.** [462]

Dear Wife, I will write to you one time more to let you know that I am on this land and among the living. We have had a powerful time. We commenced on the 5th day of May and have been fighting ever since. We have had some of the hardest fighting ever, we have had the hottest fighting in common to be seen. I have been where the balls were as thick as hail and went through several charges. I am happy to say that God had spared my life up to this time. Owen was not hurt. I think Barney Noodles is a prisoner. He is better off than I am. We have taken a good many prisoners, but I can't tell about how many were killed. I haven't got time to write much now, but if I can be spared until October, then I'll write again. I can't tell you much now. I want you to do the best you can. It looks like my chance is bad. I write this to let you hear from me one more time. There is no telling when this fight will stop. I expect it will go on as long as there is anybody to fight. Respectfully, yours to death. W.W. Gilliland

1864, August 17
James R. Jones (*Prison Camp, Elmira, NY*) to cousin **Bryan Tyson**. General wartime correspondence. [463]

Dear Cousin, Im growing somewhat impatient for an answer I thought I would again address you there is a chance now if a prisoner has a friend or relation North that will stand his security[,] he can get out on his parole of honor untill called for to be exchanged. I wish you to consult with the authorities at Washington and see if you cannot obtain one a parole[.] I would like very much to come down and spend a while with you. This leaves me well at present and I hope may find you in the best of health. Write soon and let me know whether my request can be complied with. I remain your true cousin. Jas. R. Jones

1864, August 18
Henry Clay Brown (*Point Lookout, MD*) to **Bryan Tyson**. General wartime correspondence with brief mentions of **Neil McIntosh, Daniel C. Wilson, G.W. Tyson, Joseph M. Brady, Robert Talley, Henry Brown** and **Cornelius Shields.** [464]

Dear Sir, I received your letters of the 4th inst.some time back but could not write sooner on account of not getting any stamps as there was none on the Point. you said you want me to inform you who of your acquaintees had left hear. N. McIntosh. D.C. Wilson. G.W. Tyson J.M. Brady all the rest of the boys are hear and doing tolerable well. I want you to tell Robert Talley to send me a few dollars and by so douing he will amplely rewarded for the same as I think if he had ever called on my father. or Grandfather Shields for a favor[,] it would have been granted[.] and if it is convenient for you to send me some it will be thankfully received and be returned. if it should be the lords will write soon and fail not. give me the news and if you heare any from NC. or who is elected Govener. so no more[.] I remain yours friend until death, H. C. Brown

1864, August 19
James Tyson (*Browers Mills, NC*) to **Bryan Tyson**. General wartime correspondence with brief mentions of **Jody, Fannie, Lydia Goldston, Eleanor Spinks** and her grandchildren **Henry N. Tomlinson** and **John M. Tomlinson.** [465]

Dear Sir[,] I again attempt to write you a few lines in answer to yours that came safe to hand two weeks ago[.] I was glad to hear from you and to hear that you ware well[.] it found us all in tolerable good health[.] we are all well at this time[.] so far as health is conserned I hav not got well yet though my thigh is a good eal better than it has bin[.] I can walk about over the house with crutches[.] I hav never bin out doors yet. the health of the neighborhood is very good[.] corn and oats crops are very good wheat not so good in this neighborhood[.] Jody is nocking along doing the best she can for me during my helpless condition[.] Fannie is aflicted with the spine affection that she cant walk without help[.] Aunt Lydia Goldston and Family are all well[.] Bryan the old Lady Spinks is anxious to hear from her grandsons that ware taken prisoners[.] She has not hird from them in some time[.] if you know anything about them she would be pleased for you to write it to me[.] nothing more at present but write soon. yours respectfully, James Tyson

1864, August 19
Mary Caddell and **Joseph Caddell** to cousin **A.S. Caddell**. General wartime correspondence between cousins with brief mentions of **C.D. Caddell, Wesley Upton** and **Bill Graham**. [466]

Cousin A.S., with great pleasure I drop you a few lines from whitch you may learn that I am well hoping that these lines may reach and find you well and enjoying yourself splendid[.] I received your very kind letter yesterday that you rote me the 4 of this inst and I was truly glad to hear from you[.] I have no nuse that would interest you at the present time[.] days is dull around here[.] cousin Tim I was mighty glad to hear that you was enjoying you self so well with your jularky[.] cousin Tim I do so wish I could a herd herd you a talking too her[.] I don't expect should a laughed most powerful[.] well I wished I could see my sweet heart but I expect it will be doutful whether I ever see him anymore or not[.] an cousin Tim you know if I never see him I shall ever live remindful on him[.] I do wish this war would stop and let you all come home for their isent but one of same boy about here an that is CD an I am geting tired seeing so many galls an no boys[.] oh cousin Tim there is one thing I must tell you before I go any further[.] Bill Graham has got home and if you dont know half how glad I am[.] I do wish I could think of something funny to write to you but I am here informing you I cant[.] cousin A S is their a heap a boys up there[.] if their is I would love to be up there tho feel that I know you have fine times up there[.] I wish you good luck in all your undertaking[.] an cousin Tim I wish I knew what you did see[.] I know it must bin funny an you know that I delight very mutch in hereining anything funny and greatest more so in seeing something funny[.] well cousin Tim our Sunday school is still going on[.] I think you had better come down some sunday an see how we are geting a long[.] we are a mighty plain set when we all get up there to gather[.] you dont know half how bad miss you[.] I will close my letter for this time[.] rite as soon as you get this an give me all the nuse[.] I remain as ever your true friend an cousin till death. Mary Caddell [P.S.] oh Tim I liked to forget to tell you that Wesley Upton was lying out an had hid mamas apron binding for a belt and holleyes grass knife for his defender. Mary

Dear nephew, I drop you a line or too[.] tim you had aught to a bin her to a went to the sale at Harrells with me and Eli and we would a flew around the gals[.] come down and I will give you a drink of sider[.] Joseph Caddell

1864, August 22
Alexander M. Dunlap (*Carthage, NC*) to **A.S. Caddell**. General wartime correspondence with brief mentions of Lt. **Mills**, **Festerman**, **Tyson**, **Cockman**, **Neill Caddell**, **Jenkins**, Capt. **Pearson**, **Neill Black** and friends **Jack**, **Sue H.**(from Jonesboro), **Flora**, **Malcom** and **Maggie**. [467]

My dear friend, I recd yours two mails ago was glad to you had become better reconciled and had concluded to remain where you are untill this seige is raised[.] Nothing new, no reinforcements as you[,] but looking for them daily. There has been two or three companies ordered to this County from other county which will add 250 new to our present force, you may look out for squally times soon. They are going right into plundering & eating out the deserters families & their friends[.] Lt Mills & his company hasnt been doing anything since they were [illegible] to, except stand hicket, which has kept constantly engaged. He has several jocular fellows with him[.] Festerman in particular, he keeps Tyson's little [word cut off] & James always on the alert[.] They have sent two of the prisoners to Raleigh & will send Cockman soon[.] I saw Neill this week, he told me confidentially that some person had been stealing his wheat, but it got so heavy he couldn't carry it further than the ford of the branch, and from some unknown cause the rogue made his exit in the briar patch & left the wheat in the path[.] Neill will give you further particulars as I am not at liberty to reveal enough to say that somebody is hurt[.] Jack & I have been relieved from duty on the picket lines and have retired to a more private life, drinking hard cider, and visiting "our galls" which consumes nearly all our time. McNeill still has plenty on hand and Old Jenkins made a barrel and consequently we sleapt by it to keep the enemy from capturing it - you might guess how much vinegar Jenkins had left[.] Jack had quite a nice time yesterday & today he brought Miss Sue H from Jonesboro yesterday evening, she has stopped at Jack's house & will remain there until tomorrow[.] I have called on her 3 or 4 times since her arrival at this monotonous vilage. She seems to be very happy and enjoys herself fairly. she is the same as she was before she left this county, only she is not looking so well - I wish "Our Galls" were all Sues - I havnt seen Flora lately, but intend going soon – Malcom & [illegible]are in their usual health, Malcom still calls on Maggie[.] I see that Capt Pearson Hd Qts will be at Ashboro after this untill further orders, I hardly know where to send my letter. Since Pearson has left Ashboro, but perhaps he will leave you it[,] if so I will find it. Then I suppose you will see it come if you are at Ashboro[.] Had a letter from Dan this week, says all is well & every one of the soldiers seem to be hopeful[.] Neil Black has just returned from Weldon[,] says the "new issue" is well & doing as well as could be expected. write soon to your "Old friend" A.M. Dunlap

1864, August 22
J.L. Stuart (*Petersburg, VA*) to his mother **Mary A. Harper**. General wartime correspondence with brief mentions of **William Brewer, Henry Brewer, Sampson Brewer, John Spivey, Levi Davis, John Tucker, Isaac Cagle, Matthew Cagle, Kindred Muse** and **Edward Warner.** [468]

Mrs Mary A. Harper[.] Dear Mother[,] by the Blessing of God I am a live and well[.] yesterday Sunday 21st Aug our Brigade was in a severe fight[.] the 20 August we was relieved out of the Breastworks and sent around on the right to the Weldon rail road where the yankees had takend posession of the road some few dayes before hand[.] and yesterday morning we charged on the yankees and takend their first line of Breastworks and came very near capturing one of their Batteries[,] but the troops on our right could not or did not come up so we had to fall back to their first line[.] Cookes Brigade was on our left and Kirklands on our right. I saw Wm. & Henry and Sampson Brewer as they were marching up to go into the fight[.] I saw John Spivey last night. he told me one or two of their co. was wounded but none of our neighbor boys was hurt in that Co. I do not know whether Levi Davis was in it or not his regiment was[.] I saw him the 14th[.] John Spivey was hit with a piece of shell but was not hurt bad[.] John Tucker and Isaac Cagle and Matthew Cagle was not hurt but they was in the fight[.] it was the hottest place our Brigade has ever been[.] in our regt. had forty wounded three killed and three missing[.] the 24th lost ten killed, nineteen wounded and four missing. the 56th regt lost the use of seventy killed wounded and missing[.] the 25th and 36th regts lost about forty each. we went up before a yankee Battery and they Jest mowed us down[.] some men was torne all to pieces. Sergt. E. Warner of our co. was wounded slitely in hand and K. Muse was hit in the hip but did not Break the skin. we fell back to our main line of works last night[.] today we are resting but we do not know how long we will rest for we are looking for the yankees to Blow us up again. we takend several prisenor yesterday[.] it looks like we will all be killed and wounded before this war will end[.] I want to see you all the worst in this world[.] I hope these lines may find you all well as usual[.] give my love to all the family and respects to all friends[.] write soon[.] I do not know how soon it will be before we are in another fight[.] I hope by the mercies of God we will be permitted to see each other again. Tell Charles I found an old yankee pocket book yesterday[.] it had five cents silver and 14 stamps in it[.] I remain your affectionate son. J.L. Stuart

1864, August 26

Daniel J. Shields (*Petersburg, VA*) to brother **William Wadsworth Shields**. General wartime correspondence with brief mention of battle at Globe Tavern, VA and **Benjamin J. Shields, John Vick, Duncan P. Shields, Turquill McNeill, Flora** and **Old Ben**. [469]

Dear brother, today I received your letter and I was more than glad to here from you and to here all was well. This leaves me will and I believe I have got over the scear I got in the big charge on last Sunday and I hope these few lines will find you all well and doing well. I have know nuse of interest to write you. I wrote a letter to Father a few days ago and told all about the charge we was in last Sunday. We are now in reserve in the old corner and last night they give us mortars. I never saw the like but thank God they hurt know one. I was glad to here you had your furlough renewed. I made them all believe that your old furlough was not out till the last of this month[.] I tell you to stay at home as long as you can. John Vick sais to tell Pap and Dunk that Turtle McNeill running against the red oak in the person hunt was not a drop in the bucket to the charge last Sunday. He sais to tell old Ben that he said snaiks. I must close, tell Flora I will write to here in a few days. Give my love and best respects to all and write soon and give me all the nuse. I remain your till death. Daniel J. Shields

1864, August 26

Absalom Vick (*Petersburg, VA*) to cousin **William Wadsworth Shields**. General wartime correspondence with brief mention of battle at Globe Tavern, VA and **Timothy Goodman, Richard Goins, John D.F. Smith, H.L. McLemore**, General **U.S. Grant, Capt. Henry W. Humphrey** and **Moses**. [470]

Dear cousin, it is with pleasure that I seat myself to drop you a few lines to let you know that I am yet in the land of the living and I am enjoying very good health at present and I hope these few lines will reach you and find you enjoying the same good blessings of health. We have hard times hear yet, we are lying in the ditches yet [illegible line] day for the last two of three weeks and you may know that we have slopy time of it. We had a big old he fight the other day[.] The yankees has got the railroad again between Petersburg and Weldon[.] they taken our Brigade out of the ditches and taken us around there and we staid there one night and next morning we had to charge the durn yankees[.] we charged them and you may defend that we had a big time of it. We charged them out of two lines of here breastwork but we could not rout them out of the third time. It was the hottest fight that I ever was in since the war begun. We lost half of the men that was in our Regt in the fight. We had 4 men wounded in our Co. T. Goodman and R. Goins and J.D.F. Smith, H.L. McLemore. T Goodman had his rite arm shot off near his boddy and the rest was slightly wounded. They will be able for duty in a day or two. We haven got buy 12 men in our Co. The boys is all well at this time. I hope that they will let us stay in the ditches more. Our men has charged the yankees three times on the railroad and has not got them off yet, I don't think that our men can git them off this time. I think that old Grant has got all of his forses over on the railroad this time[.] Humphrey has not been in command of our Co in 2 or three weeks. Moses is in command of it[.] If I was you I would stay at home as long as I could. I don't think that they will be any damage of doing so. I have no news to write you at present. I must close for this time. You must write soon and give me all the news you have in old Moore County. Your till Death, A. Vick.

1864, August 28
Mary Shields to brother **John W. Shields**. General wartime correspondence with brief mentions of **Robert D. Shields, Kitty Shields, Lydia Phillips Shields, Jones, Sam Hardin** and **William Hughes**. [471]

Dear Brother: I now take the opportunity of writing you a few lines to let you know how we are. As to health, we are not all well. All are well but Kitty and Robert: Kitty is about as common, and Robert is very poorly, not able to do anything like work. Mother wants you to try to get a furlough about the middle of October to come home to stay about three or four weeks to help sow wheat. If you don't, I don't know how we are going to get along, there will be so much ploughing to do. If you don't get to come home and if Robert don't get better[,] it looks like we will have to quit farming. I want you to tell whoever you go to for a furlough how we have to get along and perhaps he will let you come home and stay awhile in wheat sowing time. Robert says to ask you what you did with his old knapsack. We have not got your things that you sent by Mr. Jones yet, but we will, I reckon, before long. We will send you a pair of socks and drawers and something to eat as soon as we get a chance. I don't know when we will. We expect bad times in Moore County now. I learn there are four or five hundred hunter men at Carthage now and several hundred about at other places. They will do something before they quit. I went up to the factory last week and got some thread (?) at $25.00 and $30.00 per bunch. The hunters were about there. The layouts had killed one hunter the evening we go there, about a mile and a half from the factory. His name was Sam Harding. They said they shot ten balls in him. William Hughs came home about one Sunday and died last Monday. He give no certain evidence of being prepared to meet his God[.] John, I thought I was nearly done my letter but I will write on another paper and put it in with this. John, you must try to be a good boy. You have no mother, brother or sister to give you advice, but you are not forgotten at home and we can pray for you, and you must pray for yourself. Your loving sister, Mary.

1864, August 31
John W. McPherson (*Point Lookout, MD*) to **Bryan Tyson**. General wartime correspondence. [472]

Hearing that you were in Washington[,] I thought I would write you a few lines to let you know that I am still one among the living and in good health, also a prisoner of war. I was taken near Petersburg VA the 20th of last May and have been at this place ever since[.] We are faring tolerable well and if I had plenty of greenbacks could live sumptuously[.] I would like to have a little money and if you think proper to send me any[,] it will thankfully be received. I would write more but one page is all we are allowed to write[.] Write soon and direct to Co K[,] 1st Division[,] Point Lookout Md[,] Care of Major Brady Provost Marshal, Very Respectfully your Friend, J. W. McPherson

1864, September 3
James R. Jones (*Elmira, NY*) to cousin **Bryan Tyson**. General wartime correspondence. [473]

Dear Cousin, I seat myself to drop you a few lines in answer to your kind favor of the 26th of Aug. which came safe to hand this morning[.] I was very glad to think that you would attend to my request. if you can obtain a parole for a short time I would be glad to come and spend the time with you and will also feel very thankfull to you. As regards to what uncle James said about you[.] I did not hear any thing that he said more than that he said if you did not sympathise with the principles of the south[,] he did not blame you for leaving. And I think that the whole neighborhood held opinions similar to his - excuse bad writing as my pen is very bad. I wish to hear from you soon. When you write put the no of Barracks (3) ward (24) – Hoping to hear from you soon[.] I remain your true Cousin. Jas. R. Jones

1864, September 4

J.L. Stuart (*Petersburg, VA*) to his mother **Mary A. Harper**. General wartime correspondence with brief mentions of **William Brewer, Sampson Brewer, Wyatt Williamson, Martin L. Nall** and **John W. Maness.** [474]

Dear Mother[,] Once more by the blessings of God I am yet alive and well and as hearty as I ever was truly hoping these lines may find you all alive and well. we are in the trenches yet we have been in the ditches so much that it all comes right to us untell the yankees get to a shelling us[.] then it is anything else but pleasant to us[.] last night I was on picket and for an hour[.] the yankees threw Mortar shells at us[.] it is impossible for me to describe the scene to you[.] the Mortar shells in the dark look like a larg star or small torch flying in the air[.] sometimes there are five or six comeing at the same time and as many of ours going over to yankeedom[.] when the shell burst it makes a terrible report and the fragments fly in ever direction. They fell very close to me but I was not hurt yesterday. I saw William and Sampson Brewer they were well. I received your letter dated the 28th Aug[.] I was very glad to hear from you all very much[.] you wanted to know where Wiatt Williamson is[.] I have not heard from him since he was sent to the Hospital[.] I suppose he was sent to Richmond. Nine of our company have been hurt since the fight of the 21st. I hope I shall get to come home and eat syrup[.] you stated you was putting up a cane mill[.] I received a letter from M.L. Nall to day dated 28th Aug. he had no news of interest more than they were all well except his wounds. there was a severe fight near Reams Station the last of August but our Brigade was not in the fight[.] it appears like Grant is not going to leave here soon but I do not think he will charge our works in front of Petersburg[.] our greatest fear is we will have them to charge instead of them charging us[.] if you can find out when John W. Maness is coming back to the Company. I will be pleased if you can send me that jug of honey and syrup[,] if you get a chance to send me a box send potatoes onions and a few grounds of flour and the jug of honey[.] do not put your self to too much trouble and unless you can send it by one of my company[,] do not send it[.] I can do with out it very well but as my mess mate got a box[.] I want to see if the Sheffield District cant do as well[.] we will draw wheat bread Bacon peas sugar and coffee this evening. give my best Love to all the family and respects to all friends[.] excuse me for not writing more[.] I hope you are all getting along well and that nothing serious has occured to any of you[.] I must close[.] I hope to see you all again but we know not what aday may bring forth[.] J.L.S.

1864, September 5
C.D. Caddell (*Fayetteville Arsenal*) to brother **A.S. Caddell**. General wartime correspondence between brothers with brief mentions of **William Graham**, **Rany Caddell** and Capt. **Holmes**. [475]

I embrace he present opportunity of answering your very kind letter which came to hand the 30 inst which found me well & at home[.] I would have bin very glad to have seen you at home while I was there, but so it is. I came back here the 3rd of this inst[.] I dont think I shal have much duty to do here, I should be verry well satisfied if I new Mother could get along well[.] I expect to get Wm. Graham to stay with her[.] tell me what you think of it[.] I am assigned as watchman to guard the Goverment Smokehouse[.] I will not have any walkin to do[.] I have your horse in here[.] They have not used him any yet[.] I let Capt Holms have him[.] he says all he wants him for is to ride about town[.] he is our Quartermaster[.] if he dont use him good I will not let him keep him[.] I am assigned here for six months[.] I think in that time this war will end & that with a bad result[.] I think I should like to be at Lexington with you[.] tell mee how to manage to get a transfer to the 7th Dist[.] I want to know if you feel any way uneasy about ever going into service anymore[.] keep out if possible[.] try to get in some office of proffit if you can[.] I saw orders when they were going to turnout all conscript officers & put details & light entied men in their place[.] if I was you I would try to get some officer of profit in the 7 Dist[.] write soon & give me all the news[.] I will close for the present by saying keep out of this war[.] Your absent & affectionate Brother, C.D. Caddell

1864, September 7
Daniel C. Wilson (*Prison Camp, Elmira, NY*) to **Bryan Tyson**. General wartime correspondence. [476]

Dear Sir, I will write you a few lines to inform you that I am well and doing as well as one could expect. Situated as I am. I have written you this makes four letters. but have not received a line from you yet I have heard that you sent me money to Point Lookout but I have not received a cent yet[.] you had better countermand the amount send me[.] perhaps you may get it back from Pt Lookout. if it is convenient – please send me some tobaco and oblige your respected friend, D.C. Wilson P.W.[,] Barracks 3, Ward 23, Care Maj Colt[,] Elmira New York[.]

1864, September 8

Joseph J. Tyson (*Point Lookout, MD*) to cousin **Bryan Tyson**. General wartime correspondence with brief mention of **Doctor C. Phillips.** [477]

Dear Cousin, From the date I place of this letter, you will perceive that I am a "Prisoner of War". I wish to ask of you through this letter to send me a suit of grey clothes, and Two, or Three dollars U.S money – by so doing you will very greatly oblige a friend and relation. Dr Phillips wishes me to say to you that he had received the little money which you sent to him for which he is under many obligations to you. He wishes you to send him a dollar, or two more if you please. Our address -- Pt Lookout M.D., Co, F"[,] 4th Div., to the care of Maj. Brady, Provost Marshal, Yours truly[,] Joseph J. Tyson.

1864, September 9

Rany G. Caddell to son **A.S. Caddell**. General wartime correspondence between mother/son with brief mentions of **Daniel McIntosh**, **William Lane Wallace, Devotion Davis** and **James N. Caddell**. [478]

Dear son[,] I take my pen in order to answer your letter whitch came to hand on the 8th day of this instance[.] I was truly glad to hear from you for I had not heard from you so long so I was feared that you was not alive for I had not heard any word from you in 23 days[.] I thought every day you would come home but I am disappointed when your letter came and your wound got worse[.] I am so troubled about you[.] I do not know what to do[.] if I only was there to wait on you[,] I would be so glad but my health I fear is too feeble to go so long a journey but Daniel McIntosh will come after you if you want him too[.] he has writen three times to you since you was wounded and wrote if you wanted anybody to come after you[,] he would come[.] we thought perhaps you could not come by yourself on the train without some help[.] write if you want help and you shall you shall have it[.] old Bill Wallice wrote in his letter that you wanted D. Davis to come after you and him but since I commence writing James N. Caddell came to see me and said you did not order it done yet[.] he said when you were well enough to travel that if you would write to[,] he would meet you at Raleigh[.] dont pay no attention to any person who you know hath dealt deceitfully with Lord[.] I would rather you come without any person than come such a one[.] I want you to be very carefull of yourself[.] put your whole trust in Lord that he may spare you to once more return home to see your poor old Mother that bin troubled so mutch about[.] come as soon as you are able and let me know if you need help[.] I hope & I trust I shall see you before long[.] I remain your affectionate mother untill death, Rany Caddell

1864, September 9

J.L. Stuart (*Petersburg, VA*) to his mother **Mary A. Harper**. General wartime correspondence with brief mentions of **Joseph P. Allen, James Morgan, John Thomas, Wiley Thomas, Wyatt Williamson,** his brother **Charles E. Harper** and **Cole.** [479]

Mrs. Mary. A. Harper. Dear Mother by the blessings of a kind Providence I am permitted to write you a line to inform you that I am well and hearty truly hoping these lines may find you all well. I received your letter of the 6th to day[.] I was very glad to hear from you all. September 11th 1864[.] I am well and hearty today[.] I hope these lines may find you all well as usual[.] I have but little news to write[.] you have already heard of the fall of Atlanta and Death of Gen. Morgan[.] sometimes there the yankees get to cheering and you never heard such yelling and our men do the same[.] I was on picket last night[.] there has not been but very few shells thrown since yesterday[.] there is a good deal of sharp shooting at night here[.] our picket line and the yankees is not over one hundred yards[.] the night of the 9th the yankees charged our picket line on the right of us about one mile and captured over one hundred of our men and our men captured about sixty of them. Joseph P. Allen was wounded the other day throe the shoulder[,] the bone was broke. James Morgan is here now[.] he is well as usual. you want to know what we get to eat[.] we get flour one pound a day one third pound of Bacon an one pound of Beef some sugar and coffee and peas. two of our company have died with sickness since we came to VA, John and Wiley Thomas[.] they were brothers[.] the most of our company was wounded and the ones that went to the Hospital have got furloughs[.] I have not heard from Wiatt Williamson since he went to the Hospital[.] I hear there is bad times in Moore[.] you said you feard the Hunters would take Charles to the war but they have no right to do it untell he gets old enough[.] it is thought Grant is waiting for reinforcements[.] if he takes

Petersburg & call the Confederacy gone up. it will be a bad come off if Mr. Cole married another man's wife. the young men will have to be careful how they marry widows. I wish I could be at home with you all but as when will that time come we are here and we know not at what moment we may receive the fatal blow to take us to that long Eternity. I must close[.] write to me and let me know how you are all getting a long and what for crop you have got and how you are getting along making syrup. give my bet love all the family and tell them to excuse me for not writing more to them[.] give my respects to all the neighbors and give me the news in full[.] I hope we will meet again on Earth to tell our troubles over[.] When this you see[,] remember me[.] your affectionate son[,] J.L. Stuart to John Harper and family[.] Direct to Petersburg Va[,] Co D[,] 49th[,] NC Troops[,] Ransoms Brigade[.]

1864, September 10
Murdo McLeod (*Morris Island, SC*) to **Bryan Tyson**. General wartime correspondence. [480]

My Dear Sir—Your kind favor was rec'd sometime ago containing $2[,] half of which I gave to Lt. Jones as you advised, for this favor I am under lasting obligations to you, and hope that I may yet have an opportunity of remunerating you[.] 600 of us were put aboard the steamship "Crescent" at Fort Delaware Aug 20th, arrived off this place the 25th[,] but were not landed until the 7th inst. – being very much crowded[,] we suffered considerably[.] We are now on this island under fire for retaliatory purposes, and you can well imagine how unpleasant our situation. I do not fully understand why we are placed here only as I learn from Northern sources. I would like indeed to know which government is in fault to say the least, it is a mode of warfare I detest. When we came we expected to be exchanged soon, but now there is not the slightest probability of it. The first pamphlet you sent me[,] I rec'd and read with interest. - I concur fully with you in your views concerning slavery – the last documents I have not rec'd – except the letters so. I shall be pleased to hear from you often, and any assistance you can, at any time, conveniently render me, will be most thankfully rec'd. I think it very probable that we shall be here for some time. My address is Morris's Island, SC. Yours Truly, Murdo McLeod

1864, September 16
James R. Jones (*Elmira, NY*) to cousin **Bryan Tyson**. General wartime correspondence. [481]

Dear Cousin, I seat myself this evening to drop you a few lines which will inform you that I am very unwell at present but I am some better than I have been[.] I have written to you some days ago but thinking that it may not have come to hand[,] I thought I would again write[.] If you cannot obtain a parole for me[,] I wish you would use your influence to get me out as a citizen of the US[.] there has been an order in force for some time prohibiting any from going out in this manner and as I have no inclination for returning South[.] I have concluded to take the oath to the U.S. Government. if an opportunity is afforded-- Write soon and let me hear from you on this subject. Your Cousin[,] Jas. R. Jones, Address Prisoners Camp[,] Elmira, NY, Ward 24[,] Barracks no 3. Care Maj. Colt[.]

1864, September 16
A.M. Dunlap (*Carthage, NC*) to **A.S. Caddell**. General wartime correspondence with brief mentions of deserters surrendering including **Burris**, church at Flint Hill with Rev. **Noah Richardson**, **Daniel M. Dunlap**, Lt. **Mills**, **Muse**, **Jack McIntosh**, **Neill Caddell**, **Ashley ?**, **Caroline D.?**, **Morris** and **Williams**. [482]

My dear friend, your last communication is at hand[.] I would have responded to it sooner, only I have busy engaged in the E.O. for the last two weeks & havnt had time to write to Dan[.] Nothing new or very strange down this way than sending off a few conscripts which is by no means a pleasant task. Good many deserters have surrendered. Barris among the crowd[.] he says he has come to repair the jail[.] We are sending some of them off nearly every day. I think it very probable that they will all surrender except it is those who was engaged in ambushing Lt. Mills & his Co[.] A great revolution is now taking place in this county. I think we will have entirely a new county in a very short time[.] every person seemes to take an interest in this hunt[.] they are punishing the friends & family of those who refuse to give up such as pressing horses wagons wheat oats etc which brings those who have property in y the swarms[.] It is having a delightful effect[.] The only way to whip the Devil is to fight him with fire[.] the deserters have had the ascending for lo these many days but I rather think their popularity & reputation is somewhat on the decline[.] We had a time baptising last Sunday at "Flint Hill", Old Noah put 21 under[.] some have a good deal of confidence in this meeting but I frankly confess that I have none[.] The same spirit seems to be prevaling among the people that inspired them in 1860. Old Miss Muse is very much rejoiced at the progress of the meeting[.] she says it will prove a fruitful campaign for her some have already spoken[.] I still call on "our gall" occasionally[.] They all enquire after Tim[.] they want Tim to come home this fall to be at partys with them[.] Jack & I had a little skirmish with the enemies pickes last night[.] we drove them in capturing the stand of colours & two splendid field pieces 24 pounds[.] I feel a little worsted today after was being on picket - all night without bing relieved, but I think without some misfortunes befall me[,] I will be on the front lines again tonight[.] come down & go on picket with us[.] I know you'd like it, if you even to get into one fight you'd be fired up with such patriotism that you could never cease firing[.] sometimes we shoot away all our ammunition, but we are not long in replenishing our shot pouches[.] What are you doing? How long do you expect to remain where you are? Do you expect to be ordered to Ashboro? I saw Neill yesterday[.] all is well. He & Ashley & Caroline D. acting in consent in this meeting[.] Neill & Jack are the "bull dogs" of the camp ground[.] I hope to see you again. Get a furlough & come down & see us. I heard from the Co last week all were well that was there[.] My respects to Morris & Williams[.] Very Respectfully[,] A.M. Dunlap

1864, September 17
J.L. Stuart to his mother **Mary A. Harper**. General wartime correspondence with brief mentions of **Neill Shields,** his brother **Charles E. Harper, John W. Maness** and **Edward Warner.** [483]

Dear Mother[,] I received your letter a few minutes ago dated 11th[.] I was very glad to hear from you all but very sorry you are so poorly[.] you said that Neill Shieldes and others said that Charles was over seventeen but they are mistaken[.] he is going on seventeen[.] when he gets old enough let him join the reserve and then he can stay in N.C. and get to go home if he gets sick[.] you said you had me some things to send by Maness but Maness is here[.] he did not bring any boxes with him but Warners says he will bring some if he can get them to the rail road[.] he said he would write and let you know if he can bring any thing for me[.] I wish I could a been at Charles candy pulling but I was here a dogin from the yankees. I am sorry times are so bad at Moore[.] they are bad ever where[.] I must stop writing[.] give my best love to John Harper and all the family[.] the yankees are diging to blow us up[.] we can here them a diging[.] I do not know what is to become of us[.] I will write to you ever week and you do the same[.] I hope you are getting along as well as you desire[.] I send this letter by Edward Warner[.] I am remain your affectionate son[,] John L. Stuart to John Harper & family

1864, September 17
J.L. Stuart (Petersburg, VA) to his brother **Charles E. Harper** and sister **Mary Ann Harper**. General wartime correspondence with brief mentions of **Edward Warner** and his stepfather **John Harper.** [484]

Charles and Mary Ann, Dear Brother and sister. I write you a letter after such a long delay to inform you that I am yet a live and well truly hoping thee few lines may find you all well. Well Charly and sis I hant got anything to send to you but a little knife and it is Broke[.] you can have it between you sis[.] if you got a heap of Butter send me some of it by Warner and I want that Jug of honeyif you have got any[.] you must let me know how you are getting along and how all the girls are getting along well if you are making sure. I want to see you the worst in the world but I cannot tell when I ever shall get to see you[.] you must be good children and be good to your pap and mother[.] I could write you a good deal but I must stop for this time[.] I was up last night from 12 oclock till day[.] sis you must tell me whom Charles goes to see and Charles do the same[.] tell all the girls howdy for me and I give my best love to your pappy[.] I must stop writing[.] be good children[.] I hope we may meet again on earth so we can go to Dover once more[.] when this you see[,] remember your Brother[,] John

1864, September 17
J.L. Stuart (Petersburg, VA) to his mother **Mary A. Harper**. General wartime correspondence with brief mentions of the death of **John A. McKinnon** and **Edward Warner.** [485]

Dear Mother[,] I embrace the oppertunity to write you a few lines to inform you that I am well truly hoping these few lines may find you all well[.] we are here at Petersburg yet and I do not know how long we will stay here[.] we are expecting a long fighton the right of the lines[.] there is skirmishing on the right ever day here where we are[.] there is but little fireing where we are[.] the yankees sometimes commence Halving and talking to us[.] they call us Johmina rebs and we call them yankees and ask each other to come over[.] I am getting mighty tired of this war[.] it looks to me that all of our men will be killed and then the yank whip us at last[.] sometimes I wish

I was at home but it will not do to come home[.] times are too bad at home[.] I wish I was at home with you but I must stay here if it is the lords will[,] I shall come out safe[.] you must all do the best you can[.] I hope you will all do well[.] I do not know when I ever shall get to come and see you all since I wrote to you. John A. McKinnon was wounded in the head and died the 15th[.] he makes the seventh man killed in our co. Edward Warner of our co. starts home this evening[.] he says he will try and Bring Boxes back[.] he said he would write to you and let you know how he is going to come back[.] if the comes to Raleigh[,] you can carry the Box to Carthage[.] he will let you know so if it will not be too much trouble[,] I would like you could send me a box by Warner if I am living such as Potatoes onions and I want about eight or ten pounds of flour and if you have plenty of sirup send a quart or half gallon and a pare of sox and some red pepper and you can send any thing else you please[.] we get one pound of flour and one third of a pound of Bacon a day[.] our rations are small[.] we spend all of our money[.] ever thing cost a good deal[.] let me know if you need any money and if you do[,] I will try and send you some[.] if you can send me a box I will be under many obligations to you[.] Warner has 18 days furlough[.] give my love to all the family and let me know how you all getting along and if you are making sirup. I hope the lord will permit me to live to see each other again but we know not what time we may be called away to eternity[.] farewell. John L. Stuart

1864, September 20
Mary E. Shields to brother **John W. Shields**. General wartime correspondence with brief mentions of **Mary Shields, Tommy Shields, Daniel Fry, Archie Shields, Neill Shields, Bryant Shields, James N. Caddell, Robert Wilson, Peter Councilman, Milo Councilman, Patrick Shields, Emerson Jones, James Dowd, Willis Jones, Emily Jones, Malcolm D. Shields, Robert D. Shields** and **William McIntosh**. [486]

I seat myself to answer your kind affectionate letter which came to hand a few days ago, and was glad to hear you are well. We are all well as common and I hope when these few lines come to hand they may find you well. Mary and Tommy came home today. They are well. Daniel (Fry) is gone to the iron works to keep out of the army. . . The boys that were lying out have all come in and were going to start off today. They were to meet at the crossroads. The hunters were going to give them their dinner. They had to carry Uncle Archie's folks to the camp before Neill came in. Oh, Brother Bryant Shields is dead. He died on the 10th of August with the yellow fever. He was out of his head twelve days before he died. Mr. James N. Caddell is dead too. He died with the fever at Petersburg. If you get sick and have to take medicine keep your (:) clean and keep it out of your teeth. Robert Wilson and Peter Councilman have been gone on a hunt ever since the 23rd of August and don't know how much longer they will have to stay. They are at Carthage and have been nearly all the time. Milow Councilman is gone to the coal fields to work. He is cutting wood and burning coal. Pad (Patrick) Shields's folks all send their love to you and to Emerson Jones, and asks you to send word how Emerson comes on and yourself[.] also cousin James Dowd came home with Mary and he sends his love to you and wishes you great success. I saw Willis Jones last Sunday and he sends his respects to you. Emily Jones wants to know if you have forgotten her. Brother, we have not cleared up our wheat yet. We don't know how much we have got. We are done with our fodder, all but our late fodder. Malcolm says tell you to come get a furlough and come home and help him sow wheat for Robert is not able to work and he has to do all himself. We are going to send you a pair of drawers and socks too. Daniel will send them by William McIntosh when he comes back. If you get to come home any time and the rest of the boys draw clothes[,] get your lieutenant to draw clothes for you. Thomas says tell you he will save you a pretty pig tail til you come home. I have no more news to write this time. I could tell you a heap if I could see you. You must write every week if you can and let me know how you are doing. I remain, as ever, your loving sister, M.E. Shields

1864, September 20
John W. McPherson (*Point Lookout, MD*) to **Bryan Tyson**. General wartime correspondence with brief mentions of **Joseph J. Tyson** and **Doctor C. Phillips.** [487]

Dear Sir, Your letter of the 2nd inst. came duly to me a day or two ago and I take the present opportunity of replying I was truly glad to once more hear from an old friend that I hadnt heard from in so long[.] I have been in prison so long that I am unable to give you any information about your friends in Moore[.] Joe Tyson came in here a few days ago and is well[;] also D.C. Phillips is well[.] I have not had the pleasure of reading or seeing any of your publications[.] I would be glad to get hold of several copies.] The tobacco chewers in camp have a pretty hard time I think[.] at any rate I know I do as well as a great many other things[.] I am well hope you are the same. Write soon in care of Major Brady[,] Point Lookout, Your affect friend[,] J.W. McPherson

1864, September 22
Rany G. Caddell (*Fayetteville, NC*) to son **A.S. Caddell**. General wartime correspondence between mother/son with brief mentions of **C.D. Caddell, Daniel McIntosh, Jane McIntosh, William A. McIntosh** and **Lany Davis**. [488]

Dear son[,] your letter came to hand this morning and I was truly glad to hear from you and hear that you was well and well satisfied[.] the of my writing to you now is because CD is not here[.] he is gone to Fayetteville to go before the borde and I thought you would be a looking for a letter from him[.] he will write to you when he comes home if he comes at all[.] he left home yesterday morning[.] I am here all alone[;] we are lonesome set[.] Daniel McIntosh has bin in the servis moor than a month with the hunters and his family is left in a helpless condition[.] he gets a furlough and comes home a day some time[.] Jane has never got a letter from you sense you went up nor has none of the family[.] the soldiers has began to hunt in earnest now[.] tha taken a great deal of pains to try to get them to come in[.] I saw the cornel the other day[.] he said he reckon tha thought he was a preacher but now tha would soon find out they are tareing them all too peaces[,] hawling off everything they have[,] there wheat and horses and wggons and takeing the women to Carthage[.] I do not know how it will end but I hope but I hope tha will never leave till tha get the last one[.] you wanted to know how about the stock, your cows is fine as to the sheep I think tho are a most all gone for some has been there all the time, the hogs looks vary well[.] I have too sows just fit to pig and old Scot is just a bout like common and david is in good condition and can caper about and his back is sound as a roach[.] I want to see you vary mutch[.] I want to see the time come for you to come home for it seems a age since you left[.] I will have you some winter pants in the corse of too or three weeks[.] I am soing them now but I get a long varry slow[.] I have so many thing to do[.] I shall look for you home in the corse of a month[.] I want you to be a good boy and gain the good will of all the people[.] William A. McIntosh wants you to write to him he is at Weldon[.] the crop here is not very good tho it is better than none[.] I have spoke for some fodder but I do not wether I can get any corn or not[.] Lany Davis has promis me his crop of fodder[.] I want to try to lay up something for Dave[.] our meeting has come to end and preacers all gone and we all have to pray for our selfs[.] I want to know if you go to meeting any up there[.] I hope you will not forget the perfestaion you have mad[.] you know the promis is to none[,] only them that hold out faithfull to end[.] live near the Lord and if we meet no more on earth[,] I hope will meet in heaven[.] I must come to a close[.] write often to your loving Mother, Rany G Caddell [P.S.] I am as well as ushall and hope this will find you in the best of health[.]

1864, September 22
J.L. Stuart (*Petersburg, VA*) to his mother **Mary A. Harper**. General wartime correspondence with brief mention of death of **Kindred Muse** and mentions of **Daniel H. Muse, Archibald Currie** and **Jacob B. Fry.** [489]

Mrs Mary A Harper[.] Dear mother[,] once more by the blessings of God I am again permitted to write you a line to inform you that I am yet a live and well truly hoping these lines may come to hand in due time and find you all well as you are usually. our regiment is in the rear line of Breastworks about one hundred yards in rear of the place that was Blown up[.] our Brigade is in the front lines about one mile to the left of where we are[.] I hear that Gen Early had a fight in the Valley a few dayes ago and had to fall back leaveing all the dead and wounded in the hands of the yankees[,] also three pieces of artillery[.] loss severe on both sides[.] yesterday morning we was aroused from our slumber about day by the whistling of yankee shells[.] there was heavy shells for a few minuts and all was over[.] there is some Mortar shelling going on now close to us on both sides[.] I must inform you of the sad news of the Death of Kindred Muse of our Company yesterday afternoon[.] while all was quite[,] all at once the yankees threw a shell striking the Breastworks and exploded and killed Kindred Muse. son of Daniel H. Muse and wounded A. Currie in the shoulder and stunned J.B. Fry. since we came in Virginia we have had eight men killed[,] two died of sickness[,] eight seriously wounded and five takend Prisoners[.] one of them was wounded[.] we have heard since making twenty three we have sixteen present now in the trenches[.] our officers have fared very well[.] we have not lost no officers killed or wounded[.] it looks as if we will all be Killed and wounded before the war is over. day before yesterday Muse came to me and asked me if I was a member of the church[.] I told him I was no professer and he asked me if I wanted to take a walk[.] I told him I would[.] he asked me if I know what[.] I told him no[.] he said he was going to have a secret prayer meeting[.] there was four of us that went to a secret place and he prayed a very nice prayer[.] he told me had profest religion since he came to the army and that he wanted to keep up a little prayer meeting in the future. but he who giveth life like some bit to call him away the very next day[.] he is gone where he will not hear any more shells and shells whistle by him but we have reason to believe he is gone to rest where all is Joy peace and love[.] he leaves a wife and family to mourn after him but they not mourn as one without hope. write soon[.] fail not give my love to all the family[.] your son[,] J.L. Stuart

1864, September 26
J.L. Stuart (*Petersburg, VA*) to his mother **Mary A. Harper** and stepfather **John Harper**. General wartime correspondence with brief mentions of the deaths of **Hugh B. Monroe** and **Angus McCallum** and mentions of **John W. Maness, Robartis D. Maness, Isaac Cagle, John Tucker, Isham Owen, Martha Nall,** his brother **Charles E. Harper** and sister **Mary Ann Harper.** [490]

Mrs. Mary A Harper[.] Dear Mother[,] I embrace the opportunity of writing you a line to inform you that I am as well as usual truly hoping these lines may come safe to hand and find you as well as usual[.] I received your letter day before yesterday dated the 18th[.] I was very glad to hear from you all but I was sorry to hear of yours and J. Harpers bad health. our company is out at the Wagon yard to day[.] our regt. is in the Rear line of works near the Blow up[.] there is some cannonading going on ever day[.] last friday the yankees opend one hundred pieces artillery on us[.] I only heard of one man killed and two wounded in our Division (Johnsons). there has been heavy fireing in the Direction of Chaffins Bluff in the James River for the last day or so and it is rumord that the yankes are advancing on that place[.] I expect the yankees will make some kind of move before much longer as they have been still for some time. I must inform you of the bad news of the Death of two more of our Company H.B. Munroe and A. McCallum. they were both takend prisoners at Bermuda Hundred in May. they both died in the hands of the yankees far away from home and friends[.] it appears like here of late ever letter that I write Brings sad news of the death of some of our company. I hope this war will soon come to a close but it appears like the war is not going to close soon. I want to see you all very bad[.] I do not Know what I would give if I could be at home[.] I am far away and I see no hopes of seeing you soon[.] I must bring my letter to a close by asking you to write soon[.] John W. Maness and his father are both back here and as well as usual. I saw Isaac Cagle today[.] he is not well. J. Tucker is well today[.] Isham Owen came to our Co. the other day as a recruit[.] I remain your affectionate son[,] John L. Stuart

Mr John Harper[.] Dear step father[,] I write you a line to inform you that I am well truly hoping these lines may find you well[.] I was very sorry to hear you was crippled up with pains in your Knee[.] I hope you will soon get well[.] I received a letter from Martha Nall yesterday[.] they are all well and said all the Deserters had give up. tell Charles & sis I want to see them very bad and wish I could be at home to help you make sirup[.] I must close by sending my love to you all and respects to inquirers[.] write ever opportunity[.] your afft[,] J.L. Stuart

1864, September 29
Mastin C. Phillips *(Winder Hospital, Richmond, VA)* to parents Rev. **Lewis Phillips** and **Nancy Phillips.** General wartime correspondence with brief mentions of **Baxter Phillips, Malphus Phillips, Horace Bridges, Doctor Chalmers Phillips, Dabney Phillips** and Sgt. **Broadway**. [491]

My Dear Parents, I seat myself to drop you a line to let you know of my whereabouts. I ought to have written before now, but have delayed hoping to have something better to say to you than that I am again sick in the hospital. I improve so slowly (if in reality I am improving at all) that I fear it will be several days yet before I can give you better news. I left the trenches near three weeks ago where I had been suffering for several weeks with dyspepsia and chronic diarrhea. I remained at the Division and Corps hospital until the 16th when I was transferred to this place. I am not suffering now as I have been but I don't think I am improving but very little. The diet and treatment here is much better than I have had before this, I think is the main reason why I do not suffer so much. My flesh and strength are nearly gone. If my disease were broken up, it would take me some time to regain what I have lost. I am going to try for a furlough to come home, but I have very little hope of getting one, so do not expect me then you will not be disappointed. I left Baxter with the Company in very bad health. I am very uneasy about him, but I hope he is better before now. I have not heard from him since I left the Corps hospital. I hope he is writing home all the time so that you may know how and where he is. I wrote him yesterday and I hope to hear in a day or two. (September 22nd)[.] I began to write this letter yesterday thinking I would be able to finish it, but before I was done I was feeling so bad that I laid it by until today. I am very weak this morning, but not in so much misery. I fear I am not improving, but do not be uneasy about me. If I get much worse I will let you know. I received letters from home written on the 5th of this month. I was glad to hear from home and that matters were no worse. I was sorry to hear that Malphus had to go. I would like to know where he is, but will have to wait a while before I can find out A boat of parolled prisoners arrived yesterday. Among them, Horace Bridges of our Company. He is in bad health, but I think a few weeks at home will cure him. He says that he left Doctor Phillips there in fine health. You will please let Uncle Dabney know it. I guess he doesn't hear very often. Sgt. Broadway of our Company, who was missing from the last had also reached them, a prisoner. I believe I have nothing more of interest to write this morning. I want you to do the best you can all the time. Direct to 79th Ward, 6th Division, Winder Hospital, Richmond, Va. Pray for me. God bless you. Mastin

1864, October 3
Henry C. Brown (*Point Lookout, MD*) to cousin **Bryan Tyson**. General wartime correspondence with brief mentions of **Joseph J. Tyson, Doctor C. Phillips, Dr. Gatlin** and **William K. Nunnery.** [492]

Dear Cousin, I received your letter date Augt 23rd stating that you would send me and Lineberry some money, you need not send me the money but I want some writing paper envelopes and some stamps. Also some flax thread and combs five and coarse one. J.J. Tyson is heare and said to tell you he written some time ago but haven received not letters yet. D.C. Phillips is well[.] this leaves me well please write and let me know if you have heard from S.W.T. and the rest of the boys. Also if you have heard anything of Dr. Gatlin. Write soon[.] all the boys are well except Nunnery[.] he has been sick for some time. Yours Truly, H.C. Brown, In care of Maj Brady, Co G. 6th Division[,] Point Lookout MD[.]

1864, October 8
Rany G. Caddell to son **A.S. Caddell**. General wartime correspondence between mother/son with brief mentions of **William Lane Wallace**. [493]

Dear son[,] I take my pen this morning to answer your letter witch came to hand too days ago bearing date Sept the 22[.] If ever I felt greatful in all my life it was when your letter came[.] I am truly glad to hear that you was mending[.] por boy I know that you have suferd a great deal and to think that I can not render you any service[.] if I could only be with you even to lay my hand on your brow if could not do any more[.] I should be glad but the allwise being that cannot evr has decreed it other ways we must ambly wait and bow to this will[.] this leaves me in ushal health but in truth when W.L. Wallice come[,] he told sutch dreadful tails about you[.] he told that he did not think you would ever come home again[.] he did not tell me so but told others and was all over the settlement in a few days[.] I never was distrest in all my life[.] I was a going to see you if I had not a got your letter but I was so glad to hear you was better[.] I give it out for it would a bin a band chance for it is a bad time to leave home now when their is so mutch michief a going on[.] you said some bones had bin taken out of your leg[.] poor fellow I know it hurt you dreadfull but I did not hear you hollow[.] I pitty you with all my heart and I try in my weake way to pray for you all time that you may get so you can come home[.] I will send for you to Raleigh any time and would be so glad to do so[.] take good care of yourself and wait with patience[.] write very soon for I want to hear from you all the time[.] I must cease for the present[.] I remain your caring Mother till death[.] Rany G. Caddell

1864, October 10
Noah Deaton (Prisoners Camp Co. I 6th Division, Point Lookout, MD) to father **William Deaton** (Caledonia, NC). Wartime correspondence between son and father with brief mentions of his sister, fellow prisoners **Madison Deaton, Martin Cagle, Isham Cagle** and **Joe Yarborough**. [494]

Dear Father, several days ago I received your kind letter of Sept 5th[.] I was much pleased to hear from home and hear you were all well[.] my health is very good[.] I am tolerable well clad for the coming winter and if my health keeps good[,] I think I will get along as well or better than I did last Winter[.] I have a snug little cracker box house 9 by 10 feet and work at engraving rings breast pins & c[.] I am glad to hear that sister is teaching school and trust she may have good success[.] there is a school going on in the prison numbering from 500 to 700 schollars conducted by Professor Morgan[.] The boys here are all well that are from your acquaintance[.] Madison Deaton is here & Martin Cagle instead of Isham, as I before said Joe Yarborough is here & well & wishes word to be sent to his people[.] I must stop for the present[.] hoping to hear from you soon[.] your affectionate son. Noah Deaton [P.S] address to Co I 6th Division, Prison Camp, Point Lookout, MD in care of Maj. A.G. Brady Provost Marshall[.]

1864, October 11
C.D. Caddell (Arsenal and Armory, Fayetteville, NC) to brother **A.S. Caddell**. General wartime correspondence between brothers with brief mentions of **Kittie McIntosh, Martha Sullivan** and Capt. **Holmes.** [495]

Dear Brother[,] I am in Receipt of yours of the 7th inst[.] I was verry glad to hear from you & that you was enjoying yourself well[.] this leaves me well & well satisfied truly hoping it may go safe to hand & find you enjoying the same blessing[.] I have no news to communicate to you[.] I dont have much duty to do[.] I am on guard 4 hours of a knight & nothing els to do at all[.] I stay in town or go where I please in the day[.] if I stay here I shal make some money for I never have to attend Rooll call nor any other duty[,] only my 4 hours duty in every 24 & a man that cant stand that is no man. Although I had rather be in the 7th Dist & I expect to try to get a transfer to the 7 Dist or in the Quartermaster Department[.] Tim I Rather expect to get maried when I go home for I never can be happy[.] if I fool Kittie & if I get to go home and two weeks furlough I shal marry her according to promise[.] I was to go home next month & bring things to a close[.] Your horse is used verry well so far[.] Capt Hoolms the Quartermaster rides him is all he has to do & if they dont use him rite[,] I will take him a way from him[.] you spoke about your jularky[.] mind that you dont get but I would not blame you to marry some of them rich refugees if you can[.] Love them but I dont count them rich that has got nothing but negro property[.] if you ever see any chance for me to be transfered[,] let me know[.] write often to your affectionate Brother, C.D. Caddell

1864, October 12
J.L. Stuart (*Petersburg, VA*) to his mother **Mary A. Harper**. General wartime correspondence with brief mentions of the death of **John A. Patterson** and mentions of **Asa McIntosh** and **Levi Monroe.** [496]

Mrs M A Harper[.] Dear Mother[,] today I am blest with the opportunity to write you a few lines to inform you that I am yet a live and well truly hoping these few lines may find you all as well as common. last night there was a good deal of fireing on our right a bout one mile from us but I have not heard the result[.] in the last three dayes there have came about forty or fifty yankees Deserted to our Brigade. there are more or less that comes over[.] ever day and night the yankees have commenced their old trade throwing Mortar shells at us[.] one of our regt. was wounded last night . another one of our company is dead[,] J.A. Patterson one of my mess mates[.] he left us the 22nd and died the 27th last month. Asa McIntosh was sent to the Hospital yesterday[.] he is one of my messmates. I was very sorry he had to go off for he is the man that gets so many Boxes from home when we left N.Carolina[.] there was six of us in a mess and I am the only one in the company[.] two is dead one takend prisoner and one gone to the Hospital and one is guarding prisoners. I received my box yesterday all right but the honey had nearly all run out and the cakes was moulded and the pork but it was not spoilt[.] Levi Munroe got a box that night[.] of it was 117 we mess together here of late[.] his Brother was sent off yesterday to the Hospital very sick[.] Levi got one gallon and a half syrup potatoes sweet bread cheese Bacon pickles onions and several things but his sweet bread was spoilt[.] we have got lots of provision[.] our company got about fifteen Boxes[.] nearly ever man got a box off.] the yankees will let us stay without interrupting us[.] we will live well[.] I was very glad to get the provision[.] I hope I shall get to come home and see you all once more but I do not know when that time will come[.] I hope this war will soon end but I do not see any prospect of peace[.] you must all do the best you can[.] give my love to all the family[.] I was truly glad to hear of so many young converts in the neighborhood[.] I think if all the people will get to doing better than we will have peace in our land. give my respects to all the neighbors[.] I want to see them all very bad[.] I must stop writing for this time[.] I also received your letter of the 30 ult. I am going to have cabbage for dinner[.] I have a fine time in my bomb proof[.] I shall live as good as Jeff Davis if the yankees would quit shooting[.] J.L. Stuart

1864, October 16
J.L. Stuart (*Petersburg, VA*) to his mother **Mary A. Harper**. General wartime correspondence with brief mentions of **E. Phillips, Thomas Fry, Neill C. Blue, Mrs. Phillips** and **Levi Davis.** [497]

Mrs Mary A Harper[.] Dear Mother[,] this beautiful sabbath I am blest with the opportunity to write in reply to yours dated the 9th which came to hand yesterday[.] I was truly glad to hear from you all and to hear you was all as well as usual. I have no news more than usual[.] there has been some fighting on the North side of James River but I have not heard no particulars[.] we are in the trenches yet and will remain here I expect for some time[.] we have a good deal of duty to do such as picket and setting up[.] we get about five or six hours sleep at night[.] we are in about one hundred and fifty yards of the yankees[.] there is the same sharpshooting as usual[.] neither side are allowed to raise our heads above the works[.] we have sand bags and logs are put up[.] we call post holes which we shoot from[.] in front of our works we have a line of stockades or (shevadefriezes) which we usually call them war horses[.] the way they are made is a log about five inches in Diameter with holes about one foot apart and then there are pegs about five feet long put into the holes so they are like the spokes in a wagon wheel[.] the beams are about ten foot long and fastend together. I wish I could come home and be at the meeting at church but I cannot. I would do anything if I could be at home to go meeting & CC[.] give my best respects to E. Phillips[.] tell him Thomas Fry is at pitch landing N.C. Lt N.C. Blue of our co is some relation to Mrs. Phillips[.] he is well. I was very sorry to hear of the death of L. Davis[.] the last time I saw him was in the latter part of August[.] he said he wanted to go home to live with his wife and little girl but he is gone never to see them again on Earth[,] but if he was prepared he is better off & how many have left their homes never to return.

1864, October 17
Richard A. Cole (Moore County, NC) to **Governor Zebulon Vance**. Petition for discharge from the Home Guard with brief mentions of **Catherine Ritter Jackson, John A. Jackson, Samuel Thomas Jackson, Martha Ritter Jackson, Elizabeth Glascock Cole, Samuel W. Humber, Rosanna Cole Humber, A.H. McNeill, Col. William B. Richardson, Thomas B. Spoon** and **Elias T. Williams**. [498]

To the Governor of North Carolina: The petition of Richard A. Cole of said county would respectfully show that he is in delicate health and has been for several years; that he is not able to endure hardships of any kind, that he has not done a regular days laboring for a considerable length of time; that exposure to cold affects his lungs[.] and then he is subject to Diarrhea which injures him very much; that although he can not stand cold and endure hardships yet by taking care of himself his is able to attend to business and have work carried on; that he has a good farm for this country and six hands to cultivate his said farm; that he usually makes good crops of grain; that he has no person to attend to his farm but himself; that he has a wife and four children[.] that in addition to his own farm his mother-in law has a good farm for this country, and five hands to cultivate it, that she has two sons both in Confederate service, one of them is at home on wounded furlough now but is ordered to report next Saturday[.] in the absence of her sons[,] your petitioner has to give all his attention to her farm, and should your petitioner be sent to Goldsboro he verily believes that his own farm and his mother-in-law's will be neglected; that his mother-in-law is an aged woman in delicate health and has no white person living with her but a single daughter. That the petitioner's own mother is a widow, aged and in very feeble health and has been for many years. She is living in Carthage, having no farm, and her little son, and a daughter, whose husband is in the war, and has been ever since 1861, are living with her and they are dependant upon your petitioner in a good measure for their support[.] in consideration of the promises your petitioner verily believes that he will be of much more service at home than he can be in the field, and thereupon prays his Excellency to grant him an exemption from service in the Home Guard. R. A. Cole
Sworn to and subscribed before me this 17th day of Octbr 1864, AH McNeill. This person A.H. McNeill appeared before me, Col. W. B. Richardson, as gentlemen of veracity and credibility who having sworn say they are acquainted with R. A. Cole and his family, and the facts set forth in this petition they believe to be true. William B. Richardson, Thomas B. Spoon. I cheerfully approve the within petition October 20th 1864, E.T. Williams, Captain.

1864, November
James C. Davis (on board the CSS Indian Chief) to **N.R. Brady**. General wartime correspondence with brief mentions of his wife and **William King**. [499]

[illegible] in despite of every thing I could do, they have at last got me in the War. Rather than go to the trenches at Petersburg at the Commencement of the winter, I concluded I would try [illegible] in Charleston. There are some 12 of us from Moore County and if I could be pleased at all in the war it would be in this service. We have

little or nothing to do on board & I think there is but little danger of a fight although the Yankee fleet is in sight & constantly bombing Charleston. What I wanted to write more particular about was for you if you would please to try and collect that money for me and for which my wife has your receipt – do if you please push it ahead and try & get it for me & give to my family as they need it. Get it if you [illegible] & my wife will satisfy you. Push up Bill King for the liquor, 5 gallons. Get his note anyhow if nothing else for me & give it to my wife. Do this for me if you please. I would do it for you. When things cool off alitte I will write you a long letter. Write me soon & direct for the present to me on Board the Indian Chief, Charleston, SC.

1864, November 3
R.P. White (*Mecklenburg, NC*) to **Mary E. Shields**. General wartime correspondence with brief mentions of **Lydia Phillips Shields, Kitty Shields, Everett** and **Robert D. Shields.** [500]

Dear friend. I received your very kind letter and we truly glad to hear from you all but I have been so very busy that I could not answer until now, and but very little time now. We have an incessant rain from the east and quite cold, and I am not very well, or I am unwilling to ride through the rain. I am completely rode down and I don't see any chance for rest unless I run off down to Moore; then very likely I will be out of the frying pan into the fire. I have amputated two arms recently[,] one off a boy and the other off a woman. Both got smashed in cane mills. I have no news of importance, only a continual call for men to go to the front. That is not very pleasant, particularly to the ladies, for thousands of them will have to live old maids the remainder of their (crossed out word) days unless the Confederacy will enact laws like the Mormons, allow a man to have as many wives as he can take care of. If that be the case I want four good industrious and pretty good looking ones, stout, willing and handy, then I am sure I could keep them in something good to eat, and they could make the coats and cook something good. Perhaps my foolishness is not interesting, but it is true. Look out, Miss E.S. Tell your mother that I will come to see her some day if I keep on living, but I can't say when. I am exempted from the service on account of my profession and I am bound to attend to it, or I would have been down long before this. Tell Kitty I am sorry to hear that she is not improving but I can't do her any good unless I was nearer. I had a case of the very same kind four miles from here. She is now in good health. I performed the same operation on her that you will have to undergo, but I am fearful your case has stood too long. Every day that rolls around brings that much further progress of that disease, although it might not be perceptible to you, but you will find that delaying time will render you incurable. Give my respects to Robert and the rest of the family. It is getting dark. Give my love to inquiring friends, if any, and be duly cautious to reserve a competency for my sake. Yours truly, friend R.P. White P.S. Write me each week whether I answer or not, for I do not have time but I would like to hear from you often. Give all the news and what the deserters are doing and how Everitt is doing.

1864, November 10
J.L. Stuart (*Petersburg, VA*) to his mother **Mary A. Harper**. General wartime correspondence with brief mentions of **Neill C. Blue.** [501]

Dear Mother[,] once more I am blest with an opportunity to write you a few lines to inform you that I am yet a live and well truly hoping these lines may find you all a live and well as usual[.] I received your letter the 8th dated the 4th[.] I was highly pleased to hear from you all but sorry your health is so bad since I wrote last[.] General Gracie charged the yankee picket line and only lost one man by accident[.] we are at the place and our picket line is in the yankee picket line[.] we moved last night to our right the length of 4 companies[.] we are where they yankees throw lots of mortar shells but I have a very good bomb proff[,] but we have to be up on duty nearly all the time[.] last night we moved about dark and Just after we had moved[,] the yankees charged Wises Brigade in our Division and was Driven back but I have not heard the result[.] there was fireing all a long the line and the yankees threw a good many mortar shells[.] two men in our regiment was wounded[.] yesterday the yankees tried another flank movement on the right but was driven back[.] I expect there will be active operations. around Petersburg for the next few dayes as the weather is warm[.] two of our regiment was killed a few nights ago and Lt Blue of our company was wounded in the shoulder with a piece of mortar shell[.] we are in danger all the time but I hope I may be permitted to see you all again[.] it is reported that Gen Lee says if we hold our lines a few days longer[,] he will commence furloughing[.] according to yankee accounts McClellan is has a major army in Kentucky New York and in Warrens and Hancocks Army Corps so I suppose he is Elected[.] we will here in a few dayes but I do not know when the war will end[.] I want to see you all very bad[.] write ever opportunity[.] I remain your affectionate son[,] John to Mrs Harper

1864, November 10
J.L. Stuart (*Petersburg, VA*) to his stepfather **John Harper,** brother **Charles E. Harper** and sister **Mary Ann Harper**. General wartime. [502]

Mr John Harper[,] after my best compliments to you I can inform you that I am well truly hoping these lines will find you in good health[.] I was sorry to hear you lost one your cows[.] it looks like bad times when people get to selling cows. I hope you will not be called out[.] try and do the best you can all of you[.] I hope I shall live to come home and see you all again[.] give my Love to all the family and write to me ever opportunity and I will do the same[.] I remain yours respectfully[,] J.L. Stuart

Dear Brother & sister[,] I was very glad to hear from you all[.] I wanted to be at home to go to the meetings but I could not[.] I was glad that Mother was well enough to go to Dover[.] and I think if I live I will get to come home after a while but we Know not how long we will stay in this world[.] I want to see you all the worst in this World[.] I often think of you and long to see the time when we can meet again[.] I must close[.] I remain your Loving Brother[,] John

1864, November 17
Alexander Pleasant Williams (Lexington, NC) to **A.S. Caddell**. General wartime correspondence with brief mentions of **Smythe, Powers, Wiley Saintsing,** Lt. **Thompson** and **Pickett**. [503]

My highly esteemed friend, sir with great pleasure seat myself down to drop you a few lines to answer yours of the 13 inst which came to hand and found me well and most sincerely hoping these few lines may come briefly to hand and find you well[.] A.S. I dont now that I have much nuse to rite at this time[.] the people are generaly well in this part of the country[.] we have lost our friend Smythe[.] he departed from this world in a day or too after you left us[.] we are all here yet except Powers and he is gone home on a ten day furlough[.] he left last night on the train[.] I can inform you that we went out and caught Mr Wiley Saintsing yesterday[.] we caught him the first time we went and we have sent him off[.] we bought 14 galons of brandy the other day for which we gave 30 dollars per galon so you ought to be up with us to drink brandy[.] our enroling has come off and we duly got 4 men from this county with the exception of a few bridge guards[.] A.S. I supose we all have to go up the spout before long. Lieut. Thompson received a letter from Pryor stating that the next Board we went before would have to send us off to our command[.] it is what we have been looking for this long time[.] Mr Picketts family is well[,] Miss T.L. is as prety as ever and Miss Symantha is as sweet as ever[.] i must close here for the present[.] rite soon and give me the nuse so I remain your true friend as ever[.] A.P.W.

1864, November 21
John W. McPherson (*Point Lookout, MD*) to **Bryan Tyson**. General wartime correspondence with brief mentions of **Daniel B. McDugald.** [504]

My Dear Cousin, Having understood that you are residing in Washington City[,] and being very anxious of obtaining my release from this prison, and take no more part in this war, I am induced to write you with a hope that you will do all in your power to assist me in obtaining that end. My particular friend Danl. B. McDougal of Moore County is also desirous of getting released. You will confer a favor upon me, for which I'll can be thankful to you. if you will procure our release, and secure for us any Employment in Washington D.C. or thereabouts, that we may have a chance of earning a lively hood after attaining our release – Any Govt work, for instance work in Gent Shops[,] We are willing & anxious to procure. I wrote you sometime ago but did not receive any reply from you, suppose my letter mis carried. Your attention to this matter at your earliest convenience will much oblige. Very Truly Your Cousin, John W. Mc Pherson. Co "K"[,] 1st Division[.] Care Major Brady, Point Lookout[.]

1864, November 21
J.L. Stuart (*Petersburg, VA*) to his mother **Mary A. Harper** and stepfather **John Harper**. General wartime correspondence with brief mentions of **John Tucker, Isaac Cagle** and his brother **Charles E. Harper.** [505]

Dear Mother[,] once more I am permitted to write you a few lines to inform you that I am well and hearty truly hoping these lines may find you all well[.] I received your letter of the 16th today which afforded me great pleasure to hear from you all[,] but very sorry your health is so bad. you said it was thought John Tucker and Isaac Cagle was at home[.] if they are[,] they left here since last Friday for they were here then[.] me and John works together at a tunnel. I wish I could be at home to go to the meeting at Chapel but I cannot be There[.] you must all do the best you can and do not trouble your self too much about me[.] I am in a good warm bomb proof[.] I work six hours a day and get to rest of a night[.] I work at a tunnel but the rest of the boys has hard duty to do[.] one of our company Willis Smith started home yesterday on furlough[.] I hope I shall get to come after a while[.] I want to see you all very much and hope we may see each other again[.] give my respects to all the neighbors[.] I would be glad to see them al[.] I have no more news worth writing[.] it is said Grants Army has been reinforced with an Army Capt. it is thought there will be a fight here shortly. Lincoln is reelected so I look for four more years war[.] I must close[.] give my best Love to all the family[.] tell Charles to send me some of the Wedding cake. I remain your Loving son. J.L. Stuart

Mr John Harper[.] Dear stepfather[,] after my best respects to you I hope these lines may find you well and doing well. I have nothing worth writing today[.] we have had rainy weather[.] we are going to be paid off tomorrow. I am very sorry you are going to lose Charles. I hear he is going to marry. I must close. write to me all of you. I remain your etc. J.L. Stuart. Tell sis we will wait on Charles at the Wedding[.]

1864, November 22
Kelly H. Trogdon (*Point Lookout, MD*) to **Bryan Tyson**. General wartime correspondence with brief mentions of **Isaac Maness, Adams Brewer, Peter Garner, James Tyson** and General **H. Wessels.** [506]

Dear Friend[,] I am well and hope this may find you in good health[.] I received your kind letter yesterday which gave me greate satisfaction to hear from you. I am much a blige to you for the greate faver you done to me. You stated in your letter to know when I left home: I left home the 20th of Sept[.] It was hard times there when I left. Isaac Manes is in the woods or was the last I heard from him. A. Brewer mooved up in the mountains[.] I heard he wer ded. Deserters killed Peater Gardner. Your Bro. James wer at home when I left[.] he wer on the mend[.] all the neighbors wer all well. I would like to see you this eavening I could tell you a grate deal[.] I cant write as much as I would like to. We will send Gen. H. Wessels a note[.] I want you to tend to it for me if you please & do the best you can for me. when you get them if you dont think it will do please fix them for me. I want you to write to me & tell me all the news you have. run my bussinss through as soon as you can write Immediately. Yours Truly, Kelly H. Trogdon

1864, November 25
Nelson Hunsucker (*Point Lookout, MD*) to cousin **Bryan Tyson**. General wartime correspondence with brief mentions of **Henry C. Tyson, James Tyson, Leonard Stutts** and **Houston W. Hunsucker.** [507]

Dear Cosin, I received yours of th 11th and was glad to hear from you. I would like to see you and talk with you and have in days pass by and gone. I left home about the 20th of Oct. I have no news of importance to give you from N.C. H.C. Tyson is a ward master in Greensboro NC. James is at home. MCH is at home and is well and is living,[.] she and her brother where Len Stutts lived at Oats/Pats. Len Stutts is liveing on the old place. and made a good crop on the came break. H.W. Hunsucker is at home and the Dr. says he will never be able for service as has a lingering deseas[.] so I will close for the present[.] write soon yours. Very Truly, Nelson Hunsucker, Co I. 8th Division, In care of Maj. Brady[.]

1864, November 25
Joseph J. Tyson (*Point Lookout, MD*) to cousin **Bryan Tyson**. General wartime correspondence with brief mention of **Doctor C. Phillips.** [508]

Dear Cousin: allow me to acknowledge the receipt of your very kind and welcome letter: which came to my hand yesterday. It found me in good health; this leaves me the same. Bryan I was glad to receive your letter. I hope you will continue to write to me. you cannot immagine the consolation it is to a poor prisoner who are deboned from all the privileges of life to receive a letter from a friend. and the next you write I want you to send me as much as one dollar to buy some smoking tobaco if you please[.] I am in a quite needy circumstances at this time[,] neither money nor friends[.] I want you to send me one of your pamphlets to read also:[.] your friend and acquaintance are well[.] D.C. Phillips sends his respects to you[.] I hope to hear from you soon. Direct your letter as before. I remain your devoted friend and cousin, J.J. Tyson

1864, November 26
John W. McPherson (*Point Lookout, MD*) to cousin **Bryan Tyson**. General wartime correspondence with brief mentions of **General H. Wessels** and **Nelson Hunsucker.** [509]

Dear Cousin, Your very kind favor of 23 inst. reached me yesterday evening – I feel truly thankful to you for your kind attention. Enclosed please find letters from my friend & myself to Genl Wessels relative to our release which you will please forward for me. I fear I am troubling you very much[,] but will take pleasure in reciprocating your kind favors. I hope my communication to the Genl are in the right form. Circumstances will not allow me to write them as I would like. Nelson Hunsucker is here in camp. and in good health. Your attention to this matter will my much oblige. Your Sincere Cousin, John W. McPherson, Co "E"[,] 56th N.C. Troops[.]

1864, November 27
Manly Brady (Garrysburg, NC) to mother **Hester Brady**. General wartime correspondence. [510]

Dear Mother, I seated myself this morning for the purpose of writing you a letter. I am well. [several lines illegible] home by Christmas. I want you to send me a suit of clothes the first chance for I am near about out. Also some bed quilts. [multiple illegible lines], your affectionate son, Manly Brady

1864, November 28
Henry C. Brown (*Point Lookout, MD*) to cousin **Bryan Tyson**. General wartime correspondence with brief mentions of **Nicholas A. Shields** and **Z. Burns.** [511]

Dear Cousin, I drop you a few lines hoping they will reach you and find you well as they leave me in tolerable good health. all the boys are in very good health. I want you to go to the old Capital and see if N.A. Shields & Z. Burns is there and let me know if they are. also please send me a roll of Black Horse hair to make some watch chains[.] gets the hair as long as possible[.] write soon and fail not. Yours Very Respect. H.C. Brown, Co G. 6th Div, Point Lookout, MD, in care of Major Brady[.]

1864, December 2
Spain Williams (*Point Lookout, MD*) to cousin **Bryan Tyson**. General wartime correspondence. [512]

Dear Cousin[,] I drop you these few lines in order to let you kno that I am in prison hear and wish to get out and take the oath of alegence to the United States goverment and becom [illegible] for I am very tierd of this war. I want you to do all in your power for me and five of my friends who wishes to go out on the same terms that I do[.] pleas write soon and let me know what you can do for us[.] do all you can for us and we will satisfy you for your trouble[.] these few lines leves me in good health hoping to find you enjoying the same etc. yours truly, Spain Williams, Co C.[,] 9 Division[,] prison camp, Point Lookout M.D., Care Major A G. Brady Prov Marshal[.]

1864, December 3
Christopher C. Harrison (*Point Lookout, MD*) to brother **Bryan Tyson**. General wartime correspondence with brief mentions of **Matthew Cagle** and **Harry Boroughs.** [513]

Dear Brother, I drop you a few lines to inform you that I am well[.] Truly hoping these lines will reach you and find you well. I fear Bryan I am without means and would like very much for you to be so kind as to send me some money[.] also I would like to have some clothing and if you will send me the clothing[,] let me know it and I will get a permit from Mr Brady for the clothing[.] also Matthew Cagle is hear, and would like to have some help. all the boys are well. I would have wrote before now but I seen the letters you sent Harry Burrows[.] write soon[.] Direct your letter to Co. E. 8th Division[,] Point Lookout Md. In care of Maj Brady[.] Your Brother, C.C. Harrison

1864, December 5
Thomas J. Hogan (*Point Lookout, MD*) to **Bryan Tyson**. General wartime correspondence with brief mentions of **James Tyson, Aaron Tyson, Henry C. Tyson, Benjamin F. Tyson, Mary Tyson Hogan, Henry Clay Hogan, John T. Hogan, Josephine Tyson** and **Mary Jane Boroughs Tyson.** [514]

Dear Bryant, Yours of the 26th and also of the 3rd of december are at hand, I was very glad to hear from you and to learn that you was well. I am very sorry that I neglected writing so long that you dispaire of me getting your first. When I left hom in the 20th of October[,] James Tysons wound was better. Aaron Tyson died at Hospital in Georgia; ? Tyson, was at home well, H.C. Tyson, was ward master at Greensboro; Ben Tyson was at Weldon N.C. and well. Your mother was well and weighs near two hundred[.] Mary & Clay and J.T. Hogan and family and friends of Orange were well. Josephine and Fanny Tyson were well. We were not surprised nor did we blame you in the least for leaving under the circumstances. I have often heard Mary say that she would have left under the circumstances and express her desire to see you. I did not receive your pamphlet, I have not a cent of money and would be very thankful to you for a little help. I will write again soon and I hope you will do so[.] I am Respectfully, T. J. Hogan.

1864, December 6
Connor D. Grose (*Old Capitol Ground Prison*) to **Bryan Tyson**. General wartime correspondence with brief mention of **Alvis Groce.** [515]

Dear Friend, This affternoon I tak the opertunity of writen you a fewe lins that you may lern that my health is not good and hasends bine since I have bin in Prison tho I hope the lins may reach you and find you well. I wish I could see you[.] I could tell you a greadel about your father and people. Thoe I have bin prison 6 month that I come from home a short time before that. Your people was well[.] one of your Brother is at home now[,] I heard from home the 27 of Oct[.] evrethang get along finely. Mr. Tyson I don't expect that you noew me for I was smal when you left Moore County thoe I think that you nowe my father. I am the son of Alvis Grose and Mr. Tyson if you will send me a pair of shoes[.] if I ever have the opertunity: you shall bea sadifide for it for I am barefooted and if you oblige me[,] the sise is 8. I muste close hopen to see you soon or hear from you. So I remain your friend, Sgt. Conner D. Grose, 44 Regt. NC

1864, December 6
John W. McPherson (*Point Lookout, MD*) to cousin **Bryan Tyson**. General wartime correspondence with brief mention of **D.B. McDugald** and **Nelson Hunsucker.** [516]

Dear Cousin, I forwarded to you on the 26th inst. petitions from my friend D.B. McDougal and myself to the authorities at Washington for our release etc. Will you be kind enough to inform me whether you have received them or not, and if so, were they correct? I am very anxious to hear from them and earnestly hope this war not last. – I know you will do all in your power for me, but cannot, without the petition I refer to. If you have not received them[,] please inform me at your earliest convenience that I may make out others and forward at once. If is it convenient[,] you will you be kind enough to send me a few dollars which I take pleasure to return to you with many thanks, when it pleases God that I get my release. Mr Nelson Hunsucker is in camp[,] also several of your friends[.] Very Respectfully, Yr Cousin, John W. Mc Pherson, Co "K"[,] 1st Division, Point Lookout[.]

1864, December 7
Daniel C. Wilson (*Elmira, NY*) to **Bryan Tyson**. General wartime correspondence with brief mentions of **D.S. Short** and **Ira Phillips.** [517]

Dear sir[,] I seat my self this long to drop you a few lines to let you know I receive you leter of 31 of Nov. I am glad to her from you. My health is getting worse[.] you said in you letr that you wanted some young man. I will come and stay with you as long as I live if you will get mee out for if I was relive I should come to you anyhow. Bryant you never said nothing about sending me anything to eat. I will sadisfy you for all you send to me. Mr. Tyson I *send note know D.S. Short. When I write he is heare yet. You wanted to know what Ira Phillips is doing[.] he is working for the gorment grating$24 a month. I here from him evry week. So no much at present. Wright soon. D.C. Wilson*

1864, December 11
James R. Jones (*Elmira, NY*) to **Bryan Tyson**. General wartime correspondence. [518]

Sir[,] this is to certify that I come in to the Southern Service under the conscript act in the month of August in the year 1861. I was deliverd to the col of the county to be sent to the conscript camp and is sent to eny company or regimnt thea saw proper and I stuck chose to go to the regimt and company I now b long to Co E 8th NC Regimt and there remain until I was taken prisoner on the 31 of May last[.] and I was caputurd with my own accord for when thea ordered thea retrete I thou down my gunn and stood still tell I was capterd[.] earnestly do desire to b come a citizen by taking the oath of allegiance to the sam having sen the evils of war[.] hav determined not to go again into the Southern service under any circumstances what ever[.] I remain vary respectfully and truly yours. Jas. R. Jones

1864, December 14
James R. Jones (*Elmira, NY*) to cousin **Bryan Tyson**. General wartime correspondence with brief mentions of **Goddin Tompkins** and **John Tompkins.** [519]

Couson Bryan, Dear sir[,] your leter of the 10 com safe to hand last night But I am vary sory that leter was not right[.] I rot another I am in hopes it is right[.] I will send you the same. I am not well but I am on thea mend hoping thes few lines will find you well. Couson Bryan I here that Cosin Goodin Tomkins' son John is in Washington and has bin for sum time. I wish if you no enything of him[,] you wod let me now bout him in your next leter if you pleas and whear he is[.] so you will find that certify on thea other sid but as I sent to him eny more then comensin with you name in thea plas off his[.] so please do all you can for me and try and git me out if you can. Rite to me just as soon as thes few lines comes to hand and let me no if it is right and if you think you can get me out purty soon[.] so I will clos this sbjt for thi time. Hopin answer soon. Jas R. Jones

1864, December 16
John W. McPherson (*Point Lookout, MD*) to cousin **Bryan Tyson**. General wartime correspondence with brief mentions of **D.B. McDugald** and Gen. **Wessels.** [520]

My dear cousin, I have written you twice to which letters I have received no answer. With my first I enclosed petitions from my friend D.B. McDougal and myself to Genl. Wessels for our release[,] expressing our desire to return to the allegiance of the United States. Not having heard from them[.] I fear you did not receive them as I enclosed them to you as you kindly offered to attend to them for me. Will you be kind enough to let me know whether you received them. and if you have not[,] I will make out others and forward at once. I anxiously desire to procure my release as well as that of my friend and any attention you will be pleased to give our petitions in my behalf will be very thankfully received and reciprocated if in my power. I am not in good health and cannot again regain my health situated as I am. I hope you ar enjoying good health. Please let me hear from you soon again. John W. McPherson, Co "K"[,] 1st Division[,] Pt. Lookout[.]

1864, December 19
Thomas J. Hogan (*Point Lookout, MD*) to **Bryan Tyson**. General wartime correspondence with brief mentions of **John Boroughs, Decia Holmes, James Harrington** and **Kelly Trogdon.** [521]

Dear Bryant, Yours of the 13th came to hand and found me well. I was more than glad to hear from you and to learn that you was well. I received the fifty cents you sent me and also the stamps you sent me in the other letter and I was very glad to receive it. You are mistaken in your belief when you say that fifty cents is all that allowed to come in camp. I can get any amount by a book on the sutter. I got a book for that fifty cents[.] I can get flour and provisions here from the sutter for a book. John Boroughs of Orange cty was married to widow Holmes of More cty. James Harrington of here was selected a member of the present legislature. I was glad to hear from

Kelly Trodgon and tell him to write to me. I have not heard from home since I have been here. Write Soon and let me know if you are in business again. I am respectfully yours[,] Thos. J. Hogan

1864, December 20
William A. Vuncannon (*Point Lookout, MD*) to **Bryan Tyson**. General wartime correspondence. [522]

Mr Tyson Sir, I take my pen to write you few lines to let you know that I want to gst out therefore I sit myself down to write you few lines asking you to gat me and my too cusins out as I am very tired fighting and never like it. I want to go north and live till the war is over or I may bring my family north if I gat out. I am married myself[.] I have been in prison for 15 month and is very tired with this please. I know you can get me out if you will. I want you to write to me as soon as you get this letter and let me know what you can do for me and if I got out[,] I will pay you for all of your trouble. I would not ask you only that I know you. Be sure and write soon. Very respectfully, W.A. Vuncannon

1864, December 21
Isaac Roberts (*Fort Delaware, DE*) to **Bryan Tyson**. General wartime correspondence with brief mentions of **W.J. Lambert** and **Hack Tyson**. [523]

Dear Sir: Having learned through Lt. Lambert that you were in Washington, I have thought proper to drop you a few lines to let you know of my whereabouts and condition[.] I have been a prisoner of war nearly seven months. I am now enjoying tolerable health though the greater part of the time I have been sick. I was at home a short time before I was captured. Your relations about Carbonton were well, Hack Tyson was at home wounded[.] I have understood that he has again returned to his company. I am in quite a destitute condition as I have no relatons or acquaintances in the Federal lines. If you can assist me I would esteem it a great favor & will assure you that the kindness shall be reciprocated as soon as circumstances permit. You can send check or money by express & I will get it. Yours truly, Lieut. Isaac Roberts, Prisoner of war, Fort Delaware Del[.]

1864, December 26
Matthew Cagle (*Point Lookout, MD*) to **Bryan Tyson**. General wartime correspondence. [524]

Dear sir[,] I now can seat myself this day to inbrase the opportunity of riting you a few lines[.] It leaves me well hoping these few lines may find you well[.] if never see you no more I shant forget you[.] I would like very well if you could help me to a little money. I will be very exceptialble of it at this time present. I hate to send to you for it but I now that you have a fealing for one of your school mates. You friend, Matthew Cagle. Direct your letters to Point Lookout MD[,] Co I[,] 8 Division[,] in care of A. J. Brady[.]

1864, December 29
John W. McPherson (*Point Lookout, MD*) to cousin **Bryan Tyson**. General wartime correspondence with brief mentions of **D.B. McDougald.** [525]

Dear Cousin, My friend D.B. McDougla recd. your favor of 22nd. I see by it his application for release was not favorably considered[.] I am exceedingly sorry to hear this, for McD[,] I can conscientiously say was opposed to the war and did not volunteer as it seems to be thought but was conscripted and did not enter to service until he was forced in by enrolling officer. I wish it was in my power to establish his loyalty. I surmise that my petition was favorably considered. Though I am not yet[,] I hope to be soon released. Please let me know how my case stands at your earliest convenience. I am exceedingly thankful to you for your attention, Write soon and direct to me in Co E, Eleventh Division, as I have been transferred. Please send me a few postage stamps. Write soon and oblige, your sincere cousin, John W. McPherson, Co "E"[,] 11th Division, Care Maj. A. G. Brady[,] Pt Lookout[.]

1865, January 4
J.L. Stuart (*Petersburg, VA*) to his mother **Mary A. Harper** and stepfather **John Harper**. General wartime correspondence with brief mentions of **Bartis Maness** and his brother **Charles E. Harper.** [526]

Dear Mother, I write you a line in reply to your letter dated 29th Dec[.] I was very glad to hear from you all. these lines I am in good health truly hoping they may find you all well[.] I Have nothing new writ more than Furloughs has increased to four for even Hundreds[.] we have one gone up for our company[.] I think I will get one after a while if I get Justice[.] I am very sorry I cannot be at home with you[.] I know it is very bad for you to give Charles up but I will not say any thing about the war as we have got enough of war. Today Bartis Maness of our company was wounded in the head with a minnie ball[.] I received my box all right and wish I could do something to pay you for it but I am worth nothing. but I think the boys all like me very well[.] the captain called me a first rate soldier[.] I think I will get a furlough in a month or two[.] take care of yourselves and do the Best you can[.] I remain your affectionate son[,] J.L. Stuart

Mr. John Harper[.] dear stepfather[,] after my best respects I can inform you that am well truly hoping these may find your in good health[.] I wish I could be at home to help you work but I cannot[.] I was very glad to hear you have got your chimney done[.] I hope you will not have to come to this war[.] excuse my hasty letter and bad writing for I am nearly without a light[.] write soon[.] Direct to Petersburg[.] give my Love to all who inquire after me[.] Yours[,] J.L. Stuart

1865, January 6
James Tyson (*Browers Mills, NC*) to **Bryan Tyson**. General wartime correspondence with brief mentions of **Jody Tyson, Fannie Tyson,** the **Waddills** and **Eliza Ann Johnson Tyson.** [527]

Dear sir[,] I again write you a few lines we are all in tolerable health. Jody is complaining some[.] Fannie gets more helpless every day[.] my thigh is improving slowly[.] it is nearly healed up at this time[.] it will nearly heal up then it will rise and run again[.] I cant bare any wait on it my knee is stiff[.] my leg is a good deal shorter than the other one[.] I hav know news to write you at this time[.] we are all geting a long as well as could be expected for war times[.] the Waddills and most of your acquaintance has gone to the Army[.] your affairs stand as they did when you left[.] the people is best satesfied the way you left it Bryan. Eliza Ann sent a letter to me to forward to you thinking that I know better how to direct it better than she did and that it would go quicker from hear[.] your affares is all rite out thare[.] I wish this crewel war would soon end and we could hav a good and lasting peace and all could once more get back to there loving homes and fire side[.] So nothing more but write soon. yours affectionately, Jas. Tyson

1864, December 8 [this letter was enclosed with the above]
Eliza Ann Johnson Tyson (*Bashi, Clarke County, AL*) to brother **Bryan Tyson**. General wartime correspondence with brief mentions of **James Tyson.** [528]

Dear Brother, I seate myself this evening to write you a few lines in anser to yours which was 9 months getting heare[.] I was glad to heare from you and learn that you were well[.] we are all well at the present[.] I wish I could write you a lenthy letter but as it is I can not. Dear Brother I still keep that which you commited to my charge. Eliza's family is still increasing and she is in no condition to be put out. This war tax is ruinous at this $16 Dolars on agrene hand. I expect to kep all together untill you come. the [next word illegible] grant it soon I entend to send this to Brother James and get him to forward it to you an I think you will get it sooner. Dear Brother write soon and after. the children all gone but I wish I could write you a letter – this is no letter, the children all James me in love to you and wants to see you very much so good by[.] may the Lord Bless you[.] I remain your affection[.] Sister Eliza A Tyson

1865, January 14
Thomas J. Hogan (*Point Lookout, MD*) to **Bryan Tyson**. General wartime correspondence. [529]

Dear Bryant, As I am near destitute of clothing, I thought I would write to you to know if there was any charitable club or society or any rich lady that would befriend me enough to send me a suit. There is a great many getting clothes here on that way. [illegible] getting any[.] write mee the name and address and I will get a permit of Major Brady and send for them. I have nothing more to write you this time. Write soon and let me hear from you often. I Remain as ever, yours respectfully, Thos. J. Hogan, Co. I 8th Division, Point Lookout Md.

1865, January 16
Thomas J. Hogan (*Point Lookout, MD*) to **Bryan Tyson**. General wartime correspondence. [530]

Dear Bryant, Yours of the tenth inst come safely to hand, and I was glad to hear you was well. I am well at the present and I hope the same of you when you receive this. I expect there could be money made on rings by sending them to you, but I have not the means to buy with. Rings being tolerable high. When you send me any more money dont send less than one dollar for there is an order here that will not allow any less sum to come in camp, I have not I have not heard anything from home yet but I hope the time wont be long before I can see my wife and child again[.] I am getting very tired of prison life and if it was not for my wife and child and friends south I would not remain here much longer[.] But as it is I will have to endure it a while longer for their sakes. Hoping to hear from you soon[.] I will close[.] I am respectfully yours, Thos. J. Hogan, Co I[,] 8th Division[.]

1865, January 16
Neill Kidd (*Point Lookout, MD*) to **Bryan Tyson**. General wartime correspondence. [531]

Mr Tyson, Dear friend[,] yours of the 12th inst came due to hand which was red with pleasure[.] I am proud to here from a friend at any time. Mr. Tyson I would have ask you for a favor before this time but I hated to impose on a good friend[.] I hope this cruel war will soon come to a close so we can all return home in peace once moor for I am geting tierd of this kind of a life I will be proud to hear from you at any time[.] address me Co. K[,] 4th Division. yours truly, Neill Kidd

1865, January 17
Spain Williams (*Point Lookout, MD*) to **Bryan Tyson**. General wartime correspondence with brief mentions of **D.J. Williamson, John R. Hall, Malcom Dove, William John Morrison** and **A.J. Walden**. [532]

Dear Sir, I rec your letter stating that you had not rec our applications. we send them now seperately[.] mybe they will be better. I wll send ther names in this letter[.] my nam first Spain Williams Co C. 9, D.J Williamson Co. B[,] 2nd D., John R Hall, Malcom Dove, Wm. John Morrison & A.J. Walden. I hope at all of thre applications will reach you soon at any rate[.] If this reaches you I hope it will answer all purposes. Yours respectfully, Spain Williams, Co. C. 9th Division, Point Lookout Md[.]

1865, January 18
J.L. Stuart (*Petersburg, VA*) to his mother **Mary A. Harper**. General wartime correspondence with brief mentions of **Alexander M. Fry**, **Emily C. Nall** and his brother **Charles E. Harper.** [533]

Dear Mother[,] in hast I drop you a line to inform you that I am well truly hoping these lines may find you all alive & doing well[.]. we hear that fort Fisher is gone up[.] in a few days I think our men will do some thing to make peace but I cannot tell. this morning A.M. Fry starts home[.] I send this letter by him to Carthage[.] he has 18 days[.] I do not want you to send me any thing only you may send me a pare of socks if you see an opportunity[.] if not it will not make any adds. I want to see you all very bad and think I will before long[.] tell sis to have her shoes Black[.] I am very anxious to hear from you the last letter from you was dated 27th Dec[.] the mail does not come in for the last few dayes on account of some Bridges being washed down[.] tell Emmy Nall to have a quilting about the 14th of next month[,] that her sweetheart in the 56th regt is taking of comeing to see her[.] give my love to all[.] write soon for I want to hear from you all very bad[.] I want to know what a wool Hat can be bought at in Moore County[.] do not send me any thing unless it is a pare of socks. I must close[.] I have not heard from Charles yet[.] give my Love to all the family[.] write soon to your son. John L. Stuart, Petersburg VA, Co. D. 49[,] N.C.T. Ransoms Brigade[.]

1865, January 19
Henry C. Brown (*Point Lookout, MD*) to cousin **Bryan Tyson**. General wartime correspondence. [534]

Dear cousin, I received your letter stating the that you had learned that I had procured means so as to be a speculating and you seemed it adviseable to help those that were needing money worse. that was very true[.] I have some money but very little though. and having put up a little shantie[,] me three or four others[.] it taken all the means. I could procure and would have been very thankful and under many obligations to you for the said amount. but n other help than one dollare is allowed to be received[.] you must excuse me for calling on you for I would not if I had not been needing it. write soon. yours truly, H.C. Brown, In care of Maj Brady[.]

1865, January 22
J.L. Stuart (*Petersburg, VA*) to his mother **Mary A. Harper**. General wartime correspondence with brief mentions of his brother **Charles E. Harper.** [535]

Dear Mother[,] to night I embrace the opportunity of dropping you a line to inform you that I am well truly hoping these lines may find you all well[.] I received your two Last letters dated 5th & 12th[.] I was very glad to hear from you all. I wish I could be at home with you but I see no prospect of peace for our ruling men say fight on as long as there are a man and shinplaster[.] I think I will get a furlough after a while[.] there are only two to go before me[.] I was very sorry that Charles could not get into work at the Iron works. if my officers find out that he is laying out[,] they will not let me go home[.] I am very sorry to hear of such bad times a bout home. I do not know what our Country will come to[.] I must close[.] write soon[.] it was over two weeks that I did not get no letter from you[.] Direct your letters as usual. I remain your son as ever[,] J.L. Stuart

1865, January 24
Murdo McLeod (*Fort Pulaski, GA*) to **Bryan Tyson**. General wartime correspondence with brief mentions of **Dr. Thomas Littig, Gen. Wessels, John E. Mulford, Thomas W. Ritter, Julia Ann Caddell, Exer L. Ritter** and **Samuel Wait Seawell**. [536]

My dear Sir, Being very bare of clothing of every kind, I have written to Dr. Thomas Littig of Emorton, Harford County Maryland, to send me a suit, including hat and shoes but it is necessary to obtain the permission of Brig. Gen. Wessels, Commissary Gen. of Prisoners, Washington D.C. before I can have the articles sent. Will you do me the kindness to get the permit from Gen. Wessels, in duplicate form, and forward one copy to Dr. Littig, and the other to me so that I can receive the articles here after they shall have arrived. also instruct Dr. L. to direct the package in care of Lt. Col. John E. Mulford, Assistant Agt. of Exchange Fortress[,] Manassas Va which will insure their safe arrival at this point. If you can do me this favor I shall be under lasting obligations to you. Clothing & money have been started to me from home but failing to reach me on account of communication being interrupted I suppose. We are living hard at this time on 10 ozs. meal & 4 ozs bread with a few pickles[.] A general exchange is now spoken of but I fear it is the same old delusion. I see no immediate prospect of an exchange. I sincerely hope these troublesome times may soon come to an end. I heard from home about two months ago – no news of interest. T.W. Ritter married Miss Julia Caddell[,] also Wayt Sewell a sister of T.W. Ritter's. Yours Truly, Murdo McLeod

1865, January 26
Bryan Tyson (*Washington, DC*) to **E.M. Stanton**, Secretary of War. General wartime correspondence requesting parole from prison for **John H. Sims, D.G. Williamson, Spain Williams, A.J. Walden, John K. Hall, A.W. Mervin, Israel Lowdermilk, B. Craven, Daniel Short, Daniel C. Wilson, William Riley Barrett, James R. Jones, E.R. Bowles, James F. Vuncannon, William Vuncannon, John W. McPherson, D.B. McDugald, Malcom David, William John Morrison** and **Christopher C. Harrison.** [537]

Sir, The following persons are desirous of becoming citizens of the United States by taking the oath of allegiance to the same and being desirous that North Carolina may be the first State to which into the union especially petition that they be permitted to do so: John H. Sims; D. G. Williamson Point Lookout; Spain Williams Point Lookout[;] A.J. Walden Point Lookout; J.K. Hall Point Lookout; A.W. Mervin Point Lookout[.] A.W. Mervin is very anxious to return to his grandfather at Milford Conn. He now has but few relatives at the South[,] his mother having died in Mississippi last Sept.; Israel Lowdermilk Elmira NY[.] Mr L. is a through unionist[,] was caught in the woods by militia officers and forced into the army; B. Craven Elmira NY; Daniel Short Elmira NY[.] Mr Short is a thorough unionist; D.C. Wilson (thorough unionist) Elmira NY; W.R. Barrett (thorough unionist) Elmira NY; James R. Jones (thorough unionist) Elmira NY; E.R. Bowles Point Lookout; James F. Vuncannon (thorough unionist) Point Lookout; William Vuncannon (thorough unionist) Point Lookout; J.W. McPherson (thorough unionist) Point Lookout; D.B. McDougal (thorough unionist) Point Lookout; Malcom Davis papers submitted (thorough unionist) Point Lookout; William John Morrison (thorough unionist) Point Lookout[,] papers herewith submitted. I believe all the foregoing to be thorough union men and am willing to be placed in their situation should any prove false to the confidence reposed in them. Hoping you will give the subject a careful consideration. I am sir, very respectfully and truly, your obedt svt, Bryan Tyson. P.S. I would also recommend for release C.C. Harrison Point Lookout having omitted his name in the foregoing list[.]

1865, January 31

Thomas J. Hogan (*Point Lookout, MD*) to brother **Bryan Tyson**. General wartime correspondence with brief mentions of **Mary Hogan** and **Henry Clay Hogan**. [538]

Dear Bryan, Yours of the 25th inst was duly received and I am glad to inform you that it found me well. And I hope when you get this it will find you well. As for me leaving the prison and going back there I will never do, for if I was to do so[,] for my property in the South that my wife & child depends on for support would be confiscated and she could have to suffer, and[,] before they should suffer on the account of my conduct[,] I will remain here and even die. But I hope the time will come when I can be permitted to see my family again. You can get me that clothing and as soon as I can get a permit I will send it to you[.] permits are only given on Mondays[.] I will try get one as soon as possible[.] I want one hat, one coat, one vest, one pair pants, one pair suspenders, two shirts, too pairs of drawers, one shoes, on each article you will have to post my name.] I was very glad to hear from James and to hear that they know at home that I am captured for I have not heard from home yet but expect a letter in the mail. You can have the articles ready as before mentioned and when I get the permit[,] I will send for them. I remain as ever, your brother respectfully, Thos. J. Hogan, Co I[,] 8th Division. P.S. the shoes should be no. 9[.]

1865, February 14

J.L. Stuart (*Petersburg, VA*) to his mother **Mary A. Harper** and brother **Charles E. Harper**. General wartime correspondence. [539]

Mrs Mary A Harper[.] Dear Mother[,] I write you a few lines to night to inform you that I am well truly hoping these lines may find you all well. I received your letter of the 4th[.] I was very glad to hear from you all. I sent out to town to day and bought you four kneedles[.] the price of kneedles are fifty cents but I bought four for one Dollar[.] I would a sent more but I am scarce of money[.] I paid out my money for some thing to eat but I will try and get you some more by the time you kneed them[.] I cannot tell you when I ever shall to come home[.] it may be shortly and it may be a long time. first The three last men that went on furlough from the company did not come back and the Colonel sayes he will not give our any more furloughs[.] I hope I may yet to come but I do not know when[.] there is no chance of peace[.] I shall look for heard fighting as soon as the weather gets warm so men can fight. I want to see you all very bad[.] you must all do the best you can[.] I thought a month ago I would be at home to night but our furloughed men would not come back[.] give my love to all the family and write soon[.] from your son[,] John L. Stuart. Dear Brother[,] I want to see you all very bad[.] you must do the best you can[.] to day one of our Brigade was shot to Death for desertion Saturday night. of none of our company went to the yankees. last night two of our regiment went[.] I hope I may see you all soon[.] you all must do the best you can. I fear this war will never end[.] give my love to all the family. John L. Stuart

1865, February 21

Thomas J. Hogan (*Point Lookout, MD*) to **Bryan Tyson**. General wartime correspondence with brief mentions of **Mary Hogan, Henry Clay Hogan, John T. Hogan** and **Nelson Hunsucker**. [540]

Dear Bryan, Yours of the sixteenth and also of the seventeenth came safe to hand and finds me very unwell though I am some better now than I have been for some time. I am very glad to hear that my clothes are on the way[.] I have not got them yet but I expect to get them soon. If they keep taking prisoners out according to date of capture[,] I will stay here two or three weeks yet[.] I received a letter from Mary and Clay and John and Family were well. She had just received a letter from her ma, and she was well. Write to me as soon as you get this and let me know whether you get clear of the draft or not, N. Hunsucker is here and well[.] I remain as ever, Yours Thos. J. Hogan, Co I[,] 8th Div[.]

1865, March 5
Matthew Cagle (*Point Lookout, MD*) to **Bryan Tyson**. General wartime correspondence with brief mention of **Alexander K. Pearce**. [541]

Dear Sir[,] I seat myself this day to drop you a few lines[.] it leavs me well as comon hoping thesee few lines may come safe to hand and find you well as yours. I can tell you that I would hav raten to you before now but I could not get any stamp to rite to you before now[.] I want you to tell me where A.K. Pearce is[.] I want to rite to him[.] tell me where he is tell me his office. Mr Tyson I rite to you again for you to help me a little fare badly need some help[.] I have nobody here[.] I dont nobody north only you if you will help mee some I will pay the det to you[.] again I remain your friend untill deth[.] rite soon. Matthew Cagle. P.S. help me if you can for I need help here[.] I hate to send to you for help but need[.] will make anybody doing thing. Matthew Cagle

1865, March 20
Thomas J. Hogan (*Point Lookout, MD*) to **Bryan Tyson**. General wartime correspondence with brief mentions of **Christopher C. Harrison, Henry C. Brown** and **John W. McPherson**. [542]

Dear Bryan[,] yours of the 17th was Duly Reacievd and found Me well[.] I Was Glad to hear you gott shrt of the draft[.] I havent Heard Eny Thing from C C Harrison sinse He Went To the hospital[.] I Wrote A note To A Friend of mine at the hospital but he Could not find him[.] Henry Brown has gone to Pierce[?] Mc furson has gone to the hospital and I think perhaps to De[rest of word illegible][.] Nothing more[.] Write soon[.] I Remain yours as Ever. Thos. J. Hogan

1865, April 4
Henry C. Smith (*Point Lookout, MD*) to **Bryan Tyson**. General wartime correspondence with brief mention of **Cornelius D. Smith**. [543]

Sir, Having heard from my Father before leaving home that you resided at Washington[,] I take the opportunity of writing those few lines to you to inform you that I am confined here as a prisoner of war. Shortly before leaving Home my Father told me that if I was ever taken prisoner by writing to you I would be befriended by you. I am tired of this war and having previously consulted my Father on the subject. I know of no greater favor you could do me than to use your endeavors to get me out of this prison. If you can accomplish my release by vouching for my being a Union Man[,] I will Readily take the oath. I will anxiously await an answer to this and remain sir yours respectfully, Henry C. Smith, Son of C.D. Smith, Carthage[,] Moore Co. N.C.

1865, April 6
Isaac Roberts (*Fort Delaware, DE*) to **Bryan Tyson**. General wartime correspondence. [544]

Dear Sir: Yours of 3rd inst is to hand, also three Pamphlets. I will endeavor to dispose of them as you request if I should be exchanged soon. I expected to have gotten off before now, but I doubt not[.] recent events will put off exchange for some time. I am very anxious to get home. I have nothing of interest to write. Hoping to hear from you again, I remain yours truly, Isaac Roberts

1865, April 20
James R. Jones (*Owego, NY*) to cousin **Bryan Tyson**. General wartime correspondence. [545]

Dear cousin[,] I this morning Do tak thea opertunity of riten you a few lines to inform you I am well and harty hoping when thes few lines comes to hand thea will find you ingoin thea saim good blesing of health. all so at present I am a working in this plas and lick vary much[.] I am vary well satisfied and I am gitin my fare wages. I wod of riten to you be for now but I did not have thea opportunity. I did not hav eny steady plase to work etc. till last weak and though I had not right till I did git a steady plas to work at and then I cud git my leters. When you riten to me I was releast on thea 23 of March[.] But When I furst com out I was sick and abut to work eny hardly and I had no mony a tall and I had to get a long thea best I cud[.] And I hav not got eny yet. I was not abut to work and I nead clos vary much[.] if you cud help me to a few dollars for a short time. I will return it to you again and I wont you to send me som of your pamphlits and book you ar making and you will confur a grat favor on me by so doin[.] I will come down and yea you as soon as I make a nuff to gite me some clos and to pay my way down[.] so I wont you to right soon. Jas. R. Jones, Owego, NY

1865, May 4
Isaac Roberts (*Fort Delaware, DE*) to **Bryan Tyson**. General wartime correspondence. [546]

Dear Sir[,] When I last wrote you I thought that I would ere this time be at hom, but I am still here. I am in very bad health & very desirous of getting off. I expect to take the oath of allegiance to the U.S. Goverment when it is offered & return home. I suppose we will be necessarily detained here for several days. Can you send me five or six dollars[?] if so you would very much oblige me. Send the money per express & I will get it. I will repay you soon as circumstances permit. Hoping to hear from you very soon, I remain yours truly, Lt Isaac Roberts, Co "E"[,] 3rd N.C. cavalry, Division 30, Fort Delaware, Del, Care of Capt J.W. Ahl[.]

1865, May 16
George W. Williams (*Point Lookout, MD*) to **Bryan Tyson**. General wartime correspondence with brief mentions of **Aaron Tyson, W.E. Johnson, Eliza Ann Tyson, Matthew Williams** and **Wesley Williams.** [547]

Dear Sir, I have just recd yours (of 15th ult) to give you better evidence of my being a brother of Matthew & Wesley Williams[,] I moved to Clarke Co Ala with your brother and lived with him & W.E. Johnson until I joined the army. I could mention other incidents but I suppose the above is sufficient. The last account of Eliza A Tyson & childrin they were well and getting along finely. I hope no further doubts will rest on you as regards my being the bonafide Geo. I remain as ever your devoted friend. Geo. W. Williams

1865, June 10
George W. Williams (*Point Lookout, MD*) to **Bryan Tyson**. General wartime correspondence with brief mentions of **Aaron Tyson, Matthew Williams** and **Wesley Williams.** [548]

Mr B Tyson. Your letter of the 5th came to hand yesterday and from what I can understand you have never received my last letter which I sent you. you say all you wish to know is that I am the G. Williams that I represent myself to be[.] I will assure you there is no mistake but what I am the won. I certainly went to Alabama with your brother A. Tyson[.] you may rest assured that I am the same a brother to Matthew & Wesley Williams. I do not know when I shall be able to go home and are in need of some money which I have stated therefore by sending me the amount asked for[,] you will oblige your friend. George W. Williams, Co. D[,] 5 Division[,] Prisoners Camp, Point Lookout MD[.]

1866, June 27
Baxter C. Phillips *(Fair Haven, Moore County, NC)* to cousin **Lucy Norton** (*Barbour County, AL*). General correspondence recounting the war and with detailed updates on the Phillips family: **Emeline Phillips, Mastin Phillips, Malphus Phillips, Ceila Gilbert Phillips, Lewis Capers Phillips, Robert Mastin Phillips, Brinkley Phillips, Dabney Phillips, Louis Spinks Phillips, Charles Dickerson Phillips, Albert Phillips, Allen Warren Phillips, Doctor Chalmers Phillips, Lydia Phillips Cheek, Rhumenia Cheek, Robert H. Phillips, Mary Ann "Polly" Phillips, Charles H. Phillips, Louis Cicero Phillips, Absalom Phillips, Fanny Thomas Phillips, Amanda Phillips, Candace Phillips Street, Richard Street, Charles Lee Street, Murdo Eugene Street, Elmira Phillips, Eliza Ann Phillips, Martha Juliet Phillips, August Louisa Phillips** and **William Phillips.** [549]

Cousin Lucy, I now recommence a correspondence which I regret very much was ever broken off. I introduce myself, for I never wrote before, nor will those write again who have written, because they are not. Neither do I know whether you live or not, but it has been so long since I heard from you that I take the task upon myself to write this letter, which may give satisfaction in one sense, but it will also be the bearer of sad tidings. Since we heard from you, dear Cousin, two of us have passed into Eternity. Emeline, my oldest sister, and one whom I loved dearly died February 3, 4864. But, Cousin Lucy, she left the testimony that all was well. I am bereaved, but still I can rejoice. Her sickness was long and painful, but she bore it with Christian fortitude, died exulting and passed from pain to happiness. Also on the 11th of March 1865, Mastin, your former correspondent, exchanged this world for Heaven. Mastin with myself volunteered in the service of our country February 5, 1862 where we spent near three years in suffering, both of us in feeble health. At the Battle of Bristow, Mastin was captured, carried to Point Look Out, Maryland where he remained until May when he was paroled. During his stay he contracted chronic dirhea in connection with liver disease which gradually sunk him until he died. Mastin was my best friend on earth and it seemed like our destinies were linked, but death has parted us. He died in faith, should I grieve when such is the case? I think not. Having suffered so much together it seemed that we were connected by a common tie and just before he died, he said to me that he wished I could go with him. Still, he was resigned to God's will. He died and I still live. He rests and I have pain yet. Such dying as this is infinite gain. Let me die the death of the righteous and let my last end be like his. Our family are all well at present. My own health was very bad for over a year, but am recovered now so that I enjoy as good health as I ever did. I passed through the war with but one wound of any consequence. I had my left arm pierced with a ball on the first days fight of the Seven Days Battle, but it is about as strong as the other. Mastin was severely wounded at Fredericksburg. Malphus, my oldest brother[,] passed untouched and is at home farming. He has a wife and two fine boys, Lewis Capers and Robert Mastin. Our vicinity suffered much in men lost by the war. I guess you wish to know something about the family connections. Well, I will tell you as well as I can. Uncle Brinkley is with Malphus this year. He is nearly 80 years old and is working a very good crop of corn. He is in good health and in fine spirits. Uncle Dabney is in tolerable good health and so is his wife. He lost three sons in the war. Louis Spinks and Charles Dickerson, both of whom were killed at the battle of Sharpsburg. Allen and ___ Doctor were also wounded, but have recovered and are married and doing well. Albert the second youngest died at home from disease contracted while in service. Uncle Dabney had ten sons, all of whom were in conscript age. Aunt Lydia Cheek is in common health though blind. All her children are married but one, the youngest, Rheuhama. Uncle Robert and his wife are well and getting along as well as could be expected of people their age. Aunt Polly is living with us. She enjoys common health. Uncle Charles is still traveling, preaching. He and his wife are well. You may trust to it, he is one of the deepest men I ever heard preach in my life. He has one son, Louis Cicero. He is traveling this year about 30 miles from here. We see him frequently. We have heard from Uncle Absalom once since the war. Aunt Fanny is dead and daughter Amanda. This I believe is as near true as I know how to state. Beside Malphus, but one of us is married. Candace, the sister younger than myself, married since the war commenced to Mr. Richard Street. She has two fine boys, one two years old, Charles Lee and one Murdo Eugene five months old. I am not married nor likely to be soon. I am spending about half my time for the present on the farm and the rest I devote to study. I am very unsettled just now though I hope I will get straight soon. I will remain at home this year and should I live[,] I can't say where I will be next. I am now 25 years old and it is high time I was doing something, is it not? The war has made nearly 4 years of my life blank by sickness and depriving me of finishing my education. And now, should I confine myself in college, I fear I would break entirely, which I want to avoid if I can. I have four sisters at home, Elmira, Eliza Ann, Martha Juliett and August Louisa. Cousin Lucy, it is so that we will never see each other? I very much desire to see you. I will go home with you if you will come to see us. I intend if I live and times will get quiet to visit you, and I want you to visit North Carolina, especially Moore County. I could write more, but excuse me, it is bed time and I am tired, so I must bid you goodnight. Please answer this as soon as you get it. Address: Fair Haven, Moore County, North Carolina. Our love to all, Yours affectionately, Baxter C. Phillips [P.S.] I forgot to state about Uncle William. He is in very feeble health. He had a slight stroke, palsy from which he never will recover. He has eight children, seven boys and one girl. All strong, healthy and intelligent.

Moore County Roster of Confederate Pensions

The following individuals received a Confederate pension or widow's pension during the time period 1885-1919. [550]

According to NCpedia, "Although the Civil War injured or killed tens of thousands of North Carolinians, not until after Reconstruction did the state begin to pass broad pension laws to provide for ex-Confederate soldiers with disabilities and the widows of deceased veterans. In 1879 the legislature passed a law granting $60 per year to Civil War veterans who had lost both arms or both legs or were totally blind. Only a dozen individuals applied for this pension. An 1885 statute expanded the program by creating a $30,000-per-year fund to pay pensions to soldiers who were at least "three-fourths incapacitated by wounds" and to Confederate widows whose husbands had died during the war. As a result, from 1879 to 1900 approximately 4,500 North Carolinians applied for benefits under the new law.

Although there was an extensive verification process, approximately three-fourths of all veterans' applications were approved in the first year. The most common reason for rejection, which could be appealed, was that the disability was not severe enough to warrant a pension. In 1887 the legislature extended pensions to widows whose husbands had died from disease, not just from wounds. However, the North Carolina pension system was poorly funded; pensioners still received approximately $60 annually, in contrast with Tennessee's system, which provided $100 a year.

At the beginning of the twentieth century, state lawmakers decided that veterans were entitled to pensions simply for suffering the infirmities of old age. In 1901 fixed pensions ranged from $30 to $72 annually, based on the extent of incapacitation, with total pension expenditures not to exceed $200,000 for veterans and widows. This amount was increased during most succeeding legislative sessions, reaching $650,000 in 1919. In addition, in 1909 the lawmakers authorized counties to levy special taxes to benefit veterans residing within their borders. Moreover, veterans' petitions were now approved for reasons that earlier would have resulted in rejection, and applications were simplified.

The most important change after 1900 was that a widow could apply for a pension even if her husband had died after the war, as long as he had never deserted. Furthermore, in 1909 the legislature allowed applications from widows who had married Confederate veterans as late as 1 Jan. 1868-two and a half years after the war ended. In the ensuing years this date was gradually moved forward; by the 1920s widows received pensions even when they had married Confederate veterans in the 1880s. Another change granted pensions to women who had remarried since the death of their veteran husbands.

Before 1901 about twice as many widows as veterans applied for pensions, as few men believed that they could meet the strict eligibility requirements of the 1885 law. After 1901, with the aging of many former Confederate soldiers, the state received roughly equal numbers of applications from veterans and widows. A total of 35,000 pension applications were filed from 1901 to 1946." [551]

Soldiers, Company/Regiment, Post Office, Years Active on Pension Roll

Allen, John C., F 3rd, Spies, 1913, 1914, 1915, 1916, 1917, 1918, 1919
Bailey, Daniel, H 26th, Pharsala/Eagle Springs, 1891, 1892, 1893, 1895, 1896, 1897, 1898, 1899, 1900, 1902, 1903, 1904, 1905, 1907, 1908, 1909, 1910, 1911
Barber, Hiram, I 2nd, Carthage, 1902, 1903, 1905, 1907, 1908, 1909, 1910, 1911, 1912, 1913
Benoy, Alex., C 3rd, Aberdeen, 1898 1901, 1902, 1903
Blue, D.A., C 35th, Southern Pines, 1914, 1915, 1916, 1917, 1918, Died 1918
Blue, M.P.N., C 35th, Lobelia, 1905, 1907, 1908, 1909, 1910, 1911, 1912, 1913, 1914, 1915, 1916, to Hoke County
Blute, Michael, A 5th, Swann Station, 1891, 1892, 1893, 1894, 1895, Died
Bobbitt, Richard M., F 50th, Forkade, 1904, 1905
Bowdin, Bryant, C 3rd, Aberdeen, 1901

Brady, Eli, E 63rd, Prosperity, 1916, 1917, 1918, 1919
Brady, Manly, F 6th, High Falls, 1915, 1916, 1917, 1918, 1919
Brewer, Martin, F 30th, Spies, 1902, 1903, 1904, 1905, 1907, 1908, 1909, 1910, 1911, 1912, 1913, 1914, 1915, 1916, 1917, 1918, 1919
Brewer, Sampson, H 46th, Spencerville, 1902, 1903, 1904, 1905
Britt, Bryant, Home Guard/Senior Reserves, Bensalem, 1901, 1902
Brown, Henry C., G 26th, Hemp, 1909, 1910
Brown, Joel M., 3rd I, Sanford, 1903, 1904, 1905
Brown, P.S., H 2nd, Queen, 1896, 1897, 1898, 1899, 1900
Browning, Wm. H., G 5th, Carbonton, 1900
Buchanan, S.R.B., F 50th, Sanford, 1904, 1905
Burns, H.H., G 48th, Sanford, 1901, 1902, 1903, 1904
Burns, William, I 2nd, Spies, 1902, 1903, 1904, 1905, 1907, 1908, 1909, Died Spring 1909
Burt, Wiley Patrick, D 26th, Pinebluff, 1905, 1907, 1908, 1909, 1910, 1911, 1912, 1913, 1914, 1915, 1916, 1917, 1918, 1919
Caddell, Neill B., D 49th, Carthage, 1905, 1909, 1910, 1911, 1912, 1913, 1914, 1915, 1916, 1917, 1918, 1919
Cagle, Henry C., F 2nd, Carthage, 1897 1900, 1901, 1902, 1903, 1904, 1905, 1907, 1908, 1909, 1910, 1911, 1912, 1913, 1914
Cagle, Matthew, H 26th, Leaman, 1910, 1911, 1912, 1913, 1914, 1915
Campbell, John A., E 11th, Jonesboro, 1891, 1892, Died March 18, 1893
Clegg, W.B., M 15th, Hemp, 1907, 1908, 1909
Cole, J.D., B 66th, Cameron, 1908, 1909, Dead 1910
Connell, F.M., E 32 [SC], Carthage, 1916, 1917, 1918, 1919
Cox, George, E 8th, Sanford, 1904, 1905
Cox, John A., D 49th, Carthage, 1891, 1892, 1893, 1894, 1895, 1896, 1897, 1898, 1899, 1900, 19011903
Cox, John L., H 30th, Jonesboro, 1891, 1893, 1894, 1896, 1897, 1898, 1899, 1900, 1904, 1905
Currie, H.B., A 27th, Eagle Springs, 1915, 1916, 1917, 1918, 1919
Currie, J.A., C 35th, Jackson Springs, 1895, 1896, 1897, 1898
Davidson, Aaron, C 35th, Carthage, 1914, 1915, 1916, 1917, 1918, 1919
Davis, Baxter, D 48th, Hemp, 1909, 1910, 1911, 1912, 1913, 1914
Davis, John L., E 70th, Steeds, 1916
Deaton, J.M., D 48th, Spies, 1916
Dowdy, A.B., C 35th, Carthage/Hallison, 1891, 1892, 1893, 1894, 1895, 1896, 1897, 1898, 1899, 1900, 1901, 1902, 1903, 1904, 1905, 1907, 1908, 1909, 1910, 1911, 1912, 1913
Dowdy, J.M., G 48th, Sanford, 1903, 1904
Drake, Dallas P., H 1st, Aberdeen, 1909, 1910, 1911, 1912, 1914, 1915, 1916, 1917, 1918, Died July 1919
Drake, Mathew H., D 35th, Sanford, 1902, 1903, 1904
Drake, W.R., D 35th, Aberdeen, 1911, 1912, 1914, 1915
Dunn, James, E 1st, Steeds, 1913
Ellington, S.J., M 74th, Manly, 1912, 1913, 1914, 1915
Ellis, William A., C 24th, Sanford, 1905
Ferguson, Archibald, H 46th, Roseland, 1904, 1905
Foster, John A., E 44th, Jessup, 1898, 1899, 1900
Freeman, William M., H 30th, Carthage/Southern Pines, 1899, 1900, 1903, 1904, 1905
Fry, A.B., H 26th, Manly/West End, 1891, 1892, 1893, 1894, 1895, 1896, 1897, 1898, 1899, 1900, 1901, 1902, 1903, 1904, 1905
Fry, G.T., H 26th, Carthage, 1891, 1892, 1893, 1894, 1895, 1896, 1897, 1898, 1899, 1900, 1901, 1902, 1903, 1904, 1905
Fry, Jacob B., D 49th, Carthage, 1902, 1908, 1909, 1910, 1911, 1912, 1913, 1914, 1915, 1916, 1917, 1918, Died 1919
Fry, Nathan L., H 26th, Carthage, 1901, 1902, 1903, 1904, 1905, 1907, 1908, 1909, 1910, 1911, 1912
Fry, T.M., D 49th, Carthage, 1902, 1903, 1904, 1905, 1907, 1908, 1909, 1910, 1911, 1912
Fry, W.A., E 70th, Hemp, 1909, 1910, 1911, 1912, 1913, 1914, 1915, 1916, 1917, 1918, 1919
Gaster, John M., I 2nd, Swann Station, 1891, 1892, 1893, 1894, 1895, 1896, 1897, 1898, 1899, 1900, 1901, 1902, 1903, 1904, 1905

Gilchrist, John T., G 8th [SC], Pinehurst, 1905, 1917, 1918, 1919
Gilliam, James, D 26th, Carthage, 1892, 1893, 1894, 1895, 1896, Died
Goins, William, 26th, Carthage, 1911, 1912, 1913, 1914, 1915
Goodman, Jacob, C 35th, Cameron, 1891, 1892, 1893, 1894, 1895, 1896, 1897, 1898, 1899, 1900, 1901, 1902, 1903, 1904, 1905, 1907, 1908, 1909, Dead 1910
Goodman, Timothy, C 35th, Cameron, 1891, 1892, 1893, 1894, 1895, 1896, 1897, 1898, 1899, 1900, 1901, 1902, 1903, 1904, 1905
Graham, D.A., H 26th, Cameron, 1902, 1904, 1905, 1907, 1908, 1909
Gunter, J.A., Jr., Marine Corps, Jonesboro, 1902, 1903, 1904, 1905
Harrington, T.H., I 19th, Carthage, 1911, 1912, 1913
Hatcher, Martin G., H 3rd, Manly, 1913, 1915, 1916, 1917, 1918, Died 1918
Howell, Shadrach, B 6th, Cameron, 1908, 1909, 1910, 1911, 1912, 1913, 1914, 1915, 1916, 1917, 1918, Died 1919
Hughes, Spencer, F 50th, Jonesboro, 1902, 1903, 1904, 1905
Johnson, A., D 49th, Euphronia, 1891, 1892
Johnson, Ben J., G 27th, Sanford, 1901, 1902, 1903, 1904, 1905
Johnson, Charles A., H 46th, Cameron, 1909, 1910, 1911, 1912, 1913, 1914, 1915, 1916, 1917, 1918, Died 1919
Johnson, John, H 30th, Cameron, 1902, 1903, 1904, 1905, 1907, 1908, 1909, 1910, 1911, 1912
Johnston, David, F 50th, Sanford, 1902, 1903, 1904
Jones, Christopher, K 2nd, Mt. Carmel, 1891, 1892, 1893, 1894, 1895, 1896, 1897, 1898, 1899, 1900, 1901, 1902, 1903, 1904, 1905, 1907, 1908, 1909, 1910, 1911, 1912, 1913, 1914, 1915, 1916
Jones, Elkin, D 49th, Carthage, 1899, 1900
Jones, T.A., I 10th, Cameron, 1914, 1915, 1916, 1917, Died 1917
Kelly, Elias B., E 3rd, Gilbert, 1899, 1900
Kelly, John B., H 26th, Carthage, 1915
Kelly, Noah R., E 38th, Pinehurst, 1908, 1909, 1910, Died 1910
Kelly, Sandy, H 30th, Sanford, 1905
Kennedy, Robert, E 1st, Steeds, 1913 1918,
Kimball, W.B., E 3rd, Gilbert, 1900
Lawhon, J.J., H 26th, Cameron, 1896, 1897, 1898, 1899, 1900, 1901, 1902, 1903, 1904, 1905, 1907, 1908, 1909, 1910
Lewis, George H., C 35th, Carthage, 1914, 1915, 1916, 1917, 1918, 1919
Lewis, James H., D 48th, Carthage, 1913, 1914, 1915, 1916, 1917, Died Dec 1917
Long, Edwin, I 32nd, Carthage, 1915, 1916, 1917, Died 1918
Luck, Henry, F 70th, Seagrove, 1905, 1907, 1908, 1909, 1910, 1911, 1912, 1913, 1914, 1915, 1916, 1917, 1918,
Malone, Aaron, H 26th, Carthage, 1891, 1892, 1893, 1894
Maness, Alfred, I 10th, Carthage, 1891, 1897
Maness, Enoch N., A 8th, Browers Mills, 1908
Maness, J.S., H 26th, Fair Haven, 1893, 1894, 1895, 1896, Died
Maples, D. McD.., H 46th, Cameron, 1903, 1911, 1912, 1913, 1914, 1915, 1916, 1917, 1918, 1919
Maples, D.T., H 46th, Cameron, 1891, 1892, 1893, 1894, 1895, 1896, 1897, 1898, 1899, 1900, 1902, 1904, 1905, 1907, 1908, 1909, 1910, 1912, 1913, 1914, 1915, 1916, 1917, 1918, 1919
Mashburn, John, E 44th, Carbonton, 1899, 1900 1903, 1904, 1905
Mashburn, Thomas, B 2nd, Glendon, 1908, 1909, 1910, 1912, 1913, 1914, 1915, 1916, 1917, 1918, 1919
Mashburn, W.H.H., E 44th, Carbonton, 1903, 1904, 1905, 1907, 1908, 1909, 1910, 1911, 1912, 1913, 1914, 1915, 1916, 1917, 1918, 1919
McDonald, A.B., E 38th, Coffer, 1903, 1904, 1905
McDonald, D.L., C 35th, Manly/Thaggard Mill/Vass, 1894, 1896, 1897, 1898, 1899, 1900, 1918, 1919
McDonald, J.F., G 33th, Carthage, 1917, 1918, 1919
McDonald, John, C 35th, Cameron, 1909, 1910, 1911, 1912, 1913, 1914, 1915, 1916, 1917, 1918, 1919
McDonald, John A., C 54th, Aberdeen, 1900, 1902, 1903, 1904, 1905, 1907, 1908, 1909, 1910, 1912, 1913, 1914, 1915, 1916, 1917, 1918, 1919
McLean, Angus, H 36th, Keyser, 1907, 1908, 1909, 1910, 1911, 1912, 1913, 1914

McLean, C.C., H 26th, Carthage, 1918, 1919
McLean, James, D 19th, Cameron, 1914
McLean, Peter, H 46th, Cameron, 1905
McPherson, J.D., 5th, Cameron, 1907, 1908, 1909, 1910
McRae, G.A., G 5th, Quiet, 1897, 1898, 1899, 1900
Monroe, J.D., H 46th, Carthage, 1894, 1897, 1898, 1899, 1900
Monroe, J.T., H 46th, Cameron, 1891, 1892, 1895, 1896, 1902, 1904, 1905, 1907, 1908, 1909, 1910, 1911, 1912, 1913, 1914, 1915, 1916, 1917, 1918, 1919
Monroe, John C., F 6th, Eagle Springs, 1918, 1919
Monroe, W.D., H 3rd, Niagra, 1913, 1915, 1916, 1917, 1918, 1919
Monroe, W.E., H 46th, Cameron, 1901 1910, 1911, 1915, 1916
Moore, William C., H 26th, Carthage, 1907, 1908, 1909, 1910, 1911, 1912, 1913, 1914, 1915, 1916, 1917, 1918, 1919
Morgan, George T., D 15th, Tyra, 1891
Morris, William B., E 56th, Swann Station, 1902, 1903, 1904, 1905
Muse, S.J., C 35th, Carthage, 1915, 1916, 1918, 1919
Myrick, M.E., E 26th, Tyra/Big Oak, 1891, 1892, 1893, 1894, 1895, 1896, 1897, 1898, 1899, 1900, 1901, 1902, 1903, 1904, 1905, 1907, 1908, 1909, 1910, Died 1910
Nelson, J.O., I 2nd, Jonesboro, 1902, 1903, 1904
Nunnery, W.K., H 26th, Carthage, 1892, 1893
Oats, James A., H 46th, Manly, 1903, 1904, 1905
Oldham, Phillip, H 46th, Coffer, 1902, 1903, 1904, 1905
Parish, Jordan, I 2nd, Jonesboro, 1902, 1903, 1904, 1905
Paschal, Joseph, I 2nd, Cameron, 1899, 1900, 1901, 1902, 1903, 1904, 1905
Paschal, Robert, E 3rd, Glendon, 1907, 1908, 1909, 1910, Died 1910
Phillips, D.C., E 3rd, Bear Creek, 1908
Phillips, Ed. (Col.), D 48th, Cameron, 1914
Phillips, J.R., F 3rd, Steeds, 1909, 1910, 1911, 1912, 1913, 1914, 1915, 1916, 1917, 1918, 1919
Piner, W.J., H 46th, Cameron, 1891, 1893, 1894, 1895, 1896
Poe, James W., E 63rd, Tramway, 1904, 1905
Powers, John W., E 26th, Glendon, 1900, 1902, 1903, 1904, 1905, 1907, 1908, 1909, 1910, 1911, 1912, 1913, 1914, 1915, 1916, 1917, 1918, To Proximity Station, Greensboro
Ray, A.A., C 35th, Vass, 1917, 1918, 1919
Reynolds, E., K 34th, Carters Mills/Leaman, 1891, 1892, 1893, 1894, 1895, 1896, 1897, 1898, 1899, 1900, 1901, 1903, 1904, 1905, 1907, 1908, 1909, 1910, 1911, 1912, 1913
Riddle, George W., H 30th, Jonesboro, 1896, 1897, 1898, 1899, 1900, 1902, 1903, 1904
Riddle, Thomas, H 46th, Sanford, 1901, 1902, 1903, 1904, 1905
Salmon, Ruben, E 44th, Sanford, 1905
Sanders, Britton, F 3rd, Swinton, 1901, 1902, 1903, 1904, 1905, 1907, 1908, 1909, 1910, 1911, 1912, 1913
Sanders, Jesse, F 3rd, Swinton, 1897, 1898, 1899, 1900, 1901, 1902, 1903, 1904, 1905
Sanders, John, F 3rd, Eagle Springs, 1911, 1912, 1913 1916
Sanders, Simeon, D 48th, Inland/Eagle Springs, 1894, 1895, 1896, 1897, 1898, 1899, 1900
Sanders, William, A 5th, Clayroad, 1915, 1916, 1917, Died 1918
Scarboro, J.T., F 50th, Southern Pines, 1905, 1907, 1908, 1909, 1910, 1911, 1912
Scott, Nelson, C 10th, Steeds, 1908, 1909, 1910, 1911, 1912, 1913, 1914, 1915
Seawell, Eli P., H 30th, Carthage, 1891, 1892, 1893, 1894, 1895, 1896, 1897, 1898
Seawell, S.N., C 3rd, Bensalem, 1900, 1902, 1903, 1904, 1905
Sessoms, William, H 46th, Carthage, 1909, 1910, 1911, 1912, 1913, 1914, 1915, 1916, 1917, 1918, Died July 1919
Shaw, C.W., H 26th, Southern Pines, 1914, 1915, 1916
Sheffield, Jonathan, H 46th, Spies, 1909, 1910, 1911, 1912, 1913, 1914, 1915, 1916
Shields, John W., E 1st, Glendon, 1913
Shields, W.W., C 35th, Carthage, 1914, 1915, 1916, 1917, 1918, 1919
Sibbett, George W., C 35th, Curriesville, 1919
Sloan, David H., H 30th, Jonesboro, 1896, 1897, 1898, 1899, 1900

Sloan, David M., F 50th, Broadway, 1898 1901, 1902, 1903, 1904, 1905
Smith, Daniel, H 46th, Cameron, 1902, 1903, 1904, 1905
Smith, Hiram, F 3rd, Swinton/Spies, 1900, 1902, 1903, 1904, 1905
Smith, Malcom, H 46th, Sanford, 1908, 1909, 1910, 1911, Died
Sneed, Obediah, E 44th, Cameron, 1900, 1902, 1903, 1904, 1905
Stevens, J.C., C 50th, Lakeview, 1913, 1914, 1915, 1916, 1917, 1918, 1919
Stutts, Andrew, H 26th, Putnam, 1907, 1908, 1909, 1910, 1911, 1912, 1913, 1914, 1915
Stutts, William C., D 48th, Hemp, 1903, 1904, 1905, 1907, 1908, Died Nov 1908
Sullivan, Isaac M., D 48th, Eagle Springs, 1909, 1910, 1911, 1912, 1913, 1914, 1915, 1916, 1917, 1918, 1919
Sweatt, T.G., C 8th [SC], Cameron, 1914, 1915, 1916, 1917, 1918, 1919
Thomas, D.A., F 50th, Carbonton, 1904, 1905
Thomas, J.J., F 50th, Broadway/Jonesboro, 1891, 1892, 1893, 1894, 1895, 1896, 1897, 1898, 1899, 1900, 1901, 1902, 1903, 1904
Tillman, A.E., E 5th, Cameron, 1905
Tyson, B.F., F 70th, Eagle Springs, 1917, 1918, 1919
Tyson, B.Y., I 19th, Gilbert, 1891, 1892, 1896, 1897, 1898, 1899, 1900, 1901, 1902, 1903, 1904, 1905, 1907, 1908
Underwood, J.A., H 30th, Broadway, 1904, 1905
Underwood, W.D., E 3rd, Broadway, 1904
Vick, A.B., C 35th, Cameron, 1909, 1910, 1911, 1912, 1913, 1914, 1915, 1916, 1917, 1918, 1919
Vick, John, C 35th, Cameron/Jessup, 1916, 1917, 1918, 1919
Wadsworth, W.J., H 46th, Greenwood, 1891, 1892, 1895, 1896, 1897, 1898, 1899, 1900
Wallace, W.W., D 3rd, Carters Mills/Horners, 1891, 1892, 1893, 1897, 1898, 1900
Warner, Edward, D 49th, Carthage, 1897, 1898
White, T.A., K 43rd, Pinebluff, 1907, 1908, 1909, 1910, 1911, 1912, 1913, 1914, 1915, 1916, 1917, 1918, 1919
Wicker, Charles B., H 30th, Tempting, 1898 1901, 1902, 1903
Wicker, Thomas R., F 50th, Jonesboro, 1904, 1905
Wicker, W.G., E 7th, Sanford, 1901, 1902, 1903, 1904
Williams, Harbert, D 48th, Carters Mills/Hemp, 1900, 1901, 1902, 1903, 1904, 1905
Williams, Henry, H 26th, Pharsala/Carters Mills/Hemp, 1891, 1892, 1893, 1894, 1895, 1896, 1897, 1898, 1899, 1900, 1901, 1902, 1903, 1904, 1905, 1907, 1908, 1909
Williams, J.H., F 50th, Swann Station, 1905
Williams, John, H 26th, Carters Mills/Hemp/Eagle Springs, 1891, 1892, 1893, 1894, 1895, 1896, 1897, 1898, 1899, 1900, 1901, 1902, 1903, 1904, 1905, 1907, 1908, 1909, 1910, 1911, 1912, 1913, 1914, 1915, 1916, 1917, 1918, 1919
Williams, R.D, K 4th, Mooshanee, 1891, 1892, 1893, 1894
Williamson, Kelly, H 26th, Eagle Springs, 1914, 1915, 1916, 1917, 1918, 1919
Wilson, Hugh, F 2nd, Carters Mills/Prosperity, 1891, 1892, 1893, 1894, 1895, 1896, 1897, 1898, 1899, 1900, 1901
Wood, T.F., H 50th, Lakeview, 1905
Woodle, E.W., H 46th, Cameron, 1910, 1911, 1912, 1913, 1914, 1915
Yow, H.C., H 26th, Horners/Carters Mills/Hemp, 1891, 1892, 1894, 1895, 1896, 1897, 1898, 1899, 1900, 1901, 1902, 1903, 1904

Widows, Soldiers, Company/Regiment, Post Office, Years Active on Pension Roll

Barber, Barbara, widow, **Hiram Barber**, soldier, I 2nd, Carthage, 1914, 1915, 1916, 1917, 1918, 1919
Benoy, V.P., widow, **Alex. Benoy**, soldier, C 3rd, Aberdeen, 1903, 1904, 1905, 1907, 1908, 1909, 1910, 1911, 1912, 1913, 1914, 1915
Bishop, E., widow, **Henry Bishop**, soldier, C 3rd, Jonesboro, 1902, 1903, 1904, 1905
Black, Mary E., widow, **B.D. Black**, soldier, K 2nd, Cameron, 1905
Bolton, Mary A., widow, **Foster Bolton**, soldier, C 54th, Cameron, 1891, 1892, 1893, 1894, 1895, 1896, 1897, 1898, 1899, 1900, 1902, 1903, 1904, 1905, 1907, 1908, 1909, 1910, 1911, 1912, 1913, 1914
Brewer, Bethana, widow, **Sampson Brewer**, soldier, H 46th, Spies, 1909, 1910, 1911, 1912, 1913, 1914, 1915, 1916, 1917, 1918, 1919

Brewer, Lydia, widow, **Adam Brewer**, soldier, K 5th, Steeds, 1913, 1914, 1915, 1916, 1917, 1918, 1919
Brewer, Sallie, widow, **W.D. Brewer**, soldier, H 26th, Carters Mills/Big Oak/Hemp, 1891, 1892, 1893, 1894, 1895, 1896, 1897, 1898, 1899, 1900, 1901, 1902, 1903, 1904, 1905, 1907, 1908, 1909, 1910, 1911, 1912, 1913, 1914, 1915, 1916, 1917, 1918, 1919
Britt, Wincy, widow, **Enoch Britt**, soldier, F 3rd, Big Oak, 1887, 1888
Brown, Altrean, widow, **A.S. Brown**, soldier, H 30th, Forkade/Lonely, 1891, 1892, 1893, 1894, 1895, 1896, 1897, 1898, 1899, 1900
Brown, Julia Ann, widow, **Hiram Wallace**, soldier, D 49th, Carthage, 1911, 1912, 1913, 1914, 1915, 1916, 1917, 1918, 1919
Brown, Loretta T., widow, **Wesley Brown**, soldier, I 2nd, Hemp, 1907, 1908, 1909, 1910, 1911, 1912, 1913, 1914, 1915
Brown, Lydia, widow, **W.A. Brown**, soldier, D 49th, Gold Region/Carters Mills/Big Oak/Spencer, 1891, 1892, 1893, 1894, 1895, 1905
Brown, Mary E., widow, **Jesse Brown**, soldier, H 3rd, Carters Mills/Hemp, 1891, 1892, 1893, 1894, 1895, 1896, 1897, 1898, 1899, 1900, 1901, 1902, 1903, 1904, 1907, 1908, 1909, 1910, 1911, 1912, 1913, 1914, 1915, 1916, Died May 1917
Brown, S.J., widow, **J.S. Brown**, soldier, H 26th, Carters Mills/Spencer/Big Oak/Spies, 1891, 1892, 1893, 1894, 1895, 1896, 1897, 1898, 1899, 1900, 1901, 1902, 1903, 1904
Burns, Emeline, widow, **H.H. Burns**, soldier, G 48th, Sanford, 1903, 1904, 1905
Bynum, Mary Ann, widow, **J.H.N. Bynum**, soldier, H 46th, Vass, 1907, 1908, 1909, 1910, 1911, 1912, 1913, 1914, 1915, 1916, 1917, 1918, 1919
Caddell, Sarah Ann, widow, **Archibald B. Caddell**, soldier, D 49th, Spout Springs, 1891, 1892, 1893, 1894, 1895, 1896, 1897, 1898, 1899, 1900, 1901, 1902, 1903, 1904, 1905, 1907, 1908, 1909
Campbell, Flora A., widow, **John A. Campbell**, soldier, E 11th, Jonesboro, 1893, 1894, 1896, 1897, 1898, 1899, 1900
Campbell, Jane Murchison, widow, **D.C. Ferguson**, soldier, H 26th, Carthage, 1915, 1916, 1917, 1918, 1919
Capps, Mary L., widow, **Warner H. Capps**, soldier, C 46th, Aberdeen, 1910, 1911, 1912, 1913, 1914, 1915
Caviness, D.A., widow, **W.S. Caviness**, soldier, I 19th, Crains Creek/Gilbert, 1891, 1892, 1893, 1894, 1895, 1896, 1897, 1898, 1899, 1900, 1901, 1902, 1903, 1904, 1905, 1907, 1908
Cole, Mary Ann, widow, **Calvin C. Cole**, soldier, A 8th, Big Oak/Caledonia/Swinton, 1900, 1901, 1902, 1903, 1904, 1905, 1907, 1908, 1909, 1910, 1911
Cole, Melinda, widow, **John D. Cole**, soldier, B 66th, Cameron, 1910
Cox, C.A., widow, **H.B. Cox**, soldier, H 26th, Carthage, 1913, 1914
Cox, Jane, widow, **Thomas C. Cox**, soldier, F 50th, Jonesboro, 1891, 1892, 1893, 1894, 1895, 1896, 1897, 1898, 1900, 1902, 1903, 1904, 1905
Craven, Martha, widow, **Solomon Craven**, soldier, D 48th, Bensalem, 1890
Davis, Sarah A., widow, **Baxter Davis**, soldier, D 48th, Hemp, 1915, 1916, 1917, 1918, 1919
Dawkins, Jane, widow, **Elijah Dawkins**, soldier, D 26th, Big Oak/Candor/Eagle Springs, 1891, 1892, 1893, 1894, 1895, 1896, 1897, 1898, 1899, 1900, 1902, 1903, 1904, 1905, 1907, 1908, 1909, 1910, 1911, 1912, 1913, 1914, 1915
Dowdy, Sarah A., widow, **A.B. Dowdy**, soldier, C 35th, Carthage, 1914
Dunlap, Adeline, widow, **W.C. Dunlap**, soldier, E 70th, Spies, 1909, 1910, 1911, 1912, 1913, 1914, 1915, 1916, 1917, 1918, 1919
Dupree, Elizabeth, widow, **J.H. Dupree**, soldier, F 46th, Carthage, 1910, 1911, 1912, 1913, 1914, Dead
Estes, Matilda, widow, **Wm. T. Estice**, soldier, E 2nd, Curriesville, 1891, 1892, 1893, 1894, 1895, 1896, 1897, 1898
Evans, Effie, widow, **Henry Evans**, soldier, D 48th, Swann Station, 1891, 1892
Fields, Phoebe J., widow, **James Yeargin Fields**, soldier, G 48th, Parkwood/Mooshanee, 1891, 1892, 1893, 1894, 1895, 1896, 1897, 1898, 1899, 1900
File(Foil), E.F., widow, **J.F. File**, soldier, E 4th, Keyser, 1901, 1902, 1904, 1905
Freeman, Elizabeth, widow, **James A. Freeman**, soldier, D 48th, Carthage, 1891, 1892, 1893, 1894, 1895, 1896, 1897, 1898, 1899, 1900, 1901, 1902, 1903, 1904, 1905, 1907, 1908, 1909, 1910, 1911, 1912, 1913, 1914, 1915
Freeman, Nicy Ann, widow, **William M. Freeman**, soldier, H 30th, Southern Pines, 1908, 1909, 1910

Freeman, Sarah, widow, **Isaac Freeman**, soldier, D 48th, Big Oak/Spencer, 1891, 1892, 1893, 1894, 1895, 1896, 1897, 1898, 1899, 1900, 1902, 1903, 1904, 1905, 1907, 1908, 1909, 1910, 1911, 1912, 1913, 1914
Fry, Elizabeth, widow, **A.B. Fry**, soldier, H 26th, West End, 1916, 1917, 1918, 1919
Fry, Emily, widow, **Nathan L. Fry**, soldier, H 26th, Carthage, 1913, 1914, 1915, 1916
Fry, Fannie, widow, **A.M. Fry**, soldier, D 49th, Carthage, 1903, 1904, 1905, 1907, 1908, 1909, 1910, Died April 1910
Fry, Martha, widow, **T.M. Fry**, soldier, D 40th, Carthage, 1913
Fry, Martha J., widow, **John McDonald**, soldier, C 35th, Carthage, 1914, 1915, 1916, 1917, 1918, Died 1919
Fry, Minnie, widow, **George Thomas Fry**, soldier, H 26th, Carthage, 1909, 1910, 1911, 1912, 1913, 1914, 1915
Gale, Sarah, widow, **J.H. Gale**, soldier, E 8th, Swann Station, 1887, 1888
Gilmore, Elizabeth, widow, **J.H. Gilmore,** soldier, F 50th, Jonesboro, 1891, 1892, 1893, 1894, 1895, 1896, 1897, 1898, 1899, 1900, 1902, 1903, 1904, 1905
Goins, Rachel, widow, **Andrew Goins**, soldier, C 35th, Manly/Carthage/Cameron, 1891, 1892, 1893, 1894, 1895, 1896, 1897, 1898, 1899, 1900, 1901, 1902, 1903, 1904, 1905
Goldston, L.A., widow, **R.W. Goldston**, soldier, H 26th, Quiet, 1892, 1893, 1894, 1895, 1896, 1897, 1898, 1899
Graham, Alice, widow, **A.W. Graham**, soldier, G 24th, Cameron (removed to Laurinburg), 1887, 1888
Haithcock, Martha J., widow, **Levi Haithcock**, soldier, C 42nd, 1899, 1900
Hancock, Elizabeth, widow, **Matthew Hancock**, soldier, H 44th, Steeds, 1907, 1908, 1909, 1910, 1911, 1912, Died Dec 1912
Herring, Cynthia, widow, **Lewis Herring**, soldier, F 50th, Broadway/Lonely, 1891, 1892, 1893, 1894, 1895, 1896, 1897, 1898, 1899, 1900, 1901, 1902, 1903, 1904, 1905
Hornaday, Margaret A., widow, **Louis D. Hornaday**, soldier, H 30th, Sanford, 1902, 1903, 1904, 1905
Hunsucker, Elizabeth, widow, **James Hunsucker,** soldier, D 48th, Hemp, 1901
Hunter, Ann S., widow, **John G. Hunter**, soldier, F 50th, Jonesboro, 1902, 1903, 1904, 1905
Hurley, Penny R., widow, **Winship M. Hurley**, soldier, D 61st, Manly (removed to Chatham), 1891, 1892, 1893, 1894, 1895, 1896, 1897, 1898
Jackson, Mary L., widow, **John Jackson**, soldier, D 22nd, Crains Creek, 1891, 1892, 1893, 1894, 1895, 1896, 1897, 1898
Jackson, Nancy E., widow, **S.T. Jackson**, soldier, A 63rd, Carthage, 1894, 1913
Johnson, Rilla, widow, **A. Johnson**, soldier, H 49th, 1894, 1895, 1896, 1897, 1898, 1899, 1900
Jordan, Mittie A., widow, **John B. Jordan**, soldier, H 26th, Swann Station, 1888, 1890
Kelly, Mary A., widow, **John B. Kelly**, soldier, H 26th, Coles Mill, 1916, 1917, 1918, 1919
Kelly, Sarah, widow, **Daniel M. Kelly**, soldier, B 3rd, Cameron/Carthage, 1900, 1901, 1902, 1903, 1904, 1905
Kelly, Sarah G., widow, **John B. Kelly**, soldier, F 50th, Sanford, 1901, 1902, 1903, 1904, 1905
Key, Tempy, widow, **Rials Key**, soldier, D 48th, Swinton, 1891, 1892, 1893, 1894, 1895, 1896, 1897, 1898, 1899, 1900, 1901, 1902
Lawhon, Mary F., widow, **J.J. Lawhon**, soldier, H 26th, Cameron, 1911, 1912, 1913, 1914, 1915, 1916, 1917, 1918, 1919
Lawrence, Isabella C., widow, **J.T. Lawrence**, soldier, F 50th, Sanford/Forkade, 1901, 1902, 1903, 1904, 1905
Long, Nannie, widow, **Edwin Long**, soldier, I 32nd, Carthage, 1918, 1919
Luck, Caroline, widow, **Henry Luck**, soldier, F 70th, Steeds, 1919
Luck, Lucinda, widow, **Elijah Luck**, soldier, F 46th, Noise/Rise/Spencerville, 1891, 1892, 1893, 1894, 1895, 1896, 1897, 1898, 1899, 1900, 1901, 1902, 1903, 1904, 1905
Mashburn, Nancy, widow, **James Mashburn**, soldier, E 44th, Carbonton, 1901, 1902, 1903, 1904, 1905
Mashburn, Winnie, widow, **John Mashburn**, soldier, E 44th, Haw Branch/Vass, 1907, 1908, 1909, 1910, 1911, 1912, 1913, 1914, 1915, 1916, 1917, 1918, 1919
Mathews, Nancy, widow, **John Mathews**, soldier, C 7th, Broadway, 1891, 1892, 1893, 1894, 1895, Died
McCallum, Sarah E., widow, **Angus McCallum**, soldier, D 49th, Carthage/Ingram, 1891, 1892, 1893, 1894, 1895, 1896, 1897, 1898, 1899, 1900, 1901, 1902, 1903, 1904, 1905, 1907, 1908, 1909, 1910, 1911, 1912, 1913, 1914, 1915, 1916, 1917, 1918, 1919
McInnis, Nancy, widow, **John McInnis**, soldier, D 49th, Curriesville/West End, 1891, 1892, 1893, 1894, 1895, 1896, 1897, 1898, 1899, 1900, 1901, 1902, 1903, 1904, 1905, 1907, 1908, 1909, 1910, 1911, 1912, 1913
McIver, Flora C., widow, **John W. McIver**, soldier, H 30th, Sanford, 1891, 1892, 1893, 1894, 1895
McIver, Isabella McK., widow, **D.M. McIver**, soldier, H 30th, Cameron, 1907, 1908, 1909, 1910, 1911, 1912

McLean, Sarah, widow, **Angus McLean**, soldier, H 36th, Keyser, 1915, 1916, 1917, 1918, 1919
McMillan, Christian C., widow, **Archibald McMillan**, soldier, D 49th, Jackson Springs, 1891, 1892, 1893, 1894, 1896, 1897, 1898, 1899, 1900, 1902, 1903, 1904, 1905, 1907, 1908, 1909, 1910, 1911, 1912, 1913, 1914, 1915, 1916, 1917, 1918, 1919
McNeill, Ann Eliza, widow, **Hector McNeill**, soldier, A 25th, Broadway, 1901, 1902, 1903, 1904, 1905
McNeill, D.M., widow, **Neill McNeill**, soldier, F 50th, Broadway, 1902, 1903, 1904, 1905
McNeill, Elizabeth, widow, **Hector McNeill**, soldier, D 48th, Carthage/Mt. Carmel, 1887, 1890
McNeill, Jane, widow, **Archibald McNeill**, soldier, H 26th, Swinton, 1901, 1902, 1903, 1904, 1905
McNeill, R.A., widow, **Neill A. McNeill**, soldier, F 50th, Broadway, 1891, 1892, 1893, 1894, 1895, 1896, 1897, 1898, 1899, 1900, 1902, 1903, 1904, 1905
Melton, Mary E., widow, **James Melton**, soldier, D 15th, Spies, 1912, 1913, 1914, 1915
Moore, A.A., widow, **John J. Riddle**, soldier, G 48th, Pocket, 1903, 1904, 1905
Moore, Margaret, widow, **Aaron Moore**, soldier, A 5th, Crains Creek, 1891, 1892, 1893, 1894, 1895, 1896, 1897, 1898, 1899, 1900
Morgan, Elizabeth, widow, **Joseph B. Morgan**, soldier, I 57th, Swinton/Spies, 1891, 1892, 1893, 1894, 1895, 1896, 1897, 1898, 1899, 1900, 1901, 1902, 1903, 1904, 1905, 1907, 1908, 1909
Morgan, Elizabeth A., widow, **George T. Morgan**, soldier, D 15th, Tyra/Swinton, 1899, 1900, 1901, 1902, 1903, 1904, 1905, 1907, 1908, 1909
Muse, M.A., widow, **W.B. Muse**, soldier, E 63rd, Cameron, 1905, 1907, 1908, 1909, 1910, 1911, 1912, 1913, 1914
Muse, Martha J., widow, **A.B. Muse**, soldier, E 63rd, Hallison, 1904, 1905
Nelson, Tabitha, widow, **John C. Thomas**, soldier, D 49th, Big Oak, 1903, 1904, 1905, 1907, 1908, 1909, 1910, 1911
Nicholson, E.J., widow, **John Nicholson**, soldier, H 26th, Jonesboro, 1904, 1905
Paschal, Mary, widow, **Joseph Paschal**, soldier, I 2nd, Cameron, 1907, 1908, 1909, 1910, 1911, 1912, 1913, 1914, 1915, 1916, 1917, 1918, 1919
Patterson, Tillie A., widow, **R.D. Patterson**, soldier, A 1st, Lakeview, 1916, 1917, 1918, 1919
Pearce, A.G., widow, **James Pearce**, soldier, H 46th, Crains Creek, 1891, 1892, 1893, 1894, 1895, 1896, 1897, 1898
Pearce, Nancy, widow, **Allison D. Pearce**, soldier, C 35th, Cameron, 1888
Phillips, Candace A., widow, **Jeremiah Phillips**, soldier, E 44th, High Falls, 1910
Phillips, Elizabeth A., widow, **L.S. Phillips**, soldier, C 3rd, Prosperity/Fair Haven/Glendon, 1891, 1892, 1893, 1894, 1895, 1896, 1897, 1898, 1899, 1900, 1902, 1903, 1904, 1905, 1907, 1908, 1909, 1910, 1911, 1912, 1913, 1914
Pierce, Eliza, widow, **Archie Pierce**, soldier, H 46th, Sanford, 1905
Pool, Lucy, widow, **William Pool**, soldier, D 48th, Rise/Longleaf, 1891, 1892, 1893, 1894, 1895, Died
Reynolds, M.J., widow, **Elijah Reynolds**, soldier, K 34th, Leaman, 1914
Scoggins, Jennett/Jemima, widow, **Stephen Scoggins**, soldier, E 56th, Swann Station/Jonesboro, 1891, 1892, 1893, 1894, 1895, 1896, 1897, 1898, 1899, 1900, 1902, 1903, 1904
Scott, Franey, widow, **Nelson Scott**, soldier, C 10th, Steeds, 1916, 1917, Died June 21, 1918
Sheffield, Annie R., widow, **Isham Sheffield**, soldier, H 26th, Carters Mills/Spies, 1891, 1892, 1893, 1894, 1895, 1896, 1897, 1898, 1899, 1900, 1901, 1902, 1903, 1904, 1905
Sheffield, Delitha, widow, **J. Sheffield**, soldier, H 46th, Spies, 1917, Died Dec 1917
Sheffield, Mary, widow, **Isaac Sheffield**, soldier, H 46th, Carters Mills, 1891, 1892, 1893, 1894, 1895, 1896, 1897, 1898, 1899, 1900
Short, Martha A., widow, **Brinkley Short**, soldier, G 63rd, Carthage, 1909, 1910, 1911, 1912, 1913, 1914, 1915, 1916
Smith, Flora Margaret, widow, **Whitson Smith**, soldier, B 6th, Cameron, 1912
Smith, Mary A., widow, **Hiram Smith**, soldier, F 3rd, Spies, 1907, 1908, 1909
Smith, Mary Jane, widow, **Daniel Smith**, soldier, H 46th, Cameron, 1908, 1909, 1910, 1911, 1912, 1913, 1914, 1915
Starling, Mary C., widow, **W.R. Starling**, soldier, I 19th, Vass, 1903, 1904, 1905, 1907, 1908, 1909, 1910, 1911, 1912
Steadman, M.A., widow, **William A. Steadman**, soldier, D 48th, Sanford, 1901, 1902, 1903, 1904, 1905
Stone, Jane, widow, **Archibald Stone**, soldier, F 50th, Sanford, 1901, 1903, 1904, 1905

Stutts, Clarky, widow, **William Stutts**, soldier, D 48th, Hemp, 1909, 1910, 1911
Stutts, Lydia Jane, widow, **Cornelius Stutts**, soldier, D 48th, Hemp, 1903, 1904, 1905, 1907, 1908, 1909, 1910, 1911, 1912, 1913, 1914, 1915, 1916, 1917, 1918, 1919
Stutts, Martha A., widow, **Andrew Stutts**, soldier, H 26th, Putnam, 1916, 1917, 1918, 1919
Teague, Polly, widow, **Isaac Teague**, soldier, H 26th, Noise/Longleaf, 1891, 1892, 1893, 1894, 1895, 1896, 1897, 1898, 1899, 1900, 1901, 1902, 1903
Thomas, Ann W., widow, **Wiley Thomas**, soldier, D 49th, Jackson Springs/Charles Mills, 1891, 1892, 1893, 1894, 1895, 1896, 1897, 1898, 1899, 1900, 1901, 1902, 1903, 1904, 1905
Thomas, Delilah, widow, **Jesse Thomas**, soldier, D 49th, Caledonia, 1891, 1892 1897, 1898, 1899, 1900
Thomas, Rosa, widow, **H.T. Thomas**, soldier, H 30th, Cameron, 1905, 1907, 1908
Thomas, S.J., widow, **Jasper Thomas**, soldier, F 50th, Sanford, 1902, 1903, 1904, 1905
Thomas, Sarah M., widow, **M.C. Thomas**, soldier, H 46th, Lonely, 1901, 1902, 1903, 1904, 1905
Thompson, Sarah, widow, **Gilbert Thompson**, soldier, C 35th, Cameron, 1902, 1903, 1904, 1905, 1907, 1908, 1909, 1910
Tucker, Margaret E., widow, **John Tucker**, soldier, F 24th, Rise/Longleaf/Spencerville, 1891, 1892, 1893, 1894, 1895, 1896, 1897, 1898, 1899, 1900, 1901, 1902, 1903, 1904, 1905, 1907, 1908, 1909, 1910, 1911, 1912, 1913, 1914, 1915, 1916, 1917, 1918, 1919
White, Isabella, widow, **Weston White**, soldier, H 5th, Cameron, 1902, 1903, 1904, 1905
Wicker, Mamie J., widow, **J.J. Wicker**, soldier, H 30th, Greensboro, 1913
Wicker, Susanna, widow, **David W. Wicker**, soldier, F 50th, Sanford, 1903, 1904, 1905
Williams, Catharine, widow, **Richard D. Williams**, soldier, K 4th, Putnam/Carthage, 1895, 1905, 1907, 1908, 1909, 1910, 1911, 1912, 1913, 1914, 1915, 1916
Williams, Catharine, widow, **George Williams**, soldier, I 5th [AL], Hemp, 1904, 1905, 1907, 1908, 1909, 1910, 1911, 1912, 1913, 1914, 1915
Williams, Lucy J., widow, **Marshal Williams**, soldier, D 26th, Rise/Steeds, 1891, 1892, 1893, 1894, 1895, 1896, 1897, 1898, 1899, 1900, 1901, 1902, 1903, 1904, 1905, 1907, 1908, 1909, 1910, 1911
Williamson, Elender, widow, **Isaac Williamson**, soldier, C 46th, Swinton, 1891, 1892, 1893, 1894, 1895, 1896, 1897, 1898, 1899, 1900, 1901, 1902, 1903, 1904, 1905, 1907, 1908, 1909, 1910, 1911, 1912, 1913, 1914, 1915, 1916, 1917, 1918, 1919
Wilson, Sarah, widow, **Hugh Wilson**, soldier, F 2nd, Leaman, 1902, 1903, 1904, 1905, 1907, 1908, 1909, 1910, 1911, 1912, 1913, 1914, 1915, 1916, 1917, 1918, 1919

Lee County Roster of Confederate Pensions in 1908

Soldiers, Company/Regiment, Post Office

Andrews, George W., E 5th, Carbonton
Avent, W. Marshall, H 70th, Sanford
Booker, H.J., D 26th, Osgood
Brafford, Atlas, E 26th, Moncure
Buchanan, S.R.B, F 50th, Sanford
Burns, Bennett, Bryant
Burns, S.M., E 63rd, Jonesboro
Churchill, J.R., C 31st, Glenaloon
Cox, George, E 8th, Sanford
Cox, John L., H 30th, Jonesboro
Dalrymple, Malcom, F 50th, Jonesboro
Gaster, J.M., I 2nd, Swann Station
Gilmore, G.W., D 48th, Sanford
Godfrey, H.A., F 50th, Jonesboro
Godfrey, John, F 50th, Jonesboro
Grose, C.D., E 44th, Sanford
Gunter, A.A., F 50th, Lockville
Gunter, J. Riley, E 8th, Osgood
Gunter, J.A., Jr., Marine Corps, Jonesboro
Gunter, W.W., G 16th
Hall, L., D 2nd, Lemon Springs
Hawley, M.H., E 70th, Jonesboro
Hilliard, Joseph, E 26th
Howell, J.W., E 1st, Sanford
Hughes, Spencer, F 50th, Jonesboro
Johnson, Benjamin, G 27th, Sanford
Johnson, Josiah J., B 6th, Lockville
Johnson, Michael G., I 32nd, Sanford
Jones, H., I 51st, Lemon Springs
Jones, W.H., E 10th, Osgood
Kelly, Arch. A., F 50th, Sanford
Kelly, Joseph D., F 50th, Lockville
Kelly, Sandy, H 30th, Sanford
Lawrence, J.W., H 30th, Jonesboro
Luther G.W., F 50th, Sanford
Malone, Benj., D 48th, Lockville
Mann, J.H., D 35th, Jonesboro
McBryde, Thomas, F 50th, Lemon Springs
McDuffie, J.W., C 35th, Tramway
McFarland, J.B., F 50th, Jonesboro
McNeill, John, F 50th, Sanford
McNeill, N.A., E 8th, Sanford
Moore, J.D., G 48th, Sanford
Morris, T.W., H 46th, Swann Station
Morris, William B., E 56th, Swann Station
Nall, Ira L., E 26th, Sanford
Nelson, J.O., I 2nd, Sanford
Oldham, Phillip, H 46th, Coffer
Pattishall, J.R., G 5th, Lockville
Paul, A., E 51st, Sanford
Petty, J.W., G 63rd, Cumnock
Phillips, J.H., H 30th, Jonesboro
Pipkin, John E., F 50th, Lockville
Pittman, J.B., F 51st, Sanford
Poe, James W., E 63rd, Tramway
Riddle, Cato, H 46th, Sanford
Rigsbee, W.H., E 5th, Colon
Salmon, R., E 44th, Sanford
Sloan, Alexander, D 61st, Bynum
Smith, Fred, G 48th, Lockville
Smith, William, G 5th, Bryant
Spivey, Wilson, E 8th, Lockville
Stedman, D.L., E 8th, Jonesboro
Tally, James K., E 44th, Tramway
Thomas, D.A., F 20th, Carbonton
Thomas, Jefferson, H 30th, Jonesboro
Thomas, Luther R., F 50th, Lockville
Tyson, B.Y., I 19th, Gilbert
Underwood, J.A., H 30th, Broadway
Underwood, W.D., E 3rd, Jonesboro
Watson, Garner, F 50th, Jonesboro
Weldon, J.J., F 50th, Sanford
Wicker, J.D., E 44th, Sanford
Wicker, T.R., F 50th, Jonesboro
Williams, J.H., F 50th, Swann Station
Womble, Joe B., F 25th, Lockville

Widows, Soldiers, Company/Regiment, Post Office

Buchanan, L.C., widow, **A.J. Buchanan,** soldier, F 50th, Jonesboro
Burns, Emeline, widow, **H.H. Burns**, soldier, G 48th, Sanford
Caviness, D.A., widow, **W.S. Caviness**, soldier, I 2nd, Gilbert
Clark, Dicy, widow, **Joshua Clark**, soldier, E 32nd, Colon
Cox, Jane, widow, **T.C. Cox**, soldier, F 50th, Jonesboro
Dickens, Affiah, widow, **John Loyd**, soldier, E 8th, Colon
Gilmore, E., widow, **J.H. Gilmore,** soldier, F 50th, Jonesboro
Herring, Cynthia, widow, **Louis Herring**, soldier, F 50th, Lonely
Hunter, Ann S., widow, **John G. Hunter,** soldier, F 50th, Jonesboro
Kelly, S.G., widow, **John B. Kelly**, soldier, F 50th, Sanford
Lawrence, Isabella, widow, **Joseph T. Lawrence**, soldier, F 50th, Forkade
Mashburn, Nancy, widow, **James Mashburn**, soldier, E 44th, Carbonton
McFarland, Fannie E., widow, **W.M. McFarland**, soldier, F 50th, Jonesboro
McNeill, A.L., widow, **Hector McNeill**, soldier, A 25th, Broadway
McNeill, D.M., widow, **Neill McNeill**, soldier, F 50th, Broadway
McNeill, Mahala, widow, **William McNeill**, soldier, D 22nd, Sanford
McNeill, R.A., widow, **Neill A. McNeill,** soldier, F 50th, Broadway
Moore, A.A., widow, **John J. Riddle**, soldier, G 48th, Pocket
Muse, M.A., widow, **W.B. Muse**, soldier, E 5th, Cameron
Nicholson, E.J., widow, **John Nicholson**, soldier, H 26th, Jonesboro
Oliver, Lanie, widow, **M.T. Oliver,** soldier, F 50th, Sanford
Pearce, Eliza, widow, **Archie Pearce**, soldier, H 46th, Sanford
Riddle, Rebecca J., widow, **George W. Riddle**, soldier, H 30th, Jonesboro
Stedman, M.A., widow, **W.A. Stedman**, soldier, D 48th, Sanford
Stone, Jane, widow, **Arch Stone**, soldier, F 50th, Sanford
Thomas, Elizabeth, widow, **M.A. Thomas**, soldier, H 30th, Glenaloon
Thomas, Rosa, widow, **H.T. Thomas**, soldier, H 30th, Cameron
Thomas, S.J., widow, **Jasper Thomas**, soldier, F 50th, Sanford
Thomas, Sarah Anne, widow, **M.C. Thomas**, soldier, H 46th, Lonely
Watson, Julia O., widow, **M.K. Watson**, soldier, F 50th, Broadway
Webster, Lanie, widow, **R.B. Webster**, soldier, D 35th, Colon
Wicker, Catherine, widow, **W.W. Wicker**, soldier, F 50th, Jonesboro
Wicker, Susanna, widow, **David W. Wicker**, soldier, F 50th, Sanford

The Carthage Blade [November 8, 1905] [552]

List of Pensioners.

Mr. D. A. McDonald, clerk of court handed us the following list of pensioners for Moore county. The pensions will be paid about the 20th of December. If any of this list are dead the information should be reported to Mr. McDonald so that the pension board may be informed. Here is the list as it stands:

SOLDIERS.

A. B. Dowdy, Tim Goodwin, M. E. Myrick, Willie P. Burt, Wm. M. Cheek, Jacob Goodwin, Jesse Saunders, J. T. Monroe, D. T. Maples, Richard M. Bobbit, S. R. B. Buchanan, William Burns, Daniel Bailey, Martin Brewer, Sampson Brewer, Hyrum Barber, Joel M. Brown, M. P. W. Blue, George Cox, John L. Cox, Henry C. Cagle, Matthew Drake, J. M. Dowdy, Wm. A. Ellis, Archibald Ferguson, William Freeman, A. B. Fry, Nathan L. Fry, T. M. Fry, J. M. Gaster, D. A. Graham, J. A. Gunter, Jr., Spencer Hughes, Christopher Jones, Ben Johnston, John Johnston, Sandy Keely, J. J. Lawhorn, Henry Luck, Peter McLean, W. H. H. Mashburn, John Mashburn, J. A. McDonald, William B. Morris, James A. Oats, Philllp Oldham, Jas. W. Poe, Jordon Parish, John W. Powers, E. Reynolds, Britton Sanders, David M. Sloan, Daniel Smith, S. N. Seawell, Hyrum Smith, William C. Stutts, R. Salmon, J. T. Scarboro, A. E. Tillman, D. A. Thomas, B. Y. Tyson, J. A. Underwood, Thomas R. Wicker, Henry Williams, John Williams, Herbert Williams, J. H. Williams.

WIDOWS.

Mary E. Brown, Sallie Brewer, Mary Bolton, E. Bishop, V. P. Benoy, Emeline Burns, Mary E. Black S. A. Caddell, D. A. Caviness, M. A. Cole, Jane Cox, Jane Dawkins, E. E. File, E. Freeman, Sarah Freeman, Fannie Fry, E. Gilmore, Cynthia Herring, Ann S. Hunter, Margaret A. Hornaday, S. G. Kelly, Sarah Kelly, Lucinda Luck, Isabella Lawrence, Nancy Mashburn, A. L. McNeill, N. McInness, Jane McMcNeill, S. E. McCullum, F. A. Morgan, Eliz Morgan, Christian C. McMillan, D. M. McNeill, R. A. McNeill, A. A. Moore, M. A. Muse, Tabitha Nelson, E. J. Nicholson, E. A. Phillips, Eliza Pierce, M. A. Stedman, Jane Stone, A. R. Sheffield, Mary C. Starling, Lydia J. Stutts, M. M. E. Tucker, S. J. Thomas, Sarah M. Thomas, Sallie Thompson, Rosa Thomas, Sarah Wilson, Catherine Williams, L. J. Williams, Elander Williamson, Susana Wicker, Catharine Williams.

SIXTY NAMES ON THE PENSION LIST

Confederate Veterans and the Widows of Veterans Will Get Their Checks from the State Next Week.

Clerk of Court J. Alton McIver will pay out between $1,800 and $1,900 in pensions to the Confederate veterans and widows of veterans in Moore county this week. The checks represent the semi-annual payment by the state. Of the sixty names on the pension roll, 56 of them—37 men and 19 women—receive only $60 per year, or $30 every six months. The other four receive slightly larger amounts, the highest being $100 per year.

The sixty veterans and widows of veterans who are paid through Clerk McIver are either residents of Moore county or have moved out of the county since the pension was granted. The list is as follows:

Soldiers

First class—
Sibbett, G. W., Pinehurst.
Second class—
Maples, D. T., Cameron.
Third class—
Burt, Willie P., Pinebluff.
Fourth class—
Brady, Eli, Prosperity.
Brady, Manly, Bear Creek.
Brewer, Martin, Spies.
Caddell, Neill B., Carthage.
Clegg, B. F., Carthage.
Connell, F. M., Carthage.
Cottingham, Dinwiddie, Carthage.
Currie, H. B., Eagle Springs.
Dalrymple, John G., Carthage.
Fry, W. A., Hemp.
Gilchrist, John T., Pinehurst.
Gulledge, William, Route 2, Cameron.
Lewis, George H., Carthage.
Mashburn, W. H. H., Carbonton.
McDonald, J. A., Aberdeen.
McLean, C. C., Carthage.
Maple, D. D., Rockingham, Box 75.
Mashburn, Thomas, Glendon.
McDonald, John, Cam[illegible]
Moore, W. C., C[illegible]
Monroe, John, Eagle Springs.
Monroe, W. D., Niagara.
Muse, S. J., Carthage.
Ray, A. A., Vass.
Phillips, J. R., Steeds.
Sessoms, W. M., Vass.
Shields, W. W., Carthage.
Sullivan, Isaac M., Biscoe.
Stevens, J. C., Lakeview.
Sweatt, T. G., Cameron.
Tyson, B. F., Eagle Springs.
Tyson, B. Y., Carthage.
Vick, A. B., Cameron.
Vick, John, Jessup.
White, T. A., Pinebluff.
Williamson, Kelly, Eagle Springs.
Williams, John, Eagle Springs.

Widows

Williamson, Eleander, Spies, R. F. D. No. 2.
Brown, Julia Ann, Carthage.
Bynum, Mary Ann, Vass.
Brewer, Lydia, Steeds.
Dunlop, Adeline, Spies.
Fry, Eliz., West End.
Kelly, Mary, Carthage.
Lawhon, Mary F., Cameron.
Long, Nannie, Carthage.
Luck, Caroline, Steeds, R. F. D. 1.
McLean, Sarah, Keyser.
McCallum, S. E., Southern Pines.
McMillan, Christina C., Jackson Springs.
Mashburn, Winnie, Haw Branch.
Paschal, Mary, Cameron.
Patterson, Tillie A., Lakeview.
Parrish, Julia, Raeford.
Stutts, Martha A., Putnam.
Tucker, M. E. Steeds, R. F. D. 1, Box 8.
Wilson, Sarah, Leaman.

The Moore County News [June 16, 1921] [553]

The Moore County News [June 21, 1928] [554]

14 VETERANS OF CIVIL WAR LIVE IN MOORE COUNTY

Oldest is 95 But Still Able To Travel Around And Enjoy Life; 25 Widows Survive.

PENSION CHECKS READY

Clerk of Court Willcox has received the pension checks for the civil war veterans and widows and has them ready for distribution. Those who are unable to call or send for their checks may get them by mail. Five names have been erased from the pension list as it stood this time last year and at least one veteran has answered the last roll call since the pension moneys came in, passing away Tuesday morning.

Mr. Martin Brewer, of Bensalem township, probably the oldest veteran in the county, being 95 years of age, came to Carthage for his pension check one day last week. He expressed his intention of again attending the annual reunion this year. He is blind in one eye, but otherwise remarkably well preserved, still hale and hearty and gets about like a boy.

There are 25 widows of veterans who will draw pensions. Checks for the 14 surviving veterans are in the amount of $182.50. Disabled widows draw $150.00, while those not disabled receive $50.00.

Mr. Willcox states that he has received several inquiries as to where the reunion of veterans will be held this year. For the benefit of those seeking this information, he requests The News to announce that he has ascertained from General Smith, of Ansonville, that the gathering will be in Tarboro, N. C., from the 7th to the 9th of August. He has already mailed the information to the veterans. Arrangements to furnish the old soldiers with free transportation to and from the reunion city have been made, with all expenses paid. They will also be accompanied by some younger relative or friend, to see to their needs while making the journey. Where two or three veterans go from the same community, probably only one person will be needed to go with them, but where the veterans are scattered each one will have an attendant, with his expenses paid, as well.

The 14 Moore county veterans of the war between the states are:

Charles Brady, Highfalls; Martin Brewer, Spies; F. M. Connell, Carthage; Dinwiddie Cottingham, Carthage; John G. Dalrymple, Carthage; Wm. Gulledge, Cameron, R. 2; C. C. McLean, Carthage; G. A. McRae; Thomas Mashburn, Glendon; John Monroe, Eagle Springs, RFD; B. D. Caviness, Sanford, RFD; T. H. Caviness, Carthage.

VETS GET THEIR PENSION CHECKS

John Willcox is Distributing Semi-Annual Vouchers to Soldiers and Widows

Semi-annual pension checks, ranging from $50 to $182.50, were received here Saturday by John Willcox, clerk of the superior court, and are being distributed among as many Confederate veterans and widows of veterans. The veterans get $182.50 each. Class A widows get $150 each and Class B widows are allowed $50 each. Negro servants of Confederates received $100 each but there are none in this county.

Checks for the following veterans and widows of veterans were received;

Veterans—Charles Brady, Martin Brewer, F. M. Connell, Dinwiddie Cottingham, John G. Dalrymple, William Gulledge, C. C. McLean, G. A. McRae, Thomas Mashburn, John Monroe, B. D. Caviness, T. H. Caviness, and John B. Cameron.

Widows—Mesdames Margaret Alexander, Sarah A. Seawell, Mary A. Barrett, Sarah H. Davis, Adeline Dunlop, Lucy A. Edwards, Mary A. Ferguson, Anne Elizabeth Fry, Fannie M. Howard, Caroline Luck, Lucy McCallum, Margaret McLean, Mary Jane Monroe, Rosanna Lee Moore, Priscilla J. Nall, Jane Sullivan, Elizabeth C. Thompson, Mary C. Williams, Laura Jane Whitaker, Nora Lawhon, Nancy McKenzie Blue, Mrs. A. J. Keith, Mary Kennedy and Tabitha Martin.

The Moore County News [June 20, 1929] [555]

The Sanford Express [December 9, 1910] [556]

PENSIONS FOR VETERANS.

The List of Lee County Confederate Soldiers and Widows of Soldiers Who Will Receive Pensions from the State.

Following is a list of the Confederate soldiers and widows of Confederate soldiers who will receive a pension in Lee county this year;

Third Class—G W Andres, W M Avent, Bennett Burns, S R Buchanan, H J Booker, Atlas Brafford, S M Burns, H A Bridges, J R Churchill, George Cox, John L Cox, A A Gunter, J M Gaster, J A Gunter, Jr, C D Grose, G W Gilmore, Thos Grose, J W Howell, M K Hawley, T H Harper, J J Johnson, Benjamin Johnson, G Jackson, Joseph D Kelly, Sandy Kelly, A A Kelly, J W Lawrence, G W Luther, Ben Malone, John McNeill, J D Moore, T W Morris, J H Mann, J W McDuffie, J B McFarland, N A McNeill, W B Morris, Ira L Nall, J W Oldham, John F Pipkin, J R Pattishall, J W Petty, J W Poe, J B Pitman, J H Phillips, W H Riggsbee, Wilson Spivey, R Salmon, D L Stedman, J F Sloan, T J Savage, B Y Tyson, J K Tally, Jefferson Thomas, D A Thomas, J A Underwood, W D Underwood, J B Womble, T. R. Wicker, J H Williams, J J Wicker, J D Wicke, R M Womack, H Jones.

Widows of Soldiers—L C Buchanan, D A Caviness, Jane Cox, Decy Clark, M S Dalrymple, E Gilmore, Nancy Godfrey, E J Gilliam, Cynthia Hering, Ann S Hunter, Emeline Jones, Isabella Lawrence, Nancy Mashburn, A L McNeill, Mahala McNeill, D M D M McNeill, R A McNeill, A A Moore, M A Muse, Fannie E McNeill, Jeanette Morris, Mary E McIntosh, Bettie Medlin, E J Nicholson, Lanie Oliver, Sallie Oldham, Mary J Patterson, Virginia R Palmer, Tobitha Paul, D C Poe, Rebecca J Riddle, M A Stedman, Jane Stone, Amanda A Smith, M M Shields, Sarah Salmon, Elizabeth Thomas, S J Thomas, Sarah M Thomas, Rosa Thomas, M E Thomas, Susana Wicker, Catharine Wicker, J O Watson, Mary J Webster.

The Sanford Express [December 15, 1916] [557]

CHRISTMAS PRESENTS.

Lee County Confederate Veterans and Widows Who Will Receive Pensions from the State.

The vouchers for pensions to Confederate veterans and widows of deceased veterans are now in the hands of Clerk of the Court Campbell. Following is a list of the pensioners in Lee county:

SOLDIERS.

W. Marshall Avent, S. R. B. Buchanan, Atlas Brofford, S. M. Burns, Matthew Cagle, J. N. Cole, J. R. Churchill, George Cox, A. A. Gunter, J. A. Gunter, Jr., C. D. Gross, Thomas Gross, J. D. Hart, Jr., J. W. Howell, T. H. Harper, J. C. Harkey, J. R. Hunter, Josiah J. Johnson, Joseph D. Kelly, Sandy Kelly, Arch A. Kelly, G. W. Luther, A. G. Marks, J. D. Moore, J. W. McDuffie, Ira L. Nall, J. W. Oldham, J. B. Pittman, J. H. Phillips, William H. Riggsbee, J. F. Sloan, T. J. Savage, L. H. Sutton, B. Y. Tyson, James K. Tally, D. A. Thomas, W. D. Underwood, Jos. B. Womble, J. H. Williams, J. J. Weldon, J. D. Wicker, J. A. Willett, J. A. Foster, J. M. Bruton.

WIDOWS.

Mrs. L. C. Buchanan, Mrs. D. A. Caviness, Mrs. Jane Cox, Mrs. Dicy Clark, Mrs. Malinda Cole, Mrs. Catherine Cole, Mrs. E. Gilmore, Mrs. Nancy Godfrey, Mrs. Quincey Johnson, Mrs. Mary J. Jones, Mrs. Delilah Kelly, Mrs. Flora A. Kimball, Mrs. V. P. Lasater, Mrs. Mary E. Lawrence, Mrs. Isabella Lawrence, Mrs. Nancy Mashburn, Mrs. D. M. McNeill, Mrs. M. J. Maddox, Mrs. Mary J. McNeill, Mrs. A. A. Moore, Mrs. Fannie E. McFarland, Mrs. Jennette Morris, Mrs. Mary E. McIntosh, Mrs. Elizabeth Malone, Mrs. E. F. Marks, Mrs. Sallie Oldham, Mrs. Alice L. Poe, Mrs. Martha Pattishall, Mrs. Virginia R. Palmer, Mrs. Tobitha Paul, Mrs. C. C. Poe, Mrs. Mary L. Petty, Mrs. Rebecca J. Riddle, Mrs. M. A. Steadman, Mrs. Mary E. Stedman, Mrs. Sarah Salmon, Mrs. Sarah M. Thomas, Mrs. Rosa Thomas, Mrs. M. C. Thomas, Mrs. Tiney Thomas, Mrs. Sarah J. Underwood, Mrs. Susana Wicker, Mrs. Catherine Wicker, Mrs. Mary J. Webster, Mrs. Elizabeth Wicker, Mrs. Laura Fitchett.

The Sanford Express [December 21, 1917] [558]

PENSIONS FOR VETERANS

And Their Widowds"—Nearly Four Thousand Dollars Paid Out.

North Carolina's half million dollars for Confederate veterans and their widows this year will be split up into larger amounts for the beneficiaries, and at a time when this is peculiarly desirable, on account of the high cost of living. There is a flat addition to each pension of $13 for the year.

The pensions for Lee county veterans and their widows are now available in the office of the clerk of the court, and a few of the checks have been paid out. Clerk Campbell wishes all those who are entitled to pensions to apply for them at once.

The list of soldiers and widows of soldiers who are entitled to pensions follows:

SOLDIERS.

Alexander Sloan, Marshall W. Avent, S. R. Buchanan, Atlas Brafford, J. M. Bruton, S. M. Burns, Matthew Cagle, J. N. Cole, J. R. Churchill, Geo. Cox, A. A. Gunter, A. H. Gunter, J. A. Gunter, Jr., C. D. Gross, Thomas Gross, J. D. Hart, Jr., J. W. Howell, T. H. Harper, J. C. Harkey, Josiah J. Johnson, Joseph D. Kelly, Sandy Kelly, Arch A. Kelly, G. W. Luther, J. D. Moore, J. W. McDuffie, J. W. Oldham, J. H. Phillips, William H. Riggsbee, J. F. Sloan, T. J. Savage, L. H. Sutton, B. Y. Tyson, James K. Tally, D. A. Thomas, W. D. Underwood, J. H. Williams, J. J. Weldon, J. D. Wicker, J. A. Willett, Solomon Womble.

WIDOWS.

Mesdames Eliza Booker, D. A. Caviness, Dicy Clark, Malinda Cole, Catherine Cole, Laura Fitchett, Parmelia Foster, E. Gilmore, Nancy Godfrey, Rebecca J. Hunter, Quincey Johnson, Mary J. Jones, Delilah Kelly, Flora A. Kimball, V. P. Lasater, Mary A. Lawrence, Isabella Lawrence, Nancy Marshman, D. M. McNeill, M. J. Maddox, Mary J. McNeill, A. A. Moore, Fannie E. McFarladd, Jennette Morris, Mary E. McIntosh, E. F. Marks, Sallie Oldham, Alice L. Poe, Martha Pattishall, Virginia R. Palmer, Tabitha Paul, Salina Pendergrass, C. C. Poe, Mary L. Petty, Rebecca J. Riddle, M. A. Steadman, Mary E. Steadman, Sarah Salmon, Sarah M. Thomas, Rosa Thomas, M. C. Thomas, Tiney Thomas, Sarah J. Underwood, Susana Wicker, Catherine Wicker, Mary J. Webster, Jane Cox.

Pensions are paid out in graduated amounts. One man in Lee county, Mr. Alexander Sloan, of Moncure, drew $55 this year. This is provided for those who lost a leg below the knee or an arm below the elbow. Soldiers drawing $45 a year number 41; and widows drawing the same amount number 47. Last year this pension was $32 each. The total amount to be paid out to soldiers and their widows this year is $3,970 00. Several soldiers have died during the year but the pension money goes to their nearest relatives for burial expenses.

The Sanford Express [December 14, 1923] [559]

MONEY FOR VETERANS

List of Lee County Men and Women Who Receive Pensions From State.

There are seventeen Confederate Veterans and twenty-seven widows of veterans in Lee county who receive pensions from the State government. The pension money is sent to these men and women in two installments—one in June and the other in December. The money will be in the hands of the Clerk of the Court, D. E. McIver, some time within the next few days, and those who are entitled to pensions will receive them within the next two or three weeks.

As will be seen from the list given below, the widows of Confederate veterans on the pension list outnumber the veterans almost two to one. Many of the men who followed Lee and Jackson and fought the great civil war of the sixties have died within the past few years, leaving widows to receive the small yearly pension which the State provided for them. When Lee county was created fifteen years ago there were 150 Confederate veterans living within its bounds. We do not know how many of these men are still living, but the list of names on Camp Ranson's roster has greatly diminished within thes years.

There are a few Confederate Veterans in the county who do not receive pensions, not because they do not deserve pensions, but because the State does not provide pensions for those who have means and are able to support themselves. The United States Government provides pensions for all Federal soldiers who fought in the civil war, and each one receives a dollar a day or more as long as he lives. If Confederate soldiers received this much they could be fairly comfortable the balance of their days, but they have only the State to look to for help and the State is not able to do very much as compared with the United States.

Confederate Pensioners.

George W. Avent.
W. Marshall Avent.
Atlas Brofford.
S. R. Buchanan.
J. N. Cole.
George Cox.
A. M. Harrington.
J. C. Harkey,
J .D. Hart, Jr.
Jos. D .Kelly.
Arch A. Kelly.
T. J. Savage.
Jas. K. Tally.
J. D. Wicker.
J. D .Willett.
A. H. Grose.

Widows of Confederate Veterans.

Mrs. Dicey Clark.
Mrs. Milanda Cole.
Mrs. Samantha Gilmore.
Mrs. Rebecca J. Hunter.
Mrs. Mary J. Jones.
Mrs. V. P. Lasater.
Mrs. D. M .McNeill.
Mrs. Mary J. McNeill.
Mrs. E. F. Marks.
Mrs. Nancy Mashburn.
Mrs. Virginia R. Palmer .
Mrs. Tobitha Paul.
Mrs. Salina Pendergrass.
Mrs. C. C. Poe.
Mrs. Fannie Smith.
Mrs. Mary E. Stedman.
Mrs. Margaret A. Sutton.
Mrs .Rosa Thomas.
Mrs .Tiney Thomas .
Mrs. Sarah J. Underwood.
Mrs. Susan Wicker.
Mrs. Caroline Wicker.
Mrs. Bettie Matthews.
Mrs. Delilah Jane Morris.
Mrs. W. D .Underwood.
Mrs. Mary E. McIntosh.

The Sanford Express [December 19, 1924] [560]

VOUCHERS FOR VETERANS AND WIDOWS.

Clerk of the Court McIver has received the pension vouchers for Confederate veterans and widows of veterans in this county and by calling at the court house they can get same.

This payment is for the half year ending June 15, 1925. The sum of $60 is given each veteran in the fourth class, or a widow of a veteran. The vouchers call for a little more each six months period on account of deaths among the pensioners. Pensioners rated above the fourth class receive still larger amounts. The number of widows receiving pension benefits in Lee county is far in excess of the veterans, there being 31 widows and 20 veterans. Their names are as follows:

Soldiers

George W. Avent, W. Marshall Avent, I. D. Boyd, Redin Bryan, S. R. B. Buchanan, W. R. Campbell, George Cox, Atlas H. Gross, Thomas Gross, A. M. Harrington, J. C. Harkey, J. D. Hart, Jr., Joseph D. Kelly, Arch A .Kelly, J. J .Peele, R. G. Reid, T. J. Savage, James K. Tally, J. D. Wicker, J. A. Willett.

Widows.

Mrs. Mary E. McIntosh, Mrs. Maggie Boseman, Mrs. Mary Ann Brooks, Mrs. Dicey Clark, Mrs. Malinda Cole, Mrs. Sallie I. Cox, Mrs. Emeline Everett,' Mrs. Samantha Gilmore, Mrs. Mary F. Gunter, Mrs. Rebecca Hunter, Mrs. Mary J. Jones, Mrs. D. M .McNeill, Mrs. Mary J. McNeill, Mrs. Nancy A. McNeill, Mrs. M. J. Maddox, Mrs. E. F. Marks, Mrs. Nancy Mashburn, Mrs. Bettie Matthews, Mrs. Virginia R. Palmer, Mrs. Tobitha Paul, Mrs. Salina Pendergrass, Mrs. C. C. Poe, Mrs. Fannie Smith, Mrs. Margaret Sutton, Mrs. Rose Thomas, Mrs. M. C. Thomas, Mrs. Samantha Thomas, Mrs. M. A. Underwood, Mrs. Sarah J.Underwood, Mrs. Susanna Wicker, Mrs. Catherine Wicker.

CONFEDERATE VETERANS AND WIDOWS GET CHECKS.

Five hundred thousand dollars in checks to Confederate Veterans and widows of veterans were mailed out from Raleigh Mondy to the Clerks of the court of the various counties for distribution among those who are entitled to them. Clerk of the Court Gunter Watson received checks for eleven veterans and twenty-eigh widows. These checks for the veterans were for $100 each and for the widows $50.00 each. The total amount for the veterans was $1,100, and for the widows $1,400, making a grand total of $2,500.00. The following veterans received checks:

W. Marshall Avent, I. D. Boyd, Redin Bryan, George Cox, Thomas Grose, J. D. Hart, Jr., Joseph D. Kelly, Arch A. Kelly, J. J. Peele, R. G. Reid, J. D. Wicker

Widows: Mrs. Mary Ann Brooks, Mrs. Malinda Cole, Mrs. Margaret V. Cox, Mrs. Sallie I. Cox, Mrs. Emaline Everette ,Mrs. Samantha Gilmore, Mrs. Jackie B. Grose, Mrs. Mary F. Gunter, Mrs. Rebecca J. Hunter, Mrs. Mary J. Jones, Mrs. Kate N. Lasater, Mrs. M. D. McNeill, Mrs. Nancy A. McNeoll, Mrs. M. J. Maddox, Mrs. S. F. Marks, Mrs. Margaret Mashburn, Mrs. Nancy Mashburn, Mrs. Bettie Matthews, Mrs. Margaret L. Phillps, Mrs. C.C. Poe, Mrs. Annie M. Ross, Mrs. Nannie Smith, Mrs. Margaret A. Sutton, Mrs. Barbara Thomas, Mrs. Rosa Thomas, Mrs. Samantha Thomas, Mrs. M. A. Underwood, Mrs. Sarah J. Underwood.

Veterans will get a dollar a day out of the next pension fund, which will be distributed December 15th. The last General Assembly increased the pension fund from $1,000,000 a year to $1,4400,000. The fund for the second year of the next biennium is about $1,000,000. The fund distributed during the fiscal year closing amounted to one million dollars.

The Sanford Express [June 16, 1927] [561]

VOUCHERS BEINS ISSUED TO VETS AND WIDOWS

Total Amount Paid to Veterans and Widows, $3,475--Veterans Get an Increase.

Lee county Confederate veterans and widows are now receiving pension vouchers for the last half of this year from Clerk of the Court Gunter Watson. Some of the vouchers were called for last week and others are being called for this week. They will probably be in the hands of those for whom they were issued before Christmas. The total amount for which the checks were issued is $3,475.

Confederate veterans get the benefit of the increased pension allowance voted by the last General Assembly in this semi-annual payment, the checks being based on a dollar a day from this time on. Ten Confederate veterans receive a total of $1,825, and 23 widows receive a total of $1,650, making a grand total of $3,475. Two Confederate veterans and three widows of veterans have died during the year in the county. The widows of veterans, who are in the ordinary class, receive $50 as a semi-annual payment. The allowance for this class of pensioners was not increased by the last General Assembly which advanced the amount received by the veterans from $100 each six months to a dollar a day.

The last legislature is said to have gone back to the year 1880 to qualify widows for pensions. Unti la few years ago it was required that only widows who had married veterans prior to 1880 might qualify as pensioners, but later thas was changed to include those marrying prior to 1898. The widows of veterans who dwied since the pension roll was last made up in July, will receive the pension checks due their husbands for a whole year. If the pensioner left no widow but died since September 10th, the next of kin may draw the current voucher.

The following Confederate veterans who are in class A draw $182.50 each: W. Marshall Avent, I. D. Boyd, Redin Bryan, George Cox, Thomas Groce, J. D. Hart, Jr., Arch A. Kelly, Joseph D. Kelly, J. J. Peele, and J. D. Wicker. Widows who are in class B. Mesdames Geo. W. Avent, Mary Ann Brooks, Malinda Cole, Margaret V. Cox, Sallie I. Cox, Temperance Dalrymple, Emeline Everette, Samantha Gilmore, Jackie B. Groce, Mary F. Gunter, Rebecca J. Hunter, Mary J. Jones, N. Kate Lasater, B. J. Luther, D. M. McNeill, Nancy A. McNeill, M. J. Maddox, E. F. Marks, Margaret Mashburn, Nancy Mashburn, Bettie Matthews, Margaret L. Phillips, C. C. Poe, Nancy A. Robertson, Annie M. Ross, Elizabeth Savage, Fannie Smith, Margaret A. Sutton, Barbara Thomas, Rosa Thonias, Samantha Thomas, M. A. Underwood and Sarah J. Underwood.

The Sanford Express [December 22, 1927] [563]

PENSIONS HERE FOR VETERANS AND WIDOWS

Two Thousand Five Hundred Dollars Will be Paid Before Christmas to Confederate Soldiers and Widows.

Clerk of Court Gunter Watson will play Santa Claus to Confederate veterans and widows of veterans. The popular clerk has in hand some $2,500 to be dispensed among Lee county pensioners in order that they may enjoy Christmas to the fullest.

Twenty years ago when Lee county was created from parts of Moore and Chatham there were 150 Confederate veterans in the new county. Now there are only six who survive. These six men receive from the state of North Carolina pensions of the first class or one dolar per day, making a total for the year of $365 for each pensioner. The six men who receive pensions are, Marshal Avent, Redin Bryan, George Cox, J. D. Hart, Joseph D. Kelly and J. J. Peele. The pensions are paid semi-annually, one-half in July and one-half in December. Three veterans, J. D. Wicker, I. D. Boyd, and Joseph D. Kelly, have died within the year.

There are twenty-nnie widows of Confederate soldiers in the county who receive pensions. None of these are in class A. All of the widows who are in class B., receive $100 each, $50 semi-annually. They are Mesdames G. W. Avent, Mary Ann Brooks, Malinda Cole, Margaret V. Cox, Sallie I. Cox, Emeline Everette, Samantha Gilmore, Jackie B. Groce, Mary F. Gunter, Rebecca J. Hunter, Mary J. Jones, Kate Lassater, B. J. Luther, Nancy A. McNeill, M. J. Maddox, Nancy Mashburn, Bettie Matthews, Margaret L. Phillips, Nancy A. Robertson, Annie M. Ross, Elizabeth Savage, Margaret A. Sutton, Barbara Thomas, Rosa Thomas, Samantha Thomas, M. A. Underwood, Sarah Underwood, Kate F. Brown.

The Sanford Express [December 20, 1928] [562]

PENSION CHECKS FOR VETERANS

Four Veterans and Twenty-Seven Widows to Receive Vouchers—One Veteran Died This Year

State pension vounchers for Confederate veterans and widows of veterans, to the total of $2,080.00, arrived last week at the office of Clerk of Court, Gunter Watson and are now being delivered.

Clerk Watson requests that those entitled to the pensions call for them as promptly as possible. Those unable to come in person should send their duly authorized agent.

Four veterans are on the pension roll and these each receive the sum of $182.50, which is at the rate of one dollar per day, including Sundays, for the half year. One veteran, J. D. Hart, Jr., died April 28th. He was the only Confederate veteran to die in the county this year. His voucher goes to his estate. Following are the names of the veterans who draw pensions under class A: W. Marshall Avent, Redin Bryan, George Cox, Joseph D. Kelly.

The following widows, class B, draw $50.00 semi-annually: Mrs. George W. Avent, Mary Ann Brooks, Malinda Cole, Margaret V. Cox, Sallie I. Cox, Emeline Everette, Samartha Gilmore, Jackie B. Groce, Mary F. Gunter, Rebecca J. Hunter, Mary J. Jones, N. Kate Lasater, B. J. Luther, Nancy A. McNeill, M. J. Maddox, Nancy Mashburn, Bettie Matthews, Margaret L. Phillips, Nancy A. Robertson, Annie M. Ross, Elizabeth Savage, Margaret A. Sutton, Barbara Thomas, Rosa Thomas, Samantha Thomas, M. A. Underwood, Sarah J. Underwood.

The Sanford Express [June 20, 1929] [564]

LEE CONFEDERATE VETS GIVEN PENSION CHECKS

Twenty-Seven Widows of Confederacy Receive Semi-Annual Pensions—Total of $1,897.50 Sent to Lee Survivors of Confederacy.

Thirty Confederate pension checks, twenty-seven of which were for widows of Confederate veterans, were received last week by W. Gunter Watson, clerk of court, from Baxter Durham, state auditor, for distribution. Three Confederate veterans and twenty-seven widows are shown on the December pension roster, their vouchers aggregating $1,897.50.

Each veteran received $182.50, while the widows, all of whom were in class B, received $50 checks.

The three Confederate veterans in Lee to receive pensions were:

W. Marshall Avent, Sanford.

Redir Bryant, Jonesboro.

Joseph D. Kelly, Lockville.

Widows of Confederate veterans receiving pensions are: Mrs. Geo. W. Avent, Jonesboro; Mrs. Mary Ann Brooks, Jonesboro; Rt.2 ; Mrs. Kate F. Brown, Sanford; Mrs. Malinda Cole, Sanford; Mrs. Margaret V. Cole, Jonesboro; Mrs. Jackie B. Groce; Sanford; Mrs. Mary F. Gunter, Sanford; Mrs. Rebecca J. Hunter, Sanford; Mrs. Mary J. Jones, Lemon Springs; Mrs. Kate Lasater, Jonesboro; Mrs. B. J. Luther, Sanford; Mrs. Nancy A. McNeill, Sanford; Mrs. M. J. Maddox, Corinth; Mrs. Nancy Masburn, Carbonton; Mrs. Bettie Matthews, Jonesboro; Mrs. Margaret L. Phillips, Sanford; Mrs. Nancy A. Robertson, Jonesboro; Mrs. Annie M. Ross, Sanford; Mrs. Elizabeth Savage, Sanford; Mrs. Margaret A. Sutton, Jonesboro; Mrs. Barbara Thomas, Broadway; Mrs. Rosa Thomas, Sanford; Mrs. Samantha Thomas, Sanford; Mrs. Burline Womble, Sanford; Mrs. N. A. Underwood, Sanford; Mrs. Mary E. Poole, Sanford.

The Sanford Express [December 25, 1930] [565]

VETERANS AND WIDOWS GET SEMI-ANNUAL PENSION SUM

State pensions amounting to $1,652.50 for civil war veterans and widows of veterans have been received in the county by 24 men and women have all been called for at the office of the clerk of superior court. The checks arrive semi-annually on December 12 and June 15.

The only veteran in this county, Reddin Bryan, received half of his annual pension of $365. Stokes Judd, Negro of the Deep River section, received $100 last month because he served as body guard to Captain Davis during the war.

Widows of class A, five in all received checks for $100 each. They are Mrs. Mary Gunter, Mrs. Mary J. Maddox, Mrs. Nancy Mashburn, Mrs. Mary E. Poole, and Mrs. Burline Womble.

Class B widows number 17 and receive $100 a year which made their checks last month amount to $50 each. Those receiving the money are Mrs. George W. Avent Mrs. Mary Ann Brooks, Mrs. Kate F. Brown, Mrs. Margaret V. Cox, Mrs. Jackie B. Groce, Mrs. Thomas L. Lasater, Mrs. George W. Luther, Mrs. Martha E. Maples, Mrs. Nancy A. McNeill, Mrs. Bettie Andrews, Mrs. Sallie J. Pittman, Mrs. Minnie M. Ross, Mrs. Margaret A. Sutton, Mrs. Barbara Thomas, Mrs. Samantha Thomas, and Mrs. Annie R. Wicker.

The name of Mrs. Emma C. Cheek, a member of this class who passed away last year, will be taken off the list this year. Her last check went to her heirs.

The Sanford Express [January 5, 1933] [566]

Confederate Conscription Papers

The collection includes official records of the successive chief enrolling officers of the 7th North Carolina congressional district (Anson, Chatham, Davidson, Montgomery, Moore, Randolph, and Stanly counties). Files include individual applications for exemptions, correspondence, general and special orders received from Raleigh, N.C., and Richmond, Va., reports and lists from each county, and papers relating to deserters, manpower for essential industry, senior reserves, and details for men on limited service. [567]

Kendrick H. Hare

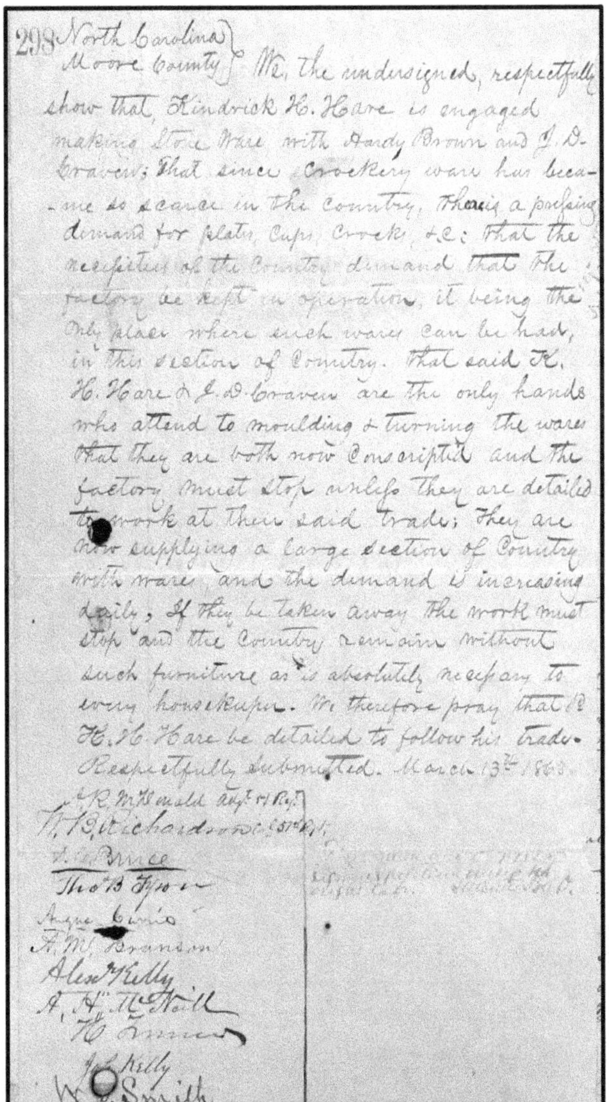

298 North Carolina }
Moore County } We, the undersigned, respectfully show that, Kendrick H. Hare is engaged making Stone Ware with Hardy Brown and J. D. Craven; That since Crockery ware has became so scarce in the country, there is a pressing demand for plates, cups, crocks, &c; That the necessities of the Country demand that the factory be kept in operation, it being the only place where such wares can be had, in this section of Country. That said K. H. Hare & J. D. Craven are the only hands who attend to moulding & turning the wares that they are both now Conscripted and the factory must stop unless they are detailed to work at their said trade; They are now supplying a large section of Country with ware and the demand is increasing daily, If they be taken away the work must stop and the Country remain without such furniture as is absolutely necessary to every housekeeper. We therefore pray that K. H. Hare be detailed to follow his trade. Respectfully Submitted. March 13th 1863.

A. R. McDonald Adjt. 1st Regt.
W. B. Richardson Col. 51st Regt.
J. W. Bruce
Thos B. Tyson
Angus Currie
A. M. Branson
Alexr Kelly
A. H. McNeill
H. Turner
J. L. Kelly
W. O. Smith

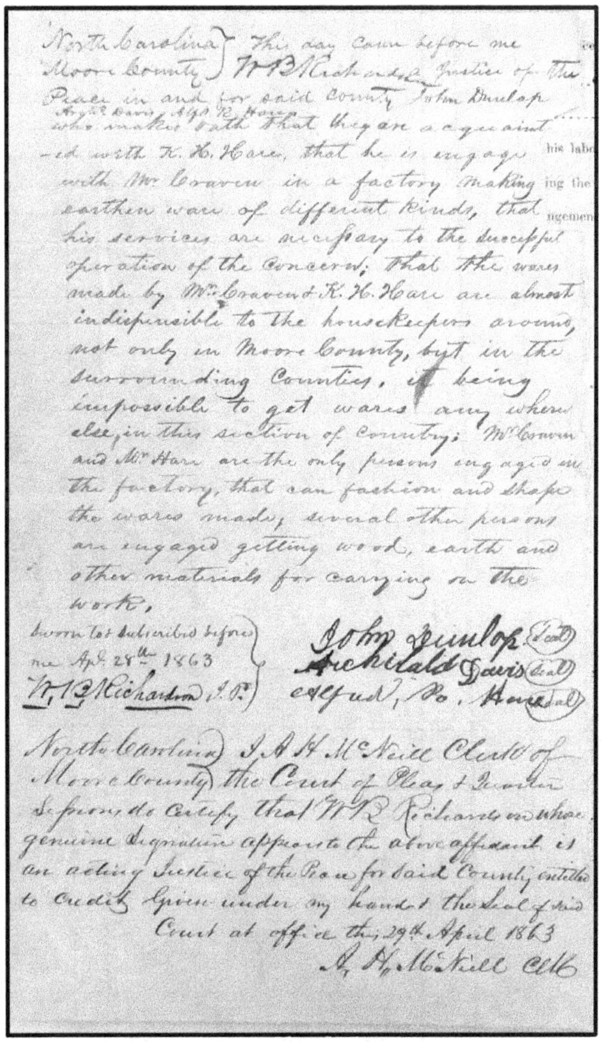

North Carolina }
Moore County } This day came before me W. B. Richardson a Justice of the Peace in and for said County John Dunlop Archd Davis, Alfd R. Hare who makes oath that they are acquainted with K. H. Hare, that he is engaged with Mr Craven in a factory making earthen ware of different kinds, that his services are necessary to the successful operation of the concern; That the wares made by Mr Craven & K. H. Hare are almost indispensible to the housekeepers around, not only in Moore County, but in the surrounding Counties, it being impossible to get wares any where else, in this section of Country; Mr Craven and Mr Hare are the only persons engaged in the factory, that can fashion and shape the wares made, several other persons are engaged getting wood, earth and other materials for carrying on the work,

Sworn to & subscribed before me Apl. 28th 1863
W. B. Richardson J. P.

John Dunlop (Seal)
Archibald Davis (Seal)
Alfred, R. Hare (Seal)

North Carolina } I A H McNeill Clerk of
Moore County } the Court of Pleas & Quarter Sessions do Certify that W. B. Richardson whose genuine signature appears to the above affidavit is an acting Justice of the Peace for said County entitled to credit. Given under my hand & the seal of said Court at office this 29th April 1863
A. H. McNeill Clk

North Carolina } This day Came before me
Moore County } Wm Brewer a Justice of
the Peace in Moore County, Henry Cagle, Martin
Sheffield, W. B. Owen, & John Brewer who being duly
sworn deposes and says that they are acqua-
-inted with K. H. Hare; that he is engaged working
in a factory making earthen wares of diffeunt
Kinds. that he is skilled in fashioning & shaping
the wares, that ~~without~~ his services, ~~are~~ neces-
-sary to the successful prosecution of the
establishment; that himself & Mr. Craven are
the only persons engaged in the establishment
skilled in shaping the diffeaent Kinds of
wares, and both working together cannot
supply the demand, as the whole country for
thirty miles around is dependant on this estab-
-lishment to furnish them their wares, in
place of Crockery & China ware formerly purchased
out of Stores; several persons are engaged in
getting wood and preparing the matrial
for making the wares but none can supply
the place of Mr. Hare in the factory, without
considerable practice and experience, and
the ~~public demand~~ for wares, is too great to
wait untill new hands can be learned the
trade.

Henry Cagle (Seal)
Marten his x mark Sheffield (Seal)
W. B. Owen (Seal)
John Brewer (Seal)

I certify that I am acquainted with the
above Affiants, that they are Citizens of respectab-
-ility, and worthy of faith and credit, and I believe
the facts set forth in their affidavit to be true
and I am disinterested.

Wm Brewer J. P. (Seal)

[10-1-63]

North Carolina } To the Honorable R R Heath one of
Moore County } Judges of the Superior Courts of said
Carolina

The petition of R. H. Hare of said County respectfully showeth unto your Honor that under the draft held in Moore County in Feby 1862 for men to go into the Confederate service for three years or the war. Your petitioner was Drafted said Draft was conducted by Genl B. Richardson Col 51st Regt [illegible] M. who was authorised so to do, after being drafted your petitioner Volunteered in the Confederate service for three years or the war under Capt N. McR. McNeill of 26th Regt N.C.T. Your petitioner after having volunteered tendered to said Capt [illegible] Archd Pierce as a substitute in his stead, said substitute was accepted by said Capt McNeill and duly sworn and Mustered into the service of the Confederate States; and your petitioner was duly discharged by said Capt McNeill on the 26th of [illegible] 1862. All this occured before the enactment of any Conscript Law by the Confederate Congress [illegible] Your petitioner substitute was aged about 33 [illegible] Under the last Call for men up to 40 years of age your petitioner was enrolled by the Enrolling officer of 7th Cong Dist N.C and ordered to the Camp of Instruction near Raleigh. Notwithstanding the above cause for exemption under the order [illegible] the general order to all Militia officers to arrest Conscripts your petitioner has been arrested by

Wm B. Owen 1st Lt Dist N.C 12 (Moore County) 51st Regt N.C. M. and held in durance illegally and against his will by the said Lieut Owens for the purpose of being sent to the Camp of instruction near Raleigh. Therefore your petitioner prays your Honor to grant to him the Writ of Habeas Corpus to be directed to the said Lt W.B. Owen or any other person having your petitioner in Custody requiring him to bring before your Honor the body of your petitioner with the Cause of his caption and detention that the same may be enquired into and relief may be afforded to your petitioner

J. C. Davis & A. H. McDonald
Attys for Petitioner
R. H. Hare

Sworn to & Subscribed before me this 1st day of October 1863

J. H. Brown Clk &
Comr of Affidavits

North Carolina

To Wm B. Owen 1st Lt 51st Regt N.C. M.

You are hereby Commanded to have the body of R H Hare in your Custody detained illegally as alleged before me R R Heath one of the Judges of Law & Equity in North Carolina together with the Cause of his Caption and detention at Ashboro N.C immediately after the receipt of this writ then and there to receive what shall be considered in his behalf.

Oct 1st 1863

R R Heath
Judge N C [illegible]

North Carolina } To the Hon R. R. Heath one of the Judges
Randolph County } of said State

In obedience to a writ of Habeas Corpus directed to me from your Honor, returnable this day I have here the body of R. H. Hare and allege as cause of his Caption and detention that I am 1st Lt Dist 12 – 51st Regt N.C. M. (Moore County) and in taking into my custody said R H Hare I acted in compliance with the orders of superior officers – I am acquainted with the facts stated in the petition and know that the said R. H. Hare volunteered in Capt McNeills Co for the war and started with the Company to Raleigh and then presented Archy Pierce as substitute in his stead and was discharged said substitute was between 31 and 40 years of age

W. B. Owen 1st Lt
October the 1st 1863

I certify that I have received Archy Pierce as a substitute for R. H. Hare and I hereby release said Hare as a volunteer in my Company March 20th [illegible]

N. McR. McNeill Capt

North Carolina } This day M. D. McNeill personally
Moore County } appeared before me Clerk of the Court of Pleas & Quarter Sessions for said County and made oath that he is acquainted with the hand writing of N McR McNeill Capt and that his name subscribed to the above certificate was his proper signature

Sworn to & Subscribed before at office the 30 day of May 1863

M. D. McNeill

J. H. McNeill Clk

North Carolina } In the matter of R. H. Hare brought before me at Ashboro N.C. on a writ of Habeas Corpus

It appearing to my satisfaction from the evidence and [illegible] brought before you that the said R. H. Hare ought to be discharged. It is therefore ordered that the said R. H. Hare be discharged from the Custody in which he now is with liberty to go where he will. It is further ordered that the Clerk of the Superior Court of Moore County file the papers in this proceeding among the records of his office and give copies to parties requiring the same

Oct 1st 1863

R R Heath. Judge &c [illegible]

North Carolina }
Moore County } I J. H. Caddell Clerk of the Superior Court do certify that the forgoing is a true Copy of the papers and discharge of R H Hare on a Writ of Habeas Corpus all of which remain [illegible] in my office

In testimony whereof I hereunto set my hand and affix the seal of said Court at Carthage Oct 1st 1863

J. H. Caddell C.S.C

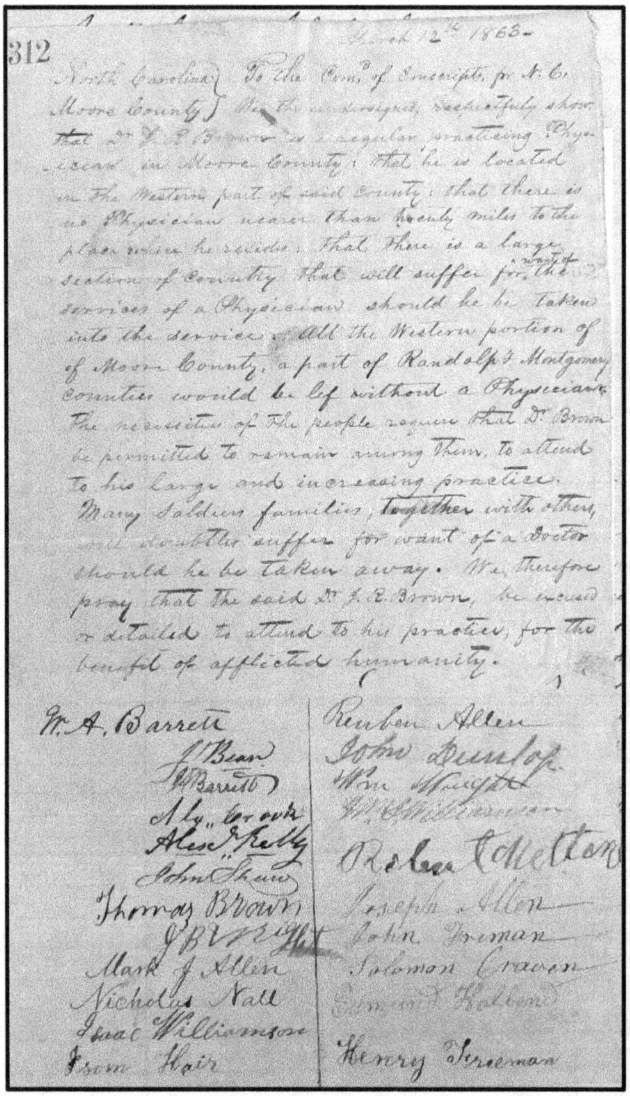

312

March 12th 1863-

North Carolina } To the Com.d of Conscripts for N. C.
Moore County } We the undersigned, respectfully show that Dr J. R. Brown is a regular practising Physician in Moore County: that he is located in the Western part of said County: that there is no Physician nearer than twenty miles to the place where he resides: That there is a large section of country that will suffer for want of the services of a Physician should he be taken into the service. All the Western portion of of Moore County, a part of Randolph & Montgomery counties would be left without a Physician. The necessities of the people require that Dr Brown be permitted to remain among them, to attend to his large and increasing practice. Many Soldiers families, together with others, will doubtless suffer for want of a Doctor should he be taken away. We therefore pray that the said Dr J. R. Brown, be excused or detailed to attend to his practice, for the benefit of afflicted humanity.

W. A. Barrett
J Bean
W Barrett
Aly. Crook
Alexd Kelly
John Shaw
Thomas Brown
J B [illegible]
Mark J Allen
Nicholas Nall
Isaac Williamson
Isom Hair

Reuben Allen
John Dunlop
Wm Wright
W. C. Williamson
Robert Collett
Joseph Allen
John Freeman
Solomon Craven
Edmond Holbert
Henry Freeman

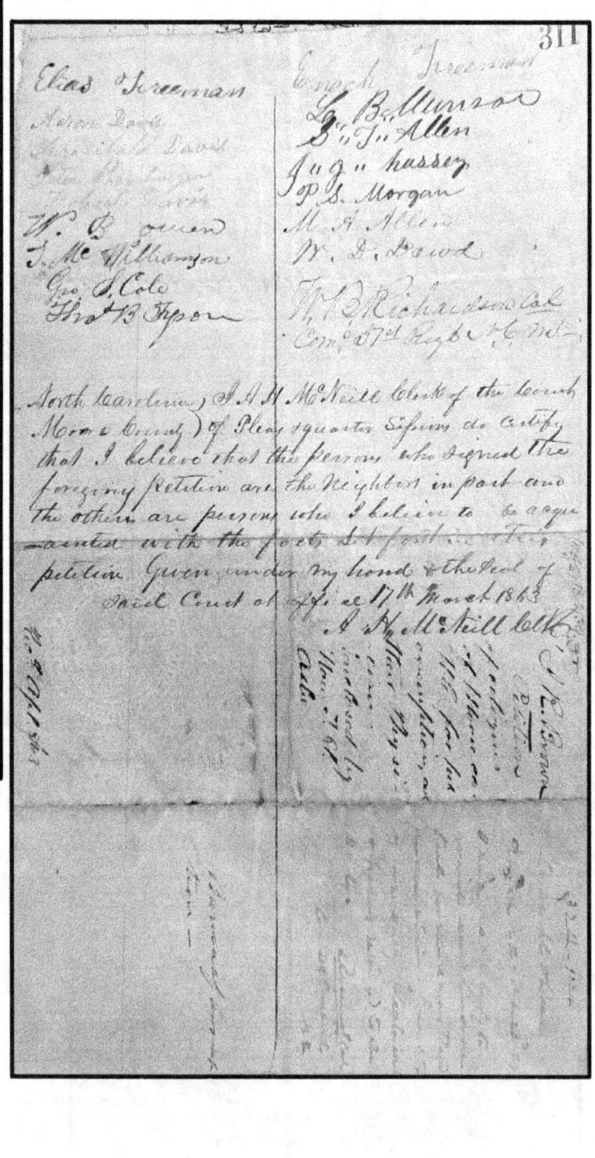

311

Elias Freeman
Aaron Davis
Archibald Davis
[illegible]
[illegible]
W. [illegible]
T. Mc Williamson
Geo. S. Cole
Thos B. Tyson

Enoch Freeman
L. B. Munroe
D. T. Allen
Jno. J. Hussey
P. S. Morgan
M. A. Allen
W. D. Dowd
W. B. Richardson Col.
Comd 57th Regt N. C. M.

North Carolina } I A H McNeill Clerk of the Court
Moore County } of Pleas & quarter Sessions do certify that I believe that the persons who signed the foregoing Petition are the Neighbors in part and the others are persons who I believe to be acquainted with the facts set forth in the petition. Given under my hand & the seal of said Court at office 17th March 1863

A H McNeill Clk

Daniel Fry

State of North Carolina) To the Honorable
Moore County } R M. Pearson Chief
Justice of the Supreme Court of North Carolina:
The Petition of Daniel Fry of said County showeth
unto your Honor - That your Petitioner is a public
Miller and was a public Miller at the time of the
last Enrollment in Moore County under the Call for
men up to 40 years of age. Your Petitioner was a
Miller in October of the year 1862 - The Enrollment
in Moore County did not take place until March
1863 - Notwithstanding your Petitioner was Enrolled
by the Enrolling Officer for this Dist (7th) after
he had been a Miller from October 1862 and still
Continued to be a public Miller until the time of
Enrollment. Your Petitioner took charge of the
Public Mill about the 27th of October 1863 and still
Continues to have Charge of said Public Mill -
All these facts were set forth before the Enrolling
Officer of this Congressional District (7th) But
said Enrolling Officer Enrolled your Petitioner
and ordered him to the Camp of Instruction near
Raleigh - Under this order and the general order
to all Militia Officers to arrest Conscripts your
Petitioner has been arrested by Murdoch Black
first Lieut in Dist No 3 Moore County N.C. M
As a Conscript to be sent to the Camp of Instruction
and held in duress illegally and against his
will by said Black 1st Lieut - Therefore your
Petitioner prays your Honor to grant unto your

Col who still holds it
May 26th 1863
At Richmond Hill
Sworn to & subscribed
before me
R M. Pearson Ch J.S.C

Daniel Fry

North Carolina
In the Matter of Daniel Fry -
The facts are - Fry is thirty three years of age - he
is skilled in the trade of a Miller and was on
the 27th of October 1862 & has been ever since actually employed in his trade habitually engaged
there as his regular vocation & has made the affidavit required by the act of Congress - he was not
Enrolled and ordered into service until 13th March
1863 - having been exempted in July 1862 from the
Conscription under the act of April 1862 on the ground
that he was then employed in teaching a public school
at which he continued until just before he commenced Keeping a public Mill
The facts of this case bring it within the decision
made by me in the matter of Mills a Tanner,
Ames a wagon maker and Nicholson a Miller.
The Exemption act applies to persons under thirty five
who are actually employed at their trade at the
time they are ordered into service - I am therefore
of opinion that Fry is entitled to exemption -

It is Considered by me that Daniel Fry be forthwith
discharged with leave to go where he will - It is
further Considered by me that the Cost allowed
by law to be taxed by the Clerk of the Superior
Court of Moore County according to the act of the
General Assembly be paid by Murdoch Black
as he did not produce the Order of Col Richardson
The Clerk will file the papers in this proceeding
among the papers in his office & give Copies to the
persons applying therefor
R M Pearson Ch J.S.C
May 26th 1863
At Richmond Hill

North Carolina)
Moore County } I J. R. Caddell Clerk of the
Superior Court do certify that the foregoing is a
true Copy of the papers and discharge of Daniel Fry
on a Writ of Habeas Corpus. all of which remain
entire in my Office
In testimony whereof I have unto set my
hand and affix the seal of said Court at
office in Carthage Nov. 30th 1863
J. R. Caddell C.S.C

William D. Warner

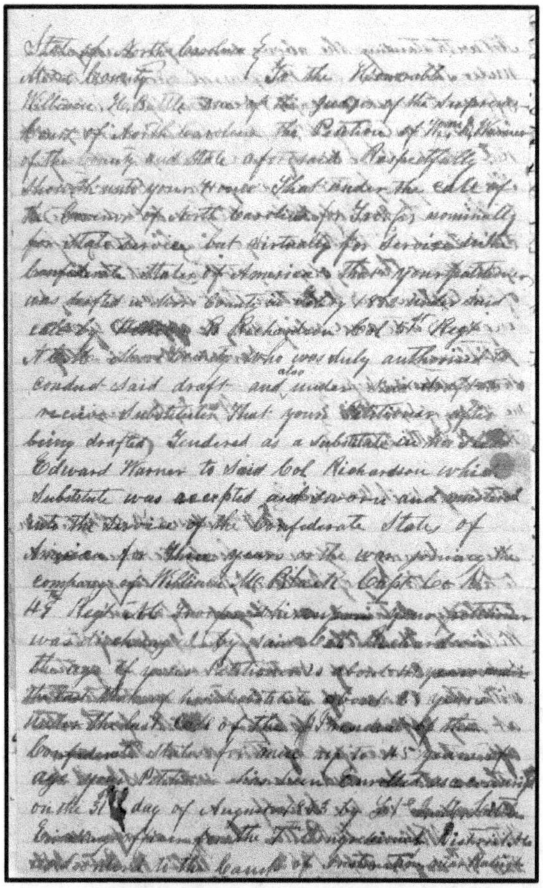

State of North Carolina [illegible]
Moore County } To the Honorable
William H. Battle one of the Judges of the Supreme
Court of North Carolina The Petition of Wm. D. Warner
of the County and State aforesaid Respectfully
Showeth unto your Honor That under the call of
the Governor of North Carolina for [illegible] nominally
for State service but virtually for service in the
Confederate States of America That your petitioner
was drafted in Moore County [illegible] said
call by [illegible] B Richardson Col 5th Regt
N C M [illegible] who was duly authorized to
conduct said draft and also under [illegible] to
receive substitutes That your Petitioner after
being drafted Tendered as a Substitute [illegible]
Edward Warner to said Col Richardson which
Substitute was accepted and sworn and mustered
into the Service of the Confederate States of
America for three years or the war [illegible] the
company of William M Black Capt Co [illegible]
49 Regt [illegible]
was discharged by said Col Richardson [illegible]
[illegible]
[illegible]
[illegible] of the President of the
Confederate States for men up to 45 years of
age your Petitioner has been Enrolled as a conscript
on the 31 day of August 1863 by [illegible]
[illegible]
[illegible] to the Camp of Instruction near Raleigh

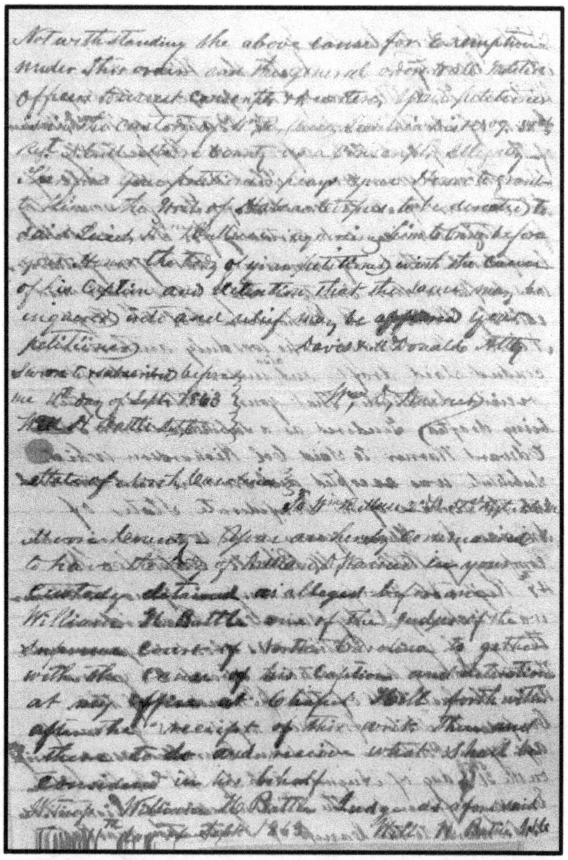

Notwithstanding the above cause for Exemption
under this order and the general orders [illegible]
Officers [illegible] conscripts [illegible]
[illegible]
[illegible]
[illegible] your petitioner prays your Honor to grant
to him the Writ of Habeas Corpus to be directed to
said [illegible] commanding him to bring before
your Honor the body of your petitioner with the cause
of his Caption and detention that the same may be
enquired into and relief may be afforded your
petitioner [illegible] McDonald Atty
Sworn & subscribed before
me 11th day of Sept 1863 Wm. D. Warner
Wm H Battle [illegible]
State of North Carolina
To [illegible]
Moore County [illegible] are hereby commanded
to have the body of William D Warner in your
Custody detained as alleged by [illegible]
William H Battle one of the Judges of the
Supreme Court of North Carolina together
with the cause of his Caption and detention
at my office at Chapel Hill forthwith
after the receipt of this writ Then and
there to do and receive what shall be
Considered in his behalf [illegible]
Witness William H Battle Judge as aforesaid
[illegible] Sept 1863 Wm H Battle [illegible]

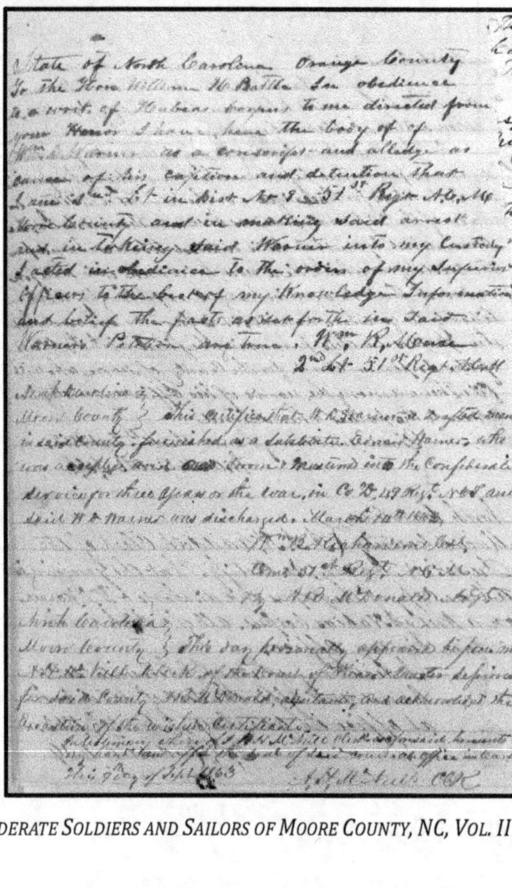

State of North Carolina Orange County
To the Hon William H Battle In obedience
to a writ of Habeas Corpus to me directed from
your Honor I [illegible] the body of
Wm D Warner as a conscript and allege as
cause of his caption and detention that
I am 2nd Lt in Dist No 8 51st Regt N C M
Moore County and in making said arrest
and in taking said Warner into my Custody
I acted in obedience to the orders of my Superior
Officers to the best of my Knowledge Information
and belief the facts as set forth in said
Warner's Petition are true. Wm R [illegible]
2nd Lt 51st Regt [illegible]

North Carolina }
Moore County } This certifies that W D Warner a drafted man
in said County furnished as a substitute Edward Warner who
was accepted and sworn & mustered into the Confederate
service for three years or the war, in Co D 49 Regt N C T and
said W D Warner was discharged March [illegible] 1862
Wm B Richardson Col
Comd 51st Regt N C M
[illegible] A H McDonald Atty
North Carolina }
Moore County } This day personally appeared before me
A H McNeill Clerk of the Court of Pleas & Quarter Sessions
for said County A H McDonald, [illegible] and acknowledged the
[illegible] of the within Certificate
In testimony whereof I A H McNeill Clerk aforesaid have set
my hand and affixed the seal of said court at office in Carthage
this 9 day of Sept 1863 A H McNeill CCK

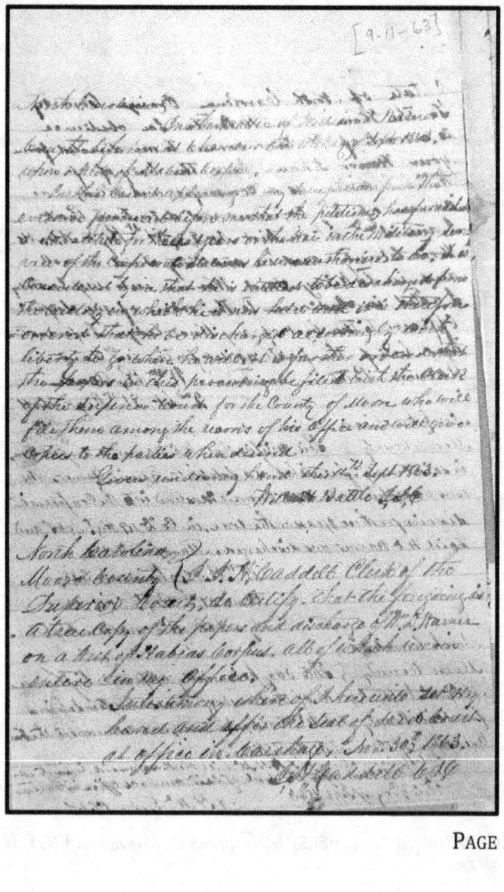

[9-11-63]

[illegible]
[illegible] William D Warner
[illegible] 11th day of Sept 1863
upon a writ of Habeas Corpus [illegible]
[illegible]
[illegible] the petitioner [illegible]
[illegible] for three years or the war in the Military service
of the Confederate States [illegible]
[illegible]
[illegible]
[illegible] discharged accordingly [illegible]
liberty to go where he will [illegible]
the papers in this proceeding be filed with the Clerk
of the Superior Court for the County of Moore who will
file them among the records of his office and will give
copies to the parties when desired
Given under my hand this 11th Sept 1863
Wm H Battle [illegible]

North Carolina }
Moore County } I A H Caddell Clerk of the
Superior Court, do certify that the foregoing is
a true copy of the papers and discharge of Wm D Warner
on a Writ of Habeas Corpus. all of which are now
on file in my office.
In testimony whereof I have set my
hand and affixed the seal of said Court
at office in Carthage, Jan 30 1863.
A H Caddell CSC

John Kenneth McKenzie

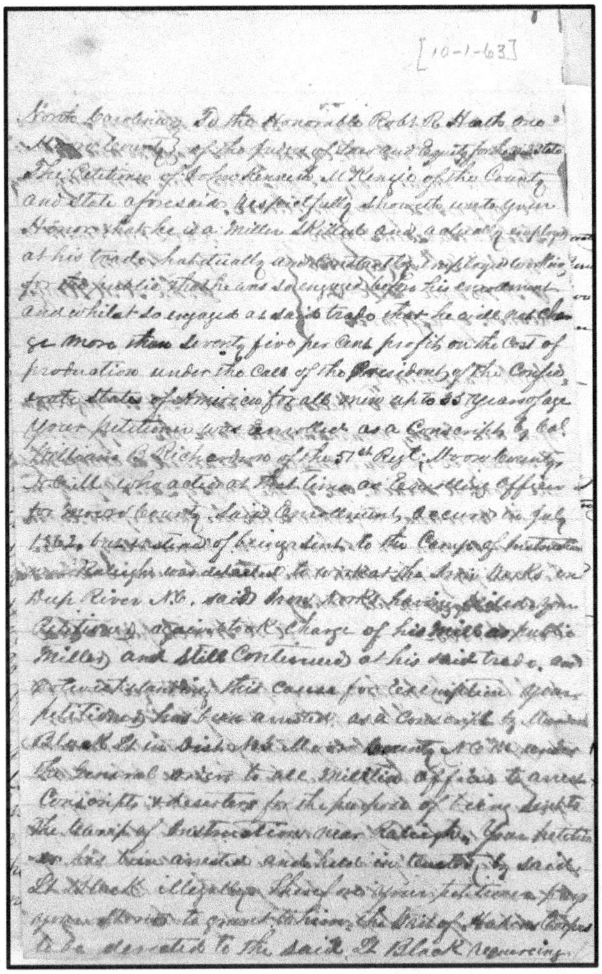

[10-1-63]

North Carolina } To the Honorable Robt. R. Heath one
Moore County } of the Judges of Law and Equity for said State
The Petition of John Kenneth McKenzie of the County
and State aforesaid, respectfully showeth unto your
Honor that he is a Miller skilled and actually employed
at his trade habitually and [illegible] employed working
for the public that he was so engaged before his enrolment
and whilst so engaged at said trade that he will not charge
more than seventy five per cent profit on the cost of
production under the Call of the President of the Confederate
States of America for all men up to 35 years of age.
Your petitioner was enrolled as a Conscript by Col.
William B. Richardson of the 51st Regt. Moore County
Militia who acted at that time as Enrolling Officer
for Moore County. Said enrollment occurred in July
1862, but instead of being sent to the Camp of Instruction
near Raleigh was detailed to work at the Iron Works on
Deep River N.C. said Iron Works having [illegible] your
petitioner's [illegible] took charge of his mill as public
Miller and still continued at his said trade, and
notwithstanding this cause for exemption your
petitioner has been arrested as a Conscript by Murdock
Black Lt. in Dist. No. 8 Moore County N.C.M. under
the General orders to all Militia officers to arrest
Conscripts & deserters for the purpose of being sent to
the Camp of Instruction near Raleigh. Your petitioner
has been arrested and held in custody by said
Lt. Black illegally. Therefore your petitioner prays
your Honor to grant to him the Writ of Habeas Corpus
to be directed to the said Lt. Black requiring

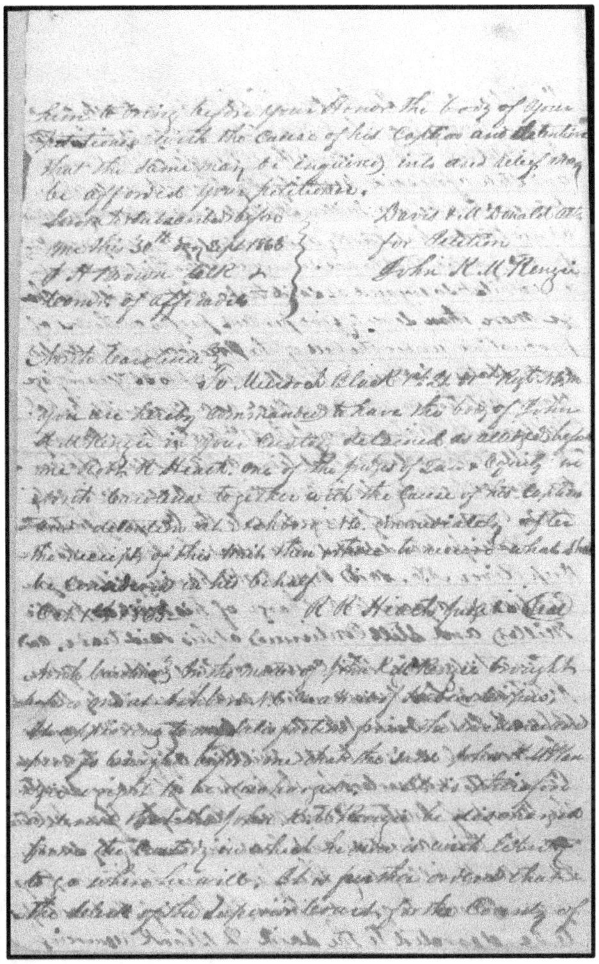

him to bring before your Honor the body of your
petitioner with the cause of his caption and detention
that the same may be inquired into and relief may
be afforded your petitioner.

Sworn & subscribed before } Davis & McDonald Attys
me this 30th day Sept 1863 } for Petition
J. H. Brown Clk } John K. McKenzie
[illegible] of affidavit

North Carolina }
To Murdock Black 1st Lt. [illegible] Regt. N.C.M.
You are hereby commanded to have the body of John
K. McKenzie in your custody detained as alleged before
me Robt. R. Heath one of the Judges of Law & Equity in
North Carolina together with the cause of his caption
and detention at [illegible] N.C. immediately after
the receipt of this writ then & there to receive what shall
be considered in his behalf [illegible]
Oct 1st 1863 R. R. Heath Judge & Seal

North Carolina } In the matter of John K. McKenzie brought
before me at [illegible] on a writ of Habeas Corpus:
[illegible]
[illegible] that the said John K. McKenzie
[illegible] that the said John K. McKenzie be discharged
from the custody in which he now is with liberty
to go where he will. It is further ordered that
the Clerk of the Superior Court for the County of
[illegible]

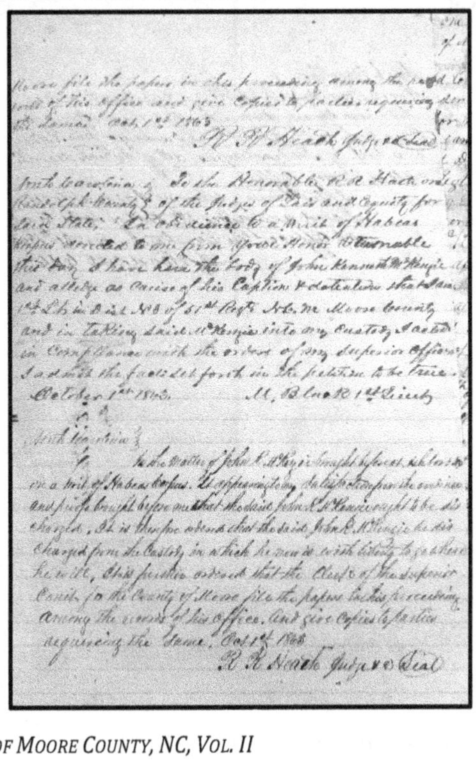

Moore file the papers in this proceeding among the [illegible]
of his office and give copies to parties requiring
the same. Oct. 1st 1863
R. R. Heath Judge & Seal

North Carolina } To the Honorable R. R. Heath one
Randolph County } of the Judges of Law and Equity for
said State. In obedience to a Writ of Habeas
Corpus directed to me from your Honor returnable
this day, I have here the body of John Kenneth McKenzie
and allege as cause of his caption & detention that I am
1st Lt. in Dist. No. 8 of 51st Regt. N.C.M. Moore County
and in taking said McKenzie into my custody I acted
in compliance with the orders of my superior officers.
I admit the facts set forth in the petition to be true.
October 1st 1863. M. Black 1st Lieut.

North Carolina }
In the Matter of John K. McKenzie brought before me at [illegible]
on a writ of Habeas Corpus. It appearing to my satisfaction upon the evidence
and proofs brought before me that the said John K. McKenzie ought to be discharged.
It is therefore ordered that the said John K. McKenzie be discharged
from the custody in which he now is with liberty to go where
he will. It is further ordered that the Clerk of the Superior
Court for the County of Moore file the papers in this proceeding
among the records of his office and give copies to parties
requiring the same. Oct 1st 1863
R. R. Heath Judge & Seal

P.A. Gillis

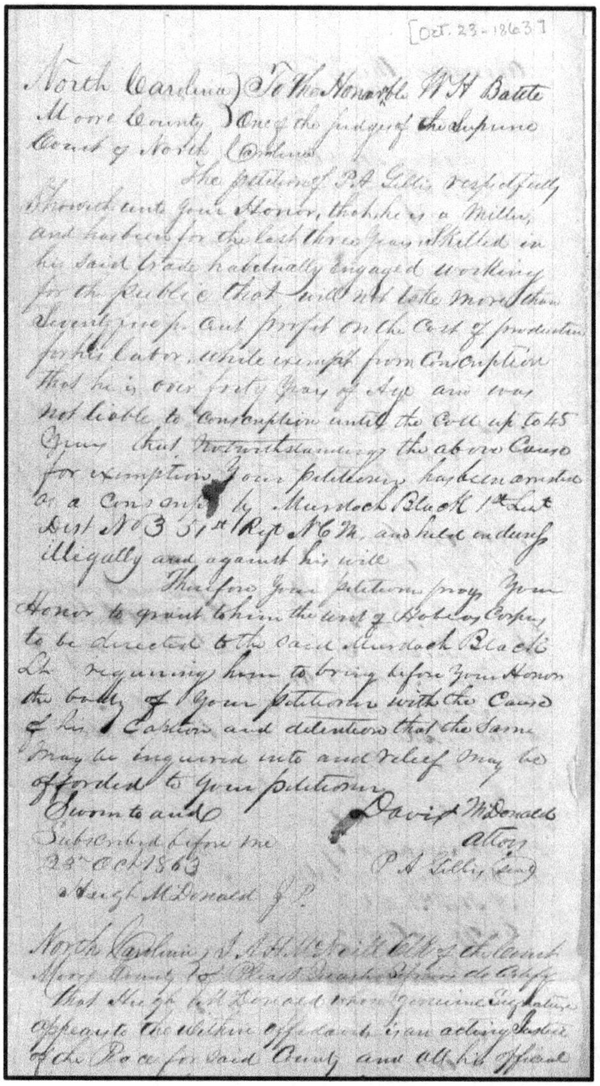

[Oct. 23 - 1863]

North Carolina) To the Honorable W H Battle
Moore County) One of the Judges of the Supreme
Court of North Carolina

The petition of P.A. Gillis respectfully showeth unto your Honor, that he is a Miller, and has been for the last three years skilled in his said trade habitually engaged working for the public that will not take more than seventy five per cent profit on the cost of production for his labor, which exempts from Conscription that he is over forty years of age and was not liable to Conscription until the Call up to 45 years that notwithstanding the above Causes for exemption your petitioner has been arrested as a Conscript by Murdoch Black 1st Lieut Dist No 3 51st Regt N C M. and held in duress illegally and against his will

Therefore your petitioner prays your Honor to grant to him the writ of Habeas Corpus to be directed to the said Murdoch Black Lt requiring him to bring before your Honor the body of your petitioner with the Cause of his Caption and detention that the same may be inquired into and relief may be afforded to your petitioner

Sworn to and
Subscribed before me
23rd Oct 1863
Hugh McDonald J P.

David McDonald attorney
P. A. Gillis (Seal)

North Carolina) I A H McNeill Clk of the Court
Moore County) of Pleas & Quarter Sessions do certify
that Hugh McDonald whose genuine signature appears to the within affidavit is an acting Justice of the Peace for said County and all his official

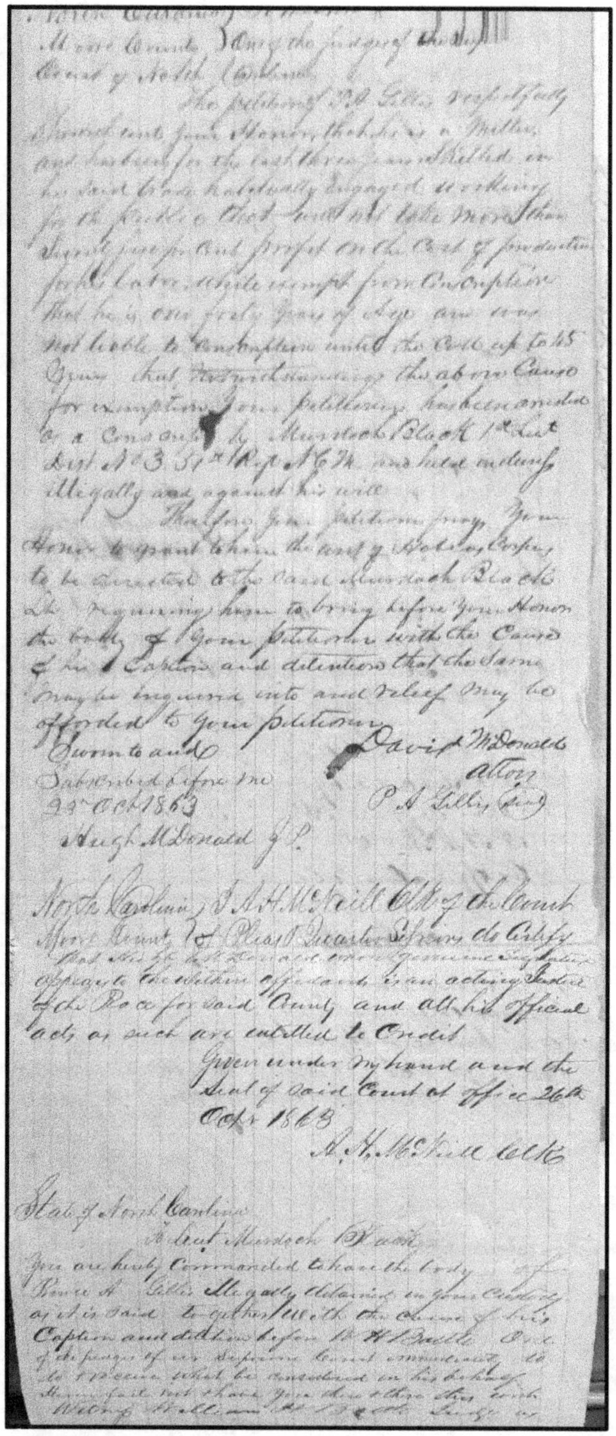

North Carolina) To the Honorable W H Battle
Moore County) One of the Judges of the Supreme
Court of North Carolina

The petition of P.A. Gillis respectfully showeth unto your Honor, that he is a Miller, and has been for the last three years skilled in his said trade habitually engaged working for the public that will not take more than seventy five per cent profit on the cost of production for his labor, which exempts from Conscription that he is over forty years of age and was not liable to Conscription until the Call up to 45 years that notwithstanding the above Causes for exemption your petitioner has been arrested as a Conscript by Murdoch Black 1st Lieut Dist No 3 51st Regt N C M. and held in duress illegally and against his will

Therefore your petitioner prays your Honor to grant to him the writ of Habeas Corpus to be directed to the said Murdoch Black Lt requiring him to bring before your Honor the body of your petitioner with the Cause of his Caption and detention that the same may be inquired into and relief may be afforded to your petitioner

Sworn to and
Subscribed before me
23rd Oct 1863
Hugh McDonald J P.

David McDonald attorney
P. A. Gillis (Seal)

North Carolina) I A H McNeill Clk of the Court
Moore County) of Pleas & Quarter Sessions do certify
that Hugh McDonald whose genuine signature appears to the within affidavit is an acting Justice of the Peace for said County and all his official
acts as such are entitled to Credit.

Given under my hand and the Seal of said Court at office 26th Oct 1863

A. H. McNeill Clk

State of North Carolina
To Lieut Murdoch Black

You are hereby Commanded to have the body of Pierce A Gillis illegally detained in your Custody as it is said together with the Cause of his Caption and detention before W H Battle one of the Judges of our Supreme Court immediately to do & receive what be considered in his behalf. Herein fail not & have you then & there this writ. Witness William H Battle Judge of

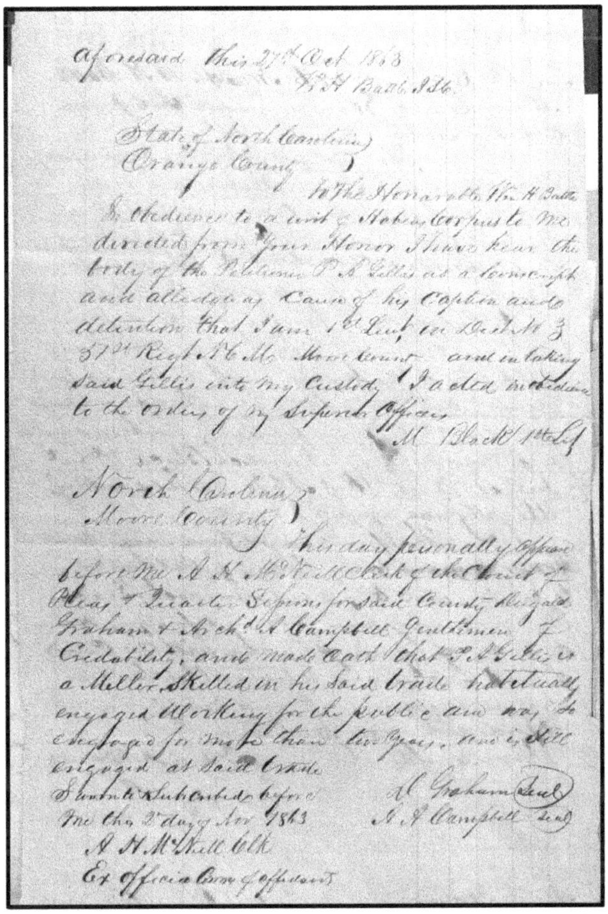

aforesaid this 27th Oct 1863
W H Battle JSC

State of North Carolina)
Orange County)

To the Honorable Wm H Battle
In Obedience to a writ of Habeas Corpus to me directed from your Honor I have here the body of the Petitioner P. A. Gillis as a Conscript and allege as Cause of his Caption and detention that I am 1st Lieut in Co. N [illegible] 3 57th Regt N C M Moore County and in taking said Gillis into my Custody I acted in obedience to the orders of my Superior Officer
M Black 1st Lt

North Carolina)
Moore County)

This day personally appeared before me A. H. McNeill Clerk of the Court of Pleas & Quarter Sessions for said County [illegible] Graham & Archd A Campbell Gentlemen of Credibility, and made oath that P. A. Gillis is a Miller Skilled in his said trade [illegible] engaged working for the public and was so engaged for more than ten years, and is still engaged at said trade
Sworn to & Subscribed before me the 3d day of Nov 1863
A. H. McNeill Clk
Ex Officio Com of affidavits

[illegible] Graham (Seal)
A. A. Campbell (Seal)

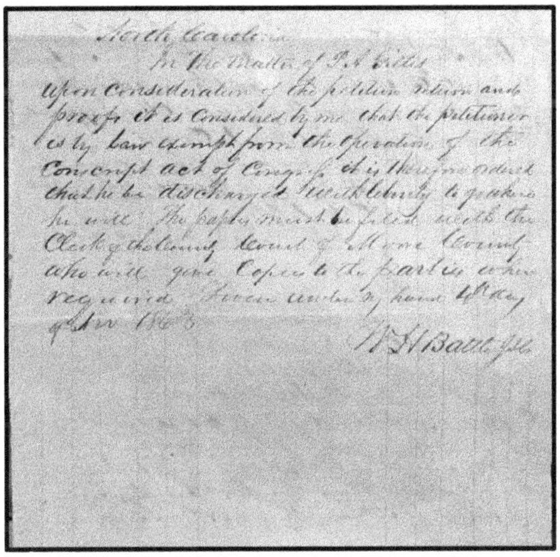

North Carolina
In the Matter of P. A. Gillis
Upon Consideration of the petition return and proofs it is Considered by me that the petitioner is by law exempt from the operation of the Conscript act of Congress it is therefore ordered that he be discharged with liberty to go where [illegible] he will. The papers must be filed with the Clerk of the County Court of Moore County who will give Copies to the parties when required. Given under my hand 4th day of Nov 1863
W H Battle JSC

Anderson Jones, Neil McIntosh, J.H. Harrington, Malcom Blue and John McKinnis

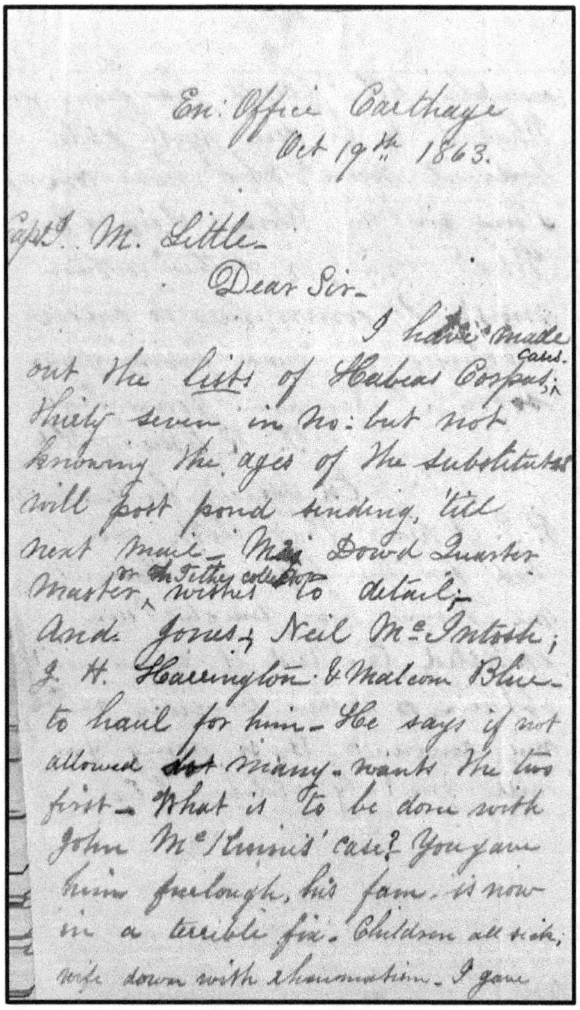

En: Office Carthage
Oct 19th 1863.

Capt J. M. Little

Dear Sir

I have made out the lists of Habeas Corpus cases; thirty seven in No: but not knowing the ages of the substitutes will post pond sending, till next mail— Maj Dowd Quarter master or Tithe collector wishes to detail; And. Jones; Neil McIntosh; J. H. Harrington & Malcom Blue— to haul for him— He says if not allowed ~~so~~ many— wants the two first— What is to be done with John McKinnis' case? You gave him furlough, his fam. is now in a terrible fix— Children all sick; wife down with rheumatism— I gave

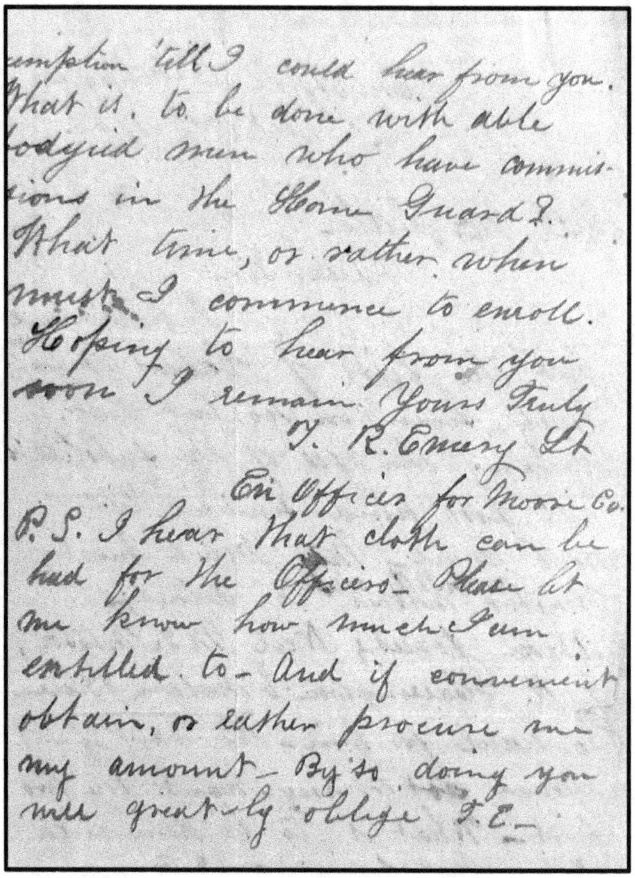

emption till I could hear from you. What is to be done with able bodyied men who have commissions in the Home Guard? What time, or rather when must I commence to enroll. Hoping to hear from you ~~soon~~ I remain Yours Truly

T. R. Emery Lt
En Officer for Moore Co.

P. S. I hear that cloth can be had for the Officers— Please let me know how much I am entitled to— And if convenient obtain, or rather procure me my amount— By so doing you will greatly oblige T. E.—

Lemuel W. Muse

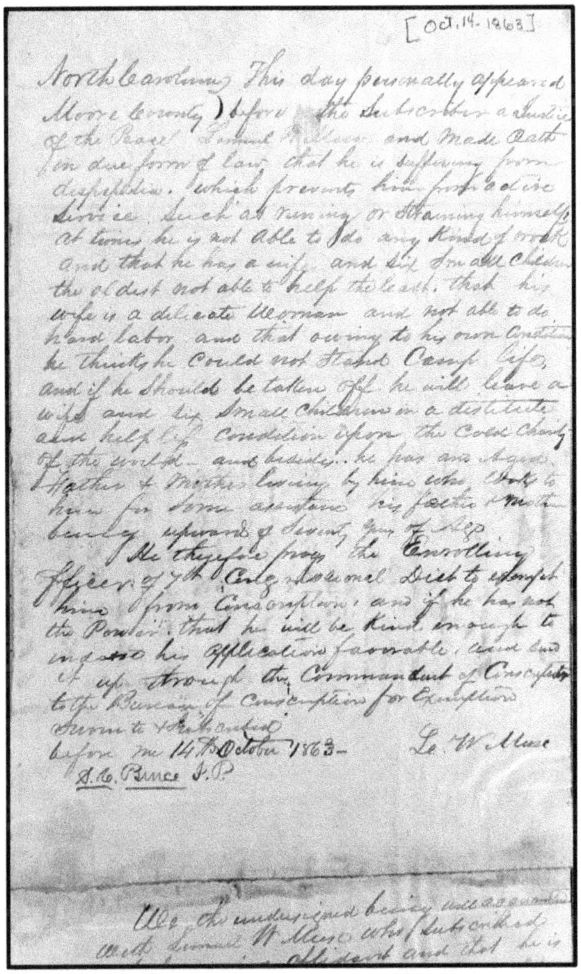

[Oct. 14. 1863]

North Carolina } This day personally appeared
Moore County } before the Subscriber a Justice
of the Peace Lemuel W. Muse and Made Oath
in due form of law that he is suffering from
dispepsia which prevents him from active
service such as running or straining himself
at times he is not able to do any kind of work
and that he has a wife and six small children
the oldest not able to help the least. that his
wife is a delicate woman and not able to do
hard labor and that owing to his own condition
he thinks he could not stand Camp life,
and if he should be taken off he will leave a
wife and six small children in a destitute
and helpless condition upon the cold charity
of the world and besides he has an aged
Father & Mother living by him who look to
him for some assistance his father & mother
being upwards of seventy years of age
He therefore prays the Enrolling
officer of 7th Congressional Dist to exempt
him from Conscription and if he has not
the Power that he will be kind enough to
endorse his application favorable, and send
it up through the Commandant of Conscripts
to the Bureau of Conscription for Exemption
Sworn to & subscribed
before me 14th October 1863 — L. W. Muse
S. C. Bruce J.P.

We the undersigned being well acquainted
with Lemuel W Muse who subscribed
[illegible] affidavit and that he is

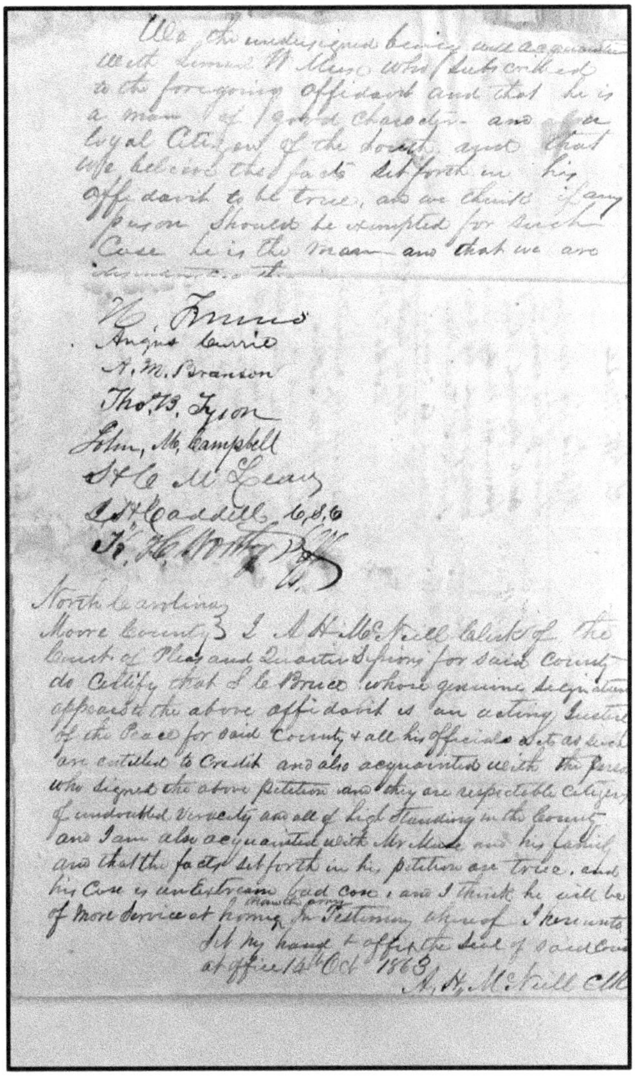

We the undersigned being well acquainted
with Lemuel W Muse who subscribed
to the foregoing affidavit and that he is
a man of good character and a
loyal citizen of the South and that
we believe the facts set forth in his
affidavit to be true, and we think if any
person should be exempted for such
case he is the man and that we are
[illegible]

[illegible]
Angus Currie
A. M. Branson
Thos. B. Tyson
John, M, Campbell
S & C McLeary [illegible]
L. H. Caddell C.S.C
[illegible]

North Carolina }
Moore County } I A H McNeill Clerk of the
Court of Pleas and Quarter Sessions for said County
do Certify that S C Bruce whose genuine signature
appears to the above affidavit is an acting Justice
of the Peace for said County & all his officials acts as such
are entitled to Credit and also acquainted with the persons
who signed the above petition and they are respectable citizens
of undoubted veracity and all of high standing in the County
and I am also acquainted with Mr Muse and his family
and that the facts set forth in his petition are true, and
his case is an extreme bad case, and I think he will be
of more service at home than in the army. In Testimony whereof I hereunto
set my hand & affix the seal of said Court
at office 14th Oct 1863
A. H. McNeill Clk

William Underwood

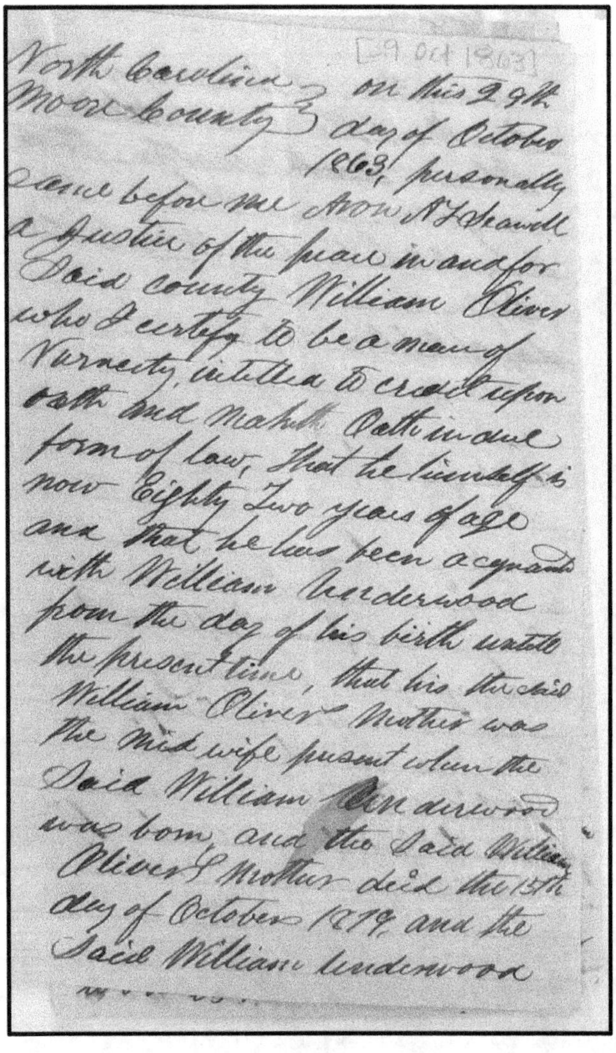

[29 Oct 1863]

North Carolina } on this 29th
Moore County } day of October
1863, personally
came before me Aron A. F. Seawell
a Justice of the peace in and for
Said county William Oliver
who I certify to be a man of
Varacity, intitled to credit upon
oath and makith Oath in due
form of law, that he himself is
now Eighty Two years of age
and that he has been acquainted
with William Underwood
from the day of his birth untill
the present time, that his the said
William Oliver Mother was
the Mid wife present when the
Said William Underwood
was born, and the Said William
Olivers Mother died the 15th
day of October 1819, and the
Said William Underwood
was ...

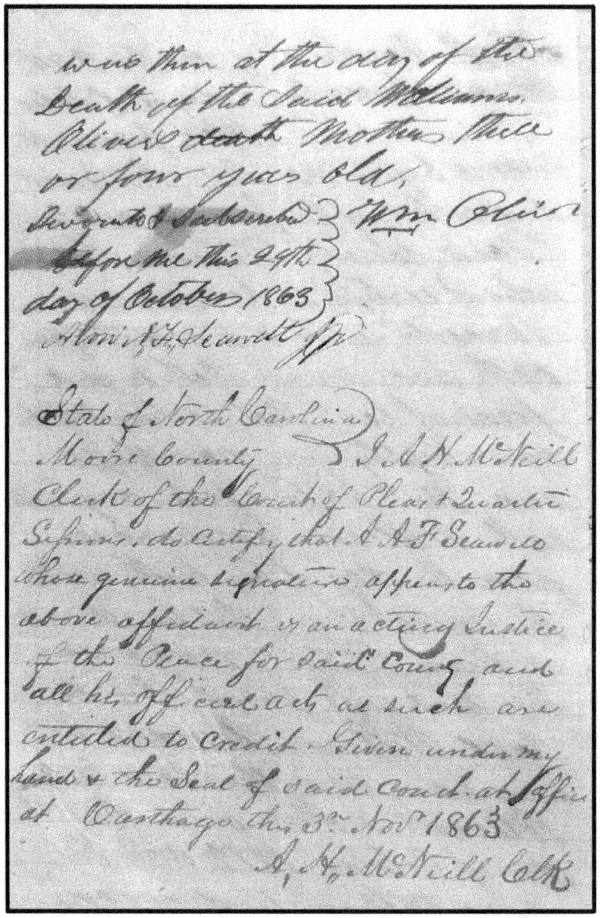

was then at the day of the
Death of the Said William
Olivers ~~death~~ Mother three
or four years old,
Sworn to & Subscribed } Wm Oliver
before me this 29th }
day of October 1863 }
Aron A. F. Seawell J.P.

State of North Carolina }
Moore County } I A H McNeill
Clerk of the Court of Pleas & Quarter
Sessions, do certify that A A F Seawell
whose genuine signature appears to the
above affidavit is an acting Justice
of the Peace for said County and
all his official acts as such are
entitled to credit. Given under my
hand & the Seal of said Court at office
at Carthage this 3rd Nov 1863
A. H. McNeill Clk

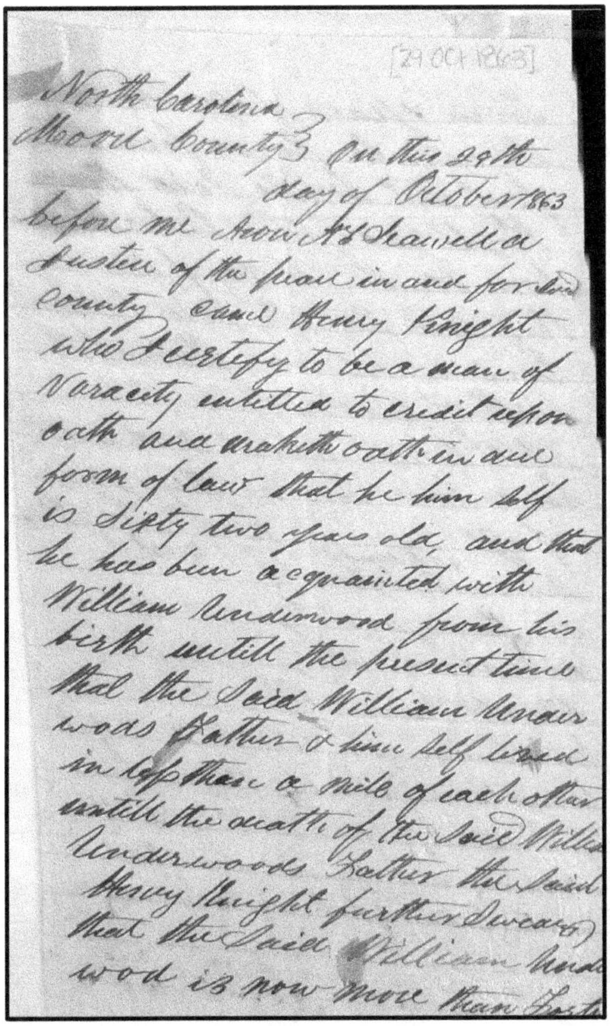

[29 Oct 1863]

North Carolina
Moore County } On this 29th
day of October 1863
before me Aron A. F. Seawell a
Justice of the peace in and for said
County came Henry Knight
who I certify to be a man of
Varacity entitled to credit upon
oath and maketh oath in due
form of law that he him self
is Sixty two years old, and that
he has been acquainted with
William Underwood from his
birth untill the present time
that the Said William Under
woods Father & him self lived
in less than a mile of each other
untill the death of the Said William
Underwoods Father the Said
Henry Knight further Swears
that the Said William Under
wod is now more than Forty

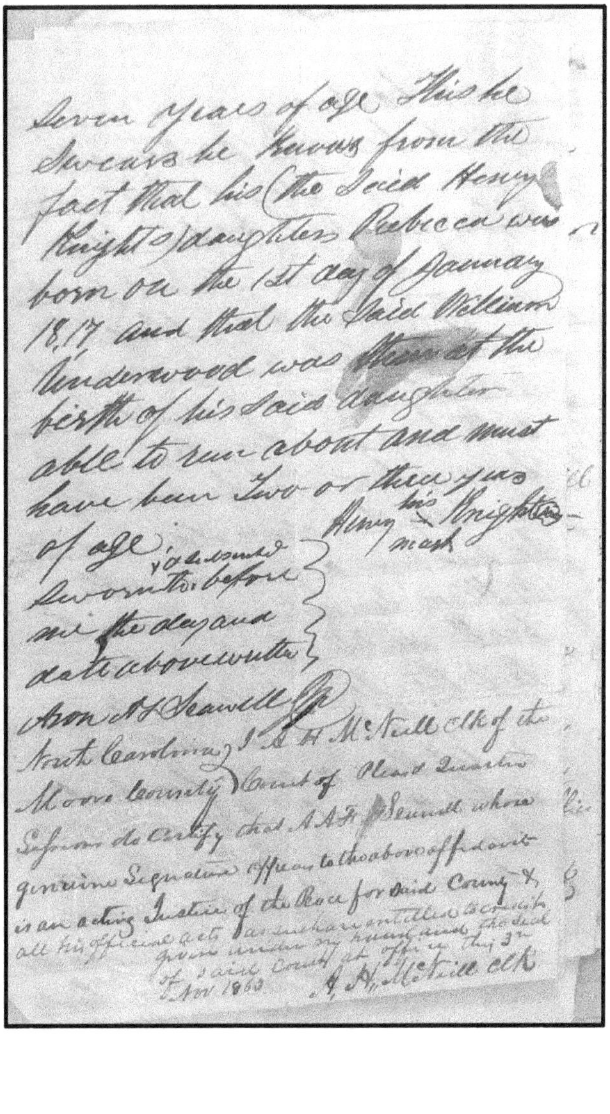

Seven years of age This he
Swears he knows from the
fact that his (the Said Henry
Knights) daughter Rebecca was
born on the 1st day of January
1817 and that the Said William
Underwood was then at the
birth of his Said daughter
able to run about and must
have been two or three years
of age

Henry his X mark Knight

Subscribed & Sworn to before
me the day and
date above written
Aron A. F. Seawell JP

North Carolina } I A H McNeill Clk of the
Moore County } Court of Pleas & Quarter
Sessions do Certify that A A F Seawell whose
genuine Signature appears to the above affidavit
is an acting Justice of the Peace for said County &
all his official acts as such are entitled to credit
given under my hand and the seal
of said Court at office this 3rd
Nov 1863
A. H. McNeill Clk

James Beal

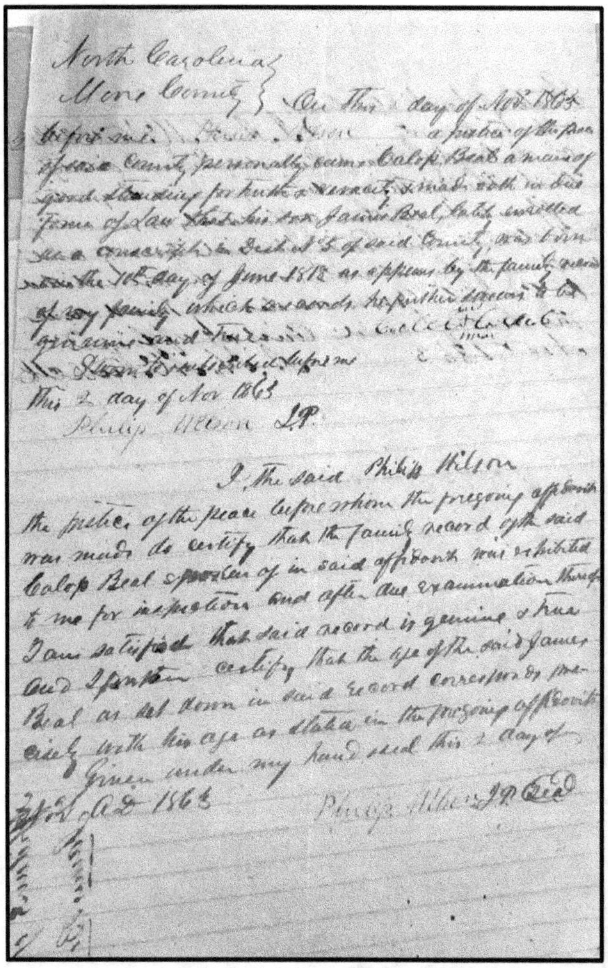

North Carolina
Moore County } On this day of Nov 1863 before me [illegible] a Justice of the Peace of said County personally came Caleb Beal a man of good standing for truth & veracity & made oath in due form of Law that his son James Beal lately enrolled as a conscript in Dist. [illegible] of said County was born on the 10th day of June 1848 as appears by the family record of my family which records he further swears to be genuine and true [illegible] Caleb (his mark) Beal
Sworn to and subscribed before me this 2 day of Nov 1863
Philip Wilson J.P.

I the said Philip Wilson the Justice of the peace before whom the foregoing affidavit was made do certify that the family record of the said Caleb Beal spoken of in said affidavit was exhibited to me for inspection and after due examination thereof I am satisfied that said record is genuine & true and I further certify that the age of the said James Beal as set down in said record corresponds precisely with his age as stated in the foregoing affidavit. Given under my hand seal this 2 day of Nov AD 1863
Philip Wilson J.P. (Seal)

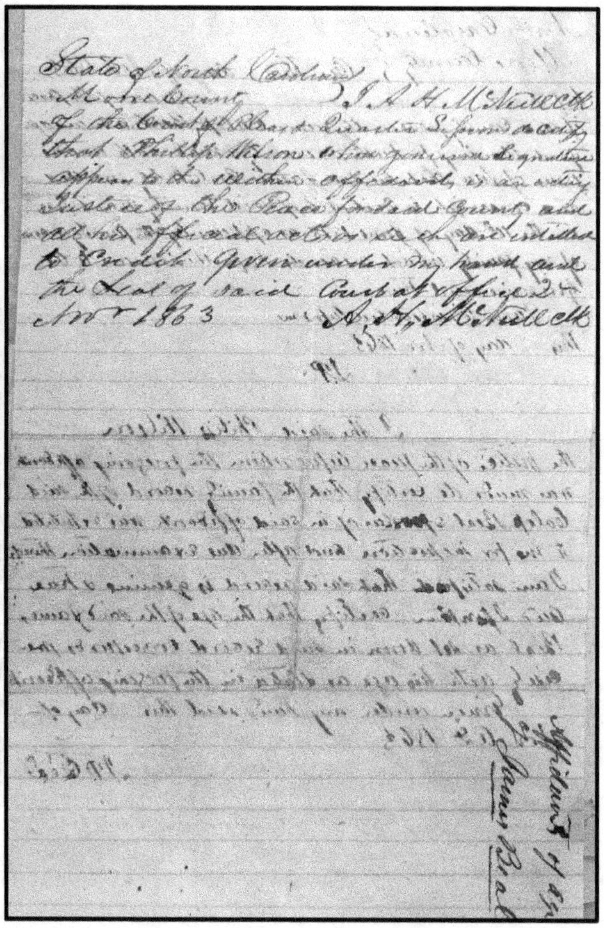

State of North Carolina
Moore County } I A H McNeill Clk of the Court of Pleas & Quarter Sessions do certify that Philip Wilson whose genuine signature appears to the within affidavit is an acting Justice of the Peace for said County and all his official acts are entitled to credit. Given under my hand and the Seal of said Court at office 2nd Nov 1863
A. H. McNeill Clk

Affidavit of James Beal

Neill McIntosh

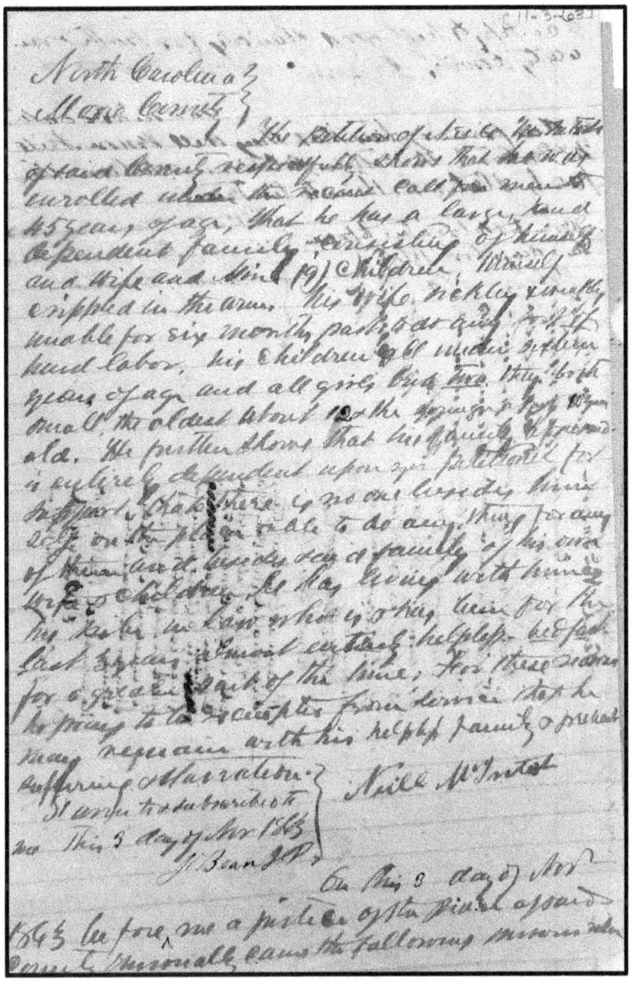

North Carolina }
Moore County }

The petition of Neill McIntosh of said County respectfully shows that he is enrolled under the recent call for men to 45 years of age, that he has a large and dependent family consisting of himself and a wife and nine (9) children. Himself crippled in the arm. His wife sickly & wholly unable for six months past to do any kind of hard labor, his children [illegible] years of age and all girls but two. They both small, the oldest about 12 & the youngest [illegible] years old. He further shows that his family is entirely dependent upon your petitioner for support. That there is no one besides him self on the place able to do any thing for any of them and besides [illegible] family of his own wife & children he has living with him [illegible] who is [illegible] for the last [illegible] years almost entirely helpless bedfast for a greater part of the time. For these reasons he prays to be exempted from service that he may remain with his helpless family & prevent suffering & starvation.

Sworn to and subscribed this 3 day of Nov 1863
J. Bean J.P.

Neill McIntosh

On this 3 day of Nov 1863 before me a justice of the Peace of said County personally came the following [illegible]

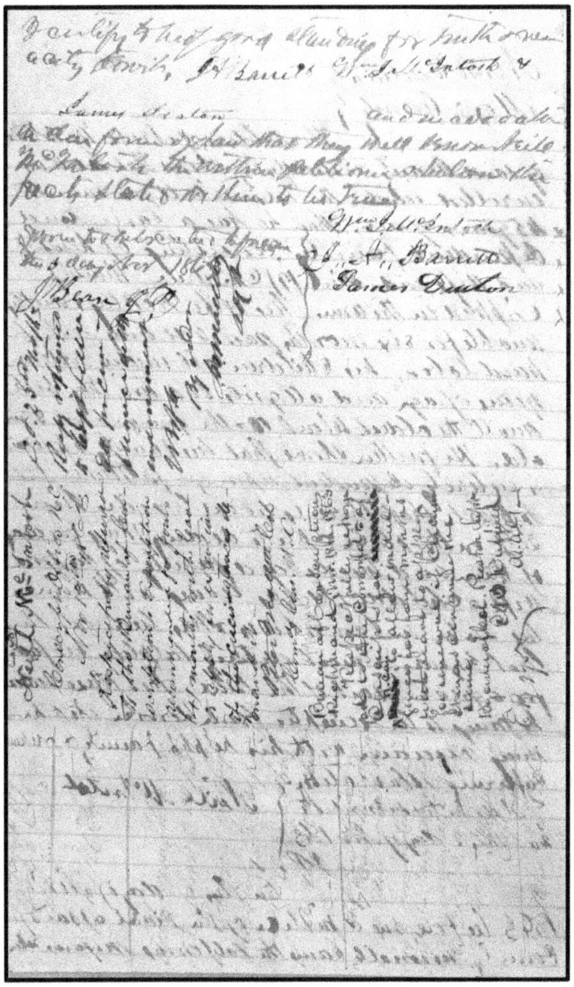

I certify that [illegible] good standing for truth & veracity [illegible] J. Bean [illegible] McIntosh

James Deaton [illegible]

[illegible]

Wm. [illegible] McIntosh
A. Barrett
James Deaton

J. Bean J.P.

Requests as of January 1864

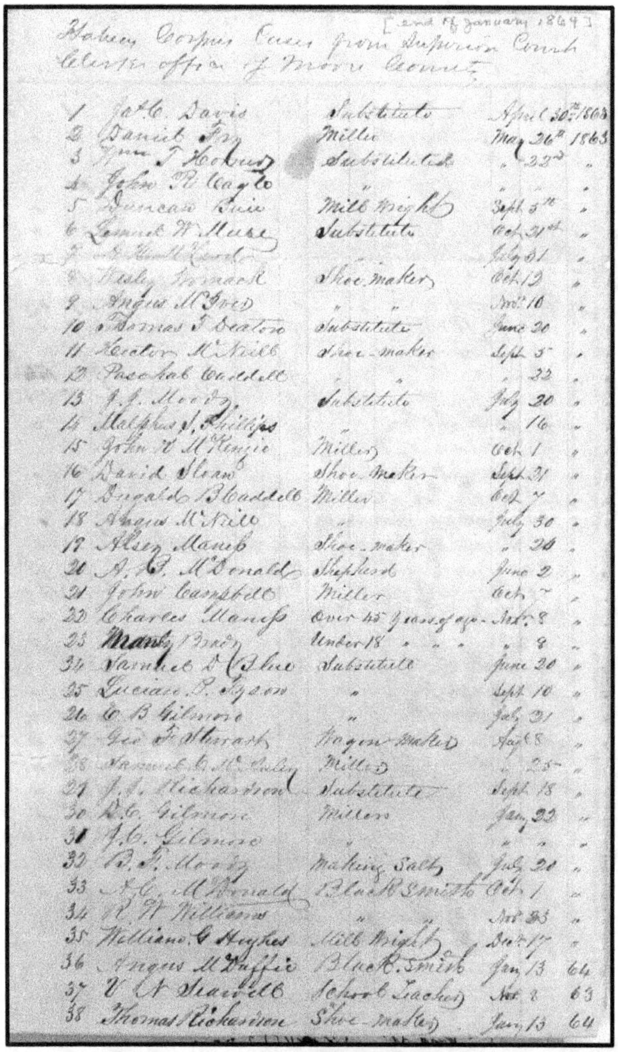

[end of January 1864]

Habeas Corpus Cases from Superior Court Clerk's office of Moore County

1	Jas. C. Davis	Substitute	April 30th	1863
2	Daniel Fry	Miller	May 26th	1863
3	Wm. T. Hobus	Substituted	" 22nd	"
4	John R. Cagle	"	" "	"
5	Duncan Buie	Mill Wright	Sept. 5th	"
6	Samuel W. Muse	Substitute	Oct. 31st	"
7	[illegible]		July 31	"
8	Wesley Womack	Shoe maker	Oct. 12	"
9	Angus McIver	" "	Nov. 10	"
10	Thomas T. Deaton	Substitute	June 20	"
11	Hector McNeill	Shoe-maker	Sept. 5	"
12	Paschal Caddell	" "	" 22	"
13	J. J. Moody	Substitute	July 20	"
14	Malphus J. Phillips	"	" 16	"
15	John R. McKenzie	Miller	Oct. 1	"
16	David Sloan	Shoe Maker	Sept. 21	"
17	Dugald B. Caddell	Miller	Oct. 7	"
18	Angus McNeill	"	July 30	"
19	Alsey Manes	Shoe-maker	" 24	"
20	A. B. McDonald	Shepherd	June 2	"
21	John Campbell	Miller	Oct. 7	"
22	Charles Manes	Over 45 years of age	Nov. 8	"
23	Manly Brady	Under 18 " " "	" 8	"
24	Samuel D. Blue	Substitute	June 20	"
25	Lucian P. Tyson	"	Sept. 10	"
26	C. B. Gilmore	"	July 21	"
27	Geo. F. Stewart	Wagon maker	Aug. 8	"
28	Samuel C. McAuley	Miller	" 25	"
29	J. A. Richardson	Substitute	Sept. 18	"
30	R. C. Gilmore	Miller	Jany. 22	"
31	J. C. Gilmore	"	" "	"
32	B. F. Moody	Making Salt	July 20	"
33	A. C. McDonald	Black Smith	Oct. 1	"
34	R. W. Williams	" "	Nov. 23	"
35	William G. Hughes	Mill Wright	Dec. 17	"
36	Angus McDuffie	Black Smith	Jan. 13	64
37	V. A. Seawell	School Teacher	Nov. 8	63
38	Thomas Richardson	Shoe-maker	Jany. 13	64

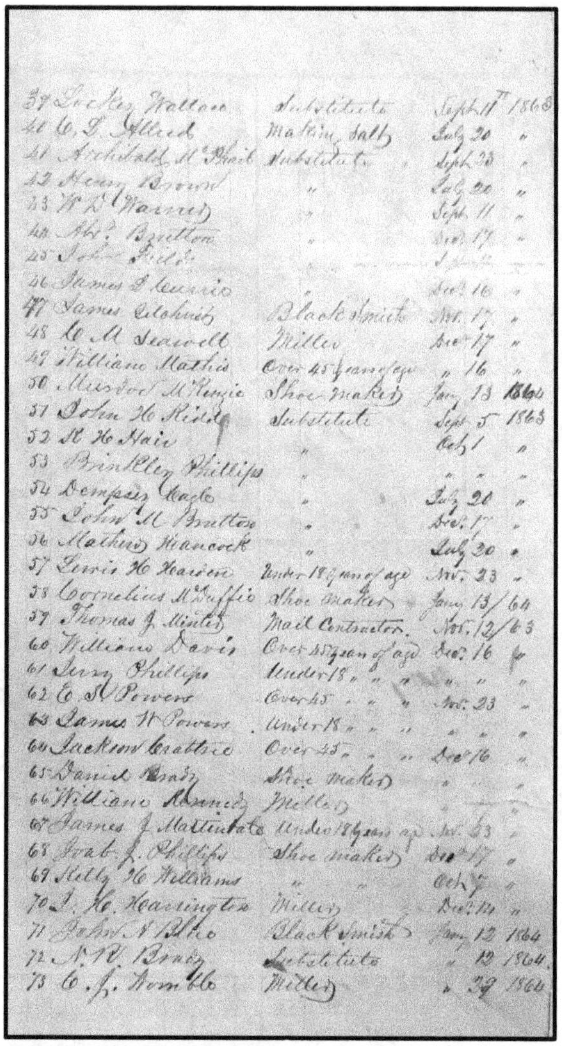

39	Lockey Wallace	Substitute	Sept. 11th	1863
40	C. G. Allred	Making Salt	July 20	"
41	Archibald McPhail	Substitute	Sept. 23	"
42	Henry Brown	"	July 20	"
43	W. D. Warner	"	Sept. 11	"
44	Alex. Britton	"	Dec. 17	"
45	John Fields		[illegible]	
46	James S. Currie	"	Dec. 16	"
47	James Cloaninger	Black Smith	Nov. 17	"
48	C. M. Seawell	Miller	Dec. 17	"
49	William Mathis	Over 45 years of age	" 16	"
50	Murdoch McKenzie	Shoe maker	Jany. 13	1864
51	John H. Kidd	Substitute	Sept. 5	1863
52	H. H. Hair	"	Oct. 1	"
53	Brinkley Phillips	"	" "	"
54	Dempsey Cagle	"	July 20	"
55	John M. Britton	"	Dec. 17	"
56	Mathew Hancock	"	July 20	"
57	Lewis H. Hearne	Under 18 years of age	Nov. 23	"
58	Cornelius McDuffie	Shoe maker	Jany. 13/64	
59	Thomas J. Minter	Mail Contractor	Nov. 12/63	
60	William Davis	Over 45 years of age	Dec. 16	"
61	Jerry Phillips	Under 18 " " "	" "	"
62	E. S. Powers	Over 45 " " "	Nov. 23	"
63	James W. Powers	Under 18 " " "	" "	"
64	Jackson Crabtree	Over 45 " " "	Dec. 16	"
65	Daniel Brady	Shoe maker	" "	"
66	William Kennedy	Miller	" "	"
67	James J. Martindale	Under 18 years age	Nov. 23	"
68	Joab J. Phillips	Shoe maker	Dec. 17	"
69	Kelly H. Williams	" "	Oct. 7	"
70	J. H. Harrington	Miller	Dec. 14	"
71	John N. Blue	Black Smith	Jany. 12	1864
72	N. R. Brady	Substitute	" 12	1864
73	C. J. Womble	Miller	" 29	1864

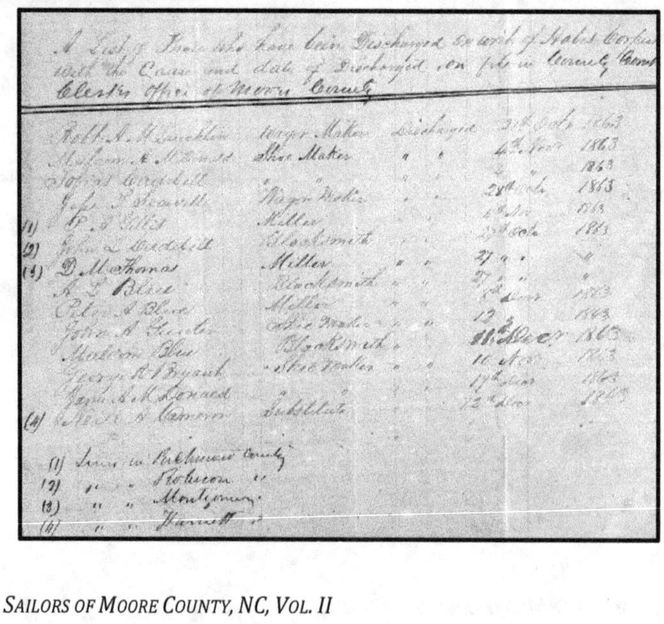

A List of Those who have been Discharged on writ of Habeas Corpus with the Cause and date of Discharged, on file in County Court Clerk's Office of Moore County

	Robt. A. McLauchlin	Wagon Maker	Discharged	31st Octo.	1863
	Malcom A. McDonald	Shoe Maker	" "	4th Nov.	1863
	Tobias Caddell	" "	" "	" "	1863
	Jeff. T. Seawell	Wagon Maker	" "	28th Octo.	1863
(1)	R. A. Gillis	Miller	" "	4th Nov.	1863
(2)	John L. Caddell	Blacksmith	" "	27th Octo.	1863
(3)	D. M. Thomas	Miller	" "	27 " "	"
	A. L. Blue	Blacksmith	" "	27 " "	"
	Peter A. Blue	Miller	" "	5th Dec.	1863
	John A. Gunter	Shoe Maker	" "	12 "	1863
	Malcom Blue	Blacksmith	" "	11th Dec.	1863
	George R. Bryant	Shoe Maker	" "	10 Nov.	1863
	Jas. A. McDonald	" "	" "	17th Dec.	1863
(4)	Neill A. Cameron	Substitute	" "	12th Dec.	1863

(1) Lives in Richmond County
(2) " " Robeson "
(3) " " Montgomery
(4) " " Harnett "

H.R. Cox, W.W. Williams, Daniel McIntosh, Lindsay Cagle and Quimby Wallace

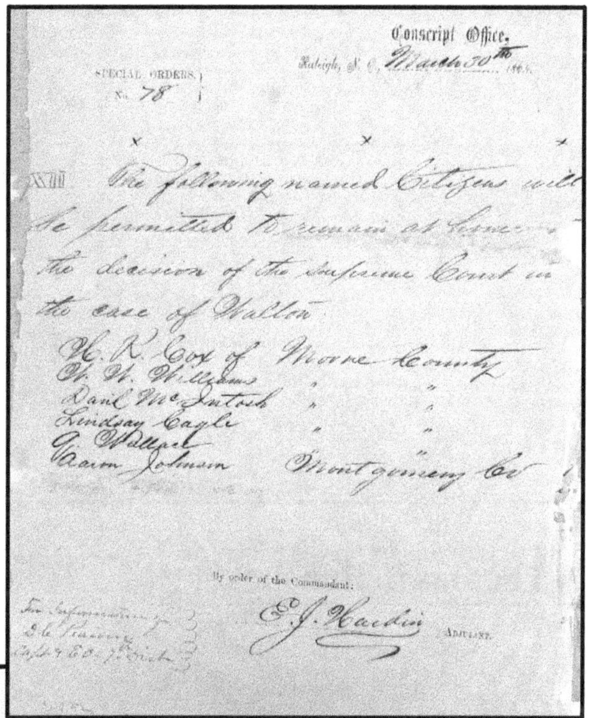

Conscript Office.
Raleigh, N.C., March 30th 186

SPECIAL ORDERS, No. 78

XIII The following named Citizens will be permitted to remain at home [illegible] the decision of the Supreme Court in the case of Walton

H. R. Cox of Moore County
W. W. Williams " "
Danl McIntosh " "
Lindsay Cagle " "
Q. Wallace " "
Aaron Johnson Montgomery Co

By order of the Commandant:
E. J. Hardin Adjutant.

John S. Ritter

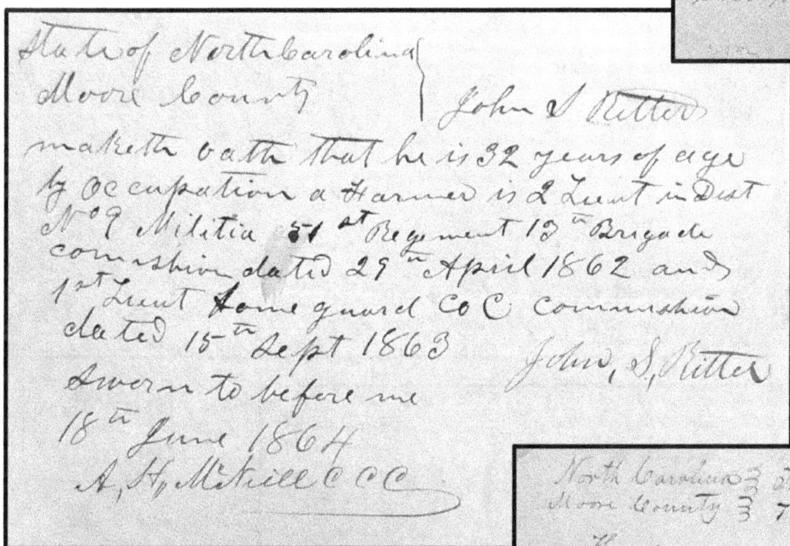

State of North Carolina } Moore County } John S Ritter maketh oath that he is 32 years of age by occupation a Farmer is 2 Lieut in Dist No 9 Militia 51st Regiment 13th Brigade commission dated 29th April 1862 and 1st Lieut Home guard Co C commission dated 15th Sept 1863

John, S, Ritter

Sworn to before me 18th June 1864
A, H, McNeill C C C

Rev. Murdoch M. Thomas

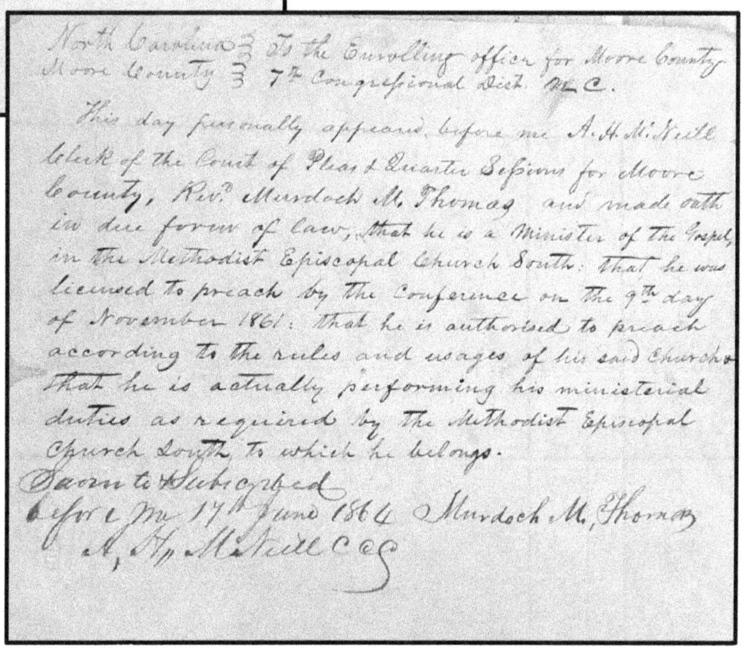

North Carolina } To the Enrolling officer for Moore County
Moore County } 7th Congressional Dist. N C.

This day personally appeared before me A. H. McNeill Clerk of the Court of Pleas & Quarter Sessions for Moore County, Revd Murdoch M. Thomas and made oath in due form of law, that he is a Minister of the Gospel, in the Methodist Episcopal Church South: that he was licensed to preach by the Conference on the 9th day of November 1861: that he is authorised to preach according to the rules and usages of his said Church & that he is actually performing his ministerial duties as required by the Methodist Episcopal Church South, to which he belongs.

Sworn to & subscribed before me 17th June 1864 Murdoch M, Thomas
A, H, McNeill C C C

Robert W. Barrett

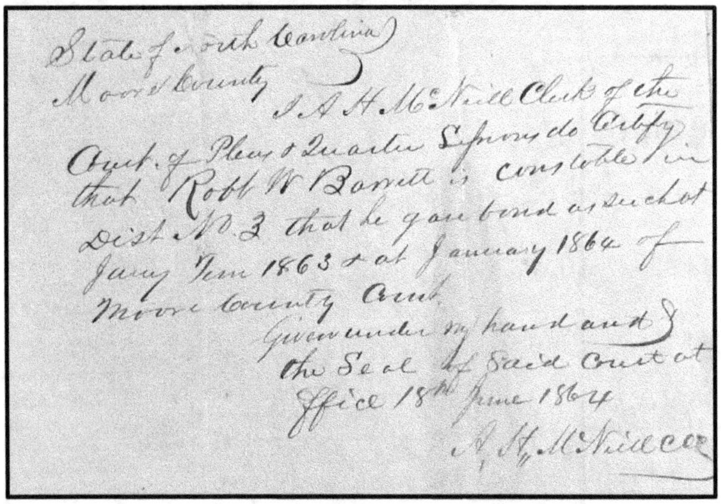

State of North Carolina
Moore County } I A H McNeill Clerk of the Court of Pleas & Quarter Sessions do Certify that Robt W Barrett is constable in Dist No 3 that he gave bond as such at Jany Term 1863 & at January 1864 of Moore County Court.

Given under my hand and the Seal of Said Court at Office 18th June 1864

A. H. McNeill CCC

Thomas B. Hunsucker

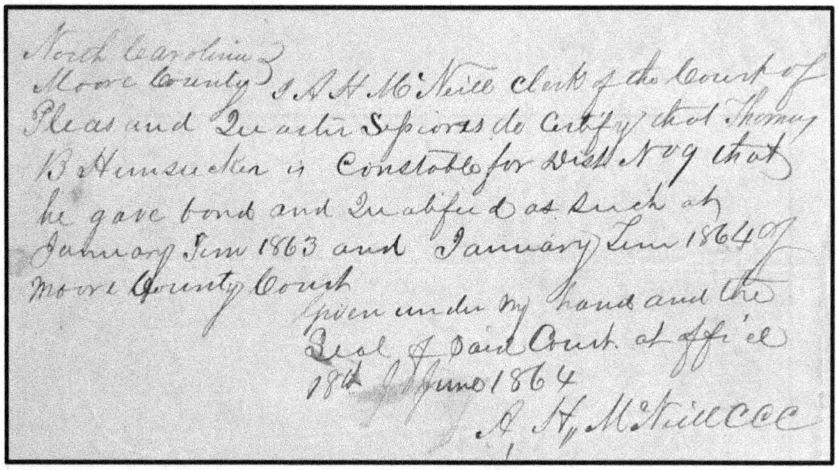

North Carolina
Moore County } I A H McNeill Clerk of the Court of Pleas and Quarter Sessions do Certify that Thomas B Hunsucker is Constable for Dist No 9 that he gave bond and qualified as such at January Term 1863 and January Term 1864 of Moore County Court

Given under my hand and the Seal of said Court at office 18th of June 1864

A. H. McNeill CCC

John Campbell

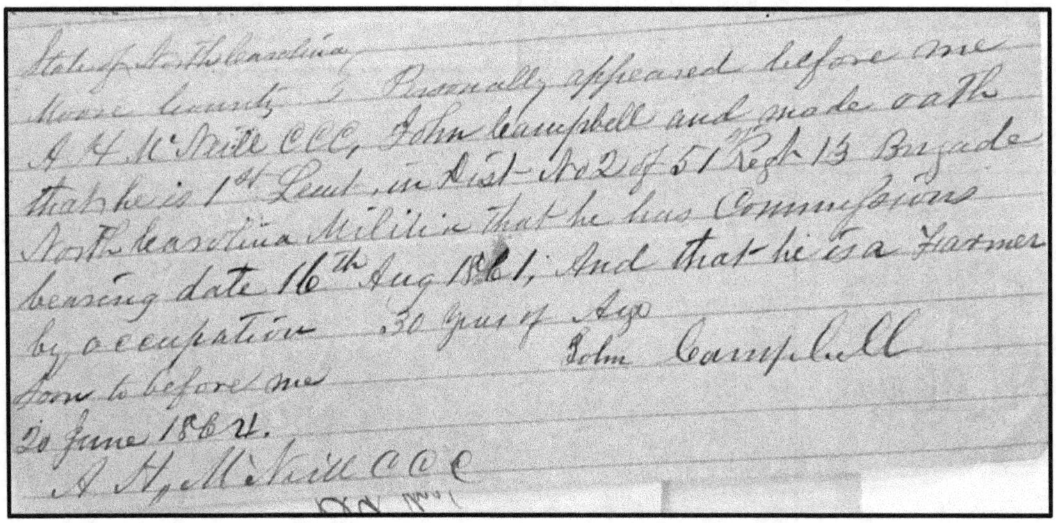

State of North Carolina
Moore County } Personally appeared before me A H McNeill CCC, John Campbell and made oath that he is 1st Lieut. in Dist No 2 of 51 Regt 13 Brigade North Carolina Militia that he has Commissions bearing date 16th Aug 1861, And that he is a Farmer by occupation 30 yrs of Age

John Campbell

Sworn to before me 20 June 1864.
A. H. McNeill CCC

M.M. Buie

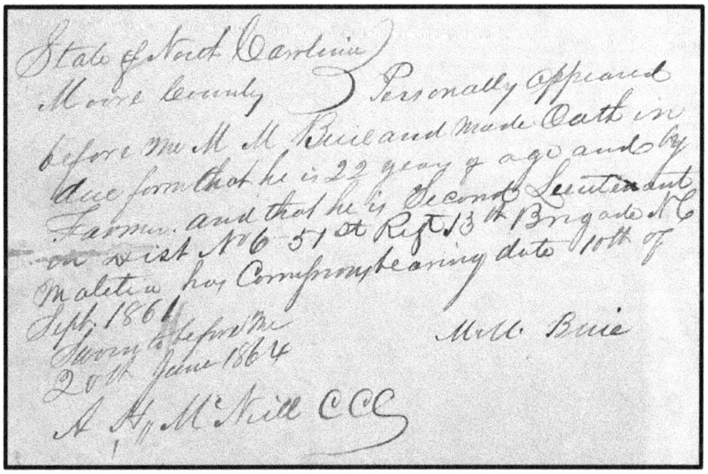

State of North Carolina)
Moore County) Personally appeared
before me M M Buie and made Oath in
due form that he is 22 years of age and by
Farmer and that he is Second Lieutenant
in Dist No 6 51st Regt 13th Brigade N C
Malitia has Commission bearing date 10th of
Sept 1861
Sworn to before me
20th June 1864
A. H. McNeill CCC

M M Buie

Lewis H. Ritter

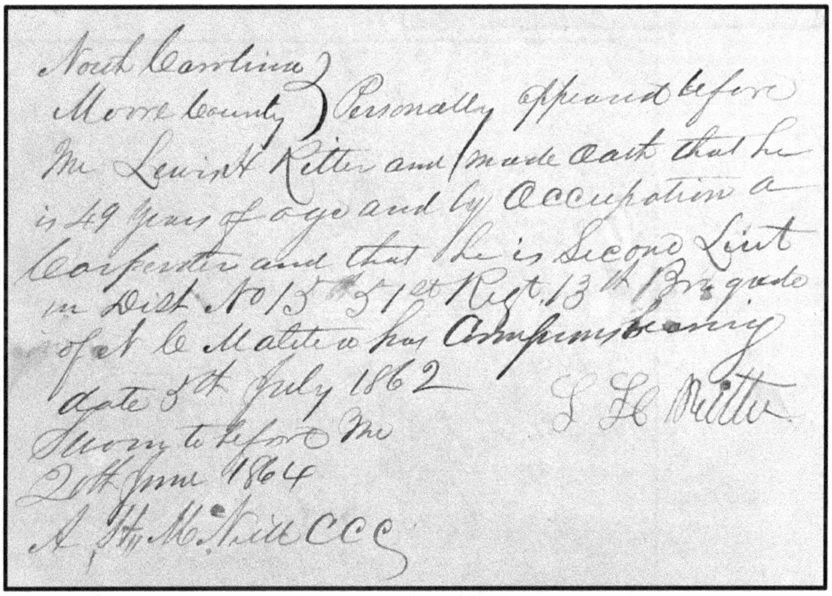

North Carolina)
Moore County) Personally appeared before
me Lewis H Ritter and made oath that he
is 49 years of age and by Occupation a
Carpenter and that he is Second Lieut
in Dist No 15 51st Regt 13th Brigade
of N C Malitia has Commission bearing
date 5th July 1862
Sworn to before me
20th June 1864
A. H. McNeill CCC

L H Ritter

A.M. Branson

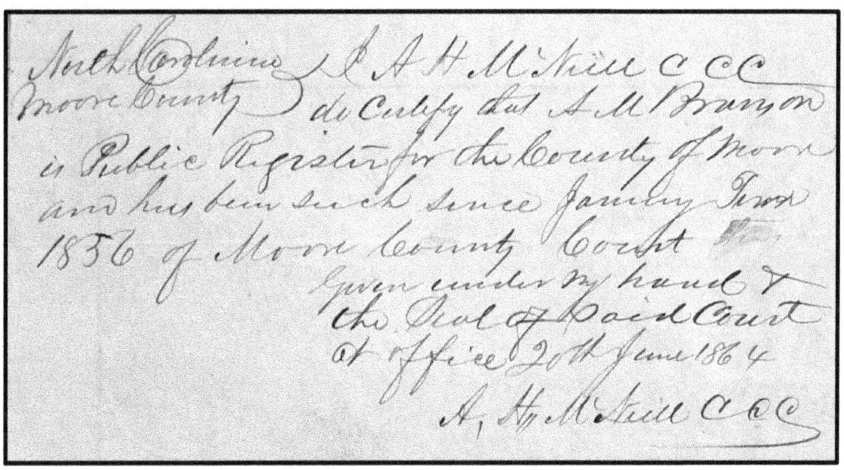

North Carolina) I A H McNeill C CC
Moore County) do Certify that A M Branson
is Public Register for the County of Moore
and has been such since January Term
1856 of Moore County Court
Given under my hand &
the Seal of Said Court
at office 20th June 1864
A. H. McNeill CCC

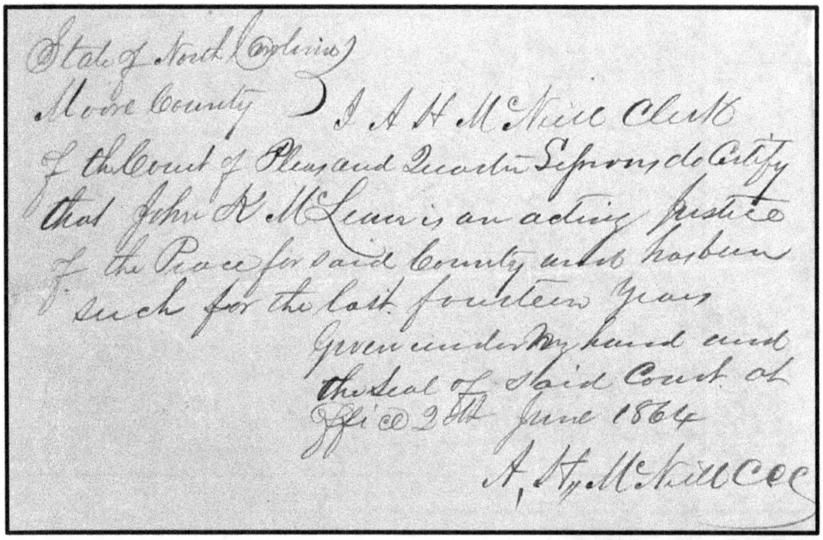
State of North Carolina }
Moore County } I A H McNeill Clerk
of the Court of Pleas and Quarter Sessions do Certify
that John K McLean is an acting Justice
of the Peace for said County and has been
such for the last fourteen years
Given under my hand and
the Seal of Said Court at
Office 20th June 1864
A. H. McNeill CCC

John K. McLean

Dr. William A. Hays

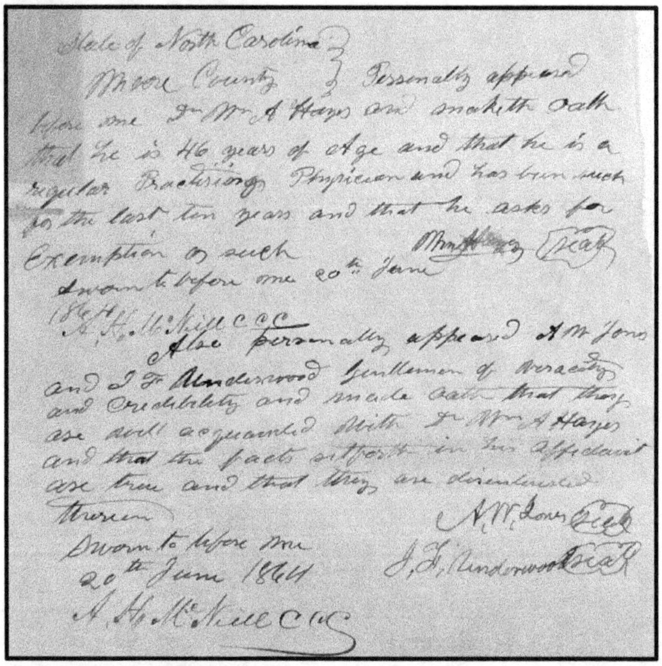
State of North Carolina }
Moore County } Personally appeared
before me Dr Wm A Hays and maketh oath
that he is 46 years of Age and that he is a
regular Practising Physician and has been such
for the last ten years and that he asks for
Exemption as such Wm A Hays (Seal)
Sworn to before me 20th June
1864 A. H. McNeill CCC
Also personally appeared A W Jones
and J F Underwood Gentlemen of Veracity
and Credibility and made oath that they
are well acquainted with Dr Wm A Hayes
and that the facts set forth in his Affidavit
are true and that they are disinterested
therein A. W. Jones (Seal)
Sworn to before me
20th June 1864 J. F. Underwood (Seal)
A. H. McNeill CCC

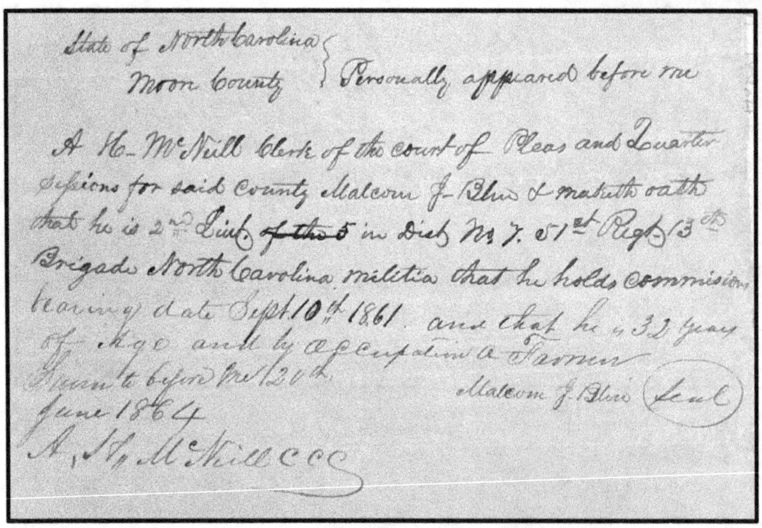
State of North Carolina }
Moore County } Personally appeared before me
A H. McNeill Clerk of the court of Pleas and Quarter
Sessions for said County Malcom J. Blue & maketh oath
that he is 2nd Lieut ~~of the~~ in Dist No 7. 51st Regt 13th
Brigade North Carolina militia that he holds commission
bearing date Sept 10th 1861. and that he is 32 years
of Age and by occupation a Farmer
Sworn to before me 20th
June 1864 Malcom J. Blue (Seal)
A. H. McNeill CCC

Malcom J. Blue

Archibald Ray

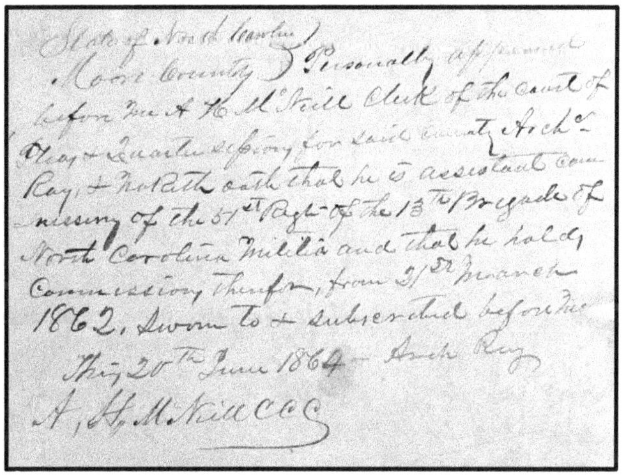
State of North Carolina
Moore County } Personally appeared
before me A H McNeill Clerk of the Court of
Pleas & Quarter Sessions for said County Archd
Ray, & maketh oath that he is assistant Com-
missary of the 51st Regt of the 13th Brigade of
North Carolina Militia and that he holds
Commission therefor, from 21st March
1862. Sworn to & subscribed before me
this 20th June 1864 — Arch Ray
A, H, McNeill CCC

Rev. Hiram Rodgers

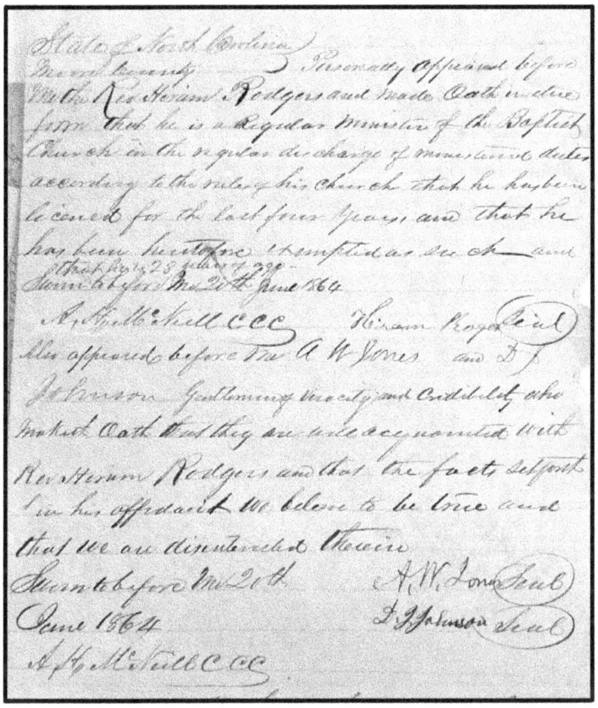
State of North Carolina
Moore County } Personally appeared before
Me the Rev Hiram Rodgers and made Oath in due
form that he is a Regular Minister of the Baptist
Church in the regular discharge of ministerial duties
according to the rules of his church that he has been
licenced for the last four years, and that he
has been heretofore exempted as such and
that he is 28 years of age
Sworn to before me 20th June 1864
A, H, McNeill CCC — Hiram Rodgers (Seal)
Also appeared before me A W Jones and D J
Johnson Gentlemen of veracity and Credibility who
maketh Oath that they are well acquainted with
Rev Hiram Rodgers and that the facts set forth
in his affidavit we believe to be true and
that we are disinterested therein
Sworn to before me 20th — A.W. Jones (Seal)
June 1864 — D J Johnson (Seal)
A, H, McNeill CCC

A.R. McDonald

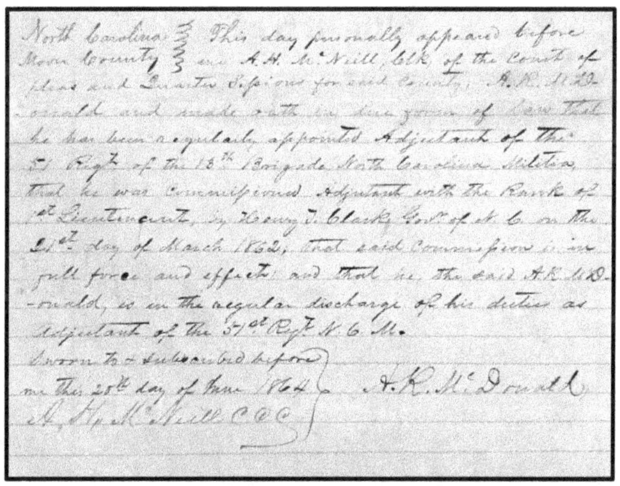
North Carolina } This day personally appeared before
Moore County } me A.H. McNeill, Clk, of the Court of
pleas and Quarter Sessions for said County, A.R. McD-
onald and made oath in due form of law that
he has been regularly appointed Adjutant of the
51 Regt of the 13th Brigade North Carolina Militia,
that he was commissioned Adjutant with the Rank of
1st Lieutenant, by Henry T. Clark, Govr of N. C. on the
21st day of March 1862, that said Commission is in
full force and effect, and that he, the said A.R. McD-
onald, is in the regular discharge of his duties as
Adjutant of the 51st Regt N. C. M.
Sworn to & subscribed before
me this 20th day of June 1864 — A.R. McDonald
A, H McNeill CCC

Dr. Jesse D. Graves

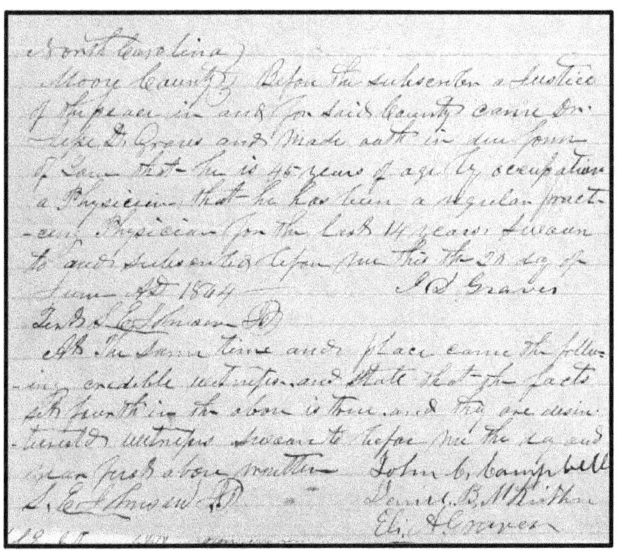
North Carolina
Moore County } Before the subscriber a Justice
of the peace in and for said County came Dr
Jesse D. Graves and made oath in due form
of Law that he is 45 years of age by occupation
a Physician that he has been a regular pract-
-cing Physician for the last 14 years. Sworn
to and subscribed before me this the 20 day of
June AD 1864 — J D Graves
Test L E Johnson JP
At the same time and place came the following credible witnesses and state that the facts
set forth in the above is true and they are disinterested witnesses Sworn to before me the day and
year first above written — John C. Campbell
L E Johnson JP — Daniel B. McKeithen
Eli A Graves

Rev. Angus N. Ferguson

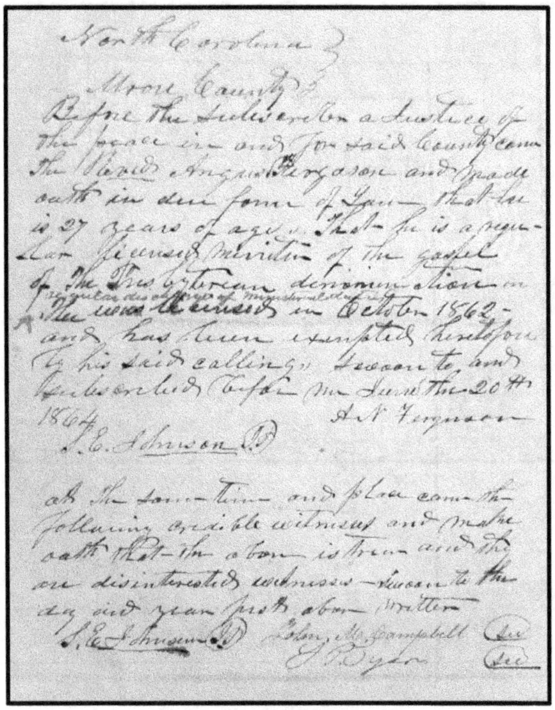

North Carolina
Moore County
Before the Subscriber a Justice of the peace in and for said County came the Revd Angus N. Ferguson and made oath in due form of Law that he is 27 years of age. That he is a regular licensed minister of the gospel of the Presbyterian denomination in regular discharge of ministerial duties. He was licensed in October 1862 and has been exempted heretofore by his said calling. Sworn to and subscribed before me June the 20th 1864
A N Ferguson
J. E. Johnson JP

At the same time and place came the following credible witnesses and make oath that the above is true and they are disinterested witnesses. Sworn to the day and year first above written
J. E. Johnson JP
John M. Campbell (Seal)
J. P. Dyer (Seal)

John McIver

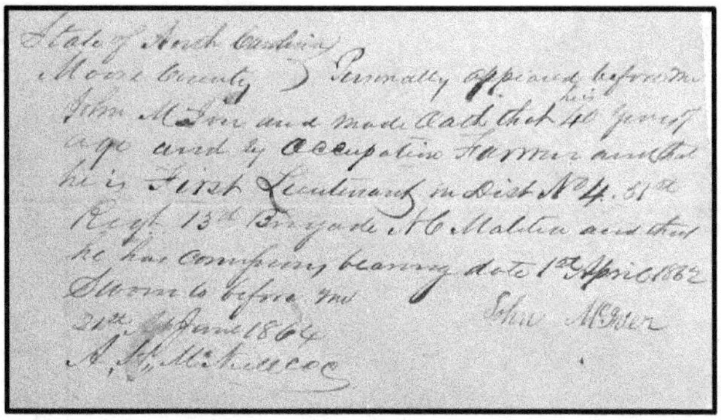

State of North Carolina
Moore County } Personally appeared before me John McIver and made oath that his 40 years of age and by occupation Farmer and that he is First Lieutenant in Dist No 4. 51st Regt 13th Brigade N C Militia and that he has Company bearing date 1st April 1862
Sworn to before me 21st June 1864
John McIver
A. H. McNeill CCC

Rev. Stephen Gilmore

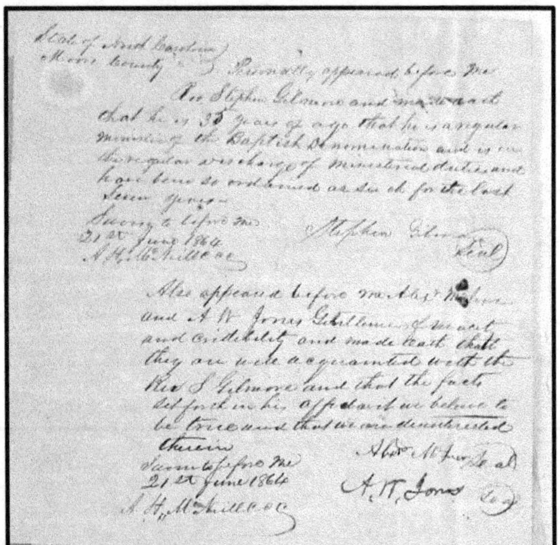

State of North Carolina
Moore County } Personally appeared before me Rev Stephen Gilmore and made oath that he is 38 years of age that he is a regular minister of the Baptist Denomination and is in the regular discharge of ministerial duties and have been so ordained as such for the last Seven years.
Sworn to before me 21st June 1864
Stephen Gilmore (Seal)
A. H. McNeill CCC

Also appeared before me Abr McIver and A W Jones Gentlemen of veracity and credibility and made oath that they are well acquainted with the Rev S Gilmore and that the facts set forth in his affidavit we believe to be true and that we are disinterested therein
Sworn to before me 21st June 1864
Abr McIver (Seal)
A. W. Jones (Seal)
A. H. McNeill CCC

A.A. Harrington

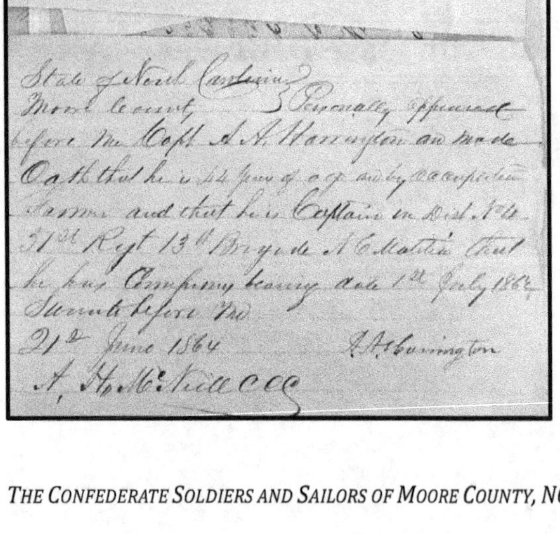

State of North Carolina
Moore County } Personally appeared before me Capt A. A. Harrington and made Oath that he is 44 years of age and by occupation Farmer and that he is Captain in Dist No 4 51st Regt 13th Brigade N C Militia that he has Company bearing date 1st July 1862
Sworn to before me 21st June 1864
A A Harrington
A. H. McNeill CCC

K.F. McIntosh

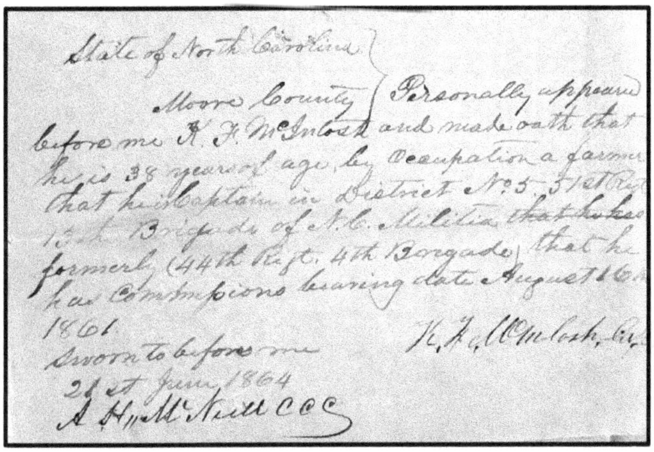

State of North Carolina }
Moore County } Personally appeared before me K. F. McIntosh and made oath that he is 38 years of age, by occupation a farmer that he is Captain in District No. 5. 51st Regt 13th Brigade of N.C. Militia ~~that he has~~ formerly (44th Regt. 4th Brigade) that he has Commissions bearing date August 16th 1861.
K. F. McIntosh, Cap.
Sworn to before me
21st June 1864
A. H. McNeill CCC

Wesley McIver

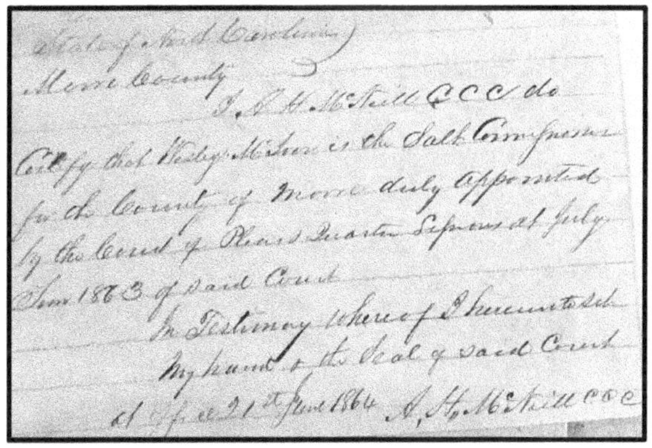

State of North Carolina }
Moore County }
I, A. H. McNeill CCC do Certify that Wesley McIver is the Salt Commissioner for the County of Moore duly appointed by the Court of Pleas & Quarter Sessions at July Term 1863 of said Court
In Testimony whereof I hereunto set my hand & the seal of said Court at office 21st June 1864 A. H. McNeill CCC

Various Reports from Enrolling Officers

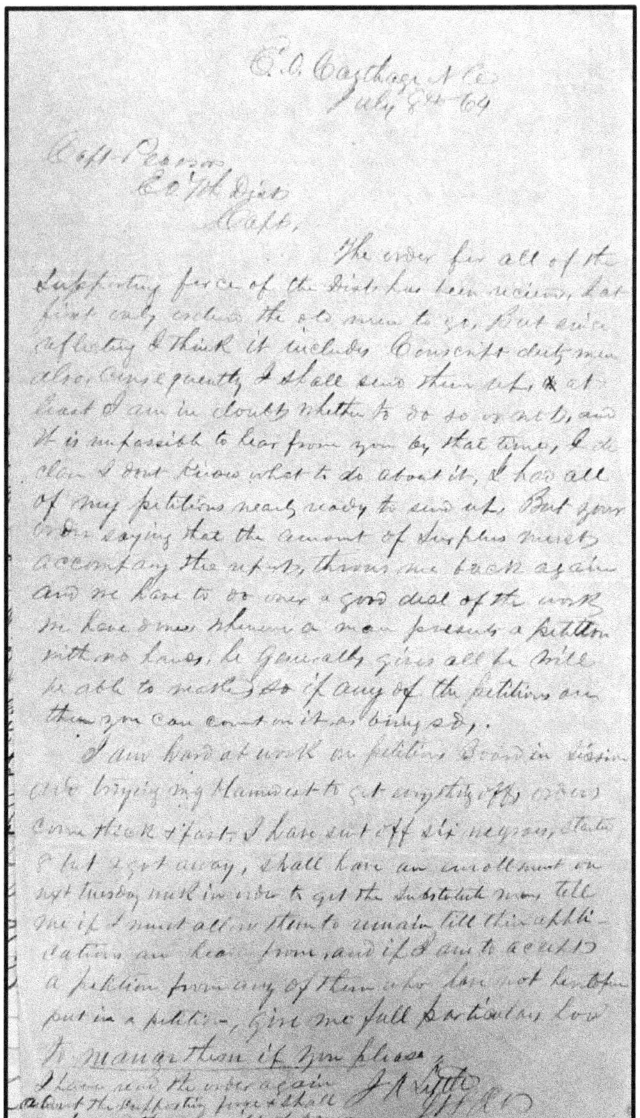

E.O. Carthage N.C.
July 8th 64

Capt. Pearson
E.O. 7th Dist
Capt,

The order for all of the Supporting force of the Dist. has been recieved, I at first only reckoned the old men to go, But since reflecting I think it includes Conscript duty men also. Consequently I shall send them up, & at least I am in doubt whether to do so or not, and it is impossible to hear from you by that time, I declare I dont know what to do about it, I had all of my petitions nearly ready to send up. But your order saying that the amount of Surplus must accompany the reports, throws me back again and we have to do over a good deal of the work we have done. Wherever a man presents a petition with no hands, he generally gives all he will be able to make, so if any of the petitions are thus you can count on it as being so,

I am hard at work on petitions Board in Session and trying my blamedest to get everything off, orders come thick & fast. I have sent off six negroes, [illegible] & but I got away, shall have an enrollment on next tuesday week in order to get the Substitute men, tell me if I must allow them to remain till their applications are heard from, and if I am to accept a petition from any of them who have not heretofore put in a petition - Give me full particulars how to manage them if you please.

J. A. [illegible]
[illegible]

I have read the order again about the supporting force & shall not send the conscript duty men,

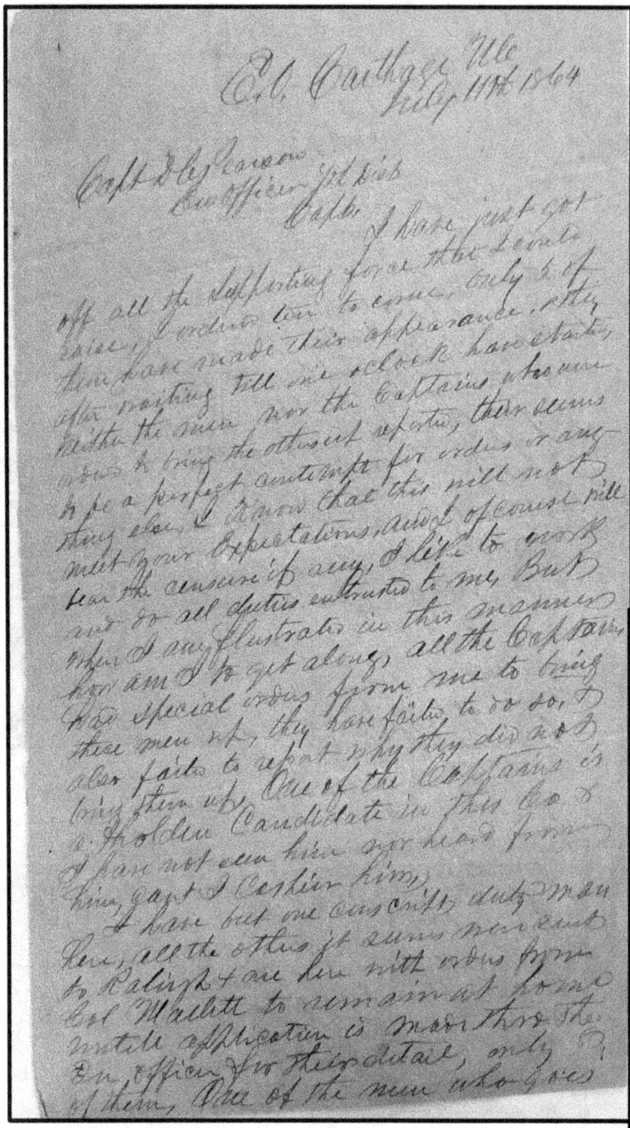
C. C. Carthage NC
July 11th 1864

Capt D. C. Pearson
Enr Officer 7th Dist
Capt.
I have just got off all the supporting force that I could raise, I ordered ten to come, only 5 of them have made their appearance, & they after waiting till one o'clock have started. Neither the men nor the Captains who were ordered to bring the others up reporting, there seems to be a perfect contempt for orders or any thing else. I know that this will not meet your expectations and of course will bear the censure if any, I like to work and do all duties entrusted to me, But when I am illustrated in this manner how am I to get along, all the Captains had special orders from me to bring these men up, they have failed to do so, & also failed to report why they did not bring them up. One of the Captains is a Holden Candidate in this Co & I have not seen him nor heard from him, cant I Cashier him.
I have but one conscript duty man here, all the others it seems were sent to Raleigh & are here with orders from Col Mallett to remain at home until application is made thro the En. Officer for their detail, only [illegible] of them, One of the men who goes

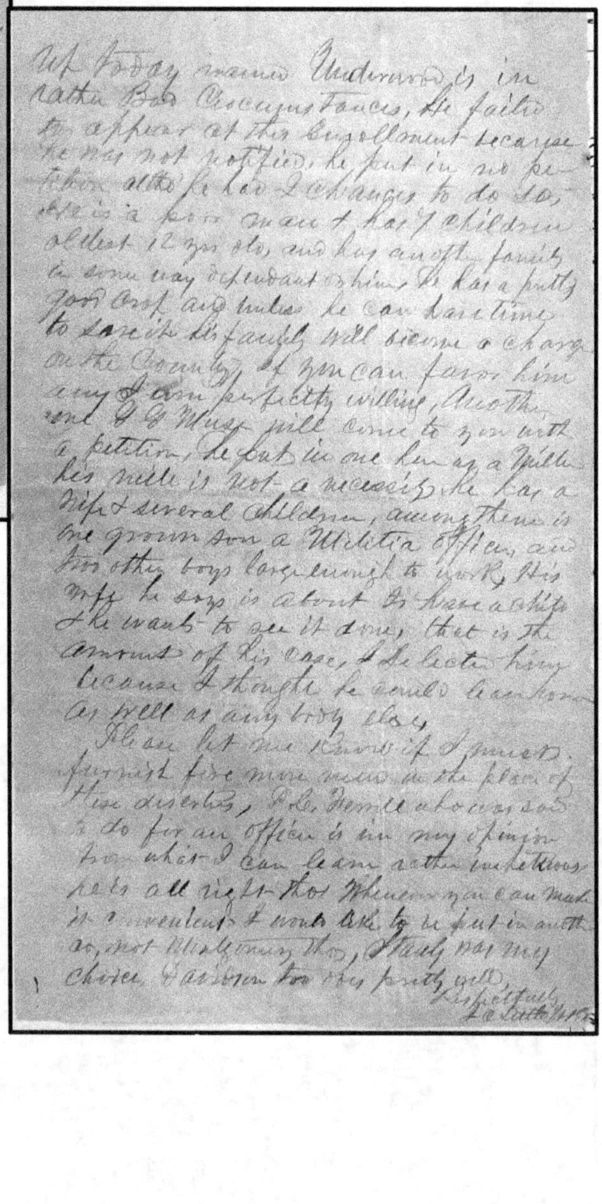
up today named Underwood is in rather Bad Circumstances, he failed to appear at the Enrollment because he was not notified, he put in no petition altho he had 2 chances to do so, He is a poor man & has 7 children oldest 12 yrs old, and has another family in some way dependant on him, he has a pretty good crop and unless he can have time to save it his family will become a charge on the County, if you can favor him any I am perfectly willing. Another one J. G. Muse will come to you with a petition, he put in one here as a Miller his mill is not a necessity, he has a wife & several children, among them is one grown son a Militia Officer, and two other boys large enough to work, His wife he says is about to have a child & he wants to see it done, that is the amount of his case, I selected him because I thought he could be at home as well as any body else,
Please let me know if I must furnish five more men in the place of these deserters, P. C. Merrill who was said to do for an Officer is in my opinion from what I can learn rather [illegible] he is all right tho. Whenever you can make it convenient I would like to be put in another Co, not Montgomery tho, Stanly was my choice, Davidson too does pretty well,
Respectfully
[illegible]

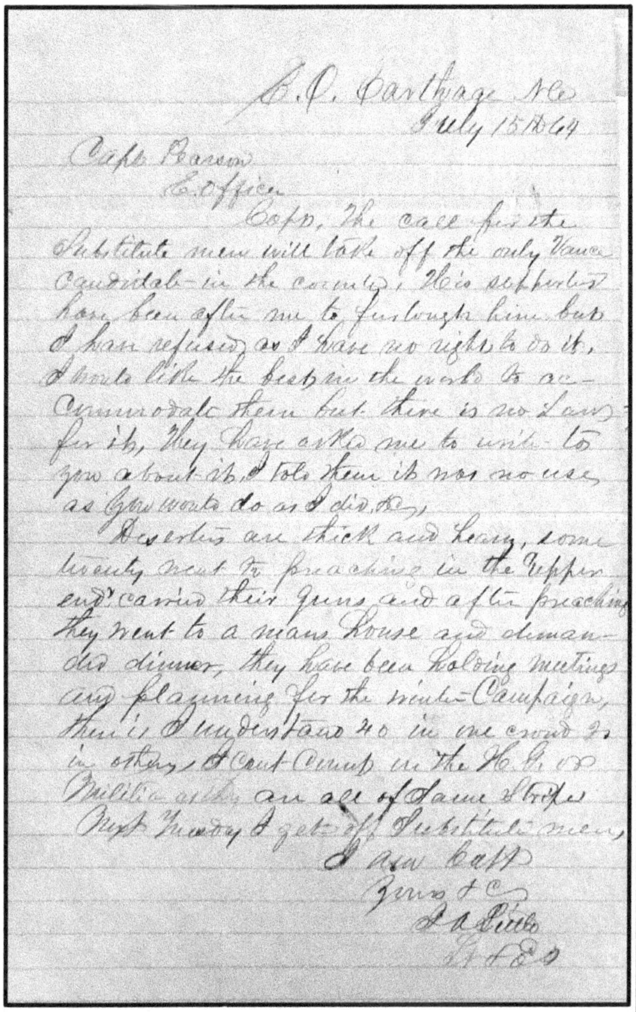

B. O. Carthage N.C.
July 15th 64

Capt Pearson
E. Officer

Capt, The call for the Substitute men will take off the only Vance Candidate in the county. His supporters have been after me to furlough him but I have refused as I have no right to do it. I would like the best in the world to accommodate them but there is no Law for it, they have asked me to write to you about it. I told them it was no use as you would do as I did, &c.

Deserters are thick and heavy, some twenty went to preaching in the Upper end carrying their guns and after preaching they went to a mans house and demanded dinner, they have been holding meetings and planning for the winter Campaign, there is I understand 40 in one crowd 25 in other, & can't Crush in the H. G. or Militia either are all of same stripe

Next Monday I get off Substitute men,

I am Capt
Yours &c
J. A. Pitts
Lt. E. O.

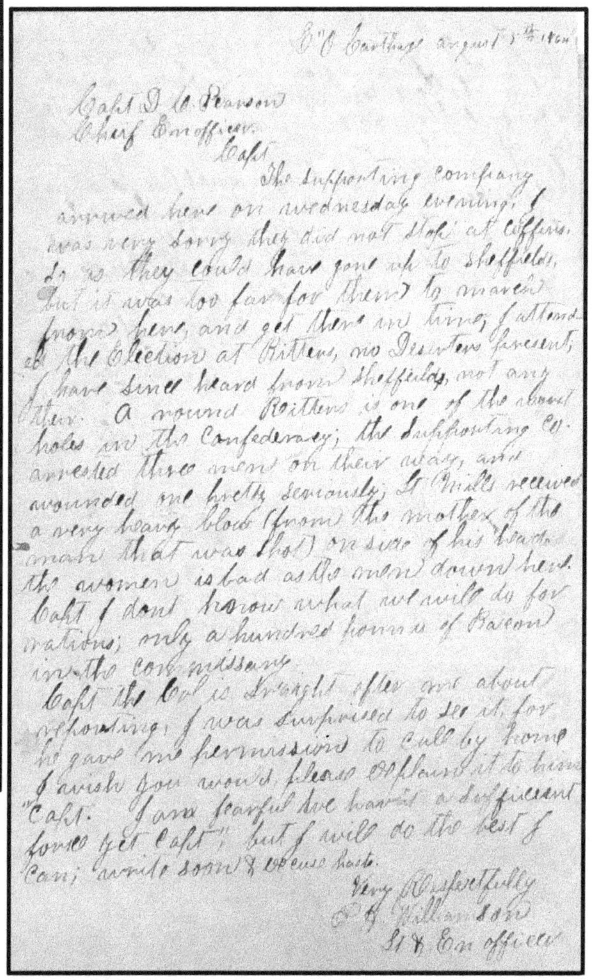

E. O. Carthage August 5th 1864

Capt D. C. Pearson
Chief En officer.
Capt

The supporting company arrived here on wednesday evening; I was very sorry they did not stop at Coffins, so as they could have gone up to Sheffields, but it was too far for them to march from here, and get there in time, I attended the Election at Ritters, no Deserters present, I have since heard from Sheffields, not any there. A round Ritters is one of the worst holes in the Confederacy; the supporting Co. arrested three men on their way, and wounded one pretty seriously; Lt Mills received a very heavy blow (from the mother of the man that was shot) on side of his head the women is bad as the men down here. Capt I dont know what we will do for rations; only a hundred pounds of Bacon in the commissary.

Capt the Col is straight after me about reporting; I was surprised to see it, for he gave me permission to call by home I wish you would please explain it to him "Capt. I am fearful we havnt a sufficient force yet Capt", but I will do the best I can; write soon & excuse haste.

Very Respectfully
P. H. Williamson
Lt & En officer

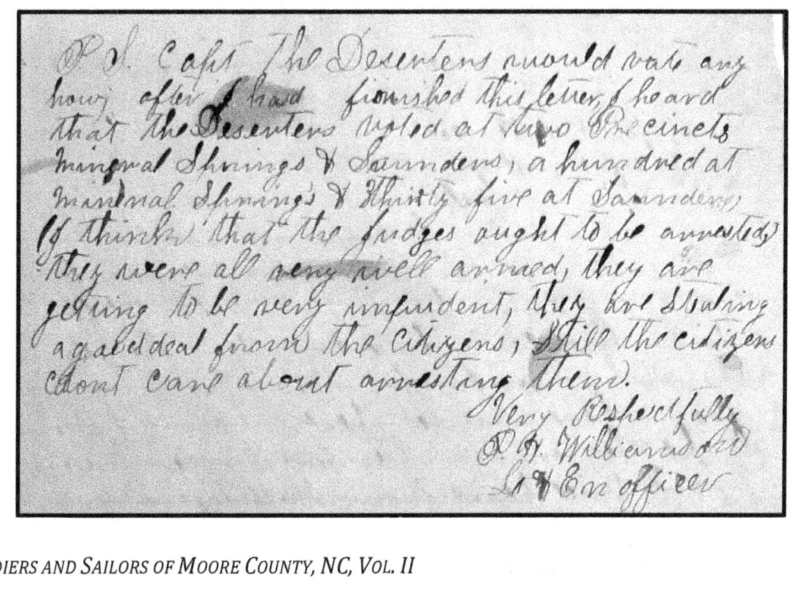

P. S. Capt The Deserters would vote any how; after I had finished this letter, I heard that the Deserters voted at two Precincts Mineral Springs & Saunders, a hundred at Mineral Springs & Thirty five at Saunders; I think that the Judges ought to be arrested; they were all very well armed, they are getting to be very impudent, they are stealing a good deal from the citizens, still the citizens dont care about arresting them.

Very Respectfully
P. H. Williamson
Lt & En officer

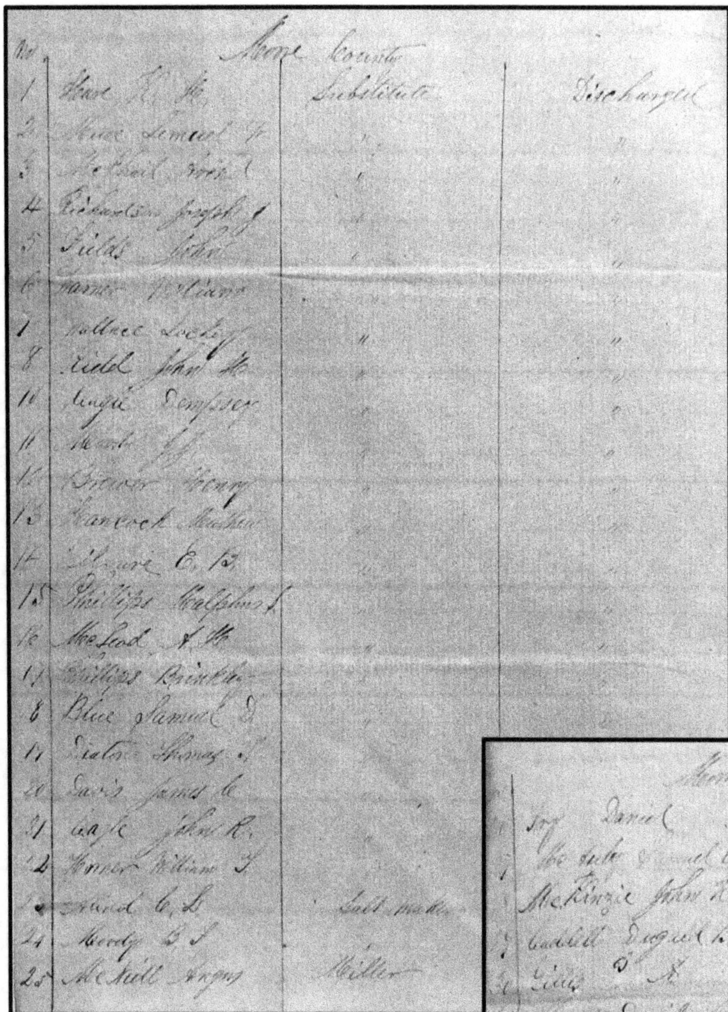

Moore County

No		Substitute	Discharged
1	Shaw R. M.	Substitute	Discharged
2	Muse Samuel J	"	"
3	McNeill [illegible]	"	"
4	Richardson Joseph J	"	"
5	Fields John	"	"
6	Harris William		"
7	Wallace Lodey	"	"
8	Riddle John M.	"	"
10	Tingle Dempsey	"	"
11	Monk J J	"	"
12	Brewer Henry	"	"
13	Hancock Matthew	"	"
14	Moore E. B.	"	"
15	Phillips Ralph	"	"
16	McLeod A. M.	"	"
17	Phillips Brinkley	"	"
18	Blue Samuel D.	"	"
19	Deaton Thomas J.	"	"
20	Davis James C.	"	"
21	Cagle John R.	"	"
22	Horner William J.	"	"
23	[illegible] C. L.	Salt maker	
24	Moody G. S.		
25	McNeill Angus	Miller	

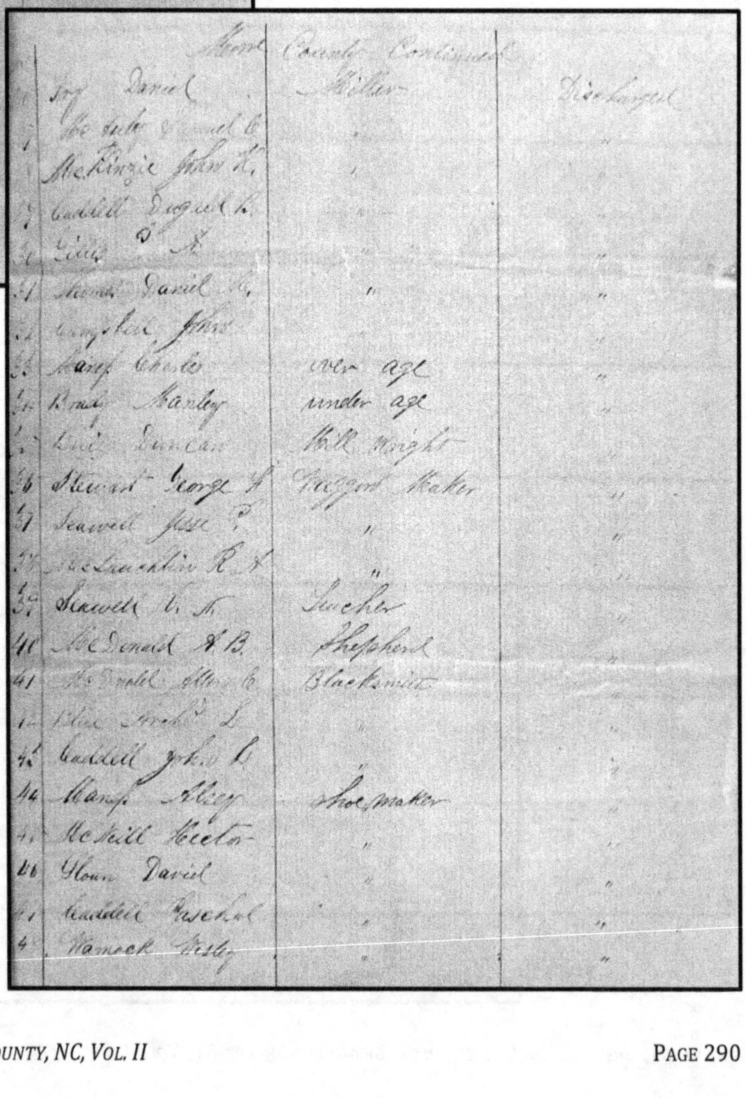

Moore County Continued

	Ivey Daniel	Miller	Discharged
	McIntosh Samuel C.		"
	McKinzie John H.	"	"
	Caddell Duguel H.	"	"
	Fields D. A.		"
31	Harris Daniel H.	"	"
	Cunningham John		"
33	Kemp Charles	over age	"
34	Brady Manley	under age	"
35	Blue Duncan	Mill Wright	"
36	Stewart George W	Waggon Maker	"
37	Seawell Jesse P.	"	"
38	McLauchlin R. A.	"	"
39	Seawell C. M.	Teacher	"
40	McDonald A B.	Shepherd	"
41	McDonald Allen C	Blacksmith	"
42	Blue Archd L		"
43	Caddell John C		"
44	Kemp Alsey	Shoemaker	"
45	McNeill Hector	"	"
46	Sloan David		"
47	Caddell Joshua	"	"
48	Hancock Wesley	"	"

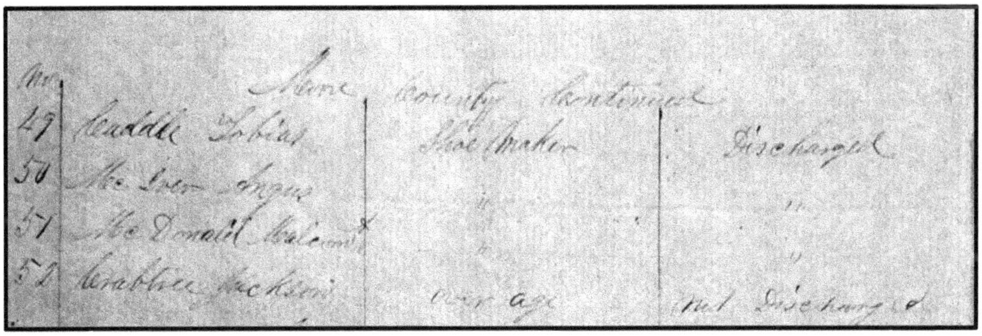

No.	Name	Moore County Continued	
49	Caddle Tobias	Shoe Maker	Discharged
50	McIver Angus	"	"
51	McDonald Malcom	"	"
52	Crabtree Jackson	over age	not Discharged

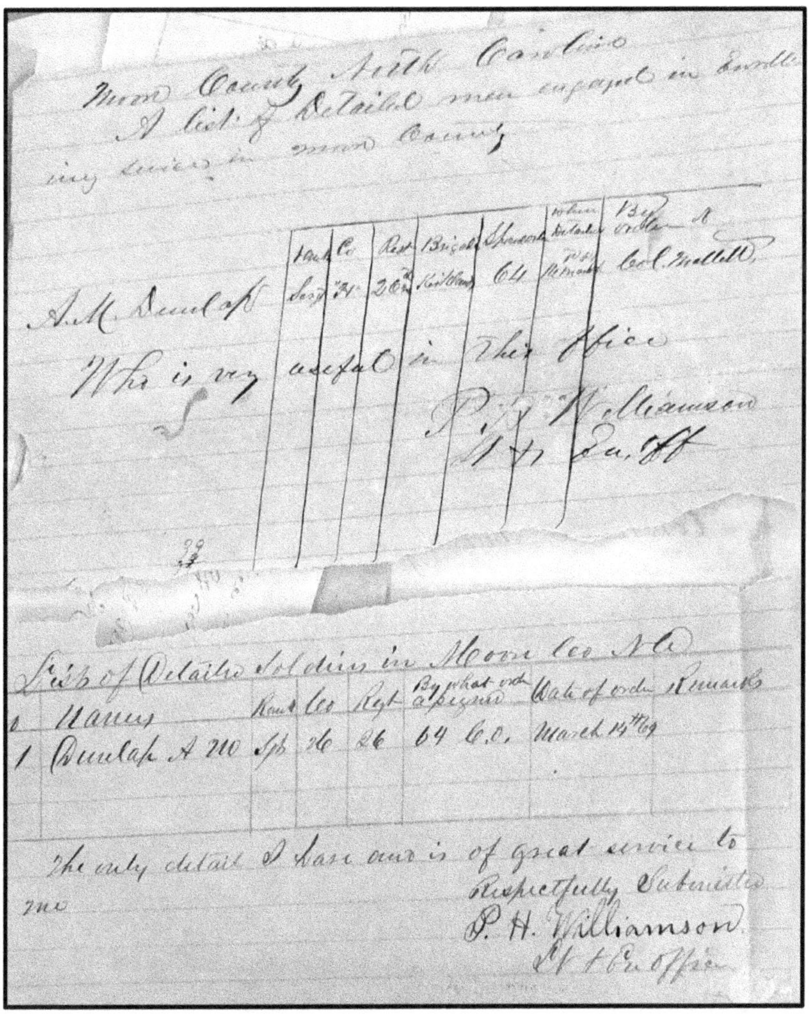

Moore County North Carolina
A list of Detailed men engaged in Enrolling service in Moore County

	Rank	Co	Regt	Brigade	Special	When detailed	By order of
A M Dunlap	Sergt	"H"	26th	Kirkland	64	[illegible]	Col. Mallett

Who is very useful in this office
P. H. Williamson
E. O. Enl Off

List of Detailed Soldiers in Moore Co N C

No	Names	Rank	Co	Regt	By what order assigned	Date of order	Remarks
1	Dunlap A M	Sgt	H	26	64 C.O.	March 14th 64	

The only detail I have now is of great service to me
Respectfully Submitted
P. H. Williamson
E. Enl Officer

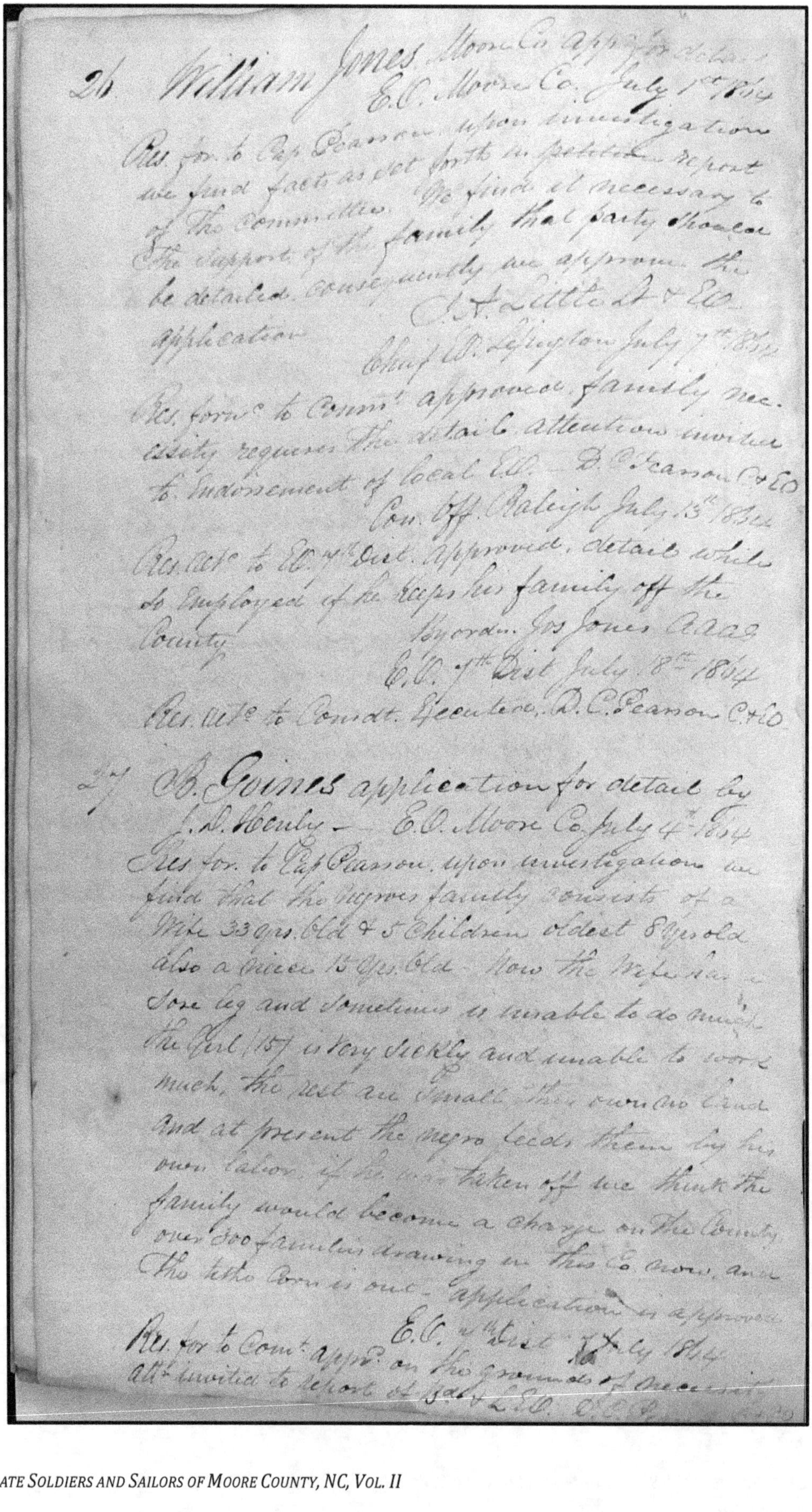

26 William Jones Moore Co. appn for detail
E.O. Moore Co. July 1st 1864
Res. for. to Cap Pearson. upon investigation
we find facts as set forth in petition report
of the Committee. We find it necessary to
the support of the family that party should
be detailed. consequently we approve the
application J. T. Littleton & E.O.
Chief E.O. Lexington July 7th 1864
Res. forwd to Commt approved. family nec-
essity requires the detail. attention invited
to Endorsement of local E.O. — D. C. Pearson C & E.O.
Con. Off. Raleigh July 13th 1864
Res. retd to E.O. 7th Dist. Approved. detail while
so Employed if he keeps his family off the
County. By order Jos Jones AAAG
E.O. 7th Dist July 18th 1864
Res. retd to Comdt. Executed. D. C. Pearson C & E.O.

27 B. Goines application for detail by
J. D. Hemby — E.O. Moore Co. July 4th 1864
Res for. to Cap Pearson, upon investigation we
find that the negroes family consists of a
Wife 33 yrs. old & 5 Children oldest 8 yrs old
also a niece 15 yrs. old. Now the wife has a
sore leg and sometimes is unable to do much
the Girl (15) is very sickly and unable to work
much, the rest are small they own no land
and at present the negro feeds them by his
own labor if he was taken off we think the
family would become a charge on the County
over 500 families drawing in this Co now and
the tithe corn is out — application is approved
E.O. 7th Dist July 16 1864
Res. for to Comt. appd. on the grounds of necessity
attn invited to report of said E.O. [illegible]

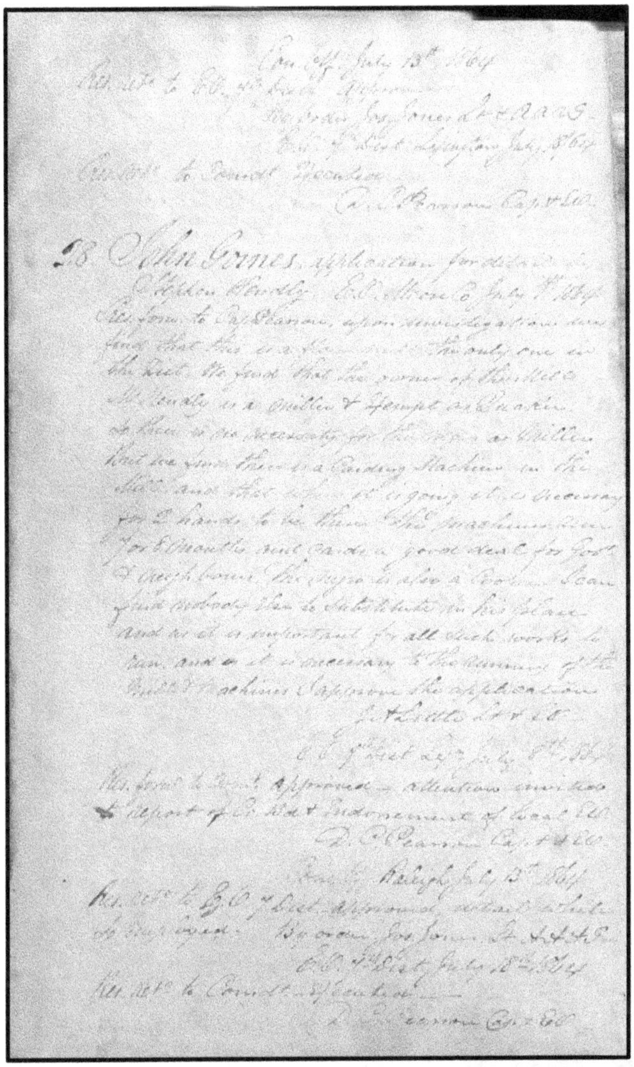

Con. Off. July 13th 1864
Res. wd to E.O. 4th Dist. Approved
By order Jos. Jones Lt & AAAG
E.O. 4th Dist Lexington July 18th 1864
Res. wd to Comdt. Execution
D. C. Pearson Capt & E.O.

28 John Goines application for detail [illegible]
Stephen Hendley. E.O. Moore Co. July 7th 1864
Res. forw. to Capt Pearson, upon investigation we find that this is a [illegible] the only one in the Dist. We find that the owner of the Mill is Hendley is a Miller & Exempt as Quaker so there is no necessity for the negro as Miller but we find there is a Carding Machine in the Mill and that [illegible] it is going it is necessary for 2 hands to be there. The machine [illegible] for 6 months and Cards a good deal for Govt & neighbours the negro is also a [illegible] I can find nobody else to substitute in his place and as it is important for all such works to run, and as it is necessary to the running of the Mill & Machine I approve the application
J. A. Little Lt & E.O.

E.O. 7th Dist [illegible] July 8th 1864
Res. forw. to Comdt. Approved — attention invited to report of [illegible] & Endorsement of Local E.O.
D. C. Pearson Capt & E.O.

Com. Off. Raleigh July 13th 1864
Res. wd to E.O. 7 Dist. Approved. detail [illegible] as [illegible]. By order Jos. Jones Lt & AAAG
E.O. 7th Dist. July 18th 1864
Res. wd to Comdt. Execution
D. C. Pearson Capt & E.O.

John Goins and Stephen Hendley

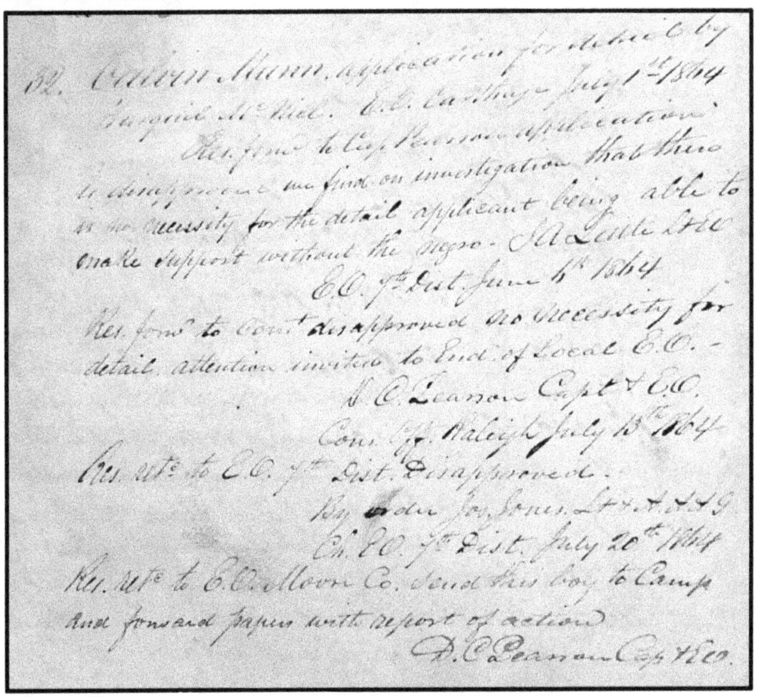

32. Calvin Munn, application for detail by Turquil McNeill. E.O. Carthage July 1st 1864
Res. forw. to Capt Pearson application is disapproved we find on investigation that there is no necessity for the detail applicant being able to make support without the negro. J. A. Little Lt & E.O.
E.O. 7th Dist. June 4th 1864
Res. forw. to Comdt. disapproved no necessity for detail. attention invited to End. of Local E.O. -
D. C. Pearson Capt & E.O.
Com. Off. Raleigh July 13th 1864
Res. wd to E.O. 7th Dist. Disapproved.
By order Jos. Jones Lt & AAAG
Ch. E.O. 7th Dist. July 20th 1864
Res. wd to E.O. Moore Co. Send this boy to Camp and forward papers with report of action
D. C. Pearson Capt & E.O.

Calvin Munn and Turquil McNeill

Ben Tuck

Thomas Goins

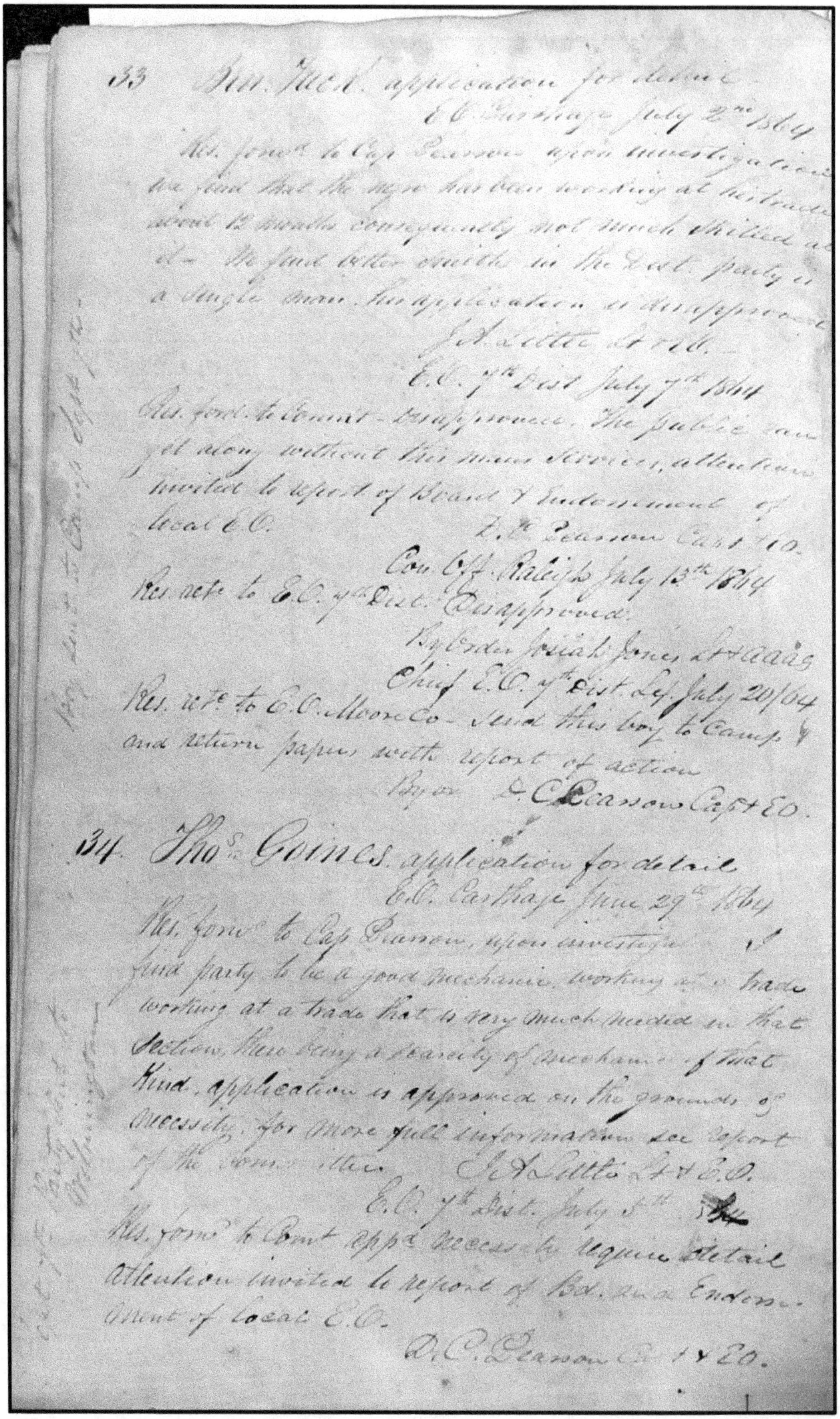

33 Ben Tuck application for detail

E.O. Carthage July 2nd 1864

Res. forwd to Capt Pearson upon investigation we find that the negro has been working at his trade about 12 months consequently not much skilled at it — We find other smiths in the Dist. party is a single man. The application is disapproved.

J.A. Little Lt & E.O.

E.O. 7th Dist July 7th 1864

Res. forwd to Comdt - disapproved. The public can get along without this man's services, attention invited to report of Board & endorsement of local E.O.

D.C. Pearson Capt & E.O.

Con. Off. Raleigh July 13th 1864

Res. retd to E.O. 7th Dist. Disapproved.

By Order Josiah Jones Lt & AAG

Chief E.O. 7th Dist. Ral. July 20/64

Res. retd to E.O. Moore Co - Send this boy to Camp & and return papers with report of action

By or D.C. Pearson Capt & E.O.

34. Thos Goines application for detail

E.O. Carthage June 29th 1864

Res. forwd to Capt Pearson, upon investigation I find party to be a good mechanic, working at a trade working at a trade that is very much needed in that section, there being a scarcity of mechanics of that kind. application is approved on the grounds of necessity. for more full information see report of the committee. J.A. Little Lt & E.O.

E.O. 7th Dist. July 5th 64

Res. forwd to Comdt app'd necessity requires detail attention invited to report of Bd. and Endorsement of local E.O.

D.C. Pearson Capt & E.O.

John Tuck

Ellis Hicks

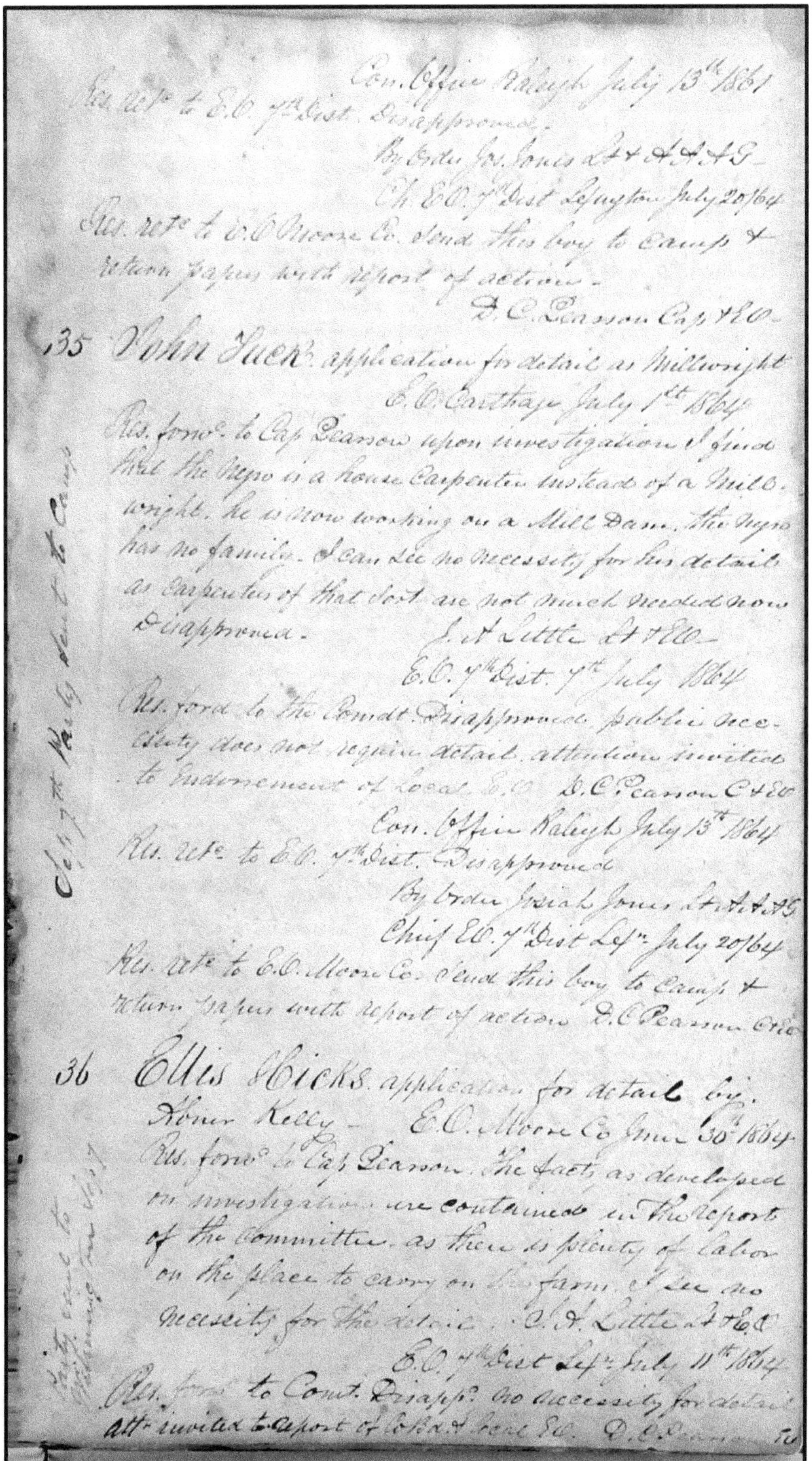

Con. Office Raleigh July 13th 1864
Res. retd to E.O. 7th Dist. Disapproved.
By order Jos. Jones Lt & A.A.G.
Ch. E.O. 7th Dist Lexington July 20/64
Res. retd to E.O. Moore Co. Send this boy to camp & return papers with report of action.
D.C. Pearson Cap & E.O.

35 John Tuck application for detail as Millwright
E.O. Carthage July 1st 1864
Res. forwd to Cap Pearson upon investigation I find that the Negro is a house Carpenter instead of a Mill-wright. he is now working on a Mill Dam. the Negro has no family. I can see no necessity for his detail as Carpenters of that sort are not much needed now Disapproved.
J. A. Little Lt & EO
E.O. 7th Dist. 7th July 1864
Res. forwd to the Comdt Disapproved. public necessity does not require detail. attention invited to Endorsement of Local E.O. D.C. Pearson C & EO
Con. Office Raleigh July 13th 1864
Res. retd to E.O. 7th Dist. Disapproved
By order Josiah Jones Lt & A.A.G.
Chief EO. 7th Dist Lexn. July 20/64
Res. retd to E.O. Moore Co. Send this boy to Camp & return papers with report of action D.C. Pearson C & EO

Copy 7th Kerly sent to Camp

36 Ellis Hicks application for detail by Abner Kelly. E.O. Moore Co June 30th 1864
Res. forwd to Cap. Pearson. The facts as developed on investigation are contained in the Report of the Committee. as there is plenty of labor on the place to carry on the farm. I see no necessity for the detail. J. A. Little Lt & EO
E.O. 7th Dist Lexn. July 11th 1864
Res. forwd to Comt. Disapp. no necessity for detail att. invited to Report of Comm & Local EO. D.C. [illegible]

[illegible]

Ellis Hicks, contd.

William Tuck

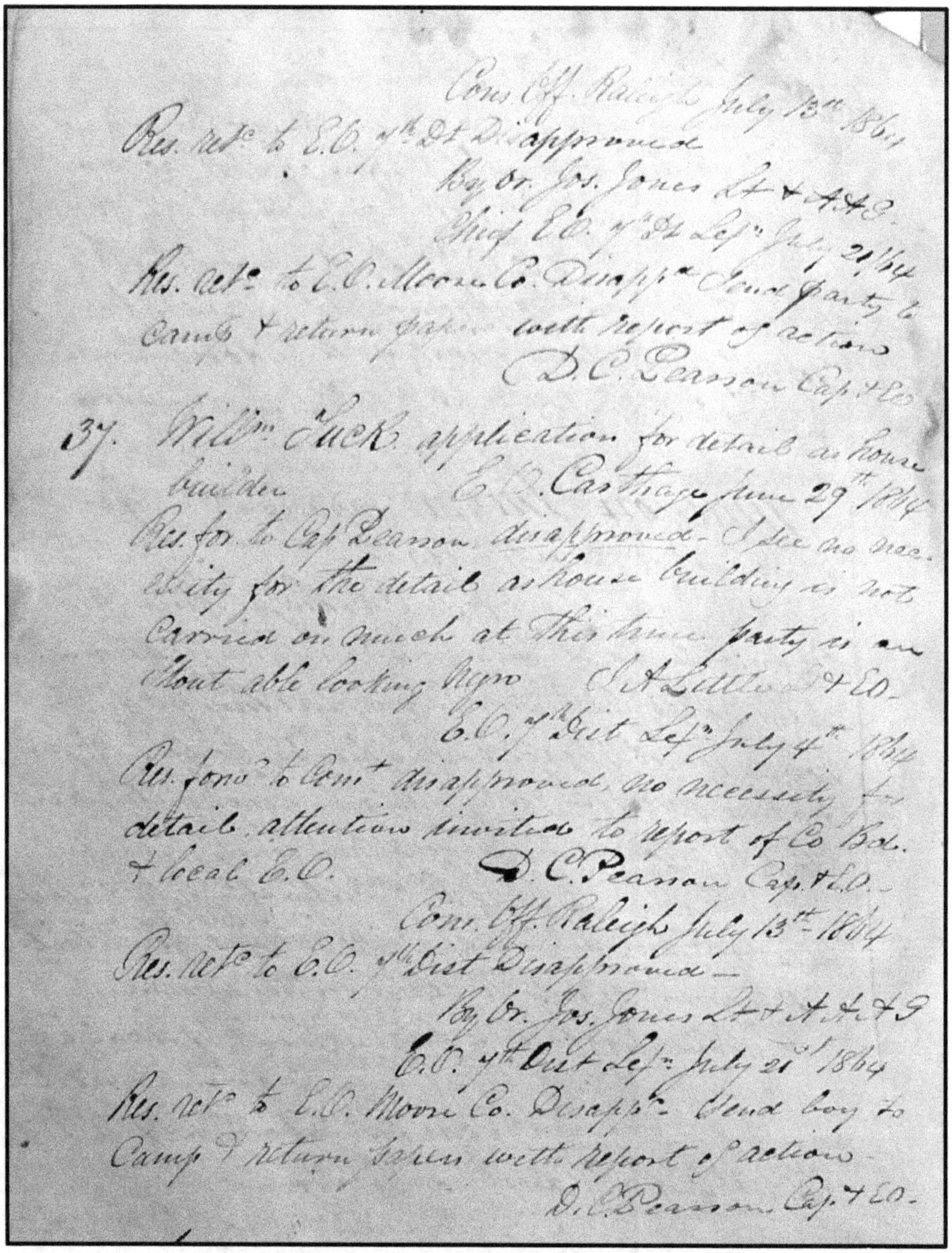

Com. Off. Raleigh July 13th 1864
Res. retd to E.O. 4th Dt Disapproved
By Or. Jos. Jones Lt & A.A.G.
Chief E.O. 4th Dt Lefr July 21/64
Res. retd to E.O. Moore Co. Disappd Send party to
Camp & return paper with report of action
D.C. Pearson Cap. & E.O.

37. Willm Tuck application for detail as house
builder E.O. Carthage June 29th 1864
Res. fowd to Capt Pearson disapproved - I see no nec-
essity for the detail as house building is not
carried on much at this time party is an
stout able looking negro J.A. Little Lt & E.O.
E.O. 4th Dist Lefr July 4th 1864
Res. fowd to Comt disapproved, no necessity for
detail attention invited to report of Co Bd.
& local E.O. D.C. Pearson Cap. & E.O.
Com. Off. Raleigh July 13th 1864
Res. retd to E.O. 4th Dist Disapproved -
By Or. Jos. Jones Lt & A.A.G.
E.O. 4th Dist Lefr July 21st 1864
Res. retd to E.O. Moore Co. Disappd - Send boy to
Camp & return papers with report of action -
D.C. Pearson Cap. & E.O.

William Thigpen

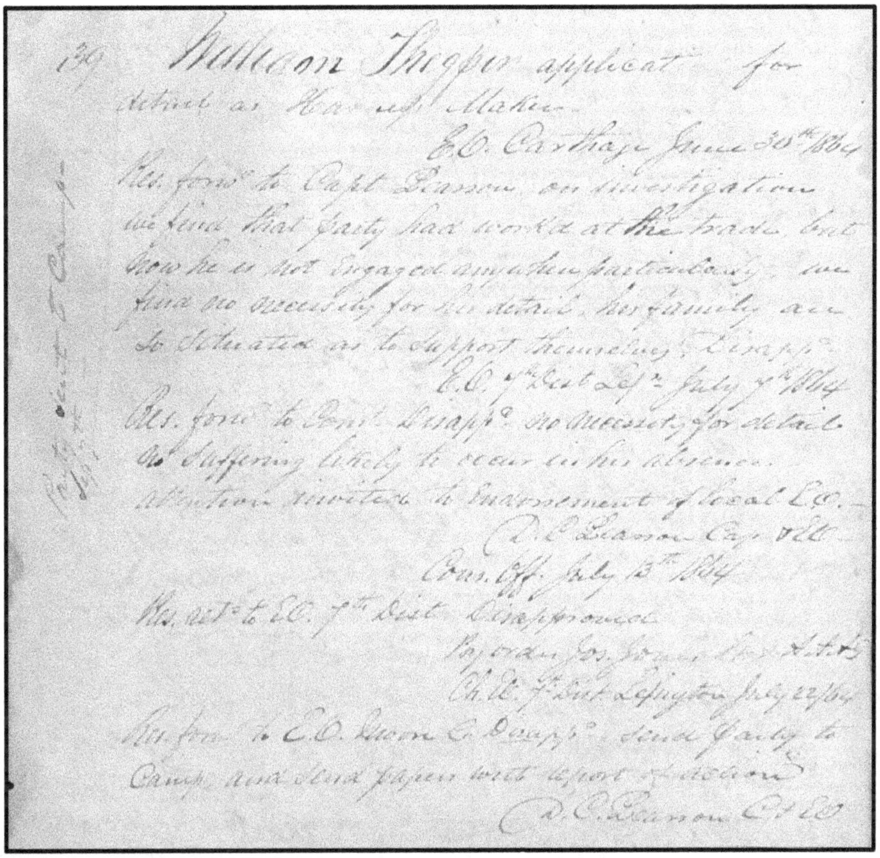

39 William Thigpen applicat for
detail as Harness Maker
E.O. Carthage June 30th 1864
Res. forwd to Capt Pearson, on investigation
we find that party had worked at the trade but
now he is not engaged anywhere particularly, we
find no necessity for his detail, his family are
so situated as to support themselves, Disappd
E.O. 7th Dist Lexn July 7th 1864
Res. forwd to Comdt. Disappd no necessity for detail
no suffering likely to occur in his absence.
Attention invited to endorsement of local E.O.
D. C. Pearson Capt & EO
Com. Off. July 13th 1864
Res. retd to E.O. 7th Dist Disapproved
By order Jos. Jones Maj & A.A.G.
Ch. E. 7th Dist Lexington July 22/64
Res. forwd to E.O. Moore Co. Disappd Send party to
Camp and send papers with report of action
D. C. Pearson Capt & EO

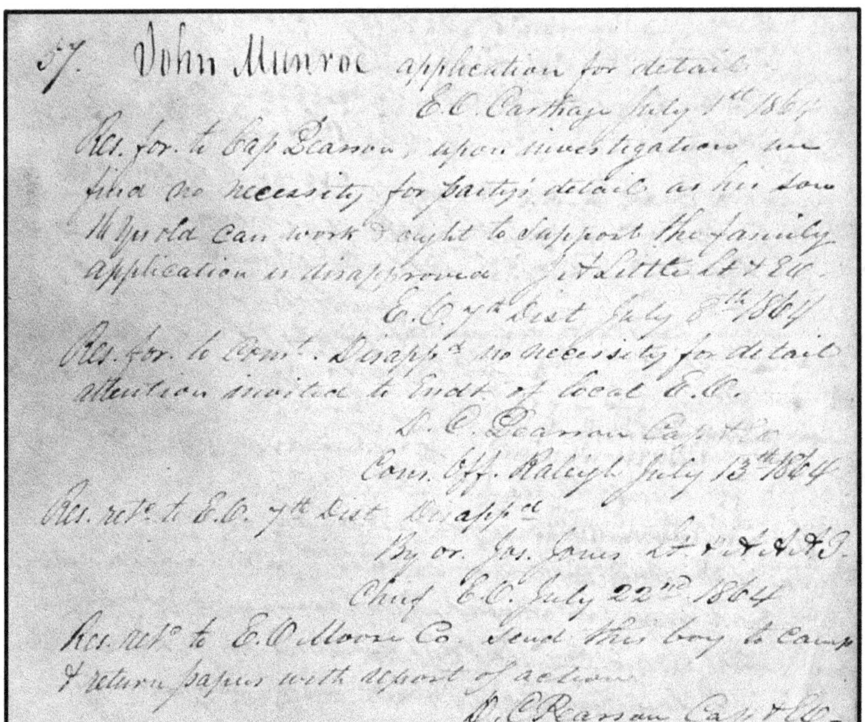

57. John Munroe application for detail
E.O. Carthage July 1st 1864
Res. for. to Cap Pearson, upon investigation we
find no necessity for party's detail as his son
14 yrs old can work & ought to support the family
application is disapproved J. A. Little Lt & EO
E.O. 7th Dist July 8th 1864
Res. for. to Comt. Disappd no necessity for detail
attention invited to Endt of local E.O.
D. C. Pearson Capt & EO
Com. Off. Raleigh July 13th 1864
Res. retd to E.O. 7th Dist Disappd
By or. Jas. Jones Lt & A A A G
Chief E.O. July 22nd 1864
Res. retd to E.O. Moore Co. Send this boy to camp
& return papers with report of action
D. C. Pearson Cap & EO

John Munroe

Confederate Petitions for Amnesty

The following individuals from Moore County requested pardons from the United States government for their service as government officials during the Confederacy.

John McF. Baker [568]

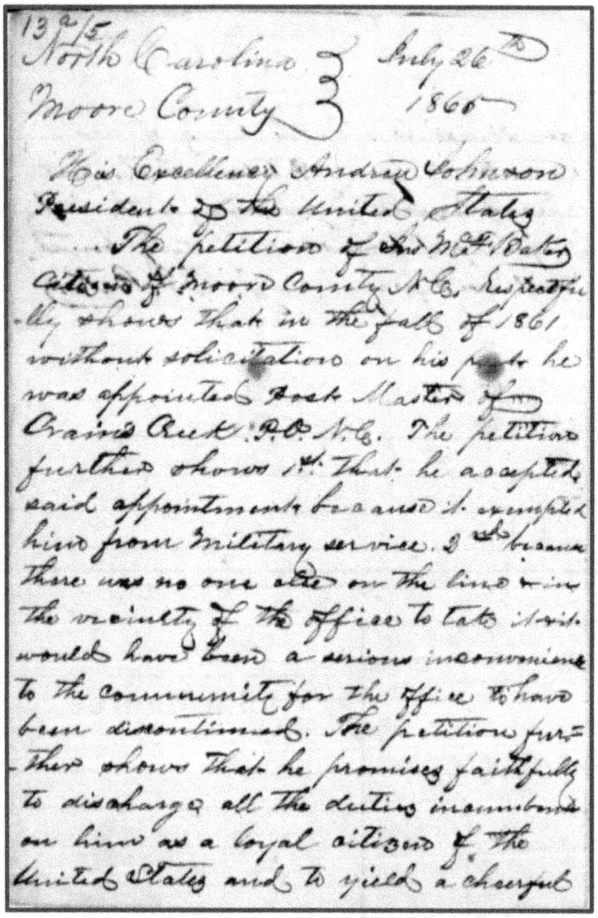

13a/15
North Carolina } July 26th
Moore County } 1865

His Excellency Andrew Johnson
President of the United States
The petition of Jno McF Baker citizen of Moore County N.C. respectfully shows that in the fall of 1861 without solicitation on his part he was appointed Post Master of Crain's Creek P.O. N.C. The petition further shows 1st That he accepted said appointment because it exempted him from military service. 2nd because there was no one else on the line & in the vicinity of the office to take it & it would have been a serious inconvenience to the community for the office to have been discontinued. The petition further shows that he promises faithfully to discharge all the duties incumbent on him as a loyal citizen of the United States and to yield a cheerful

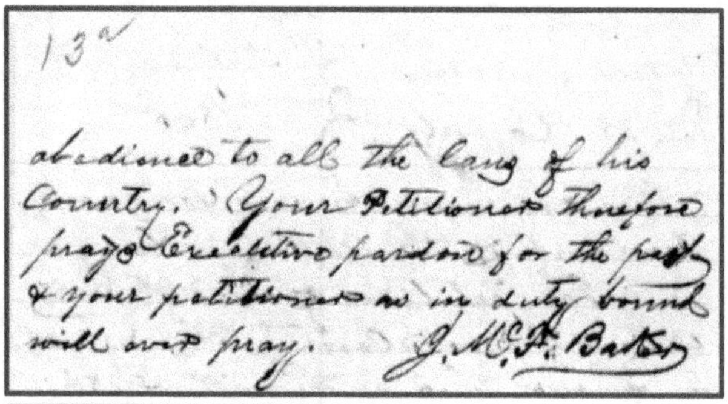

13a

obedience to all the laws of his Country. Your Petitioner therefore prays Executive pardon for the past & your petitioner as in duty bound will ever pray. J. McF. Baker

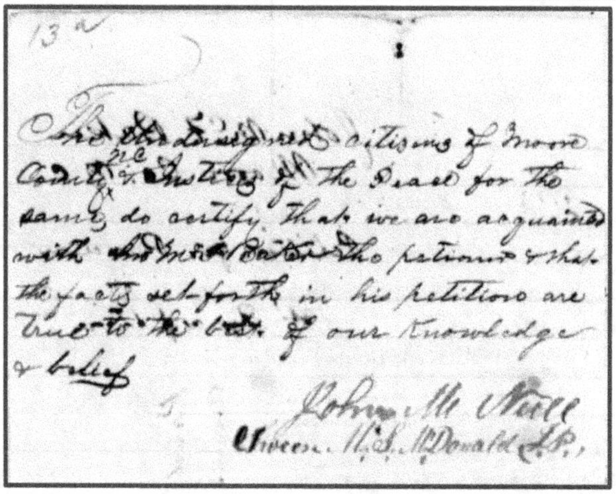

13a

The undersigned citizens of Moore County N.C. & Justices of the Peace for the same, do certify that we are acquainted with Jno McF Baker the petitioner & that the facts set forth in his petition are true to the best of our knowledge & belief

John McNeill
[illegible] McDonald J.P.

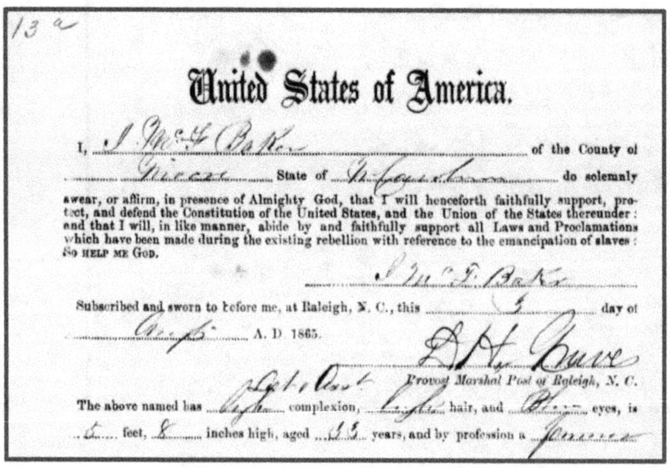

13a

United States of America.

I, J. McF Baker of the County of Moore State of N. Carolina do solemnly swear, or affirm, in presence of Almighty God, that I will henceforth faithfully support, protect, and defend the Constitution of the United States, and the Union of the States thereunder: and that I will, in like manner, abide by and faithfully support all Laws and Proclamations which have been made during the existing rebellion with reference to the emancipation of slaves: So HELP ME GOD.

J McF Baker

Subscribed and sworn to before me, at Raleigh, N. C., this 3 day of Aug A. D. 1865.

D. H. [illegible]
Capt & Asst Provost Marshal Post of Raleigh, N. C.

The above named has light complexion, light hair, and blue eyes, is 5 feet, 8 inches high, aged 33 years, and by profession a farmer

William C. Campbell [569]

130/3

Watsons Bridge N.C.
July 4th 1865

To His Excellency Andrew Johnson
President of the U. S.

your petitioner Wm C. Campbell humbly show that he accepted the Office of Post Master at Watsons Bridge Moore County State of N.C. under the so called Confederate Government in Sep. 1863 for his own Convenience and that of a few neighbours. now respectfully ask to be pardoned for the same and allowed to take the oath of allegiance to the U States. your obt servt.

Wm C. Campbell

We the undersigned citizens of said County have been acquainted with your petitioner for many years, and do hereby certify that he is a good and loyal citizen and was always opposed to secession

G. W. Hughes
W. D. Harrington

130

United States of America.

I, William C. Campbell of the County of Moore State of North Carolina do solemnly swear, or affirm, in presence of Almighty God, that I will henceforth faithfully support, protect, and defend the Constitution of the United States, and the Union of the States thereunder; and that I will, in like manner, abide by and faithfully support all Laws and Proclamations which have been made during the existing rebellion with reference to the emancipation of slaves. So help me God.

W. C. Campbell

Subscribed and sworn to before me, at Raleigh, N. C., this 7th day of July A. D. 1865.

[illegible]
Provost Marshal Post of Raleigh, N. C.

The above named has fair complexion, dk. hair, and blue eyes, is 5 feet, 10 inches high, aged 37 years, and by profession a farmer

J.L. Caveness 570

157
North Carolina
Moore County

November 7th 1865

To His Excellency, Andrew Johnson,
President of the United States

The petition of J. L. Caveness, of Moore County North Carolina, aged fifty three years, and by Occupation a Miller, would respectfully show, that he was over age, and did not volunteer, or take any part in the war, had one son in the service, sent him some clothing and something to eat: that he was appointed Post Master, at Brownsville, Mi, about the commencement of the war, and continued to be postmaster untill May 1862, when the Office was vacated in consequence of the Advance of the U. S. Army, and your petitioner returned to North Carolina. In thus holding the office of Post Master your petitioner is informed that his case comes under the 1st Clause in the Amnesty Proclamation of May 29th 1865

Your petitioner would further show that he has taken the Amnesty Oath as prescribed by the Presidents Proclamation of May 29th 1865, that he intends to observe the same a copy of which is hereunto appended

Your petitioner therefore prays for Executive Clemmency.

J. L. Caveness

We the subscribers are acquainted with the Petitioner J. L. Caveness and know him to be a respectable citizen, and believe the facts set forth in his petition to be true, and recommend that his pardon be granted

A. R. McDonald
S. C. Barrett

157

I J L Caveness of Moore County, State of North Carolina, do solemly swear or affirm in presence of Almighty God, that I will henceforward faithfully support, protect & defend the Constitution of the United States, & the Union of the States thereunder; and that I will in like manner abide by & faithfully support all laws & proclamations which have been made during the existance rebellion with referance to the emancipation of Slaves. So help me God,

J. L. Caveness

Sworn and subscribed to this 9th day of Nov A D 1865 — before

S. C. Barrett J.P.

George W. Clark [571]

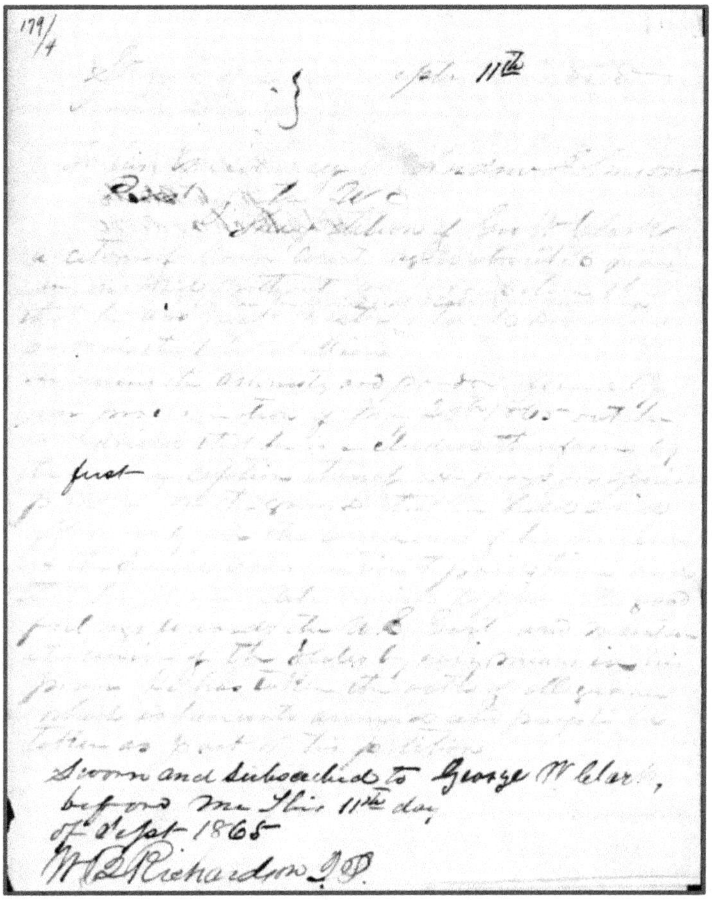

179/4

Sept 11th

first

Sworn and subscribed to George W Clark, before me this 11th day of Sept 1865

W B Richardson J.P.

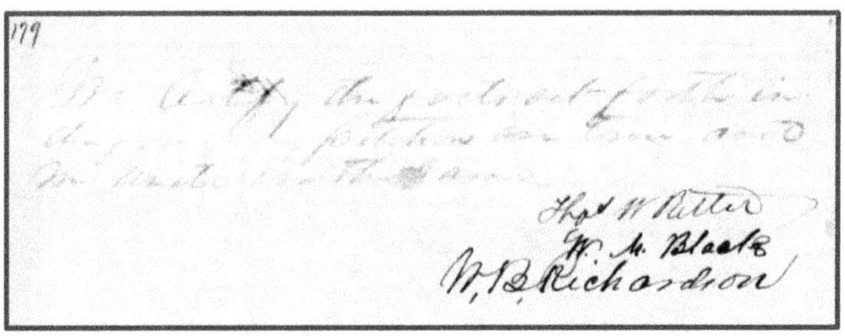

179

Thos W Ritter

W. M. Black

W B Richardson

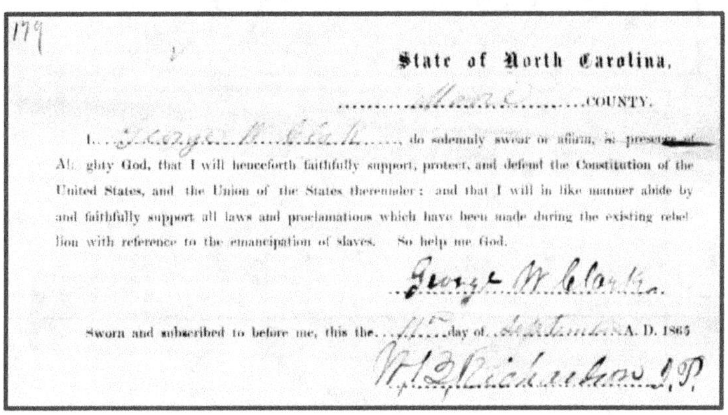

179

State of North Carolina,

Moore COUNTY.

I, George W Clark, do solemnly swear or affirm, in presence of Almighty God, that I will henceforth faithfully support, protect, and defend the Constitution of the United States, and the Union of the States thereunder; and that I will in like manner abide by and faithfully support all laws and proclamations which have been made during the existing rebellion with reference to the emancipation of slaves. So help me God.

George W Clark

Sworn and subscribed to before me, this the 11th day of September A. D. 1865

W B Richardson J.P.

John B. Cole [572]

237

4 North Carolina }
Moore County } To His Excellency the President of the United States through Governor W. W. Holden —

The Petition of John B. Cole of said County would respectfully show, that he was Post Master under the Confederate States; that he had been Post Master under the United States and continued to discharge the duties of the Office under the Confederate Government, for the benefit of his neighbours. that it was of service to him in keeping him out of the military service of the State:

That he was opposed to secession, and voted against a Convention in 1861. and now desires to enjoy the protection of the United States Government, and live under its laws: To this end he prays for Executive Clemency, that he may be pardoned, and permitted to take the oath of amnesty — And your petitioner as in duty bound will ever pray &c.

Sworn & subscribed to before me this 17th July 1865 — John B Cole

W. B. Richardson J.P.

237

North Carolina }
Moore County } We the undersigned citizens of said County being well acquainted with John B. Cole the petitioner certify that the facts set forth in his petition we believe to be true and we are disinterested therein.

W. B. Richardson
A. R. McDonald

237

United States of America.

I, John B Cole of the County of Moore State of N C do solemnly swear, or affirm, in presence of Almighty God, that I will henceforth faithfully support, protect, and defend the Constitution of the United States, and the Union of the States thereunder; and that I will, in like manner, abide by and faithfully support all Laws and Proclamations which have been made during the existing rebellion with reference to the emancipation of slaves: So help me God.

John B Cole

Subscribed and sworn to before me, at Raleigh, N. C., this 3 day of August A. D. 1865.

R. D. Graves
1st Lt & Capt, Provost Marshal Post of Raleigh, N. C.

The above named has dark complexion, dark hair, and dark eyes, is 6 feet, — inches high, aged 18 years, and by profession a farmer

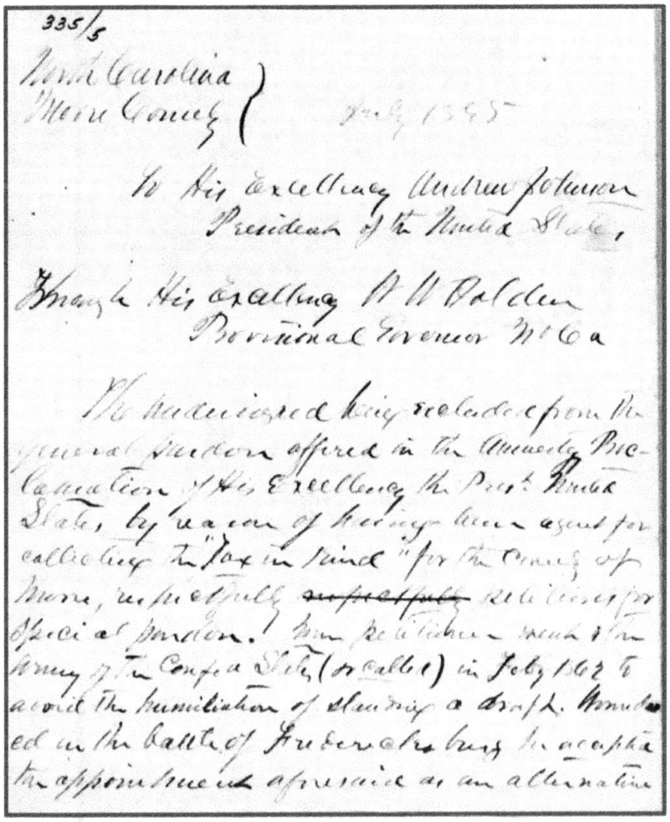

335/5

North Carolina
Moore County

July 1865

To His Excellency Andrew Johnson
President of the United States,

Through His Excellency W W Holden
Provisional Governor N C a

The undersigned being excluded from the general pardon offered in the Amnesty Proclamation of His Excellency the Prest. United States, by reason of having been agent for collecting the "Tax in kind" for the County of Moore, respectfully ~~respectfully~~ petitions for special pardon. Your petitioner went to the Army of the Confed States (so called) in Feby 1862 to avoid the humiliation of standing a draft. Wounded in the battle of Fredericksburg he accepted the appointment aforesaid as an alternative

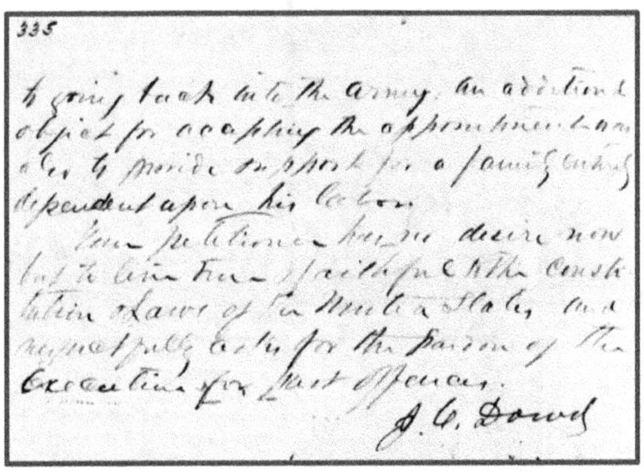

335

to going back into the army. An additional object for accepting the appointment was also to provide support for a family entirely dependent upon his labor.

Your petitioner has no desire now but to live true & faithful to the Constitution & Laws of the United States, and respectfully asks for the pardon of the Executive for past offences.

J. C. Dowd

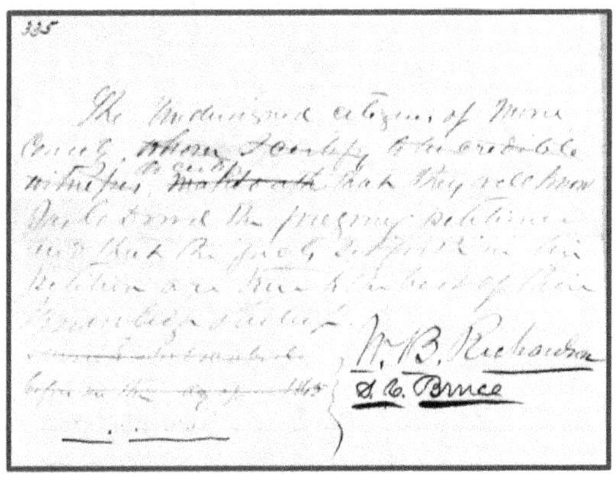

335

The undersigned citizens of Moore County ~~whom I certify to be credible~~ witnesses ~~make oath~~ that they well know Jas. C. Dowd the foregoing petitioner and that the facts set forth in the petition are true to the best of their knowledge & belief.

W. B. Richardson
A. C. Bruce

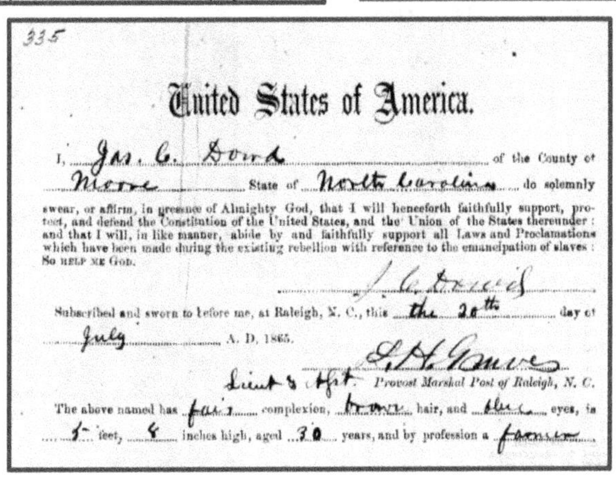

335

United States of America.

I, Jas. C. Dowd of the County of Moore State of North Carolina do solemnly swear, or affirm, in presence of Almighty God, that I will henceforth faithfully support, protect, and defend the Constitution of the United States, and the Union of the States thereunder: and that I will, in like manner, abide by and faithfully support all Laws and Proclamations which have been made during the existing rebellion with reference to the emancipation of slaves: So help me God.

J. C. Dowd

Subscribed and sworn to before me, at Raleigh, N. C., this the 20th day of July A. D. 1865.

L. H. Graves
Lieut & Adjt. Provost Marshal Post of Raleigh, N. C.

The above named has fair complexion, brown hair, and blue eyes, is 5 feet, 8 inches high, aged 30 years, and by profession a farmer

Edmund Garner [574]

463/4

State of North Carolina
Moore County

To His Excellency Andrew Johnson
President of the U States

The Petition of Edmond Garner of said County and State respectfully Sheweth that he is Forty Years of Age and by Occupation a Miller and that he has been informed that he belongs to One of the excepted Classes of the President's Amnesty Proclamation Say Class No 1. That your Petitioner acted as Post Master at Prospect, NC for about 12 Months say fall 1863 till Fall 1864 that your Petitioner was a Union man until the State identified her self with the So Called Confederacy and then he accepted the appointment of Post Master thinking thereby that it would Keep him out of the army that he done nothing for or against the U.S until he was Conscribed in the Month of Oct 1864 and he stayed in Service until March 1865 at which time he got disgusted with the So Called Confederacy and Come home, and that your Petitioner was always willing to have a just Compromise made between the two Sections and that without Shedding blood And further he has taken the Amnesty Oath as prescribed by the President as aforesaid and that his intention is to Keep and Observe

463

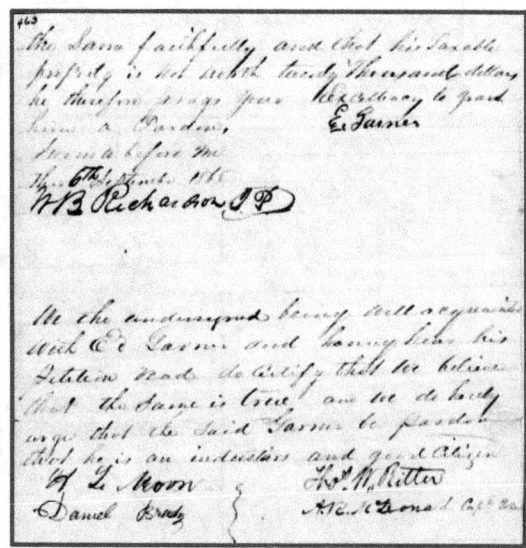

the same faithfully and that his Taxable property is not worth twenty Thousand dollars he therefore prays your Excellency to grant him a Pardon, E. Garner

Sworn to before me
this 6th September 1865
W B Richardson J P

We the undersigned being well acquainted with E. Garner and having heard his Petition read do Certify that we believe that the same is true and we do hereby urge that the said Garner be pardoned that he is an industrious and good Citizen

J L Moore — Jno W. Ritter
Daniel Brady — A. R. McDonald Capt [illegible]

463

State of North Carolina.

Moore COUNTY.

I, Edmund Garner do solemnly swear or affirm, in presence of Almighty God, that I will henceforth faithfully support, protect, and defend the Constitution of the United States, and the Union of the States thereunder; and that I will in like manner abide by and faithfully support all laws and proclamations which have been made during the existing rebellion with reference to the emancipation of slaves. So help me God.

E. Garner

Sworn and subscribed to before me, this the 6th day of Sept A. D. 1865

W B Richardson J P Clk

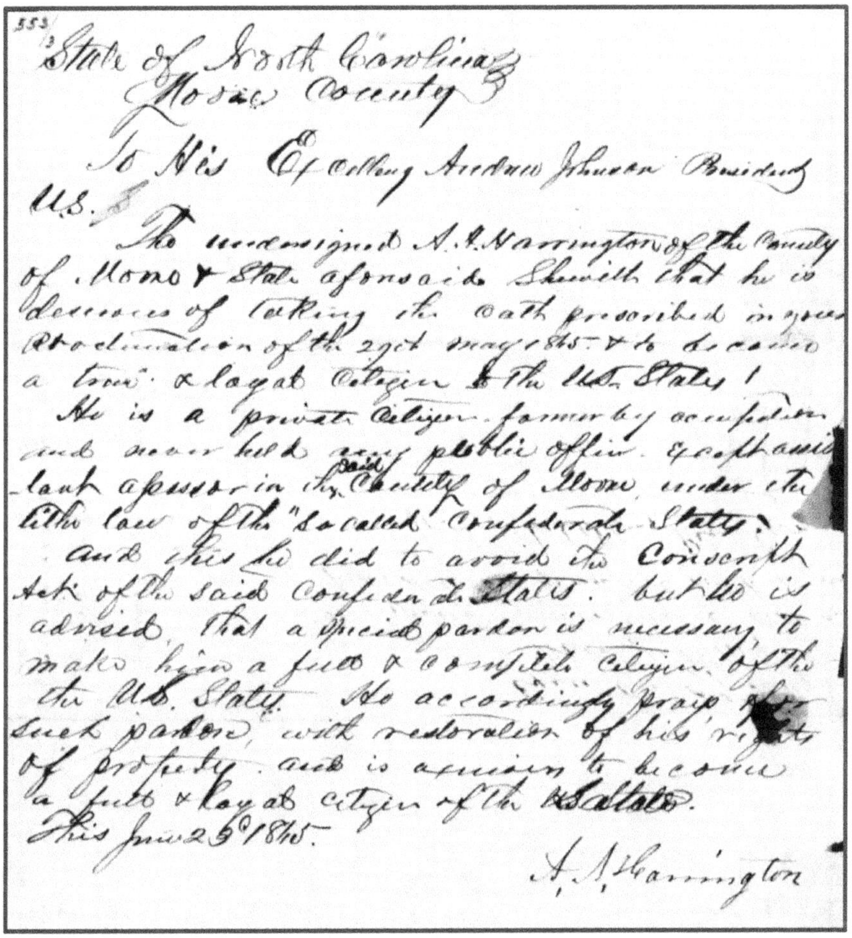
553

State of North Carolina
Moore County

To His Excellency Andrew Johnson President U.S.

The undersigned A.A. Harrington of the County of Moore & State aforesaid Sheweth that he is desirous of taking the oath prescribed in your Proclamation of the 29th May 1865 & to become a true & loyal Citizen of the U.S. States!

He is a private citizen farmer by occupation and never held any public office Except assistant assessor in the said County of Moore under the tithe law of the "so called Confederate States".

and this he did to avoid the Conscript Act of the said Confederate States. but he is advised that a special pardon is necessary to make him a full & complete citizen of the the U.S. States. He accordingly prays for such pardon, with restoration of his rights of property. and is anxious to become a full & loyal citizen of the U States.

This June 25th 1865.

A.A. Harrington

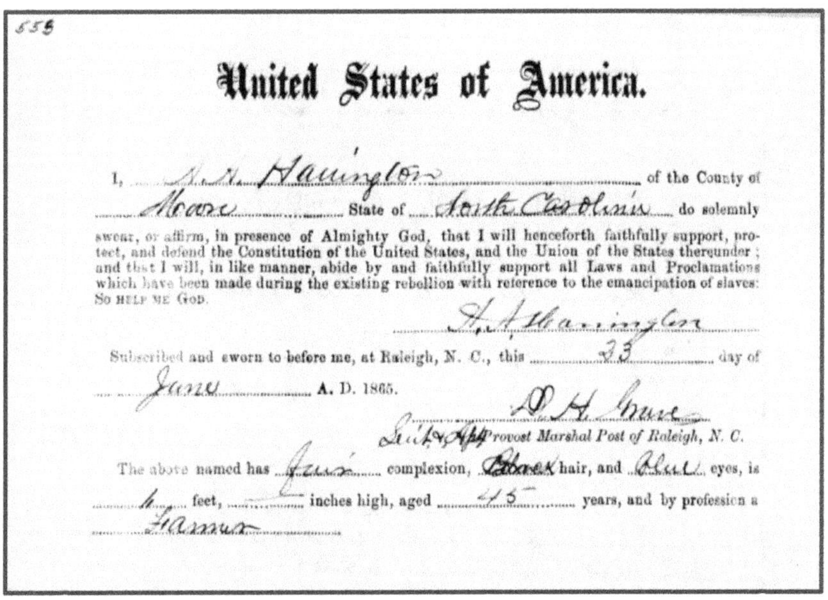
558

United States of America.

I, A. A. Harington of the County of Moore State of North Carolina do solemnly swear, or affirm, in presence of Almighty God, that I will henceforth faithfully support, protect, and defend the Constitution of the United States, and the Union of the States thereunder; and that I will, in like manner, abide by and faithfully support all Laws and Proclamations which have been made during the existing rebellion with reference to the emancipation of slaves: So help me God.

A.A. Harrington

Subscribed and sworn to before me, at Raleigh, N. C., this 23 day of June A. D. 1865.

D. H. Grove
Lieut & Asst Provost Marshal Post of Raleigh, N. C.

The above named has fair complexion, Black hair, and Blue eyes, is 6 feet, — inches high, aged 45 years, and by profession a Farmer

John C. Jackson [576]

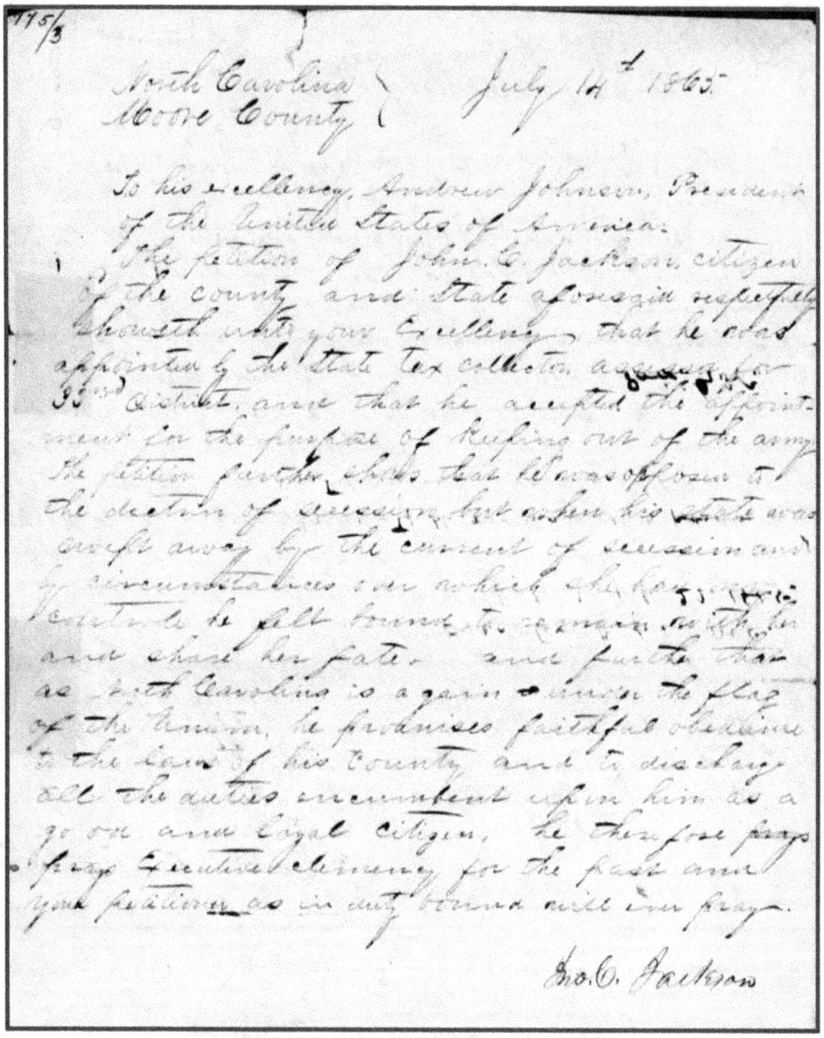

775/3

North Carolina } July 14th 1865
Moore County }

To his excellency, Andrew Johnson, President of the United States of America.

The petition of John C. Jackson citizen of the county and State aforesaid respectfully showeth unto your Excellency that he was appointed by the State tax collector assessor for 33rd district, and that he accepted the appointment for the purpose of keeping out of the army the petitioner further shows that he was opposed to the doctrine of secession but when his state was swept away by the current of secession and by circumstances over which he had no control he felt bound to remain with her and share her fate and further that as North Carolina is again under the flag of the Union, he promises faithful obedience to the laws of his county and to discharge all the duties incumbent upon him as a good and loyal citizen, he therefore prays prays Executive clemency for the past and your petitioner as in duty bound will ever pray.

Jno. C. Jackson

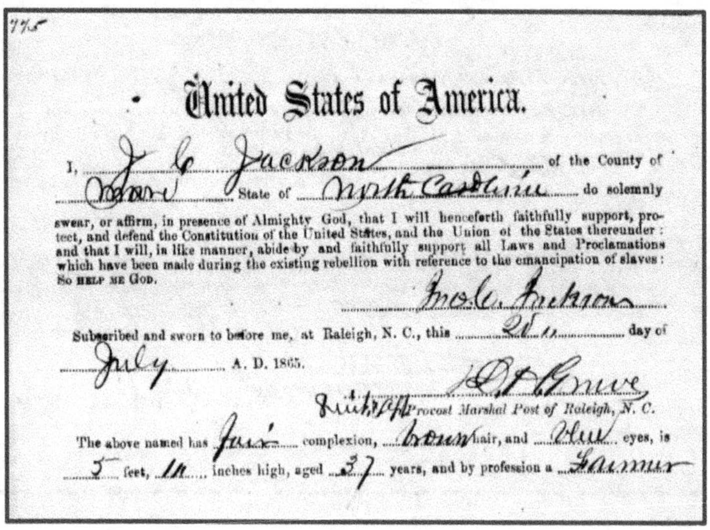

775

United States of America.

I, J. C. Jackson of the County of Moore State of North Carolina do solemnly swear, or affirm, in presence of Almighty God, that I will henceforth faithfully support, protect, and defend the Constitution of the United States, and the Union of the States thereunder: and that I will, in like manner, abide by and faithfully support all Laws and Proclamations which have been made during the existing rebellion with reference to the emancipation of slaves: So help me God.

Jno. C. Jackson

Subscribed and sworn to before me, at Raleigh, N. C., this 20th day of July A. D. 1865.

H. D. Grove
Lieut. & Provost Marshal Post of Raleigh, N. C.

The above named has fair complexion, brown hair, and blue eyes, is 5 feet, 10 inches high, aged 37 years, and by profession a Farmer

W.T. Jenkins [577]

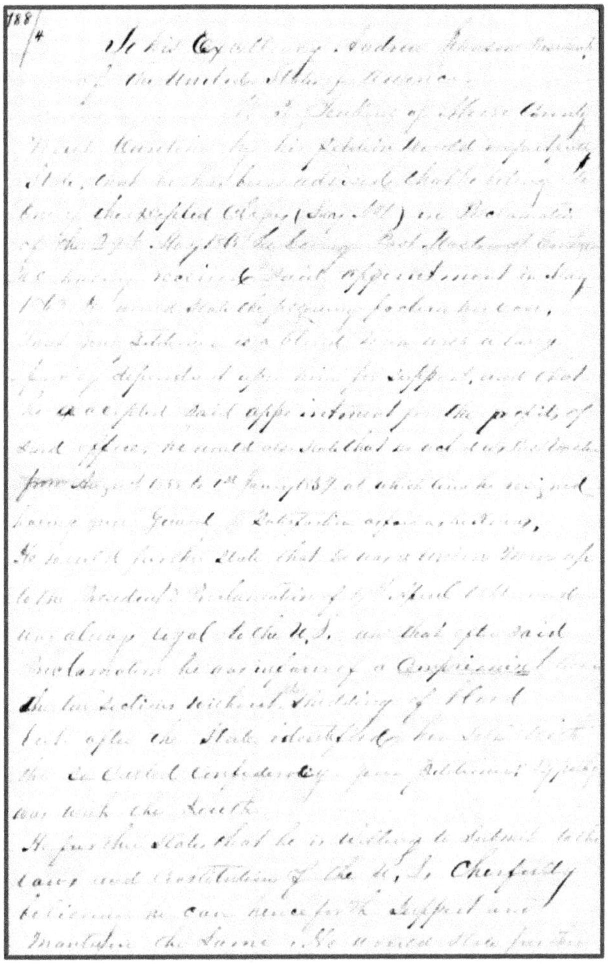

788

To his Excellency Andrew Johnson President of the United States of America

W. T. Jenkins of Moore County North Carolina by his petition would respectfully state, that he has been advised that [illegible]

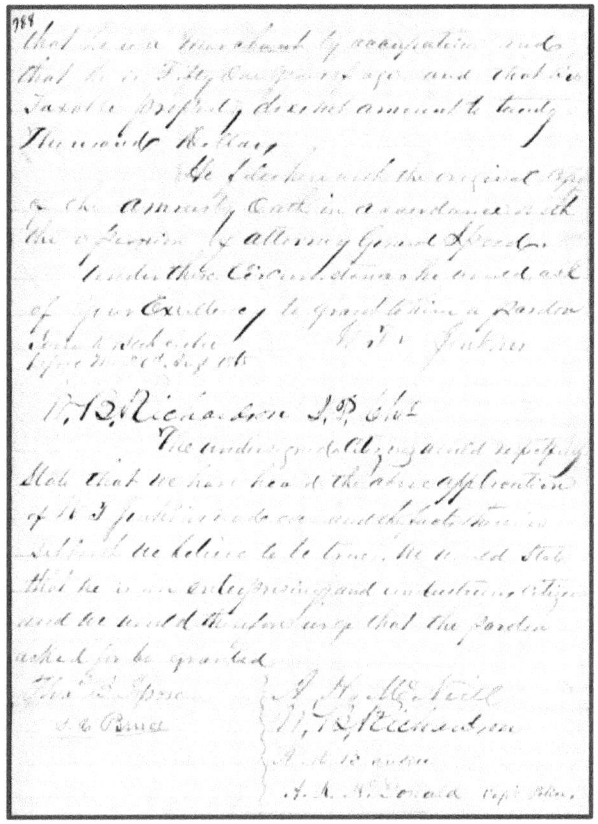

788

that he is a Merchant by occupation and that he is Fifty One years of age and that his Taxable property does not amount to twenty Thousand Dollars

He [illegible] here with the original copy of the amnesty Oath in accordance with the decision of attorney General Speed.

Under these circumstances he would ask of your Excellency to grant to him a pardon

W. T. Jenkins

W. B. Richardson J.P. Chl

The undersigned citizens would respectfully state that we have read the above application of W T Jenkins [illegible] and the facts therein set forth we believe to be true. We would state that he is an enterprising and industrious citizen and we would therefore urge that the pardon asked for be granted

A. H. McNeill
W. B. Richardson
[illegible]
A. K. McDonald [illegible]

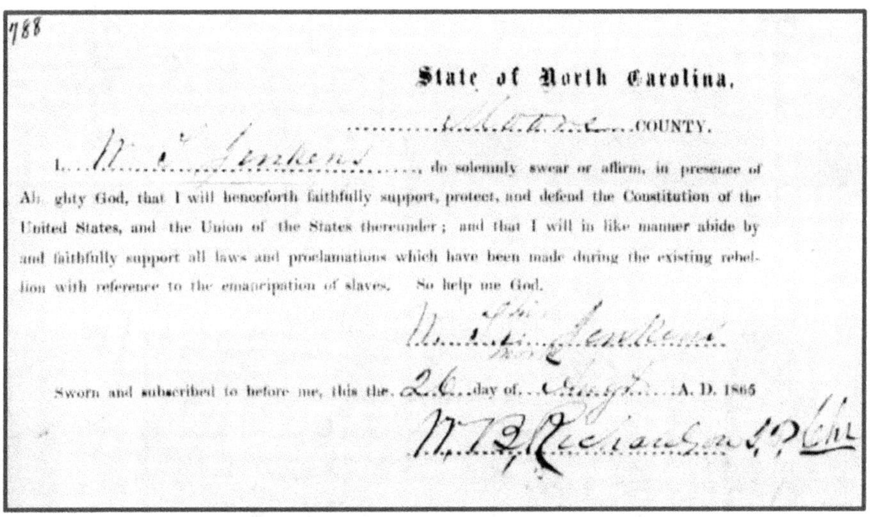

788

State of North Carolina.

..........Moore..........COUNTY.

I, W. T. Jenkins, do solemnly swear or affirm, in presence of Almighty God, that I will henceforth faithfully support, protect, and defend the Constitution of the United States, and the Union of the States thereunder; and that I will in like manner abide by and faithfully support all laws and proclamations which have been made during the existing rebellion with reference to the emancipation of slaves. So help me God.

W. T. Jenkins

Sworn and subscribed to before me, this the 26 day of Aug A. D. 1865

W. B. Richardson J.P. Chl

Alexander Kelly 578

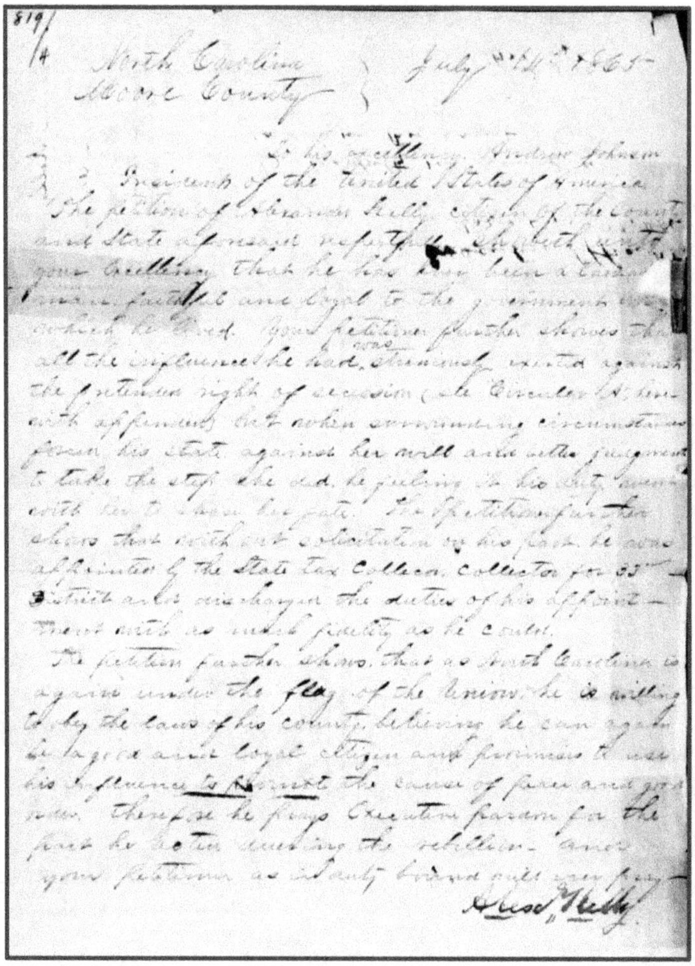

819/4

North Carolina } July 14th 1865
Moore County }

To his excellency Andrew Johnson
President of the United States of America
The petition of Alexander Kelly citizen of the county and State aforesaid respectfully sheweth unto your Excellency that he has ever been a law abiding faithful and loyal to the government under which he lived. Your petitioner further shows that all the influence he had, was strenuously exerted against the pretended right of secession (see Circular A, herewith appended) but when surrounding circumstances forced his state against her will and better judgment to take the step she did, he feeling it his duty went with her to share her fate. The petitioner further shows that with out solicitation on his part he was appointed by the State tax Collector, collector for 33rd District and discharged the duties of his appointment with as much fidelity as he could.
The petition further shows that as North Carolina is again under the flag of the Union he is willing to obey the laws of his county, believing he can again be a good and loyal citizen and promises to use his influence to promote the cause of peace and good order. Therefore he prays Executive pardon for the part he acted during the rebellion. And your petitioner as in duty bound will ever pray.

Alexd. Kelly

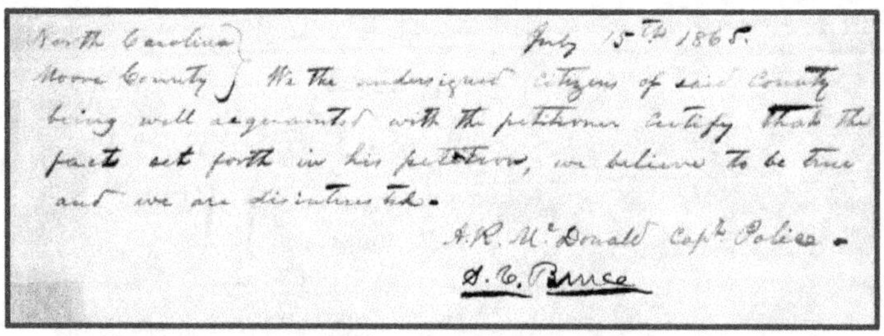

North Carolina } July 15th 1865
Moore County } We the undersigned citizens of said County being well acquainted with the petitioner certify that the facts set forth in his petition, we believe to be true and we are disinterested.

A.R. McDonald Capt. Police
A. C. Bruce

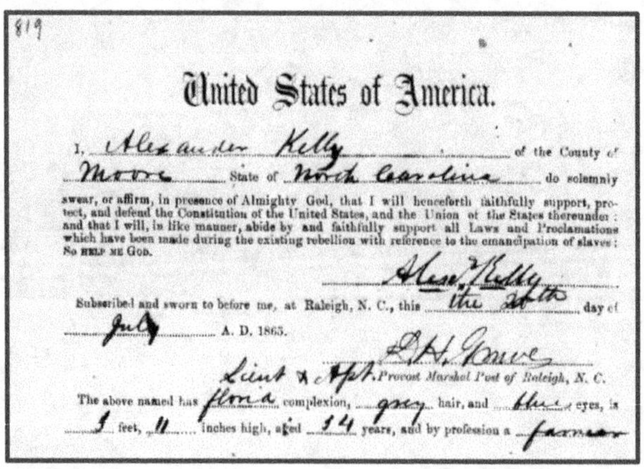

819

United States of America.

I, Alexander Kelly of the County of Moore State of North Carolina do solemnly swear, or affirm, in presence of Almighty God, that I will henceforth faithfully support, protect, and defend the Constitution of the United States, and the Union of the States thereunder: and that I will, in like manner, abide by and faithfully support all Laws and Proclamations which have been made during the existing rebellion with reference to the emancipation of slaves: So help me God.

Alexd. Kelly

Subscribed and sworn to before me, at Raleigh, N. C., this the 20th day of July A. D. 1865.

D.H. Bruce
Lieut & Apt. Provost Marshal Post of Raleigh, N. C.

The above named has florid complexion, grey hair, and blue eyes, is 5 feet, 11 inches high, aged 54 years, and by profession a farmer

L.W. Lawhon [579]

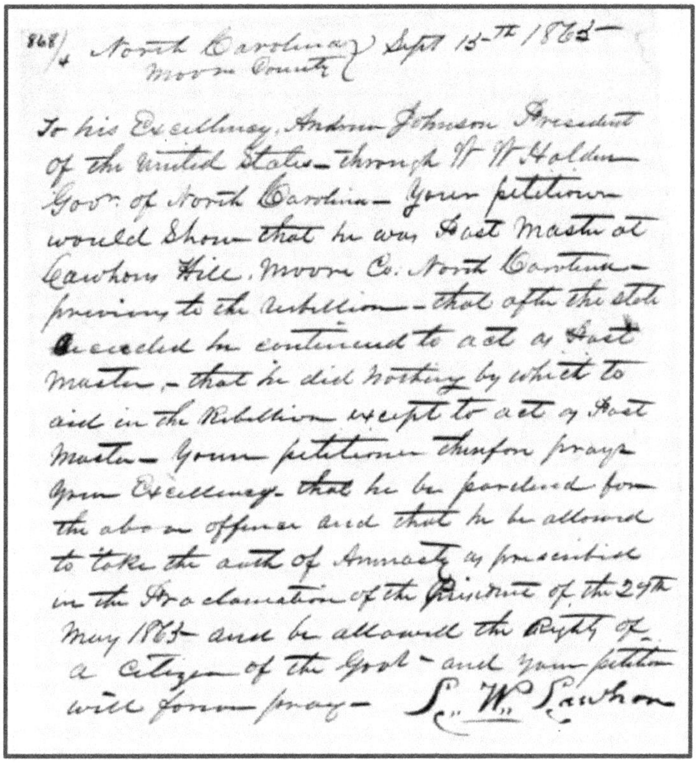

868/4 North Carolina } Sept 15th 1865
Moore County }

To his Excellency Andrew Johnson President of the United States through W W Holden Gov. of North Carolina — Your petitioner would show that he was Post Master at Lawhons Hill, Moore Co. North Carolina — previous to the rebellion — that after the State seceded he continued to act as Post Master — that he did nothing by which to aid in the Rebellion except to act as Post Master — Your petitioner therefore prays your Excellency that he be pardoned for the above offence and that he be allowed to take the oath of Amnesty as prescribed in the Proclamation of the President of the 29th May 1865 and be allowed the Rights of a Citizen of the Govt — and your petitioner will forever pray — L. Wm Lawhon

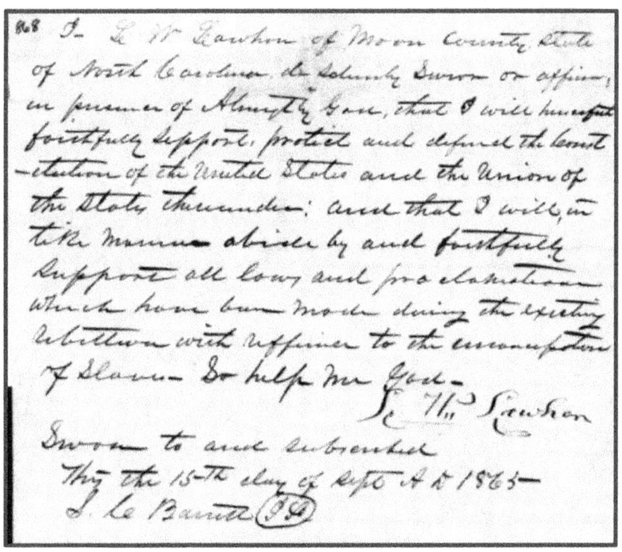

868 I, L W Lawhon of Moore County State of North Carolina do solemnly swear or affirm, in presence of Almighty God, that I will henceforth faithfully support, protect and defend the Constitution of the United States and the Union of the States thereunder; and that I will, in like manner abide by and faithfully support all laws and proclamations which have been made during the existing rebellion with reference to the emancipation of Slaves. So help me God.

L. Wm Lawhon

Sworn to and subscribed this the 15th day of Sept A D 1865 —
S. C. Barrett (JP)

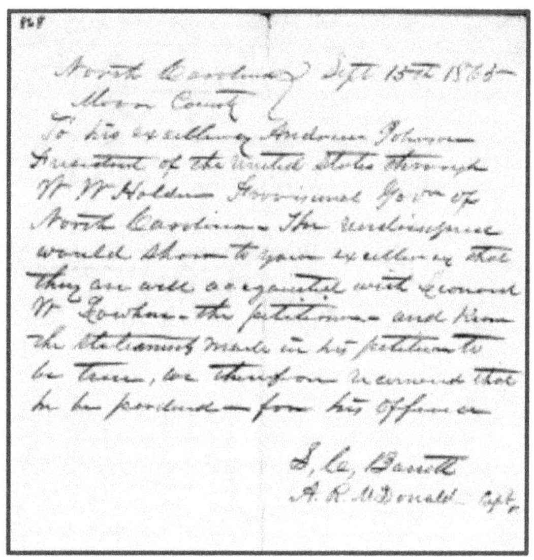

868

North Carolina } Sept 15th 1865
Moore County }

To his excellency Andrew Johnson President of the United States through W W Holden Provisional Gov of North Carolina. The undersigned would show to your excellency that they are well acquainted with Leonard W Lawhon the petitioner and know the statements made in his petition to be true, we therefore recommend that he be pardoned for his offences

S. C. Barrett
A. R. McDonald Capt

A.D. McDonald [580]

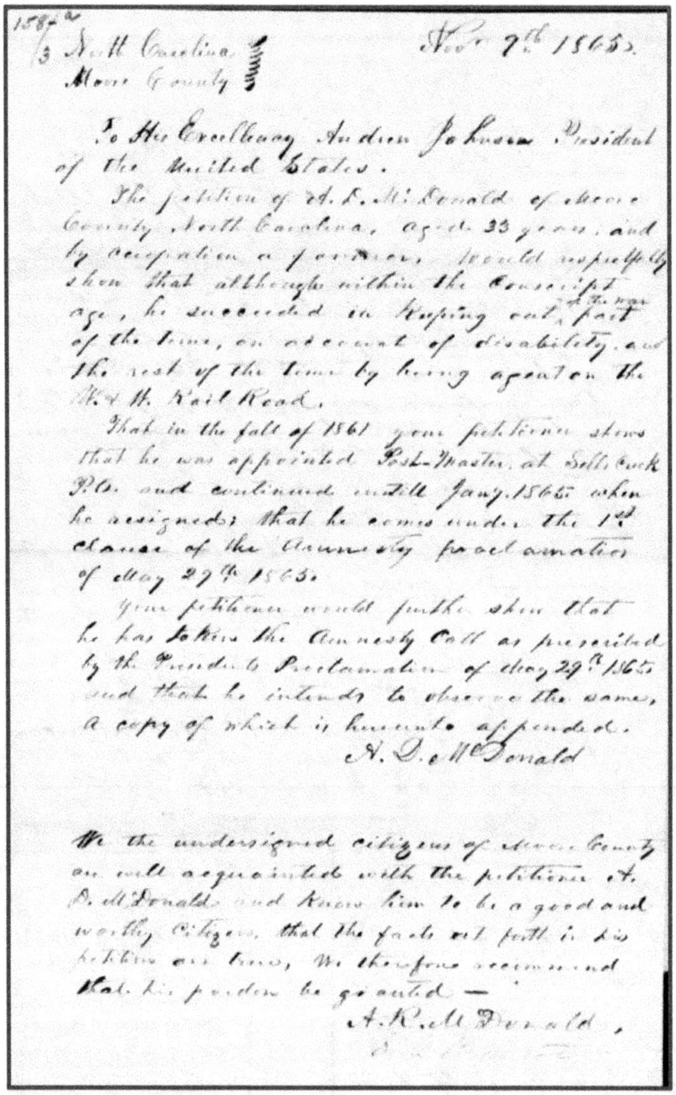

158a

3 North Carolina }
Moore County }

Nov 7th 1865.

To His Excellency Andrew Johnson President of the United States.

The petition of A. D. McDonald of Moore County North Carolina, aged 33 years, and by occupation a farmer, would respectfully show that although within the Conscript age, he succeeded in keeping out of the war part of the time, on account of disability, and the rest of the time by being agent on the W. & W. Rail Road.

That in the fall of 1861 your petitioner shows that he was appointed Post-Master at Sells Creek P.O. and continued untill Jany. 1865 when he resigned; that he comes under the 1st clause of the Amnesty proclamation of May 29th 1865.

Your petitioner would further show that he has taken the Amnesty Oath as prescribed by the President's Proclamation of May 29th 1865 and that he intends to observe the same, a copy of which is hereunto appended.

A. D. McDonald

We the undersigned citizens of Moore County are well acquainted with the petitioner A. D. McDonald and know him to be a good and worthy Citizen, that the facts set forth in his petition are true, We therefore recommend that his pardon be granted —

A. R. McDonald,

[illegible]

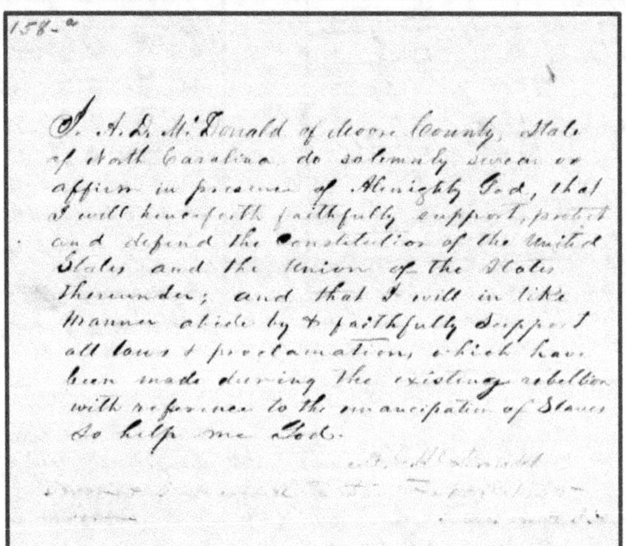

158-a

I, A. D. McDonald of Moore County, State of North Carolina do solemnly swear or affirm in presence of Almighty God, that I will henceforth faithfully support, protect and defend the Constitution of the United States and the Union of the States thereunder; and that I will in like manner abide by & faithfully support all laws & proclamations which have been made during the existing rebellion with reference to the emancipation of Slaves So help me God.

A. D. McDonald

[illegible]

174-a/3

North Carolina } To His Excellency Andrew Johnson
Moore County } President of the United States.

The petition of Evander McGilvary would respectfully show that he was appointed assessor for the County of Moore, that he was appointed without his solicitation and probably would not have accepted the appointment, had it not been that the office would exempt him from military service in the Confederate States. that he was opposed to secession and does not yet believe in the doctrine: but when North Carolina seperated from the U.S. and joined the Confederacy he felt it to be his duty to obey the laws of the Government under which he lived and consiquently acted accordingly: that as he is now in the United States again, he feels bound to obey the laws and give that government his support. To this end he prays that he may be pardoned by the president, and permitted to take the oath of amnesty; and your petitioner as in duty bound will ever pray &c.

E. McGilvary

We the undersigned citizens of Moore County, Certify that we are acquainted with the petitioner, Evander McGilvary, and that the facts set forth in his petition above, are true to the best of their knowledge and belief.

A.R. McDonald
W. P. Richardson
H. Harrington

174-a

United States of America.

I, Evander McGilvary of the County of Moore State of North Carolina do solemnly swear, or affirm, in presence of Almighty God, that I will henceforth faithfully support, protect, and defend the Constitution of the United States, and the Union of the States thereunder: and that I will, in like manner, abide by and faithfully support all Laws and Proclamations which have been made during the existing rebellion with reference to the emancipation of slaves: So help me God.

E. McGilvary

Subscribed and sworn to before me, at Raleigh, N. C., this [illegible] day of August A. D. 1865.

[illegible] Provost Marshal Post of Raleigh, N. C.

The above named has fair complexion, light hair, and blue eyes, is 5 feet, 10 inches high, aged 50 years, and by profession a farmer

Daniel M. McIntosh [582]

179-a/3

North Carolina } To His Excellency Andrew Johnson
Moore County } President of the United States.

The petition of Daniel M. McIntosh of said County would respectfully show that he was appointed Post-Master at Pocket P.O. in the year 1832 and continued to be Post-Master untill North Carolina seceded. He was then requested to act as Post-Master under the Confederate Government, and consented to do so for the convenience of himself and his neighbours: that he was opposed to Secession; did not vote for the Convention in Febry 1861. that he is now desirous to take the oaths prescribed, and to become a loyal citizen of the United States: To this end he prays that Executive Clemmency may be extended to him; that he may be pardoned and permitted to take the oath of Amnesty and your petitioner will ever pray &c.

D. M. McIntosh

United States of America.

I, D M McIntosh of the County of Moore State of N C do solemnly swear, or affirm, in presence of Almighty God, that I will henceforth faithfully support, protect, and defend the Constitution of the United States, and the Union of the States thereunder: and that I will, in like manner, abide by and faithfully support all Laws and Preclamations which have been made during the existing rebellion with reference to the emancipation of slaves: So help me God.

D M McIntosh

Subscribed and sworn to before me, at Raleigh, N. C., this [illegible] day of August A. D. 1865.

D H Pruce
Lt & Apt Provost Marshal Post of Raleigh, N. C.

The above named has fair complexion, gray hair, and blue eyes, is 6 feet, — inches high, aged 62 years, and by profession a farmer

The undersigned citizens of Moore County being acquainted with the petitioner D. M. McIntosh certify that the facts set forth in his petition above are true to the best of our knowledge and belief.

A. K. McDonald
W. R. Richardson
J. A. Harrington

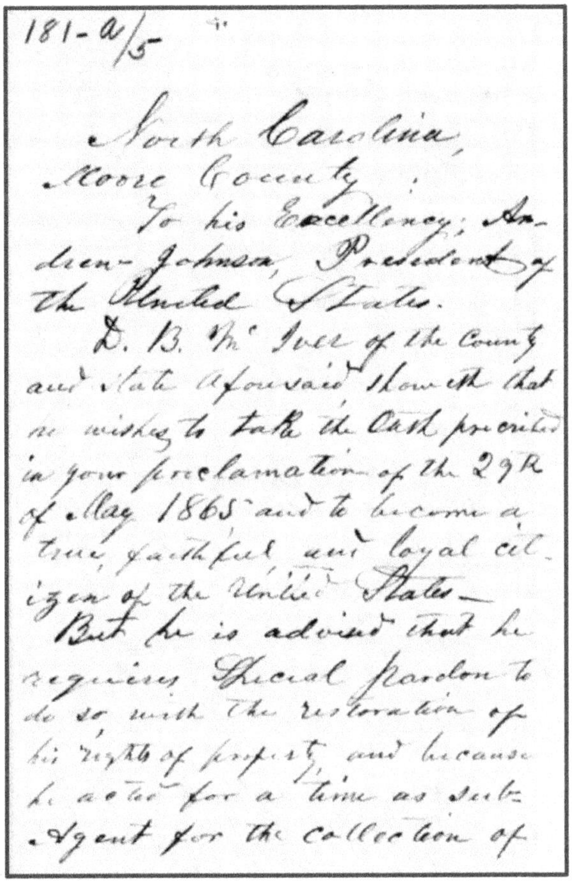

181-a/5

North Carolina,
Moore County:
To his Excellency: Andrew Johnson, President of the United States.
D. B. McIver of the County and State Aforesaid showeth that he wishes to take the Oath precribed in your proclamation of the 29th of May 1865 and to become a true, faithful and loyal citizen of the United States—
But he is advised that he requires Special Pardon to do so with the restoration of his rights of property and because he acted for a time as sub-Agent for the collection of

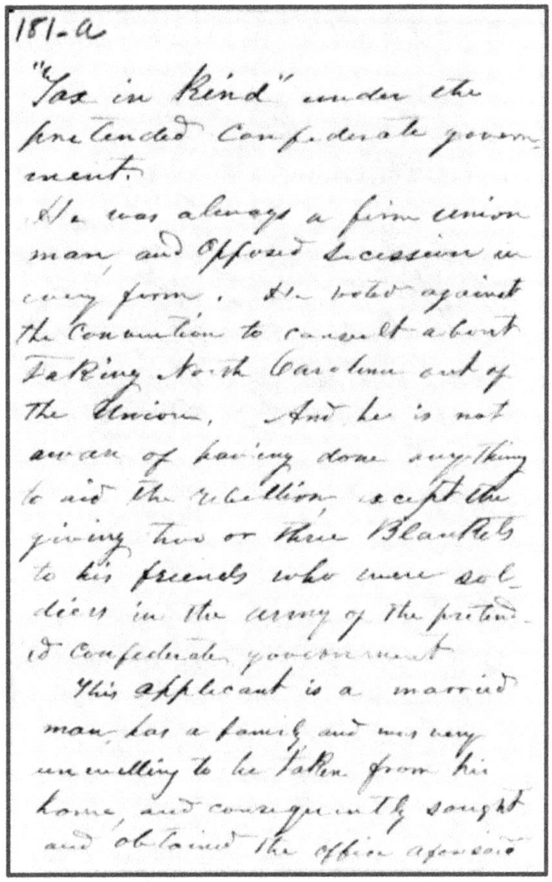

181-a

"Tax in Kind" under the pretended Confederate government.
He was always a firm union man, and Opposed Secession in every form. He voted against the Convention to consult about taking North Carolina out of the Union. And he is not aware of having done anything to aid the rebellion except the giving two or three Blankets to his friends who were soldiers in the army of the pretended Confederate government
This applicant is a married man has a family and was very unwilling to be taken from his home, and consequently sought and obtained the office aforesaid

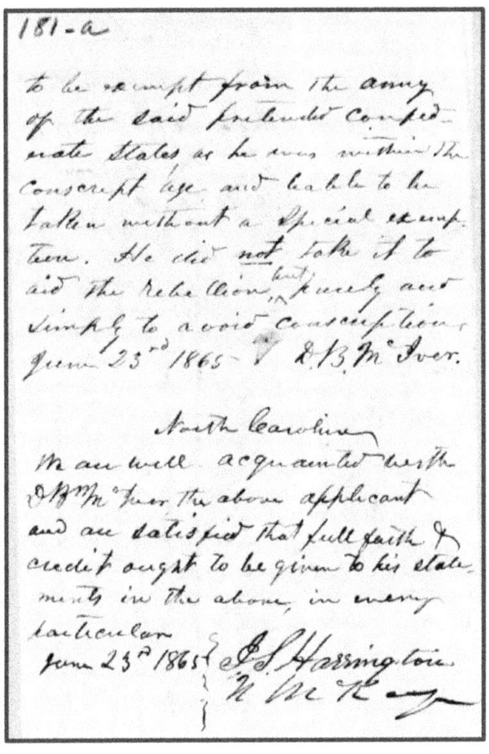

181-a

to be exempt from the army of the said pretended Confederate States as he was within the Conscript age and liable to be taken without a special exemption. He did not take it to aid the rebellion, but purely and simply to avoid conscription
June 23rd 1865 D. B. McIver.

North Carolina
We are well acquainted with D. B. McIver the above applicant and are satisfied that full faith & credit ought to be given to his statements in the above, in every particular
June 23rd 1865 J. S. Harrington
N. McKay

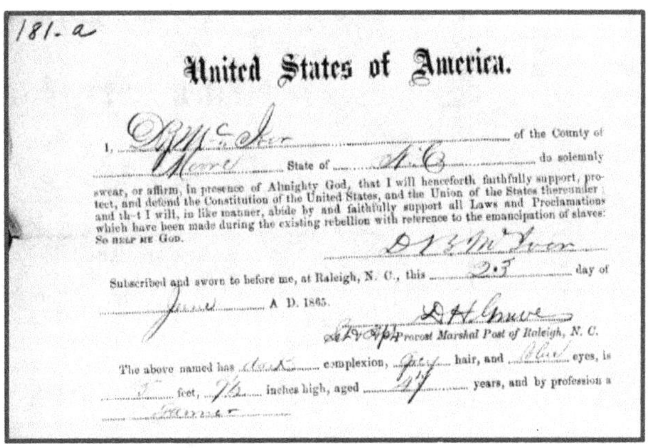

181-a

United States of America.

I, D. B. McIver of the County of Moore State of N. C. do solemnly swear, or affirm, in presence of Almighty God, that I will henceforth faithfully support, protect, and defend the Constitution of the United States, and the Union of the States thereunder; and that I will, in like manner, abide by and faithfully support all Laws and Proclamations which have been made during the existing rebellion with reference to the emancipation of slaves: So help me God.

D. B. McIver

Subscribed and sworn to before me, at Raleigh, N. C., this 23 day of June A. D. 1865.

D. H. Grave
Capt. & Pro. Provost Marshal Post of Raleigh, N. C.

The above named has dark complexion, grey hair, and blue eyes, is 5 feet, 7½ inches high, aged 47 years, and by profession a farmer

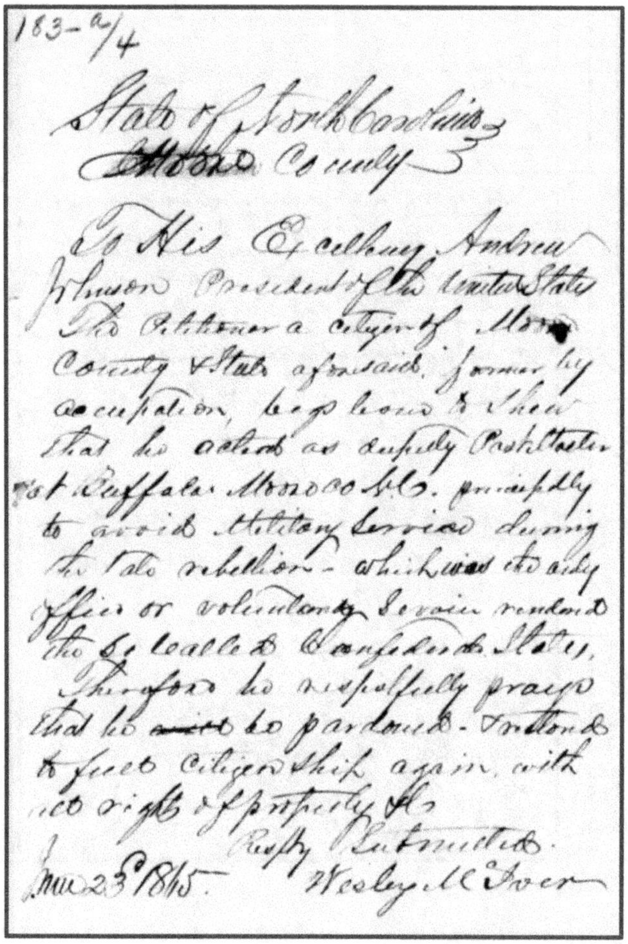

183-a/4

State of North Carolina }
~~Moore~~ County }

To His Excellency Andrew Johnson President of the United States
The Petitioner a citizen of Moore County & State aforesaid, farmer by occupation, begs leave to shew that he acted as deputy Post Master at Buffalo Moore Co N.C. principally to avoid Military service during the late rebellion - which was the only office or voluntary service rendered the so called Confederate States,
Therefore he respectfully prays that he ~~may~~ be pardoned - & restored to full citizenship again, with all rights of property &c

Respy Petitioner

June 23rd 1865. Wesley McIver

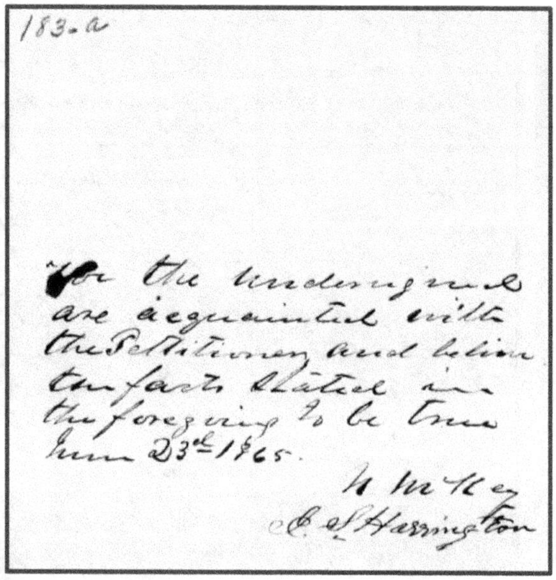

183-a

We the undersigned are acquainted with the Petitioner and believe the facts stated in the foregoing to be true
June 23rd 1865.

W McKey
E S Harrington

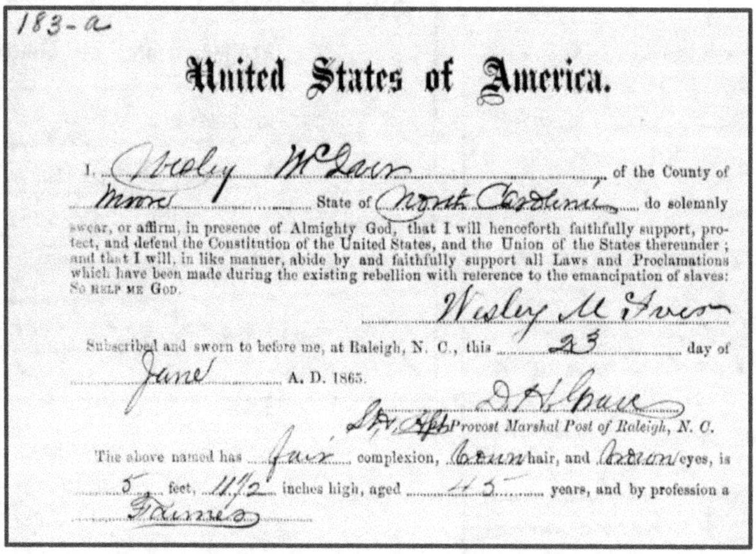

183-a

United States of America.

I, Wesly McIver of the County of Moore State of North Carolina do solemnly swear, or affirm, in presence of Almighty God, that I will henceforth faithfully support, protect, and defend the Constitution of the United States, and the Union of the States thereunder; and that I will, in like manner, abide by and faithfully support all Laws and Proclamations which have been made during the existing rebellion with reference to the emancipation of slaves: So help me God.

Wesley McIver

Subscribed and sworn to before me, at Raleigh, N. C., this 23 day of June A. D. 1865.

D H Gave
Provost Marshal Post of Raleigh, N. C.

The above named has fair complexion, brown hair, and brown eyes, is 5 feet, 11½ inches high, aged 45 years, and by profession a Farmer

191-a/4

Sept 11th

Daniel McKenzie

Sworn & Subscribed to before me this 11th Sept 1865
W. R. Richardson J.P.

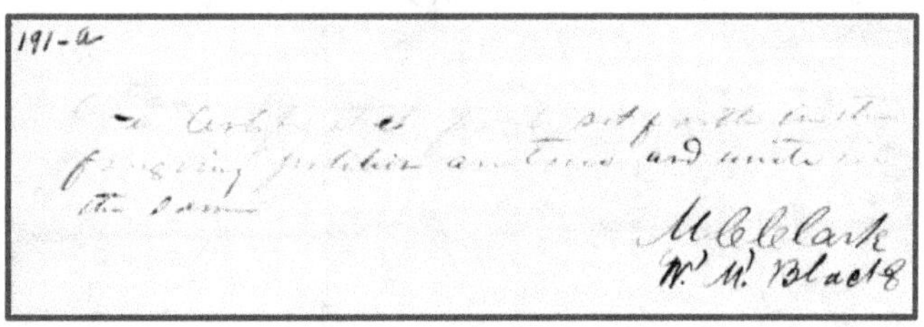

191-a

M C Clark
W. M. Black

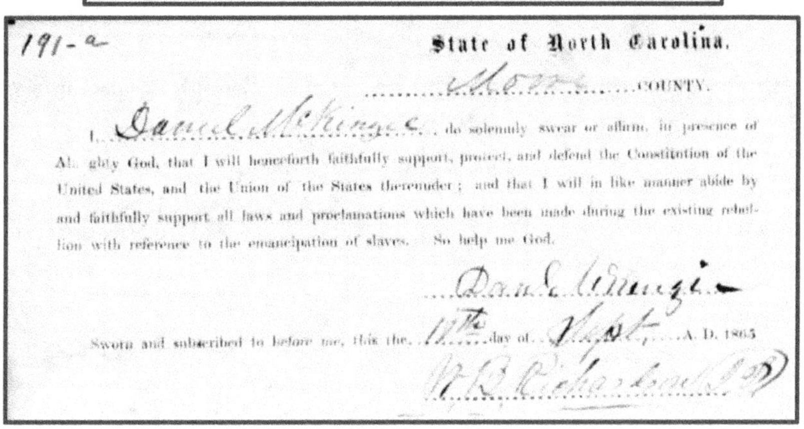

191-a

State of North Carolina.

Moore COUNTY.

I, Daniel McKenzie do solemnly swear or affirm, in presence of Almighty God, that I will henceforth faithfully support, protect, and defend the Constitution of the United States, and the Union of the States thereunder; and that I will in like manner abide by and faithfully support all laws and proclamations which have been made during the existing rebellion with reference to the emancipation of slaves. So help me God.

Daniel McKenzie

Sworn and subscribed to before me, this the 11th day of Sept, A. D. 1865

W. R. Richardson J.P.

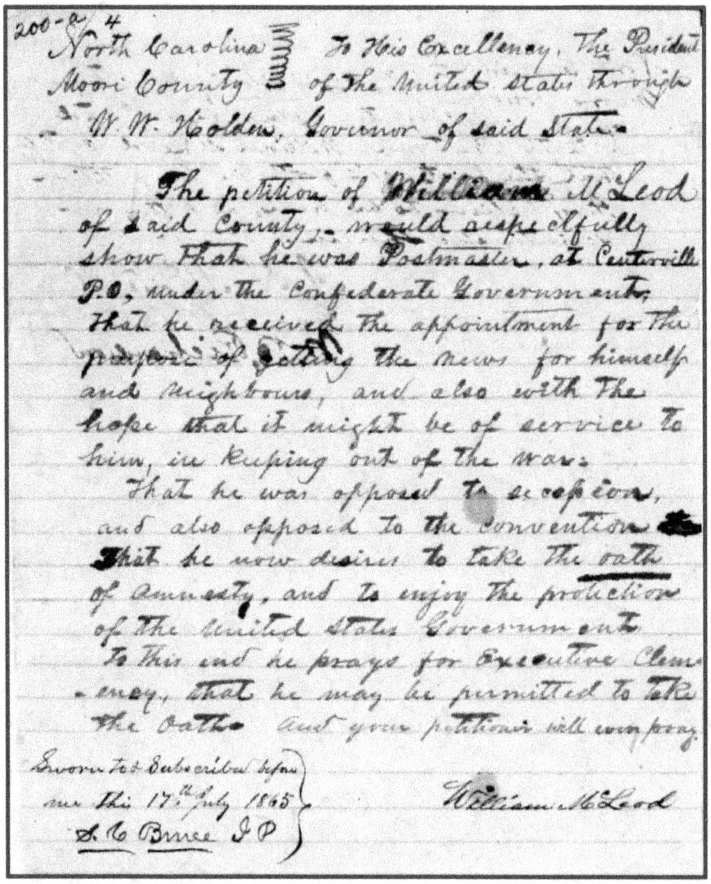

200-a 4

North Carolina } To His Excellency, The President
Moore County } of the United States through
W. W. Holden, Governor of said State.

The petition of William McLeod of said County, would respectfully show that he was Postmaster, at Centerville P.O. under the Confederate Government. That he received the appointment for the purpose of getting the news for himself and neighbours, and also with the hope that it might be of service to him, in keeping out of the war.

That he was opposed to secession, and also opposed to the convention. That he now desires to take the oath of amnesty, and to enjoy the protection of the United States Government. To this end he prays for Executive Clemency, that he may be permitted to take the oath. And your petitioner will ever pray.

Sworn to & Subscribed before me this 17th July 1865
S. C. Bruce J.P.

William McLeod

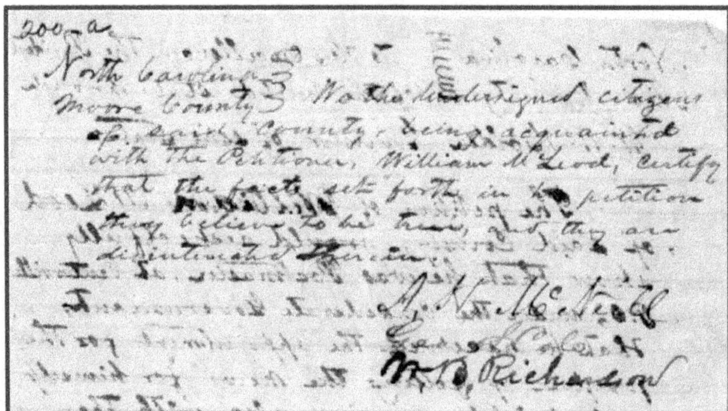

200-a

North Carolina } We the undersigned citizens
Moore County } of said County, being acquainted with the Petitioner, William McLeod, certify that the facts set forth in his petition they believe to be true, & that they are disinterested therein.

A. H. McNeill
[illegible]
W. B. Richardson

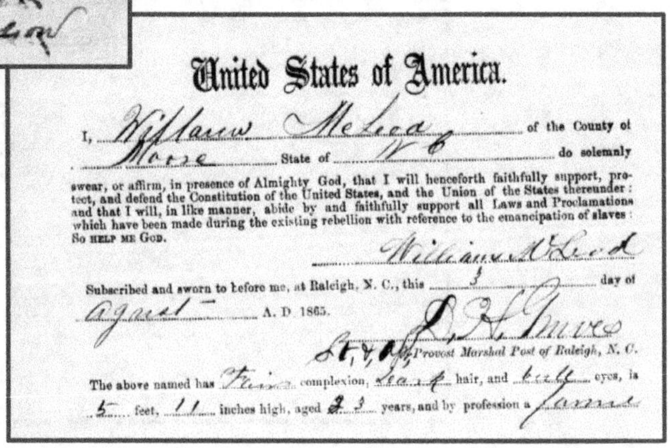

United States of America.

I, William McLeod of the County of Moore State of N C do solemnly swear, or affirm, in presence of Almighty God, that I will henceforth faithfully support, protect, and defend the Constitution of the United States, and the Union of the States thereunder: and that I will, in like manner, abide by and faithfully support all Laws and Proclamations which have been made during the existing rebellion with reference to the emancipation of slaves: So help me God.

William McLeod

Subscribed and sworn to before me, at Raleigh, N. C., this 3 day of August A. D. 1865.

[illegible], Provost Marshal Post of Raleigh, N. C.

The above named has Fair complexion, Dark hair, and Grey eyes, is 5 feet, 11 inches high, aged 23 years, and by profession a farmer

Eli N. Moffitt [587]

255-a

255-a

Sworn & subscribed before me
12th August 1865
W. B. Richardson J.P.

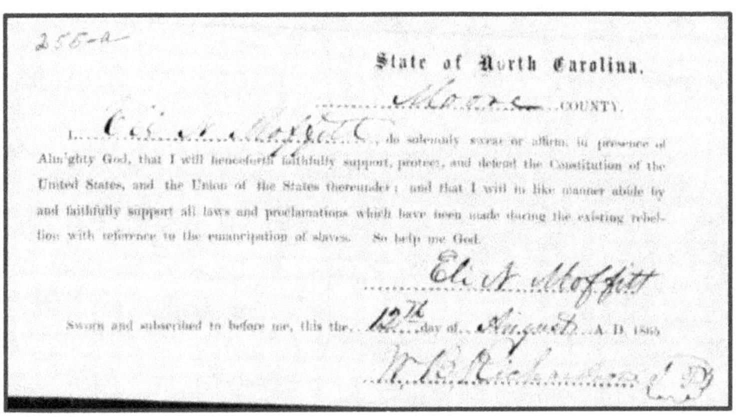

255-a

State of North Carolina.

Moore COUNTY.

I, Eli N. Moffitt, do solemnly swear or affirm, in presence of Almighty God, that I will henceforth faithfully support, protect, and defend the Constitution of the United States, and the Union of the States thereunder; and that I will in like manner abide by and faithfully support all laws and proclamations which have been made during the existing rebellion with reference to the emancipation of slaves. So help me God.

Eli N. Moffitt

Sworn and subscribed to before me, this the 12th day of August A. D. 1865

W. B. Richardson J.P.

John Munroe [588]

302-a/4

Petition for Pardon

To

His Elency Andrew Johnson President of the United States

Sir your petitioner is John Munroe Sixty three years of age a resident of Moore County N.Carolina by occupation a farmer your petitioner during the rebelion took no active part he paid his taxes and at diferent times Sent Some provisions to his sons who were in the So called Confederate army your petitioner pleads gilty under the first class of your amnesty Proclamation of May the 29 1865 having accepted the appointment of Post Master under the So called Confederate States

your petitioner has taken the oath of Amnesty as prescribed by the Presidents Proclamation of 29 May 1865 and do intend to observe the Same

your petitioner prays you to take his case into consideration and if consistant with your Sence of right you will grant him a pardon for which as in duty bound he will forever pray

John Munroe

302-a

I J. Munroe of Moore County State of North Carolina do Solemly Swear or affirm in presence of Almity God that I Will henceforth faithfully Support protect and Defend the Constitution of the United States and the States thereunder and that I Will likewise Manner abide by and faithfully Support all Laws and proclamations Which have been Made during the Existing Rebellion With Referens to the emancipation of Slaves So help Me God

John Munroe

Sworn and Subscribed to this this the 10th Day of Nov. AD1865 John M. Neill [illegible]

302-a

We the undersigned Citizens of Moore County Certify that the petitioner John Munroe is a worthy and respectable Citizen and the facts set forth in his petition we believe to be true and recommend that his pardon be granted —

A.R. McDonald

Alex Kelly

Thomas Rollins [589]

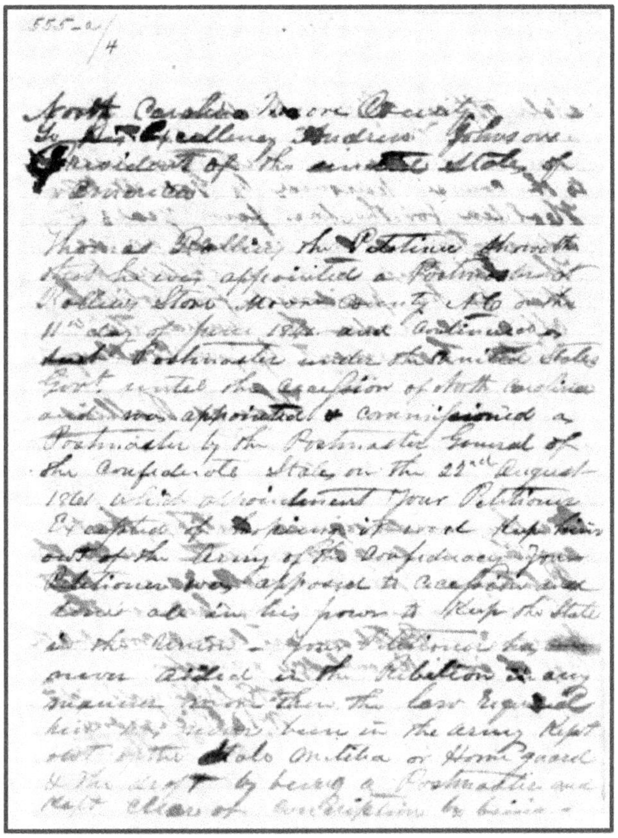
555-a
/4

North Carolina Moore County
To His Excellency Andrew Johnson
President of the United States of
America

Thomas Rollins the Petitioner showeth
that he was appointed a Postmaster at
Rollins Store Moore County N.C. on the
11th day of June 18[illegible] and continued as
such Postmaster under the United States
Govt. until the secession of North Carolina
and he was appointed & commissioned a
Postmaster by the Postmaster General of
the Confederate States on the 22nd August
1861 which appointment your Petitioner
Excepted of [illegible] it would keep him
out of the Army of the Confederacy. Your
Petitioner was opposed to secession and
done all in his power to keep the State
in the Union. Your Petitioner has
never aided in the Rebellion in any
manner more than the law required
him [illegible] never been in the army kept
out of the State Militia or Home guard
& the draft by being a Postmaster and
kept clear of conscription by being

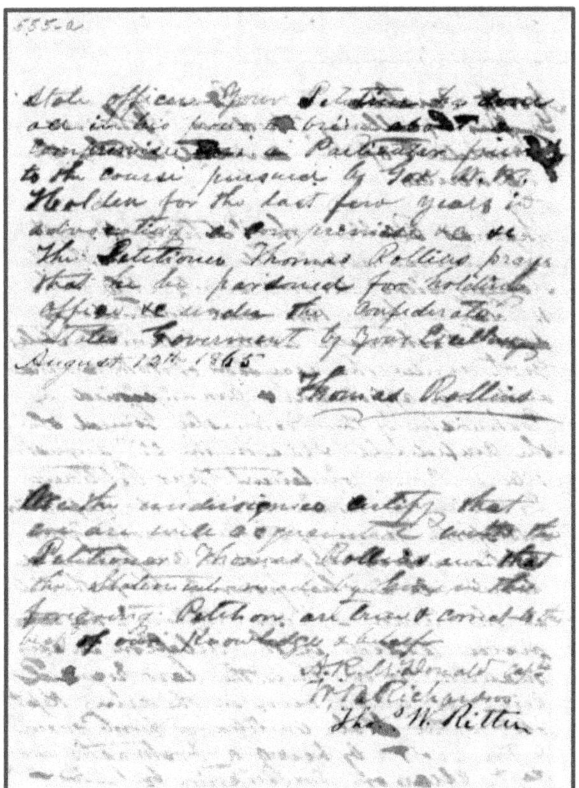
555-a

State officer. Your Petitioner has done
all in his power to bring about
compromise [illegible] a Particular friend
to the course pursued by Gov. W. W.
Holden for the last four years in
advocating a compromise &c &c
The Petitioner Thomas Rollins prays
that he be pardoned for holding
office &c under the Confederate
States Government by your Excellency
August 12th 1865

Thomas Rollins

We the undersigned certify that
we are well acquainted with the
Petitioner Thomas Rollins and that
the statements made by him in the
foregoing Petition are true & correct to the
best of our knowledge & belief

A. R. McDonald
W. R. Richardson
Thos. W. Ritter

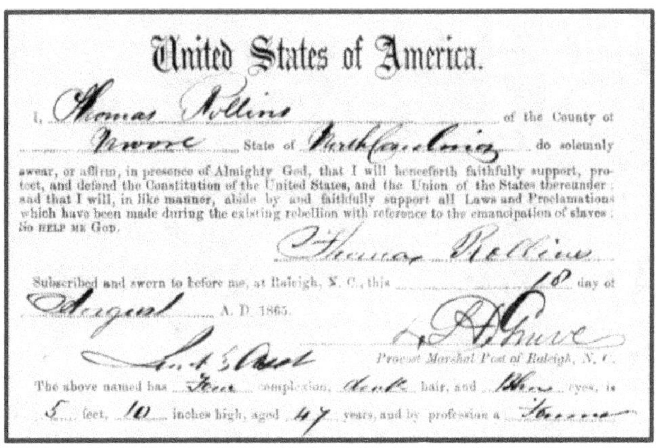
United States of America.

I, Thomas Rollins of the County of Moore State of North Carolina do solemnly swear, or affirm, in presence of Almighty God, that I will henceforth faithfully support, protect, and defend the Constitution of the United States, and the Union of the States thereunder; and that I will, in like manner, abide by and faithfully support all Laws and Proclamations which have been made during the existing rebellion with reference to the emancipation of slaves; So help me God.

Thomas Rollins

Subscribed and sworn to before me, at Raleigh, N. C., this 18 day of August A. D. 1865.

[illegible] Provost Marshal Post of Raleigh, N. C.
[illegible]

The above named has Fair complexion, dark hair, and blue eyes, is 5 feet, 10 inches high, aged 47 years, and by profession a Farmer

John Sheppard [590]

628-a
14

State of North Carolina }
Moore County }

To His Excellency
Andrew Johnson President of the United States
The Petitioner John Sheppard respectfully sheweth that he desires to be permitted to take the benefit of the amnesty oath in the Proclamation of May 29th 1865

Your Petitioner states that, he was sub Post Master at Long Street Post Office Moore Co. which was a very small office the mail being received only once a week

Your Petitioner further shows that he is an aged man and in very feeble health, and that the office of sub Post Master was the only office he held during the Rebellion and that he never voluntarily approp[r]iated or aided in the same

Your Petitioner further states that he has never been in the Military service of the Confederate States, and he prays that a Special Pardon be granted to him and that by taking the oath he be restored to the rights of Citizenship

July 1865

[illegible] Sheppard

628-a

[illegible]
[illegible] County
[illegible]
John Sheppard
[illegible]
[illegible] Absalom Kelly J.P.

628-a

State of N Carolina }
Moore County }

We the undersigned are acquainted with the Petitioner John Sheppard and believe the facts set forth in the foregoing petition to be true

J. S. Harrington
Absalom Kelly

D.M. Sinclair [591]

645-a/3

State of North Carolina
Moore County

To His Excellency Andrew Johnson
President of the U.S.

The petitioner D. M. Sinclair would respectfully show that he is a citizen of Moore County North Carolina – That he was appointed Tax assessor by the so called Confederate States – That he accepted the same for the purpose of keeping out of the Confederate army – That he acted in that capacity from Sept 1864 till Feby 1865

The petitioner prays that Your Excellency will pardon him for having acted in the position shown above and allow him to take the oath of allegiance to the United States

As in duty bound will ever pray

D. M. Sinclair

We the undersigned citizens of Moore County N.C. have been acquainted with the petitioner for many years and do hereby certify that he is a good and loyal citizen & that he was opposed to Secession

W. B. Cleg[illegible]

G. W. [illegible]

645-a

United States of America.

I, D. M. Sinclair of the County of Moore State of North Carolina do solemnly swear, or affirm, in presence of Almighty God, that I will henceforth faithfully support, protect, and defend the Constitution of the United States, and the Union of the States thereunder: and that I will, in like manner, abide by and faithfully support all Laws and Proclamations which have been made during the existing rebellion with reference to the emancipation of slaves: So help me God.

D. M. Sinclair

Subscribed and sworn to before me, at Raleigh, N. C., this 5th day of July A. D. 1865.

D. H. [illegible]
Lieut. & Asst. Provost Marshal, Post of Raleigh, N. C.

The above named has Dk complexion, Dk hair, and Dk eyes, is 5 feet, 6 in inches high, aged 47 years, and by profession a Farmer

Conscripts, Deserters, Outliers and Conflict

The following narratives tell of the hardships faced by deserters, outliers and their families on the home front. They were written by Lacy Garner as told to him by Thurman Maness. [592]

"During the Civil War many Moore County residents refused to join the Confederate Army, for various reasons, and became what was known as "Outlyers": These men hid out in the woods and eluded the Confederate soldiers (The Hunters) that came looking for them. The following account is of one such Outlyer, Emsley Moore, and his day-to-day struggle to avoid capture. This story was handed down to Thurman Maness from his father, Reuben Maness. Reuben's father was Thomas Maness who also was an Outlyer.

THE HUNTERS

Emsley had been on the run all day. The Outlyers had been dispersed earlier in the morning when the Hunters surprised them down on Bear Creek. All his friends had scattered to the four winds to avoid capture. Now he was all alone and exhausted. He decided to stop by the Ol' Spring before night fall to get one last drink of water before taking refuge for the night. In the distance he could hear the rumble of thunder and he thought to himself, "What else can go wrong today?" Drops of rain began falling on the leaves around him. The sound of the rain on the leaves made him nervous. They muffled and distorted the sounds around him. His only chance of eluding capture was being able to detect the soldiers before they detected him. Now the weather threatened that security. The soldiers could easily sneak up on him with the falling rain concealing their approach. He couldn't stay here long. He would have to stay on the move. He lay down on his stomach at the mouth of the spring. Cupping his hands, to act as a dipper, he scooped water into his mouth. After every handful he turned his head, watching his back-trail. He didn't trust this weather and he certainly didn't trust the Hunters who were probably still on his trail. Maybe if the weather took a turn for the worse, they would give up looking for him today. The Outlyers had managed to stay one step ahead of the Hunters but he knew it was just a matter of time before he slipped-up and blundered into them. He was feeling like an animal. "If I ever get out of this mess, I'll never hunt another creature as long as I live!" He had been running so long and he was quickly running out of places to run to. The soldiers had been watching his mother's house for weeks and the houses of his friends too. The sun was almost below the horizon as the storm continued to roll in from the west. This miserable war had disrupted the lives of so many men. He had once almost decided to join the Confederate Army but then news started arriving of all the young men in the community who had been killed in battle. It didn't take a genius to conclude that the South was not going to win this war. Even if he didn't get killed in battle, he would probably end up in some Yankee POW camp and from all the stories he had heard about them he figured he had a better chance surviving out here in the woods than in there. At least if he died here, he would be at home. He had learned to detest the color Gray more than Blue. The Yankees were not the ones hunting him like some rabid animal. He had even entertained the thought of joining up with the Blue, but there was no way he could take aim on one of his own. Right now his only option was to hide-out until the war was over. The sound of a snapping twig brought him back to his senses. A flash of lightening suddenly lit up the woods revealing a thousand silhouettes, any one of which could be mistaken for one of the Hunters. His feet took flight again. These days it seemed they had a mind of their own. He was running aimlessly. Suddenly he stopped in his tracks, giving reasoning a chance to catch up. "I've got to take time to figure this thing out! What I really need right now is some sleep." He remembered the lean-to he had built last week over on the south side of Deep River. "If I can get there tonight, I can get a few hours' sleep before sunrise." He knew these woods like the back of his hand. That was the one advantage he had over the Hunters. The rain was coming down hard now. There was no way the Hunters could track him in this weather. He took a few deep breaths to calm his nerves and set a course northeast. After another hour or so he spotted the lean-to during a flash of lightening. He crawled up under the makeshift shelter and covered himself with wet leaves. He drifted off to sleep while cursing the men in Gray. The dawn ushered in a new day with little change of heart. He was awakened again by the intense itching on his back and stomach. He had contracted the so called "Ground Itch" from months of exposure to nature's elements. The "Ground Itch" is a hookworm infestation. The young larvae live in the soil and bore their way into human flesh, leaving an ulcer at the site of entry with intense itching. His entire body was becoming covered with these "blessings in disguise". Emsley's stomach was gnawing at his backbone. It had been two days since he had last eaten, and he was getting weak. Instinct told him he must have food, at any cost. Standing and brushing the debris from his still wet clothing he headed south, towards home.

Crawling on his stomach, he was within 200 yards of home. From his vantage point across the field he could see that the shutters over the kitchen window were closed; a sign that he and his mother had devised to signal danger. "The Hunters must be near." He retreated into the woods to wait for a better sign. Nothing to do but wait. He sat cradled within the up-heaved roots of an old White Oak, thinking about his mother and all the sacrifices she had made for him. It was a shame he had to put her through this. She had never complained but he was well aware of the increasing burden he was becoming. The Hunters were constantly popping in, searching the house for him. He was afraid that his mother was going to become an unexpected causality of war—the same war he refused to be a part of. Hours slowly passed. Finally, he crept back to the edge of the field for another look. This time the shutters were open. He circled the house from a distance of about a hundred yards before making his final approach. There was no sign of the Hunters. His mother met him at the front door. "Get in here before someone sees you!" She grabbed his arm and yanked him across the threshold, closing the door behind them. "Sit down for a minute Emsley and let me fix you something to eat." "I can't stay long mama; the Hunters have been on my trail since early yesterday. Throw me some jerky and dried apples in a sack. I must be on my way." His mother glanced out the window just as the two soldiers stepped out of the woods onto the road. "Oh, my Lord, Emsley, here they come!" "How many mama?" "Two of them son, quickly, out the back door!" The Hunters rushed around back just in time to level their weapons at Emsley who was about sixty yards down into the woods. They pulled their triggers simultaneously, sending a hefty double load of buckshot in his direction. At that very moment his foot became entangled in a grape vine which sent him tumbling head over heels. He could hear the buckshot breaking brush over top his head. The fall knocked the wind from his lungs and the Hunters rushed in upon him as he lay gasping for breath. Rolling him over, they ripped open his shirt. They mistakenly took the "Ground Itch" lesions for buckshot wounds, immediately concluding that they had poured enough lead into him to kill any mortal man. Emsley could not decide if he was dead or alive. He could hear what the Hunters were saying, but he felt no pain. Then, suddenly it dawned on him. "They think they have killed me!" The truth was -- not a single shot had touched him. They picked him up like a slaughtered hog and carried him into the house; throwing him on the bed. "Here is the coward you call a son. He is shot up pretty bad. He'll probably be dead by morning. Anyway, it'll save us the trouble of hanging him. We would love to stay around and watch the varmint die but we just shoot 'em, we don't bury 'em." She watched from the window until the soldiers were out of sight then buried her face in her apron and sobbed uncontrollably. Suddenly she heard sounds coming from the bedroom. She rushed to what she thought was her dying son's bedside only to find him up dancing a jig! "Emsley! I thought you were dead! Let me tend to those wounds." "No need mama, unless you got a cure for the Ground Itch!" Emsley remained in bed for weeks, getting some badly needed rest. About once a week the Hunters would stop by to check on him, expecting to find him dead each time. He lay around the house until his lesions started to heal, and he was forced to take to the woods again. The Hunters never managed to capture Emsley again. The War was soon over, and life returned to normal, but Emsley Moore never forgot how a case of the "Ground Itch" once saved his life.

THE REVENGE OF THE OUTLYERS

The Civil War was never truly embraced by residents of upper Moore County. A statement by the late Dr. Henry B. Shields pretty well summarizes the sentiments of many southerners: "It was a rich man's war and a poor man's fight." Very few inhabitants of northern Moore County owned slaves and to go off and fight for the preservation of the institution of slavery was something that many felt reluctant to do. Many men outright refused to join the Confederate Army and were thrust into the category of "Outlyers". Today's terminology would be that of "Conscientious Objector". These men spent their days and nights hiding out in the surrounding woodlands, dodging the soldiers that came looking for them. Many a wife and mother in Moore County have sneaked a biscuit to a husband or son who was hiding out. Rounding-up Outlyers soon became a full-time preoccupation for the Confederate Army. Many men were Outlyers from the beginning. Others initially joined the CSA, became disillusioned and deserted. No matter the reason, if the Confederated Army called upon you and you refused to fight you became a fugitive and were aggressively pursued. Concerning my ancestors, I am afraid that many would fall into the category of "Outlyers"; refusing to die for something they had no interest in. There was heartfelt sympathy for the Confederacy, but sympathy alone never won a war. The following story centers on one such group of Outlyers and their struggle to maintain their freedom. There were times when that struggle escalated to the point of becoming a war within a war. Thurman Maness recalls the story as his father told it to him. I shall not sit in judgment of these men nor their cause but simply wish to tell the story as it actually happened. The year was 1864 and things were looking bad for the Confederate States of America. The futility of fighting a losing war was weighing heavy on everyone's mind. In a desperate attempt to bolster its devastated ranks, the CSA began to turn up the heat on "The Outlyers". Three deserters were apprehended in the upper end of the county and marched to the jail at Carthage for safe keeping during the night. "The Outlyers" were a very tight knit group and they quickly rallied to the defense of their captured comrades. The communication network maintained by these men intrigues me. Those said to have been involved were: John Henry Ritter, William D. (Big-Foot Bill) Ritter, Green Bailey, Thomas Maness, Isaac Maness, Ira Maness, Emsley Moore and William Cockman. I am sure there were many more but these are the names that Thurman recalls. His late father Reuben Addison Maness (son of Thomas Maness) pointed out the exact location of the skirmish to Thurman. That location would be just east of Carthage across the road from the present-day Hardee's. It was about midnight when Lieutenant Mills stepped out of the jailhouse door and ordered the first change of guards. John Henry had to squint to make out the figures in the doorway, but he could tell one was an officer. A fresh sentry was posted, and the door closed again. He had been hiding in the woods across from the jail since the detachment's arrival before sunset. He would fancy getting closer but did not dare, for fear of being discovered. The guards worked two-hour shifts and by sunrise he had witnessed four changes. A thick fog was descending, and John Henry reckoned they could use it to their advantage. As the first light of day urged the cocks into crowing, he saw Lieutenant Mills step out into the morning air. He began shouting orders to his subordinates indicating that they were ready to move. The three prisoners' hands were tied, and they were forced to walk sandwiched in the middle of a column of soldiers. John Henry was getting restless. He had to know which way they were going. After all, that is why he stayed here all night. His job to determine the route taken out of Carthage and to relay that information to the appropriate group of Outlyers laying-in-wait at each end. of town. They were headed EAST. John Henry ran a wide loop around the soldiers to avoid detection and was soon ahead of them. He ran like the wind until he heard a gun cock. In a low whisper he said, "It's me, John Henry, they're coming this way, get ready!" With that he ducked into the woods to join his friends. Seconds ticked away like hours. Suddenly there was the sound of footsteps along the road. They could hear the soldiers talking but the dense fog concealed their image. The group had changed their location several times that morning before settling on the present one. The fog had made it very difficult to get the proper prospective. Green Bailey motioned for the men to get ready, but very few could see him. Bailey had become sort of the captain of the group. Everyone sat with weapons cocked listening to their own breathing, waiting to hear the first shot. At that moment it was difficult determine if the fog was going to be a friend or foe. The soldiers were now directly in front of them, silhouetted against the breaking day. Who fired that first shot is not known, but fired it was. The others joined in with a barrage of gunfire that left three soldiers dead on the spot. Two of the three prisoners quickly took leave of absence. Members of the group severed their friend's bonds with their knives as they passed by them. The remaining soldiers took cover and returned fire from the roadside ditch. The Outlyers quickly dispersed and retreated. They were deep into the woods but could still hear gunfire from the road. One Outlyer, William Cockman, for some unknown reason, had chosen to hide near the scene and was captured. Lieutenant Mills would later testify that he captured Cockman crouching behind a tree near the scene of the ambush. His weapon was not loaded and was still warm to the touch. Upon that evidence alone Cockman was tried and convicted of killing soldier John C. Howard. Judge R.B. Gillian sentenced Cockman to be hanged for the crime. As luck would have it, the war soon broke and miraculously Cockman escaped the sentence imposed upon him. That part remains a mystery. It most likely had something to do with the Yankee occupation of the county after the war. I am certain the Yankees had little sympathy for a slain Confederate soldier. As for the rest of the group of Outlyers, they maintained their silence concerning the matter for years. Some thirty years later several members of the group finally acknowledged their involvement in the skirmish. Thomas Maness said he was there, but always insisted he never fired a shot. William D. (Big-Foot Bill) Ritter said both barrels of his double-barreled shotgun snapped that day, failing to discharge their loads of buckshot. Ira Maness on the other hand always suggested that if everyone had shot like him that day there wouldn't have been any soldiers remaining. Ira had deserted the CSA after the battle of New Bern and had already had a taste of war prior to this engagement...Concerning their loyalty, one must ask; "Whose side were they really on?" The answer is NEITHER. They had families to care for and not the time nor the resources to devote to sparring with their northern brothers. War encourages men to survive by whatever means necessary. Many a domestic dog will bite you if you happen to step on his tail."

Dr. Henry B. Shields recounted the incident in the book, *Country Doctor for a Half Century*: [593]

Three Confederate Soldiers Murdered: The local outstanding event during the closing days of the war between the states was the willful murder of three Confederate soldiers by a group of Moore County men in a wooded spot not far from the present McLaughlin home on the Sanford highway, and close to the site of the once famous Trogdon's barroom. As I have said before, sympathy was often with the deserters from the Confederate army, because the poor folks hereabouts had little patience with the fight for slavery, since they owned no slaves themselves. Several times to my personal knowledge, a band of soldiers would encamp in the county, alert for possible draft evaders. One such group, commanded by a Lieutenant Mills, captured three deserters in the upper end of the county. They brought their prisoners to Carthage for the night, and early next day made off on foot for either Raleigh or Fayetteville, little dreaming that they themselves were walking into sudden and violent death. Meanwhile, a group of men, all friends and possibly relatives of the prisoners, had banded together to affect their rescue. They lay in ambush close by the old Plank Road, in a wooded thicket, and as the small unsuspecting group of soldiers and prisoners approached, they took expert aim and fired. Three soldiers fell dead; and in the resulting excitement and confusion, two of the prisoners managed to make their escape. One of them, who lived about eight and a half miles above Carthage later recounted that he reached home on foot, late that night, without having crossed a stream wider than he could jump--which meant that he had made a wide detour around by Eagle Springs, in order to avoid crossing Richlands and McLennon's creeks. The lieutenant, as soon as he could recover from the sudden and unexpected onslaught, made a search through the woods for the men responsible for the crime. He found one man: the Lieutenant's story on the witness stand later being that this person was discovered sitting under a tree, with an unloaded gun lying across his knees. On this slight, and very unreasonable bit of evidence, the unhappy man was brought to trial. But more of that later. The three dead soldiers were brought back to Carthage and their bodies laid in the old Tyson house, a deserted dwelling house that had formerly been used by John Tyson's widow. This same house was afterward moved further up the block and added to the old Tyson store. Everybody in town flocked up to see them; and boy-like, I was among them. The men were laid out on what looked like rough work benches. The excitement in the town was great, but feeling was divided between sympathy for the outliers who had killed them, and patriotic feeling for the dead soldiers. The rest of this story concerns the trial of the one man found near the scene of the killing, according to the sworn testimony of the Confederate Lieutenant in charge. I shall not give this man's name; I do not for a moment believe him guilty, and I see no reason for causing embarrassment to any of his descendants now living. However, the record of his trial and sentence is on file at the courthouse, where any interested reader may peruse it. He was charged with killing a soldier named John C. Howard...He was tried at Carthage, found guilty and sentenced to be hanged. The judge who pronounced sentence was R.B. Gillian, and the solicitor was R.P. Buxton, later judge of this district...He was sentenced to be hanged on September 23rd of that year. Here there appears to be a discrepancy between the records at the courthouse. The supreme court record gives the year 1864, and the county record the date of 1865. But be that as it may, the prisoner appealed to the supreme court. For fear that the jail in Carthage was not safe for him, the court, on motion, suggested that he be carried to Fayetteville and kept in jail there until called for. The supreme court of the state of North Carolina affirmed the decision of the lower court; yet- the prisoner was never hanged! The question is how did he escape this fate, for escape it he did. After the close of the war he married the above mentioned widow Howard, settled down about five miles outside of Carthage, and raised a family of eight children. He died in 1906.

The following letters, newspaper articles, letters and personal memories detail the conflict that took place in Moore and surrounding counties as the war raged on.

1862, November 26
Mother **Mary A. Harper,** stepfather **John Harper** and brother **Charles Harper** to **J.L. Stuart**. General wartime correspondence with brief mentions of **Granny Shields, Levi Davis, Marshal Williams, Stephen Davis, Dempsy Sheffield, Peter Shamburger, Isaac Cagle, Hamon Miller, Bill Owens, James W. Stephens, Cynthia Teague, Lydia Comer, S.L. Davis, Lutitia Davis, Mathany Teague, L.F. Teague, M.S. Teague, Sinthia Davis, M.P. Nall, Emily C. Nall, N.N.P.N., Aletha Owen, D. Spivy, P. Spivy, S. Spivy, Anlisa Davis** and **Susan Teague**. [594]

Mr. J.L. Stuart[.] Dear Son[,] I again rite in an Swore to your letter dated 17th[.] I was glad to see you was well and I truly hope these few lines will reach you in good health[.] we are all about like common in common health[,] but granny Shields took her bed with bowel complainte and dos like she used to[.] I was truly glad to here yesterday that you remembered your mother advice not to curse and not to play cards[.] it filled my heart with such joy that the tears fell from my eyes as by as big as bullets. I truly hope you will not let your morals splayed with wicked associates as a great many men will not keeping in vice that they hav to dec and giv an accounte for he deeds done in the boddy[.] I now you are wore out with the fatigue of work and being away from your home. I wish you could come home but you do not want to do it if you cant get to come other ways. Levi Davis & Marshall Williams has deserted[;] one has got home and are lying out Stephen Davis & [?] Allen has deserted and come home[.] they was paroled. Dempes Shuffel is trying to get clear of going by his house[.] the men here keeps on hunting conscripts. Peter Shamburger has had about 35 men garding him & Isaac Cagle and Hamon Miller & Bill Owens[,] it is said threatened to kill them and burn there property for hunting him and his crowd and abusing his wife[.] we are looking for the cavalry to make a hunt. Peter Shamburger sent to the court house for the cavalry to help hunte[.] they has not come yet we think these will be some were in our land before long[.] James W. Stephens sent me a letter this morning[.] he wishes to now when you are here are Petersburg. He want you to rite to him[,] 26 Reg[.] I never wanted to see anybody so bad as I want to see you[.] it looks like I cante stand it mutch longer[.] I am wore out with the horribles of this war. I never was so sorry for anybody in my life as I am for you and I pity you with all my heart and I can not find in the nuse any hopes of peace[.] and god only knows when it will be and if all the soldiers would lay down their arms and come home[,] there might be peace but if the Yankey holds on they will perish us all out after a while[.] the people in our State will not sell corn at any price now and the governor & legislature is laying the embargo on a great many [?] in our state[.] and he says in his message that the state must raise 10 regiments to defend the state[.] they are to leave 4 months and to go home and make there corps[.] this is part of his message[.] I must conclude my letter to a close[,] to remain your loving mother on till death. Mary A. Harper. If you got back to Petersburg or Richmond[,] I will go and see you or send you any things that you want if I have it. John Harper.

Dear brother[,] it is with much pleasure for me to seat[.] I am as well as common[.] you wanted to now if we thought Jin was with food or no. I dont think she is. You wanted to no what girls talked about you. I will tell you of a few but I cant name half a quarter of them[,] forget all of them[:] C. Teague, L. Comer, S.L. Davis, Lut. Davis, Thany Teague, L.F. Teague, M.S. Teague, Sinthia Davis, M.P. Nall, E.C. Nall, N.N.P.N., Aletha Owen, D. Spivy, P. Spivy, S. Spivy, Anlisa Davis, Susan Teague[.] that about half[.] no more at present[.] rite to me as soon as you can[.] Charley E. Harper to J.L. Stuart

1863, January 21

R.P. Buxton (*Fayetteville, NC*) to **Governor Z.B. Vance**.

Correspondence regarding offenses committed by outliers and deserters in Moore, Randolph, Montgomery and Chatham counties. [595]

Sir: In compliance with your request I proceeded to Moore County to make inquiry about the depredations recently committed up there, and to take steps towards arresting the offenders. I returned home last evening. Your excellency has been corrected informed as to the character of the offences committed in Moore and Randolph counties – the extent of them is however, probably greater than you have been advised of. There appears to be a pretty thoroughly organized gang, consisting at present of some fifty men, but their number augmenting constantly by deserters & others, who roam about in the upper end of Moore and the lower end of Randolph committing all manner of misdemeanors – they have been guilty of no felonies yet, so far as I heard of – tho they have attempted to take the lives of several militia officers by shooting at them. Most of their operations have hitherto been carried on in Randolph Co – to which county the members of the gang principally belong. By the way, your correspondent, Jos. S. Dunn, from Dunn's Xroads, is a citizen of Randolph, and not of Moore, as you supposed – and most of the matters referred to by him occurred in his county – which

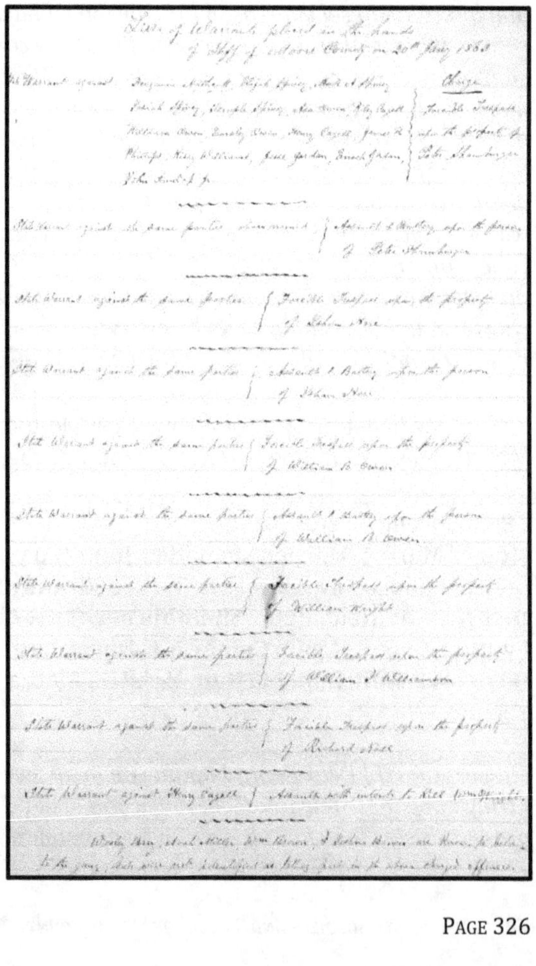

is out of my jurisdiction. While up in Moore I recd precise information of nine district offences committed by the depredators against the persons and property of citizens of that county – I also ascertained that names of 15 of the gang that perpetrated the offences. I accordingly took out warrants for their apprehension in each case, and placed them in the hands of the shff of Moore for service. Being satisfied, your excellency, that the Sheriff was unable with any force that he could command, to effect the arrests, and aware that it was of the utmost importance to the sufferers in that section, that there should be no failure when the attempt was made – I directed the Sheriff not to proceed under the warrants, or even disclose that he had them in his hands, until I communicated with you and recd advice as to the course you thought best to pursue. The militia officers in that section, who were disposed to do their duty – and I am sorry to have to say I was informed that there were many who were not so disposed – have been intimidated by the threats and acts of violence to which they have been subjected. They have been hunted, captured and parolled (!) with the distinct threat that any further effort on their part to enforce the law or any disclosure of what had occurred would be punished with death. Such being the state of things, how are these offenders to be arrested? Evidently the Sheriff of one county cannot do it – for they have accomplices and places of rendezvous in several counties, and when hunted from one, will take refuge in another. The Sheriffs of the counties (Moore, Randolph, Montgomery and Chatham) will have to cooperate with each other and with the military force, which your excellency proposes to call out. It has been suggested to me, and I think it proper to bring the suggestions to your attention – that a company of calvary, is such could be detailed for that service, would be most effective in scouring the county and making these arrests. Capt. Jesse L. Bryan's Co 2d Regt. Calvary – I understand, was raised in that section – his men are personally acquainted with the offenders and know the county. Accompanying is a list of names with the offences charges in the State Warrants now in the hands of the Shff of Moore. Very Respectfully, Your Obedient Sevt., R.P. Buxton.

List of Warrants placed in the hands of Shff of Moore County on 20th January 1863: **Benjamin Northcutt**, **Elijah Spivey**, **Mark A. Spivey**, **Josiah Spivey**, **Temple Spivey**, **Asa Owen**, **Riley Cagell**, **William Owen**, **Emsley Owen**, **Henry Cagell**, **James R. Phillips**, **Kisey Williams**, **Jesse Jordan**, **Enoch Jordan** and **John Dunlap Jr**. for forcible trespass, assault and battery, and assault with the intent to kill against **Peter Shamburger**, **Isham Hare**, **William B. Owen**, **William Wright**, **William J. Williamson** and **Richard Nall**. Separately, **Wesley Bray**, **Noah Miller**, **Wm. Brown** and **Joshua Brower** are known to belong to the gang but were not identified in the above offenses.

1863, February 20

Mary A. Harper and **John Harper** to son (and stepson) **J.L. Stuart**. General wartime correspondence with mentions of deserters, conscripts, **Elijah Spivey, Temple Spivey, Murphy Owens, William Deaton, Willis Aaron Nall, Levi Deaton, John Brewer, Polly Brewer, John Teague, Permelia Teague** and the death of a deserter **Morgan.** [596]

Dear son[,] I again rite in answer to your letter 15th this instant[.] I was glad to find that you was well but I sorry to here that you can not get letter from me for I make one to you every week but some times two[,] and I fear they keepe the money and letter[.] I took it the poste office[.] if they was sent rite[,] you wonte get them[.] my health is bad and it fore days but I keep trying So all I can[.] it is gitting to be hard times here[.] the people has got very little corn to sell in the contry and at the price 2 to 3 dollars a bushel and there is about one horse in cavalry[.] men in our neighborhood hunting conscripts and Deserters and they are to feed and they are taking all the horses from the deserters and the men that Joins them deserters[.] they took two from Lige Spivey[,] 3 from Temple Spivey[,] from Murphy Owens and 3 from Wm Deaton[.] and they say they will take all the horses from the Deserters if they dont come in and giv themselves up[.] they say they will hunt for year or get them[.] The deserters is close[.] they hav not got none in our neighborhood yet. I saw 42 of the cavalry yesterday morning a paste our house[.] they look poorly. you State that you thought you would be a long after a while to see us[.] I want to see that time come mity bad So that I can get to see you for I cante got to a letter to you[,] and that upsets me because a letter from Oren [Aaron] Nall yesterday an[.] he say he is well and hearty and sends his best respects to you and tells you not to griev for too hard bout you[.] he thinks we will see him and you at home before long and he thinks he will be man soon. He is at Fredericksburg yet and says if the yankeys will come over they will get them a worser whipping than they got before. the rest of our family is all well as common. I stated in a letter to you 2 weeks ago that about 3 weeks past there come a deserter from Raleigh home with Levi Deaton[,] both deserters. Deaton left the man names Morgan at John Brewers in the nite. Seek and gave out and he went home. Morgan stayed all nite at John Brewers[.] he complained of the matris and say nothing else about him.

Brewer had him near my house next day and he beg to Stay all nite and I can not get shot of him[.] he begs me to let him lye in the home and I don ot but he could not walk and in the nite I brought him in and let him ly on a bed in the shed that nite[.] about 2 oclock I heard him praying and calling me[.] I wente to him and saw a braking out in his fase[.] I gav him some tea and Started him with mair and got him to Bill Deatons and Deaton let him stay all nite and next morning[.] Deaton took him to (illegible) on his way home and that nite he died and they said they did not now what else from[,] but the truth is he had the small pox for one of Deatons children has dyed with pox and Polly Brewer has got the pox now. We have escaped the pox yet and 20 days has passed and I hope we may not take it but if we escape it will be good luck. Morgin told us nothing but lyes. He said he had not been in the army and he was run away from the (illegible) in Raleigh, I must tell you my dreem. I dreamed last Wednesday nite that I saw my poor son come home from the army and you comin and sat down by the fire and I was lying on the bed and John Teagues wife was setting by the fire and you and her was talking and I did not now who you was and you talked awhile[,] and I said Meary ant that John my son and she said yess. I sprang from the bed and came to you and you looked at me and I fell on my nees at your chare and threw my arm around your neck[.] and I thot you dropped your head on your nees and your color changed and the dollars stove in your eyes like sparkles but you never spoke to me and I waked crying and I happen asked you what was the matter. I saw you as plain as I ever did. I was in hopes you had (illegible)...a dream but if we don't meet again no more on this earth but hav to meet in heaven and there we will part no more. I must close by hoping you may get this letter. Your absent mother. M.A. Harper. [followed by short and illegible note from John Harper]

1863, March 22
Mary A. Harper to son **J.L. Stuart**. General wartime correspondence with brief mentions of clashes between deserters and of **Haywood Nall, Elijah Spivey, Murphy Owens, James Phillips, Bill Owens, Mark Spivey** and **John Brewer.** [597]

Mr J.L. Stuart[.] Dear son[,] I now rite and answer to your letter dated 12[.] I was glad to find that you was well[.] I am on foot but along with all my complaints[,] my eyes is getting so that I cant see but little and I fear they will loose site in time. the rest of the family is as well as common and I truly hope these few lines may find you well and doing well. Haywood Nall is at the salt works at Wilmington[.] the cavalry and foot troops is still in our neighborhood hunting deserters. Elige Spivey has 2 sons & Murphy Owens and his two sons, James Phillips and Bil Owen is the crowd that is hunted & Bill Owens with a company of about 12 men is all that the men is hunting for & they say they will halt them if they see them[,] and if they do not halt[,] they will shoot them down[.] if they fetch them[,] they mean to appoint a day for their execution and for all to come in out of the neighborhood that has had anything stole from them and see them whip these deserters to death and make them tell all they has stole from. they shot at Lige Spivey & Mark. Constable went and did not hit them. I hear they take them in after awhile but I fear not soon enough. We hav had a cold streak for the last 4 days heavy enough to brake the limbs of our [illegible] trees and dead trees. John[,] my Son[,] I do want to see you come home mity bad[.] I often fear I never shall but hold up your leave. There is a better day a coming when the soldiers will get to return home. The small pox has not spred none from John Brewers. His family is all so that they can do about home but they are not allowed to visit ther neighbors yet. No neighbors has went to Brewers house yet but they do his milling and take it to his house and he gets[,] but we have kept clear of the pox and I hope we wont yet by taking care of ourself. We are trying to farm a little[.] we hav planted a big batch of [illegible] potatoes and hav planted our garden with onions and [illegible] beans and hav commenced taking up corn ground and hav cabbag plants growing and if the war would stop and you could get to come home[,] I think we could be yet. you stated you thought you could get a furlow and come home soon[.] I wish you could for I want to see you as bad as ever said and if I can not get to see you[,] I muste keepe riting to you and you must do as you hav done for it is some satisfaction to here from you[,] but I am mity bad you will be in a fite at new bern soon[.] I donte want you to be in no moor fites if it can be helped[.] I am out of paper now and must conclude and Stop my letter by saying I am your affectionate Mother on till death. M.A. Harper

1863, April 14
Phillip Wilson on behalf of **Jeremiah Phillips** (*Moore County, NC*) to **Governor Z.B. Vance**. Correspondence regarding offenses committed by the militia in Moore and Randolph counties. [598]

To his Excellency Z.B. Vance Governor of North Carolina. In reply to a request made of me, Jonathan J. Martindale and other by David M. Barnes aid de camp to his Excellency concerning the arresting of a certain man Jeremiah Phillips of the county and state aforesaid that said Jeremiah Phillips has this day made oath before me, Phillip Wilson one of the acting justices of peace in said county that his horse was taken from him by B.G. Campbell Lt Col of sixty-fourth Regmt. NCM of the county of Randolph. That on Tuesday the seventeenth of March, that or Wednesday, the eighteenth, he was taken himself by the said Campbel of the county and regmt. Before named, that he was taken to the camp in Randolph County about eight miles from his home, that on the same knight he was in the guard house, that a man by the name of Thomas tied a rope round his neck threw it over the post, drew him up and choked him hurting his neck very bad. That after letting him down they abused him bad with a lightwood knot, that the said B.G. Campbell was an eyewitness to all, that no man interfered in his behalf, that on Friday the twentieth they sent him and his hors home. The militia officer and Campbell are one and the same person. Jeremiah Phillips and Phillip Wilson

1863, April 26
John Harper to stepson **J.L. Stuart**. General wartime correspondence with brief mention of deserters stealing from **John Comer, Adam Comer** and **Aaron Davis.** [599]

I now rite in answor to our letter Dated 12[.] We are all on foot and able to ete our allowance[.] I hope you are well and may stay well and I hope you may still has good luck[.] and I hope you may still hav good luck[,] the good mercy of god to return home[.] I am now starting off after corn and will be gone this week[,] and I will rite you more when I return. the Deserters is very troublesome in our neighbourhood[.] they come about 30 of them on friday night to John Comers house and asked to now where Adam Comers bacon was and it was in John Comers house[.] left and they went up and took about 500 lbs of all of it and Say they in tend to kill him yet they stole Aron Davis corn last week[.] and they are getting bold enough to goe and take what they want before peoples faces[.] I donte think the people can shame them and I hope they will be taken up and punished no more[.] only I am trying to doe the best I can[.] trust in god[,] John Harper

1863, June 24
Chesley Jones, JP (*Fall Creek Post Office, Chatham County, NC*) to **Governor Z.B. Vance**. Correspondence reporting the murder of a young man **Phillips** accused by the local militia of being among Confederate outliers and deserters. His parents requested that a warrant be taken out on the murderers. [600]

Mr. Z.B. Vance Governor of NC. Dear friend, I am with you inauguration but I envy you as a friend. I take this opportunity to write you a few lines to let you know what has occurred in one part of the county. Presently I am acting justice of the peace for the county of Chatham and living in the southwest corner of said county near Moore and Randolph Countys where there is a great many Lincolnists deserters and conscripts but my motif is inform you what took place recently. The militia was ordered by you or some other person to search for those outlyers[.] they went on one night and came across some four or five conscripts[.] they say they holted them they ran some of them, shot and killed one of them, a young man by the name of Phillips. The parents of this young man came to me for a warrant to arrest thos men who was a hunting that night for killing their son and I do not feel like to giving them warrant they say they will report to you if do not give them a warrant to arrest them and have them put in jail for trial and now I want you to write to me what I must do shortly to appease those persons for they are after me to arrest them[.] they threaten very much[.] I told them that I would write to you and whaever you sed do I would as to the characters of those that was a hunting that night is good tet are good loyal sitisons to there county. As to character to of the young man that was kild, there is not but they state case belaid to his charge, one is that he has disobeyed the laws of this county in lying out, another is that he was found in bad and very company bad at least for they outliers has done a great deal in some of mischief in that secsion of county in stealing...hiding working tools, and such but I want you to writ to me soon a few lines and let me know what I must do but I do not feel like arresting good setisens for anything they do to chase outliers who are doing all the mischief they can[.] as to the father of this young man he is a real Lincolnite incouraging his boys and others to ly out and is accuse of harboring them and if I were to arrest I should haald a Lincolnite and a tory by all good sitisons of the county and I had rather suffer a most anything than to be called a tory or a Linconite and so I must end by giving my best respects to you as a friend I remain at present[.] Direct your letter to the Fall Creek Post Office, Chatham County. Chesley Jones, JP

Semi-Weekly Standard [August 4, 1863] "PUBLIC MEETING IN MOORE COUNTY." [601]

"At a meeting of the Conservative party of Moore county, held in District No. 16, on Friday the 24th of July, 1863, on motion of T. W. Ritter, Capt. Elias Maness was called to the chair, and Elias T. Williams appointed Secretary. The chairman in a few appropriate remarks, having stated the object of the meeting, on motion, of T. W. Ritter, James Garner, Lewis G. Maness, Peter S. Moody and C. L. Allred were appointed a committee to draft resolutions expressive of the same, who reported through their chairman the following resolutions, which were unanimously adopted: WHEREAS, The time has arrived when the people of North-Carolina should guard with jealous care their rights and their liberties, and look with an eye single to their interests. We deem it our duty as freemen of North-Carolina, to meet in public council and express our views in regard to the policy the Confederate government has thought proper to pursue towards North-Carolina, and take a position upholding and defending the liberties of the people of the State, pledging our lives, our fortunes and our sacred honor in her defense, whether against kings abroad or tyrants at home; therefore, be it Resolved, That the course of the Confederate government towards North-Carolina from the beginning of the war, has been any thing but fair and honorable, and that, let her blood flow ever so freely, not a word is said, or charitable act done, to honor the valor or patriotism of her sons. Resolved, That notwithstanding North-Carolina has furnished more men in proportion to her inhabitants than any other State to prosecute this war, she has fewer Brigadiers or Major Generals to command them than any other State; of the injustice of which the people have long complained, but as yet their complaints have been utterly disregarded. Resolved, That while North Carolina has able and skillful physicians and officers, competent to perform the duties assigned them, the Confederate government has sent to this State physicians and officers from Richmond, to examine and enroll her conscripts, thus treating with contempt the intelligence of the State. Resolved, That the appointment of one Bradford, (a Virginian,) chief Tithingman for North Carolina is an insult to the State, and that we demand his removal, and that some North-Carolinian be appointed in his stead Resolved, That North-Carolinians are capable of performing any duties assigned them by the Confederate government, and we protest against the practice of appointing men from other States to perform duties within her borders which her own sons can do as well. Resolved, That the Davis administration, having called upon the Governor for seven thousand militia, we deem it unjust to the best interests of the State that any more troops be furnished, until other States have furnished their just quota of men. Resolved, That in view of the bad treatment this State has received at the hands of the Confederate government, and the insults constantly heaped upon her, we deem it the duty of all North-Carolinians to demand their discontinuance, or we shall in self defense be compelled to take a position where we can take care of ourselves; and we call upon the people of North-Carolina to hold meetings in their respective counties, and declare whether they shall be freemen or slaves. Resolved, That in our opinion, W. W. Holden is one of the ablest and boldest defenders of the rights of the people in the State, and that the stand which he has taken in their defense, is a just cause of pride to every true North-Carolinian; and that we recommend the Standard, under his control, to every lover of freedom, and to all those who hate tyranny and oppression. Resolved, That these proceedings be published in the Raleigh Standard and Fayetteville Observer." Elias Maness, Ch'm.

1863, September 28
Cornelius Dowd (*Carthage, NC*) to Col. **S.G. Worth**. Correspondence regarding deserters in Randolph and Moore. [602]

My dear friend: Having been honored with the command in chief of the Home Guards of this county and having learned with great pleasure that you had been similarly honored in Randolph. The only regret being that having more companied than me, your rank is higher. I desire an interchange of views with you and would like to make some arrangements and hear suggestions in regard to future movements and among other things to request you to keep your deserters and excusant conscripts from coming down into Moore lest they injure this county's fair fame! The Home Guards of this, Randolph, Chatham and Montgomery are ordered to report for duty to Col. Faison 56 Regt. but I understand he has been ordered back to Virginia. So what are we to do if we are to operate on our separate responsibility we must act in concert else when I get after the conscripts from your county who are disgracing the upper end of the this [county], they will run over the line homeward and I shall have accomplished nothing. So let me hear from you right away and lets make arrangements such as will at least present the evil from growing if we could do no more. I regret very much sir, to hear of so many deserters in your county and beg to assure you that it will at all must afford me great pleasure to lend you the aid of my loyal forces in apprehending them. Hoping to hear from you by return mail. I am as ever, very truly yours, C. Dowd.

The Greensboro Patriot [October 15, 1863] "ROBBERY** and **INCENDIARISM." [603]

"We regret to learn that on the night of the 23d Sept. the Barn and School House of Harris Tysor, Esq. of Fair Haven, Moore county, were consumed by fire, with nearly all his Winter feed for stock. He had fortunately moved his wheat from the barn a day or two previously. His tannery was entered at the same time and nearly all his leather taken. As a friend in that neighborhood writes, "Mr. Tysor is one of the best, most energetic, industrious, and charitable citizens in that section." This mischief has been done him by a band of vile outlaws, deserters and cowardly conscripts. We trust that a speedy retribution will overtake them – Fayetteville Observer"

1863, December 3
Alexander K. Pearce (*Old Capitol Prison*) to **Bryan Tyson**. General wartime correspondence with brief mention of the deaths of **Neill McDonald, Benjamin Northcut** and **Phillips, John Garner, Alfred Brower, Noah Richardson, Merritt A. Sugg, Lewis Spinks, Reuben Maness, William Maness** and **James Tyson**. [604]

Mr Tyson sir I received your letter of Nov 30 I now try to answer it Neill McDonald was killed as I before stated by a party of cecesh and soldiers it was because he was working for the union cause and as he had but one arm he would be nothing lost and they thought it would stop the union cause but alas they were mistaken[.] the more they kill the more union ther was[.] John Garner was shot in the arm so that he lost the benifitt of it[.] This was for nothing but becaus he was aiding in the union cause[.] Another horble murder was committed in Chatham one Phillips was shot while traveling along the road he was an innocent man never did any man any harm but because he was aiding in the union cause he was shot[.] Another horable act was committed near Ashboro in Randolph by shooting an old grey headed man[.] this one for nothin but because he was a union man and would not yield to the cecesh party [.] Another murder was committed at Ashboro the man executed was Benjamin Northcut if he ever did anything but what was right I do not no it[.] he was well thought of by the union party as he was on that said what he saw would do the union good and because he had much influence over the people he was killed but all this don no good[.] the more they killed the more union ther was four men they said or some of them said just before being killed that they were dying in a good cause that they had rather die at home then to die in the Rebel cause[.] all thes murders is true[.] Thes men was fighting from the union cause when they could they would defend themselves more than thes would have been if the union had not been so strong often would they take a man to kill him but the union men would go and take him by force of arms in one of thes acctions[.] there was one Rebel officer killed this was near Christian union. A. Brower's property was taken because he used the union men and wives with shame[.] he is a strong cecesh he dos all he can against the union but they are too strong for him[.] ther has been several such cases Noah Richardson was treated with the same M.A. Sugg, Lewis Spinks and many others all by the union men just because of their abuse[.] Ther has been many union meetings held in Randolph and adjoining countys and if they could only have help they would soon put down this Rebelion[.] when I left ther they were whiped and even I heard some say that they never had been cecesh but alad it is recorded[.] ther is no doubt in my mind they will be remembered by the union[.] I believe if nothin else will not stop the rebellen that famine will for when I left hom every thng was high and not any to be bought and ther are many poor wives and children suffering at this time for somethng to eat and rear but I hope that the time is not far distant when peace wil flot over our country and instead of hearing the roaring cannon we wil hear the blessful sound of the gospel and the farmer will return to the fields to make provision for the poor that are suffering[.] if I could be with you I could tell you many things that would be interesting to you for the tim is close at hand when we can talk freely together[.] Reuben Maness is in the Rebel army he belongs to the 46th Regt. Co. G. he is strong for the south and his brother Wm. is strong for the union cause he is going to school at Jackson Springs in Moore[.] I hope you will succeed in helping me in the union cause anything you or any other man can do I am willing[.] your brother James' legg was no amputated the last I heard but he was badly wounded in his thigh but I think his leg or thigh was not broken write soon, respectfuly yours, A.K. Pearce

1864, January 1
Thomas W. Ritter (*Carthage, NC*) to **Governor Z.B. Vance**. Correspondence reporting the killing of two of the

local ring leaders (**Joseph Brewer** and **Davis**) by the home guard. He also reported that **Adams Brewer** and **Peter Garner** killed **George Moore** and wounded two others. [605]

His excellency Governor Vance, Dear sir, I received yours of the 23rd December 1863 as for Maj. Dowd having given orders to burn those still houses I know nothing about as I stated to you that the men that burned the houses stated that they were acting under orders from the Maj. And Maj. Dowd said that he give no such order. I don't know that Maj. Dowd knew anything at all about it. I was asked to state the facts to you which I did and as for the two men that was shot, Davis & Brewer, as for their being shot trying to escape from the guard that I do not think is so. They certainly were parted from the other two conscripts that were taken at the same time and carried a different road to the camp and before they got to the camp they Davis & Brewer were parted and found shot and were fast tied when found and no doubt were separated an purpose to be shot. Davis I suppose was found shot by a log as if he was setting on the log when shot and fell over by the side of the log with his brains shot out and as for being ring leader of a band of robers I no nothing about I have no doubt from report that they were both bad men and were concerned in a great deal of the stealing that has been don in this county[.] There has been a man by the name of George Moore killed since by Adams Brewer. Moore was a poor man with a large family, was conscripted under the last call and did not choose to go to the war and took the thicket[.] there was some bad reports on Moore but I think he was accuse of moore that he was guilty, he was just trying to keep out of the way because he did not want to go to war and Brewer and a man by the name of Peter Garner slipped up to Moore & two others and without saying a word presented and fired killing Moore and wounding one of the others there was a man standing talking to them when they were short who give the facts as they were[.] Brewer shot Moore and had swore before on several occasions I suppose that he would shoot him if he ever come up with him Brewer is an old man don't belong to the army nor the militia and Peter Garner is a conscript himself and has so managed to be detailed I believe to cetch conscripts and deserters. He shot the other and wounded him very badly. They had no arms nor nothing to fight with[.] I suppose and could have been taken very easy without shouting shooting the people are getting tired of Peter Garner condict any way and want him gone. Sent to the army where he should be and as for Brewer the majority of people want him delt with as a murderer should he Moore lived in Moore County but was shot just over the line in Randolph County. It is two and for man to be murdered up in that style. Any other information that is wanting in the premacies can be had at anytime. Most respectfully yours, Thos. W. Ritter.

1864, January 7

Maj. Clement Dowd (*Carthage, NC*) to **R.P. Buxton** (*Fayetteville, NC*). Correspondence reporting local skirmishes between the home guard and outliers with brief mentions of **Sam Barrett, Gen. Hoke, William R. Bryant, Franklin Muse, George Williams, Charley McLean, James N. Caddell, Z.B. Moore, Alexander McLeod, Capt. Ramsey, Dr. Hector Turner**, the killing of two of the local ring leaders (**Joseph Brewer** and **Davis**) by the home guard. He also responded to accounts of **Adams Brewer** and **Peter Garner** killing **George Moore** and wounding two others. [606]

My dear sir; Yours of the 6th is in hand and in reply I take pleasure in giving you such information as I have, in reguard to the matters inquired of – Old Sam Barretts distillery (in which four stills were running day & night) was burned about 10th Nov by a squad of soldiers, as his son, the distiller, says, from Hoke's Brigade. The detachment of Genl. Hokes Brigade on duty in this county at that time were ordered away soon afterwards, and I have never learned to what Reg or Co they belonged, nor whether they burned the distillery under orders or not. A still house owned, by Wm. R. Bryant, a young militia officer of this county, was burned about the same time, and to was a still house owned and operated by Franklin Muse and George Williams, both worthless characters, by a party of citizens while out on duty as Home Guards. That however was no part of the duty assigned by the commander of the H.G., who as you may or may not know, is myself. An attempt has been made by the distillers of this county, of whom I am sorry to say there is an incredible number, that I ordered the burning of these distilleries, because of a push which I made against them as our last county court because of my known opposition to such lawlessness. The militia who did the burning did not disavow the act nor pretend that they were acting under orders from anyone. The principal actors I believe were Charley McLean, son of your landlord, James N. Caddell, a paroled prisoner, Z.B. Moore, Alexr. McLeod & some others whose names I have not heard. These men, I am sure, acted from the very best of motives, and I doubt not also with a [illegible] sense of duty and ignorance of the law. Brewer & Davis were shot by a squad of Capt. Ramsay's men (detailed from the 59th Regt. I believe to arrest deserters in this county) while going from their camp in the woods to Ramsay's camp near Deep

River. They are desperate characters and ring leaders of the worst band of robbers and plunderers that ever infested any community. It has been said, by their friends & shelters exclusively I think, that they were wantonly murdered. But this I do not believe. A piry of inquest was held over Davis & the verdict was that "the decd. Came to his death by being shot through the head," by whom & under what circumstances does not appear. I think I may apply say that the most intelligent & respectable of our citizens were disgusted at the attempt to hold an inquisition, and I am informed by Dr. Turner who was summoned as surgeon, that but for a few [illegible] female characters present, the jury would not have been impaneled. Even the brother of the decd. Was willing that the jury should not be sworn as Ramsay's men attempted no concealment whatever in regard to the matter. Dr. Turner also informs me that he made inquiries concerning the whole affair of a young man belonging to Ramsay's Co who must from this county and whom he knew to be in everyway reliable and truthful who informed him that he himself was on of the guards who had these men in charge, that they attempted to escape by darting off into the thicket, were fired upon & Davis instantly killed, the other ran nearly a mile, were pursued & halted again & again & at length coming in range of one of the men, still running, was fired upon and killed. I am not so well informed as to the killings of George Moore, another notorious robber & escaped conscripts, but have heard that he was shot by Peter Garner, a detailed soldier from Mallett's Battalion to hunt deserters & c. and by a citizen named Adam Brewer who has been completely broken up by the robbers & who has been very active lately in arresting & apprehending these desperados. Moore & another were found in the woods with guns, were fired upon by Garner & Brewer, Moore was killed & the other wounded. There is much for you to do in this county. We have a real retched state of things here and if I am not run off or murdered before court I hope to be able to give you assistance & c. Would it not be well to ask Mr. Hale to publicize the act of assembly entering the court...Very truly yours, C. Dowd

1864, February 16
Maj. Clement Dowd to **Governor Zebulon B. Vance**. Correspondence reporting problems with deserters with brief mention of Capt. **Jesse S. Bryant**. [607]

Governor: Since the withdrawal of Capt Ramseys Compy from this County the deserters & skulkers have renewed their acts of violence and robbery. Not a week, and scarcely a night, passes without some smoke house being robbed of its entire contents or some act of violence done to families and property of loyal people. I have had the Home Guard out for nearly a month and am sorry to say I have accomplished but very little with them. They cannot be relied on. Those who know the Country are the friends of the delinquents almost to a man. They profess a willingness, many of them, to obey orders but take care to do nothing substantial. If they shoot it is purposely to miss. About one third of them are true and reliable, but they are ignorant of the localities which the deserters frequent and the news of their approach is always in advance of them. Capt. Jesse S. Bryant of Co I 2nd NC Cavalry has been at home for a long time on detail to buy horses for the Regt. He is an experienced huntsman, well acquainted with the various parts of this County, is a man of unusual energy and dash. With 10 or 15 men from his company he could catch more deserters than the whole of the Home Guard. Nay, I have no doubt could with the assistance of the H G soon rid the County of these cutthroats. I have no doubt but that every month with 15 men he could return to duty a like number of delinquents & deserters and then he would keep down this frightful plundering. So far as regards the expense, the Home Guard of this County has already expended enough to feed him & his men for six months. It would be infinitely cheaper, better for the County and better for the service to detail Capt Bryant and his Compy or a portion of it for permanent duty in this County. Will you not ask for his detail for this purpose. We are sadly in need of assistance. Very Respfy Your obt Servt, C Dowd Comdg Home Guards

The Daily Confederate [February 27, 1864] "Murder, Violence** and **Treason." [608]

"The following letter from Randolph county, will give some idea of the mischief which the Agitators in North Carolina are producing. And this will be but the beginning if stern and prompt measures be not taken to arrest the evils. We call the attention of the Confederate. We call the attention of the Confederate and State authorities to the enormities and outrages. reported by our correspondent: RANDOLPH Co, N. C., Feb. 22, 1864. Messrs. Editors: On last Wednesday, the 17th, several deserters went to the house of Mr. Pleasant Simons, of Montgomery county. Some four of them entered his house after the family had retired to bed and demanded bacon of him. He concluded to give them some and ordered his daughter to get it. She brought then two hams: they said that

would not do, they must have more. They then went to the smoke-house, broke the door open and begun to cut down the meat; when an acquaintance, Mr. Jacob Sanders, who was lodging with Mr. Simons that night, got up and went out to them, with Mr. Simons. The deserters ordered them back in the house, or they would shoot them. They went back, but Mr. Sanders got a gun and repeater from Mr. Simons and went out armed, when the wretches fired on them, killing Mr. Sanders and mortally wounding Mr. Simons. Mr. Sanders fired twice or three times before he expired, and it is believed he killed the noted Bill Owens, and probably one other. Mr. Sanders died in fifteen minutes; Mr. Simons survived some twenty-four hours. Mrs. Simons came out of the house to her Husband, when the devils ordered her back in the house or they would put lead in her: that they had sent their sons to the war, and they were all a d--d set of secessionists, and took up a rock to put an end to Mr. Simons, as they said he was not quite dead. His daughter interceded, and they left to take off their wounded or dead. Six or eight balls went through the smoke-house door, and one ball through the dwelling house door. The yard was strewn with human gore: it stood in some places in puddles, where the men lay. I attended the funeral of my friend Mr. Simons, who was a very respectable citizen, as was also Mr. Jacob Saunders-both men over 60 years of age, and leave large families, having sons in our army. Only a few days previous, a Mr. Cagell was shot in the same neighborhood, but not mortally. Can nothing be done to put a stop to those acts of murder and treason?"

1864, February 27
Lauchlin McKinnon *(Moore County, NC)* to **Governor Zebulon B. Vance**. Correspondence reporting problems with deserters and requesting leave for his son-in-law, **W.S. McDonald** and brief mention of **General Pettigrew.** [609]

Dear Sir. I am constrained to write one more concerning my Son-in law W. S. McDonald who is now at home on parole. he was wounded at Gettysburg P.a. & taken prisner & cared to Davids Island NY wher he Remained about three months. he is now Exchanged & cald for again & if you take him you may take me also for I am Surrounded with theivs & Robers & I can not Sleepe for fear of being deprived of all my living as severl of my Nabors has Sufferd by the deserters as a great meny got close as mechanics & for meny other Resons. I think prope to say that I have a mill on a neer failing Strem & I also a vary good Black smith shop as I am not able to do anything my selfe. Mr. McDonald tends to both & if he is taken away Both must go to naught perhaps you would be told that I have blackies. I ha one black man on the deal and a Sickley black woman 2 half grown Black girles all told. five /of my sons/ has fell in this war. I have neither son no daughter with in 40 miles of me except McDonald wife & if he leavs She will be a charge to me. Dear Sir I do not know that you have full power to discharge my Son in law But I do Know you have Some influence & hope you will excercise it in my favor. W.S. McDonald Served in Co. D 26 Regt NC Troop. he was in listed October the 9 1862. it may be nesesary for me to say that McDonald was discharged by his cpt. & Col. also by Gen petagrew an in conclusion I disposed of the moast of my stock to furnish the market. I have funded the money & never expect to se a sent of it for my foot is on the brink of the grave & I care not if we can Gain our independence. I have the pleasure of SubScribing my name as your well wisher Farewell. Lauchlin McKinnon

1864, April 23
Henry K. Trogdon (*Carmel Post Office, Hamilton County, IN*) to **Bryan Tyson**. General wartime correspondence with brief mention of the murder of **Neil McDonald** by **Stephen Brewer**, son of **Adams Brewer.** [610]

I will write you a short letter to night. Im well and enjoying myself fine. I have had my health very well ever since I came to this state. I hope this will find you in good health and doing well. I have not wrote to you as soon as I had aught to on the acount of writing what you requested me to answer. This is about McDaniels affares which I wanted to find out something more about it before I wrote to you. So that is the reason I have not wrote to you some well I dont no as I can tell you a greate deal about it. Only they went there at his House and took him out and tryed to make him tell wher some of the boys wer that wer in the woods he refused to tell them anything about them. they swor if he dident tell wher they wer they would shoot him[.] he told them he dident no wher they wer. They says you have to tell or die he says you will have to kill me then for I dont no anything about them he could do anything with them they shot him through the boddy. I cant say how long he lived after he wer shot but I dont think it was more than a day. his foalks heard the gun they went out in the woods wher they taken him and found him shot[.] they had all left him when they got to him[.] I dont no wher they wer any but one ball went *in him or not I think it wer Stephen Brewer shot him, that is Addams son. So I think that is as near how it wer don as I no of[.] Bryant I received a letter from home about a week a go[.] it wer wrote the 12 of Feb. they wer all wel but dident say anything about Pa. They sayed they had quilting last night had a fine time dident say anything about the tin. The boys are well as far as I no of at this time[.] pleas excuse me for not writing sooner I shall have to close for it is geting late. So I will close by Saying I hope to heare from you soone, from your affectionate, H.K. Trogdon P.S. I forgot to tell you what I am doing Im working on the Farm[.] I'm geting $26 per month board & washing in write to me what you are doing*

Fayetteville Semi-Weekly Observer [April 28, 1864] "Capture of a Noted Outlaw." [611]

"For the Observer. Asheboro, April 25, 1864. Messrs. Editors: Believing it will be pleasing to the Home Guards and others of the counties of Randolph, Moore and Montgomery, as well as the loyal citizens and soldiers everywhere, I have to state that the notorious Bill Owens has at last been captured and is now confined in Randolph jail. The Sheriff of Randolph having in his hands a capias against said Owens for burglary, on Saturday evening last received information of his whereabouts. On Sunday morning he summoned his posse, consisting of nearly all the men in Asheboro and others, and marched to a place some two miles southeast of Col. Jesse D. Cox's, where, upon breasting the woods for some half a mile, two camps were discovered, but appeared to have been deserted only a short time before, and on continuing the search further, some two hundred yards from one of the camps, the notorious Owens was discovered in a brush with his wife – no arms about him, and none of his associates to be seen. He has a dangerous wound, received as he says, in that affray at Simmons' last February. He is now where, it is to be hoped, justice will reach him. Peter Garner, a detailed soldier from the army, was met and summoned by the Sheriff, and was one of the Sheriff's posse when Owens was taken, and Garner was the first man that "bearded the lion." There were no remains of any property or goods about the deserted camps, save part of a newspaper – The Raleigh Standard.'

1864, July 15
Lt. and Enrolling Officer **J.A. Little** (*Carthage, NC*) to **Capt. D.C. Pearson**, Chief Enrolling Officer, 7th Congressional District. General wartime correspondence regarding deserters. [612]

Capt., the call for the substitute men will take off the only Vance candidate in the county. His supporters have been after me to furlough him, but I have refused as I have no right to do it. I would like the best in the world to accommodate them but there is no law for it. They have asked me to write to you about it. I told them it was no use as you would do as I did. Deserters are thick and heavy, some twenty went to preaching in the upper end, carried their guns and after preaching they went to a man's house and demanded dinner. They have been holding meeting an planning for the winter campaign. There is I understand 40 in one crowd, 20 in another. I can't count on the H.G. [Home Guard] or Militia as they are all of the same stripe. Next Tuesday I get off substitute men. I am your, J.A. Little.

1864, August 5
Lt. and Enrolling Officer **P.H. Williamson** (*Carthage, NC*) to **Capt. D.C. Pearson**, Chief Enrolling Officer, 7th Congressional District. General wartime correspondence regarding deserters. [613]

The supporting company arrived here on Wednesday evening. I was very sorry they did not stop at Coffins so as they could have gone up to Sheffields, but it was too far for them to march from here, and get them to march from here, and get them in time. I attended the Election at Ritters, no deserters present. I have since heard from Sheffields, not any of theirs, around Ritters is one of those worst holes in the Confederacy, the supporting company arrested three men on their way and wounded one pretty seriously. Lt. Mills received a very heavy blow (from the mother of the man that was shot) on side on his head. The women is bad as the men down here. Capt. I don't know what we will do for rations, only a hundred pounds of bacon in the commissary. Capt., the Col. Is straight after e about reporting. I was surprised to see it, for he gave me permission to call by home. I wish you would please explain it to him. Capt. I am fearful we haven't a sufficient force yet Capt., but I will do the best I can. Write soon & excuse haste. Very respectfully, P.H. Williamson. P.S. Capt. The deserters would vote any how after I had finished this letter, I heard that the deserters voted at two precincts, Mineral Springs and Saunders, a hundred at Mineral Springs & thirty-five at Saunders. I think that the judges ought to be arrested. They were all very well armed. They are getting to be very imprudent, they are stealing a good deal from the citizens, still the citizens don't care about arresting them.

Fayetteville Semi-Weekly Observer [August 11, 1864] "OUTRAGES IN MOORE." [614]

"For the Observer. Carthage, NC, Aug. 9. Messrs. Editors: We had a dreadful tragedy in this vicinity last Saturday morning. A detachment of the "Supporting Force" (Senior Reserves,) for this Congressional District had started to the "railroad with a squad of deserters and recusant conscripts whom they had apprehended. They were ambushed four miles below this place by a gang of deserters, fired into and 3 men killed, -to-wit: D. R. Rush of Randolph, J. C. Dodd and John Howard of Chatham and another, E. Womble of Chatham, wounded in the abdomen, died this morning at 2 o'clock. One of the prisoners escaped and one of the wretches was captured. He had in his pocket packages of minnie balls and powder, carefully wrapped up in the Raleigh Standard of the 18th July, which contains the celebrated "Hecuba" article in defense of the "Red String Party," declaring that that party is not worse than the Vance party and of course the latter is legitimate game for the bullets of the former. This fellow denies being a member of the "Red String," but gave us the names of a number of his comrades who do belong to it. We have a deplorable state of things in this county. Ever since the election large gangs of armed deserters have been roaming over the country, inquiring who of the citizens voted for Vance and who for Holden, swearing that they had been deprived of their rights and intended to have revenge. Within the last few days several large gangs have been seen in the vicinity of this village on different roads, some of the gangs numbering 20 to 30, and one estimated at 200, all acting in concert no doubt. Our Home Guard and citizens are under arms acting on the defensive. We are not quite ready yet for an aggressive movement. This, sirs, is the legitimate fruits of the seeds that have been sown. The blood of these murdered citizens is upon the hands the traducers of our Government. When men are taught that the war is unrighteous on our part; that the poor are forced by unconstitutional laws to fight for the property of the rich; that our Gov't is a despotism and our President a tyrant, and that "resistance to tyrants is obedience to God," no wonder they band together to resist the laws. It has been proclaimed by prominent men, on our streets and highways, that Jeff Davis and his cabinet and Congress ought to be hung, that the only way to settle our difficulty is to kill all the Secessionists (meaning all who do not join in the tirade against the Gov't.) and that fathers will not submit to have their sons hunted up and carried into the army, and a thousand other things calculated to inflame the minds of ignorant men and make them believe that it is their sacred duty to resist rather than obey the laws of the country. If there is power in the Government it ought to vindicate itself. This fire in the rear must be put out. These organized and armed traitors, their counsellors, aiders and abettors; must be crushed, and that speedily."

The Weekly Intelligencer [August 16, 1864] "DESERTERS ATTACK THE HOME GUARD." [615]

"We are reliably informed that a body of Home Guard, (forty in number,) dispatched for the purpose of carrying deserters to Raleigh, were attacked by a party of seventy or more deserters, near Carthage, in Moore county on Monday or Tuesday last. Four of the Home Guard were killed and it is said seventeen wounded. One deserter was captured after being wounded, and was lodged in Carthage jail. The frequency of such acts of outrage calls loudly to both the State and Confederate authorities, to capture and execute every deserter found, with a gun in his possession. The case calls for prompt and vigorous measures, and we trust that the authorities will arouse themselves to the importance of this matter, and act promptly and decidedly."

Fayetteville Semi-Weekly Observer [August 25, 1864] "DESERTED CAPTURED." [616]

"Some dozen or two of deserters have been captured and sent through this place to the army within the past week or two. Eleven were carried to Raleigh on the 20th from Moore county, and 2 have been captured near Greensboro."

The Daily Progress [September 2, 1864] "Murder in the First Degree" [617]

*"**Cockman**, the deserter, arrested for killing four citizens of Moore County, member of the Home Guard, near Carthage, was tried at Moore Court last week and convicted of murder in the degree. His attorney took an appeal to the Supreme Court, but the prisoner objected preferring to be hung rather than remain in prison in his wounded condition. The appeal was however taken." [Editor's Note: **William McSwain Cockman**]*

The Daily Progress [September 5, 1864] "Moore County" [618]

"The Carolinian of Friday says: We have heard from our brave soldier boys at Moore county. They are enjoying themselves hugely. We are enabled to announce authoritatively that there has been no "general engagement as yet." Our troops are maneuvering for a position. We like the tactics of our "General in command." So soon as he has foraged sufficiently in one quarter, he changes his base to a more eligible locality. We understand that a few deserters have been captured by "our forces," and that deserters from "the enemy" are coming into our live. We learn that Capt. Owens, who has been a sort of a leader among the deserters, is. now doing good service, bringing in three and four of his party at a time. In one instance he is said to have brought two in, in irons. Some of the prisoners are expected to arrive here tomorrow. Moore county will soon be rid of deserters."

Fayetteville Semi-Weekly Observer [September 8, 1864] "HORSE THIEF KILLED." [619]

"The notorious horse thief Fry was killed by the Home Guard in Moore county a few days ago. He rode a fine horse up to where the Guard were posted, without seeing them, and on being ordered to halt, endeavored to escape, and was shot, four balls equipping his body"

Fayetteville Semi-Weekly Observer [September 12, 1864] "Jones** and **Evans." [620]

"Jones and Evans.-We have received reliable intelligence, through a citizen of this place, who has received a letter from a Quartermaster in the service in Moore county, of the capture of the notorious murderer, Henderson Jones, and of the supposed killing of the burglar, Fry, alias Evans, who was in jail here awaiting his trial. Jones was tried for the murder of Stephenson at Alamance Superior Court, when he was convicted; he appealed to the Supreme court, and at the last June Term of that court, the judgment of the court below was confirmed. The gallows was full before him, and in his desperation to escape and with the help of some outside friends he broke our jail and made forthwith for the haunts of the deserters and outlaws in Randolph and Moore. We are glad to announce his apprehension, and congratulate the law abiding people, who so much regretted his escape and who so desired to see him pay the extreme penalty of the law. We suppose he will be returned to the Sheriff here to await condemnation at Alamance, where he will be exerted should he live and not again break jail. – Greensboro Citizen"

Fayetteville Semi-Weekly Observer [September 12, 1864] "SAD CASUALTY." [621]

"On Friday last, Alex'r Spence, of this county, one of the Home Guard on duty in Moore county, was instantly killed by the accidental discharge of a gun in the hands of a comrade. His body was brought here for interment."

Fayetteville Semi-Weekly Observer [September 19, 1864] "Returned to Jail." [622]

"Jones, convicted of the murder of Stephenson, and who broke Guilford County jail on the night of the 18th of July last; was returned to his old quarters yesterday, he having been captured in Moore county. Evans, who escaped at the same time with Jones, was not killed as has been reported, and is yet at large-Greensboro Citizen."

The Daily North Carolinian [September 21, 1864] "Deserters** and **Home Guards." [623]

"Speaking of deserters and Home Guards reminds us of a fact that should be noted. Although Moore county has become notorious for its many deserters we are pleased to be able to state authoritatively, that our citizens now upon duty in that county, speak in the highest terms of the citizens and the kindness they have received at their hands. The citizens of Moore are a free-hearted, generous people, and we are pleased to be able to do justice to them by this simple statement."

The Daily North Carolinian [September 26, 1864] [624]

"We understand that our Home Guards at Moore county arrested an escaped Yankee prisoner during last week. He belongs to the 14th Indiana infantry, and says he escaped with eight hundred others from Florence, where he

was confined. A number of these 'deserters' are now loose, and our people should keep a good lookout for them. They are easily secured, and recollect that every one is, in exchange, worth one of our brave men now confined in Northern prisons."

The Daily Progress [September 26, 1864] "Deserters Coming In." [625]

"The Observer says: We learn authentically that up to Tuesday night last 106 deserters had come in to the home Guard now in Moore county, and there is a good prospect of more coming in or being caught. Tomorrow is the last day allowed for an assurance of pardon upon voluntary return. We hear of many more in other counties who have come in. Among those caught the Salisbury Watchman mentions one man in Rowan county who had been a deserter for nearly two years."

1864, September 8
Alexander K. Pearce (*Washington, DC*) to **Bryan Tyson.** General wartime correspondence with brief mentions of **Neil McDonald's** murder and **Adams Brewer.** [626]

I received your letter today I am glad to hear from you after so long a time I am well and have been since I left Philadelphia[.] you wanted to know something concerning Niel McDonalds death[.] I almost forgetten the particulars of the rumors concerning his death but he was killed and ther is no doubt but by the soldiers[.] Adam Brewer was the cause of this cruel act and would serve me and you the same if he had the opportunity – but this was don more on account of his character then being in the union case if Neil had have been an honest man proably he might have been living yet—he was taken for a [illegible] as it was said[.] now this I do not know to be so only rumors but he was found dead with several bullets holes through his body[.] if I am not mistaken he was killed on Saturday night - and found Monday evning and I suppos his oaath was cruly don for the party was drunk. I do not know wither Neil a union man or that it was don more in the account of his robing and pilfering than anything else. Mr Bryant you know the clan of men in Moore County - better than I do and you can give and idea how they do if some more of them had served the same it would proably been better for the poor honest people this took place in Moore County. I would like to see one of Wilson books[.] wil you please send one wil you write where this Wilson came from[.] I think that he or any other man that can muster for the union can had [illegible word] better take his muskett in hand and come in front of Petersburg then to be printing such things as occurred in North Carolina[.] after this war wil be plenty time to publish such things there is no good in such[.] now is the tim to save the union first at this moment then let every man lay hold of the wheel and shove and the Rebellion wil soon be closed there will be time plenty to talk about politicks if all the biblical man was here[.] I think they could do more good[.] the soldiers are much split concerning the election I think on get is may as the other if anything Lincoln is the strongest[.] most all the officers are for him I would be very glad to see you[.] I could tell mor concerning this part than I can write. wil you please write when John Tomlinson is with you, have heard from him[.] lastly tell him where I am and to write to me pleas write soon and give me all the news. Very Respectfully Your friend until Death, Alex K Pearce. direct letter to Battery B. 4th US arty. 5 army corps, Washington D.C. P.S. all our letters are mailed to Washington thence to the corps

Fayetteville Weekly Observer [January 23, 1865] "Turner Fry." [627]

"Will the Fayetteville Observer please describe the personnel of the man calling himself William Turner Fry. We have a suspicion It is not the horse thief. Fry. Only two or three weeks ago he was in this county; and about that time a horse was stolen near Gold Hill. True, he may have gone to Fayetteville, but we are of opinion there are other persons passing in the name of Fry, when caught in a "scrape." Turner Fry is about 5 feet 7 inches high, black (or nearly black) hair, dark skin, heavy eye brows, seldom if ever looks any one straight in the face, is nervous and uneasy when spoken to, and shows it by moving his feet or changing position. Inclines his head forward-is stout built and will weigh about 150 lbs. If they have the veritable Turner in jail in Fayetteville, we warn the keeper of the prison to keep a sharp look out; for we believe he has broken out of almost every jail in 50 miles of this place - Salisbury Watchman
We never saw Fry, but there is no doubt about it that the man arrested here is he. He was recognized when arrested by a gentleman from Moore county at whose house he was married; and eventually confessed his identity. That he should be in Rowan county one day and in Cumberland the next, need not surprise any one who

reflects that he kept a horse in every man's stable, and when he rode down one, had only to take another. He has been removed from this jail, to that of Richmond county, from which he formerly escaped. Sheriff Long says he will "try to keep him this time."

The Morning Post [August 17, 1905] "Reminiscences from Moore County." [628]

"Our home was in the little village of Carthage, NC...Just outside the yard was a beautiful grass plot, and here it was for several months before the war broke out, that the soldiers practiced their drills and rehearsed all the maneuvers of the battle field. My father, an old line Whig, was bitterly opposed to secession, saying that the slavery questions should have been settled in the halls of Congress, but when the war broke out his sympathies of course were all with the South, and though exempt by age of shouldering arms, he did everything he could to make our fight victorious. Every afternoon for months before the war was declared I used to sit on the porch and listen to the rollcall and watch the assembling of the soldiers, and hear the tamp, tramp, tramp of their feet as they marched up and down, back and forth, to the rap, tap, tap of the drum. When the time came for our company to enlist, a good dinner was prepared by the ladies of the village, and served in a new a capacious carriage house belonging to Mr. T.B. Tyson. Then began the activity of preparations for departure, and in good style our men left us, armed cap-a-pie in the handsome accoutrements furnished by "Uncle Sam," and, as was natural under the circumstances, some things were forgotten among which may be mentioned a generous box of edibles I had prepared for my husband, and which I succeeded in sending to him by a trustworthy servant named Isam, who carried it to Cameron. The first encounter in which our men took part was at Bogue Sound, Captain Martin being in command; and being so eager to see all that was transpiring in the enemy's camp, he raised his head too high above the ambush and was shot and killed, leaving my husband in command. There were some deserters and outlyers among the ignorant classes in the upper edge of Moore, Randolph and Montgomery counties, and twice they threatened to burn our village, their attempts being frustrated by the constant vigil, day and night, of those who were left among us for our protection. My faithful servant, Isam, with his gun, slept, or rather watched, every night, under my window, on the porch, thus enabling me to get some good sleep, which otherwise I would have been unable to get. And in this connection, I will say that while at one time we had been fearful of the attitude of the negroes, they behaved well and, in many instances, proved good friends. Naturally we were in constant dread of the enemy coming into our village, and all sorts of precautions were taken to keep our valuable in places where they would escape the vigilant eyes and ruthless hands of the enemy. One of my faithful servants assisted me in burying deep down in our chicken house my gold and silver money. One wealthy lady fled with her husband to Greenville, and being determined that her property should neither be enjoyed nor demolished by the enemy, armed herself with a stout cane, went to her elegant mahogany sideboard and deliberately broke her costly glass and chinaware. She then took a hatchet and destroyed her handsome furniture. Her husband concealed his gold and silver money in his bots, and while his feet must have felt decidedly uncomfortable, he was willing to submit to a little inconvenience in order to smuggle his wealth in safety. One of my daughters, who had been in hourly terror of the enemy, and who determined not to surrender to them a ring she prized very much, sat day after day with her precious treasure in her mouth, afraid to speak lest her jewel be discovered, and equally afraid to swallow lest it disappear down her throat. Meanwhile the war continued, and government supplies giving out, the ladies had to knot socks, make caps (by a pattern ordered from Fayetteville), and as best they could keep our men as comfortable and presentable as possible...Mrs. L.J. Dowd, Charlotte, NC [Lydia Josephine Bruce Dowd, wife of Clement Dowd]

Isham Wallace [1801-1882] had seven sons that were eligible to serve in the war but only one, **Sampson Delaney Wallace**, served in the Confederate army. My grandfather, **Mallie Wallace**, remembered his grandfather, **Emsley Wallace**, saying that he and his brother would hide in the creek beds to avoid the conscription officers. He often wondered if Lane volunteered or was just caught and forced to join. The following excerpt is from **Bryan Tyson** and was written in 1864. [629]

"In Moore County, there was one Mr. Isham Wallace, who had several sons on the dodge. So, one day, some dozen militia officers, all mounted, went to the house of this gentleman and informed him that he must accompany them to camp, he told them he had a camp of his own and should therefore not go to theirs alive. The excitement soon became intense. At length one of the officers made a movement as if he were going to dismount for the purpose of taking him by force. Our hero dared him, telling him the moment he struck the ground he would shoot

him, if he died and went to hell the next minute. Seeing they could not take him without killing him, or running a great risk of getting some of their own men killed, they desisted from any further attempt, and rode off, leaving him conqueror. As they were riding away this officer asked a brother officer if he thought the old devil would have shot him if he had got down. He answered that he would have soon found out by trying it."

The following account was written by Maxine Williams McNeill regarding her great- grandfather, **Noah Williams** [1826-1904]. [630]

"Noah was sent to Petersburg, Virginia to serve with the confederate army. He was listed as a deserter after he ran off and went home. When the officers came looking for him, Noah hid in the hollow of an old tree not far from his house. It came a big snow while he was hiding out. The family was unable to take food to him because their tracks would lead the officers to his hiding place. The officers tried to make "Polly" tell where he has hiding, but she refused, because they had told her they would kill him when they found him. They took James "Jim" the youngest son with them, thinking it would make her talk, but she still refused to tell them anything. An hour or so later Jim came running home, they had released him. Knowing that they would come back "Polly" gathered up the chickens, pigs, and what supplies that she could load in the wagon and tied the milk cow to the back. She took the children and went back into the hills. It is not known how long she hid out, or when Noah joined them, but he was never caught. The old oak tree still stands on the land owned by H. Taft Williams, a grandson of Noah. Taft has refused to let anyone cut down the tree. It was a landmark of the Williams family history. The tree was the hiding place of his grandfather Noah, but it was also the rally point for the wagon train to Tennessee in 1872."

Civil War Veteran Reunions in Moore County

The Moore County Confederate Veteran's Association was organized on July 4, 1889, in Carthage. The following article provided an account of the event.

***The Carthage Blade*, July 11, 1889** [631]
***Jonesboro Leader*, July 17, 1889** [632]

*"**Moore Co. Confederate Veterans' Association**. We extract the following from the Carthage Blade's report: Pursuant to the call of Julian S. Carr, President of the NC Veteran.' Association, one hundred and twenty-two of Moore county's old soldiers met in Carthage and organized a permanent Veterans' Association on the 4th inst.*

Charles A. McNeill, Esq., read the call and explained the object of the meeting, and on his motion, Capt. Jas. D. McIver was elected president. Capt. W.M. Black was elected vice-president, and L.P. Tyson, Esq. secretary. The following Executive Committee was appointed: Capts. Geo. Wilcox, J.O.A. Kelly, E. McN. Blue, W.H.H. Lawhon, and D.O. Bryan. The president and secretary were added to the Executive Committee.

All of the old soldiers present were requested to come forward and enroll their names, company and regiment. One hundred and twenty-two were enrolled. The meeting then adjourned to meet at 2 o'clock, pm. On reassembling, the Declaration of Independence was read by C.A. McNeill, Esq., and addresses were delivered by W.J. Adams, Esq., Capt. Jas. D. McIver, W.C. Douglass Esq., Capt. Geo. Wilcox and Capt. W.M. Black.

On motion, it was ordered that all ex-Confederates in Moore County, who have not had their names enrolled, be earnestly requested to send their names, starting company and regiment, ay once, to L.P. Tyson, Sec'y, Carthage. NC."

Moore Co. Confederate Veterans' Association.

We extract the following from the Carthage Blade's report:

Pursuant to the call of Julian S. Carr, President of the N. C. Veterans' Association, one hundred and twenty-two of Moore county's old soldiers met in Carthage and organized a permanent Veterans' Association on the 4th inst.

Charles A. McNeill, Esq., read the call and explained the object of the meeting, and on his motion, Capt. Jas. D. McIver was elected president.

Capt. W. M. Black was elected vice-president, and L. P. Tyson, Esq., secretary.

The following Executive Committee was appointed: Capts. Geo. Wilcox, J. O. A. Kelly, E. McN. Blue, W. H. H. Lawhon, and D. O. Bryan. The president and secretary were added to the Executive Committee.

All the old soldiers present were requested to come forward and enroll their names, company and regiment. One hundred and twenty-two were enrolled. The meeting then adjourned to meet at 2 o'clock, p.m.

On re-assembling, the Declaration of Independence was read by C. A. McNeill, Esq., and addresses were delivered by W. J. Adams, Esq., Capt. Jas. D. McIver, W. C. Douglass, Esq., Capt. Geo. Wilcox and Capt. W. M. Black.

On motion, it was ordered that all ex-Confederates in Moore county, who have not had their names enrolled, be earnestly requested to send their names, stating company and regiment, at once, to L. P. Tyson, Sec'y, Carthage, N. C.

A reunion of Company F 50th Regiment was organized on June 20, 1890, in Jonesboro. The following article provided an account of the event.

***Jonesboro Leader*, June 25, 1890** [633]

*"**Reunion of Co. F. 50th Regiment.** The survivors of this Company were requested by their Captain, J. O. A. Kelly, to meet together in Jonesboro, on Friday, June 20th, for the purpose of effecting a permanent organization, and to provide for a festive occasion, at as early a day as possible. In response to this call, nineteen of the rank and file of said Company gave their attendance on the appointed day, prepared to enjoy themselves. Upon arrival, they were captured by the citizens of the town, but released after short imprisonments in the dining rooms of their captors. At 3 o'clock p.m., they gathered at the town hall, and proceeded to business by calling Capt. J. O. A. Kelly to the chair, and requesting Mr. W. E. Murchison to act as secretary. Upon a call of the Company roll, the following were*

found to be present, biz.: Captain J. O. A. Kelly, Lieutenant M. M. Watson, Lieutenant James Dalrymple, Sergeant W. M. Brooks, Sergeant Garner Watson, Sergeant W. J. Kelly, Corporal Henry Cox, Corporal W. M. McFarland, Privates R. M. Bobbitt, J. T. Brooks, A. J. Buchanan, Spencer Hughes, David Johnson, J. B. McFarland, D. M. Sloan, J. M. B. Thomas, J. J. Thomas, Neill T. Watson and Thomas Wicker.

Upon motion of Lieut. M. M. Watson, it was determined that there be a reunion of the Company, and a dinner, on Saturday, August 2d, 1890, at Jonesboro; the exercises of the occasion to commence at 10 o'clock a.m.

Upon motion, the following committee of arrangements was appointed: Lieut. James Dalrymple, Lieut. M. M. Watson, J. T. Brooks, B. W. Hunter, J. M. Stephens. The following resolution was introduced and adopted:

Resolved: That it is the sense of this meeting that an association of veterans should be formed and organized; and for the purpose of effecting such, every ex-Confederate soldier, residing within the limits of Moore County, is invited to be present and participate with the survivors of Co. F. 50th NC Regiment, in their reunion and celebration at Jonesboro, on the 2d day of August 1890, when and where it is hoped that a permanent organization may be effected.

Also, the following, to-wit: Resolved: That a general invitation be, and is hereby, tendered to all soldiers, wheresoever dispersed, to attend, with their families, the reunion of this Company, at Jonesboro, on Saturday, the 2d day of August 1S90, and participate in the festivities of the occasion.

Upon motion, it was ordered that the ladies of the community be invited to cooper ate with the committee of arrangements, in arranging for the reunion and festivities. The thanks of the meeting were, upon motion, tendered the citizens of Jonesboro for the display of their hospitality on this occasion. Upon motion of Lieut. James Dalrymple, it is ordered that the proceedings of this meeting be published in the Jonesboro Leader with request to the Sanford Express and Carthage Blade to copy. The meeting then, upon motion, adjourned. J. O. A. Kelly, chm'n. W. E. Murchison, sec."

The Moore County Confederate Veterans organized in 1900 and met on September 6, 1901 in Jonesboro. The following article provided an account of the event.

The Free Press, September 13, 1901 [634]

"Moore County Veterans. *An interesting story of their organization and reunion told by one of them. Squire C. W. Shaw spent last Thursday in Jonesboro, NC, attending the reunion of the Moore County Confederate Veterans of that place. The organization is known as Camp William P. Martin, so named in honor of the man who organized and led to the front in the first year of the war, 1861, the first company that went out from this county, Company H. 26th Regiment, North Carolina Volunteers. He was killed that same year at the battle of Newbern. In February of last year, 135 members of different companies from Moore County met at Jonesboro, organized the camp and elected the following officers: Commander, Daniel O'Brien; 1st Lieutenant, George Wilcox; 2nd Lieutenant, A. Vant; Adjutant, C. W. Shaw. The citizens of Jonesboro invited the veterans to meet in their city this month and provided the entertainment in their honor About 200 veterans attended and all enjoyed the day thoroughly. The following program was rendered. Address of Welcome. A. A. F. Seawell, Jonesboro. Response lor the Veterans. Judge J. D. McIver, Carthage. Speeches. Hon. Daniel Hugh, Dunn. Gen. Julian Carr, Durham. Hon. W. A. London, Pittsboro. Music. The Old North State. Sung by the pupils of the high school.*

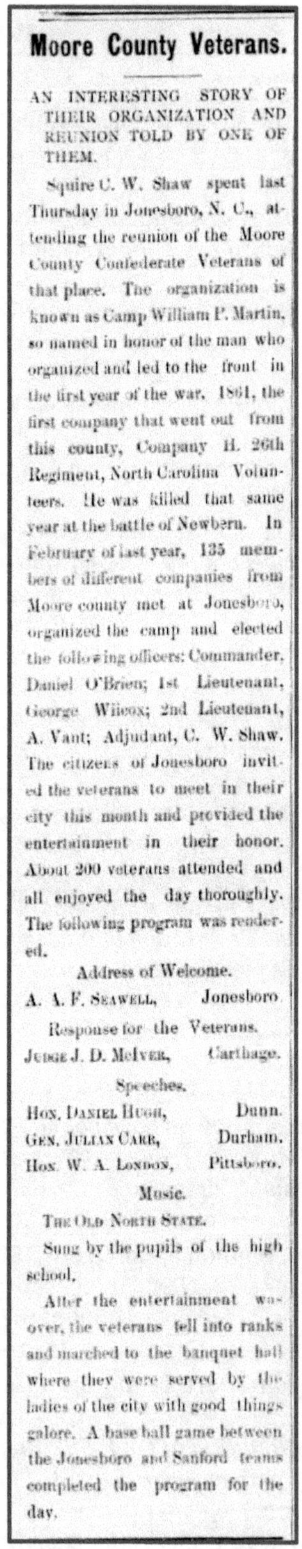

Moore County Veterans.

AN INTERESTING STORY OF THEIR ORGANIZATION AND REUNION TOLD BY ONE OF THEM.

Squire C. W. Shaw spent last Thursday in Jonesboro, N. C., attending the reunion of the Moore County Confederate Veterans of that place. The organization is known as Camp William P. Martin, so named in honor of the man who organized and led to the front in the first year of the war, 1861, the first company that went out from this county, Company H. 26th Regiment, North Carolina Volunteers. He was killed that same year at the battle of Newbern. In February of last year, 135 members of different companies from Moore county met at Jonesboro, organized the camp and elected the following officers: Commander, Daniel O'Brien; 1st Lieutenant, George Wilcox; 2nd Lieutenant, A. Vant; Adjudant, C. W. Shaw. The citizens of Jonesboro invited the veterans to meet in their city this month and provided the entertainment in their honor. About 200 veterans attended and all enjoyed the day thoroughly. The following program was rendered.

Address of Welcome.

A. A. F. Seawell, Jonesboro.

Response for the Veterans.

Judge J. D. McIver, Carthage.

Speeches.

Hon. Daniel Hugh, Dunn.

Gen. Julian Carr, Durham.

Hon. W. A. London, Pittsboro.

Music.

The Old North State.

Sung by the pupils of the high school.

After the entertainment was over, the veterans fell into ranks and marched to the banquet hall where they were served by the ladies of the city with good things galore. A base ball game between the Jonesboro and Sanford teams completed the program for the day.

Alter the entertainment was over, the veterans tell Into ranks and marched to the banquet hull where they were served by the ladies of the city with good things galore. A baseball game between the Jonesboro and Sanford teams completed the program for the day."

The first reunion of the Blue and Gray in North Carolina was held on February 24, 1906, in Southern Pines. The following articles provide a comprehensive account of the event.

***The News and Observer*, February 17, 1906** [635]

"The Blue and Gray. First Reunion Ever Held in North Carolina. Veterans of Opposing Armies Called to Meet at Southern Pines on Saturday, the Twenty-Fourth of February. *There will be a reunion of the Blue and Gray at Southern Pines on Saturday, the 24th of February, and invitations have been sent to the Confederate veterans in this city to attend. The invitation reading as follows "The Association of the Blue and the Blue and Gray especially invite you to attend a reception and Camp Fire of the Blue and the Gray at Clark's Opera House, Southern Pines, North Carolina on Saturday the twenty fourth day of February nineteen hundred and six, all day. We want you with us, particularly the Veterans of the Blue and Gray. Let us make this the great day of old North Carolina. Yours for Harmony, Capt. A.M. Clark, President of the Association of the Blue and Gray, Southern Pines, North Carolina. L.P. French, Sec. and Treas.*

THE BLUE AND GRAY

First Reunion Ever Held in North Carolina.

Veterans of Opposing Armies Called to Meet at Southern Pines on Saturday, the Twenty-Fourth of February.

It is announced that Governor Glenn, General Julian S. Carr and many others of note will be present and a special letter sent out with the invitation says: It is hoped that all Veterans, their families and friends will join in making this meeting a memorable one, as it will be the first time the Blue and the Gray have met in union within the borders of North Carolina. As the years roll by and our fellow comrades are passing away, we should hold sacred the ties of friendship which so strongly bound us together during the war. We greet our late opponents with the glad hand of welcome, and all rejoice that we are again a reunited people. Let the Reunion at Southern Pines be a joyous one, where the memories of our service can be retold, and where old-time friendships can be renewed. We trust you will urge a full attendance from your part of the State."

***The Carthage Blade*, February 21, 1906** [636]

"Gov. Glenn to be present. At Reunion of the Blue and Gray at Southern Pines on Saturday, Feb 24. *An event of interest to the veterans of the south will be the union meeting of the Blue and Gray, which is to be held at Southern Pines N.C. Saturday February 24. Among the guest of honors will be Gov. R.B. Glenn and Gen. Julian Carr. A number of others have signified their intention of being present and delegations will be in attendance from all parts of North Carolina as well as other bear by states and a large delegation of Union Veterans from different state will be present and this will no doubt be the most interesting soldier's reunion ever held in North Carolina as it is the first time the Blue and Gray have met in the North State. This reunion should be largely attended and it is hoped that the old veterans will all join in making this a memorable occasion. Southern Pines is a grand meeting place, for its many hotels and boarding places will afford ample room for the accommodation of all who may visit and which the reunion of veterans creates. There is much to interest visitors*

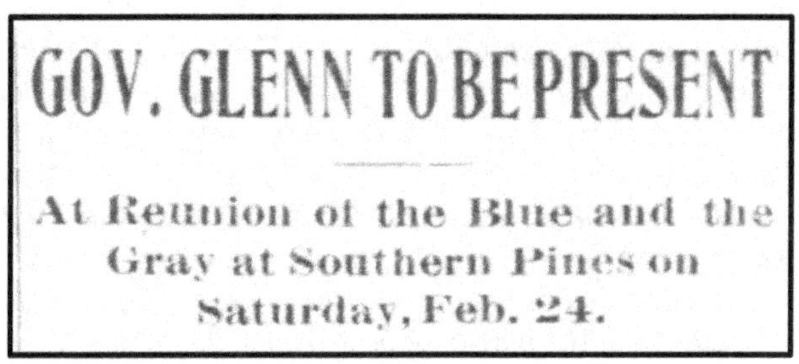
GOV. GLENN TO BE PRESENT

At Reunion of the Blue and the Gray at Southern Pines on Saturday, Feb. 24.

from all parts of the state, who will find Southern Pines a wide-awake Yankee settlement as a number of the boys who wore the blue have made it their home and they will gladly extend a hearty welcome and greeting to those who were during the civil war their antagonists. Capt. A.M. Clarke of the Union Army and Capt. C.W. Shaw of the Confederate Amry of Southern Pines are the committee of arrangements for this event."

***The News and Observer*, February 25, 1906** [637]

"Warm Grip of the Blue and Gray. The Reunion of the Civil War Veterans. A Great Gathering. Between 2,000 and 3,000 People at Southern Pines. Addresses by Governor Glenn, General Carr, Captain Clark** and* ***Others, Permanent Organization. *No such scene has ever been witnessed in North Carolina as that which occurred near the end of Governor Glenn's magnificent address this afternoon at the close of the camp fire of the Blue and Gray Association. He spoke from the piazza of the residence of Dr. W.P. Swett, in the heart of this splendid town which has blossomed as the rose in the sandhills of Moore County, and over two thousand people hung spell bound on his words, while over three hundred men and women used handkerchiefs to dry tears which flowed as he told of pathetic incidents in the war. He has made great speeches in the past, but as one of who has heard many of them. It is my opinion that he has never made a greater address than that of today, and with all of his eloquence, it was practical and full of advertisement of North Carolina's possibilities to the thousands of Northern visitors who heard him. Immediately after the address I heard hundreds of Northern men and women who pressured about him to grasp his hand and that it was the greatest speech they had ever heard, and they would vote for him if they had a chance.*

WARM GRIP OF THE BLUE AND THE GRAY

The Reunion of the Civil War Veterans.

A GREAT GATHERING

Between 2,000 and 3,000 People at Southern Pines. Addresses by Governor Glenn, General Carr, Captain Clark and Others. Permanent Organization.

By EDWARD E. BRITTON.
Southern Pines, N. C., Feb. 24.—

50 Federal and 130 Confederate Veterans. *The exercises began shortly before 12 o'clock. In Clark's Opera House, the hundred and fifty members of the Blue and Gray Association having escorted Governor Glenn and his staff, and from the Confederate Veterans General Julian S. Carr, commanding the North Carolina Division of Confederates, and Major W.A. Smith, of Andersonville from the Piney Woods Inn to the hall having cheered Governor Glenn to the echo as he joined them. With Governor Glenn were Adjutant General Robertson, Brigadier General Francis A. Macon, Colonel Wescott Roberson, and Colonel D.L. Ward, and in the procession were fifty Federal Veterans and a hundred Confederate Veterans, the entire party walking.*

Eloquence at Elegant Banquet. *At the opera house a banquet had been spread by the ladies, and it was a splendid one; but with tables all spread nothing was eaten till the speech making of the morning session was over. Captain Clark made the opening address, declaring it was a greatest honor of his life to preside of the greatest meeting ever held in the State. The welcome address by Mayor Ferguson was a gem, He declared that the North and South are indispensable to each other and paid a tribute to the soldiers of each side in the Civil War. His reference to Lieutenant Bagley as a Confederate soldier and his son, Midshipman Worth Bagley as a United States Officer lying side by side in Oakwood cemetery, one in gray, the other in blue, was a beautiful one, and was cheered to the echo. The response was by Col. Julian K. Carr, and it was one that was alive with tribute to North Carolina, to the bravery of the blue and the gray and endorsing the happy idea of reunion of soldiers from contending armies. He told of the magnificent bravery of North Carolina soldiers and closed with a tribute to the Stars and Bars. Dixie" was then sung by the daughter of a Union solider, Miss Clara Sitz, the audience joining, in the chorus. After this, Captain J.J. Kane, chaplain United States Navy, retired, in a splendid address spoke for a reunited country and for a stronger army and navy. His remarks were worthy and tributes were paid to the blue and gray. After this Mrs. Joe Person, amidst great applause, rendered "Dixie" and "Yankee Doodle" in a brilliant piano number and Major J.T. Harrington, of Carthage, led in the rebel yell. Mrs. G.T. Bacon, next admirably recited "The*

Drummer Boy," and after music by the orchestra Col. W.E. Murchison, of Jonesboro, spoke as a Confederate soldier endorsing the joint reunion, saying all Confederates would favor it. Mrs. Person next rendered "The Girl I Left Behind Me," and Captain A.O. Laufman, Federal veteran, sang an original song "Army Beans" that was a gem.

Meeting in the Open Air. *Then came the dinner and it was a feast enjoyed by a great crowd. After the meeting was adjourned to the open air and from Dr. Swett's piazza Major A.B. Adams, past commander of W.S. Hancock Post, of New York, spoke and said that having believed the reunion of the sections was accomplished and that he could not blame Southern men for being Confederate soldiers: that if he had been in the North would have fought for the Union. His remarks were a splendid tribute to the South and full of loyalty to the North.*

The Governor's Speech Charms. *Then came the great address of the day. Governor Glenn being introduced by Captain Clark as "Our Governor." It was an address that must have been heard to get its great features or reported word for word to do it justice. He spoke of the bravery of the soldiers of the North and South and the State's great record in war. In no word did he apologize for the South's part in the war, but gloried in his father as a Confederate soldier, saying that in like circumstances, he would do the same. The loyalty of North Carolina to the flag was told in glowing words and of proof given by the death beneath its folds of Worth Bagley and Lieutenant Shipp. Peace between the sections was the thought of his address and he told plain truths to his Northern hearers, but this so splendidly that he was cheered to the echo. He advertised the State's splendid possibilities and invited Northern friends to live and marry here. He took occasion to tell our splendid treatment of the negro; in closing told of the devotion of a negro servant in his family, a man who had seen his father die in battle, and his hearers wept as he told it. His audience was won completely and applauded him time and again. Tonight, there is going on a splendid banquet at Piney Woods Inn and among the toasts and responses to Governor Glenn, General Carr, and Captain Kane were delightful.*

The reunion of the Blue and Gray may be safely writ down as one of the most happy events in the State. The fraternizing of the Confederate and Federal veterans whose white hair marks the swiftly passing years since the war telling truly that among brave men North and South the war is over, and that General Grant's "Let us have peace" has come to pass".

Time brings its changes, and the conflicts of years past are forgot in the pleasant days of the present. Men who face one another on the battlefield can clasp hands in friendship in these piping times of peace, for war and discord are forgot in the common love of the South and the North for the "Flag of the Free" which floats over a reunited country.

A happy thought it was for these soldiers of two opposing armies to meet in Southern Pines in a reunion of the "The Blue and the Gray." It was a fitting place for this for here are the men by hundreds who fought 'neath the "Star and Stripes" as well as many whose hands were raised in salute to the "Stars and Bars," and these latter were reinforced in great numbers by "Old Confeds" from many parts of North Carolina, who gathered here today to meet in fraternal union those with whom in other day they contested every inch of advance on the Southland.

The idea of a reunion meeting of "The Blue and the Gray" in North Carolina began with Capt. A.M. Clark, a brave Union soldier who makes Southern Pines his home. He and other Federal soldiers found ready response from the Confederate veterans in this section, and the great meeting of today was the result. It was a glorious sight, this mingling of men once bitter enemies, and it was evidence of the high spirit which ennobles and lifts the Caucasian above all races, for men of this blood can differ and war. And then find common ground on which to clasp hands and to stand in league for the glorification and the progress of the land which is the home of both. The good will, the camaraderie, the fellowship, the respect and the esteem which were seen here today are the proofs that North and South we are of one people in the United States.

Character of the Addresses. *The splendid gathering today had its distinctive features and each was a class to itself. The Governor of the State, Robert P. Glenn, spoke, and his address breathed a spirit of the highest patriotism, in a tribute to the soldiers of the North, yet with no hint of apology for the soldier of the South. Brave men came from each section and each class he gave praise as patriots, not forgetting to say that the women had proved to be the grandest womanhood of the world because of their actual contact with the misery and suffering which had come to the war-deluged South, the theatre of the bloody conflict and had experienced sorrows and* *privations which had not come to the womanhood of the North. He portrayed the struggle in vivid terms, telling the honesty of each section and saying that the years and taught the better lesson of peace and that now in the South another invasion from the North is invited, that the money, the men, the women, the industry of the North is invited to our borders. In General Julian S. Carr's remarks, the same spirit was found, and he, a Confederate soldier, paid tribute to the men against whom they had fought, and giving the soldiers of the North credit of the same devotion to country as the soldiers of the South, spoke for the better union of the North and the South, and for the better knowledge the one of the other. Chaplain Kane, of the United States Navy, a Union veteran, spoke splendidly of the South, and paid a tribute to the bravery of its soldiers, and to the gallantry of its soldiers, its men and its women, and to the loyal allegiance now given to the flag of a reunited country.*

***Meeting and Banquet.** There were thousands here today, and at eleven o'clock in the opera house a great meeting began at which there were addresses from soldiers who once who wore the Gray and soldiers who fought in uniforms of Blue. The meeting began at eleven o'clock and was presided over by Capt. A.M. Clark, who is the president of "The Blue and Gray" Association, in the afternoon Governor Glenn made his great address for a better knowledge of the sections one of the other, and addresses were made by men of the South and of the North, the meeting closing with a reception to Governor Glenn in which hundreds pressed forward to clasp his hand.*

At night there was a splendid banquet at the Piney Woods Inn, the splendid hotel which is the pride of Southern Pines and all this section. The event was a delightful one and has not been surpassed for genuine good fellowship and enjoyment. The Piney Woods Inn proved itself a place of the real sort of hospitality, and the proprietors, Messrs. St. John & Son, were ever on the alert to give every attention to the party which met at the tables. The hotel is one that is splendidly kept, and which attracts great throngs of guests, but it is certain that there has been in it no more happy gathering than that which sat in its splendid dining room tonight and enjoyed the feast spread. It has been one of the pleasures of this day to meet the Messrs. St. John who are ever in evidence when attention to their guests to be considered.

***A Brotherhood of Blue and Gray**. In preparation for the reunion held here today there was yesterday effected a permanent organization of "The Blue and the Gray" for North Carolina, and the association proposes to make the event an annual one. In the organization Capt. A.M. Clark, Federal veteran, was made president; Capt. J.E. Buchanan, of Manly, was made vice-president, and Capt. L.P. French was elected secretary and treasurer. As delegate to the national "Blue and Gray" meeting in Atlanta on the 28th and 29th of March, the association selected Capt. A.M. Clark, of the Union Army; Capt. C.W. Shaw, of the Confederate army, and Capt. G.T. Bacon, of the Union army.*

There were between two and three thousand people here today and at the morning session the opening address was made by Capt. A.M. Clark, the welcome address being by the Mayor of Southern Pines, Dr. K.M. Ferguson, the replies by General Julian S. Carr, commander of the North Carolina Division of Confederate Veterans, and by the Chaplain Kane, of the United State Navy, who also made an excellent address. In the afternoon the address of Governor Glenn was applauded of the echo, and there were interesting short talks by Confederate and Union veterans."

***The Carthage Blade*, February 28, 1906** [638]

***"Blue and the Gray. The Reunion of the Civil War Veterans a Great Gathering.** Saturday was a great day at Southern Pines, when from 2,000 to 3,000 people assembled there to celebrate the reunion of the Blue and the Gray, and when some hundreds of old Federal and Confederate veterans grasped each other with the grip of warm hands and hearts.*

*"**Local News.** Those who attended the reunion from Carthage on Saturday at Southern Pines were: Chas. Monroe, V.V. [W.W.] Fry, Fred Womack, Miss Beulah Way, J.M. Way, Mrs. J.M. Way, Jack Sullivan, J.L. Currie, T.H. Harrington, Sheriff Kelly, T.M. Fry, J.B. Currie, S.H. Humber, A.M.D. Williamson, G.H. Humber, R.W. Pleasant, Misses Florence Ackiss and Mary Worthy."*

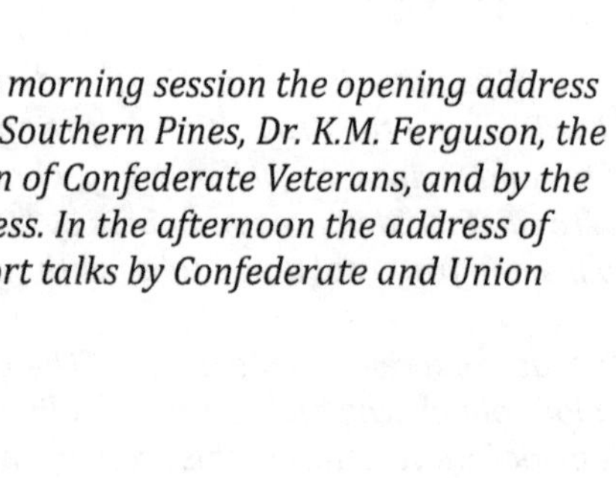
Those who attended the reunion from Carthage Saturday at Southern Pines were: Chas Monroe, V V Fry, Fred Womack, Miss Beulah Way, J M Way, Mrs J M Way, Jack Sullivan, J L Currie, T H Harrington, Sheriff Kelly, T M Fry, J B Currie, S H Humber, A M D Williamson, G H Humber, R W Pleasants, Misses Florence Ackiss and Mary Worthy.

***The Carthage Blade*, March 28, 1906** [639]

*"**Happy Conception.** Squire Wash Shaw, of Southern Pines, was in Carthage Thursday and was looking well. He is enthusiastic regarding the reunion of the Blue and Gray, the first occurrence of which came off at Southern Pines recently. The squire says that the reunion of the old veterans of the two armies was a happy and most fortunate conception and is proving already of immense power for good in bringing about a sympathy and respectful regard for each other among the old soldiers and in mollifying the last of the far-faded bitterness. So may it be. Squire Shaw said that the contributions were very liberal and met even expenses for the dinners of the occasion and all other expense, and that $65 to the credit of the association was left over and is now in the bank and will be supplemented by more than enough to meet the demands for the reunion next year."*

The second reunion of the Blue and Gray in North Carolina was held on March 28, 1907, in Southern Pines. The following articles provide a comprehensive account of the event.

The Opera House in Southern Pines decorated for the Blue and Gray reunion.
(*Photo courtesy of the Moore County Historical Association*)

Southern Pines Tourist, March 29, 1907 [640]

SOUTHERN PINES TOURIST

VOL. IV, No. 18. SOUTHERN PINES, N. C., FRIDAY, MARCH 29, 1907. 5c. COPY. $1 YEAR

THE BLUE AND THE GRAY

The Second Reunion of the Veterans of the Two Grand Armies and Their Sons

Those who enjoyed the first Blue and Gray Reunion and Campfire, which was held February 24, 1906 have been eagerly looking forward to the second gathering.

The time spent in active preparation was much less this year than last but when the committees did set about making final arrangements they worked with a will and accomplished a vast amount in a short time.

The initial idea of a Blue and Gray Reunion in this vicinity is said to have originated in the mind of Mr. White, of Pinebluff, but no sooner had the suggestion been made than it was most enthusiastically taken up and pushed forward by a large number to a most satisfactory issue.

Of course if such a gathering were to be held Southern Pines was the logical place, for it has among its residents and guests a goodly number of men who wore the blue, while living side by side with the Yanks was a still larger number of Johnnies, who remember very tenderly the years in which they wore the gray, while they fought a losing fight for their conception of the wisest governmental policy. On Blue and Gray Day last year some people saw the Confederate uniform for the first time, General Carr and two or three others appearing thus clad, while to others it was simply a reminder of the four years during which they chased gray backed soldiers or, about as often, were chased by them.

The reunion was a veritable love feast with Governor Glenn and General Julian S. Carr as the chief figures, both of whom made addresses that were most strikingly appropriate to the occasion, eloquent, broad and brotherly and yet true to their personal convictions.

It was thought by those best situated to know that the reunion of the veterans of both the great armies proved distinctly conducive to deep and lasting fraternity.

Reunion of 1907

The following committees were charged with the preparation for and the conduct of the Second Reunion, which was held on Thursday, March 28.

Executive Committee—A. M. Clarke (Chairman), C. W. Shaw, P. P. Whitehouse, S. S. Thomas and Lee Nutting.

Finance Committee—L. P. French (Chairman), J. R. Buchan, D. A. Blue, George A. Kimball and George H. Humber.

Committee on Invitation, Printing and Program—L. P. French (Chairman), F. H. Weaver and A. M. Clarke.

Committee on Transportation—Lee Nutting and A. M. Clarke.

Committee on Refreshments and Decoration—Mrs. Geo. W. Gould (Chairman), Mrs. M. W. D. Watson, Mrs. S. S. Thomas, Mrs. F. H. Weaver, Mrs. J. R. Buchan, Mrs. Lyman Merrill, Mrs. Jerry Hall, Mrs. L. P. French, Mrs. Cornelius Teal, Miss Clyde Stewart, Miss Agnes Thomas, Miss Ruby Evans, Lyman Merrill, Jerry Hall, C. W. Shaw, Reese Evans, S. N. Whipple, M. Abbott, Mr. Manlove, Walter Blue, S. S. Thomas, Edward Newton and George W. Gould.

Committee on Reception—J. R. Buchan (Chairman), Lee Nutting, A. M. Clarke, C. W. Shaw, William T. Stout, B. H. Butler, George H. Humber, George A. Kimball, L. P. French, H. E. Hotchkiss, Cornelius Teal, Mrs. G. A. Kimball, Mrs. Reese Evans, Mrs. A. M. Clarke, Mrs. Manlove, Mrs. D. A. Blue, Mrs. Ball, Mrs. Wheeler, Mrs. Hotchkiss, Miss Effie Butler, Miss Effie McCallum and Miss Margaret Blue.

Committee on Music—Mrs. F. H. Weaver (Chairman), Miss Ruby Evans, the Misses Hotchkiss and the Farrey brothers.

Committee on Badges—L. P. French.

The program as prepared by the committee, subject to slight changes, was as follows:

PROGRAM

Wednesday evening

The Governor will be met at the station and escorted to the Piney Woods Inn.

Thursday

At 11 o'clock the Governor and Commander-in-Chief will be escorted to the Opera House by the veterans.

From 11 to 12, Reception by the Governor to those who will not be able to attend the reception in the evening.

12 M., Dinner.

Music.

Address of welcome, the Mayor.

Music.

Address, the Commander-in-Chief, Gen. Julian S. Carr.

Music.

Address, the State Auditor, Hon. B. F. Dixon.

Music.

Address, Gov. R. B. Glenn.

Confederate Battle Cry, T. H. Harrington and Comrades.

Music.

General remarks.

Thursday evening

8.30, Reception at the Opera House, with refreshments and music. The public is invited.

The guests of honor were the Honorable R. B. Glenn, Governor of North Carolina, and General Julian S. Carr, Commander-in-Chief of the National Veterans of the Blue and Gray Association and their Sons, both charter members of the First Battalion, of Southern Pines.

Governor Glenn is a chief executive of whom any state in the Union might well be proud, and North Carolina has a strong admiration for her brainy governor and loves him for his fine personal qualities. It is sometimes said that no man who is radical in his moral ideas can be elected to high office, because the average voter is supposed to fear such men. Governor Glenn however, an influential member of the Presbyterian Church; a Sunday School teacher; a lay preacher, often heard in various pulpits; a temperance man of such pronounced views that he has declared that he would retire to private life, well satisfied, if he could see an effective prohibitory law enacted and enforced in North Carolina, gives the lie to this oft repeated statement. His present position and his great popularity speak well for the moral fibre as well as the intelligence of the people of the Old North State.

General Carr is as fine a sample of the old school Southern gentleman as one could desire to meet. Of attractive personal appearance,

THE HONORABLE R. B. GLENN
Governor of North Carolina

a little below the medium height but well set up, with a good sized head, well shaped and full of the finest kind of brains, developed and enriched by wide reading and with a natural gift of eloquence, he makes a strong appeal to any audience of intelligent people.

At an early hour Thursday morning veterans from the surrounding country began to come in in the family conveyances, while the trains brought those who could readily reach nearby railroad stations.

The Opera House was profusely and tastefully decorated, while stores and residences made such displays as could be made in the short time available, showing at least an interest in the reunion and a desire to do their part in welcoming the distinguished guests and their humbler but still highly honored comrades, the veterans.

The visitors spent the forenoon looking about town while the various committees of arrangement were busy doing last things and tying up any loose ends that could be found.

Then came the dinner and little need be said save that it was worthy the ladies of Southern Pines, reflected credit upon the committee and fully satisfied the needs of the veterans and their guests. Congenial comradeship is always the best of sauces and while the dinner needed no such enhancement the supreme charm of the feast was added by the good cheer that prevailed about the well filled board.

Adlutant General Clarke called the Associon to order precisely at noon calling upon Rev. Dr. Foss to invoke the divine blessing after which Mayor Ferguson delived the address of welcome which will be found in full on page 3. It was given impressively and was one of the best he has given on similar occasions during his official career.

SPEECH OF GENERAL CARR

General Carr, pleasantly introduced, said—Ladies and gentlemen and veterans of the Blue and the Gray; I was a private in Lee's army. I wore no stars nor braid but was content to serve in the ranks and often when human endurance could accomplish no more was glad to cast myself upon the ground to dream of home and loved ones. My first-born daughter was given in wedlock to the son of a captain in the Union Army. This is typical of the new spirit of unity.

It is within our memory when the ruthless hend of war despoiled our altars and destroyed everything save honor.

Veterans of the Blue and Gray uniting present an unparalleled spectacle. Once we faced each other in deadly strife and fought each other to a finish, but to-day we look into each other's faces in friendship.

No matter on which side we fought, we wrote such history as was never written before and in this record our children's children may rejoice.

The rusty saber hangs upon the wall; and every soldier, whether he wore the blue or the gray, is now proud that we are American citizens, with one flag, one nation and one destiny.

I represent a section which sent 800,000 soldiers to the field of battle, but a section which loves Old Glory as it is loved on Boston Common or in Independence Square.

We need have no fear for the coming generation.

Senator Daniels once said "We cannot see the hand upon the dial move but it does move." So, unseen but surely, the misconceptions and bad feelings of the old days have passed away. I feel that as he was in war so he is a hero now and is the bravest Knight who lays aside the animosities of a bygone generation.

Our highest aim is to develop our common country to the limit of its splendid possibilities.

In his speech at the bier of Jefferson Davis, General John B. Gordon said: "It is fitting that around his body should have been wrapped the flag for which he stood for four years. It was also right that the stars and stripes should wave above his body. In that flag there is not a star that has not been made brighter by the courage of Southern soldiers." Gen. Fitzhugh Lee said, on the same occasion, "If the occasion should demand, there is no Confederate soldier who would not fight as bravely for the stars and stripes as he did for the stars and bars."

Great things face this country, but they will be achieved by united

GENERAL JULIAN S. CARR

citizens. No braver men ever wore uniform or carried musket than the Union soldiers who fought at Lookout Mountain, Chicamauga and Gettysburg. Not until the last day will their courage be forgotten.

Young man, son of a Union soldier, do not be afraid to take the hand of the daughter of a Confederate soldier who fought in these same great battles with equal heroism and sacrifices.

The first blood in the Spanish war was shed by a Southern boy, handsome Worth Bagley.

Over the silent sleeping places of the wearers of the Blue and Gray let us stand in silent reverence. Let us teach our children to love the old flag and to protect it with their lives if need be. Let us teach them that the noblest death one can die is where men die for their fellow men.

At this point a telegram was read from Governor Glenn stating that he could not be present and regretting his absence.

State Auditor B. F. Dixon was introduced and opened with the statement that he had served under the Stars and Stripes and the Stars and Bars.

Mr. Dixon caught the attention of all by a few witty remarks and a story or two. We are nearing the border land: the mist that never rises is settling before us and hence I appreciate these gatherings.

Wearers of the Blue, if we couldn't beat you in fighting you can't beat us in telling lies about it.

Mr. Dixon spent some minutes qualifying as an expert in lying and proving that he is a worthy member of the Ananias Club. Mr. Dixon said the Southerners are a great people. He wittily alluded to the claim of a New Yorker that New York thought of the Nation and not of the State, and said that to find true Americanism you must come South. We have been Americans so long that we can't remember when we were anything else.

During the siege of Petersburg, nine months, under indescribabaly horrible conditions, these men dodged the shells and raised their hats on bayonet points, handled bombs hissing before their fatal explosion, kept their nerve and played with death. They complained not at hardship, short rations or bad food. These men were the peers of any soldiers that ever fought on any battlefield. Let me say a few things. When I think of the brave men who marched up to the cannon's mouth, on either side, and who died without a murmur, I hate the very name of war. "War is hell," said Sherman, and the men who lead a nation into war are devils. The time has come when wars may cease.

There are 7,000,000 of armed men in Europe and as many reserves. War picks the best. Think what this drain means. In Christendom there are 14,000,000 of men whose chief business is war. It's the clash of passions and not of principles.

How much loss of productiveness this means! In addition to this, the direct cost of maintaining these armies is estimated to be more than two billions of dollars.

In the world $90 are spent for war and the support of armies to $1 spent in preaching the Gospel. What have the wars of two hundred years gained for the world that might not have been gained with infinitely less of money and men? Is it a question of honor? It's the Devil's honor.

Teach your children that we must not have war. Send them through the schoolhouse and in the larger education of head and heart and hand the spirit of war will drop out, and, doing justice to all men, there will be no need of war and no excuse for it.

We want no Napoleon to lead us but the man who will give us the glories of peace and not the splendors of war. To save human life and not to destroy it is the highest achievement.

Mr. Dixon's address was a magnificent plea for peace and came with added force from the lips of a soldier of two wars. It was not a dissonant note but a sign of the progress of the spirit of peace and good will.

At this period Mr. P. P. Whitehouse read a poem written by himself forty years ago and today read, in public, for the first time.

OUR BOYS

BY OBSCURUS

By the Rappahannock's water,
On that bloody field of saughter,
Where full many a dame and daughter
Buried hope, and pride, and joy,
In the fiercest of the fighting,
Where the charge was most exciting,
With the bravest ones uniting
Fell our best, our first-born boy.

Weeping o'er the dear departed,
For the front another started,
One as brave and manly hearted
As were David's mighty three.
Soon another year is dying,
And the chilly winds come sighing
The sad tale that he is dying
'Neath the sod in Tennessee.

"Mary! can we spare another?"
Said I to the sorrowing mother;
"Shall he leave his only brother?
Must he hear the cannon's roar?"
Yes! he bore the stary banner -
Far o'er many a bright savanna,
Back along the dark North Anna,
And was never heard of more!

One remains—a boy so slender,
He would be a poor defender;
Shall we make a last surrender?
"Let me hasten!" was his cry.
E'er another moon was waning,
Not a hope had we remaining;
Weak and pale, yet uncomplaining,
Came our Willie home to die!

Noble sons! so true and fearless,
They have left our hearthstone cheerless;
We have wept till eyes are tearless,
From the load of grief we bear.
Father! still our heart's wild beating!
We forget that life is fleeting—
Heaven is near! What joyous greeting,
When we meet our darlings there!

As the Tourist goes to press brief speeches are being made by Mr. J. E. Buchan, of Maule; Mr. Fuller, of New York, and others.

The reception this evening will begin at 8.30. There will be music and refreshments.

The esteem in which Governor Glenn is held in Southern Pines is indicated by the regret at his absence, which was deep and universal. His presence and address last year are still among the most cherished memories of Southern Pines. It is to be regretted that visitors from the North could not see and hear this splendid man.

Features of the Day

The weather could hardly have been better. It was warm and genial, but tempered by an invigorating breeze from the Southwest. Last year the sky seemed partial to the Yanks as the Union color only was in evidence, monotonously blue, but this year the soft blue was mottled with a gray as soft as the blue.

Few people were astir when the veterans and their friends began to arrive. Thirty breakfasts were served to the early comers, a courtesy that was most heartily appreciated.

The vets were a grizzled and generally bearded lot. It was good to see them. Their aging faces and forms, a bit bent with the burdens of the years, spoke with impressive eloquence of the greatest war of all history between brothers and their good fellowship now was a sight no other nation could parallel. It gave one a new sense of pride to look at these men and recall the things for which they stand—once divided but now united.

Among the early arrivals was Mrs. Joe Persons without whose presence no Blue and Gray gathering would be complete. Her piano war songs last year aroused great enthusiasm.

The band of the Institute for the Blind at Raleigh furnished music during the day and were heard with great pleasure. Considering their physical disabilities their execution was quite wonderful. Their presence added much to the occasion.

Hon. B. F. Dixon, State Auditor of North Carolina, is a brother of Rev. Thomas Dixon, the famous author of the Leopard's Spots, the Clansman and the One Woman and Rev. A. C. Dixon, D. D., a prominent clergyman, of Boston. The Auditor is pronounced the most eloquent of the distinguished trio.

A scarred and aged veteran handed the Tourist the following sentiment:—"It brought tears of joy to the eyes of an aged veteran to see

Continued on seventh page.

Continued from second page.

such a large gathering of the Blue and Gray come so joyously, so lovingly together—fulfilling the prophecy of Henry Clay, "No North, no South, but one united country."

By noon the heat of one the hottest days of an unusually warm March had become oppressive, but all preserved their good nature. The meeting is held just about a month too late.

The success of this reunion, with its short time for preparation and inadequate advertising, clearly shows that the reunion should be an annual event, and proves conclusively that it may easily be the great occasion of the season. The visitors from the North are always the most interested of attendants.

The first forms of this issue were sent to press late Wednesday afternoon and early Thursday morning, and one or two advance references to Governor Glenn prove to be a bit previous, as the Governor, suffering from a severe cold, was unable to be present as eqxected to give leading address of the day. At this writing it is hoped but hardly expected that he will be present for the evening reception.

A large number of the Veterans were accompanied by their wives and children, and there was a vast deal of family fellowship during the hours of waiting.

After the dinner had been disposed of there was an hours intermission, during which the old soldiers smoked their pipes, renewed old friendships and fought their battles over again: and these social hours are among the most salutary features of the Blue and Gray gatherings, for it is in these informal hours that the old fellows get nearest to each other.

At 2.20 Captain Clarke announced that Mrs. Joe Persons would open the exercises with "Dixie," which she did with unabated spirit and unstiffened fingers, following "Dixie" with "Yankee Doodle," while the vets beat time with their feet and shouted in their enthusiasm, until she was obliged to respond with another selection, preceded by the "Rebel Yell," given on Captain Clarke's demand. These selections put everybody in the right spirit for patriotic addresses.

The Blue and the Gray

Address of Welcome by Mayor Ferguson

It has been the proud distinction of our city to have been the favored spot where the first reunion of the Blue and the Gray was held, and to us, and to the country in general, it is a matter of the profoundest congratulation to see the great public heart beat in unison with the spirit exemplified in the inception of this organization.

The vestal virgins of ancient times kept ablaze the sacred fires of their deity. We shall never in this section of our common country forget to do honor to the memory of the heroes of the Confederacy whose devotion to a cause they believed was right made glorious many a battle field. Their call to arms was neither by vengeance nor hatred; no unholy love of conquest, nor consuming love of martial glory summoned them from their peaceful homes to the tented fields.

The participants in that contest, whether they wore the Blue, or whether they wore the Gray, battled for a principle in which they believed with all their hearts, with all their souls and with all their minds and no irreverence shall be done their memory. From the standpoint of human nature it requires a broader spirit of charity for the defeated antagonist to come with the olive leaf than if upon his brow rested a crown of victory. More than forty years have now been added to the silent centuries of the past since the sword was sheathed at Appomattox and the great general of the Federal army said "Let us have peace."

We are not unmindful of the honors that belong to the Federal soldier and we would not detract one iota from the glories which they have won. The spirit exemplified in this reunion of the Blue and the Gray by the actual participants in that contest and their sons, as we understand it, is this; the rightful recognition of duties well performed, the impartial bestowing of honors for heroic acts. These principles have been, are and will continue to be the strongest props of men and states and kingdoms of the earth. This reunion today is not to exemplify maturity's stern manhood, hardened by the bitter recollections of war, but rather in the spirit of one who has fought life's conflicts, and in a material sense won or lost and as the setting sun of his life nears the horizon he wraps about him the spirit, the tenderness and the recollections of childhood's early lessons, a life ripening for higher and nobler and diviner things, a purpose to take something from the great tide of human sorrow and add something to the sum total of human happiness; a spirit of peace on earth and good will toward men.

It is related, that when Jenny Lind was just beginning her life of sweetest song, and Madam Grisi, then at the height of her great fame, was the favored idol of all true lovers of her art, there came to be the greatest jealousy of the older woman toward the younger. It so happened during the stay of both in London, that Queen Victoria, knowing already of the fame of Madam Grisi and wishing, too, to hear the sweet voiced Swedish girl, commanded them to sing at one of her assemblages. Grisi sang first, and sang most beautifully; the notes poured forth from out her golden throat in richest harmony, and swelled and swelled till all the air about seemed bursting into song, and then came Jenny Lind, the blushing maid, barely sixteen. Too timid yet to face a royal throng, too shy to know her power, she tried to sing and failed; the sounds would not come forth. Embarrassed and wounded in her pride, as she turned away, she met her rival's stare, triumphant and full of hatred; stung, and at the same time calmed by one quick touch of woman's soul and strengthened by some word of sympathy, she asked the Queen if she might try once more. Receiving assent, to her own accompaniment, she began to sing a childhood's prayer she learned to sing when, by her little bed at night, she asked to be forgiven. A simple song of purest faith and love. Slowly and sweetly she began, each note as pure and clear and as full of music as Scheppen's chimes, and every word forgiving and as full of love as the gentle heart from which they flowed; and then, as if she sought some help from God, her face lit up and from her slender throat there rushed a mighty tempest of divinest melody, which thrilled and awed, as higher yet, her heavenly voice arose, until from out the skies above, the angels seemed to come and join with her in one glorious song. Her breath grew soft and low again with suppliant murmurings, plaintive as the moanings of the distant sea, and then, as if some hovering spirit whispered that the day of peace had dawned, were heard the song of gladsomeness and music, joyous as the babbling of a summer's brook. She rose and from a hush, as silent as the stars at night, there came the victory. The little prayer had done what woman's will had set at naught, and child-like words in simple song had tied the bonds of sweet accord twixt those who had been enemies. This incident in some sense possibly typifies the spirit which has made possible this reunion of the Blue and the Gray.

The old North and the old South forget their dead issues in the holier love and broader charity which an intervening generation has taught.

The new South and the new North, standing together beneath the stars and stripes, with glowing memories of that wonderful legacy of heroism, splendor and courage won by the Blue and Gray, have no differences, for their identity in creed is the proud spirit of Americanism.

Photo of veterans from the Blue and Gray Reunion in 1907 at Southern Pines
(Courtesy of Moore County Library)

The soldiers in the photo as identified by James V. Comer and A.E. "Tony" Parker, Dec'd.

(Front Row, L-R) Seated
2nd person is believed to be John Alexander Muse
3rd person is Captain Rev. William Henry Harrison Lawhon
6th person is believed to be Charles Chalmers McLean
7th person is William Christopher Moore
8th person is believed to be John Bethune Currie "Jack"
9th person is believed to be Samuel Jones Muse

(2nd Row, L-R) Seated
1st person is Eli P. Seawell
4th person is Captain Alpha M. Clarke, Union Veteran of Company K, 8th Regiment, PA Volunteers who moved to Southern Pines, NC in 1886 (with air horn for hearing)
5th person is believed to be a Union Veteran wearing medals,
6th person is 1st Lt. William T. Jones

(3rd Row, L-R) Standing
5th person is believed to be Samuel Washington Humber
8th person is Thomas Henry Caviness
12th person is Evander McNair Blue
16th person is believed to be Virgil Newton Seawell, M.D.

The third reunion of the Blue and Gray in North Carolina was held on March 19, 1908, in Carthage. The following articles provide a comprehensive account of the event.

THE BLUE AND THE GRAY

The Third Annual Reunion at Carthage a Great Success—Attendance Estimated at Three Thousand

***Southern Pines Tourist*, March 20, 1908** [641]

"The Blue and Gray. The Third Annual Reunion at Carthage a Great Success – Attendance Estimated at Three Thousand. *The annual reunion of the National Association of the Blue and the Gray Veterans and their Sons took place this year at Carthage, the county seat and the oldest town of Moore County. On Thursday March 19, a multitude from Southern Pines, Pinehurst, Manly, Niagara, Lakeview, Vass, Cameron and the country around Carthage, came together for a day of inspiration and pleasure.*

The exercises of the morning and of afternoon were held in the auditorium at the courthouse. The front of the room was attractively decorated with patriotic colors. In the center, back of the judge's desk, hung the red, white and blue flag of North Carolina, bearing on buff scrolls two suggestive dates—May 20, 1775 and April 12, 1776—while national bunting adorned the desk, the mantelpieces and the piano and wound in and out among the palings of the court rail.

Shortly after eleven all seats in the hall were occupied and late-comers were beginning to look for advantageous standing room. Presently the band opened with "Yankee Doodle" and followed with "Dixie." When the audience had sung "America," the assembly was led in prayer by the Rev. J. K. Roberts, who gave thanks to God for preserving a common country for the people of the North and the South.

After the gathering had sung the Star-Spangled Banner," Adjutant General Clarke spoke briefly concerning the association and its work. The organization is trying to file a record of the services of each Civil War veteran with the adjutant general of his State, and it is endeavoring to bring the Boys in Blue and the Boys in Gray together in a far different way than that in which they met during me early 60's.

The address of welcome was given by Mr. George H. Humber, son of a Confederate soldier. Mr. Humber believed that the victories of peace were greater than the victories of war and that what could not be wrought by war had been accomplished through peace. Grant's noblest saying was, "Let us have peace." Lee was at his best when he exclaimed: "Boys in Gray, the sublimest word in the language is duty; go home and do your duty to a reunited country."

The speaker mentioned the causes of the era of good feeling now prevailing between the North and the South. In this condition, as in all events of American history, men might see the hand of God. Among human agencies were Vance, Grady, McKinley (who wove a chain of love about all sections of the country), Theodore Roosevelt (the son of a Southern woman), and he who, excepting George Washington, towers above all men oi the Nation—Abraham Lincoln, the friend of North and South. The Spanish War was a powerful cementing force.

Mr. Humber asserted that America had no better patriot than the Confederate veteran, Joe Wheeler and Fitzhugh Lee exemplified his thought, while Victor Blue and Worth Bagsley, of North Carolina, heroes of the Spanish War, evinced the patriotism of the South.

Col. John R. Lane, of the renowned 26th North Carolina Regiment, appeared in a faded yet priceless Confederate uniform. He said that he was attending for the first time a Blue and Gray assembly, though he had been one of the first to advocate organization.

The Colonel declared that of all men he ever knew he loved the Boys in Gray best, but that he would ever respect the men who wore the Blue. Some had said that Yankees could not fight; he felt sure that the North sent out some of the worthiest warriors that he had ever seen.

Moore County gave the Confederacy some of its best soldiers. Company H contained more Macs than any other company in the Southern army.

Colonel Lane declared that he must he allowed a privilege. The Men in Blue might honor their Grant and their Lincoln, but they must not deny him the right to eulogize his Lee and his Davis.

Col. Lee Nutting, of the 61st New York Regiment, followed. He held that war was the worst method by which to settle a disagreement. War seemed to him both savage and un-Christian. If the rulers of England and of Germany wished to fight, they might be given opportunity, but they should never be allowed to bring poverty and ruin upon innocent men, women and children.

Col. George D. Bisbee, of the 16th Maine Regiment, was the next speaker. He had had the privilege of engaging in the first day's fight at Gettysburg. He maintained that if the Confederate troops had followed up their victory that first night there would have been no second day of conflict.

Lincoln's Administration gave birth to a terrible war— a war terrible on account of the loss of life, blood and treasure; yet it was because of this war that Americans now possessed a great and common country.

Judge James D. McIver, of the 26th North Carolina Regiment, extended a cordial greeting to both the Blue and the Gray and said that he considered the men of each army his friends. Though he might never be permitted to attend another union gathering, he hoped that the commendable work would go on.

After the old soldiers and their relatives had partaken of a bounteous dinner prepared by the women of Carthage, the exercises were continued at the courthouse. Mr. P. P. Whitehouse, the Yankee bard, read an original poem descriptive of camp life and of the horrors of battle. It was the story of an eye-witness.

General Clarke followed with letters from Senator Lee S. Overman and Congressman Robert N. Page, regretting that affairs of the Nation prevented their participation in the program of the day. Mr. Page closed as follows: "The object of your association commends itself to me with great force, and if such organizations were formed all over this Union, they would do much toward wiping out sectionalism and sectional strife. God speed the day when we shall be a reunited people, not in name only, but in spirit and in truth."

Hon. John E. Buchan said that the Civil War had a lesson for young people. The world had never seen a greater struggle, nor had it known greater heroism than that shown by the soldiers in the field and by the women that stayed at home. It behooved the descendants of these noble men and women to live in such a manner as to cast fresh honor on the worthy names they had inherited.

After the singing of "God Be with You Till We Meet Again," the Rev. W.H.H. Lawhon pronounced the benediction and brought to a close the third annual reunion of the Blue and the Gray."

Photo of veterans from the Blue and Gray Reunion in 1908 at Carthage
(Courtesy of Carthage Historical Museum)

***The News and Observer*, March 21, 1908** [642]

THE BLUE AND GRAY

Inspiring Celebration at Carthage Yesterday

Happy Comradeship of the Boys of the '40's—Address by Several Prominent Men on Both Sides

Gen. Carr Absent.

"The Blue and Gray. Inspiring Celebration at Carthage Yesterday. Happy Comradeship of the Boys of the '60s – Address by Several Prominent Men on Both Sides. Gen. Carr Absent. *Carthage, NC. March 19 – Celebrated here today was the reunion of the blue and the gray. The day has been an ideal one, and the happy comradeship of the soldier boys of 61-65 seems to have inspired the whole town. On account of illness of this wife, General Carr could not be present, but Capt. A.M. Clark, of Southern Pines, adjutant general of the National Association of the Blue and Gray, was present and represented General Carr. The address of welcome was made by Carthage's gifted orator, Geo. H. Humber after eulogizing both, the blue and the gray, extended to all a hearty welcome and made every one present feel glad that they were privileged to attend and accept of Carthage's hospitality. Capt. Clark was master of ceremony and then in his happy style introduced several other speakers, among whom was Col. John R. Lane, the famous Colonel of the 26th NC Regiment; Col. Nutting, 61st, New York; Col. Bisbee, of Maine; Col. Whitehurst; Judge Jas D. McIver.*

Senator Overman was invited to speak on this occasion but press of business detained him. Gov. Glenn was also asked to be present but he also had to decline. There was one of the largest crowds assembled in Carthage in many a day and every one pronounced this one of the happiest and most successful reunions ever held. Each and every one was served with a bountiful dinner. "

Photo of Colonel John R. Lane and Major Thomas H. Harrington at the 3rd reunion on March 19, 1908. [643]

Jim Jones and Sue Pockmire of the Moore County Historical Association located a list of Moore County veterans that attended the third reunion in Carthage. The list is shared below with great appreciation.

Confederate Veterans:
John E. Buchan
Jonathan Sheffield
Henry Cagle
William B. Clegg
John B. Kelly
John McNeill, Sr.
James D. McIver
Robert A. McLaughlin
M.E. Myrick
Daniel M. Sinclair
Malcom Smith
David A. Graham
William W. Fry
Thomas H. Harrington
William T. Jones
Henry M. Kelly
George A. McRae
Charles W. Shaw
Henry Williams
John Williams
Benjamin G. Womble
William Allen Fry

Union Veterans:
Asaph Milton Clarke
Lee Nutting
William T. Stout
Milo J. Corliss
George L. Walker
Jason Levi Coffin
Charles S. Martin
Jacob Benner McCracken
Edwin Newton
Charles Edward Benton

The fourth reunion of the Blue and Gray in North Carolina was held on March 25, 1909, in Carthage. There was very little coverage of the event in local newspapers.

***Southern Pines Tourist*, March 19, 1909** [644]

*"**Local Pickups**. The Annual Blue and Gray Reunion will be held at Carthage, Thursday, March 25. A large party will go from Southern Pines."*

The national encampment of the Blue and Gray was scheduled to be held on April 18, 1910, in Southern Pines. It was later cancelled amid local disagreements.

***Charlotte Observer*, March 14, 1909** [645]

*"**Southern Pines Chosen. Veterans of the Civil War will hold their next encampment at the Moore County resort.** Fitzgerald, GA, March 13 – The Blue and Gray Association at its annual encampment here today selected Southern Pines, NC, for the next reunion.*

***The Southern Pines Tourist*, January 7, 1910** [646]

"Blue and **Gray National Encampment.** *The National reunion and encampment of the Blue and the Gray and Their Sons is to be held in Southern Pines, in March, provided that we wish to entertain the organization. That these men will be heartily welcomed goes without saying, on the grounds of both hospitality and business. The men who fought the great war are always welcome anywhere. Southern Pines and its immediate vicinity, in the season, has a large number of men who wore the blue, and a still larger number of those who were clad in gray. In a way it is neutral ground. Tins tact lends added interest to such meetings. Two State reunions have been held in Southern Pines and both were successful events, anticipated with pleasure and enjoyed by all.*

The National organization of the Blue and the Gray is not a large body and can be entertained easily and satisfactorily oy this community. The matter should be taken up at once. Of course, the first step is to decide if the veterans are to be bidden to come That matter decided the necessary committees should be appointed at once, for the time is none too great to make such preparations as will do credit to the town. Such a date should be selected as will insure the presence of Governor Kitchin. who would doubtless be glad to honor the occasion. Former Governor Glenn set a high mark in Southern Pines for appropriate and eloquent addresses upon such occasions, but Governor Kitchen will not fall below the standard of his distinguished predecessor, for he is a man of fine personality and great oratorical ability. Dr. B.F. Dixon the head of the State organization, is a very popular speaker and one who always lends interest to any assembly of which he is a member. A meeting of the National organization would bring other men of reputation and ability; the committee should see to that.

In March the season is at its flood, and while the entertainment problem would present more difficulties than at any other time, it is the month when Southern Pines shows at its best. With the Phillies here, to afford pleasure for those who are fond of sports a game or two with one of the strong college teams which last season gave the professionals such stiff battles, sandwiched in between the serious work of the Blue and the Gray, and with other interesting features added, at least three days might be so arranged as to attract large crowds—to the benefit of business and to the delectation of our guests, for whom as many entertaining events as possible should be arranged.

The whole town should take a deep interest in this matter. If the veterans assume the responsibility, constitute the committees, exclusively, and do the work, they should have the earnest and helpful co-operation of every citizen in such ways as the veterans may wish. If they wish to divide the care and labor all should join with them in making the whole affair one of common interest and responsibility."

***The Southern Pines Tourist*, February 11, 1910** [647]

*"**Blue and Gray Reunion is off**. A letter received on Thursday night from National Commander Dixon, of Raleigh, settles the Blue and Gray matter so far as Southern Pines is concerned and is herewith printed because it gives the reason, in a nutshell, for Dr. Dixon's action. The Tourist believes Southern Pines could have met all demands, and that the outcome is decidedly unfortunate, if Mayor French represents the true and general feeling of the town in this matter, discovered by a careful and extensive investigation, he has acted wisely. If he has misinterpreted the spirit of the community or acted on less than a searching inquiry or has spoken on partial information he has taken some chances of criticism. The Tourist has made no canvass to discover what the sentiment is, but from the straws that have drifted past the office it thinks there is much dissatisfaction with what has been done without specific authorization. There is a quite general feeling that no one had a right to speak for Southern Pines until the people had been definitely consulted in some assembly where all sides of the question could be presented and discussed. The exact conditions of entertainment had not been ascertained, and hence it is assuming considerable to send the news abroad that Southern Pines could not care for an organization that wished to meet within its borders. The writer believes that the whole community, residents, business men, landlords, visitors, churches, Civic Club, King's Daughters, Country Club and everybody else, would have measured up to the demands of the occasion and that the town would have acquitted itself with credit—but that's only an unofficial opinion and may be taken for what it is worth. The letter follows:*

Dear Captain: On account of the following paragraph in a letter received from Mayor French, Feb. 8th, I think it advisable to call off the meeting of the Blue and the Gray scheduled to meet in Southern Pines March 17, 18 and 19: "I have called on a large number of the business men here; also, some veterans, and have conferred with the town commissioners regarding the meeting of the Blue and the Gray. The commissioners with one exception said they did not believe that the organization could be properly entertained and cared for during March, 1919, and I have found very few who favored this meeting here in March." In the face of that I do not see how we can have this meeting, because any friction is what we want to avoid, and I have written to French calling off this meeting, and beg to hereby notify you of the same. Yours fraternally, B. F. Dixon, Commander-in-Chief"

***The Southern Pines Tourist*, February 25, 1910** [648]

*"**Good for Carthage. The County Capital would like to entertain the National Reunion of the Blue and Gray**. My Dear Captain Clarke: Since seeing that your town has "flunked" on the entertainment of the reunion of the Blue and the Gray. I have talked to several of our leading citizens in reference to inviting the Blue and the Gray to have their reunion here in Carthage, I have met with no opposition so far—in fact, they all say they will be glad to entertain the "old fellows" as best they can.*

D.A. McDonald. George H. Humber, John L. Currie. A.C. Kelly and others have asked me to write you, extending, through you, a cordial invitation to hold the reunion in Carthage. We would be glad for you to suggest a date when it will be most convenient for you to meet here, if you can; and don t put it too late, as we expect a great many of the "Yanks" will want to return home when the weather warms up. We want as many of them to attend as possibly can.

You know our people here, and we want you to tell them we are not dangerous in times of peace. Hoping to have a favorable reply from you, I am. Yours for a united country and for a good time, Gilbert McLeod. February 22, 1910

***The Southern Pines Tourist*, March 4, 1910** [649]

*"**The Blue and Gray fiasco**. There are several things about the Blue and Gray fiasco in Southern Pines that are to be regretted—the loss of business; the passing up of a good opportunity to extend the fame of the town; the acknowledgment that we could not do what our sister town of Carthage, with one hotel to our dozen, will do handsomely and with great credit to herself; the intensifying of that factional spirit which is the curse of Southern Pines—but the thing that hurts is the idea that has gone abroad that sectional feeling played some part in Southern Pines' refusal to accept the honor that, had been tendered, for it would have been a high honor to entertain these rapidly passing veterans.*

We are positive that those who have read into this unfortunate affair the slightest sectional feeling are laboring under a grave misapprehension. We do not believe that such a sentiment had anything to do with the action that was taken. Certain acts have been very severely criticized. We are not defending any person from just condemnation but we think it only fair to say that suspicions of the nature suggested above are very unjust and criticisms based upon those suspicions are wholly unfair.

There may be an individual exception here and there but they are rare who would not have had great pleasure in welcoming the soldiers of Grant and of Lee to a town where such a gathering would seem to be singularly fitting because of its admixture, in its permanent population and winter visitors, of the two elements. The Tourist is informed that the decision of the Blue and the Gray to meet this spring in Southern Pines came about in this way: A Confederate veteran arose and said, "Our State Reunion was held for two years in Southern Pines. They seemed so glad to see us and treated us so handsomely that I am moved to suggest that we meet there next year." The veterans did not dream that they would not be welcome, and in this we have no notion that they were wrong. The invitation was withdrawn or withheld, not because the old solders were not wanted but because some persons had too little faith in the hospitality of their town, a pessimism possibly somewhat confirmed and aggravated by an unfortunate personal feeling, confined to a very limited area but sufficiently positive to be felt in the air by Major Dixon, who at once called the meeting on."

A regional veterans' reunion was scheduled to be held on August 15, 1908, in Jackson Springs for the veterans of Richmond, Montgomery, Moore and Lee counties.

***The Montgomerian*, August 6, 1908** [650]

*"**Old Soldiers' Reunion at Jackson Springs, August 15, 1908.** All the old soldiers in the counties of Richmond, Montgomery, Moore and Lee, their wives and children, widow and friends, everybody in general, are invited to be present at the grand joint reunion of the old soldiers at Jackson Springs, Saturday, August 15, 1908.*

Everybody is expected to bring full baskets (as on picnic occasions) with edibles and fruits, and those who will are asked to assist liberally, so that none may be unprovided for. Arrangements will be made to spread a table especially for the old soldiers, and great care will be taken that none of the veterans shall go away without having been fed.

The managers will try to secure prominent speakers and provide music. Let everybody come and be sure to bring your basket full, take one day off and have a good time. For more information write the chairman or any of the undersigned committee, Jackson Springs, NC. W.D. Blue, Chm., Fred McKenzie, E.A. Currie, A.J. McLeod, J.P. Clark, W.A. Clark, Robert Auman, Committee of Arrangements.

Photo of Montgomery County veterans from the 1912 Blue and Gray Reunion held at the First Methodist Church at Troy, NC. It is likely some Moore County veterans were in attendance as well.
(Courtesy of Kevin Brown and Mike Kellis)

Civil War Veteran Reunions in Lee County

Lee County Confederate Veterans organized Camp Ransom No. 1669 on April 9th, 1908. Annual reunions and regular meetings were held for several years.

The Sanford Express
June 12, 1908
651

THE GLORIOUS FOURTH.

It Will be Made a Red Letter Day Here—Good Speaking, Ball Games and Other Amusements—A Picnic Dinner.

On April the 9th last, when the Confederate soldiers of Lee County met here and organized Camp Ransom, an invitation was extended them by the people through Mayor Chisholm to meet in Sanford again on July the Fourth and engage in an all-day patriotic celebration. The invitation was accepted. So the members of Camp Ransom will be here in a body on that day.

The day promises to be the biggest celebration ever held in this section and the united effort being put forth by the business men assures the success of the undertaking. At a meeting of citizens of the town this week the following committees were appointed to look after the different features of the day:

Committee on indoor entertainment and speakers: D. E. McIver, chairman; E. D. Nall, J. D. Wicker; J. R. Jones.

Committee on outside entertainment: S. V. Scott, chairman; D. M. Gurley, F. Y. Hanner.

Committee on dinner: R. D. Covington, chairman; S. M. Jones, S. C. Moffitt, W. A. Monroe, J. L. Gilmore, H. M. Williams, O. P. Makepeace.

Committee on advertising: D. L. St. Clair, chairman; C. R. Preddy, W. S. Weatherspoon.

An invitation is extended to the entire citizenship of Lee and adjoining counties to spend the day here. Dinner will be furnished the old soldiers free by the people of the town. Let other people bring picnic baskets along and all come prepared to have a general good time. There will be many interesting attractions and plenty of interesting amusements to guarantee a pleasant day.

A prominent speaker from a distance will be invited to deliver the principal address and good speaking may be expected.

Base ball games by strong and evenly balanced teams will be arranged, besides a program of outdoor sports to consume the entire afternoon. Such amusements as foot races, wheelbarrow and bag races, catching the greasy pig and climbing the greasy pole will be provided.

The merchants and others will decorate their buildings in the national colors—red, white and blue bunting.

It will be a true celebration of the "Glorious Fourth."

The Sanford Express
August 20, 1909
652

CAMP RANSOM.

Roster of the Officers and Men.

Following is the roster of Camp Ransom, Confederate veterans, which was organized in this county about two years ago:

J. O. A. Kelly—Captain.
Geo. W. Avent—Adjutant.
M. H. Hawley—1st Lieutenant.
Redin Bryan—2nd Lieutenant.
J. W. Lawrence—3rd Lieutenant.
Rev. J. D. Wicker—Chaplain.
S. P. Kimball—Orderly Sergeant.
W. J. Kelly—Color Guard.
J. W. Howell—Assistant Color Guard.
Dr. J. L. Sheppard—Surgeon.
Garner Watson—Quarter Master.
C. D. Grose—Com. Sergeant.

Privates: W M Avent, Capt D O Bryan, H J Booker, Atlas Brafford, Bailey Buie, S R B Buchanan, T C Campbell, George Cox, Dr J L Cox, J M Cole, M Dalrymple, R B Douglass, S R Dickens, J M Fitts, John M Gaster, C A Gilchrist, G W Gilmore, A H Grose, Thomas Grose, J A Gunter, J R Gunter, A M Harrington, T R Harper, J C Hawley, D M Hawley, Alex Hall, Spencer Hughes, W H Humber, G Jackson, A H Jones, Josiah Johnson, B J Johnson, H M Kelly, A A Kelly, Hugh Kelly, John T Kelly, Sr, Sandy Kelly, J D Kelly, Geo W Luther, J H Mann, N A Matthews, D Malone, John McNeill, N A McNeill, J W McDuffie, J B McFarland, John D McIver, D N McIver, J H McRae, T W Morris, W. B. Morris, Col W E Murchison, J D Moore, Ira L Nalls, J W Oldham, J W Pattishall, C H Pattishall, G B Page, A Paul, J W Petty, A Pendergrass, B C Pearce, J E J Pipkin, J H Phillips, A D Phillips, J B Pitman, J W Poe, R H Poe, Geo Poe, D B Robertson, Bright Roberts, T J D D. Seymore, J F Sloan, W G Sloan, A H Sloan, W M Smith, J H Smith, Fred Smith, W M Spivey, Wilson Spivey, B W Strayhorn, D L Steadman, Porter Steadman, C T Stone, J R Tally, C W R Thomas, D A Thomas, J M B Thomas, Jeff Thomas, A G Thomas, B Y Tyson, James Wood, J J Weldon, T B Wicker, J A Willett, Capt Geo Willcox, J H Williams, N. R. Williamson, J H Wicker, E M Wicker, R M Womack, J B Womble, J M Wicker, J A Underwood, W D. Underwood, W R Campbell.

All but a few of the members of Camp Ransom were at Jonesboro on Wednesday of last week to attend the annual reunion. Some of those who were present will hardly be able to attend another reunion. From the above roster it will be seen that there are yet a large number of veterans in this section, notwithstanding it has been 44 years since with Gen. Lee they stacked arms at Appomattox. Some of these men who followed the stars and bars to many a bloody victory are still strong and active and able to do daily labor. Here is hoping that they may be able to attend many more reunions.

The Sanford Express, July 8, 1910 [653]

MEN WHO WORE THE GRAY

The Members of Camp Ransom Celebrate the Fourth in Sanford and Enjoy the Day.

While no elaborate preparations were made yet quite a crowd of people were here from the surrounding country to celebrate the glorious Fourth. The day was an ideal one for the Fourth of July, just enough breeze stirring to make the day pleasant and comfortable. By 9 o'clock in the morning many had arrived and mingled with them were members of Camp Ransom, also a number of Confederate veterans from Chatham, Moore and Harnett.

Here and there on buildings were to be seen United States flags and decorations in national colors. Tin horns were brought into play and helped to furnish noise for the occasion. About all the shops, factories and mills were closed for the day. The stores closed at noon.

About 10:30 the members of Camp Ransom formed on Main street and headed by their Commander, Capt. J. O. A. Kelly, marched to the City Hall where the exercises of the day were to be held. When the exercises opened most of the seats in the large auditorium were occupied. Rev. G. R. Underwood, who was master of ceremonies, came forward and announced that Hon. D. E. McIver would make the address of welcome. Mr. McIver, who is always equal to the occasion, bid the old soldiers welcome in a short appropriate speech. He took occasion to pay the men who carried the stars and bars through one of the bloodiest wars of history a handsome tribute. He declared that the true story of that great struggle should be printed in the school books so that generations that come after us will know that the Confederate soldier was not a traitor, but a patriot. The speaker felt that the State owed the veterans a debt and should furnish ample provision to make them comfortable in their declining years. He said that this should be done quickly, that while there are still many of them living, yet they are fast "passing over the river to rest under the shade of the treers."

Mr. Underwood responded in behalf of the veterans in a few appropriate remarks. A string band composed of the following musicians furnished music for the occasion: Messrs. "Doug" Harden, Herman Turner, Tom Maness and W. H. Turnage. When they struck up Dixie the veterans, in their minds were carried back to the days of the sixties when they were struggling for the mastery on the battlefields of Virginia.

At the conclusion of the speech-making and music, Capt. Kelly called the roll of Camp Ransom, the following members answering to their names: John M. Gaster, C. A. Gilchrist, G. W. Gilmore, A. H. Gross, Thos. Gross, A. M. Harrington, M. H. Hawley, Adjutant J. W. Howell, G. Jackson, J Jackson, H. M. Kelly, Capt. J. O. A. Kelly, (Commander), W. J. Kelly, (color bearer), A. A. Kelly, Sandy Kelly, J. D. Kelly, G. W. Luther, (1st. Sergeant), John McNeill, N. A. McNeill, John B. McFarland, D. N. McIver, John D. McIver, Wm. B. Morris. J. W. Oldham, J. W. Petty, A. Pendergrass, J. H. Phillips, J. B. Pittman, J. F. Sloan, A. H. Sloan, Wilson Spivey, J. L. Sheppard, (Surgeon), Garner Watson, J. H. Wicker, E. M. Wicker, J. D. Wicker, J. D. Womack, J. M. Wicker, W. D. Underwood, James Wood, W. Marshall Avent, Atlas Brafford, S. R. B. Buchanan, Dr. J. L. Cox, Neill A. Matthews, John W. Lawrence, D. L. Stedman, B. W. Strayhorn, J. K. Tally, C. W. R. Thomas. J. M. B. Thomas, Jeff Thomas, A. G. Thomas, J. J. Weldon, T. R. Wicker and J. B. Womble. The following veterans arrived after the roll was called: Bennet Burns, L W Lasater, J D Wart, J A Gunter and J Jackson:

Each veteran was given a blank by Mrs. T. M. Cross, president of the chapter of Lee county Daughters of the Confederacy, which will entitle him to a cross of honor to be delivered on Aug. 23rd. At the conclusion of the exercises at the City Hall, the old soldiers, headed by the band, marched to the Gem Cafe, in the Bailey-Lutterloh building, where a sumptuous dinner was served. There were 81 covers. 75 of these were for the old soldiers. Mrs. Cross, assisted by the following ladies, served the veterans at the table and did everything possible to make them comfortable: Mrs. D. M. Fairley, Mrs. T. L. Bass, Mrs. Neill Gilchrist, Mrs. O. M. Goodwin, Mrs Robert Wicker and Miss Addie St. Clair.

The Sanford Express, November 20, 1914 [654]

At the call of the commander, Camp Ransom held a meeting at Broadway last Friday, Capt. J. O. A. Kelly resigned as Commander and J. W. Howell as Adjutant of the Camp. Rev. Daniel Wicker, of this place, was elected Commander and Mr. Redin Bryan, of Jonesboro, Adjutant. Mr. Garner Watson was elected Surgeon to succeed the late Dr. J. L. Sheppard. Camp Ransom was organized in 1908 and now has about 60 members. Twelve members of the camp died during the past two years. Capt. Kelly and son, Mr. Charles Kelly, furnished the veterans a sumptuous dinner. It was served by Mrs. Kelly and granddaughter. The following veterans were present: Capt. J. O. A. Kelly, Redin Bryan, J. W. Howell, Geo. W. Luther, N. A. Matthews, J. H. Phillips, W. D. Underwood, J. M. B. Thomas, Garner Watson, Jordan F. Sloan, D. D. Seymore, E. M. Wicker.

The Sanford Express, May 7, 1915 [655]

The Veterans Express Their Appreciation.

The Confederate Veterans of Camp Ransom met at Sanford April 28th and were called to order by the commander, Rev. J. D. Wicker, at 11 o'clock a. m. The religious exercises were conducted by Rev. G. R. Underwood.

Mr. James Pardo, learning that we had no one to deliver a welcome address, very kindly went out and brought in D. B. Teague, who delivered a nice address in behalf of Sanford.

We were under obligations to Mrs. Pardo for securing Mrs. Clark to play the piano for us, and the music that was so appropriate to the occasion was thoroughly enjoyed by all.

The camp was very much indebted to Mrs. G. R. Underwood and Mrs. B. F. Rush, who raised the money to pay for their dinner. We had a very nice dinner prepared at the Maness House for the 48 who were present.

After dinner Mr. Maness took us to the L-Ma Theatre where we enjoyed the moving pictures at his expense. As we came from there we found a train of automobiles in readiness to give the old boys a spin. We went out as far as C. H. Smith's farm and back through Sanford.

While in session we elected a delegation of 10 to attend the general reunion that meets at Richmond the 1st, 2nd and 3rd of June. We also appointed a committee to assist Adjutant Bryant in writing some obituaries for our dead who died since our last meeting.

The camp went away well pleased with their entertainment at Sanford, and felt that Sanford never fails in her hospitality toward them. The boys are looking forward to meeting there again.

The camp returned their thanks to Sanford for the pleasant manner in which they entertained the veterans.

J. D. Wicker, Com.,
Redin Bryant, Adj't.

The Sanford Express, August 9, 1928 [656]

Mr. Wm. M. Avent, Sanford, R. 2, left Tuesday morning for Tarboro to attend the North Carolina Confederate Veterans' Reunion now being held at that place. Mr. Avent is one of only five or six Confederate veterans left in Lee county. Soon after Lee county was created Camp Ransom was organized in the county with about 100 members with the late Captain Kelly, of Broadway, as commander. In about 20 years' time death has depleted the company till there's hardly a corporal's guard left. Rev. J. D. Wicker, the last commander of Camp Ransom, died a few months ago. The Lee County Chapter Daughters of the Confederacy manifest an interest in the welfare of the few veterans left by seeing that they have an opportunity to attend the annual reunions and by serving a dinner some time during the year.

The Sanford Express, June 1, 1923 [657]

MEMORIAL AT BUFFALO

Daughters of Confederacy Decorate Graves and Col. Olds, A. A. F. Seawell and Others Make Addresses--Dinner Served.

Memorial Day, May 30, was fittingly observed at Buffalo church. Heretore memorial services were held at Buffalo on some Saturday, but this year it was decided that National Memorial Day should be made the permanent date for the holding of memorial services at Buffalo, and if we are to judge by the number of people present the decision was a wise one. More people attended than we have ever seen at that church on memorial day.

Much work has been done in the cemetery and many of the graves and plots are in good shape. We have never seen a more beautiful collection of flowers at a cemetery on memorial day and they were placed on many of the graves by relatives and friends. Some came and decorated the graves and returned home before the exercises opened.

The services at the church opened at 11 o'clock with a song by the choir. This was followed with a prayer by Rev. M. A. Ray, pastor of the church, who had charge of the program. He also made a short talk on the observance of memorial day and the significance of it.

Col. F. A. Olds, who has charge of the Hall of History and State Museum in Raleigh, and who knows more about the history of North Carolina than any other man in the State, then entertained the audience with an address that had to do with the Civil War. The many facts and figures that he gave of the great war between the States and the the part that North Carolina took in it held the attention of both old and young. He exhibited a number of relics of the war period, among other things a pair of home made stockings worn by a war bride, a pair of crude looking shoes, the rivets of which were made in England, an envelop, brown with age, home made cloth, of which women made their dresses and other things that carried the older [illegible] called on to make a sacrifice for a cause they loved. The speaker told how the people substituted parched wheat for coffee and "long sweetening" for sugar. He said that the love that the people of the South had for the men who suffered and died for a great principle, helped to make them a great and noble people. He mentioned the names of Avery, Burgwyn and Lane and gave a brief history of the famous 26th Regiment which made the charge at Gettysburg with 900 men and came out with 70.

Col Olds also paid the boys who fought in the World War a splendid tribute. He pictured how the 30th division, which was composed of troops from North and South Carlina and Tennessee broke the Hindenburg line after the Germans had pronounced it impregnable.

At the conclusion of Col. Old's address, the Daughters of the Confederacy, led by their president, Mrs. J. R. Ingram, formed in front of the church and with their arms full of flowers marched to the cemetery to decorate the graves. They were assisted by other ladies. "How Firm a Foundation Ye Saints of the Lord" was sung after which Rev. T. E. White led in prayer. The graves were then decorated. This was the most impressive part of the services.

Then followed dinner on a long table in the shade of the trees near the church and a splendid dinner it was. The table was decorated with small Confederate flags and the Daughters of the Confederacy pinned miniature flags on the lapels of the coats of the Confederate veterans. The following veterans were present: Rev. J. D. Wicker, Commander of Camp Ransom; Sam Kimball, M. A. Harrington, Thomas Groce, J. C. Harkey, J. M. Cole, J. K. Tally, W. R. Campbell and A. B. Austin. The Daughters of the Confederacy and Confederate veterans assembled near the church and had a group picture made.

All then assembled in the church to hear an address by Hon. A. A. F. Seawell. Mr. Seawell never addresses an audience without saying something that is worth while. On this occasion he was both practical and sentimental. He had a subject that admitted of both. Old Buffalo where he worshipped when a boy was sacred to him. He said that the custom of holding memorial services was a beautiful one and that when we failed to honor the memory of the dead civilisation would be lost. In talking of the "Mother Church" Mr. Seawell grew reminiscent. He told of the great influence many of the men and women who worshipped there in years gone by, but who are now taking their last long sleep in the cemetery near by, had over the generation that came after them. In

[Continued on Page Four.]

Memorial at Buffalo.

[Continued from Page One]

this connection he spoke of the McIvers, McIntoshes and other leaders in that church of Scotch forbears. He pictured a neglected cemetery—a cemetery inhabited by owls, whippoorwills and other denizens of the forests and wanted to see Sanford, the living city give more attention to the "city of the dead." He advocated an all-time keeper for Buffalo cemetery.

Short and appropriate talks were also made by Rev. T. E. White, Rev. Walter M. Gilmore and Rev. T. E. Wyche.

While at Buffalo church on memorial day Mr. A. M. Harrington, who fought through the Civil War, showed Col. Fred Olds a furlough which was issued to him while he was a patient in a hospital at Columbia, S. C., during the war. Mr. Harrington was taken prisoner by the Yankees before he had an opportunity to use it. This bit of paper which is now brown with age, is highly prized by Mr. Harrington on account of its associations and history. Mr. Harrington belonged to 50th North Carolina Regiment. The flag of this regiment is now in the Hall of History in Raleigh. Col. Olds says this old flag had been of assistance to him in collecting many war relics.

The Sanford Express, June 8, 1923 [658]

Photo of the Memorial Day Event at Buffalo Presbyterian Church, May 30, 1923 [659]

The following have been identified: [Back Row L-R] Claude Pernelle Rosser (wearing hat and short pants), Thomas Groce, four Confederate Veterans, Col. Fred A. Olds, Hall of History and State Museum, three Confederate Veterans, A.M. Gunn, one Confederate Veteran [Front Row R-L] Kate Robinson Matthews Rosser, Loula Frances Matthews Cox Rush, two United Daughters of Confederacy ladies, Mrs. J.R. Riley and other ladies from Lee County Chapter of the United Daughters of the Confederacy [fourth from the left is Lillian Campbell Bell]

Confederate Veteran Cemetery Census

Moore County, NC

Acorn Ridge Baptist Church Cemetery, Robbins
Maness, John Lewis, H 26th
Moore, William Spinks, D 49th
Williams, Levi, K 38th
Williamson, James G., D 10th Battalion

Allen Cemetery #92
Allen, John Calvin, F 3rd
Allen, Raleigh S., D 48th

Bascom Chapel United Methodist Church Cemetery
Brewer, Sampson, H 46th
Freeman, Alexander, E 70th/1st Jr. Reserves

Bensalem Presbyterian Church Cemetery
Bailey, John, C 3rd
Brewer, Henry, M 22nd
Britt, Bryant, H 6th/Sr. Reserves
Campbell, Daniel B., 51st Militia
Copeland, William Baxter, 59th Home Guard
Currie, Henry B., A 27th
Kennedy, Duncan M., H 6th/Sr. Reserves
McIntosh, Neill, H 26th
McKenzie, Kenneth Sidney, H 6th/Sr. Reserves
Monroe, Benjamin Franklin, D 49th
Monroe, John Calhoun, F 2nd / Local Defense
Morrison, John C., Mallett's Battalion, D
Morrison, Malcolm P., 51st Militia
Morrison, Samuel N., Marine Corps
Tyson, Benjamin Franklin, F 1st / Jr. Reserves

Bethesda Cemetery, Aberdeen
Adams, Jacob White, C 47th
Benoy, Alexander, C 3rd
Blue, Daniel S., A 63rd /5th Calvary
Blue, John Archibald Baxter, H 46th
Bowden, Bryant, F 15th
Buchan, James A.J., H 26th
Buchan, Jonathan Edward, G 40th
Campbell, John, A 63rd /5th Calvary
Drake, William R., D 35th
Ferguson, Archibald, H 46th
Graham, John Bethune, H 6th/Sr. Reserves
Hurley, Winship Marshal, D 61st
McDonald, John Alexander, C 54th
McLeod, Alexander, D 41st
McLeod, Evander, C 1st Battalion
McNeill, Malcolm, H 6th/Sr. Reserves
Shaw, Charles Washington, H 26th
Shaw, Daniel W., H 26th

Bethlehem Baptist Church Cemetery
Barrett, David Samuel, D 49th
Caddell, Artemus S., H 26th
Caddell, Cornelius Dowd, H 26th
Caddell, Neill Branson, D 49th
Caddell, Tobias B., Unknown
Cagle, Henry C., K 54th
Cox, Thomas F., H 26th
Dowdy, James, C 35th
Dupree, James Hailey, G 46th
Hannon, Daniel, 51st Militia
Hannon, Neil, C 35th
Lawhon, Lemuel, D 19th
Lawhon, William Henry Harrison, D 48th
McCallum, Duncan A., F 2nd / Local Defense
Ritter, Thomas Wesley, 51st Militia
Seawell, Eli Pleasants, H 26th
Sullivan, William Lindsey, B 53rd

Big Oak Christian Church Cemetery
Sheffield, Elijah, I 19th /2nd Calvary

Brown Cemetery #280
Morgan, John Martin, F 3rd

Brown's Chapel Christian Church Cemetery
Brewer, Martin, F 3rd
Key, Riland, D 48th
McNeill, Archibald, H 26th
McNeill, John Robert, 59th Home Guard
Nall, John Nicholas, H 10th [Alabama]
Sanders, Brittan, F 3rd
Sanders, Jesse, F 3rd
Sanders, John, F 3rd
Sanders, Simon, D 48th
Sheffield, Jonathan, H 46th
Smith, Hiram, F 3rd
Williamson, J. Kelly, H 26th

Calvary Baptist Church Cemetery
Dowdy, Archibald Bannister, C 35th [buried at Dowdy Cemetery #338 – CSA Marker located at Calvary]

Cameron Presbyterian Church Cemetery, Cameron

Arnold, Neill Thomas, I 19th /2nd Calvary /H 46th
Ferguson, Murdock, 51st Militia
Ferguson, Neill M., C 35th
Goodman, Timothy, C 35th
Howell, Shedrick Register, Unknown
Jones, Charles E., H 26th
Keith, Andrew Jackson, C 35th
Lawhon, Joel J., H 26th
MacFadyen, Gideon, Unknown
Maples, Duncan Thomas, H 46th
McDonald, Angus, H 6th/Sr. Reserves
McDonald, John, C 35th
McDonald, Murdoch McSwain, D 49th
McNeill, Neill Augustus, H 46th
McPherson, James D., Unknown
Monroe, James Hector, E 70th/1st Jr. Reserves
Muse, John Campbell, F 2nd / Local Defense
Phillips, Burnice Bender, E 44th
Turner, Hector, 59th Home Guard
Vick, Absalom B., C 35th

Carthage Presbyterian Church Cemetery, Carthage

Blue, John Calvin, F 2nd / Local Defense
Currie, John Bethune, A 30th
Fry, Thomas M., D 49th
Fry, William Wade, C 35th
Hunsucker, William Wesley, D 49th
Jones, John, H 6th/Sr. Reserves
Lewis, George H., C 35th
Lewis, James H., D 48th
Long, Edwin, M 15th / I 32nd
McDonald, Archibald Ray, 51st Militia
McIver, James D., H 26th
McLean, Charles C., H 26th
McLean, Hugh C., H 6th/Sr. Reserves
McLeod, Duncan M., H 26th
McLeod, Murdoch, H 26th
McLeod, William, Marine Corps
Shaw, John, 51st Militia
Shields, Neill M., E 3rd
Shields, W.W., C 35th
Tyson, Lucian Person, H 26th
Wicker, Jesse Johnson, H 30th

Carthage United Methodist Church Cemetery, Carthage

Cox, Hugh B., H 26th
Davis, Stephen, D 49th
Jenkins, John R., C 35th
Maness, Alexander, I 19th /2nd Calvary
Muse, George Glascock, I 6th/Sr. Reserves
Vick, John, C 35th
Waddill, Edmund, Marine Corps

Cool Springs Methodist Church Cemetery

Edwards, Isaac N., E 26th
Fields, Henry, H 6th/Sr. Reserves
Shields, John W., E 70th/1st Jr. Reserves

Crains Creek Cemetery, Cameron

Graham David A., H 26th
Medlin, Neill, C 35th
Thompson, Gaston, H 46th

Cross Hill Cemetery, Carthage

Barber, Hiram, I 19th /2nd Calvary
Cagle, Thomas Branson, I 19th /2nd Calvary
Hannon, Archibald, C 35th
Harrington, Thomas Henry, I 19th /2nd Calvary
Humber, Samuel Washington, C 35th
Jones, William Thomas, C 35th
Kelly, John B., H 26th
Kennedy, Kendrick, F 46th
McIntosh, Asa Seawell, D 49th
Muse, Howard James, 51st Militia
Muse, Samiel Jones, C 35th
Phillips, Malphus Spain, C 61st
Rose, Elisha, C 35th
Seawell, Joseph Parker, H 26th
Sinclair, Daniel M., D 48th
Williamson, Alexander McDonald, H 26th

Culdee Presbyterian Church Cemetery

Black, William Martin, C 35th
Freeman, William, H 30th
McDonald, Malcolm Alexander, Marine Corps
Moore, William Christopher, H 26th
Wicker, William Fordham, H 30th

Currie Family Cemetery # 256

Currie, James Lauchlin, C 35th

Davis Cemetery #106

Davis, Archibald, H 46th

Davis Cemetery #172

Davis, Devotion, H 26th

Davis Cemetery #210

Davis, James, H 6th/Sr. Reserves

Davis Cemetery #415

Davis, Aaron, 51st Militia

Davis-Melton Cemetery #414

Melton, James, D 15th

Doubs Chapel United Methodist Church Cemetery
Cole, Richard A., 51st Militia
Short, Brinkley H., G 63rd /5th Calvary

Dover Baptist Church Cemetery
Davis, John Lafayette, E 70th/1st Jr. Reserves
Dunn, James Harrison, E 70th/1st Jr. Reserves
Dunn, William, H 46th
Melton, Neill, D 15th
Phillips, James Riley, F 3rd

Dowdy Cemetery #338
Dowdy, Archibald Bannister, C 35th [buried here but CSA Marker located at Calvary]

Dunlap Cemetery #43
Dunlap, William C.D., E 70th/1st Jr. Reserves

Eagle Springs United Methodist Church Cemetery, Eagle Springs
Bailey, Angus E., 59th Home Guard
Bailey, Burrel, C 35th
Bailey, Daniel, H 26th
Bailey, Jesse, C 3rd

Eureka Presbyterian Church Cemetery
Blue, Cornelius Calvin, D 49th

Fair Promise Methodist Church Cemetery
Paschal, Robert, E 3rd
Phillips, Albert R., D 61st
Phillips, Allen W., E 3rd
Phillips, Baxter Clegg, D 48th
Phillips, Berry, E 44th
Phillips, Charles D., E 3rd
Phillips, Doctor C., E 3rd
Phillips, John W., E 3rd
Phillips, Lewis Spinks, E 3rd
Womble, Cornelius Hugh, M 15th / I 32nd

Flint Hill Baptist Church Cemetery
Yow, David Derrick, D 48th

Freeman Cemetery #408
Freeman, Elias K., E 70th/1st Jr. Reserves

Freeman Cemetery
Freeman, Enoch N., H 46th

Friendship Baptist Church Cemetery
Dowd, Henry Clay, F 2nd / Local Defense
Muse, Archibald Buckley, E 63rd /5th Calvary
Muse, William Riley, 51st Militia
Seawell, Samuel Waite, 51st Militia
Seawell, Virgil Newton, E 18th
Stutts, Andrew, H 26th
Williams, Richard D., K 4th

Fry Cemetery #185
Crabtree, Andrew Jackson, H 26th

Fry Cemetery #204
Fry, George Thomas, H 26th
Fry, Lockhart, I 6th/Sr. Reserves

Fry Cemetery #394
Fry, Absalom B., H 26th

Fry Cemetery #398
Fry, Walter A., E 4th

Fry Cemetery #407
Fry, Jacob B., D 49th
Fry, Murdoch Person, D 49th

Frye Cemetery #240
Gilchrist, John Thomas, G 8th [South Carolina]

Frye Cemetery #42
Frye, Madison M., 51st Militia

Hare Cemetery #413
Hare, William James, I 19th /2nd Calvary

Harris Cemetery #45
Bryant, William Richard, 51st Militia

High Falls United Methodist Church Cemetery, High Falls
Jones, James Rigdon, K 2nd
Maness, Isaac W., E 4th

Isaac Cagle Cemetery
Cagle, Isaac, B 56th

Jackson Cemetery #172
Jackson, John A., H 26th

Jackson Springs Cemetery, Jackson Springs
Brown, Alexander Watson, C 3rd
Clark, Nevin D.J., 51st Militia
Currie, Angus McNeill, C 35th
Ray, Archibald Joseph, K 34th

Jackson Springs Presbyterian Church Cemetery, Jackson Springs
McInnis, Duncan, D 49th
McKenzie, John, H 6th/Sr. Reserves

James M. Wright Cemetery
Wright, James M., E 70th/1st Jr. Reserves

Johnson Grove Cemetery, Vass
Bynum, Joseph H.M., H 46th
Cameron, John B., B 2nd / Local Defense
Thompson, Bryant, H 46th
Thompson, Gilbert, C 35th
Thompson, Isaac, H 46th

Kennedy/Cagle Cemetery #110
Cagle, Dempsey, H 44th

Kenneth Black Family Cemetery #116
Black, Malcolm Alexander, D 48th

Kitchen Cemetery #138
Maples, John M., C 35th
McDonald, John A., C 35th
Monroe, Duncan Manning, H 46th
Monroe, John Thomas, H 46th
Monroe, William Evander, H 46th
Monroe, William Washington, H 46th

Lakeview Cemetery, Lakeview
Hatcher, Martin George, H 3rd / Jr. Reserves
McDonald, Hiram Duncan, E 70th/1st Jr. Reserves
Monroe, W. David, Unknown
Stevens, John Charles, C 50th

Malcolm Leach Cemetery #295
Leach, Daniel, C 23rd

Martin Family Cemetery #195
McDonald, Kenneth M., D 49th

Martindale Cemetery #218
Cheek, Lewis, 59th Home Guard

McDonald Cemetery #194
McDonald, Allen C., H 6th/Sr. Reserves

McDonald Cemetery #200 near Cameron
Ferguson, Daniel Campbell, H 26th

McNeill Cemetery #102, Robbins
McNeill, Alexander, H 6th/Sr. Reserves

McNeill Cemetery #154
McNeill, Hector, D 48th
McNeill, Noah, D 48th

Morgan Cemetery #275
Morgan, Nathan, D 48th

Morgan Cemetery #418
Morgan, George Troy, D 15th

Mount Carmel United Methodist Church Cemetery
Jones, Christopher M., K 2nd

Needham's Grove Baptist Church Cemetery
Maness, Enoch N., A 10th Battalion
Scott, Nelson, C 10th
Williamson, Matthew, D 49th

Oaklawn Cemetery, Whispering Pines
Thagard, William Calvin, H 46th

Old County Home Cemetery, Carthage
Maness, Enoch, B 52nd

Old Scotch Graveyard
Stutts, Henry W., D 48th

Parrish Cemetery #298
Parrish, John B., 51st Militia

Patterson Family Cemetery
Patterson, Duncan, 51st Militia

Perry Gravesite #217
Perry, Benjamin, H 26th

Phillips Cemetery #249
Phillips, Albert R., D 61st

Phillips Cemetery #253
Paschal, Nathan D., D 48th
Phillips, Mastin Crawford, D 48th

Phillips Cemetery #62
Phillips, William Briscoe, 51st Militia

Pine Grove Baptist Church Cemetery
Deaton, John M., D 48th
Myrick, Moses Emsley, E 26th

Pinebluff Cemetery, Pinebluff
White, Theodore A., K 43rd

Pineywood Baptist Church Cemetery, Cameron
Bunnell, Durham P., H 46th

Pleasant Hill Freewill Baptist Church Cemetery, Carthage
Goins, Sidney, I 19th /2nd Calvary

Pleasant Hill United Methodist Church Cemetery
Cagle, Matthew, H 26th
Hunsucker, Nelson, H 26th
Maness, Ira Lane, H 26th
Maness, Reuben, G 46th
Maness, Thomas Swain, H 26th
Reynolds, Elijah, K 34th
Riddle, John W., H 6th/Sr. Reserves
Williams, George W., I 5th [Alabama]
Wilson, Hugh F., F 2nd

Powers Cemetery #290
Powers, Enoch Spinks, H 6th/Sr. Reserves

Prosperity Friends Meeting Cemetery, High Falls
Brady, Charles Underwood, I 19th /2nd Calvary
Brady, Eli, E 63rd /5th Calvary
Brady, Nimrod, H 6th/Sr. Reserves
Councilman, Peter, 51st Militia
Moore, J.J., E 14th
Wilson, Robert W., 51st Militia

Richardson Cemetery #214
Richardson, William Brantley, 51st Militia

Seawell Cemetery #127
Seawell, Simon McNeill, C 3rd

Shamburger Cemetery #210
Brewer, Adam, K 63rd /5th Calvary
Shamburger, Peter, 51st Militia

Sheffield Cemetery #344
Sheffield, Isaac E., F 3rd

Shields Cemetery #221
Shields, Robert D., E 3rd

Short Family Cemetery #177
Short, Daniel, G 63rd /5th Calvary

Smyrna United Methodist Church Cemetery
Garner, Eli, E 5th
Garner, Elias, C 11th
Garner, James F., H 6th/Sr. Reserves
Maness, Elias, 51st Militia
Maness, John Wesley, D 49th
Maness, Lewis Grant, H 6th/Sr. Reserves
Maness, Shadrach, D 49th
Myrick, Matthew P., A 10th Battalion
Ritter, Francis Marion, 51st Militia
Ritter, John, H 6th/Sr. Reserves
Williams, Elias Terrell, 51st Militia
Williamson, Henry Clay, C 11th

Street Family Cemetery #239
Street, Murdoch G., H 26th
Street, Richard, H 26th

Stutts Cemetery #82
Stutts, Cornelius Alexander, D 48th

Tabernacle United Methodist Church Cemetery, Robbins
Brown, Henry Clay, G 26th
Brown, William Wesley, I 19th /2nd Calvary
Clegg, William Baxter, M 15th / I 32nd
Davis, Baxter, D 48th
Frye, William Allen, E 70th/1st Jr. Reserves
Garner, Atlas William, I 19th /2nd Calvary
Hunsucker, Bethuel Coffin, Unknown
Maness, Marshal G., K 10th
Marley, James Ruffin, E 70th/1st Jr. Reserves
Mathews, James, E 70th/1st Jr. Reserves
Rouse, Enoch, D 48th
Shields, James Martin, 51st Militia
Stutts, William C., D 48th
Williams, John Spanker, H 26th
Williamson, Jesse, D 15th

Union Presbyterian Church Cemetery
Arnold, John, H 46th
Blue, Daniel, C 35th
Blue, Duncan Alexander, C 35th
Blue, Evander McNair, C 35th
Blue, Malcolm Jasper, 51st Militia
Britton, Moses, C 35th
Currie, Daniel M., C 35th
Currie, Neill R., 51st Militia
Deaton, Noah, H 26th
Ferguson, John Campbell, C 35th
Ferguson, John McNeill, H 6th/Sr. Reserves
Kelly, Duncan, H 26th
Kelly, Evander, H 6th/Sr. Reserves
Kelly, Malcom, H 6th/Sr. Reserves
Leach, Martin, 51st Militia
McCaskill, John W., C 35th
McDonald, John Ferguson, G 33rd
McIver, Duncan Murchison, H 30th
McLean, James, D 19th
McLean, Peter, H 46th
McNeill, Henry Josephus, H 30th
McNeill, John K., H 26th
Ray, Archibald Alexander, C 35th
Snead, Obediah, E 44th
Wadsworth, William J., H 46th

Wallace Cemetery #68,

Wallace, Isham, D 49th

Wallace Gravesite #78
Wallace, Sampson Delaney, I 19th /2nd Calvary

Warner Cemetery #188
Warner, Levi S., B 3rd

West End Cemetery, West End
Sibbett, George W., C 35th

Williams Cemetery #183
Williams, Noah R., K 38th

Williams Cemetery #84
Williams, Henry, H 26th
Williams, Lindsay, M 22nd
Wood, Westley William, D 49th

Williams/Morgan Cemetery #86
Williams, Harbert, D 48th

Wright Cemetery #334
Wright, William, 51st Militia

Yow Cemetery #155
Yow, Henry Clay, H 26th

Lee County, NC

Baptist Chapel Church Cemetery, Sanford
Pittman, James Benjamin, F 51st
Thomas, Henry Tillman, H 30th
Thomas, Jefferson, H 30th
Thomas, John Martin Benton, F 50th
Thomas, Macklin C., H 46th
Thomas, Sackfield F., B 2nd / Local Defense

Bethlehem United Methodist Church Cemetery, Sanford
Palmer, Alexander Wesley, D 41st
Thomas, David Anderson, F 50th

Broadway Town Cemetery, Broadway
Matthews, John, C 7th
Thomas, Henderson B., I 19th /2nd Calvary
Thomas, William Otis, 51st Militia

Buffalo Cemetery, Sanford
Arnold, William, H 46th
Bryan, Daniel O., I 19th /2nd Calvary
Bryan, Redin, F 50th
Campbell, Thomas Cole, D 61st
Clegg, Benjamin R. Franklin, M 15th / I 32nd
Cole, Green Berry, H 30th
Cox, Alexander H., F 50th
Dalrymple, James, F 50th
Dennis, Henry J., H 6th/Sr. Reserves
Dye, John M., A 63rd /5th Calvary
Dye, William W., H 6th/Sr. Reserves
Harkey, Jacob Cicero, C 1st
Matthews, John Berryman, H 30th
McGilvary, Evander, H 6th/Sr. Reserves
McGilvary, William M., E 70th/1st Jr. Reserves
McIntosh, David G., H 30th
McIntosh, John, C 8th
McIntosh, William David, A 2nd / Local Defense
McIntyre, Daniel, 59th Home Guard
McIver, Daniel Newton, H 30th
McIver, John, 51st Militia
McNeill, William, M 22nd
Oldham, James Wesley, F 2nd / Local Defense
Phillips, John Atlas, E 63rd /5th Calvary
Phillips, John Henry, H 30th
Reid, Richard G., F 15th [Virginia]
Ross, John Montgomery, G 14th
Seawell, Aaron Ashley Flowers, 51st Militia
Stedman, William Alexander, D 48th
Tally, James K., E 44th
Wicker, Alexander Monroe, 51st Militia
Wicker, John Martin, A 63rd /5th Calvary
Wicker, Thomas, H 30th
Williamson, Noah R., H 26th

Butler Cemetery, Sanford
Bean, John M., F 44th

Cameron Grove Cemetery
Graham Henry White, C 54th
Graham, William David, E 70th/1st Jr. Reserves
Monroe, John P., H 30th
Morris, William B., E 56th

Center United Methodist Church Cemetery, Sanford
Caviness, Benjamin Darris, G 63rd /5th Calvary
Caviness, Thomas Henry, I 19th /2nd Calvary
Caviness, William S., I 19th /2nd Calvary
Davidson, Aaron, C 35th
Kimball, William Benjamin, E 3rd
Monger, Joseph J., H 6th/Sr. Reserves
Paul, Abraham, E 51st
Salmon, Reuben, E 44th
Thomas, Green W., H 6th/Sr. Reserves
Tyson, Bartlett Y., I 19th /2nd Calvary

Chestnut African Methodist Episcopal Church Cemetery
Judd, Stokes Parrish, Unknown

Cool Springs Baptist Church Cemetery, Sanford
Bridges, Joseph William, I 19th /2nd Calvary
Burns, Headen H., G 48th
Gilmore, George Washington, D 48th
Gilmore, John Jackson, H 6th/Sr. Reserves
Groce, Connor Dowd, E 44th
Gross, Thomas, H 1st / Jr. Reserves
Gunter, Thomas B., D 35th
Hornaday, Louis Daniel, H 30th
McIntosh, Daniel W., H 30th
Pendergrass, Alvis, D 1st
Petty, John Wesley, G 63rd /5th Calvary
Poe, James Warren, E 63rd /5th Calvary
Rogers, Joseph, H 26th
Salmon, James Thomas, E 44th

Cox Family Cemetery, Sanford
Cox, Duncan Merchant, Griswold / Local Defense
Cox, John Lewis, H 30th

Cumnock Community Cemetery
Goins, Duncan, H 30th

Dickens Cemetery, Sanford
Kelly, Archibald A., F 50th

Ephesus Baptist Church Cemetery, Sanford
Smith, Malcolm, H 46th

Euphronia Presbyterian Church Cemetery
Alexander, John Smith, F 63rd /5th Calvary
Campbell, Angus McDonald, C 35th
Campbell, Duncan C., E 63rd /5th Calvary
Campbell, Peter M., H 26th
Harrington, Elam James, A 63rd /5th Calvary
McRae, George Alexander, G 63rd /5th Calvary
McRae, Roderick M., C 35th
Sinclair, Duncan Murchison, 51st Militia
Underwood, John Fordham, 59th Home Guard

Flat Springs Church Cemetery, Sanford
Boyd, Isaac David, X 18th [South Carolina]

Gaster Family Cemetery, Sanford
Gaster, John M., I 19th /2nd Calvary
Gaster, William, H 6th/Sr. Reserves
Hunter, John G., F 50th
Williams, James H., F 50th

Grace Chapel Church Cemetery
Foster, John A., E 44th
Medlin, Benjamin J., D 49th
Oldham, Phillip, H 46th
Riddle, Thomas, H 46th
Willet, John Alexander, H 3rd / Jr. Reserves

Harrington-McDonald Graveyard
Harrington, Joseph H., Unknown

Hunt Family Cemetery
Hunt, George F., H 6th/Sr. Reserves

J.O.A. Kelly Cemetery, Broadway
Kelly, James Oscar Abner, F 50th
Sloan, David M., F 50th

John Walker Cemetery, Sanford
Walker, John A., I 19th /2nd Calvary

Johnson Family Cemetery, Lemon Springs
Johnson, Daniel, 51st Militia

Jones Chapel Church Cemetery, Sanford
Bridges, Horace Amos, D 48th
Pattishall, John Rhodes, G 63rd /5th Calvary
Smith, Joseph John, G 63rd /5th Calvary

Jonesboro Cemetery, Sanford
Avent, George Washington, D 35th
Brooks, Joab Terrell, F 50th
Cole, George S., 59th Home Guard
Dalrymple, Malcolm, F 50th
Hawley, David Morris, E 70th/1st Jr. Reserves
Kelly, William Joseph, F 50th
Partridge, Elbert R., H 6th/Sr. Reserves
Robertson, D.B., C 3rd
Stephens, John Marshall, F 50th

Juniper Springs Baptist Church Cemetery, Sanford
Thomas, William John, E 56th

Kelly Cemetery
Kelly, John B., F 50th

Kelly Family Cemetery, Sanford
Harrington, Abner Flynn, H 30th

Lemon Springs Methodist Church Cemetery
Jones, Hayes, I 51st
Seawell, Asa Jones, H 46th
Sutton, Loyd Holmes, B 56th
Watson, Elisha, Marine Corps

Love Family Cemetery, Sanford
Love, William Andrew, D 61st

Matthews Family Cemetery
Morris, Joseph, E 56th
Wicker, Green B., F 50th

McFarland Family Cemetery, Sanford
McFarland, John Baker, F 50th

McNeill Family Burying Grounds, Broadway
Cox, William A., I 19th /2nd Calvary
McNeill, Hector, Unknown

McNeill Family Cemetery
McNeill, Neill Archibald, F 50th
McNeill, Neill Jr., F 50th

Moore Christian Church Cemetery, Sanford
Burns, Spence M., E 63rd /5th Calvary

Osgood Cemetery
Booker, Henry Judson, D 26th
Kelly, Alexander D., H 30th

Pocket Presbyterian Church Cemetery, Sanford
Gilliam, William Henry, Unknown
Nall, Ira Lane, E 26th

Poplar Springs Methodist Church Cemetery, Sanford
Brown, Alexander Hinton, H 30th
Harrington, Archibald A., 51st Militia
Hunter, John Reaves, H 30th
Luther, George W., F 50th
Oliver, John M., 51st Militia
Sloan, William George, Griswold / Local Defense
Stone, Archibald, F 50th
Thomas, Benjamin Wicker, F 50th
Wicker, David Warren, F 50th
Wicker, Elijah Martin, F 50th
Wicker, Elisha, F 50th
Wicker, Thomas R., F 50th

Saint Andrews Presbyterian Church Cemetery, Sanford
Buie, Bailey, E 56th
Dalrymple, John, I 19th /2nd Calvary
Johnston, David M., F 50th
Kimbell, Samuel P., E 70th/1st Jr. Reserves
McBryde, John, H 6th/Sr. Reserves
McBryde, Thomas, F 50th
McBryde, William H., E 56th
Morris, Daniel, E 8th
Morris, Joseph D., 59th Home Guard
Morris, Martin V., E 8th
Morris, Thomas W., H 46th
Munn, John A., E 8th
Nicholson, John, H 26th
Shaw, Dougald C., H 30th
Thomas, Asa Grissom, E 56th
Thomas, Charles Wesley Ruffin, E 70th/1st Jr. Reserves
Wicker, John A., H 46th

Salem Presbyterian Church Cemetery, Sanford
Kelly, Henry Myrover, B 2nd / Local Defense
Sheppard, James L., F 50th
Sloan, Jordan F., Griswold / Local Defense
Weldon, John J., F 50th

Shallow Well Cemetery, Sanford
Campbell, John A., E 11th
Campbell, William R., H 26th
Cox, George, E 8th
Godfrey, Henry A., F 50th
Godfrey, John, F 50th
Hart, James David, G 48th
Hawley, Marshall H., E 70th/1st Jr. Reserves
Hughes, Spencer, F 50th
Hunter, Stanford, H 30th
Kelly, William A., H 30th
Lasater, William Gilbert, E 10th
Mann, James H., D 35th
McFarland, William M., F 50th
McIver, John J., 51st Militia
Oliver, Willis M., F 50th
Salmon, Bedford R., 59th Home Guard
Underwood, John A., H 30th
Underwood, William Daniel, E 70th/1st Jr. Reserves
Wadsworth, Alexander, H 26th
Watson, Malcolm McFarland, F 50th
Wicker, John Daniel, E 44th

Thomas Cemetery
Dalrymple, John G., E 70th/1st Jr. Reserves

Turners Chapel Church Cemetery
Dowdy, James Madison, G 48th
Wicker, William Gaston, E 7th

White Hill Presbyterian Church Cemetery
Cameron, Alexander Hamilton, Marine Corps
Cole, James M., 51st Militia
Cole, John B., 51st Militia
Cole, John D., B 2nd / Local Defense
Ferguson, Daniel Monroe, H 46th
Jackson, Gorrie, I 19th /2nd Calvary
McLeod, Duncan, I 19th /2nd Calvary
Riddle, Able, H 46th
Riddle, Cato, H 46th
Wicker, Kenneth, H 46th

Womack Family Cemetery, Broadway
Womack, William Rorie, Unknown

Zion Christian Church Cemetery, Sanford
Gunter, John Ambrose Jr., Marine Corps

Kelly, Joseph David, F 50th
Kelly, Thomas M., F 50th
Marks, Abner Gunter, E 5th
Spivey, Jordan, F 50th
Spivey, Wilson E 8th
Webster, Thomas Alexander, D 35th

Chatham County, NC

Asbury Methodist Church Cemetery
Burns, Elisha H., G 48th
Pattishall, William R., E 8th
Rowe, Allen McLennon, I 19th /2nd Calvary
Stedman, David Lawrence, E 8th

Bonlee Baptist Church Cemetery, Bonlee
Causey, Joshua, H 46th
Cheek, Charles Christmas, H 15th

Buchanan Cemetery
Buchanan, Ethelbert, F 50th
Buchanan, Hilliard S., F 50th

Carbonton United Methodist Church Cemetery, Carbonton
Malone, Benjamin, D 48th
Mashburn, James, E 44th
Mashburn, John, E 44th
Mashburn, Thomas, B 2nd / Local Defense
Mashburn, William Henry Harrison, E 44th
Phillips, George W., E 26th

Christian Chapel Cemetery
Carpenter, Robert, E 3rd

Clegg Family Cemetery
Clegg, Thomas J., D 48th

Douglass Family Cemetery
Douglass, R.B., F 50th

Edwards Hill Friends Meeting Cemetery, Siler City
Willett, Aaron Evans, H 46th

Fall Creek Baptist Church Cemetery, Bennett
Brady, Lucas, I 19th /2nd Calvary
Brady, Manly, F 2nd / Local Defense
Stokes, John Jackson, K 56th

Goldston United Methodist Church Cemetery, Goldston
Ausley, John Fletcher, Navy

Gulf Presbyterian Church Cemetery, Gulf
McIver, John McMillan, A 63rd /5th Calvary
Willcox, George W., H 26th

Gum Springs Church Retirement Site, Moncure
Lasater, Thomas Lambeth, H 47th

Hanks Chapel Christian Church Cemetery, Pittsboro
Thomas, John Wesley, F 50th

Haywood Baptist Church Cemetery, Moncure
Drake, Matthew H., D 35th
Fitchett, Milton Luther, D 35th
Harrington, A.M., F 50th

Loves Creek Baptist Church Cemetery, Siler City
Moore, Albert James, A 5th

Lystra Baptist Church Cemetery, Farrington
Drake, Dallas Polk, H 1st, Jr. Reserves

Merry Oaks Baptist Church Cemetery, Moncure
Womack, John B., F 50th

Moons Chapel Baptist Church Cemetery, Siler City, Chatham County, NC
Brown, Cornelius Shields, E 70th/1st Jr. Reserves

Mount Pleasant Baptist Church Cemetery
Williamson, William J., 59th Home Guard

Mount Pleasant United Methodist Church Cemetery, Pittsboro
Harris, Elias H., E 63rd /5th Calvary

New Elam Christian Church Cemetery
Thomas, Hugh C., E 10th

Old Tick Creek Cemetery, Siler City
Dunlap, Bryan Green, E 63rd /5th Calvary

Pleasant Hill United Methodist Church Cemetery

Cockman, Alexander, I 19th /2nd Calvary
Cockman, Mark A., I 19th /2nd Calvary

Poe Family Cemetery, Gulf
Poe, Logan, G 48th

Providence Church Cemetery, Pittsboro
Marks, Thaddeus S., D 35th

Providence United Methodist Church Cemetery, Bear Creek
Caviness, John A., M 22nd

Purvis Cemetery #291
Purvis, Andrew Jackson, A 10th Battalion

Saint Bartholomew's Episcopal Church Cemetery, Pittsboro
Torrence, Richmond Pearson, M 15th / I 32nd

Sandy Branch Baptist Church Cemetery, Bear Creek
Burke, Thomas Brooks, H 46th
Dunn, George Washington, E 63rd /5th Calvary
Murray, John Wesley, I 19th /2nd Calvary
Womble, Solomon W., Mallett's Battalion, D

Tysons Creek Baptist Church Cemetery, Bear Creek
Smith, Nicholas P., H 26th

Tysor Graveyard, Gulf
Gardner, Thomas Jefferson, I 19th /2nd Calvary

Wilkie Family Cemetery
Wilkie, Thomas J., H 26th

Cumberland County, NC

Big Rockfish Presbyterian Church Cemetery, Hope Mills
Wallace, John Mack, D 48th
Warner, Edward, D 49th

Brafford-Hall Cemetery, Fayetteville
Brafford, Eli, H 30th

Church of the Covenant Cemetery, Spring Lake
McFarland, James A., E 70th/1st Jr. Reserves
McFarland, John Ambrose, H 30th

Cross Creek Cemetery #1, Fayetteville
Cole, William W., C 54th
Warwick, John Thomas, H 26th

Cross Creek Cemetery #2, Fayetteville
Hollingsworth, Benjamin G., H 26th

Cross Creek Cemetery #3, Fayetteville
Scoggins, James, E 56th

Cumberland Cemetery, Fayetteville
Pardue, William, H 46th
Yarborough, Elias Gaston, F 50th

Evergreen Baptist Church Cemetery, Beaver Dam
Hales, Daniel D., C 35th

Gilliland Cemetery
Kennedy, W.M., E 52nd

Holt-Morgan Cemetery, Fayetteville
Hales, Giles, H 46th

Hope Mills Cemetery, Hope Mills
Kelly, Spencer, F 50th
Williams, Andrew Jackson, H 26th

Marvin United Methodist Church Cemetery
Graham, William H., H 26th

Mount Gilead Baptist Church Cemetery, Fayetteville
Burton, John Morehead, H 44th
Hales, Bunyan, H 46th

Russell Family Cemetery, Fayetteville
McDougald, Daniel B., E 56th

Harnett County, NC

Antioch Baptist Church Cemetery, Mamers
Fuquay, John F., F 50th
Hawley, J.A., F 50th
Stewart, John Benjamin Franklin, F 50th

Baptist Grove Baptist Church Cemetery, Chalybeate Springs
Knight, John L., F 50th

Barbecue Presbyterian Church Cemetery
Brafford, Aaron Archie, E 40th
McDonald, John Alexander, H 30th
Oliver, John, F 50th

Cool Springs United Methodist Church Cemetery
Gilchrist, Charles Abel, F 50th
McAuley, James D., F 50th
Wood, Archibald B., F 50th

Cypress Presbyterian Church Cemetery
Blue, Malcom P.N., C 35th
Cameron, Benjamin F., H 46th
Cameron, John F., C 3rd
Cameron, Neil Beaver, Unknown
Darroch, Daniel R., H 46th
Keith, Hugh, H 26th
Kelly, John M., C 35th
Martin, Wiliam P., H 26th
McCallum, Archibald D., H 26th
McKeithen, Daniel B., 51st Militia
Medlin, Shadrach, H 46th
Monroe, John, C 35th
Smith, William, D 41st
Starling, William R., I 19th /2nd Calvary

Harnett Chapel Cemetery
McNeill, Malcom, E 56th

Lauchlin McNeill Cemetery
McNeill, Lauchlin, H 30th

Matthews Cemetery
Matthews, Neill A., C 36th

McNeill Family Cemetery
McNeill, Neil Archibald, E 8th

Morris Chapel United Methodist Church Cemetery
Grose, Atlas H., H 1st / Jr. Reserves
Harrington, A.M., Unknown
McLeod, Louis H., H 30th
Thomas, Robert B., F 50th

Mount Pisgah Presbyterian Church Cemetery
McNeill, Alexander, F 50th
McNeill, Malcom, E 8th

Summerville Presbyterian Church Cemetery
McDonald, John A., F 50th

Montgomery County, NC

Bethel Baptist Church Cemetery, Mount Gilead
Barrett, William Ashley, D 49th

Candor Cemetery, Candor
Leach, Neill, D 48th

Dennis Cemetery
Williams, Upshur, I 19th /2nd Calvary

Forks of Little River Baptist Church Cemetery, Troy
Atkins, William Martin, B 14th
Martin, Allen Daniel, H 44th

Green Family Cemetery
Greene, Calvin R., E 70th/1st Jr. Reserves

Greene Cemetery, Candor
Dawkins, William Kathay, Marine Corps

Hamer Creek Baptist Church Cemetery, Mount Gilead
Tedder, Roland Mumford, E 70th/1st Jr. Reserves

Haywood Cemetery, Mount Gilead
Stutts, Andrew John, D 48th

Historical Montgomery County Home Cemetery, Troy
Brown, Pinkney Spinks, A 2nd
Jackson, Noah R., C 35th

Lassiter Cemetery
Owen, Emsley H., C 23rd

Laurel Hill Baptist Church Cemetery, Troy
Johnson, Dillon Lindsy, E 70th/1st Jr. Reserves

Leach/Star Town Cemetery, Star
Owen, William Bailey, 51st Militia
Stuart, John Lane, D 49th

Lucas Family Cemetery
Hogan, Zacheus, H 26th

Macedonia Presbyterian Church Cemetery, Candor
McCaskill, Malcolm, D 49th

Pleasant Hill United Methodist Church Cemetery
Campbell, David Allen, B 36th
Campbell, John H., C 23rd
Whitlock, William, H 26th

Sharon Cemetery, Mount Gilead
Byrd, John M., E 70th/1st Jr. Reserves
Stuart, Robert Bruce, D 48th

Southside Cemetery, Troy
Williamson, Cornelius Dowd, D 15th

Wadeville Baptist Church Cemetery, Wadeville
Hurley, John Bradley, E 70th/1st Jr. Reserves
McAulay, John T., E 70th/1st Jr. Reserves

White Oak Springs Baptist Church Cemetery, Star
Tucker, Nathaniel, H 44th

Zion Methodist Church Cemetery, Mount Gilead
Matheson, Malcolm Daniel, E 28th

Randolph County, NC

Asheboro City Cemetery, Asheboro
Burns, Solomon, I 19th /2nd Calvary
Hunsucker, Gaston DeBerry, E 3rd
Morris, Parsons Harris, E 70th/1st Jr. Reserves

Beulah Baptist Church Cemetery
Howard, William Henry, E 70th/1st Jr. Reserves
Myrick, John Montgomery, A 10th Battalion
Purvis, Joseph, 51st Militia

Cedar Falls United Methodist Church Cemetery, Asheboro
Hurley, William Elias, 51st Militia

Denson Family Cemetery, Franklinville
Denson, David, I 19th /2nd Calvary

First Baptist Church Cemetery, Franklinville
Dickens, John T., F 50th

Flag Springs United Methodist Church Cemetery, Asheboro
Williams, Aulie Spain, B 52nd

Franklinville United Methodist Church Cemetery, Franklinville
Ritter, John Spinks, I 19th /2nd Calvary

Giles Chapel United Methodist Church Cemetery, Asheboro
Howell, John W. B 36th 2nd Company
Jordan, Enoch, F 46th

Holly Spring Friends Meeting Cemetery, Ramseur
Stout, William McKenzie, H 46th

J.E. Groce Memorial Cemetery, Worthville
Johnson, Bradley B., D 48th
Martin, Kenneth Alexander, H 44th

New Hope United Methodist Church Cemetery, Asheboro
Tucker, Edmund Deberry, F 46th

Old Mount Olivet Cemetery, Randolph County, NC
Gatlin, William N., H 6th/Sr. Reserves

Parks Crossroads Christian Church Cemetery, Ramseur
Parks, Thomas B., I 19th /2nd Calvary

Pleasant Grove Christian Church Cemetery, Coleridge
Brady, William Wesley, D 48th
Maness, Robartis, D 49th

Pleasant Hill United Methodist Church Cemetery, Seagrove
Owens, Brantly, D 6th / Sr. Reserves
Upton, John Lewis, D 6th / Sr. Reserves

Union Grove Baptist Church Cemetery, Seagrove
Comer, William C., K 63rd /5th Calvary
Freeman, Aaron, F 46th
Luck, William Henry, F 1st / Jr. Reserves
McNeill, Daniel A., E 4th

Whites Chapel United Methodist Church Cemetery, Liberty

Yow, Isaac, D 15th

Whynot Cemetery
Tucker, Henry, F 46th

Richmond County, NC

Bear Branch Cemetery
Graham, William Watson, 51st Militia

Cole Family Cemetery, Ellerbe
Cole, Duncan, D 49th

Cox Bruton Cemetery, Ellerbe
Cox, McDonald, D 49th

Eastside Cemetery, Rockingham
Dowd, William James D., H 26th
Moore, Zaccheus B., 51st Militia
Nicholson, Archibald B., I 19th /2nd Calvary

Great Falls Cemetery
Riddle, Wiley, Rencher's Battalion, A

John Thrower Cemetery
Thrower, William Norris, E 8th

Marks Creek Presbyterian Church Cemetery, Hamlet
McDonald, Archibald Blue, E 38th
McLean, Angus, H 36th

Mary Love Cemetery, Hamlet
Brown, John Monroe, K 56th

Mizpah Cemetery, Rockingham
Godfrey, Pleasant G., E 10th

Mount Pleasant United Methodist Church Cemetery, Ellerbe
Key, Pleasant Troy, 51st Militia

Scottish Cemetery, Rockingham
Denson, William T., H 26th

Stevan Gibson Cemetery, Hamlet
Sinclair, Daniel F., D 48th

Thrower Cemetery, Rockingham
King, William Jerome, 51st Militia

Williams Cemetery
Williams, Alfred W., B 14th

Zion Methodist Church Cemetery, Rockingham
Maples, Dugald McDougald, H 46th

Scotland County, NC

Currie-Cameron Cemetery
Cameron, John Archibald, 8th Sr. Reserves

King Cemetery, Laurel Hill
Sinclair, Duncan F., C 3rd

McFarland Cemetery
Thrower, John Thomas, D 49th

Old Hillside Cemetery, Laurinburg
Muse, John Alexander, C 35th

Rowe, William Brandy, I 19th /2nd Calvary

Stewartsville Cemetery, Laurinburg
Chisholm, Alexander, I 19th /2nd Calvary

Alamance County, NC

Carolina Christian Church Cemetery, Burlington
Tyson, Henry Clay, H 26th

Linwood Cemetery, Graham
Stutts, George Dumas, D 48th

Anson County, NC

Deep Creek Baptist Church Cemetery
Gulledge, William M., K 26th

Pleasant Hill Cemetery

Cottingham, Dinwiddie, B 6th

Bladen County, NC

Carvers Creek United Methodist Cemetery
Gilliam, James Daniel, H 26th

Brunswick County, NC

Benfield-Chinnis Cemetery
Moore, Francis M., H 30th

Cabarrus County, NC

Coldwater Baptist Church Cemetery, Concord
Black, William James, E 70th/1st Jr. Reserves

Concord Baptist Church Cemetery, Concord
Bedsole, Duncan, H 46th

New Gilead Reformed Cemetery, Concord
Foil, John F., E 59th

Oakwood Cemetery, Concord
McInnis, John, E 70th/1st Jr. Reserves

Catawba County, NC

Oakwood Cemetery, Hickory
McIntosh, Archibald, H 30th

Craven County, NC

Cedar Grove Cemetery, New Bern
Gordon, Thomas, I 19th /2nd Calvary
Monroe, William B., C 35th

New Bern Battlefield Park, New Bern
Tysor, Lewis Brock, H 26th

Davidson County, NC

Fair Grove Methodist Church Cemetery, Thomasville
Yow, Simeon Jones, D 15th

Davie County, NC

Wesley Chapel United Methodist Church Cemetery, Mocksville
Roberts, Isaac, E 41st

Durham County, NC

Cedar Hill Cemetery, Durham
Sloan, David Hornsby, H 30th

Fowler and Proctor Cemetery
Lynn, William, H 30th

Maplewood Cemetery, Durham
Cagle, Matthew, F 1st

Tyson, James, H 26th
Walker, Tandy, H 30th

Mount Sylvan Methodist Church Cemetery
Cole, Solomon N., C 35th

Woodlawn Memorial Park, Durham
Melton, George W., D 48th

Forsyth County, NC

Salem Cemetery, Winston-Salem
Hall, Joseph O., H 26th

Sharon United Methodist Church Cemetery, Lewisville
Yow, William Andrew, E 70th/1st Jr. Reserves

Guilford County, NC

Green Hill Cemetery, Greensboro
Siler, Thompson, Mallett's Battalion, C
Sullivan, Isaac McLendon, D 48th

Pleasant Garden United Methodist Church Cemetery, Pleasant Garden
McDonald, William Henry Harrison, H 26th

Proximity Cemetery, Greensboro
Powers, John Walker, E 26th

Tabernacle United Methodist Church Cemetery, Pleasant Garden
Hanner, Robert, I 19th /2nd Calvary

Halifax County, NC

Weldon Confederate Cemetery, Weldon
Edwards, John, E 63rd /5th Calvary
McDonald, Evander, E 38th

Henderson County, NC

Patty's Chapel Methodist Cemetery
Wallace, Everett W., I 22nd

Hoke County, NC

Lucille McLeod Family Cemetery, Hoke County, NC
McLeod, William Johnson, C 1st Battalion

Johnston County, NC

D.A. Overbee Cemetery
McFatter, James, E 70th/1st Jr. Reserves

Maplewood Cemetery, Clayton
Bedsole, Calton, H 46th

Lenoir County, NC

Fairview Cemetery, La Grange
McDonald, Hugh M., C 35th

Maplewood Cemetery, Kinston
McNeill, Neill T., E 56th

McDowell County, NC

Oak Grove Cemetery, Marion
Bledsoe, John Allen, B 22nd

Mecklenburg County, NC

Arlington Baptist Church Cemetery, Charlotte
Connell, Francis Marion, E 22nd [South Carolina]

Elmwood Cemetery, Charlotte
Deaton, James P., H 30th
Dowd, Charles Dickerson, E 70th/1st Jr. Reserves
Dowd, Clement, H 26th
Dowd, James Cornelius, D 48th
Woodley, William Thomas, K 10th

New Hanover County, NC

Oakdale Cemetery, Wilmington
Swann, William Mercer, H 30th

Onslow County, NC

Family Burying Ground
Mathews, Hardy, H 30th

Orange County, NC

Bethel Baptist Church Cemetery
Lloyd, Manly C., H 30th

Hillsborough Old Town Cemetery, Hillsborough
Huske, Benjamin R., D 48th

Hillsborough Town Cemetery, Hillsborough
Love, Edmond, D 49th
Maddox, George Wesley, D 48th

Orange United Methodist Church Cemetery, Chapel Hill
Hogan, Thomas J., H 26th

Pender County, NC

Point Caswell Cemetery
Black, Murdock, 51st Militia

Robeson County, NC

Ashpole Presbyterian Church Cemetery, Rowland
Medlin, John Andrew, H 26th

Great Marsh Baptist Cemetery, Saint Pauls
Baggett, William M., F 25th

Mount Moriah Baptist Church Cemetery, Maxton
Norton, William Thomas, C 35th

Oak Grove Cemetery, Maxton
McKenzie, Murdock Gaston, H 26th

Regan United Methodist Church Cemetery
Graham, Neill Cameron, H 26th

Rockingham County, NC

Lawson Cemetery, Eden
Maness, Jonas Sedberry, H 26th

Rowan County, NC

Calvary Baptist Church Cemetery, Salisbury
Henderson, George Washington, E 70th/1st Jr. Reserves

Chestnut Hill Cemetery, Salisbury
Nelson, John R., I 19th /2nd Calvary

Old Lutheran Cemetery, Salisbury
Haltom, Reubin J., E 70th/1st Jr. Reserves
Luck, Elijah, F 46th
Sheffield, Isham, H 26th

Sampson County, NC

Avery Cemetery
Moore, John D., G 48th

Lawhon Cemetery, Ingold
Lawhon, Archibald Francis, A 30th

Salemburg Baptist Church Cemetery, Salemburg
Roberts, Bright, E 63rd /5th Calvary

Stanly County, NC

Meadow Creek Primitive Baptist Church Cemetery, Locust
Harvell, John Wesley, D 28th

Norwood Cemetery, Norwood
Ledbetter, Alphonso L., C 3rd

Palestine Methodist Church Cemetery, Albemarle
Talbert, Davidson Samuel, E 70th/1st Jr. Reserves

Silver Springs Baptist Church Cemetery, Norwood
Dunn, J.R., E 70th/1st Jr. Reserves

Vance County, NC

Elmwood Cemetery, Henderson
Judd, William Jefferson, I 19th /2nd Calvary

Wake County, NC

Oakwood Cemetery, Raleigh
Barrett, William Riley, D 49th
Cameron, Evander McNair, C 14th
Center, Charles H., H 30th
Currie, John Henry, Navy
Evans, Henry, D 48th
Goins, William Daniel, I 19th /2nd Calvary
Hagler, Hiram, H 30th
Jones, Thomas Allen, K 10th
McDonald, Malcolm A., C 3rd
McNeill, Daniel, H 46th
Morris, Benjamin J., E 8th
Morris, Daniel, D 48th
Parrish, Uriah R., I 19th /2nd Calvary
Peal, Turner, H 26th
Sasser, Philemon H., I 19th /2nd Calvary
Shaw, Thomas B., H 26th
Stone, David W., E 70th/1st Jr. Reserves
Willcox, Harmon H., H 26th

Wayne County, NC

Willow Dale Cemetery, Goldsboro
Black, Duncan B., I 19th /2nd Calvary
Davis, George W., H 46th
Lawhon, Isaac R., H 46th
Moore, Bryant, D 49th
Ray, William A., D 49th
Sheffield, John, H 46th
Stewart, C.E., F 50th

Wilson County, NC

US Army General Hospital Civil War Memorial, Wilson
Gilmore, Jasper H., F 50th
Goodman, Jacob, C 35th
Teague, William M., H 26th

Alabama

Asbury United Methodist Church Cemetery, Elba, Coffee County, AL
Dalrymple, William M., F 50th

Lincoln City Cemetery, Lincoln, Talladega County, AL
Dye, David Turner, A 63rd /5th Calvary

Saint Andrews Cemetery, Prairieville, Hale County, AL
Dunlap, Alexander M., H 26th

Smiths Chapel Cemetery, DeKalb County, AL
Freeman, John W., D 48th

Arkansas

Beard Cemetery, McCrory, Woodruff County, AR
Wright, Edward B., E 70th/1st Jr. Reserves

Choctaw Cemetery, Monroe County, AR
Campbell, George W., H 30th

Fairview Memorial Gardens, Fayetteville, Washington County, AR
Phillips, Charles Wesley, F 1st / Jr. Reserves

Walters Chapel Cemetery, Carlisle, Lonoke County, AR
Melton, William, E 8th

California

Anaheim Cemetery, Anaheim, Orange County, CA
Moody, William H., I 19th /2nd Calvary

Florida

Rosewood Cemetery, Rosewood, Levy County, FL
Walden, Eli P., G 63rd /5th Calvary

Georgia

Chauncey Cemetery, Chauncey, Dodge County, GA
Tillman, Aaron Evans, E 63rd /5th Calvary

Laurel Grove Cemetery North, Savannah, Chatham County, GA
Baker, Neill A., F 50th

New Hope Cemetery, Jasper County, GA
Cox, Andrew L., E 3rd

Old Field Cemetery, Fitzgerald, Ben Hill County, GA
Hurt, William M., E 70th/1st Jr. Reserves

Old Vidalia Cemetery, Vidalia, Toombs County, GA
McIntosh, Kenneth F., 51st Militia

Peterson Cemetery, Ailey, Montgomery County, GA
Riddle, James Alvis Jr., D 61st

Westview Cemetery, Moultrie, Colquitt County, GA
McNeill, Neill McKay, H 46th

Indiana

Back Creek Friends Cemetery, Fairmount, Grant County, IN
Burns, Virgil A., I 19th /2nd Calvary

Kansas

Fairview Cemetery, Grandview Plaza, Geary County, KS
Britt, Joseph, D 48th

Haviland Cemetery, Haviland, Kiowa County, KS
Barns, Daniel Brian, E 70th/1st Jr. Reserves

Pleasant Center Cemetery, Butler County, KS
Morgan, James Goodwin, D 48th

Saylor Cemetery, Kansas City, Wyandotte County, KS
McFatter, Onslow, C 3rd

Maryland

Loudon Park Cemetery, Baltimore, Baltimore County, MD
McCaskill, Daniel D., H 26th
Moore, Aaron, A 5th

Mount Olivet Cemetery, Frederick, Frederick County, MD
Baker, Henry C., H 30th
Eason, James, H 30th
Kelly, Daniel M., B 3rd

Point Lookout Confederate Cemetery, St. Mary's County, MD
Bethune, Murdock, E 70th/1st Jr. Reserves
Cameron, Daniel T., C 35th
Freeman, Isaac, D 48th
Harrison, Christopher C., H 26th
Kelly, David W., H 30th

King, W.H., H 30th
Lett, Green H., H 46th
Maness, Lewis Washington, K 10th
Matthews, Nathan, H 30th
McKinnon, William, H 26th
McPherson, John W., E 56th
Morris, David P., H 30th
Morris, Lockey, F 21st
Warner, John H., H 26th
Womack, James Rufus, H 30th

Minnesota

Evergreen Cemetery, Brainerd, Crow Wing County, MN
Buie, Martin M., 51st Militia

Itasca Calvary Cemetery, Grand Rapids, Itasca County, MN
Maness, Francis, D 30th

Mississippi

Natchez City Cemetery, Natchez, Adams County, MS
Jackson, Daniel, C 35th

Nelson Cemetery, Lamar County, MS
Frye, William Henry Harrison, C 35th

Oaklawn Cemetery, Hattiesburg, Forrest County, MS
Ferguson, Fergus, H 46th

Woodlawn Park Cemetery, Stone County, MS
Hall, John Green, C 35th

Missouri

Hickman Cemetery, Clarksburg, Moniteau County, MO
Seawell, Jesse P., H 26th

New Jersey

Evergreen Cemetery, Camden, Camden County, NJ
Keith, John Ross, H 26th

Finn's Point National Cemetery, Pennsville, Salem County, NJ
Smith, Angus, C 3rd
Williams, Marshall, D 26th

New York

Cypress Hill National Cemetery, Brooklyn, Kings County, NY
Morris, David C., C 35th

Woodlawn National Cemetery, Elmira, Chemung County, NY
Barber, William R., E 3rd
Campbell, Abner T., H 30th
Campbell, Charles J.E., B 36th
Fields, A.M., C 3rd
Gordon, James M., I 19th /2nd Calvary
Green, James L., H 30th
Horne, Pleasant, H 30th
Muse, Comodore G., I 19th /2nd Calvary
Ray, Angus J., C 3rd
Rayner, Henry M., E 8th
Stewart, James, C 35th
Voncannon, William, C 3rd
Wilson, Daniel C., E 41st

Oklahoma

Fairlawn Cemetery, Oklahoma City, Oklahoma County, OK
Burns, Hardy A., I 19th /2nd Calvary

Oakland Cemetery, Poteau, Le Flore County, OK
Utley, John William, H 30th

Pennsylvania

Gettysburg National Cemetery, Gettysburg, Adams County, PA
Muse, Ashley F., H 26th

Saint Mary's Cemetery, Lebanon, Lebanon County, PA
Malone, William M., H 26th

South Carolina

Beaver Dam Cemetery, McColl, Marlboro County, SC
McLemore, H.L., C 35th

Clifton Cemetery, Clifton, Spartanburg County, SC
Maness, Windsor M., A 10th Battalion

Manship Cemetery, Marlboro County, SC
Williams, Alexander Pleasant, H 26th

McBee Cemetery, McBee, Chesterfield County, SC
Bolin, Alexander, F 50th

Mount Hope Cemetery, Florence, Florence County, SC
McLeod, Samuel, K 38th

Peele Cemetery, Marlboro County, SC
Peele, John James, D 46th

Saint Pauls Methodist Church Cemetery, Little Rock, Dillon County, SC
Wallace, William Lane, H 26th

Tatum Cemetery, Tatum, Marlboro County, SC
Barber, William, E 3rd

Tennessee

Bethesda Memorial Gardens, Selmer, McNairy County, TN
Baker, Daniel Malcolm, E 70th/1st Jr. Reserves

Carnes Cemetery, Whiteville, Hardeman County, TN
Chappell, Levi, E 70th/1st Jr. Reserves

Maplewood Cemetery, Ripley, Lauderdale County, TN
Campbell, John M., 51st Militia

Old Friendship Cemetery, Chester County, TN
Rouse, John M., H 6th/Sr. Reserves

Texas

Alvord Cemetery, Alvord, Wise County, TX
Hardin, Patrick Winston, I 19th /2nd Calvary

Athens Cemetery, Athens, Henderson County, TX
Webster, William J., 51st Militia

Bethel Cemetery, Katemcy, Mason County, TX
Hurley, George Freeman, E 70th/1st Jr. Reserves

Daingerfield Cemetery, Daingerfield, Morris County, TX
Hare, Alfred Roy, 51st Militia
Hare, John Russell, I 19th /2nd Calvary

Dalby Springs Cemetery, DeKalb, Bowie County, TX
Baker, William Hamilton, D 48th

Greenleaf Cemetery, Brown County, TX

McIntosh, William Alexander, E 70th/1st Jr. Reserves

Hickory Grove Cemetery, Rusk County, TX
Sheffield, Levi, C 35th

Jaybird Cemetery, Reno, Parker County, TX
Williams, Edward A., H 26th
Williams, Elias W., I 19th /2nd Calvary

Kay Cemetery, Hawkins, Wood County, TX
Shamburger, William Jefferson, K 3rd [Texas]

Liberty Cemetery, Bebe, Gonzales County, TX
Hancock, Noah, F 46th

Liberty Cemetery, Hawkins, Wood County, TX
Shamburger, Edwin, [Texas]

Live Oak Cemetery, Purves, Erath County, TX
Sinclair, James S., C 1st [Arkansas]

Matagorda Cemetery, Matagorda, Matagorda County, TX
Currie, Archibald, D 49th

Mount Hope Cemetery, Anson, Jones County, TX
Munroe, Calvin Jones, G 25th [Alabama]

Myrtle Springs Cemetery, Cherokee County, TX
Dunlap, Daniel M., H 26th
Stewart, Angus Lorenzo, K 28th [Alabama]

Old Colony Cemetery, Abilene, Taylor County, TX
McDougald, Archibald, H 46th

Pecan Gap Cemetery, Pecan Gap, Delta County, TX
Sullivan, Lemuel Lecke, C 11th [Arkansas]

Rose Hill Cemetery, Texarkana, Bowie County, TX
Cagle, George Harrison, C 35th

West Memorial Cemetery, Quinlan, Hunt County, TX
Moffitt, Adam B., E 70th/1st Jr. Reserves

Virginia

Arlington National Cemetery, Arlington, Arlington County, VA
Williams, Asa, I 19th /2nd Calvary

Barton Heights Cemeteries, Richmond, VA
Gaster, John C., H 30th

Blandford Cemetery, Petersburg, VA
Brown, William Alston, D 49th
Caddell, Archibald B., D 49th
Cameron, Daniel P., E 56th
Comer, Peter, H 26th
Cook, William R., H 26th
Cox, Thomas C., F 50th
Deaton, James M., C 35th
Ferguson, James, H 46th
Ferguson, John A., H 46th
Harrington, John M., D 48th
Johnson, Duncan M., D 48th
Lashley, John L., F 50th
Love, John Wesley, D 61st
McMillan, Archibald, D 49th
McNeill, Andrew J., F 50th
Medlin, Angus, H 46th
Pipkin, William F., F 50th
Teague, Isaac, H 26th
White, Weston Gibson, H 50th

Confederate Cemetery, Fredericksburg, VA
Oates, John P., E 3rd
Pierce, Archibald, H 46th

Greenlawn Memorial Park, Newport News, VA
Parish, Thomas, D 48th

Hampton National Cemetery, Hampton, VA
McIver, Kenneth, A 63rd /5th Calvary

Hollywood Cemetery, Richmond, VA
Allen, Joseph P., D 48th
Barber, Jeremiah, E 3rd
Black, L.C., D 15th
Brady, William M., E 3rd
Britt, Merrimon C., D 21st
Caddell, James N., H 26th
Comer, Adam, H 46th
Davis, Charles, D 48th
Dye, Evander J., E 70th/1st Jr. Reserves
Fields, James Yergan, G 48th
Freeman, Aaron, F 46th
Graham, Samuel W., H 30th
Johnson, Alexander Jr., D 49th

Johnson, Daniel A., H 46th
Jordan, John B., H 26th
Kennedy, Neill, D 49th
McIntosh, William A.J., E 63rd /5th Calvary
McIver, Murdock A., H 30th
McKinnon, D.R., C 3rd
McRae, Alexander, H 26th
Medlin, Jacob, H 46th
Medlin, James A., H 46th
Parish, Nelson H., F 3rd
Patterson, John A., D 49th
Patterson, William D., E 52nd
Phillips, Stephen, D 48th
Pool, William, D 48th
Ray, A.A, C 3rd
Ray, Malcom, C 35th
Scoggins, Stephen, E 56th
Thomas, B.A., C 3rd
Thomas, John Covington, D 49th
Thomas, John West, H 30th
Thomas, Wiley F., D 49th
Tyson, Dawson P., H 26th
Wicker, John J., H 30th
Wicker, Louis M., H 30th
Williamson, Isaac, H 46th
Williamson, Wyatt, D 49th

Maplewood Cemetery, Gordonsville, Orange County, VA
Cook, Anderson, H 30th

Massanutten Cemetery, Woodstock, Shenandoah County, VA
Black, Malcolm, D 48th

Montgomery White Sulphur Springs Cemetery, Montgomery County, VA
Smith, Elias, D 48th

Oak Grove Cemetery, Portsmouth, Portsmouth City, VA
McPherson, Hugh, E 70th/1st Jr. Reserves

Oakwood Cemetery, Richmond, VA
Brady, Isaac, D 48th
Estis, William, E 2nd
Gilmore, William, D 48th
Jones, Milton, C 35th
Mathis, Malphus, D 48th
McFatter, Alexander, H 30th
Ray, Malcom, C 35th
Steadman, David B., H 30th

Old City Cemetery, Lynchburg, VA
Buchanan, C.B., H 30th
Buchanan, Joseph, H 30th
Jackson, William R., K 38th
McLean, Allen C., D 48th
McPherson, D.K., H 30th
Yow, Andrew C., D 48th

Our Soldiers Cemetery, Mount Jackson, Shenandoah County, VA
Britt, Enoch, F 3rd
Jackson, Samuel, D 48th

Prospect Hill Cemetery, Front Royal Warren County, VA
Voncannon, Henry T., F 46th

Spotsylvania Confederate Cemetery, Spotsylvania Courthouse, Spotsylvania County, VA
Jackson, Archibald A., H 30th

Stonewall Confederate Cemetery, Winchester, VA
Blue, Duncan Ferguson, H 46th
Person, William M., H 26th

Thornrose Cemetery, Staunton, VA
Buchanan, Thomas, H 30th
McDonald, Alexander, C 35th
Patterson, Samuel D., D 49th
Sloan, John Alexander, H 30th

Woodbine Cemetery, Harrisonburg, VA
McIver, Williamson, C 45th

West Virginia

Corbin Cemetery, Waverly, Wood County, WV
Deaton, James Madison, D 21st

Bibliography

MANUSCRIPTS / DOCUMENTS

Department of Cultural Resources, Division of Archives and History, Raleigh, NC
William Hyslop Sumner Burgwyn Papers
Civil War Collection
Governor Henry Toole Clark Papers
Richard A. Cole Papers
Alexander Hamilton McNeill Papers
Record of Pensions, 1883-1919, Moore County, NC
Governor Zebulon Baird Vance Papers
James Oscar Abner Kelly Papers

Moore County Library, Carthage, NC
Civil War Letters
Melvin, Katherine Shields. The Armory Guards at Fayetteville.
The Phillips Family and the Civil War, Vol. I
Street Papers
Vertical Files

Duke Manuscript Collection, David M. Rubenstein Library, Duke University, Durham, NC
Artemus S. Caddell Papers
Bryan Tyson Papers
John Lane Stuart Papers
Nevin Ray Papers
Noah Deaton Papers
Wyatt Williamson Papers

Southern Historical Collection, Wilson Special Collections, University of North Carolina at Chapel Hill, Chapel Hill, NC
CSA Bureau of Conscription, 7th NC Congressional District Records, 1862-1865
Marmaduke Swaim Robins Papers

John L. Nau Civil War Collection, Albert and Shirley Small Special Collections, University of Virginia, Charlottesville, VA
John Lane Stuart Papers
Noah Deaton Papers

James S. Schoff Civil War Collection, William L. Clements Library, University of Michigan, Ann Arbor, MI
Noah Deaton Papers

PRIVATE COLLECTIONS

Deaton Papers in possession of Richard Weiner
Fry Papers in possession of Amy Caddell Sadler Seitz
Kelly Papers in possession of Jim Kelly
McLeod Papers in possession of John A. Cameron
McNeill Papers in possession of Barry McNeill
Shields Papers in possession of David McCallum
Sloan Papers in possession of Mark Sloan and Judy Gore Heath

WEBSITES

26th NC Company H (companyh26th.com no longer active – accessed via Internet Archive)

Ancestry (Ancestry.com)
Family Trees and Photos
North Carolina Death Certificates
South Carolina Death Certificates
Alabama Confederate Pension Applications
Texas Confederate Pension Applications
Virginia Confederate Pension Applications
US Federal Census, Mortality Schedules 1850-1885
NC Historical Records Survey, Cemetery Inscription Card Index
US Headstone Applications for Military Veterans

The Civil War in the East (Civilwarintheeast.com)

Family Search (Familysearch.com)
Arkansas Confederate Pension Applications
North Carolina Confederate Pensions 1885-1953

Find A Grave (Findagrave.com)

Fold3 (Fold3.com)
Alabama Civil War Service Records
Arkansas Civil War Service Records
Confederate Amnesty Papers
North Carolina Civil War Service Records
South Carolina Civil War Service Records

Moore County Wallaces (MooreCountyWallaces.com)
Newspapers (Newspapers.com)

North Carolina Digital Collections (digital.ncdcr.gov)
1885 Confederate Pension Applications
1901 Confederate Pension Applications
Various Newspapers

North Carolina Genealogy Trails (genealogytrails.com/ncar/index.html)

Oklahoma Digital Prairie (digitalprairieok.net)
Oklahoma Confederate Pension Applications

Spared & Shared (sparedshared23.com/home; sparedshared22.wordpress.com; sparedcreative21.art.blog)
Wikipedia

BOOKS

Auman, William T. *Civil War in the North Carolina Quaker Belt: The Confederate Campaign Against Peace Agitators, Deserters and Draft Dodgers.* Jefferson, NC: McFarland & Company, 2014.

Barrett, John G. *The Civil War in North Carolina.* Chapel Hill, NC: The University of North Carolina Press, 1983.

Brown, Matthew M. and Michael W. Coffey, *North Carolina Troops 1861-1865 A Roster, Vol XVII. Junior Reserves.* Raleigh, NC: Office of Archives and History, 2009.

Brown, Matthew M. and Michael W. Coffey, *North Carolina Troops 1861-1865 A Roster, Vol XVIII. Senior Reserves Detailed Men.* Raleigh, NC: Office of Archives and History, 2013.

Brown, Matthew M. and Michael W. Coffey, *North Carolina Troops 1861-1865 A Roster, Vol XIX. Miscellaneous Battalions and Companies.* Raleigh, NC: Office of Archives and History, 2013.

Brown, Matthew M. and Michael W. Coffey, *North Carolina Troops 1861-1865 A Roster, Vol XX. Generals, Staff and Militia.* Raleigh, NC: Office of Archives and History, 2017.

Brown, Matthew M. and Michael W. Coffey, *North Carolina Troops 1861-1865 A Roster, Vol XXI. Militia and Home Guard.* Raleigh, NC: Office of Archives and History, 2022.

Bynum, Victoria E. *The Long Shadow of the Civil War: Southern Dissent and its Legacies.* Chapel Hill, NC: The University of North Carolina Press, 2010.

Cameron, John B. *Tar Heels in Gray: Life in the 30th North Carolina Infantry in the Civil War.* Jefferson, NC: McFarland & Company, 2021.

Carter, Kathryn Blevins. *Thompson: A Family History.* Cameron, NC: K.B. Carter, 1993.

Clark, Walter. *Histories of the Several Regiments and Battalions from North Carolina in the Great War 1861-65, Vol. IV.* Goldsboro, NC: Nash Brothers, 1901.

Comer, James V. *The Bountiful Legacy of a Mother: Buffalo Presbyterian Church, Buffalo Community / Sanford, NC.* Sanford, NC, 1997

Comer, James V. *Central North Carolina Collection Vol. I.* Sanford, NC, 2015

Comer, James V. *Central North Carolina Collection Vol. II.* Sanford, NC, 2016

Comer, James V. *Central North Carolina Vital Statistics.* Sanford, NC, 2001

Comer, James V. *Jonesboro, Moore Couty, NC, Vol. II 1908-1947*, Sanford, NC, 1990

Comer, James V. *Moore County Bible Project Vol. II.* Pinehurst, NC: Moore County Genealogical Society, 2001

Comer, James V. *Old Moore County Vital Statistics 1784-1890*. Sanford, NC, 1999

Comer, James V. *White Hill Presbyterian Church: A History of Church and Community (1881-2006)*. Sanford, NC, 2007

Garner Jr., Lacy A. *Thurman Maness Remembers: Tales from the Upper End of the County*. Robbins, NC: Lulu.com, 2009.

Hairr, John. *Stories From Deep River*. Erwin, NC: Averasboro Press, 1999.

Hatton, Katelynn A. and Alex Christopher Meekins, *North Carolina Troops 1861-1865 A Roster, Vol XXII. Confederate States Navy, Confederate States Marine Corps and Charlotte Navy Yard*. Raleigh, NC: Office of Archives and History, 2024.

Holt, Nancy Yow. *I Hope You Will All Remember Me: The Civil War Letters of Matthew C. Yow 48th North Carolina Infantry*. Jacksonville, FL, 2024. Original letters in possession of Larry R. Yow.

Hussey, Elizabeth Purvis and Carol Reynolds Purvis, *Descendants of Robert L. Purvis*. Asheboro, NC, 2020.

Jordan Jr., Weymouth T. and Louis H. Manarin. *North Carolina Troops 1861-1865 A Roster, Vol IV. Infantry*. Raleigh, NC: Office of Archives and History, 1973,1989.

Jordan Jr., Weymouth T. and Louis H. Manarin. *North Carolina Troops 1861-1865 A Roster, Vol V. Infantry*. Raleigh, NC: Office of Archives and History, 1975,1990.

Jordan Jr., Weymouth T. and Louis H. Manarin. *North Carolina Troops 1861-1865 A Roster, Vol VI. Infantry*. Raleigh, NC: Office of Archives and History, 1977,1990.

Jordan Jr., Weymouth T. and Louis H. Manarin. *North Carolina Troops 1861-1865 A Roster, Vol VII. Infantry*. Raleigh, NC: Office of Archives and History, 1977,1991.

Jordan Jr., Weymouth T. and Louis H. Manarin. *North Carolina Troops 1861-1865 A Roster, Vol VIII. Infantry*. Raleigh, NC: Office of Archives and History, 1981.

Jordan Jr., Weymouth T. and Louis H. Manarin. *North Carolina Troops 1861-1865 A Roster, Vol IX. Infantry*. Raleigh, NC: Office of Archives and History, 1983.

Jordan Jr., Weymouth T. and Louis H. Manarin. *North Carolina Troops 1861-1865 A Roster, Vol X. Infantry*. Raleigh, NC: Office of Archives and History, 1985.

Jordan Jr., Weymouth T. and Louis H. Manarin. *North Carolina Troops 1861-1865 A Roster, Vol XI. Infantry*. Raleigh, NC: Office of Archives and History, 1987.

Jordan Jr., Weymouth T. *North Carolina Troops 1861-1865 A Roster, Vol XII. Infantry*. Raleigh, NC: Office of Archives and History, 1990.

Jordan Jr., Weymouth T. *North Carolina Troops 1861-1865 A Roster, Vol XIII. Infantry*. Raleigh, NC: Office of Archives and History, 1993.

Jordan Jr., Weymouth T. *North Carolina Troops 1861-1865 A Roster, Vol XIV. Infantry*. Raleigh, NC: Office of Archives and History, 1990.

Kelly, Kenneth L. *McIver Family of North Carolina*. Washington, DC: McIver Art and Publications, 1964.

Kitchel, Margaret Cockman. *Cockman Family History*. Knoxville, TN: Tennessee Valley Publishing, 1990,

Manarin, Louis H. *North Carolina Troops 1861-1865 A Roster, Vol I. Artillery*. Raleigh, NC: Office of Archives and History, 1966,1988.

Manarin, Louis H. *North Carolina Troops 1861-1865 A Roster, Vol II. Calvary*. Raleigh, NC: Office of Archives and History, 1966,1988.

Manarin, Louis H. *North Carolina Troops 1861-1865 A Roster, Vol III. Infantry*. Raleigh, NC: Office of Archives and History, 1971,1989.

Manarin, Louis H. *North Carolina Troops 1861-1865 A Roster, Vol V. Infantry*. Raleigh, NC: Office of Archives and History, 1975,1990.

McNeill, Maxine Williams. *The Williams Family*. West End, NC: TM Custom Graphix, 1999.

Moore County Heritage Book Committee and County Heritage, Inc. *Moore County Heritage Book.* Waynesville, NC: County Heritage Inc., 2005.

Parker, A.E. "Tony". *A Guide to Moore County Cemeteries*, Southern Pines, NC: Moore County Historical Association, 1976.

Phillips, Lois Smith and Carol Smith Purvis. *The Brady Family of Moore and Chatham Counties.* Charlotte, NC: Herb Eaton Historical Publications, 1987.

Saunders, Elizabeth A. *The Search for Thomas Maness.* Archdale, NC: Tannery Books, 2024.

Shields, Henry B. *Country Doctor for a Half Century*. Southern Pines, NC: The Pilot, 1975.

Tyson, Bryan. *Object of the Administration in Prosecuting the War.* Washington, DC: McGill & Witherow, 1864.

Venner, William Thomas. *The 30th North Carolina Infantry in the Civil War: A History and Roster.* Jefferson, NC: McFarland & Company, 2018.

Watford, Christopher M., Ed. *The Civil War in North Carolina: Soldiers and Civilian's Letters and Diaries, 1861-1865, Volume 1: The Piedmont.* Jefferson, NC: McFarland & Company, 2003.

Wellman, Manly Wade. *The County of Moore 1847-1947.* Southern Pines, NC: Moore County Historical Association, 1962.

Wellman, Manly Wade. *The Story of Moore County.* Southern Pines, NC: Moore County Historical Association, 1974.

Willcox, George W. *History of the Street Family of Moore County, NC and GA, MS and TN, Vol I.* Glendon, NC: Candace Street Simmons, 1992,1996.

Yearns, W. Buck and John G. Barrett, Eds. *North Carolina Civil War Documentary*. Chapel Hill, NC: The University of North Carolina Press, 1980.

NEWSPAPERS

Abilene Daily Reporter (Abilene, TX)
The Anglo-Saxon (Rockingham, NC)
The Asheville Weekly Citizen (Asheville, NC)
The Biblical Recorder (Raleigh, NC)
Brainerd Tribune (Brainerd, MN)
The Carthage Blade (Carthage, NC)
The Caucasian (Raleigh, NC)
The Charlotte Democrat (Charlotte, NC)
The Charlotte News (Charlotte, NC)
The Charlotte Observer (Charlotte, NC)
The Chatham Record (Pittsboro, NC)
The Chrisitan Sun (Elon College, NC)
Clarion-Ledger (Jackson, MS)
The Concord Register (Concord, NC)
The Concord Times (Concord, NC)
Confederate Veteran (Nashville, TN)
The Courier (Asheboro, NC)
Courier-Post (Camden, NJ)
The Daily Confederate (Raleigh, NC)
The Daily Herald (Biloxi, MS)
The Daily Journal (Wilmington, NC)
The Daily North Carolinian (Fayetteville, NC)
The Daily Progress (Raleigh, NC)
The Daily Progress (Charlottesville, VA)
The Daily Review (Wilmington, NC)
The Daily World (Helena, AR)
The Davidson Dispatch (Lexington, NC)
The Durham Recorder (Durham, NC)
The Free Press (Southern Pines, NC)
Gainesville News (Gainesville, GA)
The Galveston Daily News (Galveston, TX)
The Gonzales Inquirer (Gonzales, TX)
Grand Rapids Herald-Review (Grand Rapids, MN)
The Greensboro Patriot (Greensboro, NC)
The Greensboro Record (Greensboro, NC)
Greensboro Telegram (Greensboro, NC)
The Eagle (Fayetteville, NC)
Fayetteville Daily Observer (Fayetteville, NC)
Fayetteville Index (Fayetteville, NC)
Fayetteville Observer (Fayetteville, NC)
Fayetteville Semi-Weekly Observer (Fayetteville, NC)
Fayetteville Weekly Observer (Fayetteville, NC)
The Herald-Sun (Durham, NC)
The Jackson Sun (Jackson, TN)
Jonesboro Leader (Sanford, NC)
The Junction City Tribune (Junction City, KS)
Kiowa County Independent (Haviland, KS)
The Messenger and Intelligencer (Wadesboro, NC)
The Montgomerian (Troy, NC)
The Moore County News (Carthage, NC)
The Morning Post (Raleigh, NC)
The News and Observer (Raleigh, NC)
The News and Record (Greensboro, NC)
North Carolina Argus (Wadesboro, NC)
The North Carolina Presbyterian (Fayetteville, NC)

Our Mountain Home (Talladega, AL)
The Pilot (Southern Pines, NC)
Raleigh Christian Advocate (Raleigh, NC)
The Raleigh News (Raleigh, NC)
The Raleigh Register (Raleigh, NC)
The Raleigh Sentinel (Raleigh, NC)
Richmond Enquirer (Richmond, VA)
The Robesonian (Lumberton, NC)
Rockingham Post Dispatch (Rockingham, NC)
Rockingham Rocket (Rockingham, NC)
Salisbury Evening Post (Salisbury, NC)
The Salisbury Post (Salisbury, NC)
The Sampson Democrat (Clinton, NC)
The Sampson Independent (Clinton, NC)
The San Angelo Weekly Standard (San Angelo, TX)
The Sandhill Citizen (Southern Pines, NC)
The Sanford Express (Sanford, NC)
The Sanford Herald (Sanford, NC)
The Savannah Morning News (Savannah, GA)
Semi-Weekly Standard (Raleigh, NC)
Semi-Weekly State Journal (Raleigh, NC)
The Siler City Grit (Siler City, NC)
The Southern Pines Tourist (Southern Pines, NC)
The Stanly News and Press (Albemarle, NC)
The State (Columbia, SC)
Statesville Record and Landmark (Statesville, NC)
The Times Journal (Eastman, GA)
The Troy Times (Troy, NC)
The Union Republican (Winston, NC)
The Weekly Intelligencer (Fayetteville, NC)
The Weekly Standard (Raleigh, NC)
Weekly State Journal (Raleigh, NC)
Western Enterprise (Anson, TX)
Wilmington Journal (Wilmington, NC)
The Wilmington Messenger (Wilmington, NC)
The Wilmington Morning Star (Wilmington, NC)

---

1 "Letter, Mastin C. Phillips to Emeline Phillips", *The Phillips Family and the Civil War Vol. I*, Moore County Library, Carthage, NC

2 "Letter, Donald Street to Richard Street", *Street Papers*, Vertical Files, Moore County Library, Carthage, NC

3 "Letter, Donald Street to Richard Street", *Street Papers*, Vertical Files, Moore County Library, Carthage, NC

4 "Letter, N.A. Ray to Sarah Ray, 17 May 1861", *Nevin Ray Papers*, Sec. A Box 110 items 1-30 c.1, David M. Rubenstein Library, Duke University, Durham, NC

5 "Letter, Artemus Caddell to Martha Sullivan, 18 May 1861", *Artemus S. Caddell Papers*, RUB Bay 0037:04 items 1-84 c.1, David M. Rubenstein Library, Duke University, Durham, NC

6 "Letter, Mastin C. Phillips to Rev. Lewis Phillips Jr. 6 Jun 1861", *The Phillips Family and the Civil War Vol. I*, Moore County Library, Carthage, NC

7 "Letter, W.B. Clegg to Richard Street 9 Jun 1861", *Street Papers*, Vertical Files, Moore County Library, Carthage, NC

8 "Letter, Noah Deaton to William Deaton, 23 July 1861", *Noah Deaton Papers*, John L. Nau Civil War Collection, Albert and Shirley Small Special Collections Library, University of Virginia, Charlottesville, VA

9 "Letter, Noah Deaton to S.B. Deaton, 28 Jul 1861", *Noah Deaton Papers*, John L. Nau Civil War Collection, Albert and Shirley Small Special Collections Library, University of Virginia, Charlottesville, VA

10 "Letter, Christian Ray to Hugh M. Ray, 30 Jul 1861", *Nevin Ray Papers*, Sec. A Box 110 items 1-30 c.1, David M. Rubenstein Library, Duke University, Durham, NC

11 "Letter, John Parsons to Rev. Lewis Phillips Jr., 31 Jul 1861", *The Phillips Family and the Civil War Vol. I*, Moore County Library, Carthage, NC

12 "Letter, Richard Street to Candace Phillips, 31 Jul 1861", *The Phillips Family and the Civil War Vol. I*, Moore County Library, Carthage, NC

13 "Letter, C.D. Caddell to A.S. Caddell, n.d. Aug 1861" *Artemus S. Caddell Papers*, RUB Bay 0037:04 items 1-84 c.1, David M. Rubenstein Library, Duke University, Durham, NC

14 "Letter, Noah Deaton to Sarah J. McDonald, 7 Aug 1861", *Noah Deaton Papers*, John L. Nau Civil War Collection, Albert and Shirley Small Special Collections Library, University of Virginia, Charlottesville, VA

15 "Letter, C.D. Caddell to A.S. Caddel, 9 Aug 1861l", *Artemus S. Caddell Papers*, RUB Bay 0037:04 items 1-84 c.1, David M. Rubenstein Library, Duke University, Durham, NC

16 "Letter, A.S. Caddell to C.D. Caddell, 9 Aug 1861", *Artemus S. Caddell Papers*, RUB Bay 0037:04 items 1-84 c.1, David M. Rubenstein Library, Duke University, Durham, NC

17 "Letter, W.L. Sullivan to A.S. Caddell, et al, 10 Aug 1861", *Artemus S. Caddell Papers*, RUB Bay 0037:04 items 1-84 c.1, David M. Rubenstein Library, Duke University, Durham, NC

18 "Letter, C.D. Caddell to A.S. Caddell, 11 Aug 1861", *Artemus S. Caddell Papers*, RUB Bay 0037:04 items 1-84 c.1, David M. Rubenstein Library, Duke University, Durham, NC

19 "Letter, A.S. Caddell to Martha Sullivan, 14 Aug 1861", *Artemus S. Caddell Papers*, RUB Bay 0037:04 items 1-84 c.1, David M. Rubenstein Library, Duke University, Durham, NC

20 "Letter, unknown soldier to Baxter Clegg Phillips, 14 Aug 1861", *The Phillips Family and the Civil War Vol. I*, Moore County Library, Carthage, NC

21 "Letter, Jane McIntosh to A.S. Caddell, 19 Aug 1861", *Artemus S. Caddell Papers*, RUB Bay 0037:04 items 1-84 c.1, David M. Rubenstein Library, Duke University, Durham, NC

22 "Letter, Lydia Seawell to A.S. Caddell, 20 Aug 1861", *Artemus S. Caddell Papers*, RUB Bay 0037:04 items 1-84 c.1, David M. Rubenstein Library, Duke University, Durham, NC

23 "Letter, Mary E. Moore to A.S. Caddell, 24 Aug 1861", *Artemus S. Caddell Papers*, RUB Bay 0037:04 items 1-84 c.1, David M. Rubenstein Library, Duke University, Durham, NC

24 "Letter, C.D. Caddell to A.S. Caddell, 25 Aug 1861", *Artemus S. Caddell Papers*, RUB Bay 0037:04 items 1-84 c.1, David M. Rubenstein Library, Duke University, Durham, NC

25 "Letter, Noah Deaton to Hiram Deaton, 26 Aug 1861", *Noah Deaton Papers*, John L. Nau Civil War Collection, Albert and Shirley Small Special Collections Library, University of Virginia, Charlottesville, VA

26 "Letter, N.F. Muse to A.S. Caddell, 26 Aug 1861", *Artemus S. Caddell Papers*, RUB Bay 0037:04 items 1-84 c.1, David M. Rubenstein Library, Duke University, Durham, NC

27 "Letter, Richard Street to Lewis Phillips, 2 Sep 1861", *The Phillips Family and the Civil War Vol. I*, Moore County Library, Carthage, NC

28 "Letter, A.S. Caddell to Wm. Caddell, 3 Sep 1861", *Artemus S. Caddell Papers*, RUB Bay 0037:04 items 1-84 c.1, David M. Rubenstein Library, Duke University, Durham, NC

29 "Letter, J.A. Jackson to R.A. Cole, 3 Sep 1861", *Richard A. Cole Papers*, PC. 1609, Private Collections, State Archives of North Carolina, Raleigh, NC

30 "Letter, C.D. Caddell to A.S. Caddell, 3 Sep 1861", *Artemus S. Caddell Papers*, RUB Bay 0037:04 items 1-84 c.1, David M. Rubenstein Library, Duke University, Durham, NC

31 "Letter, Mary A. McIntosh to A.S. Caddell, 4 Sep 1861", *Artemus S. Caddell Papers*, RUB Bay 0037:04 items 1-84 c.1, David M. Rubenstein Library, Duke University, Durham, NC

32 "Letter, A.S. Caddell to C.D. Caddell, 8 Sep 1861", *Artemus S. Caddell Papers*, RUB Bay 0037:04 items 1-84 c.1, David M. Rubenstein Library, Duke University, Durham, NC

33 "Letter, Noah Deaton to S.B. Deaton, 14 Sep 1861," *Noah Deaton Papers*, John L. Nau Civil War Collection, Albert and Shirley Small Special Collections Library, University of Virginia, Charlottesville, VA

34 "Letter, Wm. A. McIntosh to A.S. Caddell, 16 Sep 1861", *Artemus S. Caddell Papers*, RUB Bay 0037:04 items 1-84 c.1, David M. Rubenstein Library, Duke University, Durham, NC

35 "Letter, Louis H. McLeod to Eliza McLeod, 19 Sep 1861", *Louis H. McLeod Collection*, in possession of John Cameron, Broadway, NC

36 "Letter, E. Caddell and B.A. Caddell to A.S. Caddell, 22 Sep 1861", *Artemus S. Caddell Papers*, RUB Bay 0037:04 items 1-84 c.1, David M. Rubenstein Library, Duke University, Durham, NC

37 "Letter, Noah Deaton to William Deaton, 22 Sep 1861", *Noah Deaton Papers*, John L. Nau Civil War Collection, Albert and Shirley Small Special Collections Library, University of Virginia, Charlottesville, VA

38 "Letter, Mastin C. Phillips to Emeline Phillips 23 Sep 1861", *The Phillips Family and the Civil War Vol. I*, Moore County Library, Carthage, NC

39 "Letter, Julia A. Caddell to A.S. Caddell. 25 Sep 1861", *Artemus S. Caddell Papers*, RUB Bay 0037:04 items 1-84 c.1, David M. Rubenstein Library, Duke University, Durham, NC

40 "Letter, Jesse Muse to A.S. Caddell, 27 Sep 1861", *Artemus S. Caddell Papers*, RUB Bay 0037:04 items 1-84 c.1, David M. Rubenstein Library, Duke University, Durham, NC

41 "Letter, A.F. Muse to A.S. Caddell, 27 Sep 1861", *Artemus S. Caddell Papers*, RUB Bay 0037:04 items 1-84 c.1, David M. Rubenstein Library, Duke University, Durham, NC

42 "Letter, N.F. Muse to A.S. Caddell, 28 Sep 1861", *Artemus S. Caddell Papers*, RUB Bay 0037:04 items 1-84 c.1, David M. Rubenstein Library, Duke University, Durham, NC

43 "Letter, Louis H. McLeod to Eliza McLeod, 28 Sep 1861", *Louis H. McLeod Collection*, in possession of John Cameron, Broadway, NC

44 "Letter, C.D. Caddell to A.S. Caddell, 2 Oct 1861", *Artemus S. Caddell Papers*, RUB Bay 0037:04 items 1-84 c.1, David M. Rubenstein Library, Duke University, Durham, NC

45 "Letter, Louis H. McLeod to Eliza McLeod, 2 Oct 1861", *Louis H. McLeod Collection*, in possession of John Cameron, Broadway, NC

46 "Letter, Louis H. McLeod to Eliza McLeod, 5 Oct 1861", *Louis H. McLeod Collection*, in possession of John Cameron, Broadway, NC

47 "Letter, Jane McIntosh to A.S. Caddell, 6 Oct 1861", *Artemus S. Caddell Papers*, RUB Bay 0037:04 items 1-84 c.1, David M. Rubenstein Library, Duke University, Durham, NC

48 "Letter, Noah F. Muse to A.S. Caddell, 6 Oct 1861", *Civil War Letters*, Vertical Files, Moore County Library, Carthage, NC

49 "Letter, Noah Deaton to Christian Ray, 7 Oct 1861", *Noah Deaton Papers*, James S. Schoff Civil War Collection, William L. Clements Library, University of Michigan, Ann Arbor, MI

50 "Letter, Louis H. McLeod to Eliza McLeod, 8 Oct 1861", *Louis H. McLeod Collection*, in possession of John Cameron, Broadway, NC

51 "Letter, C.D. Caddell to A.S. Caddell, 12 Oct 1861", *Artemus S. Caddell Papers*, RUB Bay 0037:04 items 1-84 c.1, David M. Rubenstein Library, Duke University, Durham, NC

52 "Letter, N.A. Ray to Christian Ray, 13 Oct 1861", *Nevin Ray Papers*, Sec. A Box 110 items 1-30 c.1, David M. Rubenstein Library, Duke University, Durham, NC

53 "Letter, Jane McIntosh to A.S. Caddell, 14 Oct 1861", *Artemus S. Caddell Papers*, RUB Bay 0037:04 items 1-84 c.1, David M. Rubenstein Library, Duke University, Durham, NC

54 "Letter, Wm. A. McIntosh to A.S. Caddell, 14 Oct 1861", *Artemus S. Caddell Papers*, RUB Bay 0037:04 items 1-84 c.1, David M. Rubenstein Library, Duke University, Durham, NC

55 "Letter, Jane, Nancy and Mary Caddell, to A.S. Caddell, 15 Oct 1861", *Artemus S. Caddell Papers*, RUB Bay 0037:04 items 1-84 c.1, David M. Rubenstein Library, Duke University, Durham, NC

56 "Letter, M.P. Davis to A.S. Caddell, 21 Oct 1861", *Artemus S. Caddell Papers*, RUB Bay 0037:04 items 1-84 c.1, David M. Rubenstein Library, Duke University, Durham, NC

57 "Letter, Noah Deaton to sister, 23 Oct 1861", *Noah Deaton Papers*, John L. Nau Civil War Collection, Albert and Shirley Small Special Collections Library, University of Virginia, Charlottesville, VA

58 "Letter, M.A. Caddell to A.S. Caddell, 24 Oct 1861", *Artemus S. Caddell Papers*, RUB Bay 0037:04 items 1-84 c.1, David M. Rubenstein Library, Duke University, Durham, NC

59 "Letter, Hugh M. Ray to sister, 28 Oct 1861", *Nevin Ray Papers*, Sec. A Box 110 items 1-30 c.1, David M. Rubenstein Library, Duke University, Durham, NC

60 "Letter, C.D. Caddell to A.S. Caddell, 30 Oct 1861", *Artemus S. Caddell Papers*, RUB Bay 0037:04 items 1-84 c.1, David M. Rubenstein Library, Duke University, Durham, NC

61 "Letter, Louis H. McLeod to Eliza McLeod, 30 Oct 1861", *Louis H. McLeod Collection*, in possession of John Cameron, Broadway, NC

62 "Letter, Friend to A.S. Caddell, n.d. Nov 1861 (est.)", *Artemus S. Caddell Papers*, RUB Bay 0037:04 items 1-84 c.1, David M. Rubenstein Library, Duke University, Durham, NC

63 "Letter, H.M. Ray and William Whitlock to Nevin Ray, n.d. Nov 1861 (est.)", *Nevin Ray Papers*, Sec. A Box 110 items 1-30 c.1, David M. Rubenstein Library, Duke University, Durham, NC

64 "Letter, Noah Deaton to William Deaton, 1 Nov 1861", *Noah Deaton Papers*, John L. Nau Civil War Collection, Albert and Shirley Small Special Collections Library, University of Virginia, Charlottesville, VA

65 "Letter, Louis H. McLeod to Eliza McLeod, 3 Nov 1861", *Louis H. McLeod Collection*, in possession of John Cameron, Broadway, NC

66 "Letter, Mastin C. Phillips to Malphus S. Phillips 6 Nov 1861", *The Phillips Family and the Civil War Vol. I*, Moore County Library, Carthage, NC

67 "Letter, W.W. Edwards to Emeline Phillips, 6 Nov 1861", *The Phillips Family and the Civil War Vol. I*, Moore County Library, Carthage, NC

68 "Letter, Eliza McLeod to Louis H. McLeod, 14 Nov 1861", *Louis H. McLeod Collection*, in possession of John Cameron, Broadway, NC

69 "Letter, Louis H. McLeod to Eliza McLeod, 17 Nov 1861", *Louis H. McLeod Collection*, in possession of John Cameron, Broadway, NC

70 "Letter, Mary E. Moore to A.S. Caddell, 19 Nov 1861", *Artemus S. Caddell Papers*, RUB Bay 0037:04 items 1-84 c.1, David M. Rubenstein Library, Duke University, Durham, NC

71 "Letter, Sarah McIntosh to A.S. Caddell, 20 Nov 1861", *Artemus S. Caddell Papers*, RUB Bay 0037:04 items 1-84 c.1, David M. Rubenstein Library, Duke University, Durham, NC

72 "Letter, Louis H. McLeod to Eliza McLeod, 20 Nov 1861", *Louis H. McLeod Collection*, in possession of John Cameron, Broadway, NC

73 "Letter, W.L. Sullivan to A.S. Caddell, 21 Nov 1861", *Artemus S. Caddell Papers*, RUB Bay 0037:04 items 1-84 c.1, David M. Rubenstein Library, Duke University, Durham, NC

74 "Letter, Noah Deaton to Sarah B. Deaton, 23 Nov 1861", *Noah Deaton Papers*, John L. Nau Civil War Collection, Albert and Shirley Small Special Collections Library, University of Virginia, Charlottesville, VA

75 "Letter, Eliza McLeod to Louis H. McLeod, 24 Nov 1861", *Louis H. McLeod Collection*, in possession of John Cameron, Broadway, NC

76 "Letter, Malcom Ray to brother, n.d. Dec 1861 (est.)", *Nevin Ray Papers*, Sec. A Box 110 items 1-30 c.1, David M. Rubenstein Library, Duke University, Durham, NC

77 "Letter, Mary Caddell to A.S. Caddell and James N. Caddell, 1 Dec 1861", *Artemus S. Caddell Papers*, RUB Bay 0037:04 items 1-84 c.1, David M. Rubenstein Library, Duke University, Durham, NC

78 "Letter, John A. Walker to Tandy Walker and Louis H. McLeod, 1 Dec 1861", *Louis H. McLeod Collection*, in possession of John Cameron, Broadway, NC

79 "Letter, Eliza McLeod to Louis H. McLeod, 1 Dec 1861", *Louis H. McLeod Collection*, in possession of John Cameron, Broadway, NC

80 "Letter, Louis H. McLeod to Eliza McLeod, 2 Dec 1861", *Louis H. McLeod Collection*, in possession of John Cameron, Broadway, NC

81 "Letter, Harrison Davis to A.S. Caddell, 5 Dec 1861", *Artemus S. Caddell Papers*, RUB Bay 0037:04 items 1-84 c.1, David M. Rubenstein Library, Duke University, Durham, NC

82 "Letter, C.D. Caddell to A.S. Caddell, 6 Dec 1861", *Artemus S. Caddell Papers*, RUB Bay 0037:04 items 1-84 c.1, David M. Rubenstein Library, Duke University, Durham, NC

83 "Letter, Eliza McLeod to Louis H. McLeod, 8 Dec 1861", *Louis H. McLeod Collection*, in possession of John Cameron, Broadway, NC

84 "Letter, Louis H. McLeod to Eliza McLeod, 10 Dec 1861", *Louis H. McLeod Collection*, in possession of John Cameron, Broadway, NC

85 "Letter, William P. Martin to Hugh Leach, 11 Dec 1861", *Civil War Letters*, Vertical Files, Moore County Library, Carthage, NC

86 "Letter, Alexander McDonald to brother, 11 Dec 1861", *Spared & Shared*, accessed 27 Jul 2024, https://sparedshared23.com/2023/01/01/1861-alexander-mcdonald-to-his-brother

87 "Letter, N.A. Ray to Mary A. Ray, 14 Dec 1861", *Nevin Ray Papers*, Sec. A Box 110 items 1-30 c.1, David M. Rubenstein Library, Duke University, Durham, NC

88 "Letter, Malcom Ray to Christian Ray, 15 Dec 1861", *Nevin Ray Papers*, Sec. A Box 110 items 1-30 c.1, David M. Rubenstein Library, Duke University, Durham, NC

89 "Letter, Noah Deaton to Sarah B. Deaton and William Deaton, 19 Dec 1861", *Noah Deaton Papers*, John L. Nau Civil War Collection, Albert and Shirley Small Special Collections Library, University of Virginia, Charlottesville, VA

90 "Letter, Duncan C. Blue to F.A.V. Patterson, 20 Dec 1861", *Civil War Letters*, Vertical Files, Moore County Library, Carthage, NC

91 "Letter, Noah Deaton to William Deaton and Flora Deaton, 22 Dec 1861", *Noah Deaton Papers*, John L. Nau Civil War Collection, Albert and Shirley Small Special Collections Library, University of Virginia, Charlottesville, VA

92 "Letter, Noah Deaton to Sarah J. McDonald, 24 Dec 1861", *Noah Deaton Papers*, John L. Nau Civil War Collection, Albert and Shirley Small Special Collections Library, University of Virginia, Charlottesville, VA

93 "Letter, N.A. Ray to Christian Ray, 28 Dec 1861", *Nevin Ray Papers*, Sec. A Box 110 items 1-30 c.1, David M. Rubenstein Library, Duke University, Durham, NC

94 "Letter, Malcom Ray to Flora Jane Ray, 28 Dec 1861", *Nevin Ray Papers*, Sec. A Box 110 items 1-30 c.1, David M. Rubenstein Library, Duke University, Durham, NC

95 "Letter, John A. Walker to Tandy Walker and Louis H. McLeod, 31 Dec 1861", *Louis H. McLeod Collection*, in possession of John Cameron, Broadway, NC

96 "Letter, A.S. Caddell to Martha Sullivan, 5 Jan 1862", *Artemus S. Caddell Papers*, RUB Bay 0037:04 items 1-84 c.1, David M. Rubenstein Library, Duke University, Durham, NC

97 "Letter, Louis H. McLeod to Eliza McLeod, 9 Jan 1862", *Louis H. McLeod Collection*, in possession of John Cameron, Broadway, NC

98 "Letter, W.W. Fry to Daniel and Lydia Fry, 11 Jan 1862", *Civil War Letters*, Vertical Files, Moore County Library, Carthage, NC

99 "Letter, Eliza McLeod to Louis H. McLeod, 14 Jan 1862", *Louis H. McLeod Collection*, in possession of John Cameron, Broadway, NC

100 "Letter, C.D. Caddell to A.S. Caddell, 14 and 18 Jan 1862", *Artemus S. Caddell Papers*, RUB Bay 0037:04 items 1-84 c.1, David M. Rubenstein Library, Duke University, Durham, NC

101 "Letter, Louis H. McLeod to Eliza McLeod, 15 Jan 1862", *Louis H. McLeod Collection*, in possession of John Cameron, Broadway, NC

102 "Letter, W.M. Black to Christian Ray, 17 Jan 1862", *Nevin Ray Papers*, Sec. A Box 110 items 1-30 c.1, David M. Rubenstein Library, Duke University, Durham, NC

103 "Letter, John E. Phillips to Mary E. Shields et al., 17 Jan 1862", *Civil War Letters*, Vertical Files, Moore County Library, Carthage, NC

104 "Letter, Noah Deaton to Sarah B. Deaton, 21 Jan 1862", *Noah Deaton Papers*, John L. Nau Civil War Collection, Albert and Shirley Small Special Collections Library, University of Virginia, Charlottesville, VA

105 "Letter, Eliza McLeod to Louis H. McLeod, 21 Jan 1862", *Louis H. McLeod Collection*, in possession of John Cameron, Broadway, NC

106 "Letter, J.A. Jackson to R.A. Cole & M.A.M. Cole, 24 Jan 1862", *Richard A. Cole Papers*, PC. 1609, Private Collections, State Archives of North Carolina, Raleigh, NC

107 "Letter, Louis H. McLeod to Eliza McLeod, 26 Jan 1862", *Louis H. McLeod Collection*, in possession of John Cameron, Broadway, NC

108 "Letter, A.S. McIntosh to A.S. Caddell, 27 Jan 1862", *Artemus S. Caddell Papers*, RUB Bay 0037:04 items 1-84 c.1, David M. Rubenstein Library, Duke University, Durham, NC

109 "Letter, William P. Martin to George W. Foushee, 29 Jan 1862", *Civil War Letters*, Vertical Files, Moore County Library, Carthage, NC

110 "Letter, Eliza McLeod to Louis H. McLeod, 30 Jan 1862", *Louis H. McLeod Collection*, in possession of John Cameron, Broadway, NC

111 "Letter, Noah Deaton to Sarah Jane McDonald, 31 Jan 1862", *Noah Deaton Papers*, John L. Nau Civil War Collection, Albert and Shirley Small Special Collections Library, University of Virginia, Charlottesville, VA

112 "Letter, Jane, Wm. A. and Daniel McIntosh to A.S. Caddell, 1 Feb 1862", *Artemus S. Caddell Papers*, RUB Bay 0037:04 items 1-84 c.1, David M. Rubenstein Library, Duke University, Durham, NC

113 "Letter, Neill R. Kelly to Rachel Gilchrist, 1 Feb 1862", *Civil War Letters*, Vertical Files, Moore County Library, Carthage, NC

114 "Letter, Eliza McLeod to Louis H. McLeod, 9 Feb 1862", *Louis H. McLeod Collection*, in possession of John Cameron, Broadway, NC

115 "Letter, D.L. McDonald to Sarah Jane McDonald, 10 Feb 1862", *Noah Deaton Papers*, John L. Nau Civil War Collection, Albert and Shirley Small Special Collections Library, University of Virginia, Charlottesville, VA

116 "Letter, D. Frank Wilkie to Emeline Phillips, 13 Feb 1862", *The Phillips Family and the Civil War Vol. I*, Moore County Library, Carthage, NC

117 "Letter, A.S. Caddell to Martha Sullivan, 15 Feb 1862", *Artemus S. Caddell Papers*, RUB Bay 0037:04 items 1-84 c.1, David M. Rubenstein Library, Duke University, Durham, NC

118 "Letter, C.D. Caddell and W.L. Sullivan to A.S. Caddell, 19 Feb 1862", *Artemus S. Caddell Papers*, RUB Bay 0037:04 items 1-84 c.1, David M. Rubenstein Library, Duke University, Durham, NC

119 "Letter, Louis H. McLeod to Eliza McLeod, 23 Feb 1862", *Louis H. McLeod Collection*, in possession of John Cameron, Broadway, NC

120 "Letter, Eliza McLeod to Louis H. McLeod, 25 Feb 1862", *Louis H. McLeod Collection*, in possession of John Cameron, Broadway, NC

121 "Letter, Lizzie Skeen Phillips to Emeline Phillips, Feb/Mar 1862 (est.)", *The Phillips Family and the Civil War Vol. I*, Moore County Library, Carthage, NC

122 "Letter, Louis H. McLeod to Eliza McLeod, 2 Mar 1862", *Louis H. McLeod Collection*, in possession of John Cameron, Broadway, NC

123 "Letter, Eliza J. Berryman to Louis H. McLeod, 3 Mar 1862", *Louis H. McLeod Collection*, in possession of John Cameron, Broadway, NC

124 "Letter, Louis H. McLeod to Eliza McLeod, 5 Mar 1862", *Louis H. McLeod Collection*, in possession of John Cameron, Broadway, NC

125 "Letter, Jane, Wm. A. and Daniel McIntosh to A.S. Caddell, 12 Mar 1862", *Artemus S. Caddell Papers*, RUB Bay 0037:04 items 1-84 c.1, David M. Rubenstein Library, Duke University, Durham, NC

126 "Letter, Martha M. Sullivan to A.S. Caddell, 13 Mar 1862", *Artemus S. Caddell Papers*, RUB Bay 0037:04 items 1-84 c.1, David M. Rubenstein Library, Duke University, Durham, NC

127 "Letter, W.L. Sullivan to A.S. Caddell., 13 Mar 1862", *Artemus S. Caddell Papers*, RUB Bay 0037:04 items 1-84 c.1, David M. Rubenstein Library, Duke University, Durham, NC

128 "Letter, Mary E. Moore to A.S. Caddell, 13 Mar 1862", *Artemus S. Caddell Papers*, RUB Bay 0037:04 items 1-84 c.1, David M. Rubenstein Library, Duke University, Durham, NC

129 "Letter, Richard Street to Candace Phillips, 13 Mar 1862", *The Phillips Family and the Civil War Vol. I*, Moore County Library, Carthage, NC

130 "Letter, Noah Deaton to William Deaton, 20 Mar 1862", *Private Collection*, in possession of Richard Weiner, https://sparedshared12.wordpress.com/2017/12/17/1862-noah-deaton-to-william-deaton

131 "Letter, C.D. Caddell to A.S. Caddell, 25 Mar 1862", *Artemus S. Caddell Papers*, RUB Bay 0037:04 items 1-84 c.1, David M. Rubenstein Library, Duke University, Durham, NC

132 "Letter, Noah Deaton to William Deaton, 26 Mar 1862", *Noah Deaton Papers*, John L. Nau Civil War Collection, Albert and Shirley Small Special Collections Library, University of Virginia, Charlottesville, VA

133 "Letter, Noah Deaton to William Deaton, 30 Mar 1862", *Noah Deaton Papers*, John L. Nau Civil War Collection, Albert and Shirley Small Special Collections Library, University of Virginia, Charlottesville, VA

134 "Letter, Louis H. McLeod to Eliza McLeod, 30 Mar 1862", *Louis H. McLeod Collection*, in possession of John Cameron, Broadway, NC

135 "Letter, Louis H. McLeod to Eliza McLeod, 4 Apr 1862", *Louis H. McLeod Collection*, in possession of John Cameron, Broadway, NC

136 "Letter, Sallie E. Moore and Mary E. Moore to A.S. Caddell, 4 Apr 1862", *Artemus S. Caddell Papers*, RUB Bay 0037:04 items 1-84 c.1, David M. Rubenstein Library, Duke University, Durham, NC

137 "Letter, C.D. Caddell to A.S. Caddell, 4 Apr 1862", *Artemus S. Caddell Papers*, RUB Bay 0037:04 items 1-84 c.1, David M. Rubenstein Library, Duke University, Durham, NC

138 "Letter, W.L. Sullivan to A.S. Caddell, 6 Apr 1862", *Artemus S. Caddell Papers*, RUB Bay 0037:04 items 1-84 c.1, David M. Rubenstein Library, Duke University, Durham, NC

139 "Letter, Abel Douglas to Louis H. McLeod, 13 Apr 1862", *Louis H. McLeod Collection*, in possession of John Cameron, Broadway, NC

140 "Letter, Louis H. McLeod to Eliza McLeod, 13 Apr 1862", *Louis H. McLeod Collection*, in possession of John Cameron, Broadway, NC

141 "Letter, Eliza McLeod to Louis H. McLeod, 15 Apr 1862", *Louis H. McLeod Collection*, in possession of John Cameron, Broadway, NC

142 "Letter, W.S. Chaffin to Lewis Phillips, Jr., 15 Apr 1862", *The Phillips Family and the Civil War Vol. I*, Moore County Library, Carthage, NC

143 "Letter, Eliza Moore to A.S. Caddell, 17 Apr 1862", *Artemus S. Caddell Papers*, RUB Bay 0037:04 items 1-84 c.1, David M. Rubenstein Library, Duke University, Durham, NC

144 "Letter, Mastin Phillips to Emeline Phillips, 18 Apr 1862", *The Phillips Family and the Civil War Vol. I*, Moore County Library, Carthage, NC

145 "Letter, M.C. Yow to family, 20 Apr 1862" Nancy Yow Holt, *I Hope You Will All Remember Me: The Civil War Letters of Matthew C. Yow*. (Jacksonville, IL: 2024), 4-5. Original letters in possession of Larry R. Yow.

146 "Letter, Lydia Brown to Wm. A. Brown, 20 Apr 1862", *John L. Stuart Papers*, David M. Rubenstein Library, Duke University, Durham, NC

147 "Letter, Louis H. McLeod to Eliza McLeod, 20 Apr 1862", *Louis H. McLeod Collection*, in possession of John Cameron, Broadway, NC

148 "Letter, H.B. Bryan to N.R. McDonald, 21 Apr 1862", *Noah Deaton Papers*, John L. Nau Civil War Collection, Albert and Shirley Small Special Collections Library, University of Virginia, Charlottesville, VA

149 "Letter, H.B. Bryan to Ann McDonald, 23 Apr 1862", *Noah Deaton Papers*, John L. Nau Civil War Collection, Albert and Shirley Small Special Collections Library, University of Virginia, Charlottesville, VA

150 "Letter, Catharine Sloan to D.H. and J.A. Sloan, 25 Apr 1862", *Private Collection*, in possession of Judy Gore Heath, 25, Apr 1862, https://www.ancestry.com/mediaui-viewer/collection/1030/tree/15527994/person/1408344976/media/b033c9f5-4c35-4c20-aaff-c08c1a1447a9?galleryindex=9&sort=-created

151 "Letter, M.C. Yow to Catherine Yow and children, 26 Apr 1862", Nancy Yow Holt, *I Hope You Will All Remember Me: The Civil War Letters of Matthew C. Yow*. (Jacksonville, IL: 2024), 5-6. Original letters in possession of Larry R. Yow.

152 "Letter, Martha M. Sullivan to A.S. Caddell, 25 Apr 1862", *Artemus S. Caddell Papers*, RUB Bay 0037:04 items 1-84 c.1, David M. Rubenstein Library, Duke University, Durham, NC

153 "Letter, Wm. L. Sullivan to A.S. Caddell, 26 Apr 1862", *Artemus S. Caddell Papers*, RUB Bay 0037:04 items 1-84 c.1, David M. Rubenstein Library, Duke University, Durham, NC

154 "Letter, Noah Deaton to Sarah Jane McDonald, 27 Apr 1862", *Noah Deaton Papers*, John L. Nau Civil War Collection, Albert and Shirley Small Special Collections Library, University of Virginia, Charlottesville, VA

155 "Letter, Eliza McLeod to Louis H. McLeod, 28 Apr 1862", *Louis H. McLeod Collection*, in possession of John Cameron, Broadway, NC

156 "Letter, Louis H. McLeod to Eliza McLeod, 28 Apr 1862", *Louis H. McLeod Collection*, in possession of John Cameron, Broadway, NC

157 "Letter, Baxter C. Phillips to Emeline Phillips, n.d. May 1862 (est.)", *The Phillips Family and the Civil War Vol. I*, Moore County Library, Carthage, NC

158 "Letter, A.S. Caddell to Martha Sullivan, 2 May 1862", *Artemus S. Caddell Papers*, RUB Bay 0037:04 items 1-84 c.1, David M. Rubenstein Library, Duke University, Durham, NC

159 "Letter, Raney G. Caddell to A.S. Caddell, 5 May 1862", *Artemus S. Caddell Papers*, RUB Bay 0037:04 items 1-84 c.1, David M. Rubenstein Library, Duke University, Durham, NC

160 "Letter, Daniel McIntosh to A.S. Caddell, 6 May 1862", *Artemus S. Caddell Papers*, RUB Bay 0037:04 items 1-84 c.1, David M. Rubenstein Library, Duke University, Durham, NC

161 "Letter, C.D. Sullivan to A.S. Caddell, 7 May 1862", *Artemus S. Caddell Papers*, RUB Bay 0037:04 items 1-84 c.1, David M. Rubenstein Library, Duke University, Durham, NC

162 "Letter, Lydia Sowell to A.S. Caddell, 7 May 1862", *Artemus S. Caddell Papers*, RUB Bay 0037:04 items 1-84 c.1, David M. Rubenstein Library, Duke University, Durham, NC

163 "Letter, Jane McIntosh to A.S. Caddell, 11 May 1862", *Artemus S. Caddell Papers*, RUB Bay 0037:04 items 1-84 c.1, David M. Rubenstein Library, Duke University, Durham, NC

164 "Letter, Sarah McIntosh to A.S. Caddell, 11 May 1862", *Artemus S. Caddell Papers*, RUB Bay 0037:04 items 1-84 c.1, David M. Rubenstein Library, Duke University, Durham, NC

165 "Letter, Mary E. Moore to A.S. Caddell, 11 May 1862", *Artemus S. Caddell Papers*, RUB Bay 0037:04 items 1-84 c.1, David M. Rubenstein Library, Duke University, Durham, NC

166 "Letter, Eliza McLeod to Louis H. McLeod, 11 May 1862", *Louis H. McLeod Collection*, in possession of John Cameron, Broadway, NC

167 "Letter, J.F. Williamson to Wyatt Williamson, 13 May 1862", *Wyatt Williamson Papers*, Library Service Center Box 1, c.1, David M. Rubenstein Library, Duke University, Durham, NC

168 "Letter, John A. Sloan to Catherine Sloan, 14 May 1861", *Private Collection*, in possession of Judy Gore Heath, 14 Mar 1862, https://www.ancestry.com/mediaui-viewer/collection/1030/tree/15527994/person/1408387486/media/a8b99a93-73af-4ee2-8c6e-05cfdc27857e?galleryindex=29&sort=-created

169 "Letter, J.L. Stuart to Mary A. Harper and E.C. Nall, 16 May 1862", *John L. Stuart Papers*, David M. Rubenstein Library, Duke University, Durham, NC

170 "Letter, M.C. Yow to Simeon Jones Yow, 17 May 1862", Nancy Yow Holt, *I Hope You Will All Remember Me: The Civil War Letters of Matthew C. Yow*. (Jacksonville, IL: 2024), 6-7. Original letters in possession of Larry R. Yow.

171 "Letter, A.S. Caddell to Martha M. Sullivan, 19 May 1862", *Artemus S. Caddell Papers*, RUB Bay 0037:04 items 1-84 c.1, David M. Rubenstein Library, Duke University, Durham, NC

172 "Letter, A.S. McIntosh to A.S. Caddell, 21 May 1862", *Artemus S. Caddell Papers*, RUB Bay 0037:04 items 1-84 c.1, David M. Rubenstein Library, Duke University, Durham, NC

173 "Letter, M.C. Yow to Catherine Yow and children, 23 May 1862", Nancy Yow Holt, *I Hope You Will All Remember Me: The Civil War Letters of Matthew C. Yow*. (Jacksonville, IL: 2024), 7-9. Original letters in possession of Larry R. Yow.

174 "Letter, Louis H. McLeod to Eliza McLeod, 23 May 1862", *Louis H. McLeod Collection*, in possession of John Cameron, Broadway, NC

175 "Letter, Mary A. Harper to J.L. Stuart, 24 May 1862", *John L. Stuart Papers*, David M. Rubenstein Library, Duke University, Durham, NC

176 "Letter, Louis H. McLeod to Eliza McLeod, 26 May 1862", *Louis H. McLeod Collection*, in possession of John Cameron, Broadway, NC

177 "Letter, Louis H. McLeod to Eliza McLeod, 27 May 1862", *Louis H. McLeod Collection*, in possession of John Cameron, Broadway, NC

178 "Letter, C.D. Caddell to A.S. Caddell, 27 May 1862", *Artemus S. Caddell Papers*, RUB Bay 0037:04 items 1-84 c.1, David M. Rubenstein Library, Duke University, Durham, NC

179 "Letter, R.G. Caddell to A.S. Caddell, 28 May 1862", *Artemus S. Caddell Papers*, RUB Bay 0037:04 items 1-84 c.1, David M. Rubenstein Library, Duke University, Durham, NC

180 "Letter, Baxter C. Phillips to Emeline Phillips, 2 Jun 1862", *The Phillips Family and the Civil War Vol. I*, Moore County Library, Carthage, NC

181 "Letter, James Kelly to Rachel Gilchrist, 2 Jun 1862", *Civil War Letters*, Vertical Files, Moore County Library, Carthage, NC

182 "Letter, M.C. Yow to Catherine Yow and children, 8 Jun 1862", Nancy Yow Holt, *I Hope You Will All Remember Me: The Civil War Letters of Matthew C. Yow*. (Jacksonville, IL: 2024), 9-10. Original letters in possession of Larry R. Yow.

183 "Letter, Louis H. McLeod to Eliza McLeod, 10 Jun 1862", *Louis H. McLeod Collection*, in possession of John Cameron, Broadway, NC

184 "Letter, R.B. Stewart to William Stewart, 11 Jun 1862", *Bryan Tyson Papers*, David M. Rubenstein Library, Duke University, Durham, NC

185 "Letter, M.C. Yow to Simeon Jones Yow, 11 Jun 1862", Nancy Yow Holt, *I Hope You Will All Remember Me: The Civil War Letters of Matthew C. Yow*. (Jacksonville, IL: 2024), 11. Original letters in possession of Larry R. Yow.

186 "Letter, Louis H. McLeod to Eliza McLeod, 15 Jun 1862", *Louis H. McLeod Collection*, in possession of John Cameron, Broadway, NC

187 "Letter, Martha Sullivan to A.S. Caddell, 15 Jun 1862", *Artemus S. Caddell Papers*, RUB Bay 0037:04 items 1-84 c.1, David M. Rubenstein Library, Duke University, Durham, NC

188 "Letter, J.L. Stuart to Mary A. Harper and Charles Harper, 16-17 Jun 1862", *John L. Stuart Papers*, David M. Rubenstein Library, Duke University, Durham, NC

189 "Letter, M.C. Yow to Catherine Yow and children, 19 Jun 1862", Nancy Yow Holt, *I Hope You Will All Remember Me: The Civil War Letters of Matthew C. Yow*. (Jacksonville, IL: 2024), 12-13. Original letters in possession of Larry R. Yow.

190 "Letter, L.W. Lawhon to Gov. Henry T. Clark, 22 Jun 1862", *Governor Henry Toole Clark Papers*, G.P. 158, Governor's Papers, State Archives of North Carolina, Raleigh, NC

191 "Letter, Louis H. McLeod to Eliza McLeod, 15 Jun 1862", *Louis H. McLeod Collection*, in possession of John Cameron, Broadway, NC

192 "Letter, Jane McIntosh to A.S. Caddell, 22 Jun 1862", *Artemus S. Caddell Papers*, RUB Bay 0037:04 items 1-84 c.1, David M. Rubenstein Library, Duke University, Durham, NC

193 "Letter, A.S. Caddell to Martha M. Sullivan, 22 Jun 1862", *Artemus S. Caddell Papers*, RUB Bay 0037:04 items 1-84 c.1, David M. Rubenstein Library, Duke University, Durham, NC

194 "Letter, M.C. Yow to Catherine Yow and children, 19 Jun 1862", Nancy Yow Holt, *I Hope You Will All Remember Me: The Civil War Letters of Matthew C. Yow*. (Jacksonville, IL: 2024), 12-13. Original letters in possession of Larry R. Yow.

195 "Letter, W.W. Shields to D.P. Shields, 22 Jun 1862", *Private Collection*, in possession of David McCallum, Carthage, NC

196 "Letter, M.C. Yow to Catherine Yow and children, 22 Jun 1862", Nancy Yow Holt, *I Hope You Will All Remember Me: The Civil War Letters of Matthew C. Yow*. (Jacksonville, IL: 2024), 13-16. Original letters in possession of Larry R. Yow.

197 "Letter, J.J. Lawhon to D.P. Shields, 22 Jun 1862", *Private Collection*, in possession of David McCallum, Carthage, NC

198 "Letter, Daniel McIntosh and Wim. A. McIntosh to A.S. Caddell, 23 Jun 1862", *Artemus S. Caddell Papers*, RUB Bay 0037:04 items 1-84 c.1, David M. Rubenstein Library, Duke University, Durham, NC

199 "Letter, M.C. Yow to Catherine Yow and children, 4 Jul 1862", Nancy Yow Holt, *I Hope You Will All Remember Me: The Civil War Letters of Matthew C. Yow*. (Jacksonville, IL: 2024), 19-21. Original letters in possession of Larry R. Yow.

200 "Letter, Noah Deaton to William Deaton, 8 Jul 1862", *Noah Deaton Papers*, James S. Schoff Civil War Collection, William L. Clements Library, University of Michigan, Ann Arbor, MI

201 "Letter, J.L. Stuart to Mary A. Harper, 10 Jul 1862", *John L. Stuart Papers*, David M. Rubenstein Library, Duke University, Durham, NC

202 "Letter, M.C. Yow to Catherine Yow and children, 10 Jul 1862", Nancy Yow Holt, *I Hope You Will All Remember Me: The Civil War Letters of Matthew C. Yow*. (Jacksonville, IL: 2024), 21-23. Original letters in possession of Larry R. Yow.

203 "Letter, A.S. Caddell to Martha M. Sullivan, 10 Jul 1862", *Artemus S. Caddell Papers*, RUB Bay 0037:04 items 1-84 c.1, David M. Rubenstein Library, Duke University, Durham, NC

204 "Letter, J.L. Stuart to Mary A. Harper and John Harper, 13 Jul 1862", *John L. Stuart Papers*, David M. Rubenstein Library, Duke University, Durham, NC

205 "Letter, J.L. Stuart to Emily C. Nall, 13 Jul 1862", *John L. Stuart Papers*, David M. Rubenstein Library, Duke University, Durham, NC

206 "Letter, J.L. Stuart to William and Nancy Teague, 13 Jul 1862", *John L. Stuart Papers*, David M. Rubenstein Library, Duke University, Durham, NC

207 "Letter, J.L. Stuart to Charles Harper, 13 Jul 1862", *John L. Stuart Papers*, David M. Rubenstein Library, Duke University, Durham, NC

208 "Letter, J.L. Stuart to Cynthia Teague and Lydia Comer, 13 Jul 1862", *John L. Stuart Papers*, David M. Rubenstein Library, Duke University, Durham, NC

209 "Letter, W.L. Sullivan & C.D. Caddell to A.S. Caddell, 14 Jul 1862", *Artemus S. Caddell Papers*, RUB Bay 0037:04 items 1-84 c.1, David M. Rubenstein Library, Duke University, Durham, NC

210 "Letter, R.G. Caddell to A.S. Caddell, 19 Jul 1862", *Artemus S. Caddell Papers*, RUB Bay 0037:04 items 1-84 c.1, David M. Rubenstein Library, Duke University, Durham, NC

211 "Letter, Mastin C. Phillips to Lewis & Nancy Phillips. 19 Jul 1862", *The Phillips Family and the Civil War Vol. I*, Moore County Library, Carthage, NC

212 "Letter, C.D. Caddell to A.S. Caddell, 20 Jul 1862", *Artemus S. Caddell Papers*, RUB Bay 0037:04 items 1-84 c.1, David M. Rubenstein Library, Duke University, Durham, NC

213 "Letter, H.F. Craven to Emeline Phillips, 24 Jul 1862", *The Phillips Family and the Civil War Vol. I*, Moore County Library, Carthage, NC

214 "Letter, Lydia Fry to A.S. Caddell, 26 Jul 1862", *Artemus S. Caddell Papers*, RUB Bay 0037:04 items 1-84 c.1, David M. Rubenstein Library, Duke University, Durham, NC

215 "Letter, Jane McIntosh to A.S. Caddell, 26 Jul 1862", *Artemus S. Caddell Papers*, RUB Bay 0037:04 items 1-84 c.1, David M. Rubenstein Library, Duke University, Durham, NC

216 "Letter, William and Raney Caddell to A.S. Caddell, 26 Jul 1862", *Artemus S. Caddell Papers*, RUB Bay 0037:04 items 1-84 c.1, David M. Rubenstein Library, Duke University, Durham, NC

217 "Letter, Lizzie Phillips to Emeline Phillips, 26 Jul 1862", *The Phillips Family and the Civil War Vol. I*, Moore County Library, Carthage, NC

218 "Letter, C.D. Caddell to A.S. Caddell, 27 Jul 1862", *Artemus S. Caddell Papers*, RUB Bay 0037:04 items 1-84 c.1, David M. Rubenstein Library, Duke University, Durham, NC

219 "Letter, Mastin C. Phillips to Lewis Phillips, Jr.," 27 Jul 1862", *The Phillips Family and the Civil War Vol. I*, Moore County Library, Carthage, NC

220 "Letter, M.C. Yow to Catherine Yow and children, 4 Aug 1862", Nancy Yow Holt, *I Hope You Will All Remember Me: The Civil War Letters of Matthew C. Yow*. (Jacksonville, IL: 2024), 23-24. Original letters in possession of Larry R. Yow.

221 "Letter, M.C. Yow to Catherine Yow and children, 6 Aug 1862", Nancy Yow Holt, *I Hope You Will All Remember Me: The Civil War Letters of Matthew C. Yow*. (Jacksonville, IL: 2024), 24-26. Original letters in possession of Larry R. Yow.

222 "Letter, W.L. Sullivan to A.S. Caddell, 7 Aug 1862", *Artemus S. Caddell Papers*, RUB Bay 0037:04 items 1-84 c.1, David M. Rubenstein Library, Duke University, Durham, NC

223 "Letter, Jesse Brown to Mary E. Brown and Isaiah Brown, 12 Aug 1862", *Civil War Letters*, Vertical Files, Moore County Library, Carthage, NC

224 "Letter, J.L. Stuart to Mary A. Harper, Charles Harper, Mary Harper, Nancy Nall and John Harper, 12-14 Aug 1862", *John L. Stuart Papers*, David M. Rubenstein Library, Duke University, Durham, NC

225 "Letter, Daniel McIntosh to A.S. Caddell, 13 Aug 1862", *Artemus S. Caddell Papers*, RUB Bay 0037:04 items 1-84 c.1, David M. Rubenstein Library, Duke University, Durham, NC

226 "Letter, Raney G. Caddell to A.S. Caddell, 13 Aug 1862", *Artemus S. Caddell Papers*, RUB Bay 0037:04 items 1-84 c.1, David M. Rubenstein Library, Duke University, Durham, NC

227 "Letter, C.D. Caddell to A.S. Caddell, 13 Aug 1862", *Artemus S. Caddell Papers*, RUB Bay 0037:04 items 1-84 c.1, David M. Rubenstein Library, Duke University, Durham, NC

228 "Letter, A.S. Caddell to Martha Sullivan, 15 Aug 1862", *Artemus S. Caddell Papers*, RUB Bay 0037:04 items 1-84 c.1, David M. Rubenstein Library, Duke University, Durham, NC

229 "Letter, Sarah McIntosh to A.S. Caddell, 19 Aug 1862", *Artemus S. Caddell Papers*, RUB Bay 0037:04 items 1-84 c.1, David M. Rubenstein Library, Duke University, Durham, NC

230 "Letter, Archibald McNeill to Jane McNeill, 20 Aug 1862", Mary McNeill & Murdock McKenzie", *Lacy Garner*, accessed 8 Jul 2024, https://web.archive.org/web/20200812225857/https://www.companyh26th.com/last-names-g-j.html

231 "Letter, J.L. Stuart to Mary A. Harper, John Harper, Charles Harper, Mary Harper and Nancy Nall, 25 Aug 1862", *John L. Stuart Papers*, David M. Rubenstein Library, Duke University, Durham, NC

232 "Letter, Neill A. Ray to friend, 22 Aug 1862" *Nevin Ray Papers*, Sec. A Box 110 items 1-30 c.1, David M. Rubenstein Library, Duke University, Durham, NC

233 "Letter, J.L. Stuart to Mary A. Harper, 27 Aug 1862", *John L. Stuart Papers*, David M. Rubenstein Library, Duke University, Durham, NC

234 "Letter, J.L. Stuart to Mary Harper, 18 Aug 1862", *John L. Stuart Papers*, Accession 44539, Albert and Shirley Small Special Collections Library, University of Virginia, Charlottesville, VA

235 "Letter, Jane McIntosh to A.S. Caddell, 4 Sep 1862", *Artemus S. Caddell Papers*, RUB Bay 0037:04 items 1-84 c.1, David M. Rubenstein Library, Duke University, Durham, NC

236 "Letter, Daniel McIntosh to A.S. Caddell, 5 Sep 1862", *Artemus S. Caddell Papers*, RUB Bay 0037:04 items 1-84 c.1, David M. Rubenstein Library, Duke University, Durham, NC

237 "Letter, Wm. A. McIntosh to A.S. Caddell, 5 Sep 1862", *Artemus S. Caddell Papers*, RUB Bay 0037:04 items 1-84 c.1, David M. Rubenstein Library, Duke University, Durham, NC

238 "Letter, M.M. Sullivan to A.S. Caddell, 16 Sep 1862", *Artemus S. Caddell Papers*, RUB Bay 0037:04 items 1-84 c.1, David M. Rubenstein Library, Duke University, Durham, NC

239 "Letter, J.L. Stuart to Mary A. Harper, 21 Sep 1862", *John L. Stuart Papers*, David M. Rubenstein Library, Duke University, Durham, NC

240 "Letter, J.L. Stuart and J. Nall to Mary A. Harper and E.C. Nall, 23 Sep 1862", *John L. Stuart Papers*, David M. Rubenstein Library, Duke University, Durham, NC

241 "Letter, M.C. Yow to Catherine Yow and children, 5 Oct 1862", Nancy Yow Holt, *I Hope You Will All Remember Me: The Civil War Letters of Matthew C. Yow*. (Jacksonville, IL: 2024), 26-27. Original letters in possession of Larry R. Yow.

242 "Letter, J.L. Stuart to Mary Harper and family, 6 Oct 1862", *John L. Stuart Papers*, Accession 44539, Albert and Shirley Small Special Collections Library, University of Virginia, Charlottesville, VA

243 "Letter, B.G. Dunlap to R.B. Paschal" *Spared & Shared*, accessed 27 Jul 2024, https://sparedshared23.com/2023/12/10/1862-bryant-green-dunlap-to-richard-bray-paschal

244 "Letter, David H. Sloan to Catherine Sloan, 14 Oct 1862", *Private Collection*, in possession of Judy Gore Heath, 14 Oct 1862, https://www.ancestry.com/mediaui-viewer/collection/1030/tree/15527994/person/1408344976/media/81397f4d-50ac-4efb-94a4-92d0d1763109?galleryindex=2&sort=-created

245 "Letter, M.C. Yow to Catherine Yow and children, 28 Oct 1862", Nancy Yow Holt, *I Hope You Will All Remember Me: The Civil War Letters of Matthew C. Yow*. (Jacksonville, IL: 2024), 27-28. Original letters in possession of Larry R. Yow.

246 "Letter, Neill R. Kelly to Rachel Gilchrist, 14 Nov 1862", *Civil War Letters*, Vertical Files, Moore County Library, Carthage, NC

247 "Letter, Noah Deaton to Sarah Jane McDonald, 16 Nov 1862", *Noah Deaton Papers*, James S. Schoff Civil War Collection, William L. Clements Library, University of Michigan, Ann Arbor, MI

248 "Letter, Noah Deaton to friend, 16 Nov 1862", *Nevin Ray Papers*, Sec. A Box 110 items 1-30 c.1, David M. Rubenstein Library, Duke University, Durham, NC

249 "Letter, Charles A. Gilchrist to Catherine Gilchrist and Randall Gilchrist, 21 Nov 1862", *Civil War Letters*, Vertical Files, Moore County Library, Carthage, NC

250 "Letter, Mary A. Harper, John Harper and Charles Harper to J.L. Stuart, 26 Nov 1862", *John L. Stuart Papers*, David M. Rubenstein Library, Duke University, Durham, NC

251 "Letter, M.C. Yow to Catherine Yow and children, 30 Nov 1862", Nancy Yow Holt, *I Hope You Will All Remember Me: The Civil War Letters of Matthew C. Yow*. (Jacksonville, IL: 2024), 29-31. Original letters in possession of Larry R. Yow.

252 "Letter, W.A. Ray to Mary A. Ray, 19 Dec 1862", *Nevin Ray Papers*, Sec. A Box 110 items 1-30 c.1, David M. Rubenstein Library, Duke University, Durham, NC

253 "Letter, Noah Deaton to William Deaton, 19-20 Dec 1862", *Noah Deaton Papers*, James S. Schoff Civil War Collection, William L. Clements Library, University of Michigan, Ann Arbor, MI

254 "Letter, Henry W, Stutts to Kenneth B. Kelly, 25 Dec 1862", *Private Collection*, In possession of Jim Kelly, https://www.ancestry.com/mediaui-viewer/collection/1030/tree/43429376/person/300172669830/media/a686c942-15d3-4adb-919e-0b7288240f8a?galleryindex=11&sort=-created

255 ""Letter, J.L. Stuart to Mary A. Harper, John Harper, Charles Harper, Mary Harper and Nancy Nall, 11 Jan 1863", *John L. Stuart Papers*, David M. Rubenstein Library, Duke University, Durham, NC

256 "Letter, Mary A. Harper and John Harper to J.L. Stuart, 12 Jan 1863", *John L. Stuart Papers*, David M. Rubenstein Library, Duke University, Durham, NC

257 "Letter, M.C. Yow to Catherine Yow and children, 18 Jan 1863", Nancy Yow Holt, *I Hope You Will All Remember Me: The Civil War Letters of Matthew C. Yow*. (Jacksonville, IL: 2024), 35-36. Original letters in possession of Larry R. Yow.

258 "Letter, Mastin C. Phillips to Emeline Phillips, 31 Jan 1863", *The Phillips Family and the Civil War Vol. I*, Moore County Library, Carthage, NC

259 "Letter, Neill A. Baker to Sarah Jane Baker, n.d. Feb 1863", *Spared & Shared*, accessed 27 Jul 2024, https://sparedshared22.wordpress.com/2021/12/17/1864-neill-archibald-baker-to-sarah-jane-parham-baker/

260 "Letter, M.C. Yow to Catherine Yow and children, 1 Feb 1863", Nancy Yow Holt, *I Hope You Will All Remember Me: The Civil War Letters of Matthew C. Yow*. (Jacksonville, IL: 2024), 36-38. Original letters in possession of Larry R. Yow.

261 "Letter, W.A. Nall to John Harper, Mary Harper, Charles Harper and Mary Ann Harper, 6 Feb 1863", *John L. Stuart Papers*, David M. Rubenstein Library, Duke University, Durham, NC

262 "Letter, J.L. Stuart to Mary A. Harper and John Harper, 8 Feb 1863", *John L. Stuart Papers*, David M. Rubenstein Library, Duke University, Durham, NC

263 "Letter, William H. Patterson to F.A.V. Patterson, 9 Feb 1863", *Civil War Letters*, Vertical Files, Moore County Library, Carthage, NC

264 "Letter, Baxter C. Phillips to Emeline Phillips, 15 Feb 1863", *The Phillips Family and the Civil War Vol. I*, Moore County Library, Carthage, NC

265 "Letter, J.L. Stuart to Mary A. Harper, John Harper, Charles Harper, Nancy Glass Nall and Mary A. Harper, 15 Feb 1863", *John L. Stuart Papers*, David M. Rubenstein Library, Duke University, Durham, NC

266 "Letter, David H. Sloan to Catharine Sloan, 15 Feb 1863", *Private Collection*, in possession of Judy Gore Heath, 15 Feb 1863, https://www.ancestry.com/mediaui-viewer/collection/1030/tree/15527994/person/1408344976/media/57ef3385-6f1b-4a46-a7a9-2a47e80c2ac9?galleryindex=5&sort=

,267 "Letter, M.C. Yow to Catherine Yow and children, 15 Feb 1863", Nancy Yow Holt, *I Hope You Will All Remember Me: The Civil War Letters of Matthew C. Yow*. (Jacksonville, IL: 2024), 38-39. Original letters in possession of Larry R. Yow.

268 "Letter, Mastin Phillips to Emeline Phillips, 17 Feb 1863", *Street Papers*, Vertical Files, Moore County Library, Carthage, NC

269 "Letter, Mary A. Harper and John Harper to J.L. Stuart, 20 Feb 1863", *John L. Stuart Papers*, David M. Rubenstein Library, Duke University, Durham, NC

270 "Letter, M.C. Yow to Catherine Yow and children, 27 Feb 1863", Nancy Yow Holt, *I Hope You Will All Remember Me: The Civil War Letters of Matthew C. Yow*. (Jacksonville, IL: 2024), 39-41. Original letters in possession of Larry R. Yow.

271 "Letter, Mastin C. Phillips to Rev. Lewis Phillips Jr., 28 Feb 1863", *The Phillips Family and the Civil War Vol. I*, Moore County Library, Carthage, NC

272 "Letter, J.L. Stuart to Mary A. Harper, 28 Feb 1863", *John L. Stuart Papers*, David M. Rubenstein Library, Duke University, Durham, NC

273 "Letter, Baxter C. Phillips to Elmira Phillips, n.d. Mar 1863", *The Phillips Family and the Civil War Vol. I*, Moore County Library, Carthage, NC

274 "Letter, J.L. Stuart to Mary A. Harper, John Harper, Charles Harper, Nancy Glass Nall and Mary A. Harper, 1 Mar 1863", *John L. Stuart Papers*, David M. Rubenstein Library, Duke University, Durham, NC

275 "Letter, William H. Patterson to F.A.V. Patterson, 7 Mar 1863", *Civil War Letters*, Vertical Files, Moore County Library, Carthage, NC

276 "Letter, M.C. Yow to Joseph and Nancy Albright, 8 Mar 1863", Nancy Yow Holt, *I Hope You Will All Remember Me: The Civil War Letters of Matthew C. Yow*. (Jacksonville, IL: 2024), 41-42. Original letters in possession of Larry R. Yow.

277 "Letter, J.L. Stuart to Mary A. Harper and Charles Harper, 18 Mar 1863", *John L. Stuart Papers*, David M. Rubenstein Library, Duke University, Durham, NC

278 "Letter, M.C. Yow to Catherine Yow and children, 19 Mar 1863", Nancy Yow Holt, *I Hope You Will All Remember Me: The Civil War Letters of Matthew C. Yow*. (Jacksonville, IL: 2024), 43. Original letters in possession of Larry R. Yow.

279 "Letter, J.L. Stuart to Mary A. Harper and Charles Harper, 21 Mar 1863", *John L. Stuart Papers*, David M. Rubenstein Library, Duke University, Durham, NC

280 "Letter, J.L. Stuart to Mary A. Harper and Charles Harper, 22 Mar 1863", *John L. Stuart Papers*, David M. Rubenstein Library, Duke University, Durham, NC

281 "Letter, J.L. Stuart to Mary A. Harper, John Harper, Mary A. Harper and Charles Harper, 22 Mar 1863", *John L. Stuart Papers*, David M. Rubenstein Library, Duke University, Durham, NC

282 "Letter, David H. Sloan to Catharine Sloan, 22 Mar 1863", *Private Collection*, in possession of Judy Gore Heath, 22 Mar 1863, https://www.ancestry.com/mediaui-viewer/collection/1030/tree/15527994/person/1408387486/media/11b0b7fd-4cb3-4d9f-bf0a-f5f68b4a3484?galleryindex=30&sort=

283 "Letter, J.L. Stuart to Mary A. Harper, 24 Mar 1863", *John L. Stuart Papers*, David M. Rubenstein Library, Duke University, Durham, NC

284 "Letter, J.L. Stuart to Mary A. Harper, John Harper and Charles Harper, 1 Apr 1863", *John L. Stuart Papers*, David M. Rubenstein Library, Duke University, Durham, NC

285 "Letter, J.L. Stuart to Mary A. Harper, John Harper and Charles Harper, 4 Apr 1863", *John L. Stuart Papers*, David M. Rubenstein Library, Duke University, Durham, NC

286 "Letter, M.A. Harper to Capt. William M. Black, 5 Apr 1863", *John L. Stuart Papers*, David M. Rubenstein Library, Duke University, Durham, NC

287 "Letter, Mary A. Harper to J.L. Stuart, 5 Apr 1863", *John L. Stuart Papers*, David M. Rubenstein Library, Duke University, Durham, NC

288 "Letter, M.C. Yow to Catherine Yow and children, 5 Apr 1863", Nancy Yow Holt, *I Hope You Will All Remember Me: The Civil War Letters of Matthew C. Yow*. (Jacksonville, IL: 2024), 44-45. Original letters in possession of Larry R. Yow.

289 "Letter, David H. Sloan to Catherine Sloan, 5 Apr 1863", *Private Collection*, in possession of Judy Gore Heath, 5 Apr 1863, https://www.ancestry.com/mediaui-viewer/collection/1030/tree/15527994/person/1408344976/media/babb10bd-cb0c-4697-ba43-f5a7328295ef?galleryindex=4&sort=

290 "Letter, J.L. Stuart to Mary A. Harper, John Harper and Charles Harper, 9 Apr 1863", *John L. Stuart Papers*, David M. Rubenstein Library, Duke University, Durham, NC

291 "Letter, N.A. Ray to Sarah Ray, 12 Apr 1863", *Nevin Ray Papers*, Sec. A Box 110 items 1-30 c.1, David M. Rubenstein Library, Duke University, Durham, NC

292 "Letter, Mary A. Harper, John Harper and Charles Harper to J.L. Stuart, 15 Apr 1863", *John L. Stuart Papers*, David M. Rubenstein Library, Duke University, Durham, NC

293 "Letter, J.L. Stuart to Mary A. Harper, 17 Apr 1863", *John L. Stuart Papers*, David M. Rubenstein Library, Duke University, Durham, NC

294 "Letter, J.L. Stuart to Mary A. Harper and John Harper, 19 Apr 1863", *John L. Stuart Papers*, David M. Rubenstein Library, Duke University, Durham, NC

295 "Letter, J.L. Stuart to Charles Harper and Mary A. Harper, 19 Apr 1863", *John L. Stuart Papers*, David M. Rubenstein Library, Duke University, Durham, NC

296 "Letter, James O.A.. Kelly to Nannie Sloan Kelly, 19 Apr 1863", *James Oscar Abner Kelly Papers*, PC. 1760, Private Collections, State Archives of North Carolina, Raleigh, NC

297 "Letter, Noah F. Muse to A.S. Caddell and W.H.H. Davis, 20 Apr 1863", *Artemus S. Caddell Papers*, RUB Bay 0037:04 items 1-84 c.1, David M. Rubenstein Library, Duke University, Durham, NC

298 "Letter, M.C. Yow to Catherine Yow and children, 21 Apr 1863", Nancy Yow Holt, *I Hope You Will All Remember Me: The Civil War Letters of Matthew C. Yow*. (Jacksonville, IL: 2024), 45-46. Original letters in possession of Larry R. Yow.

299 "Letter, John Harper to J.L. Stuart, 26 Apr 1863", *John L. Stuart Papers*, David M. Rubenstein Library, Duke University, Durham, NC

300 "Letter, Charles Harper to J.L. Stuart, 26 Apr 1863", *John L. Stuart Papers*, David M. Rubenstein Library, Duke University, Durham, NC

301 "Letter, J.L. Stuart to Mary A. Harper, 1 May 1863", *John L. Stuart Papers*, David M. Rubenstein Library, Duke University, Durham, NC

302 "Letter, James O.A.. Kelly to Nannie Sloan Kelly, 4 May 1863", *James Oscar Abner Kelly Papers*, PC. 1760, Private Collections, State Archives of North Carolina, Raleigh, NC

303 "Letter, J.L. Stuart to Mary A. Harper, John Harper and Charles Harper, 5 May 1863", *John L. Stuart Papers*, David M. Rubenstein Library, Duke University, Durham, NC

304 "Letter, J.A. Jackson to Martha R. Jackson, 9 May 1863", *Richard A. Cole Papers*, PC. 1609, Private Collections, State Archives of North Carolina, Raleigh, NC

305 "Letter, J.A. Jackson to S.T. Jackson, 11 May 1863", *Richard A. Cole Papers*, PC. 1609, Private Collections, State Archives of North Carolina, Raleigh, NC

306 "Letter, Noah Deaton to Sarah Jane McDonald, 14 May 1863", *Noah Deaton Papers*, James S. Schoff Civil War Collection, William L. Clements Library, University of Michigan, Ann Arbor, MI

307 "Letter, Baxter C. Phillips to Elmira Phillips, 18 May 1863", *The Phillips Family and the Civil War Vol. I*, Moore County Library, Carthage, NC

308 "Letter, J.L. Stuart to Mary A. Harper, 21 May 1863", *John L. Stuart Papers*, David M. Rubenstein Library, Duke University, Durham, NC

309 "Letter, J.L. Stuart to John Harper, 21 May 1863", *John L. Stuart Papers*, David M. Rubenstein Library, Duke University, Durham, NC

310 "Letter, William H. Patterson to F.A.V. Patterson, 25 May 1863", *Civil War Letters*, Vertical Files, Moore County Library, Carthage, NC

311 "Letter, Mastin C. Phillips to Lewis Phillips Jr., 26 May 1863", *The Phillips Family and the Civil War Vol. I*, Moore County Library, Carthage, NC

312 "Letter, J.L. Stuart to Mary A. Harper, 26 May 1863", *John L. Stuart Papers*, David M. Rubenstein Library, Duke University, Durham, NC

313 "Letter, J.L. Stuart to Mary A. Harper, John Harper and Charles Harper, 27 May 1863", *John L. Stuart Papers*, David M. Rubenstein Library, Duke University, Durham, NC

314 "Letter, William H. Patterson to F.A.V. Patterson, 2 Jun 1863", *Civil War Letters*, Vertical Files, Moore County Library, Carthage, NC

315 "Letter, Baxter C. Phillips to Elmira Phillips, 3 Jun 1863", *The Phillips Family and the Civil War Vol. I*, Moore County Library, Carthage, NC

316 "Letter, Lizzie Skeen Phillips to Emeline Phillips, 6 Jun 1863", *The Phillips Family and the Civil War Vol. I*, Moore County Library, Carthage, NC

317 "Letter, David H. Sloan to Catharine Sloan, 9 Jun 1863", *Private Collection*, in possession of Judy Gore Heath, 9 Jun 1863, https://www.ancestry.com/mediaui-viewer/collection/1030/tree/15527994/person/1408344976/media/a242c0bb-b4a3-4993-88cf-1b5893b778e9?galleryindex=7&sort=

318 "Letter, Exer L. Ritter and Mary M. Ritter to A.S. Caddell, 14 Jun 1863", *Artemus S. Caddell Papers*, RUB Bay 0037:04 items 1-84 c.1, David M. Rubenstein Library, Duke University, Durham, NC

319 "Letter, M.C. Yow to Catherine Yow and children, 17-18 Jun 1863", Nancy Yow Holt, *I Hope You Will All Remember Me: The Civil War Letters of Matthew C. Yow*. (Jacksonville, IL: 2024), 49-51. Original letters in possession of Larry R. Yow.

320 "Letter, Jane McIntosh to A.S. Caddell, 18 Jun 1863", *Artemus S. Caddell Papers*, RUB Bay 0037:04 items 1-84 c.1, David M. Rubenstein Library, Duke University, Durham, NC

321 "Letter, Mastin C. Phillips to Emeline Phillips, 18 Jun 1863", *The Phillips Family and the Civil War Vol. I*, Moore County Library, Carthage, NC

322 "Letter, Isaac Thompson to N.G. Cameron, 20 Jun 1863", Kathryn Blevins Carter, *Thompson: A Family History*. 167-169.

323 "Letter, Noah Deaton to Sarah Jane McDonald, 23 and 30 Jun 1863", *Noah Deaton Papers*, James S. Schoff Civil War Collection, William L. Clements Library, University of Michigan, Ann Arbor, MI

324 "Letter, J.L. Stuart to Mary A. Harper, John Harper, Charles Harper, Mary A. Harper and Nancy Glass Nall, 30 Jun 1863", *John L. Stuart Papers*, David M. Rubenstein Library, Duke University, Durham, NC

325 "Letter, M.C. Yow to Catherine Yow and Elizabeth Randall Maness Yow, 3, Jul 1863", Nancy Yow Holt, *I Hope You Will All Remember Me: The Civil War Letters of Matthew C. Yow*. (Jacksonville, IL: 2024), 51-53. Original letters in possession of Larry R. Yow.

326 "Letter, J.L. Stuart to Mary A. Harper, 4 Jul 1863", *John L. Stuart Papers*, David M. Rubenstein Library, Duke University, Durham, NC

327 "Letter, Noah Deaton to Sarah Jane McDonald, 8 Jul 1863", *Noah Deaton Papers*, James S. Schoff Civil War Collection, William L. Clements Library, University of Michigan, Ann Arbor, MI

328 "Letter, Mary Patterson to Duncan A.W. Patterson, 10 Jul 1863", *Civil War Letters*, Vertical Files, Moore County Library, Carthage, NC

329 "Letter, Joseph C. Fry to Absalom and Cherry Fry, 11 Jul 1863", *Private Collection*, in possession of Amy Caddell Sadler Seitz, Southern Pines, NC

330 "Letter, Mastin C. Phillips to Emeline Phillips,11 Jul 1863", *The Phillips Family and the Civil War Vol. I*, Moore County Library, Carthage, NC

331 "Letter, M.C. Yow to Catherine Yow and children, 18 Jul 1863", Nancy Yow Holt, *I Hope You Will All Remember Me: The Civil War Letters of Matthew C. Yow*. (Jacksonville, IL: 2024), 53-54. Original letters in possession of Larry R. Yow.

332 "Letter, J.L. Stuart to Mary A. Harper, John Harper, Charles Harper and Mary A. Harper, 22 Jul 1863", *John L. Stuart Papers*, David M. Rubenstein Library, Duke University, Durham, NC

333 "Letter, William H. Patterson to F.A.V. Patterson, 25 Jul 1863", *Civil War Letters*, Vertical Files, Moore County Library, Carthage, NC

334 "Letter, M.C. Yow to Catherine Yow and children, 30 Jul 1863", Nancy Yow Holt, *I Hope You Will All Remember Me: The Civil War Letters of Matthew C. Yow*. (Jacksonville, IL: 2024), 55. Original letters in possession of Larry R. Yow.

335 "Letter, Jacob Gaster to Surgeon, Chimborazo Hospital, 30 Jul 1863", John C. Gaster, *Civil War Service Records*, accessed 2 Sep 2024, https://www.fold3.com/image/47473128/gaster-john-c-page-15-us-civil-war-service-records-cmsr-confederate-north-carolina-1861-1865

336 "Letter, M.C. Yow to Catherine Yow and children, n.d. Aug 1863", Nancy Yow Holt, *I Hope You Will All Remember Me: The Civil War Letters of Matthew C. Yow*. (Jacksonville, IL: 2024), 55-56, 58-59. Original letters in possession of Larry R. Yow.

337 "Letter, Baxter C. Phillips to Emeline Phillips, 3 Aug 1863", *The Phillips Family and the Civil War Vol. I*, Moore County Library, Carthage, NC

338 "Letter, J.L. Stuart to Mary A. Harper, 9 Aug 1863", *John L. Stuart Papers*, David M. Rubenstein Library, Duke University, Durham, NC

339 "Letter, Baxter C. Phillips to Rev. Lewis Phillips Jr. and Nancy Philips, 11 Aug 1863", *The Phillips Family and the Civil War Vol. I*, Moore County Library, Carthage, NC

340 "Letter, Noah Deaton to sister, 12 Aug 1863", *Noah Deaton Papers*, Sec. A Box 34 items 1-4 c.1, David M. Rubenstein Library, Duke University, Durham, NC

341 "Letter, M.C. Yow to Catherine Yow and children, 15 Aug 1863", Nancy Yow Holt, *I Hope You Will All Remember Me: The Civil War Letters of Matthew C. Yow*. (Jacksonville, IL: 2024), 56-58. Original letters in possession of Larry R. Yow.

342 "Letter, J.L. Stuart to John Harper, Mary A. Harper, Charles Harper, Mary A. Harper and Nancy Glass Nall, 16 Aug 1863", *John L. Stuart Papers*, David M. Rubenstein Library, Duke University, Durham, NC

343 "Letter, M.C. Yow to Catherine Yow and children, 21 Aug 1863", Nancy Yow Holt, *I Hope You Will All Remember Me: The Civil War Letters of Matthew C. Yow*. (Jacksonville, IL: 2024), 59-60. Original letters in possession of Larry R. Yow.

344 "Letter, M.C. Yow to Catherine Yow and children, 23 Aug 1863", Nancy Yow Holt, *I Hope You Will All Remember Me: The Civil War Letters of Matthew C. Yow*. (Jacksonville, IL: 2024), 60. Original letters in possession of Larry R. Yow.

345 "Letter, M.C. Yow to Catherine Yow and children, 24 Aug 1863", Nancy Yow Holt, *I Hope You Will All Remember Me: The Civil War Letters of Matthew C. Yow*. (Jacksonville, IL: 2024), 60-61. Original letters in possession of Larry R. Yow.

346 "Letter, J.L. Stuart to Mary A. Harper, 29 Aug 1863", *John L. Stuart Papers*, David M. Rubenstein Library, Duke University, Durham, NC

347 "Letter, J.L. Stuart to Mary A. Harper, 29 Aug 1863", *John L. Stuart Papers*, David M. Rubenstein Library, Duke University, Durham, NC

348 "Letter, J.L. Stuart to Mary A. Harper, 30 Aug 1863", *John L. Stuart Papers*, David M. Rubenstein Library, Duke University, Durham, NC

349 "Letter, M.C. Yow to Catherine Yow and children, 30 Aug 1863", Nancy Yow Holt, *I Hope You Will All Remember Me: The Civil War Letters of Matthew C. Yow*. (Jacksonville, IL: 2024), 61-62. Original letters in possession of Larry R. Yow.

350 "Letter, J.L. Stuart to Mary A. Harper and John Harper, 3 Sep 1863", *John L. Stuart Papers*, David M. Rubenstein Library, Duke University, Durham, NC

351 "Letter, Daniel McIntosh to A.S. Caddell, 7 Sep 1863", *Artemus S. Caddell Papers*, RUB Bay 0037:04 items 1-84 c.1, David M. Rubenstein Library, Duke University, Durham, NC

352 "Letter, M.C. Yow to Catherine Yow and children, 10 Sep 1863", Nancy Yow Holt, *I Hope You Will All Remember Me: The Civil War Letters of Matthew C. Yow*. (Jacksonville, IL: 2024), 77-78. Original letters in possession of Larry R. Yow.

353 "Letter, M.C. Yow to Catherine Yow and children, 17 Sep 1863", Nancy Yow Holt, *I Hope You Will All Remember Me: The Civil War Letters of Matthew C. Yow*. (Jacksonville, IL: 2024), 78. Original letters in possession of Larry R. Yow.

354 "Letter, M.C. Yow to Catherine Yow and children, 17 Sep 1863", Nancy Yow Holt, *I Hope You Will All Remember Me: The Civil War Letters of Matthew C. Yow*. (Jacksonville, IL: 2024), 79-80. Original letters in possession of Larry R. Yow.

355 "Letter, William J. McNeill to Angus McNeill, 18 Sep 1863", *Lacy Garner*, accessed 8 Jul 2024, https://web.archive.org/web/20200812225857/https://www.companyh26th.com/last-names-g-j.html

356 "Letter, Baxter C. Phillips to Elmira Phillips, 20 Sep 1863", *The Phillips Family and the Civil War Vol. I*, Moore County Library, Carthage, NC

357 "Letter, M.C. Yow to Catherine Yow and children, 20 Sep 1863", Nancy Yow Holt, *I Hope You Will All Remember Me: The Civil War Letters of Matthew C. Yow*. (Jacksonville, IL: 2024), 80-81. Original letters in possession of Larry R. Yow.

358 "Letter, M.C. Yow to Catherine Yow and children, 28 Sep 1863", Nancy Yow Holt, *I Hope You Will All Remember Me: The Civil War Letters of Matthew C. Yow*. (Jacksonville, IL: 2024), 82. Original letters in possession of Larry R. Yow.

359 "Letter, J.L. Stuart to John Harper and Charles Harper, 8 Oct 1863", *John L. Stuart Papers*, David M. Rubenstein Library, Duke University, Durham, NC

360 "Letter, M.C. Yow to Catherine Yow and children, 11 Oct 1863", Nancy Yow Holt, *I Hope You Will All Remember Me: The Civil War Letters of Matthew C. Yow*. (Jacksonville, IL: 2024), 83-84. Original letters in possession of Larry R. Yow.

361 "Letter, Noah Deaton to William Deaton, 17 Oct 1863", *Private Collection*, in possession of Mark Love, Sanford, NC

362 "Letter, William H. Patterson to F.A.V. Patterson, 17 Oct 1863", *Civil War Letters*, Vertical Files, Moore County Library, Carthage, NC

363 "Letter, M.C. Yow to Catherine Yow and children, 18 Oct 1863", Nancy Yow Holt, *I Hope You Will All Remember Me: The Civil War Letters of Matthew C. Yow*. (Jacksonville, IL: 2024), 84-86. Original letters in possession of Larry R. Yow.

364 "Letter, J.L. Stuart to Mary A. Harper and Charles Harper, 20 Oct 1863", *John L. Stuart Papers*, David M. Rubenstein Library, Duke University, Durham, NC

365 "Letter, M.C. Yow to Catherine Yow and children, n.d. Oct 1863", Nancy Yow Holt, *I Hope You Will All Remember Me: The Civil War Letters of Matthew C. Yow*. (Jacksonville, IL: 2024), 86. Original letters in possession of Larry R. Yow.

366 "Letter, M.C. Yow to Joseph Albright, 23 Oct 1863", Nancy Yow Holt, *I Hope You Will All Remember Me: The Civil War Letters of Matthew C. Yow*. (Jacksonville, IL: 2024), 86-88. Original letters in possession of Larry R. Yow.

367 "Letter, Baxter C. Phillips to Elmira Phillips, 24 Oct 1863", *The Phillips Family and the Civil War Vol. I*, Moore County Library, Carthage, NC

368 "Letter, J.L. Stuart to Mary A. Harper, 24 Oct 1863", *John L. Stuart Papers*, David M. Rubenstein Library, Duke University, Durham, NC

369 "Letter, M.C. Yow to Catherine Yow and children, 25 Oct 1863", Nancy Yow Holt, *I Hope You Will All Remember Me: The Civil War Letters of Matthew C. Yow*. (Jacksonville, IL: 2024), 88-89. Original letters in possession of Larry R. Yow.

370 "Letter, J.L. Stuart to John Harper, 25 Oct 1863", *John L. Stuart Papers*, David M. Rubenstein Library, Duke University, Durham, NC

371 "Letter, Henry C. Brown to Bryan Tyson, 26 Oct 1863", *Bryan Tyson Papers*, David M. Rubenstein Library, Duke University, Durham, NC

372 "Letter, J.L. Stuart to Mary A. Harper, 29 Oct 1863", *John L. Stuart Papers*, David M. Rubenstein Library, Duke University, Durham, NC

373 "Letter, William H. Patterson to F.A.V. Patterson, 2 Nov 1863", *Civil War Letters*, Vertical Files, Moore County Library, Carthage, NC

374 "Letter, W.K. Nunnery & Thomas Needham to Bryan Tyson, 3 Nov 1863", *Bryan Tyson Papers*, David M. Rubenstein Library, Duke University, Durham, NC

375 "Letter, J.L. Stuart to Mary A. Harper, John Harper, Charles Harper and Mary A. Harper, 4 Nov 1863", *John L. Stuart Papers*, David M. Rubenstein Library, Duke University, Durham, NC

376 "Letter, H.M. Tomlinson to Bryan Tyson, 7 Nov 1863", *Bryan Tyson Papers*, David M. Rubenstein Library, Duke University, Durham, NC

377 "Letter, Matthew Manis to Bryan Tyson, 10 Nov 1863", *Bryan Tyson Papers*, David M. Rubenstein Library, Duke University, Durham, NC

378 "Letter, Matthew Manis to Bryan Tyson, 14 Nov 1863", *Bryan Tyson Papers*, David M. Rubenstein Library, Duke University, Durham, NC

379 "Letter, William H. Patterson to F.A.V. Patterson, 14 Nov 1863", *Civil War Letters*, Vertical Files, Moore County Library, Carthage, NC

380 "Letter, M.C. Yow to Catherine Yow and children, 19 Nov 1863", Nancy Yow Holt, *I Hope You Will All Remember Me: The Civil War Letters of Matthew C. Yow*. (Jacksonville, IL: 2024), 89-90. Original letters in possession of Larry R. Yow.

381 "Letter, M.C. Yow to Catherine Yow and children, 20 Nov 1863", Nancy Yow Holt, *I Hope You Will All Remember Me: The Civil War Letters of Matthew C. Yow*. (Jacksonville, IL: 2024), 90-91. Original letters in possession of Larry R. Yow.

382 "Letter, Baxter C. Phillips to Emeline Phillips, 20 Nov 1863", *The Phillips Family and the Civil War Vol. I*, Moore County Library, Carthage, NC

383 "Letter, J.L. Stuart to Mary A. Harper, John Harper, Charles Harper and Nancy Glass Nall, 20 Nov 1863", *John L. Stuart Papers*, David M. Rubenstein Library, Duke University, Durham, NC

384 "Letter, J.L. Stuart to Mary A. Harper, 20 Nov 1863" *John L. Stuart Papers*, David M. Rubenstein Library, Duke University, Durham, NC

385 "Letter, William H. Patterson to F.A.V. Patterson, 24 Nov 1863", *Civil War Letters*, Vertical Files, Moore County Library, Carthage, NC

386 "Letter, Henry C. Brown to Bryan Tyson, 25 Nov 1863", *Bryan Tyson Papers*, David M. Rubenstein Library, Duke University, Durham, NC

387 "Letter, A.K. Pearce to Bryan Tyson. 26 Nov 1863", *Bryan Tyson Papers*, David M. Rubenstein Library, Duke University, Durham, NC

388 "Letter, M.C. Yow to Catherine Yow and children, n.d. Dec 1863", Nancy Yow Holt, *I Hope You Will All Remember Me: The Civil War Letters of Matthew C. Yow*. (Jacksonville, IL: 2024), 91. Original letters in possession of Larry R. Yow.

389 "Letter, M.C. Yow to Catherine Yow and children, n.d. Dec 1863", Nancy Yow Holt, *I Hope You Will All Remember Me: The Civil War Letters of Matthew C. Yow*. (Jacksonville, IL: 2024), 91-92. Original letters in possession of Larry R. Yow.

390 "Letter, J.L. Stuart to Mary A. Harper and John Harper, 18 Dec 1863" *John L. Stuart Papers*, David M. Rubenstein Library, Duke University, Durham, NC

391 "Letter, J.L. Stuart to Mary A. Harper, John Harper, Charles Harper, Mary A. Harper and Nancy Nall, 21 Dec 1863", *John L. Stuart Papers*, David M. Rubenstein Library, Duke University, Durham, NC

392 "Letter, William H. Patterson to F.A.V. Patterson, 21 Dec 1863", *Civil War Letters*, Vertical Files, Moore County Library, Carthage, NC

393 "Letter, Baxter C. Phillips to friend 30 Dec 1863", *The Phillips Family and the Civil War Vol. I*, Moore County Library, Carthage, NC

394 "Letter, J.L. Stuart to Charles E. Harper, 3 Jan 1864", *John L. Stuart Papers*, David M. Rubenstein Library, Duke University, Durham, NC

395 "Letter, Doctor Franklin Wilkie to Lewis Phillips Jr., 4 Jan 1864", *The Phillips Family and the Civil War Vol. I*, Moore County Library, Carthage, NC

396 "Letter, M.C. Yow to Catherine Yow and children, 5 Jan 1864", Nancy Yow Holt, *I Hope You Will All Remember Me: The Civil War Letters of Matthew C. Yow*. (Jacksonville, IL: 2024), 95-96. Original letters in possession of Larry R. Yow.

397 "Letter, William H. Patterson to Iver D. Patterson, 10 Jan 1864", *Civil War Letters*, Vertical Files, Moore County Library, Carthage, NC

398 "Letter, Thomas Needham to Bryan Tyson, 11 Jan 1864", *Bryan Tyson Papers*, David M. Rubenstein Library, Duke University, Durham, NC

399 "Letter, Henry C. Brown to Bryan Tyson, 11 Jan 1864", *Bryan Tyson Papers*, David M. Rubenstein Library, Duke University, Durham, NC

400 "Letter, A.K. Pearce to Bryan Tyson, 16 Jan 1864", *Bryan Tyson Papers*, David M. Rubenstein Library, Duke University, Durham, NC

401 "Letter, H.A. Bridges to Bryan Tyson, 16 Jan 1864", *Bryan Tyson Papers*, David M. Rubenstein Library, Duke University, Durham, NC

402 "Letter, M.C. Yow to Catherine Yow and children, 16 Jan 1864", Nancy Yow Holt, *I Hope You Will All Remember Me: The Civil War Letters of Matthew C. Yow*. (Jacksonville, IL: 2024), 96-97. Original letters in possession of Larry R. Yow.

403 "Letter, J.L. Stuart to Mary A. Harper, 17 Jan 1864", *John L. Stuart Papers*, David M. Rubenstein Library, Duke University, Durham, NC

404 "Letter, J.L. Stuart to Mary A. Harper and John Harper, 18 Jan 1864"[,] *John L. Stuart Papers*, David M. Rubenstein Library, Duke University, Durham, NC

405 "Letter, William H. Patterson to F.A.V. Patterson, 19 Jan 1864", *Civil War Letters*, Vertical Files, Moore County Library, Carthage, NC

406 "Letter, J.L. Stuart to Mary A. Harper, 21 Jan 1864 and 1 Feb 1864", *John L. Stuart Papers*, David M. Rubenstein Library, Duke University, Durham, NC

407 "Letter, M.C. Yow to Catherine Yow and children, 27 Jan 1864", Nancy Yow Holt, *I Hope You Will All Remember Me: The Civil War Letters of Matthew C. Yow*. (Jacksonville, IL: 2024), 97-99. Original letters in possession of Larry R. Yow.
408 "Letter, William H. Patterson to F.A.V. Patterson, 2 Feb 1864", *Civil War Letters*, Vertical Files, Moore County Library, Carthage, NC
409 "Letter, M.C. Phillips to Bryan Tyson, 6 Feb 1864", *Bryan Tyson Papers*, David M. Rubenstein Library, Duke University, Durham, NC
410 "Letter, J.L. Stuart to Mary A. Harper, 5 Feb 1864", *John L. Stuart Papers*, David M. Rubenstein Library, Duke University, Durham, NC
411 "Letter, J.L. Stuart to Mary A. Harper, 7 Feb 1864", *John L. Stuart Papers*, David M. Rubenstein Library, Duke University, Durham, NC
412 "Letter, M.C. Yow to Joseph Albright, 14-15 Feb 1864", Nancy Yow Holt, *I Hope You Will All Remember Me: The Civil War Letters of Matthew C. Yow*. (Jacksonville, IL: 2024), 100-101. Original letters in possession of Larry R. Yow.
413 "Letter, J.L. Stuart to Charles Harper **and** Mary A. Harper, 19 Feb 1864", *John L. Stuart Papers*, David M. Rubenstein Library, Duke University, Durham, NC
414 "Letter, J.L. Stuart to Mary A. Harper, John Harper, Charles Harper and Mary A. Harper, 22 Feb 1864", *John L. Stuart Papers*, David M. Rubenstein Library, Duke University, Durham, NC
415 "Letter, M.C. Phillips to Bryan Tyson, 26 Feb 1864", *Bryan Tyson Papers*, David M. Rubenstein Library, Duke University, Durham, NC
416 "Letter, H.C. Brown to Bryan Tyson, 26 Feb 1864", *Bryan Tyson Papers*, David M. Rubenstein Library, Duke University, Durham, NC
417 "Letter, D.J. Shields to B.J. Shields, 29 Feb 1864", *Private Collection*, in possession of David McCallum, Carthage, NC
418 "Letter, Duncan Cole to John Harper, 3 Mar 1864", *John L. Stuart Papers*, David M. Rubenstein Library, Duke University, Durham, NC
419 "Letter, M.C. Yow to Catherine Yow and children, 7 Mar 1864", Nancy Yow Holt, *I Hope You Will All Remember Me: The Civil War Letters of Matthew C. Yow*. (Jacksonville, IL: 2024), 101. Original letters in possession of Larry R. Yow.
420 "Letter, James O.A.. Kelly to Nannie Sloan Kelly, 9-10 Mar 1864", *James Oscar Abner Kelly Papers*, PC. 1760, Private Collections, State Archives of North Carolina, Raleigh, NC
421 "Letter, M.C. Yow to Catherine Yow and children, 12 Mar 1864", Nancy Yow Holt, *I Hope You Will All Remember Me: The Civil War Letters of Matthew C. Yow*. (Jacksonville, IL: 2024), 102-103. Original letters in possession of Larry R. Yow.
422 "Letter, Neill A. Baker to Sarah Jane Baker, 15 Mar 1864", *Spared & Shared*, accessed 27 Jul 2024, https://sparedshared22.wordpress.com/2021/12/17/1864-neill-archibald-baker-to-sarah-jane-parham-baker/
423 "Letter, William H. Patterson to F.A.V. Patterson, 15 Mar 1864", *Civil War Letters*, Vertical Files, Moore County Library, Carthage, NC
424 "Letter, J.L. Stuart to Mary A. Harper, 20 Mar 1864", *John L. Stuart Papers*, David M. Rubenstein Library, Duke University, Durham, NC
425 "Letter, J.L. Stuart to John Harper, 20 Mar 1864", *John L. Stuart Papers*, David M. Rubenstein Library, Duke University, Durham, NC
426 "Letter, Moore Co. Citizens to 7th Congressional District, 25 Mar 1864", *Artemus S. Caddell Papers*, RUB Bay 0037:04 items 1-84 c.1, David M. Rubenstein Library, Duke University, Durham, NC
427 "Letter, J.L. Stuart to Mary A. Harper, John Harper and Charles E. Harper, 3 Apr 1864", *John L. Stuart Papers*, David M. Rubenstein Library, Duke University, Durham, NC
428 "Letter, M.C. Yow to Joseph Albright, 4 Apr 1864", Nancy Yow Holt, *I Hope You Will All Remember Me: The Civil War Letters of Matthew C. Yow*. (Jacksonville, IL: 2024), 103-105. Original letters in possession of Larry R. Yow.
429 "Letter, John Harper to D.S. Barrett, 10 Apr 1864", *John L. Stuart Papers*, David M. Rubenstein Library, Duke University, Durham, NC
430 "Letter, J.L. Stuart to Mary A. Harper, 12 Apr 1864", *John L. Stuart Papers*, David M. Rubenstein Library, Duke University, Durham, NC
431 "Letter, J.L. Stuart to Mary A. Harper, John Harper and Charles E. Harper, 14 Apr 1864", *John L. Stuart Papers*, David M. Rubenstein Library, Duke University, Durham, NC
432 "Letter, J.L. Stuart to Mary A. Harper and Charles E. Harper, 17 Apr 1864", *John L. Stuart Papers*, David M. Rubenstein Library, Duke University, Durham, NC
433 "Letter, J.L. Stuart to John Harper, 18 Apr 1864", *John L. Stuart Papers*, David M. Rubenstein Library, Duke University, Durham, NC
434 "Letter, R.E. Perry to C.E. Harper, John Harper and Charles E. Harper, 14 May 1864", *John L. Stuart Papers*, David M. Rubenstein Library, Duke University, Durham, NC
435 "Letter, J.L. Stuart to Mary A. Harper, 23 May 1864", *John L. Stuart Papers*, David M. Rubenstein Library, Duke University, Durham, NC
436 "Letter, J.L. Stuart to Mary A. Harper, 29 May 1864", *John L. Stuart Papers*, David M. Rubenstein Library, Duke University, Durham, NC
437 "Letter, A.S. Caddell to Martha Sullivan, 3 Jun 1864", *Artemus S. Caddell Papers*, RUB Bay 0037:04 items 1-84 c.1, David M. Rubenstein Library, Duke University, Durham, NC
438 "Letter, William R. Jackson to Catherine Jackson, 6 Jun 1864" *1885 Confederate Pension Application*, accessed 27 Feb 2025, https://digital.ncdcr.gov/Documents/Detail/william-r.-jackson-harnett-county/306013?item=306020
439 "Letter, William R. Jackson to William McLeod, 6 Jun 1864" *1885 Confederate Pension Application*, accessed 27 Feb 2025, https://digital.ncdcr.gov/Documents/Detail/william-r.-jackson-harnett-county/306013?item=306022
440 "Letter, H.M. McDonald to Sarah Jane McDonald, 7 Jun 1864", *Spared & Shared*, accessed 27 Jul 2024, https://sparedshared22.wordpress.com/2022/04/08/1864-hugh-m-mcdonald-to-sarah-jane-mcdonald/
441 "Letter, S.W. Brewer to R.B. Paschal, 12 Jun 1864", *Spared & Shared*, accessed 27 Jul 2024, https://sparedcreative21.art.blog/2020/03/29/1864-stephen-wiley-brewer-to-richard-bray-paschal/
442 "Letter, J.L. Stuart to Mary A. Harper, 14 Jun 1864", *John L. Stuart Papers*, David M. Rubenstein Library, Duke University, Durham, NC
443 "Letter, J.H. Siddons to Catherine Jackson, 19 Jun 1864" *1885 Confederate Pension Application*, accessed 27 Feb 2025, https://digital.ncdcr.gov/Documents/Detail/william-r.-jackson-harnett-county/306013?item=306024
444 "Letter, W.R. Barrett to Bryan Tyson, 27 Jun 1864", *Bryan Tyson Papers*, David M. Rubenstein Library, Duke University, Durham, NC
445 "Letter, D.C. Wilson to Bryan Tyson, 27 Jun 1864", *Bryan Tyson Papers*, David M. Rubenstein Library, Duke University, Durham, NC
446 "Letter, F.B. Fry to Lydia Shields Fry, 28 Jun 1864", *Civil War Letters*, Vertical Files, Moore County Library, Carthage, NC
447 "Letter, Murdo McLeod to Bryan Tyson, 6 Jul 1864", *Bryan Tyson Papers*, David M. Rubenstein Library, Duke University, Durham, NC
448 "Letter, Murdo McLeod to Bryan Tyson, 6 Jul 1864", *Bryan Tyson Papers*, David M. Rubenstein Library, Duke University, Durham, NC
449 "Letter, Baxter C. Phillips to Nancy Phillips, 12 Jul 1864", *The Phillips Family and the Civil War Vol. I*, Moore County Library, Carthage, NC
450 "Letter, Mastin C. Phillips to Lewis Phillips Jr., 12 Jul 1864", *The Phillips Family and the Civil War Vol. I*, Moore County Library, Carthage, NC
451 "Letter, Murdo McLeod to Bryan Tyson, 27 Jul 1864", *Bryan Tyson Papers*, David M. Rubenstein Library, Duke University, Durham, NC
452 "Letter, unknown to John B. Ray, 29 Jul 1864", *Nevin Ray Papers*, Sec. A Box 110 items 1-30 c.1, David M. Rubenstein Library, Duke University, Durham, NC
453 "Letter, Jas. R. Jones to Bryan Tyson, 1 Aug 1864", *Bryan Tyson Papers*, David M. Rubenstein Library, Duke University, Durham, NC
454 "Letter, Matthew Maness to Bryan Tyson, 2 Aug 1864", *Bryan Tyson Papers*, David M. Rubenstein Library, Duke University, Durham, NC

455 "Letter, Noah Deaton to William Deaton, 2 Aug 1864", *Noah Deaton Papers*, Sec. A Box 34 items 1-4 c.1, David M. Rubenstein Library, Duke University, Durham, NC

456 "Letter, C.D. Caddell to A.S. Caddell, 2 Aug 1864", *Artemus S. Caddell Papers*, RUB Bay 0037:04 items 1-84 c.1, David M. Rubenstein Library, Duke University, Durham, NC

457 "Letter, A.M. Dunlap to A.S. Caddell, 2 Aug 1864", *Artemus S. Caddell Papers*, RUB Bay 0037:04 items 1-84 c.1, David M. Rubenstein Library, Duke University, Durham, NC

458 "Letter, N. McIntosh to Bryan Tyson, 8 Aug 1864", *Bryan Tyson Papers*, David M. Rubenstein Library, Duke University, Durham, NC

459 "Letter, Jas. R. Jones to Bryan Tyson, 9 Aug 1864", *Bryan Tyson Papers*, David M. Rubenstein Library, Duke University, Durham, NC

460 "Letter, Baxter C. Phillips to Elmira Phillips, 10 Aug 1864", *The Phillips Family and the Civil War Vol. I*, Moore County Library, Carthage, NC

461 "Letter, J.L. Stuart to Mary A. Harper, 10 Aug 1864", *John L. Stuart Papers*, David M. Rubenstein Library, Duke University, Durham, NC

462 "Letter, W.W. Gilliand to Charity Gilliand, 16 Aug 1864", *Civil War Letters*, Vertical Files, Moore County Library, Carthage, NC

463 "Letter, Jas. R. Jones to Bryan Tyson, 17 Aug 1864", *Bryan Tyson Papers*, David M. Rubenstein Library, Duke University, Durham, NC

464 "Letter, H.C. Brown to Bryan Tyson, 18 Aug 1864", *Bryan Tyson Papers*, David M. Rubenstein Library, Duke University, Durham, NC

465 "Letter, James Tyson to Bryan Tyson, 19 Aug 1864", *Bryan Tyson Papers*, David M. Rubenstein Library, Duke University, Durham, NC

466 "Letter, Mary Caddell and Joseph Caddell to A.S. Caddell, 19 Aug 1864", *Artemus S. Caddell Papers*, RUB Bay 0037:04 items 1-84 c.1, David M. Rubenstein Library, Duke University, Durham, NC

467 "Letter, A.M. Dunlap to A.S. Caddell, 22 Aug 1864", *Artemus S. Caddell Papers*, RUB Bay 0037:04 items 1-84 c.1, David M. Rubenstein Library, Duke University, Durham, NC

468 "Letter, J.L. Stuart to Mary A. Harper, 22 Aug 1864", *John L. Stuart Papers*, David M. Rubenstein Library, Duke University, Durham, NC

469 "Letter, Daniel J. Shields to W.W. Shields, 26 Aug 1864", *Private Collection*, in possession of David McCallum, Carthage, NC

470 "Letter, A. Vick to W.W. Shields, 26 Aug 1864", *Private Collection*, in possession of David McCallum, Carthage, NC

471 "Letter, Mary Shields to John W. Shields, 28 Aug 1864", *Civil War Letters*, Vertical Files, Moore County Library, Carthage, NC

472 "Letter, J.W. McPherson to Bryan Tyson, 31 Aug 1864", *Bryan Tyson Papers*, David M. Rubenstein Library, Duke University, Durham, NC

473 "Letter, Jas. R. Jones to Bryan Tyson, 3 Sep 1864", *Bryan Tyson Papers*, David M. Rubenstein Library, Duke University, Durham, NC

474 "Letter, J.L. Stuart to Mary A. Harper, 4 Sep 1864", *John L. Stuart Papers*, David M. Rubenstein Library, Duke University, Durham, NC

475 "Letter, C.D. Caddell to A.S. Caddell, 5 Sep 1864", *Artemus S. Caddell Papers*, RUB Bay 0037:04 items 1-84 c.1, David M. Rubenstein Library, Duke University, Durham, NC

476 "Letter, D.C. Wilson to Bryan Tyson, 7 Sep 1864", *Bryan Tyson Papers*, David M. Rubenstein Library, Duke University, Durham, NC

477 "Letter, Joseph J. Tyson to Bryan Tyson, 8 Sep 1864", *Bryan Tyson Papers*, David M. Rubenstein Library, Duke University, Durham, NC

478 "Letter, Rany G. Caddell to A.S. Caddell, 9 Sep 1864", *Artemus S. Caddell Papers*, RUB Bay 0037:04 items 1-84 c.1, David M. Rubenstein Library, Duke University, Durham, NC

479 "Letter, J.L. Stuart to Mary A. Harper, 9 and 11 Sep 1864", *John L. Stuart Papers*, David M. Rubenstein Library, Duke University, Durham, NC

480 "Letter, Murdo McLeod to Bryan Tyson, 10 Sep 1864", *Bryan Tyson Papers*, David M. Rubenstein Library, Duke University, Durham, NC

481 "Letter, Jas. R. Jones to Bryan Tyson, 16 Sep 1861", *Bryan Tyson Papers*, David M. Rubenstein Library, Duke University, Durham, NC

482 "Letter, A.M. Dunlap to A.S. Caddell, 16 Sep 1864", *Artemus S. Caddell Papers*, RUB Bay 0037:04 items 1-84 c.1, David M. Rubenstein Library, Duke University, Durham, NC

483 "Letter, J.L. Stuart to Mary A. Harper, 17 Sep 1864", *John L. Stuart Papers*, David M. Rubenstein Library, Duke University, Durham, NC

484 "Letter, J.L. Stuart to Charles E. Harper and Mary A. Harper, 17 Sep 1864", *John L. Stuart Papers*, David M. Rubenstein Library, Duke University, Durham, NC

485 "Letter, J.L. Stuart to Mary A. Harper, 17 Sep 1864", *John L. Stuart Papers*, David M. Rubenstein Library, Duke University, Durham, NC

486 "Letter, Mary Shields to John W. Shields, 20 Sep 1864", *Civil War Letters*, Vertical Files, Moore County Library, Carthage, NC

487 "Letter, J.W. McPherson to Bryan Tyson, 20 Sep 1864", *Bryan Tyson Papers*, David M. Rubenstein Library, Duke University, Durham, NC

488 "Letter, Rany G. Caddell to A.S. Caddell, 22 Sep 1864", *Artemus S. Caddell Papers*, RUB Bay 0037:04 items 1-84 c.1, David M. Rubenstein Library, Duke University, Durham, NC

489 "Letter, J.L. Stuart to Mary A. Harper, 22 Sep 1864", *John L. Stuart Papers*, David M. Rubenstein Library, Duke University, Durham, NC

490 "Letter, J.L. Stuart to Mary A. Harper and John Harper, 26 Sep 1864", *John L. Stuart Papers*, David M. Rubenstein Library, Duke University, Durham, NC

491 "Letter, Mastin C. Phillips to Lewis and Nancy Phillips, 29 Sep 1864 ", *The Phillips Family and the Civil War Vol. I*, Moore County Library, Carthage, NC

492 "Letter, H.C. Brown to Bryan Tyson, 3 Oct 1864", *Bryan Tyson Papers*, David M. Rubenstein Library, Duke University, Durham, NC

493 "Letter, Rany G. Caddell to A.S. Caddell, 8 Oct 1864", *Artemus S. Caddell Papers*, RUB Bay 0037:04 items 1-84 c.1, David M. Rubenstein Library, Duke University, Durham, NC

494 "Letter, Noah Deaton to William Deaton, 10 Oct 1864", *Noah Deaton Papers*, Sec. A Box 34 items 1-4 c.1, David M. Rubenstein Library, Duke University, Durham, NC

495 "Letter, C.D. Caddell to A.S. Caddell, 11 Oct 1864", *Artemus S. Caddell Papers*, RUB Bay 0037:04 items 1-84 c.1, David M. Rubenstein Library, Duke University, Durham, NC

496 "Letter, J.L. Stuart to Mary A. Harper, 12 Oct 1864", *John L. Stuart Papers*, David M. Rubenstein Library, Duke University, Durham, NC

497 "Letter, J.L. Stuart to Mary A. Harper, 16 Oct 1864", *John L. Stuart Papers*, David M. Rubenstein Library, Duke University, Durham, NC

498 "Letter, R.A. Cole to Gov. Zebulon Vance, 17 Oct 1864", *Richard A. Cole Papers*, PC. 1609, Private Collections, State Archives of North Carolina, Raleigh, NC

499 "Letter, James C. Davis to N.R. Brady, Nov 1864. Lois Smith Phillips and Carol Smith Purvis, *The Brady Family of Moore and Chatham Counties.* (Charlotte, NC: Herb Eaton Historical Publications, 1987), 4-13

500 "Letter, R.P. White to Mary E. Shields, 3 Nov 1864", *Civil War Letters*, Vertical Files, Moore County Library, Carthage, NC

501 "Letter, J.L. Stuart to Mary A. Harper, 10 Nov 1864", *John L. Stuart Papers*, David M. Rubenstein Library, Duke University, Durham, NC

502 "Letter, J.L. Stuart to John Harper, Charles Harper and Mary A. Harper, 10 Nov 1864", *John L. Stuart Papers*, David M. Rubenstein Library, Duke University, Durham, NC

503 "Letter, A.P. Williams to A.S. Caddell, 17 Nov 1864", *Artemus S. Caddell Papers*, RUB Bay 0037:04 items 1-84 c.1, David M. Rubenstein Library, Duke University, Durham, NC

504 "Letter, J.W. McPherson to Bryan Tyson, 21 Nov 1864", *Bryan Tyson Papers*, David M. Rubenstein Library, Duke University, Durham, NC

505 "Letter, J.L. Stuart to Mary A. Harper and John Harper, 21 Nov 1864", *John L. Stuart Papers*, David M. Rubenstein Library, Duke University, Durham, NC

506 "Letter, Kelly H. Trogdon to Bryan Tyson, 22 Nov 1864", *Bryan Tyson Papers*, David M. Rubenstein Library, Duke University, Durham, NC

507 "Letter, Nelson Hunsucker to Bryan Tyson, 25 Nov 1864", *Bryan Tyson Papers*, David M. Rubenstein Library, Duke University, Durham, NC

508 "Letter, J.J. Tyson to Bryan Tyson, 25 Nov 1864", *Bryan Tyson Papers*, David M. Rubenstein Library, Duke University, Durham, NC

509 "Letter, J.W. McPherson to Bryan Tyson, 26 Nov 1864", *Bryan Tyson Papers*, David M. Rubenstein Library, Duke University, Durham, NC

510 "Letter, Manly Brady to Hester Brady, 27 Nov 1864". Lois Smith Phillips and Carol Smith Purvis, *The Brady Family of Moore and Chatham Counties.* (Charlotte, NC: Herb Eaton Historical Publications, 1987), 4-38.

511 "Letter, Henry Brown to Bryan Tyson" *Bryan Tyson Papers*, David M. Rubenstein Library, Duke University, Durham, NC

512 "Letter, Spain Williams to Bryan Tyson, 2 Dec 1864", *Bryan Tyson Papers*, David M. Rubenstein Library, Duke University, Durham, NC

513 "Letter, C.C. Harrison to Bryan Tyson, 3 Dec 1864", *Bryan Tyson Papers*, David M. Rubenstein Library, Duke University, Durham, NC
514 "Letter, T.J. Hogan to Bryan Tyson, 5 Dec 1864", *Bryan Tyson Papers*, David M. Rubenstein Library, Duke University, Durham, NC
515 "Letter, Connor D. Groce to Bryan Tyson, 6 Dec 1864", *Bryan Tyson Papers*, David M. Rubenstein Library, Duke University, Durham, NC
516 "Letter, John W. McPherson to Bryan Tyson, 6 Dec 1864", *Bryan Tyson Papers*, David M. Rubenstein Library, Duke University, Durham, NC
517 "Letter, D.C. Wilson to Bryan Tyson, 7 Dec 1864", *Bryan Tyson Papers*, David M. Rubenstein Library, Duke University, Durham, NC
518 "Letter, James R. Jones to Bryan Tyson, 11 Dec 1864", *Bryan Tyson Papers*, David M. Rubenstein Library, Duke University, Durham, NC
519 "Letter, James R. Jones to Bryan Tyson, 14 Dec 1864", *Bryan Tyson Papers*, David M. Rubenstein Library, Duke University, Durham, NC
520 "Letter, John W. McPherson to Bryan Tyson, 16 Dec 1864", *Bryan Tyson Papers*, David M. Rubenstein Library, Duke University, Durham, NC
521 "Letter, T.J. Hogan to Bryan Tyson, 19 Dec 1864", *Bryan Tyson Papers*, David M. Rubenstein Library, Duke University, Durham, NC
522 "Letter, W.A. Vuncannon to Bryan Tyson, 20 Dec 1864", *Bryan Tyson Papers*, David M. Rubenstein Library, Duke University, Durham, NC
523 "Letter, Isaac Roberts to Bryan Tyson, 21 Dec 1864", *Bryan Tyson Papers*, David M. Rubenstein Library, Duke University, Durham, NC
524 "Letter, Matthew Cagle to Bryan Tyson, 26 Dec 1864", *Bryan Tyson Papers*, David M. Rubenstein Library, Duke University, Durham, NC
525 "Letter, J.W. McPherson to Bryan Tyson, 29 Dec 1864", *Bryan Tyson Papers*, David M. Rubenstein Library, Duke University, Durham, NC
526 "Letter, J.L. Stuart to Mary A. Harper and John Harper, 4 Jan 1865", *John L. Stuart Papers*, David M. Rubenstein Library, Duke University, Durham, NC
527 "Letter, James Tyson to Bryan Tyson, 6 Jan 1865", *Bryan Tyson Papers*, David M. Rubenstein Library, Duke University, Durham, NC
528 "Letter, Eliza Ann Tyson to Bryan Tyson, 8 Dec 1864" *Bryan Tyson Papers*, David M. Rubenstein Library, Duke University, Durham, NC
529 "Letter, Thomas J. Hogan to Bryan Tyson, 14 Jan 1865", *Bryan Tyson Papers*, David M. Rubenstein Library, Duke University, Durham, NC
530 "Letter, Thomas J. Hogan to Bryan Tyson, 16 Jan 1865", *Bryan Tyson Papers*, David M. Rubenstein Library, Duke University, Durham, NC
531 "Letter, Neill Kidd to Bryan Tyson, 16 Jan 1865", *Bryan Tyson Papers*, David M. Rubenstein Library, Duke University, Durham, NC
532 "Letter, Spain Williams to Bryan Tyson, 17 Jan 1865", *Bryan Tyson Papers*, David M. Rubenstein Library, Duke University, Durham, NC
533 "Letter, J.L. Stuart to Mary A. Harper, 18 Jan 1865", *John L. Stuart Papers*, David M. Rubenstein Library, Duke University, Durham, NC
534 "Letter, H.C. Brown to Bryan Tyson, 19 Jan 1865", *Bryan Tyson Papers*, David M. Rubenstein Library, Duke University, Durham, NC
535 "Letter, J.L. Stuart to Mary A. Harper, 22 Jan 1865", *John L. Stuart Papers*, David M. Rubenstein Library, Duke University, Durham, NC
536 "Letter, Murdo McLeod to Bryan Tyson, 24 Jan 1865", *Bryan Tyson Papers*, David M. Rubenstein Library, Duke University, Durham, NC
537 "Letter, Bryan Tyson to E.M. Stanton, 26 Jan 1865", *Bryan Tyson Papers*, David M. Rubenstein Library, Duke University, Durham, NC
538 "Letter, Thomas J. Hogan to Bryan Tyson, 31 Jan 1865", *Bryan Tyson Papers*, David M. Rubenstein Library, Duke University, Durham, NC
539 "Letter, J.L. Stuart to Mary A. Harper and Charles E. Harper, 14 Feb 1865", *John L. Stuart Papers*, David M. Rubenstein Library, Duke University, Durham, NC
540 "Letter, Thomas J. Hogan to Bryan Tyson, 21 Feb 1865", *Bryan Tyson Papers*, David M. Rubenstein Library, Duke University, Durham, NC
541 "Letter, Matthew Cagle to Bryan Tyson, 5 Mar 1865", *Bryan Tyson Papers*, David M. Rubenstein Library, Duke University, Durham, NC
542 "Letter, Thomas J. Hogan to Bryan Tyson, 20 Mar 1865", *Bryan Tyson Papers*, David M. Rubenstein Library, Duke University, Durham, NC
543 "Letter, Henry C. Smith to Bryan Tyson, 4 Apr 1865", *Bryan Tyson Papers*, David M. Rubenstein Library, Duke University, Durham, NC
544 "Letter, Isaac Roberts to Bryan Tyson, 6 Apr 1865", *Bryan Tyson Papers*, David M. Rubenstein Library, Duke University, Durham, NC
545 "Letter, Jas. R. Jones to Bryan Tyson, 20 Apr 1865", *Bryan Tyson Papers*, David M. Rubenstein Library, Duke University, Durham, NC
546 "Letter, Isaac Roberts to Bryan Tyson, 4 May 1865", *Bryan Tyson Papers*, David M. Rubenstein Library, Duke University, Durham, NC
547 "Letter, G.W. Williams to Bryan Tyson, 16 May 1865", *Bryan Tyson Papers*, David M. Rubenstein Library, Duke University, Durham, NC
548 "Letter, G.W. Williams to Bryan Tyson, 10 Jun 1865", *Bryan Tyson Papers*, David M. Rubenstein Library, Duke University, Durham, NC
549 "Letter, Baxter C. Phillips to Lucy Norton, 27 Jun 1866", *The Phillips Family and the Civil War Vol. I*, Moore County Library, Carthage, NC
550 "1883-1919 Record of Pensions" *Moore County Records*, CR.068.923.001-CR.068.923.003, State Archives of North Carolina, Raleigh, NC
551 Garrett Jones and Robert C. Kenzer. "Confederate Pensions." *NCpedia*. State Library of NC. Revised by SLNC Government & Heritage Library. accessed 21 Jun 2025. https://www.ncpedia.org/confederate-pensions
552 "List of Pensioners" *The Carthage Blade*, 8 Nov 1905, https://www.newspapers.com/image/61598356
553 "Sixty Names on the Pension List" *The Moore County News*, 16 Jun 1921, https://newspapers.digitalnc.org/lccn/sn92074101/1921-06-16/ed-1/seq-9
554 "14 Veterans of Civil War Live in Moore County" *The Moore County News*, 21 Jun 1928, https://newspapers.digitalnc.org/lccn/sn92074101/1928-06-21/ed-1/seq-1
555 "Vets Get Their Pension Checks" *The Moore County News*, 20 Jun 1929, https://newspapers.digitalnc.org/lccn/sn92074101/1929-06-20/ed-1/seq-1
556 "Pensions for Veterans" *The Sanford Express*, 9 Dec 1910, https://www.newspapers.com/image/1181313460
557 "Christmas Presents" *The Sanford Express*, 15 Dec 1916, https://newspapers.digitalnc.org/lccn/sn89071020/1916-12-15/ed-1/seq-3
558 "Pensions for Veterans" *The Sanford Express*, 21 Dec 1917, https://www.newspapers.com/image/1181747058
559 "Money for Veterans" *The Sanford Express*, 14 Dec 1923, https://www.newspapers.com/image/1181072136
560 "Vouchers for Veterans and Widows" *The Sanford Express*, 19 Dec 1924, https://www.newspapers.com/image/1181079132
561 "Confederate Veterans and Widows Get Checks" *The Sanford Express*, 16 Jun 1927, https://www.newspapers.com/image/1181542107
562 "Pensions Here for Veterans and Widows" *The Sanford Express*, 20 Dec 1928, https://www.newspapers.com/image/1181543025
563 "Vouchers Being Issued to Vets and Widows" *The Sanford Express*, 22 Dec 1927, https://www.newspapers.com/image/1181542313
564 "Pension Checks For Veterans" *The Sanford Express*, 20 Jun 1929, https://www.newspapers.com/image/1181372598
565 "Lee Confederate Vets Given Pension Checks" *The Sanford Express*, 20 Jun 1929, https://www.newspapers.com/image/1181405576
566 "Veterans and Widows Get Semi-Annual Pension Sum" *The Sanford Express*, 5 Jan 1933, https://www.newspapers.com/image/1181404533
567 "7th NC Congressional District Records, 1862-1865", *CSA Bureau of Conscription*, Southern Historical Collection, Wilson Special Collections, University of North Carolina, Chapel Hill, NC (#170), https://catalog.lib.unc.edu/catalog/UNCb2366595

568 "John McF. Baker" *1865-1867 Confederate Amnesty Papers*, accessed 14 Jun 2024, https://www.fold3.com/file/22575138/baker-john-mcf-us-confederate-amnesty-papers-1865-1867

569 "William C. Campbell" *1865-1867 Confederate Amnesty Papers*, accessed 14 Jun 2024, https://www.fold3.com/file/22572393/campbell-william-c-us-confederate-amnesty-papers-1865-1867

570 "J.L. Caveness" *1865-1867 Confederate Amnesty Papers*, accessed 14 Jun 2024, https://www.fold3.com/file/22573252/caveness-j-l-us-confederate-amnesty-papers-1865-1867

571 "George W. Clark" *1865-1867 Confederate Amnesty Papers*, accessed 14 Jun 2024, https://www.fold3.com/file/22560508/clark-george-w-us-confederate-amnesty-papers-1865-1867

572 "John B. Cole" *1865-1867 Confederate Amnesty Papers*, accessed 14 Jun 2024, https://www.fold3.com/file/22562057/coles-john-b-us-confederate-amnesty-papers-1865-1867

573 "James C. Dowd" *1865-1867 Confederate Amnesty Papers*, accessed 14 Jun 2024, https://www.fold3.com/file/22569764/dowd-jas-c-us-confederate-amnesty-papers-1865-1867

574 "Edmund Garner" *1865-1867 Confederate Amnesty Papers*, 29 Nov 2023, https://www.fold3.com/file/22613410/garner-edmond-us-confederate-amnesty-papers-1865-1867

575 "A.A. Harrington" *1865-1867 Confederate Amnesty Papers*, accessed 14 Jun 2024, https://www.fold3.com/file/22618685/harrington-a-a-us-confederate-amnesty-papers-1865-1867

576 "John C. Jackson" *1865-1867 Confederate Amnesty Papers*, accessed 14 Jun 2024, https://www.fold3.com/file/22583971/jackson-john-c-us-confederate-amnesty-papers-1865-1867

577 "W.T. Jenkins" *1865-1867 Confederate Amnesty Papers*, accessed 14 Jun 2024, https://www.fold3.com/file/22584677/jenkins-w-t-us-confederate-amnesty-papers-1865-1867

578 "Alexander Kelly" *1865-1867 Confederate Amnesty Papers*, accessed 14 Jun 2024, https://www.fold3.com/file/22587351/kelly-alexander-us-confederate-amnesty-papers-1865-1867

579 "L.W. Lawhon" *1865-1867 Confederate Amnesty Papers*, accessed 14 Jun 2024, https://www.fold3.com/file/22588582/lawhon-l-w-us-confederate-amnesty-papers-1865-1867

580 "A.D. McDonald" *1865-1867 Confederate Amnesty Papers*, accessed 14 Jun 2024, https://www.fold3.com/file/22591241/mcdonald-a-d-us-confederate-amnesty-papers-1865-1867

581 "Evander McGilvary" *1865-1867 Confederate Amnesty Papers*, accessed 14 Jun 2024, https://www.fold3.com/file/22591557/mcgilvary-evander-us-confederate-amnesty-papers-1865-1867

582 "Daniel M. McIntosh" *1865-1867 Confederate Amnesty Papers*, accessed 14 Jun 2024, https://www.fold3.com/file/22591725/mcintosh-daniel-m-us-confederate-amnesty-papers-1865-1867

583 "D.B. McIver" *1865-1867 Confederate Amnesty Papers*, accessed 14 Jun 2024, https://www.fold3.com/file/22591760/mciver-d-b-us-confederate-amnesty-papers-1865-1867

584 "Wesley McIver" *1865-1867 Confederate Amnesty Papers*, accessed 14 Jun 2024, https://www.fold3.com/file/22591803/mciver-wesley-us-confederate-amnesty-papers-1865-1867

585 "Daniel McKinzie" *1865-1867 Confederate Amnesty Papers*, accessed 14 Jun 2024, https://www.fold3.com/file/22591980/mckinzie-daniel-us-confederate-amnesty-papers-1865-1867

586 "William McLeod" *1865-1867 Confederate Amnesty Papers*, accessed 14 Jun 2024, https://www.fold3.com/file/22592406/mcleod-william-us-confederate-amnesty-papers-1865-1867

587 "Eli N. Moffitt" *1865-1867 Confederate Amnesty Papers*, accessed 14 Jun 2024, https://www.fold3.com/file/22545244/moffit-eli-n-us-confederate-amnesty-papers-1865-1867

588 "John Munroe" *1865-1867 Confederate Amnesty Papers*, accessed 14 Jun 2024, https://www.fold3.com/file/22547121/munroe-john-us-confederate-amnesty-papers-1865-1867

589 "Thomas Rollins" *1865-1867 Confederate Amnesty Papers*, accessed 14 Jun 2024, https://www.fold3.com/file/23926511/rollins-thomas-us-confederate-amnesty-papers-1865-1867

590 "John Sheppard" *1865-1867 Confederate Amnesty Papers*, accessed 14 Jun 2024, https://www.fold3.com/file/23927636/sheppard-john-us-confederate-amnesty-papers-1865-1867

591 "D.M. Sinclair" *1865-1867 Confederate Amnesty Papers*, accessed 14 Jun 2024, https://www.fold3.com/file/23927827/sinclair-d-m-us-confederate-amnesty-papers-1865-1867

592 Lacy Garner, Jr, *Thurman Maness Remembers: Tales from the Upper End of the County*. (Robbins, NC: Lulu.com, 2009), 78-84.

593 Henry B. Shields M.D., *Country Doctor for a Half Century*. (Southern Pines, NC: The Pilot, 1975), 27-28.

594 "Letter, Mary A. Harper, John Harper and Charles Harper to J.L. Stuart, 26 Nov 1862", *John L. Stuart Papers*, David M. Rubenstein Library, Duke University, Durham, NC

595 "Letter, R.P. Buxton to Gov. Zebulon B. Vance, 21 Jan 1863" *Governor Zebulon Baird Vance Papers*, Jan 1863 Correspondence, Governor's Papers, State Archives of North Carolina, Raleigh, NC

596 "Letter, Mary A. Harper and John Harper to J.L. Stuart, 20 Feb 1863", *John L. Stuart Papers*, David M. Rubenstein Library, Duke University, Durham, NC

597 "Letter, J.L. Stuart to Mary A. Harper and Charles Harper, 22 Mar 1863", *John L. Stuart Papers*, David M. Rubenstein Library, Duke University, Durham, NC

598 "Letter, Phillip Wilson to Gov. Zebulon B. Vance, 14 Apr 1863" *Governor Zebulon Baird Vance Papers*, Apr 1863 Correspondence, Governor's Papers, State Archives of North Carolina, Raleigh, NC

599 "Letter, John Harper to J.L. Stuart, 26 Apr 1863", *John L. Stuart Papers*, David M. Rubenstein Library, Duke University, Durham, NC

600 "Letter, Chesley Jones to Gov. Zebulon B. Vance, 24 Jun 1863" *Governor Zebulon Baird Vance Papers*, Jun 1863 Correspondence, Governor's Papers, State Archives of North Carolina, Raleigh, NC

601 "Public Meeting in Moore County" *Semi-Weekly Standard*, 8 Aug 1863, https://www.newspapers.com/image/144020483

602 "Letter, C. Dowd to S.G. Worth, 28 Sep 1863" *Marmaduke Swaim Robins Papers*, Folder 4 1863, Southern Historical Collection, Wilson Special Collections, University of North Carolina, Chapel Hill, NC

603 "Robbery and Incendiarism" *The Greensboro Patriot*, 15 Oct 1863, https://www.newspapers.com/image/62981640

604 "Letter, A.K. Pearce to Bryan Tyson, 3 Dec 1863" *Bryan Tyson Papers*, David M. Rubenstein Library, Duke University, Durham, NC

605 "Letter, T.W. Ritter to Gov. Zebulon B. Vance, 1 Jan 1864" *Governor Zebulon Baird Vance Papers*, Jan 1864 Correspondence, Governor's Papers, State Archives of North Carolina, Raleigh, NC

606 "Letter, C. Dowd to R.P. Buxton, 7 Jan 1864" *Governor Zebulon Baird Vance Papers*, Jan 1864 Correspondence, Governor's Papers, State Archives of North Carolina, Raleigh, NC

607 "Letter, C. Dowd to Gov. Z.B. Vance, 7 Feb 1864" *Governor Zebulon Baird Vance Papers*, Feb 1864 Correspondence, Governor's Papers, State Archives of North Carolina, Raleigh, NC

608 "Murder, Violence and Treason" *The Daily Confederate*, 27 Feb 1864, https://www.newspapers.com/image/118485959

609 "Letter, Lauchlin McKinnon to Gov. Z.B. Vance, 27 Feb 1864" *Governor Zebulon Baird Vance Papers*, Feb 1864 Correspondence, Governor's Papers, State Archives of North Carolina, Raleigh, NC

610 "Letter, H.C. Brown to Bryan Tyson, 23 Apr 1864" *Bryan Tyson Papers*, David M. Rubenstein Library, Duke University, Durham, NC

611 "Capture of a Noted Outlaw" *Fayetteville Semi-Weekly Observer*, 28 Apr 1864, https://www.newspapers.com/image/63257822

612 "Letter, J.A. Little to D.C. Pearson, 15 Jul 1864" *CSA Bureau of Conscription, 7th NC Congressional District Records, 1862-1865*, Southern Historical Collection, Wilson Special Collections, University of North Carolina, Chapel Hill, NC (#170)

613 "Letter, P.H. Williamson to D.C. Pearson, 5 Aug 1864" *CSA Bureau of Conscription, 7th NC Congressional District Records, 1862-1865*, Southern Historical Collection, Wilson Special Collections, University of North Carolina, Chapel Hill, NC (#170)

614 "Outrages in Moore" *Fayetteville Semi-Weekly Observer*, 11 Aug 1864, https://www.newspapers.com/image/63258070

615 "Deserters Attack the Home Guard" *The Weekly Intelligencer*, 16 Aug 1864, https://www.newspapers.com/image/64702643

616 "Deserters Captured" *Fayetteville Semi-Weekly Observer*, 25 Aug 1864, https://www.newspapers.com/image/63258103

617 "Murder in the First Degree" *The Daily Progress*, 2 Sep 1864, https://www.newspapers.com/image/58162130

618 "Moore County" *The Daily Progress*, 5 Sep 1864, https://www.newspapers.com/image/58162138

619 "Horse Thief Killed" *Fayetteville Semi-Weekly Observer*, 8 Sep 1864, https://www.newspapers.com/image/63258120

620 "Jones and Evans" *Fayetteville Semi-Weekly Observer*, 12 Sep 1864, https://www.newspapers.com/image/63258129

621 "Sad Casualty" *Fayetteville Semi-Weekly Observer*, 12 Sep 1864, https://www.newspapers.com/image/63258129

622 "Returned to Jail" *Fayetteville Semi-Weekly Observer*, 19 Sep 1864, https://www.newspapers.com/image/63258135

623 "Deserters and Home Guards" *The Daily North Carolinian*, 21 Sep 1864, https://www.newspapers.com/image/54044234

624 "Article" *The Daily North Carolinian*, 26 Sep 1864, https://www.newspapers.com/image/54044264

625 "Deserters Coming In" *The Daily Progress*, 26 Sep 1864, https://www.newspapers.com/image/58162207

626 "Letter, A.K. Pearce to Bryan Tyson, 8 Sep 1864" *Bryan Tyson Papers*, David M. Rubenstein Library, Duke University, Durham, NC

627 "Turner Fry" *Fayetteville Weekly Observer*, 23 Jan 1865, https://www.newspapers.com/image/63246081

628 "Reminiscences from Moore County" *The Morning Post*, 17 Aug 1905, https://www.newspapers.com/image/57473673

629 Bryan Tyson, *Object of the Administration in Prosecuting the War*. (Washington, DC: McGill & Witherow, 1864), 7.

630 Maxine Williams McNeill, *The Williams Family*. (West End, NC: TM Custom Graphix 1999), 7-8.

631 "Moore Co. Veterans' Association" *The Carthage Blade*, 11 Jul 1889, https://www.newspapers.com/image/60438655

632 "Moore Co. Veterans' Association" *Jonesboro Leader*, 17 Jul 1889, https://newspapers.digitalnc.org/lccn/sn91068774/1889-07-17/ed-1/seq-4

633 "Moore County Veterans" *Jonesboro Leader*, 25 Jun 1890, https://newspapers.digitalnc.org/lccn/sn91068774/1890-06-25/ed-1/seq-5

634 "Moore County Veterans" *The Free Press*, 13 Sep 1901, https://newspapers.digitalnc.org/lccn/sn92061679/1901-09-13/ed-1/seq-4

635 "The Blue and the Gray" *The News and Observer*, 17 Feb 1906, https://www.newspapers.com/image/75789806

636 "Gov. Glenn to be present" *The Carthage Blade*, 21 Feb 1906, https://www.newspapers.com/image/61598411

637 Britton, Edward E., "Warm Grip of the Blue and Gray" *The News and Observer*, 25 Feb 1906, https://www.newspapers.com/image/75790087

638 "Blue and the Gray" *The Carthage Blade*, 28 Feb 1906, https://www.newspapers.com/image/61598416

639 "Happy Conception" *The Carthage Blade*, 28 Mar 1906, https://www.newspapers.com/image/61598433

640 "The Blue and the Gray" *Southern Pines Tourist*, 29 Mar 1907, https://newspapers.digitalnc.org/lccn/sn92061730/1907-03-29/ed-1/seq-1

641 "The Blue and the Gray" *Southern Pines Tourist*, 20 Mar 1908, https://newspapers.digitalnc.org/lccn/sn92061730/1908-03-20/ed-1/seq-2

642 "The Blue and Gray" *The News and Observer*, 21 Mar 1908, https://www.newspapers.com/image/75790087

643 "Old Soldiers" *The Pilot*, 24 Aug 1989, Civil War Photos, Vertical Files, Moore County Library, Carthage, NC

644 "Local Pickups" *Southern Pines Tourist*, 19 Mar 1909, https://newspapers.digitalnc.org/lccn/sn92061730/1909-03-19/ed-1/seq-7

645 "Southern Pines Chosen" *Southern Pines Tourist*, 14 Mar 1909, https://www.newspapers.com/image/616494217

646 "Blue and Gray National Encampment" *Southern Pines Tourist*, 7 Jan 1910, https://newspapers.digitalnc.org/lccn/sn92061730/1910-01-07/ed-1/seq-1

647 "Blue Gray Reunion is off" *Southern Pines Tourist*, 11 Feb 1910, https://newspapers.digitalnc.org/lccn/sn92061730/1910-02-11/ed-1/seq-1

648 "Good for Carthage" *Southern Pines Tourist*, 25 Feb 1910, https://newspapers.digitalnc.org/lccn/sn92061730/1910-02-25/ed-1/seq-1

649 "The Blue and Gray Fiasco" *Southern Pines Tourist*, 4 Mar 1910, https://newspapers.digitalnc.org/lccn/sn92061730/1910-03-04/ed-1/seq-1

650 "Old Soldiers' Reunion at Jackson Springs" *The Montgomerian*, 6 Aug 1908, https://www.newspapers.com/image/67817588

651 "The Glorious Fourth" *The Sanford Express*, 12 Jun 1908, https://www.newspapers.com/image/1181312578

652 "Camp Ransom" *The Sanford Express*, 20 Aug 1909, https://www.newspapers.com/image/1181312976

653 "Men Who Wore the Gray" *The Sanford Express*, 8 Jul 1910, https://www.newspapers.com/image/1181313270

654 "Local Briefs" *The Sanford Express*, 20 Nov 1914, https://www.newspapers.com/image/1181314501

655 "The Veterans Express Their Appreciation" *The Sanford Express*, 7 May 1915, https://www.newspapers.com/image/1181314884

656 "Local Briefs" *The Sanford Express*, 9 Aug 1928, https://newspapers.digitalnc.org/lccn/sn89071020/1928-08-09/ed-1/seq-5

657 "Memorial at Buffalo" *The Sanford Express*, 1 Jun 1923, https://newspapers.digitalnc.org/lccn/sn89071020/1923-06-01/ed-1/seq-1

658 "Local Briefs" *The Sanford Express*, 8 Jun 1923, https://newspapers.digitalnc.org/lccn/sn89071020/1923-06-08/ed-1/seq-3

659 James V. Comer, *The Bountiful Legacy of a Mother: Buffalo Presbyterian Church, Buffalo Community / Sanford, NC.* (Sanford, J.V. Comer, 1997)

INFANTRY. UNIFORMS OF REGULAR CONFEDERATE TROOPS. CAVALRY. ARTILLERY. Louisiana Zouave.

Volunteer Infantry of Virginia. 1st Regiment Maryland Line. South Carolina Light Infantry. Hampton Legion. Rockingham Rangers Artillery. Gentlemen of the Road Independent Cavalry. Black Horse Cavalry.

UNIFORMS OF THE CONFEDERATE A

Louisiana Zouaves. Washington Artillery of New Orleans. Mississippi Rifles. Heavy Infantry of Georgia. Alabama Light Infantry. Marine Battery, Manassas Junction.

Black Horse Cavalry. Dragoon Guards, 14th Regt., Va. Cavalry. Mounted Rifles, North Carolina. Virginia Cadets. Grayson Dare-devils. Kentucky Rifle Brigade. Tennessee Sharp-shooters.

IFORMS OF THE CONFEDERATE ARMY.

www.ingramcontent.com/pod-product-compliance
Lightning Source LLC
Chambersburg PA
CBHW080451100526
44581CB00003B/105
* 9 7 9 8 9 9 3 2 0 2 9 2 1 *